Experience and Artistic Expression
in Lope de Vega

The Making of *La Dorotea*

Alan S. Trueblood

Harvard University Press
Cambridge, Massachusetts
1974

Publication of this book has been aided by a
grant from the Andrew W. Mellon Foundation.

Library of Congress Catalog Card Number 73–82349
SBN 674-27670-1
Printed in the United States of America

Experience and Artistic Expression
in Lope de Vega

To the memory of Amado Alonso

Contents

Preface

In writing this book I have had in mind the reader who is not a Hispanist or a student of Romance literature quite as much as the reader who is. I have accordingly provided translations for all quoted material and have translated, the first time given, the titles of all works by Lope de Vega. Unless otherwise indicated, the translations are my own; the titles of published translations of works by Lope have been retained, however. In translating poetry and prose, other than the dialogue of *La Dorotea* and certain other passages of familiar dialogue, my aim has been to stay as close as possible to the order of the original and to its exact sense. With the dialogue of *La Dorotea* and dialogue from other works, a more literary form of translation has been attempted in an effort to catch their colloquial flavor, though not at the expense of exactness.

In those cases where I have directly transcribed passages of older Spanish, I have adopted the principles of transcription followed by Edwin S. Morby in his edition of *La Dorotea*: modernization of punctuation and accentuation, retention of original spelling (save the long *s*), supplying of omitted nasal consonants, and writing out of conventional abbreviations for "que" and "etc."

This book has been long in the making and during its gestation many more persons than I am now able to recall specifically have helped me by words spoken and written to develop whatever powers of insight into its subject I may possess. Since the key faculty of the literary critic is the ability to perceive what the text before him is saying, in and between the lines, my indebtedness to the friends, colleagues, and associates who have helped sharpen my powers of perception is large indeed. It is no fault of theirs if these powers still have their limitations.

I was first led to the subject of this book nearly twenty-five years ago in the graduate school of Harvard University by the late Amado Alonso. The orientation provided by this master of Hispanic letters, whose rare gifts as teacher and mentor quite matched his stature as scholar and critic, proved decisive in shaping my approach to this subject and indeed to all literary inquiry. Though his active guidance was of lamentably short duration because of his premature death, his example has been a constant resource and stimulus. To him this book owes its first and greatest debt.

Some indication of my further indebtedness is given in the introductory chapter and in the notes. But I should like to mention here how much I have benefited over the years from Edwin S. Morby's fellow concern with Lope and *La Dorotea*, which has complemented and constantly enriched my own. His expertise and his sustained interest in this book have been a constant encouragement, while his careful reading and critique of the manuscript have been a valuable aid. The specialized knowledge of two of my colleagues at Brown University, William L. Fichter and A. David Kossoff, fellow students of Lope de Vega and the Golden Age of Spanish literature, has come to my assistance on numerous occasions, while the critical acuity of Edwin Honig and his innate understanding of the processes of literary creation have constantly widened my horizons. The perceptions and challenges of my students at Brown and Harvard have repeatedly stimulated my thinking.

I am grateful to the Guggenheim Foundation for the opportunity to pursue research for this book in Europe and to Brown University for several summer grants which helped it toward completion.

At various points in the book, as indicated in the notes, I have adapted in my exposition materials which first appeared in earlier essays of my own. The essays are: "The Case for an Early *Dorotea*: a Reexamination," *PMLA*, 71 (1956), 755–798; "Role-Playing and the Sense of Illusion in Lope de Vega," *Hispanic Review*, 32 (1964), 305–318; "'Al son de los arroyuelos': Texture and Context in a Lyric of *La Dorotea*," in *Homenaje al Profesor Rodríguez-Moñino* (Madrid: Castalia, 1966), II, 277–287; "Masters and Servants: *La Dorotea* vis-à-vis the *Comedia*," *Kentucky Romance Quarterly*, 16 (1969), 55–61; "Lope's 'A mis soledades voy' Reconsidered," in *Homenaje a William L. Fichter: Estudios sobre el antiguo teatro hispánico*, ed. A. D. Kossoff and J. Amor y Vázquez (Madrid: Castalia, 1971), pp. 713–724. To the editors and publishers of these essays I am most grateful for permission to reprint and adapt materials from the sources cited.

To the following persons and publishers I am also deeply grateful for their kind permission to quote from the works indicated: To Edwin S. Morby, for extensive citations from his edition of *La Dorotea*, 2nd ed. rev. (University of California Press, Berkeley, and Editorial Castalia, Madrid, 1968). To Editorial Planeta, Barcelona, for permission to quote a number of poems from *Obras poéticas de Lope de Vega*, ed. J. M. Blecua (Barcelona: Planeta, 1969). To the Royal Spanish Academy for permission to cite extensively from a work published under their sponsorship, *Epistolario de Lope de Vega Carpio*, ed. Agustín G. de Amezúa, vols. III and IV (Madrid: Artes gráficas "Aldus," 1941 and 1943, respectively). To Indiana University Press for permission to cite lines from a poem on p. 81 of *"Poesías barias y recreación de buenos ingenios": A Description of MS 17556 of the Biblioteca Nacional Matritense, with Some Unpublished Portions Thereof*, by John M. Hill, *Indiana University Studies*, vol. X, no. 60 (December 1923).

My particular thanks go to my mother, Louise N. Trueblood, who typed all drafts of the book and helped with aspects of the research; to Mrs. Harriet G. Mayerson, who typed the definitive draft; and to Mrs. Vivienne A. Lipps, who typed several sections and assisted in other ways. To Mrs. Nancy Clemente of the Harvard University Press my deep appreciation for her invaluable assistance in preparing the manuscript for the press.

The Hedgerows
Little Compton, Rhode Island

Abbreviations

Works by Lope de Vega

Ac.	*Obras de Lope de Vega*, ed. Real Academia Española, 15 vols. (Madrid: Sucesores de Rivadeneyra, 1890–1913)
Ac. N.	*Obras de Lope de Vega*, ed. Real Academia Española, new ed., 13 vols. (Madrid: Tipografía de la Revista de Archivos, Bibliotecas y Museos, 1916–1930)
Comedias escogidas	*Comedias escogidas de Frey Lope Félix de Vega Carpio*, ed. J. E. Hartzenbusch, 4 vols. (Madrid: Hernando, 1923–1925)
Epistolario	*Epistolario de Lope de Vega Carpio*, ed. Agustín G. de Amezúa, 4 vols. (Madrid, 1935–1943); see Principal Works Cited for publishers of individual volumes
Morby	*La Dorotea*, ed. E. S. Morby, 2nd ed. rev.; published jointly by University of California Press, Berkeley, and Editorial Castalia, Madrid, 1968
Obras escogidas	*Obras escogidas de Lope Félix de Vega Carpio*, ed. F. C. Sainz de Robles, 2nd ed., 3 vols. (Madrid: Aguilar, 1958–1962)
Obras poéticas	*Obras poéticas de Lope de Vega*, ed. J. M. Blecua (Barcelona: Planeta, 1969)
OS	*Colección de las obras sueltas, así en prosa como en verso, de don Frey Lope de Vega Carpio del hábito de San Juan*, 21 vols. (Madrid: A. de Sancha, 1776–1779)

Works by Others

Covarrubias
Sebastián de Covarrubias, *Tesoro de la lengua castellana o española, según la impresión de 1611, con las adiciones de Benito Remigio Noydens publicadas en la de 1674*, ed. M. de Riquer (Barcelona: Horta, 1943)

Estudios
J. de Entrambasaguas, *Estudios sobre Lope de Vega*, 3 vols. (Madrid: C.S.I.C., 1946–1958)

Estudios sobre Lope
J. F. Montesinos, *Estudios sobre Lope*, new ed. (Salamanca: Anaya, 1967)

Fuentes
Las fuentes del Romancero General, ed. A. Rodríguez Moñino, 12 vols. (Madrid: Real Academia Española, 1957)

Morley and Bruerton
S. G. Morley and C. Bruerton, *The Chronology of Lope de Vega's "Comedias"* (New York: Modern Language Association of America, 1940)

Proceso
A. Tomillo and C. Pérez Pastor, *Proceso de Lope de Vega por libelos contra unos cómicos* (Madrid: Fortanet, 1901)

Rennert and Castro
H. A. Rennert and Américo Castro, *Vida de Lope de Vega*, 2nd ed. with additions by Castro and F. Lázaro Carreter (Salamanca: Anaya, 1968)

Introduction

I

The first task of the critic who would pursue the artistic consequences of a key experience in the life of a writer like Lope de Vega is to clarify the premises on which he is proceeding. Lope is a *mare magnum* in which it is all too easy to founder. His vast range, his varied production, his huge output leave one wondering what compass can assure a safe passage over so trackless an ocean. Besides four hundred surviving plays out of a considerably larger total, Lope produced in his seventy-three years (1562–1635) a huge body of nondramatic writing—pastoral novels; a Byzantine novel; Italianate epics, serious and burlesque; narrative poems on contemporary history and on mythological and other subjects; short stories; and a steady stream of lyric poetry spanning more than fifty years and including over sixteen hundred sonnets alone. When one recalls the intensity with which Lope lived—his rich love and family life; his full if spasmodic religious life (as a priest during his last two decades); the restless comings and goings all over Spain and even to the shores of England in the Armada; his share in every representative aspect of the life of his day, official and unofficial, at every level from royalty to roguedom; his responsiveness to the most popular as well as the most select artistic stimuli—one understands why his contemporaries dubbed him the Phenomenon of Nature ("Monstruo de la Naturaleza") and used the phrase "good as Lope" as we now say "good as gold."

Lope in short is an "involved" artist, much of whose production envisages particular audiences and is conditioned by them: the popular public of the *comedias* whose tastes in the course of a half century he slowly refined, the cultivated or learned *cognoscenti* to whom he addressed his more ambitious nondramatic projects and whose approbation he eagerly sought, the religious congregations who commissioned plays on saints' lives or biblical subjects, the national community for whom he dramatized the latest victories in Flanders or Brazil or chronicled in verse the trials of Mary Stuart or the depredations of Drake.

This vast "public" sector of Lope's production is not my concern. With equal fervor and equal constancy Lope lived and wrote in the private sphere. It is a vein of his production in this sphere, perhaps the most significant since it culminates in his masterpiece, *La Dorotea* (1632), which I propose to explore. The origin is a resounding episode of his youth, Lope's trial for libel of certain actors (1587–88), an event which marks the end of his four-year liaison with Elena Osorio, daughter of the theatrical producer who brings the charges after Lope responds with slander to the preferment of a wealthier rival. The whole experience is traumatic in both psychological and esthetic senses. It stirs him to the core, psychically and emotionally, leaving wounds very slow to heal; it molds definitively his conception of relations between the sexes. At the same time his creative imagination is stirred by it as by no other episode in his life, and a need is aroused for relief and release in artistic expression. The experience is rich in artistic consequences in lyric and dramatic forms in the ten or fifteen years following 1588 and there are numerous signs of its continued "submerged" existence thereafter until it resurfaces in 1632 with *La Dorotea* in what might be considered definitive form, a form which Lope calls *acción en prosa* (action in prose), created ad hoc, lyric in temper, dramatic in conception and structure, though not intended for the stage. In a dedicatory note Lope remarks that the work is based on a personal experience and had been completed in 1588 but mislaid, adding that in publishing it now, "la corregí de la lozanía con que se auía criado en la tierna mía,"[1] that is, that he has toned down its lusty youthful exuberance.

It will be useful to pause at this point to summarize the action of this work. Dorotea and the penniless poet Fernando have been lovers for five years. Her mother, Teodora, at the behest of her friend Gerarda, a go-between of sorts, decides to break up the liaison in order to clear the way for a more profitable lover, the wealthy *indiano* (Spaniard returned from the New World) Don Bela. After some soul-searching, Dorotea informs Fernando that she has no choice in the matter, he takes umbrage, they quarrel, and Fernando rides off desperately to Seville after prevailing on a former mistress, Marfisa, with a rigged-up story of having killed someone, to let him have her jewels. Dorotea attempts suicide, convalesces, and eventually accepts Don Bela.

Three months after his departure Fernando returns to Madrid still obsessed with Dorotea, finds Don Bela in possession, meets him by chance under her windows and wounds him in a brief exchange of swordplay. Some days later he encounters the disguised Dorotea in the Prado, tells her his life story, and when she reveals herself, is reconciled with her. Arriving home in triumph, he encounters Marfisa, by now disabused, and is bitterly denounced by her. Fernando then reveals to his servant, Julio, that reconciliation has killed his ardor for Dorotea and that he proposes returning to Marfisa. He shares Dorotea surreptitiously with Don Bela for two more months, however, before abandoning her altogether. Dorotea, as much in love as ever, plays disconsolately with the thought of taking the veil. The accidental deaths of Don Bela and Gerarda bring the work to a close.

It is on the afterlife of the creative nexus which culminates in *La Dorotea*, as manifested in pastoral and Moorish ballads, sonnets, the play *Belardo el furioso* (*Belardo Mad*), and above all, the *acción en prosa* itself, that I shall focus. My aim is to reach a fuller understanding of Lope's creative processes, and signally of the meaning of *La Dorotea*, by examining the interaction of substance with form, *historia* or *Erlebnis* with *poiesis*, in the artistic products of the experience.[2] The acquisitions of Lopean criticism, particularly in the twentieth century, have gone a long way toward providing both the data and the critical instruments to make such an undertaking feasible. One may preface an examination of these acquisitions by indicating their underlying assumption: namely, an unusual proximity between the spheres of personal history and artistic creation in Lope, and unusual ease in the passage from experience to art. I shall seek in all the exposition that follows to explore the character and consequences of this intimate symbiosis. It constitutes the main grounds for my choice of a biographical approach to my subject.

It goes without saying that in Lope as in any other artist truth and poetry, however close, are wholly distinct domains; the passage from one to the other is not a transposition of key but an absolute change of medium. No one understood this better than Lope himself: "No me han hallado otra pasión viciosa fuera del natural amor, en que yo, como los ruiseñores, tengo más voz que carne" ("They've not been able to find any other vicious passion in me than natural love and in this, like nightingales, I have more voice than flesh"), he remarks in a private letter apropos of gossip about one of his love affairs.[3] It would be hard to convey more vividly awareness of the disproportion between voice and flesh, of their essential distinctness. Nor was he ever tempted to make a cult of esthetic sensibility, husbanding experience for the sake of art in the manner of a latter-day literary decadent. Lope lived first and wrote afterward—often directly afterward, to be sure—but the expression never took precedence over the event.[4]

Nonetheless, the persistence and ease with which private experience becomes the substance of Lope's art and the providential existence of an unusual mass of significant documentation of his private life mean that the biographical approach should be capable of providing access to the nerve centers of his *poiesis*. As an artist Lope is most compellingly possessed by what lies closest to his psyche—love, jealousy, anger arising in the private sphere; family ties; his highly emotional relationship with his God; the immediate sensory impact of the physical world. Ideology is no guide at all; as Karl Vossler notes, "It would be taking a wrong approach to attempt to identify Lope with any particular logical viewpoint . . . or to classify him from the standpoint of any particular school."[5] "An attempt to enclose him in any formula is like trying to make one pair of boots fit a centipede," remarks Ezra Pound.[6] Open any page of Lope's critical or expository prose and you soon come up against the vagaries of a mind quick but undisciplined, inquisitive but lacking in intellectual rigor, incapable of resisting the chance association, the provocative image, the stray idea, the picturesque but irrelevant detail. Even when writing what he called "serious things" to impress the "científicos" (learned), Lope slips from subject to subject with a notable lack of discipline; his pretentious erudition comes to life only when it hits on an idea or opinion that illuminates some area of his sensibility and provokes a personal response. As for broader questions pertaining to the moral, social, political, and theological orders, to his nation's historical role and destiny, they are not open ones for Lope at all. He simply makes his own the values and beliefs of his national and religious community, affirming them his whole life through in the action of his plays, in particular dramatic situations, but offering no private perspective upon them. Though in particular personal contingencies Lope may lose his sanguinity, his fundamental outlook is well conveyed in a letter drafted, probably in 1618, for his patron, the Duke of Sessa: "I laugh at those who think that the state of things in our time is the worst, since history and experience provide us with proof to the contrary."[7]

The present-day evaluation of the impact of *Erlebnis* on artistic expression in Lope was long in evolving. To many of his contemporaries, it was obvious that vicissitudes of his sometimes scandalous personal life were being turned into poetry and even finding their way into his plays. His own attempts to hide the fact are curiously ambivalent. None of his intimates could have understood the disproportion between flesh and voice, however, and after his death the connections between art and life were soon lost sight of altogether, in part as a result of the tendency to apotheosize the poet, a tendency already evident in the fulsome tone of the panegyrics spoken and penned on the occasion of his exequies.[8] Thus the nexus of experience to which I have been referring—the four-year love affair with Elena Osorio, the scandalous rupture that ended it, and the imprisonment, trial, and exile that followed for the poet—was first hushed up, then forgotten. When interest in *La Dorotea* revived in the early nineteenth century with the concern of the Romantic era for the *grandeur et servitude* of the artist, the work was put to use overzealously to document Lope's life. The trend of biographers and critics was to read fiction as if it were autobiography; only rarely was it thought of as possessing any degree of autonomy.[9] When C. A. de La Barrera composed his new biography of Lope in 1864, to introduce the Spanish Academy edition of his plays, he drew at length on Fernando-Lope's story of his life and on the forecast of his future in *La Dorotea*.[10] Discrepancies with other sources of information were accounted for by postulating an intention on Lope's part to mislead the reader and disguise the real character of events.

Concern with the autobiographical aspect of *La Dorotea* inevitably led critics to raise questions regarding its morality. Julius Leopold Klein decided that it was a "monkish catharsis" in which a pious old author mortified himself by pitilessly exposing youthful errors; he was distressed, however, by what he saw as a failure on Lope's part to bring his protagonist to justice.[11] John Ormsby, too,[12] betrayed impatience with the work's morality and dismissed Fernando as a "paltry scoundrel." In the twentieth century we will still find Ludwig Pfandl passing adverse judgment on Fernando on moral grounds.[13]

The nineteenth century had gradually become aware that *La Dorotea* belonged to a family of Lopean works. Claude Fauriel had suggested links with Lope's artistic balladry and Ormsby identified Filis, the subject of the pastoral ballads, with the heroine of the *acción en prosa*. M. Menéndez y Pelayo[14] in 1895 pointed to the analogies in text and situation between *La Dorotea* and the *comedia Belardo el furioso* and wondered whether the play is the early version of *La Dorotea* referred to by Lope.

Documentary substantiation of the autobiographical basis postulated for a century was finally achieved in 1901 by C. Pérez Pastor's discovery of the transcript of Lope's trial for libel in 1587–88.[15] The spotlight suddenly turned on an episode of Lope's youth picks out the flesh-and-blood prototypes of figures present in fictional versions of the episode and in many cases connects fictional situations with live circumstances, though not in all, for some points remain in shadow. With the further aid of new documents and by drawing on works of Lope, Pérez Pastor reconstructs the story of Lope and Elena Osorio and leaves no doubt that the ballads stem from the same matrix of experience as the *acción en prosa*. His interest does not extend, however, to evaluating these artistic products in their own right.

This is the contribution of Américo Castro, whose translation and amplification of H. A. Rennert's biography of Lope [16] had incorporated the discoveries of Pérez Pastor. Castro turns his attention to the question which is central for the literary critic as against the literary historian: that of the transmutation occurring when experience is turned into art. It is obvious to him that there is no given correlation between art and life, and while he still discerns an intention to disguise real events, he notices a much more significant process of "contamination," that is, conflation, whereby attributes of more than one live or fictional prototype enter into the characterization of certain figures of *La Dorotea*. He also observes its opposite, a dispersion of attributes. In short, he finds Lope guided by artistic, not autobiographical directives, by the desire to make *La Dorotea* bear permanent witness to the abiding passions of his life: literature and love. The exceptionally strong personal flavor of Lope's art he sees as the stamp of a temperament rather than the result of any particular correlation with data of experience, and he warns against overzealous attempts to disentangle "everyday facts" from the "permanently valid elaboration" to which they have been subjected.

Subsequent critics have followed Castro's guidelines in their reassessment of *La Dorotea* and related works as artistic entities. For the *acción en prosa* in particular, a major contribution was made by Karl Vossler in 1924 in his *Spanischer Brief an Hugo von Hoffmansthal*, later incorporated, with some additions, into *Lope de Vega und sein Zeitalter* (1932).[17] Vossler sees *La Dorotea* as Lope's most personal work and finds the key to its poetic sense in the strain of *desengaño* (disillusionment), a product of the fusion of the early adventure with a lifetime's experience of evanescence and mutability, and itself a reflection of the baroque spirit. Castro had raised the question of the date or dates of composition, viewing the work essentially as a work of old age and suggesting that there was perhaps no early version at all. Vossler, however, takes Lope at his word—correctly in my view—and sees it as the product at once of youth and of maturity: it is youth viewed indulgently but clairvoyantly through the eyes of old age, and though the author puts something of himself into all of his characters and is sympathetic toward the amorous and literary fever that possesses them, for Vossler he stands fundamentally apart and sees beyond them. Literature occupies a special place in *La Dorotea*, as it had in Lope's life; particularly characteristic is the *Literarisierung*, or literary stylization of attitude, expression, and behavior, which Vossler sees as a contagion characteristic of the baroque. He finds the characters devoid of individual moral conscience but of necessity subject to a superpersonal national and religious ethic. Vossler emphasizes Lope's solidarity with his times and he sees *La Dorotea* as exemplary of a particular stage in the development of Spanish culture, as an embodiment of the baroque Zeitgeist. Though my emphasis is elsewhere and though I shall be less concerned with the baroque as such, my fundamental debt to Vossler's penetrating and suggestive evaluation of *La Dorotea* will be constantly evident. It includes his conception of the *acción en prosa* as a *creación lírica teatral*—lyric theatrical creation—a designation which catches the work's fusion of lyric and dramatic modes, the strongly personal temper and the objectification in dramatic structure.

To the already established links of *La Dorotea* with Lope's artistic balladry, Vossler adds a connection with *La Arcadia*, the pastoral novel Lope published in 1598, which he views "as a first thwarted attempt, caught in the blind alley of virtuosity, an unsuccessful effort to give poetic expression to his own experience of *desengaño*." [18]

As significant as Vossler's are the insights the following year (1925) of J. F. Montesinos both into the form and meaning of *La Dorotea* and into its connections with other Lopean works, especially lyrics and plays. [19] Of fundamental importance is Montesinos' view of the early ballads as a poematic series, equivalent to "una *Dorotea* sentimental," and amounting to "la superación de una vida mezquina" ("the transcending of a paltry life"). Equally important is his emphasis on the role of the poetic motif in Lope's *poiesis*, its tendency to take hold in its own right, capturing Lope's imagination and undergoing free elaborations in which links with an original stimulus are lost. Montesinos points to two motifs stemming from the experience with Elena Osorio which give rise to sonnet series particularly significant for this inquiry: the ruins motif and that of the straying sheep. He also explores the relationship of *La Dorotea* with the world of Lope's plays, finding fundamentally divergent in the *acción en prosa* a dimension of everyday reality, with its concrete objects and spontaneous feelings which constitute a counterweight to *Literarisierung*. Lope's own stance he sees as that of the *figura del donaire* (jokester) of his plays, whose down-to-earth viewpoint the author here makes his own, albeit in a generous and no longer anti-heroic spirit. He sees the work as devoid of both petty vindictiveness and romantic self-pity, the ultimate step in the absorption of experience into the sphere of art, a product of prior literary elaboration as well as of *Erlebnis*.

Mention must be made of Leo Spitzer's monograph *Die Literarisierung des Lebens in Lope's "Dorotea,"* [20] despite the fact that his failure to reprint it suggests later misgivings about the absoluteness with which he fits *La Dorotea* into the pigeonholes of baroque categorization. Its value lies in the analyses of speech styles of characters whom he views as "conversation spirits" and in the emphasis on an element of "ambition to be rhetorically victorious" in their verbal intercourse.

Alda Croce in the extensive introduction to her Italian translation of *La Dorotea*[21] sees as its key the conversion of a personal experience into a generalized *trattato d'amore*. What for Spitzer was a baroque consciousness that expression cannot fit content, and for Vossler was an effect of *Literarisierung*, for her is a double presentation of sentiment, at once as "effusion" and as "judged and defined." In his eagerness to generalize, the author is seen as puncturing moods and intervening to place his own comments on the lips of his characters. The latter are simply embodiments of passions, "undifferentiated humanity," whose links with real prototypes are purely external. Action and psychology reflect the arbitrary laws of love of the *comedia* world.

While I agree with Miss Croce that Lope's capacity "to live an artistic life outside the self" makes his stance essentially nonromantic (Castro's characterization of him as a Romantic of genius is too hasty), I am far from convinced, as will become plain later, by her assimilation of *La Dorotea* to the *trattato d'amore*, her extension of its so-called definitions into a system, the playing down of the lyric element and personal temper of the work, the view of the characters as disembodied and the action as arbitrary. With regard to the interpolated lyrics, Miss Croce's analysis is the most thorough yet made, but its results are disappointing: she finds them conventional and superficial and sees Lope as intentionally refraining from expressing himself in depth. *La Dorotea* for her is exclusively a work of Lope's old age, and she usefully enlarges the context of its *desengaño* by tracing the roots of this sentiment in his later life and noting other artistic reflections.

The repertory of occurrences within Lope's work of the "complex of motives constituting the argument of *La Dorotea*" was significantly enlarged and closely analyzed by Edwin S. Morby in a penetrating study published in 1950 and subsequently supplemented.[22] Morby's concern is with those instances in which one may discover, sometimes only in embryonic form, patterns of plot structure and relationship among the principal characters which suggest experimentation, different combinations of possibilities, varyings of setting and milieu. The instances include three plays, among them the already mentioned *Belardo el furioso* (1588) and *La prueba de los amigos* (The Testing of Friends) (1604)—a version of the Timon of Athens story into which the biographical strain is worked episodically—and a number of marginal and apologetic excurses in longer works. There is striking evidence here of Lope's lifelong involvement with the literary consequences of the experience with Elena Osorio, of the persistence of motifs and details, but little, as Morby notes, of "gradual enrichment, of development from more superficial to more profound treatment." To rediscover such development seems indeed beyond the scope of any critical method, and in following a different path from Morby, who has surely gone as far as possible along his own, I do not presume to have recovered it, though I hope to uncover further evidence of its nature and direction. In confining myself to artistic entities in which the experiential substance has a central place (one of them, *Belardo el furioso*, among those treated by Morby), I hope to be better able to focus on the interaction of substance and form, the give-and-take between the will to expression and the medium in which it operates. For an inquiry of this kind, a group of sonnets, even a single sonnet, is the qualitative equivalent of a play, while an appended episode, however close in plot or configuration of characters, remains formally a fragment.

Without the brilliant and exhaustive elucidation of the text of *La Dorotea* furnished by Morby in his definitive critical edition[23] the present study would not have been carried out. In addition, Morby's introduction and annotation thoughtfully reappraise the principal critical issues already noted and in particular refine the much discussed question of the work's dating. I have set forth elsewhere[24] my view that the character of the work published in 1632 is best accounted for by taking Lope at his word, as did Vossler, and seeing in it the play of a mature outlook upon rediscovered material; as well as my hypothesis that original composition belongs to the period of service with the Duke of Alba (1590–95), while the subsequent stage is to be placed in the 1620's. Morby offers new evidence that Lope may also have been at work on the *acción en prosa* in the intervening years. There is no way of going on to a systematic delimitation of different stages of composition; if there were, further light might be shed on the development of *La Dorotea*. As it is, I am convinced that Lope's revision is a thorough reshaping, a reworking from beginning to end, and it will prove sufficient for my purpose to approach the *acción en prosa* as a mature expression, making allowance where pertinent for possible earlier stages of composition.

This brief survey of significant scholarship devoted to *La Dorotea* may appropriately conclude with the names of José Manuel Blecua and his disciple, Félix Monge. Blecua produced, three years before Morby, the first extensively annotated edition of the work, including with it a comprehensive study.[25] Particularly perceptive are his insights into the author's perspective on the characters and his self-contemplation in them, and his indications concerning the character of the dialogue, its rambling discursiveness and its dialectical tensions. The latter are taken up by Félix Monge in his monographic study,[26] which also pursues usefully the approach of Montesinos and other modern critics to *La Dorotea* in terms of its relation to the *Celestina* tradition and to Lope's *comedia* practice. The analysis brings out distinctions between Fernando and Dorotea in regard to their respective *comedia* counterparts and shows certain parallels between the master-servant "polemics," or prose repartee, of *La Dorotea* and those in verse in the plays. Monge makes useful additions to Spitzer's analysis of individual speech styles. He finds differences more of degree than of kind between the *comedia* and *La Dorotea* in regard to *Literarisierung* and the view of love, a point in which I do not follow him. Nor do I read as readily as he a serious moralizing tendency on Lope's part into the characters' *sententiae*. His monograph, however, contains useful stylistic observations and he justly notes the importance of the pastoral novel as a point of reference for Fernando and Dorotea's literary ideal and its expression.

As I reexamine the area of Lope's production in question in the light of the critical insights of the twentieth century, I shall be keeping in mind certain fundamental qualities of imagination, sensibility, and temperament which are constant conditioning factors of his *poiesis*. Though Lope is able to make the most trivial surface details artistically functional, his creative processes in the long run operate of necessity at a deeper level. It is with the inward extensions of experience that the artist's creative imagination becomes engaged, and when it does so, only its inherent power, its native depth and scope, limits its freedom of action.

Lope perfectly exemplifies an observation of Wallace Stevens about the mind of the poet: "A poet's natural way of thinking is by way of figures, and while this includes figures of speech, it also includes examples, illustrations and parallel cases generally." [27] His is par excellence a nonconceptualizing poetic mind in which image, metaphor, example are constantly being generated, or inseminated by literary suggestion, assuming a paradigmatic value as touchstones for a whole nexus of associations, then entering upon an independent existence and evolving on their own to the limit of their expressive capacity, untrammeled by set correlations with given experiences. Lope is endlessly resourceful in discovering and exploiting the expressive potentialities of poetic ideas. For this reason an effective measure of his creative achievement will be to observe the rise, recurrence, and relative longevity of certain key images and motifs associated with his experience with Elena Osorio, analyzing in the process their evolution and metamorphoses. Some, like the motif of the straying sheep, already mentioned, are fertile in artistic consequences only for a brief span; others, like the ruins motif, are more persistent. After figuring in ballads and sonnets, they can still exfoliate subsequently, or can "go underground," so to speak, and eventually inform or permeate the *acción en prosa* in new ways. Fire imagery, the motif of the moth and the flame, the figure of the labyrinth are among those with which I will be concerned. Even as obvious an association as Elena (Osorio)–Helen of Troy, already made in one of the libelous poems,[28] will be drawn into the orbit of the ruins motif by further expansion (Helen of Troy—the ruins of Troy—any ruins) and acquire new symbolic accretions. We shall even find Lope's imagination lighting upon and exploiting a purely legal fact, not an image at all, the proviso in the sentence of 1588 that "[no] pase por la calle donde viven las dichas mujeres" ("he is [not] to go down the street on which the said women live") and developing it in both ballad and *acción en prosa*.

Lope's creative imagination, as is well known and as I will have occasion to point out more fully later (Chapter IX), was in its element in both lyric and dramatic modes: the *acción en prosa*, its most original vehicle, was to become a fusion of both. One notes some tendency for the poetic figures by which this imagination is guided to move from the lyric to the dramatic mode, from a stasis marked by a particular emotional timbre, by inward orientation of feeling, sometimes by a rhetorical tendency toward amplification of mood, to the activation of figures in terms of situation, event, and a clash of words and wills. Yet the lyric and the dramatic are by no means discrete categories for Lope: his technique in the lyric form of the artistic ballad, for example, will often prove dramatic, while in the *acción en prosa* there often occurs a kind of dramatic overlaying of lyric figures. In this case we find figures moving from the representational to the presentational. I use the latter term, which originated with Susanne K. Langer,[29] to indicate the expansion of an image beyond the verbal level through its integration into the total dramatic situation. The serpent imagery of *Antony and Cleopatra*, for example, after "seeding" the play at the verbal level, becomes presentational when Cleopatra presses adders to her bosom at the end.[30]

As the expression of an individual sensibility, Lope's imagery characteristically tends toward the organic; his vigorous vitalism finds in natural life-processes one of its favorite expressive vehicles. At his most informal and spontaneous, in his private correspondence, he tosses off definitions of love—probably original with him—vividly couched in organic terms: "El amor . . . creze en los enojos, a la traza de algunas yerbas, que, maltratadas en las manos, huelen" ("Love thrives on irritations, like certain herbs that grow fragrant when you crush them in your hands"); "Bien sé que amor es planta que ninguna fuerza humana la ha sacado con rayzes y bien es fuerza que queden muchas" ("I know very well that love is a plant that no human power has ever pulled out by the roots and there must be many left").[31] His typical vitalizing touch constantly imparts vibrancy, a kind of pulsating immediacy, to his style. Abounding vital energy, impatient of channels, also helps to account for a tendency of Lope's sensibility to dovetail or conflate seemingly discrete and unrelated images: ruins and fading flowers, for example. In a portrait of himself by a Florentine artist whom Lope calls Francisco Yaneti, in 1625, Lope can see "las ruinas de los días al declinar la tarde, cuyas primeras flores, *aut morbo, aut etate deflorescunt*" ("the ruins of the days as evening comes on, with their first flowers *withering through infection or age*").[32] This tendency will help to explain certain characteristic shifts of image or situation in texts to be studied. It expresses an avid embracing of life, an impulse to accumulate rather than simply distill sensations. It is true that in the long run one detects in Lope a trend toward increasing purity and refinement of poetic expression, one which will culminate in the exquisite diction and imagery of certain lyrics of *La Dorotea*. This trend, however, contends with a certain impatience and tumultuousness of manner which translates Lope's eager and unrestrained responsiveness to the multifarious stimuli of the world.[33] The sacred and the profane become all one for Lope's "undissociated" sensibility, capable as it is of shuttling between the spheres of the divine and the human with no change of tone or inflection.[34] He lives the life of all the senses with particular keenness, at the sensuous as well as the sensual level. As a poet he is, like Lorca, a professor of the five bodily senses; his sensory alertness extends to the kinesthetic and the organic; at times sensory association can be observed setting his memory processes in motion. Moreover, Lope's responsiveness embraces products of nonverbal art as well as those of nature. His aural and musical sensitivity is keen. His imagination often has a noticeable pictorial and plastic cast. Struck, for example, by Isaiah's organic imagery, he underscores its lesson in chiaroscuro terms: "And the same prophet says that all flesh is grass, for just as the skilled painter, when he wishes some color to set off the figure, sets its opposite against it, like bright against dark . . ." so, he goes on, Isaiah opposes God's mercy to man's misery.[35]

Not only does Lope maintain his vitalizing touch and his keenness of sensory response undiminished down to the end of his life, but the range and power of his creative imagination seem to grow, so that certain of his last works, plays like *El caballero de Olmedo* (*The Knight from Olmedo*), *El castigo sin venganza* (*Justice without Revenge*), *Las bizarrías de Belisa* (Belisa's Mettle), are among his indisputable masterpieces, while his mock-epic, *La Gatomaquia* (The Battle of the Cats) (1634), is as brilliant a display of comic inventiveness as he ever provided. Lope's secret is an unusual capacity for self-renewal. His life is a constant series of fresh starts, somehow consonant with a sense of continuity: new beginnings in love—new marriages, new liaisons that last for years, new broods of children. In art he moves into new spheres—*Rimas sacras* (Sacred Rhymes) after *Rimas humanas* (Human Rhymes), a pastoral novel *a lo divino* after one *a lo humano*—into new narrative modes in prose or verse or new cultural styles, like the Neo-Platonism which he earnestly cultivates in both life and art in his last two decades. He acquires new patrons, takes up new places of residence, changes his status from secular to religious—shedding his old skin but not acquiring a new nature. Belardo becomes Tomé de Burguillos but continues to appear as Belardo. Never content simply to stand pat, to rest on achievement, Lope seems always on the move. After each crisis, a remarkable temperamental resiliency enables him to accommodate to changing circumstances, settle into a new pace and go on living. He is a creature of fresh starts but not of clean breaks. Just as he keeps the children of earlier unions gathered about him as he grows older, so he is propelled by currents out of the past as he moves into the future.

Everything new and different attracts Lope. He even flirts inquisitively with *cultearnismo* despite his fundamental opposition to its esthetic. At the same time, and not without a certain ambivalence, Lope needs the reassurance of the tried and familiar. As a prolific and popular playwright he is extraordinarily dependent on his public. He writes with their reaction in mind, counts on it, and one can see him reaching out for audience response even in the uncongenial medium of narrative fiction.[36] For all his philandering, in his private life he repeatedly settles into a comfortable domesticity; he can tell a common-law wife, Micaela de Luján:

> ... Si tienes, Lucinda, mi deseo,
> hálleme la vejez entre tus brazos
> y pasaremos juntos el Leteo.[37]

> If you share my desire, Lucinda, let old age find me in your arms and we will cross Lethe together.

In short, the familiar and the new make parallel claims on him and Lope characteristically manages to reconcile them and respond to both. If there is ambivalence in his attitude, it acts not as a block but as a stimulus, and as we shall see, is fertile in artistic consequences.

Because Lope is continually impelled to take in and amalgamate in his art the most diverse and heterogeneous materials, because also his life is constantly starting up afresh in new directions, the esthetic principle of variety has a natural appeal for him. His championing of it in the *Arte nuevo de hacer comedias* (*New Art of Writing Plays*) has been justly emphasized by Menéndez Pidal.[38] As a principle of artistic form, we shall find variety touched upon in the prologue to *La Dorotea* and reflected in its formal configuration. When the artistic avatars of the experience with Elena Osorio are considered as a single series, variety appears as variability, a tendency to experiment with the possibilities of the material in different lyric and dramatic conventions and forms. And as an articulated theme, variability becomes increasingly significant during the artistic afterlife of the experience of 1587–88, shading off into inconstancy on the one hand and mutability on the other and developing from a minor to a major strain.

In the next and in subsequent chapters we will discover further factors that affect Lope's reshaping of experience: temperamental traits, tendencies rooted in egotism, impulsiveness, a histrionic streak, a sense of subservience; incentives such as compensation, retaliation, sublimation; a seeming obsessiveness in regard to real or imagined junctures of the events; a confessional urge.[39] Operating on all of these are purely artistic forces—free movements of fantasy, a deeper need of the imagination to explore creative possibilities, a ludic sense, a capacity manifest from the start and at bottom histrionic not only to adopt different personal masks but to "live an artistic life outside the self" by projecting himself into the roles of other participants in the affair. How conscious is the operation of these forces? The question implies another not easily answerable: the degree of deliberateness with which any creative artist acts. We may observe that Lope, like so many artists, is in some degree both possessor and possessed. If, for example, he seeks compensation in art for frustrations experienced in actuality, his *métier* comes to his assistance with expressive resources beyond his immediate need which probably come into play without his full awareness. His creative imagination leads him in directions not originally envisaged. To view the matter in terms of the artist's intention is inadequate; if an idea is truly creative, it will create of its own accord. The compensation in question is effected at more levels than the artist knows; he becomes a collaborator with his medium. Such collaboration seems essential to artistic achievement; when it fails to develop, though the artist's intention remains operative, it will not have become engaged with other creative forces. It is such collaboration that distinguishes the poetic outgrowths of the experience with Elena Osorio, as formally integrated artistic entities, from the more or less random treatments in which Lope experiments with substance, combining and recombining, but not with form. In such sketches developments may indeed arise that provide milestones along the road to the *acción en prosa* of 1632 or hint at the creative substratum in which it is taking shape. As such they deserve to be noted, though experiments of this type, as already observed, are not my central concern. Where collaboration between substance and form has indeed been effected—even if not realized in full, as is the case with certain lyrics and *Belardo el furioso*— some objectification is of necessity involved. In the course of creation the experience has been taken out of the poet's hands, so to speak, and he becomes in some sense an outsider in the face of the result. Creation may begin in involvement but it ends in detachment.

Varying degrees of self-consciousness seem nevertheless to mark the poetic process. Though the intention involved is not all the artist's and though it may be polarized by subliminal factors whose role and complexity will vary with temperament and sensibility, the term "deliberateness" may still be applied, I believe, to an artistic intention which functions in full awareness of itself. In this sense it may be said that Lope does not appear as an artist exerting deliberate control until he writes *La Dorotea*, but that he is an artist conscious of himself, watching himself perform, from the beginning. One may probe for the degree of intention operative in cases where Lope produces memorable poetry; one does not discover the artist fusing self-awareness and intention to achieve the measure of deliberate control possible to him until *La Dorotea*. It follows that the many reworkings of the experience with Elena Osorio comprise variations on a theme, sometimes indeed only outlines for variations; they do not constitute its organic development, though in some one may find seeds that will develop in others. They are an artist's studies, freely produced, samples of an art that takes many directions and finds each satisfying. Lope's conviction that variety in art, as in nature, is a property of beauty carries as a corollary the enjoyment of variation for its own sake as a source of esthetic pleasure. As Vossler saw,[40] Lope is more the *rhetor* than the *vates* as poet, more virtuoso than seer. He is a pathfinder rather than a trailblazer, alert and inquisitive but not irresistibly drawn in a given direction.

The creation of *La Dorotea* is the one exceptional artistic endeavor in Lope's life on which we find him deliberately and persistently engaged, sustained as man and artist by a will to expression that impels him in a given direction and holds him to it. Having originated in a specific context of his emotional life, its raw materials emotions of love and anger, it transmutes these emotions into a comprehensive view of human life, personal yet suprapersonal, in which the interaction of art and experience which was a central truth of Lope's *Erlebnis* is incorporated as a phenomenon and contemplated for its own sake. Lope has no dramatic solution to offer here and the moral evaluation is mostly an afterthought. What he seeks is to express in order to see clearly.

Lope's progress toward *La Dorotea* is an acquisition of esthetic distance. The lucidity of his outlook, the strength of his hold on this artistic microcosm are an indication of how far removed he is in time and spirit from the events of his youth. An unusual capacity for esthetic detachment in the midst of emotional involvement had been a feature of Lope's *poiesis* from the start. Alfonso Reyes aptly comments: "When we are expecting to hear him break out in a *De Profundis* like any snobbish modern sinner, he turns up, practically smiling, describing his own experiences with great good sense and great objectivity, kept on an even keel by that Spanish realism which . . . retains a clear view of down-to-earth things and a keen sense of the ridiculous." [41]

Here and there in his writings there are indications of his awareness of such a capacity for detachment. Although it is viewed in a more circumscribed way in earlier references than in later ones, from the beginning it is evidently fortified by his virtuosity and his impulse to alleviate in art the tensions of actuality. In the early play *Los celos de Rodamonte* (Rodamonte's Jealousy), Belardo, a stand-in for the author, remarks on his ability to resurrect and relive vanished emotions:

> que en un tiempo fui querido,
> fe mantuve y tuve fe,
> olvidóme y olvidé,
> aborrezco, aborrecido.
> Y ansí, con aquella gloria
> digo a veces mi razón;
> que aunque perdí la ocasión,
> no he perdido la memoria. [42]

There was a time when I was loved, when I kept faith and had it; she forgot me and I forgot her; hated, I hate. And so, thinking of that bliss, at times I break into song; it has not gone from my memory just because I have lost the occasion for it.

In another, *Ursón y Valentín*, he vaunts his capacity to maintain a false front between art and life:

> Si lisonjeo la hermosa
> la vendo como el amigo
> y en lo mismo que la digo,
> estoy sintiendo otra cosa . . .
> Si encarezco penas mías
> no me han llegado al vestido;
> si digo que no he dormido,

he dormido quince días . . .
Aquesto y más aprendí
de aquella que yo adoré:
¡buen discípulo quedé!
¡bien puedo matar por mí![43]

If I flatter a beauty, I'm running her down as I do a friend and in the very act of speaking I'm feeling something else . . . If I play up my suffering, it's not even skin-deep; if I say I've not slept, I've slept for two weeks . . . This and more I learned from that woman I adored: I learned the lesson well! Now I can kill on my own!

Later there are signs of a capacity to stand aside and observe in its totality, as if Lope were an outsider, a situation in which he has a vital part. Writing to his patron in the early days of the liaison with Marta de Nevares, he coolly analyzes a spat: "We've had a falling-out over a certain trifle and each of us has been holding out: a silly way of acting familiar enough among lovers, when the cause is no offense either to loyalty or to keeping faith with each other (sounds like drafts for Your Excellency)."[44] The final remark shows him viewing his own life with the same detachment that he brings to the direction of his patron's affairs. An exchange in *La Dorotea* concerning a sonnet of Fernando's which Dorotea has just read to her maid points to the same capacity to divorce poetic expression from its immediate context of truth:

> *Cel.:* . . . ¿Cómo, queriéndole tanto, se quexaua de tu condición?
> *Dor.:* Estaua enojado entonces.
> *Fer.:* ¡Y enojado te alabaua y encarecía! Esse sí que es poeta . . .
>
> (p. 431)

> *Cel.:* Why, if you loved him so much, did he complain of your attitude?   *Dor.:* He was angry then.   *Cel.:* And while angry he praised and exalted you! That's a real poet . . .

Even when it is only himself who is involved, as in 1628 when he is caught by the devaluation of the copper coinage, his reaction is to cast a sardonic eye in his own direction and write himself a sonnet![45]

While these examples are not sufficient to justify an inference of steadily increasing capacity for esthetic detachment, I would still suggest that *poiesis* generated by reactions, fantasies, and moods associated with an experience not fully lived through (and traumatic effects of Lope's experience are discernible long after 1588) is more likely to be redolent of its emotional climate and coloring, to be conditioned by it in some perceptible way, than creation carried out at a greater remove; and that the sense of esthetic fulfillment and release attendant upon such creation will be correspondingly more tentative, less lasting.

In any case, the persistent hold of the artistic material in question on Lope's imagination would appear ascribable in part to an additional factor: to a sense of possibilities not fulfilled, a desire to make the material yield the full artistic harvest which he sensed it held. Though Lope seems to have been content at first to follow the lead of his virtuosity or heed promptings of his emotions, a proneness to self-examination in both the esthetic and the human spheres, a heightened reflectiveness brought by the years, must have gradually opened his eyes to the presence in his *Erlebnis* of expressive possibilities so far missed. Here and there, in the course of his artistic reworkings, as we shall find when we examine them, unrealized possibilities had been cast up, the seeds of which were to remain in his mind—a turn or a tone suggestive of the shaping which a definitive *Dorotea* might receive. Eventually precedents established by artistic treatment of the material would merge with actual recollections, themselves subject to all the vagaries of memory. The stimulus for the final reworking of the *acción en prosa* may have been the rediscovery of an earlier draft in the 1620's after an interval during which Lope had reached the threshold of old age, mellowing as a human being and maturing artistically. Only then could the cycle be brought to completion. "Aristotle holds and so does nature that all things in motion, on reaching their proper place, quiet down and rest," Lope remarks in a private letter of 1626.[46] Spoken in another connection, his words still suggest the final transformation which the substance of his experience of long ago with Elena Osorio was undergoing—the coming realization of the avatar which would bring definitive release from the cycle of creation.

My desire to concentrate on the interaction of substance and form explains the arrangement of the following chapters. I seek first to set forth what can definitely be learned from the record of Lope's affair with Elena and its stormy climax. I then take up in turn, as prolegomena to a study of *La Dorotea*, the other art forms in which the material is elaborated: ballads, sonnets, and *Belardo el furioso*. Because of the long lapse of time between these early works and the publication of the *acción en prosa* I have found it advisable before examining the work to describe in a separate chapter certain developments of the intervening years which, in my view, are important formative influences on *La Dorotea*. One of these is the experience of writing the pastoral narrative *La Arcadia* for his patron, the Duke of Alba; another, the evolution of Lope's ludic sense; a third, the religious crises that began around 1612 and the increasing experience of *soledad* (solitude) of his final years; a fourth, the Neo-Platonic trend growing out of his relationship with his last mistress, Marta de Nevares. The remaining chapters are concerned with aspects of the *acción en prosa*: history and poetry, the character of the action and the psychology of love which it embodies, dramatic and lyric aspects of form, style and literary stylization, *desengaño*. In a concluding chapter I set forth my view of the work's meaning.

While it might have been possible to take particular images and themes as an organizing principle and pursue their evolution from 1588 or earlier to 1632, this would not have permitted me to respect the integrity of each artistic form. I shall attempt to draw thematic threads together as I encounter them, to bring out accretions and permutations of meaning, establishing connections, making comparisons, suggesting analogies, counting on the reader's recollection of earlier stages of the exposition and making frequent use of stylistic analyses of particular poems, sequences, and scenes. In this way I hope to show that *La Dorotea* is not merely the final manifestation but a summation and culmination of the strain I am examining. I may also be able to account for the seemingly anomalous morality of the work, to which nineteenth-century critics objected so strongly.

The desirability of treating literary texts as such and avoiding their use for purposes of documentation is self-evident. I have therefore made the transcript of the hearings of 1587–88, with supporting documents and the texts of the libelous verse itself,[47] more raw revelation than *poiesis*, the basis of the exposition in the next chapter of the original events and of the depiction of the participants in them. Though often examined, these materials have not yet yielded all the revelations they have to make. In addition it seems appropriate to draw on certain of the epistles addressed by Lope at different stages of his life to correspondents of varying degrees of intimacy. Though sometimes destined for publication in the end, they are often in effect informal chronicles of his life, thoughts, activities. The early verse correspondence with Liñán de Riaza, a poetic confrère in Madrid,[48] falls into this category and merits more attention than it has received as a piece of self-revelation. Even more revealing and of cardinal importance as a source of information on what Lope was thinking and feeling over the thirty-year span between 1604 and 1633 are private letters written mainly to the Duke of Sessa, whom he served as secretary, but also addressed to other correspondents and often very intimate in tone. The seven *Soliloquios amorosos de un alma a Dios* (Amorous Soliloquies of a Soul to God), finally, confessional outpourings which reflect, often with anguishing immediacy, the religious crises of the fifth and sixth decades of his life, offer significant evidence of the emotional and spiritual storms which Lope had to weather before he could reach the serenity of outlook that made *La Dorotea* possible. They enable us to see more clearly into the significance of certain themes, situations, and aspects of characterization in the work.

Lope and Elena Osorio
II

When Lope was jailed in December 1587, on a charge of libeling certain actors, he was already attracting attention as a writer. His plays were in demand by acting companies and their producer-directors and he was becoming known as a poet. Asked during his cross-examination about his means of livelihood, he states that "till now he's been employed as secretary by the Marquis de las Navas and now he lives at home with his parents, because the Marquis has gone to Alcántara and he didn't wish to accompany him."[1] As for writing plays, he says "que tratar no trata en ellas, pero que por su entretenimiento las hace como otros muchos caballeros de esta corte" ("that he doesn't write them to make money, but that he does so for his amusement like many other gentlemen of this capital city") (p. 47). Lope classes himself with gentlemen of leisure, disguises the fact that he does indeed write plays for money, and admits only to the respectable position of private secretary to a high-ranking noble. In point of fact, Lope was a native of Madrid of modest background and straitened circumstances. His father, who had died in 1578, had been only a skilled craftsman, a master-embroiderer. Besides early schooling in Madrid, which seems to have included a couple of years (1572–1574?) at the recently opened Jesuit school, where he began the study of Latin authors[2] and possibly had his first contact with the stage in the theatricals which formed part of the Jesuits' educational program, Lope had spent four years at the University of Alcalá. His already marked vocation as a writer and his amorous inclinations made him, by his own admission, an indifferent student, but in these years he surely broadened his literary and humane culture. He may also have attended the University of Salamanca briefly during the year prior to his participation in the naval expedition (1583) of Philip II against the Azores. Though he may have known Elena Osorio before this time, it seems more likely that their liaison began when he returned to Madrid in the autumn. Elena's father, Jerónimo Velázquez, was a producer-director with whom Lope, as a rising playwright, would have come in contact. He states at the hearings (p. 47) that he has known Velázquez more than four years and has supplied him with *comedias* during this period. The transcript of the testimony at the hearings—December 29, 1587, to February 7, 1588—and the related documents, including the libelous verse, may profitably be drawn on for the sequel.

Reading this transcript, we are able to view the climactic stage of Lope's relations with Elena Osorio and her family—the stage most significant for his artistic creation—through the eyes and in the words of witnesses and participants, beginning with Lope himself. We are also able to draw inferences about the character of this relationship. We not only hear events being recalled from a recent past; we hear testimony on actions still unfolding. In this transcript, as in a film script, we may visualize the young Lope in action. Behavior, character, temperament, revealed under stress, stand out in sharp relief. The libelous poems speak with a blunt psychological truth, for all the lurid and disfiguring light which they cast on persons and events. Inartistic abuse poured out to relieve seething feelings and sting adversaries, they constitute the uncensored record of a wrought-up emotional state.[3]

The transcript and the libelous verse shed light not only on Lope in 1587–88 and on Elena and her family, but on secondary figures on both sides of the case, the circumstances and atmosphere surrounding it, the milieu in which it transpired. Of course they do not tell us all we would like to know, and they are sometimes silent or nearly so on matters of substance and in areas rich in artistic consequences. One must tread lightly at such times, although a persistent and especially a markedly unconventional motif offers grounds for assuming some basis in experience, and it may prove illuminating to make such an assumption. The slapping of a lady by her lover in a fit of jealousy, for example, suggests a tempestuous emotional climate in Lope's affair with Elena.[4] Sometimes even a nonrecurrent detail may be so special or peculiar as to suggest an ultimate context of experience. Such will be the case with many of the particulars given by Fernando–Lope regarding vicissitudes of his liaison with Dorotea (Act IV, scene 1, and Act V, scene 3). The origin of such persistent or peculiar details could of course be purely subjective, could be powerful feelings and convictions rather than facts. One assumes this to be the case with the repeated insistence on envy as the cause of the troubles of

Lope-figures, for which it is hard to find substantiation in the record (see below, pp. 59, 112, 151, 210). The question in such cases is one of psychological, not of objective, fact. Knowing that Lope rationalized his troubles by attributing them to envy gives us a significant psychological datum which carries its own truth.

The transcript begins (p. 3) with an undated plea of Lope, presumably from 1595, requesting that he be relieved of serving the two remaining years of his eight years' banishment from Madrid. He has already carried out the two years' exile from Castile, he says, as well as six of the additional eight years from Madrid to which he had been sentenced in 1588. (His arithmetic seems elastic.) The grounds given are, among others, "que el dicho Jerónimo Velázquez le tiene perdonado" ("that the said Jerónimo Velázquez has forgiven him") and "que su culpa fue muy poca" ("that his guilt was very slight"). This is followed (p. 4) by the transcript of Velázquez's appearance on March 18, 1595, requesting the lifting of the sentence "for the sake of God, our Lord, and from his wish to serve Him as a Christian." There follows (p. 6) the testimony of various witnesses brought by Lope's attorney to show that Lope had indeed been carrying out the sentence. Then comes (pp. 12–80) a copy requested by Lope of the entire transcript of the original hearings.

The transcript shows that on December 29, 1587, Jerónimo and his brother Diego Velázquez, the former in the name of his wife, son and daughter as well as his own, the latter in the name of his daughter, lodged a charge against Lope for having insulted and defamed them ("por los injuriar e ynfamar") in libelous verse. He is jailed the next day and all his papers are seized (p. 45). By January 3, incriminating testimony has been received from nine witnesses produced by Jerónimo Velázquez. Lope, declaring, with intentional or unintentional inaccuracy, that he is less than twenty-five years old, has requested and received a guardian (curador) and has been imprisoned. On January 9, Lope is interrogated at length. On January 15, four earlier witnesses ratify their testimony, three of them adding to it, and sentence is pronounced, condemning Lope

> en quatro años de destierro desta corte, y cinco leguas ... y en dos años de destierro del Reino ... y en que de aquí adelante no haga sátiras ni versos contra ninguna persona de los contenidos en los dichos versos e sátiras e romance, ni pase por la calle donde viven las dichas mugeres ...   (p. 60)

> to four years of exile from this capital city and a radius of five leagues ... and to two years of exile from the Kingdom [Castile] ... and to writing no other satires or verse against any of the persons

mentioned in said verse and satires and ballad, nor is he to go down
the street where the said women live . . .

Three weeks later, on February 4, particularly incriminating testimony is
given by three more witnesses, and on February 5, Velázquez and his brother
appear, this time with Elena Osorio, to lodge a complaint about new libelous
acts of Lope against them. Since his imprisonment, they charge, Lope not
only "has composed and said very offensive words against them and defamatory satires and sonnets" (p. 66); he has also forged a compromising
letter signed "Elena" and addressed to him, which is to be forwarded to her
absent husband if Elena does not withdraw the charges, "para que la corte la
cabeza" ("so he will cut off her head") (p. 67). Evidence to support this complaint is adduced in testimony taken the next day from several witnesses, including two women involved. A new sentence is pronounced on February 7,
doubling the period of banishment from Madrid to eight years.

Elena's father, Jerónimo Velázquez, after starting in life as a mason and
contractor, had become connected with the then developing theater, perhaps first as a builder of simple stages and sets on movable carts. He soon
graduated to staging and directing his own productions and acquired his own
company of players. He must also have acted himself: he is often referred
to as "Velázquez the actor." As early as 1570, we find him signing contracts
to stage autos (one-act plays) for Corpus Christi festivities in Segovia; his
career as a much sought-after producer of plays and autos sacramentales in and
around Madrid lasted into the late 1590's. From his marriage to Inés Osorio
two children were born: Elena, who retained her mother's name when she
married (1576) a Cristóbal Calderón, subsequently and perhaps even then a
member of her father's company; and Damián, who already had a degree in
law at the time of the trial and later became an officer of the Crown in the
New World. The latter, together with his parents and sister, is attacked in the
satirical verse. Elena's husband on the other hand is not a plaintiff. He is
alluded to only in passing in the libels and the only reference to him in the
transcript shows him to be absent from Madrid. The other plaintiff, Ana
Velázquez, Elena's cousin (represented by her father Diego Velázquez), was
married to a bookseller, Pedro Martínez. Both Jerónimo and Diego
Velázquez lived in their own houses on the Calle de Lavapiés in one of the
more popular quarters of Madrid. The former, increasingly prosperous,
owned three houses on that street by 1595: "dos juntas, cuyas espaldas dan a
la calle de la Comadre, y una enfrente de éstas, que linda con casas de Pedro
Maldonado, ministril, y con casas de Pedro de Ribera" ("two together, that
go through to Comadre Street, and one opposite these, which adjoins houses

belonging to Pedro Maldonado, an officer of the law, and houses of Pedro de Ribera"), as a mortgage document states (*Proceso*, p. 148). A contemporary map of Madrid locates Diego Velázquez's house at the beginning of Lavapiés Street, two of Jerónimo's a little further on, with one belonging to the heirs of Pedro de Ribera just beyond, and a second one belonging to Diego Velázquez opposite (*Proceso*, pp. 157–158).

The "heirs of Pedro de Ribera" include a certain Juana de Ribera, the single target of Lope's libelous verse outside the Velázquez family. She is identified in the record (p. 67) as a "muger enamorada amiga suya [of Lope]" (lit., "woman in love, and a friend of his").[5] The phrase is redolent of promiscuity, if not prostitution, and it bluntly ignores the pose of respectability maintained in most of the testimony. The record makes plain that this Juana de Ribera was an acquaintance of Elena's as well as a friend of Lope's, and suggests that not quite all is vituperative fabrication on Lope's part when he characterizes Elena, "Doña" Juana, and "Anilla" Velázquez in the ballad called "Sátira" as captain, sergeant, and corporal, respectively, of a team of prostitutes who have besmirched Lavapiés Street. Besides abundant obscenities, there are allusions, not wholly clear, to previous lovers of Elena (including Vicente Espinel and another who chronicled "the virtues of the lady" in ballads). Juana de Ribera's "doña" is explained saracastically and her name "Ribera" is called "un linaje montañés, / tan antiguo que se acuerda / de aquel profeta Moisés" ("a family line from La Montaña, so ancient that it recalls the prophet Moses")—an imputation of Jewish blood.[6]

Lope reserves almost five times as many lines for Ana as for either of the others; she is for some reason a particular object of his anger. (A witness in the trial reports [p. 33] having heard Lope denigrate all the Velázquezes, but "principally . . . the said Ana Velázquez.") One has the impression that he blamed her in some special way for his troubles. In "Sátira" she is accused of taking customers away from her cousin (C. Pérez Pastor, on p. 33 of *Proceso*, notes that the location of their respective grilled windows would have made this possible), evidence of ingratitude, the scurrilous poem goes on, since she owes her expertise to Elena's example. The imputations about her character, past and present, are particularly gross and have the peculiarity of linking her to actors—"the beard of the fool in the interlude," for instance. Behind the abuse, however gratuitous, one senses the rowdy and promiscuous atmosphere in which the acting companies of the day lived and realizes that the inhabitants of Lavapiés Street were at home in it.

This is the poem most constantly brought up during the hearings. Copies of it are produced and six witnesses confirm having seen or heard it. They describe its contents in some detail, three of them quoting bits of it from memory. The circumlocution used in referring to Elena particularly struck these three, all of whom single out the line "hija de la sabia Inés" ("daughter of the wise Agnes"), which they all give as "hija de la santa Inés" ("daughter of Saint Agnes"), probably the original form of the phrase. One of them adds moreover (p. 34) that Lope used to refer to Elena's mother "before the aforementioned satires came out" as "mi madre santa Inés" ("my mother St. Agnes"). The phrase may be a tag from a ballad then current.[7]

Jerónimo Velázquez bases his case against Lope likewise on a macaronic Latin satire since lost. It is produced in court, and its title, "In doctorem Damianum Velázquez" ("Against Dr. Damián Velázquez"), as well as three concluding lines, apparently the promise of a sequel, are read into the record. Five witnesses have seen or heard it but the only fragments actually quoted come from Lope himself (p. 54). It is reported (pp. 17–18) as branding Elena's father and mother, as well as her brother, as go-betweens ("alcagüetes") in her affairs.

Regarding the dates of composition of these poems, of interest for the dating of developments between Lope and Elena, one may infer from what is said in the record that Lope wrote the "Sátira" at the beginning of December 1587. He is quoted by a witness (p. 29) as having called the other poem a "Sátira nueva" (new satire) around the middle of the same month. But a third incriminating poem referred to in the record, a sonnet against Damián Velázquez known to three witnesses though not produced at the hearing, is evidently older than either of the other two libels. Testimony of two witnesses would place its composition around October 15–November 1, 1587. Although it is mentioned in some detail by Jerónimo Velázquez's first witness, the others seem to have forgotten about it, for it is not brought up again until two of them remember it on December 31, their memories apparently jogged by Jerónimo Velázquez, when certifying their original testimony on the day Lope is sentenced. The sonnet in fact ridicules and abuses Elena's brother, stating that his legal competence is as farcical as his father's profession, but that this is of no importance since his sister is supporting her relatives.

Lope thus appears to have been writing defamatory verse against the Velázquez family from mid-October 1587 on; very possibly he began sooner. There is no way of dating three other surviving sonnets, which do not figure specifically in the record. Possibly they belong rather with the "defamatory satires and sonnets" which Jerónimo and Diego Velázquez and Elena Osorio on February 5, 1588, claim (p. 66) Lope has written "since he has been jailed at their request," that is, since December 30. Their contents, as will be seen, lend some credence to this supposition.[8]

First, however, other aspects of the testimony require consideration, principally the matter of Lope's guilt. A reading of the transcript leaves no doubt in this regard. As Pérez Pastor notes (p. 154), the very full and explicit testimony against Lope by Velázquez's first witness, Rodrigo de Sayavedra, an actor in his company, must have been particularly damaging because of the intimate friendship between them. Several witnesses seem only too happy to implicate Lope and add that he is in the habit of writing defamatory verse of this type. They report having heard him speak slanderingly of Jerónimo Velázquez: "he boasts and prides himself and has told this witness that he is going to do all the harm he can to Jerónimo Velázquez and his family," says Rodrigo de Sayavedra (p. 16); on another occasion, Lope is reported defiantly going to a performance by Velázquez, with the remark: "Now is when Velázquez says he doesn't want me attending his performance, but I intend to tell him that, like it or not, by paying my half *real*, I'll get in" (p. 45).

Despite this recklessness in speech and behavior, Lope's tactic, when interrogated, is blandly to deny everything. He and Velázquez are the best of friends, he says; Velázquez opposes him because, since Velázquez has been away, he has stopped supplying him with plays. Velázquez had indeed gone to Seville in mid-1587 with a contract to put on *autos* for Corpus Christi, but Lope could have sent him plays there just as he later sent plays from Valencia to Gaspar de Porras in Madrid during his first years of exile. Asked if he knows Elena, Lope replies "que sí conoce y que la ha hablado en casa de su padre las veces que allí ha entrado en conversación, como otros, y que sabe que es casada y la tiene por mujer muy honrada" ("that he does know her and that he has spoken to her in her father's house those times when he's gotten into conversations there, as others also have, and that he knows she is married and considers her a very honorable woman" (p. 47). Presented with the allegations of witnesses against him, Lope responds by throwing the blame back at his accusers. When asked who he thinks wrote the ballad, Lope "said Castillo [the bailiff who had named Lope as the author] . . . because he was soft on Ana Velázquez, who is mentioned in the satire and is the one most offended in it, and because it is public knowledge that she has been pursued by him, though she is an honorable woman, and this bailiff fled this court after arresting this witness" (p. 50). This does not carry conviction and one wonders whether Lope's marked animosity toward Ana Velázquez stems from a belief that her connection with Castillo enabled the Velázquez family to have him jailed. Resentment against Castillo for arresting him probably explains Lope's deflecting the charge in his direction. Similarly he pins the macaronic Latin satire on a certain licentiate Ordóñez, who had unequivocally stated that Lope was the author. He alleges the very grounds of handwriting and known ill-will that had been used against him, adding with disingenuous scorn: "que por otra parte le parece que quien la escribió no es posible sepa latín ni escribirle, por no tener buena ortografía, ni vírgulas, ni comas, ni diptongos" ("that he moreover considers it impossible that the writer of it could know or write Latin, because it doesn't have good spelling, or commas and such marks, or diphthongs") (p. 52). (These defects would presumably be a copyist's rather than Lope's own.) But Lope is not consistent, for he soon says that "Ordóñez knows how to write such macaronic verse and has done so many times" (p. 53). When pressed for examples, however, he can only reply "many years ago in the Teatinos school this was said, but since these are childhood things, he doesn't remember."

Like many other parts of Lope's testimony, the passage reveals him a ready but not a skilled liar, adept at improvising a quick reply out of what is said to him but unable to avoid entanglement in his own improvisations. He falls with ease and nonchalance into the role of the aggrieved party but fails to sustain this role effectively.

He can be remarkably devious, as when he remembers only those two lines of the satirical ballad in which he is mentioned. He writes them down for his examiner: "conocido por Belardo / como Juan de Leganés" ("known to Belardo as Juan de Leganés") (p. 50). He takes it for granted that everyone will connect the pastoral sobriquet Belardo with himself, but apparently is confident all will conclude he is not the author because the third person is used. On another occasion Lope himself disingenuously takes the lead in bringing up the subject of the satirical verse. A witness, the licentiate Simeón Castaño, reports having called a week before Christmas, 1587, at the house of the "muger enamorada" Juana de Ribera at night, to be told that Lope was upstairs with his friend Melchor de Prado in the company of Juana and one Catalina de Castro. With Lope's acquiescence, "they went up and began to chatter about this and that and among other things the said Lope de Vega asked them: what do you gentlemen think of the new Latin satire that's going about? They say it's very witty and the person who wrote it is very clever" (p. 29). Lope's casual manner seems designed to avert suspicion.

What is lacking in Lope's behavior is steadiness and consistency, evidence of forethought and a planned line of defense. He is all impulse and hasty verbalization, as if he were improvising an unstudied part. At several points during the trial the effect becomes one of outright histrionism. We touch here on a complex area, as modern schools of psychology have shown, with their emphasis on the varieties and gradations of role-playing, deliberate or unconscious, in the daily lives of everyone. In the case of the young Lope something more seems to be involved: one detects a clear tendency to the exaggerated egocentricity and the sort of play-acting characteristic of the personality type known to modern psychology as the hysteric (a term not to be confused with its pathological counterpart).

> The hysteric reacts very briskly . . . to emotional stimuli but in a superficial way and with little staying quality. The hysteric tends to be egocentric; the whole external world is seen only in the light of how it affects him, a clear grasp is maintained of his own rights and the obligations of others towards him, but his own duties are forgotten. In affection the hysteric is possessive . . . The hysteric feels at home in stormy situations. Attendant circumstances are manipulated to enhance effects to their fullest extent and a stagy dramatic quality emerges. The hysteric lacks the capacity to distinguish between the genuine and the assumed. He deceives himself and is easily deceived by others . . . The incapacity for insights, either in himself or others, is at the root of the hysterical personality.[9]

Insofar as the capacity of Lope's particular brand of creative genius to foster an "artistic life outside the self" presupposes a degree of insight, one must modify the last statement in his case. Yet it seems perfectly clear that the dramatic bent of Lope's imagination, which in the last analysis underlies this ability to fashion new situations out of his own circumstances, to enter into the roles of others in his life and create new roles for himself, carries him to a degree of objectivity in art of which he is not capable in life in any consistent way. The spectacle provided by the trial for libel offers a bewildering mixture of self-knowledge and self-delusion, of lucidity and illusion; the poetry deriving from it at times suggests that Lope has been able to objectify his emotions without getting to the bottom of them, or working them through, has indeed found it natural to do so, so accessible is the sphere of artistic expression to the impulses of actuality.

In the analysis of Lope's patterns of behavior and artistic expression, certain distinctions between the dramatic, the theatrical, and the histrionic will prove useful analytical instruments. From the standpoint of the spectator, Vossler reminds us:

> The theatrical sense looks toward staging, exhibition and visual appeal, whereas the dramatic sense finds its outlet in a struggle of wills and in action by the characters . . . A dramatic way of feeling is oriented toward the key moment and, always on the alert, awaits the

critical instant, the decisive event, the thing to come, whereas for the person who feels in a theatrical way every happening is condensed into a visual effect, everything becomes converted into a spectacle for leisurely contemplation.[10]

The theatrically oriented actor or individual will correspondingly be concerned with making a show in awareness of being watched, putting on a display, calculating his effects, while the person or actor with a strong dramatic sense will focus on and express himself through the action, through following out a line of motivation, pitting himself against whatever resists, doing the deed. As for the histrionic sensibility, a faculty which specifically refers to the art of acting, the actor's expressive resources and techniques, his means of projecting emotion and creating given effects, it involves what Francis Fergusson, taking a suggestion from Aristotle, calls "a primitive and direct awareness . . . of things and people 'before predication,'" the kind of non-cognitive apperception which the Moscow Arts Theater has sought to foster in our day, teaching the actor to "make his own inner being 'an instrument capable of playing any tune,'" to "learn to make-believe situations, emotionally charged human relationships, and to respond freely within the imagined situation."[11]

Though, as a practicing playwright, Lope had been in intimate contact with the theater since the early 1580's—with actors, companies, directors, stages, audiences—we have no evidence that he was ever himself an actor. Insofar as the acting profession attracts, as it frequently does, individuals who find compensation on the stage for an inability to assert themselves in life, it is understandable why he should not have been. Though intimacy with the theater world (if the term is applicable to the nascent institution of Lope's day) undoubtedly affected his perspective on the life around him, Lope's spontaneous tendency was to take vigorous hold of life. He had no need to perform on a stage; his role-playing was grafted directly onto living.

In the record of the hearings, it is not always possible to tell to what extent Lope is behaving theatrically, deliberately staging an act for an effect; and to what extent he is carried away by his own performance so that the role is momentarily the reality for him. The uncertainty arises particularly at those points in the record where anger breaks through. The most striking instance is reported by a certain Amaro Benítez, who, on January 3, says that some six or seven days previously at a performance of Italian players, he remarked to Lope that he had been told that Lope was the author of the satirical ballad:

> y el dicho Lope de Vega le respondió a este testigo: ¿a quién le ha oído decir v.m^{d.}? y este testigo le dixo: por ahí lo dicen y helo oído a

tantos, que me lo hacen creer, porque dicen que es vuestro estilo, y a esto el dicho Lope de Vega le respondió a este testigo que votaba a Dios que qualquiera que a este testigo lo hubiese dicho mentía, porque no era él hombre que hacía semejantes cosas, y que se matara a cuchilladas con ellos aunque fuese amigo o enemigo. (p. 42)

And the said Lope de Vega answered this witness: who told you that? And this witness answered: that's what's going around and I've heard it from so many people that I begin to believe it, because they say it's your style. Thereupon the said Lope de Vega answered this witness that he swore to God that anyone who had told this witness such a thing was a liar, because he wasn't the sort of man who would write such things, and that he'd slash it out to the death with anyone who said he was, whether friend or enemy.

The anger displayed here may be partly put on for the benefit of persons overhearing the conversation. Certainly Lope overreacts; his denial is too vehement and above all too violent. The incident occurred on the eve of the judicial proceedings: "All I needed was to have you come and tell me this because a complaint has already been lodged against me with Judge Espinosa, and there's an order to collect evidence against me in the matter" (p. 43). The violence of Lope's reply may therefore be a sign of apprehensiveness.

Certainly a studied unconcern, the sort of bland disclaimer Lope makes when he is actually cross-examined, would have been more effective in allaying suspicion. Yet is there not real indignation here underneath the anger staged to hide the truth? Nowhere is there evidence that Lope considered himself seriously at fault: in 1595, as has been seen, he dismisses his guilt as "very slight" and the *mea culpas* we shall encounter in the ballads have a hollow or conventional ring and tend to minimize his fault. He does not think of himself as the sort of "man who would write such things" even if in this one instance he has happened to do so. He is jealous of his reputation—that is, of an honor dependent on the esteem of others—but his self-esteem is not affected. It is wounded vanity that makes him angry. A letter from Lope to his intimate friend Rodrigo de Sayavedra, produced at the hearings but not further quoted, is described as beginning with the phrase "Because I can't take any longer what is being said about me hereabouts" (p. 54), an indication that Lope indeed felt not guilt but outrage at the imputations on his character.

Such outbursts of anger are reported by at least two other witnesses and in each case they create the same impression of an amalgam of real anger and staged indignation. In one instance (p. 36), Lope first "acted very surprised," then, when shown the Latin poem, "blew up at this witness [Pedro de Moya] and told him he was not the sort of man who would write such satires and that if this witness were anybody else, he'd give him a piece of his mind." In another (p. 57), when accused of having written the sonnet against Damián Velázquez, Lope "se enojó con este testigo [Jusepe Enríquez de Ercilla], y juró con *grandísimas veras*, que a no ser tan su amigo, tomara muy mal que dél sospechara este testigo" ("got mad at this witness and swore *with a great show of truth* that he'd take it very hard being suspected by him were he not such a good friend") (emphasis mine). The same witness reports that Lope, accused of having written the Latin satire, replied "that this satire would be the cause of his doing something very foolish to anyone who came and told him he'd written it" (p. 58).

Thus Lope's response on feeling so many fingers pointing accusingly at him is to hurl back threats in return. He does not stop at minor officers of the law. "I swear to God that some day Judge Espinosa will be sorry he kept me here," he remarks (p. 78) to the constable searching him in his cell. Vague threats of this kind are of course a sign of powerless frustration. But they show that by this time Lope has come to feel himself actually victimized, persecuted by Espinosa out of sheer malevolence. "I can't imagine what this hatred is that Espinosa has conceived against me," he remarks in exasperation (p. 72) after he has been hauled out of his cell on February 5 at eleven o'clock at night and forced to wait outside in a freezing courtyard in his nightclothes. "Just to take some papers away from me, was it necessary to bring me out into the patio to freeze?" (p. 69). And he adds (p. 70) "con enojo y superbia . . . ¿qué me quiere ya el señor alcalde? pues demás de sacarme como a los que sacaron hoy . . ." ("with haughtiness and indignation . . . what does the bailiff want of me now anyway, since, besides dragging me out like those they dragged out today . . ."). The phrase is not finished but Lope is clearly outraged at being treated like some common criminal stripped and exposed to public scorn, and he says so haughtily and heatedly.

How is one to interpret Lope's most dramatic display of recklessness, the crude stratagem involving the compromising letter signed "Elena"? The new charge against Lope is:

> que particularmente ha ordenado y finxido una carta, diciendo que la
> dicha Elena Osorio se la invió, donde la infama y ofende de nuevo
> con palabras falsas de grande injuria y ofensa, siendo la dicha Elena
> muger casada y honrada, y la ha enviado a poder de Juana de Ribera,
> muger enamorada amiga suya, para que ella la publique, amenazán-
> dola que si no le perdona y hace soltar libremente, ha de enviar

a su marido de la dicha Elena Osorio la dicha carta para que la corte
la cabeza, y la dicha Juana de Ribera por su orden la ha mostrado y
dicho que lo perdonen, si no que tiene orden y dineros para envialla
a su marido, el cual si tuviese desto noticia la mataría . . . (p. 66)

that in particular he put together a trumped-up letter, saying that the
said Elena Osorio had sent it to him, in which he defames and offends
her once again with false words very injurious and offensive, when the
fact is that the said Elena is a married and honorable woman, and that
he sent the letter to Juana de Ribera, a loose woman and friend of his,
so that she would broadcast it, threatening Elena in it that if she
doesn't pardon him and have him set free, he will send the said letter
to the said Elena's husband so that he will cut off her head, and the
said Juana de Ribera at his order showed it to her and told her to
have him pardoned, otherwise she has directions and money to send it
to her husband, who, if he heard about this, would kill her . . .

Everything points to the conclusion that the letter is indeed a forgery, as
Elena alleged, for she stood to lose greatly if it could be proved authentic. A
witness subsequently recalls that the letter contained the words "si me viese
libre me casaría con vos" ("if I became free, I would marry you") (p. 74).
Lope's haste to destroy it in the end is decidedly suspect. Exasperation at his
enforced confinement, particularly galling on one of his restless and
energetic temperament, has set his dramatic imagination working on this
new stratagem, just as his anger had exploded in the new libels. Here we see
a new and still inchoate version of events emerging from an obscure zone
between fiction—here literally falsehood—and fact. Lope apparently
genuinely hopes to frighten Elena into pardoning him, to affect in this way
the real course of events. (If her testimony is to be trusted, he has even gone
so far as to provide money for sending the letter on.) Lope is writing a new
role for an antagonist, pushing a nagging situation of conflict in real life to an
imagined breaking point where violence will resolve the issue. Just as with
the already quoted threat of a duel to the death, the dramatic tendency of
Lope's imagination is plainly visible here in the embryonic *drama de honor* it
casts up, placing Cristóbal Calderón in the theatrical role of outraged
husband. While husbands indeed had the legal right to take the lives of
offending wives, such a right was exercised far more in dramatic practice
than in fact.[12]

This is the only point in the entire testimony at which Elena's husband is
even mentioned, though his name comes up in passing in one of the sonnets
that do not figure in the record. He seems highly unqualified for the role of

vengeful husband. He had presented no obstacle during the previous years of the liaison and it is unlikely that Elena feared him as much as she professes to.

The episode of the letter does not end here. The testimony shows (p. 73) that Lope persuaded the same Juana de Ribera whom he had so vilified in the ballad to take the letter home and show it to a friend of hers and Elena's, María de Robles, "muger soltera" ("a single woman"). A scuffle for the possession of the letter ensued; it was snatched away and snatched back, María de Robles fetched Elena Osorio—to no avail, since Juana was being pressed to return the letter by Lope, who by now could see the whole matter backfiring and was urgently sending for her. When she does go to his cell on February 5, Lope is beside himself:

> la pidió a voces que le diese su billete, y esta testigo [Juana de Ribera] le dixo: señor, dejalde que hecho está pedazos, y él le decía que le quemase en su presencia, y como esta testigo le metió en los pechos y le guardaba el dicho Lope de Vega arremetió a esta testigo y por fuerza se le quitó y le tomó. (p. 76)

> he shouted at her [Juana de Ribera] to give his letter back to him and this witness answered: sir, forget about it, it's torn to shreds; and he kept telling her to burn it in his presence, and when this witness put it in her bosom to save it, the said Lope de Vega grabbed this witness and forcibly took it away from her.

These petty details of squabbles and scuffles, besides showing up the character of the milieu which Lope and Elena frequented, bring out sharply the emotional instability and volatile behavior of Lope himself.[13]

It was in order to find this letter that Lope's cell was searched—in the event, fruitlessly, since he had destroyed it. The account furnishes a revealing glimpse of Lope, defenses down, half-naked and shivering, with no stomach for histrionics, blurting out the truth:

> ¿Quiere saber, señor San Juan, lo que es? Yo quise bien a Elena Osorio y le di las comedias que hice a su padre, y ganó con ellas de comer, y por cierta pesadumbre que tuve, todas las que he hecho después de la pesadumbre las he dado a Porras, y por esto me sigue, que si yo le diera mis comedias no se querellara de mí. (p. 70)[14]

> Señor San Juan, do you want me to tell you the real story? I was in love with Elena Osorio and I gave her father the plays I wrote, and he earned his living with them. And as a result of an unpleasant thing that happened to me, all those I've written since I've given to Porras,

and that's why he's after me. If I gave him my plays, he'd have no quarrel with me.

It is not the *whole* truth: Lope does not elaborate on the unpleasant thing but it is hard to see in it anything but the break-up of his liaison with Elena. Velázquez's actor Sayavedra had said on December 29 that "for six months now more or less, he's seen how the said Lope de Vega has been showing hostility toward the said Velázquez and trying to cut into his earnings, depriving him of co-workers and getting them to join other producers" (p. 15). The falling-out can plausibly be placed around the middle of 1587, several months before the first defamatory poems known to us began to circulate.

Lope viewed Velázquez's suit as retaliation for the loss of his plays. If he thought he had also provoked Velázquez into legal action through the libels, he naturally does not say so. He must have felt, to judge by the lack of evidence of any sense of guilt, that such a motive could not in any case be the important one. His entire production attests to his belief that "los yerros por amores / dignos son de perdonar" ("errors occasioned by love deserve to be forgiven").[15] The specific "error" in question here is pointedly pardoned in a passage of Lope's *Las burlas de amor* (Tricks of Love) (dated 1587–95 by Morley and Bruerton) in which Montesinos very plausibly sees an allusion to Lope's own case:

> *Relator:* Este es un mozo que amaba
> una mujer por extremo,
> que su afición le pagaba.
> . . . Después de muchos celos
> le ha escrito muchos libelos.
> *Reina:* ¿Pruébase que se han querido?
> *Rel.:* Y que su nombre ha subido
> otras veces a los cielos.
> *Reina:* Todo es pasión amorosa.
> Quitadle aquesa cadena
> y rasgad su verso y prosa,
> que si hoy dice que no es buena,
> mañana dirá que es diosa.[16]

Reporter: This is a youth who greatly loved a woman who returned his affections . . . After great jealousy, he wrote many libels against her. *Queen:* Is it proven that they were in love? *Reporter:* Yes, and that on other occasions he praised her to the skies. *Queen:* It's simply a passionate love. Take him out of those chains and tear up his verse and prose. If today he says she's not good, tomorrow he'll call her a goddess.

If Lope stopped to review events it could well have appeared to him that Elena's father, after taking no exception to her relationship with him as long as the supply of plays kept up—four years perhaps—was now hypocritically objecting to the satires, when his real objection was to the loss of income.

In any case the arrangement between Lope and Jerónimo Velázquez seems to have been one of mutual convenience. In effect, it made Lope a member of the household, unofficial son-in-law to "mi madre santa Inés," and it assured Jerónimo Velázquez first refusal of his already much sought-after plays. Through the documentation of Pérez Pastor in the *Proceso*, Jerónimo Velázquez appears not only enterprising but socially and financially ambitious. There is nothing in the satires or the transcript to explain why a rival was presumably allowed to supplant Lope or what Elena's feelings were in the matter. As already noted, the "unpleasant thing" had happened around the middle of the year, at which time Jerónimo Velázquez would have been in Seville with his company for the Corpus Christi festivities, Elena and her mother having presumably stayed behind in Madrid as on other occasions. It may be that the decisive step of terminating Elena's relations with Lope was taken at this time, possibly with the connivance of her brother. It was her father, after all, who had the most to lose by antagonizing Lope. Perhaps he was simply presented with a *fait accompli* on his return and persuaded that a particular rival's wealth could make up for the loss of Lope's plays. "La bella Filis" would indeed be "supporting her relatives," as one of Lope's satires alleged.

By the time Velázquez began performances in Madrid again, he and Lope were enemies. One presumes that a rival's wealth had by then made an impact on the father as well as on the rest of the family. Nevertheless, there is no reference to a specific rival in the trial record; in the libels, amidst much abuse, we find only passing references to a "Teuton".[17] Thanks to Pérez Pastor, however, we can identify him as a Perrenot de Granvela, one of two brothers, Francisco and Juan Tomás, nephews of Cardinal Perrenot de Granvela and members of a wealthy and powerful family highly connected at both the Austrian and the Spanish Hapsburg courts: there is some question as to which one. I find convincing Américo Castro's identification of him as Francisco, the elder, although Pérez Pastor had believed him to be Juan Tomás.[18] Both brothers were in Madrid in 1586–87; Francisco, however, was the more prominent. Born about 1558 and some four years Lope's senior (Juan Tomás would have been some four years younger than Lope), he had inherited his father's title in 1571, apparently spent a long period in Naples, and served, some time between 1575 and 1587, as ambassador of Rudolph II of Austria to the Venetian republic. He had come to Spain in the early 1580's, participated, apparently with his brother, in the 1583 Azores expedition, and had been admitted to the aristocratic military order of Alcántara that year. There is documentary evidence of his presence in Madrid in October and November 1586. The testimonials supporting his admission to the Order of Alcántara in 1583, adduced by Américo Castro (Rennert and Castro, pp. 52–56), picture a person of cultivation and sensibility "muy entendido en las letras y música e instrumentos de tañer, en la pintura y las lenguas francesa, italiana, latina, alemana, flamenca y en todos otros ejercicios honrados y virtuosos" ("well versed in letters and music and plucked instruments, in painting and in the French, Italian, Latin, German, and Flemish languages, and in every other honorable and virtuous exercise"). Inheritance of the bulk of the Granvela fortune had made Francisco wealthy; he was evidently a person of refinement as well. A later family historian says of him that he had "an infinite taste for furnishings and was crazy about pictures, with which he was perfectly at home" (Rennert and Castro, p. 54).

Américo Castro points to Fernando's description, in his account of his life (La Dorotea, pp. 301–302), of a "foreign prince" who was Dorotea's lover when he first met her five years before 1587–88, the fictional time of the work. This dangerous competitor is providentially removed from the scene by a mission for the king "befitting his high rank." Castro sees therein a possible allusion to Francisco Perrenot de Granvela's ambassadorial mission to Venice. The foreign prince and Don Bela would thus derive from the same prototype, a case of dispersion of biographical data in poiesis. The hypothesis would make Perrenot de Granvela the predecessor as well as the successor to Lope as lover of Elena Osorio. While Castro's conjecture rests on fiction, not fact, the "foreign prince" in question is not a figure for whom there is any special artistic rationale, there being no necessity to mention him at all. An abundance of sharp and uncommonplace detail makes an inference of more than usual proximity to some reality plausible here, as throughout Fernando's account.

Was the advent of Perrenot de Granvela the "unpleasant thing" that caused Lope to break with Elena and her father, presumably in mid-1587? Or was this rather a definitive rejection of Lope after a period of sharing Elena with his rival? Again, an account in La Dorotea, which relates (p. 410), among other episodes, how Fernando lay beneath Dorotea's grilled window, disguised as a beggar, while waiting for her official lover, Don Bela, to leave the field free, is gratuitously, almost perversely, circumstantial; again one can sense correlation with some truth.[19] Within the fictional frame of *La Dorotea* this period of sharing the lady's favors falls between April and June 1587, just where one would postulate its occurrence in reality. But it comes after a three-month break between the lovers which there is no way of substantiating and ends with Fernando's repudiation of Dorotea rather than vice versa. Given the details that ring true, and allowing for what in an original *Dorotea* could have been a compensatory inversion of roles, one is tempted to see in Lope's virulent defamation of Elena and her family a delayed reaction of outrage at his own baseness—at the humiliation of having acquiesced in a compromising arrangement only to be subsequently dislodged outright. This would be particularly true if, as appears to be the case, he still cared deeply for Elena. It may be anticipated that Fernando does indeed describe a reaction of this kind.[20]

Whatever credence may be placed in these conjectures, the remaining libels which have come to light, three vituperative sonnets, probably to be identified with the new libels launched from Lope's prison cell, permit us to gauge further his responses to the break and perhaps to the initial judgment won against him by Elena and her family. It is striking to find the repudiation of Elena—her real name is used—asserted as a fact in the conclusion of a sonnet[21] directed against her father:

> una niña más blanda que la cera,
> con quien Belardo estuvo malcasado
> y ya la repudió por no ser buena.

> a girl softer than wax with whom Belardo was ill-matched and whom he has now repudiated because she wasn't good.

Here, in embryo, is a rearrangement of events crucial to *La Dorotea*. At this point it seems a spontaneous effect of pique, purely verbal retaliation reflecting perhaps a need to save face, yet also indicative of fantasy given free rein and taking over, unharnessed to any creative idea. Only in 1632 will this revision of events come into full artistic meaning, though there will be signs of it earlier in certain of the lyric poems.

The sonnet against Elena's brother mentioned earlier had concluded with the assertion: "Trabaja la bella Filis para los parientes" ("the lovely Filis supports her relatives"). In both cases Lope ultimately reaches his real preoccupation, Elena; she is the center of his attention in the remaining two of the three sonnets presumably written in prison. In one of these, "Una dama se vende a quien la quiera" ("A lady is selling herself to whoever wants her"),[22] a lady is auctioning herself off with her parents' blessing:

Su padre es quien la vende que, aunque calla,
su madre la sirvió de pregonera.

Her father is the salesman and, though she keeps mum, her mother
was the hawker.

The parents' role is that of procurer, as it allegedly is in the lost Latin satire,
and the lady is their willing accomplice. A variation on such allegations,
which are destined to be fertile in artistic consequences, occurs in the correspondence with Liñán de Riaza, where a rival is also mentioned. The reference there is to venality:

Rondar esquinas, cohechar parientes,
estoy, como Calixto, con la escala,
entre un espadachín y dos valientes.[23]

Prowling around corners, bribing relatives, I am like Calixto and his
ladder, between a braggart and two bullies.

Does Lope perhaps mean by this "bribing of relatives" that he has tried—
unsuccessfully—to regain Elena through the good offices of Ana Velázquez,
who becomes in consequence the particular object of his abuse? One is
struck, in any case, by the invoking of the hero of *La Celestina*, the classic
Spanish literary presentation of procuration and venality. The *amores de Elena*
are perhaps even now beginning to be vaguely associated with this precedent,
as they will be so markedly later on in *La Dorotea*.

I may of course be reading these associations into the material through
hindsight. More noticeable, in any case, in the sonnet "Una dama," is the
lady's collaboration with her family. Neither here nor anywhere in the
satires or the transcript is there evidence that Elena had to be pressured; from
the record at least it is impossible to say that Lope then saw her as victimized.

Equally significant in the sonnet is evidence of literary inclinations on
Elena's part. Bids of money, clothing and dress fabrics are rejected because:

un galán llegó con diez canciones,
cinco sonetos y un gentil cabrito,
y aquéste respondió ser buena paga.

a suitor appeared with ten songs, five sonnets, and a fine little goat
and she told him this would be fair payment.

A weakness for poetry on Elena's part may reasonably be deduced from
these lines, in which J. de Entrambasaguas plausibly sees an allusion to Lope

himself. The "five" and "ten" reduce even art to the level of haggling, however, and poetry to a sort of currency, which in the end proves ineffectual against a friar's thirty doublons. There are germs here of a contest between material and poetic riches, another subsequently fertile motif.

Not to be overlooked is the "fine little goat" that has strayed into this unlikely context, bringing reminiscences of the pastoral, of song contests and the prizes and gifts offered by shepherds from Theocritus on. Nor is this the only place in the record where two such unlikely worlds meet. Two lines quoted from the Latin satire, supplied by Lope himself when asked to write down what he can remember of it (p. 74), read:

> Vidente Ordóñez, amico,
> et cantare pares et respondere parati.

> With friend Ordóñez looking on, ready to match one another in song and in reply.

The second line, lifted from Virgil's seventh eclogue, carries associations of a kind of amoebean song between Lope and his erstwhile school friend, turned witness against him, upon whom Lope now is trying to fix the authorship of the satire. A third line quoted, "qui bonis verbis solet trunkare ropillas," meaning apparently "who is in the habit of exchanging articles of clothing for fine words," though obscure, seems to strike the same literary note as the ending of the sonnet. One wonders if it may not allude to material sacrifices on the lady's part for the benefit of her indigent poet-lover—a motif significant in artistic sequels.

How conscious, one wonders, is the impulse that leads Lope to single out in the Latin satire two lines with a pastoral tinge and another possibly alluding to a literary sort of bond between Elena and himself? The record shows that on numerous other occasions he had recited the ballad in whole or in part from memory. Beneath the puerile attempt to implicate Ordóñez, there must have been deeper associations in the lines he now comes up with, seemingly at random. One is tempted to see evidence here, as in the sonnet, that traces of a pastoral and poetic atmosphere surrounding himself and Elena are surviving in the midst of all the abuse, impervious to it.

This is certainly not the case with the remaining sonnet, one beginning "Angel almacigado" ("You hothouse angel"),[24] which constitutes some sort of highwater mark for ingenuity in slander. With impassioned energy, Lope heaps coarse and picturesque invective on Elena. The twelfth line— "Avaja la bandera quenarbolas" ("Lower the banner you're flying")—gives the reason for such compulsive agitation: he visualizes her gloating in triumph. Before reaching this point, he has, amidst other slurs, called her "espíritu sin carne, picaresco" ("picaresque spirit without flesh"). Perhaps real thinness—lack of flesh on her bones—is caricaturized here.

The most important lines, however, are:

> troyana Elena, querreliquias solas
> heres de lo que fuiste . . .
>
> Trojan Helen, a mere remnant of what you once were . . .

Here, devoid of lyricism, we see the core of the pregnant poetic motif of ruins already alluded to. In this abusive context the traditional connection of Helen with supreme beauty is subjoined to that of Troy with ruins, making Elena a remnant ("reliquias") of her former beauty. For the moment it is spitefulness, not artistic suggestion, that motivates the involution. That such aspersions on Elena's beauty figured among Lope's actual reactions is evident from the blunt remark quoted by a witness: "Solamente le ha oído decir que la dicha Elena Osorio iba a vieja, e que no es tan hermosa como solía" ("He's only heard him say that the said Elena Osorio is showing her years and is not as pretty as she used to be") (p. 57). Purely vindictive at this point, Lope's assertion is the outer shell of what is to become a richly expressive theme in sonnets and *acción en prosa*: the theme of evanescence. In Lope's first epistle to Liñán we will similarly find him telling Filis–Elena to gather her rosebuds, not wait till she hates to look in the mirror, "pues, como dice el sabio: / es la hermosura breve tiranía" ("since, as the wise man says, beauty is a short-lived tyranny").[25]

The glimpses afforded by texts and documents into the lives of those involved with Lope and the milieu from which some of his early work sprang reveal a kind of demimonde on the fringes of conventional society inhabited by theatre people and women of loose lives and frequented by law students, aristocrats, and others, a world in which Lope and Elena seem quite at home. The latter we see only in passing: all injured respectability when she appears in court with angry new charges; hobnobbing with María de Robles and Juana de Ribera; displaying a weakness for receiving verse tributes—this on the persuasive evidence of Lope's sonnet—one for which there will be artistic analogues; given to writing herself, if not verse, at least love-letters. Lope pointedly asks a bailiff sent to confiscate his papers (p. 45) not to examine one bundle "because they were letters of Elena Osorio . . . written to him in her own hand," thereby assuring that he will do so. A penchant of Elena for giving her relation with Lope a literary flavor, not to say projection, is probably reflected here. As for her character, it evidently takes adultery as a matter of course. The only question is how far one can believe the allegations in the libels about the succession of lovers: Entrambasaguas supposes that both Vicente Espinel and Luis de Vargas Manrique, an intimate of Lope's, preceded him in her affections.[26] For a long period, however, the sole extramarital connection must have been with Lope. The depth of his passion may be gauged from the explosion that ended the affair; Elena evidently reciprocated his feelings. Whether she eventually tired of him and for this reason was receptive to Perrenot's riches, whether she really suffered a conflict between love and cupidity, whether she favored the expedient of the two lovers at once, we cannot know.

Nor does one gather from our sources much information about the course of the affair over its four- or five-year span. Elena was probably older than Lope, since in 1583, when he was twenty or twenty-one, she had already been married seven years. Her close relationship to her family despite this marriage is evident. She lives in her father's house, perhaps because her husband is absent, and it is her father who lodges the original complaint. Lope, however, supposes her honor to be in her husband's keeping when he conceives the crude stratagem of the forged letter.

The picture of Lope is clearer, since, as the accused, he is constantly a center of attention. Despite impetuousness and emotional instability, he displays the streak of calculation and showmanship which I have noted. The connecting link is perhaps an extraordinary self-suggestibility, sometimes kept under control, sometimes not, and a ready and vivid imagination. Lope's poses of casual unconcern are repeatedly upset by bursts of anger or surges of vanity, yet there is also a sense of staging about his rages; he is calculating effects even as he lets himself go. The mixture of calculation and improvisation spells histrionism and the tendency to make a spectacle of himself, theatricality. With all this there are the sudden frank avowals, disarmingly direct.

His capacity for dramatic projection of feeling coexists with an over-riding egocentricity which in the long run restricts Lope's perspective. There is a noticeable disparity between his ability even now to "live an artistic life outside the self" and his incapacity for sustained and consistent role-playing in life. Channeled into artistic creation, his imagination can deliver him from emotional turmoil; on the level of behavior and action, its schemes are still-born or counterproductive—the backfiring stratagem of the forged letter, the compounding of folly in the new libels. His egocentric view of his situation shuts out all other perspectives. The inability to realize his guilt is a failure of objectivity as well as of conscience, and the same is true of his conviction that he is being singled out for persecution and mistreatment.

Besides the insight it offers into Lope's individual character, the transcript of the hearings lets us see him in the group of his friends and gather some idea of his relationships with them. Melchor de Prado, about whom little else is known, appears as his most intimate companion. We repeatedly find Lope in his company and his name is linked by one witness with that of Elena's cousin, Ana Velázquez (p. 22). Lope himself says of Rodrigo de Sayavedra (p. 54) that "they treated each other like brothers," and refers to the law student Ordóñez as a schoolmate (p. 53). He evidently expected unconditional loyalty from them all, though only Prado appears to have stood by him. (His lifelong companion Claudio Conde does not figure in the record of the hearings for libel.) From the persistent references to "envy" and "betrayal" encountered later, it is a fair inference, as already noted, that Lope felt Sayavedra and others had conspired to betray him,[27] his ego finding this way of rationalizing his misfortune.

The relationships with poetic confrères are of particular interest. The names of both Liñán and Vargas Manrique, members with Lope of a literary coterie that shared one another's secrets, supported one another's literary efforts, and appreciated the allusions behind the pseudonyms and fictions of one another's verse, figure in the record.[28] Vargas Manrique, who belonged to an important aristocratic family, is reported as having remarked after reading the satirical ballad:

> Este romance es del estilo de quatro o cinco que solos lo podrán hacer: que podrá ser de Liñán y no está aquí, y de Cervantes y no está aquí, pues mío no es, puede ser de Vivar o de Lope de Vega, aunque Lope de Vega no dixera tanto mal de sí si él lo hiciera. (p. 41)

> This ballad is in the style of only four or five who write in this way: it could be Liñán's but he's not in town, or by Cervantes and he isn't in town. It's not mine. It could be by Vivar or by Lope de Vega, although Lope wouldn't say such bad things against himself if he had written it.

Though the style in question is that of vituperation and the friendly relations between Cervantes and Lope were not destined to last, Vargas's reaction to the ballad suggests easy familiarity among members of a group of literati. His remarks could well have given Lope grounds for feeling that even "Lisardo," as Vargas called himself, had joined in the conspiracy against him.

The verse correspondence with Liñán de Riaza ("Riselo") (in *Estudios*, vol. III) seems to reflect moods during the final stages of the affair when Lope chafed at the bit, took refuge in cynicism and in coarseness approaching that of the libels, and professed to be thoroughly sick of it all, to find it hopelessly overblown.

> ¿Piensa Filis que soy tan cojo o manso,
> que he de morir por ella derretido?

> Does Filis think me so halt or meek that I'm going to waste away
> for her sake?

he asks (p. 433). Like Pérez Pastor (*Proceso*, p. 124), Entrambasaguas (*Estudios*, III, 431) places the composition of this correspondence around 1587. Lope's two epistles read, indeed, as if written after the advent of the rival, at a time when he is only half-heartedly attempting to cling to Elena.

> ¡Cuerpo de mi linaje! ¿Soy yo buho?
> A oscuras veo y ciego al medio día,
> al lado del rival paseo y rúo.

> God in heaven—am I blind? I see in the dark and I go blind at noon,
> and walk the streets alongside my rival.

he remarks (p. 458). He begins his first letter to Liñán by asserting that he is ready to terminate the whole thing: he has had enough of "dando mentiras y tomando engaños" ("giving out lies and taking in deceits") (p. 431). He is annoyed at his own conventional obsequiousness and he has no stomach for the role of complaisant cuckold being reserved for him because of his poverty:

> Que, sabido mi poco patrimonio
> y el poquísimo suyo, se me guarda
> para vivir en santo matrimonio.

> (p. 436)

> Since, in view of my scant resources and her scantier ones, I am being
> reserved for holy wedlock.

He is determined to "mudar de amores y de estilo" ("shift loves and style"), to sell "cien sonetos y diez pares de elegías" ("a hundred sonnets and ten pairs of elegies") like cast-off shoes (p. 417), and to take up with scullery maids and washerwomen. He does confess, in the second epistle: "Enfermo estoy, y el alma disimula / un tósigo que tengo apostemado" ("I am ailing and am concealing a festering toxin inside me") (p. 454), but presently he adds:

Mas ya que me cerraron la rotura
del pobre pecho, estimo en un ochavo
que sea me[l]cocha blanda o piedra dura.
Cuanto [cuando?] yo te escribí, ya estaba al cabo;
acabé de morir y a vivir vuelvo;
de Filis un pregón busque el esclavo.

(p. 456)

But since they've closed the wound in my poor breast I don't care a
whit whether it's a sugarplum or a hard stone. When I wrote to you
I was about to expire; I did and now I'm revived. Let a crier locate
Filis's slave.

While these last lines seem to suggest that between the first and second
epistles Lope has turned a critical corner in a process of emancipation, the
earlier ones of the same second epistle give the opposite impression. The disparity clearly indicates warring feelings: beneath Lope's disgruntled tone and
pose of indifference one detects in the end the same emotional turbulence
that explodes in open vituperation in the libels.

This early demonstration of Lope's down-to-earth manner thus reveals not
so much his capacity for esthetic detachment as an unproductive ambivalence
of feeling. It nevertheless presages the tone of some of the so-called *romances
de desamor* (ballads of nonloving), likewise products of frustration and pique,
in one of which Lope will write: "Quien ama prendas bajas / lo más de su
pena finge" ("Anyone loving cheap women puts on most of his suffering").[29]
Once such confining sentiments have been transcended, Lope will be able to
move beyond cynicism to the matter-of-fact perspective of the *figura del
donaire* of his plays and ultimately to the stance of Tomé de Burguillos, the
jocular persona of the last two decades of his life, who will, in effect, be en-
amored of a washerwoman. At this stage the dominant tone is sour, sardonic,
disabused. Lope has not yet acquired the buoyancy and verve of his later
years.

In concluding, one must mention an area significant to the artistic elaboration of the experience on which the materials under discussion are silent: the
second feminine figure, called Marfisa in *La Dorotea*, the hero's former
mistress who remains true and comes to his aid despite his disaffection.
Morby has noted[30] how persistent her role is in different versions of the
affair. Her absence from the historical record is scarcely surprising since there
is no place in it for a rival to the heroine. Attempts to connect her with
known figures in Lope's life, such as his first wife, Isabel de Urbina, are
unconvincing.[31]

Whatever the meaning of the lack of documentary evidence for the existence of a flesh-and-blood prototype of the Marfisa-figure, the significance of a second near-silence on Lope's part seems clearer. The very prominence which makes documentation of Francisco Perrenot de Granvela's life and person possible must explain Lope's noticeable reticence in regard to him, his refraining from direct verbal assault, so far as is known, and the vague obliqueness of the passing references ("rival," "Teuton").[32] The thought of his power and position apparently inhibited Lope and curbed his tongue; his own lack of economic security and social standing must have made him wary of tangling directly with one so highly placed. His circumspection, like the streak of calculation in his histrionics, shows him capable of restraint and self-control when it behooved him to exercise them. It also points to a permanent strain in Lope's nature, namely, an attitude of subservience and humbleness, of timidity in the face of rank and authority. Effects of this attitude are frequently observable in both his correspondence and his art, sometimes appearing as obsequiousness and deviousness, with frequent overtones of insincerity or resentment; sometimes as baseness, productive in turn at times of a counter-movement of indignation; sometimes as a prizing of *humilitas* in style and of Christian humility, as opposed, for example, to a *venganza de honor* (honorable revenge). We find Lope telling the Duke of Sessa:

> Vna diferencia hallo yo, Señor excm., de los grandes a los pequeños: y es que ellos dizen todo lo que sienten sin miedo, y estos otros lo callan porque le tienen; pero, sin duda, canonizan a solas a quien les pareze y tienen la opinión que se les antoja.

> I find one difference between high and low, Sir, and that is that the former say whatever they think without being afraid, while the latter keep it to themselves because they *are* afraid. But no doubt within themselves, they call anyone they want whatever names they choose, and hold the opinions they please about them.

And he observes, also to his master: "La mayor discreción es hazer de los enemigos amigos y humillarse como el caldero al pozo para sacar el agua. La comparación es de San Bernardo" ("The smartest course is to turn enemies into friends and to lower oneself like the pail to the well to draw water. The comparison is St. Bernard's").[33] This strain in Lope's nature has important artistic consequences, often perceptibly affecting characterization, shaping of the action, and other artistic elements in the products of his experience with Elena Osorio.

A final display of recklessness and impetuosity on Lope's part at this stage in his life comes in the episode of his marriage, which emerges as a new intrigue unrelated to the conflict with Jerónimo Velázquez and his family, though apparently simultaneous with it. Some time before his departure for Valencia to begin his exile from Castile, which would have occurred in the fortnight following the judgment against him on February 7, 1588, Lope manages to persuade Isabel de Urbina to elope with him; he seems to have taken up with her when the storm was brewing over the quarrel with Elena. He adopted the course of elopement, suppose Rennert and Castro (p. 61), on the assumption that Isabel's highly placed family would not consent to their marriage, in view of Lope's circumstances. Although a record exists of a charge against Lope for her abduction (*ibid.*, p. 60), it seems to have been subsequently dropped, there being instead a marriage by proxy in Madrid on May 10, 1588, after Isabel had presumably been returned to her family. Not long thereafter, on May 29, Lope gives a remarkable display of inconstancy by forsaking his new wife to embark on the *San Juan*, a galleon of the Spanish Armada, at Lisbon. He may have been fired with patriotic fervor and a spirit of adventure. It seems likely (*ibid.*, p. 522) that he also hoped by this patriotic act to avoid punishment for having violated the terms of his exile and returned unlawfully to Madrid, possibly in connection with his marriage (*ibid.*, p. 60).

By the beginning of the year 1589 he is back in Valencia, where Isabel joins him, and the next year, having fulfilled the two years of exile from Castile, he moves on to Toledo and enters the service of the Duke of Alba as secretary, spending most of his time at the ducal estate of Alba de Tormes. With the remitting of the final years of exile Lope returns to Madrid in 1595.

The Artistic Ballads:
Moorish and Pastoral Masks
III

While Lope and Elena were lovers a stream of artistic ballads flowed from his pen, reflecting with varying degrees of proximity the smooth or stormy course of their relations. The break-up of the affair does not arrest this flow; it goes on unabated throughout much of the period of exile, its tone not even always reflecting the alteration that has occurred. This artistic balladry, along with Lope's production in the sonnet form, is the major channel for the lyric expression of the *amores de Elena* and it is these two lyric media that will occupy us in this chapter and the next.[1]

Along with others of his generation—Góngora, Juan de Salinas, Liñán de Riaza, Gabriel Lasso de la Vega, and so on—Lope found in the ballad a form traditionally conceived as a vehicle of collective experience or of individual experience elaborated in anonymity. They were to treat it with conscious artistry, poetic and rhetorical, cultivate personal tones and manners, and make it a reflection of private experience.[2] Looking back years later, in his account of the poetic contests held in honor of the canonization of San Isidro, patron of Madrid (1622), Lope writes of the ballad:

> Es [composición] envidiada de otras lenguas, por la suavidad, dulzura
> y facilidad que tiene, y porque es capaz de cuantas locuciones y
> figuras puede tener la más heroica y épica; comenzó en España con
> humildad notable: ya describiendo sus historias, ya los pensamientos
> de los amantes; contaba los grandes hechos de la guerra . . . y en
> nuestros días la han levantado tanto los Españoles, que no hay cosa
> más agradable al oído, particularmente en relaciones.[3]

It is a [composition] which other languages envy for its smoothness, sweetness, and ease and because it can accommodate all the locutions and figures of the most heroic, epic type of verse. It started out most humbly in Spain, describing historical subjects or the thoughts of lovers, relating great deeds of war . . . and in our time the Spanish have so elevated it that there is nothing pleasanter to listen to, particularly in stage narratives.

The ballad evidently appeals not only in isolation but as a display piece in dramatic *relaciones*. Lope justifies on patriotic as well as artistic grounds its lack of a classical or Italianate pedigree. Elsewhere he affirms: "Soy tan de veras español que por ser en nuestro idioma natural este género, no me puedo persuadir que no sea digno de toda estimación" ("I am so truly Spanish that, since this form is native to our language, I feel it worthy of nothing but the highest esteem").[4] Lope acknowledges the original "humbleness" of the ballad but affirms a rise in stylistic level in his day, an aptness for "locutions and figures," and even declares it capable of the same artistic refinement and elevation as more venerable poetic forms.[5] In fact, as I shall have occasion to point out, he draws upon the same resources of poetic and rhetorical craftsmanship in elaborating his artistic ballads as in writing the sonnets, odes, elegies, and eclogues whose humanistic pedigree was secure. It is true that a certain defensiveness clings to all of Lope's justifications of ballad-writing as a pursuit for serious poets. His respect for established literary hierarchies and his sensitivity to the opinions of preceptists and arbiters of literary taste cause a lingering ambivalence in his attitude. For ballad-writing never attained prestige with the *cognoscenti*—"los que saben," as Lope called them. As his contemporary, Juan Rengifo, put it in 1596: "The problem is to keep the material such and to handle it in such language that it will arouse, stir, and impress listeners. Failing this, since assonance does not by itself carry the ear along, I don't see what value there can be in the ballad."[6] Luis Carballo similarly observed in 1602: "More than other forms, the ballad requires dressing up, elegance, adornment: to be decked out and enriched with many sayings, figures and conceits, and natural grace. Otherwise anyone can write Condeclaros ballads."[7]

The popularity of the artistic ballads in their heyday—1580–1610—soon led to a superficial faddishness. Ballads had been noticeably scarce in the most elevated form of the pastoral, the novel: there are only two in Jorge de Montemayor's *Diana* (c. 1559); none at all in Cervantes' *Galatea* (1585). Even in his own *Arcadia* (1598) Lope included only a handful and these quite different in character from those inspired by Elena Osorio. Despite the refined artistry of a few of his ballads, Lope evidently took fewer pains with them than with more select Italianate compositions like the sonnets. He never bothered to collect or publish them and sometimes he allowed the ductility of the form to lead him into a run-on improvisatory manner. Yet ballad-writing clearly stimulated Lope's creative powers, and his best ballads are imbued with the overflowing vitalism and the sensory keenness that are peculiarly his own. Along with certain compositions of Góngora, these minor masterpieces constitute the lasting achievement of the artistic balladry of this period.

The "ease" Lope prized in the ballad—fluidity and metrical simplicity— particularly favored the chronicling in them of personal affairs. The main new conventions, the pastoral and the Moorish, threw only a thin veil of disguise over "the thoughts of lovers," reducing the authentic anonymity produced by long collective elaboration to pose and masquerade. The new ballads, insofar as they are truly artistic, are products of individual craftsmanship, pseudonymous but not anonymous. Poetic names are adopted, partly in sport, partly through cliquishness. The poets speak back and forth to one another as well as to ladies presented in Moorish or pastoral guise. Appropriation of one another's names and manners and imitation by epigones often create nearly insoluble problems of attribution. On the other hand, the very notoriety of certain episodes, like that of Lope and Elena, makes certain names and references open secrets even beyond the circles for whom the ballads were intended, while new musical settings facilitate their diffusion and popularity. More elaborate and tuneful than the simple accompaniments of the older ballads, these settings add a further artistic dimension to the new ones and likewise affect their form, since they encourage the division of the traditionally nonstrophic, on-running compositions into four-line stanzas. According to Carballo:

> The main charm of the ballad is in the tune. And this is rounded out and ended every four lines; whence, since it is complete, it is not proper for the sense to remain incomplete, because while the last verse is being repeated or the instrument played or the singer resting, the mind wanders and the thread of what is being said is lost.[8]

The element of play and masquerade noticeable in the ballads reflects the pastimes of an age which finds it increasingly difficult to channel energies into vigorous patterns or activity or the free exploration of ideas and directs them more and more toward pageantry and diversions, often literary in tone. Though by the 1590's the Moorish and pastoral modes have become the property of every aspiring balladeer or lyricist in city or university, at the ducal court of Alba de Tormes they still retain an aristocratic flavor and a note of distinction. Lope contributed to the atmosphere of this provincial "poetic" court by creating pageants in which his titled patrons and the ladies they courted, the latter often of dubious status, idealized their emotions and stylized their loves and intrigues by casting themselves in the role of shepherds and shepherdesses, or of Moors and their ladies. The stimulus provided by this atmosphere helps to account for Lope's continuing to reflect his own experience with Elena in ballads and lyrics. In Madrid he had written for the inner circle of his poetic confrères; his stay in Valencia had coincided with a burst of ballad-writing there reflected in the publication of the first *Flores* (Selections), later to be incorporated in the *Romancero general* of 1600.[9] Now in Alba de Tormes he finds himself in the service of a pleasure-loving duke with literary pretensions. His secretaryship made him keeper of the Duke's secrets and ultimately the chronicler of his amorous adventures in *La Arcadia*, as well as his poet and playwright in residence.

The traditional harmony of the static world of the Renaissance pastoral with its idle suffering shepherds, its Neo-Platonic idealization of sentiment, its archetypal bucolic landscapes where nature responds to the shepherd's moods, its abstraction from temporal and spatial reality, and its probing into the inward projections of feeling, will inevitably be jarred by the impact of Lope's handling of the pastoral. With the Moorish mode, on the other hand, the disparity between convention and temperament is much less.

Literary morophilia had grown out of the jousts, tourneys, and games which in the sixteenth century convert the warlike spirit that prevailed along the Granadine frontier in the fifteenth century into pageantry and pastime. These games link the frontier ballads of the fifteenth and the early sixteenth centuries, in which an epic spirit is still alive, with the *romances moriscos* (Moorish ballads) of the 1580's and 1590's, which have lost it altogether. The sense of sportsmanship, already present in skirmishing along the frontier in the fifteenth century, the assumption of the outlook of the adversary in some of the border ballads are inherited by the Christian cultivators of the Moorish mode in balladry, having been kept alive in the interim by the so-called games of Christians and Moors. These were pageants that reenacted scenes, real or imagined, of the struggle with Islam, making an elaborate display of emblems, costumes and trappings, music and fanfare. They were linked with local traditions and even reflected the internal dynastic struggles within the Granadine kingdom. Still very much alive in Lope's day at both aristocratic and popular levels, they survive even today at the latter.

When the first ballads in the Moorish style appear in the 1570's, they are often descriptions of actual games.[10] Even when the mode becomes predominantly literary, the ballads retain much action and movement and much sense of spectacle. From the more aristocratic games, the literary ballads took, often to the exclusion of all else, a note of gallantry and an element of masquerade, with costumes, emblems, devices, and roles alluding to the participants' hopes or fortunes in love.[11] It was not too long before both pastoral and Moorish conventions lost their appeal. "The springs were not very rich and soon ran dry," notes Montesinos.[12] Mockery and parody begin to appear and in the end the burlesque tone becomes the rule.

In examining Lope's ballad art in the compositions stemming from the experience with Elena, I shall dwell in detail only on the outstanding examples. However, I shall glance also at other compositions illustrative of the tonal range of his balladry or of motifs and artistic ideas destined for reelaboration in La Dorotea, though perhaps only passing suggestions at this stage. The uncertainty of chronology rules out a presentation of the ballads in strict order of composition, and uncertainties of attribution preclude treating Lope's ballad production exhaustively, something in any case beyond my purposes. Though broad chronological inferences will be made and while authorship in some instances is presumed rather than definitive, the difficulties arising in these connections are offset by the fact that Lope at his best is hard to imitate and that simultaneity rather than sequence is the rule with regard to many of the attitudes and responses reflected in the ballads, just as it was in the transcript of the hearings. Lope's changeability and impetuosity, his virtuosity and his penchant for artistic role-playing are the decisive factors, although one can observe certain trends in mood and tone developing over the years up to 1595. One finds in the ballads an array of attitudes ranging from the conventional submissiveness of the pastoral lover to sarcastic repudiation, with the two attitudes sometimes contending; one encounters tones ranging from the lachrymose to the vituperative.

It was the climax of the relationship with Elena that brought out Lope's full powers as a balladeer. Yet his characteristic manner already tempers the conventionality of the ballads that may plausibly be ascribed to the earlier years. In "El lastimado Belardo" ("Injured Belardo"), for example (ed. Montesinos, I, 3), where the shepherd laments "humbly" to "the most beautiful Filis," other feelings are entertained which would be quickly disowned by Arcadian shepherds: jealousy, doubts of her faithfulness. Belardo-Lope may catch himself up apologetically, but only after he has given expression to these feelings. Another ballad which appears to be early, "Por las riberas famosas" ("Along the famous banks") (ed. Montesinos,

I, 5), is a projection of the real extramarital situation between Lope and Elena into an imagined culmination in marriage.

Another sort of wish-fulfillment occurs in a couple of ballads, "De una recia calentura" ("From a high fever") (ed. Montesinos, I, 15) and "Después que acabó Belardo" ("After Belardo finished") (ed. Montesinos, I, 16), which Montesinos characterizes as "imaginaciones de adolescente dolorido" ("fantasies of a suffering adolescent").[13] Belardo is dying from an "amoroso acidente . . . el frío de unos celos" ("accident of love . . . the coldness of jealousy"). As he dictates his will, Filis comes to watch, at first indifferent but finally moved to tears by love she can no longer hide. The reconciled lovers are too overcome for words, but Filis's eyes tell Belardo: "Tuya soy mientras viviere" ("I am yours as long as I live"). These ballads evidently stem from some early lovers' quarrel; nothing about them suggests the atmosphere of the crucial falling-out. A fantasy of dying of love and thus forcing the lady to repent her cruelty is realized in them. The tone is injured and reproachful, tinged with bitterness. The climate is not one of long-suffering compliance with the lady's will, as commonly in pastoral tradition. Belardo's attitude, for all his passivity, is fundamentally self-centered: Filis is the cause of his suffering, but it is Belardo's wounds that are nursed, the spectacle of Belardo wronged and dying that Lope dwells on, the rightness of his cause that finally prevails over Filis's injustice. There is no diminution of self here.

Lope's capacity to project himself artistically into roles at variance with his actual one is seen to advantage in two ballads depicting the departure of Perrenot de Granvela–Almoralife to join a royal naval expedition (corresponding probably to the Azores expedition of 1583) and his return.

> El mayor Almoralife,
> de los buenos de Granada
>
> . . . .
> el sobrino de Zulema
>
> . . . .
> en socorro de su rey,
> se va a la mar desde Baça.[14]

> The principal Almoralife among the good men of Granada . . . the nephew of Zulema . . . in support of his king was going off to sea from Baza.

is a pendant to

> De la armada de su rey,

> a Baça daua la buelta
> el mejor Almoralife,
> sobrino del gran Zulema.[15]

From his king's navy the best Almoralife, nephew of the great Zulema, was returning to Baza.

The mission proper is ignored in the two ballads and the heroic note is overshadowed by the picturesque and sentimental: the Almoralife on departure wears a green burnous and a velvet hood decorated with green lilies,

> por mostrar que allá en la guerra,
> que cubre con esperança,
> los lirios que ya son verdes
> y fueron flores moradas.

to show that when away at war he covers over in hope the lilies now green that had been purple.

The color symbolism signifies that with the lovers' separation love will depend on hope rather than certainty.[16] In the first ballad, the Almoralife draws away from his men as they depart and engages in a prolonged dialogue with Filisalva's portrait (the name is clearly linked with Elena's pastoral name). He deplores his martial duty:

> ¡ Hay pundonor que me lleuas
> a meterme en vna barca
> entre las ondas y el cielo,
> cargado de azero y malla !

Oh honor that leads me to embark in a craft between waves and sky weighted down with steel and mail !

He shows no misgivings about her constancy, however. In the second ballad his confidence is somewhat shaken. He would be happier, he says,

> si de mi alma quitasses
> los recelos que le quedan,
> y algunas facilidades
> que de tus gustos me cuentan.

If you would just relieve my spirit of its lingering misgivings and of certain indulgences of your pleasure which I've been told about.

But the reunion is charged with deep emotion: as in "Después que acabó Belardo," words fail the lovers until the silence is finally broken by Filisalva with banter about misgivings of her own. Despite the ironic touches of the second ballad, the rival is depicted in both with respect and artistic sympathy. He is

> el de más seguro alfange,
> y de más temida lança,
>
> . . . .
>
> gran consejero en la paz,
> fuerte y brauo en la batalla.

> the one with the surest cutlass and the most feared lance . . . a great counselor in peace, strong and doughty in war.

Lope is impressed with his eminence and perhaps restrained as well by the thought that the allusions of the ballad could be easily pierced. His assumption of his rival's role is carried out with a curious mixture of imaginative empathy and subjective projection into the part. The emotion-charged reunion of the lovers seems a new fantasy of wish-fulfillment. In stepping into his rival's role Lope has not entirely relinquished his own.

In these ballads we are clearly face to face with the crucial triangle Lope–Elena–Perrenot de Granvela. If the reference, as seems likely, is to 1583, when Lope is presumably succeeding Perrenot de Granvela rather than vice versa, this situation would explain the serene tone of the ballads, the fact that no jarring emotions distract the poet from his absorption in a particular creative idea.

In the Zaide–Zaida ballad, "Por la calle de su dama" ("Down his lady's street"), the serenity, on the other hand, begins to be jarred.[17] The ballad appears to recreate a moment of the affair to which we will find Lope returning insistently. The experience of being informed by Elena that she was to be his (or exclusively his) no longer clearly cut deep. Zaide–Lope here takes the initiative, asking Zaida "si es mentira lo que dizen / tus criadas y mis pages" ("if what your maids and my pages are saying is untrue"): that she is intending to give him up and marry a newly-arrived Moor. Zaida's "humble" answer is noteworthy in that, while she places the blame on Zaide's verbal indiscretions—to this the libels are usually reduced in the ballads—she makes it clear that she is yielding reluctantly to pressure from her family:

> Alhá save si me pesa,
> y quanto siento en dexarte:

bien saves que te he querido
a pesar de mi linage;
y saves las pesadumbres
que [sic] tenido con mi madre

. . . .

Dizen que quieren casarme.

Allah knows how much it pains me, how much I regret leaving you.
You are well aware that I have loved you despite my family and
you know the disagreements that I've had with my mother . . . They
say they want to marry me.

Though Zaide replies in a tone more of pained reproach than of anger, he
bursts out against his rival, whom he calls "un Moro feo y torpe, / indigno
de un bien tan grande" ("an ugly and stupid Moor, unworthy of so great
a boon"). The unusually specific references to family and maternal pressures
which place Zaida–Elena in the position of victim and thus present her in a
sympathetic light would be exceptional even in pastoral ballads. Possibly
Lope, wrongly or rightly, did see Elena in this light for a time. In any case
the ballad provides the first hint of a perspective on the Elena-figure destined
to be taken up again only in *La Dorotea*.

   With "El tronco de ovas vestido" ("The trunk covered with river-
weeds"), we approach the climactic stage of the affair with Elena.

1 El tronco de ovas vestido
   de un álamo verde y blanco,
   entre espadañas y juncos
   bañaba el agua del Tajo,
2 y las puntas de su altura
   del ardiente sol los rayos,
   y todo el árbol dos vides
   entre racimos y lazos.
3 Al son del agua y las ramas
   hería el céfiro manso
   en las plateadas hojas,
   tronco, punta, vides, árbol.
4 Este con llorosos ojos
   mirando estaba Belardo
   porque fue un tiempo su gloria
   como agora es su cuidado.
5 Vio de dos tórtolas bellas
   tejido un nido en lo alto

      y que con arrullos roncos
      los picos se están besando.
6 Tomó una piedra el pastor
      y esparció en el aire claro
      ramas, tórtolas y nido,
      diciendo alegre y ufano:
         Redondillas.
7 —Dejad la dulce acogida,
      que la que el amor me dio,
      envidia me la quitó
      y envidia os quita la vida.
8 Piérdase vuestra amistad
      pues que se perdió la mía,
      que no ha de haber compañía
      donde está mi soledad.
9 Tan sólo pena me da,
      tórtola, el esposo tuyo,
      que tú presto hallarás cuyo,
      pues Filis le tiene ya.
         Sigue el romance.
10 Esto diciendo el pastor,
      desde el tronco está mirando
      adónde irán a parar
      los amantes desdichados.
11 Y vio que en un verde pino
      otra vez se están besando;
      admiróse y prosiguió,
      olvidado de su llanto:
         Redondillas del fin.
12 —Voluntades que avasallas,
      Amor, con tu fuerza y arte,
      ¿quién habrá que las aparte,
      que apartallas es juntallas?
13 Pues que del nido os eché
      y ya tenéis compañía,
      quiero esperar que algún día
      con Filis me juntaré.[18]

(1) The trunk covered with river-weeds of a green and white
poplar, amidst cattails and rushes, the water of the Tagus was bathing;
(2) and the tips of its crown, the beams of the burning sun; and the
whole tree, two grapevines, amidst clusters and tendrils. (3) To the
accompaniment of the water and the branches, the mild zephyr was

striking on the silvered leaves, trunk, tip, vines, tree. (4) This last, with tearful eyes, Belardo was gazing upon because it was once his glory as it is now his pain. (5) He saw, woven at the top, a nest of two pretty turtledoves and saw them rubbing beaks with throaty cooings. (6) The shepherd took up a stone and dispersed in the bright air branches, turtledoves, and nest, saying gay and proud: (*Redondilla verse.*) (7) "Leave off your sweet welcomes, since the welcome that love gave me I was deprived of by envy, and envy deprives you of life. (8) Let your friendship be severed just as mine was severed and let there be no company where my loneliness is. (9) I only feel sorry, lady-dove, for your sweetheart, for you will soon find someone, since Filis already has." (*The ballad continues.*) (10) Thus speaking, the shepherd is watching from the trunk to see where the unfortunate lovers will land. (11) And he saw them, on a green pine kissing once again; he was amazed and continued, forgetful of his tears: (*Final redondillas.*) (12) "The wills that you subjugate, Love, with your strength and art, who could possibly separate them, since to separate them is to join them? (13) Since I put you out of your nest and you are back together again, I want to hope that one day I will be back with Filis."

The ballad transforms an experienced affective state into an emblematic situation and vividly demonstrates what is most individual in Lope's treatment of the pastoral: the sudden violent act which shatters the pastoral calm, precipitating out in dynamic and dramatic fashion the emotion permeating the ballad. Such flare-ups of violence were not entirely unknown in Spanish pastoral tradition, where the harmonizing power of convention had never been as absolute as in Italy. There was a climactic suicide in Juan del Encina's "Egloga de tres pastores" ("Eclogue of Three Shepherds"), an incursion of savages in Montemayor's *Diana*, while Cervantes' *Galatea* opens with an "onstage" murder. Yet there can hardly be a precedent for what we find in this ballad.[19]

The ballad falls naturally into quatrains, thirteen in number. These in turn are broken into groups by the changes in meter: the *redondillas* of the seventh, eighth, and ninth and of the twelfth and thirteenth quatrains.[20] While the assonating quatrains are not sharply segmented, their distinctness from one another being often lessened by the initial copulative "y," meter makes the *redondillas* inherently self-contained. Moreover, the effect of the metric shifts and of the broken movement of the passages in *redondillas* is unsettling; in this way it is correlated with the restlessness and impulsiveness of Belardo. The effect is not noticed at first, however, since in the first three quatrains Lope is intent on accumulating suggestions of harmony in nature through paired correspondences centering on the poplar tree: the river bathing the base of the trunk, the sun the tip, river-weeds clinging to the base, vines to the tree, the vines two and interwoven. The suggestions culminate in the tremolo of the third quatrain where the sense of the two colors "verde y blanco" is unraveled in a metaphor of musical harmony (*son* suggests an instrumental accompaniment) concluding with an artistic recapitulation.[21] Only now does Lope bring Belardo onto the scene, at first as a passive onlooker, a Virgilian *pastor otiosus*. The pace quickens with the shift in the fifth quatrain from the descriptive imperfect to a preterit suggestive of something impending: "Vio de dos tórtolas bellas . . ." All prior expressions of harmony are subsumed in the paired turtledoves; at this point, however, Belardo's destructive impulse breaks startlingly onto the scene. (Three initial explosives in "Tomó una piedra el pastor" accentuate the irruption.) He vents his feelings in action before they have been articulated; his act transforms the doves' concord into a taunt. Although events are being related, not enacted, the technique of presentation makes for a highly dramatic effect. A noticeable departure from pastoral convention is Belardo's awareness of nature as not only out of key with his feelings but hostile and mocking. In pastoral tradition, the nature to which the solitary lovesick shepherd unburdens himself is one responsive to his plight, attuned to his mood, distressed at his distress. If a contrast does exist between the shepherd's pain and the continued harmonious functioning of the natural order (as for example in Salicio's lament to Galatea in the first eclogue of Garcilaso, ll. 71–84), it produces pathos, not drama.[22] Here the echo of the well-ordered "tronco, punta, vides, árbol" of the third quatrain that comes toward the end of the sixth, "ramas, tórtolas, y nido," is ironical, referring, as it literally does, to a dispersal.

Belardo not only strikes out vengefully but taunts in his turn. In the dramatic rhetoric of the apostrophe that now verbalizes his hostility (quatrains 7 to 9), iteration ("envidia me la quitó / y envidia os quita la vida"; "piérdase . . . / se perdió") and antithesis ("compañía"—"soledad") mark a rhetorical build-up intensified by *redondilla* stanzas which pile up rather than fuse. But Belardo's hostility is now finally spent and drama with it. The rest of the ballad forms a more conventional corollary in which the doves' renewed concord becomes a parable of Belardo's hopes for reconciliation with Filis.[23]

In this ballad the aggressive and retaliatory impulses that produced the libels have been brought under artistic control and given poetic form. But Lope has not shed his egocentricity. Nature's harmony, characteristically depicted with intimate sensory vividness rather than in standard pastoral images and epithets, in the end symbolizes the harmony of a single relationship. The tree "was once his glory as it is now his pain"; the spectacle of the doves is intolerable because "there is to be no company where my solitude is." The extraordinarily possessive character which jealousy assumes in Lope is evident here.[24] The restored harmony of the ending seems limited and fragile, for the reverberations of Belardo's destructiveness are still felt. But the ending coincides with the opening in viewing love in terms of harmony. From the biographical point of view, the ballad leaves little doubt that Perrenot de Granvela is already the possessor of Elena's person. The unanswerable question is whether Lope really still felt at this time that the harmony of his own relationship might be restored.

A similar rechanneling of aggressiveness can be felt in a number of other Lopean ballads, both Moorish and pastoral. "Una estatua de Cupido" ("A statue of Cupid") bears the brunt of Belardo's anger in a ballad opening with these words. The golden statue, removed from the temple where the shepherds had worshiped it, is hung on a branch. Belardo takes out his sling, and the statue is smashed.[25] But it is in Lope's most famous Moorish ballad, "Sale la estrella de Venus" ("The star of Venus comes out"), that his anger finds its most forceful artistic outlet, for here the hostility vents itself not on a nonhuman surrogate—dove or statue—but on a mask for the rival himself. Since the imprimatur of the *Flor* of Andrés de Villalta in which the ballad first appears is dated Valencia, August 2, 1588, its composition possibly belongs somewhere in the twelve months preceding, perhaps in the period immediately following the definitive break with Elena when Lope was also launching the libelous verse. Its popularity is attested by numerous reprints, a whole cycle to which it gave rise, and innumerable references to the ballad for many years following.

> 1   Sale la estrella de Venus
>   al tiempo que el sol se pone
>   y la enemiga del día
>   su negro manto descoge,
> 5   y con ella un fuerte moro,
>   semejante a Rodamonte,
>   sale de Sydonia ayrado,
>   de Xerez la vega corre
>   por do entra Guadalete
> 10 al mar de España y a donde
>   Sancta María del Puerto
>   recibe famoso nombre.

Desesperado camina,
que siendo en linaje noble,
15 le dexa su dama ingrata
porque se suena ques pobre,
y aquella noche se casa
con vn moro feo y torpe
porque es Alcayde en Seuilla
20 del Alcaçar y la Torre;
quexándose tiernamente
de vn agrauio tan inorme,
y a sus palabras la vega
con dulces hecos responde:
25 —Zayda, dize, más ayrada
que el mar que las naues sorbe,
más dura e inexorable
que las entrañas de vn monte,
¿cómo permites, cruel,
30 después de tantos fauores,
que de prendas de mi alma
agena mano se adorne?
¿Es possible que te abraces
a las cortezas de vn roble
35 y dexes el árbol tuyo
desnudo de fruta y flores?
Dexas tu amado Gazul,
dexas tres años de amores,
y das la mano a Albençayde,
40 que aun a penas le conoces.
Dexas vn pobre muy rico
y vn rico muy pobre escoges,
pues las riquezas del cuerpo
a las del alma antepones.
45 Alhá permita, enemiga,
que te aborrezca y le adores,
y que por zelos suspires
y por ausencia lo llores,
y que de noche no duermas
50 ni de día no reposes,
y en la cama le fastidies
y en la mesa le enojes,
y en las fiestas ni en las zambras
no se vista tus colores,
55 ni aun para verlas permita

que a la ventana te assomes;
y menosprecie, las cañas,
para que más te alborote,
el almáyzar que le labres
60 y la manga que le bordes,
y se ponga el de su amiga
con la cifra de su nombre,
a quien le dé los captiuos
quando de la guerra torne;
65 y en batalla de Christianos
de velle muerto te assombres,
y plegue Alhá [*sic*] que suceda,
quando la mano le tomes,
y si le has de aborrecer,
70 que largos años la gozes,
que es la mayor maldición
que pueden darte los hombres.
Con esto llegó a Xerez
a la mitad de la noche;
75 halló el Palacio cubierto
de luminarias y bozes,
y los moros fronterizos
que por todas partes corren,
con sus achas encendidas
80 y con libreas conformes.
Delante del desposado,
en los estribos alçóse,
arrojóle vna lançada,
de parte a parte passóle.
85 Alborotóse la plaça,
desnudó el moro vn estoque,
y por mitad de la gente,
hazia Sidonia boluióse.[26]

(1) The star of Venus comes out at the time the sun sets and the enemy of day spreads out its black mantle, (5) and with it a strong Moor, akin to Rodamonte, leaves Sidonia in anger, rushes over the plain of Jerez, past where Guadalete flows (10) into the sea of Spain and where Saint Mary of the Port receives its famous name. He rides in despair for, though he is of noble lineage, (15) his ungrateful lady is leaving him because it is rumored that he is poor, and that night she is marrying an ugly and stupid Moor because he is the warden in Seville (20) of the Alcázar and the Tower. He tenderly

bemoans so great an injustice and the plain with soft echoes answers his words. (25) "Zaida," he says, "angrier than the sea that swallows up ships, harder and more unyielding than the bowels of a mountain, how can you, cruel woman, (30) after so many favors, allow someone else's hand to flaunt my soul's belongings? Is it conceivable that you should clasp the bark of an oak (35) and leave your own tree barren of fruit and flowers? You give up your beloved Gazul, you give up three years of love, and give your hand to Albenzaide, (40) though you scarcely know him. You give up a very rich pauper and choose a very poor rich man, all because you put the riches of the body ahead of those of the soul. (45) May Allah grant, enemy of mine, that he shall hate you and you adore him, that you shall sigh with jealousy and weep over his absence, not sleep at night (50) nor rest by day, that you shall bore him in bed and annoy him at table, that at fiestas or celebrations, he shall not wear your colors (55) nor, just to have a glimpse of them, allow you to appear at the window; and in the reed-spear games, to make you more upset, may he scorn the gauze veil that you sew for him (60) and the bag you embroider for him, and put on his mistress's instead, with the monogram of her name, and give her his captives when he returns from war; (65) and in battle with the Christians, may you be overcome to find him dead. And may it happen when you take his hand, if you are going to hate him, (70) that you enjoy long years with him, which is the greatest curse that men can give you." On this, he reached Jerez in the middle of the night. (75) He found the palace filled with torches and voices and the Moors of the frontier rushing about everywhere with their lighted flares (80) and livery to match. Before the bridegroom he stood up in his stirrups; he thrust his lance at him and pierced him through and through. (85) The town was thrown into an uproar, the Moor bared a rapier and through the throng made his way back toward Sidonia.

One's awareness of quatrains in the structure of this ballad is all but annulled by an effect of onrushing motion which makes even the larger divisions unimportant. A build-up begins in the first quatrain toward a climax (the rival's murder) reserved for almost the last moment, over eighty lines later. The long rhetorical *imprecatio* which comes in the middle and occupies over half the ballad does not slow up the pace. Since the setting, sketched in at the outset, presently functions as interlocutor, Gazul's tirade grows naturally out of the opening and is equally naturally fused with the sequel. The rapid, energetic effect of the dactylic octosyllable with its decisive initial downbeat is felt in over a third of the lines, beginning with the opening one.[27] Even the cosmological references of the first quatrain are expressive portents. That Venus's star presides over Gazul's departure proves no chance. The periphrastic "black mantle of day's enemy" is commonplace enough, but it becomes in this case more than a conventional artifice, since it gives hostility at the start the broadest scope; the rest of the ballad will narrow the focus and finally concentrate it on a single target.[28]

Gazul rides forth under cloak of night. The phrase "con ella" (l. 5) links the night's hostility to the dark mission. His anger is compounded with despair (l. 13). The reasons are rapidly enumerated (ll. 14–20): noble but poor, Gazul is being cast aside by Zaida in favor of an "ugly and stupid" but highly placed and influential rival. He pities himself audibly and nature commiserates: the plain, involving itself in his plight, replies "with soft echoes" (l. 24). The rhetoric of Gazul's reproachful apostrophe to Zaida is loose-knit and haphazard, symmetry and complexity being subordinated to dynamism and momentum.[29]

The long tirade carries Gazul right into Jerez, the line "Con esto llegó a Xerez" turning discourse into narrative. By the end of the apostrophe his hostility has begun to focus upon the thought of his rival's death, but only as a vague hope that he be killed in battle, one of several calamities wished on him. The subsequent murder is evidently unpremeditated; Gazul's entire behavior is impulsive and improvised, like his creator's. He is certain only of the compelling emotions that drive toward discharge in the wild cavalcade, uncertain how the release is to occur. But he is not a simple stand-in for his creator. The effect of control noticeable at times behind Lope's histrionism and scheming in the transcript of the hearings here becomes esthetic control channeled into creation. Lope has detached himself from his impulsive emotions long enough to become their observer, to redirect and reshape them. Gazul does not know why he is riding forth; Lope does. He provides the reader or listener from the beginning with clear signs of the impending catastrophe, though he leaves Gazul oblivious of them. He also magnifies his abiding preoccupation with self by projecting it into a sentient nature which acts as a sounding-board for the protagonist's distress, filling the whole night with its repercussions.

The particular fiction of this ballad may have been suggested to Lope by a characteristic feature of the games of Christians and Moors. In a common form of the games a wooden "castle" was erected and after a messenger rode up with a challenge, either the Christian occupants successfully repelled attack, or, if the defenders were Moors, the castle was taken. The messenger's appearance constituted the *estafeta* (embassy) and included a *desplante*, or arrogant challenge. María Soledad Carrasco thus describes the *estafeta*:

"This consists of a rapid dash and a challenge by the horseman bearing the summons, whose arrogant and spirited manner must make up for the verbal boasting which is a characteristic note of the 'embassy.' The messenger hands over a folded paper which the leader of the opposing side makes a great show of tearing up."[30]

Lope had undoubtedly witnessed such games.[31] He has taken over in the dynamism of Gazul's ride the swift dramatic action of the messenger's embassy, and in his tirade, the messenger's arrogant boasting. (There is perhaps a transcription of real acoustic and kinesthetic impressions, a pounding crescendo of approaching hoofs, in the strong dactylic rhythms, the swift succession of end-stopped lines connected by "y" and the other iterative devices of the harangue.) Gazul flings at the echoing plain claims of superiority over his rival in everything except wealth. He clearly reflects the histrionic and theatrical proclivities of his creator, delivering his harangue to the plain as to an empty theater and nourishing his rage on his rhetoric. The frenzy that culminates in violence is not only a result of the headlong pace and staccato rhythms of the ride; it is also self-induced. When he finally reaches the palace of Albenzaide, Lope passes over the traditional presentation of the written challenge at the castle gates. Gazul dispenses with words and without even dismounting does the deed on the spot. This sudden snapping of tension once more draws out of the narrative all the drama of which it is capable. With only one more quatrain the ballad is terminated. The ending has an abrupt dramatic finality quite distinct from the truncated type of suspension that sometimes marks the close of traditional ballads.[32]

In a pair of ballads inspired by the provision in the judgment—"He is [not] to go down the street on which the said women live"—anger is almost completely put aside. Lope is already guided by the spirit of play which is to figure so largely later on, and notably in *La Dorotea*.

1   Mira, Çayde, que te digo
     que no passes por mi calle,
     no hables con mis mugeres
     ni con mis cautiuos trates,
5   no preguntes en qué entiendo
     ni quién viene a visitarme,
     qué fiestas me dan contento
     ni qué colores me aplazen.
     Basta que son por tu causa
10   las que en el rostro me salen,
     corrida de auer mirado
     moro que tan poco sabe.

Confieso que eres valiente,
que hiendes, rajas y partes,
15   y que as muerto más christianos
que tienes gotas de sangre,
que eres gallardo ginete,
que danças, cantas y tañes,
gentilhombre, bien criado
20   quanto puede imaginarse;
blanco, rubio, por estremo,
señalado entre linajes,
el gallo de los brabatos,
la nata de los donayres;
25   que pierdo mucho en perderte,
y gano mucho en ganarte,
y que si nacieras mudo,
fuera possible adorarte.
Mas por esse inconviniente
30   determino de dexarte:
que eres pródigo de lengua
y amargan tus liuiandades.
Aurá menester ponerte,
la que quisiere llevarte,
35   vn alcaçar en los pechos
y en los labios vn alcayde.
Mucho pueden con las damas
los galanes de tus partes
porque los quieren briosos,
40   que hiendan y que desgarren;
mas con esto, Çayde amigo,
si algún banquete les hazen,
del plato de sus favores,
quieren que coman y callen.
45   Costoso me fue el que heziste;
¡qué dichoso fueras, Çayde,
si conservarme supieras
como supiste obligarme!
Mas no bien saliste apenas
50   de los jardines de Atarfe,
quando heziste de la mía
y de tu desdicha alarde.
A vn morillo mal nacido
e sabido que enseñaste
55   la [trenza] 33 de mis cabellos

que te puse en el turbante.
No quiero que me la buelvas,
ni que tampoco la guardes,
mas quiero que entiendas, moro,
60   que en mi desgracia la traes.
También me certificaron
cómo le desafiaste
por las verdades que dixo,
que nunca fueran verdades.
65   De mala gana me río,
¡qué donoso disparate!
No guardaste tu secreto
y quieres que otro lo guarde.
No puedo admitir disculpa,
70   otra vez torno avisarte [*sic*]
que ésta será la postrera
que te hable y que me hables.—
Dixo la discreta Çayda
al gallardo Abencerraje,
75   y al despedirse replica:
Quien tal haze que tal pague.

(1) "Look here, Zaide, I'm telling you that you are not to go down my street, nor talk with my women, nor have dealings with my captives; (5) don't inquire what I am up to nor who comes to visit me, what festivities I enjoy nor what colors give me pleasure. It is enough that you are the cause (10) of the color that flushes my cheeks from anger at having set eyes on a Moor who is so unknowing. I confess that you are valiant, that you can slit, slash, and split, (15) that you have slain more Christians than you have drops of blood, that you are a dashing horseman, that you dance, sing and play, a gentleman as well-bred (20) as one could ask, fair, blond in the extreme, distinguished among the noble lines, top swaggerer among the boasters, pick of the wits; (25) that I lose a great deal in losing you and win a great deal in winning you, and that if you had been born dumb, it would be possible to adore you. But on account of this drawback, (30) I am determined to leave you: that you have a wagging tongue and your carelessness is embittering. The woman who wants to put up with you will have to place (35) a fortress on your chest and a warden on your lips. Gallants with your assets can go far with the ladies because they like them spirited, (40) able to slash and rip. But, along with this, friend Zaide, if they offer you some banquet, they want you to eat from the plate of their favors

and keep still. (45) The one you gave me was costly. How happy
you would be, Zaide, if you had known how to hold me as well as
you knew how to put me in your debt! But you had scarcely
emerged (50) from Atarfe's gardens when you boasted of my
misfortune and yours. To an ill-born little Moor I have learned that
you showed (55) the [braid] of my hair that I placed on your turban.
I don't want you to return it, nor keep it, but I want you to realize,
Moor, (60) that you are wearing it to my sorrow. It has also been
relayed to me how you challenged him on account of the truths he
spoke—if only they weren't truths! (65) In spite of myself I must
laugh: what a delightful absurdity! You didn't keep your secret and
you want someone else to. I can admit no excuse, (70) once again I
inform you that this will be the last time I speak to you and you to
me." So said the wise Zaida to the gallant Abencerraje, (75) and on
taking leave she taunts: "People must pay for what they do."

 1   Di, Çayda, ¿de qué me avisas?
     ¿Quieres que muera y que calle?
     No des crédito a mugeres
     no [fundadas] [34] en verdades,
 5   que si pregunto en qué entiendes
     o quién viene a visitarte,
     son fiestas de mi tormento
     ver qué visitas te aplazen.
     Si dizes que estás corrida
10   de que Çayde poco sabe,
     no sé poco, pues que supe
     conocerte y adorarte.
     Si dizes son por mi causa
     las que en el rostro te salen,
15   por la tuya con mis ojos
     tengo regada tu calle.
     Confiessas que soy valiente,
     que tengo otras muchas partes;
     pocas tengo, pues no puedo
20   de vna mentira vengarme;
     mas si a querido mi suerte
     que ya el querer te canse,
     no pongas inconvinientes
     mas de que quieres dexarme.
25   No entendí que eras muger
     a quien novedad aplaze,
     mas son tales mis desdichas

que en mí lo impossible hazen;
anme puesto en tal estremo
30 que el bien tengo por vltrage:
alábasme para hazerme
la nata de los pesares.
Yo soy quien pierdo en perderte
y gano mucho en ganarte
35 y aunque hablas en mi ofensa,
no dexaré de adorarte.
Dizes que si fuera mudo,
fuera [possible] 35 adorarme;
si en tu daño no lo e sido,
40 enmudezca el desculparme.
Si te a ofendido mi vida,
[¿quieres], 36 señora, matarme?
Basta dezir que [hablo mucho] 37
para que el pesar me acabe.
45 Es mi pecho caloboço
de tormentos immortales,
mi boca la del silencio,
que no ha menester alcayde.
Que el hazer plato y banquete
50 es de hombres principales,
mas dalles de sus fauores,
sólo pertenece a infames.
Çayda cruel, que dixiste
que no supe conseruarte,
55 mejor te supe obligar
que tú as sabido pagarme.
Mienten los moros y moras
y miente el infame Tarfe
que si yo le amenazara,
60 bastara para matalle.
A ese perro malnacido
a quien yo mostré el turbante,
no fío yo [de] 38 secretos,
que en baxos pechos no caben.
65 Yo le e de quitar la vida
y he de escrivir con su sangre
lo que Çayda replicó:
Quien tal hizo que tal pague.39

(1) Say, Zaida, what are you informing me of? Do you wish me to

die and keep still? Don't believe women so free and easy with the truth: (5) if I ask what you are up to or who comes to visit you, it's a celebration of torture for me to see what visitors give you pleasure. When you say that you are angry (10) that Zaide is so unknowing, I know no small amount since I knew enough to meet and love you. When you say that I am the cause of the color that flushes your cheeks, (15) it is on your account that I have soaked your street with tears. You admit that I am valiant, that I have many other assets; I have few, since I can't (20) take revenge for a lie. But if my luck wills that you have tired of loving, don't invent any pretexts beyond wanting to leave me. (25) I didn't realize you were a woman fond of novelties, but my misfortunes are such that they work the impossible in me. They have reduced me to such straits (30) that I consider a blessing an insult: you praise me and call me the pick of nuisances. It is I who lose in losing you and win a great deal in winning you (35) and though you speak offensively about me, I will not cease to adore you. You say that if I were mute, it would be [possible] to adore me. If I have not been so about what might discredit you, (40) may I utter no further word of excuse. If my life has been offensive to you, [would you like] to kill me, madam? It is enough to say [I talk too much] for grief to put an end to me. (45) My breast is a cell of endless tortures, my mouth is that of silence, with no need for a warden. Giving meals and banquets (50) is something for outstanding men, but to make a dish of favors received belongs only to the infamous. Cruel Zaida, who said that I didn't know how to keep you, (55) I was better able to put you in my debt than you to pay me. The Moors, men and women, are liars, that infamous Tarfe is a liar; if I were to threaten him, (60) it would suffice to kill him. That ill-born cur that I showed the turban to I entrusted with no secrets: they have no place in base hearts. (65) I'm going to take his life and I'm going to write with his blood what Zaida taunted: "People must pay for what they have done."

In no mood to take the matter to heart, yet not feeling disgruntled as, for example, in the correspondence with Liñán, Lope follows his theatrical instinct and here writes new parts for Elena and himself. Wholly in the second person, except for a brief expository prop in the last quatrain of the first ballad, the poems are a confrontation of opposing viewpoints, accusation and defense; though not actually interlocutory, they have the colloquial ring of Lope's most naturalistic stage dialogue. One has no difficulty supplying the histrionic complementation: mimicry and pantomime, laughter, raised voices, shifting intonations. In the first ballad, "Mira, Çayde, que te digo /

que no passes por mi calle" ("Look here, Zaide, I'm telling you that you are not to go down my street"), Elena–Zaida is allowed her say without interference. In "Di, Çayda, ¿de qué me avisas?" ("Say, Zaida, what are you informing me of?"), Lope-Zaide replies and defends himself against her charges. Though Lope's detachment goes far, its limits are visible in a persistent undertone of mockery. We meet here, also, for the first time, the judicial atmosphere which memories of the hearings sometimes inject into the artistic treatments (although the irreverent tone suggests nothing so much as the trial of the Knave of Hearts). Courtroom procedure and features of forensic rhetoric are engagingly parodied. Zaida tries to appear stern as she reels off her complaints but she is amused in spite of herself (ll. 65–68). She begins with interdictions (ll. 1–12), makes many concessions (ll. 13–28), then comes to the charge, again reduced simply to indiscretions ("eres pródigo de lengua / y amargan tus liuiandades") following on acknowledged intimacies (ll. 29–36). An account of the offense emerges, with much "editorializing" (ll. 37–72): his boasting of the rendezvous, for example, and, to make matters worse, his challenging the bearer of the story. No appeal is to be allowed.[40]

Zaide's reply skims over the list of charges, at times stopping to refute them and exonerate himself. In each of the opening quatrains (ll. 1–16) he echoes an accusation and replies. He then refers to Zaida's concessions and dismisses them as screens for her decision to leave him (ll. 17–32). He protests his enduring love (ll. 33–36) and vigorously defends himself against the charge of verbal indiscretions (ll. 37–40). His tone grows more reproachful (ll. 49–56) and the ballad concludes with angry abusive denials (ll. 57–68).

In these ballads the forensic *relatio criminis* (ll. 37–68) of "Mira, Çayde," trivial to begin with, is interspersed with further trivia; the *concessio* (ll. 13–28) is so full a catalogue that it nearly undermines Zaida's case. Zaide's attractiveness and attainments are underscored by Lope and the Moorish disguise is even playfully lifted for a moment in l. 21: "blanco, rubio por estremo." But at the end of "Di, Çayda," when we reach the *remotio*, the shifting of the burden of guilt (ll. 57–60), with a suggestion of *purgatio* (admission but justification, ll. 61–64), anger suddenly breaks through. Like Gazul, Zaide has worked himself into a rage and the emphatic "mienten" and "miente," the abuse of the alleged culprit, Tarfe—"infame," "malnacido"—dispel playfulness amid a gathering storm of threats. A limit to esthetic detachment has been reached, though Lope's own histrionic tendencies make it hard to define exactly. One recalls the angry denials and threats in the transcript of the hearings. Perhaps still inflammable emotions were beginning to blaze again as Lope wrote. Or one might say that Zaide is staging an act as his creator had, except that Zaide–Lope's capacity for self-suggestion soon blurs the line between staged and authentic feeling. In any case, while we see self-awareness and detect self-observation behind Lope's depiction of Zaide, we do not find any creative deliberateness. Art is content to play around the edges of experience here despite the esthetic coherence which analysis is able to uncover.

The play-spirit and ironic undertone evident in these ballads are present also in "Contemplando estaba Filis" ("Filis was contemplating") but experience has been sifted much finer and the poem no longer stands so close to reality.

> 1 Contemplando estaba Filis
>   a la media noche sola
>   una vela a cuya lumbre
>   labrando estaba una cofia,
> 5 porque andaba en torno della
>   una blanca mariposa,
>   quemándose los extremos
>   y cerca de arderse toda.
>   Suspendióse, imaginando
> 10 el avecilla animosa,
>   tomóla en sus blancas manos
>   y así le dice, envidiosa:
>   —¿Adónde tienes los ojos
>   que desta luz te enamoras,
> 15 la boca con que la besas
>   y el gusto con que la gozas?
>   ¿Adónde tienes tu ingenio
>   y dónde está la memoria?
>   ¿Con qué lengua la requiebras?
> 20 ¿Con qué despojos la adornas?
>   ¿Qué le dices cuando llegas,
>   cuando en su fe presurosa
>   le dejas alguna prenda
>   de la afición que [la] adoras?
> 25 Y sin haberte ido vienes
>   y después a volar tornas
>   hasta el punto que tu vida
>   entre las llamas despojas.
>   Viendo que no será justo
> 30 dilatar su muerte y gloria,
>   en diciendo estas razones,

llegóse al fuego y quemóla.
—Dichosa fuiste, avecilla,
—Filis prosigue—pues gozas
35 en los brazos de tu amigo
vida y muerte gloriosa;
que la vida sin contento
mucha falta y poca sobra
y sólo el sosiego es bueno
40 adonde el alma reposa.
Mas ¿cómo yo con tu ejemplo
no me doy la muerte ahora?
Morir quiero, pues me anima,
y acabar con tantas cosas.
45 He sabido que Belardo
su vida pasa con otra,
porque le enojan mis celos
y mis desdichas le enojan.—
Del paño de su labor
50 un corto cuchillo toma
y dijo toda turbada:
—Oh Belardo, aquí fue Troya.—
Pero primero que fuese
puesto el intento por obra,
55 quiso probar el dolor,
que es mujer y temerosa.
Con la aguja que labraba
picóse el dedo y turbóla,
de su muy querida sangre
60 el ver salir una gota.
Pide un paño a la criada,
intento y cuchillo arroja;
lloró su sangre perdida,
que su amante no la llora.[41]

(1) Alone at midnight, Filis was contemplating a candle by whose light she was embroidering a coif, (5) for wheeling about it was a white moth, singeing its wing-tips and close to burning itself completely up. She paused, her mind on (10) the spirited little creature, took it in her white hands, and envious, speaks thus to it: "What has happened to your eyes that you should be falling for this light, (15) the mouth you kiss it with, the pleasure you take in it? What has happened to your wits and where is your memory? What tongue do you court it with? (20) What offerings do you adorn it

with? What do you say to it when you come close, when hastily you reward its faith with some token of the fond feeling with which you adore it? (25) And without having gone you come back and then fly away again, till finally you lose your life in the flames?" Seeing that it will not be right (30) to put off its death and salvation, on speaking these words, she reached over to the flame and burned it up. "You were fortunate, little creature," Filis goes on, "since now (35) in the arms of your lover you enjoy life and glorious death; for life without happiness, if long, is not enough and, if short, is too much and repose alone is good (40) where the soul may rest. But how is it that I, following your example, do not kill myself now? I wish to die, since it rouses me to, and put an end to so many things. (45) I have learned that Belardo is spending his time with another woman, because my jealousy irritates him and my misfortunes also." From her sewing-kit (50) she takes a short knife and, all upset, says: "Oh Belardo, here Troy happened." But before carrying out her aim, (55) she wanted to test the pain, for she is a woman and timid. With her sewing-needle she pricked her finger and became upset on seeing a drop of her much beloved blood (60) emerge. She asks the maid for a cloth, puts aside knife and aim. She cried over her spilt blood, something her lover isn't doing.

To a motif of great expressive power, the moth and the flame, Lope has brought all his resources of craftsmanship and dramatic imagination; the result is the masterpiece of his artistic balladry. He is working here with a motif common in European poetry since Petrarch, and in fact older, the symbolic possibilities of which cluster about the dual properties of the flame, light-giving and heat-giving, and the paradox of voluntary self-destruction. Traditionally the light suggests spiritual illumination, ideal aspiration, and everlastingness, the heat physical passion, destructiveness, and death, though sometimes the dazzlement of the light becomes as destructive as the heat of the flame.[42] Through the fabulists, the motif eventually reached the medieval bestiaries and the troubadours until, with Petrarch, it enters the mainstream of European poetry. From his Sonnet 19, "Rassomiglia se stesso alla farfalla, ch'è arsa da quel lume che sì la diletta" ("He likens himself to the moth, which is burned by that light that so delights it"), one may trace a line of descent down to Fernando de Herrera, the last Iberian poet to work directly within the Petrarchan configuration of the motif.[43] Lope's ballad, though it belongs in this line, departs from it fundamentally in both treatment and meaning. Mood and feeling are expressed not only through Petrarchan absorption in self but by actions noticeably dramatic in character. The alternatives implied by the ambiguity of the motif are no longer spiritual and sensual but passion that destroys and passion that glorifies. The delicacy of Lope's treatment derives from a play of interlocking perspectives upon the central situation. The fascination of the moth with the flame in turn fascinates Filis, who steps in to change its direction. The spectacle of this intimate drama is in turn observed and relayed to the reader by an all-knowing narrator, Belardo–Lope, who has his own stake in it and gradually injects his view of it into his account.

The pastoral convention survives here only in the names of Filis and Belardo. The atmosphere is domestic and nocturnal, the scene an interior where Filis sits at her needlework; at the end a maid puts in a fleeting appearance. The time is the midnight hour when Filis feels most keenly her abandonment by Belardo. (The word "sola" attracts attention in the first assonantal position.) The interaction between setting and subject is not one of consonance or pathos as in the pastoral; they are connected through fascination exercised and felt. The combination of restless wheeling and fixation in the insect corresponds to the movement of Filis's thoughts as they revolve around the image of Belardo. The opening word "contemplando" puts the emphasis at the beginning on inner attunement to the outer scene, an affinity reaffirmed in the common whiteness of the moth and the hands that pick it up (l. 11). When Filis reacts, catches the moth and stops the flight, her apostrophe to it interposes between her and the insect sentiments of a more complex kind that tend to set her apart from it, yet do not break its spell. Filis's conflict is dramatized in terms of her ambivalent attitude toward the insect. Insofar as she envies the moth its dalliance with the flame (l. 12), she has ceased to identify with it and is verbalizing her own forlornness. But the note of remonstration in her monologue reveals apprehensiveness over the moth's fate, a fate which she feels as her own. The dual meaning of the flame as consummation of desire and death lies behind Filis's ambivalence; her abrupt immolation of the creature is both a vindictive gesture and a fantasy of fulfillment: "muerte y gloria." The traditional spiritual content of the symbol is here not only secularized but overladen with eroticism, since "gloria" implies sexual fulfillment, a connotation made plain in the resumption of the apostrophe (ll. 33–36). The startling impact of Filis's act is underscored by the strong stresses of the symmetrically placed preterits in l. 32—"llegóse al fuego y quemóla"—and the halt one automatically makes after this line, the exact midpoint of the ballad.

The effect of the moth's death is to destroy Filis's identification with it irrevocably. Her feeling of abandonment is intensified, and the futile attempts she makes in the rest of the ballad to emulate the moth's example only drive home her inability to elude her suffering. The renewed apostrophe to the vanished moth quickly turns into a soliloquy in which her concern is exclusively herself. Lope's irony now makes itself increasingly felt. The last traces of Filis's pride are removed in the lines (45–48) in which she explains her grounds for suicide. The disparity between her banal motives and the suicide resolve is the opening wedge of the irony. The exclamation "Oh Belardo, aquí fue Troya" (l. 52) is comically out of scale with the instrument chosen, the short knife from the sewing-kit, and has in addition a mischievous biographical allusiveness. The second thoughts which follow and the consequent staging of a dress rehearsal with an even more minute instrument —the needle—only intensify the irony and bring out, as well, the theatrical side of Filis's behavior. Her faint-heartedness in regard to both instruments, the faltering and abandonment of the suicide attempt gradually cut Filis's resolve down to size and reinstate a prosaic reality, while the contrast between Filis's agitation over a single drop of her "much beloved blood" and her lover's lack of concern brings the ballad to a close with the most sharp-edged irony of all. Lope's composure never is jarred, however, as it is in other cases; nothing interferes with the art of miniature practiced here. Restraint, understatement, a sure sense of scale and proportion and a remarkable ear for the rhythm of octosyllabic verse characterize his esthetic control and transform an elemental fantasy of compensation into an artistic achievement.[44] The restrained handling of eroticism in the ballad entails no sacrifice of Lope's characteristic sensory vividness. The central situation in fact reinvigorates a poetic cliché, the worn metaphor of the flame of passion, inherited by the Golden Age from Petrarch through the *cancioneros* (song books). By writing a miniature drama with the candle flame as its core, Lope restores the life of the figure.

The dramatization of fire imagery as a symbol of passion is an important link between this ballad, a group of sonnets on the ruins theme, and *La Dorotea*. In other ways also the present ballad is a particularly significant avatar in respect to the *acción en prosa*. The focus on the feminine protagonist, viewed as the forsaken and wounded party, though still not devoid of partiality, achieves full artistic empathy. Mood is explored and emotional conflict brought out with exceptional subtlety. The domestic atmosphere and interior setting make their appearance here. The cryptic reference to "my misfortunes" (l. 48) suggests pressures like those mentioned in "Por la calle de su dama" and perhaps the sacrifices for the lover's sake which we find alluded to in *Belardo el furioso* and spelled out in *La Dorotea*.

The restraint which characterizes what might have been an impulse to retaliation in this ballad is notably absent in others. In "Al pie de un roble escarchado" ("At the foot of a frosty oak"),[45] a sequel to "El tronco de ovas vestido," Filis, on an appropriately frosty day, utters fourteen quatrains of *mea culpas*; every other one repeats in self-accusation the tag used by Zaida against Zaide: "Quien tal hace, que tal pague" ("People must pay for what they do"). Chiasmus figures point up the retaliatory situation as she catalogues her faults.[46] She had been the first offender, she avows:

> Desamé a Belardo un tiempo,
> y el amor, para vengarse,
> quiere que le quiera agora
> y que él me olvide y desame.
>
> (ll. 25–28)[47]

I ceased to love Belardo for a while, and love, for revenge, wills that I should love him now and that he should forget me and cease to love.

Losing control, Filis starts to rave ("dando de coraje voces / que revienta de coraje" ["shouting with rage, for she is bursting with rage"]) (ll. 37–38), and in the last pair of quatrains vents her bitterness and frustration on one of Belardo's love-notes which she crumples up, tears, and destroys. The histrionic impulse is uppermost here, to the detriment of true dramatic effects. Lope humiliates Filis–Elena without granting her any artistic sympathy.

Among the so-called *romances de desamor*, there are others based like "Contemplando estaba Filis" and "Al pie de un roble escarchado" on a reversal of Lope's situation vis-à-vis Elena.[48] In still another group of ballads Lope omits the fiction of Elena's being in love. Abuse creeps in: Elena is a ruthless persecutor who has legalized her ill will, leaving Lope no recourse but retaliatory vituperation, as in the libels. In still other ballads *desamor* becomes part of a disabused and detached attitude. In a playful mood as in the Zaide–Zaida poems, or disgruntled as in the correspondence with Liñán, Lope surveys his own balladry, half amused, half impatient. In all these compositions a few final aspects of the Lope-Elena relationship may be noted, but no ballad merits detailed attention as an artistic entity; states of feeling are more verbalized than transmuted or recreated in them. Lope in exile continues to cultivate pastoral attitudes but certain pastoral ballads show his strong temperament growing restive in the role of long-suffering lover and his tone exceeding the conventional tearful remonstrations of spurned shepherds. In "¿Cuándo cesarán las iras?" ("When will the anger cease?") (ed. Montesinos, I, 11), an apostrophe of Belardo to Filis from the banks of the Tormes dating presumably from the years of exile in Alba, pointed reproaches alternate with protestations of fidelity. Filis is called "cobarde enemiga mía / que no perdonas y puedes" ("my cowardly enemy, who could forgive and won't")—a hint of the reason why resentment contends with stock adoration. In the end Belardo, nonetheless, proclaims the timeless omnipotence of beauty:

> que mientras fueres hermosa,
> no dejaré de quererte,
> y seráslo siempre, ingrata,
> porque pene eternamente.

> for so long as you are beautiful, I shall not cease to love you, and you will be so ever, ungrateful one, so that I may suffer forever.

And then he dissolves in a bath of tears.

Elsewhere the pendulum swings back and forth more sharply. In "Después que rompiste, ingrata, / de amor el estrecho nudo" ("After you broke, faithless one, the tight knot of love") (ed. Montesinos, I, 12), it goes from Belardo's assurance that after three years love is still alive to the accusation

> ...Acuden a tu casa
> más galanes al descuido
> que caben ríos y arroyos
> en el reino de Neptuno,

> ... More lovers slip into your house than rivers and streams into Neptune's realm,

a slur of a piece with the libels, then back to his "steadfastness," and finally to the sardonic conclusion:

> Y si va a decir verdades
> aunque de falsa te acuso,
> a manos de tu ira muera
> si fuere de otra y no tuyo.

> And if truth be told, though I accuse you of being false, let me die at the hands of your anger, if I am anyone else's but yours.

The love proclaimed is by now largely lip-service to a pastoral attitude; the most personal note is the abusive one. Perhaps traces of real ambivalence survive. Lope at any rate cultivates the paradox of simultaneous love and hate in the tradition of the "Odi et amo" ("I hate and love") of Catullus and the "Saepe refer tecum sceleratae facta puellae" ("Often think over to yourself the wicked girl's deeds") of Ovid's *Remedia amoris*, though it can be seen that more than paradox is involved. Until we reach the subtly shaded amatory psychology of *La Dorotea*, no inherited mold will, in fact, be capable of reconciling the vauntedly polarized feelings of one who could coin for himself the formula: "Yo nací en dos extremos, que son amar y aborrezer; no he tenido medio xamás" ("I was born at two extremes, namely, loving and hating; I've never known any midpoint").[49]

Even while Lope is writing these ballads of mixed feelings, he continues to produce others completely submissive in tone, overflowing with injured devotion. In them, Filis has parted company with Elena and survives as a purely poetic ideal, before which Belardo prostrates himself. In the ballad beginning:

> Ay amargas soledades
> de mi bellísima Filis,
> destierro bien empleado,
> del agravio que la hice,
>
> (ed. Montesinos, II, 8)

Oh bitter separation from my fairest Filis, exile well deserved for the wrong I did her,

Belardo makes a rare acknowledgment of guilt. In the nostalgic "Oh gustos de amor traidores" ("Oh treacherous pleasures of love"),[50] after six years (if "Seys años ha que porfío / para memorias de quatro" ["I have kept going six years on the strength of four of memories"] is what Lope really wrote) Belardo still can proclaim:

> Quise bien y fui querido
> y después que me oluidaron,
> tanto más la causa quiero
> quantos son más los agrauios.

I loved truly and was loved and since being forgotten, I love the cause all the more, the more she wrongs me.

In the *estancias* (song) "En un campo florido" ("In a flowery field"), written at Alba de Tormes, Belardo celebrates his martyrdom in antithetical conceits:

> Dulce destierro mío,
> querido agravio, sinrazón dichosa,

> agradable desvío
> nacido de una causa tan hermosa . . .

(ed. Montesinos, II, 8)

> Sweet exile of mine, beloved hurt, blessed wrong, pleasant aversion arising from so beautiful a cause . . .

He ends with the acknowledgment "que me priva mi culpa de mi gloria" ("my guilt deprives me of my glory"). It is the virtuoso's pleasure in writing variations on a theme, seizing upon fantasies and reminiscences to do so, that explains the poetic afterlife of this love. Or could Lope, knowing that the ballads would be repeated, copied, and set to music, have also thought that Belardo's flattering tributes and appeals might reach not merely Filis but Elena and move her to ask for a lifting of the sentence of exile? In his epistle to Fernando de Vega y Fonseca, the President of the Council of the Indies, written from his Valencian exile, he had asked the latter's intervention, fruitlessly, as his sarcastic reference to "esa casta Penélope o Diana, / que no quiso humillarse a vuestro ruego" ("that chaste Penelope or Diana who would not bow to your request") shows.[51] He could scarcely have entertained serious hopes for a pardon after this. (In the end it appears to have been the thought of his plays rather than his welfare that moved Jerónimo Velázquez to relent.)

Any hopes, in any case, are cast aside when he writes the ballads in which abuse is given free rein.

> Eras tú la que ganabas,
> mas al fin no mereciste
> tanto bien siendo tan mala.

> You were the one who gained but in the end, being so bad, you didn't deserve such a boon.

he tells her in "¿Apártaste, ingrata Filis?" ("Are you withdrawing, ungrateful Filis?") (ed. Montesinos, I, 13), repeating four times the refrain:

> Filis, mal hayan
> los ojos que en un tiempo te miraban,

> Filis, cursed be the eyes that once were set on you,

while he elsewhere tells Belisa (Isabel de Urbina):

> El cielo me condene a eterno lloro
> si no aborrezco a Filis y te adoro.[52]

Heaven condemn me to eternal tears if I don't hate Filis and adore you.

In "Pues ya desprecias el Tajo" ("Since you now spurn the Tagus"), we are inclined to see Lope's hallmark: savage satire and scandalously explicit personal abuse:

> Que yo callaré verdades
> aunque me muerda la lengua,
> y diré virtudes suyas
> tantas como tiene agenas,
> poniendo su castidad
> tan alta que no se vea,
> y que mataré a quien diga
> que es parienta de los Cerdas
> pues tenellas por el cuerpo
> no es de floja, ni de necia.[53]

For I'll keep back truths though I bite my tongue and I'll recount her virtues, all that don't belong to her, raising her chastity so high it won't be seen and I'll kill anyone who says she is a relative of the Cerdas, since having them on her body is not due to laziness or stupidity. [*Cerda* is lit. a coarse hair, bristle.]

The tone is mocking; Lope is remembering the provision "he is to write no satires or verse against any of the persons referred to in the said verse and satires and ballad" (*Proceso*, p. 60) and angrily defying it.[54]

The occasional ballads written in a spirit of detachment from the mode illuminate Lope's changing attitudes toward his ballad production. In "Mil años ha que no canto" ("I have not sung for a thousand years") (ed. Montesinos, I, 29), it can be seen that the mode is losing its appeal. Lope is as much out of sorts with his imitators as with Filis herself. "Ciertos pastores mozos / dan en llamarse Belardos" ("Certain young shepherds have taken to calling themselves Belardos")—they revoke his wills, add codicils to them: "Dios sabe lo que me corro" (God knows how angry it makes me). Lope has to take the blame for all their bad writing. Years later Lope will similarly protest against the pirating of his plays by unscrupulous producers and publishers. Ballad-writing has entered the public domain and lost its possibilities as a personal vehicle of expression:

> Los estrelleros de Venus
> me dan más priessa que al otro

que de Sidonia salía
a impedir el matrimonio.

The star-of-Venus people give me a harder time than they gave the
other fellow who left Sidonia to prevent the marriage.

It is only a step from such petulance to downright deflation of the convention
and denial of his part in it:

Aquella estrella de Venus,
compuse por cierto eclipse
y agora por agradalla,
que fue por su causa dize.

I composed that star of Venus as a result of a certain eclipse and now
it was on her account she says, in order to please her.

he remarks sourly in "Mirando estaba Lisardo" ("Lisardo was looking").[55]
The claim expresses a mood, not a fact and so does what follows:

Las tórtolas que decían
que maté nunca tal hize,
que quien ama prendas bajas,
lo más de su pena finge.

The turtledoves they claimed I killed, I never did: anyone loving
cheap women puts on most of his suffering.

From such disconcerting cynicism, recurrent if not definitive, one turns
with some relief to "Este traidor instrumento" ("This treacherous instrument") (ed. Montesinos, I, 19), where, with greater equanimity, adopting an earthy and playful manner that anticipates Tomé de Burguillos,
Lope reviews his motivation. He writes out of pique:

[Digo] mal del bien que adoro
no más de porque me falta;

[I speak] badly of the object I adore simply because she is unavailable
to me;

anger:

Mil cosas dice la lengua
que no se las manda el alma
por agradar a la ira
que ha engendrado tu venganza;

The tongue says a thousand things that the heart doesn't direct it to,
just to flatter the anger that your revenge has aroused;

to save face:

> Quien alguna cosa pierde,
> quando no espera cobralla,
> con la boca la desprecia
> y quiérela con el alma.

Someone losing something which he doesn't expect to recover
scorns it with his lips and loves it with his heart.

On the other hand,

> Cuando pienso en tu hermosura,
> mi prosa y verso te ensalzan . . .

When I think of your beauty, my prose and verse extol you . . .

Tongue in cheek he points out the debt Filis owes him,

> pues diciendo mal de ti,
> te he dado en el mundo fama.
> Mira qué buen enemigo
> que aprovecha en lo que daña.

since by speaking ill of you I've spread your fame abroad. Think
what a good enemy I am, benefiting you even as I harm you.

He makes a quite matter-of-fact plea for a reprieve:

> No te pido que me quieras
> si te condenan mis ansias,
> sino que digas que vuelva
> adonde adoré tu cara,

I don't ask you to love me if my tribulations provoke you, only to
say I may return to where I worshiped your face,

and at the end catches himself up with mock-seriousness:

> Mas triste de mí ¿qué digo?
> Muera yo, pues tú me matas,

que no merece perdón
el rendido que no calla.

But, poor wretch that I am, what am I saying? Let me die since you
are killing me: no forgiveness is owed to one who surrenders and
does not keep mum.

This frank self-appraisal, though casually tossed off, is evidence of how
clear-sighted Lope's view of his activity as a balladeer had by now become.
His point of view as he surveys what he has written is of course not that of
the critic, yet he shows awareness in his own way of psychological and
esthetic factors involved in the artistic process. His saving grace is an inability
to take himself with unrelieved seriousness; this allows his comic spirit to
play over the situation between Elena and himself, the actuality and the
poetry, sizing it up candidly and not refraining from debunking it. The
irony is restrained, however, and one notes here the same spirit of play as
in the Zaide–Zaida and other ballads, as well as a characteristic detachment
which reveals the down-to-earth side of Lope's nature, the strain that enables
him in the end to keep life distinct from art, to keep literary styles and
esthetic patterns from distorting a spontaneous response to experience.

By the end of the exile Lope has largely exhausted the expressive possibilities of the *amores de Elena* in balladry, a fact of which he appears himself
aware. The ballad has proved a malleable vehicle, however. It has reflected a
wide range of moods, accommodated his ludic, histrionic, and dramatic
tendencies, furnished him masks and, more noteworthy still, allowed him
to extend his capacity for role-playing in directions beyond the self. It has
given his virtuosity free play even after its exercise has become purely
rhetorical. In the ballads we sometimes find traits of temperament counterpointed against creative drives, as when an ironic *parti pris* progressively
weights the scales in favor of the creator's persona. But we also find temperamental characteristics—self-centeredness, impulsiveness, aggressiveness,
and so on—being harnessed to creative ideas and leading Lope to a high
degree of esthetic control. He succeeds in standing away from his own
violent impulses long enough to make them respond to purely creative
directives. Implicit in the exercise of his art there is thus a surprising degree
of insight into himself. Certain perspectives on events destined for a fertile
afterlife are already assumed in the ballads: the view of the Elena-figure as
victim, as the object of pressures; the attenuation of the retaliatory or
compensatory impulses through imaginative empathy; the possibilities of
the judicial associations of the material. Real or imagined junctures of
events that are objects of artistic concern in the ballads—learning of the

rival's preferment, languishing in self-pity and expiring, being forbidden passage down the lady's street—will also inform scenes or sequences of the *acción en prosa*. Lope does not yet give the impression of being a deliberate artist moving knowingly toward a definitive elaboration of the material. Nevertheless, his experience as a balladeer clearly produces a sedimentation which will enrich future artistic outgrowths of the *amores de Elena*.

Thematic Trends in
Sonnet Cycles
IV

As the subject of Lope's artistic ballads, Elena rode the wave of a new poetic fashion which Lope was helping to set, with characteristically dramatic emphasis, but which he felt a need to justify and defend. To sonnet-writing, on the other hand, he brought his whole life through a sense of craftsmanship applied to the precepts of an exacting form, of following in the footsteps of Spanish and Italian masters; classical themes, diction, and figures echoed in his ears. As Walter Mönch observes, the sonnet was the most prized poetic form of the educated man and woman during the Renaissance and baroque periods.[1]

Despite certain dramatic and theatrical effects in Lope's sonnets, their temper is essentially lyrical. States of feeling remain pervasive and rarely crystallize in act and gesture. The mood is often reflective, the presentation discursive. Some twenty out of the more than sixteen hundred surviving sonnets by Lope may be connected with the adventure with Elena. Chronology, as uncertain as with the ballads, is here again an aid but no sure guide. Variant readings in a few cases, including some sonnets which appeared first in plays and some found in a copybook started in 1593, shed light on their elaboration. Many, however, we know only because Lope decided to preserve them in his *Rimas* of 1602, a collection of two hundred published by the poet as a display of his mastery of the sonneteer's art. More than half of the sonnets in question, and the finest ones, reflect the crisis of the love affair. They comprise the two thematic groups mentioned earlier. In one, the destruction of Troy symbolizes the climax in its totality; in the other, the separation of a favorite sheep from its master alludes to a crucial stage. The sonnets which fall outside these two cycles are noticeably inferior in quality, often perfunctory and sometimes seemingly dashed off in haste. When one recalls that there were also libelous sonnets, one is struck by the disparities in tone and level of artistic achievement among these compositions. My principal concern is with the two thematic groups mentioned.

As Mönch points out, Lope seeks to combine in his sonnets the brilliance, musicality, and rhetoric of the Italian manner with the Spanish tradition of the conceit.[2] Even in certain Petrarchistic compositions of the *Rimas* of 1602, the forcefulness of Lope's conceit-laden language adds a distinctive note. It is precisely the conceptual aspect of the sonnet which Lope and his contemporaries stress above all else. They see as its heart a thought which may be a witticism or conceit but need not be a poetic idea in the modern sense, that is, a particularized state of feeling, an insight, impression, or perception. "Alguna sentencia ingeniosa i aguda, o grave" ("Some saying, sharp and witty, or serious") is Herrera's prescription for the conceit,[3] and Lope's way of defending a sonnet on the death of Henry IV of France, for which he had been criticized, is to point out how ingeniously he has embodied in it the specific thought with which he began.[4]

The unitary character of the sonnet was strongly felt: "Usually it has only a single thought and this so set forth that there is nothing left over or lacking," says Rengifo.[5] "A serious and elegant composition, on a single thought" is Francisco Cascales' definition,[6] and Herrera follows his prescription with the stipulation that the *sentencia* "should be worthy of taking up the whole extent." The resultant compactness explains the common equating of the sonnet with the classical epigram by these and other preceptists and by Lope himself.[7]

The self-contained and tectonic character of the sonnet made each one a discrete unit, a property repeatedly noted by preceptists: "On a given subject, there can only be one of these sonnets ... A story should not be related in sonnets," wrote Miguel Sánchez de Lima in 1580,[8] and Carballo is even more forceful: "Extended material cannot be continued from sonnet to sonnet; each thought must be contained in one sonnet and a sonnet can have only one thought."[9] In contrast to the favor which narrative cycles found in balladry, narrative sonnet sequences were proscribed. The proscription is respected by Lope. His cycles are variations on lyric themes; they cluster about thematic nuclei, their arrangement not sequential but centripetal.

The suitability to the sonnet of the highest levels of poetic and rhetorical style is repeatedly affirmed. Herrera writes: "There shine forth in it with superb clarity and brilliance of figures and poetic adornment, learning and propriety, gaiety and keenness of wit, magnificence and spirit, sweetness and jocundity, harshness and vehemence, sympathy and emotions."[10] Rengifo particularly stresses the sonnet's rhetorical aptness: "It allows comparisons, similes, questions and answers, and it serves whatever ends one may wish: praising or castigating, persuading or dissuading, counseling and arousing."[11]

Lope's practice and occasional comments show him alive to all these possibilities. In the introduction to the *Rimas*, he stresses—somewhat loosely —imagery, sonority of diction, and sublimity of concept.[12] That Lope was especially concerned with the various techniques of execution open to the sonneteer is made plain in the following passage from the *Laurel de Apolo* (1630):

¡O quán ricos sonetos,
de erudición y estilo! con qué llave
cerraban sus concetos!
¡qué conclusión, qué admiración, qué grave!
porque no es Epigrama
el que por varias sendas se derrama,
o que la conclusión tiene tan fría,
que burla al que la espera, y desconfía,
o ha de acabar con verso
tan dulce, hermoso y terso,
que deleyte y admire su harmonía
el gusto y el oído,
que también se deleyta en el sonido.

(*OS*, I, 203)

Oh, such sonnets rich in learning and style; the keys they locked up
their thoughts with! The conclusions, the wonder, the gravity! For
the epigram is not a form to spill over into different channels, or
have so chilly an ending that it cheats the expectant listener and puts
him on guard. Or else it should end in so sweet, lovely, and smooth
a line that its harmony delights and amazes the taste and the ear, for
the ear also has its delight in the sound.

The ending is crucial as is the maintenance of tone and tautness down to the end. The *concepto*, *grave* or *agudo*, may be driven home only in the conclusion, or alternatively, there may simply be a subsiding to a euphonious close, one designed for the ear more than the mind. The need to hold to a single line of development (instead of following "varias sendas") and to avoid a descent in style is affirmed elsewhere also.[13]

In every way the sonnet involved greater esthetic calculation on Lope's part than the ballad. Yet it appears that he only gradually conceived the idea of collecting and publishing his sonnets, and that originally, despite his sense of a difference in artistic category, he treated them as casually as his ballads and plays. Where the sonnets linked with Elena Osorio were concerned, this change of attitude meant a playing down of their links with his personal history, an outward depersonalizing which aimed at broadening their scope and universalizing their appeal. The criteria for inclusion in the *Rimas* of 1602 must have been esthetic in the first place: Lope selected those sonnets by which he wished to confirm and perpetuate his reputation as a sonneteer. But caprices of preservation are a factor also, and the criterion of artistic quality, even when one allows for differences in taste between Lope and ourselves, does not always explain the presence or absence of given sonnets centering on Elena in the collection.

Elena was recipient as well as subject of sonnets during the days of their liaison, if one may judge by the favor with which, in Lope's depiction, she looks on the offering of "ten sonnets" in the auctioneering libel. But the sonnets were not only tributes; sometimes they read as authentic appeals. The contemporaneous references in the correspondence with Liñán stress neither of these aspects, however. Lope's concern is not with addressee or function but with origin, with what the sonnets signify as self-expression. In his first epistle he writes:

> Ayer con mis papeles hice cuenta,
> y hallé, sin otras muchas niñerías,
> cuyo perdido tiempo me atormenta,
> cien sonetos, diez pares de elegías,
> como zapatos viejos desechados,
> vivos retratos de pasiones mías.[14]

> Yesterday I totaled up my papers and found, in addition to numerous other trifles, the time lost on which galls me, a hundred sonnets and ten pairs of elegies, like cast-off old shoes, live portrayals of my feelings.

Beneath an ensuing fiction of their sale to a spice merchant to wrap his wares in, one reads some indifference at this point to their eventual fate. Moreover, the stress is on the fidelity with which the sonnets portray his feelings—not, as will later be the case, on the disparity between the voice and the flesh. In the second epistle Lope is even more explicit:

> No por cristal o vidro transparente
> se ven desotra parte las figuras

que retrató la mano diligente,
como las amorosas desventuras
por tus coplas, Riselo, y mis sonetos,
testigos de tu llanto y mis locuras.

Through crystal or transparent glass the figures which the careful
hand has portrayed within cannot be so well seen as can misfortunes
in love through your rhymes and my sonnets, Riselo, witnesses to
your tears and my madness.

Fifteen years later when Lope writes the prologue to the *Rimas* of 1602,
he still alludes to the personal relevance of the Troy sonnets and the
turtledoves (though the latter do not figure in this collection):

> Las *tórtolas* y *Troya* no es justo que las culpe nadie por repetidas,
> pues lo fuera en el Petrarca haver hecho tantos Sonetos al Lauro y el
> Ariosto al Sinebro, y el Alemani de la Pianta: que si los nombres de
> las personas, que amaron, les dieron essa ocasión, yo havré tenido la
> misma.

(OS, IV, 168)

There is no reason for anyone to criticize the recurrence of the
turtledoves and Troy, since the same criticism would apply to
Petrarch for having written so many sonnets to the Laurel and
Ariosto to the Juniper, and Alemani to the Plant: for if the names of
the persons they loved were the occasion for so doing, I also have
had my motive.

But the introductory sonnet to the collection shows how much his point of
view has changed:

> Versos de amor, conceptos esparcidos,
> engendrados del alma en mis cuidados;
> partos de mis sentidos abrasados,
> con más dolor que libertad nacidos;
>   expósitos al mundo en que, perdidos,
> tan rotos anduvistes y trocados,
> que sólo donde fuistes engendrados,
> fuérades por la sangre conocidos;
>   pues que le hurtáis el laberinto a Creta,
> a Dédalo los altos pensamientos,
> la furia al mar, las llamas al abismo,
>   si aquel áspid hermoso no os aceta,
> dejad la tierra, entretened los vientos:
> descansaréis en vuestro centro mismo.[15]

Love verse, scattered conceits, fathered by the heart in my sufferings; offspring of my burning senses, born with more pain than freedom; abandoned to the world in which, like lost children, you went about so tattered and altered that only by the one who fathered you could you be recognized through blood; since you have appropriated the Cretan labyrinth, the lofty thoughts of Daedalus, the fury of the sea, the flames of hell, if that lovely asp does not accept you, leave earth, hold forth to the winds: you will thus be resting in your true center.

Lope now writes to salvage his sonnets from his own neglect and to fix their texts; his words are particularly apposite to the sonnets linked with Elena. Equally important, he is no longer casually thinking of these lyrics as mirror images of personal history; he sees them as poetry distilled from it. Though originally driven to expression by emotional pressures, he understands that his "offspring" now have an independent existence in a new realm. The pangs of creation have lifted them off the hard ground of history to float in the upper air of poetry, transcending the contingencies from which they arose. The shift in viewpoint between the two passages represents a gain in insight and a deepening understanding of his own creativity, the prelude to a more deliberate art.

Before turning to the two principal cycles, certain other sonnets relating to Elena Osorio may be glanced at briefly. Two of those included by Lope in the *Rimas* and another which had appeared in *La Arcadia* were exercises in the Petrarchan manner, of so conventional a type that it sufficed to replace the name Filis by another in order to dissociate the sonnets entirely from Elena.[16]

Entrambasaguas has connected with Elena Osorio four more sonnets entirely unpublished, which he found attributed to Lope in a notebook begun in 1593.[17] Two of these begin by speaking out spontaneously and naturally to Filis, then fall into literary conventionalities; another is purely conventional and the fourth of dubious relevance to Elena Osorio. One of the significant sonnets begins:

> Lo que temí llegó, siendo llegado
> mill veces a mi grave sentimiento.
> Que me dejáis no creo; sólo siento
> que ya por vos la vida me ha dejado.

What I feared has happened, after having happened a thousand times to my heavy heart. I don't believe you are leaving me; I sense only that on your account life has left me.

In all probability these lines record insecurity and foreboding in advance of the rupture and a stunned initial reaction to it. In the rest of the sonnet the direct and vivid tone of this opening is smothered by the perfunctory development already beginning in the fourth line. The sonnet is noticeably free of bitterness, however, as if Lope as yet felt only incredulity. The other sonnet, "Huyendo voy de ti por no ofenderte" ("I am fleeing you so as not to offend you"), sounds like an immediate comment on the sentence, composed as Lope goes into exile. In its resigned and restrained tone we may perhaps read, beside a cultivation of submissiveness, relief that the ordeal has ended, however unfavorably; the tone is also perhaps a sign that, for the time being at least, Lope is prudently curbing his tongue, and refraining even from reproaches. Commonplace antitheses—"te dejo—vas conmigo" ("I leave you—you come with me"), l. 2; "vida-muerte" ("life-death"), l. 8—perhaps here express genuine bewilderment.[18]

With the seven sonnets that develop the symbolism of ruins, we find Lope more closely involved in exploring a particular vein of expression and conveying, when most effective, a complex of feeling not reducible to particular affective components.

We have certain external chronological points of reference for the composition of these sonnets, yet while they may thus presumably be placed close in time to the events of 1587–88, or at a certain remove from them, the evidence is neither precise nor definitive. In some cases variant versions give important indications of the direction Lope's reelaboration was taking, though again within a rather imprecise chronological range. In my presentation of these sonnets (and of two ballads linked with them) I have therefore also been guided by supplementary considerations: key details, recurrent motifs, matters of technique, point of view, tone, handling of symbolism and imagery. I have arranged the sonnets in a plausible sequence of development: from groping and imperfectly realized versions to full realization and beyond to rhetorical reworkings.

The ruins motif must have appealed to Lope because of the chance it gave his imagination, drawing on its visual and plastic powers, to develop rhetorical *enargeias* that offered vivid and detailed depictions of spectacles or scenes as if from the standpoint of an eyewitness. A venerable motif derived from Petrarch's "Trionfo del tempo" and passed on by Sannazaro in his famous sonnet on Rome, "Superbi colli," is thus given a new lease on life. At the same time, Lope accentuates a tendency already present in Sannazaro to attach a personal meaning to the spectacle, to focus on its relevance to his individual situation, as against the broader traditional lesson in mortality, *vanitas vanitatum* and stoic resignation.[19]

Hindsight enabled us to discern in the lines

> Troyana Elena, querreliquias solas
> heres de lo que fuiste

> Trojan Helen, a mere remnant of what you once were

of the abusive sonnet the germ of future developments. A clearer suggestion of what the symbolism of ruins came to mean during the years of exile is seen in *La Arcadia*, where we find Lope interweaving his own sentiments into the account of Amphryso-Alba's "amores con desdichas" ("unhappy love").[20] As the protagonist is about to be led into the Temple of Disillusionment, his guide, the wizardess Polinesta, remarks that

> de aquella historia apenas se ven memorias en tus discursos, ni en el mar de tu entendimiento los edificios de aquella antigua Troya. Consumido ha el tiempo las ruinas de la española Sagunto, y el olvido las reliquias de la africana Cartago.[21]

> memories of that story are scarcely visible in your discourse nor are the buildings of that ancient Troy in the sea of your understanding. Time has consumed the ruins of the Spanish Saguntum, and oblivion the remnants of African Carthage.

The "historia" is personal history. To evoke a total experience of disillusionment in love, Lope falls back on the symbolism developed in the sonnets. In these we shall find it also associated with the fire imagery noticed in the ballads. A direct personal impression of the ruins of Saguntum, outside Valencia, probably received at the beginning of the exile in early 1588, had helped Lope to breathe new life into the literary theme. This must be, as Montesinos suggests,[22] the point at which the literary elaboration begins, and it is a ballad, "Mirando está las cenizas" ("Looking at the ashes"),[23] in which Saguntum, not Troy, figures, that surely marks the point of inception. Certain aspects of the sonnet treatments are already anticipated here: the lesson in temporality—"del tiempo tantos ejemplos" ("so many examples of time"), l. 10—the then-and-now stressed insistently; a theatrical apostrophe by the onlooker, here the lachrymose goatherd Belardo, who from a commanding vantagepoint addresses the empty amphitheater; keen aural impressions (ll. 33–36):

> y sólo de sus balidos
> por derribados cimientos
> estas bóvedas escuchan
> tristes y espantables ecos;

and of their bleatings alone, among the collapsed foundations, do
these vaults hear sad and frightening echoes;

the assimilation of the onlooker's situation to that of the ruined city, worked
out in all particulars (ll. 45 ff.):

> Ya fuiste ciudad insigne
> y fui yo dichoso un tiempo . . .

Once you were an illustrious city and once I was happy . . .

the balance of adversity tipped toward the onlooker (ll. 53–56):

> Sobra de malos amigos
> en este lugar me han puesto;
> tu muerte fue honrada vida,
> pues fue de enemigos buenos.

An excess of bad friends has landed me in this spot; your death
meant a life of honor, since it was at the hands of good enemies.

(Noticeable here is the persistent conviction of betrayal by friends already
evident in the trial record.)

In what may be the earliest sonnet in the group, "Vivas memorias,
máquinas difuntas," it is still Saguntum rather than Troy that figures:

> Vivas memorias, máquinas difuntas
> que cubre el tiempo de ceniza y hielo,
> formando cuevas donde el eco al vuelo
> sólo del viento acaba las preguntas;
>   basas, colunas y arquitraves juntas,
> ya divididas oprimiendo el suelo,
> soberbias torres que al primero cielo
> osastes escalar con vuestras puntas:
>   si desde que en tan alto anfiteatro
> representastes a Sagunto muerta
> de gran tragedia pretendéis la palma,
>   mirad de sólo un hombre en el teatro
> mayor ruina y perdición más cierta,
> que en fin sois piedras y mi historia es alma.[24]

Live memories, dead structures that time covers with ash and ice,
forming concavities where only a fleeting echo completes the wind's
questions; pedestals, columns, and architraves all of a piece, now

broken apart and burdening the ground; proud towers that dared to scale the first heaven with your tops: if, ever since you performed the death of Saguntum in so lofty an amphitheater, you have aspired to the trophy of great tragedy, behold in the theater the greater ruin and surer downfall of a single man, for you after all are stones and my story is spirit.

The carefully managed gradation proceeds from a single apostrophe in the first quartet to two in the second, the protasis of a condition in the first tercet and the apodosis in the second. Between octet and sextet comes the turn from expectation to fulfillment, expansion to contraction, which, as Mönch observes, is the essential inner law of the form.[25] Lope's handling of the subject is unquestionably affected by the precedent of Sannazaro in "Superbi colli, e voi, sacre ruine" ("Proud hills and you, sacred ruins"). From this prototype—or one of a train of imitations and adaptations, Italian and Spanish—stems the architectonic scheme of apostrophes, then condition; the postponement till the end of the link between speaker and ruins toward which all the preceding sections lead; the reflection on temporality.[26] Nevertheless Lope recreates the theme rather than simply restating it, and not unexpectedly the effect is more theatrical. In "Superbi colli," the speaker turns away from the ruins and moralizes to himself in the tercets, concluding:

Che se'l tempo da fine a ciò ch'è in terra,
darà forsi anchor fine al mio tormento.

For if time puts an end to everything on earth, it will perhaps also put an end to my torture.

In Lope, on the other hand, the apostrophe continues to the end.

A second sonnet (found in a version copied c. 1593 as well as in the version of the *Rimas*) also shows links with the ballad:

Contendiendo el Amor y el Tiempo un día,
señor don Luis, sobre su fiero estrago,
la destruición de Roma y de Cartago
el viejo en voz cansada repetía.
    Amor, con vanas fábulas, quería
cifrar en muerte su fingido halago,
y en Troya, cuando fue sangriento lago
las cenizas de Helena revolvía.
    "Bien sabes," replicó por pasatiempo

al ignorante niño el viejo sabio,
"que con sola una ausencia te enflaquezco."
    Pidió un testigo Amor, trújome el Tiempo;
yo juré que en un hora, habiendo agravio.
no sólo sé olvidar, pero aborrezco.[27]

Love and Time disputing one day, Sir Louis, about their fierce
ravages, the old man kept referring, in a tired voice, to the
destruction of Rome and of Carthage. Love, with empty fables,
kept trying to reduce its pretended appeal to death, and kept stirring
up the ashes of Helen in Troy, when it was a lake of blood. "You
well know," the wise old man, by way of pastime, answered the
ignorant child, "that with a single absence I weaken you." Love
asked for a witness, Time produced me: I swore that in an hour, if
there was an offense, I not only am able to forget but to hate.

The sonnet is built on the rhetorical pattern of the debate, disputants or
forces being set against one another in a contest of strength. Memories of
schoolboy or university disputations here appear reinforced by fresher
impressions of the tribunal before which Lope had appeared. Like the
Zaide–Zaida ballads, the sonnet has a forensic cast. Lope addresses by personal
name ("señor don Luis"), not pseudonym, Luis de Vargas Manrique, the
intimate friend and fellow balladeer in whose company we find him in
testimony given at the hearings. Lope seems to have thrown away the mask
of Belardo as well. The legalistic framing of the disputational situation is
confirmed in the production of a witness (Lope himself) whose testimony
is given on oath (ll. 12–13).

    The germ of the disputational pattern is the long prosopopeia of Belardo
to the empty amphitheater in the ballad, beginning:

¿Quién se ha de poner contigo
a fuerza, tiempo ligero,
teniendo tantos testigos
de tus poderosos hechos?

Who would match strength with you, swift time, when he has so
many witnesses of your powerful deeds?

In the sonnet Love takes up the challenge. When Time in the earlier version
cites "la destruición de Troya y de Cartago" (l. 3), Love claims Troy for
himself (ll. 7–8):

y de que Troya fue sangriento lago,
la causa principal se atribuía.

and claimed for himself the principal credit for Troy's being a lake of blood.

After Time retorts that he needs only an absence to weaken Love and the latter calls for a witness, Lope's decisive testimony is given in a blustering, defiant manner reminiscent of the transcript: he promises more than was asked—hatred, not simply forgetting. What this overassertiveness points to is an actual state of ambivalence—passion and hostility, love and hate. To make hatred rather than forgetting the end-point suggests emotional involvement, not indifference, and the vehemence of tone confirms this. Agustín G. de Amezúa reads in the same way a profession of Lope to his patron, the Duke of Sessa, in 1616, even though he speaks there simply of forgetting and not of hating: "Puedo lo que quiero conmigo . . . y assí, en mis mozedades nunca se me dio nada de querer, porque sabía que estaua en mi mano el oluidar" ("I can do what I wish with myself . . . and so, in my youth I never worried much about being in love, since I knew that it was in my power to forget").[28]

Though in the sonnet we find the idea of destruction beginning to center on the particular case of Troy, it does so rather impersonally. We do not yet feel Lope drawn to the symbol as a focal point; the emotions behind the sonnet are not yet sufficiently refined to permit this.

When the sonnet was revised for publication in 1602, such emotions had become less inflammable. Lope salvages what he could of artistic value from the mixture of rhetoric, perfunctory personification, and raw feeling. He substitutes Rome for Troy in Time's reference to destroyed cities, as if consciously looking back to the literary antecedent of "Superbi colli." (The change also draws the lines of the contest more sharply by eliminating the use of the same example in the claims of both contestants.) Troy is still cited by Love in the revised version of ll. 7–8, but now, after perhaps ten years, Lope has lost his reticence about referring outright by given name to his mistress. If he departs from tradition by implying Helen's death in Troy, it is perhaps because the coherence of the *exemplum* has been sacrificed to a new concern, namely, to make the case of Troy expressive of a phenomenon which has occurred in the course of revision: the stirring up of old memories. With the change in these lines, "Troy" becomes evocative of the totality of an experience and it is perhaps significant that "revolvía" ("stirring up") has further connotations of stirring up trouble.[29] Lope is in a reminiscent mood, as man and artist, but distance in time has placed him at a greater esthetic remove. Love's defeat in the contest now carries an additional sense of final deliverance: the stirring up of memories no longer threatens his composure. We detect here the beginning of a movement leading beyond expression of feeling to its contemplation. The "olvidar" ("to forget") of the last line has become a reality, humanly speaking.

The thirteenth line originally read: "Yo juré la verdad porque en tres días" ("I swore the truth because in three days"). The introduction of "agravio" as a motive for forgetting and hating in the 1602 version—the term, as Lope uses it, suggests both insult and injury, both a specific grievance and the state of being aggrieved—abstracts a new element from the complex of emotions, reduces the gratuitousness of Lope's original swagger, and converts the situation of the sonnet into a generalized definition of steps toward *desamor*: absence, a grievance, forgetting, and hatred. This skeletal codification is of interest as an early pointer toward *La Dorotea*; the *acción en prosa* will correct the still-standing incongruity of placing forgetting before hatred.

A radical ambivalence toward Elena is still felt in a third sonnet:

> Cayó la Troya de mi alma en tierra,
> abrasada de aquella griega hermosa:
> que por prenda de Venus amorosa
> Juno me abrasa, Palas me destierra.
>
> Mas como las reliquias dentro encierra
> de la soberbia máquina famosa,
> la llama en las cenizas vitoriosa
> renueva el fuego y la pasada guerra.
>
> Tuvieron y tendrán inmortal vida
> prendas que el alma en su firmeza apoya,
> aunque muera el troyano y venza el griego.
>
> Mas, ¡ay de mí!, que, con estar perdida,
> aun no puedo decir: "Aquí fue Troya,"
> siendo el alma inmortal y eterno el fuego.[30]

The Troy of my soul fell to earth, set on fire by that beautiful Greek woman: for, as a pawn of amorous Venus, Juno sets me on fire, Pallas exiles me. Yet, since it contains within it the traces of the proud and famous construction, the flame, victorious in the ashes, renews the fire and the past war. Pledges that the soul bases on its steadfastness have had and will have everlasting life, though the Trojan die and the Greek win. But wretch that I am, though Troy is lost, I still cannot say: "Here Troy happened," since the soul is immortal and the fire eternal.

A state of emotional conflict for which Lope has not yet found an adequate formal correlative is again evident here. While a conceptual link is made between ruins, Troy, Helen, and Elena, poetic coherence is lacking. The opening line hovers between two meanings: Elena's fall from Lope's pedestal and the collapse of Lope's world. Lope settles on the latter, making Troy the metaphorical equivalent of his own soul and thus restricting the scope of the image. New uncertainty arises with the introduction of fire imagery. The conflagration that consumes the soul both reduces it to ruin and inflames it with passion. Here, in contrast to the ballad "Contemplando estaba Filis," the ambiguity in the flame imagery is unmanageable; the unwieldiness of the conceit increases when Lope makes the remains of the Greeks' wooden horse in the burnt city stand for the resurgence of passion within his heart (second quartet) and from this twist in the conceit derives the point of the concluding paradox. He is perhaps struggling here to express a turbulent emotional state, but he does not succeed in incorporating it in an esthetic order.[31]

One is tempted to connect with this sonnet a ballad, "Ardiendo se estaba Troya" ("Troy was burning"), in which the emphasis is also upon the spectacle of the city's destruction by fire, while ruins, their contemplation and the lessons usually associated with them, are even more noticeably absent.[32] Except for the allusiveness of the ballad's refrain:

> Fuego dan bozes, fuego suena,
> y sólo Paris dize abrase a Elena,

> "Fire," they shout, "Fire" sounds, and only Paris says: "May it burn up Helen,"

which is pointedly quoted in *La Dorotea* (p. 432),[33] the treatment is objective and sententious. It could mark a first and still largely unassimilated injection of flame imagery into the Troy theme.

The assimilation is achieved in the sonnet "Ardese Troya y sube el humo escuro" ("Troy is burning and the dark smoke rises")—again in two versions, one copied c. 1593 and that of the *Rimas*—

> Ardese Troya, y sube el humo escuro
> al enemigo cielo, y entretanto,
> alegre, Juno mira el fuego y llanto:
> ¡venganza de mujer, castigo duro!
>   El vulgo, aún en los templos mal seguro,
> huye, cubierto de amarillo espanto;
> corre cuajada sangre el turbio Janto,
> y viene a tierra el levantado muro.

> Crece el incendio propio el fuego extraño,
> las empinadas máquinas cayendo,
> de que se ven ruinas y pedazos.
>   Y la dura ocasión de tanto daño,
> mientras vencido Paris muere ardiendo,
> del griego vencedor duerme en los brazos.[34]

Troy is burning and the dark smoke rises to hostile heaven and meanwhile Juno looks happily on at the fire and lamentation: woman's revenge, a harsh punishment! The masses, unsafe even in the temples, flee, possessed by yellow terror; the turbid Zanthus runs curdled with blood and the lofty wall crumbles to the ground. The conflagration within increases the fire from without, felling the lofty structures, of which ruins and segments can be seen. And the hard-hearted cause of all this harm, while vanquished Paris burns to death, sleeps in the arms of the conquering Greek.

Here a purely descriptive technique is employed. The viewpoint is that of an eyewitness to the burning of Troy and Lope's mastery of the *enargeia* is evident. No correlation is made between the narrator's situation and that of the city, yet the objectivity is more apparent than real, and the limitations of Lope's so-called Parnassian manner are evident. The description is too agitated to be pictorial and there is no steady angle of vision. Moreover, the narrator's sympathies clearly lie with the beleaguered city. His account accentuates the presence of hostile forces banded together against Troy: "el enemigo cielo" ("hostile heaven"), toward which the smoke rises (l. 2); Juno's vengeful delight (l. 3), generalized into universal feminine vindictiveness in the revised version (l. 4 originally read: "Armado el pecho de su temple duro"—"Her breast armed with its hard temper"); and the indifference of "la dura ocasión de tanto daño" ("the hard-hearted cause of all this harm") (l. 12). Though Lope evidently identifies himself with Paris (as in the sonnet just analyzed and the ballad "Ardiéndose estaba Troya"), the diffuse hostility reflects, in a less obvious way, the conviction of being unjustly singled out and persecuted so noticeable in the transcript. The ambiguity inherent in the fire imagery is no longer jarring. L. 9 balances the passion which inflames—"incendio propio" ("conflagration within") against the "fuego estraño" ("fire from without")—passion which destroys —and both are subsumed in the intense "muere ardiendo" ("burns to death") of l. 13. With the initial "y" of the last tercet a release of accumulated tensions begins. The full impact of the sonnet comes without stridency in these final three lines in the contrast of Helen's hardness, fickleness, and indifference with the destruction she has caused. The artistic control is sure and the correlation between personal history and literary theme unlabored. The epic associations of the subject impart a certain grandeur of tone to Lope's lyrical adaptation; intimacy, by the same token, is lacking.

In "Entre aquestas colunas abrasadas" ("Among these burned-up columns"), substance is flawlessly wedded to form and mastery attained:

> Entre aquestas colunas abrasadas,
> frías cenizas de la ardiente llama
> de la ciudad famosa, que se llama
> ejemplo de soberbias acabadas;
>   entre éstas, otro tiempo levantadas
> y ya de fieras deleitosa cama;
> entre aquestas ruinas, que la fama
> por memoria dejó medio abrasadas;
>   entre éstas ya de púrpura vestidas
> y agora sólo de silvestres yedras,
> despojos de la muerte rigurosa,
>   busco memorias de mi bien perdidas
> y hallo sola una voz que entre estas piedras
> responde: "Aquí fue Troya la famosa." [35]

Among these burned-up columns, cold ashes of the burning flames of the famous city, which is considered an example of extinguished pride; among these [columns], once erect and now a pleasant lair for wild beasts; among these ruins which fame left half-burned as remembrances; among these [ruins], once dressed in purple and now only in wild grasses, the spoils of relentless death, I seek lost memories of my happiness and find only a voice amid these stones which replies: "Here was famous Troy."

The contemplative attitude probably signifies a greater recoil in time. The sonnet is composed in a moment of elegiac retrospection. The vision of the past summoned up by a vision of ruins is calm and unhurried: the first person, as in Lope's sonnet on Saguntum and in "Superbi colli," is postponed till the final tercet, and even so the relevance of the spectacle to the beholder, almost entirely implicit, remains understated. The destructiveness of the conflagration is all in the past and the overgrown ruins themselves have been absorbed back into the landscape. Lope expresses a sense of life as an ongoing process which may be trusted to cover over and heal the wounds of any past.[36] The experience with Elena has been assimilated as an esthetic totality and in artistic recreation is seen as over. The lone voice that responds from the ruins expresses nostalgia or melancholy but no pain and certainly no claim of love to outlast time. Not even memories are stirred and the phrase "Aquí fue Troya" expresses, with overtones of wonder (*admiración*), not violence or catastrophe but the definitive pastness of the past. In "Cayó la Troya de mi alma en tierra" ("The Troy of my soul fell to earth"), on the other hand, the phrase still could not be pronounced; in "Contemplando estaba Filis" it was spoken mockingly. The appended epithet "la famosa" rounds out the quiet and euphonious close of the sonnet.[37]

In another sonnet,[38] the ruins have disappeared without a trace beneath flowery fields:

> El ánimo solícito y turbado
> como se ve en el mar la inquieta boya,
> miraba Albano el campo en que fue Troya,
> de fuego un tiempo y de dolor cercado.
>   Adonde el Ilión se vio fundado,
> que ya en la fama su grandeza apoya,
> y estuvo la greciana hurtada joya,
> vio la ceniza convertida en prado.
>   Estuvo un rato así, mas dijo luego:
> "¡Oh campos ya de fuego, en mis dolores
> y en vuestro ejemplo mis consuelos fío!
>   Que si en lugar que cupo tanto fuego
> agora veo verde hierba y flores,
> también podrá tener templanza el mío."

His spirit preoccupied and uneasy, like a restless buoy one sees in the sea, Albano was looking at the fields where once Troy was beset by fire and pain. Where that Ilium had stood which now entrusts its greatness to fame, and where the stolen Greek jewel once had been, he saw ash converted into meadow. He stood awhile thus but then said: "Oh fields once aflame, seeing my sufferings and your example, I have hope of consolation! For if in a place that held so much fire I now see green grass and flowers, my [fire] may also find assuagement."

The name of the protagonist, Albano, almost certainly marks this composition as an occasional piece written to celebrate an attachment of the Duke of Alba during the period of Lope's secretaryship to the Duke at Alba de Tormes in the early 1590's. But Lope's remark regarding the personal relevance of the Troy image and his avowed tendency to identify the Duke's love affairs with his own mark the sonnet also as bearing on Elena Osorio. Whatever residual personal expressiveness may cling to the subject, it is evident that Lope here is now more consciously following the pattern

of "Superbi colli," as in his sonnet on Saguntum, and that the theme of
ruins is entering the rhetorical domain. The sonnet is facile but perfunctory,
based on an obvious and eloquently verbalized contrast, as in "Superbi
colli," not on a subtle communion of mood between scene and onlooker.
Unlike the overgrown ruins of the previous sonnet, the meadows that
Albano gazes on are purely conventional. The lesson in hope drawn in the
tercets simply echoes that of "Superbi colli," as a comparison of the final
lines reveals: "[Il tempo] dará forsi anchor fine al mio tormento" ("[Time]
will perhaps also put an end to my torture") and "también podrá tener
templanza el mío [fuego]" ("my own [fire] may also find assuagement").
Lope, however, has pushed to extremes the effects of time: it has not merely
produced ruins, as in "Superbi colli," but swallowed them. His trial and
imprisonment, as experiences, have been lived through and are receding
into the past.

Even more of an exercise in virtuosity is the final sonnet of the group:

> Fue Troya desdichada, y fue famosa,
> vuelta en ceniza, en humo convertida,
> tanto, que Grecia, de quien fue vencida,
> está de sus desdichas envidiosa.
>   Así en la llama de mi amor celosa,
> pretende nombre mi abrasada vida,
> y el alma en esos ojos encendida,
> la fama de atrevida mariposa.
>   Cuando soberbia y victoriosa estuvo,
> no tuvo el nombre que le dio su llama:
> tal por incendios a la fama subo.
>   Consuelo entre los míseros se llama
> que quien por las venturas no la tuvo,
> por las desdichas venga a tener fama.[39]

Troy was unfortunate and Troy was famous, turned to ash,
converted into smoke, so much so that Greece, by whom it was
conquered, is envious of its misfortunes. Thus in the jealous flame of
my love, my burning life aspires to renown, and my soul, set afire
by those eyes, [seeks] fame as a daring moth. When it was proud and
victorious, it did not have the renown which its flame gave it: thus
through conflagrations I ascend to fame. It is considered a consolation
of the unfortunate that one who failed to win fame through good
fortune should attain it through ill.

The treatment is here purely conceptual; the theme—fame as compensation
for misfortune—is abstractly handled; there is no *enargeia*. The sonnet is

obvious in structure and chilly in its symmetry. The first quatrain makes Troy the vehicle of a metaphor, of which the self appears as the tenor in the second, introduced by "así." Reduced in compass, the same equation appears in the first tercet, while the second makes the natural sententious inference. Flame imagery is predominant but indiscriminate: the holocaust of the self in the flame of jealous love also appears as the immolation of the moth in the light of the lady's eyes, a case of virtuosity behind which one may sense the common psychic core of all Lope's fire imagery.[40] The fame professed to be a source of consolation is a conventionalized equivalent of the notoriety which was perhaps secretly a source of satisfaction to Lope.

While it is instructive to observe advances in technical mastery and artistic control as one examines the group of sonnets on the ruins motif, one finds a fully effective blending of substance and form in only one instance. With the four sonnets on the theme of the straying sheep, on the other hand, Lope's touch is sure and his mastery evident from the start. Traditional motifs of the literary pastoral divested of the modishness and masquerade effects present in the ballads, as well as peculiarly Hispanic touches of realistic rusticity, are combined with personal reworkings of the biblical theme of the Good Shepherd. Timoneda's *Auto de la oveja perdida* (published in his *Ternario espiritual* in 1558 and again in 1575 in his *Primer ternario sacramental*) probably lies behind Lope's cultivation of this theme, which we find appearing in his own *auto, La oveja perdida* (The Lost Sheep), as well as in episodes of the *comedias La buena guarda* (The Good Guardian) and *La fianza satisfecha* (*A Bond Honored*). It was perhaps as a pupil of the Jesuits in Madrid that Lope had first witnessed or taken part in dramatic representations of the Good Shepherd and the lost sheep.[41] Of the four sonnets, one recounts an incident, now in the past, between the shepherd and a favorite lamb, while the other three present the voice of the shepherd, who has lost his bellwether, speaking out in urgent distress. All involve esthetic exploration as well as expression of intense feeling and exemplify Lope's capacity to attain momentary esthetic detachment even when his emotions are most deeply engaged.

The chronological sequence of the sonnets is highly uncertain. As Edwin Morby has shown, one cannot safely assume from the distinctness of "Silvio a una blanca corderilla suya" ("Silvio [threw his crook] at one of his little white she-lambs") that it necessarily antedates the other three, although, to judge from the underlying situation, my hypothesis would be that this is in fact the case.[42] It must reflect a stage before the rival's advent, while the other sonnets as certainly postdate this development, though preceding the definitive rupture. That we cannot be sure of their sequence is not a vital matter, for it seems essentially fortuitous: they are to all intents and purposes products of separate but proximate moments of formal esthetic vision, complementary but not interdependent, each with its own perspective.[43] The bereft shepherd speaks in one, "Suelta mi manso, mayoral extraño" ("Let my bellwether go, strange head shepherd"), to the head shepherd who is detaining the bellwether, asking him to let it go; in another, "Querido manso mío que venistes" ("Beloved bellwether of mine"), the appeal is directly to the bellwether, which has strayed to another master; in a third, "Vireno, aquel mi manso regalado" ("Vireno, that pet bellwether of mine"), the grieving shepherd tells one of his fellows of the theft of the bellwether.

In "Silvio a una blanca corderilla suya," the sonnet which probably marks the inception of the cycle, the familiar violent act by the Lope-figure appears:

> Silvio a una blanca corderilla suya
> de celos de un pastor tiró el cayado
> con ser la más hermosa del ganado.
> ¡Oh amor! ¿qué no podrá la fuerza tuya?
> Huyó quejosa, que es razón que huya,
> habiéndola sin culpa castigado;
> lloró el pastor buscando el monte y prado,
> que es justo que quien debe restituya.
> Hallóla una pastora en esta afrenta,
> y al fin, la trajo al dueño, aunque tirano,
> de verle arrepentido enternecida.
> Diole sal el pastor, y ella contenta
> la tomó de la misma injusta mano,
> que un firme amor cualquier agravio olvida.[44]

Through jealousy of a shepherd, Silvio threw his crook at one of his little white she-lambs, no less than the prettiest of his flock. Oh love! of what is your strength not capable? She fled plaintively, and well she might, seeing that he had punished her without blame on her part; the shepherd wept, searching through the mountain and meadow, for it is only right that a debt should be repaid. A shepherdess found her in the midst of this affront and eventually brought her to her owner [where she was] softened to see him repentant, even though a tyrant. The shepherd gave her salt and she happily took it from his selfsame unjust hand, for a firm love forgives any offense.

In a fit of unfounded jealousy the shepherd has thrown his crook at the pet lamb, which has fled, then returned, forgiven its master and been reconciled with him. We have here the familiar motif of the lovers' spat rather than the destructive violence that expressed Lope's anger at the climax of the affair. Though the impulsive violence is still unconventional for the pastoral, a lachrymose apology suffices to close the incident, and the shepherd is all reasonableness and self-accusal as he relates what happened in understanding phrases: "es razón" ("well she might") (l. 5); "es justo" ("it is only right") (l. 8). The acknowledgment of guilt seems as much authentic anxiety to return to the good graces of a mistress as conformity with literary convention. It inverts the roles of Good Shepherd and straying sheep, making the former the errant and repentant party, the latter the forgiving one. The rustic touch of the salt which seals the reconciliation, stemming probably from the earthy pastoral tradition of Timoneda, where it denotes reconciliation through the sacrament of confession, is given a profane and sensual meaning by Lope's undissociated sensibility.[45] By stressing that the salt is taken from the master's very hand, Lope adds overtones of intimacy and makes of the act an expressive sexual symbol.[46] In the firm love of the lamb for its master, "a love which forgets any offense" (l. 14), there is an echo, inverted, secularized, and perhaps unconscious, of the all-forgiving love of the Good Shepherd for his sheep, and the same is true of the contrition in l. 11 ("de verle arrepentido enternecida").[47]

This sonnet was perhaps once offered to Elena as a memento of an incident over which both could smile. But when the final crisis came, stirring Lope to the core, wounding him psychically, and arousing a need for more than virtuosity—for the release and relief that the exercise of his art could bring—he must have begun to reach out for the deeper possibilities of the theme. Eschewing incident and explanation, speaking with new urgency as his own advocate, the shepherd now only insists and challenges, entreats and remonstrates, or feelingly reports his loss. The sheep in question is no longer "one of his white lambs" ("una blanca corderilla suya"): it is a particular, special bellwether ("aquel mi manso"). Identities and relationships are taken for granted, as if the sonnets fitted into a known background situation. In "Querido manso mío," of which we have two versions, aberration, not wilful straying, is attributed to the bellwether:

> Querido manso mío, que venistes
> por sal mil veces junto aquella roca,
> y en mi grosera mano vuestra boca
> y vuestra lengua de clavel pusistes,
>   ¿por qué montañas ásperas subistes

que tal selvatiquez el alma os toca?
¿Qué furia os hizo condición tan loca
que la memoria y la razón perdistes?

    Paced la anacardina porque os vuelva
de ese cruel y interesable sueño
y no bebáis del agua del olvido.

    Aquí está vuestra vega, monte y selva;
yo soy vuestro pastor y vos mi dueño;
vos mi ganado, y yo vuestro perdido.[48]

Beloved bellwether of mine, you who came up to that rock for salt
thousands of times and put your mouth and your carnation-like
tongue on my rough hand: up what rough mountains have you gone,
that such wildness should affect your soul? What frenzy put you in
so mad a state that you have lost memory and reason? Graze on
anacardium so that it may bring you out of that cruel and self-
interested sleep and don't drink the waters of forgetfulness. Here
is your plain [vega], mountain, and wood; I am your shepherd and
you my master [also: mistress]; you the creature of my flock [also:
what I have earned or won] and I am one who has lost himself
over you [also: one you have lost].

The sonnet is created in a moment of conviction or protective fantasy when
any explanation besides aberration is rejected as too unpalatable. The
technique—plea of shepherd to sheep—and the attitude—the forsaken
shepherd is pained and sorrowful but not angry, and is ready to forgive—
recall Lope's dramatic presentations of the Good Shepherd; the theme is
humanized but the roles are no longer inverted. Profane echoes of sacred
details are more noticeable in this sonnet than in the other two.

    The appeal begins by evoking the past in lines whose rough-smooth
texture is expressive of urgent carnal nostalgia. From evocation and
rationalization (in the second quatrain), Lope shifts in the climactic first
tercet to exhortation, wrenching the pastoral framework, then restores an
uneasy balance in the final tercet. The literally aberrant behavior of the
sheep becomes an unaccountable moral and emotional aberration in the
second quatrain. Echoes of the religious allegory are noticeable here.
Two of the faculties of the soul have been "lost" (l. 8): memory, to
which the appeal was made in the first quatrain, and reason (understanding), appealed to in the tercets, while the sheep's wilfulness implies
wrong use of free will as well.[49] In the profane pastoral context the
aberrancy is ascribed to some irrational and abnormal impulse: "selvatiquez,"
"furia" ("wildness," "madness").[50] In secularizing the subject, Lope's

this-worldly outlook inverts the direction of the straying. The easily accessible pastures of plains and valleys, snares of the devil to which Christ must descend in the religious allegories to take the sheep back up his steep slopes, are here the natural abode of love, from which the sheep has strayed up into "montañas ásperas." The strong dactylic downbeat of *ásperas*, coming amidst iambs, is arresting in its roughness, as if there were submerged bitterness surfacing.

After the faint pedantry of the "anacardina" of l. 9, the tenth line is a direct outcry, with its "cruel" and "interesable," the former a reproach, the latter a barb that puts us in emotional proximity to the libels. Both terms are appropriate only to Elena, not to her bellwether mask. The tone of the ending becomes pleading and cajoling. In l. 12, Lope does not stop with the obviously allusive "vega" but heightens the entreaty, sweepingly adding "monte" and "selva." The antithesis of l. 13 gains point by implicit contrast with a religious context where "pastor" and "dueño" would be identical, not opposed.[51] So they had been in the earlier version of this line: "Yo soy vuestro pastor y vuestro dueño" ("I am your shepherd and your master"). If the antithesis indicates heightened polish, it also has a more refined poignancy. The paradox that makes the weaker of the pair the dominant one brings us back to the pastoral world, and in this context the play of the last line, though trite, has a forlorn ring.

Under the pastoral cloak of "Suelta mi manso, mayoral extraño," Lope issues a summons, which is also an appeal, to the one party not denounced or addressed, scarcely even alluded to, in the satires:

> Suelta mi manso, mayoral extraño,
> pues otro tienes de tu igual decoro;
> deja la prenda que en el alma adoro,
> perdida por tu bien y por mi daño.
>   Ponle su esquila de labrado estaño,
> y no le engañen tus collares de oro;
> toma en albricias este blanco toro,
> que a las primeras hierbas cumple un año.
>   Si pides señas, tiene el vellocino
> pardo encrespado, y los ojuelos tiene
> como durmiendo en regalado sueño.
>   Si piensas que no soy su dueño, Alcino,
> suelta, y verásle si a mi choza viene:
> que aún tienen sal las manos de su dueño.[52]

Let my bellwether go, strange head shepherd, since you have another equal in status to you; give up the prize that I adore in my soul, lost [to me] to your joy and my sorrow. Put its bell of hand-worked tin on it and don't let your gold collars mislead it; taken in exchange this white bull that will be a year old when the first grass turns green. If you want markings, it has curly brownish fleece and little eyes that seem to be sleeping in peaceful slumber. If you think that I am not its master, Alcino, let it go and you will see whether or not it comes to my hut: for the hands of its master still have salt [to offer].

Though the poem grows out of a fantasy of things being once again as they were, yearning is strangely compounded with an arrogance reminiscent of the transcript of the hearings—an arrogance never directly expressed toward the real prototype. The result in the two opening quatrains is a tone that oscillates between the peremptory and the conciliatory. However, the unsteady arrogance gradually decreases through the quatrains and in the tercets becomes coaxing, suasory, and wistful. A mood of tender confidence has been achieved through a process of artistic transmutation.

The shifting tones of the sonnet are a product of sure technical control made even surer in the revision of the earlier (by 1593) version for the *Rimas* of 1602. In the quartets there are brusque imperatives every other line, beginning with the blunt opening "Suelta" ("Let it go"); in the intervening lines one encounters softening amplifications. The combination is rhythmically underscored: each imperative produces a strong initial dactylic downbeat in an otherwise even iambic texture. The effect, one of boldness with little to back it up, a brave front in danger of collapsing, is not unlike the impression produced by the blustering passages in the transcript. The fading-out of the arrogance is due to the progressively less peremptory meaning of the imperatives. In the tercets the bereft shepherd anxiously anticipates objections and removes them. He no longer commands. Each tercet is a condition, in the protasis of which the shepherd foresees reluctance, while in the apodosis he seeks to offset it in advance, in the first case furnishing a delicate description, in the second expressing a willingness to put his case to the test.

The sonnet further reflects the juncture at which it was presumably written in a series of transparently allusive details, skillfully analyzed by Fernando Lázaro, who has also noted the tendency in the revised version to remove biographical immediacy and create a purer pastoral atmosphere.[53] The puerilely abusive tone of the "pastorcillo extraño" ("wretched strange shepherd") of the opening line in the earlier version is a familiar symptom of spite and frustration, but such depreciation is out of key with the "igual decoro" ("equal in status") of the second line, which acknowledges the rival's superior rank. The discordance is corrected in the new reading, "mayoral extraño" ("strange head shepherd"); the allusion to the rival's being an outsider remains. Emotional disengagement, corresponding to increased distance in time from the experience, makes Lope more attentive to artistic considerations. The more dispassionate view of the rival, as Lázaro suggests, points in the direction of the Don Bela of *La Dorotea*.

In the earlier version of l. 5, "Ponle su esquila y su grosero paño" ("Put its bell and its coarse cloth on it"), Lázaro sees an allusion (more explicit than that already noted in "Contemplando estaba Filis") to drabness of dress resulting from real sacrifices of Elena for her indigent lover. The recurrence and elaboration of the unconventional detail in *La Dorotea* makes one presume some foothold in reality, as I earlier pointed out. In the definitive version of this line the pastorally anomalous detail gives way to a perfectly bucolic one, as Lázaro notes. The slight anomaly of "collares de oro" ("golden collars") (l. 6), a transparent allusion to the rival's wealth, stands, but gains greater artistic point through contraposition with the rustic "estaño" ("tin").

The details of the description of the bellwether, Lázaro observes, are subtly evocative of real physical features of Elena.[54] The change in the color of the hair from the *negro* of the earlier version to the *pardo* of 1602 is further illustrative of stylization tending toward purer bucolicism: the color *pardo*, as Lázaro notes, quoting Covarrubias, is "el propio que la oveja o el carnero tiene" ("that proper to the sheep or ram"). One may further note that the name "Alcino," a vocative directed to the rival which replaces in 1602 the colorless adjective "indino" ("unworthy") applied to the bereft shepherd in the earlier version (l. 12), is one which Lope gave in *La Arcadia*, a work presumably composed in the interval between the two versions, to a minor character, an older shepherd of noble rank.[55] The seniority and nobility presumably associated with the name, and destined to be retained by Don Bela, accord well with the new status of "mayoral" attained by the rival.

In the revised version of the sonnet a conscious craftsman has been at work smoothing away raw adhesions and sharp edges, stylizing with a certain deliberateness. In the earlier text, the process of artistic transmutation, operating at a deeper psychic level, had appeared to take hold almost by itself. There was already progressive refinement within the fourteen lines and this process is consciously carried on in the new version. Noticeably absent is any overt expression of the jealousy Lope must have been feeling. He achieves the surprising feat of opening at a peak of emotional intensity, yet maintaining an onward development, a progression of feeling, by means of shifts of tone, as the intensity diminishes. The resultant tenseness is relaxed only with the last line, in which the imagery of salt held out in the hand is not only an enticement to a carnal reconciliation but also a gesture of supplication.

Contrasting in technique with "Suelta mi manso" is the remaining sonnet of the group, "Vireno, aquel mi manso regalado":

> Vireno, aquel mi manso regalado,
> del collarejo azul; aquel hermoso
> que con balido ronco y amoroso
> llevaba por los montes mi ganado;
>   aquel del vellocino ensortijado,
> de alegres ojos y mirar gracioso,
> por quien yo de ninguno fui envidioso,
> siendo de mil pastores envidiado;
>   aquél me hurtaron ya, Vireno hermano;
> ya retoza otro dueño y le provoca,
> toda la noche vela y duerme el día.
>   Ya come blanca sal en otra mano;
> ya come ajena mano con la boca,
> de cuya lengua se abrasó la mía.[56]

Vireno, that pet bellwether of mine, with the blue collar; that pretty one with the deep, loving bleat that led my flock among the hills; the one with the curly fleece, the merry eyes, and charming glance, on whose account I was envious of no one and was envied by thousands of shepherds: that one has now been stolen from me, brother Vireno; now it titillates another master and arouses him; it stays up all night and sleeps in the day. Now it eats white salt from another hand; now it eats someone else's hand with the mouth whose tongue set mine on fire.

The emotional pitch, kept deliberately low at the beginning, rises steadily and reaches a peak in the last word. Up to the end of the quartets the tone is subdued. The initial vocative catches the ear of an intimate friend to whom something is to be confided, but the speaker lingers over the preliminaries, describing in detail a favorite animal with whom the addressee is already familiar, as the casual demonstrative of "aquel mi manso regalado" ("that pet bellwether of mine") shows; the speaker has become lost in amorous recollection. His evocation mingles adjectives more affective than descriptive —"regalado," "hermoso," "amoroso," "gracioso" ("pet," "pretty," "loving," "charming")—with others in which Fernando Lázaro sees allusions to real attributes of Elena Osorio: "collarejo azul," "balido ronco," "vellocino ensortijado," "alegres ojos" ("blue collar," "deep bleat," "curly fleece," "merry eyes"). In the eighth line, as the shepherd recalls how he was envied, his composure begins to be shaken. As is usual with Lope, envy, while considered a tribute to one's pride of possession, is also potential disloyalty, and as such gives rise to resentment.[57] The long-postponed and blunt predicate of the ninth line makes theft the result of such envy and breaks the hold of evocation. The bare flat statement still exhibits a certain restraint, but in the rest of the sonnet this disappears as the speaker turns to visualizing the present, reopening his wound and stirring up his jealousy.

Architectonically speaking, the sonnet is organized around two anaphoric series: the four *aquel*'s (ll. 1, 2, 5, and 9) and the three *ya*'s (ll. 10, 12, and 13), to which one may add a fourth enclitic *ya* placed emphatically at the end of the first series (l. 9) and providing transition between the two, since it punctuates the evocative mood and looks ahead to the statement about the present. The stylistic level of the sonnet is low enough to keep this rhetoric close to the natural patterns of colloquial speech, from which the familiarly used *aquel* and *ya* come. The appositive anaphora of the first series, with its repeated returns to a starting point before anything has been predicated, conveys, with a minimum of artifice, a mood of fond lingering. The second anaphoric sequence, on the other hand, carries a series of flat statements in end-stopped lines. The decreasing intervals between the *ya*'s, as against the spacing out of the intervals in the earlier series, the insistent staccato emphasis of the word *ya* itself convey both mounting agitation and fixation; the agitation is metrically underscored in the first tercet by marked anapestic and dactylic departures from the iambic pattern that had prevailed unbroken through the first nine lines, the only exception being an introductory dactyl in l. 8 at the point where, with the thought of envy, retrospection begins to grow unsettling.

Lope's attention to contour and sensitivity to tone is further demonstrated by the amplified echoing vocative "Vireno hermano" ("brother Vireno") placed at the end of l. 9, to close off the long statement it had introduced. It reestablishes the opening context of a confiding intimacy, from which the speaker had lapsed into private reminiscence. The new request for attention and sympathy, an informal *captatio benevolentiae*, is underscored by the appended, ingratiating "hermano." The sonnet falls into a framework of intimate friendship; Entrambasaguas suggests that this Vireno, who appears also in several ballads, may be Melchor de Prado.[58] The silent interlocutor, in any case, is noticeably not himself the object of a summons or appeal, as in the other two sonnets. His role is passive; he is asked only to lend a willing ear. The speaker needs to feel the reassuring presence of someone who will stand by him (the term "hermano" sets Vireno apart from the other envious shepherds), but he is not so much communicating with his friend as letting himself be overheard. Much more than in the other two sonnets Lope is looking inward here, at his own feelings. He cannot attain untroubled contemplation, however, and in giving emotions artistic form, he does not end by sublimating them, as in "Querido manso mío."

A vivid visualizing of intimacies from which he is excluded marks the last five lines of the sonnet. Creative imagination and literary craftsmanship have gained ascendancy over such fantasies, but raw feelings can be felt not far beneath the surface. The allusion to Perrenot de Granvela in "Toda la noche vela y duerme el día" ("It stays up all night and sleeps in the day") (l. 12) is also unusually pointed. But the poem is not aimed at a target, as the satires were, and the vituperation and obscenity emphasized by Lázaro seem only incidental. It is Lope's egocentricity, which will reappear in exacerbated form in the Fernando of La Dorotea, that prevails here. The references to the rival are, in truth, curiously impersonal: "me hurtaron," "otro dueño," "otra mano," "ajena mano" ("has been stolen from me," "another master," "another hand," "someone else's hand"). The vagueness of this "otherness" locates the real source of the irritation in the speaker's ego, not in his relationship with anyone else. To whatever prurient visions Lope's vivid imagination may have led him—play and provocation (l. 10), salt-eating (l. 12), and fantasies more carnal still in the last two lines—the self that returns in the last two words of the sonnet gives us the key. Lope here sees himself as a victim not simply of robbery but of rejection. His obsession is twofold: with another's enjoyment of what was once his and with his own repudiation by this same lost possession. With his characteristic sensory acuteness, he sees his rejection at the most basic level—the sexual—and it is this view, not pornography or calumny, that accounts for the seeming pruriency of the sonnet.

But it is not the question of taste or moral tone nor is it clinical interest that matters here; rather the fact that these psychic nuances in Lope's attitudes will help to explain, mutatis mutandis, the character, temperament, and behavior of Fernando in La Dorotea. And it needs to be stressed that while an almost physical anguish can be felt behind this sonnet, it is born, like the others, of an esthetic impulse. An opaque state of emotional turmoil, in which anger, jealousy, resentment, insecurity, a sense of rejection, deprivation, longing, desire, nostalgia warred confusingly, is here given order, illumination, and focus. The shape, direction, and control of the emotions are new, although their essential character remains to a surprising extent unchanged. The sonnet shows how close the realm of artistic expression may come to that of experience in Lope, how easily he crosses the threshold from one to the other. The informality of the style and the intimacy of the tone underscore this proximity.

Noticeably absent in this, as in the other sonnets on the straying sheep, are indications of the histrionic sensibility so much in evidence elsewhere. There is no striking of attitudes; there are no self-generated accesses of emotion. No doubt Lope never intended his poetic summons to reach Perrenot de Granvela; he nevertheless writes as gravely as if he really expected that that sonnet, or his appeal to Elena, would bring her back. When he wrote the third sonnet he perhaps had lost all hope, but even this is not certain. Moments of despair and hope, moods of anguish and confidence surely came and went, each with its own temporary truth. It is in such moments that we see Lope addressing his appeal to the *manso* (bellwether), his summons to the rival, his confidences to his fellow swain, impelled at once by human urgencies and by a love of artistic experimentation, a wish to assay a diversity of approaches to a particular poetic idea. With the *manso* theme the experimental field is narrower than with the sonnets on ruins because the perspective remains constant: the situation is always seen from the angle of the despoiled or forlorn shepherd, even when the account is in the third person, as in "Silvio a una blanca corderilla suya." This consistent proximity to the human viewpoint of Lope is perhaps the reason for the emotional intensity of these poems and for the focus on the self which reaches its height in "Vireno, aquel mi manso regalado." With the poems on the ruins motif, on the other hand, one does not usually sense such immediacy of personal involvement; when one does, as in the contest between love and time, the artistic control is less sure. Nevertheless, in the ruins poems, the thematic range of Lope's experimentation is wider and the implications for the *acción en prosa* more significant. As Lope returns to the subject and reworks it, the symbolism of ruins grows more comprehensive. Its sphere, less personal, embraces mutability, with its corollaries of evanescence and change and also of evolving life; and disintegration, in the form both of fragmentation and of conflagration, the latter with the further expressive resources of fire imagery.

Certain sequences of the *acción en prosa* will possess the power of the pastoral sonnets to move us at a basic human level. The masterwork will also probe more deeply into the broader reaches of human experience evoked in the sonnets of the other group. For the moment, however, the remaining early avatar, a more striking and extensive antecedent to the *acción en prosa*, the dramatic embodiment of Lope's experience in *Belardo el furioso*, must be considered.

Belardo el Furioso
V

The special interest of *Belardo el furioso*, as one looks ahead to *La Dorotea*, lies in its directly dramatic shaping of the experiential material. For all the differences in the dramatic species and destination of the two works, generically *Belardo el furioso* was the closest of any of the antecedents to *La Dorotea*, and perhaps for this reason the play provides it with the largest number of specific precedents in episode and situation, even in word and phrase. These have been studied since Menéndez y Pelayo, most profitably by Edwin S. Morby. I shall be drawing on their findings, insofar as they relate to aspects of the play of concern here, occasionally even supplementing them.[1]

It is desirable to begin by summarizing the play's action. The setting is Arcadia and the characters are all shepherds. A brief opening dialogue between two rejected suitors of Jacinta underscores her extraordinary freedom from cupidity (*interés*) and her obstinate devotion to the poor, "threadbare" ("roto") Belardo. The next scene shows the lovers swearing eternal fidelity. Immediately thereafter Jacinta's uncle, Pinardo, appears and proposes that she replace her penniless poet by the wealthy Nemoroso. Jacinta unhesitatingly agrees; Pinardo introduces Nemoroso and Jacinta signifies acceptance by giving him her hand even before he has offered his. Belardo, having witnessed the entire scene, comes forth in a jealous rage. Jacinta confirms the *fait accompli*, they quarrel violently, Belardo starts off in desperation, threatening to hang himself, she retains him with a feigned swoon which he exposes by making a pass at her with his dagger. He rails at her, delivers himself of a tirade against the power of money, and storms off. With a story that he has killed a man and must flee Arcadia, he prevails on Cristalina, a former mistress, to give him jewels and money. He proposes to destroy Jacinta's letters and keepsakes but lingers over them and puts them away instead.

The second act opens in Italy three months later. Unable to forget Jacinta, Belardo is persuaded to return to Arcadia by his companion Siralbo. The grasping Jacinta is seen extracting rich gifts from Nemoroso. Belardo and Siralbo, having returned, encounter Pinardo and learn that Jacinta is about to marry Nemoroso. The news drives Belardo mad. Armed with a bulrush, he duels with Siralbo, believing him Nemoroso, and convinces himself that he has vanquished his rival. He then goes in search of Jacinta and, finding her with Nemoroso, gives the latter a thrashing. In the opening scene of Act III, a day later, Belardo overtakes the fleeing Jacinta. She pacifies him, then slips away. His madness takes a new turn: he decides she has died, like Eurydice, and resolves to descend into hell after her, like Orpheus. Siralbo, however, appeals to Jacinta, who plays a Eurydice-like part and restores Belardo to his senses by acknowledging her wrongdoing and promising to forget Nemoroso. The reconciliation drives Nemoroso and Cristalina half mad with jealousy. Both rivals have murderous designs but decide, on learning from Pinardo that he has joined Jacinta and Belardo in marriage, to marry instead themselves.

Though the date of *Belardo el furioso* cannot be fixed definitively within the period 1585–95 postulated by Morley and Bruerton, Montesinos is surely correct in placing it close to the year 1588. The first act and the beginning of the second seem literally written with a vengeance, like the libelous verse and the *romances de desamor*. The ensuing mad scenes (Acts II and III), in which the rejected and frustrated Belardo acts out his resentment, shift the action to a domain where literary precedent—Ariosto, Garcilaso, and the Orpheus myth—come into play amidst effects of improvisation and burlesque. In the coda of reconciliation and marriage, which restores order and harmony in conformity with the convention of the *comedia*, a fantasy of wish-fulfillment is also at work. There is an analogy with the ballads in which Belardo permits himself to denounce Filis but ends by protesting enduring love.

The rough and precipitate character of the play makes one wonder if Lope did not compose it in haste to fulfill a commitment to a producer— conceivably the same Porras to whom he had turned after the *pesadumbre* (unpleasantness) with Velázquez. He evidently saw theatrical aspects capable of artistic development in his own story and on this occasion may have decided to go no further afield for dramatic material. The very choice of subject thus exemplifies his paradoxical capacity for self-observation and esthetic detachment even when emotionally involved, his ability to separate the artistic from the personal self.

This capacity, as we shall see, is nevertheless decidedly limited in this instance. To a striking degree, during much of the play, Belardo is simply a mask for Lope, and while he is inevitably viewed disparagingly by his adversaries, his perspective on events, not theirs, has the playwright's sympathy and is vindicated in the end. The play is often redolent of emotions raw and rankling and makes strange material for Arcadia. The pastoral fabric is indeed largely a smokescreen. Though chastened by the outcome of the action for libel, Lope is at heart unregenerate. He resumes the attack from behind the façade of a stage fiction, retaining the pastoral name which, as the transcript of the hearings shows, he assumed everyone would connect with his own, even using it in the title to make the personal relevance unmistakable. If the play was written in the early stages of his Valencian exile and was indeed intended for Porras, it would have been sent to the latter in Madrid and its allusions would have been plain to those in the know, whether in the audience or backstage.

A vindictive impulse can be most plainly seen and studied in the manner of slanting the familiar autobiographically conditioned pattern of events in Act I and the beginning of Act II. The significance of the play would not be very great if it were merely a vehicle for retaliation, however. Of particular interest is the madness which supervenes and which in fact is foreshadowed in the earlier sequences of the play. Madness is the source of the play's thematic unity, for Belardo's movement toward madness, his mad exploits and his emergence from it constitute the only development embracing the play's three acts. Belardo's madness, moreover, is largely an intensification of two significant strains in his make-up: his marked poetic bent and the histrionic element in his behavior. The former strain gives his character a decidedly literary cast and raises, however haphazardly, the issue of the interaction between poetic expression and real conduct and experience. Histrionic behavior, for its part, is not confined to Belardo in the play. I shall consider the two strains as they arise, pointing out the histrionic in examining the action prior to the onset of madness, and later in connection with the madness proper. In the same way Belardo's poetic vocation is first noticeable prior to the stage of madness, then in conjunction with it. Both the poetic and the histrionic elements suggest that Belardo's madness is less a psychosis than a heightened reflection of elements in the make-up of Lope the man and artist.

The other significant *leitmotiv* of the play is the power of wealth, treated by Lope now from the angle of need (*necesidad*), now from that of cupidity (*interés*). It may most easily be examined in connection with the action that follows the quarrel of Belardo and Jacinta.

If one compares the principals in the action for libel with the *dramatis personae* of *Belardo el furioso*, a striking simplification becomes evident. The multiple targets of the satires—father, mother, brother, cousin—are reduced to the single figure of an uncle. The procuring alleged in the libels occurs before the spectators' eyes in the play. The action is streamlined in keeping with the depiction of an Elena-figure who has no need for so many persuaders and intermediaries. Perhaps some lingering sense of prudence as well as considerations of dramatic decorum make the intermediary an uncle, rather than a parent. (Lope may even have been remembering that Elena's uncle was a plaintiff at the hearings, though there is evidently little connection between Pinardo and Diego Velázquez; the latter, not a butt of the libels, had appeared only in the name of his daughter, Ana Velázquez.) Pinardo realizes in full the role Lope ascribed to Elena's family; as he begins to speak, he tells Jacinta he does so:

> como experimentado y como amigo,
> como piadoso padre, y como viejo.[2]

> as a man of experience and as a friend, as a tender father and as an old man.

Later Belardo flings the charge of procuring at him with a savagery reminiscent of the satires:

> *Belardo:* Este ha sido el alcahuete
>   del negocio sucedido.
> *Pinardo:* . . . .
>   ¡Yo alcahuete!
> *Belardo:*   ¡Tú, mal viejo,
>   que aquella hechicera vendes!

>   (p. 682b)

> *Belardo:* Here is the procurer in this business. *Pinardo:* . . . I, a procurer? *Belardo:* Yes, you, you evil old man, you put that sorceress up for sale!

Pinardo's behavior as procurer is demonstrated in a key scene, whose equivalent Lope must have visualized with obsessive frequency: the pressuring of Elena by her family. Possibly Lope had an account of such pressure from his mistress, as Zaide does in the ballad "Por la calle de su dama" and as Fernando does in *La Dorotea*. The present version in any case is crudely caricaturesque. The familiar motif of Belardo's public indiscretions, so prevalent in the ballads, is here devoid of its usual playfulness:

> *Pinardo:* . . . Al fin se alaba.
> *Jacinta:* ¿Se alaba?
> *Pinardo:*   Y yo, por Júpiter lo juro,
>   que cierto día en esa fuente estaba
>   en un corrillo de otros de tal seso
>   donde por dicha algún papel mostraba.
>   No digo yo, Jacinta, que este exceso
>   ni la murmuración del valle todo,
>   a quien es tan notorio tu suceso,
>   te obliguen a dejalle de algún modo;
>   mas solamente a no vivir tan loca
>   si algún sano remedio te acomodo.
>
> (p. 671a)

> *Pinardo:* . . . In short, he is boasting. *Jacinta:* Boasting? *Pinardo:* By Jove, I swear that one day he was at that fountain in a group of other giddy spirits to whom he was no doubt showing a love-note or two. I do not say, Jacinta, that this overstepping and the gossiping of the whole valley, to whom your affairs are so thoroughly known, require you to drop him completely: only to not lead such a senseless life if I arrange some sensible remedy for you.

The familiar features recur with the thinnest of pastoral coverings: the coterie of intimates; the displaying of the lady's love-notes (one recalls the disingenuous references to letters from Elena in the trial record); the notoriety of the affair, acknowledged by Lope himself in the transcript; finally, Pinardo's suggestion that it would be feasible for Jacinta to divide her favors between two lovers, the only trace in the play of the arrangement quite possibly adopted for a while in reality and destined to reappear in *La Dorotea*.

The suggestion falls on deaf ears in the play because Jacinta is only too ready to listen to her uncle's case against Belardo and does not stop at halfway measures:

> Cualquiera cosa de ésas me provoca,
> Pinardo, a aborrecelle y que en mi vida
> su nombre escuche nadie de mi boca.
>
> (p. 671a)

> Any one of these things incites me, Pinardo, to detest him and to keep his name from ever crossing my lips again.

The promptness of this about-face exemplifies Lope's indifference to plausibility of motivation. More seems involved here than the primacy of action over character, however. For the *comedia* stage, to be sure, the saga of himself and Elena was bound to turn into a rapidly paced sequence of surprises, deceptions, volte-faces, and bravura passages that would appeal to the undiscriminating tastes of the audiences Lope was writing for at this period. Here, however, we encounter an intentional deformation, not merely conventional typing of character: behind the caricaturization there are clearly vindictive and angry impulses.

Jacinta is disconcerted when Belardo, whose name she had resolved never to speak again, appears and denounces her, prompting some brief second thoughts. She shows no concern for his poetry but she does for the pleasure (*gusto*) he gave her.

> ¿Por dicha hallaré
> en el talle y con el oro
> el gusto que en éste hallé?
>
> Will I perchance find in good looks and gold the pleasures I found with him?

she asks herself (p. 673a). *Gusto*, not further defined, suggests attractions on the order of the shepherd's salt-filled hands, a kind of appeal surely flattering to Lope's ego. However Jacinta soon resumes (p. 673a).

> Este es pobre, luego es malo
> . . . .
> sin duda el rico es mejor;
> con el mismo amor le igualo.
>
> He's poor, therefore bad . . . No doubt the wealthy one is better: I equate him with love itself.

Underlying this crude reasoning is the assumption that Jacinta still loves Belardo, and the same is true of a reference in the same speech to "seis años que le he querido y le quiero" ("Six years that I have loved and [still] love him"). But nothing comes of this love in the play: at no point does it cause Jacinta any pangs and it does not really anticipate the love that automatically shows up at the end when Jacinta takes Belardo back. Artistically infertile and belied by Jacinta's behavior, it is an incongruous carry-over from those ballads that depict the Elena-figure as suffering some inner conflict, and ultimately a sign of Lope's inability to conceive that Elena could have ceased to care for him.

Lope rounds out Jacinta's verbal rejection of Belardo by putting the two through a number of feints at physical violence in which they seem to give vent to hostility but tacitly collaborate as in a game. First, Belardo's threatened suicide:

> *Jacinta:*   Tente: ¿dó vas?
> *Belardo:* A buscar alguna rama
>   en que dejase la fama
>   que Ifis dejó en la reja.
>
> (p. 673b)

Jacinta: Hold on, where are you going? *Belardo:* In search of some branch on which I can repeat Iphis's famous act at the grilled window.

Then, Jacinta's pretended swoon: she sits down rather than keeling over:

> *Belardo:* ¿Desmáyaste?
> *Jacinta:*   ¿No lo ves?
> *Belardo:* El suelo está ahí . . .
> *Jacinta:* ¿En el suelo me has dejado?
> *Belardo:* Muy buen lugar has hallado
>   para desmayo fingido . . .
>
> (p. 673b)

Belardo: Are you fainting? *Jacinta:* Can't you see I am? *Belardo:* The ground is here. *Jacinta:* You'd leave me lying on the ground? *Belardo:* You've found the proper spot for a fake faint.

Belardo's further exposure of the swoon as faked:

> *Belardo:* . . . ¡Pero yo, con esta rabia
>   y esta daga, estoy aquí
>   sin matar a quien me agravia!
>   ¡Muere, cruel!
> *Jacinta:*   ¡Ay de mí!
> *Belardo:* ¡Oh, Medea astuta y sabia!
>   ¿Ves cómo todo es fingido?
>   Como la daga has sentido,
>   sin ayuda en pie te has puesto.
>
> (p. 673b)

Belardo: But, with this rage and this dagger, am I just to stay here without killing my offender? Cruel woman, die! *Jacinta:* Woe is

me! *Belardo:* Oh cunning, clever Medea! See how it was all a fake?
As soon as you felt the dagger, you got to your feet with no help.

The lines here approach simple stage directions; they spell out what is to
occur in performance. Jacinta's running description of her swoon makes
indisputable Lope's burlesque intention. The careful avoidance of the
extremes threatened aims at an audience reaction of hilarity rather than
anxiety. The lines of both characters underscore the play-acting Lope has
built into their roles, the effect of pantomime or shadowboxing, ultimately
a product of his ludic sense. The mixture of spontaneity and control points
to histrionism of the sort displayed by Lope in the transcript of the hearings,
although the tone here is lighter.

After a further harmless pass at Jacinta—"¿Es esto justo? / ¡Que no te
doy!" ("Is this right? And I don't stab you!")—the interview reverts to the
verbal level (p. 674a).[3] Presently Belardo exits, threatening a vengeance he
will not take. Left alone, Jacinta is exultant: "Ya no más necesidad" ("At
last free of want") (p. 674b). Emancipation from Belardo will mean
freedom from want. Then follows a demonstration of how Jacinta takes
advantage of this freedom to prey on Nemoroso's riches. Increasing
prominence is given to *interés*, a concept which includes both individual
cupidity and the universal corrupting power of wealth. Poverty stands out
by the same token as the single count against Belardo. This elementary
simplification guarantees the audience's sympathy and bypasses any question
of guilt, aside from the inconsequential verbal indiscretions already noted.
More ingenuous than his creator, Belardo is characterized by a blamelessness
that reflects Lope's failure to grasp his own responsibility.

Undoubtedly one of the lasting effects of the experience with Elena was
to bring home to Lope, as a fact of life, the traditional views of moralists on
the corrupting power of wealth, a subject particularly insisted on in his day
in sermon, emblem, and disquisition.[4] Lope's relative poverty had early
made him feel the unevenness of the contest between money and poetry, a
point instinctively grasped by so many lackeys in his plays and even by some
masters, like the Count in *La moza de cántaro* (The Girl with the Water Jar),
who states succinctly that "el oro . . . es excelente poeta" ("gold . . . is an
excellent poet").[5] Speaking a little like a lackey himself in a 1611 letter to the
Duke of Sessa, Lope deflates pastoral idealism along the same cynically
material lines:

Restituyo a Vex.ᵃ las canciones de Tirsi y Galatea sin respuesta, por
no ofender con mi mal humor la cándida limpieza de dos amantes,
que sólo en Portugal pudieran hallarse en este tiempo; pero si

conociera a Tirsi le aconsejara enviara a Galatea vn brinco de
diamantes y vna libranza a los Cruzes para alguna seda y passamanos;
que ella entendiera mal que él le pudiera decir más.[6]

I return to Your Excellency the songs of Tirsi and Galatea without
comment, in order not to offend with my ill humor the innocent
purity of two lovers who in these days could only be found in
Portugal. But if I knew Tirsi, I would advise him to send Galatea
a diamond clasp and an order on the Cruzes for some silk and lace
edgings; she would surely feel this was the best message he could give
her.

Viewed more penetratingly and less simplistically, the conflict between
gold and verse, materialism and poetry, would become a central theme of
La Dorotea. Embryonically it had already been present in the situation of one
of the libelous poems in which the friar's gold crowns prevail over another
suitor's verse-offerings, and it is similarly discernible in Pinardo's outlook:

> Y es lo peor que llega tu trabajo
> a que te pague en versos y papeles,
> y tales, que a Virgilio le aventajo.
> ¿Posible es que con esto te consueles,
> con papeles discretos? Ve a la plaza
> para comprar lo que otras veces sueles:
> no es moneda que corre . . .
> ¿Cómo piensas pasar el frío invierno,
> a lumbre de papeles y palabras?
>
> (p. 671a)

And the worst part is that your misfortune has reached the point
where he pays you in verse and love-notes, and such verse! Why,
I'd put him ahead of Virgil anytime! Is it possible that you can be
satisfied with this, with clever notes? Go to the market to get what
you usually buy: it's not a coin that circulates . . . How do you
expect to get through the cold winter by the light of notes and
words?

Later (p. 686a), Belardo himself laments that Nemoroso

> . . . Con el son de unos doblones sólo,
> ha derribado del primero cielo
> mis papeles, mis versos y mis lágrimas.

. . . With the mere sound of doubloons, has knocked down from the
first heaven my notes, my verse, my tears.

Yet, even if Lope opens this perspective on the conflict between poetry and wealth, he does not explore it artistically; *Belardo el furioso* did not provide a suitable framework for emphasizing any issue besides the obvious and easily dramatized one of wealth versus poverty. As he dramatizes this issue, however, *interés*—cupidity, material-mindedness—begins to be abstracted from the experiential material as a superior force that holds sway over human wills. While it does not become an allegorical figure like that of Wealth in numerous *autos sacramentales*, its power is recognized in a curiously impersonal way by characters who stand aside from their roles to acknowledge it. Thus when Belardo exclaims: "¡O interés!" during the quarrel with Jacinta, she replies matter-of-factly (p. 673a): "Las piedras gasta" ("It wears down stones"). Soon thereafter (p. 674a) Belardo himself interrupts his storming to remark almost understandingly:

> Ahora bien, necesidad,
> aquesta crueldad te obliga.

> Now then, it is need that forces you to this cruelty.

Later on, in Act III, Jacinta, though impelled now by greed, not need sententiously remarks (p. 689b), "Es sin ley la estrecha necesidad" ("Strict need knows no law"), while Belardo turns from denouncing her to admit (p. 690a):

> ... El oro, ¿a quién no obliga?
> ¿A cuál César no rindió?

> ... Gold, on whom is it not binding? What Caesar has it not overcome?

At the moment of reconciliation (p. 697b), Jacinta noticeably steps out of her role to excoriate the

> maldito interés infame
> que a tal maldad me obligó.

> damned filthy lucre, forcing such wrongdoing on me!

Not even now is Lope done with this *leitmotiv* of the play. Jacinta-Elena may repudiate it in the end but Pinardo, behind whom stand all of Elena's relatives, stays in its clutches. With what can the lovers overcome his expected objection to their marriage?

Jacinta: Yo sé con qué podrás.
Belardo: ¿Más que es interés?
Jacinta: No es más.

(p. 699a)[7]

Jacinta: I know with what. *Belardo:* I'll bet it's cupidity. *Jacinta:*
Exactly.

Pinardo's facile change of heart leaves intact the profiteering core of his
nature, and is perhaps even a jibe at Elena's family, while the unusual
clairvoyance of the two principals in regard to *interés* reflects an obsessive
conviction on Lope's part that the venality of Elena and her family was the
root of all his trouble.[8] Such insistence on the irresistibility of *interés* ought
by rights to have absolved Jacinta of responsibility for her behavior. This is
not the conclusion one draws from the play, however, because Jacinta is
depicted as willingly giving in to her greed and carried to caricaturesque
extremes by her avidity for money. In Act II, for example, three months
after she has accepted Nemoroso, she is shown fleecing him so cynically
that Pinardo himself cautions her:

Hija, enmiéndate en pedir
porque la caza no alteres . . .

Child, hold back on what you ask so as not to alarm the game . . .

To which she answers:

Calla, que ya está en el lazo;
gaste, deshaga, consuma
en joyas, cadena y saya;
no haya miedo que se vaya
aunque no le quede pluma.

(p. 681a)

Hush, he's already in the snare. Let him spend, ruin himself, wear
himself out on jewels, necklaces, and dresses. No danger of his leaving
even though he hasn't a feather left.

Lope's animosity is obvious. With a slight change of focus he might have
shown Jacinta in the much more sympathetic role of victim of forces too
strong for her. He stands so squarely behind his own persona, Belardo, that
he is unable to respond to the richer possibilities implicit in a less one-sided
view of the Elena-figure. Any inclination to transcend resentment and
broaden the scope of the experience by extrapolating a meaning in terms of

the forces that govern it is nullified by continuing emotional involvement.
The stark assertion of the libels—"The lovely Filis supports her relatives"—
and the imputations about earlier lovers reappear, hardly disguised, in such
a passage as the following:

> Pobres parientes tienes en el valle,
>
> solían comer de tu favor, solían;
> déjaslos ya; ¿quién ha de haber que calle?
> Otro tiempo sus casas guarnecían
> de los ricos presentes de tu mano,
> con que los mayorales te servían;
> agora ¡por Apolo soberano!
> y yo el primero, de hambre están muriendo
> por un rapaz, por un rapaz villano.
>
> (p. 671b)

You have poor relatives in the valley, they used to eat thanks to you,
they used to. Now you've abandoned them: who would not protest?
They used to decorate their homes with lavish gifts from you, which
the head shepherds presented you with. Now, by sovereign Apollo!
they're dying of hunger, I first of all, on account of a boy, a
wretched boy.

Yet when one looks closely, one discovers, overshadowed by this garish
emphasis, ingredients for a more sympathetic depiction of Jacinta–Elena:
the present passage in fact, like the opening dialogue, reveals that, out of
love for Belardo, she has for a long time renounced promiscuity and its
profits. Pinardo, in praising Nemoroso, disparages the extremes of sacrifice
Jacinta has gone to for Belardo:

> Este es amor, aquésta sí que es prenda;
> y no que por seguir a un pobre y roto,
> una loca mujer las suyas venda . . .
>
> (p. 671a)

This is love, this is a real lover; and not for a poor woman to sell her
belongings in order to stick to a tattered pauper . . .

There is a similar allusion in one of Jacinta's letters reread by Belardo:

> Si te parece que eres pobre y que no puedes acudir a mis cosas,
> cuando yo gaste mis galas en tu servicio, no he de parecerte mal con
> una pellica parda. (p. 677a)

If you think you are poor and cannot provide things for me, while
I am spending my finery for your sake, I won't look bad to you in a
drab sheepskin.

Jacinta had sold her finery to support her poverty-stricken lover, a form of
devotion peculiar enough to imply some root in the reality of Lope's
experience with Elena. Though the emphasis of the play is on Jacinta's
reversion to type, still, in these intrusive details indicative of a side of her
character which we do not see, lie possibilities for another view of the
Elena-figure, for the depiction which will in fact appear in *La Dorotea*.

   The prominence of the theme of wealth and poverty reduces the figure of
the rival, Nemoroso, to little more than a colorless embodiment of wealth.
He has the rival's usual attributes: riches, status, and power; he is a *mayoral*,
"de los que ahora son más principales" ("one of those of highest standing
today") (p. 671a), a longtime resident of their Arcadian valley, says Pinardo,
who emphasizes his vast holdings and the pastoral wealth which he is placing
at Jacinta's disposal.[9] Belardo, on the other hand, calls his rival "un extraño
pastor de ayer venido" ("a strange shepherd who arrived only yesterday")
(p. 683a). This inconsistency, like the later gifts "más de rey que de pastor"
("more like a king's than a shepherd's"), shows that conventional pastoral
traits have not been reconciled with the attributes of Perrenot de Granvela;
the rival's figure is clearly still uncrystallized artistically in Lope's mind.

   In contrast to this powerful *mayoral*, as in the sonnets, stands the small,
humble figure of the boyish shepherd Belardo. Lope allows a hostile case to
be made against him, as in the Zaide-Zaida ballad, but the charges are
manifestly minor or distorted ones: he is called "un mozuelo aborrecible
y bajo" ("a hateful, base brat"), "un llorón cual otro Adonis tierno" ("a
sissy cry-baby like Adonis"), "un rapaz villano" ("a lowly boy") (pp. 670b,
671a), one of

> estos mozalbillos
> pobres, rotos y loquillos,
> propios zánganos de amor.
>
> (p. 681b)

these beardless youths, poor, tattered, and madcap, who are sheer
spongers of love.

Poverty, indiscretion, social inferiority, madcap youthfulness, unmasculine
sensibilities: the counts cannot be too far removed from views which Lope
must have experienced or presumed on the part of Elena's relatives. Here is

perhaps an indirect justification, on the ground of immaturity, of his own conduct. In any event, we have here an indication that Belardo is too young to assume an adult and manly role vis-à-vis his rival and a rationale for his escaping instead into poetic and histrionic madness. Unlike Lope's usual valorous and limitlessly self-confident heroes, Belardo seems to reflect his author's basic timidity in the face of rank and authority. To counteract the demoralizing power of wealth, Belardo has only the personal attractiveness already alluded to, his poetic vocation, and his madness. The first is peripheral to the action of the play, having been capable of pushing Jacinta to sacrifices before the play begins and to renunciation in the coda, but remaining practically ignored during the drama proper.

Similarly, the effect on Jacinta of Belardo's poetic vocation is hardly more than routine, deducible from passing remarks like Pinardo's, but not demonstrated directly. Nevertheless, Belardo's behavior and speech constantly underscore a vocation for poetry of a different order from the conventional versifying capacity of Arcadians. Clearly this is a matter of special concern to Lope: though he does not find a way to make Belardo's poetic vocation dramatically functional, he is unwilling to dispense with it. From his first appearance, Belardo expresses himself in dense and elaborate poetic rhetoric distinct in stylistic level from the common idiom of the play. I will pause a moment to note characteristic features of this language and manner.

Belardo favours, in the first place, the drawn-out hyperbolic conceit:

> No es tan delgada mi fe,
> que a cualquier viento se doble;
> que aunque en altura compite
> con los cielos, y le imite
> el valor que en ti se encierra,
> tiene un tronco acá en la tierra
> que no hay valor que le quite.
>
> (p. 668b)

My faith is not so slight as to bend with every breeze; even though it rivals heaven in height and the worth you possess is no greater, it has a trunk down here on earth which no power can remove.

His hyperbolic *attitudes* carry to extremes the conventional Platonic-Petrarchan idealization of the beloved:

> ... ¡Oh, traidor de mí!
> Tu hermosura presumí

igualar con mi firmeza;
siendo inmortal tu belleza,
sin duda al cielo ofendí.

(p. 669a)

... Oh, traitor that I am! I presumed to equate your beauty with my fidelity. Since your beauty is immortal, doubtless I offended heaven.

He displays learning of an unusual or pedantic kind, characteristic of the *bachiller* (the ostentatiously pedantic recent graduate).[10] The metaphors describing Jacinta's role in restoring him to his senses provoke the comment "Eres necio y bachiller" ("You're silly and a show-off") (p. 698a) from his retainer, Siralbo:

Como la víbora fuiste,
que es antídoto y veneno.
Fue mi seso como hielo,
que a tu sol se desató,
y luego suelto corrió;
y yo, el hacha vuelta al suelo
muy al vivo me retrata,
que lo mismo con que tiene
sustento, eso mismo viene
a ser después quien la mata.
Ya el hacha volvió a su ser,
y la cera a sustentalla.

(p. 699a)[11]

You were like the viper, which is antidote and poison; my wits were like ice which melted in your sun and then ran free; and I ... the torch held upside down is my exact likeness: the same thing that sustains it turns out to be what puts it out. Now the torch has come back to rights and the wax is nourishing it.

Belardo's *métier* is revealed also in his fondness for reeling off *historias* and *exempla* more profusely and more indiscriminately than is usual in the *comedia*. Contemplating the return to Arcadia, he tells Siralbo (p. 687b) he will be a Hercules in resisting Jacinta, a Narcissus to her Echo, and that no Calypso or lotus-flower will detain him in Italy. In the continuation of this scene, it is as a poet versed in *historias* that Belardo, with Siralbo's help, solemnizes the burial of Jacinta's portrait. Precedents as strange as the act itself are invoked to magnify the occasion:

> *Siralbo:* . . . De Alejandro se dice
> que hizo enterrar su caballo.
> *Belardo:* De la culpa me reservo,
> pues Tiberio, emperador,
> dio noble sepulcro a un cuervo.
> *Siralbo:* Y Troya le dio mejor
> de Silvia al famoso ciervo.
>
> (p. 679a) [12]

Siralbo: . . . It is told of Alexander that he gave his horse a burial.
Belardo: I hold myself blameless since the Emperor Tiberius gave a
noble tomb to a crow.   *Siralbo:* And Troy a better one to the
famous stag of Silvia.

Belardo tends, finally, to passages of bravura rhetoric which include self-maledictions contingent on *impossibilia* and copious catalogues of obloquy.
In one of the self-maledictions, after several stanzas of provisional self-castigation, he calls down upon himself as a penalty for disloyalty:

> . . . a mis ojos, abrazada
> como tórtola casada,
> le des [to a rival], con arrullo, besos
> en su falsa boca, impresos
> con esa tuya dorada.
>
> (p. 669a)

. . . before my very eyes, clasped like a wedded turtledove, may you
give him kisses, cooingly, on his false mouth, imprinted by that
golden [mouth] of yours.

This metaphorical invoking of the kind of situation found in the ballad
"El tronco de ovas vestido," one of the many in the play, is symptomatic
of their similar emotional climate with its pattern of jealousy, violent anger,
and forgiveness. [13]

In the catalogues of abuse the personal thrust is less obvious, the traditional
commonplaces of invective more in evidence, than in the libels and *romances
de desamor.* Lope is thinking of effectiveness in stage declamation, not merely
venting anger:

> Quédate, Circe, sirena,
> viento, puñado de arena,
> áspid, sierpe, mar nublado,
> mal eterno, bien prestado,
> mujer al fin y no buena . . .
>
> (p. 674a)

Stay, Circe, siren, wind, handful of sand, asp, serpent, overclouded
sea, eternal ill, borrowed good, in a word woman and no good . . .

More theatrical is a denunciation of Jacinta nearly four *octavas* long following
the news that she is to marry Nemoroso. After a copious invoking of baleful
omens for their wedding day, the climax is reached:

Maten un hombre en tus umbrales, y ande
toda tu casa en alboroto grande.

(p. 683a)

May they slay a man on your threshold and may the whole household
be thrown into a turmoil.

These startling lines, irrelevant to the action of the play, suggest the motif
that climaxes the ballad "Sale la estrella de Venus" and link the whole
passage to Gazul's denunciation of Zaida. Belardo, however, pours into a
wild verbal fantasy the emotional energy that Gazul discharged physically,
ranting instead of acting.[14]

While there is little response by others in the play to Belardo's poetic
vocation, it is a significant factor in his madness, which partakes of both the
Platonic-Ficinian *furor poeticus* and the *furor amatorius*. Long before Belardo
crosses the threshold of madness in Act II, climaxing his flight from reality,
his joy in Jacinta's love has been expressed in imagery of insanity:

. . . Esto escucho de ti
sin dar voces como loco.
¿Cómo en poder me detengo
este seso que me culpa,
cuando a tanta dicha vengo?

(p. 670a)

. . . How can I hear such words from you without shouting like a
madman? How can I keep control of these wits that accuse me,
when I come into such bliss?

Fury at being repudiated understandably conjures up images of madness also.
Belardo threatens: "Te mataré como loco" ("I'll kill you like a madman")
(p. 672b); and Jacinta reflects: "Este está loco . . . / y será terrible estrago /
si el propósito no mudo" ("This man is mad . . . and there'll be terrible
havoc if I don't change my mind") (p. 673a). At one point (p. 674a) Belardo
declares: "Loco soy" ("I am mad"). The histrionic as well as the poetic
strain in his madness is anticipated in these passages. The turning point comes

when Pinardo enumerates Nemoroso's lavish gifts to Jacinta, "more like a king's than a shepherd's"—jewels, finery, furnishings decidedly non-Arcadian—and Belardo bursts out:

> ¡Calla, viejo mal nacido!
> que me has quitado el sentido
> ¡como si yo le tuviera!
>
> (p. 682a)

> Quiet, ill-born old man! You have deprived me of my wits—as if I had any!

A blurring of the line between rhetoric and reality will persist as a characteristic of this poet's madness. One is never sure how much hyperbole, how much real insanity is present. Though he seems on the verge of actual mental alienation when, after furiously denouncing Jacinta, he asks in a daze, "Siralbo, ¿quién hablaba aquí?" ("Siralbo, who was talking here?") (p. 683a), this hint of a split personality is never taken up and Belardo is not again confused about his identity. The distinctive feature of his madness, in fact, is the self-consciousness with which he proceeds to imitate models; he may be distinguished from those he selects, Orlando and the Albanio of Garcilaso, by this very fact. It is his creator's histrionic streak, his propensity for staging improvised scenes, that lies behind this noticeable self-awareness. The Lope who can work himself up, then turn off his performance, is present in the shifting directions and changing fictions Belardo adopts.

Links of various kinds had been formed in literary and medical tradition between love and madness. Unlike the medieval *loco amor*, with its moral overtones, the Platonic-Ficinian view of love as one of the forms of God-given frenzy was associated with the commonplace picture of the lover as a victim of madness, pleasurable or painful but essentially innocuous.[15] Madness might also be a product of the malady of *hereos*—melancholy caused by frustrated love—to which unrequited lovers fell prey.[16] Neither form of love-madness describes that of Belardo, however, for the hints in the early scenes do not indicate a routine lover's affliction, and in the second act madness is precipitated not by unrequited love but by rejection after six years of reciprocation. His madness is a wild frenzy whose main components are jealousy and anger, and its model is, of course, that of Orlando: madness choleric, not melancholic, which Ariosto ascribes to an "insopportabil some tanto di gelosia, che se ne pèra" ("such an unbearable burden of jealousy that he succumbs to it") (XXIII, 114) and to "odio, rabbia, ira e furore" ("hate, rage, ire, and frenzy") (XXIII, 129). In the exordium to

Canto XXIV, Ariosto distinguishes Orlando's from the ordinary lover's madness:

> che non è in somma amor, se non insania,
> a giudizio de' savi universale:
> e se ben come Orlando ognun non smania,
> suo furor mostra a qualch'altro segnale.

> love, in short, is nothing but insanity in the universal judgment of
> the wise; and while everyone does not go out of his head like
> Orlando, he shows his madness by some other sign.

Manifesting itself in deeds of violence rather than in brooding and moping, Orlando's madness was clearly more suited to dramatic treatment. For all Ariosto's undertone of mockery, it had an affective basis to which Lope felt a temperamental affinity.[17]

Between Belardo's verbal blast at Jacinta and his outburst of mad behavior, the literary cast of his madness reasserts itself. Belardo proclaims as a reality the topsy-turvy world of poetic *impossibilia*:

> Todo está lleno
> el mundo de un confuso barbarismo,
> ya las abejas dan por miel veneno,
> furias el cielo, estrellas el abismo,
> el principio del bien malos sucesos,
> amor desdenes y Jacinta besos.

(p. 628b)[18]

The whole world is full of confused barbarity, with bees producing poison instead of honey, heaven furies, the abyss stars, the beginnings of good bad sequels, love disdain, and Jacinta kisses.

Belardo then applies the universal disintegration to himself in a lengthy elaboration of Orlando's "Amor con che miracolo lo fai, / che 'n fuoco il [his heart] tenghi, et nol consumi mai?" ("Love, by what miracle are you able to keep my heart in flames and never burn it up?") (XXIII, 127):

Belardo: ¿Sabes qué pienso?
Siralbo: ¿Qué?
Belardo: Que estoy abierto,
> según el aire y el dolor recibo,
> desde el cuello hasta el pie y que dentro el pecho
> se me parece el corazón deshecho.
> ¿Está Jacinta en él, por vida mía?

> ¿Cómo está el corazón con tanta mengua?
> ¿Hay fuego, o sola la ceniza fría?
> . . . .
> *Siralbo:* . . . El pecho con un golpe se ha cerrado.
> *Belardo:* Dices verdad: de golpe el pecho tengo,
> pues tantos he sufrido y no me vengo.
> ¿No me vengo? ¿Qué es esto? ¡Viva el cielo!
> ¡Que tengo de escribir el desafío!
> Daca papel, Siralbo.
>
> (p. 683a)[19]

Belardo: Do you know what I think? *Siralbo:* What? *Belardo:* That I am opened up from head to foot, to judge by the air and pain I feel, and that inside my chest my ravaged heart is visible. Is Jacinta perchance in it? How is the heart so eaten away? Is there fire or only cold ash? . . . *Siralbo:* Your chest has slammed shut. *Belardo:* You are quite right. I feel my chest slammed, since I have suffered so many slams without taking revenge. Not taking revenge? How can this be? By the living heaven, I shall write the challenge. Give me paper, Siralbo.

Orlando's spontaneity gives way in the Lopean passage to a sense of make-believe, already indicated in the opening words "¿Sabes qué pienso?" Siralbo joins in a game, play-acting along with his master. But the thought of revenge takes hold of Belardo, redirecting his energies toward action, and literary by-play is momentarily forgotten. Though we are in the mock-heroic world of *Orlando furioso*, the challenge to the rival carries overtones of Lope's own resentment:

> A ti, ruin hombre, rico, vil y avaro,
> tirano de aquel bien que adoro y quiero,
> yo solo en padecer único y raro,
> con armas blancas de lustroso acero
> te desafío, espero y matar pienso.
>
> (p. 684a)

Despicable man, rich, vile and grasping, tyrannizing over that treasure that I adore and desire, I, unique, and extraordinary in my suffering, challenge you with white arms of glistening steel, await you and intend to kill you.

Though Belardo has written the challenge on the ground, he demands that Siralbo deliver it to Nemoroso. There follows a series of farcical mad scenes that covertly express resentment of Perrenot while appealing to the least refined sector of the audience. When Belardo next appears, he is "armado graciosamente con una caña por lanza" ("comically armed with a reed for a lance") (p. 685b). Siralbo poses undisguised as Nemoroso, letting himself be defeated in a mock duel and promising to surrender Jacinta. The result is the only scene in the play in which *furia* is allowed an outlet in unrestrained physical aggression as in *Orlando furioso*. Belardo comes upon the real Nemoroso in the company of Jacinta and gives him a drubbing with a stick. On this transparent note of retaliation the second act ends.

In the third, Belardo's madness takes a new turn: the chivalric framework of the delusion is replaced by a mythical one. Belardo first applies poetic *historias* to his situation, then goes on to recast it in poetic patterns.

> Párate un poco, Atalanta,
> pues paraste tu decoro
> a las tres manzanas de oro
> de aquel pastor extranjero.
>
> (p. 689b)

> Stay a little, Atalanta, since you stayed your dignity for the three golden apples of that foreign shepherd.

Belardo calls after the fleeing Jacinta as the act opens.[20] In order to escape him, Jacinta looks up at the sky and directs an appeal to his poetic imagination:

> ¿No ves, adonde el Oriente
> las nubes esmalta y dora,
> bañándose en una fuente
> sus hermosos pies la aurora?
>
> (p. 690b)

> Do you not see over there where the East is enameling and gilding the clouds, as the dawn bathes her lovely feet in a spring?

As if taking the metaphorical for a real possibility, Belardo looks and Jacinta slips away. The situation is reminiscent of Camila's escape from the mad Albanio in Garcilaso's second eclogue, but an activated metaphor is the pretext instead of a lost trinket. While Albanio is a case of *hereos*, he harks back, like Belardo, to Orlando, an association that may explain the present reminiscence of Garcilaso. It is visible also in the use of the name Nemoroso, the superfluous temporary recapture of Jacinta in anticipation of the definitive one (traceable to the recovery of Camila by Albanio before her definitive loss), the enactment of an Orpheus role by the mad Belardo, which appears to stem from the evocation of Orpheus in the eclogue (ll. 938–945) and the suggestion there of a new descent into hell.

After a futile search for Jacinta, Belardo becomes convinced that she is "otra Eurídice que queda / del áspid muerta en el prado" ("another Eurydice killed by the asp in the meadow") (p. 691a) and that he must descend to hell after her. Belardo's imitation of Orpheus, though loose and improvised from the start and soon turned to burlesque by Lope, is an attempt under cloak of madness to make a situation meaningful and bearable by shaping it to fit a mythic analogue. Belardo still knows that he is only imitating: Jacinta is "otra Eurídice," not Eurydice herself, and the fact that he places himself successively in two roles—Aristaeus and Orpheus—shows that he identifies with neither:

> ¡Triste yo que lo he causado
> por imitar los deseos
> de aquel pastor desdichado!
> Pero pues yo fui Aristeo,
> no dudes que seré Orfeo;
> al infierno he de bajar,
> y dél el alma sacar
> que metió mi mal deseo.
>
> (p. 691a)

Wretched me, to have caused it by copying the desires of that unlucky shepherd! But since I was Aristaeus, have no doubt that I will be Orpheus. To hell I shall descend, and deliver from it the soul that my wrong desire placed there.

What has gone astray here is a poetic imagination, transferring imitation from poetry to life: Belardo is acting out a myth and sustaining a metaphor. He builds a poetic framework around himself and selects the mythic role that best exemplifies the power of lyric art over brute reality. Thus he reasserts the dignity and the stature that he has lost at the hands of Jacinta and Nemoroso. Except for his fortuitous encounter with Nemoroso, it is in retreat from his rival, not in facing him, that Belardo embraces madness.

The complicity of Siralbo and Jacinta soon takes the direction of the Orpheus-role out of his hands and only the shell of the myth remains. Before a mountain cave purportedly the gate of hell, Siralbo summons Jacinta to come forth "no como furia mas como ángel bello" ("not like a fury but like a lovely angel") (p. 697a). She emerges, stating that she is simply her old self transformed:

Saldré de mí misma luego,
que es como fénix salir,
para de nuevo vivir
entre cenizas y fuego;
saldré de la antigua Troya
sobre los brazos de Eneas . . .

(p. 697a)

I shall now emerge from myself, as if emerging like the phoenix to
live again amidst ashes and fire; I shall emerge from the old Troy in
the arms of Aeneas . . .

We are much closer to Elena Osorio than to Eurydice with this talk of
furies, flames, angels, and leaving Troy behind.

These lines mark the point at which the denigrated Jacinta-Elena gives way
to the idealized figure of the dénouement. Jacinta's second volte-face is no
more adequately motivated than the first. Significantly, however, Lope falls
back, as in the deathbed ballads, on the fantasy of an Elena Osorio who takes
pity, acknowledges her wrongdoing, and begs forgiveness. Pity for Belardo
is supplemented by Siralbo's appeal to the histrionic spirit. Jacinta enters into
the act for curing Belardo in a spirit of make-believe and becomes carried
away by her own performance. We are closer to Beauty and the Beast than
to Orpheus and Eurydice:

Jacinta: ¡Loco mío, loco amado,
no por eso os tengo en poco;
que no fuera menos loco
quien fuera menos honrado!
Yo os he dado la ocasión,
mas no para aborreceros,
y baste para volveros
esta humilde confesión.
¡Maldito interés infame
que a tal maldad me obligó;
harélo ceniza yo
y que el viento lo derrame!
No me ha de quedar ya prenda
del tirano Nemoroso,
que en fuego honrado y celoso
no se deshaga y encienda.
Yo os quiero, mi pobrecico

. . . .

Siralbo, ¿respondo bien?

¿Hago buena furia acaso?
Siralbo: ¡Oh, Jacinta, en este paso,
de un ángel nombre te den!

(p. 697b)

Jacinta: My poor madman, my mad darling, I think no less of you for
this, for even one with less honor would be no less mad! I was the
cause of it but not in order to hate you; to restore you let this humble
confession suffice. Damned filthy lucre, forcing such wrongdoing on
me: I'll reduce it to ashes and let the wind scatter it. Not one token
of the tyrannical Nemoroso will I retain that will not be destroyed
and burned up in zealous, honorable flames. I love you, my poor
dear . . . Siralbo, am I answering right? Am I making a good fury?
Siralbo: Oh, Jacinta, in this passage, you should be called an angel.

Belardo is cured by gazing into Jacinta's eyes. The restored vision of her
beauty, which he presently describes in highly hyperbolic terms, exorcises
his madness. The pattern of his experience is now dissociated entirely from
that of Orpheus. Untrammeled poetic expression marks his return to sanity,
even as a misdirected poetic imagination had characterized his madness: he
breaks forth in the sonnet "Querido manso mío." Though obviously composed with no thought of this context—the poem reverses the situation of
the play in imputing madness to the straying sheep—its mood of reconciliation underscores in a lyrical *rallentando* the development in the play. The
situation of the opening is fully restored—"Yo soy la misma que he sido"
("I am the same as I was before"), says Jacinta (p. 698b)—except that a
marriage is now in the offing.

From the foregoing analysis it may be seen that Belardo's madness is a
poet's wilful escape into self-dramatization; it feeds on literature, converting metaphors and myths into patterns of behavior, half studied, half
improvised. Lope happened here on an area of concern most germane to his
own poetic nature but he was not encouraged by the medium to explore it
in depth as he would do in *La Dorotea*. Indeed he was surely unready to
take any view of this area more deliberate than the casual glimpses one
encounters in *Belardo el furioso*.

While the strain of madness, the poetic vocation, the histrionic tendency,
the theme of *interés* stand out when the play is scrutinized, it has been seen
how inadequately these salient aspects are interrelated. There is no single
design and there is a particular weakness in the failure closely to engage the
forces of materialism and poetry. The vacuity of the character of Jacinta-
Elena, in whom such a struggle should have centered, shows how far Lope

was from conceiving the action in these terms. Yet because the poetic vocation of Belardo forced itself upon his attention, the most suggestive aspect of the play for the critic who looks ahead to the *Literarisierung des Lebens* in *La Dorotea* is precisely this border area between experience and its poetic expression in which so many of Belardo's words and actions fall.

As a poet, Belardo is an isolated figure in the play. He does not create around him the literary atmosphere in which the characters of *La Dorotea* live; his poetic capacity does not arouse Jacinta. It is Lope's own involvement with Belardo, his making the play not only a public spectacle but a vehicle for the expression of private feelings, that has drawn Belardo's poetic sensibility into it. As the title shows, it is the situation of Belardo–Lope, not that of Jacinta–Elena, that really concerns the dramatist. He still feels too implicated as a participant to withdraw from the center of the stage: he does not attain the esthetic distance reached in lyric forms. Enriching possibilities are adumbrated, then allowed to lapse. Jacinta's enduring love of Belardo and her justification through need remain embryonic suggestions which must await *La Dorotea* for unfolding in a medium more conducive than the *comedia* to the presentation of the complexities, the dynamics, and the nuances of feeling. The few suggestions of ambivalence in the play center on Belardo's struggle to free himself from Jacinta while he yet clings to his passion, and even this conflict is presented in simple spectacular terms. Aggrievement and honor do not prove significant factors. By verbalizing and enacting his feelings, Belardo works off resentment and vindictiveness so that the wound to his ego can be healed simply by Jacinta's recantation. By the end Lope's interest has evidently shifted from Belardo to the theatrical possibilities of the comic by-play carried on at the mad character's expense. I do not share the view that the work reaches "the level of great human tragedy." [21] In the end the writing of the play has had a liberating effect more by accident than by design. The characters end up as playthings in Lope's hands. Having brought Belardo and Jacinta together again, he amuses himself by giving all the figures a final twirl, keeping the momentum up until he has paired off the rejected rivals, Nemoroso and Cristalina, whose murderous impulses subside as quickly as they have flared up.

In writing *Belardo el furioso* Lope evidently became aware of new levels of meaning, new expressive possibilities in his experience, lingered over them a little, then passed on. The abundant parallels of every kind with *La Dorotea* certainly point to a special proximity between the two works, and the hypothesis that the lost early version of *La Dorotea* which Lope mentions is simply this play cannot be dismissed lightly. Yet in the end it is not persuasive. If an early *Dorotea*, as I suppose, dates from the next few years after *Belardo*, such coincidences would hardly be surprising. The crucial differences in outer and inner form, the attainment of an esthetic impartiality which makes Dorotea-Elena rather than Belardo-Lope the center of the author's concern,[22] the depth and density of the analysis of love and literature—I do not see how *Belardo el furioso* could have undergone a sea change considerable enough to bring them about. Its role was catalytic, rather, and in a different sense the same is true of *La Arcadia,* the pastoral novel on which Lope soon found himself at work.

La Arcadia and La Dorotea

By the time Lope took up residence with his wife, Isabel de Urbina, two years after the action for libel, at the ducal court at Alba de Tormes to serve as the Duke's secretary, time must already have begun to alter his perspective on the adventure with Elena. While the exile lasted he could not of course definitively transcend the emotional and psychological consequences of the break with his mistress. Yet, as an artist, looking back with curiosity and added understanding, he might have begun to see himself and Elena in a different light and to conceive of the whole affair as material for broader artistic elaboration than was possible in lyrics and plays. I incline to believe, as already noted, that he was at work on an early version of *La Dorotea* in the 1590's, while at Alba and perhaps also after his return to Madrid in 1595; he could scarcely have been so sooner. Even if we suppose an original version to have been markedly different from the final one, it is not possible to imagine him in 1587–88 composing the *acción en prosa* as a commentary on unfolding events of his life or putting it together in the short space of time that precedes his departure for Lisbon and the Armada. This is, to be sure, what Lope in his dedicatory note of 1632 claims to have done:

> Escriví *La Dorotea* en mis primeros años, y auiendo trocado los estudios por las armas, debaxo de las vanderas del excelentíssimo señor duque de Medina Sidonia . . . se perdió en mi ausencia . . .
> (p. 48)

> I wrote *La Dorotea* in my early years, and having exchanged study
> for arms, under the banner of the most excellent lord, the Duke of
> Medina Sidonia . . . it was lost during my absence . . .

There is no question that in *La Dorotea*, as we now have it, he has made the
internal time-span of the work correspond to 1587–88, correspond, that is, to
the time of the real crisis with Elena.[1] In the 1632 dedication he would further
have both coincide with the time of actual composition. While the datable
allusions found throughout *La Dorotea* by Edwin Morby (ed. *La Dorotea*,
pp. 20–23) constitute *termini a quo* from all stages of Lope's life, it is a striking
fact that—if we except the clearly late portions of the scenes of the literary
academy—the preponderance of ballads, sonnets, *letrillas* (words to songs),
and all the prose or verse narratives by Lope or his contemporaries cited
fragmentarily or casually referred to in the dialogue belong to the 1590's or
earlier, while the full inserted poems by Lope, as Montesinos has shown, are
all from his later years.[2] Such a trend upsets the focus on 1587–88 and suggests
where we should draw the line in taking Lope's declarations at face value.
When we come upon a pointed allusion to the Alba court,

> *Dor.:* Ardese Troya.
> *Ger.:* ¡Fuego, fuego! dan voces, ¡fuego! suena
>   y sólo Paris dize: Abrase a Elena.
> *Dor.:* ¿Es canción nueua?
> *Ger.:* Esto cantan aora los músicos del duque de Alua.
>
> (p. 432)
>
> *Dor.:* Troy is burning up.   *Ger.:* "Fire, fire! they shout, fire! sounds
> and only Paris says: May it burn up Helen!"   *Dor.:* Is that a new
> song?   *Ger.:* The Duke of Alba's musicians are now singing it.

the "new song" and the "now" sound very much like spontaneous references
to a song newly in vogue at Alba de Tormes.[3] The fire imagery and the play
on Elena and Troy are suggestive of similar practices in the lyrics of that
period. One cannot be absolutely certain, of course; Lope's memory undoubtedly stored up tags of verse a whole lifetime through. Yet meticulous
pains to avoid anachronism are ordinarily not part of his artistic practice even
when he writes with as much care as he took with the *acción en prosa*. It is
plausible to suppose that at least the dialogue surrounding the apparently
early incrustations remains from an earlier version in fact written in the
1590's.

The hypothesis that an early version of *La Dorotea* was composed at this
time is appealing in that it permits us to understand the part which the

writing of *La Arcadia* at the behest of his patron, the Duke, could have had in the shaping of the *acción en prosa*. In my view, the composition of *La Arcadia* during the Alba years—the work was published in Madrid after Lope's return, in 1598—made Lope aware of the still unexplored possibilities of a long prose treatment of the experience with Elena Osorio. This incidental effect was facilitated by two circumstances: the atmosphere of the provincial court at Alba de Tormes, which offered Lope both down-to-earth realities and a literary stylization of them; and what Montesinos has called "the surprising similarity" between the stories of the Duke and of his secretary.[4]

Lope's experience with Elena had made him acutely aware, as the *romances de desamor* show, of how life in evolving can expose the gap between *historia* and *poiesis*. Before him at Alba de Tormes he had evidence of a similar disparity:

> The life that flowed along slowly and monotonously in Alba de
> Tormes or Las Navas needed a stylization of atmosphere and surface.
> This life was not rich or intense enough to model its forms itself,
> and a literary aim was superimposed upon them like a mask. A
> curious modesty on the part of the men, husbands or brothers,
> kept ladies of high station away from this commerce; amorous
> experience was tried out in quarters where there was no possibility
> of losing honor or violating family standards. The Amarilises, Filises,
> Lucindas, Anardas were ambiguous ladies, courtesans, actresses,
> women like Dorotea, sharers in the literary rage as long as their
> beauty or histrionic training equipped them for it; actresses in this
> great play that spread from boards to gardens, stripped of their roles
> by whims or years. The feelings aroused set up stimuli and bursts of
> emotion, the expression of which was entrusted to the most refined
> techniques.[5]

It is not Lope's purpose in *La Arcadia* to probe into the relations between actuality and its literary stylization. His aim is to lend a more lasting dignity than ephemeral pageantry could provide to the Duke's unedifying matrimonial and extramarital affairs by making a "libro de pastores" ("shepherd-book") out of them, casting them, that is, in a literary mold enjoying the highest prestige. Only in passing is literary love set against love as individually experienced in the work, and it is possible for the hero to be permanently cured of passion in the end by a purely external treatment: a guided tour through temples of learning and disillusionment where the wisdom of the ages is displayed for his edification.

Yet it is Lope himself who alerts us that something more is involved. "A vueltas de los agenos [pensamientos], he llorado los míos" ("Amidst the thoughts of others, I have wept over my own"), he writes in the Prologue. "Y más tratando amores con desdichas que cayeron en mí como en su mismo centro" ("All the more so for treating an unhappy love which hit home to me as to its very center").[6] His revealing excuse for *La Arcadia*'s shortcomings is "que nadie puede hablar bien en pensamientos de otro" ("no one can speak well about another's thoughts"), an indication that writing for his patron has at once stirred up feelings of his own and placed constraints on the urge to self-expression. In these statements one glimpses a creative disposition favorable to the conception of a *Dorotea*. They invite us to look beneath the surface of *La Arcadia* and when we do, we encounter restless emotional undercurrents that point toward author as much as hero. The introductory description of the rival to Amphryso–Alba, for example, reads: "Era rico como ignorante y presuntuoso como rico, atrevido como grosero, y venturoso como indigno" ("He had an ignoramus's wealth, a wealthy man's presumption, a coarse man's boldness, and an unworthy man's luck") (p. 6). There is evident here a wish to demonstrate loyalty to a patron, but the bitterness has its psychological roots in Lope's resentment of Perrenot de Granvela. The vehemence of the statement is startling.[7] One is even more struck by an unrefuted declaration toward the end that at one blow destroys the whole Neo-Platonic framework of the literary pastoral, to which Lope elsewhere in the work offers lip-service.[8]

> No se ha de llamar inmortal lo que está sujeto al tiempo. El argumento que casi todos los amantes hacéis en esto es frívolo y ridículo: porque decís que amor está en el alma, y que el alma es inmortal, y que assí puede el amor vivir eternamente: y no se deben de acordar entonces, que con qualquiera disgusto, zelos o ausencia, no sólo dejan lo que aman, pero lo aborrecen y persiguen.　(p. 386)

> What is subject to time ought not to be called immortal. The reasoning that almost all you lovers use in this is frivolous and ridiculous, for you say that love is in the soul and the soul is immortal and thus love can live forever. And you don't seem to recall that with any unpleasantness, jealousy, or absence, you not only forsake an object of love but hate and persecute it.

Here, suddenly Lope cuts through to the hard ground of experienced reality. Premises that hold in literature or moral philosophy are challenged, the power of time and the ironic unpredictability of human emotions are asserted. If the passage looks back toward Elena Osorio and the *romances de desamor*, it also looks in the direction of *La Dorotea*.

The arguments against love entrusted in the casuistry of the pastoral novel to shepherds free of this passion—the most prominent example being the "desenamorado" ("fancy-free") Lenio of Cervantes' *La Galatea*—are voiced in *La Arcadia* by Cardenio, el Rústico. They are not so much theoretical and formally structured (as in Lenio's debate with Tirsi in *La Galatea*) as practical and disabused. Cardenio recites the Neo-Platonic tenets, only to undercut them:

Dicen que amor es deseo
de hermosura en el amante,
de engendrar su semejante
con santa paz de hymeneo,
y que es del amor empleo
por quien sus discursos calma,
y que a la razón la palma
el apetito le quita,
y que donde quiere habita,
y no donde anima el alma.

Pastores, desta verdad,
aunque os parezca segura,
sabed que amor es locura,
en que da la voluntad:
el perder la libertad
es pereza, y negligencia
del remedio del ausencia,
que en los principios consiste,
que si el hábito se viste,
no hay arte, sino paciencia.

(p. 332)

They say love, in the lover, is a desire for beauty, for siring one like oneself in the peace of holy wedlock, and that this is the function of love and the way it quiets its thoughts, and that appetite gets the better of reason and that the soul lives where it loves, not where it breathes. Shepherds, as regards this truth, though it may seem certain to you, you should know that love is a madness afflicting the will; to lose one's freedom is inertia and neglect of absence as a cure, which is simply a matter of making a start, for if the habit is acquired, there is no recourse except to bear it.

Cardenio's subsequent "Amor es guerra" ("Love is war") is Ovidian, not Platonic, while assertions like "Amor de prenda mortal engendra aborrecimiento" ("Love of a mortal object engenders hatred") have an unmistakably Lopean ring.[9]

It is evident that Lope has written much of himself into the character of his protagonist; the emotions displayed by the latter are often reminiscent of the poet's responses and those of his literary personas to the experience with Elena. Jealousy, anger, violence, suggestions of madness shade into one another in a similar way. A view of love as "ira" ("anger") and "furia" ("frenzy") is dwelt upon (pp. 334–337). When Amphryso witnesses the presumed defection of Belisarda, he becomes "ciego de cólera y zelos" ("blind with rage and jealousy") on one occasion (p. 220) and on another,

> desatinado de averiguados zelos, que no hay alma tan dura que no lastimen, comenzó el pastor a decir tales palabras, y hacer tales desesperaciones y efectos, que a no se hallar Frondoso a resistille sin duda se arrojara de la primera peña.   (p. 317)

> beside himself with justified jealousy, which no soul is tough enough not to be hurt by, the shepherd began to speak such words and go through such acts of despair and put on such a show that, had Frondoso not been there to hold him back, he no doubt would have thrown himself off the first cliff.

The precedent of Orlando looms up here as in *Belardo el furioso*: "como otro Orlando desgajaba las ramas de los árboles, hauiéndose ensayado primero en los vestidos propios" ("like a new Orlando, he tore branches off the trees, having first tried his hand on his own clothes").[10] As J. B. Avalle-Arce remarks, the inordinate role of jealousy in *La Arcadia* is unprecedented in the pastoral novel, where it had hitherto been a subject of speculation, but not a mainspring of the narrative.[11]

Amphryso's anger, reminiscent of the tone of certain *romances de desamor*, can be felt welling up in the same half-dramatic, half-histrionic way as that of Lope-Fernando and the Belardo of the play. In his final confrontation with Belisarda it rises beneath the cold sarcasm of his tone until it bursts forth in a string of denunciations and taunts against her and her husband: "Y hai de ti, ingrata, falsa, perjura, desconocida, atrevida, y en fin muger resuelta, que has de vivir con él, y morir por mí" ("And woe betide you, thankless, false, oath-breaking, ungrateful, brazen and, in a word, determined woman, who will have to live with him and die for me") (p. 367). Familiar, too, are the poses of studied indifference with which Amphryso covers up a feeling of pique, which he candidly confesses almost killed him; they look back toward the Lope of the *Proceso* and ahead toward Fernando in *La Dorotea*.

Sometimes the narrative voice acquires a confidential tone and we sense that Lope is passing on what he has observed from experience, not displaying learning or engaging in casuistry or speculation:

> Pero no sé qué estrellas del cielo influyen algunas veces calidad en los amantes, que sin saber las causas, ni darse satisfacciones de las imaginadas ofensas, no cessan de agrauiarse, ni de procurar cada uno el daño del otro.   (p. 308) [12]

> But I don't know what stars in heaven at times put lovers in such a state that without looking into the reasons nor satisfying each other as to imagined offenses, they are forever giving each other offense and trying to do each other harm.

Amphryso's story, like Lope's, is one of legal entanglements, imprisonment, and exile. *La Arcadia* undoubtedly does not reflect with accuracy the involved matrimonial or extramarital affairs of the Duke. Like *La Dorotea* it is poetry, not history. But there are noticeable parallels between the arrangement Lope gives his patron's story in the pastoral novel and that he gives his own in the *acción en prosa*. Similar events and situations are similarly ordered in the two treatments of "unhappy love," the one in five books, the other in five acts. In both works a rival to a hero whose love seemed secure is introduced at the outset. By the end of Act I in *La Dorotea* and the beginning of Book II in *La Arcadia* external pressure and intrigues favoring the rival have caused a separation of the lovers. The second book or act in each case finds the lover absent. In the third book of *La Arcadia* and at the beginning of the fourth act of *La Dorotea*, we find the lover relating his life story. In both works (though at different stages) the hero is possessed by violent jealousy and, after poring over old love letters, uses the honored Lopean device of attaching himself to another lady. The fourth section of each work brings a reconciliation between the lovers. (The settings are similar, both heroes discovering their ladies seated disconsolately by marble fountains.) The last book or act brings the experience of *desamor* to the hero but leaves the lady still in love and suffering.

These broad resemblances are probably due not only to similarities in the raw material—the experiences of Lope and his master—but to the fact that these very similarities led Lope to treat situations in *La Arcadia* in terms of literary motifs which had grown out of the adventure with Elena and become common in *romances* and *comedias*. In this sense *La Arcadia* had already been drawn into the orbit of the *amores de Elena*.

Both *La Arcadia* and *La Dorotea* are exceptional in Lope's production in that they do not trace the triumph of love over obstacles, the favorite pattern of his plays, or carry it further to calamitous dénouements, as in his occasional tragedies, but record instead the decline of a settled love all the way to *desamor*, to a realistic indifference fundamentally conceived outside established tragic or comic modes. This for the hero, while the heroine is left to suffer alone. The dramatic potentiality of such love is minimal; its proper place is the pastoral novel.[13] In Sannazaro's *Arcadia*, which despite differences in external form is Lope's most obvious model, only a suggestion of this pattern is present, appearing in the form of nostalgia for a lost love and a world one has been obliged to renounce. There is also only a minimum of structured narrative. When the pastoral novel proper has its beginning with Montemayor's *Diana*, we encounter, in the story of Diana and Sireno, the elements of the scheme in question, as they will reappear, *mutatis mutandis*, in *La Arcadia* and *La Dorotea*. In *La Diana* the harmonious stage of love is already over when the story opens, as the *Argumento* that precedes the first book makes plain:

> Esta quiso y fue querida en extremo de un pastor llamado Sireno . . . Sucedió, pues, que como Sireno fuesse forzadamente fuera del reyno, a cosas que su partida no podía escusarse, y la pastora quedasse muy triste por su ausencia, los tiempos y el coraçón de Diana se mudaron; y ella se casó con otro pastor llamado Delio, poniendo en olvido el que tanto auía querido. El qual, viniendo después de un año de absencia, con gran desseo de ver a su pastora, supo antes que llegasse cómo era ya casada.[14]

> This lady loved and was passionately loved by a shepherd named Sireno . . . It so happened that, as Sireno unavoidably left the kingdom on business which made his departure imperative, and the shepherdess stayed behind very unhappy at his absence, times and Diana's heart changed, and she married another shepherd called Delio, forgetting all about the one she had so loved. Who, returning after a year's absence, longing to see his shepherdess, learned before he arrived that she was now married.

Their tearful leave-taking is retrospectively related in a lengthy song of the nymph Dorida in the second book. By the time they actually come together in the narrative (Books V and VI), their situations have been reversed; Sireno has been cured of his love by means of the magic water of the wizardess Felicia, while Diana, unhappily married, looks back nostalgically toward her love for him.

Montemayor's pattern of separation and tender leave-taking at the beginning, reunion without reconciliation at the end, is Lope's precedent for his
ordering of Amphryso–Alba's story, which undergoes in the process a
degree of modification at which one can only guess. It is a pattern not found
in other pastoral novels. There are of course significant differences. Diana is
inconstant, allowing her parents to marry her to Delio, while Belisarda
marries only as an act of desperation (*venganza*) after a series of trivial mis-
understandings, thinking Amphryso has been unfaithful. She purposely
chooses a thoroughly unattractive suitor so that the constancy of her feelings
will be manifest. The emotional relationship between Diana and Sireno has
changed completely by the time of the reunion, while that of Amphryso and
Belisarda, once the angry recriminations are over and the misunderstanding
cleared up, is unaltered. The acerbity of the conversations between Diana and
Sireno is more subtle and more telling in its restraint than Lope's extremes of
anger and lachrymosity. Amphryso's deliverance comes only afterward,
necessitated by the inalterable fact of Belisarda's marriage. But it is evident
that Lope felt the germaneness to the pastoral novel of a slow-paced story of
unrealized love. There is nothing as subtle in *La Arcadia* as the brief presentation of Diana, in the later part of the novel, as a figure who, as M. Menéndez
y Pelayo wrote, feels "an indefinable melancholy in which are intermingled
a vague love and wounded vanity." [15] The emotional states Lope shows us
are spectacular, extreme, unequivocal. In the figure of Diana, we find rather,
in a subdued key, nuances and ambivalence.

Montemayor has no interest in tracing as a process the manner in which
Diana's inconstancy and ambivalence develop; he is much more concerned
with the Neo-Platonic framework into which Sireno and Sylvano fit. Even
so, all three characters belong to only one among several "casos de amor y
fortuna" ("instances of love and fortune") presented in a comprehensive
survey. Lope on the other hand narrows his focus in both *La Arcadia* and
La Dorotea to a single case. Yet in *La Arcadia* he does not use the opportunity
to trace the dynamics of the decline of love any more than Montemayor had
in the far briefer compass of the story of Sireno and Diana. It is the element
of motivation, the processes of the emotions, that is missing in both cases:
the circumstances Lope contrives to propel the tale are as arbitrary and dis-
proportionate to their consequences as Montemayor's magic water. The
estrangement of Amphryso and Belisarda is not an outcome of conditions
inherent in their relationship. A sense of the passage from one emotional
state to another is not maintained any more than it usually is in the atemporal
world of the pastoral. All this is changed in the *acción en prosa*, and it is likely
that in depicting Dorotea Lope remembered more advantageously than in

La Arcadia the curious ambiguities present in Montemayor's heroine and saw how they might be expanded.[16]

The writing of *La Arcadia* may be looked upon as a formative experience which showed Lope both the relevance of the pastoral narrative tradition to the telling of nontragic stories of unhappy love, and its limitations. To present his story in the way he wished, it would be necessary to abandon the static pastoral order and establish a firm grounding in a world realistically conditioned by time and space. But as a result of his experiment with the pastoral novel, and as an outgrowth of the strain of pastoral stylization in the experience itself, the pastoral ideal world would last on in the prosaic world of *La Dorotea* as the supreme form of idealization cultivated by the heroine. If Dorotea is content to be the object of Fernando's poetic cult, it is not merely because she enjoys, like Elena, playing the role of Filis. It is because she aspires, through the verse of ballads and sonnets—in pastoral, Petrarchan, or Moorish modes—to join for all time a select company of literary heroines. When she gives voice to this aspiration, she significantly thinks first of Diana:

> La Diana de Montemayor fue vna dama natural de Valencia de Don Juan, junto a León. Y Ezla, su río, y ella serán eternos por su pluma. Assí la Fílida de Montaluo, la Galatea de Ceruantes, la Camila de Garcilaso, la Violante del Camoes, la Siluia de Bernaldes, la Filis de Figueroa, y la Leonor de Corte Real. Amor no es margarita para bestias. Quiere entendimientos sutiles, aborrece el interés, anda desnudo, no es para sujetos baxos. Después de muerta, quiso y celebró el Petrarca su bella Laura.   (p. 143)

> Montemayor's Diana was a lady from Valencia de Don Juan, near León. And Ezla, her river, and she herself will be made eternal through his pen. Similarly with the Fílida of Montalvo, Cervantes' Galatea, Garcilaso's Camila, Camoens's Violante, Bernaldes' Silvia, Figueroa's Filis, Corte Real's Leonor. Love is no daisy for cattle. It wants subtle minds, it hates self-interest, it goes about naked, it is not for the lowborn. After her death, Petrarch loved and celebrated his beautiful Laura.

The pastoral heroines together with Laura constitute Dorotea's supreme Platonic-Petrarchan ideal. The values prized in these words—delicacy of understanding, nonvenality, aristocratic refinement in love (and they are authentic values for her, however much her moral equivocation and her preciosity may distort them in practice)—find their true home in the world of the pastoral novel. Dorotea's aspiration to amatory refinement and exclusiveness sounds, indeed, like an echo of a standard voiced by Montemayor's Felicia:

> En estos casos de amor tengo yo una regla que siempre la e hallado muy verdadera y es que el ánimo generoso y el entendimiento delicado, en esto de querer bien lleva grandíssima ventaja al que no lo es. Porque como el amor sea virtud, y la virtud siempre haga assiento en el mejor lugar, está claro que las personas de suerte serán muy mejor enamorados que aquellas en quien ésta falta.[17]
> In these cases of love I have a rule which I have always found very true, and this is that a noble spirit and refined understanding, in this matter of loving truly, has a very great advantage over those who are not such. For since love is a virtue and virtue always settles in the best place, it is clear that persons of this kind will be much better lovers than those in whom such virtue is lacking.

A stimulus toward creating on his own, rather than as amanuensis to another, a will to expression aroused but not satisfied by the writing of *La Arcadia*, seem to me the most important implications behind Lope's references to *propios* (one's own) and *agenos pensamientos* (someone else's thoughts) in his Prologue.

More specific if less fundamental justification for the assertion that "a vueltas de los agenos pensamientos he llorado los míos" ("amid the thoughts of others I have wept over my own") may be seen in a certain cast, reminiscent of Lope's story, which he gives to Amphryso's tale of his early life (Book III, pp. 184–186), one that is suggestive also of Fernando's account of his life at the beginning of Act IV of *La Dorotea*. There is likewise the marginal figure of Belardo, through whom overt allusions to Lope's disillusioned feelings are made (pp. 357, 444). Another figure, Silvio, is also evidently bound up with the author: he is the confidant and companion of Amphryso–Alba, and is even called his "secretario," that is, the keeper of his secrets (p. 244). More intimately linked with Lope than the figure of Belardo just mentioned, he is significantly close to a different Belardo–Lope who does not appear: Silvio sings the latter's "Sola esta vez quisiera" ("I would like only this once") (p. 88) and is abreast of his affairs—his "departure" and his sufferings at the hands of envious friends as well as enemies (p. 91).[18]

The rhetorical and poetic style of expression employed by Lope's Arcadians will shed light, finally, on the elevated idiom to which Fernando, Dorotea, and others in the *acción en prosa* are partial. Whereas in *La Arcadia* such artistic prose will only occasionally give way to a more naturalistic idiom (see below, p. 387), in *La Dorotea*, everyday prose will be the touchstone serving to set in relief the cultivation of more select forms of utterance. In the interim Lope will have grown increasingly sensitive to the constraints of the pastoral mode for longer verse and prose works. He will remark in his *Filomena* (1621), "No son estas razones de pastores, / amor me los enseña, no los sabios" ("This is not the speech of shepherds, love teaches it to me, not the learned"); and in his short story "La prudente venganza" ("Prudent Revenge") (1624), will observe, "No es esta novela libro de pastores, sino que han de comer y cenar todas las veces que se ofreciere ocasión" ("This story is not a shepherd-book; rather, they are going to have dinner and supper whenever the occasion arises").[19] His dramatization of his *La Arcadia*, as we shall see presently, will prove him incapable of making of it, for the *comedia* stage at least, anything but a mock-serious display of make-believe.

The Spirit of Play

During the years at Alba de Tormes Lope still appears, for the most part, an unthinking artist, one who takes himself for granted. He seems content to let his talents play kaleidoscopically over a variety of artistic stimuli arising in his personal life; or to respond to challenges of a more professional nature emanating from patrons, the provincial court at Alba, insistent producers and audiences. Montesinos has observed that only to a limited extent, in his earlier years, can Lope be considered "an artistic conscience concerned with a particular problem."[20] While in my view this limited extent may be exemplified, during the 1590's, by a first attempt to explore at length in dialogued prose the meaning of the experience with Elena Osorio, it would take an increasing deliberateness of artistic purpose over the next decades to achieve the definitive elaboration of the experience. It would require a fuller recognition and acceptance of the nature of his creative gifts—of strengths, limitations, inclinations that could be trusted, tendencies to be mistrusted—before Lope could devise a form as personal and *sui generis* as the *acción en prosa*. While the need to defend himself against the critical assaults of Aristotelians and Gongorists may have sharpened his insights into his own poetic nature, a more significant factor, in my view, as far as *La Dorotea* is concerned, is the evolution of the theatrical spirit and the role-playing tendency already so much in evidence in life and art in the years around 1588. In tracing their subsequent development, I will set my remarks within the broad category of the spirit of play, as conceived by Huizinga, with its paradoxical conjoining of seriousness and levity, illusion and lucidity, self-surrender and self-awareness.

The ludic sense manifests itself, Huizinga reminds us, within certain prescribed limits, and follows its own order and its own rules. One knows one is playing as a child knows he is pretending, but within the confines of the game one gives oneself wholeheartedly to it. Play does not preclude seriousness; to view the world *sub specie ludi* is not to deny it meaning and importance; indeed the spirit of play often expresses just the opposite, a strong adherence to life.[21]

Samplings of Lope's writings and in particular of two plays, his dramatization of his own *Arcadia* and his *comedia de santos* (saints' play) on the actor-mime Genisus, *Lo fingido verdadero* (Fiction Become True), will be the points of reference here; in the situations or the allusions of both these *comedias* we find, moreover, echoes of the *amores de Elena*. We shall also consider Lope's latter-day persona, Tomé de Burguillos, created around 1620 and more subtly related to his creator than the Belardo of ballads and plays, the Zaides, Adulces, Gazuls, and others of *romances moriscos*, and the other incidental figures through whom Lope introduces himself into his *comedias*.[22] Tomé de Burguillos epitomizes the more supple artistic control which Lope exerts as he comes to view his tendency to don masks and play roles with more objectivity.

"Poetarum enim est ludere et lascivire, philosophorum autem veritatem subtili ratione investigare" ("It befits poets to play and wanton, but philosophers to investigate the truth with subtle reasoning"), remarks Lope at the end of the prologue to *Relación de las fiestas . . . en la canonización de . . . San Isidro* (Account of the Festivities . . . at the Canonization . . . of San Isidro) (1622).[23] These words, which seem to make light of the poet's craft, express in fact only the most obvious and least serious aspect of Lope's ludic sense, albeit a very prevalent one: the easily aroused playfulness of which his plays and private letters offer endless illustration. The *graciosos* (jokesters) are of course prone to see the ridiculous side of things most readily, but the spirit of ironic levity is not confined to them. As Valbuena Prat remarks: "The sly temperament of Lope goes so far at times as not to take the story itself seriously . . . The ironic Lope smiles on the fringes of the tragedy."[24] In Lope's letters to the Duke of Sessa, a grave or solemn tone will often trigger its opposite: a playful *reductio ad absurdum*.[25] When Lope decides to dramatize his own pastoral novel—between 1610 and 1615, according to Morley and Bruerton—his ludic spirit is clearly in command and it is the lightest aspect of this spirit that prevails. All the weightiness of the novel evaporates as Arcadian conventions become comic properties which Lope does not allow even his characters to take seriously. The clever rustic, Cardenio, is now given a much more prominent role. "¡Las cosas que hay en Arcadia!" ("The things that are found in Arcadia!"), he exclaims with feigned wonder to his simple counterpart Bato, as he reels off the wonders with comic copiousness and impropriety:

> Todos son encantamientos,
> todos son dioses y diosas,
> faunos, drías, semideos,
> sátiros, medio cabritos,
> circes, gazmios, Polifemos,
> centauros y semicapros.
>
> *(Obras escogidas*, III, 504b)

It's all magic spells, they're all gods and goddesses, fauns, dryads, demigods, satyrs, half-goatlets, Circes, pimps, Polyphemuses, centaurs, and semigoats.

Cardenio becomes a travestied *deus ex machina*. Training talking birds to proclaim his infallibility, he slips behind the altar of Venus, "la diosa Viernes" (lit., "the goddess Friday," a confusion with the name of the weekday, that is, Venus's day), to deliver oracles against Amphryso's rivals for Belisarda's hand. The troubled relationship that existed between the protagonists of the novel is thus simplified into a matter of pure trickery, a series of comic feints and counter-feints. In Cardenio's oracular prediction of death within three days for anyone marrying Belisarda, Lope is in all likelihood making sport of a solemn device used by Battista Guarini in his vastly popular *Pastor Fido* (1589).[26] The characters profess to take the oracular utterances seriously, yet are infected by the author with a spirit of make-believe and behave toward each other like players going through the moves of a game, calling each one out as they go:

> Celos, mis ojos, me diste;
> déjame que te dé celos.
>
> (p. 520a)

You made *me* jealous, my pet; let me make *you*.

When they tire of playing they can, without further ado, simply call the game off. The happy dénouement is initiated when Belisarda suddenly says to Amphryso:

> Saben los cielos
> que todo fue fingido
> por darte celos, que me diste celos;
> y si me das amores,
> amores te daré con mil favores.
>
> (p. 525a)

Heaven knows, it was all put on to make you jealous as you made me; and if you give me love, I will give you love to your heart's desire.

The rustics, strangers to traditional Arcadias, cannot take this one seriously. When the simpleton Bato puts on a wolfskin in order to gain access to his sweetheart Flora, the resultant rustic clowning has a peculiar aura of mock-seriousness and make-believe:

> Lidio: Pastores, paso, teneos;
>   que parece que habla el lobo.
> Vireno: ¿Cómo que habla?
> Lidio: Estad atentos.
> Vireno: ¿Si desde el tiempo de Isopo
>   que hablaban con los corderos,
>   se quedó este lobo aquí?
> Bato: Pastores, oídme os ruego . . .

(p. 516b)

Lidio: Shepherds, be still, hold off: the wolf seems to be talking. *Vireno:* What do you mean talking? *Lidio:* Just listen. *Vireno:* Can it be that this wolf has stayed around here since Aesop's time, when they spoke with lambs? *Bato:* Shepherds, hear me, I pray you . . .

Lope's dethroning of Arcadia is already clearly under way in the play. No more than the conventions and commonplaces is the idealism central to the pastoral able to withstand his impulse to make a game out of the whole mode. Whereas in *La Dorotea* such idealism will be earnestly embraced by the protagonists and contemplated within contingencies of ordinary living by the author, for the popular audiences of the play it finds no *raison d'être* at all.

It is curious, in view of this, to find surviving in the play stages and echoes of Lope's one-time association of his own adventure with that of his patron Amphryso-Alba. There are echoes of ballads involving Filis: namely,

> Amada pastora mía,
> de tu sinrazón me quejo;

(p. 516b)

Beloved shepherdess of mine, I protest your wrong to me;

tags that have a familiar ring:

Seis años de amor, Amphryso,
¿quieres tú que un extranjero
acabe ansí?

(p. 512a)

Would you have a stranger do away with six years of love in this
way, Amphryso?

and, particularly, "Troy" imagery which, on its third appearance in the
play begins to seem more than coincidental. A passage like the following,
in fact, is unmistakably suggestive in various details, of Dorotea's letter-
burning scene; it may be looked upon as a link between this scene and the
ballad "Contemplando estaba Filis":

Bato:	Sé que anoche me llamó
	Belisarda y me pidió
	una luz.
Amph.:	¡Luz! ¿Para qué?
Bato:	Tus papeles pienso que eran
	ciertas cosas que quemó,
	y aún un retrato vi yo.
Amph.:	Ya mis engaños, ¿qué esperan?
Bato:	"Arded, ¡pardiez!, les decía
	cuando los ojos quemaba;
	arded, pues en vos estaba
	alma tan helada y fría."
	Pero ansí, a medio quemar,
	más de una vez le besó,
	y aún presumo que lloró,
	queriendo el fuego apagar.
	No quedó cinta ni joya
	que no pereciese allí.
	Caballo de Grecia fui.
Amph.:	Y ella Elena; Amphryso, Troya.
Bato:	Pues no debió de quedar
	con gusto el papel quemando;
	que andaba después juntando
	lo que estaba por quemar ...

(p. 521a)[27]

Bato: I know that Belisarda called me last night and asked for a light.
Amph.: A light? What for? *Bato:* She burned up certain things
which I think were your love letters, and I saw a portrait, too.

Amph.: What more disabusing do I need?   *Bato:* "Burn, by heaven," she said to the eyes as she burned them; "burn, since there was so cold and frozen a soul in you." But even so, when half-burned, she kissed it more than once and I rather imagine she wept, hoping to put the fire out. There was not a ribbon or jewel that went unburned. I was a Grecian horse.   *Amph.:* And she Helen; Amphryso, Troy.   *Bato:* She can't have been very happy to be burning up the paper; afterward she began piecing the unburned parts together.

Amphryso, like his namesake in the novel, has a period of alienation, but unlike the latter and like Lope's persona Belardo "el furioso," he thinks himself in hell. Although he does not take Orpheus as a model, he is even more deliberate than Belardo in "staging" his madness, announcing methodically that he is going mad with jealousy,[28] declaring himself dead and proceeding to assume himself in hell. Over and above the freedom conventionally allowed *comedia* characters to articulate their feelings and announce their actions, the sense of play-acting stands out in this sequence. Lope's irony hovers about Amphryso as he cultivates the role of the lover crazed by jealousy, heightening the ludic effect.

More or less contemporary with this light-hearted dramatic travesty of the pastoral novel is *Lo fingido verdadero o El mejor representante* (Fiction Become True or the Best Actor), c. 1608, according to Morley and Bruerton. Here the subject, Genisus, the comic mime who makes his own the role of Christian martyr he has been playing for Diocletian, engages Lope's ludic sense at a deeper level. He characteristically turns the subject toward an exploration of the relationship between assumed roles and underlying realities. The subject inevitably leads him also to the theme of the world as stage, one especially germane to the temper of an age that emphasized, in the spirit of the Counter Reformation, an originally medieval awareness of the insubstantial quality of human existence when viewed against a transcendental Christian backdrop. Long before Calderón's culminating version of this theme, Lope's plays and those of his contemporaries are replete with instances in which characters, more especially the *graciosos*, casually puncture the dramatic illusion and let it be known they see themselves as only acting in a play.[29] What is notable in Lope's handling of the subject is that before coming around in the third act to the miracle play proper, Lope provides in the first two acts two other contexts for variations on the theme of the interplay between assumed roles and experienced feelings. For the first act he drew, as Menéndez y Pelayo notes, on Pedro Mexía's *Historia imperial y cesárea*.[30] The second, however, he built up from his own experience. Before reaching the divine amphitheater where illusion ends, we are thus led through the public and private arenas of the world.

As regards the first, the opening act shows us four Roman emperors being struck down in violent succession. It is the second act, centering on Genisus and his company, that is most revealing in regard to the author. Like the first, it was discarded by Jean de Rotrou when he recast Lope's play forty years later in the mold of French classical tragedy. Comparison with *Le véritable Saint Genest* also underscores Lope's insistence on the dual character of Genisus as both actor and author, a feature which permits him to work a *historia-poiesis* strain into this variation on the play's theme and to develop a concern with role-playing. Diocletian has commanded Genisus to "imitate" a lover and the mime has seized the occasion to write a script centering on his own jealous love for his leading lady, one which will allow him both to embrace her and to stage a burst of mad fury in which he will assault his rival, another actor of the company. Surely the figures of Lope's own youthful self and of Elena Osorio, as Karl Vossler surmised, hover somewhere in the background of this act, perhaps not consciously perceived by the playwright.[31] We need not follow the shifting planes of actuality and dramatic fiction arising around this play within a play—the tripping over names, the ad-libs, the effects of improvisation harking back to the *commedia dell'arte*, the overlapping nuances in the depiction of Genisus's anger: histrionic in the role, darkly smoldering in the actor's emotional state, furious at last in his reaction to the unexpected flight of his rival and his leading lady. Though this second act, with its expressly allusive inner drama, appears to proclaim an identity of role and actuality, it actually does the opposite through a play of irony, which Menéndez y Pelayo, for one, failed to perceive when he characterized the act as totally irrelevant.[32]

Genisus insists before he begins to perform that when acting a lover, as against, say, a king or a Persian, the player must be what he represents, a facile formula which proves wholly inadequate when the play breaks apart with the lovers' flight. But when Genisus throws his part aside and makes a direct impassioned plea to the Emperor to bring the lovers back, he finds Diocletian uncertain which world he is in:

> . . . ¿Quieres mostrar, Ginés,
> que con burlas semejantes
> nos haces representantes?
>
> (Ac., IV, 67)

Are you trying to demonstrate, Ginés, that with such pranks you can turn us into actors?

asks the perplexed Emperor. Lope seems positively to be playing with role-playing here, in a spirit quite foreign to both his source and his French successor. At the same time he is providing a thematic link with the first act and looking forward to the third, in which Genisus will indeed force Diocletian to play the role of executioner. There, however, the frame expands: Genisus feels the celestial audience watching from heavenly tiers. The human comedy, he announces, is over, the divine under way. We now see the full irony in Genisus's earlier assertion that role and reality coincide for the lover: the words are true of divine love, not of human.[33]

Undoubtedly Lope did not find the story of Genisus, as given in the contemporary *Flos sanctorum* of Pedro de Ribadeneira, adequate to maintain the action of an entire play, even with the addition of rudimentary historical background from Pedro Mexía. The complementary action he invents, however, has the effect of placing the whole matter of role-playing as much in the arena of profane love as of sacred. And it is not possible to discriminate between fiction and the context of the actors' everyday lives in this act, to avoid a sense of overlapping between the histrionic or illusory and the real, any more than it was in our observation of Lope during the hearings or of Belardo in the ballads. Only, in this case, Lope and Elena are present only peripherally; Lope is attracted by the phenomenon in itself. Without over-simplifying or seeking to delimit schematically what resists unraveling, he sets it in contexts of public life, private life, and the life beyond, a strikingly broad frame of reference. While a public context is largely eliminated from the *acción en prosa*, and the focus is on private roles and individual realities, essential to the meaning of the work is a transcendental dimension hinted at rather than dwelt upon, sensed in the background rather than, as here, at the core. Lope's focus certainly shifts toward the here and now in *La Dorotea*; his counterpoise to illusion is decidedly the reality of this world rather than that of the next. Still, *Lo fingido verdadero* and *La Dorotea* have roots in the same creative subsoil and it seems likely that Lope remembered his exploration of the ludic domain in the play when he gave the *acción en prosa* its final shaping.

Perhaps he had in mind also his contemplation of role-playing on a purely human level in a play of his final years, *Porfiar hasta morir* (Persist to the Death), which Morley and Bruerton place between 1624 and 1628. Lope is noticeably forbearing with his hero, Macías, as the latter literally acts out the medieval commonplace of the courtly lover faithful to the death to a hopeless love. Though Lope makes us feel there is madness in such literal embracing of a poetic fiction, he muffles the voice of the lackey who says so and resists the temptation to satirize or parody. He is clearly in a reflective mood, less interested in passing judgment on so quixotic a devotion to a fictional ideal than in giving it a sympathetic hearing. But Lope's nature is many-faceted and a ludic voice curbed in the play, but destined for a full hearing in *La Dorotea*, that of Tomé de Burguillos, is meanwhile growing increasingly audible in the nondramatic contexts of Lope's life and art. While this earthy and irreverent Lopean persona, a *gracioso* fashioned for his private use, comes into being after his creator enters the priesthood principally as an outlet for Lope's irrepressible playfulness, a vein of deep seriousness is sometimes interwoven with his levity, a sign that in his later years Lope found it natural to make seriousness and humor almost indistinguishable sides of the same coin.

What strikes one first in Tomé de Burguillos, however, is Lope's proneness to make light, through him, in a spirit ranging from spoofing to satire, of things usually taken seriously: his own literary *métier*, the values placed on love and honor, social pretensions of every sort. Tomé de Burguillos is a less stereotyped, more light-spirited version of the *figura del donaire* of Lope's plays, the lackey evolved from the earlier rustic and fool, who developed in Lope's hands into the embodiment of a nonheroic, unsentimentalized, practical outlook on the world. The plebeian hard-headedness of the *figura del donaire* or *gracioso* effectively contrasts with the romantic and heroic stance of his aristocratic master, and together they polarize two contrasting ways of apprehending reality: through the flesh and through the spirit. Offstage, where Lope is less bound by the expectations of an audience or the need to make the *gracioso*'s utterances "come across," he can be more leisurely, more subtle and more mischievous in the handling of his creation, and can play particularly on his relation to himself.

Though nineteenth- and twentieth-century critics insisted on beclouding the issue, there was never any doubt in the minds of Lope's own contemporaries that Tomé de Burguillos was an entirely fictional being. Part of Lope's pleasure in him comes from maintaining the fiction of his independent existence, entering him in poetic contests (his first appearance) in 1620 and 1622, making him the author of the *Rimas humanas y divinas* of 1634. No one was taken in by the pretense, nor did Lope intend anyone to be. The point was precisely the complicity of audience and readers in the game he was playing. Had he felt it necessary to do more than give lip-service to the serious front a priest was supposed to present, he could not have created so ridiculous a persona in the first place: a lowly law student, shabby, penniless, and famished, whose love for a washerwoman must vie with his yearning for a square meal, whose career moves in reverse, downward from the level of *maestro* (master) to that of *licenciado* (licentiate). Tomé is more impractical than practical, more soft- than hard-headed, a departure in these respects from the usual *gracioso* of the stage. He is the butt of Lope's humor as well as the voice of his comic spirit, Lope's to do with as he pleases, free of stage specifications and priestly proprieties. Lope's pleasure in his overlordship is evident at every turn. The whimsicality, inventiveness, lightness of touch, and cat-and-mouse relationship with his creature which characterize Lope's handling of Tomé de Burguillos are manifestations of the same play-spirit which *mutatis mutandis* informs *La Dorotea*, subordinating its characters in the last analysis to their creator's will. It is no surprise to find Tomé de Burguillos himself appearing on the periphery of the *acción en prosa*.[34]

The contributions of Tomé de Burguillos to the Justa poética (Poetic Tournament) held to celebrate the beatification of San Isidro in 1620—nine humorous poems in the nine different meters set for the contests—effectively undercut the inevitably solemn tone of the rest of the offerings. Probably such mockery was a means of making palatable an assignment as president of the affair which Lope seems to have been reluctant to assume in the first place.[35] His misgivings had to do with the expected role of the *culteranos*, but *culteranismo* is only one concern of Burguillos who, amidst laments over his poverty, lets fly at Madrid life and society. In 1622, when Isidro is canonized, Burguillos has a similar deflationary role: Lope reads a humorous commentary by him on each poem awarded a prize. The relationship between the poet and his persona now develops more subtlety. In the concluding *romance*, spoken in his own name, Lope's tone descends toward that of his mask as he reflects on whether self-praise can ever be justified:

> Mas también, señoras musas,
> es bien que los disculpemos;
> que a los que no alaba nadie,
> no es mucho que se alaben ellos;
> y más entre los amigos,
> como suelen los jumentos,
> rascándose el uno al otro
> por los bárbaros pescuezos.
>
> (OS, XII, 411)

Still though, madam Muses, it's right that we should excuse them, for it's hardly surprising if people whom nobody praises praise themselves; all the more so among friends, the way asses do, scratching away at each other's barbarous necks.

If this is grotesque, the concluding apostrophe to Burguillos is subtly ironical: Lope's incredulity at the latter's equanimity in the face of poverty, ingratitude, and ill will conceals both an apologia and a reproach.[36]

The most noticeable new note in the *Rimas* of 1634, some of which go back to the time of *La Dorotea* and earlier, is their more frequent interweaving of serious and even somber tones with the gay ones, the evidence that Burguillos's levity is hard won rather than gratuitous.[37] Lope's "Advertimiento al lector" ("Note to the Reader") mentions "los realzes de sus estudios entre las sombras de los donaires" ("the highlights of his studies amidst the shadows of his witticisms") and "entre la corteza Aristophánica la verdad Platónica" ("beneath the Aristophanic crust, the Platonic truth"). We are also told: "Aunque era naturalmente triste, nadie le comunicó que no le hallasse alegre" ("Although he was sad by nature, no one dealing with him failed to find him gay"), a bit of self-revelation of fundamental importance to the spirit of *La Dorotea*.

Burguillos's outlook, though antiheroic, stops short of the negativism and bitterness of the picaresque. The prevailing tone is mock-serious; there is outright burlesquing of literary conventions—Petrarchan, Platonic, mythological—of Lope's own repertory of themes and motifs, of the techniques of the literary craft—the art of the sonnet, for example (cf. note 13 to Chapter IV, below)—of the *culteranos*. The lofty poetic style is applied to lowly subjects: toothpicks, nail-cutting, oversize shoes, dogs and cats, a flea; to prosaic occurrences or remarks which strike the *licenciado* as funny even when the humor is at his expense, as when he is taken for a pauper, or when someone requests the privilege of preaching at his funeral:

> Mejor es que yo escriua en tales días,
> sonetos tristes a las honras tuyas,
> que no que tú prediques en las mías.

(fol. 31v)

> It is better that on occasions of that kind I should be writing sad sonnets for your funeral rather than you preaching at mine.

In those sonnets in which we are told Tomé is speaking in earnest ("en seso" or "de veras"), his range widens and his voice becomes indistinguishable from Lope's: sonnets penned on the occasion of a death or of events of some moment: the sack of Mantua, the birth of a prince; encomiums; satirical sonnets serious in tone. In the midst of these comes a heartfelt elegy to Marta de Nevares entitled "Que al amor verdadero, no le oluidan el tiempo, ni la muerte: escriue en seso" ("True love is not forgotten with time or death: he writes in earnest") (fol. 39v). Here, as if a sensitive spot had been touched, the underlying stratum of sadness is exposed. Though this is exceptional, the blending of tones in certain sonnets in which Tomé speaks for his creator gives us glimpses of Lope entire, of the man behind the verse. In "Discúlpase el Poeta del estilo humilde" ("The poet excuses himself for his lowly style") (fol. 81r), Tomé blames the stars for his misfortunes, laughs at himself, his studies, his attempts to curry favor, then discards his bantering tone as he thinks of his poverty and takes a stoic view of it.[38]

The *pièce de résistance* of the collection is a long poem, the burlesque epic *La Gatomaquia*, in which Tomé's muse turns to the affairs of cats and plays with scintillating irony and endless inventiveness over a mock-heroic tale of feline love and rivalries. Written in the midst of the domestic misfortunes of Lope's final years, the poem is an impressive demonstration of resilient vitality. As in the other *rimas* we occasionally catch hints of the therapeutic value which the writing must have had for the aging poet:

> ¡O quien para oluidar melancolías
> de las que no se acaban con los días,
> un gato entonces viera
> con bota, y calça entera!
>
> (fol. 123v)[39]

Oh, if only one could have seen a cat in boots and full-length hose then, so as to forget the melancholy that does not end with one's days.

Tomé de Burguillos comes into existence in the years which witness the deep spiritual and moral crises reflected in the *Soliloquios*; the conflicts attendant upon Lope's passion for Marta de Nevares; the personal shocks and losses occasioned by her death and that of his son, Lope, and aggravated when he is abandoned by Antonia Clara, the daughter of Marta de Nevares and the last child remaining at home, who elopes at the age of seventeen. The existence of Burguillos evinces Lope's capacity for self-renewal, his ability to shed emotional encumbrances and in gayness of spirit to take a fresh view of the world, free of blinders and devoid of bitterness. In deflating ideals, Tomé de Burguillos really affirms Lope's commitment to living. The leaven of his spirit acting upon the reflective side of Lope's nature gives *La Dorotea* its rare blend of effervescence and substantiality, its flavor at once fresh and mellow, and keeps the *acción en prosa* from affecting us tragically. In his final years Lope was sometimes impelled to write in the tragic vein of certain of his most impressive plays, such as *The Knight from Olmedo* and *Justice without Revenge*. But in a work which was to be a personal summing-up, which conjoined all the strains in his nature, the tragic note was not destined to predominate.

Melancholy and Solitude

Long before Tomé de Burguillos comes into existence to confirm the ascendancy of the life-force in Lope, one is aware, in the poet's life and writings, of those other tendencies which his commitment to the world holds in check: a reflective and melancholy strain, more and more perceptible with the years, with the inwardly assimilated experience of temporality and evanescence; and a tendency toward withdrawal and solitude. Vossler, as noted previously, could even view *La Arcadia* as a first attempt, thwarted by excessive virtuosity, to give poetic expression to the experience of *desengaño*.[40] The passage of a few years had fortified feelings of disillusionment stemming from the collapse of the relationship with Elena Osorio. The loss in 1595 of Lope's first wife, Isabel de Urbina, whom he seems to have loved with a good deal of tenderness, and of his infant daughters, had brought home the evanescence of other human attachments. As the poet neared the midpoint of his thirties, he must have begun, like most men, to feel the work of time in his bones and not merely from exposure to the pleas, fulminations, and laments of moralists, preachers, and poets. But, as I have noted, the undertones of such awareness are only faintly perceptible in *La Arcadia*. Time is not a factor in Amphryso's deliverance from love.[41] His visit to the Palace of the Seven Liberal Arts constitutes an instant cure: a complete *tabula rasa* can be made of the past and a new future constructed as swiftly as, in *La Diana*, Felicia's magic water can reverse the course of human emotions. Lope merely substitutes a cure by edification for a cure by magic. When Amphryso emerges from the Palace of the Liberal Arts the edification is complete; *desengaño* follows automatically. The visit to the Temple of Disillusionment is anticlimactic, for there all he sees, once he has passed the allegorical statuary at the entrance, is a large number of pictures hung on the walls by individual shepherds, each an emblem or device with a few lines of verse exemplifying his own *desengaño*. This is evidently a passage *à clef*: Lope apparently sought, before ending the book, to allude to as many individuals as possible in the Duke's own entourage. As a consequence, the contents of the Temple of Disillusionment appear trivial and impersonal, a series of schematic instances viewed from the outside. Lope has evidently drawn upon emblem literature as well as the Plinian natural history tradition in fashioning them.[42]

It is a far cry from the ostentatiousness of this Temple of *Desengaño*—the edifying aim of the edifice is awkwardly obvious—to the inwardly structured and genuinely affecting *desengaño* of *La Dorotea*. To trace the progress from one to the other would be to retell the story of Lope's life. We must be content to take samplings and to concentrate on one or two works particularly revealing: the *Soliloquios amorosos de un alma a Dios* (Amorous Soliloquies of a Soul to God) and the "Egloga a Claudio."

The strongly temporal cast of the Lopean *desengaño* is part of a preoccupation with time increasingly visible as his career advances, one he evidently shares with his contemporaries. Of course in no age are perceptive thinkers and artists content simply to measure time by clock or sun without reflecting on how such chronometry relates to man's awareness of time or his intuition of timelessness. In some periods, however, men are so fully taken up with the *hic et nunc* or, conversely, so oriented toward the hereafter that the time-bound character of life seems hardly worthy of notice. For the Greeks of the Periclean age, plenitude is in the present and the fullness they find in the world is not overlaid with a sense of its evanescence. St. Theresa, on the other hand, and the medieval ascetics before her belittle human time for an opposite reason. She writes characteristically: "It comforts me to hear the clock, because I seem to be drawing a little closer to seeing God when I see that that hour of life is over."[43] For many minds of the late sixteenth and early seventeenth centuries, it is the illusory and deceptive character of measurable time that is uppermost. Moments bestowed are really moments taken away; living is in fact using up life. "Por más que hagamos," says Mateo Alemán solemnly, "no podemos excusar que cada momento que pasa no lo tengamos menos de la vida, amaneciendo siempre más viejos y cercanos a la muerte" ("Do what we will, we cannot prevent every moment that passes from being one less moment of living, waking up as we do every day older and nearer death").[44] The corollary of this commonplace is not *carpe diem* but *memento mori*. If time is sometimes thought of as the revealer of truth, more often it is felt not as working toward fulfillment but as invisibly corroding, undermining:

> Mal te perdonarán a ti las horas;
> las horas que limando están los días,
> los días que royendo están los años.

> Hardly will the hours spare you, the hours that file away at the days, the days that gnaw at the years.

writes Góngora in his famous sonnet on "the deceitful brevity of life" (1623).[45] In Seneca the age finds a kindred spirit. Juan de Horozco y Covarrubias discourses in one of his emblems on the Senecan "Quotidie morimur" ("We die daily"):

Y si la vida no estuuiera reduzida al tiempo, apenas lo echáramos de
ver; mas quien considera el apresurarse las horas, llegarse la noche,
y venir la mañana, y leuantarse el Sol con tanta priessa para llegar al
medio día, y que allí no para dándose la misma priessa a cerrar el día,
no puede dexar de echar de ver, que esta misma priessa le va dando
su vida . . . Está claro que quanto el tiempo fuere dexando atrás desta
vida, tanto se acorta del término.[46]

And if life were not reduced to time, we would scarcely take notice
of it. But anyone considering the pressing-on of the hours, the
coming of night, the morning coming and sun rising in such haste to
get on to midday and not stopping there but rushing on in the same
way to close out the day, cannot fail to realize that his life is pressing
away on him in the same way . . . It is evident that the more of this
life time leaves behind, the more it reduces the remainder.

Measurement makes time perceptible, gives it a deceptive substantiality, but
cannot disguise the constant pressing on ("priessa") of the hours. The final
drop in the hourglass, he goes on, is merely the culmination of an unending
process:

Y aunque la postrera gota acabó la hora, no fue ella sola sino todas
las que antes della cayeron, desde la primera que tanta parte como
ella tiene en el fin, que desde su principio se començó. Y conforme
a esto tiene mucha razón el Séneca en lo que antes auía dicho, que
cada día morimos, y cada día se nos va quitando parte de la vida.

And although the final drop rounded out the hour, it did not do so
by itself but together with all those that fell before it, beginning
with the first, which has as much a share as the last in the end result,
which has itself been under way from the beginning. And,
accordingly Seneca is quite right in what he had earlier said: that we
die daily and that every day takes away a little of our life.

   One might continue citing such instances of almost compulsive probing
into the character of time as experienced by men in their lives; the culmination comes in Quevedo's anguished expressions of mortality:

En el hoy y mañana y ayer, junto
pañales y mortaja, y he quedado
presentes sucesiones de difunto.[47]

In today, tomorrow, and yesterday, I combine swaddling clothes
and winding-sheet, and I remain as present successions of one
deceased.

The unreliability of man's perception of time as measured both against the clock and against eternity, a heightened awareness of mutability and impermanence, a visceral and pre-existentialist sense of time as organic process, to say nothing of the attendant moral lessons, can all be felt and will all find echoes in *La Dorotea*. Before the process of aging refines Lope's sensibilities, however, there are only faint suggestions of a more than routine sensitivity to time. In *La Arcadia* Lope implies a vague incompatibility, for example, between chronometric time and its inner repercussions, in the well-worn conceits of a poem addressed to a watch:

> Poco mi tormento impiden
> tus horas, de tiempo llenas
> pues no se miden las penas
> como las horas se miden;
> éstas el tiempo dividen,
> sus partes mostrando al tiempo,
> que el humano pasatiempo
> pasa el tiempo en esta calma;
> pero las horas del alma
> no se miden con el tiempo.
>
> Si lo que paso sintieses,
> reloj, en tan largos días,
> más aprisa pasarías
> horas que ausente me vieses;
> yo aseguro que corrieses
> tan ligero por mi vida,
> que al margen de su corrida
> llegases en un momento;
> pero la pena que siento
> no hay pena con que se mida.

(OS, VI, 259)

Your hours filled with time scarcely prevent my torment since pain is not measured as are hours. These divide time, revealing to it its own parts: human pastimes pass time in this peaceful way. But the hours of the soul are not measurable by time. Watch, if you could feel what I am undergoing on such long days, you would get more rapidly through hours in which you found me absent. I wager you would run through my life so fast that you would reach the limit of its course in a moment. But there is no pain to measure the pain I feel.

Noticeably for the still youthful author of these lines the subjective experience of time is one of slowness, not rapidity. The suggested incommensurability, too, is hyperbolic, not a real attempt to express timelessness:

> Cuenta despacio los años
> de un hora que el alma llora.

> Count slowly the years of an hour which the soul regrets.

the poem also declares. The lines were apparently written for nothing more serious than a game of forfeits at the ducal court of Alba.

The words which Lope puts into the mouth of a hermit of Monserrate about a decade later in *El peregrino en su patria* (*The Pilgrim of Castile*) (1604) strike a different note. The ascetic context and evident exemplary intention of the passage do not entirely account for the insistence on the evanescent character of human life:

> Y assí la llama Santiago, vapor que a penas parece. Homero compara la vida del hombre, a las caducas hojas de los árboles. Eurípides dixo, que duraba su felicidad un día; pero reprehendióle Demetrio Phalereo, de que dixesse un día, debiendo decir sólo un instante de tiempo. Y Píndaro llamó al hombre semejante a la sombra. Caso estraño el de nuestros años, pues respeto de la inmortalidad, aunque nuestra vida fuera de muchos siglos, era corta; y siendo de tan pocos, que ya es viejo un hombre de quarenta, de cinquenta caduco, y de sesenta inútil, apenas consideramos su brevedad para estimar el tiempo, que después havemos de llorar tan mal perdido. (*OS*, V, 117)

> And thus St. James calls it a mist that is scarcely visible. Homer compares the life of man to leaves that fall from the trees. Euripides said that its happiness lasted one day; but Demetrius Phalereus reproved him for saying a day when he should have said a mere instant of time. And Pindar called man similar to a shadow. A strange case is that of our years, for in respect to immortality, although our life were many centuries long, it would be short; and being of so few that a man is already old at forty, at fifty tottering, and at sixty useless, we scarcely consider its brevity in order to prize the time which later we will be regretting as so ill-spent.

Though the concepts are derivative, the style suggests more than perfunctory echoing. The staccato phrases multiply, growing progressively shorter; the thoughts echoed in them focus more and more precisely on the idea of brevity. The accumulation and acceleration reach a climax in the characterization of a man's forties, fifties, and sixties. Lope had himself recently turned forty when he wrote these lines and in the tone of urgency one senses a growing personal stake.[48] The objective measurements—forty, fifty, sixty—are not only dwarfed by the idea of eternity but counterbalanced by a subjective apprehension of time's passage stylistically conveyed.

Still, the gloomy forecasts for the forties, fifties, and sixties were scarcely destined to be realized in Lope's experience. In his mid-fifties, his vitality undiminished, Lope meets Marta de Nevares, who inspires the deepest passion of his life; his touching devotion to her lasts until her death in his seventieth year. But towards the end of his forties, Lope begins to undergo the periods of painful soul-searching and the crises which lead him to seek closer and closer ties with the Church. In 1609 he joins the Congregation of Slaves of the Most Holy Sacrament of the Oratory of the Caballero de Gracia, in 1610 a second Congregación del Oratorio, in 1611 the third order of the Franciscans, and in 1614 he is ordained a priest. In 1611, we find him remarking: "Yo me pego lindos çurriagazos todas las noches" ("I give myself some fine lashes every night").[49] Though these spiritual crises are aggravated by painful experiences like the loss of his favorite child, Carlos Félix, in 1612, and of Doña Juana de Guardo, his second wife, after a painful illness, in 1613, they antedate these particular griefs. Their origin is an overwhelming sense of guilt, a pressing need to make amends for the offenses against God, the forgetfulness of Christ, into which the uncurbed impulses of anger and lust have led him. (In 1612, when he painfully injures an arm in a fall, he reflects: "Dios castiga agora en mis huesos los pecados de mi carne"—"God is now taking out on my bones the sins of my flesh.")[50] These feverish crises of conscience are evidently the result of introspection and retrospection more searching than before. Lope's examination of present and past makes him uncertain about the future and urges on him the need to do penance.

The *Soliloquios amorosos de un alma a Dios* offer a reflection of this continuing, anguished examination of conscience. They appeared in print under a pseudonym in 1626,[51] seven soliloquies written in *redondillas*, each twenty quatrains in length, with an introduction of sixteen quatrains to the seven. Each soliloquy is followed by a long prose commentary (seven pages on the average in the *Obras sueltas* edition). There are also one hundred *jaculatorias* (brief prayers), each a single sentence in prose, and several other poems. The first four verse *Soliloquios* had been published separately in 1612 as *Cuatro soliloquios de Lope de Vega Carpio; llanto y lágrimas que hizo arrodillado delante de un crucifijo pidiendo a Dios perdón de sus pecados, después de haber recibido el hábito de la Tercera Orden de Penitencia del seráfico Francisco* (Four Soliloquies of Lope de Vega Carpio; Weeping and Tears Which He Shed Kneeling before a Crucifix, Asking God's Forgiveness for His Sins after Having Received the Habit of the Third Order of Penance of the Seraphic Francis). The composition of these four poems may be placed in September 1611.[52] It is not entirely certain that the remaining three poems and all the prose commentaries were added only at the time the *Soliloquios amorosos* appeared. Some part of the prose at least must have been written by late 1614 or early 1615, to judge by a passage in a letter to the Duke of Sessa dating from that time:

> Los *Soliloquios* enbío en su mismo borrador; assí, quitados del libro en que estauan las *Rimas*; Vex.ª los haga copiar con cuidado; que el escritor no pierda esas ojas, porque no ay otras en el mundo; y aunque por mías no debo estimar esas prosas, por haberlas escrito con tanta deboción y lágrimas, querría que aprobechasen a otros. (*Epistolario*, III, 169)

> I am sending the *Soliloquios* in their original draft—just that way, and removed from the book that the *Rimas* were in. Your Excellency will have them copied with care: the scribe must not lose these sheets, for there are no others in the world. And while I ought not to prize these prose pieces because they are mine, having written them with so much piety and tears I should like them to be of benefit to others.

Possibly the first four prose commentaries were added by 1614, the year Lope became a priest; he may have originally destined them for publication with the *Rimas sacras* of that year. Indeed, the whole work could conceivably have been ready by then. Yet, although there are no appreciable differences in tone between the first four poems and commentaries, on the one hand, and the last three, on the other, it is plausible to presume that the latter were added later, after the gravest conflict of all, the inner struggle caused by his love for Marta de Nevares, had ended.[53] His priestly state does not seem to be the primary reason for delaying publication. Had it, in fact, prevented Lope from exposing himself as so great a sinner in 1614, it would have done so *a fortiori* in 1626, when his years supposedly demanded greater respectability. Lope must have sensed that his cup of penance was not yet full. Only when he had really crossed the threshold of old age and his relationship with Marta was entirely Platonic could he trust himself not to fall back as he had after the *Soliloquios* published in 1612. The *Soliloquios* of 1626 and especially the accompanying prose may thus be considered to reflect not only the emotional crises of Lope's forties but those of the fifties and sixties as well. They are works conceived in a religiously oriented solitude,[54] in the privacy of Lope's relationship with his God and published only as an afterthought. "Esta diligencia hice para mí sólo, después me pareció que el no comunicarle . . . era tyranía" ("This task I undertook for myself alone; afterward it seemed to me that not to share it . . . would be a crime"), Lope explains in the dedicatory epistle to the Countess of Olivares, shielding his intimacy by using a pseudonym and a fiction of translation:

> En pocas hojas doy a V. Exc. el fruto de un sentimiento santo, traducido de la Latina a nuestra lengua. Cuyo autor tomó la pluma de las alas de su amor, el papel de su corazón y la tinta de sus lágrimas. (p. xiii)

> In a few pages I am giving Your Excellency the fruit of a holy sentiment translated out of the Latin into our language. The author of which took a quill from the wings of his love, paper from his heart, and ink from his tears.

The voice we hear is now pleading, now reasoning, now tremulous with alarm. Constantly aware that it is God to whom he is speaking, Lope scarcely polishes or retouches his words for human ears. Rather than artistic utterance, we have here the spontaneous reverberations of an impulsive examination of conscience—the emotional climate, the tossing about; not, however, the confession itself. Although there are occasional intimately revealing fragments, the stream of consciousness that gushes forth is far too urgent to observe the order prescribed by St. Ignatius Loyola and presumably inculcated in Lope in his youth. The style and movement of these pieces—both verse and prose—betray an inner agitation too intense to be manageable artistically or indeed to be lived with for long: the span of each soliloquy is relatively short. Insofar as the style appears literary, it is because Lope is writing in an idiom which has become second nature: the lyricism is innate, the figures and images already ingrained in his imagination.

Lope here confronts spiritual and emotional crises whose after-effects will still be felt in La Dorotea. More exactly, the Soliloquios represent a stage in Lope's confrontation with himself and in his reaction to his past which had to be lived through before he could develop the breadth and serenity of outlook that made reelaboration of La Dorotea possible. Light is shed in them on Lope's view of himself, on the tensions he feels between self and world, on his deepening insights into temporality, on a confessional need in its most obvious nonesthetic sphere.[55] One cannot of course overlook the distorting effect of the emotional turmoil, the accesses of self-accusation, in the midst of which Lope is writing; these color his view of the past and his prefigurings of the future. Under the stress of anger,[56] shame,[57] guilt, remorse, dread, anything touched upon is capable of becoming a source of anguish. But this very process sharpens the instruments of introspective analysis; ultimately, when reassurance has been found, when world and self have been allowed to reassert their rights, such instruments will be applied, in elaborating the *acción en prosa*, to the contents of the poet's artistic consciousness. In the *Soliloquios*, moreover, we see most vividly emerging a backdrop of ascetic *desengaño* from whose starkness Lope will later retreat, an acute awareness of mortality and temporality which will inform in its own way the *acción en prosa*, and a personal attempt to envisage the infinite and juxtapose it with the finite.

The seven soliloquies are not sufficiently structured as a single entity to enable one to speak in more than a limited way of an overall movement from the first to the last, a progression from agitation to serenity, for example. Each represents a groping of the sinner toward reconciliation with his Maker, and while each ends in tentative reassurance, in each case Lope falls prey again to alarm and dismay. His insecurity imparts a peculiar restlessness to the whole sequence. There is always an afterthought to spring up and assail him; after blessing Christ for rescuing him, for example, he goes on:

> ¡Mas hai, Señor, ahora se me acuerda lo que tardé en desligarme la mortaja de las costumbres que me cercaban todo . . .!   (p. 29)

> But ah, Lord, now I recall how long I took to unwind the shroud of the habits that bound me up so tight . . .!

While I will therefore not try to analyze them in sequence, the final one may appropriately be left for the end, for here at last one does become aware of an overall cathartic effect, of a tenuous spiritual calm, and one also senses that a movement has occurred from attrition to contrition.

It goes without saying that the process of recollection is extremely painful in the *Soliloquios*:

> Como si el mar se secasse, se verían tan estraños monstros, assí, mi Dios, veo mis torpezas en las arenas de mis passados años.
> (*Jaculatoria* XVII, p. 89)

> As, if the sea should dry up, one would see such strange monsters, so, my Lord, I see my villanies in the sands of my past years.

There are things from which memory recoils:

> Por mis ojos passaron vanas hermosuras, flores que nacen al Alva,
> y a la noche mueren: por mis oídos locas palabras, y por los demás
> sentidos cosas, que por no ofender vuestra limpieza aún no las osa
> revolver mi memoria.   (p. 30)

> Across my sight passed empty beauties, flowers that are born at dawn
> and die in the night; through my ears, wild words, and through the
> other senses things which, in order not to offend your purity,
> memory dare not even turn over.

Yet the sinner must keep probing, driven by a need to recall each detail, each
occasion of sin, lest it remain unconfessed and unremitted. Lope is not
apprehensive of devious sins of the type that are hidden from the sinner himself.[58] The sheer mass of the sins he is aware or convinced of having committed is such, however, that he cannot hope to recover them all unassisted
by God's grace. Hence his pleading and his alarm:

> Suplícoos pues, Dios mío, Señor mío, deis luz a los ojos de mi
> entendimiento, para que os considere airado, y entienda las ocasiones
> que os dí para que lo estéis: si os tiemblan las colunas del cielo,
> ¿qué haré yo, pensando que sois juez de muertos y vivos, y más si
> pongo los ojos en el libro de mis maldades, donde a la pluma del
> fiscal riguroso no se le ha de olvidar un átomo? ¡Hai Dios! tantas
> obras feas, tantas palabras locas, tantos pensamientos vanos, ¿qué
> será de mí?   (p. 39)

> I beseech you, my Lord, to lend light to the eyes of my
> understanding, so that it will realize you are angry and understand
> the occasions I gave you for being so. If the pillars of heaven tremble
> before you, what shall I do, knowing you are judge of living and
> dead, especially when my eyes light on the book of my evil deeds,
> in which not an atom will escape the pen of the stern recorder?
> Oh God! So many wicked acts, so many wild words, so many vain
> thoughts: what will become of me?

If God did not pardon Lucifer, the "ángel criado en tanta belleza" ("angel
nourished in such beauty") (p. 63) and Adam, made in his image, how can
a sinner like Lope expect to be saved? Recoiling from the stern Jehovah, he
searches out the understanding Christ and, addressing the Cross, imagines
himself forgiven:

> Mirad, bandera santa, cómo tiene bajada la cabeza; ¿qué pensáis que
> es aquello, sino decir que sí? Bendita sea de los Angeles tal piedad.
> (p. 55)

> See, holy banner, how He has His head lowered. What do you
> think that can mean except to say yes? May such mercy be blessed
> by the angels.

Yet such reassurance does not hold for long and the writer is soon again
plunging into the depths of despair. Assailed as he is by remorse and self-
reproach, his retrospection inevitably produces a vision of his entire early
life as a single morass of sin, and he cannot help but shudder as he projects
back upon his heedless youth his present overwhelming awareness of
mortality:

> Mirad que los caminos del mancebo parecieron al mayor Sabio
> imposibles de ser entendidos: quando me acuerdo que entonces me
> sufristes: quando me acuerdo que de los mismos umbrales del
> infierno me sacastes: quando pienso en que, como los que van por
> el mar que llevan sola una tabla entre la vida y la muerte, yo iba por
> el golfo de mis pasiones en la nave de mi verde edad, un dedo de la
> pena eterna, y que esta tabla, vida mía, hizo tan gruessa el madero
> de vuestra Cruz, que fue poderoso a que no se rompiesse con la vida:
> no sé cómo no tiemblo y me deshago llorando.   (p. 28) 59

> Consider that the ways of a youth seemed beyond all understanding
> to the greatest Sage. When I recall that you then suffered me, when
> I recall that from the very gates of hell you drew me back: when I
> think that, like those who sail the sea with only a plank between
> life and death, I sailed the gulf of my passions in the ship of my
> tender years, a finger's breadth away from eternal damnation, and
> that this plank, life of mine, the timber of your Cross made so thick
> that it was strong enough not to break with life, I know not how I
> can keep from quaking and dissolving in tears.

Such a passage exposes the gap that has opened between the youthful Lope
and the Lope of maturity. Elsewhere he reconstructs even more explicitly
his youthful state of mind from his present angle of vision:

> El hombre debe pensar, o su mortalidad, o su inmortalidad; y nada
> desto pensaba yo: lo mortal, porque ninguna cosa estaba más lejos
> de mi memoria que la muerte; lo inmortal, porque ninguna me daba
> menos pena que el alma. ¡Hai ciegos errores de mi juventud! las

ignorancias de la qual aquel santo Rey, vuestro antecesor, os pedía
que no os acordássedes dellas.   (p. 39)[60]

Man must consider either his mortality or his immortality and I
considered neither: mortal things because nothing was further from
my memory than death; immortal ones because none gave me less
concern than the soul. Oh blind errors of my youth! The ignorances
of which that holy King, your predecessor, begged you not to
remember.

In his anguish, Lope takes refuge behind the figure of David.

When the process of recall casts up particular memories, they are never
concretized or dwelt upon. Instead Lope throws over them almost immediately a cover of *desengaño*, which here, for him, is simply a categorical
rejection of the world and the flesh, an eye-opening exposure of the hollowness and decay which underlie the world's deceptive allurements. Though
Lope here speaks the standard language of his age—of Mateo Alemán and
Juan de Valdés Leal—he gives this idiom a striking tone of self-accusation:

Ha pocos días que quisistes vos que una de las que me agradaron
viniesse a morir a donde yo la viesse, tan miserable, que no sólo
havía perdido la hermosura, mas también el entendimiento, para que
viesse yo el fuego, que me pareció luz, tan fea y abominable ceniza,
que me abriesse más de veras los ojos a la contemplación de nuestra
común miseria.   (p. 10)[61]

Not many days ago you willed that one of the women who had
pleased me should happen to die where I might see her, so wretched
that she had lost not only her beauty but her mind, in order that I
might behold the fire, which had seemed light to me, as such ugly
and abominable ash that it would open up my eyes more truly to
the contemplation of our common wretchedness.

With this vision Lope contrasts the smiling beauty in death of a young virgin
whom he had seen "in those same days," sure that God had intended a lesson
for him in the confrontation (p. 10). In another passage, he remembers his
"blind attachment to a wretched and fragile beauty" and, with mingled
fascination and horror, imagines himself and this mistress in hell cursing and
blaspheming against one another (p. 29).

From such nightmares Lope sometimes ascends to more sweeping visions
of *desengaño* which underscore the transience as well as the hollowness of this
life, intoning the age-old commonplaces with a peculiar personal urgency

and making the favorite *exemplum* of long-sufferingness, Job (7:21), a spokesman for himself:

> ¿Qué me prometía el mundo sin vos, o que me dió jamás, que
> estando presente, no me pareciesse passado por la brevedad que tuvo?
> ¡Qué engañosos deleytes! ¡qué grandes en la imaginación! ¡qué
> pequeños en el efecto! Gigantes parecen a la idea del miserable
> entendimiento que los fabrica, pero llegados a tocar con las manos,
> son vanas sombras, sueños phantásticos, oro de alchimia, cometas
> breves, flores phímeras, que al Alva salen, a medio día se extienden,
> y a la noche están marchitas, y esso mismo es el hombre: toda la
> vida es un día, amanece en la niñez, resplandece en la juventud, y en
> la vejez cierra las hojas de su flor. Por esso se daba prisa al perdón
> aquel inmortal exemplo de paciencia, porque temía que si os
> tardábades en buscarle, por ventura no le hallaríades.   (p. 62)

> What did the world ever promise me without you or what did it
> ever give me which, when present, did not seem past to me because
> of its brevity? What deceitful delights! How great in imagination!
> How small in fact! They seem gigantic in the eyes of the miserable
> mind that invents them, but when they come within hand's reach,
> they are empty shadows, fantastic dreams, alchemist's gold, short-
> lived comets, flowers of a day, that come out at dawn, spread wide
> at noon, and by night are wilted, and that very thing is man! All life
> is a day, it dawns in childhood, shines forth at noon, and in old age
> closes up the petals of its bloom. For this reason that immortal
> example of long-suffering was in a hurry to be forgiven, because he
> feared that if you delayed seeking him out, perhaps you would not
> find him.

Like Job, Lope fears that God's mercy may be too long postponed. A sense
of the immensity of his personal stake in salvation pushes him to an acute
awareness of the time-bound character of life. Whenever he scans his own
uncertain future, the natural effect of accumulating years in driving home the
brevity of life is compounded by a sensation of being pressed for time, a fear
that his days may run out before he is ready. An almost obsessive personal
awareness of temporality thus penetrates deep into his consciousness:

> Que yo no sé el preciso tiempo de mi fin, aunque sé que está ya
> estatuido y que es infalible. La brevedad de la vida, Señor, os doy en
> disculpa de pediros tan apretadamente que tengáis lástima de mí,
> porque su incertidumbre me atormenta, y estas hojas débiles, que el
> viento arrebata, no son defensa para resistir los golpes de vuestra ira.

Vos solo, Señor, sabéis los tiempos, los fines, las mudanzas, y los
progressos de las cosas: vos sus discursos de las edades, la instabilidad
de los años, y la ligera velocidad de los días.   (p. 42)[62]

For I do not know the exact time of my end, although I know that
it is already decreed and is infallible. I cite the brevity of life, Lord,
as my excuse for begging you so urgently to have pity on me,
because its uncertainty torments me and these weak leaves which the
wind snatches away are no defense for withstanding the blows of
your wrath. You alone, Lord, know the times, ends, changes, and
progressions of things: you know the passage of the ages, the
instability of the years and the swift velocity of the days.

Feverishly Lope piles up verbal barricades, as if to slow up the processes of
transience and mutability which he is invoking. There is so much lost time
to be made up for:

¡Hai mi Dios, quién te amasse estos días tan aprissa, que desquitasse
los muchos que ha vivido sin haverte amado!   (*Jaculatoria* LV, p. 85)

Oh my God, if only one could love you so speedily these days that
one might make up for the many days one has lived without loving
you.

In these instances the individual consciousness has become, or seeks to
become, the gauge of time's passage. Slowness and rapidity are felt as
subjective and relative experiences, standing apart from the external computation of time. And the other alternative to objective measurement of
time, time as seen by God, inevitably shows up the petty finiteness of man's
chronometry:

Las horas dividen en minutos los que miden desde la tierra
vanamente vuestro cielo: assí lo muestran los relojes, cuya arena
destila pequeños átomos: pero vuelve a correr, quando la mano del
dueño se la vuelve a restituir. ¡Hai de mí, Señor, que no volverán
los instantes de mis horas passando una vez, hasta que en el último
día la común resurrección me restituya este ser, de que vos fuistes
autor!   (p. 75)

Those who vainly measure your heaven from the earth divide hours
into minutes: so clocks record, whose sand distills small atoms. But
it runs back again when the hand of the owner turns it around.
Alas, Lord, the instants of my hours, having once passed, will not

return until the final day when the common resurrection restores to me this being of which you were the author.

The glimpse of timelessness is not held for long. As can be seen, Lope comes back to his obsession with the time allotted to his personal existence, to his limited and unrenewable store. This is the final soliloquy and in it we find him oscillating between the personal and the suprapersonal, the finite and the infinite, between clock time and timelessness:

> Pensando en vos desfallece la fuerza del entendimiento mortal, porque sois incomprensible; ni el sentido os percibe por invisible, ni la lengua os explica por inefable: ningún lugar os circumscribe, ni pluma os declara, ni tiempo os mide.   (p. 73)

> Thinking of you the power of mortal understanding falters because you are incommensurable; nor does sense perceive you since you are invisible, nor the tongue explain you because you are ineffable. No space encompasses you, nor pen declares you nor time measures you.

Lope continues at this level awhile, only to come round again, eventually, to his insistent question: "¿Que ha de ser de mí?" ("What is to become of me?"). The invoking of David and Job lends dignity to his plea. Following the fourteenth chapter of Job, Lope gives expression to the irrevocable transiency of human life in tones that are at last more poignant and lyrical than tense or anxious:

> . . . que el árbol cortado podía tener esperanza de reverdecer, y envegeciéndose las rayces en la tierra, tender los ramos, cuyo tronco muerto en el polvo, al olor de las aguas produciría la misma corona de hojas que tuvo luego que fue plantado; no el hombre una vez desnudo deste mortal vestido.   (p. 74)

> . . . that the tree when cut down might have hope of sprouting again and, while its root waxed old in the earth, spread forth branches, whose trunk, dead in the dust, through the scent of water would bring forth the same crown of leaves which it had right after it was planted; not so man, once stripped of this mortal garb.

These quieter lyrical notes, the protracted organic imagery of human transience—Lope follows Job closely but not perfunctorily—Lope's reaching out from immediate and personal concerns to the infinite and the timeless:

these features of the final soliloquy anticipate aspects of the mature *Dorotea*. They emerge here fragmentarily and at random; in the *acción en prosa* they will be worked into the woof of an artistic fabric.

The resigned and melancholy tone of the final soliloquy reveals that the writing of the series has indeed had in some degree a cathartic effect. Emotional turmoil and spiritual tensions have begun to be eased as Lope relives his orgies of repentance at the feet of Christ crucified. It is a catharsis of the most elemental kind—a straightforward emotional purgation, accompanied at times by a sensation of spiritual cleansing; it is not the liberation achieved through artistic sublimation. Directly soothing is the effect of the floods of tears constantly shed. "Dulce cosa es llorar; ¡o qué contenta queda el alma después de haber llorado!" ("It is a sweet thing to weep; oh how happy it leaves the soul to have wept!") (p. 60). Almost all the *Soliloquios*, verse and prose, end in such copious weeping, each one tentatively prefiguring, perhaps merely out of emotional exhaustion, the incipient calm of the last. In the ending of the sixth, we see that the purgative effect corresponds to a movement from attrition to contrition:

> Pues si vos queréis que me pese mucho de haveros ofendido, ya me pesa, Señor: echadme vuestra bendición, que no me dejan las lágrimas passar de aquí.   (p. 64)

> So if you wish me to be sorely grieved at having offended you, so I am, Lord: grant me your blessing, for tears will not let me go any further.

Earlier, too, one had sensed love timidly asserting itself over fear:

> Mas, Señor, ya que me pesa tanto de haver sido qual vos sabéis . . . y estoy corrido de no haver amado vuestra hermosura . . . decid vos que me queréis, y admitidme a vos.   (p. 42)

> But, Lord, since it grieves me so to have been as you know . . . and I am angry not to have loved your beauty . . . tell me you love me and admit me to yourself.

The *Soliloquios* reveal the functioning of Lope's psyche when he looks backward and inward in an effort to ease emotional and spiritual burdens. The examination of conscience is anguishing, though ultimately restorative, but it is sterile artistically. Yet, despite the predominance of *Erlebnis* over *Dichtung*, it must offer some analogy for the esthetically oriented process of

reexamination and recall that, in my view, would have preceded the definitive elaboration of *La Dorotea*. It is, moreover, a prelude to this process not
only in the redirecting and sharpening of insight it brings and the psychological settlement for which it clears the way, but in the emergence, in fragmentary articulation, of perceptions and perspectives which would become
basic to the masterwork.

That the emotional temper of the *Soliloquios* is in the end melancholic is
scarcely surprising when one remembers Lope's own repeated declarations
of his proneness to this mood, an aspect of his temperament which Amezúa
has justly emphasized.[63] A dark substratum shows through below the bright
surface of his personality, more and more perceptible with the years until,
at the end of his life, he can make, through his persona, Tomé de Burguillos,
the earlier noticed observation that, although naturally sad, he appeared gay
to everyone. In an epistle published in 1621 Lope had stated definitively:
"No es jovial el genio mío" ("My nature is not jovial").[64] Not jovial,
certainly not phlegmatic, and not choleric. The fiery emotionality, the drive
and energy so much in the ascendant in his youth began to abate with the
years, flaring up less and less frequently. In terms of the characterology of his
day, melancholy becomes the dominant humor, and so Lope himself clearly
perceives.

While melancholy covered a whole gamut of meanings and embraced a
wide range of phenomena, not always clearly distinguished or defined, Lope
was well aware of a fundamental distinction between melancholy as a
temperamental inclination and more or less transitory *tristezas* (sadnesses)
contingent upon specific causes:

> Es la tristeza tener
> por qué estar triste, que un hombre
> sabe de su mal el nombre
> y viénese a entristecer.
> La fiera melancolía
> es estar triste sin causa.[65]

> Sadness means having a reason to be sad, a man knowing the name
> of his affliction and falling into a sad mood. Cruel melancholy is
> being sad for no reason.

Lope often makes this distinction, though he is sometimes vague and con-
fusing in his terminology.[66] His vigorous temperament had worked out its
defenses against the assaults of melancholy; his reaction in 1631 when the
Duke of Sessa directs him to draw up a will for him is revealing. He tries to
reassure the Duke that his mood is caused by *tristezas* with remediable causes:

A fee que si yo estubiera con más salud, que no hauía de estar Vex.ª
ocioso, que de eso naze estar triste: porque la ociosidad es madre de
los pensamientos; ellos, de los cuidados; los cuidados estrechan el
corazón y hazen que parezcan ynposibles las mexorías de los sucesos.
(*Epistolario*, IV, 146)

Upon my word, if I were in better health, Your Excellency would
not be idle, for that is the reason for your feeling sad; for idleness is
the mother of thoughts; they of worries; worries constrict the heart
and make an improvement in the course of events appear impossible.

Anguish (literally, constriction), both physical and spiritual, is evoked in these
words in which the unceasing activity of a lifetime appears for a moment as a
modus vivendi with melancholy.

If Lope's *élan vital* always triumphs in the end, in his dark periods the line
between melancholy and *tristezas* becomes indistinct. Toward his fiftieth
year—c. 1612—in the midst of an illness, he writes the Duke:

No sé qué anda tras mí estos días como sombra, si este nombre se
puede dar a mis disgustos, que dellos naze hazer sentimiento el
cuerpo y está puesta [*sic*] en razón de trabaxos de espíritu . . .
Tristezas son estas mías, que otras vezes me han tenido al cabo de la
vida y de la paciencia, pero no con la fuerza que aora. Creo que si
me preguntase a mí mismo qué mal tengo, no sabría responderme,
por mucho tiempo que lo pensase. (*Epistolario*, III, 100)

Something or other is dogging me these days like a shadow, if this
name can be given to my troubles, for they are the cause of my
body's developing aches and suffering on account of spiritual
trials . . . This is the kind of sadnesses that on other occasions have
had me at the end of life and patience, but never with such force as
now. I think that if I asked myself what ails me, I would not be able
to answer, however long I thought about it.

Whatever the origin of these particular *tristezas*, they have reopened the
floodgates of melancholy and left him more than ever a prey to an indefinable
spiritual malaise only too familiar from previous bouts with it. The phrases
in which Lope describes his state—"trabaxos de espíritu" ("spiritual trials"),
"al cabo de la vida" ("at the end of life")—seem unconscious echoes of the
agonic "Anima mea tristis est usque ad mortem" ("My soul is exceeding
sorrowful, even unto death") (Matthew 26:38 and Mark 14:34). But this
suggestion of fellowship in suffering with Christ, while it reveals the depth
of his distress, does not alleviate it.[67] Ultimately, however, Lope came to

terms with his melancholy, discovering in it the richest vein of all. Despite the pedantic terminology he uses in his epistle to Don Antonio Hurtado de Mendoza, published with *La Circe* in 1624, his words ring true:

> No ponga en vuestro ardiente amor templanza
> esse humor melancólico, pues siento,
> que más contemplación con él se alcanza:
> que mejor el passible entendimiento
> percibe las especies producidas
> en el agente por tristeza atento.
> Y están mejor guardadas y esculpidas
> de la virtud phantástica en un triste
> las intenciones a su afecto asidas.
> Que la imaginación abstracta assiste
> con mayor atención a lo que emprende,
> lo que el placer con inquietud resiste.
>
> (*OS*, I, 284)

Do not let this melancholy humor cause a tempering of your ardent love, since I believe that greater contemplativeness is attainable through it. For the passive understanding better perceives the species produced in the agent made attentive by sadness. And in a sad person the intentions linked to his emotional state are better retained and etched by the power of imagination. For the abstract imagination goes about its business with greater attentiveness, whereas pleasure with its restlessness holds out against it.

At the very end of his life, in the elegy to his son, Lope Félix, Lope expresses himself more succinctly and more directly:

> Aunque es amor para los versos genio,
> más puede la desdicha que el ingenio:
> que engendra los conceptos la desdicha,
> y no suele la dicha
> disponer tan sutil naturaleza;
> que es madre del estudio la tristeza.[68]

Although love is the genius of verse, unhappiness can do more than native wit, for unhappiness fathers thoughts and happiness does not usually result in so subtle a nature. For sadness is the mother of studiousness.

More than love, so often proclaimed over the years as the supreme source of verse, more than wit, more than anger, it is misfortune that "fathers" poetic ideas, the abiding *tristeza* of a melancholy temperament. Like Dürer in the Renaissance and Burton in his own day, Lope in the end came to understand that melancholy was the natural condition of "los que saben" ("those who know"), the temperament of poets and painters, of contemplative and meditative spirits and of all who reflect deeply on the world.[69]

The calm, nostalgic tone of the "Egloga a Claudio" (actually an epistle), a poem composed when *La Dorotea* was finished but had not yet appeared in print, reveals how well Lope has come to terms with the melancholy strain in his temperament and shows the distance he has come since the crises of the *Soliloquios*. The contemporaneity of this retrospective poem with the masterwork says much about the mood of *La Dorotea*. Here Lope is speaking intimately with a lifelong friend, not pleading with his God; he is reminiscing, thinking out loud as his mind plays reflectively over the past. At peace with himself and with God, he can think of death steadily and without alarm:

> Voy por la senda del morir más clara,
> y de toda esperanza me retiro:
> que sólo atiendo y miro
> adonde todo para,
> pues nunca he visto que después viviese
> quien no murió primero que muriese.
>
> (*Obras escogidas*, II, 225)

I am most clearly going down the path of dying, and withdrawing from all hope. For my only concern and all I look toward is the ending of everything, since I have never yet seen anyone live hereafter who did not die before he died.

Lope surely overstates the extent of his withdrawal from the world, yet one of the sources of the poem's serenity is the confidence that God has, after all, allowed him enough time. Whatever remains will be a bonus, welcomed but neither counted upon nor needed:

> Fuera esperanzas, si he tenido alguna:
> que ya no he menester a la fortuna,
>
> Away with hope, if ever I had any: for I no longer have any need
> of fortune,

he ends. His phrase for *La Dorotea*—"póstuma de mis musas . . . por dicha de mí la más querida, última de mi vida" ("the posthumous one of my muses . . . perchance the one I most love, the last of my life")—suggests that he views his literary career as over and his life as ending. Now rounding out three score years and ten, a decade beyond the "uselessness" spoken of in *El peregrino*, he must feel himself living, as it were, on borrowed time. So the *acción en prosa* appears to him "posthumous" (the choice of this word rather than "postrera"—"final"—is hardly accidental), the after-product of a life now complete, at once a swan song and an artistic testament, although the paradoxical self-survival of its creator endows it, as we shall see, with the spirit of detachment and the buoyant lightheartedness of one no longer bound by the world. One may note that in a contemporaneous passage patently allusive to himself occurring in a play of 1631–32, a new meaning is found for Job's example of the old tree covered with fresh leaves:

> ¿No habéis visto un árbol viejo
> cuyo tronco, aunque arrugado,
> coronan verdes renuevos?
> Pues eso habéis de pensar,
> y que, pasando los tiempos,
> yo me sucedo a mí mismo . . .[70]

> Have you not seen an old tree whose trunk, though creased, is
> crowned with new green shoots? Well, you must think this and that,
> with the passage of time, I succeed myself . . .

Linked to the self by analogy, rather than contrast, the image signifies self-survival rather than, as in the *Soliloquios*, mortality. In the "Egloga a Claudio" Lope's detachment from the world no more precludes a retrospective savoring of the world's appeal than it does in *La Dorotea*. Although Lope promises another session of tears, as in the *Soliloquios*, when he starts to reminisce, he quickly corrects himself:

> . . . tú en reír y yo en llorar, ¡qué extremos!
> Demócrito y Heráclito seremos.
> Bien que parece reflexión suave
> traer en tanta edad a la memoria
> la juvenil historia.[71]

> . . . you laughing and I weeping—what extremes!—we will be
> Democritus and Heraclitus. Although it does seem a pleasant reflection
> to recall to mind one's youthful story at such an advanced age.

The equanimity with which Lope now looks back is not subsequently disturbed, though certain passing memories jar it a little now and then. As the account proceeds, Lope's mood gives rise to marginal reflections, one of which allows us a further glimpse into the old poet's state of mind. The image of the sea emerges as he recalls the expedition of the Armada, and by the same familiar allegorical extension that underlies the *barquillas* (boat-ballads) of *La Dorotea*, it becomes associated with the course of human life. But the handling of the traditional symbolism is anything but hackneyed:

> Así corre, así vuela el curso humano,
> cual suele navegante suspenderse,
> que pasó sin moverse
> el golfo al Oceano,
> que entre jarcias y velas voladoras
> miró las olas, pero no las horas.
> Sólo conosce de su incierta vía
> los vientos, que es lo mismo que los hombres;
> ni sabe más que nombres
> de tanta hidrografía,
> porque sólo le queda, en el oído,
> no el agua que pasó, sino el sonido.[72]

> Thus runs, thus flies the course of human life, just as a seaman will often be caught up with surprise when he has crossed the abyss of Ocean without moving and, in the midst of his riggings and flying sails, has looked upon the waves but not the hours. Of his uncertain course he knows only the winds, which is the same as knowing men; nor from so much hydrography does he retain anything but names, because there is left to him only, in his ears, not the water he has crossed but its sound.

It is the mood of the declining years that the traditional imagery subserves here. How quickly it is all over; one awakens on the other brink, having been so involved with living in each moment (looking at each "wave") that one has not perceived the drift of the years ("hours"). The moments have imperceptibly added up to a whole lifetime. Time had slowed to a standstill in youth's attachment to the moment, and now in retrospect it has suddenly speeded beyond all retention. "¿Fue cometa o vida?" ("Was it comet or life?"), Lope wonders. And what remains? A sense not of direction but of uncertainty, of drifting before shifting winds—those of the human world—a string of empty names, all one has to show for one's many reckonings, for the courses one has charted. The world is now only an echo, sounding in one's ears; its watery substance has eluded one. Lope's mood is melancholy rather than lachrymose. He is not now weeping with Heraclitus, but the Heraclitean perception of universal flux has penetrated into his view of existence. "Pues, Claudio, así se muda cuanto vive. / No sé si soy aquél" ("Well, Claudio, so everything living changes. I don't know whether I am that one"). Not even the self is immune: can he discern himself in that far-off being whom he describes? A sense of remoteness and distinctness coupled somehow with a feeling of continuity and flow gives a new problematical quality to Lope's perception of the past. In his present mood the substance of his life assumes an air of insubstantiality. In the *Soliloquios* the past had been a dead weight. Now it is lighter than air—and gone with the wind. With the reassurance that it is not unredeemable has come a movement back toward it, only to have it prove irretrievable in another sense. The memory which had unerringly found things it did not care to contemplate during the crisis of the *Soliloquios*, now that it is free to survey, finds itself unsure and inadequate.

Not surprisingly, Lope's account of the past in the "Egloga" soon turns into an *apologia* based not on deeds but on writings. The books whose titles he lists and lingers over are the true enduring substance of the past. With advancing years and the falling-off of other activities, his literary activity clearly assumed a larger place and new meaning in his eyes. As he withdrew into his private and domestic world and cultivated a personal *soledad*, emerging less often to respond to the solicitations of others, literary composition became more and more a means of personal fulfillment, a compensation and a solace. For the later years also brought him an increasing store of losses, misfortunes, and disappointments of which the blindness, insanity, and eventual death of Marta de Nevares was only the most painful. The meagerness of his economic circumstances brought an increased feeling of enslavement to play-writing, while at the same time he saw himself losing popularity to younger dramatists. He was humiliatingly dependent on the capricious benefactions of his patron, the Duke of Sessa, who ignored Lope's requests to alleviate his situation by making him chaplain as well as secretary. Other schemes for remedying his economic situation, like the repeated efforts to have himself named royal chronicler, which go back at least as far as 1611, were similarly frustrated.[73]

In the light of these rebuffs the protests of stoical contentment with his lot which we find Lope making in these years have a hollow ring; they seem at most momentary reconciliations with it. More and more his true compensation is "mis Musas." An engaging fantasy found in the "Epístola al Conde de Lemos" (published in 1621 with *La Filomena*) exemplifies this fact some ten years before the "Egloga a Claudio." As a delicate way of requesting assistance of his former master, the poet relates a dream, telling how he found himself in an unfamiliar setting of the New World being greeted by a man of gold who clearly represents the Count. Lope's admission that poverty has brought

him there causes the golden figure to exclaim in surprise, whereupon the poet
continues:

> Yo descubriendo unos Franciscos mantos,
> algunos niños le mostré pequeños,
> vergüenza tengo de deciros quántos.
> Estos, le dixe, son ahora dueños
> de toda mi mejor Philosophía,
> rompiéndome los libros y los sueños.
> Mirad si un pensamiento engendra y cría:
> ¿quién me dixera que mi edad parara
> a la vejez en tanta niñería?
> Díxome entonces con risueña cara:
> qué bien tu loco pensamiento escusas;
> mas cúyos son los niños me declara.
> Hijos, señor, le dixe de las Musas.
>
> (OS, I, 452)

Opening up some Franciscan habits, I showed him some small
children, I am ashamed to say how many. These, I told him, are now
the possessors of all my best philosophy, ripping my books and my
dreams. If it is true that a thought can be a parent and upbringer,
just think: would one ever have supposed that my life would end up
in old age with such a collection of children? With a smiling face he
answered me: how well you justify your mad thoughts; but explain
to me whose children these are. The offspring, sir, of the Muses, I
told him.

Midas-like, Lemos–El Dorado showers them with gold, but it so weights
them down that they all wake up in a bed of thistles and nettles. One sees
here that the justification Lope finds for his life is his books, the product of
his private sessions with the muses, though such products evidently cannot
make their way into the world unassisted.[74]

Even more revealing is a passage in the "Epístola a don Michael de Solís,"
printed with the Laurel de Apolo in 1630 and presumably dating from two years
before. Lope begins with the protest, common in his later years, that he is
occupied with more serious things than love poetry:

> No porque ya de amor dulces engaños
> me ocupen horas, ni me roben días,
> bien lo dirán mis blancos desengaños.
> Otros estudios por diversas vías
> al cielo de la fama me conducen,

sin que lo sepan pretensiones mías.
Dejados los domésticos, reducen
mi vida toda a soledades mudas,
si lo son los efectos que producen.
Salen tal vez de las materias rudas
como embriones, que el ingenio forma,
no siempre de arte y de valor desnudas,
máquinas, que después pule y reforma
mejor pincel de la segunda mano,
cuya alma el cuerpo bosquejado informa:
assí passe la furia del verano,
sirviéndome de fuentes de Beocia
infuso ardor, sujeto soberano.
Y como el alma en soledad negocia
más blanda y fácilmente, lo que emprende,
la Reyna martyr escribí de Escocia.

(OS, I, 261)[75]

Not that the sweet deceits of love occupy my hours or rob me of
my days any longer: my white disenchantments well attest to that.
Other studies along different lines are leading me to the heaven of
fame, without any aspirations on my part being involved. Leaving
domestic concerns aside, they reduce my life wholly to silent solitude,
if one can call silent the effects it produces. There emerge at times
from the raw materials, like embryos shaped by native talent, not
always barren of craftsmanship and worth, constructions which a
better brush subsequently polishes and reshapes with new handiwork,
the soul of which informs the sketched-out body. So it was that I
came through summer's assault, using as my Boeotian springs an
inspired ardor, a supreme subject. And since the soul carries out what
it undertakes more smoothly and easily in solitude, I wrote up the
martyr queen of Scotland.

Lope, whose writing is so often rooted in sociability and conviviality, ground
out in the midst of a turbulent existence, here insists on the importance of
creative solitude. His account of the embryonic shapes (*máquinas*) which the
writer's inventiveness fashions from his raw material (in this case a history of
the life of Mary Queen of Scots), to be subsequently reshaped ("reformed"),
rounded out, and refined, is a significant indication of what Lope is then
surely engaged in doing with *La Dorotea*. In the case of the *acción en prosa*, a
long gap separates the two stages of the process, which, Lope tells us, are best
carried out in unbroken continuity in an undisturbed solitude. In the lines of
the epistle, we catch the poet, in intimate confrontation with his *métier*,

filling his existence with literary activity in a manner out of the question earlier when writing had to compete with the multiple activities of a full life.

In these fertile hours of self-sufficient solitude, *La Dorotea* must have increasingly become Lope's dominant occupation, especially perhaps after the hot summer devoted to the unfortunate Scottish queen, alternating surely with projects less extensive in scope, such as the *Laurel de Apolo*. Good circumstantial evidence that Lope had indeed conceived the idea of revising a *Dorotea* as early as c. 1620 is provided by the *canción* "Amarilis a Belardo," published with *La Filomena* in 1621. Whoever the author of this poetic epistle may have been, whether Lope himself, an intimate of the poet's, the mysterious unidentified Peruvian poetess to whom it is attributed, or some other New World poet, the writer shows unquestionable signs of familiarity with Lope's life and affairs. I am therefore inclined to believe, with S. G. Morley, that *La Dorotea* is alluded to in these lines:

> Yo y mi hermana una santa celebramos,
> cuya vida de nadie ha sido escrita,
> como empresa que muchos han temido:
> el verla de tu mano deseamos;
> tu dulce musa alienta y resucita,
> y ponla con estilo tan subido,
> que sea donde quiera conocido,
> y agradecido sea
> a nuestra santa virgen Dorotea . . .
> De esta divina y admirable Santa,
> su santidad refiere
> y dulcemente su martirio canta.[76]

> My sister and I celebrate a saint whose life nobody has written, it being an undertaking of which many have been afraid. We wish to see it done by your hand. Rouse your sweet muse and bring her back to life and garb her in so elevated a style that it may be recognized anywhere and be welcome to our holy virgin Dorotea. Relate the sainthood of this divine and wondrous saint and sweetly sing her martyrdom.

Startling as may be this hyperbolic presentation of a Dorotea who is a martyred virgin and saint, its spirit accords well with the ironic tone of Tomé de Burguillos. The hand, if not of Lope, at least of someone who had caught his modes of expression is to be seen here. The impression conveyed is that *La Dorotea* is a literary project conceived but not yet executed ("cuya vida de nadie ha sido escrita"). The line "Tu dulce musa alienta y resucita" suggests, in addition, that the unrealized undertaking is a revival of an earlier one.

By 1623, there is a clearer hint that a presumably new *Dorotea* is in the making. In an episodic version of the Elena Osorio story found in "La prudente venganza," one of the *Novelas a la señora Marcia Leonarda* which was ready for the press by 1623, there appears as the Lope-figure's rival a "Perulero rico . . . hombre de mediana edad y no de mala persona, aseo y entendimiento" ("rich Peruvian . . . a middle-aged man of no mean figure, dress, and mind"), whose kinship with Don Bela, whether he is an anticipation or an offshoot of the *indiano* of *La Dorotea*, is inescapable.[77] In the same episode the role of the Elena-figure belongs to a courtesan named Dorotea.

The reelaboration of an early embryonic version of the *acción en prosa* would undoubtedly have filled Lope's life more richly than *La corona trágica* (The Tragic Crown), his poem on Mary Queen of Scots, had done, since the history that lay behind it was his own and the world being refashioned was that of his own past, a compensation for the actual world that had slipped away and could be recovered only through poetic reconstruction. Though the experience with Elena Osorio had not faded from his artistic consciousness, like everything that lives on ("así se muda cuanto vive"—"so everything living changes") it had evolved and changed. But in an early version Lope would have rediscovered, preserved from time and change, the artistic product of a previous stage of the process of transformation. Taking it up again, he treats this vision of another time with the same sense of remoteness and distinctness, yet of continuity into the present, of which the "Egloga a Claudio" offers evidence. But in this material, kept alive by still unrealized artistic potentialities, the winds and echoes of the past play over something more substantial than a trackless ocean.

Platonic Idealism

Behind the unrestrained emotionalism of the *Soliloquios* one could observe a wish for spiritual cleansing.

> Yo me limpiaré, si vos me laváis, y quedaré más que la nieve para cuando vos lleguéis, porque vos criaréis en mí un nuevo corazón, y un espíritu recto en mis entrañas,

> I will cleanse myself if you wash me, and will remain cleaner than snow against your coming, because you will foster a new heart in me and a righteous spirit in my breast,

Lope writes at one point (p. 31). Carried further, an impulse of the same kind, a movement toward spiritual ascesis, leads Lope to seek with increasing earnestness, as the years with Marta de Nevares go by, to lift his love for her to a Neo-Platonic plane. In the total context of his life, this is one strain only; it coexists with Tomé de Burguillos, with the opportunistic secretary of the Duke, with the breast-beating penitent. Its authenticity is beyond question, however; it has a close bearing on his handling of the evolving attitude of Don Bela toward Dorotea; it affects Lope's perspective on Fernando as well. (The process of spiritual refinement in Don Bela and the demonstration of Fernando's moral obtuseness are sides of the same coin, complementing each other and constituting, in effect, a confrontation of the aging author with his youthful self.) I wish now to observe certain steps in Lope's pursuit of a Platonic or Neo-Platonic ideal, as reflected in his writings, in the context particularly of his love for Marta. The development of this strain in his later years is a final significant aspect of the process of maturation which made La Dorotea possible. In examining the relationship with Marta, moreover, we will become aware of other aspects in which it affected the elaboration of La Dorotea.

When one follows the course of this attachment (1616–32), the longest of Lope's life, one is at first struck by his capacity to live and function in a situation fraught with moral conflict of every sort. In contrast to his attitude toward Elena Osorio, Lope is here fully alive to the fact of his wrongdoing. But in contrast also to the anguishing consciousness of sin manifest in the Soliloquios and in my view ascribable in part to this same relationship, Lope's correspondence and other writings reflect his ability in his day-to-day living to move on the surface, stifling the voice of conscience when it arises. Yet it is this voice, aided by circumstances and passing years, which in the end prevails. If Lope seeks to meet its objections by orthodox Catholic practices, he also seeks a way out in a genuine aspiration toward a Neo-Platonic sublimation of his love. This form of idealization becomes something more than the lip-service it had been in La Arcadia or the passing curiosity it constitutes here and there in other earlier works.[78] In certain poems inspired by Marta and particularly in La Dorotea, the impulse toward spiritual rebirth visible but artistically barren in the Soliloquios achieves, in a Neo-Platonic context, an artistic fulfillment more congenial to Lope's nature than asceticism or stoicism.

It may be noted that, in addition to the figure of Don Bela, the character of Dorotea is enriched by Lope's experience with Marta. As Rennert and Castro long ago saw (p. 50), in Dorotea Lope has blended the graces, physical charms, and artistic attainments of Marta with those of Elena Osorio.

Aside from Marta's beauty, Lope's verse and correspondence celebrate her intelligence and cultivation and her poetic and musical gifts. The letters reflect evenings of song and recitation in her home. The dedication to her of *La viuda valenciana* (The Widow from Valencia) sums up all her perfections: verse-writing, dancing, playing and singing, prose in which "la pureza del hablar cortesano cobra arrogancia, el donaire iguala a la gravedad y lo grave a la dulzura" ("the purity of courtly speech acquires verve, the levity is equal to the gravity and the gravity to the sweetness").[79] In addition to the four elegies, more than half of the other lyrics that found their way into *La Dorotea* appear to have been written originally for Marta. The fact that Lope makes these serve as artistic reflections of the story of Dorotea and Fernando is a further indication of the merging of the two feminine figures in his mind.

The overwhelming character of his passion for Marta for a long time shut his eyes to the compromising and shabby circumstances of their relationship. She was twenty-five years his junior, about thirty years old when they became lovers in 1616; she had been married for perhaps fifteen years to Roque Hernández de Ayala, whom she detested. Lope at once became inordinately jealous, characteristically heaping scorn and vituperation on Roque in his letters to the Duke, and continuing to do so even after the husband's death, in the dedicatory epistle to *La viuda valenciana* and in the eclogue "Amarilis." At first Roque Hernández seems to have settled amicably enough into the role of complaisant husband, enjoying the gifts and gratuities that the liaison brought his wife, from the Duke in the last analysis. After the birth of Lope's daughter, Antonia Clara, to Marta (1617), his attitude changes; he involves his wife in sordid financial and legal entanglements, becomes aggressive toward Lope, even sets attackers upon him. Marta flees from her husband's home and, at Lope's urging, is instituting proceedings for a separation when Roque Hernández dies unexpectedly after a brief illness (April 1620). Lope's jubilation over this event and the gratitude he expresses to Death for intervening strain one's moral tolerance considerably. All the while the Duke of Sessa displays inordinate curiosity about the intimate details of Lope's relationship with "Amarilis"; Feliciana and Marcela, his young daughters, are deputed to carry their love-notes and verse to the Duke.

Even before meeting Amarilis Lope had not maintained his priestly vows of continence. For a period after his ordination in mid-1614, he had indeed struggled to subdue his sensuality, as the correspondence with the Duke shows.[80] Yet in mid-1616 we find him involved in a brief and humiliating episode with an actress, Lucía de Salcedo, known for her dissolute mores, and this does not seem to have been his first lapse. The affair ended in an access of revulsion against her and himself, which, as Amezúa observes, "could as easily go in the direction of ascetic repentance as embark on a wild new love affair."[81] In this psychologically vulnerable state, conjectures Amezúa plausibly, a chance encounter with Marta, a woman of so different a type, to whom he had apparently been attracted for some time, produced the *coup de foudre*.[82] There is a brief stage of inner struggle, as is clear from the following letter, interesting as well because it offers a first, tenuous indication of the Platonic context which is later to become something more than a passing note:

> Traigo estos días mil pesares de verla [mi alma] enpleada tan baxamente y sin remedio: porque no estoy en tiempo de poder aplicarle ninguno; no porque fuera ynposible, pero porque el oficio y la reputación me ynpiden que pueda reducir esta potencia en acto. Certifico a Vex.ª que ha grandes tiempos que es este amor espiritual y casi platónico; pero que, en el atormentarme más parece de Plutón que de Platón, porque todo el ynfierno se conjura contra mi ymaginación, y que, si no estuuiera de por medio [lo] que resulta de las confesiones y sacrificios, desconfiara de hallar templanza.
> (*Epistolario*, III, 257)

> I am thoroughly put out these days to find [my heart] involved in such a low and unsatisfactory way. Because I am not at a point where I can give it any satisfaction, not because it would be impossible but because my status and reputation prevent my being able to convert this potentiality into actuality. I guarantee Your Excellency that for a long time this love has been spiritual and practically Platonic, although in torturing me it seems more suited to Pluto than to Plato, because all of hell conspires against my imagination and, if it were not for the intervention [of all] that comes of confessions and sacrifices, I would not be sure I could find relief.

This stage is soon superseded, as Amezúa observes,[83] by a triumphant outburst that does away with all moral scruples (September–October 1616). Lope surrenders and Amarilis, as he soon calls her, becomes the focal point of his life. Sometimes a flicker of conscience can be sensed:

> Aora me dizen que va *Amarilis* a la comedia del *Laberinto*; del suyo quisiera yo salir; mas no tengo ylo de oro, ni aun le quiero.
> (*Epistolario*, III, 306)

I have just been told that Amarilis is going to the *Labyrinth* play;
I'd like to get out of her [labyrinth] but have no golden thread, nor
do I even want one.

or:

Yo ando . . . en medio de posesión tan pacífica, que me toca *al arma*
el alma, y es mucha la edad, para tan poco seso. (*Epistolario*, III, 284)

I find myself . . . enjoying such peaceful possession that my soul is
sounding the alarm, and I am too old to be so lacking in sense.

In late 1616, Amarilis's pregnancy has a sobering effect. Once the child is
born, Lope writes the Duke: "Pienso y creo y solicito acogerme a mi
antiguo sagrado" ("I intend and expect and am trying to go back to my
old sanctuary")—that is, to priestly chastity (*Epistolario*, III, 311). In July 1617,
the inordinately protracted and difficult labor provokes a crisis of conscience:

Ha tres días que está en el puesto *Amarilis*, como dizen las mugeres,
con escesibos dolores, aunque no como los de mi alma; esta noche
no he dormido, aunque me he confesado; ¡mal haya amor que se
quiere oponer al cielo! (*Epistolario*, III, 325)

For three days Amarilis has been, as the women say, on the spot,
with excessive pains, although not like those of my soul. I did not
sleep last night although I made confession. Evil betide a love that
would set itself up against heaven!

But once his fears for Marta are quieted Lope's resolve begins to waver:

Va tan adelante [la gallardía de *Amarilis*], que no sé por donde halle
mi voluntad la puerta para salir, como dixo Seneca: *Amor habet
facilem ingressum, regressum vero tardum.* (*Epistolario*, III, 339)

[Amarilis's elegance] is making such strides that I don't know how
my will will find a way out; as Seneca said: Love's entrance is easy
but its exit laborious.

Without committing himself Lope writes that at his years "es justo que la
razón predomine al apetito" ("it is only right that reason should prevail over
appetite") (*Epistolario*, III, 330). The Platonic overtones of this remark are
evident from a passage in another letter, similarly noncommittal:

Yo voy en esta materia con sola el alma, dexando yr el cuerpo a viua fuerza de la razón, si bien la causa no admitirá xamás el estilo platónico. (*Epistolario*, IV, 3)

I am proceeding in this matter with the soul alone, letting the body be guided by the sheer power of reason, although the occasion will never admit of the Platonic way.

It is not until some two years later (1620) that Lope finally succeeds in transferring the relationship to a purely spiritual plane: "Hago más oficio de padre que de galán . . .," he writes the Duke, "hauiendo estas cosas llegado a ser como amores platónicos." ("I am acting more a father's than a lover's part . . . this affair now having become a sort of Platonic love") (*Epistolario*, IV, 56). Perhaps an incipient decline of his physical powers, and, as Amezúa believes, scruples on Marta's part, made the transition easier.[84] From this point on, Lope's role is one of touching devotion to his former mistress through years which saw her lose—c. 1628—her eyesight, then her mind. Circumstances confirmed and refined the spirituality of his feelings by undermining on her side, as time had on his, the physical basis of the relationship. It is in these years that a Neo-Platonic trend develops as a vital concern in Lope's writing. The trend already appears in 1621, with the volume containing *La Filomena*, in an abstruse sonnet, "La calidad elementar resiste / mi amor" ("My love resists the elementary quality"), resurrected from *La dama boba* (The Stupid Lady) of eight years before; and in an epistle to Félix Quixada y Riquelme. With *La Circe* (1624) it is more marked: besides the Platonic strain in the title poem and in epistles and sonnets included in the volume, there is a lengthy commentary on the sonnet published three years before. This had been meant, when originally included in the play of 1613, according to the plausible view of Dámaso Alonso,[85] as a learned *tour de force* that would rival the formal intricacies of Góngora. Now Lope discovers personal significance in it:

La intención deste Soneto . . . fue pintar un hombre, que haviendo algunos años seguido sus pasiones, abiertos los ojos del entendimiento, se desnudaba dellas, y reducido a la contemplación del divino amor, de todo punto se hallaba libre de sus afectos. (*OS*, I, 402)[86]

The purpose of this sonnet . . . was to paint a man who, after having followed his passions for a number of years, having opened up the eyes of his understanding, divested himself of them and, concentrating on the contemplation of divine love, found himself completely free of his inclinations.

The sonnet represents no run-of-the-mill Neo-Platonism; it is a highly technical treatment of the upward aspiration of love in terms of "tres fuegos correspondientes a tres mundos" ("three fires corresponding to three worlds"), which condenses into fourteen lines, as Dámaso Alonso notes, and Lope acknowledges, the central thought of Pico della Mirandola's *Heptaplus*. This *tour de force* of ten years before is made to support, in 1624, a line-by-line commentary replete with erudition designed to demonstrate both the philosophical depth of the poem and the breadth of Lope's learning. His commentary is necessary, Lope explains, because of the inherent difficulty of the doctrine he is expounding, a difficulty of substance (*sentencia*), not of language. Such difficulty, in contrast to the obscurity of the *culteranos*, he adds, has behind it an illustrious tradition: that of those writings meant only for the select few,

> pues Platón lo que escribió de las cosas divinas, lo envolvió en fábulas y imágenes Mathemáticas, de suerte que de ninguno o de pocos fue entendido: que alguna vez nos havemos de apartar del común y simple modo de decir.   (*OS*, I, 402)

> since what Plato wrote about divine things he shrouded in myths and mathematical imagery with the result that it was understood by none or few: sometimes, after all, we must depart from the common and simple way of speaking.

As Dámaso Alonso also notes,[87] one cannot dismiss all the learning displayed in Lope's showy commentary as derivative. Some of it comes from direct reading not only of Pico, but of Ficino, Leo Hebraeus, and others, including, I would add, Plato himself. The *Symposium* is quoted, in Ficino's Latin version:

> y entonces alaba tanto Platón a los que llegan a esta perfección de espíritu, *si cui contigerit, ut ipsum pulchrum intueatur, sincerum, integrum, purum, simplicem* con esta exageración; *Non humanis carminibus, coloribus, non aliis mortalibus nugis contaminatum, sed ipsum secundum se pulchrum divinum inspiciat.*   (*OS*, I, 408)[88]

> and then Plato so highly praises those who attain this perfection of spirit: *if it should so befall one, that he gaze upon the beautiful itself, unadulterated, whole, pure, unalloyed,* with this exaggeration: *not tainted by human charms, colors, or other mortal vanities, but that he behold the divine beauty as it is in itself.*

This citation of the climactic conclusion to Diotima's words suggests that, along with Ficino's commentary, Lope had read to the heart of the *Symposium* itself. No longer content with a superficial appropriation of Neo-Platonic thought, he is clearly now trying to reach the Platonic fountainhead. Beneath the pedantry one senses a vital stake. If the personal relevance of the sonnet (which in 1613 may have been nil) is still all but buried beneath the technicalities, it is there nonetheless.

Lope develops again and again aspects of the doctrine embodied in this sonnet, usually in a less pretentious and more patently personal fashion. In the epistle to Quixada y Riquelme (*OS*, I, 444–445), published with the *Filomena* (1621), after discounting the skepticism of others regarding the Platonic purity of his love and asserting

> . . . Yo sé que basto
> a sólo amar el alma con la mía,
> en que la vida honestamente gasto,
>
> . . . I know that I am equal to loving the soul alone with mine, something to which I virtuously devote my life,

Lope goes on to confute Augustine with Plato:

> Dice Agustín, que es el amor en balde
> de lo que no se ve, ni se conoce:
> el alma no se ve, respuesta dalde.
> El Philósopho quiere que se goce
> por lo que vemos, lo que nunca vimos.
>
> Augustine says that love of what cannot be seen or known is
> fruitless: answer him that the soul cannot be seen. The Philosopher
> would have it that we enjoy what we have never seen by way of
> what we see.

Human beauties, Lope says, are "cristales de las almas en essencias" ("crystals of souls in essence"), and he explains that

> . . . el apetito tan mal quisto
> de la razón, en femenil belleza,
> . . . es el que yo Platónico resisto.
>
> . . . the appetite so little liked by the reason, where feminine beauty
> is concerned . . . is what I Platonically resist.

Lope may here still be in the process of disengaging himself from his carnal relationship with Marta. One concludes from the epistles and poems published with *La Circe* in 1624, and from the presentation of the relationship of Ulysses and Circe in that poem itself, that such disengagement has been accomplished. "The dramatic situation that differentiates *La Circe* from its precursors is the measured resistance that Ulysses sets up, not without inner struggle, to all the charms of Circe,"[89] note recent editors of the poem, who go on to point out parallels between the Neo-Platonic cast of the sentiments Ulysses professes toward Circe:

> Yo te amo con aquel conocimiento
> que debo a tu belleza soberana
> y a tu divino y claro entendimiento,

> I love you with that recognition which I owe to your sovereign
> beauty and to your divine, bright mind,

and those Lope expresses in the other poetry in the volume.

In Lope's epistle to Fray Plácido de Tosantos, for example, the doctrine of the ladder of love is presented in an excursus beginning:

> Amor puede mover el pensamiento
> hasta llegar a Dios por la criatura,
> con alto y celestial conocimiento.
> Recibe por los ojos la hermosura,
> imagen dulce de la cosa amada,
> con su interna virtud el alma pura.

(OS, I, 291)

> Love can move the mind until it reaches God via the created being,
> with lofty and celestial understanding. The pure soul receives beauty,
> the sweet image of the loved one, through the eyes by means of its
> inner virtue.

Set forth in detail is the manner in which the soul transforms the material image of the beloved taken in by the eye into an ideal one,[90] which then prompts the soul to ascend through a "lofty and divine consideration" of other such forms to a knowledge of universal beauty. "Scorning the senses," the soul is then able to "mirar atenta la ideal belleza" ("look intently on ideal beauty") and further ascend to a contemplation of intelligible beauty, resting its thought finally in God. But Lope seems unsure of himself at such heights. Abruptly another voice in the poet speaks up:

¿Mas qué dirá la multitud profana? . . .
Dirán, señor, que si la edad enfría
el juvenil ardor, luego al terreno
el divino Cupido desafía:
y que de enigmas y aphorismos lleno
viene Platón y Venus se despide,
necio antídoto ya, pues no hai veneno.

(OS, I, 292)

But what will the profane mob say? . . . They will say, sir, that when
the years have cooled youthful ardor, then the divine Cupid promptly
assumes his challenging stand and that Plato arrives full of enigmas
and aphorisms and Venus takes her leave—a silly antidote by this
time, since there is no poison.

As always, Lope is sensitive to the response he will arouse. The counterpoint
places his Neo-Platonic aspiration for a moment in the total vital context in
which we will find it in the dialogued prose of *La Dorotea*.

This is Lope's fullest exposition of the side of Neo-Platonism that had the
greatest appeal to his spirit and his imagination. In the eight or ten Platonizing
sonnets accompanying *La Circe*, the doctrine is echoed and reechoed, most
effectively in those in which Amarilis's physical presence is not wholly
relinquished amidst the idealizing tendency:

Sin desearte yo, quiero quererte,
que si te quiero yo sin desearte,
dentro del alma no podré perderte.

(OS, I, 377)

Without desiring you, I want to love you, for if I love you without
desiring you, within my soul I can never lose you.

or:

Yo que soy alma todo, en peregrinas
regiones voy de un genio acompañado,
que me enseña de amor ciencias divinas.

(OS, I, 378)

I who am entirely soul travel through far-off regions accompanied
by a genius who teaches me divine knowledge of love.

In the sonnet on Amarilis's singing, which Lope never tired of extolling,
music becomes the agency of his ascent up the ladder of love:

Canta Amarilis, y su voz levanta
mi alma desde el orbe de la luna
a las inteligencias, que ninguna
la suya imita con dulzura tanta:
    De su número luego me transplanta
a la unidad, que por sí misma es una,
y qual si fuera de su coro alguna,
alaba su grandeza, quando canta.
    Apártame del mundo tal distancia,
que el pensamiento en su hacedor termina
mano, destreza, voz y consonancia:
    Y es argumento, que su voz divina
algo tiene de angélica sustancia,
pues a contemplación tan alta inclina.

(*OS*, I, 378)

Amarilis sings and her voice raises my soul from the orb of the moon to the intelligences, none of which can imitate the sweetness of her voice. From this number, [her voice] then transfers me to unity, which is one in itself, and, as if [her voice] were one of its choir, praises its greatness as it sings. It takes me so far away from the world that thought brings hand, skill, voice, and harmony to rest in its maker. And it is an argument that there is something of angelic substance in her divine voice that it inclines me to such lofty contemplation.

Music is here a natural way of access to cosmic harmony, a function which we shall also find it fulfilling in *La Dorotea*. In another sonnet, sound gives way to an even higher Platonic sense, seeing, in a dazzling vision of Amarilis ascendant and beyond the reach of time:

La luz primera del primero día
luego que el sol nació, toda la encierra,
círculo ardiente de su lumbre pura.

(*OS*, I, 377)[91]

The first light of the first day as soon as the sun was born, encloses her round in the burning circle of its pure glow.

It may be noted, in conclusion, that the special appeal of Neo-Platonic idealism to Lope resides in the possibility it offers of aspiring to a supreme conception of beauty and love, identifiable with the God of Christianity, without rejection of the love of earthly things and the beauty embodied in earthly creatures. The attachment to the here and now, to the world of appearances, need not be denied, as the poet comes and goes from the contemplation of higher things. Moving beyond his simple earlier curiosity, Lope can be observed reading more deeply and documenting himself more purposefully; the Neo-Platonic concern gives his culture a focus, direction, and relevance not always evident in his earlier years. It offers a way of extricating himself from the morass of carnal passion, a way that is attractive to a temperament so sensuously oriented and at the same time rich in artistic possibilities. Lope nowhere seems aware of the heterodox implications of so personal an approach to God; Neo-Platonism remains for him, long after its Renaissance flowering, a perfectly viable alternative to the accepted channels of institutionalized religion. One cannot separate his Neo-Platonic aspirations from his relationship with Marta; they clearly answer a vital need. In the end, however, the Neo-Platonic impulse transcends the context of his love for her and informs a more purely individual outlook, offering a way of reconciling himself to the transience of the world and to his own transience within it. In one of the sonnets accompanying *La Circe* he writes:

> Esto le debo al tiempo, que me ha dado
> conoscimiento de inmortal belleza,
> por lo que de la vida me ha quitado.
>
> (*OS*, I, 386)

> This I owe to time, which has brought me understanding of
> immortal beauty in return for all of life it has taken away from me.

In *La Dorotea* Lope's capacity both to celebrate life and to express his sense of its finiteness will be enhanced by Neo-Platonic tones and overtones present in the work not as conventional motifs or as doctrines but as reverberations of a personal *Erlebnis*.

Lope is noticeably anxious to make his readers aware of the personal roots of *La Dorotea*. In the Prologue the reader is told unequivocally: "El assunto fue historia y aun pienso que la causa de auerse con tanta propiedad escrito" ("The subject was fact and this too I think is the reason for its being written with such fitness") (p. 52). The same point is made by La Fama (Fame) in the brief Epilogue: "No quiso el poeta faltar a la verdad, porque lo fue la historia" ("The poet did not want to go back on the truth since it was a true story") (p. 457). On two occasions Lope goes out of his way to have Julio and Fernando remark that by their actions they have violated the unities of time and place: by their three months' trip to Seville, and by the subsequent lapse of time from April to January. In each case Fernando justifies himself on grounds of fidelity to *historia*: "Es historia verdadera la mía" ("Mine is a true story") (p. 236); "La fábula . . . por su gusto en esta ocasión se casó con la historia" ("The story . . . for its own satisfaction on this occasion wedded itself to fact") (p. 405).[1] Lope may be alluding sarcastically to the Aristotelian preceptists, with whom he has been feuding, but equally evident is the underscoring of the personal relevance of the material. (The horoscope of Fernando's future leaves no doubt about the connection between Fernando and himself.) The avowal contrasts with the screens Lope usually throws around the biographical implications—the masks adopted in the ballads, the tendency to depersonalize the sonnets, even the obliqueness of *Belardo el furioso*. Though after so many years there is no need for prudence, it is not simply a matter of writing more openly and in an avowedly personal way.

Lope is also showing the importance to him of creating an illusion of circumstantial trueness to life, of placing his characters in a world where clock time is an inescapable dimension of living and no emancipation is possible from the confining effects of space, a world of causality and practicality, where ideals are subject to material contingencies and where the uncertainties, complexities, and mixed motives present in all human relationships are respected.

Not only is Lope alert to this need; he has paused to reflect upon it more lucidly than before during the prolonged gestation of *La Dorotea*. His is the deliberate self-probing of the artist pushed to greater awareness by the accretion of experience. In *La Dorotea* he moves in new artistic directions without disavowing earlier ones. He could now look back upon a multitude of poetic variations on the experience with Elena Osorio and their very diversity must both have drawn him back toward the common ground from which all sprang and drawn his attention to the process of transmutation common to all. What distinguishes *La Dorotea* is not merely Lope's pains to present the context as well as the meaning of an experience. It is the relationship he establishes between them. The world of *historia* becomes the subsoil in which the poetry grows before our eyes. The work thus illuminates the creative process; it is not merely its product. Lope has now paused to reflect on that transmuting of personal history into poetry that had become second nature. Along with the insistence on the historical foundations of *La Dorotea*, the Prologue is no less insistent that *"La Dorotea es poesía"* (*"La Dorotea* is *poiesis"*), making it clear that Lope pursues only the effect of actuality, that is, verisimilitude, not the literal truth. There is no more thought of recreating the shabby environment of the transcript than of necessary fidelity to the actual sequence of events. In the original version the atmosphere of the artistic cosmos may well have been closer to that of the Calle de Lavapiés. Yet surely even then Lope had sifted, expanded, transformed the raw data of experience, making the "historical" aspect of the work a dimension of its *poiesis* as it is in 1632. The professed commitment to biographical truth in the references quoted is to be taken symptomatically, not as a reflection of fact. It may be true, as Lope claims, that the time lapses correspond to the real calendar of events. (The unity of place is not in any case violated by Fernando's trip to Seville, despite Julio's remark that "salir del lugar es absurdo indisculpable" ["leaving the locality is an inexcusable blunder"] [p. 236], since Fernando is simply absent and the setting remains Madrid.) In having Fernando assert that "la fábula . . . se casó con la historia," Lope expects the reader to recall Aristotle's remark (*Poetics*, IX, 9) that "some events that have actually happened conform to the law of the probable and the possible" and for that reason are already poetic. He is understandably anxious to advance the claim of the *acción en prosa* to a patent of literary distinction by suggesting that it falls into a category allowed for by Aristotle and by contemporary preceptists, but the suggestion is an *a posteriori* one.[2] Lope employs an Aristotelian idiom with characteristic looseness and expresses not a doctrinaire allegiance but a private intuition of the intimate relationship in his own art between *Erlebnis* and *Dichtung*, now itself the object of concern. Though *el assunto*—the subject of the work—was *historia*, the *acción en prosa* itself is *poesía*, the Prologue tells us. By calling it such, Lope asserts his freedom to be a fictitious chronicler of himself and his claim not to literal truthfulness but to a broader faithfulness to his whole experience of human nature.

An observation of E. C. Riley apropos of Cervantes may be of assistance here. This critic finds Cervantes concerned with an aspect of the problem of verisimilitude largely overlooked in antiquity: "the difference between what ought to be and what could be." Riley notes that "his all-embracing verisimilitude includes 'what ought to be' as part of an experience that 'could be.'"[3] While Lope does not probe so deeply into the problem of history and poetry, or range so widely, in his own way he nevertheless offers a verisimilitude of the possible, of what might have been, and makes it a vehicle of the ideal. Rather than transferring experience to the realm of romance, *La Dorotea* offers a projection of what might, under different circumstances, have taken place, a trajectory events might have followed had there not been the explosion of the libels and the lawsuit. At the same time an esthetically idealized dimension of this same relationship, a frame of the characters' own devising, enters the picture as a key element in their experience. The story of Fernando and Dorotea becomes a distillation of all the others in Lope's life in which the erotic and the creative impulses merged. It is quintessential, and while its exemplarity is, in the last analysis, experiential rather than orthodox, Lope is not troubled by any possible disparity between his insights and the moral climate of his age. His conscience is at rest, the life-span which had encompassed such wide-ranging experience is nearly fulfilled. Lope can feel his own truths to be both representative and unexceptionable.

It may shed light on the question of *historia* and *poesía* to ask, for a moment, whether *La Dorotea* could be viewed as a seventeenth-century version of the literary autobiography, or as a *Bildungsroman avant la lettre*. Merely to raise the question is to suggest the work's distinctiveness in an epoch and country in which secular autobiography was not practiced (save in the special fictionalized case of the picaresque) and personal development was not a subject of literary fiction. Evidently, as in autobiography, the decisive meaning Lope discovers in a core experience is one which went undetected at the time.⁴ But, quite aside from the question of genre, *La Dorotea* is clearly more than literary autobiography. As an artist-autobiographer Lope feels perfectly free to alter the shape and meaning of the past in order to meet expressive needs of the present. He thus circumvents the problem inherent in autobiographical writing proper: the distortion of the past through the inescapable projection upon it of the perspective of the present. In effect, by explicitly writing *poesía* rather than *historia,* he turns to advantage the autobiographer's disadvantage. While we will be able to detect traits of Lope in his protagonist, unlike the autobiographer, Lope will not suggest a continuity of development between the self depicted and the self recording. We must conclude that Fernando is only to a limited extent the author's persona.

The insistence that "el assunto fue historia," that the work is grounded in personal history, points to the fact that, as in the *Bildungsroman,* a particular formative experience has been selected out of the past and a crucial stage of development in the life of a protagonist crystallized in it, one that brings him to the threshold of maturity. Yet in the *Bildungsroman* the protagonist's experience is clearly seen by the author in a moral light and its moral import is felt by the character as well. His growth in the moral sphere, his acquisition of values, is the heart of the work. While Lope gives some indication of a moral perspective, Fernando can scarcely be said to have acquired any. At the end he is about to step onto a wider stage, but the process that has brought him to this point has been traced in psychological rather than moral terms; at most he will see his experience as governed by mutability and chance. The limits of the designation in respect to *La Dorotea* become plain also when we consider a fundamental shift of focus between *Belardo el furioso* and *La Dorotea.* As the title shows, it is the feminine figure, from the biographical point of view the antagonist, who now occupies the center of the stage. Fernando is a mask for the young Lope only to the extent that he is the poet—any poet—as a young man. We will find him going far beyond his creator in his assumption of an additional and in some sense opposing stance, that of the young man as poet.

There can be no question that Lope does share with the writers of both literary autobiography and *Bildungsroman* a concern for atmosphere, for conveying the feel of a world actually experienced in the course of living; he is not content to remain within the confines of literary convention. In the creation of such an atmosphere, a prose rather than a verse medium was, in his eyes, crucial. He shows himself in the Prologue much preoccupied with this matter. His first concern, to be sure, is to explain that the *acción en prosa,* though written in prose, is poetry, nonetheless. Meter, though traditional, is not essential, as long as the work is an imitation of truth in accordance with accepted principles of decorum: "Puede assimismo el poeta vsar de su argumento sin verso, discurriendo por algunas decentes semejanças" ("The poet may likewise present his subject without verse, proceeding by appropriate likenesses") (p. 50). There is nothing unusual in this affirmation that poetry is not dependent on metrical form, as the commentators on Arisotle's *Poetics* had often emphasized. What Lope has imitated, we are further told, are not so many individuals but the generic qualities and forces they represent: "los afectos de dos amantes, la codicia y trazas de vna tercera, la hipocresía de vna madre interessable, la pretensión de vn rico, la fuerça del oro, el estilo de los criados" ("the passions of two lovers, the covetousness and wiles of a go-between, the hypocrisy of a venal mother, the pretentiousness of a man of wealth, the power of gold, the behavior of the servants") (p. 52). In stating why *La Dorotea* was written in prose, however, Lope makes a revealing observation: "Siendo tan cierta imitación de la verdad, le pareció que no lo sería hablando las personas en verso como las demás que ha escrito" ("It being so sure an imitation of truth, he thought it would not be with the characters speaking in verse as in his other dramatic works") (p. 51).[5] Blandly Lope affirms the opposite of what he has been proclaiming: having the characters speak in prose *does* make for a surer imitation of truth than if they spoke in verse as in his plays. He probably did not even notice the critical inconsistency, for the Prologue is not an orderly exposition but a succession of almost casually associated remarks. The logical inconsistency shows that, whatever the theorists might say, Lope was intimately convinced that prose *would* be more suggestive than verse of experienced rather than fictional reality. When the Prologue speaks of the "propiedad" ("fitness") with which the work has been written, the reference is not only to alleged truthfulness but to the appropriateness of prose for representing the prosaic character of ordinary life. The peculiarly personal nature of the history Lope was here "imitating," his desire to convey not just here and there in the work, but continually, the atmosphere of an everyday world, evocative at least, for all its transmutations, of the one in which he had lived—to catch, as it were, echoes of remembered voices—made him discard the metrical convention along with the stage and actors. Prose in his mind was a guarantee of authenticity of a peculiarly personal kind: "A los demás señores hablo yo en verso, y a Vex.ª en prosa, con que he dicho la verdad de lo más interior de mi corazón" ("I speak to other gentlemen in verse and to Your Excellency in prose: and having said this, I have spoken the truth from the very depths of my heart"), he assures his patron, the Duke of Sessa.[6]

The insistent implication that in *La Dorotea* a personal past is being recaptured in all its circumstantiality, while not to be taken at face value, carries over into the sphere of art a tendency of Lope's later years which, in my view, now plays a decisive role: this is a confessional urge. The probing exhaustiveness of treatment given to the story of Fernando and Dorotea, the careful attention to the atmosphere surrounding it reveal an artist intent on exploring the furthest reaches of the material. It is as if, after repeated encounters with it his whole life through, Lope is now impelled to make a definitive confrontation. It is an esthetic settling of accounts that he is seeking, but the impulse must have been strengthened by the crises of conscience that began around his fiftieth year, the more extensive self-examinations attendant upon his priestly vocation, the daily practice of confession that marked the final years.[7] At certain points in the more markedly biographical intercalations of *La Dorotea*, we see evidence of this confessional urge in what might be called an undifferentiated form, unrefined esthetically. Such is the case with the unusual circumstantial detail of the account included in Act IV, scene 1 of Fernando–Lope's early life, the dwelling on vicissitudes of his subsequent experiences as Don Bela's competitor (V, 3); even the inclusion of the horoscope of the future is only in part redeemed by an artistic *raison d'être*. Much in these accounts belongs to a raw confessional substratum, still inchoately personal and artistically inoperative, suggestive of *pentimenti* (corrections) not wholly painted out on a finished canvas. Lope seems motivated by a need to make at last on his own terms the confession he did not make at the hearings. Fernando–Lope tells how he acquiesced in sharing Dorotea with Don Bela, accepting Don Bela's gold second-hand, disguising himself as a pauper to allay Don Bela's suspicions and brushing with the law as a consequence: details so humiliating and so out of the ordinary as to suggest some obscure urge on Lope's part to probe to the bottom and make a clean breast of things at the end of his life. The raw material is conjured up out of personal psychological and spiritual need, and we see further evidence of how easily the spheres of the sacred and the profane overlap in Lope.

These unrefined extremes are the exception, however, for *La Dorotea* is the product of an examination of conscience esthetically not religiously oriented, an examination of the consciousness of an artist, of its artistic resources and the creative possibilities of the materials it holds in store. The absolution sought is not sacramental but esthetic, not reconciliation of a soul with God but of an artist with his experience, of Lope's heart with the world. Without pressing the parallel too far, it can be seen that the process produces the profane equivalent of spiritual joy, a similar sense of personal release, a lightness of spirit, even a gaiety. The steady serenity of Lope's view, the indulgent fondness for the world he creates, and his equally plain emancipation from it seem aspects of a psychological mechanism analogous to that underlying religious confession.

Though Lope would scarcely have been aware of an analogy between his manner of recreating the "historical" dimension of *La Dorotea* and the Counter Reformation methodology of religious confession, it may be instructive, before examining this dimension, briefly to suggest such a parallel. The persistent retrospection underlying *La Dorotea* is an equivalent in the esthetic sphere of the attitude of the true penitent as prescribed, for example, by Fray Luis de Granada: he is to resemble Isaiah, "aquel sancto penitente que decía . . . Revolveré, Señor, en mi memoria delante de ti todos los años de mi vida con amargura de mi corazón" ("that holy penitent who said . . . I shall turn over in my memory, in your presence, Lord, all the years of my life, in bitterness of spirit").[8] Lope is no longer probing for sins, as he had been in the *Soliloquios*; bitterness, too, has been surmounted, yet there is a similar urge to recover the full sweep of the past. As for the more precisely delimited times and places, Lope has followed in his own way, in fashioning *La Dorotea*, the instructions of St. Ignatius for the *compositio loci*:

> Traer a la memoria todos los pecados de la vida, mirado de año en año, o de tiempo en tiempo. Para lo qual aprovechan tres cosas: la primera mirar el lugar y la casa a donde he habitado; la segunda la conversación que he tenido con otros; la tercera, el oficio en que he vivido.[9]

> Bring to mind all the sins of my life, looking through it year by year or period by period. To which purpose three things are helpful: the first, to look at the place and house where I have lived; the second, at the dealings I have had with others; the third, at the calling in which I have lived.   (trans. Joseph Rickaby)

Lope had studied with the Jesuits in his youth; in the temporal disposition of each act he has also adapted to the artistic sphere the Loyolan "examen particular y cotidiano . . . discurriendo de hora en hora, o de tiempo en tiempo, comenzando desde la hora que se levantó, hasta la hora y punto del examen presente." ("examen particular and daily . . . ranging through the time hour by hour, or period by period, beginning from the hour that he arose even to the hour and moment of the present examen") (trans. Rickaby). The prescribed exhaustiveness of recall and the sequential method which is to assure it will have their analogues in the temporal continuums of the scenes and acts of *La Dorotea* and in the characters' awareness of how they have filled them.

One should avoid, of course, attributing too absolute an efficacy to the Loyolan techniques of recall or indeed to Lope's own capacity for recollection. Quite aside from his contrasting assumption of artistic freedom, the inherent character of memory and the psychological factors that affect it necessarily condition Lope's view of the past. His creative imagination is, to begin with, at work on a past in which he had been much too deeply involved to have been able to see it originally with any objectivity. Subsequently the mechanism of memory, by nature selective and repressive rather than duplicative, had been at work, unconsciously elaborating a new version of the past. Lope himself was not unaware that memory was an *infida custos*: he cites the Augustinian phrase in discoursing on the subject.[10] The record of the *Soliloquios* reveals an intimate experience of memory's refractoriness, of limitations on the capacity for recall, on the one hand, and on the other of its jarring obtrusiveness; the "Egloga a Claudio" suggests further awareness of the inadequacies and fallibility of memory. Yet as Lope composes the final *Dorotea*, he is undoubtedly not merely recalling but recollecting the past, gathering together and reconstructing the context of an experience and intimately reliving it.[11] The "Egloga a Claudio" makes it plain that the process is pleasurable:

> . . . parece reflexión suave
> traer en tanta edad a la memoria
> la juvenil historia.

> it seems a pleasant reflection to recall to mind one's youthful story at such an advanced age.

Both works exemplify the well-known inclination of the old to dwell fondly on their youth, recalling it with greater vividness than the more recent stages of life.[12] The sharper impressions made on unencumbered minds and sensibilities are less subject to fading, and one is also free in later years, as Lope's case illustrates, to shed inhibitions and acknowledge responsibility for actions of a youthful self with whom one no longer feels closely identified. Even so, it is evident, as a recent study noted, that "the hard-won recall could be illusory."[13] While the *historia* recreated in *La Dorotea* is avowedly illusory, inasmuch as it belongs to art, not life, even if it were possible or desirable to discriminate sharply between actual and artistically molded *historia*, it is evidently not the former which an old man's intense scrutiny of the past would cast up.

Endless conflations of reminiscences of art, of life, of the two interwoven, are bound to occur, often in ways that defy unraveling, in the mind of an artist, by its nature a mind which retains memories not only of vital experience but of poetic ideas, of images, figures, patterns realized and unrealized. Especially is this true of a mind which like Lope's conceives of art as imitation and views earlier achievements as models for emulation, holding in store artistic precedents of every kind. Is the noticeable absence in *La Dorotea* of a conviction on Fernando's part that the invidiousness and treachery of friends have precipitated his difficulties—convictions once strongly held by Lope—indicative of a simple process of repression on Lope's part, of a vision now free of emotional blinders; or of a deliberate elimination of such factors in the interest of the artistic economy of the *acción en prosa*? In the work of 1632 such an absence is surely to be correlated with a view that the inner dynamics of this or any human relationship must eventually bring about its disintegration. The effect on the artistic design is to eliminate such external factors as contributing causes and focus exhaustively on the relationship itself. One can only conjecture as to the part that repression or belated clarity of insight may have played in this result. In the so-called contamination of events or characters connected with the original experience through association with later ones, that is, in the tendency toward conflation of experiences, the phenomenon known by psychologists as "retroactive interference" is undoubtedly also at work. Remembrance of an earlier event is affected by experience of a subsequent one (and in the artist's case by literary experiences as well). If Lope noticeably empathizes with Don Bela, the counterpart of his erstwhile rival Perrenot de Granvela, he is not only building upon a one-time imaginative projection of himself into the role of the same rival in the ballads on El Almoralife. The images of Perrenot and El Almoralife have in addition become overlaid in his memory by the subsequent experience of being in their position vis-à-vis a younger mistress or rival.[14]

One other aspect of Lope's memory processes deserves mention: the undoubted tendency to operate through sensory recall, a natural corollary of keenness in the sensory modes of perception and corresponding absence of any signal capacity for abstract thinking.[15] Singled out at two junctures in association with the figure of the rival in *La Dorotea* is the sensation of a disparity in level between the street and the floor of Dorotea's house, and the resultant need to stoop and step down. Surely a faculty for sensory recall extending to tactile and kinesthetic impressions is involved here (see below, p. 220). Again, too, there are undoubted blendings of sensory reminiscences: Don Bela's enraptured response to Dorotea's singing contains, beneath the flattery, recollections not only of Elena Osorio's voice but of Lope's reaction to that of Marta de Nevares (see above, p. 200). Perception surely also undergoes literary conditioning, artistic antecedents being retained along with live sensations, and eventually mingling in Lope's memory.[16] It would have been quite natural for Lope to set recollection in motion via an Ignatian *compositio loci*, but in the process other feminine voices heard over so many years evidently fused with Elena's.

With allowance made for the operation of psychological and memory processes on the substance of Lope's experience, let us see how his art creates the "historical" dimension of the *acción en prosa*, its atmosphere of everyday actuality. To be taken into account are the protagonists' family situations, social milieu, and economic level; likewise, atmospheric detail—touches suggestive of ordinary routines, domesticity, practical matters of daily life, inconsequentialities and trivia, for all of which Lope's art usually had little time. One must also notice the realistic handling of physical space and the realistic observance of clock and calendar time, as well as effects of sensory vividness and immediacy. Turning to the characters, I shall try to obtain an indication of how history and poetry have gone into their making. An exposition, in the next chapter, of the action will bring out additional aspects of the "historical" dimension of the work in the context of its total poetic design.

Since Lope is not preoccupied with fidelity to biographical fact, in laying his realistic foundation he makes use both of data presumably rooted in biographical reality and details invented or supplied.[17] Systematic discrimination between them is neither needed nor possible, though I shall point out the discernible biographical links and the recurrent patterns which have light to shed on Lope's creative processes. The most noteworthy characteristic of his realism is its avoidance of extremes. He has no desire to flaunt crudeness or excessive naturalism before the reader. Tawdriness remains but the sordidness of the libels and of the trial record is gone. Perhaps Lope's remark about the work in the dedicatory epistle—"La corregí de la lozanía con que se auía criado en la tierna mía" ("I pruned away the exuberance which it had developed at the time of my own [youthful exuberance]") (p. 49)—means that excessive licentiousness and vindictiveness once marked it but have been pruned away in his mature years. If so, few traces remain and those mostly inconsequential, tempered by gaiety and wit.[18]

Noticeable, too, is the elimination of everything pertaining specifically to the world of the theater.[19] There is nothing in *La Dorotea* about writing plays, selling or producing them, no question of Fernando's turning out dramas as Lope had done. Not even the play-writing status of a gentleman amateur, professed by Lope in the transcript of the hearings, characterizes Fernando, and he is not secretary to a great lord as Lope had been and was to be again. Fernando is simply an idle and impoverished young nobleman of a recognizable dandy (*lindo*) type,[20] the man-about-town of the day, belittled as unmanly by Gerarda:

> vn lindo, que todo su caudal son sus calçillas de obra y sus cueras de ámbar; esto de día, y de noche broqueletes y espadas, y todo virgen [i.e., not put to use], capita vntada con oro, plumillas, vanditas, guitarra, versos lasciuos y papeles desatinados. (p. 69)

> a dandy whose entire worldy goods are his needlepoint breeches and his amber-scented leather waistcoats; this in the daytime and at night bucklers and swords, without a scratch naturally, a cape dipped in gold, all feathery and ribbony, a guitar, lewd verse, and harebrained love-notes.

Fernando lives in quarters which he describes generically as "aposentos de moços, donde sólo ay espadas de esgrima, baúles de vestidos, y instrumentos de música" ("young men's quarters, where there are nothing but fencing foils, trunks of clothes, and musical instruments") (p. 100). Poor, idle, and a poet, like the Belardo of *Belardo el furioso*, Fernando is nevertheless presented as of the aristocracy. The "don" is consistently prefixed to the name of "aquel pobre hidalgo" ("that poor gentleman"), as Teodora calls him, and his own account puts him in the lesser nobility:

> Nací de padres nobles en este lugar [i.e., Madrid], a quien dexaron los suyos poca renta. Mi educación no fue como de príncipe, pero con todo esso quisieron que aprendiesse virtudes y letras. (p. 294)

> I was born of noble parents in this city, who were left without much income by their own. My upbringing was not princely, but they did want me to acquire virtues and letters.

He adds that when his parents died "vn solicitador de su hazienda cobró la que pudo y passóse a las Indias, dexándome pobre" ("someone claiming their inheritance collected what he could of it and went off to the Indies, leaving me poor") (p. 295).[21] Lope makes Fernando a nobleman, as he was not, but adheres to his own circumstances in keeping him devoid of powerful connections and poor. He indeed accentuates Fernando's poverty: lacking both profession and inheritance, Fernando has no source of income at all.

This readjustment of Lope's own situation, already visible in the Belardo of *Belardo el furioso*, is of fundamental importance. It removes the vital identification of Lope with his public which play-writing brought, despite the disdain he at times professed for it. Indifferent to such broadly based artistic expression, Fernando is the lyric artist whose poetry reflects his private life and world, not that of his society. He is out of step with his age as Lope never was. This nonconformism permits Lope, in focusing searchingly on the relationship between Fernando and Dorotea, to focus also on the question of *Erlebnis* and *Dichtung*, of vital experience and poetic creation.

Along with the theater world, Lope discards Elena's father, the impresario, and her brother, uncle, and cousin, retaining only the mother in the person of the widowed Teodora.[22] Dorotea and Teodora remain in the socially fluid urban milieu in which Lope had found Velázquez, the builder turned gentleman, but the popular lower-class atmosphere reflected in the libels and the transcript has given way to a vaguely middle-class one. Though Dorotea has become a "dama de esta corte" ("lady of this capital city"), it is plain that Marfisa "tenía más de señora" ("was more ladylike") (p. 408), and Laurencio makes Don Bela sound very foolish on the subject of Dorotea's nobility:

> *Láu.:* . . . Ella te dexara a ti si se le ofreciera mejor ocasión.
> *Bela:* No hiziera, que es muger principal.
> *Lau.:* Sí; pero es muger.
> *Bela:* Las de tan altas prendas no se comprehenden con esse nombre.
> *Lau.:* ¿Qué prendas?
> *Bela:* Su nacimiento noble y otras obligaciones.
> *Lau.:* Di que es señora de la casa de Dorotea, como aora se vsa.
>
> (p. 261)

> *Lau.:* . . . She would leave you if something better came along. *Bela:* No, she wouldn't: she's a distinguished woman. *Lau.:* Yes, but she's a woman. *Bela:* Those of such high endowments do not come under that name. *Lau.:* What endowments? *Bela:* Her noble birth and similar obligations. *Lau.:* Say that she is the lady of Dorotea's house, as the saying now goes.

Economic pressures are a reality for Teodora and her daughter, the more so because Teodora's widowhood increases the financial need of the household. The situation alleged in the satires, made a psychological reality by the strength of Lope's resentment, and demonstrated in *Belardo el furioso*— dependence on Dorotea as a source of revenue—becomes a plausible or at least a comprehensible expedient; it is no longer simply abusive. It persists but ceases to be grating. The hosts of starving relatives—the equivalent in *Belardo el furioso* of the dependent family of the libels—disappear but Dorotea's situation vis-à-vis her mother remains equivocal. Marriage between her and Fernando is out of the question. By giving him the status of a noble,

Lope has ruled out on social grounds what was in fact impossible because Elena Osorio was already married. Even if forged, the letter of the trial could quote Elena as writing: "Si yo me viese libre, me casaría con vos" ("If I became free, I would marry you"). In *La Dorotea*, Fernando blurts out at Dorotea: "Si no fuera por ti, yo pudiera estar casado" ("If it were not for you, I might be married") (p. 101).[23] It is strange that Lope has not eliminated completely the figure of the husband, who plays no part in the work and whom no one stops to consider except to take passing note of his absence (pp. 100, 301) or to report the news of his death at the beginning (p. 124) and unexpectedly again at the end, as if it had not been given before (p. 444). In the theater, as in the hare-brained scheme we found Lope concocting in the transcript, the husband would have been a threat or an obstacle, an effective element in a plot. Here he is no more of a hindrance than Cristóbal Calderón had been to Elena. It is surprising that Dorotea is presented as still very much under her mother's wing, as if she were not married at all. Whatever the inconsistency from the point of view of the real social practice—a woman's honor passed into her husband's keeping as soon as she was married—Lope seems to be reflecting the actual circumstances of Elena, who lived with her family while her husband was away and evidently came under their sway. Moreover, this figure of an innocuous husband seems intended with some irony to stand as a composite of several in Lope's experience whose existence he had resented but found no obstacle.[24] I do not see in this figure an intention to "disguise the real basis of the narrative," as do Rennert and Castro (p. 52). He is like a stray line on the fringes of a sketch which Lope, instead of eliminating altogether, as he might easily have done, has half-absently added to with a touch here and there, to end up with a bit of shadowy marginal tracery.

A large part of the action of *La Dorotea* takes place in the interior of the house where Dorotea lives with her mother. Lope makes this not simply a place where events occur but a household whose functioning must be attended to. He takes pains to create the domestic atmosphere whose absence from the pastoral he frequently remarked upon.[25] He mostly left it out of his *comedias* as well, knowing that his audiences came not to see their daily circumstances reproduced but to experience adventures and sensations out of the ordinary. It is the atmosphere which pervades his private correspondence with the Duke of Sessa.[26]

In Teodora's household the everyday matter of meals and food is not overlooked. In the midst of acrimonious reproaches to her daughter for staying away until two o'clock in the afternoon, Teodora remembers it is mealtime: "Dame de comer, Bernarda, que esta señora no vendrá en ayunas; que pasteles

y fruta no aurán faltado a aquel pobre hidalgo" ("Bring me something
to eat, Bernarda. Madam will certainly have had something—that poor
gentleman would not fail to provide pastry and fruit—") (p. 125). When
Marfisa makes her unexpected morning call, Dorotea directs Celia to see "si
ha quedado algún bizcocho de los que me embió mi confessor" ("whether
any of those biscuits my confessor sent me are left") (p. 148). (Biscuits in
wine were a morning refreshment.)[27] From the lofty empyrean of Don
Bela's Platonic-Petrarchan madrigal (V, 1), we descend—to what? A pound
of lamb, a half pound of beef, bacon, parsley, olives, and onions as Gerarda
describes her *olla* ("stew") (p. 391).

A scene consciously staged with the highest literary artifice (II, 5) is
followed by one in which the ordinary evening meal of the household is
shared by Gerarda. *La Celestina* suggested such a scene to Lope, but removal
from the brothel which is Celestina's house alters its character and changes its
atmosphere from licentious to domestic, assuring food and diet a large place
in the conversation. The tedium of Dorotea's convalescence, of her mother's
nagging, is repeatedly brought out:

> *Teo.:* No tanta fruta, Dorotea; que estás muy conualeciente. Dexa las
> ubas.
>
> (p. 190)

> *Teo.:* Less fruit, Dorotea—you're still recovering. Let the grapes go.

> *Teo.:* Dexa el tocino, Dorotea. Come tu pollo, que no estás para
> esso.

> *Dor.:* Todo lo tengo de dexar. ¡Pollo, pollo! Ya me tienen más
> cansada que castañas en quaresma.
>
> (p. 191)

> *Teo.:* Let the bacon go, Dorotea. Eat your chicken, you're in no
> shape for the other.   *Dor.:* I have to give up everything. Chicken!
> chicken! I'm sicker of it than of chestnuts in Lent.

> *Teo.:* Come dessa gallina, muchacha.
> *Dor.:* No puedo más, señora; que cocida me haze asco.
>
> (p. 192)

> *Teo.:* Take some of that hen, child.   *Dor.:* I can't manage it; it turns
> my stomach, boiled.

To the merry spectacle of Gerarda's wine-guzzling, which embroiders on motifs of the *topos* Lope found in the ninth act of *La Celestina*, he adds this insistent prosaic undertone. Food here is not the grim obsession of the *pícaro*, nor is it presented with the refined naturalism of certain Cervantine lunches—Sancho's picnic with Ricote or the meal in Monipodio's patio—it is part of a routine tiresome to the point of revulsion.[28]

In the corresponding scene of *La Celestina*, it may be noted, food is evoked but not consumed. The abundance in Celestina's rapt recollection of her vanished cornucopia—"pollos y galinas, ansaronas, anadones, perdizes, tórtolas, perniles de tocino, tortas de trigo, lechones" ("chickens and hens, great geese, mallards, partridges, turtledoves, pork hams, wheat cakes, suckling pigs")—is purely rhetorical, a symbol of her heyday, which contrasts with present hard times when "vn cortezón de pan ratonado me basta para tres días" ("a crust of bread that mice have gnawed lasts me three days").[29] In the more prosaic atmosphere of *La Dorotea*, food is all but tangibly present, and Teodora comments approvingly on her guest's appetite: "Tú me agradas, Gerarda, que hablas y comes" ("You have the right idea, Gerarda, you talk and eat") (p. 192). The meal is casual, without etiquette or decorum. "Ya está aquí la comida" ("Here's the food"), Celia says at the beginning. After Gerarda gives her comical blessing, the business of eating is settled into unceremoniously. "Alça essa mesa . . . niña" ("Clear the table . . . girl"), Teodora tells Celia at the end.

In this household the domestics really function as such. While the relationship of both Celia and Felipa with Dorotea is patterned on the stage convention which makes the lady's maid the confidante, tactician, and adviser to her mistress, the maids more noticeably than in the *comedia* have humdrum tasks to perform.[30] Celia waits on table; she also worries because "tengo que almidonar tres o quatro abaninos de cadeneta, y me reñirá tu madre" ("I have to starch three or four chain-lace ruffles and your mother is going to scold me") (p. 432). Felipa, as she tells Don Bela, must see that Roldán, the dog of the household, is rounded up and brought in for the night (p. 259).[31] Lope's concern with the ordinary mechanics of living even extends to the Negro slave girl and the scullery maid upon whose services the domestic world rests. They have no roles, as they sometimes do in the *comedia*;[32] they do not figure in the cast. Their presence is felt quite realistically, however, as a functioning part of the household: "Dame tú de beber, negra" ("Fill my glass, black girl"), Gerarda calls out in the meal scene, but Celia tells her, "La negra está en la cozina" ("The black girl is in the kitchen") (p. 196). Presently, as Teodora and Dorotea deplore the spectacle Gerarda is making of herself, Teodora observes that "Celia y la negra se están riendo" ("Celia and

the black girl are laughing") (p. 197). Their unrepressed titters contrast
vividly and naturally with their mistresses' frowns. Unlike these domestics,
the two mulatto slave girls provided by Don Bela are never more than super-
numeraries. Ludovico tells of seeing them when he goes to call and Teodora
finds them expendable at the end. In between they do not exist.[33] Even
Dorotea has household duties to perform and Teodora scolds her for
negligence: "Assí se harán las haziendas de casa. Dos meses ha que comen-
çaste esse cañamazo para los taburetes" ("A fine way to get housework done.
You began that hemp covering for the straight chairs two months ago") (p.
125). While needlework is a usual occupation for a young woman and does
not define her social rank, the reference in this case to the "haziendas de
casa" ("housework") and to two months suggests routine occupations
which would not be noticed in the case of the *dama* of a play nor opposed to
her pursuit of amorous adventure. The full sarcasm of Teodora's references,
in the same scene (I, 8) and in others, to Dorotea as "esta señora" ("Madam")
and to Dorotea and Celia as "estas damas" becomes evident in this context:
she is accusing them of giving themselves airs. Gerarda's advice to Dorotea
much later, when her poeticized world has collapsed—"Niña, niña, las
mugeres no han de saber de historias ni de lágrimas, sino de hazer vainillas"
("Child, child, women should not know about literary references or tears,
but about how to make openwork hems") (p. 424)—is more compassion-
ately calculated to reconcile Dorotea to the circumstances in which she must
live.[34]

The world of ordinary contingencies is never lost sight of for long. Lope's
means of evoking it include digressing into apparently trivial or incidental
matters, for which the meandering course of the dialogue provided ample
leeway. A good example is an exchange upon Teodora's arrival before the
dinner scene at the end of Act II:

> *Dor.:* Madre, lleno traes de lodo el manto.
> *Teo.:* Salpicóme vn cauallero destos que van desollinando las ventanas.
>   Ponle al sol en esse huerto, Celia.
> *Dor.:* Nunca sales que no te suceda algo.
> *Teo.:* El otro día caí en vna cueva.
> *Dor.:* ¿Por qué sales sin báculo?
> *Teo.:* Porque tú eres el de mi vejez, y no quieres andar conmigo.
> *Dor.:* Vas muy despacio.
>
> (p. 189)

> *Dor.:* Mother, your cloak is covered with mud.   *Teo.:* One of those
> gentlemen who go around staring the soot off the windows

spattered me. Give it a good sunning in the garden, Celia. *Dor.:*
Something is always happening to you when you go out. *Teo.:* The
other day I fell into a cellar. *Dor.:* Why don't you take a cane?
Teo.: Because you are the cane of my old age and you won't walk
with me. *Dor.:* You walk too slowly.

It is instructive to compare this passage with one at the end of Act XI of *La
Celestina* which clearly suggested it:

> *Eli.:* ¿Cómo vienes tan tarde? No lo deues fazer, que eres vieja.
> Tropeçarás do caygas y mueras.
> *Cel.:* No temo esso, que de día me auiso por do vengo de noche.
> [Que jamás me subo por poyo ni calçada, sino por medio de la calle.
> Porque, como dizen, no da passo seguro quien corre por el muro;
> y que aquél va más sano que anda por llano. Más quiero ensuziar
> mis çapatos con el lodo que ensangrentar las tocas y los cantos...][35]

> *Eli.:* What makes you so late? You shouldn't, you're too old.
> You'll trip and fall and kill yourself. *Cel.:* That doesn't bother me:
> in the daytime I look to see where I'll walk at night. [I never go
> along the benches or sidewalk but right up the middle of the street.
> Because, as they say, there's no sure footing along walls and the
> safest way is over level ground. I'd rather soil my shoes with mud
> than bloody my wimple and the stones . . .]

In *La Celestina* the words are the product of a situation: the exchange occurs
at the moment Elicia opens the door to let Celestina back into her house.
Their function is ironical: they foreshadow the catastrophe that is soon to
befall Celestina. The rhetorical and proverbial amplifications of the *tragicomedia* reinforce but do not alter the original thought. It was not the
function of the passage, however, but its detail that struck Lope, who might
have related it to Gerarda had he wished to retain its ironical force: Gerarda
will in fact die by falling into a *cueva* (cellar). But both Gerarda's character
and the chance manner of her death would have made such explicit foreshadowing unduly ponderous.[36] Lope links the detail with Teodora,
Gerarda's collaborator and the literary descendant of Inés Osorio, for
Teodora is also associated in his mind with Celestinesque activities. The mud,
not rhetorical but present and visible on the mantle, is revealing in regard to
Teodora (see p. 402 below). Details of the original which brought out
character—Celestina's self-assurance—are now merely evocative of things
trivial or routine. (This sort of thing is always happening to Teodora when
she goes out.) Lope even lets us know that, having been soiled, the garment

must be cleaned: "Ponle al sol en esse huerto, Celia." The garden—was it once Melibea's?—is never mentioned again. It exists solely for this prosaic purpose.[37]

Closely connected with these touches indicative of domestic routine and daily living is the handling of space and time, likewise planned to keep the created world of *La Dorotea* close to an actual and experienced one. Lope sees a stage in his mind's eye, visualizing it with remarkable clarity as the scene of the action and arranging the comings and goings of his characters like so many exits and entrances. Forgoing stage directions and indications of setting, he creates precise dimensions of physical space solely by means of dialogue and holds his characters within them. He renounces the liberties customary in the *comedia* with regard to drastic shifts of setting. The entire action occurs in Madrid, the larger part, as I have indicated, in Teodora's house, the rest in Fernando's or Don Bela's quarters, with a scene in the Prado and two sets of street scenes. The space through which the characters move or which their glance can take in is kept realistically in scale with their humanity. It is finite like them and it confines them. The spatial precision of the work, as already suggested, is undoubtedly reinforced by impressions of places known and experienced. Beneath the settings of *La Dorotea* are Elena's father's house in Lavapiés, Lope's own, which faced the convent of Nuestra Señora de la Victoria, and the memory of many passages from one to the other in the Madrid of Lope's faraway youth. The topography of *La Dorotea* is quite specific. Distances are respected and even within the confines of Madrid, to which the characters are held, they are not allowed to move about arbitrarily, to appear successively and uninterruptedly in widely separated places. A time interval is always realistically suggested to allow for their passage.

The place whose presence is most clearly felt is the house where Dorotea and her mother live. When the scene is here we are always in the same room—the *sala* (parlor) with its *estrado* (raised platform), into which meals are brought from the kitchen just beyond. (Teodora disappears briefly into it in one scene, and the drunken Gerarda is being led to it at the close of another.) Just "offstage," too, are the stairs down to the wine cellar, the scene of Gerarda's fatal fall and the perch from which Celia describes this accident. Outside is the yard where Teodora's soiled cloak is to be spread out in the sun. Most noticeable are the two entrances to the *sala*: like Jerónimo Velázquez's house in Lavapiés, "which goes through to Comadre Street," Dorotea's faces in two directions, a fact we are not allowed to forget. The back entrance is not merely theoretical (like the one in Gerarda's imaginary book on the deceiving of men, which has a chapter entitled "De tener dos puertas a diferentes calles" ["On having two doors onto different streets"] [p. 453]). It is put to use more than once for hasty exits: by Gerarda (I, 7) and by Don Bela, who is unceremoniously hurried out this back way (II, 5); it is used also for the entrance contrived by Marfisa to satisfy her curiosity about Dorotea:

> *Mar.:* Abierta está la puerta y el estrado enfrente.
> *Cla.:* Esta es la falsa, que la principal cae en la otra calle que
>   corresponde a ésta, aunque todas deuen de ser falsas.
> *Mar.:* ¿Aurá, señoras mías, vn jarro de agua para vna muger que
>   viene del campo y fatigada de poca salud?
>
> (p. 147)

> *Mar.:* The door is open and that's the *estrado* facing us.   *Cla.:* This is
> the getaway door [*puerta falsa*, lit., false, i.e., back, door]; the front
> one opens into the other street, parallel to this, although they must all
> be getaway doors.   *Mar.:* Ladies, might there be a jug of cold water
> for a lady arriving from the country and suffering from poor health?

The passage lets us see the two figures appearing in the doorway, still engaged in a private conversation, looking down an imaginary stage (the *sala*) to the *estrado*, then catching sight of Dorotea and Celia and making their entrances.

The other approach to the *sala* is even more clearly delineated in Lope's mind and reproduced in ours by the entrance of Don Bela when he comes to call. On hearing his timid knock, Gerarda urges him forward: "Entre, señor don Bela, entre; que no está hondo" ("Come in, Don Bela, come in; it's not a big step down") (p. 171). Clearly this is the same doorway about which we are later told that it was necessary when entering to "baxar vn passo porque la sala de aquella puerta no estaua igual con la calle" ("step down because the parlor the door opened into was not level with the street") (p. 302). The peculiar detail, as already noted, and the two entrances themselves must stem from Jerónimo Velázquez's house, kept alive by tactile memory. As Don Bela enters we visualize the resultant movements very clearly: Gerarda tugging him in, the *indiano* catching sight of Dorotea and addressing her, Dorotea rising and coming to the edge of the *estrado*, a chair being brought, the two sitting down.

These dramatically conceived entrances frame areas of space precisely for the ensuing scenes, locate characters in them, suggest their movements and the positions of objects and properties. Lope fills his spaces and arranges his settings as if for a stage, one which reproduces physical space more realistically than that of his plays. He places us in the position of onlookers or theater-goers, a gratuitous procedure insofar as he does not have performance in mind, but an accurate reflection of the fundamentally dramatic character of his vision of his created world. An initial speech like that of César opening Act V, scene 3, can have no other purpose than to create spatial depth. In order to do this Lope for once violates the conversational realism of his dialogue and allows a character who lacks an interlocutor simply to think out loud for the reader's benefit: "Templando está su instrumento don Fernando. Desde aquí, porque no le dexe, quiero escuchar lo que canta" ("Don Fernando is tuning his instrument. So as not to interrupt him, I'll listen from here to what he sings") (p. 400). By inserting this single remark ahead of the ensuing dialogue between Fernando and Julio, Lope locates César in the doorway and the other two across the imagined stage, framing the scene. On other occasions, we hear the voices of the characters before they make their entrances—"En los latines conozco a Gerarda. Demonio es esta vieja" ("From the Latin I can tell it's Gerarda. That old woman is the very devil") (p. 156)—or, when they exit, hear them talking until out of earshot.[38]

The other settings of *La Dorotea* do not so clearly produce the sense of experienced places as the interior of Teodora's house, but their location and contours are indicated with precision. Fernando's lodgings are upstairs: he thinks the climb the reason for Dorotea's breathlessness (p. 93) and Julio restrains him from jumping off the balcony (p. 102). This is the house of the "señora deuda mía, rica y liberal, que tuuo gusto de favorecerme" ("lady, a relative of mine, rich and generous, who was kind enough to help me out") (p. 295), where Fernando says he went to live at seventeen on returning to Madrid after his parents' death. (The only verifiable resemblance to Lope's circumstances is that he was living with his widowed mother in 1587.) Marfisa lives in the same house—she is the lady's niece—and both are still there five years later when the work opens, as we know from Marfisa's question to her maid Clara when we first meet them: "¿A qué hora vino a acostarse don Fernando?" ("What time did Don Fernando come home to bed?") (p. 113). That Dorotea should go to see Fernando there is an extraordinary step; understandably she comes heavily veiled and Fernando is understandably amazed to see her.

Lope is less precise about the location of Fernando's quarters on his return to Madrid. He clearly does not return to the house of Marfisa's aunt, though nothing in the scene of arrival from Seville lets us know that he is elsewhere. Marfisa is unaware of Fernando's return until he has been back a week (p. 376) and then must seek him out at his own door. It is at this house that he and Dorotea have celebrated their reconciliation earlier in the same day.[39] Where this house is and why Fernando's residence there is taken for granted is unexplained, a fact that would call for no comment in a less realistically conceived work but is surprising here. It is suggested that to maintain the fiction of being a fugitive from justice Fernando could not return to Marfisa's— "Lo que ha que vine he andado huyendo de la justicia" ("Ever since my return I've been keeping out of sight of the law") (p. 379)—but the real reason for the change is that the action is geared to bringing out the dynamics of Fernando's feelings, and for this it was necessary that exposure and denunciation by Marfisa should follow in short order the reconciliation with Dorotea.

Wherever this house may be, we are shown Marfisa and Clara posted at its door and through their eyes see Fernando and Julio talking as they approach (p. 378). Then, as if having come on stage, the latter are present and we view the situation from their perspective for a moment—"¿Mugeres tapadas a nuestra puerta?" ("What, veiled women at our door?") (p. 379)—before they reach and address the women. We share the author's total view, which focuses upon the natural perspectives of each pair of characters in turn.

The scene in the Prado, easily visualizable as centered in one spot, is given successively through different pairs of eyes: Marfisa exclaims to Clara on how empty the Prado is, suggesting a long vista; presently she spies two women approaching. Clara remarks "Hazia nosotras vienen" ("They're coming toward us") (p. 289), a dialogue with Dorotea and Felipa ensues, then Marfisa and Clara move off, leaving Dorotea and Felipa alone to discuss them. Presently the latter see Fernando and Julio entering the Carrera de San Jerónimo, step over to a fountain, and sit down to avoid being recognized. Fernando comes up and walks right by, without noticing them. When Dorotea sees he is continuing up the Carrera, she tells Felipa to call him. Only now do we hear from Fernando and Julio; the latter urges his master to answer, Fernando balks, Julio goes back, coaxes Fernando to follow, and like a focus found after much effort, the stage is at last set for the new encounter of Fernando and Dorotea. The dialogue makes all these movements and maneuverings clear without strain. The same is true of the scenes in Dorotea's street at night (Act III, scenes 5–9), in which Lope uses tactile impressions and chiaroscuro to provide spatial orientation.

By keeping all the action in Madrid, Lope probably felt he had, in essence, observed the unity of place, even if he reserved the right to shift locations freely within the city. He has this precept in mind, and the unity of time as well, because they suit his design, but he does not allow himself to be rigidly bound by them. Reasons of his own preclude taking undue liberties with his characters' movements and with the time allowed for them. There is of course no absolute equivalent between the chronometric ordering of the work and the "biological" time of the reader. Lope succeeds in making him feel, however, that the lives in this artistic microcosm are time-bound, outwardly and inwardly, in the same way as his own. He does so by adhering to his idea of the classical unity of time. Holding the total span to twenty-four hours he considered out of the question, but *La Dorotea* follows the prescription given in his *Arte nuevo de hacer comedias*:

> No hay que advertir que pase en el periodo
> de un sol, aunque es consejo de Aristóteles . . .
> Pase en el menos tiempo que ser pueda,
> si no es cuando el poeta escriba historia,
> en que hayan de pasar algunos años,
> que esto podrá poner en las distancias
> de los dos actos.[40]

> No need to specify that it should take place in a twenty-four hour period, although this is Aristotle's advice . . . Have it take place in the shortest time possible, except when the poet is writing about events that actually occurred, and some years are to elapse: he can then place these in the intervals between the acts.

Lope's characters point out, as we have seen, that the "preceptos del arte" ("rules of the craft") are inapplicable to them, since theirs is a true story; yet this purportedly true story has, as we know, become poetry, and its chronological ordering represents its double character. We shall find the happenings of each act pinned down to clock time as securely as if Lope were chronicling true events. (For artistic reasons, which will appear later, Act V is a partial exception.) Three of the acts span periods of twenty-four hours or less. Another (the last) probably does also. Only the third clearly does not. The Aristotelian precept is applied not to the work as a whole but to its divisions. The time of day is mentioned with unusual frequency. The absence of a chronicler requires that this be done within the dialogue by the characters, who thus impress us as possessing an unusual awareness of time. Moreover, Lope clearly wants to make time felt as a continuum and for this purpose he not only presents many unbroken sequences of scenes in the same location but makes it plain (again with Act V as a partial exception) that when the focus shifts from one set of characters and one setting to another, the successive though unconnected scenes really fit into a single time-sequence: that they are consecutive, not simultaneous.[41]

La Dorotea is built around three distinct periods of time. The first lasts about a year and embraces the action proper, which occurs on different days spaced at intervals over this period. This climactic period is the one focused upon most closely, not only through direct presentation but via detailed accounts covering large parts of the intervening months. Buttressing it is the five-year span of the affair, covered in retrospect, since it precedes the year presented. (The inception and unfolding are related by Fernando in Act IV, while highlights are reflected by both protagonists in rediscovered letters and verse and in reminiscences.) The third period sets the other two within the life-span of Fernando–Lope by means of extensions backward and forward: the account of his life up to his meeting with Dorotea, in Act IV, and the horoscope of his future in Act V. The projection into the future sheds light back on the dénouement and in addition closes the time gap between the aged author and the recreated world of his youth. Lope telescopes the years, connecting past with present, and points the whole work more insistently toward himself. The account of Fernando's early life contributes to the understanding of his character.

In the main this large outer sphere of past and future lies beyond the confines of Lope's artistic cosmos. The five years immediately preceding the opening provide, on the other hand, indispensable background for the presentation of the sixth year, and I will return to them in analyzing the course of the love of Fernando and Dorotea. In Fernando's account of them, Lope begins to make time a subjective and psychic *Erlebnis*, as in the rest of the work, not merely an objective, chronometric experience. Even more than in the case of spatial dimensions, Lope sets up tensions between time as objectively measured and a subjective perception of it, tensions also between both and timelessness, whether of art, of Neo-Platonic idealism, or of the Catholic hereafter.

In his handling of time during the central year, Lope places the gaps in intervals between the acts; the procedure he prescribes for historical plays is followed in this work grounded in personal history. He defines the intervals with unwonted precision and thereby anchors the acts with unusual exactness within the total lapse of time. Despite his own statements, this is surely not done out of fidelity to the timing of actual events during the climactic stage of the original experience, though undoubtedly recollecting that experience and reflecting upon it made Lope more sensitive to matters of time as measured by clock and calendar. The intervals he sets up between the acts are introduced primarily because the time covered by them is needed to bring about the affective and psychological developments on which the action depends.

Lope lets us infer that the year spanned by the action corresponds to the period between January 1587 and January 1588. The fictional time is thus pointedly made to reflect that of the real underlying events. The link with a real calendar is established toward the end (V, 3), by the reference to the entrance "yesterday" (p. 418) of the newly wed Count and Countess of Melgar into Madrid. The wedding took place at Vich in the Pyrenees on December 31, 1587; the entrance into Madrid would presumably have followed not long thereafter. Lope at that time would not have been telling a tale of deliverance from love of Elena Osorio but suffering confinement in jail on her account. Still, the event, which made a considerable impression at the time, would have remained linked by association in his mind with the days of his imprisonment, particularly in view of his own connections with the family of Vittoria Colonna, the Countess of Melgar.[42] Fernando's subsequent reference to joining the coming Armada against England provides a further link with this period. It follows that the other events of *La Dorotea* would theoretically fall in the year 1587, though there are no further links to this particular point in history. The previous April is twice mentioned as the time of the reconciliation (Act IV), Fernando's return from Seville (III, 1) had come a week earlier, his departure and the quarrel roughly three months before. This would take us back to January for Act I, while Act II occurs several weeks after Act I.[43] In Act II we find the convalescent Dorotea wearing a costume which Ludovico later relates (p. 238) she adopted only when her recovery was well advanced. The rest of the three-month interval until Fernando's return in Act III, scene 1, occupies the interim between Acts II and III. The events of scenes 4–9 of Act III fall in the middle of the week that separates the opening scenes of Acts III and IV.[44] The accounts which bridge the intervals are so unusually circumstantial, particularly about events in Madrid, that they maintain the effect of a temporal continuum, of a prosaic succession of works and days within which changes are slowly effected. Fernando tells in Act IV, scene 1, of his three months' journey and Ludovico in Act III, scene 4, gives an account of his frequent visits to Dorotea, the first the day after Fernando's departure; then none for a space while she is too ill to receive him; then a second, many days afterward as Dorotea begins to convalesce; others during the convalescence—her changing dress and appearance are mentioned—then, as she gets better: "Yo acudí algunas noches a ver si auía moros en la costa" ("I went over several nights to see whether there were Moors along the coast") (p. 239); finally the visit a week before Fernando's arrival when the signs of Don Bela's proprietorship are visible on all sides. Lope thus retrospectively places the decisive day of Act II in a context of continuity enabling us to visualize the progress of Dorotea's convalescence before and after this day and to note the effects of Fernando's supplanting by Don Bela. The longest interval in the work is that which separates the fourth and fifth acts. The first two months of this period, up to Corpus Christi Day, are spanned by Fernando's detailed account of the cooling and extinction of his love for Dorotea. Once this love is dead, there is nothing more to trace; the events of the remaining half-year are not recorded. One is left to imagine a sameness of days within which, nevertheless, the passage of time has its effect, producing in all three principal characters a disposition to break out of the routine into which their lives have uneasily settled. The fifth act presents the after-effects of the events of the others, the latter now definitely in the past. Lope includes in it two mornings, half-suggestive of the routine into which Dorotea's days have settled, before writing finis by disposing summarily of Don Bela and Gerarda.

How far do traces of the real pattern of events of the year 1587, insofar as one can know it, remain embedded in the realistic foundations of *La Dorotea*? The most one can say is that Lope has placed the definitive break between Fernando and Dorotea at about the same point—June—as the "unpleasantness" which apparently indicates the rupture with Elena and her family, now making Fernando, of course, the initiator of the break. The timing of the Epilogue, about six months later, places the further distintegration of Dorotea's world and Fernando's resolution to change his way of life at the same point in time when trial and imprisonment, after-effects of Lope's break with Elena, were in fact closing a chapter in Lope's life. The months between June and January, which saw Lope turn to vituperation and abuse, are passed over summarily in *La Dorotea*. In the earlier months of the year he places the two-month period of sharing Dorotea–Elena with the powerful rival, where it probably belonged (assuming it occurred), although it could have begun before April, since Perrenot de Granvela had probably been in Madrid since the previous year. Perhaps trouble really had begun to loom in January; Don Bela's appearance on the scene may be timed to correspond with Perrenot's emergence or reemergence as Elena's lover. Beyond this it is hardly profitable to speculate, and one can only observe that the maternal pressure to end the liaison brought by the widowed Teodora in January could correspond to pressure from Inés Osorio in June, while her husband, who might have objected, was absent.

As for the three months, January to April, during which Fernando absents himself, they may have had an analogue in actuality since they turn up repeatedly in *Belardo el furioso* and other artistic accounts of the affair. Perhaps they should be traced back to the first Valencian stage of the exile, February to May 1588. José María Cossío sees an allusion to this period[45] in a passage on absence in the *comedia Ursón y Valentín* (dated 1588–95 by Morley and Bruerton):

Fueron tres meses tan buenos,
como es tan buen cirujano,
que si no vino sano,
convaleciente a lo menos.

(Ac., XIII, 499b)

They were three such good months, since [absence] is so good a
surgeon, that if he did not come back cured, [he was] at least
convalescent.

But in *La Dorotea* absence conspicuously fails to work the usual emancipation, Fernando instead settling for reconciliation. With this and the repudiation which follows, history and poetry have clearly reached a parting of the
ways.

It is in the ordering by clock time of the scenes within the acts that the
combination of exactitude and continuity, of objectively measured time
and time experienced as a dimension of living, is most evident. In Acts I, II,
and IV, events begin in the early morning and carry on with only minimal
breaks until late in the day. In Act III, several days separate the two sequences
of scenes, but within each one the same effect of continuity is maintained.
Only in Act V will we find five segments less securely joined. Lope is at
greater pains than a chronicler or historian would be to make the reader feel
time elapsing as uninterruptedly for the characters as it does for himself.

La Dorotea opens at Teodora's house early one morning, and the first act
ends around two that afternoon. Dorotea, just arising, is arranging her hair
when she overhears the conversation between her mother and Gerarda;
Fernando has been with her much of the previous night.[46]

Fernando's exclamation as Marfisa goes to fetch her jewels—"¡Válame
Dios! ¡Y lo que ha passado por mí desde las nueue a las doze!" ("Heaven
help me! All that has happened to me between nine and twelve!") (p. 117)—
besides informing us that three hours have elapsed, records Fernando's impression of them as so full and intense as to appear speeded up and all of a
piece. His impression helps to bridge the gap between the internal time of the
work and the reader's time.

The first five scenes of the act fit into a single time-sequence. When we
leave Dorotea (end of scene 3) starting out for Fernando's, we pick up
Fernando just arising (beginning of scene 4). While he talks with Julio,
Dorotea is on her way to his house. After her arrival (beginning of scene 5)
and departure, we are with Fernando till he exits (end of scene 5). Some time
now elapses, allowed for, relatively speaking, by the conversation between
Marfisa and Clara in the first part of scene 6, while Fernando makes

preparations for his departure. Once Marfisa's jewels are in his hands, Fernando has only to have the mules brought and he is ready to start, via Dorotea's street, for Xetafe, where he has promised Julio they will lunch (p. 118). While Teodora and Gerarda talk (scene 7), Fernando and Julio are on their way to Dorotea's house and presently (scene 8) they pass by her windows. Meanwhile Dorotea has arrived home (beginning of scene 8) and been reprimanded by her mother because of the lateness of the hour (two o'clock) (p. 125). One may suppose her to have wandered about distraught, with Celia, before returning to face her mother. Gerarda, in the interval between scenes 1 and 7 has, for her part, established contact with Don Bela in La Merced.

The first scene of Act II takes place in the morning, the rest (2–6), after an interval, in unbroken sequence the same afternoon.[47] The conversation of Dorotea with Celia, Marfisa's visit, and the conversation with Gerarda (scenes 2–4) take us up to three o'clock; Don Bela's long visit (scene 5) occupies much of the rest of the afternoon; it is mealtime when Teodora returns.

Fernando's remark to Ludovico that "Yo pude ver a Dorotea muchas vezes después que vine" ("I could have seen Dorotea many times since my return") (p. 253) confirms the interval of several days between his return in scene 1 of Act III and his reunion with Ludovico (scene 4). At the same time his "many times" suggests a subjective impression that more than the few days marked on the calendar have elapsed; in this instance time has dragged for him. That it had also done so on the journey back to Madrid is made plain by Julio in the conversation that opens the act: "¿Esta era la prisa? ¿Esto dezir que se auía parado el tiempo? ¿Esto hazerme leuantar antes que supiessen los pájaros que amanecía?" ("So this was the haste? So this was why you said that time had stopped? This why you got me up before the birds even knew it was getting light?") (p. 204).

The intervening scenes—Don Bela and Laurencio (scene 2) are joined in scene 3 by Gerarda—may be understood as falling on the same day as scene 1, though Lope does not expressly say so. Don Bela's visits to Dorotea have plainly become habitual since the initial scene of Act II. The remaining five scenes of Act III occur on the evening of the same day as scene 4. The calendar interval in this act, which Lope could have avoided had he wished to, finely graduates the movement of the lovers toward reconciliation by showing Fernando yielding, insofar as he has returned to Madrid, yet holding out for a few days against the final step of going to see Dorotea. He is still impatient for reunion but his impatience must now contend not with distance but with an obstacle within himself: the barrier of personal pride.

The day on which their reunion occurs (Act IV) is presented as a single time-continuum from early in the morning in the Prado[48] until early afternoon. Lope dispenses with even the slight intervals found within Acts I and II. The emotional intensity with which Fernando and Dorotea live these few hours is never relaxed; they lose all sense of time's passage. Again time as subjectively apprehended is set against measured time. The two scenes of the literary academy (2 and 3) span the interval during which the lovers' reconciliation is physically consummated. At the end of scene 1 they are starting out for Fernando's lodgings with Julio and Celia. Ludovico and César are then shown in scene 2 as they start their discussion, regretting Fernando's absence. Some time later Julio arrives (scene 3), announcing that Fernando "queda en casa en vna ocupación notable. Embióme a que os dixesse que vendría lo más presto que le fuesse possible" ("stayed home on some important business. He sent me to tell you he would come as soon as he could") (p. 337). Much later Fernando himself bursts in with the remark: "Nadie me culpe, que más fácil me fuera dexar la vida que la ocasión que me ha ocupado" ("Let no one blame me; it would have been easier to give up my life than the business that occupied me") (p. 366). Though physically absent, Fernando is not allowed to drop out of the reader's sight between scenes 1 and 4; we are kept posted on the scene that is going on concurrently with the one we are witnessing. Lope's realism includes making a positive use of absence to bring home the continuity of the characters' lives when they are not before us, of Dorotea's of necessity along with Fernando's. Her presence in absentia is confirmed when Teodora begins the next scene (IV, 5) by remarking to Gerarda: "No ha buelto essa muchacha desde esta mañana" ("That girl has not come back since this morning") (p. 371). When Dorotea arrives flushed (scene 6) and is reproached for not being home at one o'clock (p. 372), it is clear she has come directly from Fernando's. There remains only to show Marfisa and Clara posted at Fernando's door (scene 7) while he makes his way back from the *cénacle*, to be greeted when he arrives (scene 8) by their furious denunciation.

With Act V temporal bearings become less certain. Two days are evidently involved and they are most probably successive. Scenes 1–7 appear to occur on a single day. One assumes that the morning hour of scenes 1 and 2 (Laurencio, Don Bela, joined by Gerarda in scene 2) belongs to the same day as scenes 4–7, which are clearly sequential, all being laid in Dorotea's house and the first reintroducing Gerarda, who has presumably proceeded there from Don Bela's. The lapse of time between scenes 1 and 7, indicated by the detail of Don Bela's horse, would thus also be within a single day. In scene 1 Laurencio has just informed a count's servant of Don Bela's inability to lend the promised horse and by the end of scene 7 he is reporting to Dorotea that Don Bela has received in reply "vn papel tan atreuido que está perdiendo el sesso" ("such an arrogant note that he is going out of his mind") (p. 438). Scenes 9–12, again sequential, clearly occur on another morning, Dorotea having recently arisen in scene 9. It is logical to assume that the morning of scene 3 (César with Fernando and Julio) is the same as that of the surrounding scenes. That it is morning is clear from César's parting remark: "Si no viniere a la tarde a veros, vendré mañana" ("If I should not come to see you this afternoon, I'll come tomorrow") (p. 418). We are free, if we wish, to assume that scene 8, when César returns, is in fact the next day and to identify this day with the morning of scene 9. The point in all this, however, is that the evidence is no longer incontrovertible, Lope leaves matters more vague, no specific times of day are mentioned. Scenes 3 and 8, in particular, not being securely joined to those surrounding them, have the effect of breaking the act up into five segments no longer clearly aligned. In a later chapter I will discuss the connection between the effect of disjoining present in the external form and the inner configuration of meaning in the act.

Despite this loosening-up in Act V, the realistic precision with which Lope customarily handles time and space grounds the artistic cosmos of *La Dorotea* firmly in the here and now. Another factor which contributes to this effect is the alertness of all the characters to the sights, sounds, taste, smell, even to the feel of the world in which they live.[49] Through them we are made to feel weight, mass, shape, nuances of color and light, a range of sound effects, movement, organic sensations. While the percepts of the senses and the qualities of things which they record, like everything else in this world, are seen as subject to fading, dulling, souring, there is no corollary rejection of the sensory mode of experience. Instead of spurning the world of sense and substance, Lope dwells feelingly on its impermanence.

The very universality of sensory awareness in the world of *La Dorotea* reveals it as a mode of expression of the author manifesting itself through the characters. The distinction common in the *comedia* between servants and masters—the former prone to react through the contact senses, touch, taste, and smell, the latter through the more refined "distance receptors," hearing and sight—is maintained only to a degree. But Lope's handling of sense impressions results in nuances of its own, supporting individual delineations and particular artistic effects. Something of this function has already been glimpsed in the case of taste sensations; other sense percepts are made similarly expressive. (I shall reserve the sense of smell for its natural context in the night scenes in Dorotea's street.)

It is naturally the sense of sight that most closely binds the characters to the world around them: "Hermosa Dorotea, desde que entré aquí puse los ojos en aquel harpa" ("Beautiful Dorotea, as soon as I came in I noticed that harp"), begins Don Bela as he asks her to play (p. 179). Marfisa more abruptly asks: "¿Es clauicordio aquél?" ("Is that a spinet?") (p. 151), as she piercingly surveys Dorotea's *sala*. The visual responses of Lope's characters make up for the absence of a stage décor. They are constantly noticing appearances of persons and things, clothes, fabrics, furnishings, *objets d'art*. They are unusually sensitive to color, patterns, lighting. How sharply Ludovico reacts, for example, to the changes in Teodora's house when he visits Dorotea:

> Hallé vna rica tapizería y estrado nueuo. Pedí agua para passar este susto, y vi diferente plata, y dos mulatas de buena gracia, vna con vna saluilla y otra con vn paño de manos labrado, que con extraordinario olor de pastilla de flores, no se auía contentado de la limpieza sola. Bebí vn áspid en un búcaro de oro. (p. 239)

> I found a rich tapestry and a new *estrado*. I asked for water to get over this shock and observed different silverware and two mulatto girls with gracious manners, one with a tray and the other with an embroidered hand-towel which had not stopped at mere freshness but carried a remarkable floral scent from an aromatic lozenge. I drank an asp in a gold *búcaro* [small earthenware vessel].

One has no difficulty in recognizing here the fulfillment of Gerarda's promises to Teodora (p. 72) and even the gold *búcaro* of the second act.

The fabrics and jewels brought by Don Bela when he visits Dorotea enter into an elaborate pattern of stylized behavior, to be analyzed later, but we may note here how vivid Lope makes color and design:

> *Ger.:* ¿Pintó la primavera vn prado ni le imitó vn poeta con más flores?
> *Dor.:* ¡Qué bien assientan estas clauellinas de nácar sobre lo verde!
> (p. 172)[50]

> *Ger.:* Did Spring ever paint a meadow or a poet imitate one with more flowers? *Dor.:* How well these mother-of-pearl pinks go with the green.

Don Bela brings hose of many colors "porque no me dixo la color Gerarda que priua más con vuestro gusto" ("because Gerarda didn't tell me which color enjoys most favor with your taste") (p. 177). Laurencio spreads out all the pairs at once and the different colors elicit comments from those present:

> *Dor.:* Estas de nácar son excelentes.
> *Ger.:* Llama este color los ojos.
> *Dor.:* Los ojos no, sino el gusto; que de la vista mejor objeto es lo
>   verde, y más la conserua.
> *Lau.:* ¡Qué bachillería!
>
> (p. 177)

> *Dor.:* These mother-of-pearl ones are superb. *Ger.:* That color attracts the eyes. *Dor.:* Not the eyes but the taste; for eyesight a better object is green, and more preservative of it. *Lau.:* What a piece of pedantry!

Pedantic or not, the trend of the conversation is noticeably chromatic. Celia is attracted to the white but they are not offered to her, Dorotea disdains the purple, Gerarda rejects the gold and takes the purple ("las moradillas"). The tastes in color are distinctly individualistic. The conversation passes on to other things, but presently we find Celia pouting and when Gerarda explains why, Dorotea placates her with a pair of white hose. Lope's attention to this trivial yet revealing detail exemplifies the fineness of his touch.

The world of *La Celestina* seems almost colorless in comparison with such chromatic and sensory vividness. In respect to personal appearance and dress, Lope has noticeably focused visual impressions around one character, Dorotea. The dress of the others provokes no reactions, though Fernando's is described more than once.[51] When their physical appearance attracts attention, Lope usually is pursuing comic effects through an overdose of color which results in caricature or irony. Celia exclaims over the drunken Gerarda: "¡Qué colorada está la madre! ¡Parece madroño y la nariz zanahoria!" ("How red the old girl is! She looks like a strawberry-tree and her nose like a carrot!") (p. 192). (One cannot imagine Celestina being observed in this fashion.) Later Celia remarks on Gerarda's bibulous, bloodshot lachrymosity: "En los ojos tienes esso postrero [*scil.*, arrope], como has llorado" ("You've got what you just said [boiled grape juice] in your eyes because you've been weeping") (p. 197). Dorotea greets Laurencio's theatrical grief with:

> ¡Ay, Dios, Laurencio! Si no te viera las lágrimas en los ojos, que traes más sangrientos que la más fina púrpura, no pudiera persuadirme a que no me engañauan tus palabras. (p. 454)

Oh Lord, Laurencio! If I didn't see tears in your eyes, which are more bloodshot than the finest purple cloth, I would never believe that your words were not deceiving me.

The irony behind the ineptness of such a comparison at such a moment—the most refined purple for the most heavily bloodshot eyes—is clearly the author's.

As for Dorotea, the observant eyes of her interlocutors catch her in a succession of poses and appearances that add animation and fluidity to Lope's presentation of her, making us aware of both the changing surface and the features that do not change.

Fernando greets her opening *démarche* with: " ¡Iesús! ¿Es Dorotea? ¡Bien mío! ¿El manto sobre los ojos?" ("Good Lord! Is it Dorotea? My darling! With your cape over your eyes?") (p. 93). Her return home after their quarrel draws her mother's scorn: "Miren allí cómo viene; ¡qué encendida! ¡qué descompuesta!" ("Just see the way she looks, all flushed, all disorderly!") (p. 125). Before Ludovico tells Fernando how she looked as a convalescent, Celia and Gerarda have both registered their reactions with considerable attention to nuance. Celia says

> ¡Qué hermosa te haze el hábito de conualeciente! Que fuera de la compuesta harmonía de tus faciones, como a otras lo macilento desmaya, a ti te adquiere gracia lo descolorido.   (p. 138)

> How lovely your convalescent habit makes you look! Quite apart from the blended harmoniousness of your features, whereas a faded look makes other women colorless, your lack of color gives you charm.

Celia adds that "fuera del escapulario azul sobre el hábito blanco, miras por lo condolido con tan garabatosa suauidad que prouocas a amor y lástima" ("aside from the blue scapular on the white habit, your air of injury makes you look about with such appealing gentleness that you arouse love and pity") (p. 139).[52] Gerarda, visually observant and given to unexpected mental associations, remembers her impressions of astrological charts and adds a pictorial note: "Estás abrasando el mundo con la nieue desse ábito, partido desse escapulario azul, como miran los astrólogos el cielo con la vanda de los signos" ("You're setting the world on fire with the snow of that habit, divided by that blue scapular the way the astrologers picture the heavens with the band of the zodiac") (p. 157).

In the next act Felipa produces a vignette for Don Bela:

> ¡Si la viesses con qué gracia está haziendo gestillos a los concetos, compitiendo con el papel la mano de la pluma, haziéndola más blanca la negra que está siruiéndola! (p. 259)

> If you could only see how charmingly she is making little faces at the conceits, with the hand holding the pen vying with the paper and being made whiter by the black one that is serving it.

Felipa's language, despite its involuted conceits, suggests how expressively Dorotea's face reflects the throes of literary letter-writing. The contrast of black and white, without color, reinforces the chiaroscuro of the nocturnal scenes.

In Act IV, Marfisa's exclamation on meeting Dorotea in the Prado—"Buena estáis ya del todo, Dios os bendiga. ¡Qué cara! ¡Qué colores! ¡Qué nácar!" ("So you're completely recovered, blessings on you. What a face! What color! What mother-of-pearl!") (p. 290)—reflects the hopes aroused by Fernando's presence in Madrid. The reconciliation effected, Dorotea's arrival home arouses tensions that are in part visually conveyed:

> *Dor.:* ¿Mas que me preguntas de dónde vengo?
> *Teo.:* ¿Para qué, viniendo tan colorada?
> *Dor.:* Mal si estoy colorada, mal si estoi descolorida. ¿Con qué tengo de contentarte? (p. 372)

> *Dor.:* I bet you'll ask where I've come from.   *Teo.:* Why, when you're so red?   *Dor.:* If I'm red, it's no good, if I lack color, it's no good. How am I to please you?

In the fifth act, finally, Dorotea's appearance faithfully reflects her moral disarray, as Gerarda's greeting shows: "¿Tú descompuesta? ¿Tú los cabellos desordenados? ¿Tú por labar la cara?" ("You not made up? You with disheveled hair? You with an unwashed face?") (p. 423). Understandably Gerarda is surprised the next morning: "¿Tú cantando, tú alegre, tú vestida de gala, Dorotea? ¿Tú tocada con cintas verdes, tú cadena y joyas?" ("You singing, you gay, you all dressed up, Dorotea? You with green ribbons in your hair, you [with] chain and jewels?") (p. 449).

The impression we receive of the volume and weight of things and sometimes of persons in this world rests on the tactile emphasis found in certain passages. The stoniness of Dorotea's silence may be almost palpable (Julio speaking):

Pero, señora, essa que lo es suya, ¿es muger o piedra? Porque la
pondremos en la fuente. Siéntome junto a ella como quien se arrima a
vn poste. ¡Pesia tal, y qué buen olor que tiene! No es de mala casta
lo rollizo del braço.   (p. 294)

But, mistress, is that person who is such to you a woman or a stone?
Because we could place her on the fountain. I sit down beside her like
someone hitching up to a post. God love her, how sweet she
smells! The plumpness of the arm is not a bad sign.

An object such as a *búcaro* is made to impress us tactilely as well as visually:

> *Dor.:* ¡Qué lindo es!
> *Cel.:* A ver, señora.
> *Dor.:* Déxale, que le ensucias, Celia.
>
> (p. 158)

> *Dor.:* How pretty it is!   *Cel.:* Let's see, madam.   *Dor.:* Leave it
> alone, Celia, you'll get it dirty.

When Dorotea makes a present of a *búcaro* to Marfisa, the latter handles it
with noticeable care and warns her servant not to break it. One is made to
feel its fragility (pp. 148, 151).

The sodden heaviness into which Gerarda settles following her levity
during supper graphically underscores her earthiness:

> *Ger.:* Después de comer, siempre tengo yo mis deuociones. Lléuame al
>   oratorio, Celia.
> *Cel.:* Tía, mejor es a la cama. No te cargues tanto, que pesas mucho.
> *Ger.:* *La puerta pesada, puesta en el quicio no pesa nada.*
> *Cel.:* *Topaste en la silla. Por acá, tía.*
> *Teo.:* ¡Qué golpe que se ha dado! Lléuala con tiento, ignorante.
> *Cel.:* ¿Qué tiento, si no le tiene?
>
> (p. 198)

> *Ger.:* After supper, I always see to my devotions. Take me to the
> oratory, Celia.   *Cel.:* Dame, to bed would be better. Don't lean on
> me so, you're very heavy.   *Ger.:* *The heavy door placed on its hinges
> weighs nothing.*   *Cel.:* *You've hit the chair. This way, dame.*   *Teo.:*
> What a blow she's struck herself! Feel your way with her carefully,
> silly girl.   *Cel.:* What do you mean feel, if she has no feeling?

A similar impression of the downward pull of the flesh, in terms not of weight but of sensuality, is conveyed by a remark in which Dorotea runs through a gamut of sensations:

> Mucho se precia [Don Bela] en estos versos de amante casto; pero todos los hombres tienen esta traza. Entran diziendo que quieren ver; ven, y dizen que quieren oír; oyen, y dizen que quieren gozar; y al fin los auemos de creer si no los arrojamos al principio. (p. 168)

> [Don Bela] greatly prides himself in this verse on being a chaste lover; but all men take this line. They start out saying they wish to see; they see and say they wish to hear; they hear and say they wish to enjoy; and we might as well believe them by then if we don't throw them out to begin with.

The entire trend of Gerarda's imagination is toward a suggestiveness expressed in organic and tactile terms:

> ¡Gragea a Guinea! Reuentado sea mi cuerpo si en él entrare. (p. 197)
> No acabe este moçuelo la hermosura de Dorotea, manoseándola. (p. 72)
> Los entendimientos son como los instrumentos, que es menester tocarlos para saber qué consonancias tienen. Y si el diuino tuyo pusiesse las manos en este chapetón de la Corte (que ansí llaman ellos a los modernos), yo te asseguro que él descubriesse el oro oculto. (p. 168)

> Gumdrops to Guinea! Blast my body if they ever get into it!
> Don't let this miserable youth finish off Dorotea's beauty handling it.
> Minds are like instruments, which have to be played on to find out what harmonies they are capable of. And if your divine one laid hands on this greenhorn here at Court (that's what they call the newcomers), I assure you the gold beneath the surface would show through.

Like her Celestinesque forebears Gerarda has all her senses constantly on the qui vive. She catches everything—Dorotea's looks and attitudes, Laurencio's mutterings and carpings, Don Bela's half-expressed suspicions—and over-reacts comically to them all. Precisely because she picks up before anyone else the faint sound of Don Bela's knock when he comes to call—she tells Celia: "Déxate de preguntas y mira quién llama; que parece galán en lo temeroso con que bate la puerta" ("Stop asking questions and see who's at the door; it sounds like a suitor from the timorous way he knocks") (p. 170)—her elaborate show of deafness immediately afterward when Dorotea questions and accuses her—"¡Ay, hija, que con la edad estoy destos oídos perdida! Anoche me puse en ellos vnto de conejo" ("Alas, child, with the years I am so gone in the ears! I put rabbit fat in them last night") (p. 171)—seems a staged jest rather than a serious subterfuge.

The other characters are not far behind Gerarda in aural sensitivity. At its most refined such sensitivity enhances their responsiveness to music, as their visual alertness does to pictorial art. It also makes them notice or evoke domestic and everyday sounds: the clatter of clogs and the gurgling of wine jars (p. 92), "los suspiros a medio puchero, como muchacho acabado de açotar, que ha perdido la habla" ("half-gasping sighs, like a little boy just whipped who can't get his breath"), as Gerarda disparagingly remarks of Fernando (p. 423). Sounds unpleasant, unusual, discordant, as well:

> *Iul.:* Oíd la *ronca rana* del sétimo verso.
> *Cés.:* ¿Cómo la llama?
> *Iul.:* *Mosca del agua.*
> *Cés.:* ¿Por qué causa de conueniencia?
> *Lud.:* Porque es importuna.
> *Cés.:* Luego vn carro de bueyes, la tolba de vn molino, vn órgano, quando le templan, vna pulga quando porfía, ¿serán moscas?
> *Lud.:* Por esso puso *ronca*, porque por su atributo se conociesse su importunidad. Pero no aduirtió como Virgilio llamó a los cisnes roncos, y le disculpa Ambrosio Calepino, dando la culpa al estrépito de las alas.
>
> (p. 351)[53]

Jul.: Listen to the *hoarse frog* of the seventh line.   *Cés.:* What does he call it?   *Jul.:* Waterfly.   *Cés.:* On what grounds of suitability? *Lud.:* Because it is annoying.   *Cés.:* Then must an oxcart, the hopper of a mill, an organ being tuned, a flea when it persists be flies? *Lud.:* That's why he calls it hoarse; so that one should realize its importunity by the adjective. But he overlooked the fact that Virgil called swans hoarse and Ambrogio Calepino exonerates him, putting the onus on the whir of the wings.

Characteristic of the sensory realism of *La Dorotea*, indeed, is the recording of unpleasant sensations upon all the senses: Dorotea's already noted revulsion against boiled chicken, Gerarda's acute distaste for sweets, the strong reaction of Gerarda and Laurencio to the smoke, irritating to the eyes and offensive to the nose, after Dorotea burns her mementos of Fernando (pp. 432, 436).

The sense of experienced reality, the "historical" dimension created through the techniques described, establishes the framework within which the characters move. The nature of the transformation Lope's imagination has worked in the autobiographical substance, the quality of the blend of poetry and history, can be most adequately brought out by analyzing characters and action. Because, in contrast to the *comedia*, action is here subordinated to character and is intended to make clear the psychological evolution of a relationship, a full analysis of the figures of Dorotea and Fernando, whose story *La Dorotea* is, can be made only in connection with an exposition of the action. I shall therefore at this point concentrate on the other characters and take only a preliminary view of the protagonists. Nor shall I now treat Gerarda fully, since in her case the significant factor is not "historical" roots, but, as will later appear, links with her creator based on affinities of another sort, of inner rather than external derivation. In the present context my concern will be with her relation to literary tradition and incidentally to the biographical substance, insofar as such a relation exists.

It is clear that Lope is seeking in the *acción en prosa* to delineate figures more in the round than he had previously done. He avoids caricaturesque extremes and eschews the schematized patterns of shepherd or Moor. He provides a wider range of perspectives on the characters and appears to be drawing upon a fuller recollection of the traits of their prototypes. Their affective lives are richer and they are endowed with a more complex humanity, being capable of appearing both selfish and generous, petty and magnanimous, weak and resolute.

His *dramatis personae* is a limited one: the heroine with her two maids, Celia and Felipa; her mother, Teodora, and the latter's friend, Gerarda, mother of Felipa; Dorotea's rival, Marfisa, and Clara, her maid; Don Fernando, with Julio, his mentor, adviser, friend, and servant; Don Bela, Fernando's rival, and Don Bela's servant, Laurencio; Fernando's friends, Ludovico and César. As regards the live ancestry of these figures, Dorotea, Fernando, Don Bela, and Teodora, for all the modifying influences upon them, are obviously connected with the prototypes of the 1580's; Marfisa must have had such a prototype also. Gerarda, on the other hand, has no such live antecedents. Her figure is the final repository of the charges of procuring once leveled at Elena's family, and her heritage is Celestinesque. While she comes closest to fitting the formula "umanità indifferenziata" ("undifferentiated humanity") by which Alda Croce denies any true creation of character in *La Dorotea*, I do not find this formula adequate even in her case. Much less do I believe that Lope intended Marfisa and Don Bela to be taken simply as embodiments of emotions larger than themselves. Lope aims in each case to delineate individuals, and while his domination of the characters is too absolute, his need of them for other expressive ends too great, to permit full realization of this aim, he has surely not wished to stop at "umanità indifferenziata."

The distinct effect created by each of the four principals stems in part from a distinct manner of presentation. With Dorotea, the presentation is not complete until the last page. While the core of her character may be described, the full picture emerges only with the nuances of her changing responses. This is a case of fluid and dynamic characterization without parallel in Lope. For different reasons, the picture of Fernando, immature at the beginning, on the threshold of maturity at the end, also needs to be supplemented by a drawn-out view. The traits of Marfisa's character, on the other hand, seem fixed from the beginning and admit most easily of summation. In the case of Don Bela, still another procedure is followed. He appears in a new light in the last act and the process of his development is only hinted at. Our concern here is with the Don Bela of the earlier acts; the figure of the last will occupy us later when we consider the strain of *desengaño* and the significance of the characters vis-à-vis their creator.

Dorotea, as Alda Croce has said, is "the figure most fully felt and studied, poetically speaking."[54] Literary currents out of Lope's own production and others stemming from classical antiquity converge in her with live memories; Marta de Nevares is present along with Elena Osorio. The figure that results has its own consistency, however, and while it may be viewed as a composite Lopean version of the eternal feminine, it is also that of a particular woman struggling with given material and affective circumstances. Nothing blocks Lope's empathic identification with her. The individual women who have come and gone in his life have each left some imaginative stimulus to keep her permanently close. We are quickly shown the deeper reaches of her character and never allowed to lose touch with them; it is the straining between surface and depths that brings her figure to life. In Dorotea we are constantly aware of the inner repercussions of things said and done, of aftereffects, of the making-over of experiences and emotions through their reliving.

She is constantly before us, present or absent. We see her through Gerarda's and Celia's observant eyes, through Don Bela's doting ones, in the exalted vision of Fernando and also when emotional release removes the poetic veils from his eyes, in the accusing glance of her mother, in Marfisa's and Clara's cold appraisal, and in the mirrors she holds up to herself, actually and figuratively. We know her looks, her mannerisms and idiosyncrasies, the way she thinks, feels, and reacts.

At the first opportunity Lope gives us a realistic picture of her through the eyes of Marfisa and Clara:

> *Mar.:* No es tan hermosa como dizen.
> *Cla.:* ¿Dónde la viste?
> *Mar.:* En la Merced vn día.
> *Cla.:* Pues no tienes razón; que es linda moça de gentil disposición, buen ayre y talle; los ojos son bellissímos, aunque algo desuergonçados . . . Son vnos ojos que antes que los embiden quieren . . . La boca es graciosa y no le pesa de reírse, aunque no le den causa. Pica en flaca, pero no de rostro.
> *Mar.:* Es muy de caras redondas. ¿Cómo le va de color?
> *Cla.:* Trigueño claro.
> *Mar.:* ¿El cabello?
> *Cla.:* Algo crespo, efecto de aquel color . . . Lo que es el entendimiento, es notable; la condición, amorosa; el despejo, desenfadado; el hablar, suaue, con un poco de zaceo.
>
> (p. 114)

Mar.: She's not as pretty as they say. *Cla.:* Where have you seen her? *Mar.:* In Merced Church one day. *Cla.:* Well, you're mistaken: she's a handsome girl with a genteel manner, a certain air about her and a good figure. Her eyes are very beautiful although somewhat bold. They're eyes that consent before they're asked . . . The mouth is graceful and she doesn't mind laughing, even with no reason to. She's on the skinny side, though not her face. *Mar.:* She's very round-cheeked. How about her complexion? *Cla.:* A lightish brunette. *Mar.:* Her hair? *Cla.:* Rather curly, an effect of that color . . . As for her mind, it's remarkable; her nature, warm; her vivacity, somewhat free and easy; her speech is soft, with a slight lisp.

This sharply focused view of Dorotea remains impressed on the reader's mind from the outset. The image of Elena Osorio, perhaps even the actual thinness alleged in the libelous sonnet (see p. 41 above), is surely recaptured here as a foundation for the depiction of Dorotea, in whom the traits mentioned keep reappearing. The too ready laugh is a characteristic mannerism. Dorotea laughs suggestively when Gerarda tells her she should give Cupid a good whipping with his bow-string: "que como le pintan desnudo, no fuera menester quitalle los gregüescos. ¿De qué te ríes? Niño es, no le imagines hombre" ("since they depict him naked, you wouldn't have to take his breeches off. What are you laughing at? He's a little boy, don't imagine him a man") (p. 156); defensively when Gerarda presses her about Fernando: "Cuéntame lo que ay de Fernando. Dime todo lo que passa, que por ventura me deues algunas palabras en tu fauor. ¿Qué me miras y te ríes?" ("Give me the news of Fernando, tell me everything that's happened—it would thank me for some good words I may well have put in for you. Why are you looking at me and laughing that way?") (p. 451); provocatively when Ludovico is spying: "En la reja estaua vn hombre; conocióme Dorotea, y rióse mucho" ("A man was at the grilled window. Dorotea recognized me and laughed a lot") (p. 239). She appears self-conscious, bold, a trifle salacious in these details, which bear out the "ojos . . . algo desuergonçados" ("rather bold eyes") and fit with Clara's observation that Dorotea and Celia are striding along the Prado "como si huuiera galanes que las miraran" ("as if there were young blades watching them") (p. 289), or Julio's remark that it will not be necessary to make a noise in the street to draw her to her window, "que en sintiendo que miran, ella se tendrá el cuidado" ("when she realizes there is someone looking, she'll see to that") (p. 117). (One recalls the windows on the Calle de Lavapiés, whose occupants were devastatingly depicted in the vituperative ballad.) Especially is this portrait consistent with Dorotea's forwardness in initiating the liaison with Fernando (p. 298) and her reckless public confrontation with him at its end (p. 416).

If we can see this much of Elena Osorio in Dorotea, we may surmise, remembering the hints in the documents and texts examined earlier, that something of her is present also in the "entendimiento notable," the literary tastes and cultural aspirations, the preciosity and the pride in the role of poet's lady. Delving into his past, Lope must have come up with an Elena "muerta por hemistichios" ("wild about hemistichs") (p. 133). But at this point the image of Elena Osorio fades into the figure of a woman whose accomplishments—"la habla, la voz, el ingenio, el dançar, el cantar, el tañer diuersos instrumentos" ("way of speaking, voice, mind, dancing, singing, playing different instruments") (p. 301), not to mention the writing of verse—are those of a Marta de Nevares, as Rennert and Castro pointed out; whose figure, as a whole, suggests in their words "a refined type of courtesan that arose through contact with Renaissance Italy"; and in whom Edwin Morby has recognized traits of Propertius's Cynthia, "no less of a *docta puella* [accomplished young woman] in music, dancing, and poetry, and who causes her lover no less anguish than Dorotea causes Don Fernando."[55] Lope's literary culture inevitably colored the vision of this figure drawn from life. It is not impossible that Dorotea's name, as William L. Fichter noted, was associated in Lope's mind with the courtesans of Plautus and Terence.[56] Fichter points to the fact that the Elena Osorio figure in *La prueba de los amigos,* one of the plays in which the experience is treated episodically, is named Dorotea and described as:

> discreta, pícara, grave,
> decidora, limpia, vana,
> cuanto en una cortesana
> de Plauto o Terencio cabe.
>
> (Ac. N., XI, 125b)

clever, roguish, dignified, a quick tongue, neat, vain, all that goes with a courtesan in Plautus or Terence.

Morby notes that an earlier Elena-figure, the Aurelia of *El peregrino en su patria,* is called "libre en sus costumbres y de aquel género de vida que describen en sus fábulas Terencio y Plauto" ("free in her mores and leading the kind of life that Terence and Plautus describe in their works").[57] He observes that a later one, the courtesan of an episode in "La prudente venganza," is called Dorotea.

Yet the behavior of these courtesans does not conform to the refinement of a *hetaira,* of a mistress like Propertius's Cynthia, but to the rapacity, dissoluteness, and vulgarity of the *meretrix* (whore). The Elena of the satires and the *romances de desamor* lives on in them. In Dorotea, while the "free and easy vivacity" is still there for the sharp eyes of Clara to catch, this side of her character is so far from defining it that Alda Croce can speak persuasively of her "instinctive shying away from vulgarity."[58] Possessed of discrimination and delicacy, Dorotea quickly responds to Fernando's "*délicatesse.*" Feeling and imagination are her highest values. Fernando appeals as lover and poet; he enables her to ignore the vulgarity of her circumstances, to recreate her life poetically as part of his own. The tawdry and degrading surroundings, the promiscuities of the past are transcended. Only her role, actual and idealized, in Fernando's life counts. Since her feelings for Fernando do not change, she fails to see that yielding to his rival must upset the basis of their relationship. For all her seeming boldness and the strength of character she displays in defending for so long the relationship with Fernando, there is no hardness in her. Her feelings may burst out under pressure of exasperation or despair but essentially she is weak and impressionable, liable to be overtaken and overwhelmed by events, unable to regain her balance. She is noticeably unsure of herself, unable to act with decisiveness. She cannot forget Fernando's love and she cannot resist Don Bela's gifts. One notes in her manner a peculiar languor, something low-keyed, a slow emotional pace, delayed responses. Despite the ready laugh she is without gaiety.

In all this one senses a refining of the figure of Elena Osorio as we glimpse her in the transcript of the hearings. If the moral insensitivity persists, the impressionability and vulnerability are surely greater. Dorotea's involvement in her role as mistress to a poet must correspond not to the pattern of a given prototype but to Lope's mature experience of woman's constancy and man's inconstancy, to a conviction of woman's need to give and bind herself and man's inclination to disengagement. In the end, Dorotea can only be the victim of her self-centered lover.

Between the author and this figure of himself as a young man, there is a gap of generations. Lope undoubtedly catches permanent features of his own nature in his protagonist—egotism, impulsiveness, a histrionic tendency and a contrasting capacity for detachment, a sense of insecurity, of subservience in the face of power and rank, morbidly possessive jealousy. Yet one is struck by the paradoxical fact that Fernando, whose appearance makes the least clear physical impression, is also the character into whom the author has seen least clearly and entered least empathically. When we first meet Fernando he sings "vn romance de Lope" ("a ballad of Lope's") and the lines

> Que con venir de mí mismo
> no puedo venir más lexos
>
> (p. 88)

Coming from myself, I could not have come further

are, as Blecua reminds us, a key to the distance, both psychological and esthetic, between author and character.[59] The remoteness is that of the Lope who muses in the "Egloga a Claudio": "No sé si soy aquél" ("I don't know whether I am that one"). It is impossible, also, to miss the relevance of the subsequent reminder by Julio that it is unworthy of the intelligent man to assume that in the "galán muy tierno" ("very soft-hearted gallant") of so many *comedias*

> el poeta imita sus costumbres mismas . . . Porque allí sólo se imita vn mozo desatinado que sigue a rienda suelta su apetito, y mientras mejor fuere el poeta que le pinta, más viuos serán los afectos y más verdaderas las acciones.   (p. 112)

> the poet is imitating his own customs . . . Because the only imitation there is of a wild youth who gives his appetite free rein and the better the poet is who is depicting him, the livelier will be the feelings and the truer the actions.

Noticeably ambivalent, Lope is as anxious not to be identified with Fernando as to connect him with himself. He stands away from the youthful figure, sizing him up, touching and retouching. Fernando is less his portrait of himself, of the poet as a young man, than of the young man as poet. Lope pushes to extremes both the poetic profession and the youthfulness, upsetting the balance between living and creating that existed in his own youth. He makes poetry the center of Fernando's being to a degree unmatched in the other literary projections of the experience and surely uncharacteristic even of his own career as well. The verse-writing, which had been an incidental, if troublesome, talent before, becomes Fernando's most important attribute. The lyrical powers which had appealed to Elena now become the key to Fernando's hold over Dorotea. While Lope had lived as intensely as he created, Fernando subordinates experience to expression, doing so, more-over, purely in the private sphere because of his lack of links with a broad public. In his relation with Dorotea and in the relation of each, respectively, with Marfisa and Don Bela, the *historia* focused on is characteristically personal history, but the *poiesis* is applied as much to patterns of living as to verbal art. Lope's nonconceptualizing turn of mind and his vitalism lead him to present the question of *Erlebnis* and *Dichtung* in the context of human nature as well as of art, while his histrionic inclination and dramatic practice lead him to work it out through overstating the case of Fernando and Dorotea. His concern remains art as related to life. A central phenomenon in his artistic make-up, seen more clearly with the years, demands exploration: how, in fact, does experience become poetry; does poetry constitute another order of experience, equally compelling, perhaps more binding? Or less so? Probing introspectively, the aging artist's eye catches a facet of the youthful affair that starts him off in this direction, trains his glance, highlights this aspect. The new illumination produces its own adumbrations and in the end the face and shape of experience are altered.

As for Fernando's youthfulness, he is seventeen when he meets Dorotea, while Lope we saw to have been at least twenty-one when he met Elena. Fernando in a fleeting moment of contrition exclaims: "Yo erré con pocos años" ("I erred because of youth") (p. 312). The remark surely reflects the detached and distant perspective of the creator. Lope is not distributing blame, and the real significance of the heightened youthfulness will be vis-à-vis the older and more experienced Dorotea, while its effect is to increase the distance between the seventy-year-old author and his protagonist. It is not surprising that this autobiographical character is the one who most eludes the author. Insofar as he seeks to recapture the others, Lope must reclaim them from memory and literary afterlife as best he can, resuming, if he can, the angle of vision from which he once saw them. Fernando he must look for in the depths of himself; it is understandable that he offers no precise impression of Fernando's outward appearance. "One knows more about oneself than any one else does, but one also knows less about oneself than other people may know," notes a recent student of the art of autobiography, who likewise observes that in autobiography "we can never reach the intensity and precision of view that is the prerogative of others."[60] Even if Lope could remove the accretions of the years and see Fernando whole, he would still be looking at him from without rather than lodging within him as he once had. Perhaps the more objective glimpses of himself which the capacity for role-playing gave him even in youth could be retrieved in occasional flashes. Inevitably, however, the part of Fernando is overwritten; the perspective of the old Lope distorts him more than any of the others. As I analyze the action, Fernando will appear frivolous, theatrical, vain and touchy, unprincipled, narcissistic, moody, insecure. Lope makes him not only a roleplayer like himself but a neurotic. It is here that Fernando parts company most noticeably with his creator and that the healthy equilibrium Lope enjoyed is upset. One sees this clearly when Ludovico, to alleviate Fernando's jealous obsession, urges: "Escriuid vn poema, pues sabéis que os diuertirá mucho" ("Write a poem—you know it will distract you a great deal") (p. 253). To which Fernando replies (as Lope would not have done): "Hame quitado amor el ingenio" ("Love has deprived me of my wits"). Rejecting the epic "sujeto graue" ("serious subject") proposed by Julio, he considers "vn sujeto amoroso como la hermosura de Angélica" ("an amorous subject like the beauty of Angelica") and rejects this pointedly Lopean subject also, observing presently:

> Mas, ¿por qué me canso, sabiendo claramente que para más que algunas endechas tristes que yo canto, no me ha de dar lugar esta passión zelosa, que como vna cortina de nube se opone a toda la luz de mi entendimiento? (p. 255)

> But why wear myself out, since I know perfectly well that except for a few mournful ditties that I sing, this jealous passion will leave no room for anything, and will shut out like a curtain of cloud all the light of my mind?

Sometimes as we watch Fernando, we seem to be following a case history. Nothing, we are convinced, ever blocked the channels between life and art in this fashion for Lope.

La Dorotea sums up Lope's mature view of the workings of human love, but it is not what Fernando makes of his experience that counts: it is what happens to him in spite of himself; his own view clouds instead of clarifying and only when the work is seen as a whole does the picture come clear. Fernando, to be sure, is immature; his character has not jelled; he does not know himself or the world. When we last see him, it is suggested that events have stiffened his fiber, molded him and projected him into manhood. We must take Lope's word for this, we do not see it happen. While we have noted an increase in worldliness and seen Fernando through a succession of psychological stages, Lope has not created a sense of growth behind the sharply delineated affective states. As for the already noted absence of a sense of moral or spiritual development, it is perhaps simply a faithful reflection of the character of Lope's own youth.

Lope has clearly dwelt on the figure of Marfisa, as he has on that of Don Bela. He is drawn to both of these characters for reasons that go beyond their function in relation to Fernando and Dorotea. In both cases, in different ways, we are offered portraits in the round. Though Don Bela is the *indiano* and Marfisa the constant woman—characters of a recognizable type—in each case their typical traits combine with characteristics and attitudes that give strong individual shading to their figures.

In Marfisa we sense that Lope has recaptured traits of a real woman whose strong and intense character had had a lasting impact. The forcefulness of the presentation, without complexity but not without subtlety, imprints the figure powerfully on the reader's imagination. The fact that Marfisa bears the name of the Amazonian type of woman who in Boiardo and Ariosto is distinguished by a proud, aggressive, irascible, and independent nature may mean that these literary antecedents have contributed something to Lope's conception of the figure of *La Dorotea*. There are allusions to Ariosto's Marfisa in plays of the 1590's and early 1600's, while the Amazonian type she represents certainly seemed dramatically effective to Lope, since it appears from time to time over the years in his plays. The near absence of Marfisa from *La hermosura de Angélica* (Angelica's Beauty), Lope's prolongation of Ariosto's poem (1602), however, causes Maxime Chevalier to conclude that "the poet did not like this feminine type," and he is not alone in this view.[61] Undoubtedly Lope preferred to combine the vigor of Ariosto's figure with a warm feminine nature. This he has done in the case of the character of *La Dorotea*, drawing her thereby into the orbit of personal reminiscence and gaining psychological depth.

Of Marfisa Morby writes: "She sprang full-grown from the author's pen, identical in *Belardo el furioso* and in *La Dorotea*, though more variable than either of the others [*scil.*, Dorotea and Don Bela] in the interval, and absent from *La prudente venganza*." Morby concludes from her variability—a term used in reference primarily to her role in plots—that she is "in all likelihood . . . not an accurate portrait of any real woman." [62] I would conclude rather that not until *La Dorotea* has Lope sought to close the gap between the original of this figure, whoever she may have been, and the subsequent variants, a gap caused by concern with her function rather than her character. As regards fullness of characterization, it is only Marfisa whom I would call "full-grown." The Cristalina of *Belardo el furioso* seems embryonic in comparison. [63]

While Marfisa's personality and temperament impress themselves on everything she says, Lope also gives us, as in Dorotea's case, the basis for an external view:

> *Fel.*: Bizarra es esta dama, Dorotea, aunque pica un poco en gruessa,
>   que no la haze tan gentil como lo fuera con menos bulto.
> *Dor.*: Las manos son bellíssimas, y las sacó del guante como si me
>   huuiera yo de enamorar dellas.
>
> (p. 291)

> *Fel.*: This lady cuts quite a figure, Dorotea, although she's a bit on
> the heavy side, which makes her less refined than if she were
> slenderer.   *Dor.*: The hands are very beautiful, and she took them out
> of the gloves as if I were expected to fall in love with them.

And elsewhere:

> *Cel.*: En verdad que no es tan linda, y para dama con demasiada
>   frescura.
> *Dor.*: Si es hermosa, ¿qué importa fresca?
>
> (p. 54)[64]

> *Cel.*: To tell the truth, she's not so pretty and she's too buxom for a
> lady.   *Dor.*: If she is beautiful, what does being buxom matter?

La Dorotea supplies details about this figure not found elsewhere. She was the niece, slightly younger than Fernando, of the "lady, a relative of mine, rich and generous," (p. 295) named Lisarda, with whom the orphaned Fernando went to live at the age of seventeen on returning to Madrid from Alcalá. She became "el primer sujeto de mi amor en la primauera de mis años" ("the first object of my love in the springtime of my life"). According to Fernando, this was an "amor venial" ("a minor romance"), which "por mi cortesía y poca malicia no dio fuego" ("through my considerateness and

lack of guile didn't flare up"); according to Marfisa (p. 380), it was a "martirio de mi inocencia" ("martyrdom of my innocence") and produced a love-
child. Since the child is mentioned in *Belardo el furioso* also, one may assume
that it is Marfisa who is telling the truth, Fernando who is glossing over his
behavior.[65] Marfisa's marriage to an older man would not have disturbed her
relations with Fernando, since he died on their wedding night, but at that
very point Fernando is lured away by Dorotea. Marfisa returns home and for
five years stands helplessly by, in daily contact with Fernando, disdained by
him and witnessing his attention to "aquella famosa Circe donde ha comido
sueño su entendimiento" ("that well-known Circe at whose hands his wits
have fed on sleep") (p. 376). This background enables us to see how Marfisa's
character has been formed. She is strong enough not to be undone by the
experience but its harshness does not leave her untouched. It makes her
impatient with pretense, blunt and direct in manner, and it brings out a
fundamental honesty. "Aún no he merecido más amor que la llaneza de
tratarnos sin cumplimientos" ("The only love I have ever received has been
the familiarity of our addressing each other without ceremony"), she acknowledges to Clara (p. 115). She does not disavow her love for Fernando.
Indifferent to vanity, she does not put up a front with him, yet her dignity
does not suffer; there is nothing abject or pathetic about her. She has none of
Dorotea's moral obtuseness, faint-heartedness, or weakness of will. Her
illusions are gone, she has a firm grasp of reality, yet she has not lost her need
for illusion, as analysis of the scene between her and Fernando in the first act
will show. In this scene, the full character—the skeptical exterior, the
responsive emotional core—is visible. Marfisa is as emotionally intense as
Dorotea is languid and subdued—a choleric temperament as opposed to a
phlegmatic one, to speak the language of humors. Her emotions break out at
the least provocation. She flares up at Clara when the latter rubs in Dorotea's
attractions:

> ¡Nunca tengas dicha! Aunque por ser tan necia, no te alcançará esta
> maldición [. . .] Ya se enmienda la ignorante, grosera, descortés y
> bachillera, que por hablar dize lo que no sabe. ¡Qué de parte está la
> tonta de su don Fernando! (p. 115)

> May you never be happy! Although you're so stupid that this curse
> won't cover you [. . .] Now our ignorant, rude, discourteous and
> pedantic girl, who just to keep talking goes on about things she
> doesn't understand, is making amends. The silly ninny is on Don
> Fernando's side, all right!

In Act IV, scene 8, it takes only a few words from Fernando to unleash all her pent-up indignation:

> *Fer.:* ¿Mandan vuessas mercedes alguna cosa de su seruicio? Si
>   quieren descansar, casa es de hombre moço.
> *Mar.:* Y tan moço, que aun no ha llegado la vergüenza a componer el
>   desenfado de su cara.
>
> (p. 379)
>
> *Fer.:* Is there something I can do for Your Graces? If you would like to rest, it's the house of a young man.   *Mar.:* So young in fact that shame has not yet appeared to tone down the freshness of his face.

When she visits Dorotea she seizes the initiative, throws her rival off balance and never lets up the pressure; she seems physically overpowering. Marfisa can be abusive, scathing, or ironical and also can dissolve easily into salutary tears. The sharp contrast between the two women roots their rivalry in the different manner of appeal they make to the hero. Marfisa's love offers an alternative to Dorotea's not only in its steadfastness but in its solid, quasi-matrimonial character and its absence of maternal protectiveness. She appears in four scenes, in two of which her function is to precipitate critical developments in the relationship of Fernando and Dorotea: she rouses Dorotea's jealousy in Act II, scene 3, and her denunciation of Fernando in Act IV, scene 8, shocks him into a new view of Dorotea. Her appearance in Act I, when she gives Fernando her jewels, is a prelude to her later role in disengaging him from Dorotea. Her second encounter with Dorotea (IV, 1) is merely a variation on the first. With Don Bela she has no contact at all.

The transformation of Lope's one-time rival, Perrenot de Granvela, a European nobleman unconnected with the Americas, into this Spaniard home from the New World is a natural corollary to the centering of Fernando's being in his poetic vocation. It reveals Lope's intention to develop through protagonist and antagonist the conflict between the claims of poetry and wealth as a major theme of the *acción en prosa*. The *indiano* had become a stock figure in the literature of the day, the embodiment of wealth without breeding or culture, of riches acquired rather than inherited. He is usually characterized by such traits as coarseness, a swarthy appearance, stinginess, wiliness, affectation of manner, and New World provincialisms in his speech. Lope, as Marcos Morínigo notes, avoids stereotyping the *indianos* of his plays; rather he presents figures whose character and characteristics are only in part ascribable to their New World background.[66] Don Bela is no exception, as we shall see.

As the *indiano* was the contemporary *nouveau riche*, so a metonymic association had made "las Indias" ("the Indies") a way of indicating great wealth. Don Bela's *indiano* identity may be ascribed in part to this fact. "Mi bien es de las Indias combatido" ("My treasure is being assaulted by the Indies"), Lope had written with reference to Elena Osorio, probably even before his trial for libel.[67]

At some point Lope must have realized that by making the wealthy rival in fact an *indiano*, he could fuse the literal and the metaphorical in a manner more presentationally and dramatically effective. The full exploitation of the identification comes only with the final flowering of *La Dorotea*, but Lope is already moving toward it when he makes the figure of the rival a "rich Peruvian" in the episode of "La prudente venganza" already alluded to.

Though certainly unequal to Fernando in cultural polish and verbal dexterity, Don Bela is by no means as uncouth as *indianos* often are. His background naturally explains his deficiencies. Unlike Fernando he is no perpetual student, having simply studied in his youth "enough to show off what he knows like a bachelor of letters," as his servant confides to Dorotea's (p. 176). Don Bela since then has devoted himself to the sea trade and has amassed a fortune by toiling in this productive enterprise. "Vnas pocas de canas que tiene son de los trabajos de la mar" ("The few gray hairs he has come from the hardness of the sea-life") Gerarda remarks (p. 73). Like so many *indianos*, he is disdained because self-made but considered fair game by the sharpers of the capital where he has come to seek preferment. The intrigues of Madrid confuse him and he is an easy mark for the purveyors of *aranceles* (rules of conduct). If he takes up with Dorotea, it is not for sentimental reasons only but because she provides a refuge in this bewildering world of favoritism, fortune-seeking, idleness, and ingenuity. She brings relief from "el cansancio insufrible de las contestaciones, oyendo siempre vna cosa misma" ("the insufferable discouragement of the replies, hearing always the same thing") (p. 261). In all of this we have a first indication that Lope has felt sufficiently close to this figure to transfer to him his own reaction to the repeated frustration of such hopes as that of being named royal chronicler.[68]

Don Bela becomes an *indiano* in the interest of thematic design but the origins of his character lie elsewhere. In him we can distinguish probable traces of his live prototype and evident sentiments of his creator. But he is no mere composite. He has aroused Lope's creative interest in his own right and Lope has given him a nature not ascribable simply to his origins or his significance in the total design. Don Bela's reaction to his experience with

Dorotea and Fernando plumbs unexpected depths of character and gives him in the end a dignity denied to any of the others. Unlike them, Don Bela grows spiritually. The irony with which Lope treats him is not malevolent and as the work proceeds it becomes tempered with wistfulness. Years before, Lope had been able to place himself imaginatively in the position of his rival in the ballads on the departure and return of the Almoralife, assuming the latter's viewpoint and subduing his own resentment. As I have already remarked, Lope did not then seem capable of sustaining such artistic objectivity in a major creation and in *Belardo el furioso* his animosity against the rival figure returns in full force. Now, however, the possibilities Lope sees in this figure absorb him and he transfers the hostility he no longer feels to Fernando, whose expression of it arouses as much ironical amusement in his creator as do Don Bela's own foibles. Lope certainly makes Don Bela less adept and facile than Fernando in respect to literary style worn as a social grace. Yet, for all his gaucheness, Don Bela does not entirely belie Gerarda's advance characterization of him to Teodora as "muy entendido, despejado y gracioso" ("very intelligent, alert, and charming") (p. 73). After so many years, Lope is at last able, as Edwin Morby has suggested, to acknowledge that his rival was not only a man of wealth and power, but one of some cultural attainment.[69] The vehement belittling of Nemoroso and the rival in *La Arcadia* as gross and stupid was borne out by their behavior. Now it is only the small voice of Fernando that still insists that Don Bela must not be "entendido ni de buen talle" ("intelligent or handsome") (p. 316). Lope has rediscovered a Perrenot de Granvela "well versed in letters and music and plucked instruments, in painting and languages," as the document reads. "Deuéis de saber música" ("You must know music"), Dorotea will observe, and Don Bela will reply: "Afición la tengo" ("I am fond of it") (p. 180). Don Bela, despite Fernando's boutade, will also possess, in Gerarda's words, "linda presencia" ("a handsome demeanor") (p. 73), with no hint of the usual swarthiness of the *indiano*.

Don Bela is about thirty-seven, Fernando, twenty-two. The gap of fifteen years is far narrower than the distance of nearly half a century between Fernando and the Lope of 1632 but it is still wider than the gap of some four years between Francisco Perrenot de Granvela and the young Lope. The retrospective view of the old author stretches it, for from his standpoint, the middle-aged Don Bela stands closer and looms larger than the fledgling Fernando. "A mí me parece demasiado hombre para la delicadeza de aquel tu ausente" ("He seems too much of a man to me compared to the *délicatesse* of that absent one of yours"), Celia will tell Dorotea (p. 154). The relation of Lope to Marta de Nevares during the years in which he is reworking *La*

Dorotea comes closer to Don Bela's attitude toward his younger mistress than to the sheltering of young Fernando under Dorotea's protective wing. Forced, moreover, to put up with a younger rival, Don Bela must have had a measure of sympathy from the Lope who so resented Marta's husband, Roque Hernández. In short, the years have brought a readjustment of Lope's attitude toward the figure of the rival because they have brought him experience of what it is to be in the rival's position. Don Bela receives an increasing measure of sympathy as the work advances. In the fifth act, he looks backward, like his creator, toward his early life, and pens an impressive madrigal "con la memoria de los estudios de mis primeros años" ("from memories of the studies of my early years") (p. 385). The poetic powers he displays, beyond the reach of either an *indiano* or a Perrenot de Granvela, come as something of a surprise in Don Bela, and Lope makes it plain they have not come without great effort. Lope has allowed Don Bela's struggle toward a Platonic sublimation of his feelings for Dorotea to release creative springs within him. By this time Don Bela has become the repository of the noblest feelings of Lope's old age and has been endowed with a share of his creative powers.

Long before this occurs, Lope has taken pains to indicate, beneath Don Bela's complacency, naiveté, and awkwardness, a strain of simple goodness missing in the other characters. Don Bela is devoid of the wiliness that usually characterizes the *indiano*, just as his speech is free of the *indiano*'s Americanisms. His largesse prompts Gerarda to observe: "Tú eres excepción de la generalidad con que se habla en ellos" ("You're an exception to what they generally say about them") (p. 131). His weakness is his trust in money and his desire to seal his position in Madrid by the display of a desirable mistress. Although he tells Dorotea, as she comes forward to greet him on their first meeting, "No soy tan gran señor que merezca que salgáis de la tarima" ("I'm not of such high rank as to merit your coming down from the platform") (p. 171), Don Bela possesses the greatheartedness (*generosidad*) of the genuine aristocrat. He is undoubtedly a second son who, faced with the alternatives "iglesia, mar, o casa real" ("Church, sea, or the royal household"), has taken the second option. "The hardness of the sea-life" has saved him from the aristocrat's besetting sins, haughtiness and vanity.

In Acts II and III (he does not appear in I or IV) Don Bela will impress us as naive and fatuous. Less gullible than he seems, however, he will not really be taken in by Gerarda, whom, at one point, he will call an "embustera" ("fraud"). In Gerarda's presence we will find him restrained. She will be allowed to think him unaware of being preyed upon. He will show discretion in not pressing his inquiries about his predecessor in Dorotea's affections in the face of Gerarda's tearful denials, even though not taken in by them.

The suggestion that there is more awareness in him than he cares to show enriches the depiction of Don Bela, setting him apart from the usual figure of the man of wealth, devoid of delicacy or sensitivity. As with Fernando and Dorotea we sense that surface and depths are not in entire harmony. In Don Bela Lope implies from the outset more reflectiveness than the *indiano* himself wishes to acknowledge. It is the possession of such awareness and the changing attitude of Don Bela that will determine his subsequent development toward solitude and sublimation, one closely paralleling the evolution of Lope's own attitude toward the ailing Marta de Nevares. Beneath the surface in the earlier acts the strain that will emerge in the last is already perceptible.

The presence of Gerarda in *La Dorotea* is a final effect of Lope's conviction, attested in the satirical verse, that Elena's relatives—father, mother, brother—acted as her procurers and were the engineers and beneficiaries of his supplanting by Perrenot de Granvela. The charge of "go-between," stridently made in 1587–88 and echoed angrily against Pinardo in *Belardo el furioso*, is unexpectedly fulfilled in this entertaining procuress. Lope makes the solicitation less unsavory by disengaging it from Dorotea's relatives and entrusting it to this, the most engaging of all the literary progeny of Celestina. "De Teodora, su madre, no quiero quexarme, pues sólo fue culpada en la permissión; pero las otras en la solicitud" ("I have no complaint against Teodora, her mother, since she was only to blame for giving permission; the other women were in on the solicitation"), Fernando expressly remarks (p. 409).

Laurencio's observation, "El oro siempre fue oro, y Gerarda siempre será Gerarda" ("Gold has always been gold, and Gerarda will always be Gerarda") (p. 262), views Gerarda more as an institution than an individual, a permanent, nonpersonal manifestation of the self-interested forces that bring man and woman together. In similar fashion Fernando calls her "la quinta essencia de la astucia, el término de la inuención, y la mayor maestra del concierto que ha tenido el impossible gusto de la vejez después de la lasciua mocedad" ("the quintessence of astuteness, the ultimate in fabrications, the greatest mistress of assignation ever produced by the vain desires of old age after a lascivious youth") (p. 409). Those, however, are biased views which overstate Gerarda's professional effectiveness. Their real interest lies in the hints they offer that in Gerarda we have the culmination of the vein of procuring present in the biographical material from the start, now esthetically objectified and cleansed of the bitterness and anger with which Lope once expressed it. The resentment in Fernando's words in his own; his creator, uninvolved, will now be free to turn the figure of Gerarda to other expressive purposes.

Matchmaking as such is depersonalized—or almost so, for a distinctive aspect of Gerarda's role, her relationship to Dorotea's mother, deserves comment. Despite some suggestion that Gerarda is of inferior social status, no real social distinctions separate these two women.[70] The opening lines of the work make them simply old friends: Gerarda addresses Dorotea's mother as "amiga Teodora." Gerarda comes and goes freely in Teodora's household and stays to dinner. Teodora's complicity with this go-between may once have been intended to compromise Inés Osorio, to reiterate the scurrilous charges of the satires, with sufficient obliqueness to avoid scandal yet remain clear to those who could read between the lines. Certain passages of the *acción en prosa* suggest that Lope thought of the two characters as sides of a single coin. He has allowed them to remain, like Siamese twins, not wholly disjoined, as if the actual memory of Inés Osorio and the line of descent from Celestina had become fused in his mind. It is Gerarda, not Teodora, who is pointedly associated with "Santa Inés," Lope's familiar name, it will be recalled, for Elena's mother. When Teodora returns home after Don Bela's visit and pretends surprise at finding Dorotea with Gerarda, the latter blandly explains: "Estáuale diziendo que en el repartimiento de mis monjas, de los santos deste año me auía cabido Santa Inés, y auíame enternecido con su martirio, y contáuale su vida" ("I was telling her that in the distribution made by my nuns of the saints for this year I had been assigned St. Agnes and I was sighing over her martyrdom and recounting her life to Dorotea") (p. 188). On the other hand it is a fall of Teodora's mentioned in passing— "El otro día caí en vna cueva" ("The other day I fell into a cellar") (p. 189)— that, as already noted, gives an advance hint of Gerarda's fate, of her fatal fall in Teodora's wine cellar. It is also Teodora who tells of a visit to a woman whose newborn child suspiciously resembles a friend of her husband's. Gerarda, as a descendant of Celestina, immediately recognizes that such a visit should be her prerogative: "¿Por qué no me lleuaste contigo? Pusiérale la rosa de Iericó y mi nómina de reliquias" ("Why didn't you take me along? I would have placed a rose of Jericho on her and my pouch of saints' relics") (p. 188).[71]

In providing Gerarda with a daughter, perhaps suggested by those of Celestina in sequels to the *tragicomedia*, Lope is in fact establishing between her and Teodora an additional bond quite foreign to the tradition of *La Celestina*, that of negligent but self-righteous motherhood. The daughters become as closely linked as the mothers and prove a comical bone of contention for the latter as they jointly thwart their elders' designs.

Whatever aspersions the overlapping of these two characters may once have cast on Inés Osorio, by 1632 the personal sting has gone out of the redundancy and Lope is free to exploit "la codicia y trazas de vna tercera" ("the covetousness and wiles of a go-between") and "la hipocresía de vna madre interessable" ("the hypocrisy of a venal mother"), not in spite but in fun.[72] We shall find him returning repeatedly to the humorous motifs of their opening conversation.

Plainly Lope in his old age can no longer take a Celestina seriously: only in a playful way does Gerarda hark back to her prototype. She goes through her Celestinesque paces with relish but entirely without the seriousness of her forebear. In Lope's treatment of Fabia, the Celestina of *El caballero de Olmedo* (dated 1615–1626 by Morley and Bruerton) there is already a pronounced comic emphasis, as Marcel Bataillon notes.[73] However, the dramatic function Lope finds for her—linking the comic intrigue with the tragic dénouement furnished by tradition—makes her in the end tragicomic. In *La Dorotea* the go-between is wholly a comic figure. In respect to the action, despite her officiousness, she is quite superfluous, at most its expediter, in no way its director. (Such superfluousness, I hope to show later, is the key to her significance.) Unlike Celestina she is a poor strategist. Dorotea's attempted suicide shows how little Gerarda anticipated the consequences of her opening maneuvers against Fernando. When Dorotea begins to recover, Gerarda assumes that Don Bela's gifts will sway Dorotea to him, and proclaims to Don Bela as Act II opens, a victory which is, in fact, a gamble, successful only through the chance agency of the jealous Marfisa.

The high spirits that characterize Gerarda persist in the face of advanced age. She is as noticeably Celestina's elder in years as she is her junior in gaiety. She is eighty years old, a fact that neither she nor her interlocutors ever quite forget (p. 171). Teodora brings up her age at the very beginning (p. 66); it underscores Gerarda's *carpe diem* injunctions to Dorotea and her mother (pp. 71–72, 168), and it injects an anxious note into her facile sanctimoniousness.

Lope handles Gerarda with the lightest of touches and, as in *El caballero de Olmedo*, "from the start plays the game that consists in setting up reminiscences of *La Celestina*."[74] But now the gratuitousness of these allusions is complete and they glance innocuously off her figure. Celestina's fate is more than once alluded to, only to be put aside as out of the question in Gerarda's case. Laurencio asks Don Bela what he would do if someone tried to supplant him:

Bel.: Contra el oro, más oro; contra Gerarda, azero.
Lau.: No es remedio el que trae más daño.

> *Bel.:* ¿Qué daño?
> *Lau.:* Poner las manos en una muger miserable.
>
> (p. 262)

> *Bel.:* Against gold, more gold; against Gerarda, steel. *Lau.:* It's no remedy that brings on more trouble. *Bel.:* What trouble? *Lau.:* Laying hands on a wretched old woman.

During Ludovico's account of his stewardship of Fernando's affairs during his absence, Fernando asks:

> *Fer.:* ¿Distes la cuchillada a Gerarda?
> *Lud.:* No; porque sabía que os auíades de arrepentir de auerlo mandado . . .
>
> (p. 237)[75]

> *Fer.:* Did you slash Gerarda's face? *Lud.:* No, because I knew you would regret having directed me to . . .

Helmut Petriconi saw Gerarda as the ultimate step in the refinement of a type, the *anus*, present as such in the Trotaconventos, the "convent-trotting" go-between of the medieval *Book of Good Love* of Juan Ruiz, given individuality and personality in Celestina and now more subtly and thoroughly individualized.[76] Undoubtedly Lope indulges in the pleasure of gratuitous variation on traditional traits of a typed character, proceeding selectively, not mechanically. Petriconi does not bring out what seems to me most characteristic, however: that with Gerarda the stage is reached in which the character becomes aware of itself as such, accentuating self-consciously its own fictionality because it has been endowed with a touch of the author's awareness that he is varying traditional motifs. Lope sometimes lends Gerarda Celestinesque characteristics *pro forma*, sometimes capriciously inflates them. He focuses on those most susceptible of spectacular display—sanctimoniousness, bibulousness, covetousness, addiction to a *copia verborum*—and deliberately overdoes them.[77] At the same time, he touches only lightly on other activities of Celestina. Can this garrulous old busybody really be a brothel-keeper, as a passing allusion to "las que tengo en administración" ("the girls I administer") (p. 395) suggests? As for sorcery, she plays at it, fascinated but cautious, like her creator, and deludes herself as to the results. "No me engañaron el chapín y las tixeras" ("The clog and scissors didn't deceive me"), she mutters, taking unwarranted credit for Dorotea's change in mood (p. 159).[78]

Her sanctimoniousness comes forth mechanically when Gerarda sees trouble looming. Unlike Petriconi, I find it more reflex than hypocrisy, an automatism purely comic in spirit and effect. It should be understood, of course, that Gerarda's overplaying the part of piety does not impugn an unquestioning faith and adherence to prescribed Catholic ritual. For all her levity, one need not doubt her sincerity when she tells Dorotea:

> Yo, hija de mis ojos, me leuanté buena. Di gracias al Señor de la salud y de auer nacido en tierra de christianos. Mira tú si yo fuera agora Iarifa Rodríguez o Daraxa Gonçález, muger de Zulema Pérez o de Zacatín Hernández, ¿qué fuera de mí? Pues era cierto que me auía de lleuar esta desdicha al infierno, embuelta en vna almalafa. Luego me puse el manto, y fui a missa. No la he perdido día con salud desde que tengo vso de razón.   (p. 449)[79]

> I, my darling child, got up feeling well. I gave God thanks for my good health and for having been born in Christendom. Now just think if I were Jarifa Rodríguez or Daraja González, the wife of Zulema Pérez or Zacatín Hernández, what would become of me? Why it's beyond any doubt that this misfortune would take me straight to hell, wrapped up in one of those Moorish robes. Then I put on my shawl and went to mass. I haven't missed it a single day I've been well since I reached the age of reason.

The resort to piety by way of diversion is well exemplified when Don Bela hesitantly inquires about Dorotea's attempted suicide:

> *Ger.:* ¿Matarse? ¡Para esso está el tiempo! Como que no huuiesse alma, y se huuiesse de dar cuenta a aquel justo juez de muertos y de viuos.
> *Bel.:* ¿Por esso lloras?
> *Ger.:* Soy tan deuota, que en hablando en el Señor, no puedo contener las lágrimas.
>
> (p. 137)

> *Ger.:* Commit suicide? As if these were times for that sort of thing! As if one didn't have a soul and one wouldn't be called to account by that just judge of living and dead.   *Bel.:* Is that why you are crying?   *Ger.:* I'm so devout that when I mention the Lord I can't keep back the tears.

Such an explicit accounting for tears is caricaturesque. By reflecting her creator's awareness that she has literary traits to display, Gerarda reduces them to ornamentality. Tongue in cheek, she gives away the act she is putting on. In the presence of those who know her best, she throws her transparent veils of piety over her sorcery and wine-guzzling as well as her matchmaking. "Esta bolsilla era de vna agüela mía, con no sé qué cosas en latín, que deuían de ser de sus deuociones" ("This pouch belonged to a grandmother of mine; it has some sort of Latin things in it, which must have been connected with her devotions") (p. 161), Gerarda explains when Dorotea pulls a prayer for St. John's Eve (that is, for a maiden seeking a husband) from her sleeve. "Pues, en verdad que no me he desayunado sino es de mis deuociones" ("Why, honestly, I've had nothing for breakfast except my devotions") is her automatic rejoinder when she senses the imputation of tipsiness (pp. 373, 393). The connection between piety and procuring is a persistent one. After assuring Teodora in the opening scene that she comes on God's business (p. 67), she remains unruffled later when her crony rejoins (p. 73) that it is the devil whose service she is in, one of the rare echoes of Celestina's diabolism (a purely verbal one) surviving in the *acción en prosa*. "Con esto me voy a rezar a la Merced," she goes on, "que en verdad que no me iré a casa sin encomendar a Dios vuestros negocios" ("I'm going now to Merced Church to say a prayer, for I certainly wouldn't go home without putting your affairs in God's hands") (p. 74). Returning some hours later, she reports, "En la Merced he cumplido con alguna de mis deuociones" ("At Merced Church I performed some of my devotions"), and presently gives an account of her conversation there with Don Bela (p. 120).

The root of Gerarda's fondness for the wine bottle is Celestina's *laus vini*, a *topos* prominent in two passages of the *tragicomedia:* the meal scene (Aucto IX), and Celestina's reminiscences of Claudina (Aucto III), which detail their drinking bouts. Lope must have been struck by certain comic suggestions already present in these passages, for example: "Vna sola dozena de vezes a cada comida, no me harán passar de allí, saluo si no soy conbidada, como agora" ("No more than a dozen times at each meal, no one can make me take more, unless I am not a guest as I'm not now").[80] These are more verbal than representational, for alcohol has no effect on Celestina's self-possession. Indeed there is nothing even in the meal scene to suggest her actual drinking from the jug she has placed beside her, and much less is there any suggestion of tipsiness. Celestina takes alcohol with no trace of gaiety as a substitute for bygone carnal pleasures. With Gerarda, on the other hand, Lope delights in hints that alcohol adds a supererogatory ebullience to natural gaiety. We are left in some uncertainty as to where alcoholic stimulation begins and native high spirits leave off. In the sequence suggested by the meal scene of *La Celestina*, there is no doubt: Gerarda grows tipsy before our eyes in finely delineated stages. Elsewhere Celestina's crony, Claudina, has become Gerarda's crony, Marina, and we witness the after-effects of a joint drinking bout which is related as having occurred that very morning instead of being evoked (as in *La Celestina*) in memories of times long past. More than once there are suggestions that Gerarda is tipsy; the alcoholic motif confined to two or three passages in *La Celestina* becomes pervasive. "Todo aquello es vino" ("That's all the effect of wine"), mutters Laurencio when Gerarda turns on pious tears (p. 137), and wine unquestionably adds to her verbal exuberance and contributes to her flights of comical poetic eloquence.

The servants have been described by Alda Croce as "individualized every one and sharply drawn," and she finds them "sometimes more coherent than the masters," assertions which I find in need of qualification.[81] It is true that Lope often seems concerned to distinguish the servants, particularly in their relations with their masters, from *comedia* counterparts, and that one sometimes feels his presentation of them is affected by memories of living prototypes. Certainly each displays individual traits and the parts played by Julio and Felipa are unusually prominent. Each, too, has his own way of meshing or clashing with his master in dialogue. Nevertheless, I detect no attempt to accentuate the servants' individuality as I do the masters'. The servants' personalities are in fact partly contingent on those of their masters, to which they give relief. If the servants seem more coherent (and they do not always), it is because they are less complex, less sensitive, free of inner conflict, uninvolved.

Despite the general affinities of the servants with the *graciosos* of the *comedia*, the categorical social distinctions of the *comedia* are unquestionably blurred in *La Dorotea*. In the case of Julio and Fernando, the reasons, to be mentioned in a moment, probably lie in Lope's *Erlebnis*. Among the maid-servants we find something more than the familiarity of the maids of the *comedia*, who know their places even though they are their mistresses' confidantes. Though it would be arbitrary to link Celia and Felipa concretely with the unappealing and shady women in whose company Elena is seen in the transcript—the "muger enamorada," Juana de Ribera, and her cousin, Ana Velázquez—recollection of the real environment seems to have brought the maids, especially Felipa, closer to the status of friends, the only ones that Dorotea has in the *acción en prosa*. Referring to the influence on Dorotea of Gerarda and Felipa, Julio observes "que las mugeres más yerran por los consejos de las amigas que por sus propias flaquezas" ("women go astray more at the urging of their female friends than because of their own weaknesses") (p. 408). If, in fact, Gerarda is an "amiga" to Teodora, it should not surprise us to find the same thing true of their daughters. And so we do, while the unnatural stress here and there on Felipa's (and Celia's) menial status seems a compensatory effort on Lope's part to keep history from upsetting too markedly the poetic conventions he has chosen to follow in these relationships.[82] During the meal in Teodora's household, the distance between those seated at the table and the servant who waits on it appears purely nominal.

With Fernando and Julio, the instability of the *comedia* convention is even more noticeable. Some close friend of Lope's young days evidently lives on in Julio—perhaps the Claudio Conde whom Lope in the "Egloga a Claudio" is still recalling as having stood by him faithfully in jail and accompanied him into exile.[83] Julio vainly argues against the trip to Seville, then resigns himself: "Siguiéndote cumpliré con tu amistad, no con mi obligación" ("In following you I'll be acting out of friendship for you, not from any obligation on my part") (p. 113). The unusual character of this friendship is seen, among other things, as Blecua and F. Monge note, in the attention shown Julio by Fernando's other friends.[84] They take his participation in their learned talk and their literary discussions as a matter of course and in these scenes he is indistinguishable from the others. Fernando for his part observes: "Pues por lo que toca a la verdadera amistad, assí fuera yo Alexandro como tú Ephestión" ("And as for true friendship, I wish I were as truly Alexander as you are Hephaestion") (p. 294). Again Lope feels an impulse to redress the balance and explain away departures in decorum, such as why it was Fernando, rather than his servant, who disguised himself as a pauper to receive money from Dorotea unbeknownst to Don Bela (p. 410). His explanation only confuses the matter: "Pues respondo que muchas veces podía hablarla, echándome en el suelo debaxo de la rexa de su ventana" ("Well, I answer that I could often speak to her by lying flat on the ground beneath her window-grill"). The true explanation must be that Lope had in fact done just this. He feels impelled to mention it now but attempts to square it with artistic decorum.[85]

As for Laurencio and Don Bela, the first time we meet them the former is already straining to be more than a servant, only to find himself forcibly put in his place by his master: "Ya es tarde para persuadirme: sirue y calla, Laurencio; que no te truxe para consejero, sino para criado" ("It's too late to dissuade me: serve and keep still, Laurencio; I didn't bring you as an adviser but as a servant") (p. 138). The situation recurs and Laurencio reflects: "Mal hize en hablar como amigo, auiendo de callar como criado" ("I was wrong to speak up as a friend when I should have kept still as a servant")

(p. 262). Morby (pp. 138n and 262n) notes cases in the *comedia* where an overstepping servant is similarly aware or made aware that his role is not that of friend or adviser.[86] The difference lies in the fact that Laurencio by the last act has in fact been promoted. Don Bela remarks:

> Después que te passé de criado a amigo, has perdido la condición de los que siruen, que parlan quanto saben. Pero pues ya eres amigo, como tienes licencia de reprehenderme, tenla de desengañarme.
>
> (p. 385)
>
> Since I changed you from servant to friend, you have forgotten the ways of those who serve, who spill all they know. But since you are now a friend, just as you have leave to reprimand me, assume it to disabuse me.

By this time Don Bela is growing in humaneness and spirituality and one wonders if this change in attitude may not be rooted in the Gospel: "Henceforth I call you not servants; for the servant knoweth not what his Lord doeth; but I have called you friends" (John 15:15). The touch is well suited in any case to the development of Don Bela's character and it is more plausibly associated with Lope's maturity than with the experience of his youth, as in the case of Julio. There is perhaps still another factor from which both characters benefit: Lope's lifelong experience of being in positions of subservience. He vindicates through both Julio and Laurencio the often humiliating use to which he was forced to put his talents for reasons of economic necessity. Amezúa has acutely seen in Laurencio's remark to Gerarda, "El que sirue no es tercero sino criado" ("He who serves is not a procurer but a servant") (p. 397), a defense of Lope's complicity in the Duke's sordid sex-life.[87] If, as Montesinos observes, Lope "knew very well what was expected of him as secretary to a nobleman and when he was supposed to speak 'in the style of a servant,'"[88] he felt, by the same token, that acting a servant's part did not make him in fact a servant.

A final factor modifying the master-servant convention of the *comedia* is Lope's own assumption of the stance of the *figura del donaire*, as Montesinos has put it. This relieves the servants of the need to take a point of view consistently antithetical to their masters'. By making plain his own reservations toward his principals and taking on himself at the end the function of forcing them down to earth, Lope leaves the servants free—or freer—to draw close to their masters, to act as their friends, colleagues, counselors, mentors, to be something besides reflecting or distorting mirrors or practical tacticians.

Julio's special position is due in part to his being Fernando's "ayo o pedagogo"—tutor and counselor—as well as servant. Ten years Fernando's senior, he has watched over his master during the years at Alcalá, Fernando's tenth to seventeenth, studying along with him and acquiring learning which everyone, his master included, considers phenomenal.[89] Have recollections of some fellow student here entered the picture? Or is Lope thinking of the *servus fidus* of Latin comedy in attaching this learned older servant to Fernando? (The only time we see him apart from his master is when he leaves the latter with Dorotea and comes to lead the discussion of the mock *culterano* sonnet.) Julio's intellectual equality with his master does not square well with his social inferiority or his occasional clowning with the maids as a comic understudy to Fernando. His is not a fully finished figure, though it is an overstatement to call his personality "clearly split in two."[90] He is best defined in terms of his imperturbable manner, his professorial turn of mind and his attitude—ironical, detached, alert to the absurd, yet tolerant and indulgent. If these traits do not entirely cohere, neither does Julio's personality. Lope has acted on a number of different suggestions, always entertainingly, but without feeling obliged to make them gravitate about a single core. Julio's aplomb is designed to set off Fernando's lack of equilibrium, his underplaying to show up his master's histrionics. Though he sometimes shows a servant's impatience and punctures his master's poses, he looks on his charge with a mixture of affection and forbearance. When he turns severe and speaks earnestly one detects the accents of the old Lope.

Laurencio is the clearest case of a servant designed—until he unexpectedly becomes Don Bela's friend toward the end—to set off his master's character by contrast. Tough-minded, cynical, materialistic, he is inalterably opposed to the affair with Dorotea. Implacably he opens his master's eyes to what Don Bela prefers to ignore and he takes a sardonic pleasure in exposing his master's fatuousness. There is nothing about Madrid that he does not know and he sets himself up as watchdog over the riches his master squanders, begrudging every penny he is forced to give up. He does not object to his master's loving Dorotea; like his counterparts on the stage, he has no conception of what love is. "Yo no soy [zeloso] de su amor sino de su hazienda" ("I am not [jealous] of his love but about his money"), he tells Celia (p. 176). He objects to the exploitation of his master and to the latter's neglect of the pursuit of advancement at Court. But all is not self-interest in his attitude. When Don Bela turns him into a friend and explains his Platonic madrigal, he grows solicitous and subdued; however incredulous, he seems awed by what he does not understand. Although Lope exploits him mercilessly when he delivers his wildly theatrical report of his master's death, there is pathos and pity beneath the exaggeration. Laurencio exemplifies the vigor with which Lope could delineate a secondary figure, moving with latitude within the limits of a type.

Celia and Felipa, though struck from the same mold, the soubrette of the stage, differ in both personality and role. Celia's function is to provoke her mistress into articulating her feelings when she is in conflict over Fernando, to express the voice that Dorotea is suppressing. Her probing is by no means gentle; she can be mercilessly sarcastic. In Act II, scene 2, when Dorotea is relenting toward Fernando, she taunts her with the thought that he has forgotten her until Dorotea demands (p. 147) that she stop rubbing salt in her wound. Her belittling of Fernando pushes Dorotea to a defiant exaltation of her own feelings. But in the next scene, after Marfisa has turned her mistress against Fernando, Celia at once becomes his advocate. Repeatedly she pierces Dorotea's façade, exposes her hidden thoughts, and throws her earlier words back at her. With a perverse relish peculiarly her own, she exposes in its full range Dorotea's vacillating, confused, and tormented state of mind. Occasionally we find her swathing her causticity in flattery (pp. 138–139, 445–446) but her claws do not remain sheathed long.

Lope complements this picture effectively with a gratuitous tendency to peevishness on her part. She pouts when she is not given stockings and she grows sullen when Dorotea favors Felipa.[91]

If Lope's reason for replacing Celia with Felipa in Acts III and IV is to reduce the implausibility of the encounter of Fernando and Julio with the disguised Dorotea in the Prado, a situation which really belongs in the *comedia*, he can hardly be called successful. Even a more careful arrangement could not have made plausible Fernando's telling his life story to a pair of strange women. (I pass over the fact that Fernando has actually conversed at some length with Felipa a few days previously [III, 8] at Dorotea's window.) Lope's life impinges on his character's here; he needs Felipa as a catalyst for the tale. In the capacity of friend more than maid, Felipa acts in Dorotea's stead as interlocutor to Fernando in this scene and in Act III, scene 8, bringing the lovers back together with wit and ingenuity in the best tradition of the enterprising heroines of plays like *La moza de cántaro* (The Girl with the Water Jar) and *Amar sin saber a quién* (Loving without Knowing Whom). She is Dorotea's surrogate, not her sounding-board. In their one intimate scene, she merely listens to the reading of Dorotea's letter. Though saucy, she is not caustic like Celia. She takes command of the situation in the Prado with a noticeable lack of reticence:

> *Iul.:* Dize mi amo que no habla con mugeres.
> *Fel.:* ¿Mas que si voy por él, que le quito la capa y le hago sentar
>   aquí, aunque le pese?
>
> (p. 293)
>
> *Jul.:* My master says he doesn't speak with women.   *Fel.:* And what
> if I go after him, pull off his cape, and make him sit down here
> whether he likes it or not?

By cajolery and coaxing, Felipa draws out of Fernando a story in which she manages to become as absorbed as if she were hearing it for the first time. One does not see Celia in such a role and one realizes that the lively manner of Felipa helps to mask the implausibility of the situation and to adjust it to the realistic climate of the *acción en prosa*. Felipa steps in again briefly when the reconciliation seems about to come apart (p. 316), and we catch a glimpse of her with Dorotea as they return home (scene 6), but her role—in which she ironically works at cross-purposes with her mother—is over and she is not seen again until the final scene, in which Lope plays her off against Celia.[92]

There remain Fernando's friends, César and Ludovico. The connection of the former with the husband of Lope's sister, Luis Rosicler, an embroiderer who died in 1612, is well founded.[93] That Rosicler was an intimate friend is shown, as Pérez Pastor notes, by Lope's naming him proxy for his marriage with Isabel de Urbina in 1588. He engaged in astrology like César and cast a horoscope of Lope, as César does of Fernando.[94]

In *La Dorotea* César is a fellow poet as well as a friend of Fernando's. He participates as a man of letters in the discussion of the *culterano* sonnet (IV, 2 and 3) and is made the author of Lope's topical sonnet on the marriage of Vittoria Colonna and the Count of Melgar.

The incredulity with which César listens to Fernando's account of his falling out of love with Dorotea (V, 3), the reservations he expresses about Fernando's abject behavior, the considerable familiarity with the Neo-Platonism of Ficino which his comments reveal suggest that in César Lope has added to his memories of Rosicler something of the perspective of his own maturity, which here sets César against Lope's youthful self. In making him a poet and man of letters, which Rosicler does not seem to have been, Lope may be thinking of some other member of his early verse-writing coterie. It must have been Rosicler's real interest in astrology (which got him into difficulties with the Inquisition) and Lope's desire to extend the biographical range of *La Dorotea* into the future through the casting of a horoscope that led Lope to base the figure of César on an astrologer in his own past who was also an intimate friend.

The intimacy of Ludovico with Fernando is even closer than César's but his biographical roots are not discernible. One thinks of figures like Melchor de Prado, who appears as Lope's companion in the testimony at the hearings. Ludovico's role in *La Dorotea* is dual: he is a friend in need and he is a poetic confrère. It is to him that Fernando and Julio turn first when they decide on the Sevilian trip, posting him like a sentinel at Marfisa's door to lend credence to their deception (p. 115) and borrowing his green bag. He looks after Fernando's affairs during his absence, writes him detailed reports in letters that are lost, and therefore reports verbally when Fernando returns. He knows Fernando well enough not to carry out the already noted order for stabbing Gerarda, but he returns his letters to Dorotea, keeps a vigil at her door, spies at night, and makes frequent calls during the day. Fernando first learns from Ludovico of her suicide attempt and his detailed account enables the reader to follow the course of her slow convalescence. He tries considerately to cushion the blow when he comes to the key point—"Hermano, yo os tengo de dezir la verdad; no sé qué dizen de vn indiano" ("My dear fellow, I have to tell you the truth: there's been talk of an *indiano*") (p. 239)—he shows more acumen than Fernando himself in sizing up the real nature of his friend's trouble (p. 241), and loses patience with his posturing when Fernando describes his moping days in Madrid (p. 243). The intimacy does not seem designed by the author, like the friendship of young noblemen on the stage, but inherent in the material, rooted in the past, and taken for granted.

Ludovico is a man of letters like César, and a fellow commentator. Although no verse by him is quoted, lyricism seems more ingrained in his nature than in César's to judge by his style of expression and the character of his imagination, matters to which I will return below. His intimacy with Fernando extends to artistic matters: as noted, he urges poetic subjects on Fernando as a form of therapy (p. 253), and when Fernando rejects them, promises to find others. He brings to mind members of Lope's coterie such as Liñán de Riaza, who, besides corresponding with Lope in verse, cultivated his ballad themes and even wrote in the same scurrilous manner, as the transcript of the hearings discloses (*Proceso*, p. 41).[95]

The loyalty to Fernando of Ludovico and César, as well as the "singular love and loyalty" of Julio (p. 294), is very noticeable. As already observed, the conviction of the Lope of 1587–88 that he had been betrayed by false friends leaves no traces. In the *acción en prosa* of 1632 (unlike the *romances*) Lope has no blame to distribute, no accounts to settle save with himself. The directives he follows are not temperamental but artistic.

In the foregoing survey, it has been seen that, except for a few unassimilated traces of "history," whatever of the "historical" past lies embedded in the foundations of the *acción en prosa* is there not for itself but because Lope has made it contribute to the shaping of a larger vision of experience, a vision created to reflect the full curve of his life—past, present, and brief future— and to speak lastingly to a further future as well. In this chapter I have often found myself suggesting the survival of elements of an actual personal past within the blend which makes up the history-like dimension of *La Dorotea*. In the next, as I describe the action and the forces Lope sees as governing it, I will become increasingly concerned with more purely poetic aspects of the work. Yet we shall continue to find evidence of a particular past helping to sustain the prevailing sensation of a world of actuality.

Action and Psychology
VIII

The action of *La Dorotea* is designed to present the disintegration of a love affair in terms primarily of psychological processes and only incidentally of external causes. An account of this action becomes a study in the dynamics of a relationship, in the functioning in a particular case of forces which Lope felt to be inherent in human nature, but obscure in their operation and variable in their results. Action is here evolving inner experience, and its analysis is inevitably both a revelation of character and a study in the psychology of love. In noticeable contrast to the figures Lope depicted on the stage, Fernando and Dorotea are less agents who take hold of events than sufferers who drift with them and who act only with misgivings or on the strength of impulse. Lope has not imposed on his characters an arbitrary series of outward occurrences; his concern is not with an adventure but with an experience and nothing disturbs the focus on the inner repercussions of what in fact occurs.

While a cultural heritage necessarily conditions Lope's insights into the workings of love, at heart they correspond to the dictates of his own nature. We will find them clustering, through elective affinities, in certain zones of humanistic, literary, and philosophical tradition, but their roots are in his own temperament. The order of love that emerges, if one may so style it, is a distillation of lifelong personal *Erlebnis* that has acquired in Lope's eyes broader relevance as a reflection of a general human experience. In so offering it, Lope is at pains not to minimize his sense of the uncertainties and ambiguities of human feelings or to underrate the necessary approximativeness of the poet's attempts to convey them.

It is his originality to have focused this time on the dissolution, not the genesis or ripening of love. Though the earlier phases are not overlooked, they figure only as a prelude, while the concluding stages are prolonged down to the bitter end. Concentration on a single story, that of Fernando and Dorotea, underscores Lope's intention to focus on the inner processes of love's disintegration. There is no secondary plot; Don Bela and Marfisa function in relation to the principals, not to each other. Their role is to catalyze developments or throw situations into relief by providing contrasts and alternatives. Not that Lope does not dwell on such alternatives: he has time to spare in the *acción en prosa* and Don Bela and Marfisa, as we have seen, arouse his interest in their own right. But these two never meet and a match between them, like that of their counterparts in *Belardo el furioso*, is unthinkable.

The action is polarized about two climactic moments: the quarrel (I, 5) and the reconciliation (IV, 1). Lope does not bring Fernando and Dorotea together at all except for those two confrontations. (In *Belardo el furioso*, their counterparts meet in every act, five times in all.) He has led up to these scenes with great deliberateness. Their asymmetrical placing underscores the distinctive design of an action conceived from the first scene to the last as one gradual and prolonged falling action. It is natural that the quarrel should be near the opening—it falls there in *Belardo el furioso* also—but it is clearly unusual that the reconciliation should come almost two acts before the end. This happens because the truly divisive effect of the quarrel is suspended for nearly three acts and the apparent reconciliation is made the starting point for the real disjoining of the lovers, which continues for almost two more. A total movement of disengagement underlies the action. On its surface, as on a receding tide, a slow undulation of divergence, convergence, and divergence produces the dramatic movement proper.

Lope, as I have suggested, has avoided categorical codification of forces which control the course of human emotions. But it will be possible, after examining in some detail the development of the relationship of Fernando and Dorotea, to discern where his emphasis lies and to make certain deductions about which factors he sees as decisive. As for the characters themselves, one cannot fail to be struck by the discrepancy between their theorizing and their experience. For all the addiction of Fernando and Dorotea to self-analysis, it is remarkable how infrequently their diagnoses and prognoses are correct with regard to their own and each other's feelings. While the figures surrounding them—Julio, Ludovico, César, Felipa, Gerarda— uninvolved emotionally, are more clear-sighted, even they are repeatedly surprised at the turn of events.

"Harás que me buelua loco y que diga que la filosofía de amor no está entendida en el mundo" ("You'll make me go out of my mind and say that the philosophy of love is not understood in the world"), exclaims Julio (p. 381), disconcerted by Fernando's categorical assertion that his love has suddenly evaporated. Is there then no "philosophy"—no theory—of love? Can its nature not be described in principles operative with predictable results? The characters of *La Dorotea* grope avidly for such principles and delude themselves into thinking they have found them, but they are continually proven wrong. "Conocer la naturaleza del alma, la sustancia y los accidentes es mui difícil; y assí no sabremos con certidumbre la condición de sus operaciones" ("To know the nature of the soul, substance and accidents, is very difficult; and thus we cannot know with certainty the conditions of its operations"), admits Fernando, ruefully quoting Aristotle in a flash of insight toward the end of the work (p. 413). In the end the characters are reduced to describing what has in effect happened to them, and to facing up to actual feelings, making certain limited deductions on this basis about the nature of love. In the process theories of love and the resultant codes of comportment, literary and philosophical, prove inadequate. Fernando's experience confounds Ovid and Amadís, Petrarch and Plato.

If there is no sure "philosophy" of love, is there at least an art, of which one may become a practitioner? So Fernando wants to believe: "El arte se haze de muchas experiencias, y la tenía tan grande por cinco cursos en la vniversidad de amor, peregrino estudiante" ("Art is the result of much experience, and I had a great deal of it through five years in the university of love, as an exceptional student"), he observes, as he looks back on the years of his liaison with Dorotea (p. 408). The inner nature and laws of love may not be reducible to the kind of formulation from which one might derive practical guidance, yet perhaps one can serve an apprenticeship in experience, learning rules and applying skills so as to attain a kind of Ovidian mastery in managing amatory relationships. Clearly such a view is more congenial to Lope's "operational" turn of mind. Yet by his seventieth year, when he publishes *La Dorotea*, Lope can no longer view the matter in quite so facile a way. In the end love is not a matter of rules and it proves refractory to those who would shape or project its course. Lope stands by what he had written years before:

> Dichoso el que se queda en tu gramática
> y no llega a tu lógica y retórica,
> pues el que sabe más de tu teórica
> menos lo muestra en tu experiencia prática.[1]

Happy the one who stops at your grammar and doesn't go on to
your logic and rhetoric, since he who knows the most about your
theory shows it the least in his practical experience of you.

In the situations of his own life, had experience conformed to the principles
articulated with so much facility in plays and private correspondence? Had
he really extricated himself from the entanglement with Lucía de Salcedo by
attaching himself to Marta de Nevares, for example? The formulas so
readily tossed off seem now so many castings-about and approximations,
not to be taken without reservations.

Yet if Lope chastens his characters by making them undergo the experience
of love's unpredictability, the habit of invoking general principles in particular instances is too congenial and too ingrained to be relinquished. The
generalities may be hasty, overstated, and not wholly compatible among
themselves, yet Lope has not ceased to pride himself, as the "Egloga a
Claudio" shows, on his capacity to produce "tantas de celos y de amor
definiciones" ("so many definitions of love and jealousy").[2] Nor is he
inclined to drop, in this new and, in its own way, intimate context, the
habits of his thirty-year private secretaryship to the Duke of Sessa, in the
course of which he had continually supplied his patron not only with
tactical missives but with worldly advice often couched in lapidary formulas.
The result in *La Dorotea* is a perspective that falls between art and theory,
one in which the irreducible experience of a lifetime offers Lope a corrective
to abstractions and places limits on generalities.

This stance on Lope's part has the effect of emphasizing the distance
between him and his protagonist. For the youthful Fernando tends to take
the art of love and its bookish sources solemnly. His experience, despite his
boasts, is not extensive, and his disposition to adjust his behavior to literary
patterns places him far more under the sway of precedent and authority
than his creator had ever been. Lope is not unindulgent toward such an
inclination; he acknowledges its appeal while exposing its shallowness and
unreliability. The claim made for the work in the Prologue that it shows,
"para el justo exemplo, la fatiga de todos en la diuersidad de sus pensamientos" ("as a necessary moral, the disenchantment of them all in their
various aims") (p. 52), though surely exaggerated in respect to conventional
morality, does remind us that no character of *La Dorotea* is a successful
practitioner of the art of love, not even the ubiquitous Gerarda, with her
semiprofessional manipulation of the desires of others. Fernando, driven in
unexpected ways by his emotions, can only accentuate them theatrically.
Despite Dorotea's greater worldliness, she makes miscalculations and ends

up badly wounded. Don Bela and Marfisa also come off as losers. It is only when the experience is seen as a whole, from beyond the confined perspectives of the participants, that a coherent vision of love emerges, a personal one in which theory is offset by practice, art reconciled with experience. The only master of love in *La Dorotea* is its creator. From his vantage point, that of the artist freed from the grip of the affective circumstances in which the work originated, there are no winners or losers. No longer in a mood to pass judgment, to accuse or defend, or even to take sides in the traditional polemic of the sexes, he feels equal indulgence toward the attempts of all his creatures to order their experience from within, having reserved for himself alone, as their arbiter, such absolute power. It is significant that when the embittered heroine exclaims, "¡Fiad en hombres!" ("Trust men!"), her maid replies: "Lo mismo dizen ellos, y los vnos y los otros tienen razón" ("They say the same thing and both of you are right") (p. 430).

Behind the single love story which Lope here imbues with meaning lies the whole range of his intense love-life, from the licentiousness accentuated in his private correspondence, through the domestic tranquillity enjoyed with Micaela de Luján, to the ideal sublimations of the final years with Marta de Nevares. Lope manages to hold them in balance, encompassing them all in a single broad perspective. The dichotomy Amezúa discerned, problematical at best, between the noble conception of love embodied in Lope's *comedias* and the base outlook found in the private letters ceases in my view to exist here.[3] Undoubtedly in both plays and correspondence there is a calculated appeal to particular recipients, an emphasis on romance in the theater, and on prurience and practicality in the letters. But in *La Dorotea* Lope's first audience is himself, his ear is attuned to voices within, his characters are his intermediaries, and he writes neither in a spirit of investigation like the authors of love treatises to whom Miss Croce likens him, nor as a practical Ovidian counselor, nor as a moralist who provides an exposé in order to condemn and admonish. He writes reflectively, in the spirit of one who has paused to look back in the fullness of his years, who feels impelled to have his say about human love when it is removed from the atemporal asylum of romantic art and set in the continuum of ordinary living, its grandeur and servitude, its altruism and egotism.

Love, so seen, while still subject to fortune, falls under the sway of a new power—time. Inconstancy and mutability, one the erratic effect of fortune, the other a result of time's corrosiveness, are the forces that preside over the course of love in *La Dorotea*. The design of the work reveals their operation and the characters are made to acknowledge their sway. Particular features—choruses and lyrics—accentuate different aspects of this Lopean vision of love. While the discursive character of the dialogue permits a proliferation of the most varied views and opinions, key formulations, when seen in the context of the whole, reveal the direction of the emotional currents moving beneath the surface. The significance of such formulations is underscored by reiteration or confirmed by events, and they emerge as definitive. So it is that particular states and stages in the process of love are presented and the constellations of emotion which characterize them are brought out. By following the story of Fernando and Dorotea, I hope to make these stages and constellations plain. In the process, the depth of insight and the wealth of nuance attained by Lope should become evident, and it should prove possible further to define the relation of the story presented here to the biographical substance and to the earlier versions. Finally, the salient aspects of the view of love assumed in *La Dorotea* will be analyzed apart from their fictional context, and their pertinence to Lope's views elsewhere and to given literary and cultural currents will be shown. I will examine Lope's philography in four principal aspects: love's staying-power, its admixture of warring emotions, its egotism, its dissolution. The last two aspects, common to other artistic elaborations of the experience, will now be found more probingly and subtly treated; the attention paid to the others, though not unprecedented, will prove peculiarly characteristic of *La Dorotea*.

The *acción en prosa* will emerge, I believe, as a psychological drama of a depth and subtlety surpassing any other Lope wrote. One need not take a Freudian approach to criticism to realize that he has here viewed love in terms whose modern equivalents are ambivalence, insecurity, role-playing, self-delusion, domination, dependence, obsession, suppression, compensation, and the like. Such psychological richness amply justifies Amezúa's opinion that in *La Dorotea* Lope "expressed wonderful ideas, of a deeper and more penetrating psychology than ever before, crowning his philographic doctrine in the end with admirable pages."[4]

Though *La Dorotea* presents only the final stage of a love affair, a consideration of the earlier stages is essential to the understanding of the action proper. Fernando's account of the previous years makes it clear that from the beginning their love had run a different course from the love usually portrayed in Lope's plays. Fernando's tale does not stress the vicissitudes of courtship, as in plays where the heroine is unmarried, nor is it an account of assaults on honor, as in plays dealing with married protagonists. Like Elena Osorio, Dorotea, though married, is not bound by matrimony. She has embraced her love for Fernando, the only deep and disinterested passion she has known, without reserve or calculation, as a means of redemption. Older than he, more experienced, she assumes the dominant role from the start. He relates that she first sent for him "porque en ciertas conuersaciones en que los dos nos auíamos hallado, le auía caído en gracia o mi persona o mi donaire, o todo junto" ("because in certain conversations in which both of us had participated, my person or my charm or the two together had appealed to her") (p. 298). Conversationally displayed *donaire* must have attracted Elena Osorio in the same way. (When asked how he knows her, Lope, it will be recalled, is quoted in the transcript as saying: "he has spoken to her in her father's house those times when he's gotten into conversation there, as others also have" [*Proceso*, p.47]). There being no plays and no play-producing father in *La Dorotea*, Fernando's lyric powers suffice to sweep Dorotea off her feet. Their passion, immediate and total, needs no other agency to support it than the stars: "No sé qué estrella tan propicia a los amantes reinaua entonces, que apenas nos vimos y hablamos, quando quedamos rendidos el vno al otro" ("Some star propitious to lovers must have been in the ascendant then because we had no sooner seen and spoken to each other than we were completely gone on each other") (p. 300). Fernando sees himself and Dorotea as star-crossed from birth: "Nos vimos Dorotea y yo tan conformes de estrellas, que parece que toda nuestra vida nos auíamos tratado y conocido" ("Dorotea and I found ourselves so star-crossed that it seemed that we had been on close and familiar terms all our lives") (p. 301). Yet this is not the usual case of the stars' influence as found in Lope's plays.[5] What is most significant in Fernando's words is a sensation of the familiar, as if the love in fact were already of long duration. From the beginning it appears as much under the aegis of *costumbre* (habit) as of *novedad* (novelty). And it is more than stars that make conquest easy:

> Pues yo pudiera dezir lo que el excelente poeta Vicente Espinel dixo por la facilidad de la hermosa Ero:
>> De Ero murmuráis, yo lo sé cierto,
>> Que fue muy blanda en el primer concierto.
>
> (p. 302)

> For I might say what that excellent poet, Vicente Espinel, did about the easy-goingness of beautiful Hero: "You're running down Hero, I'm sure of it, / because she was so accommodating when first approached."

Just beneath the surface is the recollection of an Elena Osorio surely similarly "blanda en el concierto" ("accommodating when approached"): the phrase is applied to Filis in one of Lope's satires; it occurs also in a ballad, probably by him and probably allusive to Elena Osorio.[6] The non-necessity of "diligencia," as Fernando puts it, for winning Dorotea, had eliminated the usual stages of intrigue and pursuit. But Dorotea, it will be recalled, though she has sent for Fernando, is not at first free to consummate their love. In her husband's absence, Fernando recalls,

> la había conquistado vn príncipe extrangero . . . que hallé en la
> possessión deste pensamiento . . . Con este gran señor que os digo,
> me sucedieron grandes auenturas, no por soberuia de mi condición,
> que bien sabía que el que se opone al poderoso con flacas fuerças es
> fuerça que alguna vez caiga en sus manos.   (p. 301)

> a foreign prince had made her conquest . . . whom I found in
> possession of her favors . . . With this great lord I am referring to I
> had quite some experiences, not out of any arrogance in my nature,
> for I was well aware that anyone opposing someone high and
> mighty with weak forces must forcibly fall at some point into his
> hands.

Fernando tells of a narrow escape from this rival which has analogues elsewhere in Lope's production.[7] The entire account of the rivalry must have an autobiographical basis, the competitor perhaps having been, as earlier suggested, Perrenot de Granvela himself. Though Fernando says, "Tengo por cierto que me huuiera quitado la vida, porque yo auía perdido el temor a su poder y a mi muerte" ("I have no doubt he would have taken my life because I had lost all fear of his might and my death") (p. 302), he acts with more rashness than valor and speaks indeed like a humble suitor awed by the power and rank of his rival, as Lope appears to have been, not like the scion of the nobility he is meant to be. It is significant that the tense situation is alleviated by chance, not by any move of Dorotea, who seems unable or unwilling to dislodge the prince from his "possession of her favors." A mission for the king removes him and all at once Fernando finds himself

> señor pacífico de tan rica possessión . . . Pero con toda esta riqueza
> en breues días me començaron a afligir y atormentar cuidados de
> verme pobre, y que no estaua seguro por serlo de alguna ofensa
> merecida de mi necessidad, no de mi culpa; y que no se podía
> conseruar nuestra amistad dentro de las esferas de la actiuidad de
> amor.   (p. 301)

the peaceful owner of so rich a possession . . . But despite all this richness, after a few days I began to be assailed and tortured by worries about being poor and on this account not being safe from some offense brought on by my poverty, not by any fault of mine, and that our friendship could not be preserved within the sphere of love's activity.

Metaphorical riches but material poverty: Fernando sees the dichotomy from the start and he knows the contest is unequal. Already he has forebodings of what will happen five years later; he knows that love, like a flame outside the sphere of fire (and their love is indisputably earthbound), must have material sustenance; it cannot feed upon itself alone.[8] For whatever reason—poverty, extreme youth, a feeling of powerlessness—Fernando shows not heroic swagger and self-assurance, prerogatives of the *galán* of Lope's plays, but deep-seated insecurity; in this he reflects Lope's own lack of an assured social status and of economic self-sufficiency. Lope has carried to an extreme in Fernando the poverty of his own situation in the 1580's in order to polarize in him and Don Bela, the rich *indiano* (anticipated in the earlier rival), a tension between the artistic and the material realms. Fernando indignantly asserts that his honor could not tolerate the idea of Dorotea's prostituting herself for his sake:

Entre tanta copia de competidores y deudos, no [auía] yo nacido con aquel linage de sufrimiento que está—según dizen los que le han leído—en el capítulo primero del libro de la infamia, que con poca distinción comprehende la opinión de los galanes y la honra de los maridos.   (p. 302)

Despite such a quantity of competitors and relatives, I had not been made with that sort of complaisance which—according to what people who have read it say—is in the first chapter of the book of infamy and which with little difference takes in the good names of lovers and the honor of husbands.

Yet Fernando quite readily accepts the fruits of her earlier affairs when Dorotea, to quiet his doubts, "quitándose las galas y las joyas con la plata de su seruicio, me las embió en dos cofres" ("removing her finery and jewels along with her silver service, sent it all to me in two chests") (p. 303). The hints of moral ambiguity in the ballad "Contemplando estaba Filis" and in the sonnet "Suelta mi manso" and the clearer allusions in *Belardo el furioso* here become explicit. Fernando not only cannot provide for

Dorotea; he is willing to let her provide for him. The hollowness of his honor is as clear as the pathetic generosity of Dorotea's action. If he feels scruples, she knows how to reassure him.[9]

The result of so self-sacrificing a love is friction with Dorotea's grasping mother. The complicity suggested by the transcript and the satires is for the first time completely displaced by conflict between the Elena-figure and her family, a situation of which I have found only stray suggestions in earlier treatments.[10] This development, along with the new prominence given the feminine protagonist, assures an enriched depiction of a heroine more victim than culprit, hungry for poetry but surrounded by tawdriness, capable of sacrifice yet beset by pressures, courageous to a point but timid, like all women, in the end.[11]

However much of Elena Osorio there may be in such a depiction, it is surely more than in a figure like the Jacinta of *Belardo el furioso*. Behind the blind conviction of Elena's complicity in 1587–88, there must have been a less simple, less lurid reality, less malevolence, more conflict. In looking back Lope may well have caught signs he had ignored previously. The only Elena who interests him at present, in any event, is an Elena who might have been, realized now in Dorotea and endowed with the secrets of other feminine hearts encountered in life and literature. Between Fernando's account and reminiscences, and the mementos (letters and verse) brought up in the dialogue, there are sufficient indications of the character and course of their love prior to January 1587 to show that its eventful moments are seized upon and lived poetically and theatrically (sometimes after the fashion of particular literary analogues), and are also recast in verse and elevated prose. One example may suffice: that of the slap already alluded to, inflicted by Fernando in a fit of jealous rage, "agrauio que tú lloraste mucho tiempo y que la misma noche me dauas tu daga para que yo me vengasse de la agressora de tan injusto delito" ("an offense that you grieved over a long time and that you gave me your dagger for [*sic*] the same night so that I might avenge myself on the perpetrator [his own hand] of so unjust a crime") (p. 316), as Dorotea later recalls. Fernando's theatrical repentance exceeds even Ovid's on a similar occasion, as his offense exceeds Theagenes' inadvertent slap of Chariclea. The very next day Dorotea had put her imagination to work on the incident, spinning conceits and allegories about it in the elaborate prose of a missive she pens for her lover as if she were writing for posterity (p. 106).[12] We catch here reflections of the emotional and esthetic climate in which Lope's early poetry flourished.

As Fernando's account approaches the point at which the action opens, he seems to dispose of the five years of love in a flash:

> Con esto duró nuestra amistad cinco años, en los quales quedó casi
> desnuda, aprendiendo labor que no sabía, para sustentar las cosas
> más domésticas. (p. 303)

> In this way our friendship lasted five years, in the course of which
> she was stripped practically bare and had to learn to do unfamiliar
> needlework in order to support the everyday needs of the household.

His brief words reveal, nevertheless, the gradual corroding of this poetic
existence through the action of time. "Finalmente," Fernando ends up
ambiguously, "ia vi de suerte que, quando considero su necessidad, la
disculpo; mas quando mi amorosa perdición, me bueluo loco" ("Finally, I
saw her reduced to such a state that, when I consider her need, I excuse her;
but when I consider how crazy about her I was, I am driven mad") (p. 303).
Time is running out on the lovers, a reckoning with the world is inevitable.
The material pressures on Dorotea have reached a critical point; *necessidad*
now plagues her as it does her lover.

> Díxome vn día con resolución que se acabaua nuestra amistad,
> porque su madre y deudos la afrentauan; y que los dos éramos ya
> fábula de la Corte, teniendo yo no poca culpa, que con mis versos
> publicaua lo que sin ellos no lo fuera tanto. (p. 303)

> One day she told me firmly that our friendship was over because her
> mother and relatives were reviling her; and that the two of us were
> the talk of the town, I being largely to blame for broadcasting in my
> verse what wouldn't have been so blameworthy otherwise.

This is all that Fernando says of the quarrel. In the acknowledgment of
undue publicizing of their love, similar to the admissions of Belardo–Lope
in the ballads, all the scurrility of the satires lies buried. The recognition of
Dorotea's state of need, far from arousing a sense of Fernando's own responsibility, is quickly swallowed up in "madness," more or less reminiscent of
that of Belardo. Fernando of course speaks figuratively, yet his expression
"me bueluo loco" suggests that the psychological blocking and acute obsession which we are shown in his case is a refinement of the histrionic alienation suffered by Belardo in the play. But Fernando is now going over ground
which the *acción en prosa* covers directly, and we shall find that his creator,
who is not his alter ego, has introduced into the quarrel all that Fernando
leaves out.

We may now turn to the opening scene and follow the unfolding action
from this point on in chronological sequence. The opening wedge between

the lovers is driven in the first scene of the first act; by the fifth scene it has produced a split; the rest of the act pursues the effects of this split on each lover: flight for Fernando, attempted suicide for Dorotea. The second act makes a fresh start some weeks later and carries on through the day that produces the decisive turn in Dorotea's drift toward Don Bela. By its end Don Bela has been accepted as her lover and the extreme point of the divergence has been reached. By the time Act III opens, with Fernando's return to Madrid, three months after Act I, the lovers' renewed pull on each other is noticeable. During the days spanned by the act the mutual attraction grows so strong, despite the obstacle of Dorotea's connection with Don Bela, that it has almost reunited the lovers by the final scene. In contrast to earlier versions, in which one of the pair had been under emotional compulsion from love, hate, self-reproach, and so on, and the other indifferent or free, both now strain toward reconciliation.

The reunion some days later (Act IV) paradoxically exposes the forces of disengagement operating beneath the surface. By the afternoon of the same day, as the act ends, the definitive drawing apart of the lovers, spurred by Marfisa, is starting. The final act recounts retrospectively the process of disengagement—more precisely, of Fernando's withdrawal—and presents its result, Dorotea forsaken.

Let us now see how Lope incorporates the substance of the story of Fernando and Dorotea into the formal structure of scenes and acts, leaving aside at this point those scenes which do not bear closely on this story. The use of so spacious a frame for so slender a story means a very slow pace. Lope proceeds by accretion, slowly building pressures, developing motives, and elaborating responses. Of prime importance is an unusual propensity of Fernando and especially of Dorotea to live through the quarrel, the reconciliation, and the related experiences in advance and in retrospect, to go over them in solitude and in company, to reenact them. The line between experience as lived and as anticipated or relived grows faint. Actuality is read in terms of anticipation, the past revised by hindsight. Through such modulations Lope in effect furnishes a number of subtly different versions of events, which, taken singly, might once have appeared as separate compositions. Viewed together, they suggest all the ambiguities inherent in human relationships.

The change of focus which has placed Dorotea instead of Belardo at the center of artistic interest is evident from the start. Instead of the rapid, shifting events that installed Nemoroso and dismissed Belardo by the middle of the first act of *Belardo el furioso*, the first three scenes of *La Dorotea* delineate the situation of the heroine in conversations that bring out the steadily rising pressures upon her. After a fourth scene devoted to Fernando, Lope is ready to proceed to the crucial interview. Beginning with Gerarda's solemn opening declaration to Teodora that she must talk to her about her daughter, Lope presents successive confrontations between Gerarda and Teodora, Teodora and Dorotea, and finally, in Dorotea's soliloquy, between conflicting voices in Dorotea herself. Dorotea is in turn subject, defendant, and self-examiner. The second scene is roughly half the length of the first, the third half that of the second. The first is leisurely, full of conversational meanderings and sham shows of resistance. The second is brisker: Teodora drops all pretense, takes over Gerarda's role, and assaults her daughter both physically and verbally. In the third scene, Dorotea, left alone, drops the front she has put up to her mother, faces herself, and ostensibly surrenders. The scenes have been designed to show Dorotea from the outset as a victim of pressure but also as lacking in inner firmness. Their increasing compression, the mounting tenseness of the dialogue, the passage from verbalization to action, from Gerarda's oblique approach to Teodora's direct one set up artistic lines of force that lead to Dorotea's capitulation with the inevitability of natural processes operating. When Dorotea turns the external pressures inward, she has to give way, though her capitulation is still hesitant, one in thought only, not definitive.

Artistic directives, not personal impulses, guide Lope in this opening. His first concern is to probe to a basic motivational level in the character of his heroine. There he uncovers a state of unresolved conflict, of indecisive decision. Only then does he show Dorotea taking action. The uncertainty of her resolve, the ambivalence of her state of mind are presentationally underscored, as if for a stage audience, by her stumbling as she sets out and again (or still) as she arrives.[13] In contrast to the strong-minded heroines of Lope's plays, including the Jacinta of *Belardo el furioso*, Dorotea is a picture of irresolution and helplessness. Moved to act, paradoxically, by a sense of futility, she formulates her dilemma as a conflict between *costumbre* and *novedad*. Her inner debate, as Leo Spitzer has observed, echoes in prose the play of the contrasting self-examining voices of a Petrarchan sonnet.[14] Her very sacrifices she sees as self-defeating. Forced into a perception of the long-range implications of her situation (against which she will soon resume the struggle), she is overcome by a sense of mutability and impermanence:

¿Para qué quiero aguardar a que te canses y me aborrezcas, a que te agraden las galas de otras . . .? No quiero aguardar al fin que tienen todos los amores; pues es cierto que paran en mayor enemistad quanto fueron más grandes. (p. 80)

Why should I wait for you to tire of me and hate me and start
looking at the wardrobes of other women . . .? I don't want to
wait for the end in store for all love, since it's certain that the greater
it has been, the greater enmity it turns into.

It is only a step from such thoughts to an open voicing of world-weary
disillusionment, and this step will be taken when she relays them to Fernando
two scenes later: "Con versos me engañas, y con tu voz, como sirena, me
lleuas dulcemente al mar de la vejez, donde los desengaños me siruan de
túmulo y el arrepentimiento de castigo" ("You are misleading me with
verse and with your voice, like a siren, sweetly taking me toward the sea of
old age, where disillusionments will serve as my tomb and repentance as
my punishment") (p. 99).[15]
    The fourth scene is devoted to Fernando. Again Lope probes inward in
order to disclose a state of mind, the instrument in this case being a device
of classical tragedy, the baleful prophetic dream, one he employed also in
plays that he considered tragedies, such as *El caballero de Olmedo*.[16] The
device is well chosen since Fernando's state of mind, unlike Dorotea's, is
ascribable to no immediate cause. Fernando has dreamt that the sea had
come up all the way to Madrid from the Indies, that a lone passenger on the
ship "vestida de velas" ("decked out in sails") was tossing down bars of
silver and ingots of gold, that Dorotea was in a boat eagerly gathering them
up, and that she came ashore and ignored him. The obvious tailoring of the
dream to the situation, in a relation of prophecy to event (a rich *indiano*,
whose name is alluded to in "velas," winning Dorotea), is not its most
significant aspect, for Lope has shifted the emphasis, traditionally on a true
or false foretelling of events, to the disclosure of character. It is not impersonal
fatality that concerns him but personal fatalism. The discussion and interpretation of the dream serve to expose the insecurity and apprehensiveness
deeply embedded in Fernando's nature. Julio's interpretation—"Como deseas
dar a Dorotea lo que no tienes, desse pensamiento y solicitud ha nacido que
la soñasses rica" ("As you wish to give Dorotea what you don't have, that
thought and desire are the reason for dreaming she was rich") (p. 83)—
cannot dispel the anxiety rooted in Fernando's dread of an "offense brought
on by my poverty, not by any fault of mine." The dream discloses in him
a feeling of helplessness similar to Dorotea's; the stage is set for misunderstanding.
    Fernando sees himself as a powerless victim of venality and cupidity
(*interés*). Lacking the will that conquers circumstances, he is plagued, like
Dorotea, by his own weakness and by the forces of the prosaic world in which

Lope has placed him. There appears in his attitude the meekness in the face
of power and authority that tied Lope's hands and restrained his tongue
vis-à-vis Perrenot de Granvela. The fatalistic attitude of Fernando toward
his dream and the paralysis of action which its apparent prompt confirmation
produces are outgrowths of the numbing effect Perrenot de Granvela's
wealth and power must once have had on the young Lope.

As Fernando utters the words "Me ha de matar el oro" ("Gold will be
the death of me") at the end of the scene, he hears steps approaching.
Dorotea's initial stumble is followed by a heavy silence on her part, then a
swoon. By its singularity in a milieu that prizes verbal facility, the silence
conveys genuine emotional distress. It arises from a level of feeling untouched by literary posing. With the swoon, such feeling grows overpowering: its authenticity gives it an expressiveness far beyond that of
Jacinta's staged swoon, its distant antecedent. A mute appeal for help, the
swoon reveals Dorotea's defenselessness. Fernando's words, meanwhile,
make plain the lasting impact of his dream. Still absorbed in this private
experience, he incongruously invokes it as if it were public knowledge:
"Pues plega al cielo, que si he mirado, visto, ni oído, ni imaginado otra cosa
de quantas él ha hecho, fuera de tu hermosura, que la mar que esta noche he
soñado me anegue y me sepulte, y el oro que te dauan te conquiste" ("Well,
may heaven grant that, if I have looked at, seen, or heard, or imagined
anything created by it outside of your beauty, the sea I dreamed of last night
may drown and bury me and the gold given to you conquer you") (p. 93).

Only when Dorotea comes to can the confrontation of the lovers begin.
Eventually this simple exchange occurs:

> *Dor.:* ¿Qué quieres saber de mí, Fernando mío, más de que ya no
>   soy tuya?
> *Fer.:* ¡Cómo! ¿Ha venido alguna carta de Lima?
> *Dor.:* No, señor mío.
> *Fer.:* ¿Pues quién tiene poder para sacarte de mis braços?
>
>   (p. 97)
>
> *Dor.:* What is there for me to say, my Fernando, except that I am
> no longer yours? *Fer.:* What? Has some letter come from Lima?
> *Dor.:* No, my lord and master. *Fer.:* Well, who would be capable
> of taking you out of my arms?

Embedded in the impassioned rhetoric with which Dorotea proceeds to
denounce her mother are simple statements, underscored by asyndeton:
"A vn indiano me entrega. El oro la ha vencido, Gerarda lo ha tratado,

entre las dos se consultó mi muerte" ("She's turning me over to an *indiano*. Gold has conquered her, Gerarda arranged it, the two of them planned my death") (p. 99). Despite the seeming finality of these words, in which Fernando at once reads the confirmation of his dream, Dorotea quickly adds: "Déxame deshazer estos ojos, pues ya no son tuyos; no ay que respetarlos, no me ha de gozar con ellos quien ella piensa, porque verá en sus niñas tu retrato, que sabrá defenderlos" ("Let me destroy these eyes, since they are no longer yours; there's no need to respect them, the person she thinks is not going to have his way with them and me, because in their pupils he'll see your likeness, which will find a way to defend them") (p. 99). The conceit renews, in the oblique form of metaphor, the appeal for protection dramatically manifested in the stumbling, the silence, and the swoon. The resisting voice, seemingly silenced in the earlier debate, speaks up again. Nothing was settled. Fernando is asked to ignore the elaborately verbalized hopelessness and listen to this voice from the heart.

In appealing for his championship, however, Dorotea is specifying for Fernando a role he has never played. He can no more be protector than she maiden. It is she, not he, who has been the shield, fending off opposition and competition.[17] Her sacrifices have made it possible for Fernando to ignore the reality of their situation. Her protectiveness toward her very young lover is that of a mother as well as a mistress. While the extreme youthfulness of the lover was similarly emphasized in *Belardo el furioso*, as if in extenuation of his failure to play a virile role, there was no complementary maternal aspect to his mistress's love, as there is to Dorotea's.[18]

Fernando ignores Dorotea's plea and his pride takes over as a cover for weakness. The studied indifference of his response—"¿Pues para ocasión de tan poca importancia tanto sentimiento, Dorotea?" ("Why, for an occasion of such slight importance, such carrying on, Dorotea?") (p. 99)—recalls the disingenuous coolness of some of the responses of Lope transcribed or reported in the libel proceedings. Fernando's flair for façade stems from Lope's, and there is a connection between the way his touchy pride takes over, eluding responsibility for Dorotea's plight, and Lope's covering over in injury and outrage any sense of guilt for his slanders. Fernando is able to maintain the pose of indifference until almost the end; then, as Dorotea prepares to leave, anger and resentment break through unexpectedly. It is a significant flare-up, as we will see later. Dorotea is unable to take in at first what Fernando's cold response means; she clearly has set her heart on a different one. She answers in a daze, totally unable to match his barbs: "Pienso que no me has entendido" ("I think you haven't understood me"); "¿Mas que piensas que te he burlado?" ("I'll bet you think I've been playing a joke on you") (p. 100). "¿Cómo lo puedo pensar, si estas veras vienen desde las Indias?" ("How can I think that if there's no joke about its coming from the Indies?"), replies Fernando, still absorbed in his dream. Finally Dorotea reacts, reciprocates Fernando's asperity and goes off convinced that he has a new mistress.

The *tu quoque*'s of this climactic stage of the quarrel have a piercing ring of psychological truth. Much more subtly conceived than that in *Belardo el furioso*, the quarrel here is over a possibility, not a *fait accompli*, a distinction all-important to Dorotea but nonexistent for Fernando. Neither a spat nor a clean break, the quarrel marks the moment when the *conformidad* (harmoniousness) that has characterized this love begins to yield to the pressure of the days and years. Its future will now hang in the balance for three months. During this interval, in which the characters turn from looking back to looking ahead, Lope makes the hold of each upon the other plain in the trend of their conversations, especially in the dialogues with servants, and in the self-revelations afforded by Dorotea's letter and Fernando's tale of his Sevilian sojourn. Following each character in turn, we will become aware of the different way in which each relives the past and moves toward the future.

The quarrel is hardly over before Dorotea is seeing it in a new light. Thoughts of suicide already hover in her mind as she arrives home distraught from Fernando's quarters (I, 8). A noise in the street draws her to the window. Fernando, departing with Julio, looks back:

> *Dor.:* El es sin duda, él se va por lo que le dixe, cómo podré
> llamarle?
> *Cel.:* No es possible, que va muy aprisa.
> *Dor.:* Qué coléricos son los zelos, muerta soy, o qué mal hize: mi
> Fernando se va, no quiero vida.
>
> (fol. 42v)

> *Dor.:* No doubt it's he, he's leaving because of what I said, how can
> I call him?   *Cel.:* It's not possible, he's riding too fast.   *Dor.:* What
> an angry thing jealousy is, I'm killed. Oh, what a bad thing I did:
> my Fernando is leaving, I don't want to live.

With this, Dorotea swallows her diamond ring.

Filis's cautious needle prick, so delicately ironical, and Jacinta's tale of having swallowed a diamond are the earlier avatars of the suicide motif which culminates here.[19] Though there is an ironical fillip in the comment Lope allows Celia, for Dorotea the attempted suicide, prefigured in her swoon, is an act of genuine despair, devoid of theatricality and rhetoric. (I have quoted her words with the original punctuation to underscore their rapidity and spontaneity. The omission of connectives is a natural affective staccato, not an asyndeton.) Fernando's departure casts a new light on everything: it shows that he has no other mistress and forces her to recognize that it is she who has done violence to their love. What seemed the voice of wisdom sounds in retrospect like that of folly. But the hard consequence stands: instead of rejecting Fernando she has found herself rejected by him.

The verbal preliminaries of "Contemplando estaba Filis" are missing in this scene; the precipitate starkness of the act has a genuinely dramatic effect. Dorotea's attempted suicide serves the important function of confirming at this early stage of the work the authenticity and depth of the feeling that underlies the posing we have already witnessed and the histrionics, concessions, and compromises to come. Lope thus makes it a significant touchstone.

Behind the departure of Fernando which provokes the suicide attempt it is not difficult to recognize traces of another familiar motif: the prohibition of Elena's street to Lope, which had led to Zaida's admonition and Zaide's mocking reply. The motif survives in Fernando's defiant panache: "Por la calle de Dorotea auemos de passar," he tells Julio, "que quiero que vea con sus ojos mi sentimiento. Tú harás ruido para que se ponga a la ventana" ("We are going to go down Dorotea's street: I want to witness her regrets with my own eyes. You'll make a noise so that she'll go to the window") (p. 117). Fernando rides noisily by, unmistakable as "aquel de las plumas, y la cadena" ("the one with the plumes and the chain") (p. 126). The allusion in *Belardo el furioso*—"De tu partida se arguya mi amor" ("My love may be gauged from your departure")[20]—shows that Lope by then had already thought of linking the departure and the attempted suicide as cause and effect, though he did not include the episode in the play. The joining and development of the two motifs was a natural sequel and the rapid sequence of the two episodes provides the most dramatic moment of the act. The tensions building for so long reach the breaking point and the protagonists rush to extremes of precipitate action. Like Filis in the ballad, Dorotea acknowledges her fault, but hers is the deeper despair because it contains no admixture of jealousy.

When we next see the convalescent Dorotea, many days later (II, 2), her conversation with Celia brings out new nuances of response to what has occurred. The prosaic process of recuperation has taken the edge off her despair; she is now resigned, melancholy, and belatedly glad to be alive. Her need for Fernando is undiminished: "La ausencia de vno que quise me atormenta" ("The absence of one in particular whom I loved is torturing me"), she admits (p. 140). She is unsparing in her self-reproach: "¡Ay de mí, que tan necia resolución tomé quando tan atreuida a mi amor dixe tales locuras a Fernando!" ("Alas for me, such a stupid course as I followed when with so little respect for my love I said such crazy things to Fernando!") (p. 139). Into this state of quiet distress Lope injects the forward and jealous Marfisa, who deceives Dorotea into thinking she is Fernando's mistress. The encounter between the rivals, insignificant and inconsequential in *Belardo el furioso*, important to plot but not to character in one of the episodic versions studied by Morby, *La prueba de los amigos*, now becomes a key link in a finely wrought chain of motivation.[21] Dorotea's self-reproach gives way to jealous indignation as she reverts to her original explanation of Fernando's coldness and tells Celia: "No he tenido primero mouimiento de rendirme, ni al indiano ni a las Indias, hasta este punto" ("I haven't had any impulse to give in either to the *indiano* or to the Indies up to this point") (p. 151).

Though the invoking of a "first movement" in extenuation of an act or thought is a commonplace in Golden Age Spain, Dorotea's present words are uncommonly revealing. The point of the "first movement," it may be observed, is that it is only a passing impulse and, being involuntary, does not incur blame or guilt.[22] Yet in this case Dorotea's spontaneous first movement plainly turns immediately into a deliberate act of will as she goes on to express a resolve to exorcise her love of Fernando: "Oy sale Fernando de mi pecho, como espíritu a los conjuros desta muger" ("Today Fernando leaves my breast, like a spirit under the conjuring of this woman") (p. 152). Her words show that she holds herself blameless whether she responds voluntarily or involuntarily.

One is also struck by a seeming inconsistency in Dorotea's assertion that only now has the thought of surrendering to Don Bela entered her head. Much earlier, during her inner debate (I, 3), Dorotea clearly implied the same thing: "¿Cómo es possible que primero mouimiento de lo que digo aya llegado a mi imaginación?" ("How is it possible that a first impulse toward what I say can have even entered my mind?") (p. 79). Since the spontaneity of Dorotea's present outburst leaves no doubt as to its sincerity, the seeming discrepancy is actually an index of the new shape which the break with Fernando has by now assumed in her mind. Her earlier "primero movimiento" had in fact been followed by the *démarche* that produced the break with Fernando. Yet all Dorotea can now see in this is an appeal for help; the rest of her role is simply suppressed. Her behavior, in her eyes, though foolish, was blameless. She can now genuinely believe that her loyalty to her lover has not wavered. We have here a first demonstration of her capacity for moral self-delusion. Resolution of the seeming discrepancy in Dorotea's assertions in fact provides an insight into Lope's subtle and fluid handling of the psychology of this figure.

Fernando of course remains lodged in Dorotea's breast even as she becomes Don Bela's mistress, which she consents to do the same afternoon. Well along in Act III, otherwise taken up almost entirely with the returned Fernando and the complacent Don Bela, Lope introduces Dorotea in a brief scene in order to probe her emotional state once more on the eve of the reconciliation. Her letter to Fernando (pp. 264–266), modeled on the epistle of the Ovidian Dido to Aeneas in the *Heroides*, illuminates the substratum of her emotions with the same directness as her scene alone in Act I and reveals subtle new accretions of feeling. It begins with a recapitulation that is actually a new view of the past and ends by looking hesitantly ahead.

The letter is a compound of rationalization and affective insight. Dorotea appeals confidently to presumed principles of love, on the strength of which she affirms with conviction that Fernando is more to blame than she; she concludes with assurance, though erroneously, that he must still be in love with her as she is in love with him. She becomes visibly worked up, reliving the experience as she writes; the calm tone with which she begins gives way to increasing agitation, reproach, and sarcasm, to be recaptured only at the end, after her emotions have spent themselves. Her letter is at once *apologia*, concession, cry of pain, and gesture of appeasement. It is surely one of the most delicate and probing examinations of the feminine heart ever penned by Lope. Serenely uninvolved, he reveals, without passing judgment and without ironical reservations, the range and the fallibility of a woman's vision. At this point, searching out the truth of the character he has created, he is wholly unconcerned with the truth of her sometime original.

The intimate tone of the letter, in noticeable contrast with the Ovidian model—Dorotea has no epic role, no reasons of state, no tragic past against which to set her present distress—stems from her total immersion in what she writes. She presents, in a summing-up, the shape of an experience formed by living with it, reliving it involuntarily, and struggling with it until it is assimilated and reduced to a semblance of meaning and order. (The sureness of Lope's touch here may be due to the fact that he is in effect describing, whether he realizes it or not, the kind of process that underlay or led up to his own *poiesis*.) In making the letter suggest the passage of an interval of time, Lope departs noticeably from his Ovidian model, for Dido writes in the heat of passion before her actual separation from Aeneas in order to prevent his departure. Dorotea manages to bridge the gap in time and space as well as the psychological distance caused by the quarrel. That she senses

Fernando very close as she writes is plain from her tendency to put words in his mouth, to supply his replies and objections, changing him from addressee to interlocutor. The straining toward dialogue conveys an emotional urgency for which the model again offers no precedent. The psychological proximity prepares the way for the appearance of Fernando under her window the moment the reading of the letter is over. The letter thus contributes to a dramatically managed gradation of suspense.

Dorotea begins by distributing blame, accepting a share, but assigning Fernando a larger one. Men have more "valor y entendimiento"—more strength and intellect—she says, again casting Fernando in a more manly role than she had expected of him for five years. Women, on the other hand, are naturally timorous and so he should have protected her. "Dirás que ¿cómo no pudo mi amor aconsejarme que nos estaua mejor a los dos morir que diuidirnos...?" ("You will ask: how could my love fail to advise me that it was better for the two of us to die than to separate...?"). With disarming sincerity she admits she has no answer: "Aquí no sé qué disculpa darte, más de que parece que me quitó [mi madre] con los cabellos el entendimiento" ("Here I have no excuse to offer you, except that my mother seems to have pulled my wits out along with my hair").

Now the earlier surmised details of Dorotea's passage from her house to Fernando's are supplied. She describes how she walked in a blind daze of tears, imagining all sorts of things except his leaving, thinking he would understand and console her. At this point the reproaches begin, for instead he responded "con tanta seueridad y aspereza, que le fue forçoso al alma esforçar mi natural flaqueza para no perder su honra" ("with such severity and asperity that my soul was forced to force my natural weakness into not losing its honor"). We are now shown the obverse side of the earlier dialogue, the face-saving and anger:

> Secásteme con tu sequedad las lágrimas, con tu aspereza el coraçon,
> y con tus palabras la voluntad; que las respuestas injustas enfurecen
> la humildad, escurecen el entendimiento y alteran con tempestades
> de ira la serenidad del alma.

> With your abrasiveness you abraded my tears, with your asperity
> my heart, and with your words my will: for unjust replies infuriate
> humility, dim the understanding, and unsettle the serenity of the soul
> with storms of anger.

Dorotea simply confirms what was already sensed; her new pleading of the case even alters it a little, converting cold anger into burning rhetoric. Yet the very process of analysis removes the proud masks that had separated the lovers and eases the way to reconciliation.

The measure of the change in her view of what had happened can be seen in her rhetorical question to Fernando: "¿Qué coraçón de fiera con tan animosa determinación en vn instante executara, con cinco años de amor, tan gran castigo?" ("What beast would be so hard-hearted as, with such vigorous resolve, to inflict in an instant so great a punishment on five years of love?"). It is the reproach she had originally leveled at herself (I, 3) for even contemplating the step she took. The heartlessness is now attributed entirely to Fernando.

Moving toward the present with reproaches to Fernando for not having written her, she returns sarcastically to his failure to play a protective role and makes him responsible for her infidelity: "¡O qué bien me has animado para sufrir tan desesperada ausencia sin ofensa tuya!" ("Oh how well you encouraged me to withstand such a desperate absence with no offense to you!"). This oblique allusion to Don Bela is the only one in her letter, so far is she from considering him a barrier between her and Fernando. She loses her composure a little and bravely asserts that by disillusioning her, he will cure her of love, a return to face-saving as psychologically acute as it is logically inconsistent. It is short-lived also, for Dorotea demonstrates forthwith, convincingly in her own eyes, that Fernando cannot have ceased to love her since she still loves him. There is dignity and assurance in her ending: "No te digo que me respondas, ni que te acuerdes de mí; que esto no se haze rogando, sino sintiendo" ("I don't ask you to answer me nor to remember me; this is done not through asking but through feeling"). She signs herself "La misma." So Jacinta had told Belardo: "Yo soy la misma que he sido" ("I am still the same one that I was").[23] For her there is no obstacle to taking up where they had broken off. Swallowing pride and writing to Fernando has proved salutary, reviving her faith in the healing and redeeming power of love. She has come full circle; the dejection, the conviction of love's transience that prompted her initial step have vanished.[24] Dorotea is now in a mood to write off the past three months and resume her relations with Fernando as before. A failure of moral sensitivity enables her to overlook the present reality of Don Bela, although it is ironically his alleviation of her want that has restored the clarity of her vision.

The only unnatural element in her revising of the past is the reasoning by which she persuades herself of Fernando's love:

> Es fácil conseqüencia que tú no me puedes auer oluidado a mí, pues yo no te he oluidado a ti; que conforme a lo que los hombres sentís,

dezís y escriuís de nosotras, con más facilidad os oluidamos. Y pues que yo, con tantas razones para aborrecerte, y con ser muger, te quiero todavía, claro está que quien es hombre me tendrá el mismo amor agora que solía tenerme; fuera de tener más que oluidar los hombres en las mugeres que nosotras en ellos. Porque siempre son mayores nuestras perfecciones y gracias.

It follows easily that you cannot have forgotten me, since I have not forgotten you. For, according to what you men think, say, and write about us, we more easily forget you. And since, despite so many reasons to hate you and despite being a woman, I still love you, it's evident that one who is a man will still feel the same love for me that he always felt, aside from the fact that men have more to forget in women that we in them. Because our perfections and charms are always greater.

Though Dorotea does not here invoke the example of Petrarch and Laura as she had, in order to reassure herself, in Act II, scene 2—"Después de muerta, quiso y celebró el Petrarca su bella Laura. Fernando me quiso en Madrid, y me querrá en Seuilla" ("After she died, Petrarch loved and celebrated his beautiful Laura. Fernando loved me in Madrid and will love me in Seville") (p. 144)—a similar literarily conditioned cast of thought helps account for the self-delusive assurance of her tone. One observes here, also, a specious syllogistic reasoning which we may suppose she has picked up from her lover. Her premises are in fact unsound and her reasoning faulty: she has injected presumed general truths of "natural philosophy"— psychological truths—into a particular private situation with which they cannot be reconciled. Even so, her reasoning is essentially *a posteriori*, a rationalization of what she wishes to believe; her mistake is as much of the heart as of the head. Reconciled to her own feelings, confident of Fernando's, she surveys the past in a broad vision that creates the illusion that she is in control of the present.

The survey of Fernando's emotional state during the same three-month interval provides a totally different picture. Rather than making over the past, he remains in a state of fixation with it. Blocked, he can only relive what has happened; he cannot get beyond it and he cannot reconcile himself to it. The struggle within him, though he does not so see it, is between the desire for emancipation from Dorotea and the need for her engendered by habit. The state of his emotions immediately after the quarrel is subjected to scrutiny much more intense than Dorotea's. Three months later, on his return from Seville, it is still being scrutinized by himself and Julio, with Ludovico soon participating also. The intervening months are covered by Fernando's narrative in Act IV, scene 1. Guided by literary and learned precedent, Fernando eventually hits on the formula love-hate, but fails to see that his love is in effect simply jealousy. It is in a discussion between Julio and Ludovico that the latter view emerges and the trend of Fernando's feelings begins to become clear. The elucidation is not complete till the end of the fifth act, by which time the state itself has been superseded.

The anger that flares up briefly at the end of the quarrel with Dorotea is submerged again as soon as she departs. The resentment which Lope vented in virulent verse, Belardo in stormy histrionics and feints with his dagger, is turned by Fernando upon himself. Suicide, which had been only a passing thought with Belardo and surely never occurred to Lope at all, is Fernando's first reaction. For Fernando is characterized not merely by egotism but by extreme self-love, the obverse side of which is self-hate.

He next turns on Dorotea's portrait and letters, but, becoming absorbed in the love-notes he had been intending to destroy, is carried back by them to the halcyon days of the affair with Dorotea and lulled into renewed worship of her. In contrast to Belardo, who stops to read only two very brief excerpts from Jacinta's letters, Fernando reads through an entire letter, then picks up verses of his own—"que me los boluió para que se los cantasse" ("she returned them to me so that I might sing them to her")—and re-captures his earlier poeticization of a moment in their relationship. The artistic narcissism present in this action becomes more marked with the third note he pauses over, a reply of Dorotea to verse he had sent her. Fernando ignores the reply and listens to Julio's recitation of the verse from memory. Refracted in his own lines, the effect of "la hermosura, la gracia, el brío, el gusto, la alegría . . . que tuuo aquel día Dorotea" ("the beauty, the charm, the spirit, the appeal, the lightheartedness . . . that Dorotea had that day") is to "poner impossibles a mi partida" ("set up barriers to my departure") (p. 111). Fernando is losing not only a mistress but a poetic subject and a rhetorical topic. He has esthetic habits as well as emotional bonds to break.

The conflict which he has been acting out is finally articulated verbally:

> ¡Ay Iulio! ¡Qué bien dixo Séneca que mientras el ánimo está
> dudoso, por instantes se muda, impelido a diuersas partes de varios
> pensamientos! ¿Soy yo quien se determina de no ver a Dorotea?
> No es possible. Pero ¿cómo puedo verla con este agrauio? Mayor
> desdicha sería quedarme a verle. (p. 108)

Ah Julio! How well Seneca put it that while the mind is uncertain, it keeps changing, pushed in varying directions by various thoughts! Can I be the one who is determined not to see Dorotea? It's not possible. But how can I see her while suffering such an offense? It would be a greater disaster to stay here and see her.

The expressions Fernando uses—"no ver a Dorotea" ("not to see Dorotea") and "¿cómo puedo verla?" ("how can I see her?")—suggest that the feeling beneath the surface is "No la puedo ver": "I can't abide her."[25] Going to Seville to avoid seeing her will be a demonstration of dislike, though Fernando verbalizes this feeling only on his return.

It is honor which he sees as motivating his flight—"Yo hago lo que manda mi honra" ("I do what honor requires of me") (p. 112)—honor which is essentially a mask for vanity and self-love. His misgivings come out in the negativeness of the "desconfianza" ("unsureness") and "desesperación" ("despair") which he says he feels.

The skeleton of the next scene, the unscrupulous deception of the doting ex-mistress by means of a fabricated tale of homicide and enforced flight, is the same as that of its counterpart in *Belardo el furioso*. But the episode is now made to reveal much about Fernando that was not present in Belardo. Fernando casts himself so emphatically in the role of Dorotea's victorious champion, playing for the gullible Marfisa the swaggering part he had in fact avoided, that he inevitably appears to be compensating histrionically for actual timidity.[26]

Fernando drops out of sight for an act and returns after three months still in emotional deadlock. The subsequent account of the Andalusian sojourn underscores the enduring obsession with Dorotea and the uselessness of absence as a cure for his love. But the ceremonial burial of her portrait, already as much an act of hostility as of revenge in *Belardo el furioso*,[27] is more ambiguous still in *La Dorotea*:

> *Fer.:* Finalmente, determiné de quitarme la ocasión de tantas penas, porque ya no me seruía de consuelo, sino desesperación, y sacando la daga . . .
> *Fel.:* ¡Iesús! ¿Matastes a Dorotea?
>
> (p. 310)

> *Fer.:* Finally I resolved to free myself of the cause of so much suffering because it was no longer a source of consolation to me but one of despair, and taking out my dagger . . . *Fel.:* Good Lord! Did you kill Dorotea?

Felipa's challenge discloses the antipathy in Fernando's tone. The sonnet he pens for the occasion, with the symbol of the obstinately renascent phoenix, softens but does not erase the implication of his tone.[28]

The only change the three months away have wrought is an advance in Fernando's capacity to verbalize his emotional impasse. His recipe is the paradox, and he follows it from the first. His opening words are: "Apenas, o Iulio, he llegado quando quisiera no auer venido" ("Scarcely have I arrived, Julio, when I wish I hadn't come") (p. 203). When Julio asks what keeps him from seeing Dorotea, he replies: "El mismo amor que me lo manda" ("The same love that directs me to") (p. 204).

He thwarts several attempts by Julio to divert him from his obsession. His reaction to Julio's reading of "Ay soledades tristes" ("Oh sad barrenness"), the most impassioned of Lope's laments for Marta de Nevares, is to wish that Dorotea too were dead (p. 215): "¡Pluguiera a Dios que yo llorara a Dorotea!" ("Would to God that I were mourning Dorotea!"). The ensuing exchange articulates Fernando's ambivalent state as love-hate and implicitly bases the latter feeling on anger at having been supplanted:

> *Fer.:* Mejor estado, Iulio, es el de esse amante que el que yo tengo.
> ¡O si pudiéramos trocar tristezas! Que él llora lo que le falta,
> y yo lo que tiene otro.
> *Iul.:* No digas tal, que no es possible.
> *Fer.:* Si ello es, como es, possible, ¿para qué lo dudas?
> *Iul.:* O quieres o no quieres a Dorotea. Si la quieres, piensa bien de lo que quieres; si no la quieres, no pienses tanto en cosa que no quieres.
> *Fer.:* Yo la quiero y la aborrezco.
> *Iul.:* Es impossible.
>
> (p. 215)

> *Fer.:* That lover's situation is a better one than mine, Julio. Oh, if only we could exchange sadnesses! Because he is grieving for what he has lost and I for what someone else has. *Jul.:* Don't talk that way, that's not possible. *Fer.:* If it is possible, and it is, why do you doubt it? *Jul.:* Either you love Dorotea or you don't love her. If you love her, think well of what you love; if you don't love her, don't think so much about what you don't love. *Fer.:* I love her and hate her. *Jul.:* That's impossible.

The connection between not seeing and not liking is also made explicit: "La quiero porque es hermosa, y no la veo porque la aborrezco" ("I love her because she's beautiful and I don't see her because I hate her") (p. 217).

Despite Julio's objections, Fernando, guided by feeling, not theory, clings to his formula, forcing Julio into a more subtle diagnosis:

> *Iul.:* Yo sé que si [Fernando] la tuuiera no la quisiera tanto.
> *Fer.:* Aquí la priuación es necio argumento.
> *Iul.:* Quando ella no sea, los zelos bastan.
> *Fer.:* ¿Cómo la puedo yo querer por lo que la aborrezco?
> *Iul.:* No la aborreces, sino que temes que te aborrezca.
> *Fer.:* Bien sabes tú que he deseado su muerte.
>
> (p. 250)

> *Jul.:* I know that if he had her, he wouldn't love her so much.
> *Fer.:* Privation is a silly argument here.   *Jul.:* If that isn't it, then jealousy suffices.   *Fer.:* How can I love her for the thing I hate her for?   *Jul.:* You don't hate her; you fear, rather, that she'll hate you.
> *Fer.:* You know very well that I've wished her dead.

Julio had earlier intimated such a view—not love but jealousy.[29] It is also given prominence in an aside between him and Ludovico. Although no consensus is reached between Fernando and his interlocutor, their positions are not in fact mutually exclusive. Love-hate and jealousy are tied together by a common basis in obsession. In the aside mentioned, Fernando's fixation in paradox finds a vivid equivalent in Ludovico's image of a magnetized needle and Julio's of a magnifying glass acting as a combustion agent.[30] There is also a common element of anger, "esta rabia de Don Fernando" ("this rage of Don Fernando's"), as Ludovico calls it. The emphasis in Julio's suggestion that Fernando's hatred of Dorotea is really fear of being hated by her, that is, fear of rejection, is shifted from fear to anger in his example from Xenophon: "Díxole Armenio a Ciro que no matauan los maridos a sus mugeres, quando las hallauan con los adúlteros, por la culpa de la ofensa, sino por la rabia de que les huuiessen quitado el amor y puéstole en otro" ("Armenius told Cyrus that husbands didn't kill their wives when they discovered them with adulterers because of their part in the offense, but from fury at their having taken their love away from them and placed it in someone else") (p. 250 and n. 105).

Thus it is concern not only with being supplanted, with yielding to a rival, but with repudiation by his mistress that emerges as the obsession of Fernando, the concern expressed in sorrow rather than anger in the sonnet "Vireno, aquel mi manso regalado," in raving madness as well as rage in *Belardo el furioso*. Here the disruptive factor is finally isolated, examined, and defined. Subsequent developments will sustain the aptness of Julio's diagnosis. Fernando admits to feeling a "passión zelosa, que como vna cortina de nube se opone a toda la luz de mi entendimiento" ("jealous passion which will shut out like a curtain of cloud all the light of my mind") (p. 255). Such jealousy, instead of spurring him to action, becomes another emotional block, as this graphic, nonliterary image shows. Fernando's fiber is not that of Lope's strong-willed stage heroes, and his so-called honor is an obstacle, not a spur. When Julio suggests that going back to Dorotea would be the cure for all his ills and Ludovico asks, "Luego ¿no pensáis verla?" ("Then you don't intend to see her?"), Fernando answers: "Esse día sea el vltimo de mi vida" ("Let that day be the last day of my life"), adding, "Siempre fue valiente la honra" ("Honor was always powerful") (p. 253).

From such an emotional and psychological impasse the only escape is an impulse such as Fernando feels as soon as Ludovico leaves: "¿Qué te parece, Iulio, de mis fortunas? Iuré a Ludouico que no vería en mi vida a Dorotea, y muérome por quebrar el juramento" ("What do you say, Julio, to my fortunes? I swore to Ludovico that I wouldn't ever see Dorotea again and I am dying to break the oath") (p. 255). In this impulsiveness that of Belardo in "El tronco de ovas" or of Gazul in "Sale la estrella de Venus" lives on, and Lope touches a permanent strain in his nature. Unlike Dorotea, who finds her way back to her lover on her own, Fernando shifts responsibility to "mis fortunas" and cushions his impulse with casuistry: to see Dorotea will not be to speak to her, to see her door is not to see her: "Veamos siquiera esta noche la caxa de aquella joya" ("Let's at least see that jewel's case tonight") (p. 257). This syllogistic hedging regarding what seeing her means suggests that hostility (being unable to stand seeing her) has not disappeared. As it turns out, Fernando does not see her, only her restless shadow, and he speaks only to Felipa, her surrogate. The movement of convergence strongly suggested at the beginning of the act,[31] then suspended, now slowly resumes, but reunion is still incomplete at the act's end and remains so for several more days between the acts. By this pacing of the action Lope suggests the difficulty of surmounting barriers to reconciliation that loom larger the closer the lovers come to reunion, obstacles not physical or moral but psychological.

Fernando's impulse is not definitive but it has an unexpected consequence. Don Bela appears and Fernando, taken by surprise, defends himself in a sudden spate of swordplay. He draws Don Bela's blood, as we learn later, and thus stumbles into a display of manly valor, coming to grips with the real obstacle to reunion with Dorotea. Don Bela's blood temporarily assuages the wound to his honor.

Fernando does not follow through on his victory, however. His touchiness does not evaporate overnight and he reverts to nursing his wounded vanity.

It is anger roused by Don Bela's sudden appearance and his proprietary manner—"No vengo a ser cortés, sino a echarle dessa puerta" ("I'm not here to be courteous but to throw you out of this doorway") (p. 286)—that has enabled Fernando to fight. The "rabia" of jealousy had come to his aid, making up for his lack of real drive. When he next appears one April morning in the Prado (IV, 1), he has recoiled so far that he is back under the sway of melancholy, so absorbed in himself that he notices nothing.[32] The interval between the acts has aggravated Fernando's earlier condition; this is one of those mornings after a fitful night described earlier:

> *Fer.:* . . . Sueño tan prodigiosas inuenciones de sombras, que me
>   valiera más estar despierto.
> *Lud.:* Efetos son de la melancolía.
> *Fer.:* Al alba salgo al Prado.
>
> (p. 242)

> *Fer.:* I dream such astounding creations of the shadows that I would do better to stay awake.   *Lud.:* Those are effects of melancholy.
> *Fer.:* At dawn I go out onto the Prado.

At Felipa's insistence, Fernando tells her and the silent, disguised Dorotea his life story. In his melancholy state, after his sleepless night, he is more sorry for himself than resentful of Dorotea. Not knowing he is in her presence, not concerned with saving face, Fernando is adroitly steered by Felipa into an acknowledgment of guilt. The thought of Dorotea's suicide attempt, which had left him unmoved when he first heard of it from Ludovico, now provokes an access of self-reproach:

> Yo erré con pocos años. Yo pudiera ser causa de la muerte de Dorotea, yo priuara a la naturaleza de su mayor milagro y al mundo de su hermosura. Suplícoos, señora mía, que me perdonéis: que se me ha cubierto el corazón y los ojos de agua.   (p. 312)

> I erred because of youth. I could have caused the death of Dorotea, I could have deprived nature of its greatest miracle and the world of its beauty. I entreat you, madam, to pardon me: my heart and eyes are being inundated.

Though we nowhere find in the early compositions such wallowing in guilt as Fernando exhibits here, abetted by his own rhetoric, it does seem at this point as if we were looking through the mature Lope's eyes at the youthful author of certain self-pitying ballads, like the deathbed fantasies

"De una recia calentura" and "Después que acabó Belardo"; or of self-accusatory lyrics like the ballad "Ay amargas soledades" and the song "En un campo florido."[33] Fernando, in the throes here of one of the "amorosos deliquios" ("amorous fainting spells") to which Julio has said he is prone,[34] reminds us of Belardo, victim for different reasons of an "amoroso acidente" ("amorous setback") in the two deathbed ballads. While the acknowledgment of guilt made in the self-accusatory poems is largely conventional, a similarity in attitude is noticeable. Belardo cultivates a sense of guilt, genuine or not, and expatiates on it rhetorically just as Fernando does here, though Belardo does so in verse and Fernando verbally and in action. The analogy makes us aware that there is also an element of posing and morose delectation in Belardo's attitude.

At this juncture, with defenses completely down, having fallen away from the high point of angry retaliation reached at the end of Act III, Fernando will be reconciled with Dorotea. This will mean resuming the relationship on the same terms of dependence as before. "Ponle la cabeça en mi regaço; seré leona que con bramidos le infunda vida" ("Put his head in my lap; I will be a lioness and breathe life into him with my roars") (p. 312), she cries. Thus cradling him, she will resuscitate him as the lioness was said to re-suscitate her stillborn cubs. Dorotea's metaphor may be pedantic but it is neither haphazard nor frivolous. The maternal suggestion is confirmed a little later when Fernando opens his eyes and utters his first words, "Viuo estoi, Dorotea; que como estuuo en tu mano mi muerte, pudo también mi vida" ("I'm alive, Dorotea: as my death was in your hands, so too was my life"); and Julio comments: "Assí la dan en los pechos a los gusanos de seda las damas de Valencia" ("So the ladies of Valencia give life in their bosoms to silkworms") (p. 313).

This episode is the ultimate reworking of those fantasies of reconciliation that gave rise not only to ballads like "Después que acabó Belardo" but to the involution of the Orpheus-Eurydice story in *Belardo el furioso*. Relenting and repenting, the lady restores her ailing lover to health. If the pattern seems reminiscent of courtly tradition, of Amadís wasting away on the Peña Pobre and reviving when Oriana's favor is restored, such parallels are misleading. In the domestic world of this psychological drama, this moment of reconciliation will prove transitory, for Lope knows of no such thing on earth as lasting love. The reconciliation comes off because the changeable hero, caught in one of his characteristic swings of mood, is covering up jealousy with self-reproach. Symptomatically, a new quarrel arises almost at once. The *quid pro quo*'s fly thick and fast, hardened positions are resumed, and all of Fernando's hostile jealousy rises to the surface. Felipa and Julio save the situation and the quarrel is patched over, but the frailty of the patching is plain.

The *tu quoque*'s give the quarrel a recapitulatory character. Themes and attitudes which I have been singling out are succinctly rearticulated. Dorotea clings to her revised version of the original falling-out. Her only offense was "auerte auisado" ("to have given you notice"); she expected Fernando to "matar a quien intentara quitarme de tus ojos" ("Kill anyone trying to take me from your eyes") (p. 314). Fernando invokes *interés*: "Contra oro no hay acero" ("Against gold there is no steel"). The exchange grows more acid and Fernando's jealousy finally explodes into anger when Dorotea calls Don Bela "discreto":

> *Fer.*: ¿Discreto, Dorotea? Vámonos, Iulio, que nos dirá sus gracias.
> *Iul.*: No te leuantes furioso, que no te ha dado causa.
> *Fer.*: Yo sé que es don Bela un necio.
>
> (p. 315)

> *Fer.*: Clever, Dorotea? Let's go, Julio, before she tells us his charms.
> *Jul.*: Don't get up in a rage, she gave you no cause.   *Fer.*: I know that Don Bela is a fool.

The reunion which began with Fernando's eclipse ends by putting him in the stronger position, riding the crest of another wave of anger. Dorotea retrieves herself and the flare-up subsides. Reconciliation begins to move toward a physical consummation and Julio remonstrates: "¡Ea, reyes míos!, que en el Prado y por abril sólo tienen licencia los rozines" ("Come, my fine ones, in April on the Prado only the nags have permission") (p. 316). In the end the reconciliation becomes a glossing over of disharmony by physical desire. So, Lope perhaps now reflected, it would have proved with Elena Osorio.

Fernando and Dorotea spend the morning together at his house while the reader is following the discussions of the literary academy. When Fernando bursts in as these are ending, he is still flushed with victory. If any strains stand out in the profuse rhetorical ornamentation of Act IV, scene 4, they are those of victory and fortune: "vitorias ... de amor," "vitorias del sufrimiento" ("victories of patience") (p. 367). Fernando is dubbed "el Doroteánico" ("the Dorotheanic") because he has "vencido los desdenes de Dorotea" ("conquered the disdain of Dorotea"), just as Scipio was called Africanus for having conquered Africa (p. 370). Along with "mudanças de la fortuna" ("changes of fortune"), Fernando credits his own firmness of will— "milagros son de la firmeza, portentos de la voluntad" ("these are miracles of firmness, prodigies of will") (p. 367)—but he ends significantly on the note of fortune: "Sentaos, y sabréis quán secretos caminos tiene la fortuna, y quánta obligación tengo de escriuir su alabança" ("Sit down and you'll learn what secret ways fortune has and how great is my obligation to write her praise") (p. 370). The paradoxical emphasis on fortune's inscrutable ways at the moment when he is proclaiming the triumph of his own will underscores the ultimate unaccountability of human feelings. In reality, it is lack of will which makes Fernando insist so much on it, while fortune will soon prove his victory as hollow as his rhetoric, one not of love, as Fernando claims, but of vindictiveness. *Vengança*, subject of the chorus that ends the act, is the implication of so much emphasis on victory. In his moment of triumph, Fernando's eloquent expression of what has happened to him misses its meaning. So far from being an embodiment of his creator, he fails to grasp what Lope's vision encompasses, as Ludovico's concluding comment on writing in praise of fortune reveals: "No lo hagáis; que dixo Tulio que alabar la fortuna era necedad, y vituperalla, soberuia" ("Don't do it, for Tully said that praising fortune was folly and censuring her, conceit") (p. 370).

In provoking awareness in Fernando of a change in his feelings, Marfisa now (IV, 8) plays a part analogous to her role in pushing Dorotea into Don Bela's arms. In Act IV, scene 4, fresh from Dorotea's embraces, the exultant Fernando had shown no signs of weariness of the flesh. Following the upbraiding from Marfisa, however, he solemnly vows:

> Iulio, hago testigo al cielo, a quanto ha criado, a ti, a mi honra, a esse poco entendimiento mío, de solicitar con todos la vengança de Dorotea, que al fin vino a despedirme, y pagar a Marfisa tan justa deuda.   (p. 381)

> Julio, I take as witness heaven and all it ever created, you, my honor, what little intelligence I have, that I will apply them all to gaining revenge on Dorotea, who after all came and dismissed me, and will pay the legitimate debt I owe to Marfisa.

He then flatly asserts that his love of Dorotea is dead:

> *Fer.:* Con verla rendida se me ha quitado.
> *Iul.:* Templado basta.
> *Fer.:* Quitado digo, Iulio.
>
> (p. 381)

> *Fer.:* Seeing her capitulate freed me of it.   *Jul.:* Moderated it will do.
> *Fer.:* Freed me, I tell you, Julio.

The three months' suspension of the habit of love, Fernando insists, has broken Dorotea's hold for good: "No me pareció que era Dorotea la que yo imaginaua ausente, no tan hermosa, no tan graciosa, no tan entendida" ("Dorotea didn't seem to me the way I imagined her when I was away, not as beautiful, not as charming, not as intelligent") (p. 381). As Julio foresaw, reconciliation and physical satiety have brought relief from obsession, a sensation so keenly felt that Fernando does not stop to stylize its expression. His psychosomatic imagery is almost prosaic—cleansing, the lifting of a weight. Behind it one senses experienced feelings; it records deliverance from obsession as a physical effect:

> Como quien para que vna cosa se limpie la vaña en agua, assí lo quedé yo en sus lágrimas de mis deseos. Lo que me abrasaua era pensar que estaua enamorada de don Bela, lo que me quitaua el juizio era imaginar la conformidad de sus voluntades. Pero en viendo que estaua forçada, violentada, aflixida, que le afeaua, que le ponía defetos, que maldezía a su madre, que infamaua a Gerarda, que quería mal a Celia y que me llamaua su verdad, su pensamiento, su dueño y su amor primero, assí se me quitó del alma aquel graue peso que me oprimía, que vían otras cosas mis ojos y escuchauan otras palabras mis oídos. (p. 381)

> Like someone who bathes something in water in order to clean it, I was bathed clean of my desires in her tears. What inflamed me was the thought that she was in love with Don Bela, what drove me out of my mind was to imagine the oneness of their wills. But when I saw that she was put upon, forced, distressed, that she ran him down, that she found flaws in him, that she cursed her mother, said terrible things about Gerarda, resented Celia and called me her truth, her one thought, her master and her first love, the dead weight that was oppressing me was lifted from my spirit, my eyes began to see other objects and my ears to hear other words.

Now that he feels relief, Fernando is able to see to the bottom of what has been troubling him: "the thought that she was in love with Don Bela"; not simply supplanting by another but repudiation by her—"la inquietud de imaginarme aborrecido" ("the distress of imagining myself hated"), as he later puts it (p. 405)—precisely as Julio had seen. The key to Fernando's tormented state of mind, as to Lope's wild actions and savage slander in 1587–88, is rejection felt on a sexual level, expressed in the "Now it titillates another master and arouses him" of the sonnet to Vireno and in the "fury at their having taken their love away from them and placed it in someone else" mentioned by Julio.

It can scarcely be the years with Elena which furnished Lope with the experience of psychological liberation so vividly described in this passage. Other junctures of his long love-life are surely remembered here and injected into Fernando's story, especially perhaps his break with Lucía de Salcedo, "the Madwoman";[35] perhaps echoes of intense religious emotionality as well, incongruous as this may seem. In the words "assí se me quitó del alma aquel graue peso que me oprimía" ("the dead weight that was oppressing me was lifted from my spirit"), some trace of the relief afforded by the sacrament of confession seems to have strayed into this profane context, some hint of that easing of spiritual burdens visible at times in the *Soliloquios*.

For all the dramatic finality of his assertions, Fernando has not yet finished with Dorotea. The world may end with a bang in the theater; offstage, Lope has discovered it ends in a whimper and sometimes a chuckle. The stage of disengagement is still to come, unflattering as it may be to the protagonist, and to Lope insofar as Fernando is his private and not merely his artistic property. Before the present act is over, Fernando has begun to waver again. His final words revert to the love-hate formula in a direct paraphrase of Catullus's "Odi et amo" (p. 382). The hold of habit has not been broken as Fernando thinks.

Months later, however, when Fernando recapitulates these same events for César, his opening declaration, "Ya no hay amor de Dorotea" ("There is no love of Dorotea any more") (p. 404), is indeed a fact. We have seen that for the two months between the April day on which the reconciliation took place and Corpus Christi in June his relations with Dorotea had continued. Honor, it will be recalled, proves no obstacle to his accepting both the humiliating role of second lover and gratuities from Dorotea's new riches. Eventually Fernando decides that Dorotea is a bad habit which must be broken. An honor more substantial than vanity or face-saving finally asserts itself and Fernando awakens to the full indignity of occupying needlessly the position of complaisant cuckold.

> Y fue tanto el corrimiento, que me parecía que todos me mirauan,
> y que todos me tenían en poco; como acontece al que ha hecho
> algún delito secretamente, que siempre imagina que hablan dél,
> aunque sea diferente la materia. Y afrentado de mí mismo—que el
> que es hombre de bien no ha menester que le digan lo que haze
> mal para que le salgan colores quando esté más solo—determiné dos

cosas: tomar vengança de la libertad de Dorotea, y curarme en salud.   (p. 407)

And such was my anger that I thought everyone was staring at me and that everyone looked down on me, as happens to someone who has committed a secret crime, who always supposes he is being talked about even though the subject is a different one. And affronted at myself—for he who is a respectable man does not need to be told what he is doing wrong in order to blush, though entirely alone—I resolved on two things: to take revenge for Dorotea's liberties and to try an ounce of prevention.

Honor here is a voice arising from within during an examination of conscience: "Vn día, César, estaua mi honra considerando la baxeza de mi pensamiento" ("One day, César, my honor was considering the baseness of my standards"), Fernando begins, and the whole passage, as we have observed earlier, cuts down to the raw confessional substratum of the *acción en prosa*.[36]

The delayed response to the indignity of sharing Elena with Perrenot, the anger that produced the satires are rediscovered here, and there are traces of the morbid touchiness ("I thought everyone was staring at me and that everyone looked down on me") which Lope manifests in the trial record. But an aging priest, not an impetuous young man, is speaking, and Fernando acknowledges his own unworthiness more genuinely than the youthful Lope had ever done. The anger ("corrimiento") which Fernando feels, unlike Lope's in 1587–88, is directed inward, at himself, since the affront to his honor is acknowledged to be self-inflicted. But the septuagenarian Lope draws away from Fernando and leaves him to act on his insight only to the limited extent that his own egocentric nature dictates. The result of the examination of conscience, one more premeditated and less scandalous than the virulent libels, will be no more edifying: a "diligencia" ("plan of action"), not a crime, a plan both curative and retaliatory—by attaching himself to Marfisa Fernando will detach himself from Dorotea.[37] It is the fixation of habit, not of passion, which he is now combatting; he has the additional spur of resentment of Don Bela, and fortune comes to his assistance as well. The extent to which Fernando has helped himself to fall out of love exemplifies, however, the limited degree to which Lope feels it possible to develop a human art of curing love.

Nevertheless, even as Fernando celebrates his triumph, through the reservations of the other characters Lope suggests its pettiness and questions its definitiveness. Julio observes acutely, when Fernando denounces Dorotea, that he is still in a state of "desesperación amorosa" ("amorous despair") (p. 401): true recovery would bring indifference. César, too, suggests that vindictiveness may mask love: "Guardaos no os engañe el gusto de la vengança y la mal curada herida reuerdezca" ("Be careful that the pleasure of vengeance does not deceive you and the badly healed wound flare up again") (p. 416). Fernando's attachment to Marfisa never seems more than perfunctory—"mi obligación a muger tan principal como Marfisa" ("my obligation to so outstanding a woman as Marfisa") (p. 415)—a debt of gratitude: "Con el mayor [amor] que puedo le agradezco auer sido el templo de mi remedio" ("With the greatest [love] that I can, I thank her for having been the temple of my salvation") (p. 416). Subsequently César calls into question the entire strategy of manipulated shifts in love: "Y para que no boluáis a Dorotea, no os enlacéis con Marfisa; que no sale del peligro el que entra en mayor peligro" ("And to avoid returning to Dorotea, don't become involved with Marfisa, for one doesn't escape danger by seeking greater danger") (p. 444).

Down to the end of La Dorotea Lope shows emotions trailing away unevenly, protracted by slow-paced routine. The neat contours which the expression of afectos (emotions) acquires in literary and rhetorical usage are blurred, the ready formulas in comedias and even in the letters to the Duke of Sessa prove inadequate, Fernando's clear-cut assertions are repeatedly undermined by his experience. Fernando finally acknowledges, in a moment of truth, that "la paz de mis pensamientos" ("my mental tranquillity") depends on his making a complete break and entering the king's service as a soldier of the Armada (p. 442). It will take positive action in a sphere transcending the personal, a manly role, not a mere shuffling of mistresses, to cure Fernando. "Vamos a oír missa, donde pidáis a Dios su diuino auxilio para reformar vuestros passos, con que os libraréis de todo" ("Let's go to hear mass, so that you may ask God's divine assistance in mending your ways; you will thereby become free of the whole thing"), César advises him on their final exit (p. 444). Again it is an old priest speaking, suggesting without sanctimoniousness that Fernando in the last analysis belongs in the hands of God and king, not in those of fortune.

One is still moved to ask whether the sense of liberation Fernando experiences on finally achieving indifference to Dorotea is merely youthful callousness. Unlike other versions of the experience, La Dorotea furnishes an answer in the negative. For here Fernando's emancipation from Dorotea is simply the condition for coming into his manhood; it is this for which he has been struggling without knowing it. The force of habit (costumbre) has early made him accept Dorotea's dominant role, enjoy her indulging of his egocentricity, welcome the maternal overtones of her solicitude.[38] Unadventurously he has settled for the familiar in preference to the novel. The foregoing analysis has emphasized Fernando's anxiety over the possibility of losing Dorotea. But as one surveys the full cycle of Fernando's feelings, it appears that his fear of losing her conceals its opposite—a desire to free himself from her. Of this Fernando is not originally aware, nor does the thought occur to Julio. But in the quarrel scene, an unrecognized wish to emancipate himself compounds the irony of Fernando's indifference: in hiding what he thinks he feels, he is inadvertently revealing something deeper. Dorotea seems to sense this: "¿Pues cómo, si te digo que se acaba nuestra amistad, tan fácilmente te has consolado?" ("But when I tell you that our friendship is over, how can you take it so lightly?") (p. 100). At the end of the quarrel Fernando suddenly veers from the subject at hand and bursts out:

> *Fer.:* . . . Si no fuera por ti, yó pudiera estar casado, con más oro que el que te han traído. Pero aún no he cumplido veinte y dos años.
> *Dor.:* Y yo, ¿tendré quinientos?
> *Fer.:* ¿Dígolo yo por esso, o porque, si Dios quiere, me queda vida para valerme della? Que de diez y siete llegué a tus ojos, y Iulio y yo dexamos los estudios, más oluidados de Alcalá que lo estuuieron de Grecia los soldados de Vlisses.
>
> (p. 101)

> *Fer.:* If it weren't for you, I could be married and have more gold than they brought you. But I'm not yet twenty-two years old.
> *Dor.:* Am I five hundred then?   *Fer.:* Am I saying it for that or because, if God wills, I still have life left to make good use of? For at seventeen I came into your life and Julio and I gave up our studies and put Alcalá further from our minds than Ulysses' soldiers put Greece.

The unaffected spontaneity of Fernando's words—"Dígolo yo por esso, o porque . . . ?" ("Am I saying it for that or because . . . ?")—points to the genuineness of the exasperation they express. When eventually Fernando becomes convinced that he has not been repudiated, he reacts against his subjugation. The anger that pierces his studied composure during the quarrel is resentment at being kept from a man's estate: profession, marriage, wealth, a worthy life ("vida para valerme della," "life to make good use of") by captivity at the hands of Dorotea. Though not free of after-effects, Fernando is on the threshold of emancipation when last seen.

The situation is far different with Dorotea. Her immediate response to reconciliation has been an exultation impervious to the carpings and sarcasm that greet her return from Fernando's quarters (IV, 6). She is now confident of his love, determined to retain it and to discard Don Bela, in spite of her mother and Gerarda. "No quiero Indias, ni cautiuar mis años. ¿Qué oro, qué diamantes como mi gusto?" ("I don't want any Indies, nor to enslave my years. What gold, what diamonds can equal my own satisfaction?"), she tells herself (p. 374), echoing the voice overruled three months earlier.[39] Now she ignores a flash of clairvoyance, the only echo of the voice she had listened to:

> Oy, Felipa, ni pienso llorar, ni reñir; que, aunque los estremos del placer suelen ser los principios del pesar, haré agrauio a mi alma si con la memoria de tanto bien estoi triste en mi vida. (p. 373)

> Today, Felipa, I have no intention of either weeping or quarreling, for, although an extreme of pleasure is usually a beginning of pain, I will be wronging my own soul if with the memory of so much happiness I am ever sad again.

The intense emotional impact of reconciliation crowds out Dorotea's intuition of the future and leaves her as blindly exultant as Fernando two scenes earlier. At this peak of emotion all is clear-cut and Dorotea envisages a complete break with Don Bela. But as Fernando first misreads his own triumph (IV, 4), then the extent of his liberation from Dorotea (IV, 8), so Dorotea underestimates her bondage to *interés*. Old ways reassert themselves, there is no break with Don Bela: "Bien quisiera Dorotea quererme solo. Pero ya no podía ser, ni el interés la dexaua" ("Dorotea would have been only too happy to love me all by myself. But that was no longer possible, nor would her self-interest allow it"), Fernando explains later (p. 408). She is now as implicated herself as are her mother and Gerarda. The self-sufficient and all-absorbing character of their relationship is compromised on both sides. The rivals are permanently in the picture and the days of this love are clearly numbered, though it drags on out of inertia. "Conocía Dorotea menos viuos mis afectos" ("Dorotea could see my emotions becoming less ardent"), Fernando relates (p. 408), but she believes the reason is simply "el agrauio que resultaua en mi [Fernando's] honor de la amistad injusta de don Bela" ("the wrong that the unjustified friendship with Don Bela did to my [Fernando's] honor") (p. 408). A mix-up of love-notes sets her straight. On Corpus Christi Day, as Fernando wears Marfisa's blouse, Dorotea

> con súbita passión de zelos baxó a la calle, y . . . llegó adonde yo iba con otros amigos siguiendo a Marfisa, y oluidando a Dorotea.

Referiros el coloquio era cansaros. Habló con zelos, respondí sin amor;
fuésse corrida y quedé vengado.   (p. 416)

in a sudden fit of jealousy came down to the street and . . . over to
where I was walking with several friends, following Marfisa and
forgetting Dorotea. I won't bore you by relating the exchange.
She spoke from jealousy, I answered without love; she went off
indignant and I had my revenge.

In all this final stage, an ironic view of the limitations of human vision is
manifest. Intense emotion blinds the lovers, habit and routine lull them. Their
emotional tempo is too slow or too fast; they cling to what is over or rush
ahead of events. They see the handwriting on the wall but do not read it.
Meanwhile emotional relationships go on evolving at their own pace and
sooner or later individual wills are forced into step.

Though Fernando's story of himself and Dorotea has been heard out to
what for him is the end, Lope, as we know, is not yet done with his heroine,
whom he reintroduces in Act V, scene 4, and presents in seven additional
scenes, tracing as long as possible her responses to the break with Fernando,
until, by setting up the fortuitous deaths of Don Bela and Gerarda he calls a
halt. The concentration on Dorotea is broken only by the scene devoted to
the horoscope of Fernando's future (V, 8). His heroine thus occupies Lope's
particular attention at the end as at the beginning. Instead of the effect of
increasingly sharp focus produced by the early scenes, however, the concluding ones—by their multiplicity, their brevity, and the ceaseless comings
and goings about Dorotea of the other characters—suggest restlessness and
fragmentation, the formal correlative to disintegration.[40]

We must now consider the implications of the foregoing reading of the
story of Fernando and Dorotea with respect to the broad aspects of love
mentioned earlier. We may profitably view the question of love's staying-
power with reference to habit, routine, and familiarity versus novelty and
change, to subjugation versus emancipation; that of the admixture of other
emotions with reference to jealousy, anger, antipathy, and hate; that of self-
love in terms of vanity, façade, and honor; that of the dissolution of love in
terms of aggrievement, new attachments, revenge, desamor—being out of
love—and forgetting.

The rest of Lope's writing, public and private, as well as sources beyond
Lope, will serve as points of reference in this discussion. For the last three
aspects mentioned—revenge, desamor, forgetting—analogues are easier to

find outside the *comedia* than in it for the reason, noted by Amezúa (*Epistolario*, II, 644), that love is usually triumphant on Lope's stage. Moreover, even in the nondramatic productions there is not much emphasis on such aspects. Since they also raise questions of moral evaluation linked with the total meaning of the *acción en prosa*, I shall leave them for my concluding chapter.

An ambivalence rooted in Lope's nature, which I noted at the outset, leads him to stress from the beginning of the *acción en prosa* the conflicting emotional claims on the characters of the familiar and the novel, a dilemma given special point by the stress in the work on the routine and everyday aspects of living. Variety and uniformity, vital as well as esthetic principles, run counter to each other in Dorotea's first self-examination (I, 4). Her mother's jibes at her shabby dress have clearly sunk in:

> Fernando no tiene más que para sus galas. Mira las otras mugeres con ellas, ya le parecerán mejor; que el adorno y la riqueça añaden hermosura y estimación, y la pobreça del trage descuida los ojos y haze que vna muger cada día parezca la misma; y la diferencia causa nouedad y despierta el deseo.   (p. 79)

> Fernando has only enough for his fancy wardrobe. He looks at other women dressed the same way and they no doubt seem more appealing, for ornamentation and richness contribute to beauty and high regard. Poverty in dress lets the eyes wander and makes a woman seem the same every day; difference causes novelty and arouses desire.

Dorotea's wavering is presented with sympathy by an understanding Lope. In the context of human relationships variety all too easily becomes variability and inconstancy (this is what Dorotea fears) or goes to painful extremes, while uniformity may turn into sameness, a force of habit that could equally put an end to love. The first drawback sometimes looms larger for Lope: "Sin duda es el mexor de todos [los estados] el pacífico . . . ," he writes the Duke of Sessa, "porque si bien es verdad, y yo lo tengo escrito, que amor ha de estar dudoso, tanbién es fuerte caso padezer por aumentar el gusto" ("No doubt the best [situation] of all is a pacific one . . . because while it is true and I have so written, that love must be unsure of itself, it is also a terrible thing to have to suffer just to increase one's enjoyment").[41] But Lope had indeed written endlessly of the need for a pinch of what he calls "la pimienta de los celos" ("the pepper of jealousy") to keep love fresh and had also told the Duke of Sessa with characteristic sensuousness:

"No tiene salsa el amor como las pesadumbres" ("Love has no sauce like disagreements").[42] Like Dorotea he certainly saw variety in dress and *galas* as one way of counteracting routine:

> . . . Aquel estar
> siempre en una misma acción
> no mueve la inclinación
> que el traje suele obligar.
> Ver siempre de una manera
> a una mujer es cansarse . . .
>
> . . . .
>
> Porque el variar también
> da novedad a el amante.[43]

> Always to go around the same way doesn't produce the appeal that dress arouses. To see a woman always the same is to become bored . . . for variation provides the lover also with novelty.

Dorotea's idealistic reliance on the unassailability of their love has made her neglect the enticements that could have helped to preserve it. Even so, for Lope, habit is a double-edged sword; it would in any case have doomed their love affair after five years. Lope had thoroughly verified in his own experience and often repeated to the Duke of Sessa the originally Aristotelian view, long since become a commonplace, of habit as second nature (*Ethics*, sec. 1152a), hence very hard to oppose: "Yo no querría que Vex.ª de tantos actos hiziesse vn háuito, como dicen los philósophos, que no se le pudiesse desnudar cuando quisiesse" ("I would not want Your Excellency to form from so many acts a habit, as the philosophers say, which you couldn't remove when you wished").[44] In the emotional life, the effect of *hábito* or *costumbre del trato* ("a habit of association"), as far as Lope is concerned, is to strengthen the hold of love for better or for worse (more often for the latter). It may in the end take the place of love and ultimately provoke a rebellion against its own tyranny. *Hábito* often suggests a habitual sexual relationship unconnected with romantic or idealized love, and even a kind of straitjacket. One can point to places in Lope's production in which one or the other aspect prevails. Habit not in conflict with love: "[un remedio] para un amor a quien el trato ha puesto tan estrecho hábito . . . fuera impossible" ("[a cure] for a love which constant contact has clothed in so tight a habit . . . would be impossible").[45] Habit extinguishing love:

> Amor que comienza ingrato
> y el trato le da valor,

> no se ha de llamar amor,
> sino costumbre del trato.[46]

Love that starts out thankless and that association gives strength to
should not be called love but habitual contact.

Insofar as the love of Fernando and Dorotea is star-crossed and has lasted
five years, habit does not appear to be working against it. But beneath the
surface this has in fact been occurring and their love is overripe for dissolution. Julio, quoting Lope himself, immediately after the quarrel points this
out:

> *Iul.:* Amor tiene fácil la entrada y difícil la salida.
> *Fer.:* Mucho me ha de costar el deshazerme de la tenacidad de la
>   costumbre.
> *Iul.:* Assí dixo vn poeta:
>   Pintarle de colores como a loco,
>   y no llamarle amor, sino costumbre.

(p. 113)

> *Jul.:* It is easy for love to enter but hard for it to leave.   *Fer.:* It is
> going to be very hard for me to get free of the hold of habit.
> *Jul.:* So a poet said: "Deck it out in motley, like a fool, / and call
> it not love but habit."

Fernando here foresees accurately the difficulty of breaking the *costumbre del
trato*, but he will later revert to the kind of panache Lope expressed apropos
of his own youth both in one of the sonnets discussed earlier and in the
already quoted words of a letter of 1616 to the Duke of Sessa: "I can do
what I wish with myself and so in my youth I never worried much about
being in love since I knew it was in my power to forget."[47] Fernando
declares to Julio with finality, after the reconciliation with Dorotea, that his
love of her is dead, although in fact it will take him two more months of
real effort to break the force of habit, as he subsequently explains to César:
"Yo no quise esperar a la naturaleça por desconfiança de la costumbre. Y
assí me puse en manos de la diligencia" ("I decided not to wait for nature
because I was wary of habit. And so I put my trust in a concerted effort") (p.
407).

   In the end Fernando's instinct, like his creator's, is to throw off whatever
straitjacket restricts his emotional freedom—and such restriction, as we have
seen, is the ultimate effect of the relationship with Dorotea. Until the final
stages of his love for Marta de Nevares, Lope's eroticism was predominantly

acquisitive, and Lope no doubt felt confined and restive once he had enjoyed at length the satisfactions of fulfillment. Though not a Don Juan—Lope's interest is not in conquest but in forming attachments, however brief they may prove—he is polygamous and fickle by nature. Even while he is devoting himself selflessly to the ailing Marta de Nevares in 1628 (as he had years earlier to Juana de Guardo), he is capable of writing cynically to his patron: "Siempre fui de parezer que nunca las mugeres nos hazen mayor bien que quando nos agrauian, pues con eso sale la voluntad de cautiberio, el gusto de soledad y la onra de peligro" ("I have always been of the opinion that the greatest good women can do is to wrong us, because as a result the will emerges from captivity, pleasure from single-mindedness, and honor from danger").[48] One sees here clearly that for Lope in his private life "cautiverio" (captivity) is equivalent to sensual bondage, a far cry from the conventional courtly connotation of subjugation willingly and lovingly embraced.[49] Fernando's accusation against Dorotea that her love has held him down, has prevented his going on to marriage and a career, and the cold satisfaction he also takes in emancipating himself from her undoubtedly carry to an extreme a deep-seated impulse of Lope's nature.

The fate of Dorotea, on the other hand, exemplifies the iron grip of habit on a member of the weaker sex. What she misses in Fernando, she tells Gerarda, is "su talle, su entendimiento, sus caricias, sus amores; que de todos estos actos se haze al alma vn hábito tan estrecho que es impossible quitarle sin romperle" ("his figure, his intellect, his caresses, his love, for of all these acts so tight a habit is formed around the soul that it is impossible to remove it without breaking it") (p. 433). The image, including the play on *hábito* (habit as a garment that cannot be removed) is the same as in Lope's admonition to the Duke of Sessa but Dorotea, whose personal weakness compounds the frailty of her sex, has suffered the fate against which the Duke was warned. No love remains stable, Lope seems to be saying, except one which has moved to the spiritual plane on which his love for Marta de Nevares now rests. This is the meaning he now reads into his youthful experience.[50]

Once Fernando's conduct is seen as a movement toward emancipation, uneven but persistent, other elements in the depiction of love stand out more clearly. In the first place, Fernando's view of his emotional state as a compound of love and hate. Fernando backs this up in Act III by quoting Xenophon, it will be recalled, and in the last words of Act IV, by paraphrasing Catullus's "Odi et amo":

De amor y aborrecimiento
tan igual veneno tomo,

que si me preguntan cómo,
no sé más de lo que siento.

(p. 382)

From love and hate I take such equal poison that if I am asked
how, I know only what I feel.

These precedents have clearly affected his way of articulating his conflicting
feelings. The conjunction of love and hate belongs also within the Petrarchan
tradition of cultivated paradox, though such a combination is clearly not
itself Petrarchan. (The Petrarchan line "Et o in odio me stesso ed amo
altrui" ["And I feel hate for myself and love for others"] significantly
becomes "A un mismo tiempo amo y aborrezco" ["I love and hate at the
same time"] in the adaptation by Lope.) [51] But it was probably the elaboration
of the paradox in Ficino's commentary on the *Symposium* that most struck
Lope:

> Ferinus et humanus amor sine indignatione esse numquam potest.
> Quis illi non indignetur, qui ipsi abstulerit animum? Ut enim pre
> ceteris grata libertas, ita servitus onerosa. Itaque formosos odis
> simul et amas, odis tamquam fures et homicidas, tamquam specula
> caelesti fulgore micantia, mirari cogeris, et amare . . . Cum hoc esse
> non potes, qui te perdit, qui enecat. Sine hoc non potes vivere . . .
> Hunc fugere cupis . . . Huic etiam cupis herere.[52]

> Animal and human love can never exist without anger. Who would
> not be angry at one who deprived him of his soul? For as freedom is
> desirable above all things, so enslavement is unbearable. Hence you
> love and hate beautiful persons at the same time; you hate them as
> thieves and homicides; as mirrors sparkling with a celestial glitter
> you are forced to look at them and love them . . . You cannot abide
> with one who destroys you, who kills you. Without him you
> cannot live . . . You wish to flee him . . . You likewise wish to cling
> to him.

Only a sublime love will be able to escape the admixture of hatred inevitably present in love on a human plane. In the early ballads the promptings
of his violent nature had led Lope to the love-hate paradox, which he was
content to express without penetration. In Ficino he now finds it not only
elaborated but viewed in terms of a struggle between freedom and enslavement which he could readily understand. The insight this gives into his
own temperament—much more subtle than the earlier quoted formula
tossed off at one point in the correspondence with the Duke of Sessa: "I

was born at two extremes, namely, loving and hating; I've never known any mid-point"[53]—is carried over into the depiction of Fernando. In contrast to most Lopean protagonists, Fernando feels love and hate simultaneously rather than consecutively.[54] Such embracing of paradox distresses Julio, who opposes to it the more conventional view: "Eso es por lo que yo temo tu juizio y más quisiera que amaras o aborrecieras determinadamente" ("That's why I fear for your sanity and I would prefer you to love or hate one at a time") (p. 251).[55]

It is hardly necessary to remark that Lope's insight into the coexistence of love and hate in erotic passion is in advance of his time. One of the most fundamental aspects of personality for modern psychiatric theory is the principle of polarity according to which emotional trends appear in pairs and love and hate are directed toward the same person at the same time. "The more one loves another, the more the narcissistic nucleus of the personality hates the loved object."[56] While in normal circumstances one of these emotions is deeply buried, in morbid conditions—and such is Fernando's—both parts may become conscious, repressed hatred readily breaking through when one feels betrayed by someone. The admixture of hatred in love is at heart a manifestation of anger and resentment and this in turn is intimately bound up with jealousy. This constellation of emotions so characteristic of Lope, present in the ballads and prominent in *Belardo el furioso*, is now examined, analyzed, and illuminated as never before.

In regard to his own irascibility, Lope, with his customary mixture of impetuosity and self-observation, had taken full note of how combustible the "gunpowder of anger" was in him.[57] Very early, at the thought of Elena in the correspondence with Liñán, he stops himself short with these lines:

Llevado me ha el enojo por la posta,
pues hablando con vos de mi remedio,
a destruir salí como langosta.
Pongamos al enojo tierra en medio . . .[58]

Anger has gotten the better of me, since in speaking to you of my cure, I lit out about me like a swarm of locusts. Let's leave anger behind . . .

Amezúa observes (*Epistolario*, II, 250) that the irritability visible in the *Proceso*, which in 1618 still causes Lope's brother-in-law, Luis Rosicler, to remark on his "improvisae iracundiae impetus" ("sudden bursts of rage"), eventually is tempered and controlled and that by the time Pérez de

Montalbán meets him, he may not be so inaccurate in calling him "blando, perdonador, templado, humildísimo" ("mild, forgiving, moderate, very humble"). Lope unquestionably struggled harder against irascibility, resentment, and hating after he entered the priesthood; the struggle can be surmised in his private letters:

> En el estado que estoy, ni puedo aborrecer, ni tomar venganza; y aunque desto vltimo me guarde, de lo primero pareze ynposible . . .
>
> Yo pienso rogar a las canas que me enseñen donde vive la prudencia, pues dizen que son sus apossentadoras; aunque la yra sienpre haze que se yerre el camino de hallarla y el bien y descanso de posehcrla.[59]
>
> In my present state, I can neither hate nor take revenge; and even if I refrain from the latter, to do so from the former seems impossible . . .
>
> I intend to ask my grey hairs to show me where prudence lives, since it is said that they are in charge of its lodging, though anger always causes one to miss the way to finding it and the satisfaction and peace of possessing it.

Yet the violence of Lope's assaults on Roque Hernández, the husband of Marta de Nevares, in the same correspondence, and the anger so evident in the eclogue "Filis" against his daughter, Antonia Clara, and the man with whom she eloped in 1634, show that the outcome of the struggle was not as decisive as might be gathered from the panegyrics penned at the time of his death. In any case, the conflict brought this strain in his nature into sharper focus for him and gave him a clearer insight into the case of Fernando, in whom, in contrast to his creator, anger remains for the most part submerged and smoldering and encounters no opposition from the will. Unlike Lope himself or the protagonists of his plays, Fernando is a case of resentment accumulated and repressed and therefore almost pathological in its effects.

In recounting his life in *La Filomena*, Lope connects anger with love as a matter of course:

> dándome aliento los juveniles años,
> canté de amor las iras,
> verdades y mentiras.
>
> (*OS*, II, 451)
>
> my youthful years spurring me on, I sang love's rages, truths, and lies.

That Lope saw Fernando's case as an exacerbation of a common phenomenon is plain from a passage like the following from *Las bizarrías de Belisa* (1634):

> . . . Ira y amor son lo mismo,
> porque como es imposible
> que haya amor sin celos, y ellos
> venganzas de agravios piden,
> es fuerza que entre la ira
> adonde el amor la admite,
> como se ve por ejemplos
> de esposos y amantes firmes,
> que mataron lo que amaban
> por celos . . .[60]

> Anger and love are the same thing because as it is impossible for love to exist without jealousy and this demands vengeance for wrongs done, anger necessarily comes in where love admits it, as can be seen from the instances of husbands and steadfast lovers who killed the ones they loved out of jealousy . . .

Despite the hyperbolic equating of love and anger here, the basic point is their concomitance. This Dorotea herself underscores when she makes the observation (ultimately of Thomistic origin) that "la ira y el amor son nuestras dos passiones principales" ("anger and love are our two principal passions") (p. 448).[61]

As for jealousy, Fernando links it to hatred in the already cited reply to Julio:

> *Fer.:* Privation is a silly argument here.
> *Iul.:* If that isn't it, then jealousy will do.
> *Fer.:* How can I love her for the thing I hate her for?

(p. 250)

Jealousy is also linked to anger, as already seen, on the authority of Xenophon. This conjunction is further stressed in Dorotea's reaction as Fernando rides past her house without looking up—"¡Qué coléricos son los zelos!" ("What an angry thing jealousy is!") (p. 126)—and in the definition "poderosa ira" ("powerful rage"), which stands out among the many given in the Coro de Zelos (Chorus of Jealousy) (p. 287).

The fundamental characteristic of jealousy is the inacceptability of being surpassed by another; it is this which lies at the heart of Fernando's conflict. It is helpful in this connection to refer to the Thomistic distinction between constructive envy (zealousness, emulation) and the destructive kind (jealousy), a distinction familiar enough to the moral climate of the age, as Cervantes' allusion in the prologue to the Second Part of *Don Quixote* shows. Refining Gregory's definition of jealousy as "sorrow for another's good" ("tristitia in alienis bonis"), St. Thomas says that while sorrow can only refer to the self, jealousy ("zelus invidiae") arises "through one's being sorry for . . . another's good, considered, however, as one's own evil." He states also: "Recollection of past goods in so far as we have had them, causes pleasure; in so far as we have lost them, causes sorrow; and in so far as others have them, causes envy; because that, above all, seems to take away from our own glory."[62] One could hardly find a better statement of Fernando's case, and not only of Fernando's: St. Thomas's analysis also happens to illuminate sharply the operation of jealousy in Fernando's creator. Lope confesses to the Duke of Sessa in 1617 that at the thought of giving up Marta de Nevares "me muero de çelos de suçessor" ("I die of jealousy of a successor"). Earlier (1614), we find this penetrating retrospective self-analysis:

> Yo, quando en mis tiempos, trataua en esta mercadería de la
> voluntad, me rendía tanto, que como yo no pensaua en otra cossa,
> assí no quería que lo que yo amaba pensase, viesse, hablasse con otro
> que conmigo, y eran estos çelos tan desatinada pasión en mí, que
> llegaua a tenerlos de mí mismo: porque si me favorecían mucho,
> ymaginaua que lo fingían, o que yo podía ser otro, o parecerme
> entonces a alguna cosa que le agradaua o de que en otro tiempo
> había tenido gusto.[63]

> In my time when I dealt in this merchandise of the flesh, I
> surrendered myself so completely that, as I thought of nothing else,
> so I did not want the one I loved to think of, see, speak to anyone
> but me, and this jealousy was such an insane passion with me that I
> even became jealous of myself: because if I was particularly favored,
> I imagined that it was put on, or that I might be someone else or
> resemble at that point something that she liked or that she had once
> taken pleasure in.

We clearly touch here a permanent strain in Lope's nature. The self-characterization in Fernando's remark, apropos of jealousy, "Yo te confiesso, Iulio, que en mi tierno y amoroso natural tiene esta passión más fuerça" ("I admit, Julio, that this passion has the greatest power over my soft and amorous nature") (p. 112), points toward his creator as much as himself. Indeed, Fernando's characterization of his nature sounds forced on his lips;

it suggests the viewpoint of maturity projected back upon "tender" youth, as in the letter of 1614, though in fact underscoring a feature of Lope's affective make-up that would survive as long as his libido was active.

Lope's fundamental conviction that jealousy is a spur to love, so long as jealousy is without foundation in fact, helps account for the enormous role this passion plays in his works for the theater. The conflicts resulting from refusal to accept being surpassed or displaced by a rival make it a powerful dramatic resource.[64] But in *La Dorotea*, where there is almost no active clash between rivals, the emphasis shifts to the obsessive character of the emotion and its arbitrary possessiveness, the latter an aspect occasionally treated by Lope elsewhere—in *El perro del hortelano* (*The Dog in the Manger*), for example. The extreme degree of possessiveness characteristic of Fernando's jealousy has no explicit analogues in other treatments of the material, however. If Lope felt something similar in 1587–88, he probably did not pause to reflect on it, despite the fact that such possessiveness is implicit in his concern with the motif of the stolen or straying sheep. In the autobiographical account of *La hermosura de Angélica*, jealousy does indeed cause passion to revive:

> Zeloso yo, como en su fin la vela,
> vuelvo en mi fuego muerto a alzar la llama . . .[65]

> Feeling jealousy, I, like a candle at its end, send a flame up again from my dead fire . . .

But this is jealousy acting as a spur to love. The peculiarity of *La Dorotea* is the suggestion that, in its possessiveness, jealousy may actually take the place of love. The closest analogue to this relation between the two emotions comes in a letter of 1617 in which Lope thus analyzes his patron's feelings: "El [amor] que tiene no lo es sino unos çelos rebozados, como Jacob con las manos de Esau, y porque lo que trata no sea de otro, permaneze a tanta costa suya [*sic*] en su propósito" ("The [love] you feel isn't such but jealousy in disguise, like Jacob's of Esau's hands, and in order that the object of your attachment should not become someone else's, you are determined to keep it yours at so great a price").[66] Rather than as an object of love, the person in dispute is valued as a prize, a possession. As such, he or she is an enhancement of self and loss of that person is painful because it means a diminution of self. Fernando, who speaks proudly of Dorotea as "so rich a possession," is stung by her defection as by some physical loss.[67]

Lope is too preoccupied with bringing out the finer nuances of feeling and psychology to allow so clear-cut a separation of jealousy from love to stand wholly unqualified subsequently. Some passion does persist in Fernando, as we know, passion strong enough to survive for a while the clearing up of his obsession, just as passion had persisted earlier even when the *costumbre* of intimacy and carnal contact threatened it. It is a matter of shifting proportions in a total blend. Lope's neat analysis of his patron's state suffices for the common adventure of a debauched noble; when exploring human feelings in depth, as in *La Dorotea*, Lope does not so sweepingly oversimplify.

The obverse side of Fernando's jealousy is simply self-love. Of this St. Thomas, agreeing with Augustine, says: "Well ordered self-love, by which man desires a fitting good for himself, is right and natural; but it is inordinate self-love, leading to the contempt of God, that Augustine puts as the cause of sin."[68] It is evident that in Fernando self-love is of the second variety and that it affects his sense of honor as much as his jealousy, the point of contact being excessive zealousness. Vis-à-vis Dorotea, honor is a determination not to lose face, just as vis-à-vis the rival jealousy is an obsession with being outdone: "¡O mi Dorotea! ¿Cómo pudiste ser tan cruel conmigo? ¿Cómo me dixiste tales palabras que fue forçosa obligación de mi honra perderte para siempre?" ("Oh my Dorotea! How could you be so cruel to me? How could you say such words to me that my honor was inexorably bound to lose you forever?"), exclaims Fernando under Dorotea's windows in Act III, scene 7 (p. 272).[69] For once, Lope does not hesitate to pass moral judgment: Julio is the intermediary through whom he exposes the hollowness of this sort of honor:

> *Fer.:* Yo hago lo que manda mi honra.
> *Iul.:* ¡Qué amor tan honrado, para ser libre!
> *Fer.:* No toda la honra está sujeta a leyes.
> *Iul.:* La que no está sujeta a ellas no es honra.
> *Fer.:* Los hombres hazen honra de lo que quieren.
> *Iul.:* Vn hombre ha de querer lo que es justo para ser honra.
>
> (p. 112)

> *Fer.:* I do what my honor demands. *Jul.:* What an honorable love, free and all! *Fer.:* Not all honor is subject to laws. *Jul.:* That which isn't subject to them isn't honor. *Fer.:* Men make honor of what they wish. *Jul.:* A man has to wish what is right for it to be honor.

The arbitrary, egotistic, and antisocial character of Fernando's sense of honor is here made explicit. The passage brings to mind St. Thomas's statement in his discussion of self-love as the root of every sin: "Now the fact that anyone desires a temporal good inordinately, is due to the fact that he loves himself inordinately, for to wish anyone some good is to love him."[70] Fernando's honor is fundamentally *amour propre*. Until it tardily awakens to a sense of personal dignity, it does not save Fernando from the compromising situation of surreptitiously accepting gratuities from the benefactions Don Bela has bestowed on Dorotea.

The depiction of Fernando in terms of self-love carries overtones of narcissism.[71] Gerarda refers to him sarcastically as a "gentil Narciso" ("fine Narcissus") (p. 423), using a term then current in the sense of hyper-refined or dandified young man, and as a "lindo" ("fop"). Lope associated the second term as well as the first with what he liked to call by its Greek name "philautia"—"self-love."[72] The connotations of both for Lope may be gauged from two sonnets in the *Rimas de Burguillos*. Addressing a *lindo's* lady in "Descriue un lindo deste tiempo" ("He describes a fop of this age"), he writes:

> Mas es forçoso lástima teneros,
> porque sabed que tanto amor se tiene,
> que no le ha de sobrar para quereros.[73]

> But one must pity you, because you must know that he's so in love with himself that he has none left over to love you.

In another sonnet he writes:

> Quien no sabe de Amor, viua entre fieras,
> quien no ha querido bien fieras espante,
> o si es Narciso de sí mismo amante,
> retrátese en las aguas lisongeras . . .[74]

> Anyone who knows nothing of love should live among wild beasts, anyone who has not been in love should frighten beasts away, or if he is a Narcissus in love with himself, let him do his own portrait in the flattering waters . . .

That exaggerated self-love could be equivalent to madness for Lope is evident from a much earlier passage in a *comedia*:

> *Liseno:* ¿Era amante?
> *Belardo:*   No era amante.
> *Liseno:* ¿Ni Narciso?
> *Belardo:*   Ni Narciso.
> *Liseno:* ¿Ni celoso?

> *Belardo:*   Ni celoso.
> *Liseno:*   ¿Ni poeta?
> *Belardo:*   Ni poeta.
>   ¿De qué puede estar furioso?[75]

Liseno: Was he a lover? *Belardo:* He wasn't a lover. *Liseno:* Nor a
Narcissus? *Belardo:* Nor a Narcissus. *Liseno:* Nor jealous?
Belardo: Nor jealous. *Liseno:* Nor a poet? *Belardo:* Nor a poet.
What can have caused his madness?

Lope seems to grow increasingly sensitive to self-love and to see it more
decidedly as a form of moral aberration toward the end of his life, an
attitude which is perhaps the natural corollary to his earnest pursuit of a
Neo-Platonic amatory ideal.

Dorotea's rueful reflection that "Fernando no tiene más que para sus
galas" ("Fernando only has enough for his fancy wardrobe") (p. 79)—
while she must forego hers, for his sake—hints at his *philautia* from the
start. But it is Fernando's own description of his moody mornings in Madrid,
in which we see him morosely savoring his suffering, that gives the clearest
view of the self as Narcissus: "Al alba salgo al Prado, o me voy al río,
donde sentado en su orilla estoy mirando el agua, dándole imaginaciones
que lleue para que nunca bueluan" ("At dawn I go out onto the Prado or
go to the river, where, sitting on the banks, I gaze at the water, offering it
fancies to carry off, that they may never return") (p. 242). It is significant
that, as we shall see later, in opposing César's advocacy of an uplifting
Neo-Platonism (V, 3), Fernando seizes upon those very passages of Ficino's
commentary on the *Symposium* which, taken out of context, can be made to
sound like an espousing of self-love:

> El fuego no huye del agua por odio que la tiene, antes por amor
> propio, reusando que no le mate con su frialdad. Ni ella le apaga
> porque le aborrece, sino por acrecentarse a sí solicita conuertirla en
> su materia misma. (p. 410)

> Fire doesn't flee water from any hatred it bears it, from love of self
> rather, refusing to let it kill it with its coldness. Nor does water put
> out fire because it hates it; rather in order to make itself greater,
> it seeks to convert it into its own substance.

With remarkable equanimity Lope here whets his irony toward his protagonist on the same framework of Neo-Platonic thought which he had
himself been so earnestly building upon in his Platonizing sonnets.

While Lope surely took for granted a considerable degree of self-love in human beings, the extreme of narcissism displayed by Fernando is clearly aberrant in his eyes. Once more the author is standing sharply away from this free version of his youthful self. In Fernando he does not so much reflect the shape of his own egotism as push it to exaggerated consequences which, from an old man's vantage point, appear implicit in the egocentricity of the young, and particularly of the young man as poet.

The way out of love in *La Dorotea* begins in aggrievement, moves through new attachments, and ends in revenge, in being free of love (*desamor*), and in forgetting.

In the first two stages the philography derived from personal experience accords with the Ovidian formulation of the art of unloving, which Lope had thoroughly assimilated, but moves beyond it with suggestions of greater complexity. Self-centered as he was, Lope was particularly sensitive to the wound to ego and *amour propre* which *agravio* constituted (*agravio* being both the offense and the resultant state of aggrievement). Noting the Ovidian roots of the "doctrine" that aggrievement is a cure for love ("Often go over in your mind the deeds of the wicked girl"), Amezúa adds that it is a "very personal" one, particularly emphasized by Lope.[76] We saw it pinpointed early in the phrase "habiendo agravio" ("if there was an offense") inserted in the revised version of Lope's testimony in the sonnet on the contest of love and time. The correspondence with the Duke of Sessa, facile and cynical in tone, makes aggrievement, as has been seen, the means of freeing "la voluntad de cautiverio" ("the will from captivity"). It also proclaims that "El edificio de aborrecer se funda en la piedra del agrauiar" ("Hatred's building has wrongs for a foundation stone");[77] and affirms: "Yo soy de parezer que por agrauios no se ha de reñir, sino yrse" ("I am of the opinion that one should not quarrel when wronged, but leave").[78] Yet, as the case of Fernando shows, Lope knows that the matter is not so simple. Fernando does go away (acting in accord with the Ovidian advice "I procul"—"Go far off") but he continues to dwell on Dorotea's misdeeds and it is obvious that, far from helping, absenting himself exacerbates his suffering and increases his fixation. Absence and *agravio* no more cure him than they did the mad Belardo. Against the power of *agravio*, Dorotea affirms acutely during Fernando's absence: "Los hombres nunca están más inhábiles para ofendernos que quando maltratados; que mejor les va de ánimo quando están satisfechos de que los queremos" ("Men are never more incapable of offending us than when wronged; their morale is better when they are satisfied that we love them") (p. 141), a statement which ironically foreshadows the course of events more accurately than Dorotea intends. Later (IV, 7) we are given the record in verse of Fernando's examination of his feelings as he leaves Madrid. In "¿Adónde vais, pensamiento?" ("Whither bound, thought?") Lope has conflated with the youthful episode a spat with Marta de Nevares, for whom the poem was written, of a kind which his private correspondence shows in fact occurred.[79] The futility of both flight and aggrievement in putting an end to love is the subject of the poem. Among its lines are two quatrains that expand Dorotea's unwitting statement of what is to transpire between Fernando and her:

> El ver que rendido buelue
> el que se despide airado,
> cuando no yele, assegura,
> que es en amor graue daño.
> Amor, pensamiento, es miedo,
> y vna vez assegurado,
> bien puede ser que se quiera,
> mas no que se quiera tanto.
>
> (p. 378)

To see one who goes off in anger come back submissive, if it does not freeze, reassures, a serious mistake in love. Love, my thought, is fear, and once reassured, it may well be that one will love, but never that one will love as much.

The Coro de Venganza (Chorus of Revenge) at the end of this same fourth act goes even further in drawing out the implications of the action:

> Amor de ser amado satisfecho
> quando agrauiado imaginó vengarse,
> templado el fuego y el furor deshecho,
> adonde pudo arderse pudo elarse.
> Quien ama y agrauió no buelua y diga
> que fue violencia agena la mudança,
> pues quando piensa que rendido obliga,
> el agrauiado intenta la vengança.
>
> (p. 382)

Love assured of reciprocation when, wronged, it planned revenge, its fire tempered and its frenzy dissipated, proved able to freeze where it had been able to blaze. One who loves and has given offense should not come back and say that the change of heart was forced on him, for when he thinks he is tying another down by being submissive, the aggrieved party is plotting revenge.

Fernando returns physically but Dorotea capitulates morally, and it is the resultant assuaging of the wound to his pride that initiates Fernando's deliverance, not the imputed *agravio* itself.

That love should be cured by reassurance is the natural complement to "Love, my thought, is fear," or, as Lope put it spontaneously and revealingly to the Duke of Sessa: "Siempre quien ama piensa lo peor y da crédito a quanto es en su agrabio" ("A person in love always thinks the worst and will believe everything harmful to him").[80] It is instructive, however, to compare the handling of an instance of this phenomenon in *Las bizarrías de Belisa* (1634) with Fernando's case, in which, as we know, the process of *desenamoramiento* (falling out of love) is protracted. (The lines "It may well be that one will love, but never that one will love as much" seem tailored to his situation.) In the second act of the *comedia*, Belisa's rival, Lucinda, who had appeared to spurn the protagonist Don Juan, gives in and confesses to him that she loves him. Don Juan thus relates his reaction:

> Apenas, ¡oh Belisa!, vi llorando
> la que ser piedra para mí solía,
> cuando quedé como en la luz infusa
> Atlante del espejo de Medusa.
>
> . . . .
>
> Salí después de tantos sentimientos
> tan desenamorado, que pudiera
> vender olvido a la mayor constancia.
> ¡Gran cosa levantarse con ganancia!
>
> (Ac. N., XI, 453a)

> Scarcely, Belisa, had I seen the one who usually was a stone to me,
> in tears, when I became like Atlas in the light diffused by Medusa's
> mirror . . . From such varied feelings I emerged so free of love that I
> could have sold obliviousness to the greatest constancy. It's a
> wonderful thing to quit when one is still winning!

While Belisa expresses misgivings about the efficacy of the cure, Don Juan's account of his feelings proves absolutely correct; he has no subsequent relapse and in fact collaborates with Belisa in taking revenge on Lucinda at the end. The latter, however, can fall back on an erstwhile suitor of Belisa, whom she accepts with alacrity and good grace. These easy shifts and surprises in amatory allegiances are clearly intended to enhance the appeal of the play to the audience. Lope here has no interest in probing more deeply.[81]

Fernando, however, mistrusts his own assertions of absolute liberation and therefore, as we have seen, resorts to the *diligencia* of making Marfisa a means of freeing himself from Dorotea, a tactic rooted in Ovid's advice: "Hortor et ut pariter binas habeatis amicas" ("I also recommend that you keep two mistresses at the same time"). I have already alluded to Lope's presumption of having himself applied it in respect to Lucía de Salcedo and Marta de Nevares, his claim to have freed himself from the former by attaching himself to the latter. We need now to examine this claim more closely for the light it may shed on Fernando. Lope writes to the Duke:

> Ni a solas ni aconpañado me acuerdo de aquella baxeza [his affair with Lucía de Salcedo], a lo menos desde que supe las suyas; escríbenme, sienten, veo, entretengo mis pensamientos: he hallado finalmente, tan buen médico a mis heridas, que desde vna legua se me bee el parche; trabaxo y cuidado me costaron estos principios; pero, como me resoluí, todo se hizo a pedir de boca, y en perdiendo la esperanza de bolber a lo passado . . . no hay cosa mas fácil que mudarse.[82]

> Neither alone or in company do I remember that base behavior [his affair with Lucía de Salcedo], at least not since learning of hers. I am written to, there is resentment, I observe, and I keep my thoughts to myself. In short I have found such a good doctor for my wounds that my plaster can be seen for miles. It was difficult and bothersome in the beginning but, once my mind was made up, it all went like clockwork. In losing hope of resuming the past . . . nothing is easier than making a change.

In a subsequent letter Lope is even more emphatic: "Para huir de vna muger no ay tal consejo como tomar la posta en otra, y, trote o no trote, huir hasta que diga la boluntad que ha llegado donde quiere y que no quiere lo que quería" ("To escape from one woman there is no better advice than to run after another and, trot or not, flee until the flesh says that it has reached what it was after and that it no longer loves what it did").[83]

This is not a matter, strictly speaking, of "binas amicas" as with Fernando, but of substitution, yet one can still sense Ovid and his physiological reasoning in the background.[84] It is no doubt true that Lope's strong libido found this expedient congenial. Even so, matters were clearly less simple than Lope suggests and more than physiology is involved. Amezúa has correctly stressed the catalytic effect for the experience of liberation hinted at here (in the afterthought "at least not since learning of her [base behavior]"), of the eye-opening revelations about the mistress related in a letter just prior to the two from which I have quoted:

> Vino vna criada de aquella persona [Lucía de Salcedo] y contóme su vida y milagros desde que salió de aquí; y son tales que hasta oy no he buelto en mi juicio; ya estoy tan consolado, que puedo prestarle a otro quexoso.[85]

> A servant of that person came and told me her life and times since she left here, and they are such that I still haven't recovered from the shock. I am so thoroughly consoled that I have consolation to spare for some other patient.

Clearly we have here a truer reason for Lope's ability to forget the actress with whom he had been obsessed than the strategy of substitution which he says he worked. As Amezúa writes: "From this point on, as if at last he could see to the bottom of this matter, Lope will consider this affair with *La Loca* over. His joy, his satisfaction at being out of her snares . . . are unbounded."[86] Although the psychological mechanism is not the same—satiety in Fernando's case, revulsion in Lope's—it is difficult not to see in Fernando's account, overstated as it may be, of how the scales fell from his eyes and he was relieved of a great weight of oppression, a record of an analogous experience of liberation from an obsessive emotional state. Next to this, the stratagem of replacement seems only incidental.

In the letters Lope does not pause to examine closely or sort out the factors involved. In *La Dorotea* he has looked more deeply into the process of the emotions and made a subtle order of it. He has not lost his fondness for lapidary formulations; it is visible in the tendency to abstract or generalize in the choruses and at many points in the dialogue. Yet Lope knows the limitations of codifying and he is now more interested in revealing those ambiguities and puzzles in human feelings and human relationships which may be demonstrated but elude definitive formulation. The dialogue imposes some polarization of views and sorts out some of the skeins—anger, resentment, self-sacrifice, self-love, carnality, possessiveness, and so on—in a complex of feeling corresponding, if not to the actuality of his own past with Elena, to its potentiality; skeins which, in a world of might-have-been, would perhaps have assumed the configuration they do in the *acción en prosa* where, in addition, threads of Lope's subsequent affective *Erlebnis* are woven into the pattern. Yet in this final reordering of the experience Lope respects its complexity. His subject is the fate of human love in a prosaic world. He finds it doomed by egotism, by a failure of human vanity to understand human weakness, a conclusion proposed wistfully but with equanimity.

Dramatic and Lyric Aspects
of Form
IX

The blending of features of diverse literary provenience in *La Dorotea*, rather than a sign of eclecticism, is an effort to reach a unique kind of *concordia discors* in answer to expressive needs more demanding and complex than before. To study the interaction of form and substance becomes especially meaningful when the ad hoc form is expressly a function of the substance, as it is here. Integrated into this new context, each of the features required by Lope for the total artistic statement—formal delineation of acts and scenes, terminal choruses, the dialogued prose and inserted lyrics—gains enhanced meaning from the others and contributes distinctively to the meaning of the whole.

While Lope is here primarily a spokesman for himself rather than for patron, society, or nation, the substantial preface he addresses to the discriminating reader indicates that he came to view the work not only as self-expression but as a memento of the self, that is, as a *monumentum aere perennius* destined to insure his self-survival as a serious artist and literary creator in those eyes which he felt increasingly trained upon him at the end of his life, the eyes of posterity. He made *La Dorotea* impressive architectonically, supplying clean formal lines of act, scene, and chorus and creating contours mostly absent from his plays. However unsuited its subject matter might appear, the work was offered for serious thought as well as for entertainment. An encomiastic description in the Prologue challenges a potential detractor to produce:

otra imitación más perfeta, otra verdad afeitada de más donaires y
colores retóricos, la erudición más plausible y lo sentencioso más
graue; con tantas partes de filosofía natural y moral que admira
cómo aya podido tratarlas con tanta claridad en tal sujeto. (p. 53)

a more perfect imitation, truth decked out in more graces and
rhetorical colors, more commendable erudition, weightier
sententiousness, with so many aspects of natural and moral
philosophy that one is amazed that he was able to treat them so
clearly when writing on such a subject.

The weighty matters touched upon, Lope undoubtedly felt, entitled the
work to consideration by exacting and learned readers.[1]

As Edwin Morby has pointed out (ed. La Dorotea, p. 14) Lope, perhaps
recalling schoolboy experience, took the term acción, as a name for a
dramatic work, from actio, the blanket term used by the writers of Latin
plays for Jesuit schools to designate every kind of drama they wrote. In
describing the different plays, García Soriano, the authority on this theater,
finds the term equivalent at different times to comedia, tragicomedia, and
tragedia; it thus covers the main classes to which Lope thought of his own
plays as belonging. This scholar's descriptions show that much of this
production was in fact of a most mixed and heterogeneous character,
combining very disparate elements.[2] From Lope's designation of La Dorotea
as an acción en prosa one may conclude that he thought of the work as falling
outside established literary categories. In effect he acknowledges its fundamentally dramatic character yet forthrightly declares himself an innovator.
The independence of this stance goes hand in hand with the avowedly
personal character of the work and the abandonment of the usual audience.

This declaration of independence from accepted literary practice is an
unusual step both for Lope and for his age, with their customary acquiescence
in an established hierarchy of literary forms. However, Lope's so designating
La Dorotea is, in my view, an affirmation, not an evasion as Morby tends to
consider it. One senses here, as one does beneath the superficial perplexities
of Cervantes' preface to the Quixote of 1605, a conviction of the solidity of
Lope's achievement, however unconventional and unclassifiable. Morby's
definition of the work, "tragedia irónica" ("ironical tragedy") (p. 17),
stresses the presence of outward features of tragedy: choruses, the five-act
form, messengers, prophetic dreams, together with the departure from
tragic canons in regard to decorum, subject matter, and social station of the
characters. Unable to call the work a "tragedia," Lope, he suggests, settled
on "acción en prosa" as a compromise. La Dorotea would thus be the ironic

version of a Senecan type of classical tragedy. Yet is it possible, one wonders, to treat the substance and the form of tragedy ironically without converting it into something else? I am not referring to the dramatic irony which is integral to the tragic view of the limitations of human power and vision but to irony bearing on the idea of tragedy itself. This must inevitably mean destroying the spectator's (or reader's) single-minded absorption in an action destined to stir him to compassion, wonder, or awe, causing him instead to take a detached point of view, from which incongruities, ambiguities, and the author's own reservations appear. With this, the tragic spirit is dissipated.

If pressed to fit this work, which is *sui generis* like *Faust* or the *Quixote*, into a formal dramatic category, I would incline to that of comedy, it being understood that this is comedy of deeply serious intent. Ultimately the lyric temper of the work gives it an affective stamp of a personal kind which, in my view, makes the categories of comedy and tragedy in any strict sense of the terms inadequate, though surely Lope's fundamental outlook is that of the comic rather than the tragic artist.[3] I will return in my concluding chapter to this question of outlook. My principal present intention is not directed to the matter of comedy or tragedy but to the various formal features themselves as components of a total design, their provenience, the functions they fulfill, the inner form they help create.

While in fact the *actiones* of Jesuit schools were often in part or entirely in prose, it is only Lope, so far as I know, who has seen fit to append the phrase "en prosa" to his subtitle. He clearly wishes to draw attention to the prose medium, new to his dramatic writing. Its principal connotation (there will be others) is personal authenticity, as I have already noted. Prose is a guarantee of genuineness in contradistinction to the fictions of verse. In designating *La Dorotea* "acción en prosa," Lope is thus not only informing the reader that the work is set in the prosaic world of everyday (the world of comedy), but indicating that he speaks in it from the heart, speaks earnestly, for all his seeming levity.

The spectacle presented in the *acción en prosa*, we are informed in advance, will differ from those offered on the *comedia* stage, where "las demás que ha escrito" ("his other dramatic works") were presented. The subjects suited for this theater were perforce those of romance, "las cosas [que] se escriben por notables" ("things written about because they are worthy of notice").[4] Lope now suggests that the world in which the spectators ordinarily live holds dramas as compelling as any that unfold on the stage, though their paucity of incident and slowness of pace might ordinarily cause them to escape notice.

In taking drama off the stage, Lope is following a tendency of the age, for his is a period in which poetry is everywhere being drawn into closer proximity with the everyday. But he is no more able than Cervantes to stop at parody or burlesque; in dethroning the old poetry, he too produces poetry of a new kind. Beneath a traditional shell, his *creación lírica teatral* (to recall Karl Vossler's term for it) marks a new departure. Not in the direction of Cervantes, of course; there was no question of his following Cervantes' lead, even if he had been capable of discerning the way of the future opened up by his contemporary. For, as he well knew, his natural inclination lay in another direction, and by the time he brought the *acción en prosa* to fruition Lope was no longer interested in forcing himself down paths uncongenial to his talents.[5] Indifferent to the expectations of his usual audiences and readers, responding to inner directives, he fashions the form which will allow his creative energies fullest scope, while yet offering guidelines, channels, contours within which his meaning can take shape. Insight into the character of his own creativity shows him how to endow an outward dramatic structure with a lyricist's perception of human experience, how to imbue it with the bittersweet flavor of a life drained nearly to the bottom. He follows his natural bent by presenting his characters entirely through what they say, though this time they are not the usual "personas vestidas" ("costumed characters"), and by relying entirely on dialogue and representation to show what happens to them, though now the representation is only to be imagined and the speeches are not to be heard. He thus produces a work in the dramatic mode that remains this side of drama in the usual sense—that is, an action to be enacted on a stage—yet goes beyond drama in the more restricted sense—an action presented solely through spoken parts and dialogue. As has already become evident and will now be more so, habits of writing for the stage do persist and affect Lope's inner visualization of his created world.[6]

Ostensibly Lope allows himself no voice, not even the voice heard in the marginal comments of his narratives and the speeches of Belardo in his plays. (Belardo's voice, notes J. M. de Cossío, was clearly to be understood by the audience as Lope's own.)[7] Yet Lope achieves close proximity to the reader and one feels his presence everywhere. This is fundamentally because the *acción en prosa* is written *à la recherche du moi* and because the meaning which human experience acquires in it is simply a meaning Lope now reads into his own life, bodying it forth in a single recreated episode. We reach here the central source of the lyricism of the *acción en prosa*. If, as the "Egloga a Claudio" shows and Lope's view of Fernando confirms, Lope finds it hard to regain a sense of the continuity of the self, as against its fluidity, he is not troubled by any problem of identity nor is his strong sense of his own ego impaired. So strong indeed is this that we shall find him partaking of his characters' experience from within, embodying aspects of his psyche and outlook in his presentation of them. He does not simply participate through imaginative projection upon them of what he has observed of man and society, which is the method of the novelist or dramatist. He has been in at their making, and in all their voices, as I hope to show later, one perceives echoes of his own. The cosmos of the *acción en prosa* is in a special sense his and while his vision outreaches that of any particular figure in it, he expresses himself primarily in the meaning he discovers in the totality of their experience, making an original use of a dramatic structure to project the spectacle of a world that exists primarily within himself. Despite his addressing the *cognoscenti* and his concern to produce a work memorable in the eyes of posterity, the audience of the *acción en prosa* is thus really an afterthought. In the traditional manner of the lyricist, Lope is writing to be overheard; to be overseen, also, in keeping with his dramatist's vision of his world.[8]

The pervasive lyricism of *La Dorotea* crystallizes in the poems which, with great care and skill, Lope has set in the dialogue. Their form and function will occupy us in the latter part of the present chapter, although a few which have particularly significant links to the contexts in which they occur will be treated in other connections. Our initial concern is with the dramatic aspects of the *acción en prosa*. First, however, we should dispose of the question of narrative patterns and techniques.

Despite Lope's eschewing the narrative mode as uncongenial, the comprehensiveness of form of the *acción en prosa* has enabled him to adapt to it a few features usually (though not exclusively) associated with certain types of narrative prose: a slow tempo, inwardness, interpolated lyrics, tributary tales. In the pastoral novel, as earlier noted, he had become aware of the possibilities of a slow-paced action, devoid or nearly so of outward incident, free of the externally imposed vicissitudes of short stories, *comedias*, and novels of adventure, an action on which clear-cut dénouements were not imposed, the endings commonly leaving matters unresolved. This kind of action was foreign to both *La Celestina* and its sequels. Even the uneventful *Euphrosina* had a plot of sorts which brought matters to a happy ending. Moreover, unrequited love, the commonest emotional state of shepherds and shepherdesses, tended to isolate them from their physical and social surroundings, turn their concern inward, and bring the subjective world for the first time into the foreground. A natural setting amplified their feelings in concord or discord and sooner or later caused them to be poured forth in song. It was the pastoral (not the *Celestinas*) which set the precedent for the inclusion of lyrics in narrative prose, an example followed by Lope in all his prose fiction and given further and noticeably dramatic expressiveness in the *acción en prosa*.

Also employed in *La Dorotea* is another technique of pastoral fiction, the practice of suspending the main narrative to permit interpolation of a character's life history, usually through his own account to interested listeners. In the pastoral such tales constitute new "casos de amor y fortuna" ("instances of love and fortune") and have a central place in the scheme of the works. In the *acción en prosa*, however, where only a single "instance" is treated, these accounts are so disposed as to shed further light on the single history of Fernando and Dorotea. They are modeled not on the formally autonomous *relaciones* delivered as display pieces on the stage, but on the *relatos* of pastoral fiction, the life stories told by newly arrived shepherds. In the present work, however, they are interspersed with questions and comments, give rise to exchanges and repartee, and are interrupted by digressions, after which they must be set in motion again. Besides informing us of the past and future, they interrelate these with the present through the reactions and responses they provoke between speaker and listeners, in effect creating new situations. Rather than interrupting the flow of the dialogue, they are absorbed into it and carried along on the conversational stream.

The dramatic character of *La Dorotea* thus in the end governs the adaptation to the work of features of narrative prose, and we shall find it affecting the functioning of the lyrics as well. More directly it is revealed in features and techniques carried over from various dramatic traditions, which we may now examine more closely, noting how they function in the *acción en prosa* and the modifications they have undergone.

Certain aspects of the work's dramatic configuration have already been touched upon. It has been seen that the realistic spatial and temporal ordering, and the comings and goings of the characters, are tailored to imaginary stage conditions less arbitrary than those of the *comedia*, that Lope has adhered in his own way to the dramatic unities of time and space, that his conception of the servants has been affected by *comedia* conventions.

It is significant that Lope has prefaced the work with a cast of "personas que se introducen" ("characters who take part"), directed the Prologue "To the audience" ("Al teatro"), and at the end made La Fama step in with a short allocution to a "senado" ("jury") of spectators, asking for applause. These are signs that even though no actual theater or audience was ever envisaged, Lope finds it congenial to write as if they were, retaining a dramatic format, with its reassuring sense of proximity to an audience, yet overcoming the disadvantages of the actual theater conditions in which he felt increasingly constrained and unappreciated as the years passed.[9] The Prologue declares that "el papel es más libre teatro que aquel donde tienen licencia el vulgo de graduar, la amistad de aplaudir y la embidia de morder" ("paper is a freer theater than the one in which the common folk are free to pass judgment, friendship to applaud, and envy to bite") (p. 52). The audience of this freer theater is "quien lo leyere" ("anyone reading"). Lope has written this time for leisurely private perusal, emancipating himself from the requirements of stock companies, fixed roles, particular performers; dispensing, in short, with interpreters as intermediaries. In *La Dorotea*, he says, "no se ven las personas vestidas sino las acciones imitadas" ("one sees not costumed characters but actions imitated") (p. 54). Not even group reading or recitation is envisaged, as with *La Celestina* and *La Euphrosina*, works to which passing allusion is made in the Prologue. *La Dorotea* is solely for a private reader, and it is his eyes which are to look over the author's shoulder at the spectacle being offered.

The five-act structure is suggested to Lope by classical, specifically Senecan, tragedy, a fact underscored by the attempt to reproduce classical meters in the verse of the choruses. This marked departure from the form of his stage plays confirms the desire to make the *acción en prosa* a more solid and less ephemeral achievement than his *comedias*. He had found a five-part structure congenial off the stage, as the five-book arrangement of the longer narrative works—*La Arcadia, El peregrino en su patria, Los pastores de Belén*—shows.[10] Nowhere else than in *La Dorotea* do we encounter, however, the Senecan constellation of five acts, choruses, a prophetic dream (I, 5) and a messenger bearing baleful news (V, 11).[11] The fact that on one occasion when writing "al estilo español" ("in the Spanish manner") a play he expressly calls a tragedy (*El castigo sin venganza*), Lope abjures "las sombras, nuncios y coros" ("shades, messengers, choruses"), suggests that in incorporating such features he is conscious of associating himself with another tradition, demonstrably an enduring and venerable one.[12] Although his spirit and his techniques will considerably modify the meaning and function of features of this kind, as we have already seen in the case of the prophetic dream, they nevertheless stand as signs of his boldness in taking a patently nonheroic subject, drawn from purely personal history, and offering it as a modern-day equivalent, in the scope of what it seeks to express, of a Senecan tragedy. It cannot itself be a tragedy—Senecan events and issues do not arise or belong in its everyday world and Senecan tones can be made to appear singularly inappropriate— but we are not on this account to misread its seriousness. If Lope's drama of the everyday casually offers new wine in old bottles, it is wine intended for long aging.

The extensive and precise subdividing of the five acts of *La Dorotea* into formal scenes, another outward sign of its dramatic configuration, was surely in the first instance a way of keeping within bounds, through formal demarcation, the wide-ranging discursiveness of the dialogue. The precedent here is not classical tragedy, whether Seneca's plays or those of his Spanish successors; there are no scenic demarcations in the former and the Spanish epigones had only the vaguest notions of them.[13] The suggestion must have come rather from the *Comedia Euphrosina* of Jorge Ferreira de Vasconcelos (Coimbra, 1555), a work which, as I have already noted, is alluded to along with *La Celestina* in the Prologue. In *La Euphrosina* the scenic divisions served to compartmentalize a highly variegated content, fitting, however capriciously, into a five-act structure. (In *La Celestina*, by contrast, Lope found only a single succession of scene-like *auctos*.) Though in the *comedia* scenes existed, in effect, the emphasis, despite shifts of setting, time, and situation, was on the forward thrust of the action and Lope did not stop to delimit the scenes formally. The term *scena* referred simply to each new grouping of characters resulting from an exit or an entrance. While in *La Dorotea* the scenic divisions often also coincide with exits and entrances, they do not do so consistently; clearly other artistic intentions are reflected. The effects of concentration at the beginning of Act I and fragmentation in Act V have already been observed and further aspects of artistic design in the scenic arrangement will later appear. Far more skillfully than Ferreira, Lope uses scenic subdivisions to frame pointed or rambling conversations, give prominence to particular situations, pinpoint cruxes of action, or merely record variations on given motifs. The clarity of contour thus attained is consonant with the exact chronometric and spatial ordering of the work. With so uneventful an action, the scenic divisions can be used for its energetic punctuation into carefully graduated stages.

Scenes often open on a character's entrance, carrying a strong impact of physical movement, with incisiveness such as one would look for in performance resulting. Examples are the almost breathless entrance of Dorotea in Act I, scene 5; the deliberate one of Don Bela in Act II, scene 5. In these two cases, the character's approach is perceived at the end of the previous scene and the scenic division corresponds to his physical passage through a doorway, with no break in the continuity of the action. But in each case the scenes preceding and following the entrance are felt as distinct phases of the action: the exposition of Fernando's dream, then its confirmation in the interview with Dorotea; the disposing of Dorotea in favor of Don Bela, then his visit. A strong new beginning in the dialogue, which also serves as an indirect stage direction, marks the opening of the new scene:

> *Dor.:* Llama recio, si no te duele la mano. (p. 92)

> *Dor.:* Knock hard, if it doesn't hurt your hand.

> *Bel.:* No me tire de la capa, señora Gerarda . . . (p. 171)

> *Bel.:* Don't pull me by the cloak, mistress Gerarda . . .

The same combination of segmentation and continuity marks Dorotea's two arrivals home following her meetings with Fernando (beginning of I, 8, and of IV, 6). Again the scenic division is her entrance, anticipated at the end of the previous scene in the dialogue of her mother and Gerarda, and the opening lines are again incisive: Teodora's aggressive "¿De dónde vienes a las dos de la tarde, Dorotea?" ("Where have you come from at two in the afternoon, Dorotea?") (p. 125); and Dorotea's defiant "¿Mas que me preguntas de dónde vengo?" ("I'll bet you'll ask me where I've come from") (p. 372).[14]

Scene endings, whether or not involving the actual exit of a character, are often set off by the sort of striking curtain line that Lope prescribes in the *Arte nuevo de hacer comedias* (*New Art of Writing Plays*) for the *comedia:*

> Remátense las scenas con sentencia,
> con donaire, con versos elegantes,
> de suerte que al entrarse el que recita,
> no deje con disgusto al auditorio.

> (*Obras escogidas*, II, 889)

> The scenes are to be closed off with a pithy saying, with a witticism, with elegant verse, so that when the actor speaking exits he does not leave the audience dissatisfied.

An admonitory *sententia* of Ludovico, for example, closes down the talk in the scenes celebrating Fernando's triumph in winning back Dorotea: "Dixo Tulio que alabar la fortuna era necedad, y vituperalla soberuia" ("Tully said that praising fortune was folly and censuring her, conceit") (p. 370).[15]

A quip often marks the close of a scene, especially when there is no break in the action. Examples are Gerarda's "¿De qué tiene miedo? Aquí estamos tres mugeres, que entre todas tenemos ciento y veinte y cinco años; pero yo sola me tengo los ochenta" ("What are you afraid of? We're three women here, a hundred and twenty-five years all told, but by myself I account for eighty of them") (p. 171); and Julio's remark that the best sounds are those of women's clogs and wine jars, as feminine steps are heard approaching (p. 92). Closing lines often have great incisiveness even when the last word is not, strictly speaking, a witticism.[16] While there is naturally no counterpart to the "elegant verse" that Lope recommends for ending scenes on the stage, we sometimes find a line or two of quoted verse providing the kind of pithy summation that a playwright leaves with an audience. Garcilaso's line (quoted inaccurately by Fernando) "Conozco lo mejor, lo peor aprueuo" ("I know what is best, I give in to what is worst") (p. 227) catches up in a single formula paradoxes lengthily detailed in the preceding conversation.

Endings of this sort are even used at the joining of scenes too static to hold a real stage. For one of the advantages of the freer theater, as Lope could see in La Euphrosina, was the inclusion of marginal or peripheral sequences, dramatically but not ambiently or psychologically otiose, devoted to conversations and discussions which had little to contribute to the delineation of the situation and hardly affected the progress of the action. In La Dorotea this advantage is especially drawn upon in certain scenes involving Gerarda. Much of her long initial interview with Don Bela, all of the subsequent two interviews, her second conversation with Teodora, and the whole meal scene of which she is the center are structurally superfluous. They are simply a virtuoso's variations on Celestinesque motifs, which the domestic atmosphere and conversational tone of the work were able to accommodate with ease. They provide perspective on the changing course of affairs between Fernando and Dorotea and help to orchestrate certain major themes, such as those of *interés* and *desengaño*. The conversational idom and scenic compartmentation of the work made it feasible also to insert the long scenes of rambling literary commentary in Act IV, and to devote entire scenes in Act V to the successive minutiae which protract the work: a piece of information, a shift of mood, the destruction of a portrait or of a pack of letters.[17]

The projection of a mood or state of mind through the agency of an interlocutor, common enough in Lope's plays, now consumes entire scenes and is used with increased subtlety to bring out affective and psychic nuances. In their leisureliness such scenes recall the exchanges in the *Comedia Euphrosina* between Euphrosina and Sylvia de Sousa, her cousin, and between the latter and Zelotypo, all social equals, quite as much as the exchanges between masters and servants in Lope's *comedias*.[18]

Indeed it must have been *La Euphrosina*, a work which Vossler calls "the first truly modern conversational drama," which led Lope in the direction of drama of this kind.[19] Ferreira's example showed how a slender thread of dramatic action could be drawn through the luxuriant discursiveness of "apparently insubstantial conversations which seem to intoxicate and enmesh the characters."[20] Such predominance of talk over action must have caught Lope's attention. One does not find it in *La Celestina*, a work in which the diffuseness of the dialogue is more apparent than real. Recent criticism has stressed how economically *La Celestina* in fact adjusts speech to motivation, will, and action.[21] Despite rhetorical amplification, erudition, and moralizing, the dialogue of the *tragicomedia* reflects the clash of strong personalities intent on their objectives and powerfully propels a tense action toward climax and catastrophe.

If *La Euphrosina* tempted Lope in the direction of conversational drama, it scarcely offered a model to follow. The author's control of both talk and action is highly uncertain. Vossler notes the disconnectedness of all the "jokes, pranks, chattering and arguing, deceptions and surprises, feints and counterfeints and outpourings of emotion" that fill the twenty-nine scenes of its five acts.[22] Developing events end up nowhere and only the slim central love intrigue, the winning of Euphrosina by the timid and chaste Zelotypo through the prodding of his libertine friend Cariophilo and the intercession of the lady's cousin, comes to fruition. The principal lesson of *La Euphrosina* was one of unrealized possibilities. Lope's subject—the disintegration of love —and his action—one long dénouement—bear no resemblance to those of either *La Celestina* or *La Euphrosina*, but his pace is that of *La Euphrosina* and the disproportion between dramatic event and conversational commentary in *La Dorotea* is almost as great as in *La Euphrosina*. In *La Celestina* Lope had seen how prose could serve as a medium for clipped repartee, for "le vrai dialogue comique, plus agile que la conversation ordinaire" ("true comic dialogue, more agile than ordinary conversation"), which Marcel Bataillon sees as one of Rojas's major innovations.[23] *La Euphrosina* showed in addition that prose simulating the rambling talk of everyday could find a place in a dramatically conceived work. We will later see how far Lope surpasses Ferreira in the artistic quality of his conversations; we have already seen how he takes advantage of the slow tempo, which so often makes for sluggishness and drifting in *La Euphrosina*, to record psychic processes that have no counterpart in the Portuguese work.

Though Lope expressly abjured the *comedia* stage in the *acción en prosa*, he did not on that account, as we know, shed the techniques and conventions which so many years of active play-writing had made second nature. The distinctness of his new stance usually modifies the effect of such practices, however, although not always. The suggestion of verbal mimicry and visual comedy, of gesture and grimace that actors would realize for a popular audience, may be very vivid:

> *Iul.:* ¿Para essa obligación eran menester testigos?
> *Cla.:* No, por cierto, que cara tienes tú de jurar falso.
> *Iul.:* Pues, Clara, ¿a tu querido y deseado Iulio?
> *Cla.:* Pues, Iulio, ¿a tu aborrecida y oluidada Clara?
>
> (p. 379)

> *Jul.:* Would witnesses be needed for that obligation?   *Cla.:* Certainly not, you've enough gall to swear falsely all by yourself.   *Jul.:* Why, Clara, is that a way to talk to your beloved and longed-for Julio? *Cla.:* Why, Julio, is that a way to talk to your hated and forgotten Clara?

Lope clearly visualized such by-play on a stage as he wrote. Having himself assumed the position of audience, however, he does not usually stop at such obvious and standard comedy. Instead he undercuts the old conventions, carrying further a device not without precedent, indeed, in the *comedia* itself. More characteristic than sequences like the one cited, in which a *comedia* technique appears to have come through unaltered, are those in which *comedia* patterns appear hedged about with reservations and equivocations.

I have already noted the modification of the conventions governing relations of masters and servants caused by the presence of "historical" foundations and the further unsettling effect on these relationships of Lope's assumption of the stance of *figura del donaire*. Montesinos's definitive study of Lope in this role emphasized not only continuity with the *comedia* but the undermining of the scheme of values of its aristocratic protagonists which this new perspective entails. Fernando and Dorotea are not *cauallero* (gentleman) and *dama* (lady) (even though the cast so designates them), but *comedia* types *manqués*, unable to realize their aspirations to cultural and social distinction. Although subsequent scholars have tended to emphasize affinities between the *acción en prosa* and the *comedia*, it is the modifications which point more significantly to the character of Lope's dramatic art in prose.[24] While in a Lopean work dramatically conceived the practice of the *comedia* will inevitably constitute a point of reference, the effect of the *comedia* is felt, in my view, more in externals than in the substance of the work. The aspirations of Fernando and Dorotea will be governed by attitudes, values, modes of thought and feeling derived from lyric and pastoral tradition, forms of greater cultural distinction than the immediate and contemporaneous world of the *comedia* affords. While such strains also figure in the depiction of Lope's stage protagonists, they do so in a more conventionalized manner. The values emphasized there are those that spur to action: adventure, *esfuerzo* (manly endeavor), honor. The less dynamic and more reflective attitudes dominant in *La Dorotea* are present as modes of expression but not of being.

Where the voice of the *figura del donaire* is most perceptible, it does not coincide with those of its usual stage mouthpieces, the servants. What is most characteristic is the author's irony playing about this expressive pattern of the *comedia*, glancing off it, undermining it, moving beyond it. The spirit is that of Tomé de Burguillos, the Lopean mask who, unlike Belardo, does not figure in the plays. One notes how the *comedia* convention is suggested, for example, then ruled out, in the servants' comments on the theatrical attitude Fernando assumes toward Dorotea's faint ("Sol, tu luz se eclipsa" ["Sun, your light is eclipsed"], and so on):

> *Iul.:* Celia, encender quiero vn acha.
> *Cel.:* Calla, pícaro, que no estás en la comedia.
>
> (p. 94)
>
> *Jul.:* Celia, I'd like to light a flare.   *Cel.:* Quiet, rascal, you're not in a play.

More than allusiveness, it is distinctness in the handling of the convention that stands out here. That it should occur to the characters to refer themselves to *comedia* counterparts is a reflex of Lope's which he immediately counters by bringing out the inappositeness of the reference.

Much as the mood of Tomé de Burguillos will suddenly turn serious, so Lope's handling of the servants in those exchanges in which he puts them through *comedia*-like paces may acquire a serious dimension, one not merely critical, as on the stage, but moral. In their humorous imitations of their masters' actions, parody may be suddenly put aside. Julio, for example, follows Fernando's fleecing of Marfisa by a bantering bid to Clara for assistance, only to be stopped short by her impassioned denunciation of the master's ignoble behavior (p. 119). On the other hand, a long aside of Laurencio and Celia during the visit of Don Bela to Dorotea begins in criticism of Don Bela's affected and pedantic manner of expression, moves into outright slapstick and mimicry suggestive of the stage,

Cel.: Desenfádate, bobo.
Lau.: No me lo digas con la mano, discreta.

(p. 176)

Cel.: Come off it, silly.   *Lau.:* Don't tell me to with your hand, smarty.

but concludes with a gingerly skirting-about of the stage convention of love between maid-servant and manservant:

Cel.: ¿Qué sabes tú si lo [dama] quiero yo ser tuya?
Lau.: Si yo no lo sé, ¿cómo quieres serlo?
Cel.: ¿Truxiste mucha plata?
Lau.: Si leíste el aranzel, ¿cómo no sabes que nos auemos de hazer pobres?

(p. 177)

Cel.: How do you know whether I want to be your [lady]?
Lau.: If I don't know, how do you expect to be?   *Cel.:* Did you bring lots of silver?   *Lau.:* If you read the rules of conduct, how come you're not aware that we're supposed to act poor?

The *figura del donaire* behind *La Dorotea* is Tomé de Burguillos. The gratuitous ludic strain present in the latter's skepticism becomes the free indulgence of a creator's pleasure in his overlordship, an authorial attitude of amused benevolence toward his creatures, something beyond parody, comedy, or criticism.[25]

The unusual dramatic configuration of *La Dorotea*, its adjustment to an imaginary stage but renunciation of an actual one, the strict adherence to dialogue unsupported by stage directions of any kind, presented Lope with the particular problem of making the movements and gestures of his unseen characters plain to readers who could not be spectators. He found a solution by adapting what María Rosa Lida de Malkiel has called "la acotación artística," that is, the stage direction built into the dialogue.[26] Like all dramatic dialogue, dialogue not intended for staging assumes complementation in enactment. The burden on the imagination is heavier, however, since the test of performance cannot be made. Lope was no stranger to the need for oblique stage directions in the plays he wrote for performance, as their texts prove. Though he never took time to provide more than the scantiest of actual directions to actors and producers, the bare stages he wrote for and the rapid actions he composed did require some additional orientation of the players. This need could be met largely by directing movements and stage play orally; actors could also be counted on to supply "afectos" ("given emotions") and "efectos" ("given effects") in accordance with the rhetoric of histrionic convention, the gestures, vocal effects, facial expressions called for by what Lope refers to as "toda acción de personal figura" ("every action of a figure on the stage").[27] In later years the practice of writing definitive versions of his *comedias* for reading as well as performance led him to stress the importance of recreating the stage action in the imagination. The nonexistent stage of *La Dorotea* is thus less anomalous than might appear. In revising his scripts for publication, he had grown forcibly aware of the gap between the spoken and the written word, "la diferencia . . . de la acción y voz viva a la escritura, donde es fuerza que el que lee, no sólo entienda, pero se mueva con los accidentes a la conmiseración, a la alegría y a los afectos" ("the difference . . . between enactment and live voices, and the written text; with the latter the reader must not only understand but be moved by the vicissitudes to compassion, joy, and given emotions").[28]

In composing the dialogue of *La Dorotea*, Lope appears to have been particularly anxious to make up for the absence of performers and the example of *La Celestina* undoubtedly helped him to perfect the techniques of his own plays. Rojas, as Mrs. Malkiel has demonstrated, found ways of indicating through what is said, not only the movements, appearances, and facial expressions, but the states of feeling, temperament, and character of his speakers, as well as the locales and circumstances in which they found themselves. She notes that in *La Dorotea* Lope made abundant, graceful, and varied use of Rojas's techniques.[29] She finds him incorporating stage directions which she classifies as enunciative, descriptive, implicit, and related to action and character. The built-in stage direction is an important factor in producing certain effects already noticed: the sensory vividness which strengthens the "historicity" of *La Dorotea*, the comic power of a figure like Gerarda, the focus upon Dorotea. It may be added that Lope does not confine himself to Rojas's precedents; he goes further, applying skillful new artistry to ends of his own.

Let us now exemplify the more specifically histrionic side of these devices: the revelation of affective states through facial expression; the rendering of connected actions suggestive of stage-play; the underscoring of flare-ups of feeling or histrionic outbursts.

1. Unverbalized states of feeling revealed through allusions to facial expression.

   A. Anxiety.

Fer.: ¿Distes la cuchillada a Gerarda?
Lud.: No; porque sabía que os auíades de arrepentir de auerlo
  mandado, *como en el semblante mostráis agora . . .*

(p. 237; italics mine)

Fer.: Did you slash Gerarda's face?   *Lud.:* No, because I knew you
would regret having directed me to, *as I can see by your expression
you now do.*

B. Consternation.

Iul.: [to Fernando, nonplussed at Marfisa's recriminations] ¿Qué la
  miras? ¿Por qué no hablas? ¿Por qué no la consuelas?

(p. 380)

Jul.: What are you looking at her for? Why don't you say something?
Why don't you console her?

C. Tearfulness.

Teo.: Vñas de gato y hábito de beato. Haz pucheros, por vida mía.
Fel.: Calla, Dorotea. No leuantemos alguna poluareda que no se vea
  don Beltrán.
Dor.: Oy, Felipa, ni pienso llorar, ni reñir . . .

(p. 373)

Teo.: A cat's claws and a saint's habit. Start bawling, go on.   *Fel.:*
Hush, Dorotea. Let's not raise some cloud of dust and lose Don
Beltrán.   *Dor.:* Today, Felipa, I have no intention of either weeping
or quarreling . . .

(Dorotea's face evidently begins to pucker up, then clears.)

Facial expressions tend to become part of larger attitudes for which a
total nonverbalized histrionic bearing is implied. In turn, such attitudes
generate responses and an action develops. When Teodora quarrels with
Dorotea, for example, she is incited to physical violence not only by what
Dorotea says, but by the defiant attitude indicated for the reader in the
way Dorotea looks at her. All of this is conveyed through Teodora's
reaction: "¿Qué me miras? ¿Gestos me hazes? Por el siglo de tu padre, que
si te doy vna buelta de cabellos, que no has de auer menester rizos" ("Why
are you looking at me that way? Making faces at me, huh? By your dead
father's soul, if I pull out some of your hair you'll have no need of curls")
(p. 77).

2. Rapidly moving actions suggestive of stage-play.

Here one clearly sees the hand of the craftsman of the theater suggesting interconnected movements and gestures and specifying much that would have been left to the actors in a play intended for performance. (There is no equivalent in *La Celestina*, even in the love scenes in Melibea's garden, for the detail, precision, and animation of these sequences.) Fernando's restlessness, for example, provokes the following passage, just after he has thrown aside, after reading one sentence, the Heliodorus Julio has handed him:

> *Fer.:* Muestra el axedrez; jugaremos vn poco.
> *Iul.:* Bien dizes; pongo las piezas.
> *Fer.:* ¿Están puestas?
> *Iul.:* ¿Pues no lo ves? Comienza. ¿Qué has hecho?
> *Fer.:* Derribélas todas, por no ponerme a peligro de perder la dama. Muestra las espadas negras.
> *Iul.:* Quitaréles el poluo de nuestra ausencia.
> *Fer.:* De la postura angular dize Carranza que salen todas las heridas. ¿Qué postura tendría el amor quando me dio las mías?
> *Iul.:* Pregúntale a Dorotea, que le dio el arco.
> *Fer.:* Bien hiziste essa treta; que del fin del tajo salen todas las estocadas. ¡Ay, Dorotea, que no me bastan reparos contra las tuyas!
> *Iul.:* ¿Por qué arrojas la espada?
>
> (p. 205)

Fer.: Bring out the chess men; we'll play a little.   *Jul.:* Good idea; I'm setting them up.   *Fer.:* Are they all set up?   *Jul.:* Can't you see? You start. What are you doing?   *Fer.:* I knocked them all over so as not to risk losing the queen. Bring out the dueling foils.   *Jul.:* I'll remove the dust that accumulated while we were away.   *Fer.:* Carranza says that all wounds proceed from an angular stance. What can love's stance have been when it gave me mine?   *Jul.:* Ask Dorotea—she supplied the bow.   *Fer.:* That was a good thrust of yours—all gashes come at the end of a slash. Oh, Dorotea, I have no protection against yours.   *Jul.:* Why are you throwing down your sword?

In Don Bela's courting of Dorotea, a scene alive with suggestions of stage action, there is a sequence remarkable in its minute focus on hands and fingers, the play of which Lope suggests as clearly as if he were dealing with full-scale figures. Such action in miniature, too minute to be seen and followed on a real stage, is peculiarly suited to the imaginary one of the *acción en prosa:*

Ger.: Como estás conualeciente, las [manos] traes sin adorno. Por
vida de don Bela, que le prestes essas dos sortijas por vn instante,
verás lo que parecen en aquella nieue.

Dor.: Necia estás, Gerarda. ¡Iesús, qué necia! Tened, señor, las manos.

Bel.: No desfauorezcáis, os suplico, estos diamantes, siquiera por lo
que os parecen; y permitidme que yo os los ponga.

Ger.: Acaba, muchacha. ¿Qué rehuyes los dedos? ¡Qué descortesía!
¿Tú naciste en la Corte?

Bel.: En éste no vienen bien, aquí están mejor. Dadme essotra mano.

Dor.: Basta que honréis la vna.

Bel.: Quexaráse la otra si no la igualo, y no quiero yo que aya
cosa en vos que se quexe de mí.

Dor.: Ya las rindo a vuestro fauor: que no quiero que me riña
Gerarda.

(p. 175)[30]

Ger.: Since you're convalescing, your [hands] are unadorned. On
Don Bela's life, lend her those two rings for a moment, you'll see
how they look against that snow.   *Dor.:* You're silly, Gerarda.
Lord, so silly! Sir, please keep your hands to yourself.   *Bel.:* Do not
be uncharitable to these diamonds, if only because of their
resemblance to you, and allow me to put them on you.   *Ger.:* Stop
dawdling, child. Why are you hiding your fingers? Such discourtesy!
Were you born in this Court city?   *Bel.:* They don't fit on this one,
they go better on this. Give me your other hand.   *Dor.:* It's enough
for you to honor one.   *Bel.:* The other will complain if I don't
treat it the same, and I don't want anything of yours to have any
complaint against me.   *Dor.:* I give them up to your favor. I don't
want Gerarda to scold me.

In another context I will be discussing the letter-burning scene in which
the remarks of Dorotea and Celia enable the reader to follow the sometimes
circuitous, sometimes precipitous course of the slips of paper into the
candle flame. In the meal scene, the dialogue, as has been noted, evokes all
the motions associated with eating far more vividly than in the parent scene
in *La Celestina*. We are able to tell when the characters are reaching for
dishes or pushing them away, munching, chewing, savoring their food, as
the following excerpts show:

Teo.: No tanta fruta, Dorotea, que estás muy conualeciente. Dexa
las vbas.

(p. 190)

Teo.: Less fruit, Dorotea, you're still recovering. Let the grapes go.

Teo.: Dexa el tozino, Dorotea. Come tu pollo, que no estás para
esso.

(p. 191)

Teo.: Let the bacon go, Dorotea. Eat your chicken, you're in no
shape for the other.

Ger.: ¡Quál está el tozinillo!

(p. 191)

Ger.: Does this bacon ever taste good!

Teo.: Come dessa gallina, muchacha.
Dor.: No puedo más, señora; que cocida me haze asco.

(p. 192)

Teo.: Take some of that hen, child.   *Dor.:* I can't manage it; it turns
my stomach, boiled.

Teo.: Quítale essas azeitunas, negra.
Ger.: Bien puede, que vn hora aurá que estoy con el huesso de vna,
pidiendo vna consolación.

(p. 197)

Teo.: Take those olives away from her, black girl.   *Ger.:* It's about
time, I've been sucking the pit of one for at least an hour, asking
for a reward.

Though separated by segments of dialogue, these indications suffice to
fill the whole scene with the activity of eating. Against the mobility of this
background, the stratagems of Gerarda's bibulousness are steadily projected.
One particularly noteworthy for its connected stage-play is her operation on
a fig, a fruit repellent because of its sweetness. Lope plausibly lets her explain
each step as she goes along, incidentally informing the reader, a procedure
justified by the fact that she is conducting a demonstration for intrigued
onlookers:

Teo.: Toma estos higos, Gerarda.
Ger.: Por ti tomaré vno, que no lo hiziera por el padre que me
engendró. Pero es menester que sepas que con vn higo se bebe
tres vezes.
Teo.: ¿Quién lo escriue?
Ger.: El filósofo Alaexos. ¿Pensaste que era Plutarco? Abrole por
medio. Dame, Celia, la primera.

Teo.: ¿Sin comerle bebes?
Ger.: Agora le hecho vn poco de sal. Dame la segunda.
Teo.: Ya tienes las dos aparte. ¿Qué harás agora?
Ger.: Cerrar el higo, y dame la tercera.
Cel.: Bebe, y buen prouecho . . .

. . . .

Teo.: ¿El higo echas por la ventana, después de tantas preuenciones?

(p. 190)

Teo.: Have some figs, Gerarda. *Ger.:* For your sake I'll take one, though I wouldn't do it for my own father. But you must understand that with a fig one takes three drinks. *Teo.:* Who wrote that? *Ger.:* The philosopher Alaejos [the name of a wine]. Did you think it was Plutarch? *Ger.:* First I split it open. Pour me the first, Celia. *Teo.:* You're drinking without eating it? *Ger.:* Now I put a little salt on it. Pour me the second. *Teo.:* That's two down. What comes next? *Ger.:* Closing the fig; now pour me the third. *Cel.:* Drink, and more power to you . . . *Teo.:* You've thrown the fig out the window after such elaborate preparations?

3. The underscoring of flare-ups of feeling or histrionic outbursts.

In contrast to these sequences indicative of continuous but minor activity, Lope sometimes brings a scene to a dramatic climax by implying a single act in which a whole situation is condensed: the "Suéltame, que daré vozes" ("Let me go or I'll shout") (p. 380), which is at once Marfisa's exit speech and her answer to Fernando's pleadings; the "No te leuantes furioso, que no te ha dado causa" ("Don't get up in a rage, she gave you no cause") (p. 315) of Julio when Fernando's reviving resentment of Don Bela threatens the reconciliation with Dorotea. Sometimes reactions and the actions they imply epitomize a whole relationship. Dorotea's "No bebáis tanto" ("Don't drink so much") (p. 148) after Marfisa accepts a drink of water vividly indicates the latter's precipitateness and also prefigures the difference in vital pace between the two women which will presently be demonstrated in their encounter.

Impulsive or histrionic behavior on Fernando's part is indicated and sometimes mocked in a "dead-pan" manner by Julio's remarks:

¿Dónde vas, que has quebrado la guitarra por salir de prisa? (p. 93)

Where are you going—you've smashed the guitar you're in such a hurry!

Por el balcón no se baxa bien a la calle: mejor irás por la puerta.

(p. 102)

The balcony isn't the best way to the street; the door is better.

Fer.: ¡Ay paredes! ¡Ay puertas! ¡Ay rexas de la cárcel hermosa de
   mi libertad! Quiero besaros mil vezes.
Iul.: ¿Los hierros besas?

(p. 269) [31]

Fer.: Oh walls! Oh doors! Oh bars of the beautiful prison of my
freedom! I'll give you a thousand kisses.   *Jul.:* You're kissing the
bars?

What Mrs. Malkiel calls the *acotación enunciativa*, which simply reports to
the reader what has happened or who is present, as a detached fact, is never
just this in *La Dorotea*, even when a character reports his own action:
Fernando's "Ya estoy sentado" ("I'm seated") (p. 293) conveys unwilling
compliance, as if to say: "What next?" Don Bela's "Esta es la reja" ("This
is the window grill") (p. 258) suggests actual groping in the dark as well as
arrival at his goal. Fernando's "¡Desmayóse!" ("She's fainted!") (p. 94)
expresses genuine consternation. A shocked realization is conveyed by
Celia's "¡Iesús! La sortija de los diamantes se ha tragado para matarse"
("Good heavens—she's swallowed the diamond ring to kill herself")
p. 126) following the descriptive "¿Qué hazes, señora? ¿Qué has metido
en la boca?" ("What are you doing, madam? What are you putting in your
mouth?"). Finally, Dorotea's announcement: "Rompíle. ¡Vitoria!" ("I've
torn it apart. Victory!") (p. 426), climaxing her struggle with Fernando's
portrait, snaps the tension of the confrontation with a note of feverish
theatrical exultation.

   As in the last two instances, the indirect stage directions often include
references to objects which are the equivalent of stage properties. Lope has
the dramatist's knack of making them functional and expressive. Almost
palpable is a surprisingly large array, ranging from the trivial to the exquisite.
Olives and diamonds, stockings and flowered cloths, guitar strings and silver
tankards, charred love-notes and card-sized portraits become embodiments
of situations or foci of action. They reduce developments to tangible form
as if for visual apprehension. Attention is frequently drawn to them by having
the characters pause over them, hold them up, pass them back and forth.
As the work proceeds, certain objects thereby become charged with a
particular significance which is communicated as if on signal to the reader.

A conspicuous example is "aquel búcaro dorado que tiene el Cupido tirando al dios marino" ("the gilded *búcaro* with the Cupid aiming at the sea-god on it") which Don Bela gives to Gerarda (p. 132). We are able to follow its progress step by step: on Don Bela's orders, out of Laurencio's reluctant hands ("Este es el búcaro"—"Here's the *búcaro*"), into Gerarda's waiting grasp. At this point the object already is serving as a conversation piece, as commonly occurs in the *acción en prosa*, its pictorial ornamentation being supplemented by verbal adornments. Gerarda examines the *búcaro* and presently asks matter-of-factly:

> *Ger.:* ¿Qué dizen estas letras?
> *Bel.:* Omnia vincit amor, que es vn hemistichio de vn poeta latino.
>
> (p. 133)[32]

> *Ger.:* What do these letters say? *Bel.:* Omnia vincit amor, which is a hemistich of a Latin poet.

Three scenes later attention is pointedly paid to the object when Gerarda holds it up before Dorotea:

> *Ger.:* Mira, mira, ¡qué búcaro tan lindo! Aquí está Cupidillo, aquel de tu edad, aquel dulce matadorzillo. Toma, açotale por el mal que te ha hecho. Bien lo merece. Pero no, por el siglo de mi confessor; que primero me has de dar algo.
> *Dor.:* ¡Qué lindo es!
> *Cel.:* A ver, señora.
> *Dor.:* Déxale, que le ensucias, Celia. Pero ¿qué quieres que te dé, madre?
> *Ger.:* No más de recibirle. Di: "Yo le recibo."
> *Dor.:* ¿Es casamiento?
>
> (p. 157)

> *Ger.:* Look, look, what a lovely *búcaro*! Here's cute little Cupid; he's just your age, the cunning little murderer. Here, whip him for the harm he's done you. He well deserves it. But no, upon my confessor's soul, first you must give me something. *Dor.:* How pretty it is. *Cel.:* Let's see, madam. *Dor.:* Leave it alone, Celia, you'll get it dirty. But what do you want me to give you, Gerarda? *Ger.:* Just your receiving him. Say: "I receive him." *Dor.:* Is this a marriage?

The catch-all symbolism of the ornamental motif had been seized on by Don Bela in his conversation with Gerarda: "Y si quieres alegorizarle estas figuras, di que el Cupido es ella y yo el dios marino, pues vine por la mar a que me tirasse las flechas de sus ojos" ("And if you wish to allegorize these figures for her, say that she's the Cupid and I the sea-god since I came over the sea to be shot at by the arrows of her eyes") (p. 132). Now Gerarda (who has managed to bring Cupid into the conversation a few moments before) playfully but purposefully dramatizes Don Bela's static "allegory," bringing Cupid to life and making the acceptance of the vase a renunciation of the past ("Toma, açotale por el mal que te ha hecho"—"Here, whip him for the harm he's done you") and an augury of the future ("Di: 'Yo le recibo'"—"Say: 'I receive him'"), as Dorotea well understands ("¿Es casamiento?"—"Is this a marriage?"). For Gerarda the transaction simply detaches love from profit. Dorotea, hesitant but weak-willed, resorts to coy casuistry: "Este es niñería, y está aquí amor presente; y siendo suyo el agrauio, no me dize que no le tome" ("This is mere child's play, and love is right here and though he's the offended party, he doesn't tell me not to take it") (p. 159).

The conversation passes on to other things, the *búcaro*, now Dorotea's, is put down somewhere, Don Bela comes to call unexpectedly and showers Dorotea with new gifts, Teodora is heard knocking, Don Bela is hurried out, Celia hastily ordered by Dorotea to put all his presents out of sight. The *búcaro*, there all the while but not among the gifts delivered in person, escapes notice. Teodora's sharp eye does not miss it:

> *Teo.:* ¡Ay! ¿Qué búcaro es éste?
> *Dor.:* Vna amiga me le ha feriado al manteo que tú dezías que auía
>   vendido, y de rabia no he querido enseñártele.
> *Teo.:* Aunque te dixe aquellas cosas, bien sé yo tu virtud y honestidad,
>   Dorotea. ¡Qué lindo es el búcaro!
>
> (p. 189)

> *Teo.:* Oh, what is this *búcaro*? *Dor.:* A woman friend gave it to me
> in exchange for that cloak you claimed I had sold and I wouldn't
> show it to you out of spite. *Teo.:* Even though I spoke to you that
> way, Dorotea, I am well aware what a decent, respectable girl you
> are. What a lovely *búcaro*!

The *búcaro* speaks more eloquently to Teodora than any words. Its accrued meaningfulness is taken in by her in a flash. It produces an instantaneous volte-face toward her daughter and initiates a reconciliation which Lope cannot resist underscoring ironically—"Bien sé yo tu virtud y honestidad, Dorotea" ("I am well aware what a decent, respectable girl you are, Dorotea").[33]

It has already been suggested that the choruses of *La Dorotea*, another indication of dramatic craftsmanship, are only ostensibly Senecan. In fact they furnish a final example of Lope's individualistic manner of appropriating a dramatic tradition. Through their presence, the effect of segmentation without discontinuity, already noted in the case of the scene joinings, is reaffirmed. Their outward function is to accentuate the division into five acts, sharpening the definition of each one. Since, however, for a reader there is no actual interval of time between acts, the choruses constitute only the briefest of interpositions.

Undoubtedly the cultivation of classical metrical and strophic patterns in them is intended to put the weight of Senecan tradition behind them and lend authority to the sentiments they voice. Lope adheres to the Senecan practice of detaching the chorus from the action and making it a vehicle for the dramatist's moral comments, exhortations, and reflections. There was some precedent for this in his immediate model, the *Primeras tragedias españolas* of Jerónimo Bermúdez (1577), and in another writer of Senecan tragedy admired by Lope, Cristóbal de Virués. More characteristic, however, is the tendency of such ecletic dramatists to bring the chorus into dialogue with the characters, even into the action, and to respect its collective character. (In Bermúdez we have a "Chorus of Women of Coimbra," in Virués a "Chorus of the Priests of the Temple.")[34] The one hint of a choric collectivity in Lope, the choric plural of "Porque cantemos tus loores diuinos / en sáphicos himnos" ("That we may sing your divine praise in Sapphic hymns") (p. 129), is, so to speak, purely fossilized; the essential point is that a single voice is speaking. But is this a personal or an "official" voice? Examination of the choruses reveals that, characteristically and not unexpectedly, the latter voice is undercut by the former.

In the cast, the choruses are listed in order of appearance: Coro de Amor, Coro de Interés, Coro de Zelos, Coro de Vengança, Coro de[l] Exemplo (Chorus of Love, Chorus of Self-Interest, Chorus of Jealousy, Chorus of Vengeance, Chorus of Exemplarity). Lope seems to imagine them as allegorical figures stepping solemnly forth when the talking stops. But the voice that speaks in the choruses is not a philosophical one even when Lope deplores the power of love, as in the first chorus. Nor does he develop other common Senecan themes like the shortness of life and the inconstancy of fortune. Beneath their formality and ostensible admonishment, we detect an individual voice and when we take all the choruses together, the credo we find it intoning emerges as markedly personal. The noticeable diversity of the choruses in tone and style suggests that, rather than envisaging a consistent dramatic function for them, Lope saw in this feature of classical tragedy a chance to step out from behind the characters and speak on his own, either "officially" as in the first and last choruses or individually as in the others. This fact is particularly obvious in the concluding Coro del Exemplo, where the first person clearly represents an author's apologia:

> Quando del amor lasciuo
> el trágico fin contemplo,
> no sólo al deleite escriuo,
> pero sentencioso templo
> la dotrina en lo festiuo,
> y en el engaño el exemplo.
>
> (p. 458)

When I behold the tragic ending of lascivious love, I write not only for entertainment but sententiously temper doctrine with amusement and deceit with exemplarity.

In the Coro de Amor at the end of Act I the tone of the exemplary advice offered is noticeably forced: "Huid sus engaños, hazed resistencia / a tanta violencia, o locos amantes" ("Flee its deceptions, stand up against such violence, oh mad lovers") (p. 129). In this chorus, Lope is visibly following out the assertion of the Prologue that "quantos escriuen de amor enseñan cómo se ha de huir, no cómo se ha de imitar" ("everyone writing of love shows how it is to be avoided, not how it is to be imitated") (p. 52).

In the second, third, and fourth choruses he drops this admonitory stance as he focuses on the aspect of amatory psychology most prominent in the act. The focus is more pointed in each successive act, yet Lope remains dispassionate, as if in detached reflection on private experience. By the end of the Coro de Interés, which follows shortly after Don Bela buys his way into Dorotea's favors in Act II, it is Interés itself which is speaking (referring to Love): "Que mis pomas hespérides / han de vencer sus máquinas" ("For my apples of the Hesperides will outdo its machinations") (p. 202), the only occasion when the *leitmotiv* of the act is turned into a speaker in the manner of the allegorical figures found in plays of classical mold. But there is no consistency in this device. Interés, to begin with, had been spoken of, not speaker: "Al interés esplendido / son las empresas fáciles" ("For glittering wealth enterprises are easy") (p. 200), while Love, referred to in the third person, had been spoken to at the outset: "Amor, tus fuerças rígidas" ("Love, your rigorous forces") (p. 199). The true first person implied is that of the author and it was evidently an afterthought to make it coincide with Interés, the subject of the chorus. The style is appropriately ornate, Interés being a worldly force, not an intimate feeling. A succession of ancient *exempla* and *casus* dispassionately enumerates its triumph over Love.

In the Coro de Zelos, of Act III, the subject is first addressed in apostrophes that double as characteristically Lopean definitions of jealousy, then Jealousy is reproved in a series of classical *exempla* illustrative of its disastrous effects. But after so much condemnation, Lope ends in a different vein: "No passes de rezelos; / que si llegas a ofensa, no eres zelos" ("Don't go beyond misgivings, for if you become an offense, you're not jealousy") (p. 288). The implication is that jealousy is a useful spur to love, provided that it is groundless, a tenet of Lopean love-lore plainly relevant to what is to come: *venganza*. Lope is not now thinking in terms of making love abhorrent; he is making a practical observation and revealing incidentally that the indignation toward jealousy voiced from the outset is not so much moral as practical in origin. We are closer to an *ars amatoria* than to a sermon.

The Coro de Vengança (Act IV) contains purely worldly advice; moral concern is even more noticeably absent. Lope is speaking feelingly about a subject particularly close to his own psyche; he does not even bother to prop it up with *exempla* or famous case histories. He ceases to declaim or to apostrophize and speaks in confidential tones, for anyone who will listen:

> Tenga quien agrauió justos rezelos
> y nunca mire el alma por los labios;
> que amistades son dulces sobre zelos,
> pero siempre fingidas sobre agrauios.

(p. 383)

One who has given offense may well have his misgivings and should never judge the soul by the lips, for reconciliations are sweet after jealousy but always feigned after offenses.

Lope is clearly issuing a warning to lovers but he is warning how to manage love, not how to flee it. The chorus has a markedly foreboding note: it points to the inevitable consequences of what has transpired in the act, looking ahead to Act V.

Vossler calls the choruses "guirnaldas de adorno" (ornamental wreaths). Ornate they may be but they are not simply ornamental or adventitious. Although the leitmotifs singled out in them are already quite clearly articulated in the dialogue, in crystallizing these motifs formally, the choruses also reflect in capsular form the total historical-poetical character of the work. Thematically as well as formally they offer a counterposition of the personal and the traditional. (Lope's adaptation of classical metrical and strophic patterns, it may be observed, is highly idiosyncratic.) Even where the intimate tone of voice is not heard—as in the first and last choruses—one awaits its entrance or retains its echo. In the opening and concluding choruses as in the Prologue and the concluding Ciceronian epigraph—"Lectionem sine vlla delectatione negligo" ("I spurn reading a work that gives no enjoyment")—Lope establishes, so to speak, a protective shell of express exemplarity, in keeping with the moral climate of the Counter Reformation. But the small personal voice that becomes increasingly audible in the inner choruses undermines the ponderousness of the official voice and suggests a lack of solidity at the core, beneath the rigid architectonics of the choral structures. Like the artificial patterns Lope's characters impose upon their lives, the formal rigidities must be reconciled with the suppler rhythms of experience.[35]

The cultivation of effects of segmentation without discontinuity, which we have noticed several times, points to one of the lines of force governing Lope's fusion of various literary traditions. It thus leads ultimately toward the inner form of the work, which will be discussed in later chapters. At present it remains to be seen how the lyrics contribute to the *concordia discors* of the whole.

It may be noted that we shall sometimes find them interacting with their contexts in a distinctly dramatic way, throwing inner conflicts into sharp relief or contributing new elements to the representation of a total affective situation. In these cases we will have a particularly clear demonstration of the fusion of the lyric and the dramatic modes in the *acción en prosa*.

The explanation given in the Prologue for the presence of lyrics in the dialogue falls noticeably short. He has chosen this time not to write in verse, says Lope, "si bien ha puesto algunos porque descanse quien leyere en ellos de la continuación de la prosa, y porque no le falte a La Dorotea la variedad, con el deseo de que salga hermosa" ("although he has included some so that the reader may find in them resting places amidst the continuity of the prose and so that La Dorotea may not be lacking in variety, to the end that it may prove beautiful") (p. 51). The reader is thus to find in the lyrics resting places where he may enjoy the esthetic pleasure always afforded, in Lope's view, by variety. The words seem prompted by the misgivings that Lope usually felt when writing prose, narrative or not. He notes, for example, of *El triunfo de la fe en los reinos del Japón* (Triumph of the Faith in the Kingdoms of Japan) (1618) that it is not "escrito en verso, si bien lleva algunos que celebran la fortaleza de estos mártires" ("written in verse, although it contains some that celebrates the fortitude of these martyrs"); and, as at the end of *La Dorotea*, he quotes Cicero to the effect that it is discourteous, when writing, "nec delectatione aliqua allicere lectorem" ("not to allure the reader with some entertainment").[36] There was no problem of holding an audience when writing for the stage: it was right at hand and Lope knew his power over it, which his metrical skill enhanced. His prose narratives— *La Arcadia* (1598), *El peregrino en su patria* (1604), *Los pastores de Belén* (1614), the *Novelas a la señora Marcia Leonarda* (1624)—all appeared, however, with verse insertions, as if to secure their hold over a discriminating reader. In keeping with the view prevalent in his day, Lope rated verse more highly than prose and assumed that his reader would do likewise.[37]

In the case of *La Dorotea* Lope seems to have been motivated, in addition, by a desire to make the work in a special way a tribute to the mistress whose presence was already felt in the figure of the heroine and in the sentiments she inspired in Don Bela. Of the twenty-seven poems, all but three lyrical, which the work includes, some ten had been written originally for Marta de Nevares, including the four eclogues *in morte* which Lope had added upon her death (April 7, 1632), one month before the work was approved by the censor (May 6, 1632). Others represented compositions of his later years which he particularly prized and sought in this way to perpetuate. The poems were clearly added when he gave *La Dorotea* its definitive form, for, with a single possible exception, he included nothing from his early years.[38] The *acción en prosa* contains, in effect, a small anthology of secular lyrics of Lope's final period.

In discussing them it will be useful to consider first those lyrics which are played and sung, connecting them with a broader context of harmony in which they find a place. Then the lyrics read or recited will be considered. I will reserve for other connections and treat here only in passing the poems of *soledad*, manifestly expressions more of Lope himself than of the characters: "A mis soledades voy" ("I go off to my solitude") and the four elegies to Marta de Nevares. I will similarly reserve for later Don Bela's madrigal and a lyric of Dorotea's composition which she sings in Act V, scene 9. Nor are the three compositions not truly lyrical of concern here.[39]

It has already been observed that the prose of the pastoral provided Lope with the clearest precedents to follow in including lyrics spoken or sung. *La Celestina* and *La Euphrosina*, with their occasional snatches of verse, in most cases fragmentary couplets or quatrains, could not serve as a guide.[40] Yet Lope goes beyond the pastoral in the extent to which he makes the lyrics revelations of moods and affective states, poems which look away from events and toward the inwardness of singer or speaker. He neglects entirely, as might be expected, the narrative function often entrusted to them. In the pastoral, where they sometimes carry the story forward, important events, key developments in the characters' lives, may be presented in verse; tributary tales may be joined to the central line of the narrative in this way also.[41] As might be expected in a work where the real action lies so often beneath the surface, the lyrics of La Dorotea apprise us of nothing essential that happens or has happened to the characters. As far as their "story" goes, the poems could be dispensed with entirely. When they do concern some particular incident, they simply commemorate or reflect upon it subjectively, as an experience.

When we find lyrics serving dramatic functions, these are, not unexpectedly, more subdued, less spectacular than is usual on the stage. If contrasts are effected, they are not the striking shifts, the lulls before a storm, that one finds, for example, in Fuenteovejuna (The Sheep-Well), where an idealized version of events is introduced in the form of a wedding song. They give us quieter contrapositions of states of feeling or insights into character.[42] If atmosphere is being developed, it is not with the intensity and brooding sense of doom which one finds, for instance, in El caballero de Olmedo.

Much more significant in La Dorotea than in any antecedent are matters of authorship, craftsmanship, and performance, whether poems are spoken or sung. This is scarcely surprising in a milieu in which artistic connoisseurship is a distinction and the poetic métier an attainment rather than an automatic possession; where, too, there is, on the part of the characters, so much studying of effects, so much attention to performing for the benefit of others. Listeners as well as those who compose, recite, or perform vocally or instrumentally are sensitive to nuance and critically on the qui vive. For all of them these poems, rising out of prose that, unlike pastoral prose, is essentially colloquial, constitute an impulse toward a refining, stylizing, universalizing of feeling and attitude.

In this respect the contrast with pastoral convention is again striking. By birthright every shepherd is endowed with poetic and musical ability. Sooner or later almost every character who enters a pastoral narrative sings or recites—some sixteen individually in La Diana, for example, and over twenty in La Arcadia.[43] This without mentioning group performances—duos, trios, choruses, poetic games, and festivals. Moreover, there is rarely a distinction between author and performer or an insistence on authorship in the pastoral world. The poems are usually presented as the creation of those who introduce them, improvised at the moment of utterance, though they show no signs of improvisation in style. The very commonness of poetic talent causes it to go virtually unremarked; when made, comments are usually brief and conventional.

Lope, on the other hand, surrounds his lyrics with an aura of expertise and appreciation in respect to composition, stylistic refinement, quality of recitation or performance.[44] He also noticeably clusters them around Fernando and Dorotea. As performers, they sing nine of the poems included and read or recite from memory eight others (one of them ascribed to Don Bela), accounting for nearly three quarters of the twenty-four. Five more lyrics, including one of his own composition, are presented by Fernando's companion, Julio. Don Bela reads his own madrigal, and Marfisa a ballad of Fernando's.[45]

In respect to authorship, Fernando is the creator of eleven poems; of the others, one is by Dorotea, one by Julio, and four are given to Don Bela, while the rest are attributed directly or indirectly to Lope or are presented with no indication of origin.[46]

The key to the role of music and song in *La Dorotea* is given in the very first words of the Prologue: "Como nuestra alma en el canto y música con tan suaue afecto se deleita que algunos la llamaron harmonía, inuentaron los antiguos poetas el modo de los metros y los pies para los números" ("As our soul takes such delight in song and music, with such sweet enjoyment that some have called it harmony, the ancient poets invented the mode of meters and feet for measures") (p. 50). While Lope goes on to ascribe to music a morally beneficent object and to assert, as has been seen, that metrical and musical form are not necessary parts of *poiesis*, the pertinent point, in the present context, is the suggestion of an intimate connection between the human psyche and music. The view that the soul itself may be harmony, as presented in Plato's *Phaedo* (ultimately to be rejected by Socrates as grounds for affirming the soul's immortality), is based on an analogy between well-tempered bodily humors and the tuning of a lyre: "The thought, Socrates, must have occurred to your own mind that . . . when the body is in a manner strung and held together by the elements of hot and cold, wet and dry, then the soul is the harmony or due proportionate admixture of them."[47] It is clear that Lope sees both these aspects of harmony—the musical and the psychic—as elements of an all-embracing Neo-Platonic scheme of which the motive force is love. In a pointed digression, he has one of his characters, César, after hearing Fernando sing, express the view that love was the true inventor of music:

Porque la armonía es concento, el concento es concordia del son graue y del agudo, y la concordia fue instituida de amor; porque

> con aquella recíproca beneuolencia se sigue el efeto de la música, que es el deleite. Esta vnión amorosa llamó Marsilio Ficino ministra suya: assí la bella Lamia enloqueció de amor al gran Demetrio.   (p. 403)

> Because harmony is concord, concord is agreement of low and high tones and such agreement was established by love; because from that mutual attraction the effect of music, which is pleasure, follows. This loving union Marsilio Ficino called its helper: by means of it beautiful Lamia drove the great Demetrius mad with love.

Drawing perhaps on memory, Lope here fuses reminiscences of Ficino's commentary on the *Symposium* and reminiscences of the *Symposium* itself. Ficino, in the third chapter of the third speech of the commentary ("Amor est magister artium et gubernator"—"Love is the master and ruler of the arts"), surveys the different arts as works of love, devoting most attention to the first two considered, medicine and music:

> Quid enim aliud medicina considerat quam quo modo humores quatuor corporis amici invicem fiant atque permaneant . . . Idem in musica observatur. Cuius artifices qui numeri, quos numeros aut magis aut minus diligant investigant . . . Hi voces acutas et graves, natura diversas, certis intervallis et modulis suis sibi invicem magis amicas faciunt. Ex quo harmonie compositio et suavitas nascitur.[48]

> For with what else is medicine concerned than with the way the four humors of the body become well disposed toward each other and remain so . . . The same thing may be observed in music. Whose composers investigate which melodies love which others more, which less . . . They make high and low notes, by nature diverse, better disposed toward one another by means of certain intervals and measures. Whence arises the composition and smoothness of harmony.

Ficino alludes to the differing effects of the two melodic modes on the hearer, then goes on to astronomy, prophecy, and the priestly calling, and suggests that love guides all others as well. Whence his conclusion: "amorem in omnibus ad omnia esse. Omnium auctorem servatoremque existere et artium universarum dominum et magistrum" ("love is in all things for all things. It exists as the author and preserver of all things and the lord and master of all arts"). Lope's "ministra suya" may derive from a misunderstanding of Ficino's "servatorem." In any case, though Lope applies the words only to music, the references to its "divine" nature and to Ficino imply the total scheme of cosmic harmony.

The wording of the corresponding passage of the *Symposium* (which I quote in Ficino's Latin) is clearly recalled by Lope. Plato, too, makes an express parallel between bodily humors and musical notes:

> Ex his quae prius discrepabant, graui scilicet et acuto, deinde per artem musicam consonantibus, harmonia conficitur . . . Harmonia namque concentus est. Concentus vero concordia quaedam . . . Et quemadmodum humoribus medicina concordiam, ita vocibus musica consonantiam tribuens, Amorem consensumque mutuum gignet.[49]

> Harmony is formed from high and low notes which had formerly been in discord but subsequently through musical art are brought into agreement . . . For harmony is concord and concord is a certain agreement . . . And just as medicine effects agreement among the humors, so music produces consonance among notes, creating Love and mutual accord.

In *La Dorotea* we shall find singing and musical performance related more insistently and subtly than in the pastoral world to a conception of universal harmony, the creation of love, which links the natural world, the passions and humors, the souls of human beings, and the whole cosmos in a single network through reconciliation of contraries—*concordia discors*, concerted strife—or, indeed, through natural affinities.[50] In the pastoral world, a sentient nature regularly responds in consonance to the songs or moods of the shepherds who dwell in it. If it fails to respond sympathetically, its indifference, felt as a dissonance, still maintains the principle of harmony. With the shift from the conventional natural setting of the pastoral to the prosaic urban world of the *acción en prosa*, this idealistic scheme inevitably appears in a new light: as an aspiration, a vision yearned for, instead of an unquestioned possession or assumption. The framework of harmony into which the lyrics as well as the sought-for attunement of human emotions fit acquires thereby a problematical character. Its elusiveness, however, connects it more compellingly with a world of actuality, with everyday contingencies—such as those of Lope's life with Marta de Nevares, in which it had become a genuine aspiration.

If the earnest need to make the vision of a harmony underlying the scheme of things a reality for himself is a development of Lope's later years, the ideas on which it rests are not new to him, as passages cited by Morby (p. 225, n. 43, and p. 403, n. 54) dating as far back as *La Arcadia* and *La hermosura de Angélica* show. In regard to the art of music itself, there is a long excursus in *Los pastores de Belén* which, although pedantic and derivative in character, consisting as it does of "curious and philosophical things which [Aminadab] said he had read in various books," shows clearly the interrelatedness of what Lope calls divine and human music:

> Trató de que el supremo Hacedor de los cielos les había dado al principio tal templanza, que no se habían jamás destemplado de aquella armonía . . . Trató luego de la música humana, instrumental y aneja a la del cielo, como de principio de quien se deriva, y de qué suerte la música aguda llama a la grave.

> He talked of how the supreme Maker of the heavens had brought them at the beginning so into tune that they had never lost the attunement of that harmony . . . He then talked of human music, instrumental, and linked to that of heaven as the principle from which it derives, and of how high-pitched music attracts the low.

Elsewhere in the same work music is called "alma del mundo, gobierno y harmonía de los cielos" ("soul of the world, rule and harmony of the heavens").[51]

The movements of the humors that control human feelings, linked though they may be to the movements of celestial bodies, do not, unfortunately, respond to human music as the soul does to divine. Lope did not oversimplify the interaction between music and human emotions, as a disquisition in *El peregrino en su patria* makes plain:

> Es cosa certíssima que las hierbas, el harmonía, y otras muchas cosas sensibles pueden mudar la disposición del cuerpo: y por el consiguiente el movimiento de la sensualidad . . . Aristóteles en el séptimo de su *Política* . . . quiere, que diversas harmonías causen diversas passiones en los hombres.

> It is absolutely certain that herbs, harmony, and many other objects of the senses may alter the disposition of the body and consequently the movements of sensuality . . . Aristotle in the seventh book of his *Politics* . . . affirms that different harmonies produce different passions in men.

Though noting that other authorities support this view, Lope ends the disquisition with a more moderate and orthodox opinion: "Si las hierbas y el harmonía, y las cosas corporales no pueden totalmente redimir estas vexaciones con su natural virtud, a lo menos pueden aligerarlas" ("If herbs and harmony and bodily things cannot completely dispel these afflictions with their natural virtue, they can at least alleviate them").[52] But against even this moderate view, Lope acknowledges that often music merely intensifies the emotion one is already feeling. Two pages later, a character is declaring: "No quisiera que con él huviera hecho la música el efecto que todos dicen, que es entristecer más a los que lo están" ("I would not wish music to have the effect on him that they always say it has, which is to make sad people all the sadder"). Morby cites Montemayor: "La música es tanta parte para hazer acrecentar la tristeza del triste como la alegría del que más contento vive" ("Music is as likely to increase the sadness of the sad as the joy of the person happiest with the world"). Morby's abundant documentation of this commonplace in Lope proves that it was no empty formula for him.[53]

The range of responses to music and verse in *La Dorotea* goes beyond even those suggested here. Composed, sung, or heard, they may assuage or intensify feeling; they may demonstrate a performer's skill, prove his artistic attainment; they may amplify a theme, examine an emotion, reflect an experience touched on in the dialogue; they may simply stir painful memories. Through the moods they project, the feelings they underscore, they contribute to the delineation of character; in their placing and motifs, they help sustain the total thematic design.

It follows from the central place of music in the cosmos and in the human microcosm, from the fact that human music is a derivation of the divine— or, in the terminology Lope used, practical music is a derivation of theoretical —that musical expression had for him an elemental and natural authenticity, just as, for different reasons, prose did.[54] The musical climate of Lope's age is sympathetic to his personal tendency in music as in poetry, to keep the natural conjoined with the artistic. As Rafael Mitjana points out, contrapuntal polyphony is in Lope's day being superseded by expressive monody with instrumental accompaniment—precisely the combination we find in *La Dorotea*. The music is subordinated to poetic texts, the aim being to "translate intimate emotion and affective atmosphere." The development of chromatism will lead to musical drama, to an "explicit interpretation of feelings, sentiments, and passions."[55] Of such drama, which looks toward opera, Lope's own *La selva sin Amor* (The Wood without Love), written for a court festivity in 1629, is one of the earliest Spanish examples. Lope relates admiringly in his preface to the published version that at the performance:

Los instrumentos ocupaban la primera parte del teatro sin ser vistos, a cuya armonía cantaban las figuras los versos, haciendo en la misma composición de la música las admiraciones, las quejas, los amores, las iras y demás afectos. (Ac., V, 753)

The instruments occupied the forward part of the theater without being seen, to the accompaniment of which the actors sang the lines, bringing out in the very composition of the music their wonderment, lamentations, love, anger, and other emotions.

Long before, in a sonnet of the *Rimas sacras*, Lope had used music as a point of reference in evaluating spontaneity and sincerity in speech:

> La lengua del amor a quien no sabe
> lo que es amor, ¡qué barbara parece!;
> pues como por instantes enmudece,
> tiene pausas de música suave.
>   Tal vez suspensa, tal aguda y grave,
> rotos conceptos al amante ofrece;
> aguarda los compases que padece,
> porque la causa su destreza alabe.[56]

How barbaric the tongue of love seems to one who does not know what love is, for, as it falls silent at times, it has a soft music's pauses. Now dropping away, now high, now low, it offers broken thoughts to the lover; it waits on the pulsations of feeling so that the one inspiring it will praise its skill.

A speaking voice that directly records the inner pulsations of feeling ("los compases que padece") will be using a language akin to music, with its rests, its holds, its drops and rises in pitch. Such an attitude toward music is quite consonant with the tendency toward directness of expression which Jesús Bal, in his edition of Lopean songs with musical settings, finds particularly Spanish.[57] Noting that the "tendency toward the *solo* is what facilitates musical dilettantism in the Spain of that time," Bal cites Fernando in *La Dorotea* as a case in point and remarks that it was in the aristocratic salons of the age that songs like Lope's with musical settings were most frequently performed. Dorotea's salon and Fernando's quarters are those of would-be aristocrats only, but the realistic basis of the work clearly extends to its musical dimension. We shall see in fact that music becomes a retreat for the characters when words prove inadequate.

Lope gives Fernando and Dorotea the distinction of being the only characters who sing and play instruments in *La Dorotea*. Each of them sings, accompanying himself, on three different occasions. Each is seen first seeking to assuage intimate feelings in song, later offering two or three selections to a hearer, finally singing a single song in privacy. Dorotea plays refined salon instruments, the harp and the spinet (*clavicordio*); Fernando, the guitar. One of Dorotea's three harp melodies is even of her own composition (p. 186); another (p. 448), we are told, is by Juan de Palomares. Gerarda does not fail to tell Don Bela how accomplished Dorotea is on the spinet: "Pues si la viéssedes poner las manos en vn clauicordio, pensaréis que anda vna araña de cristal por las teclas" ("Why, if you saw her set her hands to a spinet, you would think a crystalline spider was running over the keys") (p. 186). It is clear that Dorotea is a musician of no mean attainments. Her statement "Sólo no tengo de música el escusarme, porque me falte todo" ("The only thing about a musician I don't do is to ask indulgence because I am deficient in everything") (p. 179) is quite exact. Marta de Nevares probably came closer than Elena Osorio to the musical skills Lope has given Dorotea, though the only instruments he alludes to in Marta's case are the guitar—"Si toma en las manos un instrumento, a su divina voz e incomparable destreza el padre de esta música, Vicente Espinel, se suspendiera atónito" ("If you pick up an instrument, the father of this music, Vicente Espinel, would stop short in astonishment at your divine voice and incomparable skill")—and the lute.[58]

Fernando is also an accomplished musician. He sings for his own delectation in the first and last acts and serenades Dorotea with songs in the third. He seems to be the composer of his own accompaniments.[59]

On only one occasion in *La Dorotea* (III, 7 and 8) is Fernando shown communicating with Dorotea through music. On this occasion, however, the intimate expressiveness attained by Spanish monody and the wider implication of musical harmony in the *acción en prosa* invest the singing and the reaction to it with a rich range of meaning. The lovers are straining toward reconciliation. Fernando, having sung "Pobre barquilla mía" ("Poor little boat of mine"), the third of Lope's elegies to Marta de Nevares, worries about the quality of his performance:

> *Fer.:* Creo que he cantado mal, porque me temblaua la voz.
>
> *Iul.:* Antes no te he oído en mi vida con tan excelentes passos y cromáticos. Divinamente passauas en las otauas de la voz al falsete.
>
> *Fer.:* Deues de consolarme; que mal puede tener la voz segura quien tiene el coraçón temblando. Cantaré otra cosa, ya que voy perdiendo el miedo.
>
> (p. 277)

Fer.: I think I sang badly because my voice was quivering.   *Jul.:*
On the contrary, never in my life have I heard such excellent trills
and chromatics from you. You went from the voice to the falsetto
superbly in the octaves.   *Fer.:* You must be trying to cheer me up,
for someone whose heart is trembling can scarcely have a firm voice.
I'll sing something else since I'm beginning to be less afraid.

In this account of Fernando's rendition of Lope's elegy, one reads the
restlessness of his emotional state—its pain, uncertainty, longing; these are
superimposed on Lope's own profound feelings of desolation. The tremulous-
ness of his voice, conveying directly (as in the sonnet of the *Rimas sacras*) the
misgivings of the heart, records also, without a jar, the still fresh grief of
Lope. The emotional blend of long ago and yesterday is complete and
through music it achieves a single ultimate authenticity. Though music does
not bring Fernando release from distress, it clearly brings some alleviation,
as his remark "Cantaré otra cosa, ya que voy perdiendo el miedo" ("I'll
sing something else since I'm beginning to be less afraid") shows. The effect
is in keeping with what Lope had written in *El peregrino:* if harmony cannot
dispel pain, it can at least assuage it.

Dorotea's response to the singing is shown when a guitar string breaks
and Fernando is forced to suspend his rendering of the remaining lament
for Marta just as he reaches (for the third time) the recurring refrain:

Mas tanto pueden tristezas
de passadas alegrías,
que obligan, si porfían,
a no estimar la muerte ni la vida.

(p. 282)

But regrets over past joys have such power that, if they keep up,
they force one to hold life and death in no esteem.

It is as if the deep disharmony of Fernando's emotions injected into the
Lopean inconsolability expressed in the ballad was momentarily too much
for even the power of music to reconcile. Behind this small occurrence there
ultimately lies the Platonic figure of the soul as the harmony of a well-
tempered body. The emotional effect of the singing, drawn out in the
lengthened last line, carries over into the pause and Dorotea is stirred to the
depths:

Dor.: Temblando me está el coraçón. Estoi por llamarle.
Fel.: Tu madre ha conocido la voz, y está mirando, aunque finje

desatención, la inquietud de tus acciones y el desasossiego de tus
mouimientos.

Dor.: ¡Ay, Felipa, que somos Fernando y yo como la voz y el eco!
El canta, y yo repito los vltimos acentos.

Fel.: Creo que andas porque te vea.

Dor.: ¿Puede ignorar su alma que la mía le escucha?

Fel.: La prima que se le quebró ha puesto, y a cantar buelue.

(p. 282)

Dor.: My heart is quivering. I feel an urge to call him.   *Fel.*: Your
mother has recognized the voice and, though she pretends not to be,
is observing your agitated behavior and restless motions.   *Dor.*: Oh,
Felipa, Fernando and I are voice and echo. He sings and I repeat the
final notes.   *Fel.*: I think you're moving about so he will see you.
Dor.: Can his soul be unaware that mine is listening?   *Fel.*: He's
replaced his broken treble string and is starting in to sing again.

Music, in this striking passage fraught with dramatic tension, prefigures
the reconciliation toward which Fernando and Dorotea are straining. Her
letter two scenes earlier had revealed the direction of her feelings; one scene
before, Fernando, despairing of words and prodded by Julio, had turned to
music:

Iul.: Señor, dexa por Dios essos desatinos. Toma el instrumento y
canta, siquiera porque diuiertas tanta tristeza . . .

Fer.: . . . Sepa o no sepa Dorotea que estoi aquí, yo le quiero dezir
mis locuras en estas cuerdas. Y quando no me escuche, no
importa; que el alma se deleita con la música naturalmente.

(p. 272)

Jul.: Sir, stop your ranting, for goodness' sake. Take up the
instrument and sing, if only to distract yourself from such
sadness . . .   *Fer.*: Whether or not Dorotea knows I am here, I want
to tell her of all my unsoundness on these sound strings. And even if
she doesn't listen, I don't care, for the soul naturally takes delight in
music.

The reconciliation will not come at once, as we know. The binding power of
music is limited. But at this moment, with a delicate sense of timing, Lope
makes music communicate the truth. Dorotea and Fernando are voice and
echo, song and refrain. The quaver in his voice becomes trepidation in her
heart and is manifested dramatically in the "inquietude" of her motions.
Music, to which the soul feels a natural affinity, is the sure meeting place of
kindred spirits. The Platonic commonplaces come to life and inform

presentationally a depiction of emotional discords struggling toward resolution.

On other occasions, noticeably more numerous and more subtly handled than in Lope's stage plays, an insistence on the tuning of a plucked instrument —a guitar or harp—refers back ultimately to the attunement of the human psyche. These passages also vividly convey the effort and skill that underlie musical mastery: "Perdonad el afinarla, que es notable el gouierno desta república de cuerdas" ("Forgive my tuning it—governing this commonwealth of strings is notoriously difficult"), Dorotea apologizes to Don Bela as she tunes her harp (p. 179). Their more significant function is to provide a presentational counterpoint to the emotional processes of the characters. The analogy is sometimes self-evident, as when Fernando tunes his guitar (V, 3):

> *Fer.:* Malas primas.
> *Iul.:* No ay cuerda buena.
> *Fer.:* Mira lo que dizes, que no es cuerda la que es mala.
> *Iul.:* ¿Desto sacas alegorías?
> *Fer.:* Dorotea fue la causa.
> *Iul.:* ¿Ya es mala Dorotea?
> *Fer.:* Tú lo sabes.
> *Iul.:* Hasta que no digas mal de Dorotea, no tengo de creer que la has oluidado.
> *Fer.:* Pues digo que es vn ángel.
> *Iul.:* Tampoco.
> *Fer.:* Pues ¿cómo ha de ser?
> *Iul.:* No dezir bien ni mal de Dorotea: que el que ha oluidado lo que amaua, no dize mal ni bien de lo que oluida.
>
> (p. 400)

Fer.: Bad treble strings. *Jul.:* No string ["cuerda" also means discreet woman] is good. *Fer.:* Careful what you say. One who is bad is not discreet. *Jul.:* Are you seeing an allegory in this? *Fer.:* It was Dorotea's fault. *Jul.:* So Dorotea is bad now? *Fer.:* You know yourself she is. *Jul.:* Until you stop speaking ill of Dorotea, I'll refuse to believe you've forgotten her. *Fer.:* Very well, I say she's an angel. *Jul.:* Not that either. *Fer.:* Well, how am I supposed to speak of her? *Jul.* Neither well nor badly, for one who has forgotten someone he loved says neither good nor bad things about the forgotten person.

We find here not only commonplace plays on *prima* and *cuerda* but an interplay between the process of tuning that Fernando is carrying on and the attuning of his feelings toward Dorotea to a desirable balance between love and dislike, which in this case means indifference. Julio's remarks are in fact a subtle comment on Fernando's lingering animosity toward his mistress (cf. below, p. 609).

On Fernando's first appearance (I, 4), the process of tuning foreshadows the impending quarrel with Dorotea. The uneasiness caused by his dream and not allayed by Julio's argument seeks alleviation in music. He calls for his guitar but it is only twenty speeches later that he begins to play. The intervening dialogue lets us visualize him bent over the instrument, impatiently replacing a broken string.[60] He had heard it snap during the night, he says, when thoughts of Dorotea kept him awake. The connection between the inner emotional process and the external activity underlies the ensuing exchange with Julio:

> *Iul.:* . . . Finalmente, son [*scil.*, las cuerdas] como algunas mugeres, que siempre es menester templarlas.
> *Fer.:* Por esso tiran de su condición, para que alcancen al punto del que las templa.
> *Iul.:* Muchas quiebran.
> *Fer.:* Buscar las finas y arrojar las falsas; que assí hazen los músicos.
>
> (p. 87)

> *Jul.:* In a word, [strings] are like women, who are always in need of tuning. *Fer.:* That's why they pull them into condition—so that they'll be pitched the same as the one doing the tuning. *Jul.:* Many break. *Fer.:* So you look for the genuine ones and discard the false. That's what musicians do.

Though the familiar allusion to tempering the human "condition" is here given facile sexual overtones, its presentational basis and its context make it prophetic. Behind it lies Fernando's vague apprehension that, unlike the attunement within reach of the guitarist, the perfect *conformidad* that has existed between him and Dorotea is about to be jarred irremediably. Lope underscores the ironical contrast by bringing out sharply Julio's reaction to the tuning:

> *Fer.:* Yo he templado.
> *Iul.:* A mi costa, que lo he oído.
>
> (p. 87)[61]

> *Fer.:* I've finished tuning. *Jul.:* At my expense—I was listening.

The song Fernando chooses to sing when the tuning is finally over, Lope's "A mis soledades voy" (Lope is explicitly alluded to as author, p. 87), expresses a disenchantment far vaster than Fernando's uneasy premonition. The full scope of the Lopean *desengaño* is beyond Fernando but he responds strongly to its temper.

> *Iul.:* ¿Cómo no has cantado alguna cosa de Dorotea?
> *Fer.:* Por la pesadumbre que me ha dado aquello del oro.
>
> (p. 91)

> *Jul.:* How come you didn't sing something about Dorotea?   *Fer.:* Because of the heavy mood that gold business put me in.

Music and poetry have crystallized Fernando's state of mind, briefly carrying him further beyond himself than he knows. ("Essos versos os dirán más de mí que lo que yo sabía cuando los hize" ["These lines will tell you more about me than I realized when I composed them"], Fernando himself remarks elsewhere of one of his own compositions [p. 376].) His mood is dignified by being caught up in a musical and poetic statement, given, as it were, an illusion of permanence. Herein lies some part of the power of music and poetry to alleviate but not to heal. We see his obsession returning when the song is over.

Dorotea too gains some assuagement of her feelings, albeit temporary, when she plays and sings in the solitude of her chamber. Music then allows her to accept them without deluding herself. An instance which also exemplifies the dramatic function the lyrics sometimes acquire comes in Act II, scene 3, shortly after Marfisa has stopped to visit Dorotea (estranged from Fernando but still attached to him) and added the pangs of jealousy to the pain of abandonment. We will later examine the intervening conversation with Celia in which Dorotea tries unsuccessfully to put up a brave front while Celia unearths her real feelings. Dorotea is plainly growing more and more distraught as they talk. Her agitation is patent in tone and gesture and she has evidently begun moving restlessly about even before the exchange that leads up to her song:

> *Dor.:* Ya no se me da nada de don Fernando.
> *Cel.:* Pareces loca.
> *Dor.:* Al clauicordio me llego a diuertirme.
> *Cel.:* Y yo escucharte.
>
> (p. 154)

Dor.: I don't care in the least about Don Fernando any more.   *Cel.:* You seem out of your mind.   *Dor.:* I'm going over to the spinet for some diversion.   *Cel.:* And I to listen to you.

The emotional pressure has built up to a point where it can be released only in poetry and music. "Al son de los arroyuelos" ("To the sound of the little streams"), the lyric that follows, transfers Dorotea's conflict to a medium in which art gives it a new shape and meaning. The painful tensions of actuality are brought to a temporary standstill, the friction of raw feelings reduced to smooth poetic and musical textures. The lyric, the most exquisite of *La Dorotea* and one of those most subtly coordinated with its context, merits a detailed examination:

 1   Al son de los arroyuelos
     cantan las aues de flor en flor,
     que no ay más gloria que amor
     ni mayor pena que zelos.

 5   Por estas seluas amenas
     al son de arroyos sonoros
     cantan las aues a coros
     de zelos y amor las penas.
     Suenan del agua las venas,
10   instrumento natural,
     y como el dulce cristal
     va desatando los yelos,
     al son de etc.

     De amor las glorias celebran
15   los narcisos y claueles;
     las violetas y penseles
     de zelos no se requiebran.
     Vnas en otras se quiebran
     las ondas por las orillas,
20   y como las arenillas
     ven por cristalinos velos,
     al son de etc.

     Arroyos murmuradores
     de la fe de amor perjura,
25   por hilos de plata pura
     ensartan perlas en flores.
     Todo es zelos, todo amores;
     y mientras que lloro yo
     las penas que amor me dio

30   con sus zelosos desvelos,
    al son de los arroyuelos
    cantan las aues de flor en flor,
    que no ay más gloria que amor
    ni mayor pena que zelos.

(p. 155)

To the sound of the little streams the birds sing from flower to
flower that there is no greater glory than love and no greater pain
than jealousy. (5) Throughout these pleasant groves, to the sound
of sonorous streams, the birds sing in choirs the pangs of jealousy and
love. The veins of the water sound (10), a natural instrument, and as
the sweet crystal begins to undo the ice, to the sound of etc. The
glories of love are celebrated (15) by the narcissi and pinks; the
violets and pansies do not court one another out of jealousy. The
waves break against one another along the banks (20) and, as they
see the fine sands through crystal veils, to the sound of etc.
Streams gossiping about love's broken faith (25) with thread of pure
silver string pearls on flowers. All is jealousy, all love. And while I
weep for the pains that love brought me (30) with its jealous vigils,
to the sound of the little streams the birds sing from flower to flower
that there is no greater glory than love and no greater pain than
jealousy.

    The theme of "Al son de los arroyuelos" appears most commonplace:
"that there is no greater glory than love and greater pain than jealousy,"
as the refrain has it. Nevertheless the lyric bears on its context as directly
as if we were to suppose it improvised in the moment of utterance. We
know, however, that Lope eschews the convention of spontaneous composition; hence Dorotea's resort to this lyric must be ascribed to an esthetic
sensitivity alive even in this moment of emotional turmoil. Nor is the
choice of the spinet, played here for the only time, accidental: the imagery
and phonic texture of the song are delicately correlated with the tonal
quality of this plucked keyboard instrument.[62]
    In her rendering of this *letrilla artística* (artistic lyric) Dorotea loses herself
momentarily in its substance, like the actor who becomes the role. Though
her only listener is Celia, there is a marked effect of performance, as so often
in the *acción en prosa*; in this case it is underscored by the imagery of the
poem. It will be noted that the opening four-line *pie*, or refrain, is followed
by three eight-line variations (*mudanzas*), the last line in each case leading
back into the refrain. Each variation has its own rhymes; each marks a new

departure but each ends up in the same place, for the refrain is not simply injected at intervals: it is the thematic center of gravity. Furthermore, the lyric is not only a set of variations on a theme; it possesses in addition a unitary thematic development which integrates the three variations into a single progression of feeling. This in turn is correlated with a process of sublimation which gradually brings assuagement to Dorotea.

The theme evidently is not simply *amor-gloria* and *zelos-pena* as polarized alternatives. It is rather the problematical distinctness or indistinctness of these emotional states viewed not as a dialectical issue capable of resolution but as a human predicament admitting of lyric formulation. The refrain simply asserts and reasserts that love and jealousy coexist. The first variation attenuates the opposition, the second sharpens it, and in the third it disappears altogether. The refrain places the variations in a concert framework: birds singing antiphonally and rivulets providing an instrumental accompaniment (*son*); behind this lie two well-established conceits of which Lope (like Góngora) was fond: the concerted strife of singing birds and the brook as a stringed instrument with pebbles for frets. Thus a delicate interplay of natural and artificial harmonies, which includes in the second variation color as well as sound, runs through the poem. It is epitomized in Lope's antithetical term for the music-making brook: *natural instrument*. The context of performance in turn links this natural instrument with the spinet on which Dorotea is playing. Lope's ear must have recalled impressions of music played upon the instrument and retained the watery quality of its tone, for he has subtly managed to suggest through the phonic, rhythmic, and prosodic properties of his text the keyboard accompaniment which one is to imagine supporting its sense: effects of modulation, dissonance, mobility of arpeggios and chromatics are given through vowel color and plays of rhythm and stress in conjunction with the imagery and sense of the poem. In the beginning of the third variation, the affective overtones grow intense. There are dark hints of perfidy clashing with suggestions of purity, but all presently gives way to a single pervasive concord: "All is jealousy, all love." In a kind of *concordia discors* love and jealousy become fused, indistinguishable, omnipresent. The tension between them is relaxed and Dorotea's conflict is subsumed into this wider scheme and subdued. But at this point, for the only time, a suffering human consciousness is introduced: "And while I weep for the pains that love brought me with its jealous vigils, to the sound of the little streams . . ." The self of the singer is by now no longer distinguishable from the *I* of the song. There is a breach in the frame of the poem, the backdrop of the performer's plight reappears for a moment, then the refrain returns and carries the singer away from her private grief back into a world where pain is balanced by joy and music leads into a universal harmonic order in which suffering becomes bearable.

Dorotea's performance is an act of lyrical soul-searching. The genuineness inherent in musical expression uncovers the core of her dilemma and leads to an avowal in song of what was denied in speech. The lyric thus functions dramatically. It constitutes not only an interlude of meditation or reflection but a confrontation by Dorotea of the conflicts with which she must live, conflicts that may be softened but not removed by the incantatory effect of music. The song ends the scene. For once the listening Celia has no sarcastic comment. One is surely to imagine an interval of silence—the silence that follows revelations—before Gerarda bustles in with shattering effect.

The meaning of the last lyric in *La Dorotea*, sung to the harp by the heroine, as we shall see later on, is as dramatically enhanced by its context as that of her first selection.[63] Like other lyrics sung in *La Dorotea*, it probes a fundamental level of feeling. The unaccompanied verse, for its part, will usually provide, with deliberate artifice, a stylized record of moments and emotions shared or solitary. The verse by Fernando, to take his poems first, consists both of the compositions that have turned Dorotea's head (there are three such) and of more self-contained lyrics which examine and dissect Fernando's emotions during his separation from Dorotea (six of these). Fernando apostrophizes personified thoughts or states, such as joy and absence, in the Petrarchan manner favored by the characters in Lope's plays.[64] Or he addresses Dorotea or Amarilis, in absentia. Four of these poems, products of particular moments, are set in Fernando's account of his sojourn in Seville and Cadiz. The other two are "sentimientos de ausencia" ("feelings of separation") composed on Fernando's outward journey.

The samples of the verse Fernando has offered to Dorotea are introduced at two points: by Fernando after the first break with Dorotea; by Dorotea after the definitive break with Fernando. The passage of time in each case has thrown a new light upon them. The contrast between the memories they arouse and the present situation of the characters rekindles emotional conflicts, and their reactions once again give a dramatic character to the reading or recitation, with effects of both irony and pathos. The new contextuality of the lyrics is made to underscore the impermanence of human feelings.

Seeking to follow Ovid's advice in the *Remedia amoris* and destroy old love-letters, neither the injured Fernando of Act I nor the abandoned Dorotea of Act V can resist the painful pleasure of re-reading them. Lyric tributes of Fernando to Dorotea appear among the love-notes. I have already mentioned Fernando's rediscovery of verse of his own in Act I, scene 5. "Çagala, assí Dios te guarde" ("Shepherd girl, so may God preserve you") (p. 107) is a pastoral version, in Lope's late manner, of a lovers' spat, its details so conventionally stylized that it can as easily refer to Fernando and Dorotea in the heyday of their love as to Lope and Amarilis, about whom it was probably written.[65] (The *Epistolario* retains traces of such spats between Lope and Marta de Nevares.) A second lyric of this scene, "Vnas doradas chinelas" ("A pair of gold clogs"), which mentions Amarilis by name, calling her a "serrana" ("mountain girl"), is written in what Leo Spitzer calls a "charming and piquant" rococo manner.[66] Julio, as has been seen, is prompted to recite a third poem of Fernando's from memory, one inspired by the sight, beneath upturned skirts, of a tiny foot leaping a brook. As Fernando listens, his mistress regains her role as his muse and he encounters a new obstacle to departure and the relinquishing of Dorotea. Independent in origin and intention, the poem acquires a dramatic edge in the new context.

In Act V, scene 5, Dorotea, coming upon a sonnet, "Quexosas, Dorotea, están las flores" ("The flowers, Dorotea, are resentful") (p. 431), sent her by Fernando, experiences, more poignantly, the same backward pull upon her feelings as had Fernando earlier.

As Fernando relates the story of his Andalusian sojourn, he explains: "Con lo que allá descansaua, descanso agora. Porque no tenía más aliuio que escriuir mis pensamientos, como agora le siento en repetirlos" ("What afforded me some respite then affords me some now. Because my only relief was to write down my thoughts, as I now find it in repeating them") (p. 306). This therapeutic view of poetic composition, the relevancy of which Lope instinctively felt, receives classical reinforcement elsewhere:

> *Fer.:* . . . Aduierte cómo parece que se hizieron los versos para
> descansar los que aman.
> *Iul.:* Y para desechar las tristezas y el temor del ánimo, como en
> Horacio aurás visto, donde dize que con las musas no temía el
> rigor de los cuidados.
> *Fer.:* Remedio del amor las llama Teócrito en su *Cíclope;* y deue de
> ser porque aliuian sus tristezas quexándose, que no porque le
> curen.
>
> (p. 224)[67]

> *Fer.:* Observe how verse seems to have been invented to afford some
> respite to those in love.   *Jul.:* And to cast sad thoughts and fears
> from the mind, as you will have observed in Horace where he says
> that with the muses he didn't fear the harshness of worry.   *Fer.:* A

cure for love Theocritus calls them in his "Cyclops"; it must be because they alleviate its sufferings by bemoaning them, not because they cure it.

Composed or recited, poetry, like music, can be a balm, though one of necessarily limited effectiveness. The play of dialogue shows Lope still of two minds.

None of the four poems with which Fernando intersperses the account of his journey is dramatic in function. The first two, ballads written for Amarilis—"Si vas conmigo, Amarilis" ("If you are coming with me, Amarilis") and "Cuidados, ¿qué me queréis?" ("Cares, what do you want with me?") (pp. 305, 306)—are conventional treatments of absence, facile compositions that dissect feelings in neatly turned conceits and hyperboles. They would fit any context of absence or separation. It must have been theme that made Lope insert them at this juncture, prompting Felipa's observation: "Por vuestros versos he creído que os acordáis de Dorotea" ("I thought from your verse that you still remembered Dorotea") (p. 307). A third ballad, "En vna peña sentado" ("Seated on a rock") (p. 307), also originating in Lope's love for Marta de Nevares, has greater depth and subtlety.[68] It exemplifies Lope's meditative manner, which here remains undramatized, and records a train of reflections set in motion by an outward sensation but gradually turning inward as introspection. Emotion is not projected upon the scene but crystallized around the inner repercussions of impressions.

> Fabio miraua en las olas,
> cómo la playa las hurta,
> a las que vienen la plata,
> y a las que se van la espuma.
> Contemplando está las penas
> de amor y de oluido juntas:
> el oluido en las que mueren,
> y el amor en las que duran.
>
> (p. 308)

Fabio was noticing in the waves how the beach steals the silver from the incoming ones and the foam from those withdrawing. He is contemplating the pains of loving and being forgotten, all at once: being forgotten in those that die, loving in those that last.

The balanced mobility of the lines carries the movement of both waves and reflections. Lope's keen eye and deft touch correlate external impressions with psychic movements in diction of stylized simplicity. Then the impressions are left behind as the setting had been, only the reflections remaining.

> Verdades de largo amor
> no hay oluido que las cubra,
> ni diligencias humanas
> a desdeñosas injurias.

> The faithfulness of a long love cannot be wiped out by any forgetting
> nor can there be any human efforts against disdainful wrongs.

From such elegiac echoes of Lope's undying love for Marta de Nevares, the poem slips into a series of epigrammatic dicta on loving and forgetting contained in quatrains of general love-lore that are no longer the property of any particular Lopean protagonist. The poem nevertheless belongs, unlike the other two, to the reflective and introspective mode of the years which culminated in *La Dorotea*, belongs in the company of the "Egloga a Claudio," the Neo-Platonic poetry (including Don Bela's madrigal), and, signally, "A mis soledades voy." But it falls on ears more curious than appreciative or understanding, just as do the other poems of its kind in *La Dorotea*. After the last quatrain:

> Tomó Fabio su instrumento,
> y dixo a las peñas mudas
> sus locuras en sus cuerdas,
> porque pareciessen suyas.

> Fabio took up his instrument and on its strings told the mute rocks
> how unstrung he was, so that there would be no mistaking who was
> unstrung [*cuerda* means "sane," as well as "string," and is opposed
> to *locura*, "madness"].

Felipa makes a comment that could not be more prosaic: "¿Qué dixo?" ("What did he tell them?").

The last composition included in Fernando's account is the already mentioned sonnet commemorating the ceremonial burial of Dorotea's portrait; it is a monument in words:

> Aquí donde jamás tu rostro hermoso
> planta mortal, diuina Dorotea,

toque atreuida, tu sepulcro sea,
sin colunas de pórfido lustroso.

(p. 310)

Here where your beautiful face will never be touched by an insolent
mortal foot, let your tomb be, divine Dorotea, without any columns
of gleaming porphyry.

The elevated diction, the severe architecture create a ponderousness dis-
proportionate to the small scale of the symbolic act. The strained metaphorical
equivalence of portrait and phoenix, sustained through much of the poem,
acknowledges in advance the uselessness of this ceremony of exorcization,
which Fernando nonetheless solemnly performs.[69]

On Fernando's return to Madrid, in response to a query from Ludovico,
"¿Y vos no auéis hecho alguna cosa a esta ausencia?" ("And how about
you? Haven't you written anything on this separation?") (p. 245), we are
given another set piece on this theme: "Ay riguroso estado, / ausencia
fementida ..." ("Oh pitiless state, treacherous absence ..."). It is a new
version of a heptasyllabic ballad written by 1621 for the enforced departure
of hero from heroine in El caballero de Olmedo. Morby aptly notes (p. 246,
n. 96) that not all the variants are due to the removal of allusions to the action
of the play. More noticeable, indeed, are additions which double the poem's
length: new quatrains of stylistic amplification, new hyperboles, new
naturalistic floral imagery for the crushing of hopes "cuando más verdes
florecían" ("when flourishing most green"), and at the end an apostrophe to
"Dulces pensamientos" ("Sweet thoughts") in the form of a glossed
seguidilla on the journey motif. The ballad thus no longer reflects a particular
dramatic situation. It is a literary and rhetorical display piece, much more
decidedly the product of a professional lyricist than in its original form as
spoken by Don Alonso, the knightly hero of the play. Despite its artistry
the poem is recited perfunctorily by Fernando, as if in his present mood it no
longer interested him. There is no preamble and it elicits no comment.

The final poem which has the separation from Dorotea as background is
the poet's apostrophe to his thoughts: "¿Adónde vais, pensamiento?"
("Whither bound, thought?") (p. 376). Written in ballad meter, it is actually
a series of four-line variations on the conceptual antithesis: flight is useless
but return impossible. Views on love to be sustained by subsequent developments are reduced to lapidary formulation as in some of the choruses:
"Nunca amor al rendido / trató bien, aunque es hidalgo" ("Love, though
honor-bound, has never treated well one who capitulates"); "Amor,

pensamiento, es miedo" ("Love, my thought, is fear"), and so on. A letter accompanying the verse details its antitheses in prose:

> Yo voy, amigo Fabricio, sin alma porque la dexé, y sin vida porque me quiere dexar, y tan acompañado de pensamientos que, como venenos diferentes, compitiendo vnos con otros, me sustentan viuo . . . Más vamos Iulio y yo en Dorotea que en el camino. No hablamos en otra cosa desde que amanece.   (p. 376)[70]

> Friend Fabricio, I go on without a soul because I left it behind, and without life because it is trying to leave me, and so accompanied by thoughts that, like different poisons, competing with one another, they keep me alive . . . Julio and I are more intent on Dorotea than on the road. We speak of nothing else from the moment it gets light.

We hear nothing more about the Fabricio to whom Fernando writes here except that he has passed the letter on to Marfisa, who reads it to Clara along with the verse. Marfisa becomes understandably furious when Julio claims (p. 380) that the poem was written for her, since the letter has already told her that Fernando wished the verse to be sung to Dorotea (evidently so that music and song should avow feelings which his coldness had masked during the quarrel). But the whole question of whom the verse really pertains to arouses the play spirit in Lope. He effects, through Clara, a *reductio ad absurdum* of the conflicting female claims, then proceeds offhandedly to disallow and admit them all:

> *Cla.:* . . . Pero dime, señora, ¿de quándo acá se llama esta señora
>   Amarilis? Dorotilis auía de dezir: que a ti, como a Marfisa, te
>   tocó siempre esse nombre.
> *Mar.:* ¡Ay, Clara! Por engañarnos a entrambas; que los poetas tienen
>   versos a dos luzes, como los cantores villancicos, que con
>   poco que les muden siruen a muchas fiestas.
>   (p. 378)

> *Cla.:* But tell me, Madam, since when has this lady been called
> Amarilis? Dorotilis he ought to have said; that other name always
> belonged to you, as Marfisa.   *Mar.:* Ah, Clara, so as to deceive us
> both, since poets have verse with double reflections as singers do
> popular songs, which with a little fixing-up can serve for many
> different festivities.

It is the spirit of Tomé de Burguillos that breaks forth here, unconcernedly revealing professional secrets while making light of prying contemporaries and, one might add, of subsequent generations unwilling to take poetry as Lope wished it taken—on its own merits.

The view of Fernando as author is not materially changed by the two already mentioned ballads, with musical settings, specifically ascribed to him. "Cautiuo el Abindarráez" ("The Abindarraez, taken prisoner") (p. 180) is a polished lyrical treatment of an established Moorish theme rather than a conventional *romance morisco* with disguises and pageantry. "Si tuuieras, aldeana" ("Village girl, if only you had"), played by Fernando to himself in Act V (p. 401) is another variation on the theme of unfounded jealousy presented in "Çagala, assí Dios te guarde." (The jealous lady, specifically Amarilis this time, must have been Marta originally.) All told, Fernando appears an accomplished rhetorical poet, dexterous in handling conceits and applying stylistic adornment. His two sonnets are impeccably turned and his ballads are light and delicate, segmentation into quatrains being subtly observed.

It is noticeable, however, that Lope has not identified as Fernando's any verse of sustained expressive power or conceptual depth or any verse with the intensity of his best ballads to Elena Osorio. Exquisite as some of Fernando's compositions are, they are essentially amplifications of slight circumstances, of well-tried conventions of feeling, reflective at bottom of immaturity of character and an egocentric nature. The single poem written by Dorotea, "Si todo lo acaba el tiempo" ("If time brings everything to an end"), is more poignant and expressive than any of Fernando's; the same is true of Don Bela's madrigal. It is especially significant that Lope has not given to Fernando but retained for himself the deeper compositions "A mis soledades voy" and the *barquillas* (boat-ballads), the latter under the transparent disguise of the "gentleman whom you know" who has lost his lady.

We have already seen how meaningful Lope makes Fernando's selection of the first ballad, at once the most personal and the most universal. The contextuality of the four piscatory idylls likewise adds a new function to their original expressive significance, one which Lope's art accommodates without friction or strain. All five poems will concern us later as expressions of Lopean *soledad;* let us here examine the contextual function of the latter four. The fact that these poems so closely reflect the harrowing impact of the loss of Marta de Nevares in no way inhibits Lope's capacity to make creative use of Fernando's response to them. In the case of the third, we have seen how, in Fernando's vocal and instrumental rendition, Lope blends his own voice of 1632 with that of his young protagonist. In the other cases, it is the distance between them that is underscored, and this in contrapuntal fashion.

Julio brings forth the first two poems as a form of diversion for his master: "A vn gentil hombre, que tú conoces, se le ha muerto su dama; yo quiero entretenerte con vnos versos suyos a manera de idilios piscatorios" ("A gentleman whom you know has lost his lady. I wish to entertain you with some verse of his in the manner of piscatory idylls") (p. 206). Besides detaching Fernando from his creator, this introduction places him midway between author and reader. Like the latter, he is a recipient of this poetic reading, but he constitutes an inner audience, and the reader who listens in from the outside is in a position to find revelations in his responses as well as to receive the impact of the poems directly.

The counterpoint between author and character begins as soon as the reading of the first elegy is over:

> *Fer.:* Con tanta acción has leído, Iulio, essos versos, que me has
> traído las lágrimas a los ojos.
> *Iul.:* Deue de ser como te halla flaco de la voluntad.
> *Fer.:* ¡O, quánto me agradan las cosas tristes! ¡Bien aya hombre
> tan firme y tan dichoso!
> *Iul.:* ¿Dichoso puede ser quien pierde lo que los versos dizen?
> *Fer.:* ¡Pluguiera a Dios que yo llorara a Dorotea!... Mejor estado,
> Iulio, es el de esse amante que el que yo tengo. ¡O si pudiéramos
> trocar tristezas! Que él llora lo que le falta, y yo lo que tiene
> otro.
>
> (p. 214)

> *Fer.:* You read that verse with so much expression, Julio, that you've
> brought tears to my eyes.   *Jul.:* You must be suffering from weakness
> of will.   *Fer.:* Oh, how I enjoy sad things! More power to so
> steadfast and fortunate a man!   *Jul.:* Can a man who has lost what
> the poem says be fortunate?   *Fer.:* Would to God that I were
> mourning Dorotea . . . That lover's situation is a better one than
> mine, Julio! Oh, if only we could exchange sadnesses! Because he is
> weeping for what he has lost and I for what someone else has.

In this exchange between two Lopean voices one recognizes echoes of the traditional debate over which plight is worse: the loss of the beloved or her failure to love in return, the same debate that figures in the early sixteenth-century *Questión de amor de dos enamorados: al uno era muerta su amiga; el otro sirve sin esperança de galardón* and in Garcilaso's first eclogue, where the two shepherds voice, as in Lope, two sides of a single self, polarizing as simultaneous, emotional states which in fact occurred successively. In *La Dorotea* the debate becomes a confrontation between the voices of the young and the old Lope, in the process acquiring an ironic edge lost in the later scenes when Fernando sings rather than listens. The irony arises because the perspective of the protagonist is so confined and his suffering, the result of ousting by a rival, so lacking in nobility.

Fernando's initial response highlights the quality of the performance: it is a rhetorical comment, a commendation of Julio's expressive delivery ("acción"), as if the poetry could not otherwise have worked its effect. As for the verse itself, it is merely a sounding-board for Fernando's own sadness: it pleases him because it intensifies his present mood, one sedulously cultivated. Like Shakespeare's Jaques, Fernando "can suck melancholy out of a song as a weasel sucks eggs." As regards his creator's *tristeza*, so impervious is Fernando that he can facetiously suggest exchanging it for his own, as if it were negotiable, then dismiss the sadness of the "gentil hombre" as of less consequence than deprivation and displacement by a rival. Julio's mildly incredulous "Can a man who has lost what the poem says be fortunate?" (p. 215) is the old Lope's only comment on Fernando's egocentricity. With surprising objectivity Lope places side by side Fernando's response, essentially his own to Elena's defection, and his reaction some forty-five years later to the loss of Marta de Nevares. There is no resolution, only contrast. Like so much else relating to Marta, the "historical" fact of her death enters the magnetic field of the *poiesis* then reaching completion. In this new medium it is indistinguishable from the poetic materials cast up by creative retrospection. Lope understands Fernando: was he not once in his shoes? He cannot, however, conceive of a Fernando capable of understanding him.

In Fernando's response to Julio's reading of the second boat-ballad, Lope allows the voices of age and youth to coincide fleetingly before again dissociating them: "¡Qué amor! ¡Qué fineza! ¡Qué verdad! ¡Qué soledad! No le ha faltado a esse amante sino beberse las cenizas de su Amarilis" ("What a love! What delicacy! What faithfulness! What loneliness! The only thing left that lover was to drink his Amarilis's ashes") (p. 223). Fernando's "¡Qué soledad!" ("What loneliness!") gives the key to Lope's mood but the frivolous pedantry which Lope allows him immediately after shows how far Fernando is from responding to it.[71] The voice of Lope comes and goes underscoring the words now of Julio, now of Fernando, but it is clearly a voice apart, separated once and for all from that of his young protagonist by the gulf that separates a manner—a self-conscious assumption of attitudes and poses ("¡O, quánto me agradan las cosas tristes!" ["Oh, how I enjoy sad things!"])—from an authentic expressive style.

An end is finally made to the counterpoint between the voices of youth and age after the singing of the last *barquilla*:

Fel.: Si otra noche venís por aquí no traigáis lamentaciones.

Fer.: Acabaldo vos con mi tristeza: que por hacerla mayor he buscado entre los versos que sé de memoria los que mejor se aplican a las que tengo.

Fel.: Paréceme que esse pescador lamentaua alguna prenda muerta. ¿Por dónde se aplica a sentimiento vuestro, pues la tenéis viua?

Fer.: Porque lo mismo es tenerla ausente, aunque se diferencian en que los ausentes pueden ofender y los muertos no. Y este pescador lloraua la más hermosa muger que tuuo la ribera donde nació, más firme, más constante y de más limpia fe y costumbres.

Fel.: Parece aprouación de libro.

(p. 285)

Fel.: If you come this way another evening, don't come with lamentations. *Fer.:* Just try putting an end to my sadness when, to make it greater, I've chosen among poems that I have memorized those most applicable to my own memories. *Fel.:* I have the feeling that that fisherman was grieving for some loved one who had died. How can this be applicable to your own feelings since yours is alive? *Fer.:* Because it's the same thing if she is away from one, although there is this difference: that people away can give offense and dead people can't. And this fisherman was grieving for the most beautiful woman that ever graced the shore where she was born, the truest, most steadfast, and the one of most spotless faith and morals. *Fel.:* Sounds like the censor's approval of a book!

The terse sarcasm of Felipa's comment brings the exchange to an abrupt halt. Fernando's present formula is as mechanical as his earlier emotional indulgence was inappropriate. Lope leaves him to the end incapable of understanding authentic grief.

While the genesis of the lyrics is largely distinct from that of the central action of *La Dorotea*, Lope has had no trouble incorporating them in a work which is in fact the expression of an entire lifetime. But he has not been content merely to interpolate them in the somewhat mechanical fashion of most writers of narrative. He has been remarkably resourceful in finding contextual functions for them, in making them support characterization, theme, artistic connoisseurship and accomplishment as well as contribute to self-expression and to other ends which will appear later. They stand as evidence of the literary dimension which the characters give to their private lives, and they function dramatically to bring out tensions and conflicts within them. Their presence in Lope's prose dialogue is symbolic of the place of his own artistic creativity in the total context of his life. Such completeness we find nowhere else in his production. We have either the rather perfunctory insertion of lyrics into the patently literary molds of narrative fiction, with its artistic prose and its contrived plots, or lyrics pure and simple, standing alone. Of particular significance for the meaning of *La Dorotea*, the lyrics, contextually considered, are the crowning manifestation of the ideal role envisaged for poetry and music in men's lives, one of attunement of body and soul within the self, of the conformity of kindred bodies and souls, in the end of an overarching Platonic order governed by love. However unattainable, it is a vision which haunted Lope and repeatedly polarized the artistic expression of his later years. He is compelled now to set it in a context of prosaic living where it inevitably appears more remote and problematical. Yet is is more compelling, more disinterested, less strained than another aspiration to an ideal order, now to be considered, which has a large place in the *acción en prosa*. This is the cultivation of artistically stylized forms of behavior and parlance, of life styles and values based on literary models. In the end the same quest for a harmony capable of resolving the dissonances and tensions of existence underlies each aspiration, and this fact both enhances the relevance of the lyrics to the total world view presented in *La Dorotea* and accounts for the indulgent, if critical eye, with which Lope surveys the *Literarisierung* of life.

Style and Literary Stylization
X

Despite the artifice so noticeable in the conversations of *La Dorotea*, the stylistic order of the *acción en prosa* reflects Lope's search for an art situated closer to the world of everyday. It is evident from the first pages that the traditional order of stylistic decorum has been abandoned. The low style—the colloquial prose of *oratio soluta*—sets the tone; different kinds of artificiality and different forms of stylistic elevation are doubly noticeable as departures from it. Though given stylistic trends predominate in particular scenes and varieties of personal style are distinguishable, there is no basic stability of stylistic level, only a downward leveling effect of colloquial speech everywhere in evidence.

Stylistic decorum, still maintained in *La Euphrosina*, no longer holds within the pervasive atmosphere of experienced reality which extends to all the characters and upsets conventional social distinctions in *La Dorotea*. It is quite impossible to sort out in Lope's work the three traditional levels of discourse corresponding to social rank and the nature of the dramatic situation which Eugenio Asensio finds in *La Euphrosina*.[1] Much less can one, with any consistency, distinguish finer stylistic gradations, such as Lope's contemporary, Juan de Robles, established in *El culto sevillano* (1631) by subdividing the three traditional categories. Indeed, the unconventionality of *La Dorotea* stands out when referred to the sensible specifications made in 1602 by Luis Alfonso de Carballo concerning "el decoro de los estados" ("appropriateness to social station").

Y differente ha de ser la plática de vna matrona graue, a la de vna
muger liuiana, y el trato de la viuda del de la religiosa, o casada, que
poco importa dezir muy buenas cosas y adornarlas con mucha
galantería de vocablos y figuras, si son impropias del estado de la
persona, que no sólo conuiene el vestido ser bien hecho, pero ha de
venir al justo del que lo ha de vestir.[2]

And the speech of a grave matron must differ from that of a giddy
woman and the conversation of the widow from that of the nun or
married woman. It does little good to say very fine things and deck
them out in much fanciness of words and figures if they are
inappropriate to the station of the person. It's not enough for the
suit to be well made: it must be a close fit for the person who is to
wear it.

Such specifications were of course already disappearing from the *comedia*.
Lope's own criterion, as expressed in the *Arte nuevo* (1614), is more flexible,
linking style much more with subject matter and intention than with social
status or character types.

Comience pues, y con lenguaje casto
no gaste pensamientos ni conceptos
en las cosas domésticas, que sólo
ha de imitar de dos o tres la plática.
Mas cuando la persona que introduce,
persuade, aconseja o dissuade,
allí ha de haber sentencias y conceptos,
porque se imita la verdad sin duda,
pues habla un hombre en diferente estilo
del que tiene vulgar, cuando aconseja,
persuade o aparta alguna cosa.

(*Obras escogidas*, II, 889)

Let him start in, then, and in pure language, not waste thoughts
and ideas on domestic matters, where he has only a conversation of
two or three to imitate. But when the person he presents persuades,
advises, or dissuades, there should be dictums and ideas, because
this is surely an imitation of truth, since a man speaks in a different
style from his everyday one, when he recommends, persuades, or
advises against something.

But even this freer criterion, which already looks away from stylistic
convention and toward living speech, is inadequate for *La Dorotea* where,
as we see in the first scene, suasory rhetoric is applied to domestic matters,

where the character of highest rank, Don Bela, is the least adept at the sublime style, and where the dialogue is characterized throughout by shifts in level from the elevated to the everyday. This is in itself a violation of the stylistic criterion of *igualdad*, consistent maintenance of level, and would strike an exigent, traditionalistic ear as bizarre.[3] Moreover, the basic level of the dialogue does not, as in *La Euphrosina*, correspond to the speech habits of "popular types"; it is not rustic but urbane, the everyday speech of an urban milieu of some sophistication employed without reference to social status.[4]

While in matters of verbal expression, as in other respects, Lope may invade the privacy of his characters, allowing his ludic spirit and his ironical attitude toward them to express themselves through their speech styles, the principle of decorum, insofar as we may speak of one in *La Dorotea*, is psychological rather than social or hierarchical. It reflects authentic impulses toward cultural refinement on the part of characters not naturally endowed with breeding, roles deliberately assumed which reflect chosen visions of themselves; and it underscores the tensions and psychic instability that inevitably ensue. While in the *Arte nuevo* Lope expressly abjures "vocablos esquisitos" ("fancy words"), for example,

> porque si ha de imitar a los que hablan,
> no ha de ser por Pancayas, por Metauros,
> hipogrifos, semones y centauros,
>
> (Obras escogidas, II, 889)

> because if he is to imitate people speaking, it oughtn't to be in terms of Panchaias, Metauruses, hippogryphs, Semos, and centaurs,

in *La Dorotea* he makes his speakers' affectation of them a mode of expression that contributes to the revelation of character. The same is true of other aspects of the self-stylization deliberately cultivated by the characters: the literary, the learned, the rhetorical, the histrionic, and so on. Their varying proclivities in these directions are effects of their particular natures and point not to more or less typed figures with expressive styles correlated to age, station, position, sex, and so forth, but to characters conceived as individuals. It will prove particularly revealing in respect to character delineation to observe the adjustments or maladjustments of style to life, the degree to which assumed styles are allowed to become second nature, the opposing reactions they provoke from within or without, the breakthroughs of spontaneity which punctuate them. For Lope's concern in *La*

Dorotea is not with artistic issues as such but with art in life. The esthetic is not viewed simply as part of the poet's *métier;* its role and effect in a world of *historia* is an equal concern.

In the discussion to follow, we will need to consider a number of preliminary matters before we can examine in an adequate perspective the question of individual styles, verbal and vital. We need first to substantiate what has been said about the prevalent colloquial nature of the dialogue, seeing it both in the context of the age and in terms of tendencies peculiar to Lope. We will note evidence of the artistic control Lope exercises over the dialogue, drawing particularly on passages of colloquial speech in this connection. We shall note characteristic locutions, idioms, and other traits of colloquial dialogue style and observe the artistic designs behind them.

Consideration of the more elevated and ambitious stylistic modes cultivated by the characters will involve us first with the standards they reveal, particularly as manifested in the faculties the speakers prize in verbal intercourse, the techniques they develop, and the skills they seek to display. Their individual styles of expression and behavior will be considered, with certain particularly revealing key scenes being analyzed by way of exemplification. Finally, moving beyond the characters' particular styles, we will consider what *La Dorotea* has to tell us of Lope's own stylistic values, how it reflects the broad movement of his art between the poles of art and nature and his preoccupation with the question of material versus esthetic values.

The Conversational Format

As a *Konversationsstuck, La Dorotea* makes the reader aware from beginning to end that he is a listener-in on a series of continuing conversations. The opening lines simply bring him into earshot: he is neither caught up in an incident as in *La Celestina,* nor placed in a situation, nor offered a *relación,* as frequently in the *comedia.* Rather he is made to understand that the first words he reads, Gerarda's "El amor y la obligación no sólo me mandan, pero porfiadamente me fuerçan, amiga Teodora, a que os diga mi sentimiento" ("Love and duty not only command me but insistently force me, friend Teodora, to tell you my feelings") (p. 63), belong to a conversation about Dorotea that has been proceeding for some time. This he realizes when Teodora very soon after the undramatic opening mentions ironically to Gerarda "el afecto con que desde el principio de nuestra plática me la auéis encarecido" ("the affectionate way you've been building her up since we started talking"). Similarly, at the end of the work, the characters' irrepressible loquacity can take in its stride the double catastrophes of Don

Bela and Gerarda and carry right on before finally running down. Symptomatically, the term *conversación* is often on the characters' lips, adding to suggestions of social intercourse seemingly deliberate connotations of verbalization:

Esto del magisterio es para las escuelas, no para las conuersaciones.

(p. 176)

This matter of lecturing is for the classroom, not for conversations.

Nunca te he visto muy deseosa de su conuersación.

(p. 188)

I've never seen you very eager for her conversation.

Fer.: . . . No hay sino tener paciencia y diuertirnos por essos campos.
Iul.: Mejor fuera por essas conuersaciones . . .

(p. 225)[5]

Fer.: Nothing to do but be patient and seek distraction in the
country.   *Jul.:* In conversations would be more to the point . . .

Though Leo Spitzer's term *Konversationsgeister*—"conversation spirits"—neglects deeper levels of characterization in *La Dorotea*, it underscores the strong interlocutory impulse of the characters, their urge to divulge what strikes their fancy, whatever is in their minds or on them, their indefatigable verbalizing. As Mrs. Malkiel has seen, they are much less given to monologues than the characters of Lope's plays, who have a real audience to take into their confidence.[6] In *La Dorotea* the characters are, in effect, one another's audiences, and with rare exceptions monologues are dispensed with by the author as a means of externalizing what they are feeling. It does not of course follow that they are always good listeners; in quite lifelike fashion we shall find them talking at cross-purposes as well as collaborating.

The underlying colloquial character of the dialogue, which is a corollary of the conversational format of *La Dorotea*, is evidently bound up with the "historical" grounding of the work. The idiom of everyday Spanish, its phrasing, rhythms, casual, approximate, or tentative tones show through—at times break through—the artifice of much of the talk, part and parcel of the realistic world in which the characters are placed. In many scenes of his plays of contemporary setting, Lope had also managed to suggest the movement of everyday conversation despite the restrictive effect of metrical structure and rhyme. Referring to the language of the *comedia*, Menéndez Pidal even finds "in its dialogue imitated from that of everyday ... all of conversational speech."[7] Only in the *acción en prosa*, however, has Lope given full play to his remarkable ear for the spoken language. That he was writing lines to be read rather than heard is immaterial; his inner ear was clearly attuned to their spoken character: "Puedo yo con sola la vista oír leyendo" ("With my eyes alone I can hear when I read"), he had once observed.[8] The point of numerous passages in the dialogue depends on an assumption of aural apprehension:

> *Mar.:* Hablauas con Dorotea.
> *Fer.:* Con esse demonio, Marfisa.
> *Mar.:* ¿Ella o yo? Que juntas el demonio con mi nombre y siempre te lo parezco.
>
> (p. 116)

> *Mar.:* You were talking with Dorotea.   *Fer.:* With that devil, Marfisa.   *Mar.:* She or I? You link the devil with my name and I always seem one to you.

In this respect, as in others, Lope shows no inclination to break with the habits formed in writing for the theater. Yet, in addressing himself to readers as he now is, he feels less restricted; he can count on a leisurely perusal suited to the unhurried discursiveness of the work, a savoring of particular exchanges, a disposition on the reader's part to explore conversational bypaths. Dramatic lines destined only for the ear, on the other hand, needed to be briskly functional, immediately graspable, sharp-edged: arresting openings, emphatic underscoring, decisive curtains. Even if the playwright strove for declamatory effectiveness and sought opportunities to set off the talents of given actors, rapidity of delivery as well as the rapid pace of the action destined much of what was said to oblivion, if the shortcomings of actors or the inadequacies of the audience had not already done so.[9]

Removal from the stage and imposition of a standard of colloquial speech have, as suggested, the important effect of focusing attention on the artifice present in the more formal and stylized sequences with an insistence foreign to the *comedia*, where such expressive styles command a more conventional acceptance. The reader of *La Dorotea*, having heard ordinary voices in offhand conversation during moments of domesticity and routine, is all the more conscious of the poses the characters strike as they aspire to speech of greater stylistic elevation. They start close to us, the sound and substance of their speaking voices highly natural, then move off to be observed on imaginary stages, from which they subsequently step down to resume their ordinary tones. The moments of artifice—poetic, erudite, ceremonious—the passages of disputational tautness, the displays of rhetoric, the rare dramatic climaxes, all are borne along on the current of a continuing conversation whose movement, noticed as soon as the grand scenes subside, is the drifting, eddying one of colloquial talk, associative, improvisatory, capricious; it picks up trivia and marginalia as it proceeds. If there is danger of losing the thread, the reason lies in these colloquial patterns rather than in pedantic developments or concentrated verbal copiousness such as one finds in *La Celestina* or *La Euphrosina*. Lope only rarely allows a speaker to hold forth at length on a given subject or go unchallenged when he disgorges learning. However rarefied or precious, the conversations of *La Dorotea* retain at bottom the vivacity, spontaneity, and interlocutory play of ordinary talk.

It is true that this dialogue is draped like an oversize garment around a very slender action; the artistry of its arrangement, however, eliminates all the actual incoherences of everyday talk. Lope knows the difference—to speak in twentieth-century terms—between the chaotic chatter of a tape-recording and an esthetic ordering of the spoken language. Even at their most banal and desultory, his conversations represent a sifting-out, not a transcription of real ones. Designs can be discerned beneath their seeming meanderings, the hand of the artist conveying nuances of mood, attitude, and atmosphere with a finesse foreign to actual conversations. There is, indeed, no need to borrow twentieth-century terms to characterize this aspect of Lope's conversational art. The *Galateo español* of Luis Gracián Dantisco, a popular manual of courtesy which had been adapted from the Italian original of Giovanni della Casa (1558) and which Lope knew well, having written two sonnets for the 1598 Lisbon edition, is quite explicit on common failings of speakers in civil conversations.[10] It makes us see how well Lope's naturalness avoids certain inartistic extremes: overobsequiousness: "el que se deleita de assegundar mucho el plazer del que le escucha, puede ser tenido por juglar, o por ventura por lisongero" ("he who takes delight in continually enhancing the pleasure of one listening to him may be considered a buffoon or possibly a flatterer") (p. 106); dullness and vulgarity: the subject matter "no deve ser fría, de poca sustancia, ni baxa y vil" ("shouldn't be dull, slight, ordinary, or indecent") (p. 120). If you are relating an anecdote, have it well in mind so that you do not hesitate, grope for words, or forget names (p. 153). To forget what you were talking about shows as little consideration for your listener as to monopolize the conversation. There are some talkers who "acabada la materia de lo que han hablado, no por esso cessan, antes buelven a referir las cosas dichas, o hablan en vazío. Y si alguno sale con su razón se la toman de la boca" ("when the subject they have talked about is concluded, don't stop talking on that account, but go back and relate all over again what they have already told, or talk in a vacuum. And if anyone tries to put in a word, they snatch it from his mouth") (p. 173). On the other hand, to remain unduly silent is also to give offense: "parece que es un quererse estar desconocido y encubierto" ("it seems an attempt to remain unnoticed and concealed") (p. 174).

Such counsels remind us that live conversation was already very much an art in its own right, one inherited by the Spaniards from Renaissance Italy, although Gracián Dantisco's cautious standards for dignified, inoffensive conversation were more hypothetical than actual, and like all such codes, were widely ignored. Quevedo's mock conversational manuals point up one sort of affectation which breached them: the pedantic and precious. His *Culta latiniparla* (published in 1631) offers a glossary for pretentious females and a supplementary vocabulary "porque si dura la visita o conversación mucho, suele acabarse a algunos cultos la cultería, y tienen conversación remendada de lego y docto" ("because if the visit or conversation keeps on long, some affected pedants tend to run out of pedantry and their conversation becomes a patchwork of learning and illiteracy"). The later *Agudeza y arte de ingenio* (1648) of Baltasar Gracián carries verbal ingenuity and dexterity far beyond the mean favored by Gracián Dantisco. The live conversations recorded in a work like the *Fastiginia* of Pinheiro da Veiga prove how agile and daring actual talk could be.[11]

The tempering of artifice with naturalness, the careful avoidance of formlessness assure the efficacy of the dialogue of *La Dorotea* as an artistic medium, one freer and more supple than stage dialogue, and more lifelike than the novelistic dialogue of Lope's contemporaries, with the natural exception of Cervantes. In its genuine colloquiality this dialogue also stands apart from contemporary forms of the nonfictional dialogue. The "compendium-like" dialogue characteristic of the age of the Counter Reformation (to borrow the term of Luis Murillo) had lost the art of live interlocutory play evident in the Erasmian dialogues of the early sixteenth century and had largely sacrificed dialectic in converting the dialogue from a medium for the genuine exploration of ideas into a doctrinal or informational vehicle.[12] We cannot, to be sure, speak of dialectic in any profound sense in connection with the dialogue of the *acción en prosa*. If we occasionally feel a certain play of minds probing for a truth (as in the diagnosis of Fernando's emotional state as jealousy, not love, reached by Julio and Ludovico in

Act III, scene 4, or in parts of the literary discussions of Act IV, scenes 2 and 3), the conversations lead in an almost incidental way to disclosures of the author's convictions about human nature, convictions which, as we have seen, resist pat formulation and definitive systematization. As for conversational art, one need only glance at dialogues of the period in which one might expect to find it exemplified to see how little they had to teach Lope. A work like the *Días geniales o lúdicros* of Rodrigo Caro (completed 1631), for example, offers its survey of ancient games and festivities in tones of gravity that belie its title. In a work of more purely recreational intent, the *Diálogos de apacible entretenimiento* of Gaspar Lucas Hidalgo (1616), a repertory of ways to tell practical jokes and make others the butt of witticisms, the tone is wooden and colloquiality is conspicuously missing.[13]

Insofar as Lope's art has a literary derivation, its affinities are clearly not with works of this kind but with *La Celestina*, the basic dialogue of which, as Mrs. Malkiel notes, in its everyday conversational tone, involves only a little stylization of spoken speech and impresses one as "natural" and "modern."[14] Its influence on Lope can be surmised from certain specific reminiscences of the *tragicomedia* which I shall have occasion to point out, but Lope's ability to profit by the example of *La Celestina* rests, in the last analysis, on his individual cast of mind and on the communicativeness native to his temperament. The flexible medium of the *acción en prosa* at last provides an artistic order capable, through the free play of conversation, of giving the heterogeneousness, the loosely knit associativeness characteristic of his mental habits an artistic rationale. By making the tangents on which the talk diverges the contributions of different speakers rather than the caprice of a single one, Lope creates a play of suggestion and association between different minds which manages to be engaging even when it fails to go deep.

Lope clearly found congenial the loose rein he allowed himself; the contrast is noticeable with the restiveness he shows when trying, more or less seriously, to hew to a single narrative line in his works of prose fiction. In his longer narratives he stops to comment in asides to the reader about the characters or events and about his role as narrator.[15] In the short stories his efforts to gain a free hand produce charming but superfluous and often distracting tracery in the margins.[16] Yet it is clear from indications in his earlier prose narratives that a gift for prose dialogue lay untapped for a long time before he devised a suitable medium for its deployment. Here and there among pages of artistic prose one comes upon snatches of colloquial conversation. In one passage from *La Arcadia*, for example, the dialogue fleetingly acquires such a colloquial cast:

No te digo estas cosas, porque han de ser parte para que tú la quieras,
mas porque son meritorias para que ella te quiera a ti, que si
comienzas a ser amado della, sin duda que lo agradecerás, y en
llegando la historia a este capítulo, haz cuenta que lo demás está
hecho. ¿De qué arte de amar, respondió Amphryso, has estudiado
estas liciones de querer? ¿De qué arte? dixo Silvio: de haver, que nunca
fuera, passado por semejantes desdichas, de que la experiencia me ha
hecho maestro. ¿Nunca has oído a Lucino los amores que tuve con
Elisa, la de los ojos tan celebrados de quantos Poetas y músicos
nuestra Arcadia ha tenido desde el primer valle hasta el
postrero monte?[17]

"I don't tell you these things because they will influence you to love
her but because they justify her in loving you; and once you begin
to be loved by her you will no doubt repay her love; and when the
story reaches this chapter, consider the rest accomplished." "In what
art of loving," answered Amphryso, "have you studied these
lessons in love?" "In what art?" said Silvio; "in having myself—I
wish it were otherwise—gone through similar mischances, of which
experience has made me a master. Has Lucino never told you about
my romance with Elisa, she whose eyes have been so celebrated by
every poet and musician that ever was in our Arcadia from the first
valley to the farthest mountain?"

More than in Lope's published works, however, it is in his private letters
to his patron that we detect signs of a trend toward live conversational
dialogue. In these letters, as in the *acción en prosa*, the written word echoes
the spoken; the style is chatty and casual. Reading the letters is like listening
to one side of an intimate conversation. "No sé quién decía," Lope writes,
"que las cartas eran oración mental a los ausentes, y decía bien, porque
mientras se escriue se habla con él en el entendimiento, en quien se representa
al viuo su ymagen" ("Whoever it was who said that letters were mental
prayers to people away, said well, because while one is writing one is talking
with a person in one's mind, in which his image is vividly reproduced").
Indeed the letters are often resumptions of actual conversations: "Señor, lo
que yo dixe a Vex.ª es lo que ynporta, y me buelbo a afirmar y confirmar en
ello" ("Sir, what I told Your Excellency is what matters and I again affirm
and stand by it"). Or: "Sin duda es el mexor [estado] de todos el pacífico,
como ya dexamos definido la otra noche" ("No doubt the best state of all
is the peaceful one, as we concluded the other night"). Or again: "Hablo
de buena gana con Vex.ª de mis pensamientos, porque no tengo a quien
decirlos en todo el mundo . . . y porque Vex.ª se halla en estado que no le

desagrada la conuersación desta materia" ("I am happy to talk to Your Excellency about my thoughts, because I have no one to tell them to in the whole world . . . and because Your Excellency is in a state of mind in which conversation on this subject is not displeasing to him").[18] Though without an interlocutor present to spur, steer, or stem the flow of ideas, real dialogue is naturally out of the question, Lope can be seen straining toward it more intently than most letter-writers, and he actually quotes in direct discourse imagined replies, sometimes mental, sometimes as if really spoken, and proceeds to supply his own rejoinders:

> Dira Vex.ª: Este me escriue en día de jubileo de la Porciúncula. Así es verdad; pero para mí, señor, cada día lo es, pues todos ellos es fuerza confessarme.
>
> Dirá V. M.: mucho deue de hablar en esto Lope, pues aún a mí lo quenta. Prometo a V. M. como hidalgo que no me han oýdo una palabra fuera de mi cassa.
>
> Dirá Vex.ª: ¡Qué ocupaciones éstas de vn ombre de bien! Y responderé yo que no puedo más.[19]

> Your Excellency will say: He is writing me on the day the Portiuncula is celebrated. So I am, but for me every day is such a day, since I am obliged to make confession every day.
>
> Your Grace will say: Lope must be talking about this a lot since he even tells it to me. I assure Your Grace as a man of honor that no one outside my family has heard a word of it from me.
>
> Your Excellency will say: What a way for a respectable man to spend his time! And I will answer that I can't help it.

Occasionally an imagined exchange is more drawn out:

> Después me boluí a su cassa, y me dieron de cenar alegremente; que entre la gente de nuestra gerarquía se ussa guardar de la comida algo fiambre, y sabe, según decía otra muger (porque esta respuesta llebe tales autores), como segunda carretilla. Parézeme que dize Vex.ª: Bueno anda este Padre; échasele de ver que trata en estas niñerías, pues parézeme que vienen fuera de propósito, que en papel y en conuersación es el más cansado estilo; porque Vex.ª, señor, está, según escriue, en estado de tanta pena, que ni ésta le será consuelo, ni dexará de traerle a la memoria passados gustos.[20]

> Afterward I went back to her house and we had a cheery supper. For among people at our level something cold is usually kept over

from a meal and it tastes, as a certain woman used to say (just so this
remark may have proper authority), just as good as the first time. I
can imagine Your Excellency saying: this father is in a fine way;
it's evident from his talking about such trivia, which, it seems
to me, are beside the point, and on paper and in conversation this
is the most annoying style. Because Your Excellency, sir, from what
you write, is in such a state of unhappiness that this will neither be a
consolation to you nor will it fail to bring past pleasure to your mind.

The Duke's imagined response (although still in the third person) shows how
close to dialogue Lope's letter-writing style can come. Recalling his master's
heavy mood, Lope grows uneasy as he imagines the Duke's reaction and
curbs his prattling. Such sensitivity to the master's mood is not mere
obsequiousness. It bespeaks a natural orientation toward the reaction of an
addressee or an audience: in the Duke's imagined reproach—"beside the
point"—Lope sees his failure to remain attuned to the Duke's mood. As if
he and the Duke were speakers drifting apart or talking at cross-purposes,
Lope restores communication by reverting to what the Duke had written
of his state of mind. Such letter-writing is more than ordinarily imaginative.
Lope creates conversational counterpoint as a way of cementing a relationship and displays the sensitivity to cross-currents of mood and feeling between
speakers which will permit him, in the dialogue of *La Dorotea*, to bind his
speakers to each other, or to suggest a failure to communicate, by means not
confined to the purely verbal.

Shaping of the Dialogue

Turning, then, to this dialogue, let us look for signs of the artistic control
exercised by Lope in the manipulation of digressions, in the technique of
transitions—especially their opportune omission—and in the creation of
effects of abruptness or of continuity.

In regard to digressions, a tendency one can observe elsewhere in Lope's
prose to mark them off sooner or later for what they are and return
deliberately to the subject is passed on to his characters. He instills in them
his own awareness of the need to put limits on discursiveness. When Lope
as narrator practices this not very subtle form of control in his longer or
shorter stories, he is often heavy-handed; the same is true when it is the
characters themselves who announce that they are about to come back to
the point.[21] On the lips of characters who set out to make an art of conversation, as do those of *La Dorotea*, the practice comes into its own, however,
and Lope uses advantageously a technique handled imperfectly elsewhere.

We shall find digressions becoming part of a game played by collaborating speakers within limits they all respect (III, 4) or creating tensions between speakers differently motivated, speakers like Gerarda who bide their time, then return to the subject (I, 1); or like César (V, 3), the Neo-Platonic trend of whose observations on Fernando's account of the cooling of his love continually diverges from the cynical course of this account. In either case the artistry evident in the perceptible pattern of the conversations has its counterpart in the speakers' consciousness of creating such patterns. Continually Lope's art tightens up the looseness of ordinary talk, creating the essentially ludic order of a game or contest.

As I have already said, and as subsequent analyses of particular scenes will bring out, Lope is adept at catching the associative movement characteristic of live conversation: a random phrase or thought becomes the hinge on which a new direction in the talk turns. But it is pertinent to note here that he sometimes dispenses with such hinges, producing the kind of abrupt or jerky movement that can reflect particular personalities or particular tensions between speakers. Marfisa's bluntness in her first encounter with Dorotea (II, 3) is illustrative on both counts. Their conversation consists less of well directed parry and thrust than of random stabs by speakers who cast about for ways to score against each other. Telling in another way is the exceptional absence of any comment by Fernando on the sonnet which Julio cites (p. 225) "apropos of your jealousy." Fernando simply proceeds with his own line of thought as if Julio had not spoken, too preoccupied to listen or too indifferent to object. In the first scene of Act V, the uneasy situation between Don Bela and Laurencio—reticence on the servant's part meeting with ironic reservations on the master's—is reflected in abrupt shifts of subject throughout the brief scene: the borrowed horse, Don Bela's rejection, ideal beauty, the rejection again, and so on. As for Gerarda, we shall find her garrulity sometimes characterized by ex-abruptos and not merely by associative rambling or self-observant digressions. Lope is especially adept at creating effects of dissociation at the beginning of scenes, when speakers are still feeling their way toward some sort of conversational alignment: cases in point are the exchange between César and Fernando near the beginning of Act V, scene 3 (pp. 402–403), in which Fernando's remarks—"Arte diuino es la música"; "¿Qué os auéis hecho estos días?" ("Music is a divine art"; "What have you been doing these days?")—break with staccato effect into a texture of courteous phrases and observations on music; or the opening dialogue of the supper scene (II, 6), to be analyzed below.

More frequent, however, are those scene openings already referred to in which we seem to be dropping in on conversations that have already taken hold. The second act, like the first, begins in this way: "No digo yo lo prometido, pero todo el oro . . ." ("Not merely that which I have promised, but all the gold . . ."). Don Bela's words not only confirm as actuality the developments for which the first act had set the stage; they clearly fit into a more immediate context of conversation left for the reader to supply, whose drift is plain from Don Bela's reference, in his next sentence, to "esta vitoria" ("this victory"). Lope creates here an illusion of talk overflowing the formal confines of the work, or, more precisely, flowing into it from beyond, reinforcing the effect of the opening of Act I. At the same time, by what he has chosen not to include, he avoids belaboring the obvious and is free to focus from the beginning on Gerarda and her acquisitive antics.

While the other act openings are all more theatrical than the first two, the characters not merely talking but responding to some immediate external stimulus—arrival home, morning on the Prado, the count's servant's call— Lope on occasion reverts to the conversational technique to open particular scenes, especially those of pure talk without dramatic tension. We happen in on conversations already proceeding and are able to imagine the context of talk from which they emanate. So with Don Bela's "Estoy contento, Laurencio, de auer conquistado la gracia de su madre de Dorotea" ("I am pleased, Laurencio, to have won the favor of Dorotea's mother") (III, 2, p. 228) and Fernando's "¿Tan infaustas cosas pronostica essa figura, que no queréis dezírmelas?" ("Does that horoscope forecast such disastrous things that you don't want to tell me what they are?") (V, 8, p. 438). (So also with the openings of II, 2 and IV, 2.) Occasionally the preceding conversation implied in the opening is an actual one just given, as in Act III, scene 6, where Dorotea's question "¿Con quién hablauas, Felipa?" ("Whom were you talking to, Felipa?") (p. 263) refers to the dialogue in the preceding scene. In this case, nothing is left out for the reader but one side of what he knows has been missed by Dorotea. There is a similar immediate link-up in Act I, scene 2. In these cases Lope shifts interlocutors but maintains the conversational momentum unbroken. As always, his scenic demarcations provide distinct contours without destroying continuity.

The analyses and expositions to follow will bring out other indications of Lope's sureness of touch in the artistic shaping and manipulation of the dialogue, beginning with the patterns discernible behind certain characteristic passages of everyday language. Before turning to these, however, let us note instances where everyday language is particularly in evidence and mention a number of specific features of usage which help to give the dialogue as a whole its familiar and colloquial cast, even though it sometimes happens that the line between rhetorical and natural usage is hard to draw.

As has been suggested, the overall effect of the sequences of familiar dialogue is to create a context of the everyday about passages of deliberately wrought stylistic artistry. Sometimes it is a matter of spontaneous colloquiality piercing artifice only momentarily: Dorotea's embarrassed "Necia estás, Gerarda. ¡Iesús, qué necia!" ("You're silly, Gerarda. Lord, so silly!") (p. 175) when Gerarda angles too aggressively for Don Bela's diamonds; Fernando's exasperated "¿Qué me dezís, Ludouico?" ("What are you telling me, Ludovico?") and the reply, "Lo que me passó con ella" ("Simply what happened to me with her") (p. 237), when Fernando hears his friend impute sorcery to Gerarda; Julio's putting aside for a moment a position he is defending to make a candid avowal:

> Fer.: No creas en sueños.
> Iul.: No sé qué te responda, pues siempre sueño que soy pobre, y
>   despierto soy lo mismo.
>
> (p. 83)
>
> Fer.: Don't trust dreams.   Jul.: I don't know how to answer, since
> I always dream I'm poor and when I wake up I still am.

Sometimes a more prolonged exchange in everyday language is placed for purposes of contrast in a context of high artifice: the noticeably offhand exchange between Fernando and Julio when Marfisa steps out to get her jewels, for example, underscores the histrionism of the preceding and following sequences. More frequently touches of colloquial language begin or end a scene, serving as a frame for the rhetoric, histrionism, or preciosity displayed in it: the second scene between Marfisa and Fernando (IV, 8) begins and ends on a colloquial level; a very brief familiar coda ends the play-acting of Gerarda and Teodora in Act I, scene 7 (p. 125); Laurencio remonstrates with Don Bela after Gerarda's exit in Act II, scene 1: "Señor, ¿tienes juizio? ¿Dessa manera gastas?" ("Sir, are you in your right mind, spending this way?") (p. 137); the dialogue of the reunion scene in the Prado subsides at the end into a coda of everyday speech (p. 316). Sometimes there is a noticeable descent in level within a scene: as soon as Ludovico exits in Act III, scene 4 (p. 255), for example, the well-wrought sophisticated dialogue of the poetic confrères is replaced by an exchange on a practical everyday level. In particular, an intervention or entrance of Gerarda produces this effect—an intervention during the visit of Don Bela to Dorotea, for example: "¿Queréis que me ponga en medio aunque lleue la peor parte? Paz, señores . . ." ("Would you like me to step in, even though I may get the worst of it? Peace . . .") (p. 172); the bustling entrance at the beginning of Act II, scene 4 (p. 156) directly after Dorotea's song in Act II, scene 3; Gerarda's presence, too, can keep the underlying level of everyday language very much in view (II, 4). It is a level which likewise becomes noticeable after Julio arrives for the second of two successive scenes of literary discussion (IV, 3), in contrast to the more formal exchanges of the first. We may also note how in both encounters of Marfisa and Dorotea the familiar style inevitably breaks through the elevated ceremoniousness with which they begin, as they lock forces in rivalry over Fernando. It is because Marfisa becomes unbearably forward that Dorotea puts courtesy aside and asks bluntly: "¿Sobre qué trato queréis vos tan aprisa mis pensamientos? Lo cierto es que, aunque más los encubráis, se os ven los vuestros" ("On the basis of what acquaintance are you asking for my private thoughts so soon? The truth is that yours are showing, no matter how much you cover them over") (p. 151). The tone of colloquial prose, finally, prevails in the scene between Don Bela and Laurencio that opens Act V, in contrast to the pretentious arguments of the master and the rapier thrusts by the servant that marked their earlier exchanges. Naturally enough it prevails also in the brief scene that ends Act III (scene 9), in which Fernando and Don Bela finally come to blows.

Among the more noticeable touches of colloquial usage we may count, besides the everyday vocabulary itself, familiar locutions and idioms of the daily language, hackneyed phrases and conversational props, repetitions of various kinds, ellipsis and staccato effects, use of diminutives, parataxis or run-on syntax. In considering samples of each,[22] we shall more than once find an element of artistry sustaining or overlaying what might otherwise appear purely familiar or offhand usage.

Colloquial Usage

Familiar Locutions and Idioms

Familiar locutions and idioms are, of course, legion. A random sampling (emphasis mine) includes: Dorotea's (to Marfisa) "Como tengo pocas fuerças, y *me lleuáis cuesta arriba*, me voy cansando" ("As I've so little strength, and *you're taking me uphill*, I'm getting tired") (p. 151). Laurencio's "*Haz cuenta* que tú estauas en Madrid" ("*Pretend* that you were in Madrid") (p. 228). César's "*Hazed cuenta* que no lo soi [amigo]" ("*Pretend* that I am not one [a friend]") (p. 403). Gerarda's "Y si *no lo has por enojo, anduue tan liberal de la taza*" ("And if *you've no objection, I made so free with the bottle*") (p. 234); or her "¿*Pensauas hazer algun peso falso* a Dorotea?" ("*Were you intending to shortchange* Dorotea?") (p. 390). Don Bela's "Y *a la cuenta* también se lo pondrá [el afeite] Dorotea" ("And *as far as one can tell* Dorotea must also put it [make-up] on" (p. 393). Fernando's "*como si ya fuéramos a la parte* del desollamiento indiano" ("as if *we were* already *going in together on* the *indiano* fleecing") (p. 409). Julio's "¿Para qué quieres *andar en pronósticos?*" ("Why do you want *to fool around with* fortune-telling?") (p. 421). Gerarda's "*mas que se ahorque* don Bela" ("*let* Don Bela *go hang*") (p. 451). Dorotea's "¿*Mas que piensas* que te he burlado?" ("*I'll bet you think* I've been playing a joke on you") (p. 100); or her "¿*Mas que me preguntas* de dónde vengo?" ("*I'll bet you'll ask me* where I've come from") (p. 372). Compare Gerarda's "¿*Cuánto va que* te arrepientes?" ("*How much do you want to bet that* you're sorry?") (p. 433); and her "Y *yo apostaré que* dize aquel bobillo . . ." ("And *I'll bet that* that silly little . . . is saying") (p. 452). Gerarda's "¿Matarse? ¡*Para esso está el tiempo! Como que* no huuiesse alma" ("Kill herself! *The time is ripe for that, all right! As if* there were no such thing as a soul") (p. 137). Celia's "¿*Cosa que sea* destos que venden agua?" ("*No doubt he'll be* one of those water-vendors?") (p. 191).

Hackneyed and Popular Phrases; Conversational Props

Quevedo's *Cuento de cuentos* provides a good point of reference for hackneyed phrases and conversational props. Of "ahora bien" ("now then"), Quevedo remarks:

> Y para ver a cuál mendiguez está reducida la lengua española, considere vuesa merced que si Dios, por su infinita misericordia, no nos hubiera dado estas dos voces *ahora bien*, nadie se pudiera ir ni se despidiera de una conversación.[23]

> And in order to see the beggarly state the Spanish language is reduced to, consider that if God, through His infinite mercy, hadn't given us the two words *ahora bien*, no one would be able to depart or take his leave from a conversation.

In *La Dorotea* the phrase is used six times in all, not for taking leave, but as an informal indication of what in rhetoric would be a *reditus ad rem* or a *transitio;* for example, Gerarda says, "Aora bien, boluamos a coger el hilo de nuestro cuento" ("Now then, let's pick up the thread of our story again") (p. 451).[24] Another cliché is "No, sino el alba" (lit., "No, just the dawn").[25] As Morby remarks (p. 371, n. 245), in Lope this set phrase is usually an ironical answer to a superfluous question and it is so used by both Teodora (p. 371) and Gerarda:

> *Bel.:* ¿Aquéllas se afeitan, madre?
> *Ger.:* No, sino el alba.

(p. 392)

> *Bel.:* Do those girls use make-up?   *Ger.:* No, wouldn't dream of it.

Other phrases of this kind mentioned by Quevedo and found in *La Dorotea* are "al cabo al cabo" ("when all is said and done"): Gerarda's "y al cabo al cabo, morir fea y nacer hermosa" ("when all is said and done, die ugly and be born beautiful") (p. 435); and the ironical "¡Gentil...!" ("A fine...!"), indicative of a reservation or reproof: Gerarda's "¡Gentil Narciso!" ("A fine Narcissus!"), apropos of Fernando (p. 423).

Also functioning essentially as popular phrases are passing snatches of traditional songs and ballads not quoted but casually encrusted in speech, as in Don Bela's remark: "Estar triste Dorotea y no ir a los toros ... *algo tiene en el campo que le duele*" ("Dorotea sad and not going to the bullfight ... *something's surely the matter with her*") (p. 392). (The emphasis is mine; cf. Morby's n. 20. The anacoluthon is itself colloquial.) Another instance is Gerarda's explanation of why she refuses to eat a fig as she drinks: "¿Pues el auía de entrar acá? *No se verá en esse gozo*" ("It go down here? *It'll never share such joy*") (emphasis mine; p. 191). Here Gerarda falls back on a line from the traditional ballad "Santa Fe, ¡qué bien pareces!" ("Santa Fe, how fine you look!").[26]

Repetitions

With repetitions the line between natural usage and forms of the rhetorical figure *geminatio* is not always easy to draw. Act V, scene 4, ends with Dorotea triumphantly calling to Celia after she tears Fernando's portrait in two (p. 426):

> *Dor.:* ... ¡Celia, Celia!
>   *Scena Quinta*
>   *Celia.—Dorotea*
> *Cel.:* Señora, señora.
> *Dor.:* ¡Vitoria, vitoria!

> *Dor.:* Celia! Celia! Scene Five. Celia. Dorotea.   *Cel.:* Madam, Madam!
> *Dor.:* Victory! Victory!

In these verbal echoes the iterations involve some degree of conscious mimicry on Celia's part and obvious theatrics on Dorotea's. At the other extreme and clearly on the colloquial level, however, are nonvocative and nonimperative repetitions expressing a slightly ironical incredulity: Dorotea's mimicry "¿Toda, toda?" ("All, all?") (p. 451) to Gerarda's "Fue menester toda [la botilla de vino]" ("The whole [wineskin] was needed"); Dorotea's "¿Tantos requiebros? ¿Tantos?" ("So many compliments? So many?"), also to Gerarda (p. 156); or, expressing an impatient concession, Gerarda's "Bueno, bueno, dexa el arpa" ("All right, all right, let the harp go") (p. 451).

Double vocatives are used colloquially mainly in admonishment (sometimes mingled with commiseration), alarm, or reproof.

Admonishment. Gerarda's "¡Ay, niña, niña! No harás casa con azulejos" ("Ah, child, child. You can't build a house with tiles") (p. 435); and "Dorotea, Dorotea, mientras eres niña, toma como vieja" ("Dorotea, Dorotea, while you're a girl, take all you can, like an old woman") (p. 168); Laurencio's "Señor, señor, a pretensiones humanas, diligencias diuinas" ("Sir, sir, for human ambitions, divine exertions") (p. 261).

Alarm. Celia's "¡Señora! ¡Señora!" (calling to Teodora after Dorotea swallows the ring, p. 126); Teodora's "¡Dorotea! ¡Dorotea!" shortly afterward.

Reproof. Gerarda's "¡Ay, Teodora, Teodora! Felipa no la pierde, sino el amor que tiene a don Fernando" ("Oh, Teodora, Teodora! Felipa isn't ruining her—it's her love for Don Fernando that is") (p. 375); Don Bela's "Gerarda, Gerarda; si hablamos de veras, no soi tan simple" ("Gerarda, Gerarda, to be truthful about it, I am not so simple-minded" (p. 394); Gerarda's "Laurencio, Laurencio, esto que agora no es [Gerarda's teeth] fue perlas algún día" ("Laurencio, Laurencio, these which are no longer, were once pearls") (p. 232).

Repeated colloquial imperatives (sometimes simply their noun objects) express impatience, ingratiation, urgency, encouragement.

Impatience. Gerarda's "Parece retrato. ¿Mas que sé de quién es? Muestra, muestra" ("It looks like a portrait. I'll bet I know whose. Let's see, let's see") (p. 424); Dorotea's "El dize verdad y tú mientes. Toma, toma, cuélgale" ("It is telling the truth and you are lying. Here, here, hang it up") (p. 139), referring to her hand mirror.

Ingratiation (blandishment, cajolery, coaxing, pleading). Gerarda's "Mira, mira, ¡qué búcaro tan lindo!" ("Look, look, what a pretty *búcaro*!") (p. 157); Dorotea's "Siéntate, siéntate, y dime de dónde vienes" ("Sit down, sit down, and tell me where you've come from") (p. 449); Gerarda's "¡Ay, hija! que no sé qué tenemos en la imaginación, que parece que siempre nos está diziendo, quando no queremos mirar '¡Míralo, míralo!'" ("Ah, child, I don't know what it is we have in our imaginations that always seems to be telling us when we don't want to look: 'look at him, look at him!'") (p. 157); Dorotea's "Este sólo, éste sólo" ("Just this one, just this one") (p. 431), as she holds a love-note of Fernando's back from the flames; Fernando's "Espera, señora, espera. Por lo menos, no te vayas llorando" ("Wait, Madam, wait. At least don't go off crying") (p. 380).

Urgency. Gerarda's "¡Agua!, ¡agua! ¡Iesús! ¿Qué incendio es éste?" ("Water, water! Heavens, what is this fire?") (p. 432); her "Tenla essa mano; que le ha dado mal de coraçón. Tenla, tenla" ("Hold her by the hand; she's had a heart seizure. Hold her, hold her") (p. 456).

Encouragement. Julio's "Canta, canta, pues has templado" ("Sing, sing, since you've finished tuning") (p. 273).[27]

Elliptical Constructions

As in ordinary conversations thoughts are sometimes conveyed without being fully formulated; they are reduced to key elements with connectives or verbs omitted. A clipped telegraphic style expresses the gist of what is thought or felt; structure reflects the order of importance to the speaker rather than logical or conventional syntax: "¡Dama Fernando, y más si es ésta!" ("A lady Fernando, and one like this, especially!"), exclaims the shocked Dorotea to Celia as soon as Marfisa departs (p. 151). "No, sino dar ocasión a que la tengan por descortés" ("No, no, go right ahead and give them grounds for considering her impolite"), says Gerarda, turning away an assumed objection of Don Bela to Dorotea's talking to "an acquaintance" (p. 438). Certain replies or retorts single out a key element and question it: Gerarda's "¿Yo siete almendras?" ("Seven almonds, me?") (p. 195); Dorotea's "¿Yo la causa?" ("I the reason?") (p. 74). Such questions may be not replies but challenges: Dorotea's "¿Tú también, Gerarda?" ("You too, Gerarda?") (p. 372); Felipa's "¿Donaires, Celia?" ("Wisecracks, Celia?") (p. 456); Gerarda's "¿Tú cantando, tú alegre, tú vestida de gala, Dorotea? ¿Tú tocada con cintas verdes, tú cadena y joyas?" ("You singing, you gay, you all dressed up, Dorotea? You with green ribbons in your hair, you chain and jewels?") (p. 449). Particularly in the last phrase of this staccato series, the breach of normal syntax is striking. Naturally, non-interrogative replies are also abridged, for instance, Don Bela's "Yo no, sino locuras" ("Not me; mad words, rather") (p. 258) to Laurencio's remark on the "stupidities" that Dorotea's suitors must have spoken through her grilled windows. When what a character has to say is reduced to one or two words, the colloquialism is often tersely expressive: Celia's "¿Zelitos?" ("Aha! Jealous?") (p. 431); Laurencio's "Buen remedio" ("Simple solution") (p. 392); Fernando's "Malas primas" ("Bad treble strings") as he tunes (p. 400); his simple opening "Escura noche" ("Dark night") (III, 7, p. 266), so strongly in contrast with the literary magnification to follow. Pithy colloquiality underscores a key development when Fernando and Julio reduce a disagreement to a single word (p. 381):

> *Fer.:* Con verla [Dorotea] rendida se me ha quitado [el amor].
> *Iul.:* Templado basta.
> *Fer.:* Quitado digo, Iulio.

> *Fer.:* Seeing [Dorotea] capitulate freed me of it [love].
> *Jul.:* Moderated it will do.   *Fer.:* Freed me, I tell you, Julio.

Diminutives

Diminutives are a noticeable feature of colloquial style in *La Dorotea*. It is equally noticeable in two thirds of the cases (roughly thirty out of forty-five) that we find them on the lips of Gerarda, often concentrated in single passages, a feature of a professionally ingratiating manner stemming evidently from Celestina and aiming at a *captatio benevolentiae*.[28] And peculiar to Gerarda is an almost technical awareness of the diminutive as such. Both these aspects of the diminutives used by Gerarda are more appropriately treated in connection with her particular style of expression. I shall mention here those other diminutives—Gerarda's and the other characters'—which contribute in more ordinary ways to the colloquiality of the dialogue, although the distinction cannot always be rigidly maintained.

In the first place, there are those diminutives particularly characteristic of colloquial speech, called by Amado Alonso "affective-active."[29] These seek to create a particular disposition of mind or feeling in an interlocutor. Thus Gerarda's disparaging references to Fernando in the opening conversation with Teodora: "este moçuelo" ("this miserable youth") (p. 72) and— generically contrasting him to Don Bela—"hombre de disculpa, y no moçitos cansados" ("a man for whom there is some excuse and not these tiresome young boys") (p. 73), another instance of colloquially anomalous syntax. In Gerarda's references to the protagonist as "Fernandillo" ("young Fernando") (pp. 73, 121, 436) such disparagement is also present, particularly when Gerarda calls him "don Fernandillo" (p. 73). On the other hand there is cajolery in the "Dorotica" ("Dotty") that first appears during Don Bela's visit: "Dale tú las gracias, Dorotica, pues que por ti me abriga este liberalíssimo príncipe" ("You thank him, Dotty, since this most generous prince is outfitting me because of you") (p. 179). Later Gerarda displays far less deference when she tries offhandedly to allay Don Bela's doubts as to which suitor is most favored by Dorotea: "Tú, bobillo" ("You, ninny")

(p. 394). Later, too, Fernando twice becomes "Fernandillo" for Teodora (pp. 371, 375). With her, however, this diminutive seems to express some admixture of affection. The same is true of Teodora's own reference to her daughter as "Dorotica," once Dorotea has accepted Don Bela (p. 197).

Entirely "emotional," as Amado Alonso calls them, are the diminutives expressive of Gerarda's delectation in drink and the accompanying food: her "jarrillo de vino" ("little jug of wine") (p. 157), the "traguecito" ("little drink") (p. 189) and "traguillo" ("little drink") (p. 451), "tozinillo" ("lovely bacon") (p. 191) and "torreznillos" ("nice little slices of bacon") (p. 450). Julio's "Papelito tendremos" ("We'll be getting a nice little love-note") (p. 93) expresses pleasurable anticipation. Noticeably familiar in their effect are the "representational-eloquent" diminutives that simply focus attention on their object: Celia's already quoted "¿Zelitos?" ("Aha! Jealous?") (p. 431), her "Otro refrancito" ("There goes another proverb") (p. 192); Gerarda's "Las [medias] moradillas serán para mí, pues que no las quiere nadie" ("These nice purple [stockings] will be for me since no one else wants them") (p. 178). These shade over characteristically into the "esthetic-valorative" when they become an element in a consciously artful depiction, one inevitably of Dorotea: Fernando's description of her "lagrimillas, ya no perlas" ("little teardrops, pearls no longer") (p. 416); Felipa's of her "gestillos a los concetos" ("little faces at the conceits") as she writes (p. 259); Ludovico's of her convalescent appearance: "muletilla, tocado bajo" ("a bit of a crutch, low headdress") (p. 238). Finally we may note those diminutives which are courteously softening: Celia's (to Laurencio): "Enojadillo estás" ("You're a bit put out") (p. 176); Don Bela's description of his actually elaborate offerings as "Vn poco de tela y unos passamanillos" ("A bit of cloth and just some gilt lace edgings") (p. 172).

Meandering Dialogue

Some of the most effective sequences of colloquial dialogue occur when the characters forget the roles they are playing or the images they are projecting and settle back into quiet or casual conversation with servants, companions, cronies. We can then sometimes observe how, under Lope's delicate touch, more sensitively than in ordinary conversations, words in an interlocutory situation seem to be indicating minute movements of thought, feeling, or fantasy, tracing them out faintly without articulating them. Sometimes these lead the speakers away from the context of the moment; we are aware of minds wandering, of thoughts running ahead of words or diverging from them altogether. The stage for which Lope wrote hardly had time for this sort of dialogue; asides and soliloquies were a more easily apprehended way of delineating what a character might be feeling or imagining. In the "más libre teatro," on the other hand, words at times seem meant to suggest inconclusively, without defining.

Act III, scene 6, for example, begins with Dorotea inquiring of Felipa about a conversation she has just been having (scene 5):

> *Dor.:* ¿Con quién hablauas, Felipa?
> *Fel.:* Con el señor don Bela.
> *Dor.:* ¿Fuése?
> *Fel.:* Díxele que estaua Teodora cuidadosa, rezando, mirando y gruñendo.
> *Dor.:* Y de mí, ¿qué le dixiste?
> *Fel.:* Que estauas escriuiéndole vn romance; y murmuraua Laurencio.
> *Dor.:* ¿Qué murmuraua?
> *Fel.:* Que sería alguna prosa dedicada a tus galas.
> *Dor.:* Todos os auéis engañado.
> *Fel.:* ¿Cómo?
> *Dor.:* Es impossible que lo adiuines.
> *Fel.:* ¿Cosa que fuesse alguna carta?
>
> (p. 263)

Dor.: Whom were you talking to, Felipa?   *Fel.:* To Don Bela. *Dor.:* Has he left?   *Fel.:* I told him that Teodora was uneasy, saying her prayers, keeping a watch and grumbling.   *Dor.:* And what did you say about me?   *Fel.:* That you were writing a ballad to him— and Laurencio kept muttering something.   *Dor.:* What was he muttering?   *Fel.:* That it was certainly something nonfictional addressed to your wardrobe.   *Dor.:* You are all mistaken.   *Fel.:* What do you mean?   *Dor.:* You couldn't possibly guess.   *Fel.:* You don't mean it was some letter?

Dorotea's mind is neither on her questions nor on Felipa's answers. It is running ahead to the revelation she is about to make. The conversation marks time in a lifelike manner by interweaving Dorotea's absent-minded questions with Felipa's matter-of-fact replies.

At the beginning of Act II, scene 6, the conversation that precedes the meal backs and fills in what seems a desultory way (p. 188):

> *Teo.:* ¿Qué hazías, Dorotea?
> *Dor.:* Aquí estaua con Gerarda.
> *Teo.:* ¿Con Gerarda? Milagro.

Dor.: ¿Por qué milagro?
Teo.: Porque nunca te he visto muy deseosa de su conuersación.
Ger.: Estáuale diziendo . . .

Gerarda spins her story about Santa Inés, then asks Teodora:

Ger.: ¿De dónde vienes?
Teo.: De ver vna amiga que estaua de parto.

Teo.: What were you doing, Dorotea?   *Dor.:* I was here with
Gerarda.   *Teo.:* With Gerarda? Miraculous.   *Dor.:* Why
miraculous?   *Teo.:* Because I've never seen you very eager for her
conversation.   *Ger.:* I was telling her [. . .] Where have you been?
Teo.: Visiting a friend who's just had a child.

The two crones speculate on the intriguing circumstances of this birth,
and Dorotea falls silent. Presently she breaks in with: "Madre, lleno traes
de lodo el manto" ("Mother, your cloak is full of mud"). This surprising
way of rejoining the conversation shows that in the interim she has not so
much been listening to her mother as observing her. It starts up another
train of inconsequentialities, with no noticeable direction, until Dorotea
quietly suggests that Gerarda stay to dinner. "¿Qué nouedad es ésta?"
("What does this mean?"), asks Teodora in feigned surprise, and the meal
is brought in. While Dorotea's eye has been on her mother's mud-stained
cloak, her mind has still been dwelling on the dazzling fabrics just received
from Don Bela. The contrast is suddenly jarring. Mollified by the gifts,
Dorotea has an unexpected movement of solicitude first for her mother,
then for Gerarda. Submerged, perhaps even entirely subliminal, the libelous
motif "Lovely Filis supports her relatives" reappears. Lope's touch is very
light as he suggests a connection between the daughter's acquisitions and
the mother's well-being. The bold reproof of Pinardo, the resultant rapaciousness of Jacinta have given way to this restrained, finely drawn
naturalistic sequence which uses trivia artistically to indicate shifting attitudes and the emergence of an accommodation among the speakers. As
Dorotea's hostility fades, Teodora catches sight of the *búcaro* on which I
have already commented, and she becomes conciliatory in her turn:
"Aunque te dixe aquellas cosas, bien sé yo tu virtud y honestidad, Dorotea"
("Even though I spoke to you that way, Dorotea, I am well aware what a
decent, respectable girl you are"). There is no hard feeling left in Lope,
only ironical amusement at Teodora's hypocrisy. This brief sequence
marks a moment of *détente* between the high artifice that fills the scene of

Don Bela's visit and the briskly paced and more exhibitionistic merriment of Gerarda in the ensuing meal scene.

Other snatches of down-to-earth dialogue occur when masters and servants size up other characters:

> *Dor.:* ¿Qué te parece desta visita, Celia?
> *Cel.:* Que nos engañó al principio.
> *Dor.:* ¡Dama Fernando, y más si es ésta! No sin causa se le dio tan poco de lo que le dixe.
> *Cel.:* Pues, ¿cómo se fue tan aprisa?
> *Dor.:* Porque ya deuía de tener preuenida su jornada.
>
> (p. 151)

> *Dor.:* What do you say to this visit, Celia? *Cel.:* That she played false with us at the beginning. *Dor.:* A lady Fernando, and one like this, especially! Now I see why he took what I said to him so lightly. *Cel.:* Then why did he leave in such a hurry? *Dor.:* Because he must already have had his journey all arranged.

The thought shared by mistress and maid but only hinted at in their first words suddenly breaks out in "¡Dama Fernando, y más si es ésta!" ("A lady Fernando, and one like this, especially!"). I have already noted how the staccato phrasing records spontaneously the order of emphasis in the speaker's mind and omits everything else. Dorotea brushes aside the implication of Celia's question—if Fernando really loved Marfisa, would he have rushed to Seville after quarreling with you?—and answers the first thing that enters her head. Her mind is elsewhere and she is incapable of seeing that Celia's point is unanswerable. She is already preparing herself for the rhetorical tirade that follows this first unpremeditated expression of indignation. But the tirade in turn will leave her shaken and disconsolate, weakly threatening reprisals against Fernando's portrait:

> *Dor.:* Sí, sí, muy tierna me dexan estos zelos; no zelos, que son de lo que se imagina, sino de lo que se prueua. Tú verás lo que passa. Con una aguxa le tengo de picar los ojos.
> *Cel.:* Quexaránse los tuyos.
> *Dor.:* No le miraré entonces.
> *Cel.:* Pues, ¿cómo verás dónde le picas?
> *Dor.:* Vn pintor tengo de llamar que le pinte vna soga al cuello.
>
> (p. 152)

> *Dor.:* Yes, yes, this jealousy leaves me soft-hearted, all right; not jealousy, which is of something you imagine, but of something you

prove. Just wait and see what happens. I'll prick his eyes out with a needle. *Cel.:* Yours will protest. *Dor.:* Then I won't look at him. *Cel.:* Then how will you see where to prick him? *Dor.:* I'll call a painter and have him paint a rope around his neck.

It is purely the verbal play between Dorotea and Celia that conveys the agitation of the former. The sequence is not dramatic. Although Fernando's portrait is before her (she has brought it out for Marfisa) Dorotea is talking about it, not addressing or assaulting it, as she will do in Act V. She flits from one fantasy to another under the goading of her maid, scarcely heeding what she is saying. The irrational trend of her thoughts is reflected in the contradictory, telescoped formulation of "Sí, sí, muy tierna me dexan estos zelos; no zelos, que son de lo que se imagina, sino de lo que se prueua." The irony is colloquial rather than rhetorical in this bit of *oratio soluta* and the afterthought is not a *correctio* but a sign of distraction. The improvisatory movement of the dialogue traces a psychic process: the attempt to repress a truth—her own jealousy—which she resists acknowledging.

In a situation not unlike Dorotea's, Marfisa is later seen (IV, 7) thinking aloud to Clara about Fernando's deceitfulness.[30]

> Aquel gentil hombre que hablé es vno de los amigos de Don
> Fernando, que el seruir a Lisena, su vezina de Dorotea, los hizo
> iguales, como en el amor, en la confiança. Preguntóme cómo me
> iba con él después que auía venido de Seuilla. Yo le respondí que
> don Fernando no auía venido, y él entonces (como en la Corte se
> vsa) me refirió la causa por qué se auía partido, que eran los zelos
> de vn cauallero indiano no mal admitido de su casa, aunque con poco
> gusto de Dorotea; que no auía muerto a nadie, en que conocí que
> fue inuención para sacarme lo que sabes que le di para que se fuesse;
> que en mi vida compré tan barato el gusto de apartalle de aquella
> ninfa, por cuya ausencia alguna promessa la obliga a vn hábito, casto
> por ironía. Sólo el escapulario azul será verdadero, por lo zeloso.
> No sé qué pretendió en esta conuersación Fabricio (éste es su
> nombre). Pero ¿para qué lo dudo? Lo que todos los hombres, que
> quanto ven codician. Deuió de querer apartarme del amor de
> Fernando; que me dio esta carta que desde el camino le auía escrito,
> con vnos versos que a su partida compuso, que todo dize assí...
>
> (p. 376)

That gentleman I spoke to is one of Don Fernando's friends. His
attachment to Lisena, Dorotea's neighbor, made them equal in love
as well as in their secrets. He asked me how I was faring with him

since his return from Seville. I answered that Don Fernando hadn't returned and he then (as is customary in this Court city) told me the reason for his leaving, which was jealousy of an *indiano* gentleman not unfavorably looked on by the family, although this wasn't much to Dorotea's liking; that he hadn't killed anyone, which showed me that this was a fabrication to do me out of what you know I gave him so he could leave. Never have I purchased so cheaply the satisfaction of separating him from that damsel; because of his absence some vow puts her under obligation to wear a habit— ironically, a chaste one. Only the blue scapular must be sincere, since it's for jealousy. I don't know what Fabricio was after in this conversation (that's his name). But how can I doubt it? The same thing as all men, who covet whatever they see. He must have been trying to make me give up my love of Fernando and he gave me this letter which he had written him on the trip, with some verse he composed about his departure, which reads like this . . .

Marfisa is speculating, not resorting to fantasies like Dorotea. Her account first preserves the live conversational exchange as indirect discourse, then slips into a string of casually connected deductions and afterthoughts. Her question "But how can I doubt it?" self-directed but addressed to Clara, is not rhetorical. The answer has occurred to her only as she begins to wonder, and the explanation emerges paratactically, in a succession of copulatives and parenthetical *que* clauses that record her on-running thoughts. Lope has refined here, in the direction of naturalness, the "pregunte y responda a sí mismo" ("let him question and answer himself") technique prescribed in his *Arte nuevo de hacer comedias*. The tentative ring of Marfisa's supposition, "Deuió de querer apartarme," like that of Dorotea's, "Deuía de tener preuenida su jornada," reinforces the effect of improvisation.

Sometimes the colloquial dialogue simply catches the flavor of ordinary living. This is the case, with an added undertone of quips from Laurencio, when Don Bela appears under Dorotea's windows (III, 5):

Fel.: ¿Es el señor don Bela?
Bel.: Yo soy, Felipa.
Fel.: Aún no está recogida Teodora.
Bel.: ¿Qué hace?
Fel.: Allí está con el rosario, dando más cabezadas que reza cuentas.
Lau: ¿Y son de la gineta o de la brida?
Bel.: ¿Y mi Dorotea?
Fel.: Compone vn romance que quiere enviarte.
Lau.: ¿No lo dixe yo? ¿Quánto va que es el romance para el

> mercader y el estriuo para tu dinero?
> *Bel.:* Habla baxo, ignorante . . .
> *Fel.:* Roldán anda suelto. Quiero hazer que le recojan. Tú, en tanto, da vna buelta, y tendré auisada a Dorotea.
>
> (p. 259)

> *Fel.:* Is that you, Don Bela? *Bel.:* Yes it is, Felipa. *Fel.:* Teodora hasn't retired yet. *Bel.:* What is she doing? *Fel.:* She's at her rosary, and her head is taking more dips than she tells beads. *Lau.:* From long or short stirrups? *Bel.:* What about my Dorotea? *Fel.:* She's composing a ballad to send you. *Lau.:* What did I say? How much will you bet that the ballad is to the tradesman and the refrain to your money? *Bel.:* Keep your voice down, idiot . . . *Fel.:* Roland is loose. I want to have him brought in. You take a turn, meanwhile, and I'll see that Dorotea is informed.

Unlike most such exchanges in *comedias*, this does not point toward action but dwells on domestic details: the nodding mother, the prowling dog, the daughter writing. The tense verbal tug-of-war between Bela and Laurencio that precedes and follows it here subsides to an undertone as Lope interposes these suggestions of an unhurried pattern of domestic life.

Frequently the colloquial conversational effect depends not on particular passages or remarks but on retention of natural movement in the dialogue despite elevated style or formal content. The initial scene—to be analyzed presently from a rhetorical point of view—provides a good example. In the underplayed conversational opening it is made plain that Dorotea is to be discussed; it is some time, however, before the "sentiments" regarding her which Gerarda has been announcing, emerge. This is because, beneath a show of formal argumentation, the grounds of the discussion are continually shifting. The dialogue moves sideways, sliding from subject to subject and slipping back as conversations do, rather than proceeding directionally in the manner of dialectic, controversy, or simple exposition. Passing phrases, as in actual conversation, unexpectedly splice one topic to another. Teodora's objection to Gerarda's "quando vos érades moça" ("when you were a girl") sidetracks the general subject of upbringing, in which the specific case of Dorotea has already been swallowed up, into a long exchange on aging. Only when this subject is wearing thin does Gerarda begin to steer the conversation back toward her "sentiments," and then only circuitously. As the scene proceeds, it becomes plain that the talk, for all its random drift, is responding to the designs of a tactician who is biding her time. Like her forebear, Celestina, Gerarda is purposeful, but unlike Celestina, she pursues her purpose not by bending her interlocutors to her will—Teodora desires exactly what Gerarda does—but by helping them to talk themselves into what she wants, saving face as they do. Lope's art shapes the conversation without disturbing its lifelike rhythm; both speakers are made alert to the drift of the talk, Gerarda more actively than Teodora, and by pressure and counterpressure they fetch up where they both desire. Gerarda knows how to pull up the slack with a tactical transition: "Nunca yo huuiera dicho aquello de *quando érades moça*, que tan fuertemente me auéis castigado. Si assí riñerades a Dorotea . . ." ("I should never have said anything about 'when you were a girl,' you've given me such a punishing for it. Now if you scolded Dorotea that way . . .").The exchange grows more animated, each speaker putting words into the other's mouth:

> *Ger.:* Pero diréisme vos que *quien tunde el paño quita la cresta al gallo* . . .
> *Teo.:* Diréis que la festeja don Fernando: ¡qué gran delito! . . .
> *Teo.:* Diréis que no la tengo [honra] porque aquel señor extrangero regaló a mi hija.
>
> (p. 66)

> *Ger.:* But you'll tell me that he who trims the cloth, removes the cock's crest . . .   *Teo.:* You'll say that Don Fernando courts her: what a terrible crime! . . .   *Teo.:* You'll say I haven't any [honor] because that foreign gentleman was kind to my daughter.

Are these "you'll say's" instances of rhetorical *anticipatio*, designed to undercut in advance an adversary's position, or simply suggestions of intimacy between speakers who enter easily into each other's thoughts and purposes (as we found Lope doing with the Duke of Sessa) while they feel their way toward a meeting of minds? Something of both, no doubt. Gerarda allows herself a trace of impatience as Teodora goes on:

> *Teo.:* Fuése a su tierra. ¿Qué milagro? También se fue Eneas de la reina Dido, y el rey don Rodrigo forçó a la Caua.
> *Ger.:* Que no me espanto desso, Teodora, que ya se sabe que *libro cerrado no saca letrado.*
>
> (p. 67)

> *Teo.:* He went back home. What's so unusual about that? So did Aeneas leave Queen Dido, and King Roderick violated La Cava.

Ger.: That's not what's upsetting me, Teodora: everyone knows that "bygones must be bygones."

Despite Teodora's resort to *exempla*, humorously inept in the circumstances, the colloquial basis of the dialogue comes out in her familiar "¿Qué milagro?" Gerarda's suddenly frank "Que no me espanto desso," and her unforced proverb. But a moment later Gerarda is embarked on the grand rhetorical finale she has been holding in reserve.

Artistic and Life Styles

If one looks on Lope's *poiesis* as varyingly drawn by the poles of art and nature, one would place this opening conversation somewhere near a mid-point. It invites the critic to view the dialogue in the context of Lope's concern with the question of naturalness and artifice in expression; in other words, with the question of style. This question poses itself in *La Dorotea* not primarily in regard to the specific esthetic issue of *culteranismo*, though that stylistic manner is noticeably a case in point in the scenes of the literary academy and is also touched on occasionally elsewhere. Instead, as part of his scrutiny of the poetic process, Lope ponders in broader and less polemical terms the appeal and the effects, beneficial or adverse, of different modes of discourse—the rhetorical, the disputational, the poetic proper—with more or less explicit suggestions of an alternative to them in artless natural utterance. The fact that the basic medium of expression of all the characters is the plain prose of everyday highlights, as I have said, the artifice involved when they adopt other speech styles, but the proximity and the juxtapositions are not merely a matter of doctrinal literary interest. They indicate a preoccupation lived with and reflected upon not merely in terms of the poetic craft but of life styles. Lope knows that art may affect the character of experience just as living affects the response to literature. His interest centers on the relevance of different types and levels of language and expression to given circumstances and, by extension, on the appropriateness of the behavior, the life styles, that accompany them.[31] The language itself, as a literary medium, is not in question. Lope's opposition to *culteranismo* reveals his essential satisfaction with the literary instrument he had inherited. It is as a phenomenon, not as a problem or dilemma, that he views the question of style. As has already been noticed, and as will be increasingly evident later, his interest extends to border zones of expression where life and art meet, to artistic naturalness and natural artifice.[32]

The phenomenon of style may be viewed in *La Dorotea* in a range of meanings extending from technique of adornment and manner of expression to way of being. It might be said that all culture, from ethical codes to standards of taste and conventions of etiquette, is a way of imparting style to living; style is clearly a product of historical acculturation and not simply a phenomenon of a given moment. It is the markedly literary derivation of style and the overlapping of literary and life styles that stand out in *La Dorotea*. Like their creator, Lope's characters consider poetry a *ciencia* (branch of learning). That it makes its own the substance of other branches of learning is an oft-repeated contention of Lope's echoed in the Prologue to *La Dorotea*.[33] While the culture of Lope's characters is primarily literary, the many "partes de filosofía natural y moral" ("aspects of natural and moral philosophy") of which the Prologue speaks naturally belong to it as a legacy of learning stemming from humanistic, patristic, and scholastic sources, more or less reelaborated. In particular, the more purely literary and rhetorical elements of the poetic production of the Greco-Latin, Italian, and native traditions, sometimes transmitted through commonplace books, constitute a fund of precedents to be borrowed or adapted. As Antonio Vilanova brings out in his survey of Renaissance and Golden Age theories of imitation,[34] this procedure is commonly seen as the incorporation into new contexts of the tropes, figures, and epithets of earlier poets, their phrasing, images, *sententiae* and *exempla*, in an attempt to emulate or surpass them. In Lope's own words: "Las imitaciones no son el mismo contexto, sino la alteza de las locuciones, términos y lugares felicemente escritos, las sentencias, el ornamento, propiedad y hermosura exquisita de las voces" ("Imitations are not the context itself but the loftiness of the expressions, terms, and passages felicitously phrased, the sententious sayings, the ornamentations, propriety, and exquisite beauty of the language").[35]

These are the materials that the characters in *La Dorotea*, who belong to an age in which culture is ceasing to be the prerogative of an intellectual, social, or creative élite, bring into their conversations in order to steep them in poetic elegance, literary sophistication, and wit. It is clear that when such a cultural style is adopted for display in an atmosphere of sophisticated sociability, there is a corresponding inattention to the scheme of values which gives it meaning. Recast as conversational currency, a cultural heritage proves more glitter than gold, intoxicating but not nourishing; it no longer has authentic guidance to offer to the judgment or the conscience. As a set of attitudes assumed or abandoned, a decorative manner and idiom, its function is essentially esthetic; ethical relevance is secondary and learning hardly serves to foster a wisdom that relates the individual to a larger order. Indeed its effect is more likely to be distorting, inasmuch as culture, conceived as a matter of form, may become too conscious and superficial a patterning of conduct on literary models, of attitude on artistic precedents.

We find Lope's personal preoccupation with *Erlebnis* and *Dichtung* reinforced in *La Dorotea* by the concern of the age of the Counter Reformation with the effects of art on life; it is a concern which engages the attention of moralists as well as of creative writers, all preoccupied in one way or another with the response of readers, listeners, or spectators to artistic stimuli. An age which questions the autonomy of art and the self-sufficiency of humanism, which enlists techniques of realism, *admiratio* (wonderment), and drama to bridge the distance between the artistic microcosm and the world inhabited by an audience so that art may contribute to the living of Christian lives, also exposes itself to an impact of art and culture which is not edifying or exemplary but histrionic and unsettling. Like Cervantes Lope approaches this problem through characters who go to extremes in taking artistically based patterns as a way of life. And like Cervantes but more obviously, since his own culture is less profound, Lope shows himself to be of two minds.

Not surprisingly, we shall only occasionally find Lope pointing the *chrias, exempla, sententiae,* and citations of precedents and authorities that abound in the characters' talk in a consistent direction which implies a moral judgment.[36] When this does occur we do well to listen, since it is his own voice behind those of the characters which is offering the moral perspective (cf. below, p. 612). Usually the erudite material simply constitutes what Lope calls "ornamento" ("ornamentation"). Of course the sense of limitations which arises from the highlighting of its esthetic role in the characters' lives does imply an evaluation which is in some sense moral. Yet, as I have pointed out, Lope is not so much concerned to pass judgment as simply to examine, in the transparency of an artistic cosmos created ad hoc, the interacting spheres of his own life as lover and creator. He is far from abjuring secular culture, however much he may be dramatizing and over-dramatizing its misappropriation.

If the handling of erudite or ornamental materials by the characters only rarely results in a moral perspective, there are occasional instances when Lope makes it psychologically revealing. We have already seen such an instance in Fernando's highlighting of self-love in his citation of Ficino. We shall find a similarly telling resort to the example of Hercules and Antaeus by Dorotea. Like their creator (see below, p. 527), Lope's characters tend to seek out classical instances in self-justification, in order to reinforce prior stands or emotionally held convictions, rather than in a disinterested search for moral guidance.[37]

Decorative Aspects of Style

Though a sharp line cannot be drawn between the decorative and the distorting effects of style as it impinges on living, the more purely decorative aspects—both the simple and the complex—and the standards they presuppose will concern us first: to begin with, the prizing of such qualities as intellectual exclusiveness, curiosity, memory, subtlety of understanding, *gracia* (charm), wit, and of words themselves. We shall note characteristic conversations in which these values are collaboratively manifested, finding in them tendencies common to all the speakers and to their age and in addition noting individual shadings in the manner of handling the common idiom, of relating to literary culture and reacting to literary values.

Underlying the cultivation of style as form is the tendency of all the characters to self-dramatization and display. In the case of Fernando and Dorotea it has already been seen that an entire relationship centers on the roles in which they cast each other and their ultimate inability to sustain them. At key junctures in the lives of the central pair of protagonists, in their dealings not only with each other but with Marfisa and Don Bela, all four of them deliberately call upon their powers of poetic and pictorial imagination, their command of rhetoric, their histrionic capacity, in order to live such moments in what might be called a grand style. In discussing this phenomenon below I shall pause particularly over certain scenes in which some or all of these artistic resources are brought into play, not excluding the comical effect of the rhetorical manner adopted even by Gerarda and Teodora.

As has been suggested, the dominant lesson of Gracián Dantisco's manual of etiquette is that in cultivating the unusual and different one is giving offense by spurning conventions adhered to by others. Fernando, his associates, and at one remove, his mistresses, make a cult precisely of standing apart from such conventions and pride themselves on a cultural distinction based on an assumed superiority in learning and poetic ability. Fernando and Julio are described as "perpetual students" by their friend César, although the University of Alcalá is five years behind them. Dorotea remarks that her lover's only vice is books, books in many languages. Fernando has pursued no activity besides literature in Madrid. He and Julio are the pace-setters in witty and learned conversation. Dorotea and Marfisa attempt to conform to their urbane standards, which alternately attract and repel the other characters. Their circle cannot be penetrated by mere wealth: Don Bela will always remain an outsider. Yet if Don Bela has studied only "lo que basta para ser bachiller, que es el peor linage de cortesanos para tratado" ("enough to show off what he knows like a bachelor of letters, which is the worst breed of courtiers to deal with") (p. 176), Fernando, for all his learning, has in truth hardly advanced much further. His manner perfectly exemplifies the showy and superfluous display summed up in the term "bachillería," originally associated with those who had reached the first stage in the study of humane letters. Suárez de Figueroa, though excessively censorious, accurately reflects the intellectual climate in which it had acquired a derogatory sense, recalling, in his *Plaça universal de todas artes, y ciencias*

> la sentencia de San Bernardo: Ay algunos (dize) que quieren saber, por saber, y es curiosidad; y otros que quieren saber, porque sepan que saben, y es vanidad; otros que quieren saber, por ganar, y es codicia; otros que quieren saber, por edificar, y es caridad.

> the dictum of St. Bernard: There are some (he says) who wish to know for the sake of knowing and that is curiosity; and others who wish to know so that people will know they know and that is vanity; others who wish to know in order to profit and that is covetousness; others who wish to know in order to edify and that is charity.

He proceeds to inveigh against the pretentious "ostentación . . . con que [los estudiantes] campean en público . . . recogiendo en sí toda la ciencia de Platón, y los documentos de todos los otros Filósofos" ("ostentation . . . with which [students] parade about in public . . . monopolizing all the learning of Plato and the teachings of all the other philosophers").[38]

It occurs to no one in *La Dorotea* to "know in order to profit." For Lope's characters learning is a matter of curiosity and, certainly, of vanity. Suárez de Figueroa's preoccupation with learning in order to edify, consistent with the moral climate of the Counter Reformation, gets scant attention in *La Dorotea* and only lip-service from Lope in his Introduction. The term *curiosidad*, however, denotes a faculty highly valued by the interlocutors of the *acción en prosa*. With them it carries the same implication of idleness as with Suárez de Figueroa, but the pejorative overtone is gone.[39] Such curiosity is a product of lives content to be inquisitive in an undirected way, to limit a spirit of inquiry to ferreting out the surprising, the unusual, and the strange. "Curiosidad" for them connotes both the inquiry and the findings. "No ay cosa de que no quieras saber algo y de todo no sabes nada" ("There's nothing you don't want to know something about, and about everything you know nothing"), Fernando tells Julio in a moment of impatience (p. 85). But Fernando begins his story of falling out of love with Dorotea by telling his friend César: "Por vuestra curiosidad y estudio en todas materias, veréis los admirables efetos de las condiciones de nuestra naturaleza" ("For your inquiry into and study of every subject, you will see the remarkable effects of the conditions of our nature") (p. 404). "Oíd vna curiosidad de Suetonio Tranquilo" ("Listen to this curiosity from Suetonius Tranquillus"), begins César (p. 348), adding in all seriousness an anecdote about Nero *qua* poet to a conversation on any poet's need for constant revision. Julio prefaces a *curiosidad* with the equivalent of a footnote: "Vna cosa hallé leyendo el libro tercero de Xenofonte, que me causó admiración, no lexos de este propósito" ("In reading the third book of Xenophon I discovered something not unrelated to this subject which amazed me") (p. 250). *Admiración*—amazement, wonder—is a natural concomitant of *curiosidad* and it takes precedence over appropriateness.[40]

The effect is pedantic in these instances. There is no ingenuity of presentation; the curiousness of the subject matter suffices and the characters do not trouble to be enigmatic or witty. Commonly, however, conversational dexterity is a way of driving home the curiosity:

> *Iul.:* Holgárame que huuieras leído, en el libro primero de los
> *Retóricos*, la causa por que los amantes, en medio de sus tristezas,
> están alegres.
> *Fer.:* ¿A qué propósito?
> *Iul.:* Dize que como los enfermos se alegran en la furia de la
> calentura pensando en que han de beber, assí los que aman,
> quando están ausentes, quando escriuen y quando desean, se
> alegran imaginando en el efeto del bien que esperan.
> *Fer.:* Ya te entiendo, Iulio: quieres dezir que espero ver a Dorotea.
> Pues, ¿cómo se ajusta esse pensamiento al mío si la quiero porque
> es hermosa, y no la veo porque la aborrezco?
>
> (p. 216)

> *Jul.:* I would be glad if you had read, in the first book of the
> *Rhetoric*, the reason why lovers, in the midst of their sadness, are
> cheerful. *Fer.:* Apropos of what? *Jul.:* He says that, as sick people
> cheer up in the height of a fever with the thought that they are
> going to drink, so those in love, when they are away, when they
> write, and when they desire, cheer up by setting their minds on the
> effects of the happiness they hope for. *Fer.:* Now I understand you,
> Julio; you mean that I am hoping to see Dorotea. Well, how does
> that thought square with mine if I love her because she is beautiful
> and don't see her because I hate her?

Julio's tactic is to perplex Fernando and provoke him into asking for the Aristotelian explanation of the paradox. But Fernando simply takes the explanation for granted and challenges Julio on the score of its relevance to himself. Julio, however, cannot forego relaying a *curiosidad* appreciable both in itself and because it constitutes an implicit rejoinder to Fernando. The latter quickly sees Julio's meaning and refutes it. The obliqueness and sophistication of the verbal sparring set off the fact that in this instance the *curiosidad* in fact applies significantly to Fernando's case.

Sometimes the superfluousness of a *curiosidad* makes its effect purely humorous:

> *Lud.:* ¿Luego no pensáis verla?
> *Fer.:* Esse día sea el vltimo de mi vida.
> *Lud.:* En su *Combite de amor* dixo Platón que solamente se reían los
>   dioses de los amantes perjuros.
> *Iul.:* Alguna vez se rieron de la música de Palas, por la fealdad con
>   que tañía.
>
> (p. 253)

> *Lud.:* You're not intending to see her then?   *Fer.:* May that day be
> the last one of my life.   *Lud.:* In his *Symposium on Love* Plato said
> that the gods laughed only at lovers who break their vows.   *Jul.:*
> On one occasion they laughed at Pallas's music because she looked
> so ugly as she played.

Ludovico is countering Fernando with an Ovidian curiosity (which Lope erroneously attributes to Plato). The grotesque humor of Julio's rectification is compounded by its gratuitousness. Lope here seems to be smiling at his own weakness for stray associations and strange bits of information.

The technique of the *curiosidad* clearly requires a good memory. Traditionally important in rhetorical training, memory had assumed so large a role in all disciplines by Lope's day that Bartolomé Ximénez Patón omits it from his *Eloquencia española en arte* (1604) on the ground that it is not peculiar to rhetoric at all.[41] While Lope echoes Cicero's characterization of memory as a "famosa joya adquirida y aumentada con la cultura" ("famous jewel acquired and enlarged by culture"), he could also see that memory was no guarantee of real learning:

> La memoria es tesoro y excelente,
> pero es, si no hay doctrina, hipocresía;
> parece ciencia, y es bachillería;
> que no hay ciencia en el mundo de repente.[42]

> Memory is a treasure and an excellent one, but without learning it is hypocrisy. It seems a form of knowledge and it's merely a parading of it, for there's no overnight learning in all the world.

With his penchant for acknowledging but not renouncing personal foibles, Lope here exposes the shallowness of much of the learning to which he, like the characters he depicts in the *acción en prosa*, felt attracted.

I have earlier alluded to Lope's experience of the uncertain operation of memory in the sphere of his own *Erlebnis*. For the more professional task of acquiring a repertory of stylistic, literary, and "scientific" materials to be drawn on for artistic elaboration, his memory seems to have served him very well, even if his hastiness sometimes precluded total accuracy. In the private correspondence with the Duke of Sessa, classical tags and allusions flow easily from his pen, in most cases evidently without consultation of the compendiums and commonplace books to which he was on occasion addicted. He does not seem to have followed the practice of writers like Marino and Herrera, who recorded in personal notebooks striking passages to be adapted at leisure, though by underlining and marginal annotations he apparently fixed in his mind what particularly struck him.[43] He makes his characters in *La Dorotea* do more than this, however. *Mutatis mutandis*, Dorotea approaches conversation as Herrera did poetic composition. The latter, according to Francisco de Rioja, customarily jotted down in notebooks "las palabras i modos de dezir, que tenían o novedad o grandeza ... para que le sirviessen cuando escrivía" ("the words and expressions which were either novel or grandiose ... so he might make use of them when he wrote").[44] Dorotea, "en oyendo vn vocablo esquisito, le escriue en vn librillo de memoria, y que venga o no venga, le encaxa en quanto habla" ("upon hearing a fancy word, writes it down in a little memorandum book and, willy-nilly, drags it into everything she says") (p. 133). Fernando and Julio also have their "little memorandum books," keep their compositions in them, and as has been noted, give evidence of trained powers of memorization.

The necessary concomitant of memory, understanding—*entendimiento*—is the truly decisive faculty for Lope's characters and the quality Fernando and Dorotea most prize in each other: "¿Qué riqueza como la de su entendimiento, persona y gracias?" ("What wealth like that of his mind, person, and charms?"), Dorotea retorts (p. 77) to her mother's disparagement of her indigent lover, while Fernando caps a catalogue of illustrious women of antiquity by finding Dorotea "superior to all of them" in *entendimiento* (p. 96).

The prizing of *entendimiento* in *La Dorotea* is consistent with the importance Lope regularly gives this quality of mind and spirit.[45] It is the basis of love in its more lasting and elevated forms, and it differentiates the crudeness of the lowborn from the refined sensibility of the noble and cultivated. The awareness it brings adds a higher element to physical attraction and gives love a basis in reason—"que entre los que le tienen [entendimiento] y aquellos a quien falta ay esta diferencia, que los vnos quieren por razón, y los otros por costumbre" ("for between those who have it and those in whom it is lacking there is this difference: that the first love with the reason and the second out of habit") (p. 312)—and thus, implicitly, in Neo-Platonic idealism. Along with these aspects, emphasis is placed in *La Dorotea* on the social manifestations of *entendimiento:* cultural distinction and intellectual superiority over the uninitiated. *Entendimiento* is both refinement of knowledge and a worldly wisdom incompatible with the simple wisdom of "Sólo sé que no sé nada" ("All I know is that I know nothing"), which Lope, unlike his characters, has come to value. It is both the capacity to understand and the ability to display that capacity, both intellect and ready learning. When Dorotea says, "Amor no es margarita para bestias. Quiere entendimientos sutiles" ("Love is no daisy for cattle. It requires subtle minds") (p. 144), she refers to both refinement of sensibility and intellectual sophistication. Opportunistically Gerarda prizes such *entendimientos.* "¡O entendimiento, dulce parte del alma!" ("Oh understanding, lovely part of the mind!") (p. 132), she exclaims with simulated rapture as she listens to Don Bela, whose *entendimiento* she extols to Dorotea both in advance of their meeting—"Los entendimientos son como los instrumentos, que es menester tocarlos para saber qué consonancias tienen" ("Minds are like instruments which have to be played on to find out what harmonies they are capable of") (p. 168)—and during its progress—"¡Mira qué sabiduría con aquel talle! Entendimiento tiene que podía ser feo" ("Look at the wisdom that goes with that figure of his! With a mind like that he could have been ugly") (p. 187).

While Lope mocks the hypertrophied intellectual snobbery of his characters, he is also acknowledging a personal weakness. One recalls the disorderly and superficial displays of learning that adorn so many of his works. But it is equally true that a strong need to believe in his own superiority in *entendimiento* comes through beneath all the exaggeration of *La Dorotea* and that the attitudes of the protagonists are rooted in the lives of Lope and Elena Osorio. Late in life when he writes his "Elogio en la muerte de Juan Blas de Castro" ("Eulogy on the Death of Juan Blas de Castro"),[46] it is still apparently Elena Osorio whom he is looking back to as "aquel entendimiento, ídolo necio de mis verdes años" ("that mind, the silly idol of my young days"). We have seen her weakness for finding herself idolized in sonnets and songs documented in the satires. It is in relation to the contest between poetry and wealth that we will find the full significance of the stress on *entendimiento* emerging.

It is already evident that the efficacy of the qualifications to which I have been alluding under the headings of curiosity, memory, and understanding hinges on techniques for activating them in social intercourse. Both rhetorical and disputational techniques are employed to this end without noticeable regard for the usual standards of aptness and propriety. There are also more particularized skills, aspects in one way or another of wit (*ingenio*): skills of *gracia*, *aplicación*, *agudeza*, all of which center on avoidance of the obvious, capturing of attention through the unexpected twist or rejoinder, or eliciting of admiration for one's ingenuity and of *admiratio* through one's ability to surprise and startle. The last capacity sometimes involves an inversion of the usual *recherché* procedures—that is, a sudden simplicity calculated to shock precisely because it is unexpected. One also notes some inclination toward pure preciosity, affectation, and verbal gymnastics, manifest in diffuse rather than pointed effects and dependent primarily on a disparity between diction and content. In addition one finds not only the already mentioned prizing of "vocablos esquisitos" but a heightened sensitivity on the part of all the characters to words in and of themselves. We shall now note in turn manifestations of these different stylistic phenomena.

Rhetoric

The domains of poetry and rhetoric—particularly epideictic or ceremonial rhetoric—were by Lope's day thought of as practically coterminous. That Lope so saw them is clear from an extended catalogue of rhetorical figures appropriate to poetry which he brings into a discussion of the *culterano* style in his reply to a "Papel . . . en razón de la nueva poesía." He observes that "de todas hay tan comunes exemplos" ("there are such common examples of all of them"), but nevertheless advises restraint: use them "raras veces y según la calidad de la materia y del estilo" ("only rarely and in keeping with the quality of the matter and style").[47]

The fact that Lope has chosen a prose medium for the *poiesis* of *La Dorotea* means that rhetorical elements have, so to speak, double entry in its dialogue. Not surprisingly, they are particularly in evidence in those situations for which rhetoric had been traditionally employed: persuasion, praise and blame, ceremony, celebration. The peculiar character of the underlying experience, with its juridical culmination, causes the arts of persuasion and praising practiced by the go-between of literary tradition to proliferate in all directions in the *acción en prosa*. We find them deployed not only very extensively by Gerarda but by others as well. While Celestina needs to sway only Melibea and can count on Satanic assistance, Gerarda, for whom sorcery is only an inconsequential curiosity, must win over Teodora as well as her daughter, must belittle Fernando as well as extol Don Bela; a choice and change of lovers is involved, not merely the forwarding of a single suit. Teodora in her turn will laud Gerarda, denigrate Fernando, excoriate her own daughter. Dorotea twice pleads her own cause to Fernando, vituperating her mother in the process. Fernando upholds his case to Dorotea; even Marfisa denounces Dorotea in absentia and Fernando to his face. Viewed in this light, *La Dorotea* seems one continuous apportioning of guilt and innocence, one long airing of charges and countercharges, as if reimmersion in the past had put the juridical stamp of long ago on the material all over again. One notes, however, that Gerarda never seriously has to exert her suasory talents in the other direction in which Celestina is obliged to operate, that is, upon the servants (see below, p. 620). While epideictic rhetoric, the branch of rhetoric most adaptable to literary expression and most assimilated by it, is naturally the form most in evidence in *La Dorotea*, one finds procedures of the suasory or deliberative branch employed and even notes overtones of the forensic.[48]

I will later have occasion to point out characteristic individual sallies and flights of rhetoric, particularly in the case of Dorotea; here I can best exemplify what is most characteristic, the transferring of rhetorical procedures to unconventional contexts, by analyzing the rhetorical aspects of the scene between Gerarda and Teodora with which the work opens. For her unedifying, domestic purpose of persuading Teodora to dismiss Fernando and admit Don Bela as Dorotea's lover, Gerarda deploys, at a middle level of style, formal rhetorical techniques, both suasory and epideictic. More than once Lope draws attention, through Teodora, to the disparity between means and ends: "¿Y para esso, Gerarda, veníades tan armada de sentencias y tan preuenida de aduertimientos?" ("And was this the reason you came so well armed with dictums and so well supplied with advice?") (p. 66); "Si traíades, Gerarda, essa correduría, ¿para qué era menester tanta retórica?" ("If that was your commission, Gerarda, why was so much rhetoric needed?") (p. 73). But Teodora uses similar means herself in her defense and counterattack. The comical impropriety of the rhetorical structures is increased by the fact that they float on the surface of the ordinary conversation, whose movement I have already traced. The levels of formalism and colloquiality are often distinct but by no means always; Lope sometimes suggests overlappings between artistic and natural utterance, like that already noted in the "diréis" ("you'll say's") of the two speakers. Gerarda's several series of questions also sometimes seem properly rhetorical, sometimes have a spontaneous ring.

From the rhetorical standpoint the scene, as a whole, may be described as follows. Gerarda opens with a brief formal exordium: "El amor y la obligación no sólo me mandan, pero porfiadamente me fuerçan, amiga Teodora, a que os diga mi sentimiento" ("Love and duty not only order me but insistently force me, friend Teodora, to tell you my feelings") (p. 63). She observes sententiously before the conversation has proceeded very far: "Desconfío de persuadiros a lo que vengo . . . que ningún juez sentencia animosamente si es culpado en el mismo delito" ("I despair of winning you over to what I've come about . . . for no judge willingly passes sentence if he is guilty of the same crime") (p. 64). She has in effect placed Teodora in the position of judge; her aim is to produce Quintilian's "iudicem benevolum, attentum, docilem" ("well-disposed, attentive, and open-minded judge").[49] For a while both speakers build on concepts put forward by Gerarda—love, duty—sparring back and forth. Gerarda expands love into friendship for Teodora and love of Dorotea (l. 9); Teodora ironically challenges the latter (l. 10). Gerarda shifts to parental love as an obstacle to parental duty (l. 12). Teodora defends parental love (ll. 15–16) and the conversation slips into the subject of upbringing. With Teodora's objection to Gerarda's passing phrase "quando vos érades moça" ("when you were a girl") (p. 64), the two become sidetracked into the long exchange on aging alluded to earlier and the issue of upbringing appears forgotten until Gerarda marks off the bypath for the digression it is and turns back to the original subject. Teodora ripostes and a series of *quid pro quo*'s follows, in the course of which disputation and rhetoric give way to bickering colloquiality. But Gerarda is ready at last to come to the point. Rising to the occasion, she delivers herself of a lengthy discourse in which the devices of epideictic rhetoric and the tone of popular speech achieve a remarkable blend. With two brief sentences of recapitulation she subsides and leaves: "Con esto me voy a rezar a la Merced; que en verdad que no me iré a casa sin encomendar a Dios vuestros negocios" ("I'm going now to Merced Church to say a prayer, for I certainly wouldn't go home without putting your affairs in God's hands") (p. 74). Six scenes later it becomes plain that she has gone there to meet Don Bela.

Both speakers show vigilant verbal and rhetorical awareness: "Más cincos auéis dado que vn juego de bolos" ("You've thrown more fives than a game of nine-pins"), Teodora quips, acknowledging a use of epiphora by Gerarda even as she mocks it. Gerarda characterizes Teodora's strong verbal barrage as a punishment (p. 66), deliberately using the word already employed in relation to Dorotea (p. 63) as a means of returning to the subject of Teodora's daughter: "Si assí riñérades a Dorotea..." ("Now if you scolded Dorotea that way..."). An examination of Gerarda's speech shows it to be studded with rhetorical devices, simple and compound:

1. Amplification: "El amor y la obligación no sólo me mandan pero porfiadamente me fuerçan" ("Love and duty not only order me but insistently force me, friend Teodora") (p. 63).

2. Isocolon and antithesis: "acercarse a morir y començar a viuir" ("to be approaching death and starting in to live") (p. 64); "o por el grande amor que los tienen, o por el poco cuidado con que los crían" ("either because of the great love they bear them or because of the lack of care with which they bring them up") (p. 63).

3. Isocolon, amplification, interrogation, anaphora: "¿Qué oficio adquirimos en la república? ¿Qué gouierno en la paz? ¿Qué bastón en la guerra?" ("What position do we acquire in the state? What governorship in peace? What command in war?") (p. 72).

4. Isocolon, anadiplosis, interrogation, and epiphora: "¿O es [la hermosura] vna primauera alegre de quinze a veinte y cinco, vn verano agradable de veinte y cinco a treinta y cinco, vn estío seco de treinta y cinco hasta quarenta y cinco?" ("Or is [beauty] a gay springtime from fifteen to twenty-five, a pleasant summer from twenty-five to thirty-five, a dry season from thirty-five to forty-five?") (p. 71).

5. Periphrasis:

> *Teo.:* ¿Tanta edad os parece que tengo?
> *Ger.:* En buena fe, que es punto el de vuestros años, que qualquiera jugador le quisiera más que la mejor primera.
>
> (p. 64)
>
> *Teo.:* Do I seem that old to you? *Ger.:* In all honesty, the score of your years is such that any gambler would prefer it to the best hand.

(This last combination of lowly content and ornate form spells affectation.)

Gerarda's climactic discourse begins with a prolonged simile, then moves on:

> Los padres, Teodora, somos como las aues; en sabiendo bolar el pájaro, ayúdele el aire y válgale el pico: pero Dorotea que no está

fuera de vuestras alas, y que cada día buelue a reconocer el nido, y que ha cinco años que este moço la tiene perdida, sin alma, sin remedio y tan pobre, por no darle disgusto, o por miedo que le ha cobrado, que ayer vendió vn manteo a vna amiga suya, y dize, que por deuoción y promessa trae vn ábito de picote, la que solía arrastrar Milanes y Nápoles en pasamanos y telas.   (fol. 4r)

We parents, Teodora, are like birds: once the young bird is able to fly, it's for the air to help him out and his beak to take care of him. But Dorotea, who hasn't yet left your wings, who comes back every day to reconnoiter the nest and who it's been five years this boy has kept her sunk on him, soulless, helpless, and so poor, so as not to put him out or because she's come to fear him, that yesterday she sold a cloak to a friend of hers and she says that out of piety and to keep a vow she is wearing a goathair habit, she who used to trail Milans and Naples after her in gilt lace trimmings and in fabrics.

The anacoluthon corresponds to a temporary abandonment of rhetoric and a descent to the level of ordinary speech. Gerarda becomes genuinely aroused at the thought of Dorotea's wasted opportunities and merely appends thought to thought paratactically as they occur to her: "Pero Dorotea, que ... y que ... y que ... y dice que ..." The opening of the next sentence does, however, patch up the anacoluthon: "¿Para qué será bueno que ande de recoleta por vn lindo, que todo su caudal son sus calcillas de obra, y sus cueras de ámbar, esto de día, y de noche..." ("What good is it for her to go around like a nun under strict rule, all for a dandy whose entire worldly goods are his needlepoint breeches and his amber-scented leather waistcoats—this in the daytime; and at night") (fol. 4r). The final offhand linking phrase is at the same time a neatly turned rhetorical *transitio*.[50] Proceeding sarcastically ("... y ella muy desvanecida" ["... and she all stuck up"]—the solecism of the omitted verb is a colloquial trait), Gerarda invokes Petrarch and Laura, Diego Hurtado de Mendoza and "la celebrada Filis" ("the celebrated Filis") to ridicule Dorotea and Fernando (pp. 70, 71). The cultivated *exempla* signal a recrudescence of rhetoric. The repeated vocative "¡Ay Teodora, Teodora!" (p. 71) is not merely colloquial but an iteration that sets a pathetic tone for the rhetorical questions that follow. Teodora breaks in with a quip, but Gerarda, in full tilt, brushes it aside and leads up to her proposition through the isocolon already noted ("¿Qué oficio...?" ["What position...?"]) and an insistent iteration ("Bolued, bolued en vos" ["Come back, come back to your senses"]) (p. 72). Having at last reached the heart of the matter—"yo he sabido que vn cauallero indiano ..."

("I have learned that an *indiano* gentleman . . .")—Gerarda drops once more into colloquialisms and popular speech patterns: parataxis (*y* and *que* as connectives), capricious associations ("y yo vi el otro día un rétulo" ["and the other day I saw a sign"] [p. 73]), and a telegraphic descriptive manner distinct from rhetorical asyndeton ("Tiene linda presencia, alegre de ojos" ["He has a handsome demeanor, bright look in the eyes"] [p. 73]). The one noticeable departure from colloquialism, a sudden touch of poetic ornamentation in the simile "dientes blancos, que luzen con el vigote negro como sarta de perlas en terciopelo liso" ("white teeth, which glow beside his black moustache, like a string of pearls against smooth velvet"), is not unmotivated: the pearls and velvet recall the silverware and tapestries, substantial and not metaphorical, which Gerarda has just mentioned to Teodora as gifts to be expected from Don Bela. The poetic simile serves a practical rhetorical end. The overornateness of Gerarda's speech is as clearly a cover for her matchmaking activity as is her cloak of sanctimoniousness.

Lope makes Teodora noticeably less adept rhetorically than Gerarda. Her inexpertise shows up especially when she attempts to make the point that hiding one's age is useless. She first establishes a general premise, with the proposition: "La tema deste mundo más general es quitarse años a sí y ponerlos a los otros" ("The most common obsession of this world is to take years away from one's own age and add them to other people's"). But she clearly becomes entangled in the expression of the consequence: "y es necedad inútil, porque lo mismo piensa a vn tiempo el que se los pone al otro, y cada vno se los quita" ("and it's useless nonsense, because the person adding them to someone else's thinks the same thing at the same time and everyone takes them away from his own") (p. 64). She confuses another thought in attempting to phrase it in the inverted symmetry of a rhetorical *inclusio:* "¿Puédese negar a la naturaleza el amor de la sangre, ni el de la criança a sus gracias . . .?" ("Can one deny to nature love of its own blood, or that of upbringing to its cuteness . . .?") (p. 63).[51]

Disputation

The alliance of rhetoric and dialectic was felt as particularly close in Lope's day; that the combination of the two sometimes gives the dialogue of *La Dorotea* a disputational cast has already become plain. Dialectic in this case means, in effect, techniques of argumentation; it is not a method of philosophical inquiry. Dialectic and rhetoric together are like "un cuchillo de hierro, y azero" ("a knife made of iron and steel"), writes Ximénez Patón:

El azero se sustenta admirablemente sobre el hierro, y corta, y no
falta: assí también la Dialéctica sobre la Rhetórica corta
admirablemente, y no falta . . . La Eloqüencia sin ayuda de la
Dialéctica no será efficaz.[52]

The steel is admirably supported by the iron and cuts and does not
fail: so also dialectic [supported] by rhetoric cuts admirably and does
not fail. Eloquence without help from dialectic will not be efficacious.

Advising teachers on the training of their students, Suárez de Figueroa
observes in his *Plaça universal:*

Sobretodo sería menester argumentassen amenudo con los otros,
porque la disputa (según Leonardo Aretino) es quien sutiliza el
entendimiento, haziéndole llegar donde el estudio, y la letura no
alcançan.   (fol. 320r)

Above all they will need to debate frequently with their fellows,
because disputation (according to Leonardo Aretino) is what refines
the understanding, taking it further than study and reading can.

The "entendimientos sutiles" ("refined understandings") prized by
Fernando, his associates, and his mistresses bear the earmarks of this sort of
training; they have retained their fondness for keeping their wits whetted
through oral controversy. Sometimes disputation is merely a pastime,
sometimes it is purposeful. In both cases it runs to extremes and clearly
reflects a trend of the times condemned by moralists like Juan de Horozco y
Covarrubias in his *Emblemas morales* in the image of the camel who muddies
the clear water where he drinks:

que ay algunos que prueuan la paciencia
buscando sin propósito questiones.
Sólo el contradezir tienen por sciencia,
y contra la razón buscan razones.

for there are some who try the patience by pointlessly raising
objections. They consider contradiction the only learning and they
hunt up reasons against reason.

Covarrubias notes in his discussion of the emblem "how great a discourtesy
it is for someone who prides himself on his learning, when he finds himself
in the company of serious persons, to try to push everything that is said too
far merely to show off, and to turn a quiet conversation or a gathering that
has other purposes into a formal disputation."[53]

Lope's own educational experience, which included early training by the Jesuits in Madrid as well as studies at Alcalá, undoubtedly exposed him to both the appeal and the abuse of these habits of verbal contention.[54]

An important part of the training of students in schools as in universities was in the holding of public contests in debating, declamation, and controversy, an outgrowth of the *controversiae figuratae* in which students were trained to uphold first one side, then its opposite. Horozco's strictures on the impropriety of introducing disputation into conversations raise the same issue as does *La Dorotea* regarding the place and function of learned practices in the full context of living. Scholarly controversy practiced as a cultural veneer does not escape Lope's scrutiny as he reflects in his maturity on the place of art in a world of experience.[55]

The proclivity for disputation noticeable in the interlocutors of *La Dorotea* goes well beyond the tendency toward a polarization of perspective observable in the *comedia*. Opposition is here expected and desired. Though the distraught Dorotea complains when Celia goes too far, "Déxame, Celia, vete a tu labor; que más me quiero estar sola, que con quien me pone en las heridas cáusticos para matarme" ("Leave me alone, Celia, go and do your sewing. I'd rather be alone than with someone who puts caustic on my wounds to kill me") (p. 147), she also complains when Celia fails to stand up to her at all: "You servant-girls are extraordinary. You go along with everything and have your flattery ready for anything" (p. 445).

An extreme case of the tendency to set up verbal but not substantial oppositions occurs in the scenes between Gerarda and Teodora. More in a spirit of opposition than through motherly instinct we have seen Teodora put up a defensive front when Gerarda in the opening scene brings up the subject of Dorotea. No sooner has Gerarda departed than Teodora shifts from defense to prosecution and turns on her daughter, using not merely Gerarda's arguments but her very words: "¿Puedes tú negar cosa alguna de quanto ha dicho, ni poner falta en vna muger honrada, que sólo pretende el seruicio de Dios y nuestra honra?" ("Can you deny a single one of the things she said or find fault with an honorable woman whose only thought is to serve God and our honor?") (p. 74). (Gerarda had claimed: "A lo que venía me mouieron dos cosas: el seruicio de Dios y vuestra honra"— "I was motivated in this matter that brought me by two things: serving God and your honor" [p. 67]). Teodora thereby assumes the burden of the charges—particularly that of hypocrisy—which she had leveled at Gerarda. But Lope is not merely exposing here, as the Prologue piously claims, "la hipocresía de vna madre interessable" ("the hypocrisy of a venal mother"), and face-saving is not a sufficient motive for Teodora's behavior. Teodora's about-face seems a positive parody of the scholastic tendency to assume first one position, then its opposite, in controversy. By extending it into such unlikely quarters Lope compounds its absurdity.[56]

Some air of disputation hangs about subsequent conversations between Gerarda and Teodora (I, 7; IV, 5 and 6), with their elaborate screens of formality that contribute to a total pattern of comically gratuitous play. As I have noted, the merits of their respective daughters become a bone of contention over which they argue interminably and with comic solemnity in the equivalent of a *controversia figurata*. When by tacit agreement they are ready to call a halt, Gerarda delivers by way of peroration a fulsome pane-gyric of her daughter's modesty and piety and elicits from Teodora the final technical comment of a dialectician or a rhetorician: "Lo más fácil es negar, y lo más difícil defender. Tomado me auéis lo fácil y dexádome lo difícil" ("The easiest thing is to deny, and the hardest to defend. You have taken the easy part and left me with the difficult") (p. 375).

Of all the characters, it is Julio, the "graduate in philosophy" and "perpetual student," who is most versed in techniques of controversy; he falls back on them as a way of diverting his master. Although books, fencing, chess, and even the reading of verse fail to draw Fernando from obsession with his passion, Julio manages to elicit a lively response when he challenges him with a debating proposition: "Either you love Dorotea or you don't love her. If you love her, think well of what you love; if you don't love her, don't think so much about what you don't love" (p. 215). Fernando is sufficiently intrigued to be drawn into an exchange out of which there emerges a humorous syllogism based on the application of an Aristotelian locus. The desire of each adversary to score against his opponent vies with a tendency to collaborative exercise of ingenuity; serious inquiry into Fernando's state is left behind, other Aristotelian loci being invoked with more ingeniousness than relevance and erudition being made subservient to wit.

Sometimes Julio deliberately provokes Fernando with casuistry and pedantic argumentation:

> *Fer.:* ... Si hasta los desmayos del ánimo es aforismo físico en casos
> que lo piden [una sangría], ¿cuál se puede ofrecer como éste?
> *Iul.:* No me agrada el argumento; porque si amor es lo mismo que
> la sangre, ningún semejante puede expugnar su semejante, que
> es impossible, como el calor al calor y el frío al frío.
> *Fer.:* Bestia, esso es por sí, pero no por accidente. ¡Qué gentil
> filósofo, sabiendo que por el mío ya son contrarios!
>
> (p. 103)

Fer.: If it is a physical aphorism that loss of consciousness in certain cases requires [blood-letting], what case could be more to the point than mine? *Jul.:* The argument doesn't impress me. Because if my love is the same as blood, no similar can expel its similar: that's impossible, like heat expelling heat and cold cold. *Fer.:* Idiot, that is in and of itself but not by accident. What a delightful philosopher, when he knows that through my accident they are now contraries!

When Fernando impulsively determines to see Dorotea despite all his contrary assurances to Ludovico, he cushions his impulse with capricious casuistry, juggling alternative arguments: to see Dorotea will not be to speak to her, to see her door is not to see her. Julio disputes the first point: "Si tú la ves, tú la hablarás" ("If you see her, you'll talk to her"); but the second catches his fancy and he begins to play with it:

> *Fer.:* . . . Esto no es ver a Dorotea; que Dorotea no es puerta.
> *Iul.:* Y es fácil silogismo.
> *Fer.:* ¿Cómo?
> *Iul.:* Toda puerta es de madera, toda muger es de carne; luego la
>   muger no es puerta.
> *Fer.:* Maldito seas, que en tanta tristeza me has mouido a risa.
>   ¡Qué gracioso silogismo!
>
> (p. 256)

Fer.: This isn't to see Dorotea; Dorotea isn't a door. *Jul.:* That's an easy syllogism. *Fer.:* How so? *Jul.:* Every door is wood, every woman is flesh; therefore woman is not a door. *Fer.:* The devil take you, you've made me laugh for all my sadness. What a funny syllogism!

There is no real disagreement; the disputational by-play is only a pastime but it serves to send Fernando off in a better humor.

Julio is a master of the dialectical and rhetorical *anticipatio*, which consists in "anticipating the objections that may be raised by our opponent" and stating them before he is able to.[57] "El discreto filósofo considera el sentido de la proposición para prevenir lo que ha de responder, conceder, o negar" ("The shrewd philosopher considers the meaning of the proposition in order to anticipate what he will answer, concede, or refute"), he remarks when Fernando puts a leading question: "Dime, Iulio, en la juuentud, ¿no es la sangre más sutil, clara, cálida, y dulce?" ("Tell me, Julio, in youth, is the blood not finer, clear, hotter, and sweeter?") (p. 267). He then reels off the explanation which Fernando was about to give, nearly verbatim from the same source Fernando was paraphrasing—Ficino's commentary on the *Symposium* (Oratio IV, cap. 7)—and replies to it. Fernando can only observe peevishly: "Parece que respondes antes que te pregunten" ("It seems you answer before you are questioned"). Nevertheless he ripostes with a further paraphrase from the same chapter of Ficino, which Julio in turn caps. The learned material is bent one way and another by speakers who wield it tactically for ends purely of the moment.

Julio, indeed, is particularly adept at employing erudition as a conversational tactic. It becomes a way of teasing out of his master the revelation of his dream which Fernando had at first refused. Fernando's evasiveness launches Julio on an exposition of Aristotelian dream theory which draws a protest—"Ya comienças a cansarme con tus filosofías. Déxame, Iulio" ("You are already beginning to annoy me with your philosophies. Leave me alone, Julio") (p. 81)—but no revelation. Julio renews the assault from the angle of dream interpretation, citing curiosities, with better results. As Fernando begins to yield, the pace of the dialogue quickens and the dream emerges little by little, helped along by Julio's crisp comments and questions. The dialogue loses its tug-of-war character. Julio has created for the dream a setting of precedent and authority flattering to Fernando's pride and into this the dream is fitted like some rare gem. Ironically, however, the real meaning of the dream never emerges from the welter of learning and speculation.[58]

Julio is adept, finally, at the *reflexio*, the device of taking the adversary's words in a sense contrary to that intended by him.[59]

> *Fer.:* Pues, ¡si vieras el entendimiento que tiene sobre tanta hermosura!
> *Iul.:* El entendimiento no se ve, antes bien se diferencia del sentido en que aquél es vna cierta potencia aprehensiua de las cosas esteriores . . .
> *Fer.:* Bestia escolástica, ¿agora me repites las palabras?
>
> (p. 105)

> *Fer.:* But if you could see the mind she has in addition to such great beauty! *Jul.:* The mind can't be seen; it differs from sense in that the latter is a certain power that apprehends outward things . . .
> *Fer.:* Scholastic beast, is this a time to throw my words back at me?

The mechanism is a willful confusion of the colloquial and technical levels of language. The aim is to provoke and thereby divert Fernando. The tone is perversely pedantic with overtones of wry irony:

Fer.: ¡Ay, sol mío! Sal a oírme, aunque me abrases, pues eres el
    mismo fuego.
Iul.: Los cuerpos celestes calientan, no porque son cálidos, sino en
    quanto son de veloz mouimiento y luminosos.

(p. 273)[60]

Fer.: Ah, sun of mine! Come out and hear me, though you set me
ablaze, for you are fire itself.   *Jul.:* Heavenly bodies produce heat
not because they are hot but insofar as they have rapid movement
and are luminous.

Although Julio has a weakness for showing off his learning, these quibbles
are provoked with tongue in cheek, as a diverting form of muscle-flexing.
He is too sophisticated to do more than play at being literal-minded. His
pedantry is not really as heavy as it appears and the verbal sparring that
accompanies its enunciation keeps it from actually palling.

Far less adept at disputation and controversy than Fernando and Julio is
Don Bela. He clearly lacks their training and although he tries to master the
the techniques, he comes off a poor second, as his exchanges with Laurencio
show. Because Laurencio is far less indulgent than Julio toward his master's
involvement with Dorotea, the tension between him and Don Bela is acute
and constant. They argue incessantly, and always in the same way, Laurencio
attacking and Don Bela on the defensive. Don Bela clings to his infatuation
as tenaciously as Fernando to his obsession, but unlike Julio, Laurencio seeks
less to diagnose and entertain than to warn; his is a voice of common sense
steadily rebuffed by Don Bela. Though the occasions for controversy are more
constant (in almost everything Laurencio says he takes issue with his master),
the speakers are less learned and their arguments less technical. Rather than
real repartee, we have a series of fatuous assertions by Don Bela and immediate retorts, usually witty and caustic, by Laurencio. No match for his
servant, Don Bela keeps shifting ground, so that the sliding movement of
conversation shows through their desultory arguments, which only
occasionally fall into disputational patterns. Lope shows Laurencio and Don
Bela in conversation together once in Act II, twice in Act III, and once in
Act V. The first exchange is very brief; it merely foreshadows the contention
to come. The last is in no sense an argument. It is in the second and fifth
scenes of Act III that Lope shows Don Bela and Laurencio contending, the
master smug, the servant cynical. We may here notice the first of these
scenes. In it Don Bela maintains that Dorotea's beauty justifies all his expense, Laurencio that Dorotea is merely out for his money. They argue
over whether beauty is an *oficio* (that is, a lucrative occupation) or a *digni-*

dad ("También las dignidades son oficios" ["Honorary positions are also lucrative ones"], notes Laurencio pointedly, p. 228); about *bienes de naturaleza* (natural gifts)—Dorotea's charms—and *bienes de fortuna* (gifts of fortune), Don Bela's wealth; about present pleasure and future pain and whether or not beauty is a weapon of assault. Laurencio cites *historias*, and Don Bela finally attempts formal disputation, setting up patently faulty syllogisms which Laurencio easily takes apart:

> *Bel.:* Dime, Laurencio: ¿Platón fue sabio?
> *Lau.:* Llamáronle diuino.
> *Bel.:* Pues él dixo que todo lo bueno era hermoso. Luego
> conseqüencia es que todo lo hermoso es bueno . . .
> *Lau.:* ¡Estremados conuertibles! Pero paréceme, señor, que a ti y a
> mí nos haze mucho daño esso poco que auemos estudiado.
>
> (p. 229)

> *Bel.:* Tell me, Laurencio, was Plato a wise man? *Lau.:* He was called
> divine. *Bel.:* Well, he said that everything good was beautiful. So
> it follows that everything beautiful is good . . . *Lau.:* Stupendous
> equivalents! But I think, sir, that the small amount we have studied
> does you and me a good deal of harm.

In the face of Don Bela's hopelessly bad logic, Laurencio is obliged to reflect on how dangerous a thing a little learning is, a reflection which opens a long perspective on the whole scene; then he plunges on, deviously applying his own learning to the task of calling his master a fool.[61]

Conversational Tactics

The *Aplicación*

Within the broad strategies of rhetoric and disputation, the tactical techniques to which I have referred take their place. There is first the *aplicación*, which may be called the capacity to establish connections between different orders of phenomena in an arresting fashion, though not necessarily a witty one. The term was used in Lope's day for moral or allegorical interpretation. Pérez de Moya, for example, in *Philosophía secreta*, his exposition and interpretation of ancient myth (1585), uses "aplicación" and "aplicación moral" interchangeably with terms like "declaración" ("explanation") and "moralidad" ("moral"). In *La Dorotea* the practice of the *aplicación* is, so to speak, secularized, fitted into a framework of sociability and human intercourse and oriented toward individual lives and relationships.

Because, unlike the rhetorical *aptum* or the poetic decorum, it supposes a criterion of ingenuity, not one of suitability, it implicitly raises questions of relevance.

Quite early in the work (II, 1), we find Gerarda remarking to Don Bela: "¡Qué discreción, qué gracia, qué aplicación tan linda!... No ay tesoros que la obliguen [Dorotea] como estas aplicaciones" ("How clever, how amusing, what a beautiful application!... No treasure will bind her to you as securely as these applications") (p. 132). She is referring to the verbal and conceptual display which Don Bela has devoted to the *búcaro dorado*:

> Si pone en él los rubíes de le boca, le boluerá diamante, digno de la ambrosía de los dioses. Y si quieres alegorizarle estas figuras, di que el Cupido es ella y yo el dios marino, pues vine por la mar a que me tirasse las flechas de sus ojos.

> If she applies the rubies of her mouth to it, she'll turn it into a diamond worthy of the ambrosia of the gods. And if you wish to allegorize these figures for her, say that she is the Cupid and I the sea-god, since I came over the sea to be shot at by the arrows of her eyes.

Despite Gerarda's show of enthusiasm, Don Bela's *aplicaciones* prove overly explicit and overly methodical. Their very long-windedness makes the mechanism plain, however, especially in the case of this "allegory," which has affinities with the device and the emblem: the motto ("Omnia vincit amor") and the depiction are made a symbolic representation of Don Bela's feelings for Dorotea.

Fernando's *aplicaciones* invariably sustain his obsessive egotism. Characteristic is the turn he gives to certain pedantries of natural history proffered by Julio:

> *Iul.:* Eliano y Plinio dizen que vn animal llamado perígono se engendra del fuego.
> *Fer.:* Esse soy, Iulio, que viuo y muero templando con mis lágrimas este viuo ardor que me consume.
> *Iul.:* Allá dixo el poeta Hesíodo que tenían larga vida las náyades: deue de serlo ya tu espíritu. Y la amphibia es vn animal que viue la mitad en la tierra y la mitad en el agua.
> *Fer.:* Todas essas fábulas son moralidades de mis penas.
>
> (p. 270)[62]

> *Jul.:* Aelian and Pliny say that an animal called perigon is engendered by fire. *Fer.:* That is what I am, Julio: I live and die tempering

with my tears this sharp burning that consumes me.   *Jul.:* It was the
poet Hesiod who said that naiads were long-lived: your spirit must
be one by now. And the amphibia is an animal that lives half on
land and half in the water.   *Fer.:* All those fables are moral
allegories for my sufferings.

For her part Dorotea will first expound, then lengthily "apply" for
Fernando, in self-justification, the fable of Hercules and Antaeus, which she
remarks she has read in a "libro de fábulas" ("book of fables"). We shall find
the cloth of "primauera de flores" ("flowering spring") offered Dorotea by
Don Bela occasioning an elaborate contest of applications allusive to themselves. The effect of the *aplicación* in all such instances is to narrow the
scope and significance of a fable, a pictorial or literary fiction, or a stray bit
of learning by capricious application in a particular instance which turns it
into a piece of sophistry, sacrificing the universalizing and dignifying power
of such recourse to symbols in ages and milieux of more profound cultural
aspiration.

The *Agudeza*

More rapid in thrust and timing, less pointedly personal but not fundamentally distinct in its mechanism from the *aplicación*, is the *agudeza*, the
art of which is soon to be codified by Gracián; the binding force here is
clearly *ingenio*, wit. More restricted in scope than metaphor, which plays at
reconstructing the world along new lines, the *agudeza* appeals to the intellect
rather than the imagination. Its effect is enhanced by *gracia*, of which quality,
in its verbal form, Lope's friend Ximénez Patón observes: "Para que las
cosas que se dicen, tengan gracia, se an de decir las nueuas como comunes,
las comunes como nueuas" ("In order for the things one says to possess
gracia [charm], novel things should be said like ordinary ones and ordinary
ones like novel").[63] To treat the novel as an everyday matter and the
commonplace as something out of the ordinary: the formula well catches
both the sophisticated offhandedness and the studied avoidance of the
obvious that the speakers of *La Dorotea* affect. That they are attuned to a
mode of the age is clear from a passage which the usually conservative
Gracián Dantisco, in his *Galateo español*, adds to his Italian original:

No menos que el saber dezir un mote gracioso o un dicho agudo y
breve, es el saber responder con presteza a qualquiera pregunta. Y hay
algunos tan ingeniosos, y dotados de gracia, que responden con
tanta brevedad a una pregunta, o aplican a lo que oyen un donaire

tan ingeniosamente, que parece que le estuvieron pensando mucho tiempo para sacalle a luz.[64]

No less than knowing how to utter an amusing *mot* or a pithy witticism, is knowing how to make a quick reply to any question. And there are some so clever and so endowed with wit, they answer a question so rapidly or make a witty remark on what they hear so ingeniously, that they seem to have been thinking it up for a long time before uttering it.

In the already noted sequence in which Julio pries out Fernando's dream, the servant greets with capricious witticisms the revelations that begin to emerge:

> *Fer.:* Soñaua, ¡o Iulio!, que auía llegado el mar hasta Madrid desde
>   las Indias.
> *Iul.:* Ahorrárase mucho porte desde Seuilla a Madrid. Di adelante.
> *Fer.:* Llegaua furioso hasta la puente.
> *Iul.:* ¡Pobre de Illescas!
>
> (p. 82)

Fer.: I was dreaming, oh Julio, that the sea had come all the way up to Madrid from the Indies.   *Jul.:* A lot of fare would be saved from Seville to Madrid. Go on.   *Fer.:* It came furiously up to the bridge. *Jul.:* Poor Illescas!

Julio keeps up the game when Fernando calls for his guitar:

> *Fer.:* Dame aquel instrumento . . . Saltó la prima.
> *Iul.:* Sería de la puente, aunque no ay río.
> *Fer.:* Yo la oí esta noche.
> *Iul.:* Desuelado estauas.
> *Fer.:* En Dorotea.
> *Iul.:* Yo pensé que en ir a la mar a buscarla.
>
> (p. 86)

Fer.: Give me that instrument . . . The treble string [*prima:* also, cousin] has sprung.   *Jul.:* It must have been from the bridge, though there's no river.   *Fer.:* I heard it last night.   *Jul.:* You were staying awake.   *Fer.:* Dorotea's fault.   *Jul.:* I thought it was because of going to the sea to get her.

Such interposed comments, which might have been made by a *figura del donaire* on the stage, do not create any particular tension in this case. In the final sequence of the work, however, the steady stream of witticisms by Celia apropos of the dead Gerarda and the fainting Dorotea becomes acutely jarring and draws protests from Felipa:

Cel.: ... ¡O miserable espectáculo! Gerarda es muerta. Mas
    ¿quién dixera que buscando agua?
Fel.: ¿Donaires, Celia? Pues no se lo deuías ...
Fel.: ¡Ay, dulce madre mía!
Cel.: Antes era salada ...
Teo.: ... ¡Niña, a niña!
Dor.: ¡Ay Dios, qué de desdichas!
Cel.: ¿A qué muger llamaran niña, que no boluiera del otro mundo?
(p. 456)

Cel.: Oh pitiful spectacle! Gerarda is dead. But who would have thought it would be while going for water?   *Fel.:* Wisecracks, Celia? She deserved better of you ...   *Fel.:* Alas, sweet mother of mine!   *Cel.:* She used to be salty ...   *Teo.:* ... Girl, girl!   *Dor.:* Oh God, so many calamities!   *Cel.:* What woman, if she heard herself called a girl, would not come back from the next world?

Through Celia's "wisecracks" Lope is deliberately setting an "agudo" ("clever") tone in order to avoid a pathetic one.

During a lengthy exchange at Dorotea's window, we find the dominant tone of *agudeza* explicitly noted:

Fel.: Los cuerpos muda la fuerça y violencia de la fortuna, no las
    almas.
Fer.: Es impossible que sin el alma se mude el cuerpo.
Fel.: Estáis engañado. Porque donde no va la voluntad, va el cuerpo
    solo, como quien lleua luz en vna linterna que alumbra la
    calle y escurece la persona.
Iul.: No he oído cosa tan aguda.
(p. 279)

Fel.: Bodies are swayed by the force and violence of fortune, not souls.   *Fer.:* It is impossible for the body to be swayed without the soul.   *Fel.:* You're mistaken. Because if the will doesn't come along, the body goes alone, like one carrying a light in a lantern which lights the street but darkens the person.   *Jul.:* I've never heard anything so clever.

Julio's admiration is caused not only by the ingeniousness of the comparison but by its novelty; he is doubly taken by surprise.[65] Fernando ripostes with a comment on the material (horn) from which lanterns are made, eliciting another admiring comment from Julio, and then plays with the implications of the lantern's dazzling light.

Despite Celia's sharp running comments in the last scene of the work, it is Felipa whom Lope particularly endows with skill at *agudeza*, which she displays again in the encounter with Fernando in the Prado, again evoking Julio's admiring comments. The same scene opens on the sharper tone of *agudeza* set by Clara:

> *Mar.:* ¡Qué solo está el Prado!
> *Cla.:* ¿Cómo no quieres que lo esté, si apenas le acompaña el día?
> *Mar.:* ¡Qué bien pintara esta mañana Fernando!
> *Cla.:* Mejor supo despintar el oro de tus joyas.
>
> (p. 289)

> *Mar.:* How alone the Prado is! *Cla.:* What do you expect if it's scarcely even accompanied by daylight? *Mar.:* How well Fernando would have painted this morning! *Cla.:* He did a better job of tarnishing the gold off your jewels.

Similarly barbed *agudezas* of Fernando set the tone of the climactic stage of the quarrel with Dorotea. In a different vein, finally, we find Gerarda parrying a proverb Teodora aims at her, "Vieja que baila, mucho poluo leuanta" ("An old woman dancing raises a lot of dust"), with "Por mi vida, que no seas aguda, sino discreta" ("For heaven's sake, don't be witty—be smart") (p. 121).

At times the most tactical *agudeza* is the most unexpectedly direct statement. We shall find Fernando climaxing his excessively theatrical fabrication about murdering someone with the sudden plain declaration: "Maté al vno y herí al otro" ("I killed one and wounded the other") (p. 116); Laurencio topping the overblown rhetoric of his account of Don Bela's death with the naked truth: "Sacaron las espadas, y entre los dos le han muerto" ("They took out their swords and between the two of them killed him") (p. 455); Dorotea descending from the histrionic heights of her first scene with Fernando to declare simply: "¿Qué quieres saber de mí, Fernando mío, más de que ya no soy tuya?" ("What is there for me to say, my Fernando, except that I am no longer yours?") (p. 97). Unlike the descents into colloquiality noted earlier, these sudden thrusts are calculated to score on an interlocutor by startling and unhinging him. In such rhetorically planned simulation of simplicity, naturalness is overlaid by artifice: the principle "ars celare artem" ("the art is to conceal art") is dominant.

Stylistic Preciosity

Affected Speech

The remark of Clara about the Prado quoted a moment ago—"¿Cómo no quieres que lo esté [solo], si apenas le acompaña el día?" ("What do you expect if it's scarcely even accompanied by daylight?")—in its circuitousness sounds precious as well as *agudo*. It in fact points to an aspect of the aspiration to cultural refinement which manifests itself particularly in matters of verbal expression: affected diction, elaborate periphrasis, far-fetched metaphor, stilted ceremoniousness—matters of stylistic rather than erudite preciosity. "¡Notable batería hizo en el muro de tu entendimiento la fisonomía liberal del rico indiano!" ("The munificent physiognomy of the rich *indiano* did a fine battering job on the wall of your understanding!"), exclaims Dorotea (p. 76), heaping coals on the fire of her mother's wrath by deliberately affecting "the language of her lover." Felipa brings Fernando back to the point with: "Bolued a engarçar la cadena de vuestro cuento, no se os pierdan algunos eslabones" ("Fasten the chain of your story again, lest you lose some links") (p. 295); she greets his catalogue of epithets for Dorotea with: "¡Con qué de injuriosos nombres desembarca essa pobre muger del mar de vuestra ira!" ("With what a quantity of abusive names that poor woman steps ashore from the sea of your anger!") (p. 297). She presents to Don Bela a picture of Dorotea as she writes, "compitiendo con el papel la mano de la pluma, haziéndola más blanca la negra que está siruiéndola" ("with the hand holding the pen vying with the paper [*scil.*, in whiteness] and being made whiter by the black one [*scil.*, the pen] that is serving it") (p. 259). More ingenuity than Don Bela possesses is required to draw out of this conceit, with its juggled antecedents and its far-fetched chiaroscuro pun, the simple meaning it contains. ("¿De tintero, Felipa?" ["With an inkwell, Felipa?"], he asks, uncomprehending.) "Es notable el gouierno desta república de cuerdas" ("The governing of this common-wealth of strings is notoriously difficult") (p. 179), remarks Dorotea solemnly as she tunes the harp. Her affected speech accords with the elaborate ceremoniousness that marks the occasion of Don Bela's visit. The over-elaborateness of the *indiano*'s remarks and of others, as Félix Monge notes,[66] goes well beyond the usual formalism of the age: "No os tengáis por desseruida de que os suplique me fauorezcáis con dos versos de lo que vos tuuiéredes más gusto" ("Do not hold yourself disobliged if I entreat you to favor me with a couple of lines of whatever your pleasure may dictate") (p. 179); "No es mi entendimiento capaz de tanta dicha que halle vuestra atención dispuesta a la música de mis palabras" ("My understanding is not capable of so much bliss as to find your attention favorably disposed toward the music of my words") (p. 172). Nor is Fernando immune to such preciosity of expression:

> *Cés.:* No dexéis el instrumento, Fernando, por mi vida.
> *Fer.:* Ya las auían dado licencia los versos a las cuerdas para que descansassen.
>
> (p. 402)
>
> *Cés.:* Don't put the instrument down, I beg you.   *Fer.:* The verses had already given the strings permission to rest.

Sometimes the verbal ingenuity affects structure and syntax in particular. One often senses fastidiousness in the verbal ordering of thought. Fernando places the pronoun before the antecedent, for example: "No bien me acostaua para esperar la mañana en que Dorotea, por el que me dieron suyo quando di a Celia el papel de Marfisa, prometía verme, quando…" ("Scarcely had I gone to bed to await the morrow on which Dorotea, through the one from her which I was given when I gave Celia the note from Marfisa, promised to see me, when…") (p. 415). (Is it by design that the involuted phrasing underscores the mix-up of the love-notes?) In the scene of leave-taking from Marfisa, the endless conceit in which Fernando professes his gratitude is impeccably turned:

> Mi alma sale a la fiança, y en prendas desta liberalidad te dexo mi memoria. Escriuiré en llegando, y escriuiré en mi coraçón la escritura deste recibo, para que la cobres dél, si Dios me dexa boluer a verte, testigos tus ojos. (p. 118)[67]
>
> My soul provides the security, and as an earnest of this generosity I leave you the memory of me. I will write upon arrival, and I will write in my heart the instrument of this receipt, so that you may collect it from it, if God grants that I see you again, with your eyes as witnesses.

A high point of such verbal play, in the manner of the famous *razón de la sinrazón* (reason of the unreason), is Fernando's remark: "Pero yo os prometo que no pude dexar de dexarlo. Pero ¿qué me importa, si lo que dexé no me dexa?" ("But I assure you that I had no leave not to leave it. But what do I care, if what I left doesn't leave me?") (p. 285). More surprising is the expressive artifice that Gerarda sometimes displays. In an anecdote she points at Teodora, popular substance is incongruously combined with extreme artifice of syntactical arrangement:

Comadre, sabed que al rey don Iuan de Portugal le truxo vna
labradora, que le pedía que le perdonasse vna muerte que su marido
auía hecho, vna cantidad de natas, no estando allí la reina, que
sentada con él a la mesa comió muchas. Echóse a sus pies la labradora,
pidiendo la vida de su marido a entrambos. El rey perdonaua, la
reina no quería; a quien él dixo, viéndola tan ayrada: "Passo,
señora; que auéis comido muchas natas."   (p. 372)

Gossip, you must know that King John of Portugal was brought,
by a peasant woman who was asking him to forgive a murder her
husband had committed, a quantity of whipped cream, during an
absence of the queen, who, seated at table with him [subsequently],
ate a good deal of it. The peasant woman threw herself at their
feet, pleading with both for her husband's life. The king was for
forgiving, the queen refused, to whom he said, seeing her so wrathful:
"Just a moment, madam, you've eaten a great deal of whipped
cream."

In this curious blend of naturalism and artifice, one notes the calculated
hypotaxis—subordinate clauses that leave a thought suspended, or, conversely,
telescope it drastically—and a total effect of pithy condensation unexpected
in Gerarda and distinct from her native paratactic utterance.

The counterpart of the tendency to preciosity and formality in verbal
expression is a hypercritical attitude toward unduly flat, long-winded, or
unimaginative diction:

> *Fer.:* . . . Y este pescador lloraua la más hermosa muger que tuuo la
> ribera donde nació, más firme, más constante y de más limpia fe
> y costumbres.
> *Fel.:* Parece aprouación de libro.
>
> (p. 285)

> *Fer.:* And this fisherman was grieving for the most beautiful
> woman that ever graced the shore where she was born, the truest,
> most steadfast, and the one of most spotless faith and morals.   *Fel.:*
> Sounds like the censor's approval of a book.

Lope, who himself knew what it was to reel off automatic phrases of
approbation as a censor, here mocks their very automatism—with remarkable detachment since, at the autobiographical level, the reference is to the
newly dead Marta de Nevares. Julio greets Fernando's overly detailed
account to Felipa of his literary and linguistic attainments with: "Parece que
informas esta dama para algún oficio" ("You seem to be giving this lady an

application for some position") (p. 295). Through the comment by Julio, Lope beats the reader to the draw and acknowledges the awkwardness of so detailed a self-revelation, more his own than his protagonist's. "Pareces hábito, que informas de limpieza" ("You seem like some insignia of knighthood, reporting on purity" [*limpieza:* cleanliness; specifically, of blood]), Gerarda observes sarcastically to Laurencio's: "Quisiera yo vn entretenimiento a medio traer, libre de polbo y de paja y de toda fullería" ("I'd like a pastime halfway submissive, free of dust and straw and of all cunning") (p. 396). The resort to "officialese"—standard legal or, in the last case, presumably commercial terminology—is here mocked as unimaginatively prosaic.[68]

The sophistication manifested in regard to techniques and styles of expression extends also to the quality and pedigree of what is expressed. Curiosity and novelty are, in this respect, at a premium; cultural commonplaces are taken for granted and something beyond them is expected. No *gracia* of enunciation will retrieve an *aplicación* or *agudeza* if its substance has become hackneyed or stale. "¡Qué cosa más triuial y vieja! Perdóneme Diógenes" ("What an antiquated, trivial thing! May Diogenes forgive me"), says Julio scornfully when Fernando remarks (p. 85) that gold is yellow through "fear at being sought after by so many people," clearly a worn-out bon mot.[69] Fernando himself (p. 417) dubs as a "dicho vulgar" ("common saying") the maxim "que las iras de los amantes son redintegración del amor" ("that the spats of lovers are a reaffirming of love").[70] For him it has clearly lost its Terentian pedigree and become indistinguishable from an ordinary proverb.

The Routine and the Select

Such reactions show the impatience of Lope's protagonists with the least select stratum of the classical heritage—the clichés, set phrases, *chrias*, *exempla*—which had become the common property of lettered and unlettered. (Sancho Panza could call his master "liberal sobre todos los Alejandros" ["more generous than all Alexanders"]; it was clearly not necessary to be able to read to pick up such tags.) We have seen Teodora offhandedly citing Dido and Aeneas apropos of Dorotea's abandonment by an earlier lover. Laurencio castigates Dorotea and Gerarda as Charybdis and Scylla; Gerarda alludes to Cleopatra as "aquella que molía perlas para brindar a Marco Antonio" ("the one who ground down pearls to drink to Mark Antony's health") (p. 158). Nor are such commonplaces confined to the least cultivated characters, for, despite the disdain of the more lettered, they could hardly be avoided; as Lope himself wrote, tags like "engaños de Ulysses, salamandra, Circe y otros" ("wiles of Ulysses, salamander, Circe, and others") had become part of a standard idiom: "Ya son como adagios y términos comunes y el canto llano sobre que se fundan varios conceptos" ("By now they're like proverbs and common terms and the ground upon which different concepts are built up").[71] Everyday speech could absorb such tags in an age when the increased circulation of books was depriving humanistic culture of its selectness and allowing it to sift down to the unlettered. For those who could read, there were the compendiums, editions, and translations that prompted Quevedo to remark in the *Sueño del infierno:* "Saben ya los tontos lo que encarecían en otros tiempos los sabios; que ya hasta el lacayo latiniza y hallarán a Horacio en castellano en la caballeriza" ("The stupid now know what the wise prized in other ages; even lackeys spout Latin and you can find Horace in Spanish in the stable").[72] For those who could not, there were the public festivities, of which one needs only to read the accounts to realize how considerably the outer trappings of classical culture had entered into the ordinary man's experience. Pagan gods and goddesses with all their retinues, every figure, subject, and episode in the repertory of ancient and modern culture that could be converted into pageantry, all were paraded before the common man on ceremonial occasions.[73]

It is against this background that one must set the noticeable desire of the characters of *La Dorotea* to back up the spoken word with the written: "¿Quién te lo ha dicho?" ("Who told you that?"), asks Clara, and Marfisa answers with finality: "Yo lo he leído" ("I've read it") (p. 115). If they do not read—and it seems clear that Felipa, like her mother Gerarda, is illiterate —they fall back on the reading and study of others: "Tengo vn hermano estudiante, y dame quando corta latín estos retales" ("I've a brother who's a student and when he trims his Latin he gives me these scraps"), explains Felipa when Julio remarks (p. 299) on her use of the word "pedagogo." Latin and Greek are indistinguishable smatterings in her pot-pourri of oral culture. Teodora even asks, "Who wrote that?" on Gerarda's remarking (p. 190) that every fig eaten requires three draughts of wine. "The philosopher Alaejos. Did you think it was Plutarch?" replies Gerarda, in a typical Lopean *reductio ad absurdum.*

The written word has sufficient prestige to provide purely nominal authorities where none exist: "el capítulo primero del libro de la infamia" ("the first chapter in the book of infamy") (p. 302); "el libro primero de amistades sobre zelos" ("the first book of making up after being jealous") (p. 313); "Los días passados vi vn libro en el estudio de vn amigo, que se llamaua *Verdades averigvadas*" ("The other day I saw a book in a friend's study called *Established Truths*") (p. 414). All women know by heart, says Gerarda, the book that tells how to deceive men (p. 452). The invention of such anonymous authorities is symptomatic of a cultural climate in which access to written sources is a mark of distinction vis-à-vis those who possess only tag ends of oral learning. But the figurative and patently apocryphal character of such sources shows that in an age of commonplace books, mere familiarity with the written word no longer means a great deal.[74] It is the rare and recondite authors, the unusual thoughts that count. In the course of Lope's parody of Góngora's commentators, their indiscriminate purveying of "quanto hallan en Estobeo, la *Polianthea* y Conrado Gisnerio y otros librotes de lugares comunes" ("everything they come upon in Stobaeus, the *Polyanthea*, and Conrad Gessner and other commonplace tomes") (p. 319) is roundly panned, and one of the characters, referring specifically to commonplaces, exclaims: "¡Malditos ellos sean! que ya no tengo cabeça para sufrirlos" ("Curse them—my head can't take any more of them!") (p. 336). While the parody of Góngora's followers carries the extraordinary to the point of absurdity and the principle "Califican mucho a los que escriuen, autores estraordinarios" ("Unusual authors give those who write great prestige") (p. 342) is formulated ironically, its relevance to the conversational standards of Lope's interlocutors is clear.

A prime source of cultural exclusiveness is words themselves. The characters display them with the self-satisfaction of connoisseurs, valuing them like collectors' items, for their properties rather than their function: for novelty, rarity, substantiality, musicality. Ceasing to be employed spontaneously as elements of a linguistic system, words turn into social and cultural symbols. Lope's keen verbal sensitivity is reflected in his characters' alertness to even the texture of the language. His strong feelings on the subject of *culteranismo*, mostly hostile despite some ambivalence, had heightened his verbal awareness when he was at work on *La Dorotea*, but even in the academy scenes the concern with words goes beyond literary polemics. It is a craftsman's delight in the materials of his craft and on occasion this may even embrace items of the *culto* lexicon, such as *afecta* in the following exchange:

> *Bel.:* Madre, quiérote dezir vn secreto para confirmar las facultades natiuas, que en qualquiera parte afecta y mórbida pone vigor . . . Toma vn pedaço de oro y métele ardiendo en vino, que es poción milagrosa.

Ger.: Ya se te ha pegado lo crespo de la lengua: *poción, natiua, afecta* y *mórbida.*

(p. 232)

Bel.: I want to give you a secret to fortify the native faculties, which invigorates any affected and morbid part . . . Take a piece of gold and put it red-hot in wine—it's a miraculous potion.   *Ger.:* You've been infected by the frills of the language: *potion, native, affected,* and *morbid.*

Gerarda pauses over Don Bela's language before addressing herself to his question. But Lope lets Don Bela reply with some justice: "¿No ves que son los propios términos?" ("Can't you see that these are the proper terms?"). At least in this technical context, the *culto* or Latinizing forms are "proper": not hyperbolic or metaphorical but literally exact.

True, Lope allows the outsider, Don Bela, to be dazzled by such terms, while making Fernando take a stand against them:

Fel.: Leuantan agora los nueuos términos a la lengua.
Fer.: Testimonios.

(p. 283)

Fel.: There are telling new terms now to elevate the language.
Fer.: To tell tales on it.

Lope is present in both characters, however, and on the whole his hostility toward *culteranismo* is swallowed up in an expansive enjoyment of the possibilities of words.

A concern with words per se as a specialized interest of literati is constantly in evidence in the dialogue. The speakers dwell on nuances of meaning and sound, for example, *çabullarse, sumergirse, somorgujarse* (all mean "plunge"), the last with Garcilaso surely in mind (p. 270). It is the women who most self-consciously collect "fancy words," however, especially literary, rhetorical, and exotic terms. Though they have developed a modish taste for reading, they are fundamentally untrained in letters and are more attuned than the men to assimilation through conversation or through the latter's writings. (Gerarda notes that men "nos han priuado el estudio de las ciencias, en que pudiéramos diuertir nuestros ingenios sutiles" ["have deprived us of the study of different branches of learning in which we could occupy our subtle minds"], p. 452.) The "vocablos nueuos, destos que no se precian de hablar como los otros" ("new words used by those who pride themselves on not speaking like everybody else") (p. 143) which, according to Celia, constitute Fernando's legacy to Dorotea, are *culterano* neologisms or precious and affected terms.⁷⁵ Like his creator, Fernando is secretly attracted to what he rejects. Exasperated, Teodora vows to destroy Fernando's love-letters and verses: "Yo visitaré tus escritorios, yo te quemaré los papeles en que idolatras, y essas locuras en que estudias vocablos que no nacieron contigo" ("I'll go through your writing-boxes, I'll burn those notes that you idolize, and that nonsense in which you study words that didn't originate with you") (p. 77).

Gerarda makes sure that Dorotea does not miss Don Bela's *abstracto*, a term Lope specifically branded as *culterano*,⁷⁶ when Don Bela first calls on her: "¿No te dixe yo que era muy discreto?" ("Didn't I tell you he was very bright?") (p. 182). Like the Nise of Lope's *comedia La dama boba* (The Stupid Lady), Dorotea has undeniable affinities with the *précieuses* of her day, who earned Quevedo's ridicule in 1629 in his already cited *Culta latiniparla*, a tract in which the invasion of conversation by *culterano* neologisms, ancient and foreign phrases, scholastic pedantry and affected periphrases is pitilessly mocked. Her literary tastes also recall the strictures of Juan de Horozco y Covarrubias on "el daño que se hazen [las mujeres] a sí, y a otros, quando presumen de saber dezir su razón, y se precian de mostrarlo, assí de palabra como por escrito" ("the harm that women do to themselves and to others when they assume they know how to give their opinions and glory in showing them off both orally and in writing").⁷⁷

From the beginning of the work words, in their own right, independently of their meaning, are made symbolic objects of derision or admiration. Dorotea's reply to Teodora's hypocritical praise of Gerarda, "Todas essas gracias tienen diuersos sentidos: y si no son ironías, no se han de entender literalmente" ("All those delightful things have various meanings, and if they are not ironies are not to be understood literally") (p. 75), undercuts her mother's words in a spirit of cool literary analysis which infuriates Teodora: "La bachillera ya comiença a hablar en el lenguage de su galán: aprouechada está de parola. ¿Es esso lo que le enseña? ¿De *ironías* quedará rica *literalmente*?" ("Our affected pedant is now starting to speak the language of her lover: she's well stocked with palaver. Is this what he teaches her? She'll be *literally* rich in *ironies*?"). Teodora wrenches the technical terms from their contexts and flings them at her daughter.

Significantly, when the writing-box Teodora has threatened to rifle is brought out, in a subsequent scene (p. 150), Dorotea refers to its contents as "bagatelas" ("bagatelles"), explaining that the word as well as the box were gifts of an Italian gentleman, presumably an earlier lover. We see that her weakness for exotic words is of long standing.⁷⁸

Gerarda, as she prompts Don Bela for his meeting with Dorotea, encourages a similar combination of verbal and material offerings. "¡Iesús, don Bela! Concertados estáis los dos; que es muerta por hemistichios" ("Heavens, Don Bela! You two are matched already: she's mad about hemistichs"), she exclaims when Don Bela drops the latter term (p. 133). His promise to offer Dorotea "hipérboles y energías" ("hyperboles and *enargeias*") is literally the "acabóse" ("be-all and the end-all") for Gerarda. Though she has no idea what he means, she equates the Greek words with the variety of exoticism she knows best: "Parecen frutas de las Indias, como plátanos y aguacates" ("They seem fruits of the Indies, like bananas and alligator pears") (p. 133). The earthy Gerarda, who reflects the sensuous side of her creator, revels in their exotic flavor and lends them bulk, shape, and color.[79]

For all her enthusiasm, Gerarda's own interest in words is not selective but practical and tactical. No more than Teodora does she equate verbal with material riches. Nevertheless she finds words amusing playthings:

> *Ger.:* Esté en buen hora la honra de las viudas, el exemplo de las
> madres, la maestra primorosa de las cortesías, la caritatiua
> huéspeda de las desamparadas, mager [*sic*] con poca dicha, que
> merecía ser princesa de Transiluania.
> *Teo.:* Notable vienes, Gerarda, hablando a lo moderno y a lo
> antiguo. ¿Cómo has casado el *Mager* y la *Primorosa*, ésta moça y
> aquél viejo?
> *Ger.:* Ya, Teodora, nuestra lengua es vna calabriada de blanco y tinto.
> *Teo.:* Con esso la hablas de tan buena gana.
>
> (p. 119)
>
> *Ger.:* Blessings upon the honor of widowhood, the model of
> motherhood, the gracious mistress of courtesies, the charitable
> benefactress of the helpless, albeit not very lucky, when she deserves
> to be the princess of Transylvania.   *Teo.:* You're something special
> today, Gerarda, speaking in modern and ancient fashion. How come
> you've matched *albeit* with *gracious*, the latter a young girl, the
> former an old man?   *Ger.:* Our language is now a blend of white
> and red.   *Teo.:* That's why you speak it so enthusiastically.

Gerarda is surely the first of Celestina's descendants to drink words as well as wine and to apply her matchmaking talents to language.[80] Her high spirits bubble over in the copious picturesqueness of her speech. Teodora's technical objection to the rhetorical solecism of combining a neologism with an archaism reveals the same hypersensitive verbal antennae which had earlier caught Dorotea's literary terms. In Teodora the impropriety of such sensitivity is more ludicrous even than among the more highly placed *hembrilatinas* (Latinized females) satirized by Quevedo.

In respect to language as in other respects the geminal relationship of Teodora and Gerarda is evident. In a continuation of the verbal by-play just quoted, Lope inverts their roles:

> *Teo.:* Ya, Gerarda, no querría más de que saliesse esta moça bien morigerada de mi educación.
> *Ger.:* Y essas dos palabritas, ¿de dónde son, Teodora? Bien digo yo que se pega la habla como la sarna.
> *Teo.: Comer a gusto, y hablar y vestir al vso.*
>
> (p. 120)[81]

> *Teo.:* The only thing I do want, Gerarda, is for this girl to emerge with great morigeration from my nurture.   *Ger.:* And those pretty little words—where are they from, Teodora? I always said that speech was as contagious as the itch.   *Teo.:* "Follow your taste in eating, follow fashion in speech and dress."

Teodora's sense of verbal propriety is clearly as elastic, despite her cavils at Dorotea and Gerarda, as her sense of moral propriety. Indeed, speech, like dress, is not a matter of decorum at all, but of fashion. Her pretentious language is as artificial as the pose of respectability it expresses. But unlike Quevedo, Lope is merely amused, not caustic. Presently he trips Gerarda up over a *cultismo:* "Amores ay honestos que se causan naturalmente por no sé qué sinfonía o simpatonía, que dizen estos que saben poco latín y mucho griego" ("There are some proper loves that are caused naturally by some sympathy, or sympathony, or other, as these people who know little Latin and a lot of Greek say") (p. 120).[82]

The two crones pause to blow these verbal smoke rings while they put up their mock smokescreens of propriety. Lope's irony glances off his creatures and the *cultos* alike. Much later there is an echo of such verbal play when Gerarda once more trips up over an elaborate word:

> *Dor.:* Y el sueño, ¿de quién nace?
> *Ger.:* De estar confortadas las partes intri . . . trínsecas.
> *Dor.:* Mucho te costó salir de essa palabra.
>
> (p. 196)[83]

> *Dor.:* And sleepiness, what causes it?   *Ger.:* Having the intri . . . trinsic parts satisfied.   *Dor.:* You had a hard time getting through that word.

This time, however, Gerarda has been imbibing something more than words. Her verbal stumbling carries inescapable overtones of a belch, and is advance notice of the real stumble that will follow when she rises from the table, stone drunk.

Patterns of Literary Stylization

The heightened sensitivity to words as objects and symbols is a particular manifestation of the concern with literary culture that pervades the entire milieu of *La Dorotea*. As we now proceed to consider more extended patterns of literary stylization, examining their manifestations in conversation and behavior and observing the individual tendencies which mark the styles of the principal characters, it should not be forgotten that beneath the facile manipulation by the characters of the showier trappings of literary ornamentation there lies a genuine professional concern on Lope's part, for which Fernando and his peers are sometimes spokesmen, with the literary *métier* itself. While the characters' penchant for novelty and display is never relinquished, in the course of their virtuosistic conversations come occasional rapid confrontations with serious literary issues. The conversation then becomes more collaborative than competitive or disputational and substance is as significant as manner. Scenes 2 and 3 of Act IV, where the friends of Fernando expressly meet as a literary "academy," mark the culmination of this tendency. To exemplify an earlier manifestation, one might cite a brief exchange provoked in Act III, scene 4, by Julio's proposal to recite an "epigrama" he has just written (p. 243). He is asked whether the poem is in Latin (a real epigram) or Castilian (that is, a sonnet) and the question is then raised as to which language one should write in. Precedents for preferring one or the other or for writing in both are cited, and while the issue is not resolved, Julio and Ludovico taking opposite views, its significance lies in the fact that all three interlocutors take it for granted that one writes in one language or the other: one does not try to Latinize Castilian. This assumption will underlie their ridicule of Góngora's commentators in Act IV, scenes 2 and 3.

Fernando is absent when the *cénacle* meets and Julio, present for the commentary on the sonnet in scene 3, misses the more generalized discussion in scene 2 of the literary issues involved. But even when Ludovico and César are alone, they are united in their opposition to *culteranismo* and in essential agreement on other literary issues. Lope has clearly introduced these scenes in order to reassert the artistic values of clarity and of lexical and syntactic "normalcy" challenged by *culteranismo* and in the process, as we shall see later, to reaffirm, as the basis of his own *poiesis*, a balance between art and nature. The issue is not dramatized, however. Not even for the sake of argument does one of the talkers espouse the cause of *culteranismo*. The speakers are made, rather, to work together in affirmation as well as in mockery. Indeed, in the first of these scenes, Lope seems so anxious to make certain points about his respect for Góngora, about poetic commentaries generally, about censoring plays, so eager to bring in a long list of "grandes poetas," that soon after the opening he allows the dialogue to degenerate for a while into a straight interrogation of César by Ludovico reminiscent in its wooden mechanism of the didactic dialogues of the age. Ludovico asks César for information which, as one of Fernando's group and on the basis of his earlier conversation, we should expect him already to possess: "¿Essos son todos los [grandes poetas] que ay aora en España?" ("Are those all the [great poets] now in Spain?") (p. 327); "¿Qué han impreso hasta aora?" ("What have they published up to now?"); "¿En qué ha parado el examen de las comedias?" ("What was the upshot of the investigation of plays?") (p. 328); "Dezid algo deste nombre *culto*, que yo no entiendo su etimología" ("Say something about this name *culto*: I don't understand its etymology") (p. 330). But when the detailed discussion of *culto* esthetics and the citation of authorities and examples in refutation begins (p. 331), a different Ludovico emerges, as knowledgeable as the confrère with whom he is now joining forces. Despite its technical subject matter, the conversation picks up momentum and begins to carry the reader along. The line-by-line commentary on the sonnet begins and eventually we are treated to Julio's procession of burlesque authorities, works, and quotations. Though the others cannot match his inventive fantasy, Lope does not confine the obvious to Ludovico, the ridiculous to Julio, or the serious to César, but mixes the different tones among the three indiscriminately, making them supplement and draw each other out endlessly. There are many gradations between the obviously serious and the obviously ridiculous in their remarks and the fact that the speakers are themselves *bachilleres* often makes it impossible to draw sharp distinctions. Though their attention is here focused on a significant literary issue, their tendency to weave webs of erudite and poetic adornment about every subject they consider is too ingrained to be put aside. Hence, even while they carry Lope's case against his professional opponents and speak as his advocates on other literary matters, in the end we find his Burguillos-like irony hovering about them. Unlike them, Lope sees that, although at this point they are applying their weakness for ornamentation to an artistic issue of real substance, the impulse involved is the same as that which governs their approach to the experiences of their own lives.

    This becomes abundantly clear when we find Fernando bursting in (scene 4) as the comments on the sonnet are concluding. Attention is thereby quickly diverted from the literary artifact to a human predicament. The adorning tendency carries on unabated, however. Jubilant at his reconquest of Dorotea, Fernando simply harnesses the imaginative energy which has been loosely expended on the sonnet to a new object: his own triumph. There is no discontinuity, merely a shift of focus and an intensification. We find ourselves witnessing a glorification of the new development which produces the tensest and most highly wrought piece of literary stylization of experience in the whole *acción en prosa*. The authorial irony diffused through the previous scenes becomes more concentrated: Lope's reservations, though unexpressed, are evident in the reckless overdoing of the whole sequence. Thus we find ourselves, with scarcely more than a shift of emphasis, moving from a level of basically serious concern with literature in its own right to a high point in the misappropriation of literature to life.

The brief scene transplants the triumph motif characteristic of baroque celebrations to the domain of personal feelings and private experience. Fernando's entrance is a triumphal entry. Recalling it months later, César remarks: "Bien me acuerdo del regozijo con que veníades de tan alegre triunfo, como si en el carro de amor fuérades vos el cónsul, y los desdenes fingidos de Dorotea los despojos de la vitoria" ("Well do I recall the jubilation with which you came back from so joyful a triumph, as if you were the consul in the chariot of love and the pretended disdain of Dorotea the spoils of victory") (p. 405). It is at once a triumph of love—a motif established in Romance literature by Petrarch—and a personal triumph. Though rhetorical pomp and circumstance replace pageantry and spectacle, this is no allegorical triumph; it is rather the directly enacted glorification of a private victory. The pace is deliberately slow and stately: "No es para dicho aprisa" ("This is nothing to be told of in a hurry"), Fernando admonishes Ludovico and César (p. 367) when they press him to explain his elation: "Vitorias son de amor, milagros son de la firmeza" ("These are victories of love, miracles of steadfastness"). There follows in a rhetorical procession a congeries of nine symmetrical members. These are adorned by Ludovico and César with *historias* centering on the motif of sudden joy—the rhetorical equivalent of the ornamental and episodic medallions with which the pictorial triumph as it developed in the sixteenth century became increasingly overladen. Lope draws a handful of incidents from Ravisius Textor[84] and distributes them among his interlocutors: the decorative intention is evident. This is an enterprise of collaborative adornment; there is no trace of controversy. César and Ludovico are perfectly aware of the reason for Fernando's joy. They have pierced Julio's enigmas at the beginning of the preceding scene but they observe the rules of the game and deliberately play into Fernando's hands in this scene, as desirous as he of staging a triumph with fitting ceremony. Their assumed ignorance merely provides the minimum divergence among the interlocutors required for the dramatic build-up of the scene. As the ornamentation proceeds, the motif of joy prolonging life becomes intertwined with that of sudden joy resulting in death and dwindles away as longevity pure and simple.[85] When Ludovico enjoins Fernando, "Sosiégate, loco, y di, si puedes, lo que te ha sucedido" ("Quiet down, you wild man, and tell if you can what happened to you") (p. 368), the answer is a "notable sarta de romanos y griegos" ("remarkable string of Romans and Greeks"), as Julio exclaims in admiration. "¿No alaban la religión de Pompilio, la constancia de Régulo, la fortaleza de Catón . . .?" ("Don't they praise the religiousness of Pompilius, the constancy of Regulus, the fortitude of Cato . . .?"), begins Fernando, and a new procession of *exempla* unwinds, made up of twenty figures, with Fernando as the twenty-first: "Pues añadan las historias a estos títulos él contento de don Fernando" ("Well, to these titles of glory, let historical records add the satisfaction of Don Fernando"). The only common note among all the varied "titles" which Fernando has evoked is their praiseworthiness: it is their rhetorical, not their ethical, potentiality that counts, for it is only on the former grounds that Fernando's "contento" belongs in this company. The *exemplum* is divorced from all moral exemplarity and its ornamental function is inordinately magnified.

The final stage of Fernando's triumph is the bestowing of a title:

> *Fer.:* ¿No llamaron a Scipión el *Africano* porque venció aquella parte del mundo?
> *Lud.:* Por lo mismo llamaron *Germánicos* o *Británicos* a sus Césares.
> *Fer.:* Pues ¿cómo se llamará quien ha vencido los desdenes de Dorotea?
> *Lud.:* Fernando el *Doroteánico*.
> *Fer.:* Pues ésse es mi nombre, mi dicha y mi historia.
>
> (p. 370)
>
> *Fer.:* Did they not call Scipio the *African* because he conquered that part of the world? *Lud.:* For similar reasons they called their Caesars the *Germanic* or the *Britannic*. *Fer.:* Then what will one who has overcome the disdain of Dorotea be called? *Lud.:* Fernando the *Dorotheanic*. *Fer.:* Well, that is my name, my joy and my story.

Ludovico's responses seem to be on cue, the exchange appears rehearsed in advance. This ceremoniousness befits the invoking of the ancient triumphs most celebrated in Renaissance art and letters: those of Scipio and the

Caesars.[86] If one compares this scene, moreover, with Lope's descriptions, in the *Triunfos divinos* (Divine Triumphs) (1625) inspired by Petrarch's *Trionfi*, of triumphal cars celebrating allegorical religious triumphs, one has evidence that it is in effect a rhetorical version of the pictorial triumph motif.[87]

Fernando's Style

Fernando's triumphant celebration of his "contento" well exemplifies the theatrical tendency which (along with an obstinately poetic vision of the world) distinguishes what might be called his personal style. Lope makes Fernando an extreme embodiment at once of the histrionic and of the esthetic sensibility. Drawing his collaborators after him, Fernando detaches himself in this scene from the emotion being glorified in order to exploit it like an actor. The intimate character of Fernando's feeling is not affected by the celebration; the ornamentation is clearly *a posteriori* and the emotion has become a pretext for its own glorification. No question is seriously raised as to the interaction between genuine and staged feelings: the actor remains unmoved by the role he is playing. This is Fernando's characteristic pattern of behavior. His role-playing is a form of self-aggrandizement that compensates for immaturity and a certain hollowness at the core. He is continually posing, continually aware of an imagined audience, never fully committed to the role he assumes. In his heightened awareness of self, he exacerbates the tendency to self-observation which we noted in the young Lope and carries to an extreme the tendency of the mature dramatist to cultivate particular effects in order to meet an audience's expectations. The spectacle Fernando offers is essentially simply himself, and its presentation presupposes detachment sufficient to see himself as others see him. The result is in the nature of a vicious circle: he deliberately fosters certain expectations, especially in his mistresses, then must behave so as to live up to them. In the process spontaneity is sacrificed and we are at a loss to know where the vital center of Fernando's being lies. In short, the histrionic streak of the young Lope reappears in him without the powerful creative gift which carries Lope beyond himself and redresses the balance. (The conventional character of the poetry Fernando writes has already been noticed.)

Lope's depiction of the histrionic sensibility in Fernando is clearly the product of a more considered art than the histrionism we find presented in the earlier lyrics and plays. But an effect of this deliberateness is, as suggested, to endow Fernando himself with the heightened objectivity in regard to role-playing that Lope acquired with advancing years. The combination of reckless youthful play-acting and mature detachment corresponds well to Lope's fascination with this ludic phenomenon, but it does so at the price of coherence and solidity in the characterization of the protagonist. At the price of humanity also: an element of calculation, chilling at times, is evident in Fernando's histrionism; it is entirely devoid of the ebullience which the play-spirit generated in Lope. Nor is Fernando's detachment accompanied by the saving grace of humor: he is quite lacking in his creator's rich comic sense and in the ultimate sense of proportion on which it rests.

The tendency to self-dramatization is so ingrained in Fernando that it appears even when he has no one but Julio to perform for. His immediate reaction to the quarrel with Dorotea is characteristic. The theatricality of his behavior here magnifies that of Lope himself vis-à-vis Elena and becomes particularly evident when contrasted with two literary precedents that have left traces upon it: Lope's Belardo in *Belardo el furioso* and the Calixto of *La Celestina*. As has already been suggested, Fernando's suicidal impulse represents a deflecting of his aggressiveness toward himself from its actual target, Dorotea. It is significant that, unlike Belardo who stormed at Jacinta directly with his dagger, Fernando lets Dorotea depart before dramatizing his despair. When Julio confirms that she is not looking back, the reaction of Fernando is undoubtedly modeled by Lope upon Calixto's behavior after Melibea dismisses him in the opening scene of the *tragicomedia:*

Fer.: Muerto soy, Iulio. Cierra todas las ventanas, no entre luz a mis ojos, pues se va para siempre la que lo fue de mi alma. (p. 101)

Cal.: Cierra la ventana, y dexa la tiniebla acompañar al triste, y al desdichado la ceguedad. Mis pensamientos tristes no son dignos de luz.[88]

Fer.: I am slain, Julio. Close all the windows, let no light reach my eyes, since she who was such to my soul is leaving forever.

Cal.: Close the window and let darkness accompany one sad and blindness one unlucky. My sad thoughts are unworthy of light.

But Calixto settles back supinely to enjoy his suffering—"Sólo quieres padecer tu mal" ("All you want is to suffer your affliction"), Sempronio tells him—whereas Fernando play-acts energetically from the beginning. (Lope's inability to take self-destruction seriously reinforces the seventeenth-century proscription of depictions of suicide.)

Fernando goes on:

Fer.: Quita de allí aquella daga, que el trato es demonio, la
    costumbre infierno, el amor locura, y todos me dizen que me
    mate con ella.
Iul.: Quedo, señor, detente. ¿Qué ceguedad es ésta?

(p. 101)

Fer.: Remove that dagger from there, for dalliance is the very
    devil, habit hell, love madness, and all tell me to kill myself with it.
Jul.: Quiet, sir, hold on. What blindness is this?

Even blindness (*ceguedad*) is acted out in Fernando's blind rush to self-destruction. But it is not in fact blindness at all: it is too carefully controlled. Fernando can count on Julio's knowing his role; Julio indeed responds with marked irony as Fernando feints at different forms of suicide: "Por el balcón no se baxa bien a la calle; mejor irás por la puerta" ("The balcony is not the best way to the street; the door is better"). "¡Qué fina locura!" ("What refined madness!") is his comment when Fernando stops to consider which poison will be most appropriate. The manner is all-important, whether in the choice of poison or the selection of another form of suicide—stabbing, bleeding to death, or self-defenestration. While Belardo really worked himself up, Fernando at this point is merely theatrical. It is the fitting gesture he has in mind; there is no substance to the idea of suicide itself. Fernando's behavior becomes more exaggerated and Lope's ironical amusement more evident when Fernando turns upon the portrait of Dorotea with the aggressiveness that Belardo directed at Jacinta herself.[89] The disparity between the fury of the assault and the minuteness of its object makes this intended display of wrath and despair caricaturesque. Belardo's turbulence quite lacked the element of calculation we find in Fernando's, though there may be a residue of Belardo's madness in the convulsive, overplayed assault on the portrait.

Fernando's most characteristic displays of theatrical behavior occur in his scenes with Dorotea and Marfisa; the presence of a woman in love with him who is both an impressionable spectator and a responsive collaborator is a strong stimulus. His performance is not staged merely for her or for the servants who observe and comment. His lines seem intoned for a wider audience supplied by the imagination. His partners are inevitably drawn into play-acting with him. In analyzing the most characteristic instances, a scene with Dorotea and one with Marfisa, we will find their roles inevitably vying with his for our attention.

The rhetorical, poetic, and pictorial playing-up of the confrontation with Dorotea in Act I is an effect of Fernando's awareness that, however painful, this moment is supreme and deserves to be dramatized to the full. During much of the scene, Fernando and Dorotea are actually collaborating rhetorically and histrionically in building up their falling-out, if one may so phrase it. Clearly not for his servant but for some vaster invisible audience, Fernando, on hearing Celia at the door, proclaims that he is going to "recibir el arco embaxador de los dioses, la aurora de mi sol, la primauera de mis años y el ruiseñor del día, a cuya dulce voz despiertan las flores, y como si tuuiessen ojos abren las hojas" ("receive the rainbow that is emissary to the gods, the dawn to my sun, the springtime of my years, and the nightingale of daytime, at whose sweet voice the flowers awaken and, as if they had eyes, open their petals") (p. 93). Giving his rhetorical tendencies a new turn when Dorotea enters, Fernando, having surmised what has occurred, anticipates charges and formulates his defense in a variation on *subiectio*, a rhetorical *figura sententiae*:

> ¿Hante dicho algo de mí? Tu madre me aurá leuantado algún
> testimonio porque me dexes. Pues plega al cielo que si he mirado,
> visto, ni oído, ni imaginado otra cosa de quantas él ha hecho, fuera
> de tu hermosura, que la mar que esta noche he soñado me anegue
> y me sepulte, y el oro que te dauan te conquiste.   (p. 93)

> Have they said something to you about me? Your mother must have
> spread some tale against me to make you leave me. Well, may
> heaven grant, if I have looked at, seen, heard, or imagined anything
> else created by it except your beauty, that the sea I dreamed of last
> night drown me and bury me and the gold you were given win you.

The *deprecatio* figure of Fernando's defense has a legalistic tinge. When Dorotea promptly faints, histrionism joins rhetoric in Fernando's overplayed despair: "¡Muerto soy, acabóse mi vida! ¡A, mi señora! ¡A, mi Dorotea! ¡A, vltima esperança mía!" ("I am slain. My life is at an end. Alas, my lady! Alas, my Dorotea! Alas, last hope of mine") (p. 94).[90]

Fernando greets her first words as she comes to—"¡Ay, Dios! ¡Ay, muerte!" ("Oh God! Oh death!")—first in refined poetic prose, then with the inopportune technical comment of a mind schooled in topics of controversy: "Pero ¿cómo la primera palabra ha sido las dos cosas más poderosas, Dios y la muerte?" ("But how is it that your first words have been the two most powerful things, God and death?") (p. 95).[91] Her eloquence quickly recovered, Dorotea unhesitatingly replies: "Porque Dios me libre de mí misma, y la muerte ponga fin a tantas desventuras" ("So that God may deliver me from myself and death put an end to so much misfortune"), citing in self-justification an Aristotelian dictum on the universal frailty of women. The issue now becomes a disputational one, between the general rule and the particular case, Fernando proclaiming a principle of exceptions, Julio collaborating with a catalogue of exemplarily strong women, Fernando capping the list with Dorotea and concluding rhetorically in a flourish of asyndeton, antithesis, anaphora, and a *sententia:* "Y esto no lo digan mis ojos, no mi amor, no mi conocimento; calle mi voluntad y hable la embidia; que no ay mayor satisfación que remitille las alabanças" ("And let this be said not by my eyes, not by my love, not by my knowledge; let my will remain silent and envy speak; for there is no greater satisfaction than to leave the praising to it") (p. 97).

Dorotea, however, systematically and spectacularly dissociates herself from Julio's *exempla,* capriciously using the strong point asserted in each case to accentuate her own weakness, a clear example of the willful and futile manipulation of humanistic commonplaces. Genuinely taken aback, Fernando in spontaneous questions protests Dorotea's deliberate building of suspense, "¿Qué es eso, mi bien? ¿Por qué me sangras a pausas?" ("What is this, my treasure? Why are you letting my blood intermittently?"), then recovers his rhetorical composure only to hear Dorotea blurt out, with the bluntness we have already noticed: "¿Qué quieres saber de mí, Fernando mío, más de que ya no soy tuya?" ("What is there for me to say, my Fernando, except that I am no longer yours?"). Such bluntness disarms him and she rushes ahead to denounce her mother in a climactic surge that draws on all her verbal and histrionic powers.

Dorotea's denunciation of her mother is an exercise in *vituperatio* that takes her present situation as subject and thereby acquires a suasory function as well. What she has to say is simple enough: "My mother upbraided me violently over what my love for you is doing to me. She is making me take a rich new lover whom Gerarda has found." Key elements in this situation are vastly amplified: the mother, the upbraiding—act and substance —the violence; others in contrast are played down: Dorotea's reply, the new lover, Gerarda's role. In time-honored fashion grandiloquence is varied with brevity to avoid the pitfall of tedium. Anaphora is deployed systematically in lengthening gradated clauses or, conversely, in short symmetrical phrases, in order to play on Fernando's feelings. In answer to Fernando's "¿Quién?" ("Who?") Dorotea starts off with five periphrastic epithets apparently stemming, as Leo Spitzer noted, from some canon of abuse;[92] she studiously avoids mentioning Teodora by name: "Essa tirana, essa tigre que me engendró . . . esse crocodilo gitano, que llora y mata" ("That tyrant, that tiger that bore me . . . that Egyptian crocodile that weeps and kills"). Then the quarrel: "Oy me ha reñido, oy me ha infamado, oy me ha dicho que me tienes perdida" ("Today she scolded me, today she vilified me, today she told me that you have ruined me")—the last clause immediately proliferating into "sin honra, sin hazienda y sin remedio" ("[leaving me] no honor, no income, and no prospect"). Next she reinforces brevity with *emphasis:* "Respondíle; pagáronlo mis cabellos" ("I answered her back; my hair paid the price"). Histrionism comes to the fore as Dorotea, holding out her torn hair, unravels the implications of the pregnant *pagáronlo:*

> Ves aquí los que estimauas, los que dezías que eran los rayos del sol, de quien hizo amor la cadena que te prendió el alma, los que llamauan red de amor tus versos, esta color que tu dezías que deseauas tener en la barba antes que te apuntasse el boço. Estos, en fin, mi Fernando, lo pagaron.

> Here you may see those [locks] which you prized, the ones you said were the sun's beams, from which love had made the chain which bound your soul, the ones your verse called love's net, this color which you said you hoped your beard would have before the down appeared. These, then, my Fernando, paid the price.

This is the climax of Dorotea's appeal, precisely bracketed between the introductory "pagáronlo mis cabellos" and the summarizing inversion "Estos, en fin, mi Fernando, lo pagaron." Unlike the rest, this climactic sequence has no informative function, only a pathetic one: Dorotea is not relating present events but evoking the private world shattered by them. The hair she clutches is a shred of this world, a dramatic prop that at the same time functions as a multivalent symbol, evoking at once the present violence and the poetry and intimacy of the past, the now powerless poetry that set their relationship apart through the transmuting power of metaphor, whether in verse or in plays of oral fancy. For all the theatricality of Dorotea's posture there is undeniable poignancy in these lines: the tender maternal character of her feeling for her beardless lover shows through. The anaphoras here fall into place more simply, there is only the semblance of an amplifying movement in the clauses, her expression seems to follow the natural trend of memory, ending in an intimate associative afterthought. The enlargement of the concluding bracket—"Estos, *en fin, mi Fernando,* lo pagaron"—transcribes verbally the lingering over the past. With evident empathy Lope allows the core of Dorotea's femininity to reveal itself, and this new blending of rhetorical and naturalistic utterance underscores the revelation.

Now Dorotea changes pace, rushing through all the rest of the story in a single breath: "Aquí te traigo los que me quitó, que los que quedan ya no serán tuyos, de otro quiere que sean; a vn indiano me entrega, el oro la ha vencido, Gerarda lo ha tratado, entre las dos se consultó mi muerte" ("I bring you here those she pulled out, since those remaining are to be yours no longer, she wants them to be someone else's; she's turning me over to an *indiano*, gold has conquered her, Gerarda arranged it, the two of them planned my death").[93] The facts come out obliquely, in the order of their importance to Dorotea, not in the sequence in which events occurred. But the oblique presentation is tactical also and, like the marked asyndeton, is a device for slipping past the real sticking-point, the new lover. The rest of Dorotea's appeal is couched in poetic prose—*dulce* and markedly metrical[94] —with rhetorical interjections—"¡O cruel sentencia!"; "¡Ay Dios! ¡Ay de mí!" ("Oh cruel decree!"; "Oh God! Woe is me!")—and is climaxed by the access of histrionism already noted in which she assaults her own eyes. Dorotea concludes as she began: "¡Ay Dios! ¡Ay muerte!" ("Oh God! Oh death!"). Julio's acid comment—"Boluió al estriuo" ("She's at the refrain again") (p. 99)—is an adverse critical appraisal of a performance. The studied indifference of Fernando's response—"¿Pues para ocasión de tan poca importancia tanto sentimiento, Dorotea?" ("Why, for an occasion of such slight importance, such carrying-on, Dorotea!")—while a cover for injured pride, is also a critique of a piece of overacting.

I have already pointed to an affinity between the cool control exhibited by Fernando in the ensuing exchange, the quarrel proper, and the flair for façade visible in the Lope of the trial record. This final part of the scene is dominated, just beneath the surface, by the sarcasm with which Fernando plays the role of indifference. I will comment later on his studied concern for esthetic composure, his attention to the disfiguring effect of Dorotea's "descompuestos afectos" ("disordered emotions"). We may here note the care for a perfect rhetorical symmetry that continues to set off, as in his opening question, perfectly turned contrasts: "¿Para tan débil causa tan fuerte sentimiento? Restitúyeme al coraçón el alegría de verte, que me auía quitado la tristeza de escucharte" ("For such a flimsy cause, such powerful grief? Restore to my heart the joy of seeing you which the sadness of listening to you had taken away") (p. 100). Then he drops, still underplaying, into the unceremonious parataxis of ordinary discourse: "Y vete en buen hora; que aguardo vn amigo para vn negocio, y no es justo que te vea; que las damas, y tan hermosas, sólo pueden estar sin sospecha en casa de juezes y de letrados" ("And now leave, and godspeed, because I'm expecting a friend about a certain matter, and it wouldn't be right for him to see you.

For ladies, and such beautiful ones, can only be found irreproachably in the houses of judges and jurists").

With this, the final phase of the confrontation begins: deliberate rhetorical schemata give way definitively to the parry and thrust of repartee; the pace noticeably accelerates. Fernando falls back on wit to fend off Dorotea's simple, uncomprehending questions and she is completely undone by his barbed *agudezas*. He seizes on her words and throws them back, twisting their meanings in flashy displays of the disputational technique of the *reflexio*:

> *Dor.:* . . . No lo [mi amor] merece quien no siente perderme.
> *Fer.:* Engáñaste, que tú sola te pierdes.
> *Dor.:* Estraños sois los hombres.
> *Fer.:* Antes muy propios; que nuestra primera patria sois las
> mugeres, y nunca salimos de vosotras.
>
> (p. 101)

> *Dor.:* One who doesn't regret losing me doesn't merit [my love].
> *Fer.:* You're mistaken; you alone are doing the losing.   *Dor.:* You
> men are strange.   *Fer.:* Rather, very at home; you women are our
> first motherland and we never get beyond you.

The pointed exchanges momentarily give the dialogue the tenseness of Senecan stichomythia. The contrast is striking between the stylistic simplicity and psychological directness which Dorotea attains in this final phase and the defensive display of puns and quips put on by Fernando as he wields verbal weapons and disputational techniques as a means of rejecting her, capping them with a *fábula:* "Que de diez y siete [años] llegué a tus ojos, y Iulio y yo dexamos los estudios, más oluidados de Alcalá que lo estuuieron de Grecia los soldados de Vlisses" ("At seventeen I came into your life and Julio and I gave up our studies, more forgetful of Alcalá than Ulysses' soldiers were of Greece") (p. 101). Through Celia's comment, "¡Qué sequedad de hombre! Dios me libre: ¿agora cuenta fábulas?" ("What a pill of a man! God save the mark, is this a time for fables?"), Lope underscores not only the stylistic impropriety but the theatrical pretentiousness of the posturing that goes with it.

Marfisa's susceptibility to Fernando's play-acting is particularly striking because she is presented as much less prone to self-delusion. A few moments after Fernando decides to resort to her for funds to go to Seville following the quarrel with Dorotea—merely telling Julio, "Marfisa . . . socorrerá nuestra necesidad liberalmente . . . con algún engaño" ("Marfisa . . . will come to our aid liberally . . . by means of some trick") (p. 105), and having no further thought to what he will say—he confronts Marfisa, confident of his ability to stage a plausible act. Belardo's deception of Cristalina in *Belardo el furioso* offers an embryonic preview of this scene; Fernando's manner even reminds us of Lope in court, unable to perjure himself without being overdramatic. Cristalina's gullibility, however, was merely mechanical, there was no collaborative interaction between her and Belardo; with Marfisa and Fernando the histrionic sensibility takes over. Marfisa sees that the act is overdone and says so several times, yet her need for illusion is such that she ends by suspending disbelief and joining in. Despite herself she is unhinged by Fernando's histrionics. In the earlier play we were not shown Cristalina's surrender of her jewels. In the *acción en prosa* Marfisa's compliance receives as much attention as the appeal. There was in the play only a brief suggestion of attitudes put on for the woman's benefit in support of the tale:

> *Bel.:* ¿Puedo llegar?
> *Sir.:*   Llegar puedes;
>   ¿qué temes?
> *Bel.:*   Que las paredes
> han visto a veces y oído.
>
>   (Ac., V, 676a)

> *Bel.:* May I approach?   *Sir.:* You may. What are you afraid of?
> *Bel.:* Walls have sometimes had eyes and ears.

Actors of course might have staged further indications of haste and alarm. In *La Dorotea* these are built into the dialogue because histrionics is not automatic offstage and Lope's aim is precisely to highlight it.

Taking Marfisa as his audience, Fernando acts out—for the first time—what he relates. He displays alarm from the outset, as Marfisa's opening words show: "¿Cómo vienes desta suerte?" ("What brings you here in such a state?") (p. 115). Pointedly posting Clara as a lookout, he winds himself up with stops and starts:

> *Fer.:* Anoche . . .
> *Mar.:* Di adelante.
> *Fer.:* Anoche, entre la vna y las dos, estaua hablando . . . no sé cómo la nombre.
> *Mar.:* Yo lo diré por ti, si se te ha oluidado. Hablauas con Dorotea.
>
>   (p. 116)

> *Fer.:* Last night . . .   *Mar.:* Go on.   *Fer.:* Last night, between one
> and two, I was talking . . . I don't know what to call her.   *Mar.:*
> I'll tell you, in case you've forgotten. You were talking with
> Dorotea.

Julio collaborates with expressions of alarm ("Señor, mira el peligro"
["Sir, consider the danger"], and so on) until Marfisa protests the over-
acting: "No hagas más efetos, por Dios . . . Di presto" ("Don't play it up
so, for heaven's sake . . . Come to the point"). With the calculated shock
technique already noted, Fernando suddenly snaps the suspense:

> *Fer.:* Maté al vno y herí al otro.
> *Iul.:* Y yo, ¿mondaua nísperos?
> *Fer.:* No se ha visto en el mundo valor como el que tuue.
> *Iul.:* Y yo, ¿quedéme en casa?
> *Fer.:* Bien lo hizo Iulio.

> *Fer.:* I killed one and wounded the other.   *Jul.:* And I—was I
> twiddling my thumbs?   *Fer.:* Valor like mine has never been seen in
> the world.   *Jul.:* And I—did I sit at home?   *Fer.:* Julio did all right.

The more and more conscious overplaying of the parts brings out the
ludic aspects of the situation; the act becomes a game. As Lope's sense of
fun is aroused, his playfulness adds its ironic edge and threatens to steal the
show.

Marfisa, already weeping, takes the game at face value. Hers are the
impartial tears of a susceptible theater-goer:

> *Fer.:* ¿Lloras por mí o por el muerto?
> *Mar.:* Lloro por entrambos.

> *Fer.:* Are you weeping for me or for the one who got killed?
> *Mar.:* I'm weeping for both of you.

Then she shifts from spectator to participant. As if on cue she and Fernando
collaborate in glossing over the unbeautiful situation with dramatic pathos.
They create a verbal context in which her diamond earrings and gold
trinkets, present as real properties, become purely poetic attributes destined
to adorn not verse, however, but acts and emotions. Made presentationally
metaphorical, diamonds underscore the value of words. With Fernando's
phrases still ringing in her ears, she removes her diamond earrings: "Quien
no ha de oír tus palabras, ¿para qué quiere galas en los oídos?" ("What good
are fine things in the ears, if one is not to hear your words?"). The transfer

of Marfisa's gold trinkets to Fernando is not merely ingeniously verbalized; it is dramatized as an allegory of binding love. The blunt terms of a commercial contract are the basis (p. 118) on which they construct and enact an elaborate conceit already noted in part: Fernando's soul is the bondsman, his memory the bond, the receipt is written in his heart, his eyes are the witnesses, his signature—at Marfisa's request—is converted into an embrace. The tears which Marfisa is copiously pouring down his cheeks brand him as her slave. Against the staged artifice of this leave-taking, the only farewell in *Belardo el furioso* was:

> *Bel.:* ¡Viva en mi alma tu nombre!
> *Cris.:* ¡Adiós, adiós!
>
> (Ac., V, 676b)

> *Bel.:* May your name live always in my soul!   *Cris.:* Farewell, farewell!

By the end of the same scene Marfisa has become thoroughly absorbed in it and all her misgivings are overcome. Though Fernando's performance has swept her off her feet, he, by contrast, has remained noticeably detached from the emotion he is depicting. When Marfisa steps out to fetch her jewels he exclaims: "Mas ¡cómo lo ha creído!" ("But how she swallowed it!") (p. 117). Such aloofness permits him to exploit the situation like an actor. The intimate character of his feelings remains unaffected by the external show and the histrionic self-stimulation.

It is only three months later that Marfisa learns the truth. Her shock and indignation enable her to resist the new deceiving act Fernando attempts to stage (IV, 8) but it is plain from his narrative in the fifth act that subsequently she falls back under his spell.[95] Indeed, even in this scene we can see the process beginning. The dialogue has a swifter movement and more dramatic tension than in Act I, scene 6. Each time Fernando and Julio begin to build upon each other's fabrications they are cut short by the angry rejoinders of Marfisa and Clara. When Marfisa's anger finally bursts its bonds, she turns the full force of her sarcasm on Fernando's theatrics. Men like you, she tells him, "assí tienen los fines, los sucessos, las desgracias, y el matar los hombres, como aquel por quien te fuiste a Seuilla, Dios le perdone. ¡Qué estocada le diste! Valiente eres de palabra" ("end up in this kind of fix, this kind of misfortune and killing of people, like the man on whose account you went off to Seville, God rest him! What a slash you gave him! You're brave in words") (p. 380). Brave in words, words without deeds, without feeling! The scathing denunciation and the sobs to which Marfisa is reduced disconcert

and all but disarm Fernando; even so, his histrionic impulse is not extinguished: "Marfisa, yo veo claramente la razón que tienes. Corrido, confuso y
arrepentido me pusiera a tus pies y te diera esta daga para que me passaras
mil vezes el pecho, *si no estuuiéramos en la calle*" ("Marfisa, I clearly see how
right you are. Put out with myself, beside myself, sorry for what I have
done, I would throw myself at your feet and give you this dagger to put
through my breast a thousand times, *if we were not in the street*") (p. 380;
emphasis mine). Lope's consummate irony makes Fernando even at this
stage concerned with audience reaction! Marfisa refuses his invitation to
come in, but the manner in which she does so, calling him "dulce enemigo
mío" ("sweet enemy of mine") and reminding him of their erstwhile
intimacy, shows that her wrath is spent and that she is on the verge of
succumbing once more.

It is noticeable that in this scene there is little rhetoric in Fernando's
diction and elocution; there is even less in the leave-taking scene of Act I.
His account there is straightforward, simple in construction, couched in
plain language. But he makes it detailed to the point of irrelevancy, cannily
aiming at an effect of unadorned truth—the truth of history, not fiction. It
is clearly not his words but his delivery and performance that are to achieve
the desired effect. The abundant detail suggests improvisation, stalling for
time. An incongruous reference to the prophetic dream (which clearly
haunts him) is a sign of padding. At the climax he forgets himself and
launches into a lengthy poetic simile while he thinks up what to say next;
it is ridiculously inappropriate to the "historical" context, as Marfisa drily
observes:

> *Fer.:* . . . Púseme en pie ligero, no de otra suerte que el toro que
> cerca de la vaca estaua echado, quando por la senda que diuide
> el prado siente latir los perros del caçador, que en confiança
> del plomo no le teme. "¿Qué quieren?", dixe.
> *Mar.:* Esso no dixera el toro.
>
> (p. 116)

> *Fer.:* I got up quickly, not otherwise than the bull who has been
> lying beside the cow when on the path that divides the meadow he
> hears the barking of the dogs of the huntsman, who, trusting in
> his bullets, has no fear of him. "What do you want?" I asked.
> *Mar.:* The bull wouldn't have said that.

The introductory litotes formula ("not otherwise than"), characteristic
of the lofty style to which such drawn-out epic-type similes belong,[96]

compounds the impropriety, but the direction of the simile is significantly self-aggrandizing. In equating himself with the bull and then proceeding to magnify his prowess in the fight, Fernando is showing that his histrionic bluster is, at bottom, a vicarious outlet for a need to assert his masculinity.

Fernando's interpolation of a poetic simile into what was to be the straightforward account of a calamity is, however mechanical, a sign of a poetic habit of mind. Noting "quán mal se juntan vna comparación y vn sobresalto" ("how badly a simile and an alarm go together"), Marfisa remarks: "Pero esso te ha quedado del curso de los versos" ("But that's left over from your practice of verse").[97] It is this second aspect of Fernando's personal style, with the prominence which it gives to the esthetic sensibility, that we will now examine in its various manifestations. For the other characters it is the key element in his make-up, as their responses show. Symptomatic are the reactions of first Marfisa, then Dorotea to early morning on the empty Prado: "¡Qué bien pintara esta mañana Fernando!" ("How well Fernando would have painted this morning!") (p. 289); "Por encarecimiento solía dezir Fernando que deuía de ser ésta tierra del Paraíso, donde fue la fábrica del primer hombre" ("Hyperbolically Fernando used to say that this must be a bit of Paradise, where the fashioning of the first man took place") (p. 292). Their eyes have grown accustomed to viewing the world through the imagined or remembered poetic vision of Fernando; they are no longer willing to forego such artistic heightening. The examination of Fernando's attitude and expression *qua* poet will once more necessarily involve us in their effects on the other characters, for art cannot, in Lope's view, be divorced from the human relationships of artists. Although Clara, as we have seen, punctures her mistress's "How well Fernando would have painted this morning!" with the sarcastic "He did a better job of tarnishing the gold off your jewels," her own vision has not always been so untouched by his, as her description of Dorotea's speech shows:

> *Cla.:* . . . El hablar, suaue, con vn poco de zaceo, con que guarnece de oro quanto dize, como si no bastara de las perlas de los dientes.
> *Mar.:* ¡Maldita seas, pintamentiras! ¡Qué pesadumbre me has dado! ¿Qué más hiziera don Fernando en sus versos?
> *Cla.:* Dellos lo he sabido más que de mis ojos.
>
> (p. 115)

> *Cla.:* Her speech is soft, with a slight lisp, so that she sets everything she says in gold as if the pearls of her teeth weren't enough. *Mar.:* Curse you, you fabricator of fibs! How bad you make me feel!

Don Fernando couldn't have done better in his verse.   *Cla.:* That's
where I learned it, more than from my own eyes.

For all Lope's reservations about Fernando, his protagonist is Lope's
portrait of the artist as a young man and not only of the young man as
artist. Lope intends us to see, beneath the exaggeration, a poetic imagination
in ferment playing over the varied panorama of man and nature. He knows
from experience that the artist's imagination, in surveying the world about
him, is already at work upon it, reshaping it, however embryonically, along
the lines of the "imitación" he intends to make. But if the artist's vision leaps
ahead, it is of course also retrospective, and draws a train of cultivated
reminiscences in its wake, guided and conditioned as it is, at times unbeknownst to itself, by earlier elaborations of similar scenes and themes.
All cultivation of sensibility involves such conditioning of vision: the
imagination of the cultivated amateur, while it may not leap into the
unknown like that of the artist, accompanies him and is oriented by him in
the backward glance. To see Whistler in a sunset or Hamlet in a person torn
between reflection and action only reveals how the artists in question have
permanently refined the vision of those coming after. Lope's age, less bent
on innovation and originality than the nineteenth and earlier twentieth
centuries, more readily recognized the place of tradition in poetic creation
when it approached the imitation of nature through the practice as well as
the precepts of earlier artists.

With Marfisa and Dorotea another factor comes into play. Their emotional attachment to Fernando, whose actual poetic gifts, as we have seen,
are not out of the ordinary, involves them, indiscriminately from the
esthetic standpoint, in his vision. Lope understood, better than most of his
contemporaries and long before the Romantics, that human emotion as
well as human art, feeling as well as form, colors the world one beholds, and
that women, in particular, are prone to adopt the angle of vision of the men
they love. To acquire so high an emotional stake in a given artistic vision
could prove rash as well as undiscriminating and might become dangerous
as well. But more disturbing in Lope's eyes was another failure of discrimination, one from which he was himself not always immune, as he well knew.
The process of imitation could degenerate into an automatic and unimaginative invoking of long established and, so to speak, prerecorded precedents
—anecdotal, verbal, imagistic, exemplary. The rhetorician and the histrion
in the poet could too easily take over from the creator. In addition, the poet
could carry his professional habits too ostentatiously and insistently into his
own life.

All these failings may be seen in Fernando. His need for Dorotea, as has been seen, is professional as well as personal. As his "muse," she becomes the object of a Petrarchistic cult and is placed at the apex of a poetic order which Fernando arbitrarily superimposes on the real order that Lope's experience has discerned in the world. It is on the poetic order willfully erected by Fernando that his *Literarisierung* of his life ultimately rests. Though Lope's presentation of this order is by no means hostile—it is marked rather by an indulgent irony and by highlights and adumbrations—he unmistakably suggests its inadequacy not only through the course events take and through intimations of the presence of a transcendent Christian framework, but through the alternative vision of a Neo-Platonic world harmony offered in the last act. The resultant contrasts, as we shall see in the final chapter, express Lope's insights into the role art may play in the totality of human experience.

Fernando's poetic order seeks both to activate in live contexts and to spin very fine, through wit, *aplicaciones*, and plays of fancy, the Petrarchistic conventions developed by more than two centuries of tradition, with their by now standardized sixteenth-century Platonic accretions. Fernando's vision and expressive powers do not extend far enough to move beyond these conventions. Instead, Fernando must simply abandon the whole enterprise in the end.

One sees the order in operation as soon as Fernando and Dorotea are presented together (I, 5). At the same time, Lope makes its artificiality plain by indicating through nonverbal "stage effects," the spontaneous and often rough impulses which it refines and overlays. Knocking strong enough to break in the door is heard and Fernando rushes forward, clumsily overturning and (Julio claims) breaking the guitar in his haste. He accompanies this brusque action with the smoothly exfoliating poetic prose quoted earlier which, through its periphrases for Celia, his mistress's messenger, invokes Dorotea hyperbolically.[98] While Dorotea's prompt stumble and swoon belong, as already observed, at a level of uncontrived natural expression, the swoon provokes in Fernando a new efflorescence of poetic diction coordinated with the preceding and the development reaches a climax when Dorotea comes to: "Ya boluió a concertarse quanto auías dexado descompuesto; ya el amor mata, ya el sol alumbra, ya la primauera se esmalta, y yo estoy viuo" ("Once again, all that you had put out of order has begun to function; once again love slays, once again the sun gives light, once again spring decks herself out and I am alive") (p. 95). Leo Spitzer has noted how Dorotea is here forthrightly made the supreme motive force on which the operation of Fernando's Petrarchan-Platonic universe depends.[99] His poetic fancy is placed at the service of this vision which conforms to the order of art and ignores the hierarchy of values implicit in the Christian order, perforce the true one. The implications of cosmic order and harmony in these words are quite without the spiritual overtones we shall discover in the far more impressive suggestions of the fifth act. They correspond, in effect, to a circumscribed secular outlook and underscore a limitation of vision in the protagonist.

While Fernando is obstinate in his truancy, it would be erroneous to view him as an anticipation of the Romantic visionary lost in a material world or of the alienated artist of the twentieth century. He does not lack awareness of the world as it is; in retreating from it, he deliberately suspends such awareness to make way for the constructions of his fantasy. When Dorotea recovers from her swoon and expounds her predicament, Fernando's response is to ask her first of all to respect the esthetic order of their relationship:

> ¿Pues para ocasión de tan poca importancia tanto sentimiento, Dorotea? Buelue a serenar los ojos, suspende las perlas, que ya parecían arracadas de sus niñas. No marchites las rosas, ni desfigures la harmonía de las faciones de tu rostro con descompuestos afectos; que te asseguro, por el amor que te he tenido, que me auías dexado sin alma. (p. 99)

> Why, for an occasion of such slight importance, such carrying-on, Dorotea! Make your eyes once again fair, hold back those pearls, which were already looking like earrings for the darlings of your eyes [*niña:* girl; pupil of the eye]. Do not crumple the roses, nor disfigure the harmony of the features of your countenance with disordered emotions. I assure you, by the love I have had for you, that you were taking my soul away.

Though this ironically offhand reply is dictated by pique, it nevertheless prefigures the coolness with which Fernando describes much later the moment of final liberation: "Vi las lagrimillas, ya no perlas, que pedían fauor a las pestañas para que no las dexassen caer al rostro, ya no jazmines, ya no cl;aueles" ("I saw the little teardrops, no longer pearls, asking the eyelashes please not to let them drop onto the countenance, no longer jasmine, no longer carnations") (p. 416). Despite the gulf that separates him from his creator, and the obstinacy with which he inverts the order of art and nature, Fernando can draw on Lope's full capacity to objectify the phenomenon of role-playing and, without emotion, drop an assiduously cultivated manner here in order to let reality reassert itself.

The Platonic-Petrarchan artistic order which places the lady at the center of the lover's idealized vision is the key to the solar imagery which Fernando persistently applies to Dorotea. Celia is the "aurora de mi sol" ("dawn to my sun") (p. 93) and presently, when Dorotea faints, Fernando builds on the image, imperturbably exploiting the possibilities of *Literarisierung* present: "Desvíale los cabellos, Celia; veámosle los ojos, pues se dexa mirar el sol por la nube de tan mortal desmayo" ("Push her hair aside, Celia; let's see her eyes, since the sun lets itself be looked at through the cloud of such a mortal swoon") (p. 94). As Fernando stands under Dorotea's balcony later (III, 7), he produces a new *aplicación* of the image: "¡Ay, sol mío! Sal a oírme, aunque me abrases, pues eres el mismo fuego" ("Ah, sun of mine. Come out and hear me, though you burn me up, since you are fire itself") (p. 273). A chiaroscuro effect presently evoked is turned by Fernando into a superfine presentational reinforcement of the sedulously cultivated world view:

> *Iul.:* Paréceme, señor, que han abierto vn poco de la ventana; sombra haze la luz. ¿Si está allí Dorotea?
> *Fer.:* Necio, ¿cómo puede ser? Que el sol no hiziera sombra en otra luz, sino mediante el cuerpo opuesto.
> *Iul.:* Dará en Celia, y ella formará la sombra.
>
> (p. 277) [100]

> *Jul.:* Sir, I think they've opened the window a little; the light is making a shadow. Can Dorotea be there? *Fer.:* Silly, how can that be? The sun wouldn't make a shadow against another light except if some body intervened. *Jul.:* It could be striking Celia and she creating the shadow.

Since Fernando turns Dorotea into the center and the informing principle of an esthetic world order, it is no surprise to find him treating his experience with her as if it were itself a poem, an attitude in which he is abetted by his kindred spirits, Ludovico and César. Ludovico urges poetic composition upon Fernando as an antidote to melancholy and even promises him subjects: "Yo os veré mañana y os traeré de mi corto ingenio vn sujeto que escriuir, que vestido de vuestros versos será admirable" ("I'll see you tomorrow and will bring you a subject of my own poor devising to write about, which will be admirable dressed up in your verse") (p. 255). The germ of ambiguity in Ludovico's words—"sujeto" is both subject and person and "vestido" will fit either—develops into a new confounding of the poetic and the real. Fernando protests that his mood is an obstacle to all but the most rudimentary creativity, and the unspecified subject Ludovico presumably provides the next day (which falls in the interim between Acts III and IV) evidently leaves him cold. But in the experience of reunion with Dorotea Fernando finds both release and subject. His friends surmise this even before the triumphant Fernando appears in Act IV, scene 4:

> *Cés.:* No vendrá esta mañana a nuestra junta don Fernando.
> *Lud.:* Deue de andar con los pensamientos de su poema, que desvela mucho la dificultad de vn principio.
> *Cés.:* No sea el poema Dorotea.
>
> (p. 317)

> *Cés.:* Don Fernando won't be coming to our meeting this morning.
> *Lud.:* He must be preoccupied thinking of his poem: the difficulty of making a start is very troublesome.   *Cés.:* I trust the poem is not Dorotea.

As already noted, his companions are aware of what has happened when Fernando appears in scene 4, since they have pierced Julio's enigmas in scene 3:

> *Cés.:* Yo asseguro que le han ocupado las musas.
> *Iul.:* No, sino la musa.
>
> (p. 337) [101]

> *Cés.:* I am sure that the muses have kept him busy.   *Jul.:* No, the muse rather.

When Fernando remarks: "Entrad conmigo en mi estudio; que no será mal principio de poema leeros mi sucesso" ("Come into my study with me: it won't be a bad beginning for a poem to read my experience to you") (p. 367), they recognize that the ambiguity they have all been nursing along is about to blossom forth. The solecism "leeros mi sucesso" ("read my experience to you")—instead of *contaros* ("relate to you")—suggests that the *historia* Fernando might have been expected to relate is already turning into a *poema*. As already seen, the "reading" starts off with a triumphant exordium. The rest of the so-called poem is left to our imagination, but by the time Fernando tells his friends at the end of scene 4, "Sentaos, y sabréis quán secretos caminos tiene la fortuna, y quánta obligación tengo de escriuir su alabança" ("Sit down and you will see how secret are the ways of fortune and what an obligation I have to write in her praise") (p. 370), it is clear that this poem will give rise to still another, that Fernando perceives in his experience the makings of a major rhetorical effort: a poem in praise of fortune.[102]

This interlacing of live poetry—Dorotea as a poem—with lifeless—the mock profession of *culterano* faith or the burlesque commentary—occurs in all three scenes of the literary academy and does not appear coincidental. It is a way of binding the purely literary discussions to the fictional fabric of the *acción en prosa* and of juxtaposing two contrasting deviations that upset an ideal equipoise of art and nature, one a distortion of the literary medium, the other a warping of *Erlebnis* itself.

Fernando's manner of giving a literary turn to experience is not always as theatrical as in the triumph scene. It is also characteristic of him to make verbal adornment a shield against experience. In their escapist function words become an anesthetic and talking an intoxicant: they deaden sensibilities in the face of an unacceptable reality.

A characteristic instance occurs in that part of the conversation between Fernando, Julio, and Ludovico in Act III, scene 4, which follows Ludovico's intimation regarding Dorotea's new lover. Though Ludovico is intentionally vague—"No sé qué dizen de vn indiano" ("There's been talk of an *indiano*") (p. 239)—Fernando recoils as if stung: "Acabóse. ¿Para qué pintó la antigüedad al amor con vn pez en la mano, y en la otra flores?" ("Stop right there. Why did antiquity paint love with a fish in one hand and flowers in the other?"). Summoning both pictorial and verbal memory, he seizes the conversational initiative, employing by way of *aplicación* an emblem he has seen in Alciatus. His question puts an abrupt end to Ludovico's account and the *indiano* is scarcely mentioned again in all the ensuing talk. (Only once, out of Fernando's hearing, do Ludovico and Julio bring him up.) Less spontaneous than it appears, Fernando's question is, in effect, a form of rhetorical *aversio*.[103] It adds to the characteristic avoiding (averting) of a particular subject a decidedly negative emotional charge (aversion). As an adept conversational tactician, Fernando not only leads away but leads into a new theme, making his *aversio*, in effect, a *transitio* by setting it up as an enigma and then improving on the answer. Equally conversant with Alciatus, Ludovico takes the cue (p. 240): love is so depicted, he answers, "porque es igual señor de mar y tierra" ("because he is joint master of sea and land").

> *Fer.:* Mejor fuera pintarle con una barra de oro.
> *Lud.:* ¡O gran virtud la del oro!
>
> *Fer.:* It would have been better to paint him with a bar of gold.
> *Lud.:* Oh the great power that gold has!

Ludovico, falling into line, is here announcing a topic; a set of variations on the theme of *interés* ensues: drinkable gold, the genealogy of gold—

pillagings of Leo Suabius and Levinus Lemnius, as Edwin Morby has demonstrated.[104] Ludovico furnishes the learned data, Fernando supplies a running counterpoint of *aplicaciones* to himself and Dorotea, while Julio, clearly conversant also with Ludovico's erudite sources, contributes to both sides of the conversation. The persistent trend of Fernando's *aplicaciones* leads his interlocutors to their aside on the obsessive character of his jealousy. Ludovico's points on metals remind Julio of others and his mind runs on to other parts of the book. Even though Lope must have had Lemnius and Suabius open before him as he wrote this part of the dialogue, he is skillful in adapting the data they furnish to the mental processes of his characters; it is not mechanically relayed but shaped to suit the dovetailing character of this collaborative conversation and thus its burden is lightened.

But Fernando becomes restive:

> *Fer.:* ¡Ay de mí! Mal me fue ausente, peor presente. No durará
> mucho mi vida.
> *Lud.:* ¿Y en qué la passáis después que venistes?

> (p. 242)

> *Fer.:* Woe is me! I had a bad time while absent, a worse one present.
> My life hasn't long to run.   *Lud.:* And how have you been spending
> it since you returned?

Ludovico's underplayed response, the casualness of his zeugma ("¿Y en qué la passáis . . .?"), turns the conversation from the *recherché* to the routine, a turn resisted by Fernando, who insists on dignifying his moping days by describing them in elevated poetic prose, as we shall see presently. Ludovico's spontaneous comment "¡Qué necia jornada!" ("What a stupid way to spend the day!") terminates the collaborative phase of the conversation. The characters pull against each other and tension rises. The trend of the talk is argumentative, with Fernando holding out against Julio and Ludovico in his diagnosis of his feelings, as described earlier. Yet, as the conversation moves through different phases—collaborative adornment, digressions, verse interludes, argumentation—it clearly carries Fernando to a state of mind distinct from that which prompted the words "Acabóse" ("Stop right there"). After Ludovico's departure, he can set off with Julio to catch a glimpse of Dorotea in full awareness that he may run up against Don Bela. A deluge of words has unblocked the way to action; Fernando has talked his way around his obsession. But if talking has proved therapeutic (as writing did to Lope), in Fernando's case this is because it has enabled him to build up a view of his situation as a product of forces vaster than himself which have occupied men's pens and eluded their control from antiquity onward—*interés*, warring emotions, fortune, the mirthful gods themselves. Rather than with a sense of his own smallness, such as the reader derives, Fernando emerges with an expanded ego, feeling no more obliged than before to assume responsibility for his own predicament. His mood shifts, his spirits revive, and Julio is even able to draw a laugh out of him as they start out for Dorotea's house.

In *Belardo el furioso*, it will be recalled, Belardo crosses the threshold of madness at precisely the juncture at which Fernando exclaims "Acabóse": namely, on being informed, after a three month's absence, of the definitive triumph of his rival. Both try to escape from the harsh fact but both end up freed for action. Shielded by madness, Belardo manages his one assault on Nemoroso, while the impulsive visit to Dorotea which follows Fernando's verbal rampage leads to his first and only skirmish with Don Bela. Though the mechanism of liberation has shifted from madness to literary auto-intoxication, one form of self-aggrandizement appears as unhealthy an evasion of reality as the other—the one abnormal, the other compulsive. If the new emphasis, however overstated, reveals a heightened concern with the artist in his relation to tradition and reality, it also leaves intact the traces of Lope's real sense of impotence in the face of a mighty rival.

Not only does Fernando reveal the mentality of a *poeta rhetor* in his manner of drawing on his literary culture and in his way of taking experience. His speech shows the professional practice of a lyricist in the choice of ornamental materials, the development of images and figures, the rhythmic patterns into which it sometimes falls. At times Fernando makes prose sing; at times, also, as already seen, his imagination works pictorially, like his creator's, with plastic and pictorial images reinforcing the poetic. Constantly Fernando feels obliged to display his professionalism by running through a series of poetic possibilities without pausing to develop any particular one, as if he were merely examining his *copiae rerum et verborum*—his store of subject matter and of words—his equivalents to Don Bela's riches.

Certain of these signs of a poet's professionalism are also visible in Ludovico, Fernando's close companion, and they sometimes produce a kind of counterpoint between them. The lyrical prose style also rubs off on Dorotea and even on Marfisa. Some indication of what prose effects were felt to be peculiarly poetic or lyrical is a necessary basis for the analysis of these professional tendencies, which stand out amidst the prevalent rhetorical flavor of the characters' noncolloquial speech. One might sum them all up by saying that in any age the rhetorician gives way to the poet when he ceases to attune his discourse to an audience with a view to making a display before it or working a particular effect upon it and pursues instead the pleasure of his own inner ear or the delight of the mind's eye. He loses himself in the expression of private feelings or in personal esthetic fruition, only as an afterthought seeking communication with a responsive auditor.[105]

Lope and his more perceptive contemporaries made a number of fine distinctions, more of degree than of kind, between rhetorical and poetic practice. Perhaps the most significant is one of tone, poetry being characterized by *dulzura*—sweetness or softness. They were also aware of divergences in regard to epithet, metaphor, rhythm, and particular vehicles of imagery. I shall briefly point out the nature of these differences (except those affecting imagery, which will be treated later),[106] then show their effects in the dialogue and note Lope's skill in using the characters' deployment of the lyrical style to illustrate aspects of feeling and attitude.

1. "*Dulzura*" *of tone*.   While Lope does not define it precisely, *dulzura* of tone always carries a suggestion of musicality with him, as in the opening words of the Introduction ("Al teatro") to *La Dorotea:* "Como nuestra alma en el canto y música con tan suaue afecto se deleita ... inuentaron los antiguos poetas el modo de los metros y los pies para los números, a efeto de que con más dulçura pudiessen inclinar a la virtud y buenas costumbres los ánimos de los hombres" ("As our soul takes such delight in song and music ... the ancient poets invented the mode of meters and feet for measures, to the end that they might with greater sweetness incline men's spirits to virtue and good morals") (p. 50).[107] *Dulzura* is an inherent quality of lyrical verse for Lope: "Mi mejor Musa [*scil.*, Marta de Nevares] ... viene a influirme no sé si dulçura para los versos o estilo para la prosa" ("My best muse ... is coming to instill in me sweetness for verse or style for prose, I'm not sure which"),[108] although he also observes: "No esté tan enervada la dulzura que carezca de ornamento, ni él tan frío, que no tenga la dulzura que le compete" ("Let the sweetness not be so flat as to lack decoration, nor the latter so cold that it doesn't have the sweetness it should") (*OS*, IV, 467). A failure of *dulzura* results in *dureza* (harshness), an effect for which Lope reproaches Góngora's imitators (*OS*, IV, 469), whereas when Góngora wrote in "aquel estilo puro ... todos aprendimos erudición y dulzura, dos partes de que debe de constar este arte" ("that pure style ... we all learned erudition and sweetness from him, two parts that this art ought to consist of") (*OS*, IV, 465). In stressing *dulzura* Lope is of course following tradition. Herrera, quoting Horace's "Non satis est pulchra esse poemata, dulcia sunto" ("It is not enough for poems to be beautiful, they should be sweet") (*Ars poetica*, 99), specifies that "las palabras suaves, llenas de afeto, traen

consigo la dulçura" ("words that are smooth and full of feeling produce sweetness").[109] Juan de Robles, in speaking of *dulzura*, evidently has the poetic prose of the pastoral in mind:

> La dulzura tiene sentencias de fábulas poéticas o de historias semejantes a ellas, y las descripciones de cosas que alegran los sentidos, como de prados, arboledas, fuentes, edificios, convites y sucesos felices amorosos . . . La dicción . . . semejante a la poética, con epítetos de ornamento.[110]

> Sweetness has sayings drawn from poetic fables or from stories similar to the latter, and descriptions of things that bring pleasure to the senses, like meadows, lanes, fountains, buildings, banquets, and happy amorous happenings . . . The diction . . . similar to the poetic, with adorning epithets.

Lope would certainly have subscribed to these words, but it should be noted that, as regards spoken discourse, he clearly warns against *dulzura*, making it equivalent to excessive refinement: "Haced, hijos, elección de un moderado hablar, que ni bien seáis notados de la dulzura del estilo, ni de la rusticidad del lenguaje" ("Settle for a moderate way of speaking, my sons, that you may neither be criticized for the sweetness of your style nor for the rusticity of your language").[111]

2. *Epithets.* The poet was to use epithets abundantly, the rhetorician sparingly, the latter preferably to praise or censure and never pleonastically. Like Robles, Lope views abundant use of adjectives as a hallmark of the poetic prose of the pastoral. After quoting Sannazaro's opening in defense of his own *Arcadia*, Lope observes:

> Aquí pone el Sanazaro altos y espaciosos árboles, hórridos montes, cultivadas plantas, doctas manos y adornados jardines. De manera que casi hay tantos epíthetos como palabras; porque la *amplificación* es la más gallarda figura en la Rhetórica, y que más majestad causa a la oración suelta; ¿y los epíthetos, por qué han de ser *Pleonasmos*?   (*OS*, IV, 166)

> Here Sannazaro has tall and wide-spreading trees, rough mountains, cultivated plants, skilled hands, and stately gardens. There are thus almost as many epithets as words, for *amplification* is the most impressive figure in rhetoric, the one which lends most majesty to ordinary prose. And why must epithets be considered pleonastic?

Herrera declares (after Quintilian, VIII, 6, 40):

> [For poets] it is enough for [epithets] to be appropriate to the word
> to which they're affixed, and thus no one ever condemned *wet wine*
> or *white teeth* in them; but in the public speaker if they create no
> effect they are superfluous, because no one is so ignorant as not to
> know that *snow* is *white*, the *sun golden*, the *moon silver*, and that these
> epithets are excessive, but in poetry they have no small charm.[112]

Juan de Robles observes:

> Epithets and appendages are used . . . for praise or condemnation;
> and although everyone follows Aristotle's rule in his *Poetics* that they
> should be the poet's dish and the public speaker's sauce, I . . . say . . .
> that they should be as much the dish of the one as of the other,
> with only this difference: that the speaker's table should be that of a
> moderate man and that nothing be served at it beyond the plates
> required by and suited to the dignity of his station; and that the
> poet's should be that of a rich and luxury-loving man on which,
> beside these plates, dishes are set for taste and display. Accordingly,
> in prose, epithets are to be used not superfluously but in such a way
> that they really accomplish something and in poetry those may be
> used that serve only for ornamentation, as the poet chooses.[113]

3. *Metaphor.* For the poet the function of metaphor is principally
decorative, and a metaphor may be spun out at length, as in the epic simile.
The rhetorician requires the metaphor to be brief, expeditious, and more
easily intelligible (that is, less far-fetched). Herrera writes (after Quintilian,
VIII, 6, 17): "Not all the metaphors admitted by poets have a place in prose.
And many of those that belong in ordinary prose do not fit in verse, because
poets have made use of them for pleasure and variety; and to keep away from
everyday speech, and forced by the requirements of verse . . ."[114] Of long,
descriptive similes in verse, Carballo notes: "This figure, very particularly,
gives ornamentation great weight."[115] On the same subject, Cipriano
Suárez states:

> Videndum est, ne longe simile sit ductum: Syrtim patrimonii,
> scopulum libentius dixerim: Charibdim bonorum, voraginem
> potius . . . Diligenter etiam cauendum est ne omnia quae poetis
> permissa sunt convenire orationi putemus: nec enim pastorem
> populi, auctore Homero dixerim, nec volucres pennis remigare, licet

Verg. in apibus, si Daedale speciosissime sit usus. Modus autem nullus est florentior in singulis verbis.[116]

One should avoid using far-fetched similes: for "the patrimony of Syrtis," I should prefer to say "rock"; for "the property of Charybdis," "whirlpool" rather . . . We should carefully avoid assuming that everything allowed to poets is suitable to a discourse: for neither would I say "shepherd of the people" on Homer's authority, nor "flying things rowing with wings" on Virgil's about bees, even if it is very brilliant applied to Daedalus. For there is no more vigorous usage with single words.

4. *Rhythm.* In *La Dorotea* Lope points out through Ludovico, as if to alert the reader, that the proscription of metrical lines in prose is hard for poets to observe:

> La causa de que los poetas escriuiendo prosa mezclen en ella versos medidos, es el vso de escriuirlos; de que se enfadan los dos filósofos [Aristotle, Cicero] y con mucha razón. Pero el que fuere poeta natural no podrá remediar este defeto, si no es con mucho cuidado.
>
> (p. 350)[117]

The reason why poets writing prose intermingle metrical lines in it is the habit of writing them, something which greatly exercises the two philosophers [Aristotle, Cicero], and understandably so. But anyone who is a born poet will not be able to correct this defect unless he takes great pains.

We may examine now the implications of a number of typical passages characterized by the presence of one or more of these features, beginning with an exchange between Fernando and Ludovico in which the procedure in all of them is made explicit:

> *Lud.:* . . . Conualeció Dorotea, huuo muletilla, tocado baxo, punto de toca los primeros días, y después algo del cabello descubierto, como que era descuido. Desta transformación resultó vn ábito azul y blanco. Aquí yo la vi vn día . . . No querría renouaros las llagas.
>
> *Fer.:* ¿No sabéis que se están frescas?
>
> *Lud.:* Más hermosa muger no la pintó el Ticiano, aunque entre Rosa Solimana, la fauorecida del Turco.
>
> *Fer.:* ¿No pudiérades dezir Sophonisba, Atalanta o Cleopatra?
>
> *Lud.:* Essas no las pintó el Ticiano.
>
> *Fer.:* Bien dezís, que este retrato le auemos todos visto.

Lud.: Suelen traer las labradoras en las texidas encellas los naterones cándidos, y caerse algunas hojas de rosa encima, de los ramilletes que también lleuan; assí auéis de imaginar en su rostro sobre la nieue legítima la color bastarda.

Fer.: Parece que escriuís versos, cuya costumbre os presta el mismo estilo para la prossa, o queréis boluerme loco.

Lud.: No vais aprisa al gusto; que presto le perderéis con lo que se sigue.

(p. 238)

Lud.: Dorotea convalesced, there was a bit of a crutch, a low headdress, a wimple that encircled the whole face the first days and after that, the hair showing a bit, as if unintentionally. The result of this transformation was a blue and white habit. I saw her here one day . . . I would not wish to reopen your wounds. *Fer.:* Don't you know they're still fresh? *Lud.:* No more beautiful woman was ever painted by Titian, and that includes Rosa Solimana, the Turk's favorite. *Fer.:* Couldn't you have said Sophonisba, Atalanta, or Cleopatra? *Lud.:* They were not painted by Titian. *Fer.:* Touché— we've all seen this portrait of his. *Lud.:* Peasant women are wont to carry in wattle baskets pure white curds and some rose petals to drop on them from the nosegays which they also carry. So you must imagine in her face the bastard color upon the legitimate snow.

Fer.: You seem to write verse, which practice lends you the same style for prose, or else you're trying to drive me mad. *Lud.:* Don't be too quick with your enjoyment; you'll soon lose it with what follows.

The vivid visual character of Ludovico's description shows that he is embellishing his account with *enargeias* (*evidentiae*), aiming in this way to stir his interlocutor by making him feel that the scene described is actually being exhibited before his eyes. Whoever can manage this figure "erit in affectibus potentissimus" ("will powerfully affect the emotions") observes Cipriano Suárez.[118] Ludovico knows that his powers of depiction will affect strongly an auditor as esthetically oriented and as impressionable as Fernando. His *correctio*, "I would not wish to reopen your wounds," shows him already anticipating effects; he displays the added esthetic refinement of refracting the visual impressions at times through a pictorial or a poetic medium. The delicate touches of detail, the suggestions of color and design in "a blue and white habit," lead naturally to analogy with a particular painter and a particular canvas. In the new *enargeia* that follows, playing as he is on the imagination of a poet, he uses metaphor as arrestingly as possible,

beginning with the vehicle of the comparison—"Suelen traer las labradoras'
("Peasant women are wont to carry")—and protracting it before establishing
contact with an immediate reality. The peculiarly poetic character of the
metaphor is evident in its deliberateness, its redundant epithets ("texidas
encellas," "naterones cándidos"), the *dulzura* produced by both content and
undulating rhythm.

As foreseen by Ludovico, Fernando reacts, strongly; Ludovico must
restrain him: "No vais aprisa al gusto" ("Don't be too quick with your
enjoyment"). Earlier in his account of Dorotea's convalescence, Ludovico
had already been playing on Fernando's esthetic sensibility with other
carefully wrought and uncommon poetic-visual metaphors: "Habló
poco ... no sin alguna lágrima, que por más que le escondía no podía
negármela; porque le sucedía como al sol quando llueue con él, que como
no se ve la nube, se ven el sol y el agua" ("She spoke little . . . not without a
tear or two, which for all her efforts to hide them, she couldn't keep back
from me; because it happened with her as with the sun when it rains with
the sun out, that as the cloud is not seen, the sun and the water are")
(p. 237).[119]

When Ludovico unravels the present climactic metaphorical *enargeia*,
Fernando clearly recognizes that his friend is reworking an image of long
standing in the European lyric. His response both underscores the poetic
cast of Ludovico's words and shows their double impact, affective and
esthetic. Ludovico, is, in effect, speaking the poetic prose of the pastoral, as
comparison with Lope's own *Arcadia* shows: "Las mexillas se rosaban, como
quando sobre pura leche cayeron claveles deshojados" ("Her cheeks flushed,
as when petals from carnations have fallen on pure white milk"), Lope
says there of the anger of a shepherdess (*OS*, VI, 32). In *La Arcadia* the
dulzura of this simile drains anger of all but an esthetic force, softening harsh
emotion in a characteristically pastoral manner. Lope is cultivating there a
particular style, "aquella prosa ... poética, que a diferencia de la historial
guarda su estilo" ("that poetic prose . . . which in contrast to the historical,
observes a certain style") (*OS*, IV, 165). In the pastoral context such a simile,
being more or less routine, attracts no particular attention and elicits no
special response; in fact it is not given to a character, it is Lope's, as narrator.
Having placed Fernando, on the other hand, in a "historial" world, Lope
makes him rise to the stimulus of such poetic diction, the more so because
the image in this case may be presumed to stir traditional associations in
him, as it did in Lope, with whom it was a favorite.[120]

Until his final experience of Dorotea's "lagrimillas, ya no perlas" ("little
teardrops, no longer pearls"), Fernando *qua* poet persistently clings to the

cult of his mistress's beauty in the face of emotions which might be expected to undermine it:

> Nunca la podré aborrecer tanto que dessee verla fea: tan dulce me será siempre la memoria de su hermosura. Ni sufrirá mi alma que el tiempo saque della vna Dorotea tan hermosa y me la ponga tan fea, ni me persuado que los años se atreuan a desluzir tanto milagro de la naturaleza.   (p. 237)

> Never will I be able to abhor her so completely that I desire to see her ugly, so sweet will the memory of her beauty be to me always. Nor will my soul suffer time to extract from her a Dorotea so beautiful and make her so ugly in my eyes, nor can I imagine that the years would dare to tarnish such a great miracle of nature.

The suggestion in these lines of a gap developing between experience and its poetic expression recalls the touches of pastoral submissiveness which alternate with the caustic tones of the ballads written to Elena in exile:

> que mientras fueres hermosa
> no dejaré de quererte,
> y seráslo siempre, ingrata,
> porque pene eternamente.

> for so long as you are beautiful, I shall not cease to love you and you will be so ever, ungrateful one, so that I may suffer for ever.

Underlying the characteristic esthetic emphasis of Fernando's lines one notes, in effect, lip-service to a pastoral nobility of sentiment such as we find expressed, for example, by the Sireno of Montemayor's La Diana: "Puesto caso que ya nuestros amores sean passados, las reliquias que en el alma me an quedado, bastan para dessearte yo todo el contentamiento possible" ("Even though our love is over, enough traces of it have remained in my soul to make me wish you all the happiness possible").[121] Fernando's attitude finds a more markedly lyric expression, coming to the verge of metrical regularity. However, the dialogue runs on and the verse fails to crystallize. Poetic prose here is a passing accommodation of the lyric impulse to the exigencies of conversational intercourse. There is clearly some declamatory tendency and the antithetical structure, marked by contrasts like *fea-hermosa* (ugly-beautiful), *nunca-siempre* (never-always), is as rhetorical as it is poetic. But the hypersensitive anticipation of *dulzura* one day to be savored nostalgically, the retreat into fantasies of beauty beyond the reach of time, makes the lyric tone dominant. Sireno's expression seems matter-of-fact by comparison.

Elsewhere the lyric impulse casts up true metrical lines. In response to Ludovico's query as to how he has spent his days since his return to Madrid, Fernando slips into a Petrarchan self-depiction and metrical lines inevitably follow. "Y si de cansado de la batalla de mis pensamientos, como el Petrarca dixo, me duermo vn poco, sueño tan prodigiosas inuenciones de sombras, que me valiera más estar despierto" ("And if, worn out by the battle of my thoughts, as Petrarch said, I sleep a little, I dream such astounding creations of the shadows that I would do better to stay awake").[122] Metrical structure appears in the parenthetical "como el Petrarca dixo," a heptasyllable, is confirmed in two further assonating heptasyllables—"sueño tan prodigiosas inuenciones de sombras"—and finally produces a full hendecasyllable. The placing of *más* in the last clause after, rather than before, "me valiera" (where its effect would have been simply colloquial) confirms the poetic cast of the diction.

Fernando continues: "Al alba salgo al Prado, o me voy al río, donde sentado en su orilla estoy mirando el agua, dándole imaginaciones que lleue para que nunca bueluan" ("At dawn I go out onto the Prado or to the river, where, sitting on its banks, I gaze at the water, offering it fancies to carry off, that they may never return"). Several segments of this already noted vision of the self as Narcissus are metrically heptasyllabic: "Al alba salgo al Prado," "sentado en su orilla," "estoy mirando el agua." Its poetic character is underscored by the forlorn conclusion, "para que nunca bueluan," contextually superfluous but answering the need of the poet's ear for a final heptasyllabic cadence.

To be noted finally is Fernando's employment of regular poetic patterns, metrical, assonantal, and correlative, in the high stylization of one of his grand scenes: the meeting with Dorotea preceding the quarrel. In the already quoted greeting to Celia as "el arco embaxador de los dioses, la aurora de mi sol, la primauera de mis años y el ruiseñor del día, a cuya dulce voz despiertan las flores, y como si tuuiessen ojos abren las hojas" ("the rainbow that is emissary to the gods, the dawn to my sun, the springtime of my years, and the nightingale of daytime, at whose sweet voice the flowers awaken and, as if they had eyes, open their petals") (p. 93), assonance reinforces the heptasyllabic-hendecasyllabic cadence of the beginning (*embaxador*, at the caesura, *dioses, sol*) and recurs in the heptasyllabic "a cuya dulce voz." "Y el ruiseñor del día" is also heptasyllabic. Poetic prose—the adjective *dulce* specifies its tone—supplements theatrical behavior here and though the metricality fades out at the end one can literally see the imagery exfoliating as Fernando lets his fancy soar.[123]

Fernando keeps his earlier quoted response to Dorotea's subsequent swoon correlated with this greeting and the theatrical activation of metaphorical commonplaces continues: "¡A, mi señora! ¡A, mi Dorotea! ¡A, vltima esperança mía! Amor, tus flechas se quiebran; sol, tu luz se eclipsa; primauera, tus flores se marchitan; a escuras queda el mundo" ("Alas, my lady! Alas, my Dorotea! Alas, last hope of mine! Love, your arrows are broken; sun, your light is eclipsed; spring, your flowers fade; the world is thrown into darkness") (p. 94). Through the lengthening phrasing of the three rhetorical apostrophes to his mistress, he leads to the more metrically cadenced *dulzura* of the following three to love, sun, and spring. The heptasyllabic "a escuras queda el mundo" again supplies a final falling cadence (one rhetorically anticlimactical, to be sure, and at once mocked by Julio), for the hendecasyllabic "primauera, tus flores se marchitan."

Perhaps the most subtle effect attained with poetic prose in *La Dorotea* is one found later in the same scene as Dorotea concludes her highly rhetorical appeal to Fernando. She ends by reporting her mother's reproach: "que con versos me engañas, y con tu voz, como sirena, me lleuas dulcemente al mar de la vejez, donde los desengaños me siruan de túmulo y el arrepentimiento de castigo" ("that you are misleading me with verse and with your voice, like a siren, sweetly taking me toward the sea of old age, where disillusionment will serve as my tomb and repentance as my punishment") (p. 99). Where but from Fernando has Dorotea acquired this way of slipping insinuatingly into meter? After the brief parenthesis of "como sirena" come three heptasyllables, then "me siruan de túmulo," which falls a syllable short, then a perfectly turned hendecasyllable to bring the series to a poetically true close. In her very style of expression, quite aside from the metaphorical resort to a "fábula poética" ("poetic myth"), Dorotea demonstrates the spell of which she is speaking and reveals a sensibility permeated with poetic *dulzura*. ("Dulcemente" is the single qualifying word she uses.) The familiar motif of the weakness of the Elena-figure for her lover's verse has in no other version the subtlety it attains here. For Dorotea, Fernando's verse is not merely a tribute, it is an intoxicant. Though no "poeta natural," she has absorbed her lover's capacity for poetic expression in prose as well as in the verse she writes.

At certain points in *La Dorotea* the poetic turn of the prose results from supersaturation with Petrarchistic commonplaces of diction, style, and imagery. Lope shows us speakers who, by *tours de force* of ingenuity and intensification, are still seeking to inject novelty into this outworn stuff of poetic adornment, be it of a sumptuary character (jewels, precious materials) or "natural" (flora, fauna, landscape), atmospheric, or celestial. As in other instances, Lope depicts practices at which he looks askance, yet for which he has a certain weakness.

Behind these sequences are critical implications reminiscent of the views of preceptists like Ximénez Patón and satirists like Quevedo. Góngora himself, in whose work such materials reach their highest degree of elaboration, sometimes—as in "Fábula de Píramo y Tisbe"—makes them the butt of his mockery. For Ximénez Patón the overuse and misappropriation of such materials in prose or verse is a particular failing of young writers or speakers, a view evidently pertinent to the situation we find in *La Dorotea*: "Es proprio este vicio [cacozelia] de ingenios loçanos de moços, assí poetas como predicadores, a quien enseña, y desengaña el tiempo y esperiencia" ("This vice [studied affectation] is characteristic of the exuberant minds of young men, poets as well as preachers, whom time and experience teach better and disabuse"). He observes: "Desto pecan algunos sonetos cargados de argentería, perlas, rubíes, diamantes, y otros vocablos tales que ai soneto que vale un infinito tesoro. Otros cargados de flores, otros de otras viçarrías . . ." ("Sinning in this are some sonnets laden with silver embroidery, pearls, rubies, diamonds, and words such that there are sonnets worth an infinite treasure. Others laden with flowers, others with other rich materials . . .").[124] Quevedo's ridicule of *cacozelia*—studied affectation—is part of a broader assault on Góngora and his followers. In the "Aguja de navegar cultos" Quevedo sarcastically gives samples of the ready-made verbal wares of the "ropería de los soles" ("ready-made clothing store of the suns")—"nácares y ostras, leche y grana" ("mother-of-pearl and oyster shells, milk and fine scarlet cloth"), and so forth—and of the "platería de los cultos . . . aunque los poetas hortelanos todo esto lo hacen de verduras" ("silversmith's shop for *cultos* . . . although truck garden poets do all this with green vegetables").[125]

Such ridicule reveals the impatience of the discriminating spirits of the age with a literary idiom that had lost its expressiveness through over-inflation and overuse. Typical of further criticisms one might cite is the summons of Bartolomé Leonardo de Argensola to moderation in the use of sumptuary imagery:

¿Será bien que sin forma y sin estilo
luzgan en la hermosura los despojos
espléndidos del Ganges y del Nilo?
¿Zafiros o esmeraldas son los ojos,

i diamante la tez, perlas los dientes,
i encendidos rubies los labios rojos?

Can it be right for the spoils of the Ganges and the Nile to be
displayed without form or style on a beauty? Are the eyes sapphires
or emeralds, the skin of diamond, the teeth pearls, and the red lips
glowing rubies?

Moderation in floral adornment is also recommended:

La verdad se lamenta de otra lista
de antiguos i modernos, que la exorna,
en este gran precepto mal prevista,
que en sus purezas de vn jardín trastorna
lleno el canasto, i con las mismas flores
la encubre cuando piensa que la adorna.[126]

Truth deplores another list of ancients and moderns that, unobservant
of this great precept, deck it out, that upon its purity pour out a
brimming garden basket and smother it in the very flowers with
which they think they are decorating it.

Lope, too, is aware that "en aquel libro [his *Arcadia*] y en éste [his *Rimas*
of 1602] . . . y en cuantos tiene el mundo de poesía, cansa a muchos que
se pinte una mujer con oro, perlas y corales" ("in that book [his *Arcadia*]
and in this [his *Rimas* of 1602] . . . and in as many as the world of poetry
holds, it irritates many that a woman should be painted with gold, pearls,
and corals").[127] Nevertheless, he cites innumerable Latin precedents in
self-justification, clearly feeling such diction to be the very marrow of
elevated poetic style.

Forman los versos altamente raros,
Fernando, las hipérboles mayores,
flores, oro, cristal, mármoles paros,

Lofty and rare lines, Fernando, are formed of the principal hyperboles:
flowers, gold, crystal, Parian marbles,

he writes in defense of poetry against the charge of being "alchemistic."[128]
His own response to the need for revitalizing poetic diction is to fall back on
his innate capacity for sensory freshness and affective vigor, bringing it to
bear on the traditional materials. But Fernando, as we know, lacks Lope's
enlivening touch; Lope has endowed him with more virtuosity than genuine

creative power. Particularly when it comes to spoken discourse, his prod-
igality with his "alchemistic" repertoire inspires ironic reservations in his
creator. Even though this repertoire largely coincides with Lope's, it is the
facile professionalism, the endless ingeniousness, the abundance of "hipérboles
mayores" that stand out, clearly setting Fernando apart among the characters
of the *acción en prosa*, with only the occasional exception of Ludovico.

Characteristic are the variations Fernando spins about the inverted or
intertwined roles of art and nature within the poetic order he centers on
Dorotea. Nature may appear as artifex—as, in effect, an alchemist or a
painter whose art has outdone itself in producing Dorotea. Or Dorotea
may be equated with the supreme products of human art. All these figures
have a "technical" flavor, carrying in their tenor suggestions of "professional" artistic processes.

Nature, for example, does the poet's work for him, producing Dorotea
by a process of refinement analogous to the poet's art and making her a
distillation, pharmacopoeial as well as alchemistic, of everything exquisite:

> *Fer.:* ... Parece que la naturaleza distiló todas las flores, todas las
> yeruas aromáticas, todos los rubíes, corales, perlas, jacintos y
> diamantes para confacionar esta bebida de los ojos y este veneno
> de los oídos.
> *Iul.:* Deuía de ser entonces boticaria la naturaleza. No te faltó sino
> mezclar aí essos simples con el tártaro.
>
> (p. 300)

> *Fer.:* Nature seems to have distilled all flowers, all aromatic herbs,
> all rubies, corals, pearls, jacinths, and diamonds to prepare this
> potion for the eyes and this poison for the ears. *Jul.:* Nature must
> have been a pharmacist at that point. The only thing you didn't do
> was mix those simples with tartar.

Julio's deflationary manner, that of a stage lackey, reduces poetic alchemy to
the filling out of a druggist's prosaic prescription.[129] Comparison of this
passage with an antecedent in *La Arcadia* underscores the inflation of hyperbole in Fernando's figure, making the antecedent seem almost pedestrian.
Amphryso catches sight of Belisarda:

> Fue su vista la medicina más famosa y la epíthima más saludable,
> porque fue una bebida compuesta de oro, esmeraldas, corales y
> perlas, y para el corazón, que toda esta confección hacían sus cabellos,
> ojos, labios y hermosos dientes.[130]

The sight of her was the most excellent medicine and the most salubrious epithem because it was a drink composed of gold, emeralds, coral, and pearls and [was meant] for the heart; all this potion her hair, eyes, lips, and beautiful teeth formed.

While in both cases the sensory is flavored with the sensual in a manner characteristic of Lope, Fernando takes for granted the correlation explicated in the earlier passage; his hyperbole operates at a further remove from nature, having a quantitatively absolute (and not only a qualitative) character ("todas las flores," and so on) and complicating the underlying conceptual paradox ("vista-bebida") by the addition of a new sense, hearing.[131]

Elsewhere it is as painter that Nature performs the supreme act of creating Dorotea:

> *Fer.:* Mil vezes he pensado que de lo que le sobró [to Nature] de la materia de que la compuso hizo después las rosas y los jazmines.
> *Iul.:* A essa cuenta, ¿primero fue Dorotea que las rosas?
> *Fer.:* No, Iulio, sino que aquello cándido y purpúreo de jazmines y rosas estaua ya gastado con el tiempo, y renouóse con las sobras de los colores de Dorotea.
>
> (p. 225)

> *Fer.:* A thousand times have I thought that out of what [Nature] had remaining from the material of which it composed her, it afterward made roses and jasmine. *Jul.:* According to that, Dorotea existed before roses? *Fer.:* No, Julio, only that the white and purplish color of jasmine and roses was already worn with the passage of time and it was refurbished with the leftovers from the colors of Dorotea.

It was standard enough praise of a painter to state that his art outdid nature. Lope in praising Rubens or his friend Juan van der Hamen, a painter of still lifes, characteristically embroiders upon the formula: Rubens, for example, finding Nature asleep with her wet paint brushes dangling from her fingers and tinting the flowers, steals them to paint the king's portrait, causing Nature to declare: "Doy por bien hurtados mis pinceles" ("I consider my brushes well stolen").[132] It is noticeable, however, that with Fernando the focus shifts from painter to painting. Nature is still the artist but something more than a purely pictorial one: painting is inseparable from her total creativity and the supreme goal of this activity is simply Dorotea. Under Julio's prodding, Fernando's fancy adjusts the conception to give Dorotea, if not absolute priority over other created things, at least the power of renewing them in a world of time and fading. He thus ends up on the rather technical note of touching up or retouching with materials that are plastic as well as pictorial. We are reminded of the *silva* in praise of painting which Lope wrote for the *Diálogos de la pintura* of his friend Vincencio Carducho, which ends by telling Painting:

> Diuina, en todo, por diuino modo,
> si no lo crías, lo renueuas todo.[133]

> Divine in everything, in divine fashion, if you do not create, you renew everything.

In essence, the divine character of the painter's art, a result of its analogousness to that of God as creator, is made by Fernando to subserve the profane fabric of his private world, in which Dorotea occupies the place of the divinity.[134]

When the tendency to see Dorotea as a work of art presumes a human artifex, Fernando's fantasy shifts with undiminished hyperbole to the realm of particular paintings and sculptures. He seizes the occasion of Dorotea's fainting, it will be recalled, to gaze upon her as if viewing supreme creations of these sister arts: "¡O Venus de alabastro! ¡O aurora de jazmines, que aun no tienes toda la color del día! ¡O mármol de Lucrecia, escultura de Michael Angel!" ("Oh alabaster Venus! Oh jasmine dawn that does not yet have the full color of day! Oh marble of Lucretia, sculpture of Michelangelo!") (p. 94).[135] Such hyperbolical and metaphorical fantasies show that Fernando is in effect making his mistress his own supreme work of art, an object of elaboration from which the flesh-and-blood mistress with the "pobreça del trage [que] descuida los ojos" ("poverty in dress [that] lets the eyes wander") (p. 79) must inevitably part company in the end. Beneath all Fernando's exaggeration is Lope's awareness that the artist is inevitably an egotist, whose pursuit of his own forms takes him away from the occasions that inspire them, whose absorption in his own image of things transcends concern with their originals, who in any case can always fall back on the knowledge that "tan dulce me será siempre la memoria de su hermosura" ("so sweet will the memory of her beauty be to me always"). While in Fernando the artistic impulse is partly misdirected, confounding *Erlebnis* and *Dichtung*, he remains an overstated case of a phenomenon which Lope sees as "normal" in the artist as a young man, indeed the artist at every age.

The objects of Fernando's "poetizing," if they become too involved in it themselves, must inevitably suffer in the end from the *décalage* between art and life. Like the musicality of his verse and prose, Fernando's image-making powers corrode Dorotea's sensibilities. Flattered at being the object of his poetic cult, she eagerly collaborates in his poetic sublimation of even the tawdry aspects of their relationship. While the intimacies and vicissitudes of their life together are celebrated in verse, as had been the case with Lope and Elena,[136] Lope especially dwells on the surrounding context of their lives together in which poetry's transforming powers are manifest. We see Fernando cultivating the attitudes and the idiom of his poetry and Dorotea eagerly collaborating until she falls into patterns of thought as misleading as the reasoning whereby she convinces herself, in her letter to her estranged lover, that she can still count on his loving her, or as deceptive as her pronouncement, after their reunion, that the memory of the event will keep her happy forever.

Nor is the spell Fernando casts *qua* poet limited to Dorotea. Supported by his contagious histrionism, it confounds Marfisa's tears and her diamonds to gloss over his ignoble action in relieving her of her jewels:

> *Mar.:* En tu rostro las estampo [tears], a efeto de que te acuerdes que las lloraron mis ojos casi en los tuyos, por engañarme de que eran tuyas.
> *Fer.:* Alguna mía se ha mezclado en ellas, y yo te juro que las que me has puesto han hecho en mi rostro las letras de tu nombre. Pero ¿qué esclauo truxo en el mundo hierros de diamantes?
>
> (p. 118)

> *Mar.:* I imprint them [tears] on your face in order that you may recall that my eyes wept them almost into yours so as to delude myself that they were yours. *Fer.:* One or two of mine have become mixed with them and I swear to you that those you have shed on me have formed the letters of your name on my face. But what slave ever wore diamond fetters?

Marfisa herself, prior to this exchange, it will be recalled, has already volunteered the thought that his words were more precious in her ears than her diamond pendants. Though, once away from Fernando, Marfisa is capable, as we have seen, of reacting abrasively against his verbal magic, in his presence not even she is immune to it.

Don Bela's Style

Between Fernando and Don Bela, his rival, there is no real competition in either aspect of Fernando's style, the histrionic or the poetic. Don Bela lacks both the natural poetic powers and the native histrionic streak of his rival. He goes through the paces and adopts the attitudes of the closed circle of Fernando and Dorotea, as he employs its idiom: for tactical reasons, not out of conviction. Having lived his life in a sphere of action and enterprise, he is adjusted to practical realities and not prone to self-delusion. In the only scene in which he is called upon to play a particular role, his visit to Dorotea, Don Bela performs without naturalness or ease. As with Fernando, we sense a nature distinct from the part being played, but for other reasons. With Don Bela the part is so palpably foreign to his native way of being that effects of outright comedy compound the usual Lopean irony. Don Bela handles literary parlance with almost truculent heavyhandedness and often loses his bearings after he has embarked upon a piece of sophistry or pedantry. His subsequent emergence as the author of the Platonic madrigal is the more remarkable in view of this earlier performance. Yet it is not wholly unanticipated, as a closer examination of Don Bela's expressive style will show.

Before turning to the scene of the meeting between Dorotea and Don Bela, we should note how Lope has brought out the differences between the rivals not only through the contrast in their behavior and conversation when in her presence but by devoting successive scenes to their poetization of a similar situation when she is not present: that of paying court to her outside her windows. It is noticeable that the poetic elaboration in these scenes centers on the olfactory sense, masters sensitive to scents being counterbalanced by servants sensitive to smells. By a *tour de force* Lope confines within a single sensory sphere the contrast between the percepts of superior and lower senses that commonly corresponds to the social distinction between masters and servants in the *comedia*. The unusual olfactory sensitivity of Lope, which made the evoking of fragrances and odors, real and imagined, a favorite form of poetic ornamentation, produces this modification of the traditional Platonic sensory hierarchy, originating in the *Timaeus*, which Lope found elaborated in detail by Ficino in his commentary on the *Symposium*.[137]

Don Bela arrives first:

> *Bel.:* En entrando por esta calle me parece que por abril estoy en alguna de la insigne Valencia.
> *Lau.:* ¿De qué suerte?
> *Bel.:* Tiene diferente olor que las otras.
> *Lau.:* Téngolo por impossible, si reparasses en los naranjos de donde sale azar tan diferente a estas horas.
> *Bel.:* ¡O, Laurencio! Acuérdate de Plauto, donde dixo que hasta los perros de sus damas lisonjeauan los amantes.

Lau.: Traes en la imaginación el buen olor de Dorotea, y está más viua quanto más te acercas a su casa; que los que aman tienen todos los sentidos en la imaginación.

(p. 257)

Bel.: Coming into this street it seems to me that I am in one of noble Valencia in April.   *Lau.:* How do you mean?   *Bel.:* It has a different odor from the others.   *Lau.:* I believe that impossible if you consider the orange trees from which such different blossoms issue at this hour.   *Bel.:* Oh Laurencio, remember Plautus where he said that lovers flattered the very dogs of their ladies.   *Lau.:* Your imagination is set on the pleasing odor of Dorotea and becomes all the more vivid the closer you get to her house; people in love have all their senses in the imagination.

If Laurencio gives his master's words a foul twist it is partly Don Bela's lame "diferente olor" that provides an opening. Unable to sustain his lofty beginning, Don Bela is reduced to explaining that he is merely trying to say what is expected of a lover, and it is Laurencio who must help him out.

Fernando's description of the street is stylistically far more accomplished than his rival's:

Fer.: A mí me parece el rocío idalio que dixo Pontano, la mirra del Orontes, y todas las yeruas aromáticas, sabeas, arabias, armenias y pancayas.

Iul.: *El poluo de la oueja alcohol es para el lobo.* Pero dixo don Luis de Góngora de las calles de Madrid, que eran lodos con peregil y yeruabuena.

Fer.: Mejor durmiera yo en ésta que en los jardines de Chipre o entre las rosas del monte Pangeo, hibleas o Elisias flores.

(p. 267)

Fer.: To me it seems the Idalian dew that Pontano spoke of, the myrrh of the Orontes and all the Sheban, Arabian, Armenian, and Panchean aromatic herbs.   *Jul.:* *The dust of the sheep is alcohol to the wolf.* But Don Luis de Góngora said of Madrid streets that they were mire with parsley and mint in it.   *Fer.:* I would sooner sleep in this one than in the gardens of Cyprus or amid the roses of Mt. Pangaeus, Hyblean or Elysian flowers.

Julio's interposed remark, literally earthy, with its mud and its home-grown herbs and odors,[138] sets off by contrast Fernando's deliberate pursuit of the most exotic epithets of the Greco-Latin poetic tradition, whose *dulzura* arises from their sonority as much as from their suggestion of exquisite scents more literary than real. Except for the myrrh and roses, Fernando does not deal in specific fragrances. He prefers to heap up rare epithets in a manner theoretically acceptable in poets (though frowned upon in rhetorical usage), but he carries even this so far that he seems merely to be suggesting a range of possibilities. His copiousness, more of words than of things, is doubtless second-hand, drawn probably from the Cornucopia section of Lope's vademecum, Ravisius Textor's *Officina*, the poet's "workshop." [139]

Don Bela deploys the poetic idiom with ostentation but without finesse. In a more literal-minded way than Fernando he treats metaphorical riches as if they were real ones and pounces on conceits as if they were possessions. In trying to compete with Fernando on his own grounds, he is, for all his shortcomings, just sufficiently successful to make his words act as a catalyst for his gifts to Dorotea. The words require material props as Fernando's do not—they are presentational as well as representational—but the props also require complementation through the words.

Already quoted in another context, the first words we hear from Don Bela's lips set the tone of his particular style: "No digo yo lo prometido, pero todo el oro que el sol engendra en las dos Indias me parece poco, y aunque se añadieran los diamantes de la China, las perlas del mar del Sur y los rubíes de Zeylán" ("Not merely that which I have promised, but all the gold that the sun engenders in both Indies seems little to me, even adding to it the pearls of the South Seas and the rubies of Ceylon") (p. 131). [140] Don Bela here makes good in advance the determination he expresses soon afterward: to say to Dorotea "tales hipérboles y energías, que no me igualen quantos agora escriuen en España" ("such hyperboles and *enargeias* that none writing in Spain today will come up to me") (p. 133). The rubies of Ceylon are not terms of comparison for Don Bela, they are simply a supplement to gold actually promised. His way of thinking is more quantitative than qualitative. After the conquest of Dorotea he becomes more blunt: "Yo sé que todo el oro del mundo no es ya poderoso, Laurencio, para conquistar a Dorotea" ("I know, Laurencio, that all the gold in the world no longer has the power to conquer Dorotea") (p. 262). He is a complacent Croesus, more partial to hyperboles and "energías," which heighten and intensify but do not transform, than to metaphors. [141]

Gerarda from the outset understands that she must coach Don Bela in the deployment of both verbal and material riches. The initial scene between them becomes an inventory of the resources, poetic as well as material, at Don Bela's command. Hyperboles, *energías*, conceits, words pure and simple, are readied for use like so many strategic weapons. I have already noted Gerarda's elaborate encouragement of Don Bela's not very subtle *aplicaciones*.

The choice he offers between a hyperbolic conceit and an allegorical one to accompany the presentation of the *búcaro* to Dorotea is characteristically both lavish and business-like.

Don Bela's style is best displayed when he passes from rehearsal to performance in Act II, scene 5, and wields verbal as well as material offerings in his campaign for Dorotea. It is plain from the earlier scene that he places reliance principally on the latter, giving Gerarda everything she asks for and silencing Laurencio's grumbling with the blunt remark: "Necio, las entradas de amor son éstas. En ganando la plaça, retiraré la artillería" ("Fool, these are the entering wedges of love. Once I take the fortress I'll withdraw the artillery") (p. 137). He knows his inadequacy in the conversational arts and secretly has little patience with them. Indeed, he approaches the meeting with some trepidation, for he must display a mastery of etiquette, a poetic touch, a knack for repartee, facile learning, artistic taste, connoisseurship, while secretly convinced that it is money that talks. We will find him in fact laying on the hyperboles, conceits, and *fábulas poéticas* thickly and indiscriminately, at times misapplying them altogether and blundering badly. But Don Bela's role cannot be seen except in the context of the whole, for his conquest of Dorotea provides the most dazzling display of the varied resources at Lope's command—verbal, pictorial, musical, histrionic, rhetorical —for the deliberate artistic playing-up by its participants of a particular event.

This meeting of Dorotea and Don Bela, the only scene we are shown between them, is also the only one in which the ceremoniousness of a formal occasion sustains the play of conversation and the effect of theater. The scene to which the imagination of the jilted lover of 1588 surely returned over and over is finally recreated without a trace of hostility. True, the situation is not without its elements of irony and the *sotto voce* of Gerarda and the servants does not let us forget this. This is no case of seduction. Dorotea is not virginal; she has a husband and is, moreover, of demonstrable corruptibility. But the willing sacrifices of five years with Fernando have brought a kind of purity. We are made to see her as a Romantic courtesan *avant la lettre*. Devoid of Jacinta's rapaciousness, she observes with some surprise at the end: "En efeto, he tomado lo que no pensaua" ("Indeed, I've taken what I hadn't expected to") (p. 188). In spite of herself, Dorotea falls under the spell of *interés* and her eyes light up at the exquisite beauty of Don Bela's gifts as she takes in the words he weaves around them. More than ever in this scene Lope presents her as uncertain of her own course, almost devoid of intentionality. She wishes neither to admit nor to reject Don Bela; she simply drifts into acceptance.

Despite the temporary assuagement brought about by music, the state of perplexity, indecisiveness, and conflict in which Marfisa's visit has left her persists. Gerarda's initiative, immediately following Marfisa's deception, comes at the moment of greatest psychological vulnerability. Yet, while more receptive to Gerarda, Dorotea is still taken aback by the suddenness of Don Bela's visit, for events have gotten ahead of her.

It is Gerarda who at once seizes the initiative, her presence marking a clear departure from the usual role of the go-between. From the beginning her aim has been to coach Don Bela in the part he is to play in order to smooth his way into Dorotea's arms. ("Si tú tienes algo de poeta, ganarásle el alma" ["If you've something of the poet about you, you'll win her soul"] [p. 133], and so on.) Far from bowing out when she hears Don Bela's timid knocking, Gerarda proceeds to direct the performance for which she has trained her client. More than her ordinary inquisitiveness and cupidity, it is a need to be not merely witness but participant that motivates her. Actually a supernumerary, she insists on stepping in as director, stage manager, prompter. Without destroying psychological verity, her comic overcompensation for her presence adds to the authorial irony with which the scene is edged and brings it to the verge of parody.

Taking over the direction at once, she makes Don Bela's first words sound like a naive stage whisper: "No me tire de la capa, señora Gerarda; que a quien trae su voluntad no es menester hazelle fuerça" ("Don't pull me by the cloak, mistress Gerarda; someone coming of his own will doesn't have to be forced") (p. 171). Then Don Bela delivers the lines he has prepared for Dorotea: "Dios guarde tanta hermosura para testigo de su poder, aunque a costa de quantas vidas mata" ("God preserve so much beauty as a testimonial to his power even at the cost of every life it slays"). This refinement of Calixto's opening greeting to Melibea does not entirely eradicate the impression that Don Bela has made a poor start. The touch of burlesque is a demarcation and a grounding for the conscious play-acting that follows. The stage for the imminent drama is precisely located in space as Don Bela advances to the *estrado*, which he entreats Dorotea not to leave, and takes a seat, while she says apologetically: "Perdonad el no auer salido más passos; que me ha cogido vuestra venida tan de súbito, que no halla el coraçón lugar donde se afirme" ("Forgive me for not coming further forward: your coming has taken me so unawares that my heart can find no place to steady itself"). Don Bela seizes the conversational initiative with a comment on this unquiet heart, Dorotea replies, and the thrust and parry of allusive repartee begins. Don Bela caps the sparring with a *fábula*. His touch is inexpert and in his eagerness he goes into the story of Argos, "aquel pastor

de Ouidio" ("that shepherd in Ovid"), in excessive detail. Dorotea is nonetheless impressed by his show of learning: "Con vos a lo menos ya no
importará guardar los ojos, si podéis robar los coraçones por los oídos"
("With you at any rate there won't be any point in guarding the eyes, if
you are able to rob hearts through the ears") (p. 172). He has won the
first skirmish with words alone.

Gerarda now decides to step in. Her cue to Laurencio—"¿Qué trae
Laurencio, que está más cargado que sardesco de conuento?" ("What is
Laurencio bringing? He's more loaded down than a convent jackass")—
is ignored by the hostile servant and Gerarda's next words suggest a caricaturesque tug-of-war as she struggles with the recalcitrant lackey: "Descoje,
descoje, muestra, desembóçate. ¡Qué atado estás! Más difícil es de sacar
esta tela de tus braços, que de la tienda del mercader" ("Open it up, open it
up, disentangle yourself. How tied down you are! It's harder to get this
cloth out of your arms than out of the tradesman's shop"). With the unfolding of the flowered Milan cloth, a world of beauty and refinement opens
out dazzlingly and temptingly before Dorotea in cloth of the very pattern,
"primauera de flores" ("flowering spring"), which, Gerarda knows,
Dorotea had recently exchanged for a "manteo de picote" ("goathair
cloak") in order to provide for her indigent lover.[142] Dorotea's admiration
is spontaneous and unaffected: "Por cierto que es bellíssima" ("It is certainly
most beautiful"). Gerarda, for her part, proposes the cloth as a conversation
piece: "Did spring ever paint a meadow or a poet imitate one with more
flowers?" The situation is presentationally sustained in the ensuing exchange,
in which the characters' fancy plays about the design of the cloth in displays
of imagery, interweaving the naturalistic, the poetic, and the pictorial
through the connecting threads of color symbolism and color harmony
in comments on the cloth which are also *aplicaciones* to the situation.
Gerarda clearly listens closely:

> *Dor.:* ¡Qué bien assientan estas clauellinas de nácar sobre lo verde!
> *Bel.:* Assí se casaran dos voluntades como estas dos colores.
> *Dor.:* Lo verde es esperança y lo encarnado crueldad.
> *Bel.:* La crueldad será vuestra color, y la esperança la mía. Pero
> ¿quién las podrá casar, siendo contrarias?
> *Dor.:* Contrarias, sí, pero no enemigas.
> *Bel.:* Dezís bien; que vna cosa es la enemistad y otra la oposición.
> *Dor.:* Tiene más esta esperança, que está esmaltada de flores, que son
> más que principios de la execución del fruto.
> *Ger.:* No has dicho cosa más a propósito.

Dor.: No tan aprisa, Gerarda; que muchos almendros se han perdido
  por auer tenido flores sin tiempo.

Ger.: Echástelo a perder, hija; mejor lo auías dicho, porque la
  producción de las flores puede ser serenidad del tiempo, y no
  atreuimiento del árbol, para merecer el castigo del yelo.

(p. 172)

Dor.: How well these mother-of-pearl pinks go with the green!
Bel.: Would that two wills might be matched as well as these two
colors.   *Dor.:* The green is hope and the flesh-color cruelty.   *Bel.:*
Cruelty must be your color and hope mine. But who can ever
match them when they're opposites?   *Dor.:* Opposites, yes, but not
enemies.   *Bel.:* Well said, for enmity is one thing and opposition
another.   *Dor.:* Another thing about this hope, it's strewn with
flowers, which are more than a beginning of the realization of the
fruit.   *Ger.:* You couldn't have said anything more to the point.
Dor.: Just a moment, Gerarda: many almond trees have been lost
because they bloomed before their time.   *Ger.:* You've spoiled
everything, child; you should have said: because producing flowers
may be a matter of fine weather and not boldness on the tree's part,
to deserve the punishment of frost.

We seem to hear a director emending a script. As the repartee continues and
Don Bela first sketches a Platonic view of love, then rejects it, an aside of
Celia evaluates the performance more caustically: "¡A Platón encaxa este
majadero!... Pero ¿qué tiene que ver aquí Platón, sino hazer a Dorotea el
plato?" ("This bore manages to drag in Plato!... But what does Plato
have to do with it except to keep Dorotea's plate full?") (p. 174). The
offstage context of *La Dorotea* makes this instance of the menial in a deflationary role more pointed than in Lope's plays. Celia's jab makes a rent in
the texture of the dialogue and presently Dorotea's deeper mood shows
through. Her mind has wandered during Don Bela's Platonic excursus and
she has no comment to make on it. When he presses her, "¿Qué respondéis
a esto?" ("What is your answer to that?"), she answers unexpectedly:
"Estoy en estremo triste" ("I'm extremely sad"). The conversational game
has palled and even the beauty of the cloth no longer holds her. With a sure
touch Lope puts before us again the conflict between surface and depths.
Dorotea has let Gerarda and Don Bela draw her away from Fernando but
the truth of her feelings reasserts itself. The characteristic ambivalence will
prompt her later, when she has been enticed back by Don Bela's gifts and
words, to choose precisely verse by Fernando to sing for his rival.

Failing to perceive Dorotea's mood, Don Bela plunges on apropos of her sadness: "En Grecia reinó vn humor en las doncellas, que se matauan todas con sus manos. Assí lo escriue Plutarco" ("In Greece something took hold of the maidens so that they all took their own lives. So Plutarch writes"). The ineptness of the *chria* is striking: besides violating Dorotea's mood, it awkwardly brings up the subject of suicide. Well-meaning but gauche, Don Bela simply hews unimaginatively to the line laid down by Gerarda and surmised by Celia: "El ha oído decir que Dorotea es perdida porque la tengan por sabia" ("He has heard that Dorotea is crazy to be considered learned") (p. 174). Gerarda hastens to intervene, displaying Don Bela's *passamanos* ("gilt lace edgings"), but Dorotea's response—"Son más ricos que de buen gusto" ("They are more showy than tasteful")—fastens on them her disaffection and her disdain for Don Bela's tastelessness. Gerarda nevertheless prompts insistently:

> Hasta con los passamanos eres ingrata por lo que tienen de manos. Hasta agora, ¿quién te las pide? Y ¡qué tales son ellas para pedirlas, para desearlas y para encarecerlas! Como estás conualeciente, las traes sin adorno. Por vida de don Bela, que le prestes essas dos sortijas por vn instante, verás lo que parecen en aquella nieue.
>
> (p. 174)

> You're even ungracious toward the gilt lace edgings because their handiwork reminds you of hands [lit.: because of the *manos* ("hands") in them]. So far who has asked for yours? And such hands to ask for, to desire and to extol! Because you're convalescing, you have no ornament on them. Upon Don Bela's life, lend her those two rings a moment; you'll see how they look on that snow.

As can be seen, Gerarda improvises a way out of the impasse, deploying puns and presentational imagery step by step. Dorotea's spontaneous response, noted earlier—"Necia estás, Gerarda. ¡Iesús, qué necia!" ("You're foolish, Gerarda. Lord, so foolish!")—suggests authentic embarrassment. Don Bela's suit is reduced momentarily to a game of hide-and-seek with Dorotea's fingers, but when it is over he has clearly won. The struggle, in which Dorotea has grown visibly less reluctant, and the dazzle of diamonds have dispelled her dark mood. But Don Bela once again spoils things by an awkward metaphor:

> *Bel.:* ¡Qué buenas están las sortijas! Parecen estrellas los diamantes
>   en vuestras manos.
> *Dor.:* Dezís muy bien, siendo las manos noche.
>
> (p. 175)

Bel.: How fine the rings look! The diamonds seem like stars on your hands.   *Dor.:* You're quite right, since the hands are night.

As if to make up for her surrender to his wealth, Dorotea taunts him on his inferiority in *entendimiento*. Don Bela hastily resorts to one of the promised hyperboles—"Nunca pensé ver estrellas a mediodía hasta que vi estos diamantes en vuestras manos" ("I never thought I would see stars at noon until I saw those diamonds on your hands") (p. 175)—but takes a worse plunge when Dorotea makes a gesture to remove the rings. They would never go on any other fingers, he says, "que el cauallo Bucéfalo de Alexandro de nadie se dexó sujetar sino de sólo su dueño" ("for Alexander's horse, Bucephalus, would let no one mount him except his master"). Laurencio's comment, "¿Qué tiene que ver el cauallo de Alexandro con los diamantes de Dorotea?" ("What does Alexander's horse have to do with Dorotea's diamonds?") (p. 176), underscores the ludicrous impropriety. The rings end up on Dorotea's fingers, nevertheless, with the comment, "Si los anillos fueron prisión, antiguamente, presas estarán mis manos de vuestra liberalidad" ("If rings were prisons in ancient times, my hands will be the prisoners of your munificence") (p. 177), which signals her capitulation. One sees clearly in such a remark how a veneer of poetry glosses over self-delusion.

There is a notable relaxation now and a drop in tone as the assault on Don Bela's bounty becomes more general. In the new display of colors provided by the hosiery it is the popular and everyday associations that are commented on (white suggests "piernas de difuntos"—"the legs of dead persons"— purple is for a bishop, gold for a soldier), not esthetic or symbolic ones, and the effect is less exquisite. Gerarda's direction is more relaxed, she has less occasion to step in. When Don Bela asks Dorotea to play the harp, a new sort of performance results. Musical "voz y destreza" ("voice and skill") supplements conversational dexterity and pictorial fantasy. Don Bela's eagerness to show himself a connoisseur complicates the performance: he steps in with technical comments, makes the musical solo a social duo, uses the music as a pretext for *aplicaciones* just as the art-objects had been.

The atmosphere of expectation, visual and aural, prior to a concert is noticeably evoked by Lope. Dorotea's hands moving on the strings, "como los diamantes, hazen diuersas luzes" ("like the diamonds, set up sparkles in all directions") (p. 179) as she tunes the harp, apologizing elaborately for the discords.

Halfway through Fernando's ballad of Rodrigo and Jarifa, Don Bela catches a pair of hyperboles, interrupts to exclaim, "¡Excelentes ocho versos!" ("An excellent eight lines!"), and asks the author's name. Dorotea answers evasively and resumes, making music her refuge from too painful a memory. A final intervention by Gerarda, which entices a "maridaje de rubí y diamante" ("coupling of a ruby and a diamond") from Don Bela, induces Dorotea to sing a second selection. In its figures and imagery, this *romance* displays poetic substances—colors, stars, flowers, precious stones— in subtle correlation with those that have been literally or figuratively present in the scene and the conversation. Don Bela's celebration of the recurrent refrain of the ballad is spoiled immediately by a new *faux pas*:

> *Bel.:* ¿Cúyo es el tono?
> *Ger.:* De la misma que lo canta. ¿Esso preguntas?
> *Bel.:* ¡O, qué mal pregunté!
>
> (p. 186)

> *Bel.:* Who wrote the melody?   *Ger.:* The same person that is singing it. Is that a question to ask?   *Bel.:* Oh, how wrong of me to ask!

When Dorotea concludes, Don Bela asserts briskly: "Es excelente; pero yo me atengo al moro" ("It's excellent but I'll stick to the Moor"). His reason is a practical one: the Moor's words furnish a readily adaptable conceit. With a heavy hand—announcing exactly what he is doing—he makes an *aplicación* of the "excellent eight lines" he has singled out, to himself and Dorotea, whom he now finds disposed to collaborate:

> *Bel.:* Sutil anduuo el poeta en dezir que antes de nacer la quiso
>   Auindarráez en la ideal fantasía de la naturaleza.
> *Dor.:* Los poetas son hombres despeñados. Toda su tienda es de
>   impossibles.
> *Bel.:* Y de sentencias grauues quando escriuen cosas serias. Valerme
>   quiero de aquel concepto, y dezir que os quise antes que tuuiesse
>   ser.
> *Dor.:* Si os valéis desso, pensaré que vuestro amor es poesía.
>
> (p. 187)

> *Bel.:* That was subtle of the poet to say that before he was born Abindarráez loved her in the ideal imagining of Nature.   *Dor.:* Poets are reckless men. Their whole stock-in-trade consists of *impossibilia.*   *Bel.:* And of solemn sayings when they write serious things. I want to take over that conceit and say that I loved you before I had any being.   *Dor.:* If you take that over, I shall think that your love is poetry.

Both Dorotea and her suitor know the deceptiveness of the poetic aura in which he is enveloping the situation. For Don Bela at this point the Platonic "ideal fantasía" is simply a verbal stratagem.[143] For Dorotea, the illusoriness of all poetic materials, as patent as that of *impossibilia*, is confirmed in this particular case by the defection of the author of this very conceit. Yet she accepts Don Bela's tribute and puts the seal on his love-making with a fantasy of her own. Behind the theatricality of this conscious confounding of life and art is a strong will to illusion and an equally strong awareness of self-delusion, evidence of Dorotea's irresoluteness. She accepts Don Bela but she does not renounce Fernando. Her embracing of illusion, as against Don Bela's simple appropriation of it, once again spells the difference between a woman's emotional stake in an esthetic vision and a man's. Dorotea perpetuates poetic forms of behavior learned from Fernando even as she acquiesces in the suit of his successor.

Styles of Dorotea, Marfisa, and Gerarda

The present scene and others already analyzed have brought out what is most characteristic in Dorotea's "style": the need to make poetry a medium of refinement for her life and the susceptibility she shows to whatever she supposes will help her do so—Fernando's tears or verse, Don Bela's *fábulas* or diamonds. There is inevitably in her attitude an element of modishness and preciosity but upon occasion there is also true dignity.

Lope has not endowed Dorotea with his own playfulness. She is highly serious in her cultural aspirations and takes poetry very much to heart; she lacks Fernando's reserves of lucidity and Don Bela's practicality. In her, as in the *hetaira* of antiquity or in the Romantic courtesan, an instinct for refinement is visible; it responds avidly to her lover's techniques of stylization. Despite misgivings, she is seduced into imagining that affective experience can be made to respond to esthetic ordering, that the patterns of art can be imposed on experience. She has insufficient tact or understanding to respect the sphere of art for itself, to avoid demeaning it by casuistry.

Dorotea's tendency to preciosity and her aspiration to the role of *femme savante* are constant attitudes, manifest under the most diverse circumstances. In answer to Marfisa's simple question, " ¿Lloran los hombres?" ("Do men cry?"), Dorotea proffers first a Petrarchistic sophistry of Fernando's: "Este era tan lisongero que dezía que ya él no era hombre; porque, transformado en su dama, auía perdido el ser" ("This one was so flattering that he said he no longer was a man, because, having been transformed into his lady, he had lost his own being") (p. 149); then a footnote of her own: "que en las mugeres . . . las lágrimas son piedad, hermosura y consuelo, como mayorazgo de su imperfección" ("and in women . . . tears are compassion, beauty, and recompense, being the inherited privilege of their imperfection"). Marfisa's pointed questions about her illness are met with a neatly evasive chiasmus: "Dixe lo que pensaua, y pensando en lo que dixe, solicité mi muerte" ("I said what I hadn't thought to, and thinking of what I said, I sought my own death") (p. 148). I have already noted how infuriated Teodora becomes when her daughter, using the terminology and techniques of a *femme savante*, dissects the mother's remarks about Gerarda. Even when she has no one but Celia or Felipa to hear her, Dorotea self-consciously celebrates her moments of triumph or outrage in what might be called grand opera style:

> ¡O, felicíssima muger, con qué dicha te leuantaste oy! Ya tus deseos se cumplieron, ya viste el sujeto de tus ansias, el centro de tus pensamientos, cierta de que te adora, cierta de que te estima . . . ¡O, muger felicíssima! (p. 374)

> Oh, most happy woman, with what good fortune you arose today! At last your desires have been fulfilled, at last you have seen the object of your anxieties, the focus of your thoughts, sure that he adores you, sure that he thinks well of you . . . Oh, woman most happy!

In this self-directed paean one observes the same carefully inverted rhetorical brackets as in the denunciation of her mother discussed earlier.

More striking still is the apostrophe expressing her indignation toward Fernando after Marfisa has deceived her:

> ¡O fementido, o falso, o cauallero indigno deste nombre! ¿A vna muger de mis prendas, ingrato, y que ha dexado por ti quanto puede atraer la hermosura, la gracia y el entendimiento en la Corte? ¿Esto merecía mi verdad? ¿Esto mis braços? ¿Esto lo que he padecido con mi madre y deudos . . . ? ¿Qué Penelope fue más perseguida? ¿Qué Lucrecia más rogada? ¿Qué Porcia más firme?
> (p. 151)

> Oh faithless one, oh deceiver, oh gentleman unworthy of this name! Is this any treatment for a woman with so much appeal, ingrate, when she has given up for your sake all that beauty, charm, and brains are capable of attracting in this Court city? Is this the reward for my faithfulness? For my caresses? For all I have suffered at the hands of my mother and relatives . . . ? What Penelope was ever more set upon? What Lucrecia more besought? What Portia more steadfast?

How are we to take this fervent invocation of exemplars of constancy and chastity? In an absolute sense it is singularly, indeed grotesquely unsuited to the context. The *exempla* are dwarfed and trivialized by being employed in such a situation. Once more we seem to hear authorial laughter in the wings. Yet in terms of Dorotea's view of her conduct—one of abnegation, sacrifice, deprivation, and, in recompense, esthetic ennoblement—such invocations are quite in order. An inflaming of the imagination as well as a warping of vision are recorded in them, in appropriately ornate style. We have here a characteristic instance of stylistic decorum become psychological rather than social.

In neither of these passages is the exalted level of utterance sustained without interruption. The second, as earlier seen, rises out of a context of colloquiality and falls back to it. In the first, thoughts of Teodora and Gerarda presently draw Dorotea down toward a more naturally vehement tone: "Será mío, aunque pese a esta vieja de mi madre y a la hechizera que la aconseja" ("He will be mine in spite of this old hag of a mother of mine and the sorceress who advises her") (p. 374). Such stylistic shifts, characteristic of the dialogue as a whole, are particularly so of Dorotea, and they bring out clearly the limits of her vocation and capacity for the role she has chosen to sustain, limits noticeably narrower than those of her more accomplished lover. It is curious to see, nevertheless, how much formalism creeps even into private conversations with Celia: in Act II, scene 2, for example, elaborately turned compliments on the part of the flattering maid and, on that of the mistress, sententious generalizations and reflections, along with the "versos, acotaciones y vocablos nueuos" ("verse, marginal notes, and new words") that Celia remarks upon. With Felipa, on the other hand, Dorotea's tone stays, for the most part, closer to the colloquial.

As Marfisa contrasts with Dorotea in character, so she does also in style of utterance. Except when she falls under Fernando's sway, she is direct to the point of bluntness, outspoken to the point of asperity. Her speech has a vividly lifelike ring and tends far less to verbal and stylistic affectation than that of the other characters. In her visit to Dorotea, though she at first responds in kind to Dorotea's hyperbolic phrases of flattery, her direct questions phrased without any ceremoniousness soon reduce the conversation to the level of everyday speech. In the scene of the leave-taking with Fernando, she punctures his theatrics repeatedly with her matter-of-fact comments and only joins him in verbal pyrotechnics in the grand climax when she gives up her jewels. When later she confronts Fernando at his door, she catches him off guard with the caustic bluntness of her assault.

In her climactic speech of denunciation (p. 380) her feelings burst forth as if a dam were breaking. The outpouring of words sweeps everything along impetuously, in pell-mell accumulations—"los tiros, los agrauios, los zelos, las competencias, las temas y los desprecios" ("the offenses, the wrongs, the jealousy, the rivalries, the obstinacy, and the scorn"); "los fines, los sucessos, las desgracias y el matar los hombres" ("the outcomes, the doings, the disasters, and the killing people"). Her verbal copiousness is the product of overabundant feeling underscored by sarcasm; there is a minimum of rhetorical ordering. When she does seek a more calculated effect, denouncing Julio, it collapses anticlimactically: "¿Comiença ya la sombra de tus maldades, el aforro de tus insolencias, el Mercurio de tus embaxadas, la capa de tus traiciones *a echarnos bernardinas?*" ("Is the shadow of your evil deeds, the sheath of your insolences, the Mercury of your embassies, the cloak of your betrayals, starting now *to pull the wool over our eyes?*") (p. 379; emphasis mine). The progression of the periphrases is uncertain enough, but the sudden colloquiality completely destroys the final effect. The tone of Marfisa's private conversations with Clara is noticeably natural; there is none of the formality one finds in Dorotea's exchanges with Celia.

Of all the characters it is Gerarda who displays the most mobile speech style. Spitzer speaks of "promiscuity of speech style," observing that her speech is a composite of the styles of all the different milieux she frequents.[144] She is greeted by remarks like the already quoted "Notable vienes, Gerarda, hablando a lo moderno y a lo antiguo" ("You're something special today, Gerarda, speaking in modern and ancient fashion") (p. 120) and "De rúa traes el gusto" ("Your taste is at street level") (p. 449). She alternates between salutations and benedictions in a macaronic Latin that Spitzer calls halfway between church and kitchen Latin (pp. 156, 190, 198), and comically over-wrought versions of the rhetorical *captatio benevolentiae*. Her "Paz sea en esta casa *et omnibus habitantibus in ea*" ("Peace be unto this house *and all dwelling in it*") (p. 156) causes Celia to comment: "En los latines conozco a Gerarda. Demonio es esta vieja" ("I can tell it's Gerarda by that Latin. That old woman is the very devil").[145] The comic impropriety of the already quoted salutation to Teodora late in the first act when she comes back exuding satisfaction from her rendezvous with Don Bela—"Esté en buen hora la honra de las viudas" ("Blessings upon the honor of widowhood") (p. 119)—reestablishes the tone of their dialogue in the first scene as a point of departure for new verbal skirmishes.

To Celestina's tactical command of speech Gerarda adds a sophisticated technical awareness and a gratuitious linguistic playfulness which notably dilute the steady purposefulness of her forebear. A natural mimic, she can

suit her utterance when she wishes to the tastes and tendencies of her inter-
locutors, but she can also quite unceremoniously expose the game, revert to
her natural colloquiality and give her fancy free rein. In writing her part
Lope perhaps remembered a cynical aside of Celestina commenting to
Sempronio on the overblown rhetoric and exaggerated deference of
Calixto's greeting:

> ¡De aquellas biuo yo! ¡Los huessos que yo roý piensa este necio de
> tu amo de darme a comer!... Dile que cierre la boca y comience
> abrir la bolsa, que de las obras dudo, quanto más de las palabras.[146]

> That's my stock-in-trade! That simpleton of a master of yours
> thinks he can feed me the very bones I've gnawed!... Tell him to
> shut his mouth and start opening his purse; I've no trust in deeds,
> let alone words.

An echo of this passage seems present in Gerarda's: "Yo no sé para que os
vais conmigo a las retóricas y habladurías, que es vender miel al colmenero;
dadme para el vino, ya que no me dais el oro" ("I don't know why you
try your rhetoric and chitchat on me—it's like selling honey to the beekeeper;
give me something for wine since you won't give me gold") (p. 233).
Spoken as they are directly to the master, Don Bela, these words acquire an
impertinent tone unthinkable in the circumspect dealings of Celestina with
her superiors; the abandonment of social decorum and the neglect of stylistic
decorum go hand in hand. (Celestina's impertinences are kept for asides, to
which Gerarda is noticeably less prone.) The same Gerarda who had simulated rapture over Don Bela's "hemistichios" and his "abstracto" here
tells him to his face to spare his honeyed words, when he discourses to *her*
on "auersiones y contrariedades naturales" ("natural aversions and con-
trarities"). It is not in this channel that Gerarda's native loquacity, assisted
or not by alcohol, naturally flows. It tends rather to verbal exuberance,
copiousness fundamentally of a popular kind, as already noted (namely, in
I, 7), though still oddly streaked with rhetorical effects. I have noted how
she slips into the run-on manner of parataxis or the staccato of a colloquial
sort of asyndeton (V, 10). We may now observe other qualities: verbal
fantasy; associations and coinings; acoustic play; the peculiar artifice that
marks her handling of as seemingly natural a feature of speech as the proverb;
the particular significance of the diminutives she uses.

"Estraña es esta vieja. Mira a los despropósitos que salta" ("Strange, this
old woman. Look at the non sequiturs she strings together"). Celia's remark
(p. 169), prompted by a whimsical leap from a Dorotea resplendent in a

manteo to the resplendent armor of Don Juan of Austria at Lepanto, articulates what is most characteristic in Gerarda's speech: its capricious variability, its indiscriminate mixing of the most diverse elements, high and low, trivial and transcendent. Gerarda's speech style faithfully reflects a nature for which everything is equally important—or unimportant—a nature without a hierarchy of values, which can speak in the same tone—almost in the same breath—of the serious and ultimate and the frivolous and sensual. The effects of such indiscriminateness remain comical down to the very moment before her death, when in the nick of time Gerarda ceases to be the gay unawakened sinner.

The "rhetoric and chitchat" professed by Gerarda combine feigned seriousness of tone with lowly content, extravagance of form with copious verbalization. The very familiarity of the term "habladurías" ("chitchat"), which she couples with "retóricas," undercuts the formality of the latter: the "habladurías" always prevail in the end. Gerarda trivializes the recourse to learned authority by suggesting alternative and even mock sources.

> No sé si lo dice Cicerón o el Obispo de Mondoñedo.   (p. 193)

> I don't know if it's Cicero or the Bishop of Mondoñedo who says it.

> *Teo.:* Who wrote that?
> *Ger.:* The philosopher Alaejos. Did you think it was Plutarch?
> (p. 190)[147]

Characteristic is the already noted anecdote in which, with striking syntactic artifice, she presents the king and queen of Portugal in the lowly act of eating cream (p. 372). Equally characteristic is a semiformal encomium of underpinnings—petticoats, footwear—upon which Gerarda launches as she drains the last drops of Don Bela's munificence. Her emphasis on the "autoridad"—standing, prestige—conferred by "buenos baxos" ("good underthings") comically caricatures the idea of decorum:

> Que, aunque vieja, no me pesa de que me digan que lleuo buenos baxos, que dan autoridad a la persona y buena opinión a la limpieza. Vn poeta dixo que los pages y lacayos eran los baxos de los señores, que, si van mal puestos, le desautorizan.   (p. 136)[148]

> For, though I'm an old woman, I don't mind being told that I have good underthings, which give standing to one's person and a good presumption of cleanliness. A poet said that pages and lackeys are the underpinnings of gentlemen; if they are poorly attired, they detract from his standing.

Just prior to this the promise of a *manteo* that would be a cover for the winter of her years has occasioned this mockery of poetic convention, of a piece with those of Lope's Tomé de Burguillos:

> Y espántome de los poetas, que quando le pintan [winter] diziendo que ya braman los ayres, las fuentes se quexan, las aues hazen defensa a los futuros yelos, no ayan dicho: "Ya se aderezan los tejados y se limpian los braseros." (p. 136)

> And I'm surprised at poets, who, when they paint it [winter], saying the winds now roar, the fountains groan, the birds seek protection against coming frosts, have never said: "Now the tile roofs are repaired and braziers are cleaned."

The *reductio ad absurdum* of the extended poetic metaphor comes in an *enargeia* depicting Dorotea at the harp:

> Si la vieras agora de sirena con el arpa, trayendo aquellos dedos de cuerda en cuerda, que parece que se reían como que les hazía cosquillas; los cabellos sueltos, que a vezes sobre el arpa, embidiosos de las cuerdas, querían serlo, porque los tocasse también a ellos; y aún pienso que las cuerdas dezían, en lo que sonauan, que les dexassen hacer su oficio, pues ellas no los iban a estorbar quando se tocaua Dorotea. (p. 393)

> If you could just see her now at the harp like a siren, running those fingers of hers across the strings, making them seem to laugh as if she were tickling them; her tresses hanging loose over the harp and at times, out of envy, wanting to be strings themselves so that she might play on them too; and I actually think the strings were saying in the sounds they made that they should allow them to do their job, since they didn't go and get in the way when Dorotea was dressing her hair.

Gerarda lets her fancy run on and on, unraveling the initial image, spinning conceits proper to verse in a tone that rapidly descends to the colloquiality of everyday. There is understandable irony in Don Bela's comment, "Madre, mui poética vienes esta mañana" ("Mistress, you're in a very poetical mood this morning"), a remark Gerarda counters by protesting that she is not drunk.

The sensuous verbal sensibility that could savor Don Bela's "hipérboles y energías" ("hyperboles and *enargeias*") like so many "aguacates y bananos"

("alligator pears and bananas") is always ready to play on the phonic properties of words, to mimic them assonantally or alliteratively: "porque
siempre la Marina viue cerca, no de quien mire, sino de quien mida"
("because Marina always lives close, not to someone who keeps tabs but to
someone who keeps taverns") (p. 451); or

> *Teo.:* ... Dale, niña, vn poco dessa gragea a Gerarda.
> *Ger.:* ¡*Gragea a Guinea*! Reuentado sea mi cuerpo si en él entrare.
>
> (p. 197) [149]

> *Teo.:* Child, give Gerarda some of those black gum drops.   *Ger.:*
> *Gum drops to Guinea!* Blast my body if they ever get into it.

When Teodora suggests that if Gerarda before eating had taken "siete
almendras amargas ... no te ofendiera el vino" ("seven bitter almonds ...
wine wouldn't harm you"), the latter ridicules the idea in capricious verbal
echoes of the *siete:* "No ay cosa como siete torreznos. ¿Yo siete almendras?
Dáselas a los siete infantes de Lara" ("There's nothing like seven slices of
bacon. Me, seven almonds? Give them to the seven princes of Lara")
(p. 195). Her propensity to play on numbers had already prompted Teodora's
earlier quoted comment, "Más cincos auéis dado que vn juego de bolos"
("You've thrown more fives than a game of nine-pins") (p. 72), and it is
seen in the already noted one-two-three technique of her demonstration of
how one should eat a fig with wine. (We have still to see—p. 573, below—
the significance it acquires in her final session of haggling with Don Bela.)

   This fondness of Gerarda for verbal and phonic play must be accounted a
factor in her addiction to proverbs. Of the 104 which Edwin Morby has
found in her speech—fully two thirds of the 153 in the work, only a handful
—some eight—fail to show any trace of rhyme or assonance. [150] And, as
Morby has noted, a certain number of brief remarks originating with
Gerarda—occasionally also with others—characterized by plays of rhyme or
assonance, [151] seem to have been erroneously taken for proverbs.

   Morby has observed how noticeably Lope makes the proverbs a monopoly
of Gerarda's (in contrast to their wide use by different characters in *La
Celestina*), how rare they are in scenes where she does not appear, how it is
almost always she who "acts as fuse" to set off exchanges with the others.
His research has also established the fact that Lope's selection of proverbs in
La Dorotea is a "deliberately unusual one," the product possibly of a combing
of written collections in pursuit of the less commonplace, that they are
"often obscure in meaning and further obscured in application." He
concludes that Lope was at the same time following a well-established

literary tradition and parodying it, "mocking at his own adherence to it," and presenting in Gerarda a "pedantry of the commonplace" which under-cuts the usual transparency and broad applicability of what the proverb expresses. This simultaneous cultivation of a literary mode and reaction against it through overstatement and parody is evidently consistent with the stylistic trends we have been observing in the *acción en prosa* as a whole.

It is ornamentality rather than function that characterizes the proverbs of *La Dorotea*. The moral intention, operating through irony, which Bataillon[152] discerned behind their perversion and misappropriation in *La Celestina* cannot be discovered here. Rather, as Spitzer observed,[153] Gerarda is a self-conscious *Volksliteratin* and her proverbs are a form of *Literarisierung* on a popular level of speech, one on occasion taken up by her interlocutors: "You have me to thank for that—I taught you how to speak," she tells Laurencio (p. 236), who had pointedly observed, "I know proverbs too." Ironically enough, Gerarda is able to articulate expertly the idealized Renaissance concept of the proverb as the embodiment of natural wisdom— "Hijo, estos son todos los libros del mundo en quinta essencia. Compúsolos el vso y confirmólos la experiencia" ("Son, these are the quintessence of all the books in the world. Usage made them up and experience confirmed them") (p. 391)—which her own practice belies. (In *Don Quixote*, on the other hand, while Sancho spouts proverbs with unself-conscious ease and aptness, except when they go to his head, it is left to Don Quixote to define their significance for him.) It is perfectly clear in the case of Gerarda and her proverbs that Lope is pushing the natural to artificial extremes and off-handedly turning one of his creatures into an instrument for his own virtuosity. Gerarda's dueling matches in proverbs with other characters— Celia during the supper scene (p. 194), Laurencio (pp. 235 and 395), Dorotea (p. 372), Teodora (p. 373)—are a novel travesty on disputational by-play. The proverbs come by twos and threes, with more rhyme than reason, sometimes through purely verbal associations or even pure caprice:

> Ger.: . . . *que no ay olla tan fea que no tenga su cobertera. Nuestro yerno,*
> *si es bueno, harto es luengo;* pues *nadie diga desta agua no beberé,*
> que suelen mudarse los tiempos.
> Lau.: *Mudança de tiempos, bordón de necios.*
> Ger.: *Assí es redonda y assí es blanca la luna de Salamanca.*
> Lau.: Gerarda, Gerarda, *la muger y el huerto no quieren más de vn*
> *dueño;* que *la donzella y el azor, las espaldas al sol.*
>
> (p. 235)
>
> Teo.: No me agrada esta nueua compañía [*scil.,* Felipa].
> Ger.: *Tocóse Marigüela, y dexóse el colodrillo de fuera.*

Teo.: Plegue a Dios, Gerarda, que sea agua limpia.
Ger.: Obispo por obispo, séalo Don Domingo.
Teo.: Las malas tixeras hicieron a mi padre tuerto.

(p. 373)

Ger.: No pot is so ugly that it doesn't have its lid. Our son-in-law, if he is good, is all he needs to be; so let no one say I won't drink of this water, for times have a way of changing. *Lau.: Changing times, the simpletons' crutch. Ger.: So the moon of Salamanca is round and so it is white. Lau.: Gerarda, Gerarda, woman and garden require only one proprietor; since maiden and hawk, back to the sun.*

Teo.: This new company is not to my liking. *Ger.: Little Mary put on her bonnet and left the back of her head showing. Teo.: God grant, Gerarda, that it be clean water. Ger.: As bishops go, let it be Don Domingo. Teo.: Bad scissors left my father blind in one eye.*

Although Teodora stands far behind Gerarda in the number of proverbs she uses (twenty), she is ahead of the other two figures—Laurencio and Celia—who accumulate a significant number (twelve and ten, respectively). Appropriateness to age and social station, as Morby remarks, is a factor here, and perhaps, one might add, the geminal relationship of the two older women. But only the proverbs of Gerarda are prompted by gratuitous mimicry:

Lau.: ¿Cómo te han de doler [las muelas] si no las tienes?
Ger.: ¿Cómo no riñe tu amo? Porque no es casado.

(p. 232)

Teo.: Tú me agradas, Gerarda, que hablas y comes.
Ger.: Esse niño me alaba, que come y mama.

(p. 192)

Lau.: How can they [teeth] ache if you don't have any? *Ger.: How come your master doesn't scold? Because he's not married.*

Teo.: You have the right idea, Gerarda, you talk and eat. *Ger.: Hold that child up to me who eats and sucks.*

Only Gerarda's proverbs show her fancy alighting on a single word:

Ger.: Prestado lo da todo la naturaleza.
Lau.: Por poco tiempo lo fía.
Ger.: Cochino fiado, buen inuierno y mal verano.

(p. 232)

Cel.: Nueue vezes has bebido.
Ger.: Escuderos de Hernán Daza, nueue debaxo de vna manta.

(p. 197) [154]

Ger.: Nature gives everything on loan. *Lau.:* On short-term credit.
Ger.: A pig on credit, good winter and bad summer.

Cel.: You've taken nine drinks.   *Ger.: Hernán Daza's squires, nine
under one cover.*

The oddness and reconditeness—in a word, the artificiality—of so many
of Gerarda's proverbs constitute a studied eccentricity. In this, as in other
respects, her variation on the role of proverb-spouting go-between is a self-
conscious one. Gerarda shares her author's awareness that she is the heir to a
literary tradition; she cultivates her role with obvious enjoyment and is
herself amused by the spectacle she offers.

Strikingly transformed by her ebullient loquacity and irrepressible comic
verve is the Celestinesque motif of regret over a vanished past. The proud
evocation of bygone days of power and prosperity becomes a capricious
recalling of questionable domestic vicissitudes with her husband, Nuflo
Rodríguez. The somber and sardonic humor characteristic of the usual
panegyric of vice is transformed into the most casual ironic understatement;
the weight of evil evaporates in effervescent gaiety. In Gerarda wine induces
merriment, not, as in Celestina, melancholy; Gerarda's tears are only
alcoholic bleariness. Everything she relates is reduced to the same level of
inconsequentiality: thefts of silver, exposure to public shame, service in the
galleys, her own infidelities (p. 193). Everything is understated with ironical
offhandedness. The very connecting thread of all the reminiscences is her
husband's own sense of humor—"¡Qué gracias! ¡Qué cuentos!" ("What
jokes! What stories!"). She recalls his bon mots as much as his equivocal
feats: "La primera vez que yo me fui de con mi Nuflo, no estuue más de
cinco meses fuera de su casa. Aun aora se me acuerda con qué gracia que me
dixo quando boluí: 'Aguardaría la señora a que fuesse por ella'" ("The
first time I left my Nuflo, I was not gone from his home more than five
months. I can still remember how amusingly he said to me when I returned:
'Madame, I suppose, was expecting me to come after her?'") (p. 194).

This tendency to minimize the importance of things, to reduce them to
childish trivialities—"aquella niñería del estudiante" ("that prank with the
student") (p. 193)—or whims—"Por curiosidad supe algo" ("Out of
curiosity I've dabbled a bit"), when sorcery is mentioned (p. 435)—gives
the diminutives used by Gerarda a special quality foreign to those of Celestina
quoted earlier, a rococo effect *avant la lettre*. The very love Gerarda deals in is

symbolized by "Cupidillo": desire, sensual but trifling, rather than consuming passion. "Aquí está Cupidillo," she tells Dorotea, turning the depiction on the *búcaro* into the child-god himself, "aquel de tu edad, aquel dulce matadorzillo. Toma, açótale por el mal que te ha hecho" ("Here's cute little Cupid; he's just your age, the cunning little murderer. Here, whip him for the harm he's done you") (p. 157). The phrase "bobilla, desconfiadilla" ("little ninny, suspicious little thing") which she uses for Dorotea in the same passage is not merely ingratiating, or, to use Spitzer's terms, a verbal expression of her function as go-between in linking the most diverse things, a function which the diminutives of Celestina also fulfilled. It also suggests how impossible it is to ascribe more than minor importance to the young and their little passions when one views them from the height of eighty years. The similarity of perspective between Gerarda and her creator is inescapable here; I shall return to it in the concluding chapter. There is something almost grandmotherly in her reference to Fernando, to his "lagrimillas mugeriles, los suspiros a medio puchero, como muchacho acabado de açotar, que ha perdido la habla" ("womanish tears, half-gasping sighs, like a little boy just whipped who can't get his breath") (p. 423). They belittle him but not without affection. Félix Monge is quite justified in calling Gerarda's use of diminutives less "teleological"—that is, purposeful —than Celestina's and noting the "matiz afectivo" ("affective shading") they sometimes acquire.[155] She may recommend Don Bela as a "hombre de disculpa, y no mocitos cansados" ("man for whom there's some excuse and not these tiresome young boys") and urge on Teodora "para todo acontecimiento . . . hombres, hombres, y no rapazes" ("for every eventuality . . . men, men and not boys") (p. 73), the emphatic repetition reminding us that Lope really stands closer to Don Bela than to Fernando. But like Lope's, Gerarda's view of Fernando is not without a certain indulgence which softens the disparaging tone of the "Fernandillo" she uses for him (pp. 73, 121, 436) and even affects the general diminutive "temper" (to use Amado Alonso's phrase) of other references: "vn lindo que todo su caudal son sus calcillas de obra . . . y de noche broqueletes y espadas . . . capita vntada con oro, plumillas, vanditas" ("a dandy whose entire worldly goods are his needlepoint breeches . . . and at night bucklers and swords . . . and a cape dipped in gold, all feathery and ribbony") (p. 69). In the same phrase in which she refers to him as "aquel bobillo, polligallo, quiérelotodo" ("that little ninny, chick-cock, grab-all") (p. 452)—slipping from a diminutive to a familiar diminutive-like word and then to what appears to be a pure invention; pare the "commíralotodo" ("gawker that you are") she uses for Don Bela (p. 392)—she can even offer to help Dorotea win him back.

There is little difference between the mixed tone of her words here and the affectionate reproach she later addresses to Dorotea: "¡Qué melindroseta eres, rapacilla!" ("How dainty and squeamish you are, my girlish one!") (p. 451).

A final and quite unprecedented aspect of Gerarda's use of diminutives is her own technical awareness of doing so, which clearly reflects Lope's, and is of a piece with her overall self-consciousness in the role of go-between: "Compraréle de camino medias y çapatos. ¿Çapatos dixe? Çapatillos, y aún no es bastante diminutiuo" ("On the way I'll pick up some shoes and stockings for her. Shoes did I say? Shoelets, and even that's not diminutive enough") (p. 134). Her comment is strictly suited to the fundamental "notional" or quantitative sense of the diminutive, but how strange the literary precision sounds in a descendant of Celestina![156]

Gerarda's manner of expression, to anticipate for a moment, confirms her affinity in spirit and outlook with her creator. Her wish to squeeze all possible expressiveness from her diminutives is what we should expect of a professional writer. The varied forms of *reductio ad absurdum*—mock-seriousness of tone, comical understatement, coupling of elaborate literary or rhetorical techniques with prosaic substance, of poetic diction, hackneyed or not, with everyday situations—are of a piece with the manner and tone of Lope's Tomé de Burguillos, whose mischievous irony is prone to undermine the exemplarity of *exempla* as Gerarda's does when it links Dorotea, for instance, with a paragon of virtue: "Si hablas en su virtud desta niña, será nunca acabar; si fuera en el tiempo de las fábulas, ya fuera piedra, como Anaxarete" ("Talk of this girl's virtue, why one could go on endlessly. If these were the days of myth, she would be stone by now, like Anaxarete") (p. 190).

Gerarda shares with her creator something of the double vision of old age: she has one wary eye on the hereafter (though we shall see that its perception, unlike her creator's, is not very clear) and the other on the world of men, whose weighty preoccupations she finds trivial and irresistibly amusing. No more than her creator does she turn from the world; instead we find her fondly trifling with it. The reduced dimensions people and things assume in her outlook are the same ones that Lope's Tomé will be dealing in when he turns from human protagonists—himself and his washer-woman sweetheart—to felines, adding *La Gatomaquia* to his *Rimas*.

There is something of Lope's virtuosity, too, in Gerarda's tendency to make words sonorous playthings that bounce off one another less in plays of wit than in free plays of fantasy devoid of any conceptual basis; indeed, the playfulness that characterizes her entire handling of language points toward her creator's ludic spirit. In her indefatigable spouting of bizarre proverbs, often willfully irrelevant, she seems to express some whimsical striving of Lope after originality at any price. Gerarda's style, in this aspect, constitutes a capricious imposition of art upon nature; in her handling of diminutives, on the other hand, and in other aspects of her expression, nature more nearly holds its own against artifice. Gerarda's affinity with her creator suggests, in any case, the need to consider the interplay of art and nature in the *acción en prosa* as a whole, as seen from the perspective of the author. In the examination of this question I hope to find a stylistic key to the work.

Art and Nature

The whole of Lope's literary career, as Menéndez Pidal demonstrated in his now classic monograph, "Lope de Vega: El *Arte Nuevo* y la *Nueva Biografía*,"[157] may be defined in terms of the power of attraction upon Lope of the twin forces of art and nature, and the increasing subtlety with which they are conjugated as his career advances. In the last analysis, as Menéndez Pidal showed, the Platonic and Renaissance idealization of nature always holds the edge over art in Lope's allegiance. Spontaneity of inspiration, inborn endowment, individual temperament, native literary tradition, modern culture took precedence over acquired craftsmanship and over the forms and standards of classical antiquity. But as Lope grew older he was less concerned to rank than to reconcile. In his style as a whole the inherited resources of the humanistic and classical tradition are fused with his native informality, simplicity, and imaginative fantasy, the proportions alone varying to suit the level of cultural sophistication of his audiences. The stylistic level of the plays, written as the years passed for an increasingly refined public, keeps rising, while the more elaborate prose and poetry destined for his most cultivated readers, under his individual enlivening touch, remains well this side of the extremes of *culterano* artifice. Art and nature, far from being discrete categories, are more and more viewed as interpenetrating. Early in his life, as Menéndez Pidal, citing him, reminds us, Lope had looked on his *romances* as pure incidentals, like cornflowers "springing up when the grain is sown" ("nacen al sembrar los trigos"); and on his plays as wildflowers—"flowers on the field of his plain ('vega') that appear without cultivation."[158] But later the metaphor, characteristically organic, is much refined:

> Mas cuando del arado el diente corvo,
> muerde la tierra en que el humor reside,

las flores que divide
no son al trigo estorbo,
y así con sus preceptos y rigores
cultiva el arte naturales flores.[159]

But when the hooked tooth of the plow bites the earth in which the moisture is found, the flowers that it pushes aside are no hindrance to the wheat; thus with its precepts and demands art cultivates natural flowers.

We find Lope resorting to such terms as "artificiosa naturaleza" ("artificial nature") and "natural arte" ("natural art").[160] From the analyses already made it is clear that in such interpenetration there may be blending as well as contrast; overlaying, overlapping, dovetailing, as well as comic incongruity. We have observed the fusion of rhetoric and colloquiality, of lowly substance and formal artifice, natural movement and elevated style, the calculated artifice of sudden bluntness and directness, the juxtaposition of colloquial speech and ornate prose. Rather than a doctrinal concern we have here a temperamental inclination. Behind the esthetic issue is a need to relate the cultivation of style and form to the process of living, to bring together the two spheres of Lope's own being: psyche and style, nature and nurture.

Amidst the literary polemics and the destructive parody of the scenes of commentary on the mock *culterano* sonnet, one finds Lope touching upon the question of art and nature in comments clearly significant for the style of the *acción en prosa*. A conversation in the first of the scenes between Ludovico and César leads the latter to remark: "Aunque es verdad que tiene principio [el arte poética] de la naturaleza, ¿qué bárbaro no sabe que el arte la perficiona?" ("Although it is true that [poetic art] has its beginnings in nature, who is so uncouth as not to know that art perfects it?") (p. 335). As Morby notes in his abundant documentation of this passage, in Lope's versions of this standard doctrine, he always assigns a large place to inborn talent. Much earlier, indeed, he had even echoed a Ciceronian statement: "que eran mejores las cosas que la naturaleza hacía que las que el arte perficionaba" ("that the things made by nature were better than those which art perfected").[161] In now conceding a larger place to artistic craftsmanship, Lope is careful to make clear what he understands by its "perfecting" of nature. His "perficiona"[162] means both improving upon (refining) and carrying to completion, that is, fulfilling a natural process: "Aquel poeta es culto que cultiua de suerte su poema que no dexa cosa áspera ni escura, como vn labrador vn campo, que esso es cultura, aunque ellos [los culteranos] dirán que lo toman por ornamento" ("That poet is cultured who so cultivates his poem that he leaves nothing rough or obscure, as a farmer does a field. This is what culture is, although [the *culteranos*] will say that they understand it to be ornamentation") (p. 330).

These words emphasize the pre-Gongorine sense of *culto* as the desired result of a process of polishing and refining of form and style, in contrast to the sense implied in "ornamento," a learned ornateness that complicates both.[163] According to Lucien-Paul Thomas, Lope's agricultural analogy echoes Juan de Robles:

> Ya se sabe que *cultivar* significa labrar y beneficiar los campos para que den fruto . . . Esto se traslada galanamente a los ingenios . . . que beneficiados con los estudios renuncian la aspereza y bronquedad de la ignorancia, y quedan hábiles para las obras y discursos convenientes a la vida humana y la policía y̆ conversación de las gentes.[164]

> It's well known that *cultivar* means to work and fertilize the fields so that they will be productive . . . This may be handsomely applied to minds . . . which, fertilized by studies, abandon the roughness and harshness of ignorance and become fit for mental and physical activities suitable to human life and for refinement and intercourse among people.

One notes that Lope changes the emphasis from cultivation of the mind to cultivation of the poem, underscoring the element of organic process in the poet's activity, that is, the collaboration of nature with art. And the "ornamento" which his speakers so casually brush aside is, ironically, applicable not only to excesses of the *culterano* type, but to their own excessive literary and erudite adornment of speech and behavior.

Besides this general comment, the question of art and nature by implication underlies certain passages of the specific commentary in the following scene. The right of nature to occasional primacy over *cultura* is asserted, for example, when Ludovico remarks: "Lo vnico, lo aplaudido, lo grande, aunque yerre sin disculpa, se ha de venerar por acierto" ("What is unique, applauded, and great, though it be hopelessly irregular, is to be venerated as a sure achievement") (p. 357). This remark is the conclusion he draws from a discussion occasioned by the epithet "ronco" (hoarse) in the sonnet being commented upon. The combination "ronca rana[,] mosca del agua" ("hoarse frog, waterfly") is ridiculed on the principle that "la metáfora ha de ser según la proporción, como el vestido" ("the metaphor should be to the measure, like a suit of clothes" (p. 357); the "causa de conveniencia" or connecting thread (the importunity of both creatures) is here too tenuous. However, a Virgilian use of the epithet, despite its novelty, is cited approvingly by Ludovico: "Virgilio llamó a los cisnes roncos, y le disculpa Ambrosio Calepino, dando la culpa al estrépito de la alas" ("Virgil called swans hoarse and Ambrogio Calepino exonerates him, putting the onus on the whir of the wings") (p. 351). Calepin (s.v. *raucus*) explains that Virgil is thinking of swans "who by the beating of their wings as they fly produce a harsh noise in the air like the sound of trumpets." [165] If there is "harshness" here, Calepin's explanation proves that this is a case not of obscurity but, for the *cognoscenti*, of "perspicuity." For Julio the unexpected novelty is an asset: "Estoy cansado desta dulçura y suauidad con que dizen que cantan" ("I am tired of that sweetness and smoothness with which they are said to sing"). Ludovico, too, decries *canoro* (melodious) and *sonoro* (harmonious) as "such commonplace attributes of theirs" (p. 356). It is the claim of the new, the fresh, the spontaneous, especially over the staid and tried, that is being advanced. As a counterpart to the condemnation in the whole scene of the "confusión de los términos mal colocados" ("disorderliness of misplaced terms"), the abuse of artifice by the *culteranos*, Lope advocates a roughness of texture of a more natural kind, the effectiveness of the occasional asperity left in the field cultivated by art. It may be noted that in an earlier scene, no doubt remembering Garcilaso (Eclogue III, l. 83), Julio had showed open-mindedness toward even as harsh a form as *somurgujóse* ("plunged"), acknowledging that "aunque es significatiuo es áspero" ("although it is expressive, it is harsh") (p. 271). Roughness may be a source of freshness, Lope seems to suggest, and the importance of the latter quality causes the modern in the end to be given the edge over the ancient by the literary discussants in Act IV, scene 3. The principle "many things are respected because they are ancient which do not equal those we see today" (p. 342) is exemplified in a well-known anecdote concerning Michaelangelo. Impatience is here expressed with the clichés of slavish literary conventionality, as it is in other parts of the work with excessively hackneyed and prosaic expression: "Estoi . . . pudrido de ver que en todos los epitafios ha de entrar el caminante" ("I am . . . sick to death of seeing that the passer-by has to be included in every epitaph") (p. 362); "Los cultos deste tiempo sabrán mucho de calças, porque todo es calçar estrellas, calçar flores, nubes, noches, soles, y aun ponelle chapines a la Luna" ("The *cultos* of this age must know a great deal about footgear, considering all they put on the feet: stars, flowers, clouds, nights, suns, and even clogs on the moon") (p. 361). The latter example ridicules the particular form of unimaginativeness which makes a routine even of the novel, indeed of the bizarre, the extreme degree of novelty.[166] On the other hand the ingenious new *agudeza* of the lighted lantern that leaves the bearer in the dark (p. 280) provokes Julio's admiration, as has been seen.

In Lope's writings on the subject of *culteranismo*, namely, his answer to a "Papel que escribió un señor destos reynos . . . en razón de la nueva poesía" ("Paper Written by a Gentleman of These Realms . . . concerning the New Poetry"),[167] we find him concerned to safeguard the principle of novelty as a means of maintaining vigor and freshness of expression, while drawing the line at what he considers the exaggeration of this principle at the expense of clarity and the continuity of stylistic tradition. In *La Dorotea* he exhibits what might be called a constructive form of novelty in a device already noted: the timely resort to the most natural type of spontaneity. We have observed the vigorous effect produced by the underscoring of key developments or remarks with the starkly simple statement or the obvious unelaborated metaphor: "Yo sé que es don Béla vn necio" ("I know that Don Bela is a fool") (p. 316); "No lo puedo sufrir, Felipa" ("I can't bear this, Felipa") (p. 312); "Mi Fernando se va, no quiero vida" ("My Fernando is leaving, I don't want to live") (p. 126); "Templado basta.—Quitado digo, Iulio" ("Moderated it will do.—Freed me, I tell you, Julio") (p. 381); "Y como quien para que vna cosa se limpie la vaña en agua, assí lo quedé yo en sus lágrimas de mis deseos" ("Like someone who bathes something in water to clean it, I was bathed clean of my desires in her tears") (p. 381); "esta passión zelosa, que como vna cortina de nube se opone a toda la luz de mi entendimiento" ("this jealous passion, which shuts out, like a curtain of cloud, all the light of my mind") (p. 255). The contrast with the common recourse by the characters to recondite or *recherché* expression is striking. When Gerarda, in the next to the last scene, criticizes Laurencio for over-acting the part of grief-stricken messenger—"Bien pudieras escusar tan encarecido estilo de contar vna desgracia; que bastauan las palabras sin las lágrimas y los sentimientos sin los sollozos" ("You could well have dispensed with so elaborate a way of relating a misfortune; the words were sufficient without the tears and the feelings without the sobs") (p. 455)—such explicit advocacy of simplicity and naturalness is a revelation by the author of the esthetic he has himself favored.

It is to be noted that Gerarda's words, addressed as they are to one who in a situation of daily life is adopting the manner and speech of a character in a Senecan play, pertain to natural spoken utterance rather than to artistic expression in writing; they complement thereby those of the members of the literary academy. It is clear that Lope's broad-ranging interest in forms of expression takes in the living language as well as the literary medium and by this very fact tends to bring them closer together. This is clearly an interest of long standing and it will be well to pause to note certain of its earlier manifestations.

What kinds of language, what levels of style, what degree of artifice, of naturalness, Lope had long been asking himself, are most appropriate and effective in given circumstances, situations, emotional states? He could give the traditional answer in terms of the rhetorical *aptum*: "Personas, tiempos y ocasiones guardo / con artificio de un hablar gallardo" ("I observe persons, times, and occasions through the artifice of elegant speech"), as Rhetoric herself had said in the Temple of Learning of *La Arcadia*.[168] But Lope needed something more subtle than so pat a formula. He had long championed natural spontaneity as the language of love, simple authenticity as the key to that of music: the already noted sonnet of the *Rimas sacras* extols both. But he also saw that the borderline between natural and artistic expression is not clear-cut. Did not Quintilian himself "attribute the art of rhetoric to nature"? So recalls a monk as he delivers a long excursus on rhetoric in *El peregrino en su patria* (1604).[169] And in 1621 we find Lope noting complementarily that "los que hablan, aunque sea en las calles, plaças y tiendas" ("people speaking, even in streets, marketplaces, and shops") make use of rhetorical figures.[170]

Helping to shape his attitudes in this whole area was his Christian piety, deep and abiding despite all his lapses. Noticeably offsetting with the years the appeal of classical and humanistic patterns of rhetoric and poetic ornamentation was the valuation the Christian faith had placed upon the *sermo humilis* in accord with its unclassical prizing of the virtue of humility. "A new *sermo humilis* is born," notes Erich Auerbach in reference to the Gospels and Augustine's *Confessions*, "a low style, such as would properly be only applicable to comedy, but which now reaches out far beyond its original domain, and encroaches upon the deepest and the highest, the sublime and the eternal."[171] As early as *El peregrino*, in the aforementioned excursus, a distinction is made by Lope between the language appropriate in talking to men and to God. Lope's monk recommends "un moderado hablar, que ni bien seáis notados de la dulzura del estilo, ni de la rusticidad del lenguaje. Esto hablando con los hombres, porque con Dios más habla la sencillez del corazón que la dulzura de la lengua" ("a moderate way of speaking, that you may neither be criticized for the sweetness of your style nor for the rusticity of your language. This when speaking with men, since with God simplicity of heart speaks louder than sweetness of tongue") (p. 152). He touches the heart of the matter when he quotes St. Gregory to the effect that "la verdadera oración es el gemido y conpunción del pecho, y no el sonido de las compuestas palabras: que es lo mismo que dixo el que nos enseñó a orar con humildad a su eterno y increado Padre" ("the true prayer is the moan and compunction of the breast and not the sound of well-composed words, which is the same thing we were told by Him who taught us to pray with humility to His eternal and increate Father"). Reinforcing the humility ingrained in his nature, Lope's humbling experiences of self-prostration and confessional outpouring before Christ crucified made him prize simplicity of utterance, even inarticulateness, for the sake of genuineness: "Si no te hablo dignamente, Jesús, perdóname," runs one of the *Jaculatorias* included in 1626 with the *Soliloquios*, "que de quien ama, más valen desatinos, que de los que están libres, cuidadosas discreciones"[172] ("If I do not speak to you as you deserve, Jesus, forgive me, for from one who loves, incoherences are worth more than clever niceties"). A sonnet published the preceding year with the *Triunfos divinos* had contrasted the susceptibility of "príncipes de la tierra" ("princes of this world") to the "conceto / que de vana rhétorica se viste" ("concept dressed up in empty rhetoric"), and God's concern with the soul, recalling to God:

> que vos no me queréis a mí discreto,
> sino turbado, arrepentido y triste.[173]

> you wish me not clever but distraught, sorrowful, and sad.

It was easy for Lope with his undissociated sensibility to make such originally Christian humility serve the expression of feeling in the secular sphere. "The tongue of love" of the already quoted sonnet of the *Rimas sacras* is in that collection the tongue of sacred love (although this becomes plain only in the sextet of the sonnet), while on Fernando's lips in *La Dorotea* (p. 247) it is exclusively that of profane love and its simplicity goes unnoticed in his allusion. Moreover, in the case of relationships purely in the secular sphere, when Lope finds himself in positions of both subservience and intimacy toward a patron who was a "prince of this world"—the Duke of Sessa, especially, and also the Count of Lemos—he is sometimes in a quandary as to how to reconcile the different aspects of the relationship on the verbal level. In articulating his uncertainties, he then airs his thoughts on the give-and-take between artistic and natural, or high and low, levels of style. Some time between 1616 and 1621 he writes his already cited epistle to ask the favor and largesse of the Count of Lemos, whom he had served as secretary and probably as valet some twenty years previously (beginning in 1598) for a short period. The opening speculations show the effect of his *Erlebnis* on stylistic decorum:

Mostrara yo con vos cuidado eterno,
mas haveros vestido y descalzado
me enseñan otro estilo humilde y tierno.
La vana ostentación de hablar pensado
no corre aquí con el honor parejas,
aunque digáis: Quin termin de criado.
No es cortesía hacer alzar las cejas
a un gran señor con estupenda Musa,
pudiendo hablar debajo de las tejas.
. . . .
Yo que en amor las dulces cuerdas pulso,
por Dios que os he de hablar como amor manda
con libertad y natural impulso.

(*OS*, I, 447–448)

I would like to display endless deference toward you but having
dressed you and removed your shoes has taught me a more humble
and affectionate style. The vain ostentation of words that are weighed
does not here keep pace with honor, although you may say: what
servant talk! It is not a courtesy to make a great lord raise his
eyebrows by a stupendous muse, when one is able to speak
offhandedly . . . I who in love pluck sweet strings, by Heaven will
talk to you as love demands—freely and with a natural impulse.

With the Duke of Sessa we do not simply have such an occasional piece,
of a type (the epistolary) sufficiently formalized to find its way into print,
but private correspondence continuing over several decades. Such correspondence belonged to a category of writing that tradition placed beyond
the pale of rhetoric, as Lope was well aware, even when the addressee was
among the high and mighty.[174] Here too he encounters stylistic dilemmas and
we can see him pondering their implications, though it is quite clear that
humility of manner and style came easily to one of Lope's modest
background, accommodating temperament and hierarchical outlook: "Si
lo más que se sabe es hablar apropósito, quien sabe acomodar su grandeza a
tanta humildad todo lo que quiere sabe" ("If the most one knows is how to
speak appropriately, one who knows how to adjust his greatness to such
humility knows all he needs to").[175]

Familiarity in the letters is often an acknowledged violation of normal
stylistic decorum. "Señor excm.º, los términos más significatiuos esos son
los que tienen mejor lugar en las epístolas familiares" ("Most excellent sir,
the most expressive terms are those most at home in familiar letters"), he
tells his patron after making a "cruel comparación" between the telltale

smell of onions and the patent unworthiness of certain purchasers of titles.[176] Such jocular allusions to matters of style and expression, indicative of a self-observant literary mind, are also signs of a lingering insecurity in his relationship with his patron, which periodically impels him to reassure the Duke that he is properly respectful despite the familiarity of his manner. But when it comes to accounting for the simple tone of the love-letters he had written to Marta de Nevares, which the morbidly inquisitive Duke demanded to read, we merely find new affirmations of what we already know. Lope offers no other justification than that "el amor . . . no quiere lo que se siente con elocuencia, sino con sencilla y descansada libertad" ("love . . . does not want to say what it feels with eloquence but with simple, easy freedom"),[177] a view elaborated upon in another letter, in which he speaks of his love-letters as "niñerías que pasan entre los gustos del trato, cuya domestiquez no es a todos notoria" ("childish trifles that occur amidst the pleasures of dalliance, the intimacies of which not everyone is privy to"), adding: "Donde habla amor puro no hay cosa más extrangera que los colores retóricos; assí me passaua, assí lo escriuía, solicitando más a la voluntad que al entendimiento" ("where pure love speaks, nothing is more alien than the colors of rhetoric; this is the way it went with me, this is the way I wrote it, drawing more on the will than on the understanding"). Lope also affirms that to anyone but his most understanding patron (!), the letters would seem "bárbaros, que la lengua de los amantes sólo la entienden los naturales de la misma prouincia" ("barbaric, since the language of lovers is understood only by natives of the same province").[178] In the back of his mind is clearly his own sonnet, a kind of personal *locus classicus* for the expression of what he is saying here: that directness is the quality most suited to the everyday intimacy of a settled love-relationship—no longer courtship, not yet satiety—and that rhetorical artifice is wholly uncalled-for.

Passages such as those cited show that it is not by chance that a letter of Dorotea's which Fernando happens upon before his reluctant departure for Seville begins: "Fernando mío, ¿para qué son buenas tantas satisfacciones? Las que me diste anoche fueron bastantes; que más me desenojaron tus lágrimas entonces, que aora tus palabras; que no ay retórica para persuadir coraçones airados, como efetos tan humildes" ("My Fernando, what is the good of so many apologies? Those you gave me last night sufficed; your tears melted my anger better then than your words now, for there is no rhetoric for persuading angry hearts like such humble effects") (p. 106). Lope is here offering a significant perspective from the standpoint of "humility" on the literary posturing of his protagonists. But Dorotea, "desvanecida de discreta" ("giddy at her own cleverness") as she is, coincides with her creator only fleetingly in this attitude. Lope remarks to his patron on his own reluctance to "desvanecer el sujeto" ("turn the head of the person concerned") in matters of love:

> Yo confiesso a Vex.ª que pudiera haber escrito estos v otros papeles con cuidado; pero parezióme y me pareze sienpre que en esta materia lo que más muebe es lo más seguro, y haziendo este efeto lo más claro más presto, y lo más dulce con mayor eficacia, nunca gusté de desbanezer el sujeto, sino de mober la potencia que estuuiese más de mi parte.[179]

> I admit to Your Excellency that I could have taken pains writing these or other notes but it seemed to me and still does that in this area the surest thing is what is most exciting, and since what is clearest has this effect most quickly, and what is sweetest most efficaciously, I never favored turning the person's head but instead arousing that faculty most favorable to me.

Here there is undeniably a note of practicality in the espousing of simple directness. The suasory purpose which rhetoric serves is best accomplished in such private amatory contexts by nonrhetorical appeals. In other instances practicality becomes outright calculation and what seems ingenious is really disingenuous. We find naturalness and artifice becoming indissolubly joined. The "llaneza" (plainness) of certain love-letters written for his master's use Lope explains on the grounds that "en tales ocasiones ha de enmudecer la bachillería y hablar el afecto" ("at such times pedantry should keep still and feeling speak").[180] He counsels "demostraciones que lleguen hasta lágrimas y obedezca, pues soy su Ouidio hasta el postrer capítulo de este *Arte amandi*" ("putting on a great show, and even weeping—now just do as I say, since I'm your Ovid down to the last chapter of this *Art of Love*"). *Mutatis mutandis*, this assumption of the role of *profane* director to the patron is an anticipation of Gerarda's role vis-à-vis Don Bela, while the care for histrionic effects befits the protagonists of both the *Proceso* and the *acción en prosa*.

In nonamatory contexts we find an even more explicitly "rigged" naturalness: "Ese estilo llanísimo . . . es el mayor artificio en tales ocassiones; que no en todas se puede lebantar el estilo" ("This very plain style . . . is the greatest artifice on such occasions; not on all can one elevate the style"), explains Lope apropos of a letter for his master to send to a duke.[181] But sometimes, when Lope's own relationship to his patron is in question, rather than simulation or cynicism, genuine ambivalence seems to lie behind the professed espousing of simplicity: "Vex.ª sabe que yo le amo como debo; pienso que lo he encarecido más que si dixera quantas enargías han hallado la Poesía y la Retórica" ("Your Excellency knows that I love you as I should; I think I have underscored it better thus than if I uttered all the *enargeias* that poetry and rhetoric have discovered").[182] How evasive the "como debo" ("as I should") sounds, pointing (perhaps unconsciously) to mixed feelings toward one who had humiliated Lope as much as he had helped him.[183] It is pointless to ask where artifice begins and naturalness ends in such a declaration, since the feelings expressed are not themselves completely crystallized or clear in the speaker's mind. The lucidity which will allow Lope, in *La Dorotea*, to move beyond such inchoate ambiguity to a constructive sort of ambivalence, one of affirmation and reconciliation, is not visible in the *arrière-boutique* of his correspondence. Yet the live tensions discernible there surely contributed to the stylistic flexibility of the prose dialogue, with its capacity to marry spontaneity and calculation; simplicity and ambiguity; manipulation for shock effect or simulated directness that disarms, on the one hand, and, on the other, brilliantly unconventional vigor of expression or adherence to the most obvious and ordinary diction. "Natural" rhetoric shades off into rhetorical artifice in the noninterrogative questions, the reiterated vocatives and imperatives, the techniques of transition, the irony and sarcasm, the asyndeton-like broken utterance. Condensed and concise expression cuts through discursiveness in all tones from the extreme artlessness of Dorotea's recurrent "Estoy en estremo triste" ("I am extremely sad"), through the natural asyndeton of her "Todo llega, todo cansa, todo se acaba" ("Everything runs its course, everything palls, everything has an end") (p. 454) and the plain straightforwardness of Fernando's "Ya no ay amor de Dorotea" ("There is no love of Dorotea any more") (p. 404), to the contrived simplicity of "Sacaron las espadas y entre los dos le han muerto" ("They took out their swords and between the two of them killed him") (p. 455) and the brevity figures openly based on rhetorical models:

> *Iul.:*   ... Sería larga de contar la historia.
> *Lud.:* Pues haz vna brachilogía, como aquel verso:
> > *Abrasa a Paris amor,*
> > *roba a Elena, el griego se arma.*
> *Iul.:*   Pues digo en essa imitación:
> > *Ausentóse Fernando,*
> > *iuró, mintió, boluió, rogó llorando.*

(p. 338)[184]

Jul.: The story is too long to tell.   *Lud.:* Well, give us a *brachylogia*, like those lines: "Love fires Paris, he steals Helen, the Greek arms." *Jul.:* Well, on that model, I say: "Fernando absented himself, swore, lied, returned, implored in tears."

Contrived simplicity characterizes figures tacitly based on rhetorical models as well: "Referiros el coloquio era cansaros. Habló con zelos, respondí sin amor; fuesse corrida y quedé vengado" ("I won't bore you by relating the exchange. She spoke from jealousy, I answered without love; she went off indignant and I had my revenge") (p. 416).

The characters' speech styles, in their variability, move thus between poles of naturalness and artifice. In the remarks leading up to the *brachylogia* just quoted, a colloquial anacoluthon is followed by high-blown rhetorical invocations of supreme governing forces; Fernando says:

Esta satisfación me pareció indigna de mi obligación a muger tan principal como Marfisa, y no auiendo remedio de otra suerte, para confirmar las pazes; de que a mí ya se me daua menos. ¡O Tiempo! ¡o Amor vengado! ¡o mudanças de Fortuna! ¡o condición humana!
(fol. 246r)

Such amends seemed to me unworthy of my obligation to so fine a woman as Marfisa, and there being no other possible hope of making up, something I was less anxious to do, anyway. Oh Time! Oh Love avenged! Oh shifts of Fortune! Oh human nature!

The concept of *mudança* (mutability) is reinforced by a citation of Camoens, then Fernando goes on with his account, proceeds straight to the *brachylogia*, and ends with the combination of conceit and *enargeia* in the already quoted passage on "lagrimillas, ya no perlas" ("little teardrops, no longer pearls").

These varied interweavings in the characters' speech styles of artistic and naturalistic expression are surface manifestations of an underlying Lopean esthetic which bases *poiesis* on the mutual permeability of art and nature. To the extent that the characters overstep, that art for them ends by perverting nature, Lope dissociates himself from their excesses. For him art perfects nature and nature reciprocates by vitalizing art. Though his characters distort this ideal balance, Lope affirms it; the stylistic phenomena we have been observing show how he has managed to reconcile an abiding trust in nature—a Renaissance faith never lost—and a whole-hearted commitment to the full resources and possibilities of art.

Art and *Interés*

It is in the light of Lope's concern with the interaction of art and nature that the theme of *interés*, so persistent during the long life of the creative nexus, acquires its full meaning. An examination of the theme in this light may therefore conclude the consideration of style in *La Dorotea*.

No doubt Lope's experience with Elena left him with a lasting conviction, rightly or wrongly derived, of the corrupting power of wealth, gave the innumerable formulations of this apparent fact of life by poets and moralists, past and present, a personal relevance, and changed even hoary common-places—like the "Ouidio dixo que más daño auía hecho el oro que el hierro" ("Ovid said that gold had done more harm than iron") scorned by Julio (p. 83)—into lapidary reflections of what personal experience had demon-strated.[185] In the design of *La Dorotea*, Don Bela, as we have seen, becomes an *indiano*, for Lope's age the very embodiment of wealth—of "las Indias"— and Fernando, the poet, is made indigent to a degree beyond even his creator's experience. Such polarization leads to a highlighting of the already noticed opposition between real and metaphorical riches, between the world's materialism and the resources of the poetic imagination. It is in the light of this conflict that the theme of *interés* may most appropriately be examined. Although the bald, elemental struggle between love and money sometimes shows through, embedded as it is in the substructure of the work as a vestige of earlier elaborations of the material, one can see on examining the contexts in which it does so how effectively Lope has now fleshed out this issue and transcended the crudeness of a simple dichotomy.

The issue is perhaps most starkly joined in the Coro de Interés of Act II, a fact which the ornate and figured style of that chorus does not conceal. From the action Lope has here abstracted a simple rivalry between money and love conceived in terms of laying siege to a prize, a conception stemming ultimately from the Ovidian view of love as warfare, with *interés* inevitably as the superior force. When we examine the actual situation between Don Bela and Fernando the oversimplification becomes apparent, for we see that Fernando's poetic vocation and its appeal to Dorotea causes *both* rivals to view their contest in terms of the claims of art as well as those of love and wealth, leads each in his own way to poeticize his suit, and thus subtly modifies the character of their contest.

Again the handling of the twin figures of Gerarda and Teodora makes them much more than mere agents of *interés*, expediters of Don Bela's claims against those of Fernando. Undoubtedly they are motivated by varying degrees of cupidity and need: in her very first words Dorotea brands

Gerarda "vna vil muger" ("a vile woman") whose incentive is simply "el interés que le han dado" ("the bribe they've given her") (p. 74), and soon she states bluntly, in reference to her mother, that "el oro la ha vencido" ("gold has conquered her") (p. 99). But from the first scene it is plain that Lope is writing variations on the functions of this geminal pair, endowing them with unprecedented verbal sensitivity, making them delight in sparring with each other and in pure play with words. In the end these features quite transform them.

A stripping down of the struggle to bare essentials in a manner reminiscent of the Coro de Interés occurs during the flare-up of recriminations that precedes the reconciliation of Dorotea and Fernando.

> *Fer.:* En no competir con el oro, pienso que fui cuerdo.
> *Dor.:* Las espadas son de azero, y el amor es loco.
> *Fer.:* Contra oro no ay azero . . .
> *Dor.:* Leí en vn libro de fábulas que luchauan Hércules y Anteo, que era hijo de la tierra, y que con sus grandes fuerças Hércules le alçaba en alto. Pero que quando boluía a poner el pie en ella, cobraua mayores fuerças quando más rendido.
> *Fer.:* ¿Qué quieres dezir en esso?
> *Dor.:* Que luchando amor y interés, que es inuencible gigante, si estuuieras presente, todas las vezes que pusiera en ti los ojos cobrara nueuas fuerças para defenderme.
>
> (pp. 314–315)

Fer.: In not competing with gold, I think I was sensible.   *Dor.:* Swords are made of steel and love is mad.   *Fer.:* Against gold there is no steel . . .   *Dor.:* I read in a myth-book that Hercules and Antaeus, who was a son of the earth, were wrestling and that Hercules with his great strength kept lifting him up. But that every time his foot touched earth again, he regained his strength, all the more the more overcome he was.   *Fer.:* What do you mean by that? *Dor.:* That when love was struggling with self-interest, which is an invincible giant, if you had been present, every time my eyes lighted on you, I would have gained renewed strength to defend myself.

Dorotea's climactic *aplicación* unravels a *fábula* similar to the *exempla* of the Coro de Interés. Yet the significant point is the psychological appropriateness of such a reduction in the emotionally charged atmosphere of the reunion. We have here the convincing and accurately observed reflection of a need for self-justification on both sides which strips differences of all complexity and ignores underlying tensions. Such a need is consistent with the view

Lope has been giving us of the characters of Fernando and Dorotea, the fatalism and passivity earlier manifested in Fernando's "Me ha de matar el oro" ("Gold will be the death of me") (p. 91) and Dorotea's weakness of will. The oversimplification is thus a reflection of individualities; the generalization formulated holds not in itself but as an expression of those who formulate it. The exemplarity is more psychological than moral.

Interés, finally, is glaringly highlighted in Fernando's final words on Dorotea and in the view of her future afforded by the horoscope. As Fernando recounts the final months with his mistress, before the definitive rupture, he declares: "Bien quisiera Dorotea quererme solo. Pero ya no podía ser, ni el interés la dexaua" ("Dorotea would have been only too happy to love me all by myself. But that was no longer possible, nor would her self-interest allow it") (p. 408). Later he states flatly: "No dexará Dorotea sus Indias...que ya sabéis que el derecho las llama género auaríssimo" ("Dorotea will not give up her Indies...for you know that the law calls them [women] a most avaricious breed") (p. 417). Dorotea's covetousness will here appear as that of women in general. We subsequently learn from the horoscope that Dorotea will in fact have become wealthy when she tries in the future to lure Fernando back and will tempt him with riches as well as love (p. 440). But we already know that the key to Dorotea's nature is ambivalence. Even in their formulation, these descriptions suggest a commingling rather than a contention of love and material-mindedness, sustaining the direct views we have of her in the course of this same Act V.

Rather than being an allegory of the contest between Love and Riches, therefore, the work, by making all the characters, in their several ways, view the issue in terms of art as well, becomes in fact a thoughtful inquiry into the *nature* of the appeal of the material and the affective and into the subtle ways in which the appeal of one may overlay that of the other. Lope's attachment to the world of things and sensations and his equal propensity for living to the full the life of the emotions are thus both drawn into the orbit of his concern with the process of *poiesis*.

Throughout *La Dorotea* we constantly notice divergent valuations of poetic and material riches, contrapositions of them, suggestions of possible reconciliations. Some of these are the facile and superficial manipulations of overworn literary clichés that run rife in an age when poets and poetasters are legion. Yet the persistence of the trend and the subtlety it attains at times show that it reflects Lope's own musings on the expressive resources of his art and of the arts in general and on their capacity to sustain authentic alternatives to material values. To what extent can talent be its own reward in an inevitably material world? What weight can it carry in the eyes of others? Ovid's blunt "Carmina laudantur sed munera magna petuntur" ("Poems are praised but fine gifts are asked for") (*Ars amatoria*, II, 275) by no means suffices as an answer. Lope's insights are far more refined and, for all his downright insistence on *interés*, the *acción en prosa* mirrors in its meaning the compensations he increasingly found with the advancing years in artistic expression.

To bring out the persistence of the thematic and stylistic trend we are observing, we need only recall certain passages already noted and indicate additional ones. In the very first words Don Bela utters, it will be recalled, he awkwardly sweeps into a single vast hyperbole the same sumptuary poetic materials—gold, rubies, diamonds, pearls—that Fernando and every other poet of the age deal in as a matter of course. Rather than constituting a display of the poet's cornucopia, however, his words place the traditional jewels in the transoceanic setting of the trader's world and are proferred not as attributes of Dorotea but as offerings to her, extensions of actual gold already promised. Even in Fernando's most lavish displays of poetic abundance, on the other hand, the wealth is always conceived qualitatively as well as quantitatively, metaphorically as well as hyperbolically.

In the scene of Don Bela's wooing of Dorotea, as we have already had occasion to see, Lope has established subtle correlations between the material properties present and their poetic equivalents in the dialogue. We may recall how Dorotea's eye is attracted by the *nácar* color of the carnations depicted with such refined naturalism on the cloth of *primavera de flores* unfolded before her. (*Nácar* may here, as commonly, suggest a whitish iridiscence, as of mother-of-pearl. It certainly suggests a rose or pink shade, as the subsequent equivalence to *encarnado* shows;[186] compare the full passage quoted above, p. 490). When Dorotea's eye is subsequently also attracted by the same *nácar* shade in the much more prosaic form of stockings, the materialistic basis of the whole sequence is underscored.

Don Bela, prompted by Gerarda, invites Dorotea to sing a second selection by offering her a "coupling of a ruby and a diamond" (p. 183), and very soon in the poem appear white and red narcissi and roses "vestidas de blanco y nácar" ("dressed in white and mother-of-pearl"). (A pink or rose shade is again clearly intended.) These details of chromatic correspondence between the poem and its immediate context—the chromatism harks back as well to the earlier *nácar* in which pink seems to overlay white or pearl-color— seem subtly attuned to the meeting of minds being effected between Dorotea and Don Bela, though here these details do not reflect a play of allusion or taste between them but simply the artistry of Lope.

In the first clash between Teodora and Dorotea (I, 2) we have already seen how the former flings Dorotea's terms "ironías" and "literalmente" back at her like so many counterfeit coins—palaver (*parola*), not *palabras* (words)—underscoring their lack of value by her sarcastic terminology: "*aprouechada* está de parola" ("she's *well-stocked* with palaver"); "de ironías quedará *rica* literalmente" ("she'll be literally *rich* in ironies") (fol. 7v; emphasis mine). Dorotea picks up her "rica" and retorts, "¿qué riqueza como la de su entendimiento, persona, y gracias?" ("what riches like those of his mind, person, and accomplishments?") (fol. 8r), to which Teodora angrily and crudely replies: "¿qué gracias, qué persona, qué entendimiento tiene, si le confiessas pobre?" ("what accomplishments, what person, what mind can he have if you admit he is poor?") (fol. 8r). Left alone, Dorotea lengthily expands on the contraposition of poetic-affective and material values: "¿Qué riqueza como oírte?" ("What riches like hearing you speak?"); "esse agrado tuyo, esse brío, esse galán despejo, essos regalos de tu boca . . . ¿qué Indias los podrán suplir, qué oro, qué diamantes?" ("that attractiveness of yours, that dash, that elegant smartness, those favors of your mouth . . . what Indies can make up for them, what gold, what diamonds?") (p. 79). Consistently with this outcry, Dorotea makes a diamond ring the instrument of her attempted suicide at the end of the act as Fernando dashes off under her windows. The conflict of the material and the poetic is thus presentationally reinforced.[187] Consistent likewise are Dorotea's jubilant words in celebration of winning Fernando back: "No quiero Indias, ni cautiuar mis años. ¿Qué oro, qué diamantes como mi gusto?" ("I don't want any Indies, nor to shackle my years. What gold, what diamonds can equal what gives me pleasure?") (p. 374).[188]

Fernando's account of the liaison relates that "Me vi mil vezes con tal vergüença y lástima, que no pudiendo cubrir aquellas hermosas manos con diamantes, las bañaua en lágrimas, que ella tenía por mejores piedras para sortijas que las que auía vendido y despreciado" ("Thousands of times I found myself so filled with shame and pity that, being unable to cover those beautiful hands with diamonds, I bathed them in tears, which she considered finer stones for rings than those she had sold and scorned") (p. 303). Dorotea has learned from Fernando that the sparkle of tears is more precious than that of diamonds. Into such metaphorical riches he transmutes her real jewels, playing on a need for self-delusion even greater than his own. The moral ambiguities implicit in their poetic existence are evident here and, at the same time, the presence of a poetic imagination spilling over into life in an attempt to compensate, however unevenly, for the tawdriness of reality. All is not seen as falsehood and deception by Lope; there is a vein of sympathy in his irony as he contemplates, perhaps reminiscently, this instance of the poetic phenomenon, in the process reinstilling a certain presentational vigor into the worn Petrarchistic adornment. But when a similar situation between Fernando and Marfisa is unfolded before our eyes, moral ambiguity has become duplicity, and susceptibility to poetry is compounded by histrionic impulses. The result is an outright subversion of poetic values by material ones, an adverse demonstration carried so far as to make the spheres of art and nature appear irreconcilable. Lope in this instance is standing at the greatest esthetic remove from his characters.

With Fernando the tendency to play at reconverting poetic properties into their material and natural realities, if a mark of facility and virtuosity, is also, as we have already observed, the sign of a poet's professionalism. When he tells us that roses and jasmines were made by nature from the leftovers of the materials out of which it had "composed" Dorotea (p. 225), or conversely that nature distilled "all flowers, all aromatic herbs, all rubies, coral, pearls, jacinths, and diamonds" in the fashioning of Dorotea (p. 300), he is running through the repertory of his riches like a miser going over his hoard. The saturation of the dialogue at certain points with an over-abundance of "rich" imagery, whether naturalistic or sumptuary, in the aggregate creates the impression of a Lope who himself is poring over his poetic store, rejoicing in its possibilities, touching it up, straining to make it as palpable as the sculptor's or artist's materials. It is noticeable that in the concession to Góngora with which the seance of the literary academy begins, it is said of his "new phrases and rhetorical figures" that they "embellish and enamel" the language and enrich it with "uncommonplace terms" (p. 317). Stopping short of Góngora's techniques himself, Lope nevertheless understands the aim—enrichment and renewal of the medium of poetry— by which they are animated.

As for Fernando, he is obsessed, as we know, by a sense of the unevenness of the struggle between material wealth and his poetic *copia*. If at first he feels wealthier than Croesus with the "tan rica possessión" of Dorotea, very quickly he is haunted by the thought of his material poverty. When he lavishly executes, with assistance from his interlocutors, his series of variations on the theme of gold, first apropos of the dream in which the metaphorical equivalence of "Indias" and wealth is worked out in all detail, later when he reacts to Ludovico's description of the new prosperity of Dorotea's house, he does so with the feverish energy of despair. While this energy derives ultimately from Lope's abiding preoccupation with *interés*, it expends itself here solely in embroidering superficial tracery. Later (p. 284), in his obsessiveness, Fernando on the contrary cuts the contest between natural poetic endowment and material wealth down to the bone:

Fel.: La fortuna, ¿no compite con la naturaleza?
Fer.: No, porque siempre la derriua.
Fel.: ¿Qué llamáis fortuna?
Fer.: Riqueza.

Fel.: Doesn't fortune compete with nature? *Fer.*: No, because it always topples it. *Fel.*: What do you call fortune? *Fer.*: Wealth.

In the next act, in a moment of anger after Dorotea has had the *maladresse* to call Don Bela *discreto*, Fernando bursts out: "Tenga plata, tenga oro, tenga diamantes, sea bien nacido; pero no sea entendido ni de buen talle" ("Let him have silver, let him have gold, let him have diamonds, let him be well-born, but he is not to have a good mind or good looks") (p. 316). The vehemence Fernando puts into insisting that his rival should not have *entendimiento* expresses as youthful petulance a conviction stated so often by Lope as to constitute an article of faith. The same vehemence and something of the same insistence were visible in the description of the rival to the hero of *La Arcadia*—"rico como ignorante y presuntuoso como rico" ("an ignoramus's wealth, a wealthy man's presumption"), and so forth—and they will still characterize the description of a rival husband in the eclogue "Amarilis" (1633): "sabio entre necio, lindo entre grosero, / mas pienso que decir rico bastaba" ("stupidly wise, foppishly coarse, but I think it's enough to say rich").[189] In intervening contexts Lope formulates the underlying thought in more general terms:

Comprar pueden los ricos la nobleza,
la autoridad y el personal respeto,
la obediencia, el deleyte y la belleza:
mas no el ingenio, el discurrir discreto,
calidad que a la tierra el cielo envía
por el don más heroyco y más perfeto.
                    ("Epístola al Conde de Lemos," *OS*, I, 454)

the rich can buy nobility, status, and respect for their persons, obedience, pleasure, and beauty, but not a good mind, clever thinking, an ability that heaven gives earth as the most heroic and perfect gift.

Conoce qualquier hombre
que hay otro más galán, más gentil hombre,
más rico y bien nacido,
más dichoso, más bravo y más querido;
pero en llegando a que confiese y diga

(tanto del alma aquella parte obliga)
que otro tiene mejor entendimiento,
las riendas perderá del sufrimiento.

(Laurel de Apolo, OS, I, 192–193)

Any man will admit that another is more elegant, a more polished
gentleman, richer, of higher birth, luckier, braver, better liked, but
when it comes to admitting and saying (so much store is set by that
faculty) that another has a better mind, he'll be beside himself.

Lope fastens with satisfaction on classical formulations which support his
views: "Pues rendirse al ingenio de otro no está visto en el mundo, por más
amigo que sea: *Qui velit ingenio cedere rarus erit.* Aunque en todas las demás
cosas se confiese inferior, como Marcial dice" ("As for deferring to another's
intellect, it's unheard of in this world, however much of a friend he may be.
Anyone willing to yield in talent will be most unusual, as Martial says").[190]
Here at last there emerges a conviction that the artist's talent has after all
an absolute value which the world's valuations cannot alter. No doubt the
youthful feelings of compensation vis-à-vis Perrenot de Granvela preserved
or recovered in Fernando's outburst no longer have the capacity to take
possession of Lope as they once had, no doubt he is now seeing the childish-
ness of Fernando's resentment and exposing it. Still, the persistence with
which he reiterates throughout the years his unwillingness to admit anyone
else's superiority in intellect and talent is surely symptomatic. Even if
Fernando, in his insistence on *being* the poet, displays more vocation than
talent, behind him stands a Lope assured of his own genius, for whom the
sanctuary of art has become vital, a Lope who, moreover, will turn the
indiano evolved from the figure of his rival of long ago away from the
material—in the end the only gold Don Bela keeps will be "el hilo de oro
de la razón" ("the golden thread of reason")—and allow him to fall back
on long neglected poetic powers.

So, in the end, the contest between art and the world is a draw. One's
fancy may speculate on the worth of the treasure trove of poetic diction
vis-à-vis that of real gold and jewels; one may even establish some sort of
exchange on which they appear mutually negotiable. Ultimately, however,
art, like one's private *soledades*, is an inviolable personal preserve. Its ultimate
value is its permanence in a world where everything else is evanescent—
wealth, beauty, life itself. True, from the absolute perspective of the
Christian afterlife, even the value of art becomes illusory. Yet Lope's mood
of *desengaño* does not extend to art as such, only to the art that perverts
instead of perfecting nature. I will examine in the final chapter his reservations

toward Dorotea's aspirations to literary immortality. Yet in the fervor of her cry, "What greater riches for a woman than to see herself made eternal?" when Celia disparages Fernando's legacy of "versos, acotaciones y vocablos nueuos" ("verse, marginal notes, and new words") (p. 143), and of her declaration that love "aborrece el interés" ("detests self-interest") (p. 144), there is a Lopean fervor as well. In the end Dorotea will not be able, in a world of "historia," to emancipate love from *interés*. This does not mean, however, that either she or Lope embraces any less fervently a vision of art's self-sufficiency and of its everlastingness.

Desengaño
XI

The artistic cosmos of the *acción en prosa*, unlike those of Lope's plays, is intended as a simulacrum of our own. In this cosmos illusion is mostly self-induced and the hard ground of reality is the ultimate place of reckoning. What the nature of this reality may be, as an epistemological problem, is not a concern of Lope's: it suffices that his world "imitates" our own, a world created by God out of matter that is solid enough. His concern, as in the "Egloga a Claudio," is with the mutable character of reality, the corrosive work of time, the instability of forms and feelings constantly in process of transformation. The world is palpable and pleasurable enough; the trouble is that its shapes and delights are forever shifting and that the man who experiences them is himself transitory. Despite the moods of withdrawal and the authentic Neo-Platonic aspirations which leave their mark in *La Dorotea*, Lope remains deeply attached to the world of matter and sense. With the years awareness of evanescence grows on him viscerally; it is no longer simply a lesson heard and repeated. Out of his attachment to what is impermanent, his growing sense of impermanence within himself, arises the wistful disenchantment peculiar to the mood of *La Dorotea*, one of *desengaño en el goce vital* (disillusionment amidst the fruition of life), like the Lucretian "amari aliquid quod in ipsis floribus angat" (something bitter that brings distress even among the flowers), a mood bittersweet, not bitter, melancholy but acquiescent. Because he knows the world is slipping away from him, he looks at it with particular fondness and insistence, sees it sharp and whole, and celebrates its joys even as he records their impermanence. This blend of delight, regret, and acceptance permeates the *acción en prosa* with an urgent yet disinterested *desengaño*, a mood less linked to particular contingencies than in earlier expressions of the *amores de Elena*.

Three principal aspects of this sense of *desengaño* merit our attention and, at the risk of some overlapping, we shall examine them in turn: its meaning as expressed in the structure of the final act, where it culminates, and in certain controlling images in terms of which that structure is conceived; its temporal aspect—the interaction of the chronometric order already observed with time as subjectively perceived and intimations of timelessness; the reflection in *La Dorotea* of the Lopean experience of *soledad*.

Desengaño in the Structure of Act V

It is lyrically, in relation to the expression of *desengaño*, not dramatically, in respect to action, that is, to the story of Fernando and Dorotea, that the Aristotelian injunction that the end must give meaning to the work has been understood by Lope. The dénouement of the story can be foreseen from the outset; the surprises and hasty endings so often improvised for his plays are discarded. Though the last act may seem an epilogue, at one remove from the rest, it is in fact closely bound to it, for this act brings to culmination the sense of disillusionment building in earlier acts as the protracted beginning of the end gives way to the bittersweet ending. The backward glance in this act over the intervening months, the direct view afforded of the aftermath are essential to the temporal shading of the Lopean vision of *desengaño*. While the phrase of the Prologue "la fatiga de todos en la diuersidad de sus pensamientos" ("the disenchantment of them all in their various pursuits") alludes to the scope of this vision, it does not adequately render its quality and does not distinguish, as I shall attempt to do, between Lope's affirmation of life, the life of this world, and the experience of undeceiving he makes his characters undergo. When this experience is examined closely we shall find that it proves, for the central pair of protagonists, to be one not of renunciation but of inescapable recommitment to life in this world; and that the sudden violent deaths of Gerarda and Don Bela, along with the end foretold for Marfisa, while reminders of *memento mori*, do not imply a corollary exposure of the world as sham and inner void. It is here that the spirit of *desengaño* in Lope stands apart from the usual baroque denunciation of the world's false appearances, deceits, and nothingness, a kind of denunciation which Lope had indeed engaged in during the crisis of self-accusation reflected in the *Soliloquios* but which he had now left behind. The characteristic image of the bitter pill deceptively gilded will prove a touchstone of this distinction.

Desengaño is of necessity an eye-opening experience, a discarding of illusion and facing of ultimate truth. But in Lope, unlike Calderón no position-taker, no builder of allegorical structures, otherworldliness is not irreconcilable with worldliness. An unreasoned but genuine reconciliation is effected through cultivation of the affective response to the conflict, which is transcended and allayed in lyric expression. Nor is Lope a Quevedo, denouncing the human flawing of the ethical order on which the social order ideally rests. He lacks Quevedo's burning moral conscience and reforming zeal and is not goaded by the world's imperfections into satirical retaliation against man and society. The libels of Lope's youth are rooted in particular personal passions and if in his mature years he inveighs against favoritism, corruption, injustice, immorality, his remarks stem largely from disappointed personal aspirations. If things go well for him, Lope has no quarrel with the world. Perhaps in *La Dorotea* he is closest, among his contemporaries, to Cervantes in affirming life even as he acknowledges its transience and its finiteness. Yet his personal stake in his world is more obvious than Cervantes' and the expression of *desengaño* has a more markedly lyrical cast. His viewpoint is less detached, his irony less kaleidoscopic, his control over his characters' destinies more decidedly asserted.

The imposing architectonics of the work are fully meaningful only in relation to the theme of permanence and impermanence central to it. Just as literary patterns of conduct and style represent vain aspirations to circumvent the work of time by molding experience in forms as fixed and lasting as those of art, so the formal features of *La Dorotea* mark off segments of time which order but do not alter the process of change implicit in the action. The precisely delimited portions of time and space, which we have found to be so carefully worked out on a human scale, appear very securely joined, very solidly grounded, very much proof against change. In the end, however, these measured portions of man's world become the measure not of stability but of change, reflecting in the formal order of the *acción en prosa* the mutability which is its meaning. Their seeming fixity, like that of the sailor in the "Egloga a Claudio" "que pasó sin moverse el golfo al Oceano" ("who has crossed the abyss of ocean without moving"), serves only to accentuate the flux of a universe where nothing living endures in the same state. "Como quita cada día tan poco," Don Bela says of the work of time, "no se siente" ("As it takes away so little each day, you don't notice it") (p. 393). Its action at any one moment eludes us, but set one block of time against another and the traces of its work become plain. Within precise coordinates of time and space Lope traces the fluctuations of the long descending curve of his *acción en prosa* and reveals the process whereby the emotional relationships at its core have slowly come apart.

In the final act the pace of this process accelerates and the formal order in which it is set forth is itself modified. As we have already seen, there is a partial disjoining of the formerly carefully aligned scenic units, there are hiatuses in the uninterrupted temporal continuums of the earlier acts, making us less certain of our bearings. In a multiplicity of brief or fairly brief scenes (the act has twelve scenes and only one is long), Lope focuses on "la diuersidad de pensamientos" ("the various pursuits") of three characters in particular: Don Bela, Fernando, and Dorotea; the first in the first two scenes, Fernando in the lengthy third and the eighth, Dorotea in scenes 4–7 and 9–10. The last two scenes precipitate the conclusion by bringing the deaths, respectively, of Don Bela and Gerarda. The sequential character of the two scenes devoted to Don Bela and the two groups of scenes devoted to Dorotea is clear, as we know. There are hiatuses between these and the scenes dealing with Fernando, however. In the latter, accounts of the past (scene 3) and the future (scene 8) are unrelated to any specific present involving Dorotea or Don Bela. A temporal order, probably of twenty-four hours, still exists, but we are no longer able to align the different groups of scenes within it as clearly as in the other acts. The arrangement which breaks the fifth act into five segments less securely joined than before reflects in the formal order the fragmentation of the world built by the characters of *La Dorotea*. Within each segment we are offered situations, not actions; there is no progression and there can be no overall dramatic resolution, since the lives of the characters, being no longer enmeshed, no longer impinge actively upon one another. Indeed, there are no confrontations, no quarrels, conquests, contests, reunions, in the fifth act, as there are in the others; the principal characters do not come together at all. Marginal circumstances and chance happenings bring about the dénouement and we must look elsewhere for the unity of the act.

The overall sense of fragmentation and disorientation which we, as readers, derive from the outward ordering—the arrangement of scenes, the temporal discontinuities—has its correlative in the characters' perception of their experience. The effect of fragmentation and disorientation is sustained and reinforced by particular actions and patterns of behavior, which I shall presently describe. Lope also makes his characters, in certain moments of heightened insight, articulate responses to their predicament in imagery and figures which provide indications of the artistic guidelines followed by him in bodying forth their experience. Two recurrent motifs stand out:

that of the labyrinth and that of the city or edifice in ruins. The latter, we know, is bound up from the beginning with Lope's artistic reworkings of his experience with Elena; the former has other antecedents in Lope of which we shall take notice in a moment. Both the figure of the labyrinth and the imagery of ruins are evidently emblematic of a stage of *desengaño* suggestive of moral and spiritual bankruptcy: of bewilderment, the collapse of values with no necessary perception of new or true ones. Deliverance from the labyrinth, reedification or at least the perception of hard ground underfoot, of a firm foundation for renewal—these are of necessity the complementary stage of the process of undeceiving.

To what extent does Lope suggest such a stage or offer such a process in *La Dorotea*? If he does not reject the world as hollow and insubstantial, what emerges in the way of affirmation from the experience of *desengaño*? Put in this form, the question scarcely admits of a specific answer; Lope's art here eschews the formulation of precise positions. Besides religious faith he has only recommitment to life to hold forth as a reagent to disillusionment for Fernando and Dorotea. As we shall see later, the dispositions he makes of these and the other characters at the end are significant mostly in terms of what these characters mean to him as aspects of self-expression. In themselves such dispositions are simply a series of more or less incidental, more or less definitive dispensations that find their place in a larger artistic scheme. It is in seeking to delineate this total order that we may hope to apprehend the wider dimensions of the Lopean sense of *desengaño*. In pursuing the artistic configuration of the *acción en prosa* as it culminates in the final act, let us focus in turn, as Lope does, on Don Bela, Dorotea, Fernando, juxtaposing in the case of the last two the separate scenes or scenic sequences devoted to them. We will need to consider to what degree the poetic figures we have mentioned are in fact controlling ones, to observe the contrasts, shifts, involutions, disjoinings, and so on, which they entail. We must also observe how particular actions, patterns of behavior, tensions, and insights find a place within the total artistic configuration. While Lope, as ordainer of the characters' destinies, will never be far from our considerations, it will be in the final two scenes, where the focus clearly shifts from specific characters to their world as a totality, that we will best see the act and the work as a whole, see beyond the characters to the author and consider more closely the nature of his participation in their experience.

By way of introduction, let us glance briefly at some antecedents of the image of the labyrinth in Lope. That it had long figured in his repertoire of poetic motifs is clear from its presence in each of the introductory sonnets which he wrote to provide overviews, respectively, of his two main collections of lyrics: the *Rimas* (1602) and the *Rimas sacras* (1614). With more facility than profundity the figure is made representative of total worldly affective or moral situations. Lope also plays, somewhat superficially, with the figure in his dramatization of the Theseus story, *El laberinto de Creta* (The Cretan Labyrinth).[1] Undoubtedly he knew the "moralizations" of this story so much in vogue during the Counter Reformation. In Pérez de Moya's *Philosophía secreta*,[2] for example, the labyrinth is interpreted as:

> el mundo lleno de engaños y desventuras, adonde los hombres andan metidos, sin saber acertar la salida o sus daños, enredados en tantas esperanzas vanas, atados en contentamientos que no hartan, olvidados de sí, embebidos en sus vicios, aficionados a su perdición; finalmente rendidos a sus desfrenados apetitos.
>
> Por Teseo es entendido el hombre perfeto que sigue el hilo del conocimiento de sí mismo; este tal sale deste peligroso laberinto, el cual, no soltándole jamás de la mano, con este conocimiento de sí, vencido el terrible Minotauro, que es su propia y desordenada concupiscencia, sale del mundo con maravillosa vitoria.

> the world full of deceptions and calamities in which men are caught without being able to discover the exit or to realize the harm they are doing themselves, enmeshed in so many vain hopes, bound by satisfactions that don't fulfill them, forgetful of themselves, absorbed in their vices, attached to their damnation: in a word, surrendering to their unbridled appetites. By Theseus is meant the perfect man who follows the thread of self-knowledge; that man gets out of this dangerous labyrinth who, never letting it out of his hand, with this self-knowledge, having conquered the terrible minotaur which is his own unrestrained concupiscence, goes out of the world marvelously victorious.

While in the opening sonnet of *Rimas* (1602) the labyrinth is simply a passing metaphor that evokes "neutrally" the Patrarchistic analyses of feeling contained in the sonnets of the collection—"le hurtáis el laberinto a Creta" ("you steal from Crete its labyrinth"), the poet says, apostrophizing the "versos de amor" ("love poems")—in the introductory sonnet to the *Rimas sacras* Lope dwells upon the figure in a more moralistic vein:

> Entré por laberinto tan extraño
> fiando al débil hilo de la vida
> el tarde conocido desengaño,
>   mas de tu luz mi escuridad vencida,

el monstruo muerto de mi ciego engaño,
vuelve a la patria la razón perdida.

I went into so strange a labyrinth, trusting the frail thread of life to
bring tardily recognized disillusionment, but your light having
conquered my darkness, the monster of my blind deception being
slain, lost reason returns to its home.

In contrast to the affirmative significance given the thread by Pérez de Moya,
Lope charges it negatively. It stands not for self-knowledge, hence safe-
conduct through the labyrinth, but for trust in the world; the "fragile
thread of life" is clearly an inadequate guide and intervention from another
quarter, divine illumination—"de tu luz mi escuridad vencida" ("your
light having conquered my darkness")—is required for deliverance, for the
tardy restoration of reason. This sudden chiaroscuro—light dispelling
darkness—takes us beyond the labyrinth and destroys the metaphorical
coherence of the sonnet. It expresses vividly Lope's sense of his human
weakness and his personal need of God's help—or rather, his assurance of
such help, for the poem is written from the standpoint of deliverance,
clearly before the final crises of the *Soliloquios* and the passion for Marta de
Nevares.

In *El laberinto de Creta* the thread becomes functional again, directly and
dramatically, as the key to the labyrinth. Lope here eschews both moral and
personal overtones.[3] However, in Theseus's account of his experience, a
sensation of groping in a labyrinth and of disorientation is conveyed:

Até el hilo de oro, y entro
dando vueltas a mil calles
por infinitos rodeos;
cuando pensaba que estaba
del laberinto en el centro,
estaba más lejos de él,
y cerca cuando más lejos.

(Ac., VI, 127b)

I tied the golden thread and entered, turning about in a thousand
avenues through endless roundabout ways. When I thought I was in
the center of the labyrinth I was furthest from it, and close when
furthest.

The thread is now gold as it will be in *La Dorotea*. The Platonic context
of the scene in which Don Bela evokes "el hilo de oro de la razón" ("the
golden thread of reason") (V, 1) makes it likely that Lope has conflated with

the labyrinth figure another: the Platonic "sacred golden cord of reason" that "every man ought to grasp and never let go" (*Laws*, sec. 645). In the play no particular significance attaches to the gold color nor are further expressive possibilities of the labyrinth figure exploited. Lope is indeed noticeably flip in the already noted remark he tosses off in a contemporaneous letter (May–June, 1617?) to his patron: "Aora me dizen que va Amarilis a la comedia del *Laberinto*: del suyo quisiera yo salir, mas no tengo ylo de oro, ni aún le quiero" ("I've just been told that Amarilis is going to the *Labyrinth* play; I'd like to get out of hers but have no golden thread, nor do I want one").[4] Only after he has himself ceased to tarry in the labyrinth, "olvidado de sí" ("forgetful of himself"), and gone through another period of painful groping for a golden thread, will the potentially dramatic lyricism of the sonnet and the casual suggestions of the play crystallize into a depiction, grounded in deep fellow-feeling, of a struggling Don Bela and convert the labyrinth into a symbol expressive of a deep human plight.

The final glimpse of Don Bela discloses, indeed, a state of feeling and, aside from the Neo-Platonic and Ficinian direction of his thought, a frame of mind similar to Lope's at the stage of spiritual development represented by the *Soliloquios*. In its brief compass, the first scene of Act V traces out a similar curve of emotional uncertainty. The phrase with which Don Bela describes his feelings at the beginning—"perdido estoy de triste" ("I am lost in sadness")—suggests utter dejection and utter disorientation. While Laurencio assigns a human cause to Don Bela's mood—"De la tristeza de Dorotea nace la tuya" ("Your sadness arises out of Dorotea's")—it clearly goes deeper. It has made him turn for relief to poetic composition but such relief has not been lasting. By opening with a dialogue that reveals his returning distress—we have noted earlier the groping, shifting character of the exchange with Laurencio—Lope forewarns of the practical inefficacy of the dazzling vision of Neo-Platonic harmony and spiritual tranquillity attained in the madrigal penned by Don Bela the previous evening. As he now proceeds to read and explain the poem, for Laurencio, we can foresee the ensuing relapse.

The poem, sixteen lines long, adapts very loosely the characteristic "circular" movement of Ficino's thought whereby the beauty of God descends as love into the created world and draws creation in delectation upward toward itself:

Miré, señora, la ideal belleza,
guiándome el amor por vagarosas

sendas de nueue cielos;
y absorto en su grandeza,
las exemplares formas de las cosas
baxé a mirar en los humanos velos,
y en la vuestra sensible
contemplé la diuina inteligible.
Y viendo que conforma
tanto el retrato a su primera forma,
amé vuestra hermosura,
imagen de su luz diuina y pura,
haziendo, quando os veo,
que pueda la razón más que el deseo;
que si por ella sola me gouierno,
amor que todo es alma será eterno.

(p. 386)

Lady, I looked upon ideal beauty, love having guided me along the
turning paths of nine heavens. And, carried away by its greatness, I
descended to look upon the exemplary forms of things in human veils;
and in your sensible form, I contemplated the intelligible divine
form. And seeing that the portrait so conforms to its first form, I
loved your beauty, the image of its divine and pure light, the effect
being that when I see you reason prevails over desire. If I am guided
by reason alone, a love that is wholly soul will be eternal.

In the first six lines the lady is told how the poet, having attained the
vision of ideal beauty (opening line) after being guided upward by love
(ll. 2 and 3) and deeply stirred by the greatness of this vision (l. 4), has
descended again to look at the "exemplary forms of things in human veils"
(ll. 5–6). The next six lines express the "conformity" between her beauty,
perceived by the senses, and the divine beauty that has been perceived by the
mind: it is the conformity of a portrait and its original ("its first form"),
of an "image" and the "divine and pure light" which it reflects (ll. 7–12).
The final four lines relate the effect on the poet of his contemplation of her
beauty: transcending of desire, perpetuation of love.

The affirmation that divine beauty is immanent in the human, the ideal
present in the particular, a premise of Ficino's Christian humanism, clearly
held a special appeal for Lope. As Don Bela now proceeds to explain, such
immanence enables love to "formar vna idea particular, que ama sin diuertir
el pensamiento fuera de los límites de la razón" ("form a particular idea,
which it loves without diverting the mind beyond the bounds of reason")
(p. 388). (Other forms of Platonic and Neo-Platonic thought saw the
contemplation of particular beauties as a point of departure for the ascent to

the idea of Beauty in the abstract, saw sentiment—love—as a means of rising to pure intellection.) For Don Bela, as for Lope in the already quoted Platonizing sonnets from *La Circe*, it is possible to rise to the universal without renouncing the particular, to cling to the beauties of this world in etherealized form.[5] When Laurencio confesses he does not understand the poem, Don Bela does not explicate it: he expounds its underlying concept by expanding upon the fifth chapter of the second discourse of Ficino's commentary on the *Symposium*: "Pulchritudo diuina per omnia splendet, et amatur in omnibus" ("The divine beauty shines throughout everything and is loved in everything"). It is the visible beauties of the earth and skies that are detailed and accentuated in this expansion, with their culmination in the beauty of woman: "Y vltimamente el hombre se admira en los rayos desta diuina belleza que en la hermosura de las mugeres sobre todas las inferiores criaturas resplandece" ("And lastly man rejoices in the rays of this divine beauty which shines forth in the beauty of women more than in any lower being") (p. 388). At the same time Don Bela's commentary articulates what is implied (but only incidentally) when the poem refers to the "divine and pure light" of the "first form" of beauty, that is, worship, as a Christian religious act, of the beauty of God manifested in the form of light descending as love upon the universe. The Ficinian circularity now appears as a lengthily elaborated downward descent of light (in the poem the descending movement is condensed into the single personalized "baxé" ["I descended"]) followed (rather than preceded as in the poem) by a briefly suggested upward movement. Descent and ascent are correlated as vehicle and tenor of a simile ("Assí como . . . assí . . ." ["As . . . so . . ."]), though their relation is properly one of complementarity, not equivalence. The equivalent descending movement is, however, implicit in the phrase "idea particular": descent necessarily comes between the vision of the ideal and the subsequent perception of it in the particular.

It is more evidently suggested in Laurencio's remark: "De manera que tú me das a entender que amas a Dorotea tan platónicamente, que de la belleza ideal suprema has sacado la contemplación de su hermosura" ("So you are suggesting to me that you love Dorotea so Platonically that from supreme ideal beauty you have deduced the contemplation of her beauty"). "Querría a lo menos quererla con este propósito" ("At least I should like to love her with this aim"), replies Don Bela, reintroducing into the conversation the melancholy uncertainty of its opening. The dazzling vision of the poem has been a deliverance not only from his own carnal desire but from the disaffection and venality of his mistress. To Laurencio's objection that the poem may be beyond her grasp, Don Bela had replied curtly: "Mira,

Laurencio, lo que ha de entender Dorotea de mi pluma son las libranças de los mercaderes para sus galas. Esto, basta que yo lo entienda" ("Look here, Laurencio, what Dorotea has to understand from my pen are orders to merchants for her wardrobe. As for this, it is sufficient if I understand it"). The ostensible addressee of the poem—the *señora* of the opening line, the second person of ll. 7, 11, 13—was never really intended to receive it; the poet is really speaking to himself, struggling for his personal emancipation. The reciprocity without which Platonic love between human beings had no meaning for Ficino scarcely enters into Don Bela's vision as he explains it; instead, Lopean *soledad* reappears. The setting casts a penumbra about the poem.

The problematical and solipsistic character given by such contextuality sets this apart from other Neo-Platonic expressions inspired by Marta de Nevares, discrete artistic entities free of shadowy contingency. But the full extent of such contingency becomes apparent only in the remainder of the scene. Memory of the struggles reflected in the *Soliloquios* clearly contributes to the sudden deepening of the shadows. Don Bela's anguish bursts all bonds and the dazzling vision of ideal beauty, of concentric spheres turning with "soft harmony," is all but obliterated. The "turning paths of nine heavens" through which Don Bela has ascended in the poem are abruptly transformed into unending involutions of the dark labyrinth of sensual attachment in which he sees himself groping:

> ¡Ay, Laurencio! ¿Quién ay que tenga entendimiento que no conozca que es mortal? Traen consigo los deleites por sombra la conciencia, como suelen dezir los que han muerto algún hombre a sangre fría que le traen siempre a cuestas. Dorotea es hermosa vnicamente, entendida, y con tantas gracias, que si el hilo de oro de la razón no me saca deste laberinto, creo que auemos de dezir al fin de la vida, como aquel rey de la Gran Bretaña, "Todo lo perdimos." (p. 389)

> Ah, Laurencio! What man with any understanding can fail to recognize that he is mortal? Pleasures bring conscience after them as their shadow, just as those who have killed some man in cold blood say that they always bear him on their shoulders. Dorotea is uniquely beautiful, intelligent, and has so many attractions that if the golden thread of reason doesn't deliver me from this labyrinth, I think we shall have to say when life is over, like that king of Great Britain: "We have lost everything."

A sense of mortality and sin overwhelms Don Bela; he is haunted, as his creator had been, by realization of the magnitude of the stakes involved.

His sense of having lost his way threatens to become absolute; he may lose his soul forever. The guidance by reason tranquilly assumed in the poem becomes a fevered groping for a fragile thread. The attenuated chiaroscuro of the scene becomes absolute, one of nearly unrelieved contrast without compenetration or penumbra; only the gold thread braves the shadows which have gathered so thickly upon Don Bela's conscience. The chiaroscuro, though still dramatic, inverts that of the opening sonnet of the *Rimas sacras*: darkness now displaces light.

The "golden thread" nevertheless constitutes the thematic link, *qua* light and *qua* reason, between the gloom of the scene's ending and the luminous vision recorded in the poem and commentary, with their assumption of governance by reason. It keeps a ray of Platonic aspiration alive even in the shadows of the labyrinth. Remembering his own struggles at the corresponding stage of his life, remembering no doubt also God's mercy to him, Lope will spare his creature the fate he had himself so feared. Not by giving him time, as it had been given to him—time to spare belongs to life, not art—but by making his death his deliverance and assuring that it does not catch Don Bela unprepared. In keeping with the reduced temporal span of the *acción en prosa*, in keeping perhaps, too, with the character of the *indiano*, less unregenerate, less caught in the backlog of sin than Lope had felt himself to be, Lope lets us understand that in the space of a week or so Don Bela has readied himself for death, for the death which he does not really expect, yet of which he seems to have a premonition, as the passage quoted shows. It is Laurencio who underscores his preparation.

> No sé qué traes de ocho días a esta parte, que no pareces el que solías. ¡Tú deuoto! ¡Tú contrito! ¡Tú melancólico! Si es diuino impulso (quiéralo el cielo), daré de albricias quanto me ha valido el ir y venir a casa de Dorotea.

> I don't know what's come over you the past week—you seem a different person. You, devout! You, contrite! You, melancholy! If this is a divine impulse (heaven grant that it is), I shall consider well spent all my time going back and forth to Dorotea's house.

A few moments later he adds: "No estás en mal estado de enmendarte, pues lo conoces" ("You're in a fair way to reform, since you see the need to").

Don Bela has attained a state of contrition, has come to understand the nature of his sin, to realize that love of creature, far from directing him toward "that sovereign artificer," is diverting him from love of God. Lope had written in one of the *Rimas sacras* (Sonnet 46):

Mas si del tiempo que perdí, me ofendo,
tal prisa me daré, que un hora amando
venza los años que pasé fingiendo.

But if I take offense at the time I have lost, I shall make such haste that
in one hour of loving I shall overcome the years I spent pretending.

The hyperbole is less extreme in the case of Don Bela. He is still caught in
the labyrinth, as the flickers of jealousy in the subsequent scene show, but
he is seeking the only way out, reaching for "the golden thread of reason,"
and he is headed for mass when we last see him. Lope safeguards him from
damnation even as he leads him to violent death. Touching but not tragic,
his death is well timed to remove him with dignity from the labyrinth of
human suffering. Far from being an act of retaliation upon an erstwhile
rival, it is a deed of mercy. The subsequent shamelessly overstaged report of
it by Laurencio merely underscores Lope's determination that it should not
affect the reader tragically.

As we have already noted, Lope lingers longest in the last act over the
depiction of Dorotea. He gives us a compelling picture of the bewilderment
and bitterness attendant upon the break-up of a cherished affective world.
Dorotea has no golden thread to grope for; the escapes she attempts prove
blind alleys and wrong turnings in the labyrinth in which she had already
(Act I, scene 3) seen herself as caught when contemplating her first move
toward a break with Fernando: "Quando aya passado lo mejor de mis
años en este laberinto amoroso, ¿qué tengo de hallar en mí sino arrepentimiento . . . ?" ("When I have spent the flower of my years in this amorous
labyrinth, what will I find in myself except repentance . . . ?") (p. 78).
Prior to her appearance in the last act, we are told through Fernando all that
has occurred: his alienation, her futile attempts to win him back. Laurencio's
remarks to Don Bela have apprised us of her unrelieved state of sadness.
Dorotea finds no deliverance, but in the culmination of the act—the final
two scenes—the labyrinth itself crumbles, so to speak, and a shocked Dorotea
is left to build a new mode of existence from the fragments. In earlier scenes,
moreover, the coming collapse of her world is anticipated in a series of small
shocks and petty destructions.

My figurative language is intentional, an attempt to suggest again the
controlling figures in terms of which Lope's dramatic imagination has
shaped the creative substance, informing it both dynamically in actions large
and small and structurally in the formal designs imposed. While it might
seem that imagery of the labyrinth and that of ruins would prove incompatible

when elaborated, this is not in fact the case. These figures are not allegorical constructs; they are embedded in the material as dramatic metaphors and they set up lines of force, not systematic conceptual patterns. Lope has combined them freely (he has also brought in suggestions of other figures), but there is no sense of their working at cross-purposes and we are unaware of logical inconsistencies because in the end all point in the same direction: toward a poetic and dramatic expression of disintegration and of the disorientation attendant upon it. I shall attempt no rigid compartmentation in my analysis, seeking rather to analyze figures in terms of context and function.

Lope's imagination turned quite naturally to "architectural" imagery for the expression of affective situations and relationships:

> El edifiçio del aborreçer se funda en la piedra del agrauiar.
>
> Las pendencias que tocan en lo viuo es como caerse la cassa sobre vn onbre.
>
> A la firmeza de un amor una buena obra sola en sazón tan triste hizo temblar y estremecer si no el dueño, la casa, si no los cimientos, las paredes, y por lo menos se cayeron algunas almenas, aunque se quedaron los muros firmes.[6]
>
> Hatred's building has wrongs for a foundation-stone.
> Quarrels that strike a tender spot—it's like the house caving in on a man.
>
> A single good deed at so sad a time made the solidity of a love quake and rocked the house, if not the owner; the walls, if not the foundations; and at least a few merlons fell off the roof although the walls remained solid.

An express articulation in the dialogue of the ruins figure (scene 3) hints at the function it is to assume in the rest of the act. From the beginning Lope's imagination had found in this motif an emblem of the experience with Elena Osorio in its totality, and it will be illustrative to look backward, for purposes of comparison, to earlier analogues. The passage in question in *La Dorotea* occurs before the heroine is reintroduced, associated not with her but with Fernando. As the latter concludes his long account of the cooling of his ardor, César remains skeptical:

> *Cés.:* ¿Es possible que no ay en vos reliquias del amor de Dorotea?
> *Fer.:* Ni apenas las señales que suelen quedar de las heridas.

Cés.: Guardaos no os engañe el gusto de la venganza, y la mal curada herida reuerdezca; que si boluéis, no ha de hauer estrago que no haga en vos. Seréis su Troya, seréis Numancia, seréis Sagunto. No ha de quedar en el edificio de vuestra vida piedra sobre piedra.   (p. 416)

Cés.: Is it possible that there are no remnants of love of Dorotea in you?   *Fer.:* Not even the scars that wounds commonly leave. *Cés.:* Be careful that the pleasure of vengeance does not deceive you and the badly healed wound flare up again. For if you fall back, there's no havoc she won't wreak on you. You will be her Troy, you will be Numantia, you will be Saguntum. Not one stone will be left on top of another in the edifice of your life.

An obvious analogue to this passage is the sonnet "Cayó la Troya de mi alma en tierra" ("The Troy of my soul fell to earth"):

> Mas como las reliquias dentro encierra
> de la soberbia máquina famosa,
> de la troyana reina victoriosa
> renace el fuego y la pasada guerra.
>
> (*Obras poéticas*, p. 96)

Yet since it contains within it the traces of the proud and famous construction, the fire and concluded war over the victorious Trojan queen are renewed.

While César's metaphor is mixed, the reference in both cases is to passion flaring up after it had seemed destroyed and receiving further punishment. In each instance the image is characteristically centered in the self, and it is not surprising that in the succeeding dialogue César specifies: "You will be her Troy, you will be Numantia, you will be Saguntum." It is the old equation city-self, here reduced to *exempla*, of which only Numantia does not echo Lope's ballads and sonnets. In César's warning, "Not one stone will be left on top of another in the edifice of your life," the

> basas, colunas y arquitraves juntas
> ya divididas oprimiendo el suelo

> pedestals, columns, and architraves all of a piece, now broken apart
> and burdening the ground,

of the sonnet "Vivas memorias, máquinas difuntas" ("Live memories, dead structures")[7] live on, and we perceive an echo of Belardo's apostrophe to Saguntum: "Ambos en el suelo estamos, / tú difunta, yo muriendo" ("Both of us are flat on the ground, you defunct, I dying"). The overpowering sense of destruction, disintegration, and ruin which had crystallized in ballads and sonnets about the examples of Troy and Saguntum has lost these specific *points d'appui* in *La Dorotea* but will gain new amplitude and power by being worked into the formal fabric of the *acción en prosa*. Lope had sensed long before 1632 that he was exhausting the conventional expressive capacity of symbols like that of Troy: "There is no reason for anyone to criticize the recurrence of the turtledoves and Troy," he observes in the preface to the *Rimas* (1602),[8] and though he bolsters himself with the precedents of Petrarch, Ariosto, and Alamanni, his tone is defensive. To be sure, the metaphorical equivalence between ruins and individual destinies, which governed the early cycle, will still provoke an occasional poetic afterthought, but only a rather perfunctory one: "the ruins of the days as evening comes on, with their first flowers *withering through infection or age*" on which I commented in the opening chapter.[9] In a sonnet (*OS*, I, 386) published in 1624 beginning

> Silvio, ¿para qué miras las ruinas
> deste edificio, fáciles victorias
> del tiempo en largos años . . .?

> Silvio, why do you look at the ruins of this building, easy victories of time in long years . . .?

the addressee is subsequently told:

> No mires piedras, donde vive y dura
> reliquia alguna de este excelso templo:
> mira, Silvio, de Phylis la hermosura.

> Don't look at stones, where no trace of this lofty temple lives on and endures; look, Silvio, at Phyllis's beauty.

Desengaño embodied in the symbolism of ruins had not been confined to lyrical expressions, however. It will be recalled that such imagery is also invoked apropos of Amphryso–Alba in the fifth book of *La Arcadia* at a stage of the story equivalent to that in which the quoted passage of *La Dorotea* occurs. In the *acción en prosa* César's words come when Fernando has completed his account of the ending of his love; subsequently he will be introduced to the horoscope of his future. In the pastoral novel the hero is similarly free of love when Polinesta tells him (to recall a passage quoted earlier):

Ya me parece . . . que estás dispuesto, Amphryso, para visitar el
templo santo del Desengaño; pues de aquella historia apenas se ven
memorias en tus discursos, ni en el mar de tu entendimiento los
edificios de aquella antigua Troya. Consumido ha el tiempo las
ruinas de la española Sagunto, y el olvido las reliquias de la africana
Cartago. (*OS*, VI, 441)

I now think . . . you are ready to visit the sacred temple of
Disillusionment, Amphryso, since memories of that story are scarcely
visible in your discourse nor are the buildings of that ancient Troy
in the sea of your understanding. Time has consumed the ruins of the
Spanish Saguntum and oblivion the remnants of African Carthage.

Here there is no tentative warning note as in César's remarks; the edifying
learning absorbed in the Palace of the Seven Liberal Arts has been a cure
for love as effective as any medicine: there is nothing left of the "buildings
of that ancient Troy." An analogue to this passage of *La Arcadia* is the
sonnet "El ánimo solícito y turbado" ("His spirit preoccupied and uneasy"),
in which the protagonist, also the Duke of Alba (Albano), finds not even a
vestige of Troy remaining on the grassy meadow where once it stood and
concludes that the flame of his love may also one day be as completely
extinguished. In neither case is there a temporal dimension: Amphryso's
visit to the Palace constitutes an instant cure and with Albano only a hypothetical future is involved. In cultivating the pastoral novel, Lope had largely
adhered to convention in such matters as atemporality and unmotivated
reversals of feeling. A *tabula rasa* is made of the past and a new future constructed as arbitrarily as Montemayor in his *Diana*, with the magic water of
Felicia, redirected the affective lives of his characters.

In contrast, there is neither *tabula rasa*, obvious edification, nor facile
reedification in *La Dorotea*. There is, instead, in César's words a personal
urgency that is absent from Polinesta's. The perfunctory ruins imagery in
La Arcadia points to nothing beyond itself; in *La Dorotea* the imagery is
revitalized by being integrated into an artistic economy directed toward the
expression of *desengaño* as a *process* of disjoining, unsettling, fragmentation,
an *orden desordenado* variously bodied forth in the work. Dramatized in
terms of fragmentation, the ruins motif is also recharged lyrically since it
now entails for Lope a heightened awareness of temporality: "the ruins of
the years" are now consubstantial with life itself for him.

Fundamentally César's figure relates to the experience of all the characters
as a representation of the author's *Erlebnis*. In keeping with the shift of the
Elena-figure to the center of the stage, however, it is more immediately

apposite to Dorotea than to Fernando. It is she, not Fernando, whose life is shattered when their joint world disintegrates. Even the labyrinthine imagery suits Fernando in no very specific way.[10]

While the whole brief presentation of Don Bela in scenes 1 and 2 is centered on his desperate attempt to sublimate his feelings and find deliverance from the labyrinth of self and world through an attempt to transcend them, with Dorotea there is no comparable movement. Despite impulsive gestures in the direction of the convent, she can only conceive of deliverance in worldly terms—*desamor*—or in terms of literary and histrionic escape. She is without resources beyond the self as she is without inner resources. She thus presents a curiously involuted picture: her attempts at escape all end up where they began.

In the two sequences of scenes in which she appears, we see her performing symbolic acts of destruction, magnified by rhetoric and feverishly overplayed, hiding behind outward show and assumed roles, resorting to artistic expression in poetry and music. But she remains trapped in the maze of her feelings and winds up in each instance in a cul-de-sac, defeated and drained. Histrionic exaltation can clearly only fleetingly deaden the awareness of truth; recourse to art cannot long suspend it.

In these sequences, Dorotea is constantly "on stage," the other characters —Gerarda, Celia, Laurencio, Teodora—coming and going about her, their entrances and re-entrances providing external grounds for beginning new scenes; such milling-about—the weaving in and out of Gerarda in particular—heightens the effect of motion directed to no end and sustains the impression of a maze surrounding the heroine. The scenic units mark off the different directions and guises Dorotea's struggle takes. The junctures will sometimes be found particularly significant in this regard.

In scene 4, Lope provides perspective for what is to come by presenting Dorotea "straight"—indifferent, defenses down and mask off—as we have not seen her before. But she rouses herself, flings about in the verbal contortions of her dialogue with the portrait, then wrenches free and destroys it. In the next scene, sustained by rhetoric, she gloats over her "victory," then turns to Fernando's love-notes and consigns them to the candle flame. But this protracted process tells on her, her spirits flag, and in the next scene it does not take much probing by Gerarda to bring out the simple truth: "Confiesso que me muero" ("I confess I'm dying"). In the last scene of this sequence Dorotea is practically silent, too dejected to speak. In the second sequence she appears to have recovered her composure and makes a show of high spirits (scene 9). Though these are belied by the song she sings, Gerarda, nevertheless, entering in scene 10, can still exclaim over her gaiety and finery. But Gerarda's probing again uncovers the truth: "Estoy tan triste que me pongo cosas alegres por huir de mí misma" ("I feel so sad that I put on bright things to escape myself") (p. 454). Dorotea voices again a resolve to enter a convent. But the next moment (scene 11) Laurencio brings the shattering news of Don Bela's death. When Dorotea comes out of her faint in the last scene, it is to learn that Gerarda too has died and to feel a world toppling about her.

The Dorotea reintroduced in scene 4 is unkempt and disheveled: "¿Tú descompuesta? ¿Tú los cabellos desordenados? ¿Tú por labar la cara?" ("You not made up? You with disheveled hair? You with an unwashed face?"), Gerarda exclaims (p. 423). As if dazed, Dorotea is indifferent to her appearance and Gerarda's words reveal that she has been so for days: "¡Tú llorando todo el día! ¡Tú inquieta toda la noche!" ("You weeping all day! You restless all night!"). The picture is one of a penitent Magdalene, that favorite baroque symbol of renunciation, a Magdalene with a difference, however, as the ensuing conversation makes plain:

> *Ger.:* . . . Bien sé yo que no lloras por penitencia, sino por no auerla hecho.
> *Dor.:* Y esso, ¿no es arrepentimiento?
> *Ger.:* Bien sé yo de qué le tienes.
> *Dor.:* ¿De qué, Gerarda?
> *Ger.:* De auer empleado mal tanta hermosura, tan rico entendimiento y tantas gracias. Pero dalas a Dios de que te ha traído a tiempo que lo conoces.
> *Dor.:* No fueran ellas mal empleadas si fueran bien agradecidas.
>
> (p. 423)

> *Ger.:* I know very well that you're not weeping out of repentance, but for lack of it. *Dor.:* And isn't that repentance? *Ger.:* I know what you're feeling it for. *Dor.:* For what, Gerarda? *Ger.:* For having made such poor use of so much beauty, so rich an understanding, and so many charms. But thank God that He has brought you to a realization of this. *Dor.:* They wouldn't have been put to a poor use if they had been properly appreciated.

Dorotea's penance remains within the worldly sphere—self-reproach over an error in sentimental judgment—and only ironically recalls the Magdalene's. The equivocal character of such penance had been sarcastically anticipated at the start of the *acción en prosa* by Gerarda's caustic "Dize que por deuoción y promessa trae vn ábito de picote" ("She says that out of piety and to keep a vow she is wearing a goathair habit") and Teodora's "¿Por quién hazes essa penitencia?" ("For whose sake are you doing this penance?"); while Dorotea had actually feared the day when "este sayal que visto sea silicio de tus brazos y penitencia de tus ojos" ("this sackcloth that I wear will be the hair-cloth of your arms and the penance of your eyes"). The "sack-cloth" which Dorotea will presently contemplate wearing as a nun will still reflect a resolution made purely on a worldly level.

But the full significance of Dorotea's present disarray is that it constitutes an esthetic as well as a moral travesty of the Magdalene. Earlier Gerarda had told Don Bela: "que como la moça es virtuosa y su madre miserable, ándase todo el año en cabello, ¡y qué cabello! Quando le peina y tiende, parece vna Madalena en el desierto" ("for as the girl is virtuous and her mother poor, she goes about all year long with her hair loose—and such hair! When she combs it and spreads it out, she looks like a Magdalene in the wilderness") (p. 134). Gerarda's *enargeia* evokes the ethereal beauty that radiates from the Magdalenes of El Greco or Ribera, betokening spirituality. The application to Dorotea is frivolous, of course, but it is a reminder of the natural beauty that has hitherto survived the plainness of her dress. (When we first see her, it will be recalled, though garbed in a sackcloth, she has been dressing her hair as she eavesdropped on Gerarda and her mother.) The present scene represents the neglect of such beauty, easily eclipsed without a minimum of art to "perfect" it. The "uncomposed" look, the unwashed face, the undressed hair, reflections of an unbeautiful state of mind, are disagreeable, almost repellent; they hinder any movement of sympathy from reader to character. Lope does not jeer as he did in his youth at Filis abandoned. There is no distortion, only unrelieved naturalism; the picture is not caricaturesque, merely bleak and painfully plain. Lope's art is too close to nature for comfort here. When Dorotea tears at her hair in the subsequent monologue with the portrait, the effect is chaotic, for she is not destroying an artful arrangement but adding disorder to dishevelment. The doubly disordered hair stands out against the intimate meaningfulness—the *orden desordenado* in miniature—of the "tousled hair" (the "cabellos rebueltos") which she evokes as once having so strongly appealed to Fernando.

Gerarda proceeds to belittle Fernando. She is unable to cheer Dorotea, who resists the disparagement, but beneath the surface of the conversation Gerarda's attempt to cut Fernando down to size is taking effect in an unexpected way. It implants in Dorotea the idea of a reprisal in miniature: she will destroy her lover's portrait and this human act of atonement will make up for the past. She sends Gerarda off on a pretext, takes out the portrait and confronts it. While Lope might have placed a scenic break at this point, he prefers first to pursue Dorotea's impulse to its dramatic climax. The continuity underscores a feverish need to act before misgivings overtake her.

Dorotea's struggle with the portrait has a dual character: she seeks in physical destruction a psychological outlet for resentment and she tries to achieve an identification of the portrait with its subject, to convert it into a true talisman. She succeeds in the first aim and gains momentary relief, but she fails in the second. The heart of the monologue is the second struggle. The vacillation between portrait and subject is fatal to play-acting and to self-delusion. The course of Dorotea's feelings, as seen in these two interacting struggles, is indeed tortuous; shifting pronouns, persons of discourse that shift with them as the portrait, Fernando, Teodora, Dorotea herself are spoken to or about in various tones indicate the changing directions. Though Lope's model is the same Ovidian Dido as in the letter to Fernando in Act III, the tone of assurance, the regained intimacy, the confident exposition, and the steady progression toward reconciliation found in the earlier letter are notably absent. The addressee—the portrait—cannot compel Dorotea's attention as could the vision of Fernando.

She starts by addressing the portrait as a likeness only: "Salid, salid, verdadero traslado del hombre más traidor que tiene el mundo" ("Come forth, come forth, faithful likeness of the most treacherous man the world knows") (p. 425). The *vos* of the second person marks the distance between portrait and subject, for Fernando is always *tú* to Dorotea. Still, the portrait exerts its fascination and, after covering it with reproaches, she begins to identify it with its subject: "Con estos ojos miráis a Marfisa, y con esta boca me engañáis a mí" ("With these eyes you look at Marfisa and with this mouth you deceive me"). Just at this point she changes direction, however, and aims her reproaches at herself. An indeterminate third person now denotes both portrait and subject: "¿A éste lleué yo los cabellos que por su causa me quitó mi madre?" ("Was it to this one that I took the hair my mother pulled out on his account?"). But rapidly she passes on and in quick succession addresses her mother and Fernando himself:

¡O madre, qué bien hazías! Tú aquéllos y yo éstos [cabellos], no quedarán en mi frente, porque te agradaron, porque dezías que nunca cosa ponía en paz tus deseos como verlos rebueltos. Y llamándome tu aurora, al salir la del cielo, con amorosos requiebros, como los pajarillos a las puertas de sus nidos me dauas, a imitación de sus vozes, los buenos días.

Oh mother, how right you were! You that [hair] and I this—there'll be none left on my brow, simply because you liked it, because you

said nothing so quieted your desires as to see it tousled. And calling
me your dawn, when heaven's appeared, with amorous serenades,
like the little birds at the gates of their nests, you said good morning
to me in imitation of their voices.

The portrait is forgotten, it is Fernando Dorotea is speaking to, tenderly.
She has strayed into a recess of memory and there she lingers, stringing out
phrase upon cadenced phrase, in her lover's poetic idiom. But she catches
herself up and recoils from this dead end. A caustic third person pushes back
the thought of Fernando: "¿Por ventura imagina que su retrato será la
espada de Eneas para la reina Dido?" ("Does he perchance think that his
portrait will be an Aeneas's sword to Queen Dido?"). Indignation at last
gives her the strength to turn violently upon the portrait and after a struggle
she tears it in two. But the resolve that follows her theatrical outcry shows
how far she still has to go: "Rompíle. ¡Vitoria! Lo mismo haré con su
exemplo del que tengo en el alma. ¡Celia! ¡Celia!" ("I tore it apart. Victory!
This is a sample of what I will do to the one in my heart. Celia! Celia!")
(p. 426).

The scenic break comes here, exactly at the point of the portrait's dis-
memberment, which it underscores; though Dorotea is left on the crest of
"victory" for a moment, the effect is ironical: the dismembering cuts deeper
than she knows. After a brief sequence celebrating her "victory," the new
scene will register the recoil toward despondency as she burns Fernando's
love-letters. Rhetoric at first sustains her at the peak of triumph, but Celia's
ironical tone as she matches Dorotea's exultantly invoked *exempla* of super-
human strength already begins to undermine them:

> *Cel.:* ¿Romper vn naipe es mucho? ¡Miren qué valiente Céspedes,
>   que rompía juntas quatro barajas!
> *Dor.:* Luego ¿no es más vn hombre?

> *Cel.:* Is it so much to tear a card apart? What a powerful Céspedes,
> the tearer in two of four packs at a time!   *Dor.:* Well then, isn't
> it more when it's a man?

Dorotea's confounding of the man with the image is bravado; Celia
by exposing the rhetorical technique destroys the effect: "¿Dónde has leído
tantas historias? Estas medras nos dexará Fernando" ("Where did you ever
read so many classical instances? These are the profits we'll be left with by
Fernando") (p. 428). The futility of confounding rhetorical possibilities with
real ones is made plain, while the sarcastic use of "medras"—tag-ends,

loose bits of knowledge—extends disintegration to the expressive medium itself. The effect meanwhile is presentationally reinforced:

> *Dor.:* ¿Qué miras? ¿Qué tanteas?
> *Cel.:* Aún se pueden juntar estas mitades.
> *Dor.:* Para juntarlas, mejor fuera no auerlas apartado.

> *Dor.:* What are you looking at? What are you groping about for?
> *Cel.:* These halves can still be fitted together.   *Dor.:* For fitting them together, it would have been better not to separate them.

It is the disjoined fragments of a way of life that Celia here holds in her hands. Dorotea is experiencing the fate against which César had warned Fernando two scenes earlier: "Not one stone will be left on top of another in the edifice of your life" (p. 416). At the same time, her ambivalence is clearly underscored as she tries to undo what she has done. The poetic tension of the scene derives from a focusing of verbal, formal, and presentational effects on a single sensibility which both abets and resists their action. Its power derives from the transformation of the persistent but limited "traditional" motif of destroyed letters and keepsakes into a broadened representation of disintegration, of a world in collapse. Poetic motifs and dramatic actions heretofore elaborated separately (ruins, destruction of mementos) are fused and jointly revitalized.

Such renewal is also evident in the following sequence, the second part of scene 5, in which Lope quite visibly shifts from fragmentation to a subtler form of disintegration, consumption by flames (p. 428):

> *Cel.:* ¿Para qué rasgas essos papeles?
> *Dor.:* Bien dizes. Trae vna vela.

> *Cel.:* Why are you tearing up those papers?   *Dor.:* You're right. Bring a candle.

This sudden turn, surely no caprice, enables him to draw on the symbolic possibilities of fire imagery. An afterthought tossed off in one of the early ballads appears now to sprout new dramatic and poetic possibilities:

> Y que rompa [Filis] por su gusto
> los desdichados papeles
> do la descubrí mi pecho,
> o por mejor, que los queme.[11]

And let [Filis] enjoy herself tearing up the unfortunate papers in which I opened up my heart to her—or better, let her burn them.

The flames that consume mementos and love-notes in artistic versions of Lope's experience, the conflagrations found in certain sonnets of the Troy sequence, the echoes in the *acción en prosa* itself of the motif of passion ostensibly extinct flaring up again, are all embedded in the substratum of the sequence that follows. So we become aware when Dorotea, apostrophizing the "falsos papeles" ("false slips of paper") as Celia is lighting the candle, promises that they are now to be "hechos ceniças para que no quede memoria de mi fuego ni reliquia de vuestro engaño" ("turned into ashes so that no memory will remain of my fire nor relic of your deceit") (p. 428). So, even more palpably, in the dialogue that opens scene 6:

> *Ger.:* ¡Agua, agua! ¡Iesús! ¿Qué incendio es éste?
> *Dor.:* ¿Tú pides agua, tía? ¿Qué nouedad es ésta?
> *Ger.:* ¡Papeles! Iuráralo yo, muchacha.
> *Dor.:* Ardese Troya.
> *Ger.:* *¡Fuego! ¡Fuego! dan vozes, ¡fuego! suena,*
>   *y sólo Paris dize: Abrase a Elena.*
> *Dor.:* ¿Es canción nueua?
> *Ger.:* Esto cantan aora los músicos del duque de Alua.
> *Dor.:* *Arded, mentiras, arded,*
>   *que yo no os puedo valer.*
>
> (p. 432)

> *Ger.:* Water, water! Heavens, what is this fire? *Dor.:* "You asking for water, mistress? What kind of novelty is this? *Ger.:* Papers! I would have sworn it, child. *Dor.:* Troy is burning up. *Ger.:* "Fire! fire! they shout; fire! sounds, and only Paris says: May it burn up Helen!" *Dor.:* Is that a new song? *Ger.:* The musicians of the Duke of Alba are now singing it. *Dor.:* "Burn, lies, burn, I cannot avail you."

The abundant smoke of this miniature conflagration fills the atmosphere of this new scene and the next. The overt allusions not only to previous artistic avatars but even to the proximate reality (Troy, Elena, the Duke of Alba's musicians singing "now") certainly lead far back. Whether they are survivals of an earlier text or later recollections, in either case they show the previous scene to be deeply rooted in the past.

The atmosphere in that scene is more poignant, less agitated than in the theatrical portrait sequence. It gathers around the flame of a single candle, all that here remains of the consuming bonfire or the burning city. An analogue to scene 5 is clearly the ballad "Contemplando estaba Filis." That earlier version of a confrontation with the past before a candle flame and its symbolic destruction in the burning of an object identified with it has surely left traces in the present scene, whose meaning can be read more easily if the ballad is made a point of reference. To be sure, the intimacy of the ballad is lacking: the heroine is no longer alone, she can no longer surrender to reverie, the ironical remarks of the maid (who in the ballad figured only at the end) constantly pull against the spell of the past now embodied in the love-letters, as earlier in the moth. The letters are less pregnant symbols than the wheeling moth, binding Dorotea as they do to specific moments and episodes, rather than evoking the past as a whole, hypnotically. It is less a mood than the conflicts attendant upon a resolve that the sequence in *La Dorotea* brings out: Lope has unraveled the dramatic possibilities latent in the lyrical ballad. As the scene progresses it becomes clear that the symbolism of the moth's flight, the inherent ambivalence, the dangerous flirtation with the flame, survives in Dorotea's dalliance with the past. There is no equivalent to Filis's sudden burning of the moth, but each letter read, then burned, is like a singeing of wings. In a strange commingling of pleasure and pain, Dorotea exacerbates the feelings she is trying to banish, causing Celia to exclaim: "¡O amantes locos! Aún en la misma pena se deleitan" ("Oh mad lovers, glorying even in the midst of their pain!") (p. 431). Yet this is the only remaining trace of a suggestion that the flame connotes the consummation as well as the destructiveness of passion, as it had in the ballad. In Celia's subsequent remark, "Más parece que te quemas tú que los papeles" ("You seem to be burning yourself more than the love-notes"), we can read into Dorotea's self-torture only the death of the moth.

The vengefulness present in Filis's destruction of the moth, whose bliss she envied, becomes vocal in the bursts of rhetoric accompanying Dorotea's burning of the love-letters. Yet these wane as the scene continues. The dominant tone is not rhetorical or theatrical and Lope avoids a climax of the sort present in the tearing of the portrait. The scene indeed ends before the whole remaining packet of letters has been thrust into the flames. Lope relegates this action to the interval that one is left to supply between this scene and the next, prior to the entering Gerarda's exclamation over the smoke and flames. It is a running-down of Dorotea's spirit in a series of small shocks that Lope records, a movement toward exhaustion, not a release. Her restlessness, her sense of frustration are suspended, not dispelled. The random and disconnected character of the excerpts Dorotea reads prolongs the effect of disarray and once more Lope's art consists in an order-ing of this disorder. The counterpoint of commentary in the surrounding dialogue, sardonic in the mistress, sarcastic in the maid, binds past to present, and there is in addition a masterly manipulation of pace, which I will discuss later.

In the next scene Dorotea's defenses are gone. She confesses her real feelings to Gerarda and tells her exactly what she misses in Fernando: "Su talle, su entendimiento, sus caricias, sus amores; que de todos estos actos se haze al alma vn hábito tan estrecho, que es impossible quitarle sin romperle" ("His figure, his intellect, his caresses, his love, for of all these acts so tight a habit is formed around the soul that it is impossible to remove it without shattering it") (p. 433). These words add to the traditional view of habit as second nature and the conceit built upon it—through another sense of habit, garment—a corollary of fragility which again brings symbolism of disruption to bear on Dorotea's life. It is herself that she has been tearing apart in all the small destructions and burnings of the preceding scene, her spirit that has been broken, herself that she has done violence to. There is nothing to add to this revealing acknowledgment. In the remainder of this scene, Gerarda's insinuating prattle leads Dorotea off on inconsequential tangents, and in the next—the last of this series of four—she remains wholly apart from the bickering of Gerarda and Laurencio, coming out of her silence only at the end to suggest that even Don Bela no longer interests her. We are back at the starting point. Dorotea's state of dejection and indifference is the same one in which we found her at the opening of scene 4.

After the interval of scene 8, Lope returns to her and presents new efforts at emancipation. Again an initially vigorous reaction rapidly spends itself, so that in the final scenes, 11 and 12, where her experience of disillusionment is swallowed up in a vaster disenchantment, we find her silent, passive, as if drained of feeling. But it is the earlier responses that now interest us. In scene 9, reasserting her *desamor* to a skeptical Celia, Dorotea strikes the note of ascetic renunciation, then seeks sublimation in song and music. In scene 10 it becomes evident that she has also sought to lift her spirits by attention to externals: appearances, dress. Before turning to the most revealing of these responses, the resort to art, let us look at the others.

In the unspecified interval allowed by scene 8 must be placed the end of a chain reaction of emotions which Dorotea, expressing herself in a prolonged anadiplosis, asserts has brought her release: "Mi amor paró en zelos, mis zelos en furia, mi furia en locura, mi locura en rabia, mi rabia en deseos de vengança, mi vengança en lágrimas, y mis lágrimas en arrojar por los ojos el veneno del coraçón" ("My love turned into jealousy, my jealousy into frenzy, my frenzy into madness, my madness into rage, my rage into a wish for revenge, my revenge into tears, my tears into expelling the poison from the heart through the eyes") (p. 444). One can trace back to the scene in the street described by Fernando when Dorotea gave way to a "sudden fit of jealousy" the beginning of this process, and place the "wish for revenge" in scenes 5 and 6 (destruction of the mementos). The urgency of the *catena* figure points to Dorotea's need to convince (and delude) herself. The tensions of the unrelieved conflict build up again to a breaking point in scenes 9 and 10.

In the first part of scene 9, Dorotea flares up touchily when Celia seconds too emphatically her protestations of world-weariness, accusing her maid of having no mind of her own: "Si te dixera que fuéramos a inquietar a Fernando . . ." ("If I were to suggest that we go and bother Fernando . . ."). Celia is on her heels at once:

> *Cel.:* Si quieres que vamos, ¿para qué me lo dizes con inuenciones?
> *Dor.:* ¡Yo, Celia! Plega a Dios . . .
> *Cel.:* No pliegues, ni jures, si quieres que te crea . . . que ha vn hora
> que estás martillando essas clauijas, templando más que las cuerdas
> del arpa, las locuras del pensamiento.
> *Dor.:* He quitado dos o tres, porque falseauan en los bemoles.
> *Cel.:* Essos deuían de ser los pensamientos de don Fernando.
>
> (p. 446)
>
> *Cel.:* If you want us to go, why don't you come right out and say so? *Dor.:* I, Celia! God fail me if . . . *Cel.:* Don't go flailing or swearing if you want me to believe you . . . You've been torturing those poor pegs for an hour, tuning not so much the harp strings as your unstrung thoughts [lit., madnesses of your thoughts]. *Dor.:* I've removed one or two because they didn't ring true on the flats. *Cel.:* Those must have been thoughts of Don Fernando.

Celia's pun—*placer-plegar* (lit., to please, to fold)—nips Dorotea's intended *deprecatio* in the bud, reducing it to an imputation as much of nervous fidgeting at the harp strings as of tuning the instrument. Dorotea has in fact been clinging to the harp since calling for it at the beginning of the scene and it will still be beside her well along in scene 10 when Gerarda tells her: "All right, all right, let the harp go and let me in on your gaiety" (p. 451). Lope uses this action to reinforce presentationally the resort to music as a shield against reality. But music, as we know, is less a shield than a palliative that makes bearable the truth it exposes. Dorotea's feverish plucking at the harp strings involuntarily acknowledges tensions she has not verbalized, and her plucking them out gives a new turn to the conventional analogy between tempering of the instrument and tempering the emotions. The total situation—words and action—connects love no longer requited with the discordance of strings that no longer vibrate in harmony. On the instrument, eradication and replacement restore harmony. On the human level this does unbearable violence to the feelings. For all Dorotea's agitation, she does manage to tune the harp. She cannot do the same with her own feelings because the "strings" of thoughts she would banish still set up an answering vibration within. The present sequence is the counterpart to the serenade scene at the end of Act III which had evoked Dorotea's outcry: "Fernando and I are voice and echo! He sings and I repeat the final notes" (p. 282). The presentational complementation of—and counterpoint to—the conceptual imagery expresses the fragility of the equilibrium on which the emotional bonds between human beings rest, the impossibility of restoring a balance that has been jarred. Implicit here is the same truth to which Dorotea had come a few scenes earlier, when she spoke of "so tight a habit around the soul that it is impossible to remove it without shattering it" (p. 433). But now she goes further and acknowledges that the true abode of harmony is in the soul alone: "que la ciencia de la música . . . no está en la facilidad de los dedos ni la voz entonada, sino el alma" ("for the science of music . . . is not in the fingers' skill nor the modulated voice, but the soul") (p. 446).[12] She now understands that only by transcending the senses can such harmony be permanently won.

Though Dorotea can conceptualize this Platonic view, she is unable to act in accord with it. It is the truth of suffering—of the broken spirit in the human realm—that emerges in the song she now sings. Once again, as in Act II, music overcomes psychic defenses and discloses the substratum of genuine feeling. Lope takes special pains in this instance to stress the bearing of the song on Dorotea's present situation. She has written the words herself and Celia's unfamiliarity with them suggests that she has just done so.[13]

The song is a series of variations on the thought: "Si todo lo acaba el tiempo, / ¿cómo dura mi tormento?" ("If time ends all things, how does my torment go on?"). The conceit proposing a contest between love and time which the youthful Lope had developed in his own name so truculently in his early sonnet is now glossed from a feminine viewpoint. Dorotea declares not the victory but the defeat of time, which the torments of her hopeless love will outlast. In contrast to the dialogue, the poem initially acknowledges her failure to free herself of passion despite "tantas dificultades como mi amor ha tenido" ("all the difficulties my love has had"). It goes further, to a purely artistic sublimation quite at odds with the dialogue: a conventional stance of glorifying hopeless love and embracing suffering. The poem is an effort to wring dignity from such suffering by assuming, in the pastoral manner, that devotion to love in any form, even unrequited, is ennobling. In effect, Dorotea still cultivates attitudes of the pastoral heroines with whom she has sought to identify. Her lyric could pass for the outpouring of a Diana or a Belisarda to a receptive listening world. Celia's reaction underscores the incongruity of Dorotea's pose by supplying, as if on cue, the response it would receive in a pastoral milieu:

> Aquí sí que entraua como nacido aquello de los libros de los pastores, que se paró el aire, que abrieron las flores los pinpollos de las hojas, y que se desató el nácar de la verde cárcel de los botones, aromatizando el aire; que callaron los sonoros cristales de los arroyos, que aprendieron las filomenas de las seluas dulces passos. (p. 448)

> Here that business of the shepherd-books would fit to a T, about the breeze dying, the flowers opening the wads of their petals, and the mother-of-pearl breaking out of the green prison of the buds and perfuming the air, the sonorous crystals of the streams growing still and the philomelas of the woods learning sweet trills.

Time should now stand still, its action defeated, as in Dorotea's song, but such an effect and the accompanying response of a sympathetic nature now seem out of touch with ordinary reality. Celia does her undermining obliquely: she does not ridicule or caricature but the automatism of her opening converts all the rest into parody of the static clichés of pastoral style and diction. The implication is that tranquillity of spirit is as inaccessible as the ideal harmony on which it rests. The truth of music is in the end out of reach. Still the old Lope contents himself with gentle irony and leaves intact, at one remove, the pastoral order which Belardo had shattered, for he respects the truth it aspires to realize.

Dorotea, for her part, takes no notice of her maid's irony. She calmly talks with Celia about her authorship of the verse and the composition of the music and finally, in the words with which the scene ends, makes the avowal she had earlier refused: "Pues dime, Celia, si dixeron los antiguos que la ira los hazía [los versos], ¿por qué no serán más fáciles al amor, que se quexa de lo que padece en dulcíssimas consonancias?" ("Then tell me, Celia, if the ancients said that anger created [verse], why wouldn't it come more easily to love, which laments its sufferings with the sweetest accords?") (p. 448). Her recourse to poetry and music has clearly wrought a change of mood. While the present poem is a more perfunctory piece than "Al son de los arroyuelos," like the earlier performance at the spinet it quiets her emotional turmoil, though powerless ultimately to resolve it. The "dulcíssimas consonancias" of music and verse create the temporary illusion of a world in which art can restore harmony to human emotion.

Brusquely Gerarda shatters this mood with her aggressive entrance and her battery of questions (scene 10): "¿Tú cantando, tú alegre, tú vestida de gala, Dorotea? ¿Tú tocada con cintas verdes, tú cadena y joyas? ¿Qué nouedad es ésta? ¿Qué te ha sucedido? ¿Qué te has hallado, niña?" ("You singing, you gay, you all dressed up, Dorotea? You with green ribbons in your hair, you chain and jewels? What novelty is this? What has come over you? What have you found for yourself, child?") (p. 449). A final trace of pride restores Dorotea's façade: "Tía, no son todos los tiempos vnos. De los nublados sale el sol, y de las tormentas la bonança" ("Mistress, not all weather is the same. From cloudy skies the sun comes forth, from storms, fair days"). Gerarda returns to the attack, lets herself be temporarily sidetracked, renews the assault. Dorotea then gives in very quietly: "No te desveles, tía, que no he tenido papel de don Fernando, ni le quiero. Vete con Dios y déxame; que esta alegría esterior es el oro de las píldoras y el membrillo de los jaraues" ("Don't get upset, mistress, I've not had any note from Don Fernando, nor do I want any. Go with God and leave me, for this outward cheerfulness is the gilding on pills and the quince in the syrup") (p. 452).

Dorotea here falls back on a commonplace that particularly appealed to the ethos of the baroque. Mateo Alemán, for instance, in exemplifying the polar opposition between falsehood and truth, writes: "Los [trabajos] que los hombres toman por sus vicios y deleites, son píldoras doradas, que, engañando la vista con apariencia falsa de sabroso gusto, dejan el cuerpo descompuesto y desbaratado" ("The [tribulations] which men take for their vices and pleasures are gilded pills which, deceiving the eyes with a false appearance of a pleasant taste, leave the body broken down and undone").[14] In Alemán such images are intended to show that, once we learn to see beyond appearances, once we become properly undeceived (*desengañados*), we will welcome the concealed truth, however unpalatable. In Dorotea's words something considerably less straightforward and quite irreducible to ideological formulation is suggested. The hollowness of the role she has been playing is acknowledged but role-playing is not repudiated. If literary histrionism began as a gilding of her existence, the role and the reality have ultimately become so fused that "it is impossible to remove it without shattering it." Love always involves self-delusion, Lope knows; who is to say where such delusion begins and ends? When she is forced to open her eyes, Dorotea can only regret the impossibility of prolonging the illusion. It is the human plights caused by the discrepancies between appearance and reality—between art and life—that concern Lope, not the discrepancies as such. It is not the world that Dorotea is fleeing, but herself: "I feel so sad that I put on bright things to escape myself," she presently confesses to Gerarda. For her, as for Don Bela, the labyrinth is as much within as without.

Her resort to bright external *galas* to escape her distress is an ironical complement to the plainness of costume that marked the heyday of her love. Fernando's enamoured imagination had had no difficulty compensating for such plainness from his poetic store, and for a long time, despite Dorotea's apprehensions, had clothed her in metaphorical finery. The real contrast to Dorotea's colorful costume in the present scene is the utter neglect of her appearance and dress in the earlier sequence. But Lope is not urging that previous vision of Dorotea as an unpleasant truth in preference to the present one, a beautiful and deceptive appearance. Unlike Quevedo he does not use repulsiveness to shock the reader into awareness; the unpleasantness of that scene has no specifically salutary aim. The contrast is not one between truth and falsehood; there is no suggestion that each extreme does not have its relative truth: the truth of human suffering and the truth of the human need for self-delusion. Between them, Lope suggests, lies another kind of truth: that of the fragile harmony engendered by love, a composure which is the true origin of beauty, capable of creating it out of apparent plainness. Objective truth is not accessible to man except in the ultimate confrontation with God. Until all human truths fade away, Lope is not willing to relinquish any.

With these observations we move beyond Dorotea's experience of *desengaño* to the author's encompassing expression of it. As occurred when Lope focused for the last time on Don Bela in the opening scene of the act and led him toward his own final situation of sublimation vis-à-vis Marta de Nevares, so here too, where Dorotea for the last time occupies the center of the stage, her attitude toward the impasse in which she struggles reflects Lope's own vital responses to the experience of living. The outward trappings of gaiety which she puts on, the show of high spirits she makes as an antidote to despair remind us of Lope's urgent summonses to the Duke of Sessa, of his playing-up of the persona of Tomé de Burguillos. We may remember Lope's admission to the Duke: "Parézeme que dice Vex.ª que estoy de humor; pues le prometo que le tengo tan diferente, que en mi vida he estado con más tristeza" ("I seem to hear Your Excellency saying that I'm in a good humor; well, I can assure you that I am in one so different that never in my life have I felt sadder").[15] As Dorotea "puts on bright things to escape" herself, so Lope writes: "Estoy tan corrido de la poca o ninguna calidad que tienen [mis pensamientos], que de mí mismo los procuro esconder, engañándome a mí mismo" ("I am so irritated at the little or no value of [my thoughts] that I try to keep them from myself, deceiving myself").[16] In such remarks Lope acknowledges the practical need for a degree of self-delusion and confirms again that his art, like that of so many comic geniuses, is a *modus vivendi* with melancholy. The already quoted remark about Tomé de Burguillos, "Although he was sad by nature, no one dealing with him failed to find him gay," is made apropos of a supposed portrait of him in the "Notice to the Reader" of the 1634 *Rimas*. Examining the portrait, one discovers the countenance of a youthful Lope (copied, as he tells us, from the portrait done by Ribalta) crowned with laurel but wearing an unmistakable expression of melancholy.

Gaiety and melancholy are sides of the same coin, complementary tendencies nourished in the same zone of the poet's psyche. The wellsprings of the comic are tapped, as if on signal, whenever the pull of despondency becomes too strong. Lope has of course not endowed Dorotea with his own resilient vitality or his reserves of creative power; her self-administered therapy inevitably fails. Where creature and creator coincide is in the impulse underlying the pattern, not only an impulse toward survival but an assertion of self, an affirmation of life. Not even pain is eternal and grief does not kill, Lope has learned, and he leaves us in no doubt, for all the burden of Dorotea's song (César's prophecy has indeed already alerted us), that Dorotea will survive the crumbling of her present world and outlive her collapsing illusions.

The last two scenes of the work, despite their seeming finality, do not close off awareness of days to follow. There stretches before Dorotea a horizon of prosaic living, for without her lover she is incapable of the self-renewal Lope found within. For all its bleakness this prospect belongs to the sense of ongoing life that reflects Lope's commitment to the world even as he comes to terms with it. The vision of corruption and hollowness conjured up in the *Soliloquios* was not native to his temperament and could not be lasting. Lope's world view admits of no crucial and definitive moment of undeceiving. If the process of living, viewed in its full cycle, is a shedding of illusions,[17] it is at the same time a continual restoring of them. Life possesses its inner dynamics: the world removes but replaces, the self surrenders but recovers. Lope's response to living must be formulated in some such terms, even though disillusions may not be so easy to surmount and illusions not so easy to restore when the life-impulse finally shows signs of waning. Lope cannot divorce living from the embracing of illusion or the playing of roles, nor can he turn his back on the world, the restorer, even though he may come and go more frequently from his solitude as he grows older and the moments of fatigue may occur more often. By bodying forth in *La Dorotea* a sense of the interplay of self and world, by counterpointing illusion and disillusion, Lope enters upon final possession of life and readies himself to relinquish it.

In the last two scenes of the work, the presentation of the dénouement is kept insistently at a human level, the backdrop of the eternal being glimpsed only for a moment in two brief curtain speeches and even then in tones more stoic than expressly Catholic. The intention is plainly to affirm life at the very moment in which the evidence of its fragility becomes overwhelming. Lope frames the two scenes between Laurencio's monstrously overplayed announcement of Don Bela's death and Celia's incongruously casual description of Gerarda's. He clearly obstructs any empathic involvement on our part. Between the extremes of Laurencio's self-conscious aping of the tragic messenger and Celia's overdoing the comical *figura del donaire* comes a point of equilibrium at the end of scene 11 in what proves to be Gerarda's swan-song: "Ah, Laurencio! You could well have dispensed with so elaborate a way of relating a misfortune; the words were sufficient without the tears and the feelings without the sobs" (p. 455).

Lope deploys the resources of his art—rhetorical, histrionic, and poetic— to underscore the toppling of a world. Seizing the unique occasion for theatrics, Laurencio in all deliberateness builds a structure of rhetoric. The grandiloquence of his exordium with its snowballing of *topoi* of inexpressibility that culminate in the periphrastic preannouncement of the greatest tragedy of all time rouses the histrionic impulses of Gerarda and the despondent Dorotea, who promise to collaborate with profuse tears. Assured of their responses, Laurencio delivers the set piece prepared in his self-styled role of "trágico y desdichado nuncio, más lloroso y con más razón de dolor que en el *Hipólito* de Séneca" ("tragic and unlucky messenger, more tearful and with more reason for grief than in Seneca's *Hippolytus*") (p. 455). Morby's apt citation of the *Arte nuevo*:

> El lacayo no trate cosas altas
> ni diga los conceptos que hemos visto
> en algunas comedias estrangeras
>
> (*Obras escogidas*, II, 889)

> Let the lackey not treat of lofty things nor utter the ideas we have seen in certain foreign plays

makes plain the intention to underscore the impropriety of Laurencio's comportment and diction. Not only is the sublime tragic manner inappropriate in the nontragic setting of the *acción en prosa*: the servant's aping of the *nuncio* is itself caricaturesque. His puns—*herrador* and *yerro* (lit., blacksmith, error)—and plays—"Acábese mi vida en acabando" ("May my life finish when I finish")—rather than functionally expressive, are distracting in their triviality. Laurencio manipulates suspense with painful obviousness by interjecting *sententiae*—"¡O, quánto yerra quien se fía de la soberbia de la ira en confiança de la razón!" ("Oh how greatly he errs who trusts in the arrogance of anger, relying on the rightness of his cause!")—and by calling attention to his own performance in further declarations of inexpressibility: "No sé cómo agora passen adelante las mías [palabras], si no desocupa el camino a la lengua para formarlas el confuso tropel de los sollozos y el espeso diluuio de las lágrimas" ("I know not how my [words] can now proceed, if the confused mass of sobs and the heavy deluge of tears do not clear a path for the tongue to form them"). He clearly manipulates his listeners' responses in preparation for the climactic revelation (p. 455):

> *Lau.:* Pero ¿qué me detengo mirando vuestro sentimiento?
> *Dor.:* Habla, Laurencio, que me matas.
> *Lau.:* Sacaron las espadas, y entre los dos le han muerto.
> *Dor.:* ¡Iesús, qué crueles hombres!
>
> *Lau.:* But why do I hesitate, seeing your emotion? *Dor.:* Speak, Laurencio, you are killing me. *Lau.:* They took out their swords and between the two of them killed him. *Dor.:* Lord, what cruel men!

This calculated shock technique—the blow with the naked truth—brings down the whole top-heavy rhetorical structure, brings down Dorotea too; she keels over to Gerarda's cry: "Tenla, tenla, que se hará pedazos" ("Hold her, hold her, she'll go to pieces") (p. 456). The downward thrust of disintegration had been anticipated in Laurencio's account of the defenseless Don Bela's descent into a patio to what proved to be ambush and death. Now it carries across the pause which marks the scenic break and ends up in Gerarda's fall down the cellar stairs. Her head is smashed but her wimple and the water jar in her hand remain intact. The singularity of these exceptions to the prevailing disintegration only heightens the effect of fragility.

There is a willfulness verging on caprice in Lope's manner of pushing these figures over one after the other. Here at the end they seem no longer to engage his full attention or concern. His imagination has leapt ahead, beyond the confines of their world, for the act of plotting their destinies in art has freed him from them and from the creative nexus to which they belong. The time has come to call a halt and Lope is more than ready. The pace quickens: the final scene becomes a spirited coda, its mood buoyant. The deaths of Don Bela and Gerarda, rather than inducing an atmosphere of gravity, seem to have cleared the air and restored a fundamental equilibrium. Neither has any tragic dimension, neither figure falls from pride. Laurencio expressly sees Don Bela's death as a case of "[la execución] del poder en la humildad" ("[the exercise] of power against humility") and speaks of modesty and truth as his only defenses. Neither character is highly enough placed to be unseated by fortune and Celia's quip about Gerarda—"Pero puédese consolar que murió cayendo, como aquellos a quien leuanta la fortuna" ("But she can take consolation in having died in a fall, like those whom fortune upraises") (p. 456)—is plainly ironical. Both deaths strike us as in fact occurring in the ordinary course of events, Bela's in consequence of a conflict between a new-found Platonic ascesis and obligations lasting over from earlier stages of worldly ambition. It is pathetic that his noble aspirations should be tripped up by so trivial a circumstance, but his death, as has been seen, is also a deliverance. As for Gerarda's, in Vossler's unforgettable phrase it is merely the ending of the pitcher that has gone once too often to the well. Both deaths are after-effects rather than climaxes; neither is central to the story of Fernando and Dorotea. They are, in short, a means of marking a stopping point, devices for breaking off with suitable definition.

Indeed, everything about Gerarda's death is calculated to prevent our taking it seriously. She is clearly tipsy as she starts down the stairs: her account of her extraordinarily bibulous breakfast with her crony Marina (pp. 450–451) is evidence enough. Teodora's reaction when Felipa explains that Gerarda was going to get water—"¿No auía de donde más cerca pudiera traerla? ¡Qué buena diligencia para vn desmayo!" ("Was there nowhere closer she could have brought it from? A fine thing to do when someone has fainted!") (p. 456)—makes sufficiently clear that in fact Gerarda seized the pretext of Dorotea's faint (which she assumes to be staged) to head for the wine cellar. (Has she not just cited the chapter title "De desmayarse a su tiempo y llorar sin causa" ["On fainting opportunely and weeping unnecessarily"] from her book of feminine deceits [p. 453]?) These developments had been anticipated in the meal scene at the end of Act II: the rejection of water, the unslaked thirst for wine, the resultant drunkenness in which she trips over a chair and Celia exclaims: "¡Qué golpe que se ha dado!" ("What a blow she's struck herself!") (p. 198). Gerarda is running true to form for the last time. Felipa begs Celia to investigate, then peers down the stairs after her, and their voices carry from imagined wings in a rapid counterpoint of observation, witticisms, and reproaches.

Cel.: ¡O miserable espectáculo! Gerarda es muerta. Mas ¿quién
   dixera que buscando agua?
Fel.: ¿Donaires, Celia? Pues no se lo deuías.

(p. 456)

Cel.: Oh lamentable spectacle! Gerarda is dead. But who would ever
have thought it would be when going for water?   *Fel.:* Wisecracks,
Celia? She deserved better of you.

And Celia launches, as Leo Spitzer notes,[18] into a negative panegyric modeled
on those of the picaresque. But the black humor and jaded disillusionment of
the picaresque evaporate in the buoyant atmosphere of this finale, leaving
only amusement at the mock-seriousness of the tribute. Dorotea suddenly
comes to without benefit of water when Teodora calls, "¡Niña, a niña!"
("My girl, my girl!"), and Celia quips, "¿A qué muger llamaran niña, que
no boluiera del otro mundo?" ("What woman, if she heard herself called a
girl, would not come back from the next world?") (p. 457). So cavalier a
treatment of a calamity is rare even in Lope; it looks ahead to the coming
mock-heroic *Gatomaquia* where the calamities will happen only to cats.
These final innings allowed the *figura del donaire* end only with the curtain
lines of Laurencio. He has been silent up to this point and now it is Lope,
suddenly serious, who speaks through him to the reader:

> para que veas qué se puede fiar desto que llaman vida, pues ninguno
> —como dixo vn sabio—la imaginó tan breue que pensasse morir el
> día que lo estaua imaginando. No hay cosa más incierta que saber el
> lugar donde nos ha de hallar la muerte, ni más discreta que esperarla
> en todos. (p. 457)

> so you may see just how much trust is to be placed in this thing
> called life, since no one—as a wise man said—imagined it so brief
> that he expected to die the same day he was imagining it. Nothing
> is more unsure than discovering the place where death will overtake
> us, nor wiser than expecting it everywhere.

Through the Senecan tones the voice of Lope reaches us, speaking *ex
cathedra* now, and revealing the significance he attaches to these seemingly
casual deaths: they show the fragility of our hold on life, the need to live in
full awareness of its precariousness. But to live. There is no renunciation of
life, merely an old man's awareness of its uncertainty. The words convey
his calm readiness to die, for all his attachment to living, the equanimity

reached through the crisis reflected in the *Soliloquios*. And they remind us that he has not delivered Don Bela or Gerarda unprepared to the beyond. Don Bela's contrition and the mass to which Lope sends him on his last exit symbolize his state of spiritual readiness; Gerarda, just before her death, has suddenly found in the brevity of life not a summons to *carpe diem*, as always previously, but grounds for something more than lip-service to *memento mori*.

The Temporal Aspect of *Desengaño*

However the characters may respond to their awareness of the brevity of life, there is no doubt that they are endowed by their creator with an unusual sense of the evanescence of the things of this world. Time itself sometimes seems to be cast in the role of antagonist. We are far from the ideal worlds of the Renaissance, of Botticelli or Garcilaso, in which the conditions of things seem fixed and pure. Here not only individual flowers fade; all floral color can be viewed as "worn with the passage of time" and in need of renewal. The artistic cosmos of *La Dorotea* is permeated with a sense of temporality in which Lope's peculiarly organic perception of time's work compounds the temporal sensitivity of his age. While transience and mutability are native conditions both of man and of all that surrounds him, there are unsettling differences in the timing and duration of their cycles. Man outlasts some things in the world of nature and fortune, others outlast him. Lope's response, as we know, is neither to cultivate insensibility nor to withdraw into otherworldliness; he is neither stoic nor ascetic. Nor does he protest or cry out in anguish; he is no Romantic. At the most fundamental level Lope makes artistic creation an antidote to evanescence. But he does so in no escapist way: he builds temporality into his artistic cosmos and by giving expression to it is reconciled with it. If, in this sense, he writes from a lyric impulse, dramatically speaking he commits his protagonists to life and leads those characters who are to die toward a sense of time's ending.

The care with which Lope sets the action in time as measured by clock and calendar, human devices for bringing the time of nature within man's grasp, needs no reiterating. The formal external units of act and scene align precise segments of clock and calendar time sequentially, as I have pointed out, forming a temporal order disturbed only in Act V. Both measured and onflowing, the time thus ordered suggests at once human chronometry and time beyond man's computation. Within the framework thus established Lope gives us time perceived as a medium of life through its effects on persons and things existing within it; endows his characters with a peculiar sensitivity to aging and suggests in them a subjective experience of time at variance with its outward measurement; and offers intimations of the confined character of human time by suggesting, through insights of the characters and through effects of pacing and symbolization transcending them, how minute and finite the temporal world appears *sub specie aeternitatis*.

As a medium of life time is perceptible in terms of the routines of living, the habitual patterns of action to which it gives rise; it is detectable also through the physical traces of its passage. Casual details that turn up in the dialogue, incidental remarks, by their recurrence, impress themselves upon our attention. In the first scene, when Teodora boasts of the smoothness of her complexion and Gerarda replies ironically, "Harto es que el tiempo no aya echado sulcos por tierra tan suya" ("It's remarkable enough that time has not traced furrows in earth so much its own") (p. 65), we are startled by the earthiness of what seems a far-fetched metaphor. Ultimately we realize that even this detail emanates from Lope's organic feeling for the action of time. This is a world, as details earlier noted show, in which things are subject to soiling and breakage, in which even the biscuits brought out for a visitor are leftovers; in which it is necessary to remove three months' accumulation of dust from foils before fencing with them; in which the "hemp coverings for the straight chairs," begun by Dorotea two months before, have stood about unfinished ever since; in which the convalescent Dorotea grows exasperated at being offered chicken because she has been able to eat nothing else for so long: "Chicken! chicken! I'm sicker of it than of chestnuts in Lent" (p. 191); in which the mud on Teodora's cloak prompts the remark that she is always having some accident when she goes out: the other day had she not fallen into a wine cellar? We not only learn the origin of the mud spots but are told that the cloak will be sunned to dry and remove them.

The ordinary action of time to which these remarks offhandedly refer is sometimes explicitly acknowledged by characters who feel it as subversive, corrosive, destructive. We have seen how Don Bela echoes the Senecan "Quotidie morimur": "Como quita cada día tan poco, no se siente" ("As it takes away so little each day, you don't notice it") (p. 393). Gerarda from the height of her eighty years presses *carpe diem* on Dorotea with an urgency in which her own experience reinforces her literary prescription: "Quando yo era moça leí en Garzilaso aquello de: 'En tanto que de rosa y açucena.' ¿Piensas que el tiempo duerme quando nosotros?" ("When I was a girl I read in Garcilaso that part about 'While of rose and lily.' Do you think time sleeps when we do?") (p. 436).

Time not only does not sleep; it carries everything existing within it from freshness to overripeness. Lope's sensory keeness brings forth tactile, olfactory, peptic, visual imagery suggestive of organic processes of spoiling and souring: "Don't let this miserable youth finish off Dorotea's beauty handling it," Gerarda cautions Teodora at the outset (p. 72). Besides a characteristic sensual suggestiveness, we detect here an allusion to fruit that loses luster and freshness on handling. Gerarda's image then becomes olfactory, and markedly disagreeable: "Que ya sabéis con qué olor dexan las flores el agua del vaso en que estuuieron" ("You know very well how flowers leave the water of the vase they have been in smelling"). In the last act, during the burning of Fernando's love-letters, Celia urges haste on Dorotea by reminding her that "también ay amores rancios como perniles" ("there are also loves as rancid as hams") (p. 432). Though love and beauty are not looked upon as vanities, human relationships are conceived as having life cycles which it is senseless to brook. Later still, Dorotea visualizes the love-notes as they came through the flames: "aquellos papeles cuyas letras quemadas, blancas entre lo negro del papel, me ponían miedo" ("those papers whose burned-out letters, white against the black of the paper, made me feel afraid") (p. 445). The white handwriting which a breath would have reduced to ashes is still impressed on her memory.

These extreme evocations of the impact of organic temporality on man and nature function as expressions of untimeliness, the inopportuneness of relationships disjoined but not severed. Beneath the level of moral imperatives and divine injunctions, a natural order brings its day of reckoning in due course unless one is able to find renewal by evolving with it.

We touch here on the subjective repercussions of temporality, on the unusual sensitivity of the characters to the role of time in their lives. From the outset of *La Dorotea* we are among old persons who long to be young again and young persons uneasy about growing old. The characters respond to the sense of transiency that haunts the old age of their creator, the old (Teodora and Gerarda) with a heightened sensitivity to life as a long past and a brief future; the young (Dorotea in Act I, scene 3) with the premature awareness, already commented upon, of the ephemerality of present bloom, with uncanny anticipations of aging.

With some surprise we find Dorotea exclaiming at the height of her exultation over regaining Fernando: "Although an extreme of pleasure is usually a beginning of pain, I will be wronging my own soul if, with the memory of so much happiness, I am ever sad again" (p. 373). She scarcely seems to be repeating a dictum, yet her misgivings are hardly explicable in terms of her experience, sounding rather like an expression of Lope's. Her immediate repression of them suspends our disbelief, however.

Only in Fernando is sensitivity to the action of time, to mortality, merely skin-deep. His hyperbole claiming immunity from time's ravages for Dorotea (quoted above, p. 476), unlike her defiance of the thought of mutability, is merely facile. Fernando's heedlessness, so distinct from the mature outlook of his creator, is of a piece, rather, with Lope's already quoted retrospective self-appraisal: "I considered neither [mortality nor immortality]: mortal things because nothing was further from my memory than death; immortal ones because nothing gave me less concern than the soul." Beneath Fernando's absorption in self, there is, in fact, a core of unthinking assurance about the future: "If God wills, I still have life left to make good use of," he tells Dorotea defiantly after they quarrel (p. 101), and at the end he has no difficulty rousing himself to join the Armada.

With the others it is different. The bickering of Teodora and Gerarda in the opening scene over their respective ages throws the temporal theme into relief from the start.[19] Despite the comic tone, the insistence with which Teodora protests her youthfulness is already suggestive of deliberate self-delusion, the ambiguity of which is made plain by her own oblique avowals: "Lo que no puedo negaros es que estoi vn poco más fresca de lo que solía; pero por esso gozaré de dos mocedades" ("What I can't deny is that I'm a little ruddier than I used to be; but that means I shall enjoy youth twice") (p. 65). Her generalizations universalize the phenomenon: "The most common obsession of this world is to take years away from one's own age and add them to other people's; and it's useless nonsense, because the person adding them to someone else's thinks the same thing at the same time and everyone takes them away from his own" (p. 64). The circuitous and elliptical formulation of the remark is appropriate to the attitude it expresses: everyone plays the game of ages, everyone sees though it, everyone continues to play. Without ponderousness, Lope in this opening dialogue suggests the ambiguities implicit in man's attitude toward time and implies that man's wavering response to his awareness of temporality stems as much from desire and need as from limitation of vision.

Gerarda, in an anticipation of "architectural" figures to come, presses the *carpe diem* argument: "La hermosura, ¿es pilar de de iglesia, o solar de la montaña que se resiste al tiempo, para cuyas injurias ninguna cosa mortal tiene defensa?" ("Is beauty the pillar of a church or a family seat in La Montaña that holds out against time, against whose offences nothing mortal has any protection?") (p. 71). She is naturally speaking out of self-interest. But as a very old woman herself—older than Celestina, for she is eighty—

Gerarda is qualified in a special way to reflect the outlook of the author's old age. As she proceeds to draw parallels between stages of human life and seasons of the year, adapting to women a *topos* long applied to men, Lope's inborn sensitivity to organic processes lends urgency and finality to her words: "Or is it a gay springtime from fifteen to twenty-five, a pleasant summer from twenty-five to thirty-five, a dry season from thirty-five to forty-five?" (p. 71). In Gerarda's scorn for Fernando's youth, there is not only a weighting of the scales in favor of Don Bela—"For every eventuality, Teodora, men, men and not boys" (p. 73)—but, superimposed on the self-interest of the go-between, a view of the very young from the standpoint of the very old, that of Lope himself.

One senses this blending of the voices of character and creator later in Gerarda's nostalgic underscoring of the difference between her stage of life and Dorotea's:

> Tú, como eres moça, estás pensando en tus galas; que, aunque dizen que *el moço puede morir y el viejo no puede viuir*, lo cierto es ir con las leyes de la naturaleza. Y es ignorante el que se persuade que puede viuir, siendo viejo, más que los que mira moços; que si esto fuera, no huuiera él llegado a la edad en que está.   (p. 160)[20]

> You, being young, are thinking of your wardrobe; for, although they say that *the young man may die and the old man cannot live*, the truth is that things go according to the laws of nature. And anyone who convinces himself that, as an old man, he can live longer than the young men he sees around him is an ignoramus. For if this were the case, he would not have reached the age he has.

The young may die but the old will die; Lope might have died before, as he was so painfully aware in the *Soliloquios;* he will surely die now. We will presently see that Gerarda's view of her own mortality is more superficial and unthinking than her creator's, but it is fundamentally an acquiescence in the "laws of nature," which are to be trusted, however regretfully, not a declaration of *vanitas vanitatum* or a dread of hellfire. These Lope has faced and superseded, while Gerarda has never seriously thought of them at all. She knows that "Prestado lo da todo la naturaleza" ("Nature gives everything on loan") (p. 232) and that her lease on life is running out: "No ayas miedo que yo sea como el moro" ("Have no fear that I will be like the Moor"), she tells Laurencio after recalling a Moor in India who lived three hundred years (p. 232). But as we shall find, she is too involved with the present to think more than perfunctorily about the hereafter.[21]

The already noted instances of *décalage* between psychic (subjective) and chronometric (objective) apprehension of time are not particularly out of the ordinary. Fernando's "Heaven help me! All that has happened to me between nine and twelve" (p. 117) and Julio's "So this was the haste? So this was why you said that time had stopped?" (p. 204) stand as subjective impressions of the speed or slowness of time's passage, given added point by the careful chronometric substructure of *La Dorotea* but not necessarily dependent on it. It is only in the fifth act that Lope's art begins to exploit to full effect the contrast between the carefully established external chronometry and the characters' perception of temporality. Although the chronometric order is no longer wholly precise, it still functions as a scale or standard of measurement. Similarly, in this act Lope makes us apprehend the disjunction between both outwardly measured and inwardly perceived human time and the timelessness of eternity.

One is more aware in the last act than previously of Lope's manipulation of the pace of the dialogue, of sudden accelerations when emotional pressures or the pressure of events break through the unhurried talkativeness in stark exposures of feeling, as earlier in Dorotea's "I am extremely sad" or in climactic disclosures like Fernando's "I killed one and wounded the other" (I, 6).

Now the more or less momentary effects noted earlier are expanded and the pacing of the dialogue, the rhythms and cadence of the characters' words are more obviously coordinated with broader temporal patterns, movements toward an adjustment of phase between inner and outer time or gropings toward an unattainable timelessness. The culmination comes in the already noted *presto* of the coda-like final scene. Leading up to it, the calculated theatricality with which Laurencio first holds back, then suddenly delivers in starkest brevity the news of Don Bela's death, thereby precipitating Gerarda's, itself marks the inevitable and definitive onrush of the time of the world, the time of clock and calendar, into the microcosm of lives lived in prolonged disdain of temporality. Prior to this, the interaction of subjective and objective apprehensions of time may best be observed by looking again at the action of the scene of the burning of the love-letters; and one may gain an idea of how Lope brings out a sense of the incompatibility between temporal and eternal by observing the particular form he gives to the sequences—four in all—in which we are shown each of the principal characters of the act for the last time.

As we saw earlier, the letter-burning scene as a whole embodies Dorotea's attempt to escape the bondage of the past represented in the scraps of paper in her hands. Despite Celia's pressure for speed, she clings to these tangible reminders, hangs back, delays. The tension between such psychic prolongation of the past and the measured, ongoing time that impinges on her in Celia's words, is the heart of the scene. The outcome is a first forcible adjustment of Dorotea's emotional pace to the ever-present chronometry of the clock. In this sense the scene constitutes a necessary awakening. But it is not a liberation. Dorotea, as we have seen, while outwardly deferring to the world's time, remains under the spell of the past, of a life style cultivated, so to speak, in defiance of time. The uncanny emergence of Fernando's written words from her candle flame will symbolize the persistence of his emotional hold. Even as she is forced into step with reality, Dorotea will still ambiguously acknowledge a need for self-delusion.

As the scene progresses the tension between mistress and maid quickens and the pace keeps accelerating. Celia grows increasingly impatient with Dorotea's inopportune pauses and the cross-purposes behind them. From the outset (p. 428) she urges speed on her mistress:

> *Dor.:* . . . Llega, Celia, la buxía.
> *Cel.:* Ponlos presto. ¿Para qué los miras?
> *Dor.:* Oye éste sólo . . .
>
> *Dor.:* Bring the candle up, Celia.   *Cel.:* Put them to it rapidly.
> What are you looking at them for?   *Dor.:* Listen to just this one . . .

The candle is forgotten as Dorotea reads. A pattern is thus set: rapid exchanges marked by increasingly urgent appeals from Celia—"No te eleues, por Dios; que estoy de prisa" ("Don't get yourself worked up, for heaven's sake; I'm in a hurry") and "Si te paras a leerlos, a la noche no auremos quemado la quinta parte" ("If you stop to read them, we won't have burned a fifth of them by nightfall") (p. 430)—and between exchanges, the lingering of the mistress over bits of verse and rhetorical prose. Under Celia's prodding, Dorotea keeps curtailing her reading and the clipped exchange "Vaya al fuego"— "Vaya" ("Into the fire with it"—"Into the fire") is heard at shorter and shorter intervals until Celia warns, "Mira que se acaba la buxía" ("Mind—the candle is burning out"), and, after allowing her mistress a few last hurried lines, urges her to burn all the rest together. Like one caught up in gathering momentum, Dorotea finally ceases to resist, as if she had at last given in to the clock that has been almost perceptibly ticking away throughout the scene.

In seeking to show how Lope conveys a sense of the limited character of the human apprehension of time, one may begin by noting that in one way or another he has sought to lead his characters at the end toward the deeper awareness he has himself attained of the permanent imminence of the Christian beyond. In the dispositions he makes of them, one can feel his hand at work, arresting, redirecting, or simply jarring the course of their lives. But he avoids dealing too arbitrarily with these creatures of his imagination, jolting them too unnaturally. The evidence of divine intervention in their lives is kept to a minimum; their different intimations of the beyond are attained strictly from within the confined perspective of the temporal world. Each, too, has his own response to the summons that reaches him.

In the earlier acts the characters had been shown existing purely within the confines of unawakened worldliness. I have noted how Fernando, when he sings ballads by Lope—"A mis soledades voy" in Act I and the elegies to Amarilis in Act III—egocentrically restricts their meaning, missing the strong sense of *vitam impendere aeterno* which permeates them. Although Dorotea, in marshaling the reasons for breaking with Fernando (I, 3), does foresee the danger of this affair to her immortal soul—"Será impossible librarle de algún fin desdichado o en la vida o en la honra; y lo que más se deue temer, en el alma" ("It will be impossible to preserve it from some end unlucky for life or honor; and, what is most to be feared, for the soul") (p. 80)—this moment of insight, soon ignored, has no more effect on her subsequent conduct than the operatic "Oh God! Oh death!" with which she emerges from her faint. It is precisely her insensitivity to the implications of what she is saying that is significant, and the effect is ironical.

The same is true on those occasions when Gerarda shows concern with the hereafter. Gerarda's years inevitably make her more sensitive to what lies beyond and, as I shall note later, there is a paradoxical element of detachment in her attachment to life. This is because she eases her conscience with external observances and naively deludes herself into believing that she will be prepared to meet her Maker whenever the moment arrives.[22] No awareness of sin dampens her high spirits and until the last moment she remains self-assured and unawakened. Although she professes alarm at the thought of death and judgment, in the very process of expression her alarm is desensitized by copious rhetoric and a histrionic imagination:

> *Ger.:* A la fe, niña, que me dio [Don Bela] no sé quántos [escudos];
> que no te los enseño, porque los dexo guardados para mi entierro.
> Allí estarán con el hábito pardo. No he de tocar a ellos, porque,
> hija, lo que importa es pensar en el fin y temer la muerte; que
> nos ha de pedir estrecha cuenta aquel Señor que sabe hasta los
> pensamientos, y no ay cabello de que no se la auemos de dar
> quando en el valle de Iosafat nos veamos todos.

Dor.: ¡Qué presto te enterneces!
Ger.: Soy pecadora, Dorotea, y temo que no ay donde huir aquel
  tremendo día.

(p. 160)

Ger.: The truth, child, is that [Don Bela] gave me I don't know how
many [crowns]. I don't show them to you because I have them put
away for my funeral. There they'll be with the drab habit. I shall
not touch them because the important thing, child, is to think of the
end and fear death; for a strict accounting will be required of us by
that Lord who knows even thoughts, and there's not a hair for
which we won't have to give it when we all meet in the Vale of
Josaphat.   *Dor.:* How easily you are moved to tears!   *Ger.:* I'm a
sinner, Dorotea, and I fear there'll be no place to hide that terrible
day.

An extratemporal concern is indeed channeled into lyrics in the early acts
but it is peculiarly the author's, remaining unmediated by the characters,
as will be seen later. Not until the opening scenes of Act V does Lope begin
to awaken the characters' perceptions. In scene 1 Laurencio suggests that
Don Bela's devout and contrite manner might stem from a "divine impulse."
The suggestion is not pursued, for Lope is focusing on the human circumstances that lead to such "impulses." But in scene 2, in which Don Bela in
fact appears to be detaching himself from the human world, the usual
process of bargaining with Gerarda takes on dimensions suggestive of the
pettiness of human calculations viewed against the background of the
infinite. Bodied forth in a dramatic situation and no longer unnerving, there
persists here something of the awareness reflected in the final *Soliloquio*:
"Thinking of you the power of mortal understanding falters because you
are incommensurable . . . No space encompasses you nor pen declares you
nor time measures you."[23] As Gerarda proceeds to nag and wheedle, Don
Bela complies meekly and absently: "Dale quatro reales, Laurencio"
("Give her four *reales*, Laurencio"); "Dale otros quatro reales" ("Give her
four more *reales*")—four, eight, twelve. The phrase recurs with increasing
frequency and we move rapidly up the numerical scale as Gerarda persists
in her demands: twelve more, six. Suddenly Don Bela remarks, "Dáselos,
y adiós, que me voy a missa" ("Give them to her, and good-bye—I'm going
to mass"), and exits for the last time. His abrupt termination of the demeaning process, the contrast between the unconcern of his "Dáselos" ("Give
them to her") and his thirst for spiritual sustenance, makes suddenly plain
to us the smallness, the ludicrous inadequacy of all these countings and

computations viewed *sub specie aeternitatis.* Don Bela's final exit prefigures
in a flash the reckoning in the beyond that now impends for Gerarda as well
as himself, the "reckoning to that just judge of living and dead" to which
Gerarda had so lightly alluded in their first scene together (p. 137), the
"strict accounting" of which she had piously spoken to Dorotea. Nor do the
echoes of Don Bela's words stop here, for they also hark back to the opening
scene, in which Gerarda, speaking opportunistically rather than understandingly, but saying more than she realized, had applied her game of fives to
the stages of feminine beauty only to end by telling Teodora: "Well,
realize that they all overshoot the mark and the game is lost" (p. 72). The
present passage throws light on the authorial irony behind Gerarda's numerical juggling and orients us to Lope's experience of how small any number
appears at the point where numbers cease. The earlier suggestion is caught
up and dramatized in the disparity between Don Bela's inner anguish and
Gerarda's continuing insensitivity.

Before Gerarda's callousness is penetrated in the nick of time in the last
moments of her life, we are given, through Dorotea, two striking formulations of the gap existing between human limitations and God's infiniteness:
they come in speeches framing the pair of scenes (V, 9 and 10) that lead up
to the final calamities. At the beginning of scene 9, with her usual ambivalence, Dorotea contemplates thoughts of the convent and the hereafter:

> Trocaré estas galas a vn hábito y daré con prudencia esto que los
> hombres llaman gracias al autor dellas, que ni puede engañar ni
> faltar, ni dexar de agradecer; que, boluiendo los ojos a lo passado,
> ¿qué tengo yo, Celia, de la amistad de Fernando, sino el arrepenti-
> miento de mi ignorancia, aquellos papeles cuyas letras quemadas,
> blancas entro lo negro del papel, me ponían miedo, y auer echado
> cinco años por la ventana de mi apetito en la calle de mi deshonra?
> La hermosura no buelue, la edad siempre passa. Posada es nuestra
> vida, correo el tiempo, flor la juuentud, el nacer deuda. El dueño
> pide, la enfermedad executa, la muerte cobra.   (p. 444)

> I will exchange this finery for a habit and will with prudence
> surrender what men call graces to the author of them, who is able
> neither to deceive nor to be found wanting, nor to be unappreciative.
> For, looking back to what is past, Celia, what do I have to show for
> Don Fernando's friendship except repentance for my ignorance;
> those papers whose burned-out letters, white against the black of the
> paper, made me feel afraid; and having thrown five years of my life
> out the window of my appetite into the street of my dishonor?
> Beauty does not return, the years move forward always. Our life is a

hostelry, time a courier, youth a flower, birth a debt. The creditor demands, illness forecloses, death collects.

Dorotea's disillusioned words at the end of scene 10 are blurted out in bitter reflection on her emotional cul-de-sac:

Ay Gerarda, si hablamos de veras, ¿qué viene a ser esta vida sino vn breve camino para la muerte? Si don Bela quiere, tú verás estos pies que celebrauas trocar las çapatillas de ámbar en groseras sandalias de cordeles; estos rizos cortados, y estas colores y guarniciones de oro, en sayal pardo. ¿Quién ay que sepa si ha de anochecer la mañana que se leuanta? Toda la vida es vn día. Ayer fuiste moça, y oy no te atreues a tomar el espejo por no ser la primera que te aborrezcas. Más justo es agradecer los desengaños que la hermosura. Todo llega, todo cansa, todo se acaba. (p. 454)

Ah, Gerarda, speaking plainly, what does this life amount to except a rapid road to death? If Don Bela is willing, you will see these feet you celebrated exchange amber-scented pumps for rough rope sandals, these curls cut off, and these colors and gilt trimmings exchanged for a drab sackcloth. Is there anyone who knows when he gets up in the morning whether he will live through the day? All of life is a day. Yesterday you were a girl and today you don't dare pick up the mirror so as not to be the first to hate yourself. It is more proper to be grateful to disillusion than to beauty. Everything runs its course, everything palls, everything has an end.

Because we know from Fernando's horoscope—and indeed from the intervening moments of scenes 9 and 10—that Dorotea will not retain the insights reached here under the pressure of despair, we are prevented from taking these outbursts as indications of a genuine reformation or shift of values. The Dorotea who, in regaining Fernando, has not been able to renounce Don Bela is scarcely capable of giving up the world. Emotional tensions, rhetorical and theatrical exaltation propel her at this point beyond her depth into visions of renunciation which it has been made plain she will not pursue. Lope lends her disillusionment all the dignity available to it by setting it against a transcendent backdrop. In the poignancy of Dorotea's anguish, beyond the conventional homiletic tone, there are undoubtedly echoes of the remembered anguish, the crushing awareness of mortality and sin which had been poured into the *Soliloquios*. In a certain sense Lope is speaking out of his own heart, giving Dorotea, with benign irony, the benefit of experience beyond her ken. As if speaking over her head for a moment, he reasserts for the reader his own hard-won sense of proportion, reminding him that after all the "real" world of man and nature is only a plaything of God's eternity.

A more limited verbal irony is present here also, especially in the first passage, throwing an equivocal light on certain of Dorotea's professions, a light in which her attitude appears quite consistent with what we already know of her. Her "gracias" plays ambiguously about the triple meaning "charms," "thanks," and "grace"; her God is peculiarly negative, an unworldly lover who will not be found wanting. How ambiguously, too, she evokes the burning of the love-letters, stressing the eerie survival of the handwriting. Lope's keen eye and subtle artistry are evident in this detail, for it also makes, more remotely, an ironical comment on the vaunted indestructibility of the poetic word, which here survives only as a travesty of itself. In both passages, as Dorotea proclaims her new ascetic role, the impression is conveyed that it intrigues her without at all binding her.

The asyndeton that concludes the first passage, with its nine brief rapid phrases five to eight syllables long, contrasts strikingly with the leisurely sinuosity and syntactic complexity of the rest; the second passage culminates in the even starker "Todo llega, todo cansa, todo se acaba." In these climactic expressions of universal evanescence, the alignment of the accumulating phrases, the rapid succession devoid of subordination or amplification, not only underscores what is signified, but forces on our awareness again a rhythmic beat, the on-running tick-tock which measures mortality down to the final limit, then fails altogether. The reiteration of this effect clearly reinforces the fundamental chronometry in anticipation of the moment now impending, when time's undermining action will eventuate in collapse and calamity.

In the clipped prose of these passages, the old strain of desolation reenters the Lopean *desengaño* and recharges the old moral and doctrinal common-places[24] with a personal intensity of feeling that does not abate until a counter-thrust of levity reasserts itself through the calamities of the final scene. The first passage closely echoes similar outpourings in the *Soliloquios*: "Toda la vida es un día, amanece en la niñez, resplandece en la juventud, y en la vejez cierra las hojas de su flor" ("All of life is a day, it dawns in childhood, shines forth at noon, and in old age closes up the petals of its bloom").[25] The anaphoric *todo* at the end of the second is sweeping indeed. There are seeds of decay in everything. Nothing escapes, there can be no renewals. There is nothing to anticipate (*todo llega*); nothing holds its appeal (*todo cansa*); nothing is lasting (*todo se acaba*).

The most notable effect of these words is to bring Gerarda suddenly to her senses:

¡Ay, hija Dorotea! Conmigo hablas, que no sé si amaneceré viua. Las lágrimas me has traído del coraçón a los ojos. Conozco, aunque tarde, mis engaños. Dios te ha puesto las palabras en la boca.   (p. 454)

Oh Dorotea, child, that you should be saying this to me, when I'm not even sure whether I'll wake up tomorrow. You've brought tears from my heart to my eyes. Late though it is, I recognize the error of my ways. God put those words in your mouth.

Here there can be no doubt that we are to understand a "divine impulse." If, as Gerarda says, "God put those words in your mouth," God has also suddenly touched Gerarda's heart and only for this reason is she moved by expressions of a type that have never roused her before. With tears at last authentic and involuntary, tears of contrition stemming from the heart, Gerarda is ready for the death of which she here has a premonition, though, as Laurencio will remark at the end of the work apropos of the brevity of life: "No one . . . imagined it so brief that he expected to die the same day he was imagining it" (p. 457). Lope is now done with Gerarda and can even let her venial bibulousness reassert itself and lead her to her death.

Dorotea's words and Gerarda's response, just preceding, as they do, the entrance of Laurencio at the beginning of scene 11 with news of his "lamentable tragedy," clearly set the stage for the calamitous turn of events which will bring the work to a close.

What, finally, of Fernando? The dialogue surrounding the *barquillas* of Act III had earlier eliminated the possibility that the youthful persona might share the sense of desolation caused in Lope by his loss of Marta de Nevares. It is no surprise to find that Fernando's account (V, 3) of the gradual break-up of his liaison with Dorotea shows no traces of the deeper disenchantment experienced by the other characters. Fernando relates accesses of shame and feelings of humiliation; he records his discovery that passion cools and scales fall from the eyes. But he also coolly registers "el gusto de la vengança" ("the pleasure of vengeance") and, along with relief at delivery from passion, shows a desire to attach himself to a new mistress. Fernando repeatedly expresses wonder at the workings of human love but the world-weariness he had earlier affected is gone; it was only a symptom of emotional turmoil, after all. When we have heard Fernando out, we find him as attached to the world, to art, to love as ever. We have seen that the warning which César voices—"Not one stone will be left on top of another in the edifice of your life"—is a false alarm as far as Fernando is concerned. Quite the contrary, he likens himself to a watch put back in working order (p. 405).

What is missing in Fernando is his creator's sense of the frailty of his hold on the world, of the infinite impinging on his life. The other characters become attuned to their creator's mood, each in his own way, though evidently none responds to the full range of Lope's *desengaño*. But Lope could no more endow Fernando with a sense of disillusionment attuned to his than instill in him a sense of guilt. The world was no more slipping away from Fernando than it had been from Lope at a comparable stage of life. Fernando has indeed grown, has acquired a clearer mastery of the realities of love as a result of his experience, but there is even less reason than there was for Lope for Fernando to feel deeply disabused. Unlike Lope, he has had the last word, has not been left smarting, and has no need for the resilience Lope had shown. At bottom Lope could not conceive of a young male, for all the temporary estrangement passion might cause, losing his grip on life, as age was forcing Lope to relax his own despite his unfaltering *élan vital*.[26] He found it natural for the young man to try to clasp the whole world in his embrace, heedless of the consequences to himself or others. Fernando is no more capable of moral responsibility—and no more fundamentally immoral —than Lope had been. Precisely because Fernando plays at being submerged by suffering, he is a greater object of amusement to his creator than any other character of the *acción en prosa*. The gulf that separates the old man from the figure of his youthful self is nowhere wider than here. Fernando is bound to bounce back in the end because the experience with Dorotea is only a temporary alienation. Lope is being profoundly true to himself in depicting Fernando's youthful egotism, however much some critics may have objected to the impunity Fernando enjoys. Conversely, Lope's depiction of an Amphryso–Alba overcome by disillusionment and in effect renouncing living fails to ring true.

Lope cannot impute authentic disenchantment to Fernando without disturbing the psychological consistency of his conception of the young man as poet. Yet Lope felt it incumbent on him to offer a moral perspective on Fernando's conduct and he also felt impelled to reach out toward him across the gap of years and in some way to draw him into the orbit of the wider *desengaño* of the work. The result is to break a second time into the block of scenes embodying the disintegration of Don Bela's and Dorotea's world in order to project Fernando's life into the future by means of a horoscope and to record his reaction to the vicissitudes and calamities foretold. In effect Lope appends his own life-span to the persona of his youthful self and injects into Fernando's response to the events foretold an inkling of the disillusionment to come. Fernando is appalled at the vision of the persecutions of which he is to be the object and the toils ("trabajos") reserved for him, while the calamitous fate of Marfisa, whose third husband is to kill her in a fit of jealousy, provokes the response: " ¡Iesús, qué tristeza me auéis causado!" ("Lord, what sadness you've caused me!") (p. 443). Fernando has no thought of Dorotea in the entire scene, but his final words (this is the last we see of him) show him profoundly stirred:

> No puedo boluer en mí, con saber que esto es incierto, de la tragedia que César promete a Marfisa. Assí es el coraçon cobarde quando ama, y la duda poderosa para temer la desdicha. ¿Yo preso? ¿Yo desterrado? ¿Marfisa muerta?   (p. 444)

> Even though I know it's not definite, I can't get over the tragedy that César promises Marfisa. So much of a coward is the heart when it loves, so all-powerful is doubt in fearing misfortune. I in jail? I exiled? Marfisa killed?

This is the closest Fernando comes to the *desengaño* experienced by the other characters. A gulf clearly remains between the *tristeza* that wells up from within Dorotea and Don Bela and the gloom that is imposed upon Fernando by the news of particular developments to come. It is perhaps not incongruous for Fernando to step into Lope's shoes with his announced intention to "trocar las letras por las armas" ("exchange letters for arms") in the Armada against England. Although he has shown little inclination for the sword and none to abandon the pen, a spirit of adventure may be conceded to this *littérateur*. The note of *desengaño* which truly fits the scene into the artistic order of the whole comes at its end, when César, after inviting Fernando to accompany him to mass, "so that you may ask God's divine assistance in mending your ways," further urges: "Bolued los ojos a tantos amigos muertos, y muchos de vuestros años" ("Stop and consider so many friends dead, many of them of your own age") (p. 444). The attempt to telescope the years is put aside here. It is clearly as an old man looking about him that Lope reflects on "so many friends dead"; as an old man looking far back and taking in a decade at a glance that he summons a hitherto unaware Fernando to think of the "many of them of your own age" —the friends like the Melchor de Prado of the *Proceso*, whose death is perfunctorily recorded in a mannered sonnet, "Ay, cuántas horas de contento llenas" ("Ah, how many hours filled with happiness"), of the *Rimas* of 1602, or Luis de Vargas Manrique, to whom Lope frivolously alludes in the ballad "Mil años ha que no canto" ("I have not sung for a thousand years") as "Lisardo, aquel ahogado, / como Narciso, en el pozo" ("Lisardo, the one drowned like Narcissus in the well"): he had died by drowning in the

Tyrrhenian Sea some time before 1600.[27] These deaths had not made much of an impression at the time, to judge by such literary records. The poignant urgency of the old man's words to a silent Fernando is Lope's true elegy to his long-lost friends. (Like every elegist, he has himself, the survivor, in mind as much as the departed.)[28]

Fernando's response is not given us; the scene ends with César's summons. We may imagine a Fernando awed to silence or one not even touched by César–Lope's voice. But that voice unquestionably picks up the poignant note of *desengaño* heard elsewhere in the act.

The Expression of *Soledad*

In the voice of César-Lope, as in the solitary struggle of Don Bela at the beginning of the act for a private emancipation, it is the *soledad* of the mature Lope that emerges. The allusion to "so many friends dead" points to experiences of loss that can only intensify the radical awareness of every man that, however close he may be to his God, humanly speaking, he is essentially alone on earth. The Lopean *Erlebnis* thus reflected links the strain of *soledad* to the expression of "disillusionment amidst the fruition of life" which culminates in the fifth act. While it is now effectively mediated through the characters, it had earlier been manifested largely independently of them in lyrics of the first and third acts, in which a poetic voice which we have seen expressly presented as Lope's own speaks.[29] Let us now look back at these lyrics, examining the nuances which they add to the expression of *soledad* in the *acción en prosa* and seeking to determine the relation in which they stand to the mood of *desengaño* which culminates later.

The poems in question are "A mis soledades voy" ("I go off to my solitude") of Act I and the four elegies to Marta de Nevares incorporated into Act III. The tone and mood of the group of four are strikingly different from those of the first poem. As I noted earlier, the poems of Act III were inserted at the last moment, in the month between the death of Lope's mistress (April 7, 1632) and the censor's approval of the work (May 6). With an emotional intensity reminiscent of the *Soliloquios* and a narrow affective range, the heptasyllabic *romances* convey a crushing sense of personal loss and utter desolation. The poem of Act I, written in octosyllabic ballad meter, on the other hand, is bound to no particular emotional contingency. The tone is reflective and Lope ranges much more broadly between self and world, between world and the beyond. In the placing of the poems a concern is evident for a certain symmetry in the configuration of *soledad*. The first poem comes near the opening of Act I, the other four in pairs at the beginning and end of Act III, and the strain is absorbed, as we have seen, in the mainstream of the action in Act V.[30]

Earlier I described a tendency in Lope toward withdrawal and solitude as a manifestation of the melancholy strain increasingly evident in the latter part of his life. Before turning to the poems of La Dorotea, let us observe more closely what the soledad of the later years entails. In a letter of 1621 Lope writes:

> Dichoso ochenta veces quien vive en Sevilla; así estaba yo cuando en un barco me iba todas las mañanas a las Cuevas y volvía a la noche alegre de haber hablado con un hombre solo y no haber topado a nadie ni a caballo ni en coche.[31]

> He who lives in Seville is eighty times blessed. So I was when I used to go off in a boat every morning to Las Cuevas and come back at nightfall, happy at having talked with a single man and not having run into anyone either on horseback or in a coach.

Whether or not these lines allude to a boatman, the suggestion is strong that this "hombre solo" is simply the responsive voice in a communion with the self sought by the poet from time to time for respite from the tensions of a world to which he still remains committed. Within Madrid, as Lope grows older, the house and garden of the Calle de Francos become his "rinconcillo, donde tantas vezes me ha oído Vex.ª disputar esta philosophía del viuir quieto" ("little nook, where Your Excellency has heard me so many times upholding this philosophy of quiet living"), as he tells his patron as early as 1615.[32] Here he finds access to soledad of the most elemental kind: isolation needed and embraced. It could not be absolute, of course, for the world inevitably intruded on Lope's consciousness: "Verdaderamente no es soledad estar vn ombre de día y de noche accompañado de tantos pensamientos, que estuuiera más solo en vn exército o en Madrid el día del Angel" ("Truly it is not solitude for a man to be accompanied day and night by so many thoughts that he would be more alone in an army or in Madrid on Annunciation Day"), he writes in 1628.[33] Still this was aloneness without loneliness, the self "all one," integrated and fulfilled, not separated and deprived.

Yet there is more to the Lopean soledad than moral self-sufficiency rooted in physical withdrawal. As the advancing years bring disappointment of hopes, personal losses, a sense of being superseded professionally, a weakening of his physical hold on the world, Lope experiences soledad in less tranquil form, as pervasive disenchantment with a world that is leaving him behind and alone. A note of forlornness may now sometimes be felt in his expression of *soledad*, a sense of the barrenness of the world itself, *soledades* as at once a physical reality and a state of mind and soul. Awareness of lonely survival, as we have already sensed it in César's words in *La Dorotea*, projects premonitions of Lope's own end on the world in heightened expressions of its evanescence, its fragility, and its approaching demise. His vital urge must increasingly contend with a desire for rest, a physical and spiritual fatigue that reach their climax in the poems of Act III, where the world-weariness reflected becomes excruciatingly intense. In "A mis soledades voy" there is less imbalance between a self-sufficient and a desolate form of *soledad*, yet no definitive fusion is achieved even there. Only in the last act, as we know, will the balance be righted.

Vossler saw "A mis soledades voy" as a dialogue of the spiritual self with the bodily, of the lone man with the world.[34] It is a dialogue of inner voices, lyrical in movement, mood, and expression, despite a persistent drift toward social criticism.[35] The presence of the poem at this point must be meant, through an articulation of tensions between the temporal and the eternal, the social and the solitary side of the self, its surface and depths, to dispose the reader in advance to the *desengaño* to come. Prolonging the introspective and meditative strain of the "Egloga a Claudio" and, further back, the *Soliloquios*, the poem stands, so to speak, halfway between them and the *acción en prosa*. On the threshold of the work it allows us a glance over the author's shoulder, as it were, as he muses over concerns that are bodied forth in it. Lacking the intense emotional temper of the *Soliloquios* and the focus of the "Egloga" on creative expression, "A mis soledades voy" gives considerable prominence to the self in society. The outer world clearly disturbs the tranquillity of the inner here.

An effect of restlessness is present from the start; it must have been this note, later verbalized in the phrase "universal movimiento" (l. 78), which caught Lope's fancy in the pattern of the popular ditty that in all likelihood was his point of departure:

> A la villa voy,
> de la villa vengo,
> que si no son amores,
> no sé qué me tengo.[36]

> I go to town, I come from town; unless it is love, I don't know what's the matter with me.

The poem's movement is fitful and inconclusive; the voices of the self answer one another in no orderly progression. They start up, fall silent, then start off in new directions, coming back at the end to the starting point with accumulated allusiveness. In the movement of these voices I see the key to the poem's form and meaning. The voice of the profounder self is heard in the three introductory quatrains, gives way in the fourth to that of the social or worldly side of the self, reenters in the eleventh, gives way again in the twelfth, reenters in the twenty-first, dies out in the twenty-second, to return finally in the last, the twenty-eighth. The poem thus falls into a pattern of shorter and longer segments—three quatrains, seven, one, nine, two, five, one—not without a certain rough tripartite symmetry.

The opening of the poem sets up a movement of withdrawal and return from *soledades* that are at once a place, like the "villa" of the folksong—a physical retreat—and a state of mind:

> A mis soledades voy,
> de mis soledades vengo,
> porque para andar conmigo
> me bastan mis pensamientos.

> I go off to my solitude, I come from my solitude, because to accompany me my thoughts are sufficient.

The scope of this solitude, which is clearly not characterized by loneliness, is enlarged in the second quatrain and proves a matter of more than simple stoic self-limitation:

> No sé qué tiene el aldea
> donde viuo y donde muero,
> que con venir de mí mismo
> no puedo venir más lexos.

> I don't know what there is about the village where I live and where I die, but coming from myself I cannot come from any further away.

The world—*el aldea* is here at once the social and the temporal world—arouses in the poet a brooding sense, caught in the expression "no sé qué," of its inadequacy, a sense bound up with its finiteness, with the finality of "donde viuo y donde muero." But it is the self, not the eternal world, that Lope then sets against the *aldea*, a self now coextensive with the *soledades* of the opening ("venir de mí mismo"—"de mis soledades vengo"). The last two lines, with their suggestion of incommensurability, evoke unfathomable depths of the self, the depths Lope has found ultimately impenetrable as he looks into them and composes the *acción en prosa*. He has come, like every man, out of his own distant past, out of depths of time and place, and, as I remarked earlier, he knows how far behind he has left the Lope–Fernando of long ago. Both the attraction and the irretrievability of the past are evoked, as they also had been in the "Egloga a Claudio."

If solitude reveals the mutability of the self and its world, it also suggests the aloneness of every human being, as Lope—not Fernando—has come to experience it. Awareness of self is awareness of *soledades*, even within the *aldea* to which one's life is bound. In its singularity the self lives alone and in the end it dies alone.

There seem to be further overtones, suggestions of Christian immortality, in these lines (7–8). They are certainly perceptible in the third quatrain, though remaining muted here as throughout the poem and the *acción en prosa*:

> Ni estoy bien ni mal conmigo;
> mas dize mi entendimiento
> que vn hombre que todo es alma,
> está cautiuo en su cuerpo.

> I am neither at ease nor at odds with myself; but my understanding tells me that a man who is purely soul is a captive in his body.

In the first line the self still speaks, though irresolutely, as something apart, as its own sole associate. Then it stops speaking and listens to a small voice from within, the voice of the understanding—not the "subtle" worldly understanding that Fernando will prize in Dorotea, but that same Christian understanding, a faculty of the soul, that is evoked by the old Lope when he speaks to Fernando through César before their last exit and tells him to thank God for "el entendimiento que os ha dado con amarle y temerle" ("the understanding he has given you in loving him and fearing him") (p. 444). The Christian implications behind the earlier expressed inadequacy of *el aldea*, a sense of the confinement it brings, here become clear.

There is an evasive answer—"Entiendo lo que me basta" ("I understand what suffices me")—then the self turns away from its *soledades*. Back in the world, it slips at once into the quibbles which play over so much of the poem's surface. The sense of apartness now turns into opposition to specific failings of society and its members, grievances strung out with a testiness that bespeaks anything but detachment. The back-and-forth movement, the restlessness fundamental to the poem, turns into a series of verbal contrasts—assertions and exceptions, paradoxes and alternatives, puns and zeugmas—that produce sudden switches from the transcendent to the trivial.[37]

The marked segmentation of the poem into quatrains, the pithiness produced by the octosyllabic units, the aphorisms sometimes coined—for example, "que humildad y necedad / no caben en vn sujeto" ("for humility and stupidity don't go together in one person"), ll. 23–24—the restless play of the stylistic devices mentioned, all are choppy and unsettling. The seven quatrains that follow the opening three trail away at last into a *boutade* of false modesty:

> No me precio de entendido,
> de desdichado me precio;
> que los que no son dichosos,
> ¿cómo pueden ser discretos?
>
> (ll. 37–40)

I don't pride myself on being intelligent, I pride myself on being unfortunate, for how can those who are not fortunate be smart?

The "entendimiento" to which Lope disclaims any pretension here is now clearly a subtle worldly understanding, one which in other moods, as we have amply seen, far from renouncing, he prized as much as do the characters he depicts in the *acción en prosa*. An unresolved ambivalence in fact underlies the disparity between the Christian "entendimiento" that speaks in l. 10 and the worldly counterpart unconvincingly disclaimed in l. 37.

One must supply a reflective pause before what follows:

> No puede durar el mundo
> porque dizen, y lo creo,
> que suena a vidro quebrado
> y que ha de romperse presto.
>
> (ll. 41–44)

The world cannot last because they say, and I believe it, that there is a sound of breaking glass about it, and that it will soon go to pieces.

With this fresh start, the fragility of the world, of all imaginable worlds, evoked and not yet evoked in the poem—of society, of nation, of man, nature, time—is caught and held in one vivid image of tinkling, splintering glass. Eerily the sound precedes the cataclysm, like the signs of imminent doomsday mentioned in the next quatrain. The inversion of shock and sound adds to the unsettling effect of the image and attunes the ear of the alert reader of the *acción en prosa* to the still faint sound of coming calamities, forewarning of the disintegration destined to overtake this created world in the last act.[38]

Lope digresses from such forebodings of Christian doomsday almost immediately by means of a zeugma:

> Señales son del juizio
> ver que todos le perdemos . . .
>
> (ll. 55–56)

It's a sign of the judgment that we are all losing ours . . .

Soon he is sniping at his age, taking economic and political conditions as his targets. Increasingly sharp aim is taken at contrasts between Spaniards and foreigners, between modern and old-time Spaniards, between Spaniards from the waist up and the waist down. The ancient ages, no longer temporally contiguous, are located in the Europe of his day, side by side; more precisely, the age of silver and a clearly topical age of copper are thus juxtaposed. The unrestrained critical tone, the consciousness of a society and a nation gone wrong are much more reminiscent of remarks in private letters to the Duke of Sessa than of sentiments intended for publication.

The subjective self noticeably present behind the image of breaking glass— "porque dizen, *y lo creo*, / que suena a vidro quebrado ("because they say, *and I believe it*, that there is a sound of breaking glass about it")—is silent for eight quatrains. It is as a social being that Lope speaks. There is no first person, only a long sequence of plurals and indefinite pronouns which end up in a condemnation of complaisant cuckolds, favoritism, and venality.

There is a new pause, then the poet speaks again in the first person (twenty-first quatrain):

> Oigo tañer las campanas,
> y no me espanto, aunque puedo,
> que en lugar de tantas cruzes
> aya tantos hombres muertos.

> I hear the bells toll and I am not alarmed, though I might be, that in a place with so many crosses there should be so many dead men.

A listening self again perceives sounds of mortality. The jarring pun on *cruzes* (crosses), the abrupt shift from the cemetery to a society where decorations have grown legion, does not wholly dissipate the atmosphere of finality that has gathered again in these lines. "Do not ask for whom the bell tolls," Lope seems to be saying, "it tolls for thee." An old man is speaking, attempting to reassure himself by recalling "lo que se dize de los tordos viejos, que no se espantan en las torres del sonido de las campanas" ("what they say about old thrushes, that they don't become alarmed in towers at the sound of bells").[39] The worldly afterthought that changes the meaning of "No me espanto" from "I am not afraid" to "I am not surprised" marks the beginning of a new movement back to the society of the day. The poet lingers a moment—"Mirando estoi los sepulcros" ("I look at the tombs")—then resumes with surprising vehemence:

> ¡O, bien aya quien los hizo!
> porque solamente en ellos
> de los poderosos grandes
> se vengaron los pequeños.
>
> (ll. 89–92)

Oh, blessings on him who made them, because only in them have the little people avenged themselves on the powerful great.

His composure is jarred, as if pent-up resentments were breaking through. Is it the obverse side of Lope's relationship with the Duke of Sessa that we glimpse here? In the four succeeding quatrains the world intrudes more and more upon the *soledad* of the self and Lope invokes in its place the impersonal self-sufficiency of "vnos hombres que no saben / quién viue pared en medio" ("certain men who don't know who lives next door"). As Spitzer notes, the *aldea* has shrunk to a country village and represents a kind of Horatian retreat, with echoes of the simple life of the *beatus ille*.[40] The envy acknowledged in this section is painted as "an ugly woman," following the traditional iconography of this figure as one who consumes and is consumed by her own bitterness.[41] So the poet's resentments have corroded his *soledades*. But in a final shift envy is transcended and *soledades* regained:

> Con esta envidia que digo,
> y lo que passo en silencio,
> a mis soledades voy,
> de mis soledades vengo.

With this envy I speak of, and what I suffer in silence, I go off to my solitude, I come from my solitude.

The pregnant phrase here is "lo que passo en silencio": at the same time "what I suffer in silence" and "what I keep to myself." On the one hand, indignities and humiliation; on the other, something even less specific than the *pensamientos* of the opening, thoughts unmentioned and beyond expressing. The poet keeps his own counsel and his own company but "lo que passo en silencio" goes further, suggesting, like the "más lexos" of the second quatrain, limitless reaches of the self and beyond the self.[42]

With this ending, despite the narrowing of scope caused immediately by the adjustment of the poem to its context through the already quoted remarks of Julio and Fernando, a way of *soledad* is opened up into the rest of the *acción en prosa*. It is true that in the ballad we are made almost obsessively aware of the pettinesses and injustices of the world of men. Under the guise of the world's finiteness, it is not its beauty and appeal or the poignancy of losing them that are stressed, but its insufficiencies and limitations. The poem oscillates between petulance and a moral and spiritual tedium, with no suggestion of the creative fulfillment that solitude brought Lope in his later years. Yet its delineation of *soledades* leading both into the self and toward the hereafter is suited to its liminal setting in the *acción en prosa*.

When the strain of *soledad* emerges again two acts later in the four so-called *barquillas*, its character, as we know, is altered. Lope's love for Marta had evidently brought him compensation for the disappointments of his later years; now, on her death, all of them seem to come flooding back. Written under the immediate impact of the loss, before Lope's natural mechanisms of recuperation could come into play, the poems are often oppressive in the intensity of feeling they convey. Nevertheless, as Lope expatiates upon the vast disenchantment which the death of his mistress precipitated, this very intensity foreshadows a more tempered fullness in the expression of *desengaño* at the end of the *acción en prosa*.

Dejection, not simply regret, at the thought of human transience, and total disillusion with men and society are the dominant notes of the *barquillas*. Nothing relieves the heavy mood. The resourcefulness of their insertion into the dialogue and the casualness with which they can be passed off there as "lamentations" (p. 285) are clearly subsequent acquisitions. Expression in the poems is essentially cathartic and inevitably reminiscent of the outpourings of the *Soliloquios*. The fourth *barquilla* records Lope's inability this time to bounce back.

> Baxa fortuna corre,
> poco la vida estima
> quien todo lo desprecia
> y a todo se retira:
> que despreciarlo todo
> es humildad altiua,

acción desesperada,
que no filosofía.
Mas tanto pueden tristezas
de passadas alegrías,
que obligan, si porfían,
a no estimar la muerte ni la vida.

(pp. 280–281)

He has fallen on hard times, he little values life who scorns everything
and withdraws from everything; for scorning everything is arrogant
humility, an act of desperation, not a philosophy. But sadness over
past joys is so powerful that, if it persists, it forces one not to value
death or life.

Lope has blended diverse literary traditions, which it will be useful to
take into account, to convey a *soledad* felt as desolation both intimate and
far-reaching, a mood most pronounced in "Ay soledades tristes" ("Oh sad
barrenness"). Since this is the first of the poems to be introduced, these
opening words affirm the thematic continuity with "A mis soledades voy,"
even though the intense intimacy of the *soledad* of these poems contrasts
with the meditative temper of the earlier ballad. Lope's *soledad* now has a
pre-Romantic cast; it brings to mind that of a Lamartine: "Un seul être
vous manque et tout est dépeuplé!" ("A single person is missing and all is
barren!"). It is loneliness, the void and yearning caused by bereavement.
Lope's disillusionment with the world, on the other hand, falls back on the
Horatian figure of the allegorical ship, traditional since the "O navis"
ode.[43]

The Virgilian pastoral provides the framework for the elegiac strain
proper, but in cultivating the piscatory or marine version of this tradition
Lope is clearly recalling Sannazaro. (The poems are introduced by Julio
[p. 206] as "versos . . . a manera de edilios piscatorios" ["verse . . . in the
manner of piscatory idylls"].) Sannazaro's first Latin piscatory eclogue,
"Phyllis," strictly speaking the only elegiac one, is Lope's clearest precedent,
though the other four have also left traces in Lope's poems.[44]

Features of the traditional pastoral elegy which reappear in Lope's poems
(along with pastoral but nonelegaic features of the idyll and eclogue) are
threnody and eulogy in the first and second, a suggestion of the apotheosis
of the departed in the second and third, a song contest with a description of
the prizes in the first, gifts to the beloved in all but the third. Tradition
clearly sustains Lope and helps him sublimate his private grief. This often
overflows traditional channels, to be sure, but it is never contorted or
theatrical.

The unrestrained character of Lope's expression does away with the segmentation into quatrains observable in "A mis soledades voy" and in other ballads of his maturity. Replacing Sannazaro's chiseled and polished hexameters, free-running heptasyllables revive the ballad manner of Lope's earlier days. (In "Pobre barquilla mía" ["Poor little boat of mine"], where the Horatian imprint is strongest, the segmentation is noticeably more marked.)

One is tempted to see something more than chance in the order of insertion of these poems, which is that of decreasing length. No doubt it seemed more appropriate to Lope that the two shorter ones should be offered as songs; both are less than half as long as the first, and the last, with its refrain, is particularly adapted to singing.[45] The order in which we find the ballads appears to be a compromise between this consideration and the probable order of composition. At least the ballad which Lope places first, "Ay soledades tristes," by far the longest (272 lines), is closest to pure threnody, and in it the sense of personal loss is keenest. The emotion keeps subsiding, then welling up again, as if Lope could not bear to come to a stop and forfeit the assuagement that he found in artistic expression. This is the ballad closest in manner to Sannazaro's; the Horatian strain is all but absent. In other ways, too, it seems to have priority, to be the point of departure for a series which tends after it toward a blending of Sannazaro and Virgil with Horace. For the ballads differ noticeably in the prominence they give to the personal elegiac strain as against the broader one of disenchantment with human society, and in the effectiveness with which they combine them. All come sooner or later to an acute sense of loss, to happy, then painful memories, to inconsolability. If we treat them according to the prominence they give to such sentiments, in the order one, four, two, three, we shall probably not be mistaking the order of composition.

Lope's _barquilla_, following the example set in Sannazaro's first eclogue, is always in these poems the skiff of a grieving fisherman. At times it also functions as a metaphor of the self in keeping with the practice of certain cultivators of the Horatian tradition.[46]

In "Ay soledades tristes" the _barquilla_ is purely decorative. Neither storm-tossed nor gratefully beached, as in the others, it exists only as an emblem of grief, to be draped in dark shrouds and adorned with funereal flowers. Fabio's long lamentation—sixty-four quatrains out of sixty-eight—is presented unbroken and without a preamble; then two quatrains beginning "Assí lloraba Fabio / del mar en las orillas" ("Thus Fabio wept on the shores of the sea") indicate his situation and tell us that he has broken down. In the last two quatrains an authorial voice breaks in to declare that only ancient exemplars can match

amores tan de veras
que ni el morir los cura
ni el tiempo los remedia.

love so true that neither death cures it nor time heals.

The "soledades" of the opening lines, at once inward and outward, link inner desolation with the desolate seaside scene. For eight quatrains Fabio invokes the sea, the night, and Venus's star. In nine more he addresses his "barquilla," once gaily adorned, now "pobre y yerma" ("poor and deserted"). He next appeals to his fellow boatmen, kept ashore, as in one of Sannazaro's eclogues, by the stormy sea, to "assist my pitiful lament with sighs." [47] He offers the traditional cups incised with mythological scenes and two woven nets for the best elegies on the "exequias / de mi querida esposa" ("exequies for my beloved wife"). (The detail may indicate composition around the time of Marta's funeral.) The formal eulogy of the deceased follows (quatrain 30), offered as a sample of how Fabio's companions are to lament—"Ya es muerta, dezid todos" ("All say: now she is dead")— no less heartfelt for the conventional hyperbolic conceits with which it covers the remembered traits of Amarilis's physical and moral beauty. The eulogy over, Fabio withdraws again into his *soledades*, rejecting consolation and company, and coveting sadness (quatrain 40):

Venid a consolarme,
que muero de tristeza.
Mas no vengáis, barqueros,
que no quiero perderla . . .

Come and console me, for I am dying of sadness, but don't come, boatmen, for I don't wish to lose it . . .

This embracing of pain, which, it will be recalled, Fernando reads as his own indulgence in suffering, suggests the need, experienced when grief is fresh, to cling to it as a means of retaining the person mourned. Chosen inconsolability of this kind, reflected with increasing feeling in the remainder of the poem, exemplifies vividly how close to the surface the vital springs of Lope's art may lie.[48] Lope brushes aside as inadequate the *topos* of the broken instrument (quatrain 42) and suggests more authentic phenomena of grief, such as the illusion of Amarilis's presence:

En este dulce engaño,
pensando que me espera,

> salen del alma sombras
> a fabricar ideas.
>
> > (quatrain 45)

Under this sweet illusion, thinking she is waiting for me, shadows come forth from the soul to form ideas.

Then he succumbs to the spell of memory:

> Qué alegre respondía,
> dividiendo risueña
> aquel clavel honesto . . .
>
> > (quatrain 48)

How brightly she would answer, smilingly dividing that virtuous carnation . . .

He is soon drawn back to desolate reality:

> Mas ya no me responde
> mi dulce, amada prenda;
> que en el silencio eterno
> a nadie dan respuesta.
>
> > (quatrain 50)

But now she answers me no longer, my sweet, beloved dear, for in the eternal silence answer is made to no one.

He wrestles with the agony of looking at her portrait:

> No miro su retrato
> y muérome por verla;
> que no pueden los ojos
> sufrir que muerta sea . . .
>
> > (quatrains 54–55)

I don't look at her portrait, though I am dying to see it, for my eyes cannot bear her being dead . . .

Even the vaunted eternity of art turns hollow:

> Lo que deseo huyo,
> porque de ver me pesa
> que dure más el arte
> que la naturaleza.
>
> > (quatrain 56)

I flee what I desire because it grieves me that art should outlast nature.

Though Fabio's lament does not conclude—it merely stops at the point where Lope tells us he breaks down—his final words reiterate his need for *soledad* in which to retain grief:

> Quando barqueros miro,
> cuyas esposas muertas
> que tanto amaron viuas
> oluidan y se alegran,
> huyo de hablar con ellos
>
> . . . .
>
> porque si alguna cosa,
> aún suya, me consuela,
> ya pienso que la agrauio,
> y dexo de tenerla.
>
> (quatrains 62–64)

When I see boatmen who forget their dead wives whom they so loved when alive, and act happy, I avoid speaking with them . . . because if anything, even a thing of hers, brings me consolation, I think I am offending her and I let it go.

The relatively orderly arrangement perceptible at the beginning of the poem—a series of apostrophes leading to a eulogy, all of roughly equal length—gives way after the midpoint (quatrain 40) as Lope struggles to express more intimate reactions to Amarilis's death. Recollection now seems unpremeditated and involuntary, the confrontation with the portrait has an urgency which the earlier literary portraiture lacked, the order of the poem is now more associative than composed. Although the imposed pattern fades, a persistent affective atmosphere preserves coherence, the *soledades* of the opening being reaffirmed in the sudden rejection (quatrain 40) of solace and companionship. Improvisation coexists with consistency of mood in a manner characteristic of Lope.

The fourth eclogue, "Gigante cristalino" ("A crystalline giant") (p. 280), is the closest to "Ay soledades tristes" in the prominence given to the personal grief of Fabio (the name figures only in these two) and the immediacy with which this grief is recorded. The effectively used refrain leads the poem back four times, at six-quatrain intervals, to its *leitmotiv*, the painfulness of memory:

> Mas tanto pueden tristezas
> de passadas alegrías
> que obligan, si porfían,
> a no estimar la muerte ni la vida.[49]

But sadness over past joys is so powerful that, if it persists, it forces one not to value death or life.

A current of worldly disillusionment enters the poem at the beginning but does not blend effectively with the intimate elegiac strain and is presently dropped. The boat is again beached at the outset, grief keeping Fabio ashore. But a storm rages to seaward, on the sea of fortune stemming from the Horatian tradition, and when it splits a ship open Fabio proclaims sententiously (p. 281):

> ¡Dichoso yo, que puedo
> gozar pobreza rica,
> sin que del puerto amado
> me aparte la codicia!

Happy I, who am able to enjoy rich poverty without covetousness taking me away from the port I love.

Morby notes (p. 281, n. 186) the evident reminiscence of the *aurea mediocritas* of Horace's "Rectius vives." But the poet seems to have lost his sense of propriety: the complacently moralizing voice and the disconsolate one are hardly reconcilable:

> La soledad me mata
> de vn bien que yo tenía,
> no los palacios altos,
> ni el oro de las Indias.
> Quando anegarse veo
> las naues y las dichas,
> consuelo en las agenas
> las pena de las mías.
> Mas tanto pueden, etc.
> Memorias solamente
> mi muerte solicitan ...

Loss of a beloved that I used to have is killing me, not lofty palaces or the gold of the Indies. When I see ships and happiness go under, I take comfort in other people's [misfortunes] for the pain of my own. But sadness over past joys is so powerful ... Memories alone are seeking my death ...

The recurrent refrain—this is its second appearance—seems now to reorient the poet. From this point on, the focus is on *soledad* as inner void; grieving memory is the only theme. Recollections come crowding in, first within the idyllic imagery of piscatory convention, then, as they grow more poignant, breaking through it—in obsessive allusion, for example, to Marta's blind eyes further eclipsed at the moment of death (p. 283):

Nunca del pensamiento
vn átomo se quitan
las luzes eclipsadas
de tu postrera vista.

Never do the eclipsed lights of the last sight of you leave my mind for an instant.

There is a fleeting echo of lengthy passages in the first eclogue on the tricks played by memory:

Intento consolarme
con ver que, fugitiua,
parece que me llamas,
y que a partir me animas.

I try to console myself when I see that as you flee you seem to call me and urge me to depart.

Then the refrain returns and the poem is terminated with a clarity of contour noticeably missing from the ballad previously analyzed.

Lope merges the elegiac and allegorical strains effectively in the other two eclogues, where the allegorical has a far larger place. In both, the seagoing *barquilla* is introduced at the start and apostrophized. A current of personal grief comes into the second, "Para que no te vayas" ("So that you should not go") (p. 217), about one third of the way through and quickly becomes dominant. In "Pobre barquilla mía," on the other hand, the figure of the beloved is introduced only close to the end, almost casually; Lope seems furthest from absorption in grief here. The poem's popularity is surely due to the thorough exploitation of the straightforward natural symbolism of ship and sea, the concentration on the trials of man in society, rather than on a single more circumscribed grief. (In this aspect the poem stands close to "A mis soledades voy.") In both these poems (the second and third in order of introduction) the allocution to the boat is in fact a dialogue with the self. The second person is introspective, like the first person of "A mis soledades voy," but more dramatically and less meditatively so.

Though far-reaching disillusionment is suggested at the beginning of "Para que no te vayas" by the professed abandonment of every hope ("De viento fueron todas" ["They were all wind"]), at first only warnings against society ("Traidoras son las aguas" ["The waters are treacherous"]) are voiced, along with a summons to withdraw:

> Ya, pobre leño mío,
> que tantos años fuiste
> desprecio de las ondas
> por Scilas y Caribdis,
> es justo que descanses . . .
>
> (p. 217)

> Now, poor boat of mine, you who for so many years were an object of scorn to the waves among Scyllas and Charybdises, it is right that you should rest . . .

No counter-movement of adherence to the world relieves the sense of fatigue; there are only exhortations to stoical resignation in the face of injustice:

> . . . vitorioso apercibe
> para injustos agrauios
> paciencias inuencibles.
>
> (p. 218)

> . . . victoriously prepare stores of unconquerable patience for unjust offenses.

Lope alludes to particular worldly contingencies: attacks of his literary enemies, his defeated hopes for royal favor, his disappointment with his patron. A persistent undertone of the long opening section is the note of transitoriness and irrevocability:

> En la deshecha popa
> desengañado escriue:
> "Ninguna fuerça humana
> al tiempo se resiste."
>
> (p. 218)

> On the broken stern write, disillusioned: "No human force resists time."

This note becomes dominant in the elegy that occupies the rest of the poem:

> Quando tu dueño y mío
> en esta orilla viste

. . . .
eras pomposo cisne
por las ocultas sendas
del reino de Anfitrite.
Ni temías tormentas
ni encantadoras Circes.

(p. 219)

When you saw your mistress and mine on this shore . . . you were a
majestic swan upon the hidden paths of the realm of Amphitrite.
You feared neither storms nor bewitching Circes.

While Marta's love emerges in these lines as compensation for disappointments, evocation soon becomes painful. The memory of Death's intrusion
brings Horatian imagery in its wake, and even an echo of the deliberate
beat of Horace's meter (second line here):

Ya la temida parca,
que con igual pie mide
los edificios altos
y las choças humildes,
se la robó a la tierra . . .

(p. 220)

Now the dreaded fate who paces out tall palaces and lowly huts
with an equal tread has stolen her from earth . . .

With increasing pathos, Fabio recalls Amarilis's physical and moral beauty
and finally he intones a threnody. Nature resounds in consonance with his
pain as in the classical elegy—waves, rocks, "the seals and dolphins." Still,
the expression of grief can now at last be contained within the traditional
molds: the breaking of the lyre (renunciation of art), the *impossibilia* of
inconsolability. In the final stanzas of envoi, nevertheless, the reversal of
mood traditional at the end of the pastoral elegy becomes simply another
expression of the *soledades* of separation:

¡O, luz, que me dexaste!
¿Quándo será possible
que buelua a verte el alma
y que esta vida animes?
Mis soledades siente . . .
Mas, ¡ay! que donde viues,

de mis deseos locos
en dulce paz te ríes.

(p. 223)

O light that has abandoned me, when will it be possible for the soul
to see you and for you to give life to this life again? Have pity on
my loneliness . . . But alas, where you live you laugh in sweet
peace at my mad desires.

Remembering as a Christian that the bliss of souls in Paradise is impervious
to thoughts of human suffering, Lope here pushes the expression of unconcern common in Christian elegiac poetry to the extreme of laughter. This
dramatic touch, which serves to heighten Fabio's sense of abandonment and
desolation, ends the poem.[50]

In "Pobre barquilla mia," the expression of disillusionment with the
ways of the world reaches a high point. Echoes of Horace's "navis," now an
object of pity and affection, as the opening line shows, are felt in the tone of
urgency and alarm and in the situation of the craft, tossed and torn by the
stormy waters of the open sea. In a long series of epigrammatic quatrains the
barquilla is exhorted to cease "inciting the waves." Its presumptuousness is
decried far less succinctly than in Horace's "Tu, nisi ventis / debes ludibrium,
cave" ("Unless you are to be a plaything of the winds, beware"). It is too
"small in its defenses," it lacks "favor astern"—favoring winds and the
winds of favor. It has no "sails of lies" or "oars of flattery." It will end up
only "amidst the rocks of arrogant envy, that shipwreck of honors." The
constant preoccupations of Lope's advancing years (some indeed, such as
envy, of his whole lifetime) emerge here in straightforward allegory. Near
the beginning there is a passing evocation of happier, more temperate days:

Quando por las riberas
andauas costa a costa,
nunca del mar temiste
las iras procelosas.
Segura nauegabas . . .

(p. 274)[51]

When you went coastwise along the shores you never feared the
stormy rages of the sea. You sailed in safety . . .

After the midpoint, the poet starts to look back again:

Passaron ya los tiempos
quando, lamiendo rosas,

el zéfiro bullía
y suspiraua aromas.

(p. 276)

The times now are past when the zephyrs billowed, caressing roses,
and breathed fragrances.

But he is once more drawn into the "fieros vracanes" ("fierce hurricanes")
of the present, before settling, two thirds of the way through, into idyllic
memories:

Contenta con tus redes,
a la playa arenosa
mojado me sacauas;
pero viuo, ¿ qué importa?

(p. 276)

Content with your nets, you brought me up on the sandy beach wet,
but alive—so what matter?

The personal self begins to be drawn into the symbolic orbit of the little
boat, which has hitherto had only the social self as referent:

Sin pleito, sin disgusto,
la muerte nos diuorcia:
¡Ay de la pobre barca
que en lágrimas se ahoga!

(p. 276)

Without a lawsuit, without a falling-out, death divorces us: alas for
the poor boat drowned in tears!

Thus, without brusqueness, the elegiac strain proper appears, although the
consistency of the allegory suffers. Then the allegory is abandoned altogether,
and the poem, like "Gigante cristalino," moves on to a concluding appeal:

Si con eternas plantas
las fixas luzes doras,
¡O dueño de mi barca!
y en dulze paz reposas,
merezca que le pidas
al bien que eterno gozas
que adonde estás me lleue

más pura y más hermosa.
Mi honesto amor te obligue . . .

(p. 277)[52]

If with eternal footsteps you gild the fixed lights, oh mistress of my boat, and repose in sweet peace, may I merit your asking the blessed one that you are enjoying eternally that He take me to where you are, purer and more beautiful. May my virtuous love prevail upon you . . .

The dead Amarilis (in this poem alone remaining unnamed) regains at last the Neo-Platonic Empyrean to which Lope had so often raised her in life. The old poet, left disconsolate, even takes comfort for once in the thought of his own mortality:

Mas ¡ay, que no me escuchas!
Pero la vida es corta:
viuiendo, todo falta;
muriendo, todo sobra.

(p. 277)

But alas, you are not listening to me. But life is short: while we live, all falls short; when we are dead, all is unneeded.

The more formal and relatively more restrained character of the last two poems analyzed is at once evident. As if the floods of feeling released in the first two had left him calmer, Lope now finds the traditional molds of the elegy more adequate. He no longer seeks so urgently to retain every thought, image, and trace of Amarilis. Falling into the apotheosis pattern of the classical elegy, he acquiesces in her deliverance from death and even casts her in the Christian role of intercessor, as Garcilaso had cast Elisa. As the final step in his mourning, he can now look ahead to his own deliverance from suffering.

In the last two lines of the final poem—"Viviendo, todo falta; muriendo, todo sobra"—Lope sums up the ultimate meaning of the *soledades* depicted in all of them and at the same time achieves as compact a formulation as one could wish of his experience of *desengaño*. In this life nothing is stable; all eventually fails one, fades, falls away. In the next, as the first line of the final quatrain confirms, one is no longer even aware of such distressing conditions. The worn antithesis "falta-sobra" is rejuvenated here. Parallel, juxtaposed, but not connected, the lines convey the absolute distinctness of the finite and the infinite, the temporal and eternal orders.

For all the imbalances among them, the three directions in which Lope's *soledades* take him—toward God, toward self, toward the world of men— suggest a complexity of attitude whose roots lie ultimately in Petrarch, the first man of modern sensibility, as he has been called. In more problematical and less rhetorical fashion than Petrarch, Lope gives expression to the same constellation of impulses that marks the latter's *De vita solitaria*, a work which modifies the absoluteness of the famous "Our heart is restless until it rests in Thee" that opens Augustine's *Confessions*. Petrarch begins by forthrightly proposing the alternatives of self and (chosen) society: "Credo ego generosum animum, preter Deum ubi finis est noster, preter seipsum et archanas curas suas, aut preter aliquem multa similitudine sibi coniunctum animum, nusquam acquiescere" ("I think that a generous spirit will never find repose save in God in whom is our end, in itself and its secret cares, or in some other spirit bound to it by a great resemblance").[53] The third alternative is, to be sure, more appropriate to Góngora than to Lope: it suggests the *cénacle* of Córdoba more than the Calle de Francos. But a larger worldliness may be sensed invading the solitudes of all three writers, and it is Lope who most unequivocally reveals it just as he most strongly affirms Petrarch's second inclination, toward a solitude of the self.

When Lope returns to *soledades* at the beginning of the last act, it will be, as we know, in the context of Don Bela's growing *tristeza* and disenchantment. On the *indiano* will be bestowed the same capacity for a compensatory creative employment of *soledad* that Lope had found for himself in his maturity. In confrontation with himself, Don Bela will now pen the Neo-Platonic madrigal which Lope had addressed to Marta-Amarilis *in vita*.[54] In the poem the beauty of Amarilis will appear as a reflection of the same *ideal belleza* of which she partakes in the Neo-Platonic heaven invoked at the end of "Pobre barquilla mía." Don Bela will make clear, as we have seen, that the poem is really centered in the self rather than directed to its ostensible recipient. In the context of the *acción en prosa*, his remark "Esto, basta que yo lo entienda" ("As for this, it is sufficient if I understand it") (p. 388) brings echoes of the mood of "Me bastan mis pensamientos" ("My thoughts are sufficient") in the *soledades* lyric of the first act.

Thus we sense the continuity of the current of *soledades* in the *acción en prosa*, flowing from outside the fictional framework, from the author's mind, to surface in the first act; broadening out and enhancing its lyricism when it appears again in the four poems of the third, still apart from the mainstream of the action; absorbed into this, finally, and into the tide of *desengaño* in the last act. This current reinforces certain notes of *desengaño* that I have analyzed and adds others. It reduces the esthetic distance at which the author stands from his creation, and its more personalized and intense form of lyric expression strengthens both the balance and the coherence of the *acción en prosa*.

The Meaning of *La Dorotea*
XII

Lope's art in *La Dorotea*, in the last analysis, is a way of assimilating and understanding an individual experience of a finite world. It exalts the personal while paradoxically subjecting it to a greater order and in this exhibits the quality which Albert Gérard in a suggestive interpretation sees as the essence of the baroque.[1] Without sacrificing the bountiful variety of nature, Lope's art subjects it to form—to shaping, design, pattern, texture—so that nature ceases to be bewildering, disorderly, unmanageable, and becomes instead an object of delight. Yet his artistic cosmos is not framed along symmetrical lines or conceived as a world in ideal repose: in this, too, it reflects the spirit of the baroque rather than the Renaissance. The richness of life is conveyed with a sense of its heterogeneousness, impurities, approximativeness, instability, yet the world is made graspable and meaningful. Tensions are confined within the lineaments of an artistic form that imposes its clarity of definition without eliminating an "atectonic" effect of openness between this artistic cosmos and a living world. Lope's exact art paradoxically preserves the continuity and flow of the natural life which nourishes it. Well-articulated segments—acts, choruses, scenes, inserted lyrics—become parts of a single voluminous whole bound together in an "ordenada confusión y apacible variedad" ("orderly confusion and pleasing variety"), to borrow a phrase of Lope's contemporary, Tirso de Molina.[2]

From the first to the last Lope succeeds in suggesting the presence of a world of actuality—that of nature and *historia*, of author and reader—at the confines of the work, flowing across them. As the *acción en prosa* opens, one is drawn into range of voices that have been conversing for some time; at its close, they are running down inconclusively before going out of earshot. Within the work the characters show a similar inclination to close in their own way the gap between the world of *historia* Lope has created for them and their experience of art. They move repeatedly from observation to participation, from the stance of beholder or listener to that of actor or critic.

The swooning Dorotea is surveyed by Fernando as if she were a piece of statuary—an alabaster Venus, a marble Lucretia, a sculpture of Michelangelo. Soon, however, he is stepping through the confines of his plastic fantasy and prying at something more than a work of art: "Push her hair aside, Celia; let's see her eyes" (p. 94). Fernando's theatrics work so strongly upon Marfisa that, from being his detached spectator, she finds herself drawn irresistibly into the act. The characters' responsiveness to the songs and poetry they hear is often intensely personal. Dorotea's reaction to Fernando's singing—"¡Ay, Felipa! ¿Quién será esta dama? Que me abraso de zelos" ("Oh, Felipa, who can that lady be? I'm burning up with jealousy") (p. 282)—catches beneath the *poiesis* of the lyric a *historia* that she assumes will critically affect her. At every turn during Don Bela's call upon Dorotea, we find characters impatiently violating the frontiers of art. We have seen Gerarda intervening like a director emending a script or a master of ceremonies. On hearing the refrain "Madre, unos ojuelos vi" ("Mother, I saw some little eyes"), she breaks into Dorotea's singing to remark: "A ti sola te sufriera villancico que entrara con madre, porque en fin la tienes y eres tan niña; pero no a vnos barbados, quando comiençan: 'Madre mía...'" ("Only from you would I put up with a ditty starting with 'Mother,' because you do have one after all and you're still such a girl, but not from one of those men with beards when they start out: 'Mother of mine...'") (p. 184). Gerarda's criticism of this convention, while scarcely original, is so intrusive and gratuitous in this context that its effect is irresistibly comical. Nor is hers the only interruption: the second time round Don Bela greets the refrain with his clumsy query, "¡Qué graciosa repetición! ¿Cúyo es el tono?" ("What a delightful repetition! Who wrote the melody?") (p. 186); in the same way he had interrupted the Abindarráez ballad with the remark: "¡Excelentes ocho versos! ¿Cúyo es este romance?" ("An excellent eight lines. Who wrote this ballad?") (p. 181).

The singing always resumes after such interventions (including that of Dorotea during Fernando's song); the selection in the end is complete, not truncated or abridged. But we do not have an intact composition. Instead, the two or three artistic segments, unlike the discrete lyrical insertions in

pastoral and other narratives, are worked into the "live" woof of the surrounding dialogue. The texture of the composition that results is rough-
grained, unlike the fabric of idealized art forms in which actuality does not
insistently intrude; it has something of the sturdy roughness of life.

The "historical" context surrounding the work is sometimes simply that
of Lope's own life. His distant past overlaps with Fernando's youth in the
account of Fernando–Lope's earlier years; his future extends beyond Fernando–Lope's present in the sketch of what is to come. Repeatedly we are
made to feel the author's presence on the fringes of the work as a person
known to the interlocutors—"este Lope de Vega que comiença agora"
("this Lope de Vega now starting out") (p. 326), "Listen to a ballad of
Lope's" (p. 87)—known not merely through his writing but in person—the
"gentleman whom you know" who has lost his lady (p. 206), the "maestro
Burguillos" (p. 356) who might easily be hobnobbing with the members of
the literary academy: "Si aquí le tuuiéramos, él nos sacara de muchas dudas
en la tremenda esfinge deste soneto" ("If we had him here with us, he would
deliver us from many doubts regarding the tremendous sphinx of this
sonnet") (p. 356).

Just as Lope brings himself, as writer, acquaintance, or confrère, into his
characters' lives, so is he prone to involve them in his through the stray bits
of unassimilated biography I have pointed out: the confusion as to Dorotea's
husband, Teodora's visit to a friend whose newborn child suspiciously
resembles "a friend of her husband's" (p. 189), Fernando's pauper's disguise
beneath Dorotea's window ledge and his brushes with the police (p. 411).
I have noted the aplomb with which Lope brazens out, as it were, the inconsistencies arising at those points where history does not mesh smoothly with
poetry, letting the characters themselves remark upon them: Felipa commenting upon the impropriety of Fernando's lamenting a dead, rather than
a live mistress (p. 285), Fernando himself invidiously comparing his *tristeza*
with that of the "gentil hombre" (p. 215), Clara surprised at Dorotea's
receiving the poetic name "Amarilis"—why not at least "Dorotilis" (p.
378)? Going a step further, Lope lets the characters think of themselves as
literary characters and measure their actions against purely literary laws.
The "inopportune laws of fiction" which had involved him in so much
controversy he now chooses to mock by this needless injection of them into
lives patterned on *historia*. We sense in all these touches the same tendency
toward the interrelating of history and poetry which led Cervantes into the
creation of the modern novel when he worked the literary issue into the
lives of his characters and the texture of their story. With Lope the basis of
the history is more markedly personal, the range correspondingly narrower,

the treatment more random, less persistent and probing. He is, however, reflecting in his own way the need of his age to let a draft of the fresh air of history into the closed atmosphere of poetry.

Lope clearly feels free to come and go as he pleases within the world of the *acción en prosa*. Having fashioned it in response not to external solicitation but to an inner compulsion, he views it as peculiarly his own possession. His absolute artistic overlordship is compensation for the subservience and humiliation which were often his lot in life. In a much more profound sense than is suggested by his overt appearances on its fringes, he makes the entire artistic cosmos a vehicle of self-expression. This is obvious enough in the total sense of "disillusionment amidst the fruition of life" with which the story is imbued. But it is also true in respect to the meaning which the four principal characters—Dorotea, Fernando, Don Bela, Gerarda—have acquired for him. Novelistic criteria of autonomy are inapplicable to them, as we know: they are not able to carry their creator beyond himself, to propel him in directions not originally envisaged, as do the characters of Cervantes, for example, or those of Thomas Mann.[3] Nor, for all the dramatic configuration of the work, do they function simply in the manner of *dramatis personae*, agents of a dramatic action set within the framework of a play. In keeping with the lyric temper of the *acción en prosa*, it becomes necessary, for a full understanding of them, to revert to their creator, whose supporting presence they require, to see them in the end in terms of their relation to him, as projections, embodiments, symbolic expressions of his responses to his experience of the world. They are oriented toward him as much as toward each other; our perspective upon them is his view, often an ironic one, rather than their circumscribed views of each other. We do not get close enough to any of them to mind their being snuffed out or to be awed by "la fatiga de todos en la diuersidad de sus pensamientos" ("the disenchantment of them all in their various aims").

Lope's attitude toward them is both sympathetic and detached. He displays more empathy with some than with others, but his attitude is not consistently empathic toward any. He has imposed on them limitations he had not suffered, limitations of talent, understanding, emotional and psychic resilience. Those aspects of the self which he does project into them are not seen without reservations. Secure in his own superiority, he dominates them, observing their predicaments with amused benevolence.

It follows that a key not only to the understanding of the characters but to the meaning of the work should be sought in a clearer definition of the relationship in which Dorotea, Fernando, Don Bela, and Gerarda stand to their creator as Lopean agents of self-expression.

In his heroine Lope has symbolized the appeal of the world he is losing, the beauty which incites to love both because "everything beautiful is worthy of being loved" and because it is the inspiration for art. The Platonism in this case is only skin-deep; the focus is on beauty time-bound, in the only medium in which it can be sensuously and sensually enjoyed. It is thereby inevitably on beauty subject to fading. Dorotea, whose changing aspect is so constantly observed by the other characters, embodies the attraction of the world of appearances, which does not cease to draw Lope even as he sees beyond. The Fernando unable to conceive "that time could extract from her a Dorotea so beautiful and make her so ugly in my eyes" (p. 237) and the Fernando who experiences, as the obverse of all his hyperboles, a "Dorotea [not] so beautiful" and "little teardrops no longer pearls" sum up between them, or together, the double vision, two sides of a single coin: the enduring pull of the world and the clear-eyed acknowledgment of its evanescence.

Because Lope has gathered up in Dorotea, as we have seen, reminiscences of several women in his emotional life and associations with others of literary extraction, she also embodies, more than any other figure in his production, the eternal feminine, the femininity which never ceased to attract him as the quintessence of the world's appeal. By the same token, because Lope is Lope, she is also woman as the muse, the object of the poet's cult, whose beauty and charm require a supplementary outlet in artistic expression: Fernando's "Me cuesta dos mil versos" ("It would take me two thousand lines") (p. 301). Fernando's cult willfully confounds the muse and the woman (p. 337):

Cés.: Yo asseguro que le han ocupado las musas.
Iul.: No, sino la musa.

Cés.: I am sure that the muses have kept him busy. *Jul.:* No, the muse rather.

With Lope, the "posthumous one of my muses, Dorotea" and the view of his works as "offspring of the muses" is only a figurative, if symptomatic, blending of voice and flesh. Yet in its very exaggeration Fernando's cult conveys the strength and persistence of Lope's lifelong commitment to his art, the personal experience of the muse which, for all its moments of servitude to the "rameras" ("whores") of the *comedia*, became the solace of his declining years.

It is because Dorotea embodies so vital an aspect of his attachment to the world he is losing that Lope finds it natural to make her voice at times his own, especially in the expressions of *desengaño* already discussed, which carry her beyond herself. At such times the mood expressed arises from depths and years of experience beyond hers. Dorotea is losing a lover but the wound inflicted by Fernando will harden over in the end and Dorotea will return to the world. Lope is losing the world itself. Still, Gerarda, wringing a laugh out of Dorotea's gloom in their last conversation, provokes a reaction that sums up her creator's commitment to life. Rather than the unflattering view given by the horoscope, we will be left at the end with a picture of a Dorotea "all dressed up . . . with green ribbons in your hair . . . chain and jewels." If she presently faints at the news of Don Bela's death, the ease with which she recovers when she hears herself called "niña" ("girl") expresses, in a final gesture of comic irony, the resilient spirit of Lope in its attachment to youth and world.

What of Fernando? Though, as already concluded, Lope's picture of the poet as a young man coincides only imperfectly with what we know of his own youth, it is still clear that Lope has pinned down and preserved in Fernando a number of permanent traits of his nature: impetuosity, inconstancy, histrionic tendencies, egotism, irascibility, a sense of humbleness and subservience. But the gap between creator and creature is vast. The difference lies not so much in psychological make-up as in the response to experience, the attitude to self and world. Lope can no longer take himself with Fernando's solemn seriousness: he clearly stands back from his protagonist when he shows him not merely following the literary life in the role of the poet as a young man but assiduously cultivating the pose of young man as poet. Lope knows how difficult it is to reach self-knowledge, how uncertain the knowledge attained is. He can only view Fernando's presumption to understand himself and his emotions with amused irony. His own egotism he pushes to narcissism in Fernando, his inconstancy to frivolity, as in Fernando's purely rhetorical responses to expressions of authentic feeling, Dorotea's in Act I, scene 5, those of the *barquillas* in Act III, scene 1. In action and in words spoken and written Fernando embodies the rhetorical side of Lope's poetic *métier*. He is the poet as rhetorician without the redeeming genius and the compensatory vitality of his creator: there is, indeed, something bloodless in Fernando's devotion to the muse. He is, in short, mannered, as Lope never was.

If Lope is at times bemused by his heroine, by his hero he is often amused. But more than amusement is involved: Lope surrounds Fernando with countering voices. Without ponderousness he makes it possible to infer from them a moral perspective not provided by the choruses and the smattering of wisdom dispersed through the dialogue. The vanity passed off as honor by Fernando is exposed by Julio in the already quoted sequence whose crux is the simple assertion: "A man has to wish what is right for it to be honor" (p. 113). The previously cited exchange on tempering and attunement also subjects the vindictiveness Fernando displays toward his former mistress to a moral critique when his sputterings against Dorotea lead Julio to observe: "One who has forgotten someone he loved says neither good nor bad things about the forgotten person" (p. 401). The real sign of *desamor* is to be oblivious and indifferent; vituperativeness betrays emotional involvement persisting.[4] Behind this elemental philographic observation lies an implicit judgment not only on Fernando's spitefulness toward his erstwhile mistress but upon the author of the libels of long ago. It sets against the cynicism of the Coro de Venganza (Act IV), with its caution that always "the aggrieved party is plotting revenge," the more humane attitude toward which Lope had been struggling in his later years.

It had been a spiritual struggle, both in orthodox Catholic terms, as the *Soliloquios* give evidence,[5] and in a Neo-Platonic sense, such as *La Circe* (1624) exemplifies. There we find fully articulated the mature evaluation of revenge:

> Venganza fue, que quando el fin alcança
> no ay hombre que contento la possea,
> que es condición de la mortal venganza
> que no sin daño de los dueños sea.[6]

> It was vengeance which, when it attains its goal, no one can be
> satisfied with possessing, for it is a condition of mortal vengeance
> that it is never unharmful to its possessor.

Have we in the counterpointed attitudes of Julio and Fernando an imposition of a late outlook upon an earlier one? One cannot let it go at that: one must avow that Lope is of two minds and that his art makes a creative use of his ambivalence, rather than forcibly resolving it. He records in the Chorus and in Fernando the fruit of experience, observation, and readings such as the *Ars amatoria*. The countering voice of Julio reflects, as does *La Circe*, an earnest aspiration of the final years, a perspective Lope cannot avoid assuming toward his hero.

It is precisely the whole aspect of Lope's *Erlebnis* represented by such aspirations that comes between him and the mask of his youthful self. The pursuit of them has made them part of his being, essential to his vision of self, and has drawn him away from the Fernando in him. Unlike Fernando he has genuinely striven for self-mastery, has sought to be more than a weak-willed observer of himself. In the *Soliloquios* we see him trying to come to terms with the impulses of lust and anger which he shares with Fernando. The *Epistolario* retains vivid echoes of the same struggle, aggravated, as we have seen, by his having taken orders. Eventually the old impulses are only fading echoes of an earlier stage of his life. With the waning of his physical powers and the self-sacrificing role in which his relationship to his ailing mistress places him, Lope is finally in a position to rise above narrow egotism. A striking judgment, dating from 1630–31, on the Duke of Sessa's behavior toward a discarded and fading beauty illuminates for us the outlook implicit in the presentation of Fernando:

> Díxome [the lady] todo lo que hauía passado con Vex.ª el domingo en el Prado, con tales quexas, que parecían justas y admiréme realmente asší de los milagros del tiempo como de la aspereza con que Vex.ª trató su voluntad, en que quisieron las lágrimas aconpañar vnos harto graciosos ojos. Lo que passó, Vex.ª lo sabe mexor: no tengo para qué repetirlo . . . Olg[u]éme de verla, y cierto que venía hermosa y que trahe muchas prendas de la opinión que ha tenido. No sé qué sienta destas cosas; lástima es gastar afectos quando no lo siente el que sintió tanto; Dios nos libre de llegar a estado que quien quiso con ydolatría desprecie con escarnio; aquello, Señor, tubo a Vcx.ª tan rendida la voluntad, que no era dueño de sí mismo; ¡qué diferentes parezen las cosas miradas a la luz de los desengaños! Acción es el respeto deuido al amor passado; no diga Vex.ª que hablo de licenciado en esto, sino perdóneme; que de ayer a oy no se me ha oluidado la lástima, y diérala mui grande a quien supiera menos que yo destos achaques.[7]

> She told me all that had happened with Your Excellency on Sunday in the Prado, with such complaints that they seemed justified and I was really taken aback both at the wonders time works and at the asperity with which Your Excellency treated her feelings, in which some tears chose to keep company with some fairly lovely eyes. What happened Your Excellency knows better than I: there's no reason for me to go into it . . . I enjoyed seeing her and certainly she looked beautiful and retains many indications of the fame she once had. I don't know what to think about these things; it is a pity to waste feelings on one who doesn't feel what he once felt so strongly; God preserve us from reaching the stage at which someone who

loved idolatrously scorns jeeringly. That affair, Sir, had Your Excellency's will so enslaved that you were not your own master. How different things appear when viewed in the light of disillusionment! Something is to be said for the respect due a past love. Your Excellency should not say that I speak like a jurist in this, but should forgive me, for since yesterday the pity has not gone out of my mind, and one knowing less about these afflictions than I would feel just as much [pity] as I do.

"I don't know what to think about these things," says Lope: his reticence scarcely masks a reproof to the Duke for an abrasive tongue and callous behavior. What Lope feels is *lástima*, pity. This heartfelt reaction colors his account of the episode from beginning to end and still has not subsided as he writes: generous pity for the victimized woman and broader feelings of regret at this evidence of the fragility of human attachments and the transience of femine beauty. Lope is carried beyond his usual circumspection to an unwonted boldness of tone not only by the strength of his compassion but because the light in which he sees the whole episode, "la luz de los desengaños" ("the light of disillusionment"), shuts his master out of the picture and delivers him up to some private wistfulness. As in *La Dorotea* moral judgment seems the by-product of an affective response and remains strongly colored by it.

It is surely Lope's voice that we hear behind Dorotea's, speaking from the same generous and altruistic perspective, on the occasion when Dorotea rises suddenly from the depths of her despair to commiserate for a moment with her triumphant rival: "Mas ¿para qué llamo yo dichosa a quien tan presto mudará de fortuna la inconstante naturaleza de los hombres? Porque si agora esta vitoria la prouoca a risa, desde los acentos della la combido a las mismas lágrimas" ("But why do I call happy someone whose fortunes the fickle nature of men will soon alter? Because if this victory now rouses her to laughter, amidst its very peals I invite her to share the same tears") (p. 425).[8] The same Lope, against the inconstancy of Fernando's youth, sets the constancy of the Fabio–Lope of the *barquillas*; it is Fernando himself who exclaims incredulously: "Bien aya hombre tan firme y tan dichoso" ("Blessings on so steadfast and so blissful a man") (p. 215). This is the steadfastness that had appeared a few years earlier, with Neo-Platonic overtones, in the attitude of Ulysses toward the blandishments of Circe, as both a conjugal virtue and a quality of the moral nature.

The detachment which marks Lope's point of view in the letter to his master subtly informs the reactions of César to Fernando's account in Act

V, scene 3, of the process by which he has cast off Dorotea's love. This is one of the infrequent instances in which we sense the author signaling to us through a trend in the remarks and erudite references of a particular character and the counterpoint they set up with other voices in the dialogue. At the very outset of the scene, before Fernando begins his story, with César's seemingly gratuitous vision of music as a divine art whose harmony is based on "mutual attraction," Lope picks up, after a hiatus of one scene, the Neo-Platonic thread of the opening scene of the act and reveals the basis of the reservations César will presently express as he listens to Fernando. The latter's claim to have executed with ease his decision to "exact revenge for Dorotea's liberties" by taking up with Marfisa is met with: "¿Fácilmente, cosa tan difícil?" ("Easily, something so difficult?") and "¡Qué inconstancia!" ("What inconstancy!") (p. 407).[9] When Fernando describes his scheme for sharing Dorotea with Don Bela, the following exchange ensues:

> Cés.: ¡O, si huuiérades empleado esse cuidado en aquel amor de la diuina belleza que en nuestra mente assiste, por cuya gracia seguimos los oficios de la piedad y los estudios de la filosofía y justicia!
> Fer.: ¡Qué metido estáis en el amor socrático! Ya de los platónicos me cupo el ínfimo.
>
> (p. 410)

> Cés.: Oh, if you had only taken these pains with that love of divine beauty that is present in our minds, by grace of which we carry out the offices of piety and the study of philosophy and justice! Fer.: How stuck you are on Socratic love! It was the baser of the Platonic ones that came my way.

As earlier seen, Fernando's acid rejoinder goes on to misappropriate the same source (Ficino) which César has paraphrased in an idealistic vein, making it underscore the self-love which, I have suggested, is the core of his character. Julio reproaches them both for "paradoxes and irrelevancies," not without supplying a Ficinian paradox of his own, and the Neo-Platonic perspective is not again supplied by the author. Yet by counterpointing César's invocation of the Socratic expansion of love in the *Symposium* into the desire for the good and the beautiful in their highest forms and Fernando's misappropriation of Ficino in the service of self-love, Lope is again providing the basis of a moral judgment even as he allows the discrepancy between the ideal aspirations and the reality of human feelings to stand. In one final echo of César's incredulity, his simple question, "Pues ¿qué teníades por vengança?" ("What did you consider vengeance, then?") (p. 415), we seem to catch again the sound of the older Lope's voice.

Fernando is the only one of the four lovers of *La Dorotea* whose love is not in the end more giving than demanding, more unselfish than self-serving. The opposite is patently the case with Dorotea and Marfisa: the extremes of self-sacrifice to which they go have been amply demonstrated. Nor, unlike Fernando, is Don Bela left untouched by Lope's ultimate generosity of spirit. It is true that he begins, like Fernando, by coveting Dorotea as a prized possession and, once he has conquered her, views her, for all his munificence, mainly in terms of pleasure and self-satisfaction. He knows the Platonic injunction to love the higher of the two Venuses but prefaces his spouting of it with the assertion that Platonic love is a "quimera en agrauio de la naturaleza" ("hopeless folly that offends nature") and then rests his case on carnal love (pp. 173–174). By the fifth act, his emphasis, as has been seen, has strikingly shifted: "No sé si he leído en el filósofo que amor puede ser de entrambas maneras, y quererla con sola el alma es el más verdadero, y para ella lo más seguro" ("I'm not sure whether I have read in the philosopher that love can be of both kinds and loving her with the soul alone is the truer and the safest way for her") (p. 388). In seeking to purge love of carnality, Don Bela is thinking of Dorotea's good as well as his own. The *soledad* into which he retreats, though solipsistic, still leaves room for unselfishness. Don Bela's retreat is not effected at the expense of others as is Fernando's cult of self, merely independently of them.[10] Like Lope's attitude toward the much younger Marta de Nevares, Don Bela's toward Dorotea has acquired a paternalistic tinge. He will provide for her and expect nothing in return except perhaps the releasing of his poetic powers. He aspires to ascend the ladder of love alone (the idealized *señora* of his poem has parted company with Dorotea), but his concern with self does not preclude concern for Dorotea.

The highest strain in the idealism of Lope's later years, an existential and not simply an artistic attitude, thus finds expression in Don Bela. The urgency of Don Bela's groping toward Neo-Platonic sublimation reflects, as we know, a stage in the struggle with the self which Lope has by now transcended. If in the end Lope leads Don Bela to God by more orthodox routes, the authenticity of the Neo-Platonic alternative is not thereby called into question. Lope's absolute faith in the sacrament of the mass does not oblige him to renounce access to "that sovereign artificer" through "that love of divine beauty that is present in our minds," to recall César's phrase. In Lope's house, as we know, there are many mansions.

Lope still does not allow Don Bela time to exchange the dark labyrinth of world and self for the harmoniously ascending spheres of the Neo-Platonic heaven. It is not a puerile retaliatory impulse that reasserts itself in the snuffing out of Don Bela's life. This decisive dramatic fact originates, rather, in the same zone of Lope's psyche as the reflection in the "Egloga a Claudio": "I have never yet seen anyone live hereafter who did not die before he died." In surviving Don Bela Lope is surviving himself, and in leaving him at a stage which he had himself transcended, he is acknowledging the fragility of his own self-survival.

Less paradoxically than at first appears, it is the two characters closest in spirit to his old age whose lives Lope extinguishes almost before our eyes. Gerarda's death leaves us, like Don Bela's, with a sensation of the Lopean "I succeed myself." Lope's readiness to put an almost accidental end to these two existences expresses his own paradoxical readiness to leave at any moment a world on whose appearances his eyes are still feasting. Especially is this true in the case of Gerarda, for the very gratuitousness of her role, the superfluity born of a conflation of literary tradition and experiential fact, has in the end turned her part in the *acción en prosa* into a celebration of the grace granted him in living on. Gerarda is the life impulse in Lope, stronger than all the promptings of *desengaño* but peculiarly dependent for prolongation on the benevolence of a creator: on the will of God in the case of Lope, on the whim of her own creator in that of Gerarda. If in the timing of her death he expresses an allegiance to life capable of lasting down to its final moment, her levity, the peculiar weightlessness of her figure, is the spirit of a Lope lighter than air who knows himself to be bound only by the most easily severable ties to the world.

Gerarda will fall, it is true, of her own weight, down the stairs of the wine cellar, as she had almost fallen over at the end of her drunken supper. But "La puerta pesada, puesta en el quicio no pesa nada" ("The heavy door set on its hinges weighs nothing"), her proverbial observation in the earlier instance, is for once singularly apt. These reminders of earth-bound mortality serve only to highlight by contrast what is most meaningful when Gerarda is viewed within her own element: her virtual exemption from laws of gravity as an expression of the Lopean spirit of play in its freest, most untrammeled form. The redundancy of her professional function left Lope free to endow her to the highest degree with his own sense both of immersion in life as in a game and of ultimate detachment from it, a combination characteristic of the ludic situation. Gerarda is able to stand away from herself to a degree unmatched by any other character. In her, as in her creator, this capacity is a product of age. Like Lope she surveys the world from the summit of advanced years and finds the spectacle of its smallness at once amusing and endearing. For one who has lived so long in it, the world can have no surprises left; nor, as the analysis of Gerarda's speech style has brought out, can anything seem of overriding importance. Yet the player does not tire of playing and the world still contrives to hold its charm.

The significant limitation imposed by Lope on this creature, the freest of his inventions in the *acción en prosa*, is that Gerarda's detachment arises from an excess of familiarity with the world and with humanity, not from the soul-searching crises of conscience through which her creator has passed. It is skin-deep, not visceral. Lope has not endowed her with the capacity to look searchingly in any direction, least of all into herself. He leaves her to the very last moment unawakened to the sense of sin with which he has himself come to grips. Her lightness of spirit is naive, not hard-won like his own. She has, to be sure, an instinctive animal-like awareness of her mortality. Though a child of nature, she knows that "nature gives everything on loan," and her lightheartedness is not oblivious of her own fragility. "Campana cascada, nunca sana" ("A cracked bell, never sound"), she tells Don Bela when he remarks how well she looks, assuring him there is no danger that she will be unnaturally long-lived (p. 232). But Gerarda is too involved with the present to give more than perfunctory thought to the hereafter. She eases her conscience with external observances and, as we have seen, can be jocularly complacent about her salvation. She dismisses as "sucessos humanos" ("human occurrences") (p. 423) what others call sins. She plays at piety without really grasping the stakes involved and thereby becomes an object of her all-seeing creator's irony. In the view of life *sub specie ludi* formulated at the very beginning when she replies to Teodora's "You've thrown more fives than a game of nine-pins" by remarking, "Well, realize that they all overshoot the mark and the game is lost" (p. 72), we sense not the weight of original sin but a self-seeking urging of *carpe diem*. It is Lope's feeling for life as a game played within prescribed limits that is revealed here —as it also is in Celia's later remark on the pointlessness of love-notes, "acabado el juego" ("when the game is up") (p. 432).[11]

But Lope's attitude is by no means consistently ironical toward this favorite child of his old age. A special congeniality draws them close and makes their voices indistinguishable at times. Vis-à-vis her creator, Gerarda has even less autonomy than the rest of the characters. The playfulness with which Lope endows her removes all traces of viciousness from her nature and converts procuring from a profession into an engaging pastime, part of a broader hedonism which no sense of sin could eradicate in him. Gerarda's role is vital in preventing the mood of disillusionment and the sense of disintegration from settling down too heavily, in making the *acción en prosa* a serene rather than an anguished expression. Though her bustling activity proves ineffectual in the end, in attempting to stem the rising tide of disenchantment she clearly emerges as Lope's affirmation of the triumphant play-element in his comic genius.[12]

How often she seems to be staging an act not to convince but to entertain, putting on a performance patently only half-genuine. The theatrical character of such sequences stands out the more sharply in the offstage setting. But unlike the role-playing of the other characters, Gerarda's is intentionally comic, and hence possesses detachment missing even from Fernando's. While the seriousness of the others in their posturings is punctured from without by the sarcasm of interlocutors, Gerarda pokes fun at herself and casually undermines her own poses:

> *Dor.:* Ni hallo cosa que se le pueda dezir a vna muger más afrentosa que llamarla echizera.
> *Ger.:* Mira que te oigo.
> *Dor.:* Pues, tía ¿éreslo tú?
> *Ger.:* Por curiosidad supe algo; pero ya, ni por el pensamiento. Y te puedo jurar con verdad que ha más de seis días que no he tomado las habas en la mano.
>
> (p. 435)

> *Dor.:* Nor do I know of anything more insulting to say to a woman than to call her a sorceress. *Ger.:* Watch out, I'm listening. *Dor.:* Then are you one, mistress? *Ger.:* Out of curiosity I've dabbled a bit, but now I wouldn't think of it for a moment. And I can swear to you in all honesty that I haven't had the beans in my hands for over six days.

The professional skills of a Celestina are reduced to paper-thin comic properties when, with an actor's flair for timing, Gerarda searches in her sleeve for the poem lifted from Don Bela with which she wants to impress Dorotea. One after another the wrong slips of paper are drawn forth and passed to her interlocutor to read. (The inference, as with her earlier question to Don Bela, "What do these letters say?" [p. 133], is that Gerarda is illiterate.) "Receta para dar sueño a vn marido fantástico" ("Recipe to put a husband with ideas to sleep"), "Oración para la noche de San Iuan" ("Prayer for St. John's Eve"), "Xaraue famoso para desopilar vna preñada dentro de nueue meses, sin que lo entiendan en su casa" ("Well-known syrup for delivering a pregnant woman within nine months without anyone at home knowing about it") (p. 161). In this flirtation with the conventional traits of a literary type, Gerarda as entertainer coincides with Lope. Although she tells Dorotea, "Creo que lo hazes adrede" ("I think you're doing it on purpose"), she gives the impression of herself guiding this *pro forma* exhibition of Celestina's professional attainments.

It is most of all gusto, unfailing vital energy, that characterizes Gerarda. Though she is never still—Spitzer calls her "the spirit of mobility"—her mobility is not nervous agitation but liveliness, responsiveness to everything in her surroundings. Her vigorous attempts to rouse Dorotea (beginning of scene 4, Act V) reflect the same ascendancy of vitality over dejection which Lope displays vis-à-vis himself and the Duke of Sessa. Later, when Dorotea's show of gaiety momentarily misleads her, there is authentic relief in her reaction: "All right, all right, let the harp go and let me in on your gaiety . . . as long as you are satisfied, let Don Bela go hang" (p. 451). Dorotea suggests that Gerarda is merely trying to probe her feelings, but Gerarda insists in earnest: "No, hija, sino aconsejarte que viuas y te gozes, que la mayor discreción es poner la capa como viniere el viento. Quiere lo que quisieres, y no repares en intereses" ("No, child, rather to advise you to live and enjoy yourself, for the wisest thing is to trim your sails to the wind. Love whatever you want to and pay no attention to profit") (p. 452). Gerarda here chooses life in preference to profit. The spirit may be opportunistic, hedonistic, pagan, but in the last analysis it is disinterested. It reveals, at the core of her nature, a Lopean hedonism convinced that a force as natural as love requires no agency beside itself for fulfillment.

This ultimate disinterestedness of Gerarda is the final sign that she is closer to her creator than to her literary prototype. Lope has made her dependent, as he was himself, on the largesse of others, with neither Celestina's self-sufficient professionalism nor her irrational and morbid cupidity. Her besetting sin is no more avarice than it was Lope's. The despoiling of Don Bela is an exercise more in gamesmanship than in greed. If she is the agency of her friends' "betterment," the demonstration of the power of gold over the frailty of women is more conclusive in the "madre interessable" ("venal mother") and the claim of *interés*, of materialism against poetry, more evident in the vacillation of the weak-willed daughter. While Don Bela is a providential windfall for Gerarda, at bottom her wants are no greater than her needs. It is only in the nature of her needs that she reverts to type, with many added baroque flourishes, to be sure. She hankers after Don Bela's gold, first in order to slake her thirst for wine—"Para comprar el vino me holgara de tener el oro" ("To buy the wine I'd be happy to have the gold"), she remarks matter-of-factly (p. 232)—and then to ease her transit to the next world. We need not doubt her sincerity in twice insisting on the latter point:

> Esso que me ha dado don Bela, hermano, está para mi entierro; que no quiero ir al cimenterio de la parroquia con vn *Quirieleison* desentonado de vn sacristán solo, que parece que pregona algún borrico perdido. Mis cofradías tengo de lleuar, y la mejor sepultura ha de ser la mía, que no quiero que me dé el agua a cielo abierto. (p. 232)

> What Don Bela gave me, my friend, is for my burial. I don't want to go to the parish cemetery with a single sexton's *Kyrie eleison* off-key sounding like some stray jackass preaching. I intend to have my sodalities and mine shall be the best tomb; I don't want to be rained on from the open sky.

Naively she wishes to gild death's pill with an elaborate burial and an ornate tomb. Sanctimoniousness aside, she genuinely believes that these doubloons will be an aid to salvation: "No he de tocar a ellos," she tells Dorotea, "porque, hija, lo que importa es pensar en el fin y temer la muerte" ("I shall not touch them because the important thing, child, is to think of the end and fear death") (p. 160). Lope smiles, indulgent and amused, dissociating himself from such baroque funerary theatricality; he expressly abjured it in the will he signed February 4, 1627: "El cuerpo mortal y miserable mando a la tierra de quien tuvo principio y quiero y es mi voluntad que se le restituya sin honor alguno de los que el mundo suele dar en tales actos" ("My miserable mortal body I commend to the earth from which it arose and I wish and so will that it be restored thereto without any of the honors which the world customarily bestows on such occasions").[13]

Though Gerarda's high good humor remains triumphant to the end, a plaintive edge creeps into her voice in the fifth act. She whines at Laurencio's baiting of her, at Don Bela's allegedly reduced largesse. The hint that the game may be losing its freshness lets us see that in holding out against the rising tide of melancholy, in asserting down to the end Lope's love of life more explicitly than any other character, she is not insensitive to the drag of disillusionment but superior to it. Her free-floating gaiety returns, more effervescent than the patterned witticisms of the servants, whose voices lose their levity in the last act. Her buoyancy, like Lope's, triumphs over down-heartedness in a contest less even, to be sure, because she is not burdened with a sense of sin.

In the end, the single figure of Gerarda is not capable of encompassing all the manifestations of Lope's ludic sense, either the more serious or the lighter. As with other expressions of his spirit in the work, no one figure suffices as a channel; one must look beyond the single intermediary.

Even the lighter side of the Lopean play spirit finds other outlets in the *acción en prosa*. It does so, first of all, in Lope's penchant for making the characters—any of them—his playthings. A sign at once of pleasure in over-lordship and of fundamental benevolence, of absolute power withheld as well as wielded, is the ease with which he breaks in upon these figures, trifles with them, puts them through standard comic paces for a moment or two, speaks out in their words. He is then as much their observer as the motor power behind them; he is the craftsman indulging his fondness for the materials of his craft, his repertory of techniques, formulas, themes for variation. He sets up *comedia* conventions like straw men as foils for the nonconventionality of these figures, he gives their conversations the ludic order of a game or contest and endows them with his own awareness of this order. Nonchalantly he makes them his mouthpieces for the exposure of the inconsistencies which, like impurities or rough spots, he has left in the warp of the work. Especially, as we know, he makes them players: players in the double sense of participants in a game and actors in a drama. He endows them, like all players, with a consciousness (his own) that they are indeed playing.

To be sure, we will here again often find Gerarda Lope's outlet. The sense that a game is unfolding before us is particularly strong when she intervenes. (It is no accident that she is the only character beside Dorotea to do so in every act.) Lope has given his ludic sense free rein in writing for her and Teodora, within very narrow limits, two gratuitous variations on their initial conversation (I, 7, and IV, 5–6). With each one the impression grows that we are witnessing a contest between adversaries opposing one another for no purpose beyond the pleasure of the game. (This was the effect also of the various passages of disputational sparring already examined.) Lope plays Teodora and Gerarda off against each other contrapuntally, in purely verbal oppositions. Out of step, yet in accord, they are propelled toward the same goal. *Quid pro quo's*, innuendo, verbal evasions, pursuits and echoes, façades that collapse and are set up again, poses suddenly abandoned mark their exchanges. With each fresh start, the contestants are less able to surprise one another and ultimately new grounds for contention have to be found: Lope takes up and spins out with endless comic ingenuity (IV, 5 and 6) the maternal motif insinuated on the first page during their initial encounter.

I have called Gerarda's fleecing of Don Bela an exercise in gamesmanship. Analysis of her visits to Don Bela, also three in number, *sub specie ludi*, would bear out this view. While not so obviously set up as encounters between equivalent and evenly matched opponents, they are essentially gratuitous epilogues to a *fait accompli* which begin where the authors of *La Celestina* left off: begin, that is, when the essential matchmaking is over. *La Celestina*, indeed, served Lope largely as a storehouse of motifs on which to write variations, and it is for this reason that so many play motifs cluster about the figure of Gerarda. Her dealings with Laurencio show this even more plainly than her relations with his master. The Celestinesque strain of the perversion of the loyal but untried retainer is transformed into a contest with a cynical, hard-bitten adversary that simply ends in a stand-off after both contestants have shouted themselves hoarse. Their quarrel significantly leaves no hard feelings, and when they meet again it is as friendly enemies, sparring partners who revert with a certain automatism to the pattern of harmless bickering in which their relationship is cast.

To observe Lope's play-spirit operating in full freedom we must turn from such virtuosistic variations on set motifs to the purely conversational context of the literary academy scenes. The discussion of the sonnet is conducted essentially as a game and what strikes us first of all is the blending of jest and earnest in its playing. Lope here takes up in a spirit of high humor a literary issue about which he felt deeply and airs esthetic concerns that stood at the heart of *La Dorotea* itself. A burlesqued rather than a serious sonnet is made the object of the commentary, however; from the outset we find ourselves in the realm of parody. Parody not of Góngora to be sure, as is made clear by the careful distinctions established at the outset, but of followers who are both epigones and commentators.[14] César and Ludovico are at pains to make distinctions between useful and useless commentators, between authentic and distorted senses of *culto*, between legitimate and unacceptable ornamentation. Such preliminary discussion in effect delimits the sphere of what is to follow, setting up the serious underlying premises, establishing the rules of the game, which will plainly exhibit the usual ludic combination of jest and earnest.

Ludovico begins by citing the first line of the sonnet: "Pululando de culto, Claudio amigo" ("Pullulating as a *culto*, Claudio, my friend"):

> Cés.: Columela nos dirá lo que es *pulular*, por ser propio de los árboles.
>
> Lud.: Assí las musas os fauorezcan, César, que no hablemos de veras, pues el soneto es de burlas. Dexad a Columela y los lugares

comunes, ¡malditos ellos sean! que ya no tengo cabeça para
sufrirlos.

Cés.: Sea como quisiéredes. Pero si se ofrece alguna cosa seria o
científica, auéisme de perdonar.

(p. 336)

Cés.: Columela will tell us what *pullulate* is since it is proper to trees.
Lud.: So may the muses favor you, César, don't let us speak seriously
since the sonnet is in jest. Forget Columela and commonplaces, curse
them; I can't take any more of them.   *Cés.*: As you wish. But if
some serious or scholarly matter turns up, you'll have to forgive me.

And César proceeds to comment not on *pulular* but on the construction in
which it occurs, in such a way as to ridicule Lope's literary adversaries by
association.[15] But in the next breath César cites in earnest a "diuiníssima
traslación de *pulular*" ("most divine metaphorical use of *pullulate*") from the
book of Ecclesiasticus.

Like this opening passage, the main body of the commentary, which
comes in the next scene, combines mockery with a varied admixture of
seriousness. If the burlesquing of the commentary as well as the sonnet
compounds the mockery, by nonetheless turning serious in the dialogue Lope
makes us sense deeper implications in the game.[16] The ludic spirit breaks out
in a kaleidoscopic play of fantasy with the arrival of Julio, who is soon
announcing: "Si algo me tocare a mí, no lo pienso prouar con la ilustre
cáfila de la antigüedad, sino con poetas exquisitos, como los autores modernos
que piensan que es erudición ensartar nombres sin leer los libros" ("If I
have any part in it, I intend to cite as proof not the illustrious band of the
ancients but rare poets, just like the modern authors who think that it's
erudition if they string names together without reading the books") (p.
340). His resourceful imagination invents, for every twist in the conversation
and every point of the commentary, a ludicrously named author or authority,
and improvises ridiculous quotations from his work. The others become
infected with his spirit:

Iul.: . . . Que por esso dixo el poeta Filondango Mocuseo . . .
Lud.: ¡Prodigioso poeta!
Iul.: En su *Lucifereida*, aunque tomado del griego Calipodio.
Cés.: ¡Qué bien se burla!
Iul.:   Cántenme buhos, no sonoras aues,
        endechas tristes, no canciones graues.

(p. 356)

Jul.: That is why the poet Filondango Sniveler said . . . *Lud.:* Astounding poet! *Jul.:* In his *Lucifereid*, although borrowing from the Greek of Calipod. *Cés.:* How well he jests! *Jul.:* Let owls, not sonorous birds, sing sad lays to me, not solemn songs.

Burla here goes beyond mockery or parody and becomes a joyous release of purely verbal energy, sheer comic inventiveness. This is the tone and the spirit of Tomé de Burguillos and it is symptomatic that Julio twice recites compositions by this persona of Lope's maturity, pieces that might have found their way into the *Rimas humanas y divinas*: a lengthy ode to a flea and a brief mock epitaph (pp. 353 and 364). As he tosses off his inventions— the *Zarambaina* of Cosme Pajarote "poeta manchego" ("a poet of La Mancha")—one suspects mimicry of Don Quixote de la Mancha—and names of authors like Zanahorio Caracola, Macario de Verdolaga, Serpentonio Proculdubio (Carroty Shell, Macarias Portulaca, Snaky Beyondquestion), we are in the same mock-heroic world of animals and vegetables as in *La Gatomaquia;* the proximity is sealed by a reference to a commentary on "la *Gaticida* de Gusarapo Magurnio" ("the *Caticide* of Waterworm Magurnius") (p. 358).[17]

Over and above other discernible links between these scenes of pure literary discussion and the surrounding context of the *acción en prosa,* it is the spirit of play in its underlying seriousness and its infectious levity that binds them. Hardly coincidentally, this spirit is also noticeable, in less free-floating form, in the scene (IV, 1) directly preceding, that of the long encounter in the Prado which culminates in the reconciliation of the lovers. Julio is here again the special channel of Lope's ludic sense, this time because, pushing Julio's characteristic detachment to extremes, Lope gives him the perspective of a disinterested spectator whose comments extrapolate the strain of play-acting present in the scene. Perhaps because this is the one scene in which Lope has not succeeded in avoiding the contrived implausibilities of *comedia* situations, the realistic perspective has to be grounded in the responses of an observer who looks on as if at some piece of make-believe and sees it all as an absorbing game. The fact that Julio himself has a supporting part does not in the least impair his lucidity: he is the bit actor keenly aware of being such. He joins the act in a sporting spirit, as zestfully as two scenes later he will help pull apart the *culterano* sonnet, and he cries out, cheers, boos at different turns in the repartee: "¡Quál es la hermana compañera!" ("Quite some sister we have with us!") (p. 294); "Bien dicho" ("Well said") (p. 297); "Parece que informas esta dama para algún oficio" ("You seem to be giving this lady an application for some position") (p. 295). He sees through the performance from the beginning but still plays along enthusiastically. Not in the least surprised at the outcome, he has in fact seen Dorotea's avowal coming and, suddenly in earnest, reproves Fernando: "No era Dorotea de mármol para no sentir a crueldad con que te partiste. Acuérdate de lo mucho que le cuestas de alma, vida y honra" ("Dorotea was not made of marble not to feel the cruelty of your leaving. Remember the price she is paying for you in soul, life and honor") (p. 311). We catch here a fleeting judgment of the old author, naturally sympathetic with the victimized woman. In the end, as the reunited Fernando and Dorotea begin to frisk about, Julio remarks: "¡Ea, reyes míos!, que en el Prado y por abril sólo tienen licencia los rozines!" ("Come, my fine ones, in April on the Prado only the nags have permission") (p. 316). A tolerant but detached observer, Lope–Julio here views the amorous by-play of the young as a form of animal spirits, and places it in a class with the love-making of nags, as he will with that of cats in the *Gatomaquia*. Humanly in sympathy with his characters, Lope is spiritually as far from them as a man from his pets. They delight and amuse him but his field of vision is so much deeper than theirs that the distance inevitably becomes marked with irony.

My analysis has imperceptibly moved from game to theater; the borderline between them is no fixed one. The essential point about the characters' role-playing is that it takes place on the stage of life, of *historia* rather than in an actual theater and avowedly as poetry. The whole artistic cosmos thus takes on dimensions of world-theater. Yet, as I have stressed, if the playwright of this theater, as of Calderón's, is ultimately God Himself, it is not from His perspective that Lope writes. We look toward the hereafter from within a temporal world and only sense its surrounding presence through finite approximations. We have indeed a sense of breakthrough when Gerarda tells Dorotea: "God put those words in your mouth" (p. 454). But it lasts only a moment: the vista is at once closed off by Laurencio's theatrics, which leave us with an overpowering sense not of prompting by God but of strings being arbitrarily pulled by a human artifex, by Lope as supreme being. The role with which Laurencio is avowedly flirting, as we know, is that of tragic *nuntius*. In removing it from the classic stage Lope makes the bearing of tragic tidings seem so preposterously out of place as to call into question the very possibility of tragedy in a world such as he is depicting.

From his perspective this is indeed the case. Rather than world-theater, this is a view of the offstage world through the playwright's eye, a view conditioned, in Vossler's words, "by the experience of the poet who always worked for the stage and, for this reason, can scarcely conceive of life offstage other than as a theater." [18] But Lope's is not the magnifying view of tragedy: his figures are not larger and grander than life. They have rather all the pettiness of this world and thus they are truer to the scale of the poet's experience. Coming between them and us, as Lope constantly does, he makes it impossible for us to look out on the world through their eyes. We end rather by looking down upon this artistic cosmos and its inhabitants through his. If when we do so its figures sometimes even appear diminished in size, smaller than life, it is because we are surveying it with him not *sub specie aeternitatis* but from the remote vantage point of old age, retrospectively, across a gap of years.

What does stand out clearly in this perspective, against a backdrop not of eternity but of humanity, is the prevalence of the histrionic sensibility, the propensity of men and women to play roles offstage as well as on: roles patterned on cultural forms, on attitudes, conventions, styles of literary and artistic derivation; roles improvised freely out of an absolute histrionic sense, the same flair for the dramatic and the rhetorical which Lope himself possessed to so marked a degree. As he watches his characters cultivate or slip into this or that part and perform with varying degrees of earnestness or detachment, Lope is not primarily impelled to pass judgment—and this for the fundamental reason that "no judge willingly passes sentence if he is guilty of the same crime," as Gerarda reminds us in the very first scene (p. 64). He wishes to isolate the phenomenon for contemplation, to define and delimit it in order to see himself as man and artist more clearly. Habits of dramatic craftsmanship inevitably lead him to highlight role-playing by overstatement; in the process his own sense of the comic is engaged and becomes the instrument for delimiting and defining, grounded as it is in a sense of proportion, of balance in the relation between art and life.

What Lope had never done, even at his most impulsive, was to lose himself completely in the role he was cultivating. The view of life *sub specie ludi* had grown on him with the years as he developed the ability to detach himself from the world, to contemplate from his *soledad* the panorama of worldly life as a spectacle, a game in which chance plays a large role, and, precisely for this reason, one cannot stake too much on worldly success. He now has no need of fortune, as he tells us in the "Egloga a Claudio." But such detachment, never absolute, does not of course entail giving up the world. Adherence to life is of necessity adherence to playing roles. What he stresses in *La Dorotea* is the need for lucidity, for maintaining a sense of proportion, something in which none of the characters is successful, neither Dorotea in her desperate seriousness, Fernando playing in cold blood,

Marfisa infected as by a contagion, Don Bela amateurishly clumsy, nor even Gerarda, aware of all accounts but the final reckoning.[19]

That the points of reference of role-playing in *La Dorotea* are largely literary follows from the importance given to Fernando's poetic vocation and its impact upon those around him, and ultimately from the importance of the poetic imagination in Lope's own life. *Literarisierung* is at bottom highly stylized role-playing. But the question is one of limits and proportion. *La Dorotea* may be viewed as a testimonial at once to the power and the waywardness not only of the histrionic sensibility but of the poetic imagination. César's affirmation that "inuención y imitación [son] . . . vna misma cosa" ("invention and imitation [are] . . . one and the same thing") (p. 320), in B. W. Wardropper's view, reflects the new attention which Lope's epoch was giving to the role of the imagination in poetic creation, consonant with the extensive revaluation of the potentialities of this faculty which the humanism of the Renaissance had undertaken.[20] J. Huarte de San Juan is convinced that "from a sound imaginative capacity arise all the arts and sciences that have to do with form, balance, harmony, and proportion; they are poetry, oratory, music . . . etc.").[21] But along with numerous moralists, Huarte also stresses the dangerous capabilities of the imagination, finding it as liable to exacerbate the passions as to strengthen the reason.

Lope is similarly aware that imagination may lead men astray as well as lead poets to new creations. In a late play, *El castigo sin venganza* (ll. 1540–1541), it is denounced as "una manera de alma / que más engaña que informa" ("a sort of spirit that deceives more than it informs") and in *La Dorotea* itself Fernando at one point (p. 203) echoes what are probably lines of a youthful ballad of Lope's:

> ¡O gustos de amor traidores,
> sueños ligeros y vanos,
> gozados siempre pequeños,
> y grandes imaginados![22]

Oh treacherous pleasures of love, light and empty dreams, when realized always small, but large when imagined!

The concern in the *acción en prosa* with both human passions and their poetic expression, with lovers who would consciously be artists, does not lead to a polarizing of beneficial and adverse effects of the imagination. It produces instead a dispassionate and nuanced examination of its processes as both an esthetic and a moral phenomenon. Lope knows from his own experience (the "dramatic" fabrications of the trial record are a case in point) that the artist's special gift of creative fantasy, his image-making and fictive power, will not be confined within the limits of written expression. Laurencio in one instance (III, 5) is not content merely to undercut his master's poeticized view of Dorotea's street by his own realistic one (as a stage lackey would do); he must explain why Don Bela perceives a—nonexistent—fragrance of orange blossom: "Your imagination is set on the pleasing odor of Dorotea and becomes all the more vivid the closer you get to her house; people in love have all their senses in the imagination" (p. 258). The poetic imagination spills over from expression to sensation and is capable of superimposing its effects on those of nature. Are these necessarily distorting effects? What of the effect of Marta de Nevares' singing on Lope: "It takes me so far away from the world that thought brings hand, skill, voice, and harmony to rest in its maker."

Lope's answer is guarded. He is of course far from any abjuring of secular artistic culture and he can only present with sympathy the aspiration to emotional and spiritual refinement which in the best sense informs the artistic stylizing of a response to feminine beauty or to music. Repeatedly in *La Dorotea* poetic and musical expression in the pastoral or Neo-Platonic or another mode eases tensions in the emotional lives of the characters and, though not removing them altogether, affords intervals of authentic sublimation. Rather than distortion of life by art, these intervals reflect nostalgia for a lost harmony, for a transcendent, atemporal world order that has room for ideal configurations of experience. The Renaissance ideal is incorporated into the lives of these post-Renaissance characters as the vision of an impossible yet compelling dream. An illusion, to be sure, but the sort of illusion one lives by, that answers the human need to cushion reality yet stops short of self-delusion. Like Cervantes, Lope has never lost his allegiance to the dream and he can only share the vision.

Along with this straining toward the ideal, however, Lope knows only too well that life is actually lived in a world in flux where prosaic contingencies and the variability of all things put strict limits on the sustaining power of illusion. His capacity for self-renewal inevitably involves a gift for the tempering of illusions. He has seen all too clearly that too mechanical a cultivation of artistic life styles may end in the distortion of experience, the pursuit of gesture and attitude for their own sake, of forms that have lost their *raison d'être* in losing their links to existential nerve centers. In short, Lope offers us mannered characters, and it is against their mannerism, not their poetic and artistic proclivities per se (or their morals, despite his reservations about Fernando), that he principally reacts—against the obstinacy with which Fernando imposes his fanciful poetic order, centered in Dorotea, upon the real face of the world, or the ease with which Dorotea pulls the wool over her own eyes (to return to a passage cited earlier):

> *Bel.:* That was subtle of the poet to say that before he was born Abindarráez loved her in the ideal imagining of Nature.   *Dor.:* Poets are reckless men. Their whole stock-in-trade consists of *impossibilia.*   *Bel.:* And of solemn sayings when they write serious things. I want to take over that conceit and say that I loved you before I had any being.   *Dor.:* If you take that over, I shall think that your love is poetry.   *Lau.:* It will soon be history and may God grant that it not be a tragic one.   (p. 187)

It is the staginess of the attitudes struck by the characters in glossing over what is in effect a seduction, not the fact of the seduction which, as Laurencio's comment shows, overcomes Lope's tolerance. (Lope's entire presentation has made the seduction comprehensible enough.) Certainly it is not his own subtle delineation of the ebb and flow between art and life which prompts him to puncture the play-acting here. It is rather the compounding of the will to illusion by deliberate self-delusion.

The pinpointing of the characters' mannerism establishes the fact that Lope's art is not itself manneristic.[23] Fed by both the idealist and the naturalist currents of the Renaissance, it conflates them in a world view properly baroque, one which both glorifies man and his works and imposes upon them a statute of limitations, acknowledging their nonprivileged position in an order which transcends them. In a perspective of such distinctions among epochal styles, one may perhaps read more clearly Dorotea's declaration of faith in the sanctity of artistic form, the capacity of art to bestow eternity, and its natural sequel, her reaction to the burning of the verse in which Fernando was "eternalizing" her. The original declaration—"¿Qué mayor riqueza para vna muger que verse eternizada? Porque la hermosura se acaba y nadie que la mira sin ella cree que la tuuo; y los versos de su alabança son eternos testigos que viuen con su nombre" ("What greater riches for a woman than to see herself made eternal? Because beauty comes to an end and no one who sees her without it believes she ever had it: and the verse in her praise is an eternal testimony that lives in her name") (p. 143)—arises suddenly in a context of trivial repartee and is as suddenly left behind, with no comment of any kind, ironic or otherwise. One has the strong impression that Lope is breaking in, underscoring Dorotea's affirmation of a Renaissance faith in the autonomy of art: "So long lives this and this gives life to thee." Yet there is irony in the sequel: "those papers whose burned-out letters, white against the black of the paper, made me afraid" (p. 445). The letters of the love-notes survive the flames but only as travesties of themselves, ready to crumble at a touch, and in their inverted form unnerving, not comforting, to the heroine. What has been forgotten by her is that the immortality accessible through art belongs exclusively to the sphere of *poiesis*. It is for Filis or Amarilis, not Dorotea, Elena, or Marta. In the act of accession the subject is removed from the realm of *historia*. The distinction brings out the note of self-glorification in the first passage, makes us aware, indeed, of a certain mannerism, an effect of posing on the part of one whose "historical" circumstances are those of Dorotea.

The corollary to such dethroning of the heroine is, however, the elevation of the artist. It is from the point of view of creator, not subject, that art is capable of circumventing the work of time and that Lope can write in an absolute sense (he mentions no specific work) at the end of his epistle to the Count of Lemos: "Sé bien que viviré por mi Poema" ("I well know that I will live through my poem").[24] In such a profession, as in the two complementary sequences of *La Dorotea*, we glimpse the faith by which Lope has been sustained in his creation of the *acción en prosa*: faith in his powers as inventor, as creator, and not merely as imitator, his capacity to transform a personal testament into a *monumentum aere perennius*. The act of creating on this scale turns him into a demigod: it is through creating and not merely in his creation that he emancipates himself from the finiteness of the human condition. It is as creator and demiurge that he makes us aware of his presence in, around, and beyond the fictional frame, as originator and prime mover of the *acción en prosa*, focal point upon which so many of its strands of meaning converge. Like the *Quixote* in Leo Spitzer's perceptive evaluation, *La Dorotea* is a testimonial to the supremacy of the artist.[25] In imitating nature as *naturans* and not merely as *naturata*, not only her handiwork but her creative processes, in adopting a stance equivalent on a smaller scale to that of God the Artifex, Lope too moves beyond the Renaissance glorification of the artist to a conception of the artist as autonomous creator that belongs properly to the baroque. Creation has become for Lope at the end of his life an act of faith in human possibilities.

Yet, insofar as Lope reflects the spirit of the baroque, he also reflects its awareness that in the last analysis all human autonomy is circumscribed and, viewed *sub specie aeternitatis*, illusory. In a world "that has a sound of breaking glass about it, and that will soon go to pieces," man's creation will be obliterated along with man himself. At the end of his career Lope is no stranger to the mood of the prophecy in which Shakespeare's Prospero foretells that, "like the baseless fabric of this vision,"

> . . . the great globe itself,
> Yea, all which it inherit, shall dissolve.

But as with Shakespeare, the sense of the ultimate insubstantiality of man and his works remains subdued and does not impose a view of life as illusion. And, as with Cervantes, a reconciliation is effected through irony.

The irony of Lope, though supple, is less rich than that of his fellow Spaniard, which can irradiate a complex world view through a thousand subtle refractions. With Lope irony is sometimes simply a corrective or an indication of reservations based on a wider vision, a purely supplementary dimension. Sometimes it cements a more complex statement or situation, showing Lope to be genuinely of two, or several minds, as for example in the presentation of Dorotea's trust in artistic immortality. Sometimes it is properly situational or dramatic, as when the characters through words or acts unconsciously foreshadow developments unforeseen by them. For the most part it appears, however, that Lope's irony is expressing not the apperception of a multifaceted reality but a reluctance to surrender any possibility. He is not uncomfortable in his ambivalence, if such it is, or multivalence, because it is one of affirmation, not indecision, an avid response to the manifold possibilities of life. "El barroco es el arte de no renunciar a nada" ("The baroque is the art of not giving up anything"), observes Montesinos.

Still, Lope's irony unquestionably operates closer to the surface than that of Cervantes and its form is often that of pure play. It ends by subserving his ludic sense and it is the latter faculty which, *mutatis mutandis*, corresponds in *La Dorotea* to the irony of Cervantes. The limitations imposed upon man by God's Providence become the demarcations of the arena in which one plays one's part as in a game of chance or a spectacle, plays in earnest yet joyously. The ludic view of life and of art is in the end a protection: it conditions one to their finiteness, to the prospect of giving them up as one eventually gives up a contest. Bodying forth this outlook in the work, Lope builds into it a sense of regulation, of rules of a game *sui generis*. He reduces the variety and formlessness of nature to the dynamic and shifting order of such a game, governed by a regime of *concordia discors*. The resultant form, baroque in its opulence, is capable of combining in a single order, in addition to the now richly representative story of Fernando and Dorotea, the personal lyricism of the strain of *soledad*, the free variations on Celestinesque motifs, the extensive airing of purely literary questions, an anthological selection of lyrics—in sum, blended voices of youth and age—without falling into a disparate heterogeneousness. With its strong suggestions of scenographic, pictorial, plastic, musical effects it makes us think of the baroque *Gesamt-kunstwerk*, the dawning opera.

That the range of Lope's vision is more restricted than Cervantes' is beyond question. Ultimately, because of the lyric temper of his expression, conditioned as it is by sensibility more than intellect and oriented as much to self as to posterity, it is through the quality of feeling which he is able to infuse into the artistic cosmos and to project through it that he makes his appeal and sets up an answering response in the reader properly attuned. The concepts Lope deals in are as old as Job, the Book of Psalms, and the stoic and classic perception of *fugit inreparabile tempus*, as prevalent and common to his age as the notion of *vitam impendere aeterno*. It is not as a thinker but as an exponent of the affective, sensory, and esthetic dimensions of experience that Lope appeals.

The morality of *La Dorotea*, too, is essentially experiential: it reflects Lope's own temperament as lover, creator, man of nature, man of the world. The equivocations of the characters are in the last analysis his own, whence his restraint in judging them and the directing of the judgment to transgressions less of the moral law than of the laws of nature. The moral evaluation unquestionably supplied in Fernando's case is in some sense a retrospective self-evaluation, the imposition of hard-won hindsight. Judgment for the most part is not passed individually but is implicit in Lope's shaping of the *acción* as a whole. Fernando's smallness shows up in contraposition to Don Bela's magnanimity; Marfisa's integrity, to Dorotea's lack of moral sensitivity. It does no harm, quite the contrary, to claim, as the Prologue does, that a principle of poetic justice is operative in this world. In fact, however, insofar as we are actually aware of a "disenchantment of them all in their various aims," our awareness is related to a mood of "disillusionment amidst the fruition of life," not to an ethical scheme: sensibility, not doctrine, is its basis.

With what a deft touch Lope's reconciliation in gaiety finally sweeps away even the *lacrimae rerum*! The catharsis is comic because, for the believer, a tragic sense of life is incompatible with a scheme of things that admits of his ultimate salvation by a personal God, making it dependent only on himself. Here at the end, like Amarilis envisaged in the beyond, Lope is in a mood to make light of earthly griefs. In the accelerated coda, as he applies his finishing touches, he finally allows the effect of make-believe to become predominant. He emerges above his shrinking artistic cosmos like a *maître des jeux* when the game is ending. It is perhaps a sense of liberation, a feeling of fulfillment on having at last reached the expressive limit of materials so long with him, that makes him appear to be pushing his figures over like so many figurines in a rush to conclude. The effect is that of Alice discovering, as her wonderland collapses, that it was peopled by nothing but a pack of cards. Though *La Dorotea* is not the final product of Lope's pen—he is destined to "succeed himself" for three more years—these last scenes have a farewell ring. The Phoenix seems to be looking ahead and beyond like Shakespeare, the "insubstantial pageant faded," in Prospero's Epilogue:

> Now my charms are all o'erthrown
> And what strength I have's mine own,
> Which is most faint . . .
>
> . . . .
>
> . . . Now I want
> Spirits to enforce, art to enchant,
> And my ending is despair
> Unless I be relieved by prayer . . .

Prayer *has* relieved Lope, his ending is the opposite of despair. Having abandoned the stage to increase his hold on the inner world of his imagination, he now releases this world too, wholly poetry at last, into the hands of posterity, and tranquilly awaits the hour when life will be relinquished.

Principal Works Cited
Notes
Index

Principal Works Cited

Abel, Lionel. *Metatheatre: A New View of Dramatic Form*. New York: Hill and Wang, 1963.

Albarracín Teulón, Agustín. *La medicina en el teatro de Lope de Vega*. Madrid: C.S.I.C., 1954.

Alemán, Mateo. *Guzmán de Alfarache*. Edited by S. Gili Gaya. 5 vols. Madrid: La Lectura, 1926–36.

Alenda y Mira, J. *Relaciones de solemnidades y fiestas públicas de España*. Madrid: Sucesores de Rivadeneyra, 1903.

Alexander, Franz. *Fundamentals of Psychoanalysis*. New York: W. W. Norton, 1948.

Alonso, Amado. "Noción, emoción, acción y fantasía en los diminutivos." In *Estudios lingüísticos: Temas españoles*. Madrid: Gredos, 1954.

———— "Vida y creación en la lírica de Lope." In *Materia y forma en poesía*. Madrid: Gredos, 1955.

Alonso, Dámaso. *La lengua poética de Góngora (Parte primera)*. Madrid: S. Aguirre, 1935.

———— *Poesía española: Ensayo de métodos y límites estilísticos*. Madrid: Gredos, 1950.

———— "Versos correlativos y retórica tradicional," *Revista de filología española*, 28 (1944), 139–153.

Alpern, Hyman. "Jealousy as a Dramatic Motif in the Spanish Comedia," *Romanic Review*, 14 (1923), 276–285.

Anacreon. *Anacreon Teius, Poeta Lyricus*. Edited by J. Barnes. Cambridge: E. Jeffrey, 1905.

Aquinas, Saint Thomas. *Summa Theologica*. Translated by the Fathers of the English Dominican Province. 2 vols. Chicago: Encyclopedia Britannica, 1952.

Arco y Garay, Ricardo del. *La sociedad española en las obras dramáticas de Lope de Vega*. Madrid: Escelicer, 1941.

Argensola, Bartolomé L. and Lupercio L. de. *Rimas*. Edited by J. M. Blecua. 2 vols. Saragossa: C.S.I.C., 1950–51.

Arias Pérez, Licenciado Pedro. *Primavera y flor de los mejores romances recogidos por el ...* [Madrid: Viuda de Alonso Martín, 1621]. Edited by J. F. Montesinos. Valencia: Castalia, 1954.

Ariosto, Ludovico. *Orlando furioso*. Edited by L. Caretti. Milan and Naples: Riccardo Ricciardi, 1954.

Aristotle. *Ethica Nicomachea*. Translated by W. D. Rouse. (Vol. IX of *Works*, edited by W. D. Rouse.) Oxford: Oxford University Press, 1949.

Aristotle. *Politics*. Translated by B. Jowett. Oxford: Clarendon Press, 1920.

────── *The Rhetoric of Aristotle*. An expanded translation by Lane Cooper. New York: D. Appleton, 1932.

────── *Rhetoric*. With an English translation, the *"Art"of Rhetoric*, by J. H. Freese. New York: G. P. Putnam's Sons, 1926.

Atkinson, W. C. "*La Dorotea*, acción en prosa," *Bulletin of Spanish Studies*, 12 (1935), 198–217.

Auerbach, Erich. *Mimesis: The Representation of Reality in Western Literature*. Translated by W. R. Trask. Princeton: Princeton University Press, 1953.

Avalle-Arce, J. B. *La novela pastoril española*. Madrid: Revista de Occidente, 1959.

Baader, Horst. "Die Eifersucht in der spanischen Comedia des goldenen Zeitalters," *Romanische Forschungen*, 74 (1962), 318–344.

Bachelard, Gaston. *La Flamme d'une chandelle*. Paris: Presses Universitaires de France, 1961.

Barrera, C. A. de la. *Nueva biografía [de Lope de Vega]*. Ac., vol. I. Madrid: Sucesores de Rivadeneyra, 1890.

Bataillon, Marcel. "*La Célestine*" selon Fernando de Rojas. Paris: Didier, 1961.

Beau, A. E. *Estudos*. Vol. I. Coimbra: Universidade de Coimbra, 1959.

Bermúdez, Jerónimo. *Primeras tragedias españolas*. In J. J. López de Sedano, *Parnaso español*, vol. VI. Madrid: A. de Sancha, 1772.

The Book of Wisdom. Translated by Joseph Reider. New York: Harper, 1957.

Bravo-Villasante, Carmen. *La mujer vestida de hombre en el teatro español (Siglos XVI–XVII)*. Madrid: Revista de Occidente, 1955.

────── "La realidad de la ficción negada por el gracioso," *Revista de filología española*, 28 (1944), 264–268.

Butterfield, Herbert. *The Origins of Modern Science, 1300–1800*. Rev. ed. New York: The Free Press, 1965.

Calepino, Ambrogio. *Dictionarium septem linguarum*. Lyons, 1581.

Cano, Melchor. *Tratado de la victoria de sí mismo*. In *Obras escogidas de filósofos*, edited by Adolfo de Castro, pp. 301–324. Biblioteca de Autores Españoles, LXV. Madrid: Sucesores de Hernando, 1922.

Carballo, Luis Alfonso de. *Cisne de Apolo*. Edited by A. Porqueras Mayo. 2 vols. Madrid: C.S.I.C., 1958.

Carducho, Vincencio. *Diálogos de la pintura*. Madrid: Francisco Martínez, 1633.

Carrasco, M. S. "Aspectos folklóricos y literarios de la fiesta de moros y cristianos en España," *PMLA*, 78 (1963), 476–491.

—— *El moro de Granada en la literatura.* Madrid: Revista de Occidente, 1956.

Carrillo y Sotomayor, Luis. *Fábula de Atis y Galatea.* Edited by P. Henríquez-Ureña and E. Moreno. La Plata: Cuadernos de *Don Segundo Sombra,* 1929.

Cascales, Francisco. *Cartas filológicas.* Edited by J. García Soriano. 3 vols. Madrid: Espasa-Calpe, 1954.

—— *Tablas poéticas.* Madrid: A. de Sancha, 1779.

Castro, Américo. "Algunas observaciones acerca del concepto del honor en los siglos XVI y XVII." In *Semblanzas y estudios españoles,* edited by Juan Marichal, pp. 319–382. Princeton: Princeton University Press, 1956.

—— *La realidad histórica de España.* Mexico City: Porrúa, 1954.

Cats, Jacob. *Emblemata moralia et aeconomica.* Rotterdam: P. van Waesberge, 1627.

Cervantes, M. de. *Persiles y Sigismunda.* Edited by R. Schevill and A. Bonilla. 2 vols. Madrid: Bernardo Rodríguez, 1914.

Charney, Maurice. *Shakespeare's Roman Plays: The Function of Imagery in the Drama.* Cambridge, Mass.: Harvard University Press, 1961.

Chevalier, Maxime. *L'Arioste en Espagne (1530–1650): Recherches sur l'influence du "Roland Furieux."* Bordeaux: Institut d'Etudes Ibériques, 1966.

Cicero, M. T. *De Oratore.* With an English translation by H. Rackham. 2 vols. Cambridge, Mass.: Harvard University Press, 1959–60.

Cioranescu, A. *El barroco o el descubrimiento del drama.* La Laguna: Universidad de La Laguna, 1957.

Collard, Andrée. *Nueva poesía: Conceptismo, culteranismo en la crítica española.* Madrid: Castalia, 1967.

Cossío, J. M. de. *Lope, personaje de sus comedias.* Madrid: Real Academia Española, 1948.

Cota, Rodrigo. "Diálogo entre Amor y un viejo." In *Cancionero castellano del siglo XV,* edited by R. Foulché-Delbosc, II, 580–587. Nueva Biblioteca de Autores Españoles, XXII. Madrid: Bailly-Baillière, 1915.

Covarrubias, Sebastián de. *Tesoro de la lengua castellana o española, según la impresión de 1611, con las adiciones de Benito Remigio Noydens publicadas en la de 1674.* Edited by M. de Riquer. Barcelona: Horta, 1943.

Croce, Alda. *"La Dorotea" di Lope de Vega, studio critico seguito dalla traduzione delle parti principali dell'opera.* Bari: Laterza, 1940.

Curiosidades bibliográficas: Colección escogida de obras raras de amenidad y erudición. Edited by Adolfo de Castro y Rossi. Biblioteca de Autores Españoles, XXXVI. Madrid: Hernando, 1926.

Curtius, E. R. *European Literature and the Latin Middle Ages.* Translated by W. R. Trask. New York: Pantheon, 1953.

Damas Hinard, J. J. S. A. de. "De quelques erreurs publiées touchant la vie et les ouvrages de Lope de Vega." Introductory study to his *Chefs-d'oeuvre du théâtre espagnol—Lope de Vega.* Paris: C. Gosselin, 1842.

Díaz Rengifo, Juan. *Arte poética española*. Barcelona: Martí, 1759.

Durán, Manuel. "Lope de Vega y el problema del manierismo," *Anuario de letras*, 2 (1962), 76–98.

Edmonds, J. M., translator. *The Greek Bucolic Poets*. Cambridge, Mass.: Harvard University Press, 1950.

Ehrmann, Jacques. "*Homo Ludens* Revisited," *Yale French Studies*, no. 41 (1968), 31–57.

Entrambasaguas, J. de. "Un amor de Lope de Vega desconocido: La 'Marfisa' de la 'Dorotea,'" *Fénix, revista del tricentenario de Lope de Vega*, 1 (1935), 455–499.

——— "Cartas poéticas de Lope de Vega y Liñán de Riaza." In his *Estudios sobre Lope de Vega*, III, 411–460.

——— *Estudios sobre Lope de Vega*. 3 vols. Madrid: C.S.I.C., 1946–58.

——— "Los famosos 'libelos contra unos cómicos,' de Lope de Vega." In his *Estudios sobre Lope de Vega*, III, 7–74.

——— "Las 'hipérboles' y 'energías' de *La Dorotea* de Lope de Vega." In *Romanica et occidentalia: Etudes dédiées à la mémoire de Hiram Peri (Pflaum)*, edited by Moshe Lazar. Jerusalem: Magnes Press, Université hébraïque, 1963.

——— "Poesías de Lope de Vega en un romancero de 1605." In his *Estudios sobre Lope de Vega*, III, 377–410.

——— "Poesías nuevas de Lope de Vega, en parte autobiográficas." In his *Estudios sobre Lope de Vega*, III, 217–375.

——— *Vida de Lope de Vega*. Barcelona: Labor, 1936.

Equicola, Mario. *Libro de Natura de Amore*. Revised by Thomas Porcacchi. Venice: Gabriele Giolito, 1562.

Erdman, E. G., Jr. "Lope de Vega's 'De Absalón,' a *laberinto de concetos esparcidos*," *Studies in Philology*, 65 (1968), 753–767.

Fauriel, Claude. "Les Amours de Lope de Vega: La Dorothée," *Revue des deux mondes*, September 15, 1843, pp. 881–924.

——— "Lope de Vega," *Revue des deux mondes*, September 1, 1839, pp. 593–623.

Fergusson, Francis. *The Idea of a Theater: The Art of Drama in Changing Perspective*. Garden City: Doubleday, 1953.

Ferreira de Vasconcelos, Jorge. *Comedia Euphrosina* (Text of the first edition of 1555 with the variants of 1561 and 1566.) Edited by Eugenio Asensio. Vol. I. Madrid: C.S.I.C., 1951.

Fichter, W. L. "Color Symbolism in Lope de Vega," *Romanic Review*, 18 (1927), 220–231.

——— *Lope de Vega's "El castigo del discreto" together with a Study of Conjugal Honor in his Theater*. New York: Instituto de las Españas, 1925.

Fichter, W. L., and F. Sánchez y Escribano. "The Origin and Character of Lope de Vega's 'A mis soledades voy,'" *Hispanic Review*, 11 (1948), 304–313.

Ficino, Marsilio. *Commentaire sur le Banquet de Platon*. Edited and translated by Raymond Marcel. Paris: Les Belles Lettres, 1956.

—— *Commentary on Plato's "Symposium": The Text and a Translation.* Edited by Sears R. Jayne. University of Missouri Studies, vol. XIX, no. 1 (1944).

Frye, Northrop. *Anatomy of Criticism.* Princeton: Princeton University Press, 1957.

Fucilla, J. "Notes sur le sonnet 'Superbi colli,'" *Boletín de la Biblioteca Menéndez y Pelayo,* 31 (1955), 51–93.

Las fuentes del Romancero general. Edited by A. Rodríguez Moñino. 12 vols. Madrid: Real Academia Española, 1957.

García Soriano, J. *El teatro universitario y humanístico en España.* Toledo: R. Gómez, 1945.

Garcilaso de la Vega. *Obras completas.* Edited by E. L. Rivers. Madrid: Castalia, 1964.

—— *Obras de Garci Lasso de la Vega con anotaciones de Fernando de Herrera.* Seville: Alonso de la Barrera, 1580.

Garcilaso de la Vega el Inca. *Comentarios reales de los Incas.* Vol. III of his *Obras completas,* edited by C. Sáenz de Santa María. Biblioteca de Autores Españoles, CXXXIV. Madrid: Atlas, 1960.

Gérard, Albert. "Pour une phénoménologie du baroque littéraire: Essai sur la tragédie européenne au XVIIe siècle," *Publications de l'Université de l'Etat à Elisabethville,* 5 (1963), 25–65.

Gillet, J. E. "The Autonomous Character in Spanish and European Literature," *Hispanic Review,* 24 (1956), 179–190.

Gilman, Stephen. *The Art of "La Celestina."* Madison: University of Wisconsin Press, 1956.

—— *Cervantes y Avellaneda.* Mexico City: El Colegio de México, 1951.

Glaser, E. *Estudios hispano-portugueses.* Valencia: Castalia, 1957.

Góngora, Luis de. *Obras completas.* Edited by J. and I. Millé y Giménez. 5th ed. Madrid: Aguilar, 1961.

—— *Sonetos completos.* Edited by B. Ciplijauskaite. Madrid: Castalia, 1969.

Goyri de Menéndez Pidal, María. *De Lope de Vega y del romancero.* Saragossa: Librería general, 1953.

—— "Los romances de Gazul," *Nueva revista de filología hispánica,* 7 (1953), 403–416.

Gracián Dantisco, Luis. *Galateo español.* Edited by Margherita Morreale. Madrid: C.S.I.C., 1968.

Green, O. H. *Spain and the Western Tradition.* 4 vols. Madison: University of Wisconsin Press, 1963–66.

Guillén, Claudio. *Literature as System: Essays toward the Theory of Literary History.* Princeton: Princeton University Press, 1971.

Hardison, O. P., Jr. *The Enduring Monument.* Chapel Hill: University of North Carolina Press, 1962.

Hatzfeld, Helmut. *Estudios sobre el barroco.* Madrid: Gredos, 1964.

Henkel, A., and A. Schöne, editors. *Handbuch zur Sinnbildkunst des XVI und XVII Jahrhunderts.* Stuttgart: J. B. Metzler, 1967.

Hermenegildo, Alfredo. *Los trágicos españoles del siglo XVI.* Madrid: Fundación Universitaria Española, 1961.

Herrero García, M. "Ideas estéticas del teatro clásico español," *Revista de ideas estéticas*, 2 (1944), 79–109.

Hidalgo, G. L. *Diálogos de apacible entretenimiento*. In *Curiosidades bibliográficas: Colección escogida de obras raras de amenidad y erudición*, edited by Adolfo de Castro y Rossi, pp. 279–316. Biblioteca de Autores Españoles, XXXVI. Madrid: Hernando, 1926.

Hill, John M. "*Poesías barias y recreación de buenos ingenios*": *A Description of MS. 17556 of the Biblioteca Nacional Matritense, with Some Unpublished Portions Thereof.* Indiana University Studies, vol. X, no. 60 (December 1923).

Horace. *The Odes and Epodes.* With an English translation by C. E. Bennett. Cambridge, Mass.: Harvard University Press, 1952.

Hornedo, Father R. M. de. "A propósito de una fecha: 1572. Lope en los estudios de la Compañía de Jesús en Madrid," *Razón y fe*, no. 108 (1935), 52–78.

——— "Lope y los jesuitas," *Razón y fe*, no. 166 (1962), 405–422.

Horozco y Covarrubias, Juan de. *Emblemas morales.* 3 vols. in 1. Saragossa: Alonso Rodríguez [for] Juan de Bonilla, 1603–1604.

Huarte de San Juan, J. *Examen de ingenios para las ciencias.* In *Obras escogidas de filósofos*, edited by Adolfo de Castro. Biblioteca de Autores Españoles, LXV. Madrid: Sucesores de Hernando, 1922.

Hudson, H. H. "Rhetoric and Poetry." In *Historical Studies of Rhetoric and Rhetoricians*, edited by R. F. Howes. Ithaca: Cornell University Press, 1961.

Huizinga, J. *Homo Ludens: A Study of the Play-Element in Culture.* Boston: Beacon Press, 1955.

Hunter, M. L., *Memory.* Rev. ed. London: Penguin Books, 1964.

Jáuregui, Juan de. *Discurso poético* [Madrid: J. González, 1624]. Edited by A. Pérez Gómez. Valencia: Tipografía Moderna, 1957.

Jones, C. A. "*Honor* in Spanish Golden Age Drama: Its Relation to Real Life and to Morals," *Bulletin of Hispanic Studies*, 35 (1958), 199–210.

Klein, Julius L. *Das Spanische Drama.* 5 vols. (His *Geschichte des Dramas*, vol. IX.) Leipzig: T. O. Weidel, 1871–76.

Klitansky, R., E. Panofsky, and F. Saxl. *Saturn and Melancholy: Studies in the History of Natural Philosophy, Religion and Art.* London: Nelson, 1964.

Kristeller, P. O. *The Philosophy of Marsilio Ficino.* Translated by Virginia Conant. New York: Columbia University Press, 1943.

Lafuente Ferrari, E. *Los retratos de Lope de Vega.* Madrid: Junta del Centenario, 1935.

Langer, Susanne K. *Philosophy in a New Key: A Study in the Symbolism of Reason, Rite and Art.* 3rd ed. Cambridge, Mass.: Harvard University Press, 1957.

Lausberg, Heinrich. *Handbuch der literarischen Rhetorik.* 2 vols. Munich: Max Hueber, 1960.

Lázaro Carreter, F. "Lope, pastor robado: Vida y arte en los sonetos de los mansos." In his *Estilo barroco y personalidad creadora.* Salamanca: Anaya, 1966.

León, Fray Luis de. *De los nombres de Cristo.* Edited by F. de Onís. 3 vols. Madrid: La Lectura, 1914–21.

Lida de Malkiel, M. R. *La originalidad artística de "La Celestina."* Buenos Aires: Eudeba, 1962.

López Pinciano, Alfonso. *Philosophía antigua poética.* Edited by A. Carballo Picazo. 3 vols. Madrid: C.S.I.C., 1953.

Loyola, Saint Ignatius. *The Spiritual Exercises of St. Ignatius Loyola.* Edited by Joseph Rickaby, S.J. London: Burnes and Oates, 1915.

Luis de Granada, Fray. *Memorial de la vida cristiana.* In *Obras de Luis de Granada,* edited by J. J. de Mora. Biblioteca de Autores Españoles, VIII. Madrid: Hernando, 1925.

McCrary, W. T. *The Goldfinch and the Hawk: A Study of Lope de Vega's Tragedy, "El Caballero de Olmedo."* University of North Carolina Studies in the Romance Languages and Literatures, LXII. Chapel Hill: University of North Carolina Press, 1966.

McCready, W. T. "Lope de Vega's Birth Date and Horoscope," *Hispanic Review,* 28 (1960), 313–318.

Macrí, Oreste. *Fernando de Herrera.* Madrid: Gredos, 1951.

Mann, Thomas. "The Making of *The Magic Mountain*," *The Atlantic,* January 1953, pp. 41–45.

Martial. *The Epigrams of Martial Translated into English Prose.* London: G. Bell, 1901.

Mayer-Gross, W., E. Slater, and M. Roth. *Clinical Psychiatry,* 2nd ed. Baltimore: Williams and Wilkins, 1960.

Menéndez y Pelayo, M. *Orígenes de la novela.* 3 vols. Buenos Aires: Espasa-Calpe Argentina, 1946.

Menéndez Pidal, R. "El lenguaje de Lope de Vega." In his *El Padre Las Casas y Vitoria.* Madrid: Espasa-Calpe, 1950.

——— "Lope de Vega: El *Arte Nuevo* y la *Nueva Biografía*." In his *De Cervantes y Lope de Vega.* 2nd ed. Buenos Aires: Espasa-Calpe Argentina, 1943.

——— *Romancero hispánico.* 2 vols. (His *Obras completas,* vols. IX–X.) Madrid: Espasa-Calpe, 1953.

Millé y Giménez, J. "Apuntes para una bibliografía de las obras no dramáticas atribuidas a Lope de Vega," *Revue hispanique,* 74 (1928), 345–572.

——— "El horóscopo de Lope de Vega," *Humanidades* (La Plata), 16 (1927), 69–96.

Mitjana, Rafael. "Comentarios y apostillas al 'Cancionero poético y musical del siglo XVII,' recojido por Claudio de la Sablonara y publicado por D. Jesús Aroca," *Revista de filología española,* 6 (1919), 14–56, 233–267.

Mönch, Walter. *Das Sonnett: Gestalt und Geschichte.* Heidelberg: F. H. Kerle, 1955.

Monge, Félix. "*La Dorotea* de Lope de Vega," *Vox Romanica,* 16 (1957), 60–145.

Montemayor, Jorge de. *Los siete libros de la Diana.* Edited by F. López Estrada. Madrid: Espasa-Calpe, 1946.

Montesinos, J. F. "Algunas notas sobre el romancero *Ramillete de flores*," *Nueva revista de filología hispánica,* 6 (1952), 352–378.

——— "Algunos problemas del Romancero Nuevo." In *Ensayos y estudios de literatura española,* edited by J. H. Silverman, pp. 75–98. Mexico City: De Andrea, 1959.

—— *Estudios sobre Lope.* New ed. Salamanca: Anaya, 1967.

—— "Lope, figura del donaire." In his *Estudios sobre Lope,* pp. 65–79.

—— "Notas a la primera parte de *Flor de romances,*" *Bulletin hispanique,* 54 (1952), 386–404.

—— "Para la bibliografía de las obras no dramáticas de Lope de Vega." In his *Estudios sobre Lope,* 279–291.

—— "Para la historia de un romance de Lope ('Una estatua de Cupido')." In his *Estudios sobre Lope,* 251–266.

—— "Las poesías líricas de Lope de Vega." In his *Estudios sobre Lope,* 129–213.

Morby, E. S. "A Footnote on Lope de Vega's *Barquillas,*" *Romance Philology,* 6 (1953), 289–293.

—— "Levinus Lemnius and Leo Suabius in *La Dorotea,*" *Hispanic Review,* 20 (1952), 108–122.

—— "Persistence and Change in the Formation of *La Dorotea,*" *Hispanic Review,* 18 (1950), 108–125, 195–217.

—— "A Pre-*Dorotea* in *El Isidro,*" *Hispanic Review,* 21 (1953), 145–146.

—— "Proverbs in *La Dorotea,*" *Romance Philology,* 8 (1955), 243–259.

—— "Reflections on *El verdadero amante,*" *Hispanic Review,* 27 (1959), 317–323.

—— "Two Notes on *La Arcadia,*" *Hispanic Review,* 36 (1968), 110–123.

Morínigo, Marcos. *América en el teatro de Lope de Vega.* Buenos Aires: Instituto de Filología, 1946.

Morley, S. G. "The Pseudonyms and Literary Disguises of Lope de Vega," *University of California Publications in Modern Philology,* 33 (1951), 421–484.

Morley, S. G., and C. Bruerton. *The Chronology of Lope de Vega's "Comedias."* New York: Modern Language Association of America, 1940.

Morley, S. G., and R. Tyler. *Los nombres de personajes en las comedias de Lope de Vega: Estudio de onomatología.* University of California Publications in Modern Philology, vol. LV, nos. 1–2 (1961).

Müller-Bochat, Edward. *Der allegorische Triumphzug: Ein Motiv Petrarcas bei Lope de Vega und Rubens.* Krefeld: Scherpe, 1957.

Murillo, Luis G. "Cervantes' *Coloquio de los Perros,* a Novel-Dialogue," *Modern Philology,* 58 (1961), 174–185.

—— "Diálogo y dialéctica en el siglo XVI español," *Revista de la Universidad de Buenos Aires,* 5th ser., 4 (1959), 56–66.

Nanni Mirabelli, Domenico. *Polyanthea, hoc est, opus suavissimis floribus sententiarum tam Graecarum quam Latinarum exornatum.* Savona: F. de Silva, 1503.

Ormsby, John. "Lope de Vega," *Quarterly Review,* 179 (1894), 486–511.

Orozco Díaz, E. *Temas del barroco en poesía y pintura.* Granada: Universidad de Granada, 1947.

Osuna, Rafael. "*La Arcadia* de Lope de Vega: génesis, estructura y originalidad," unpub. diss., Brown University, 1966.

Ovid. *The Art of Love and Other Poems.* With an English translation by J. H. Mozley. Cambridge, Mass.: Harvard University Press, 1957.

—— *Heroides and Amores.* With an English translation by Grant Showerman. Cambridge, Mass.: Harvard University Press, 1963.

—— *Metamorphoses.* With an English translation by F. J. Miller. 2 vols. Cambridge, Mass.: Harvard University Press, 1951.

Pascal, Roy. *Design and Truth in Autobiography.* London: Routledge and Kegan Paul, 1960.

Pérez de Hita, G. *Guerras civiles de Granada.* Edited by P. Blanchard-Demouge. 2 vols. Madrid: Bailly-Baillière, 1913.

Pérez de Montalbán, Juan. *Fama póstuma a la vida y muerte del doctor Frey Lope Félix de Vega Carpio y elogios panegíricos a la inmortalidad de su nombre escritos por los más esclarecidos ingenios, solicitados por el doctor Juan Pérez de Montalbán.* OS, vol. XX.

—— *Orfeo en lengua castellana.* Edited by P. Cabañas. Madrid: C.S.I.C., 1948.

Pérez de Moya, Juan. *Philosophía secreta.* Edited by E. Gómez de Baquero. 2nd ed. 2 vols. Madrid: Compañía Ibero-Americana de Publicaciones, 1928.

Petrarca, Francesco. *Prose.* Edited by G. Martellotti et al. Milan and Naples: Riccardo Ricciardi, 1955.

Petriconi, Helmut. "Trotaconventos, Celestina, Gerarda," *Die Neueren Sprachen,* 32 (1924), 232–239.

Petrov, D. K. "El amor, sus principios y dialéctica en el teatro de Lope de Vega," *Escorial,* 16 (1944), 9–41.

Pfandl, Ludwig. *Historia de la literatura nacional española en la Edad de Oro.* Translated by J. Rubio Balaguer. Barcelona: Sucesores de J. Gili, [1933]. (German original: *Geschichte der spanischen Nationalliteratur in ihren Blütezeit*; Freiburg im Breisgau: Herder, 1929.)

Pinheiro da Veiga, Thomé. *Fastiginia o fastos geniales.* Translated by N. Alonso Cortés. Valladolid: Colegio de Santiago, 1916.

Plato. *The Dialogues of Plato.* Translated by B. Jowett. 2 vols. New York: Random House, 1937.

Plato. *Divini Platonis Opera Omnia quae Exstant.* Translated by Marsilio Ficino. Frankfurt: C. Marnius et haeredes J. Aubrii, 1602.

Plutarch. *Moralia.* Vol. III. London: Heinemann, 1931.

Poetas dramáticos valencianos. Edited by E. Juliá Martínez. Vol. I. Madrid: Revista de Archivos, 1929.

Pound, Ezra. *The Spirit of Romance,* rev. ed. London: Peter Owen, 1952.

Praz, Mario. *Studies in Seventeenth Century Imagery.* 2nd ed. Rome: Edizioni di Storia e Letteratura, 1964.

Pring-Mill, R. D. F. "Sententiousness in *Fuente Ovejuna*," *Tulane Drama Review,* 7 (1962), 5–37.

Questión de Amor de dos enamorados: al vno era muerta su amiga; el otro sirue sin esperança de galardón. Edited by M. Menéndez y Pelayo in *Orígenes de la novela,* II, 41–98. Nueva Biblioteca de Autores Españoles, VII. Madrid: Bailly-Baillière, 1907.

Quevedo, Francisco de. *Obras completas*. Edited by J. M. Blecua. Vol. I (*Poesía original*). Barcelona: Planeta, 1963.

—— *Obras completas (Prosa)*. Edited by L. Astrana Marín. Madrid: Aguilar, 1932.

—— *Obras en prosa*. Edited by F. Buendía. (*Obras completas*, vol. I.) Madrid: Aguilar, 1961.

Quintilian. *Institutio Oratoria*. Translated by H. E. Butler. 4 vols. Cambridge, Mass.: Harvard University Press, 1969–1971.

Ravisius Textor, Johannes (Jean Tixier, sieur de Ravisy). *Theatrum poeticum et historicum sive Officina Johannis Ravisii Textoris*. Basel: Bryling, 1552.

Rennert, H. A. "Sobre Lope de Vega." In *Homenaje a Menéndez Pidal*, I, 455–467. Madrid: Hernando, 1925.

Rennert, H. A., and Américo Castro. *Vida de Lope de Vega*. 2nd ed. with additions by Castro and F. Lázaro Carreter. Salamanca: Anaya, 1968.

Reyes, Alfonso. "Silueta de Lope de Vega." In his *Cuatro ingenios*, 2nd ed. Buenos Aires: Espasa-Calpe Argentina, 1950.

Riley, E. C. *Cervantes's Theory of the Novel*. Oxford: Oxford University Press, 1962.

Robles, Juan de. *Primera parte del culto sevillano*. Edited by J. M. Asensio. Seville: Sociedad de Bibliófilos Andaluces, 1883.

Robortello, Francesco. *In Librum Aristotelis de Arte Poetica Explicationes*. Florence: In Officina Laurentii Torrentini, 1548.

Rojas, Fernando de. *Tragicomedia de Calixto y Melibea*. Edited by M. Criado de Val and G. D. Trotter. Madrid: C.S.I.C., 1958.

"Les Romancerillos de la Bibliothèque Ambrosienne," edited by R. Foulché-Delbosc, *Revue hispanique*, 45 (1919), 510–624.

"Le *Romancero de Barcelona*," edited by R. Foulché-Delbosc, *Revue hispanique*, 29 (1913), 121–194.

Romancero general. Edited by A. Durán. 2 vols. Biblioteca de Autores Españoles, X and XVI. Madrid: Atlas, 1945.

Romancero general (1600, 1604, 1605). Edited by A. González Palencia. 2 vols. Madrid: C.S.I.C., 1947.

Romera-Navarro, M. *La preceptiva dramática de Lope de Vega*. Madrid: Ediciones Yunque, 1935.

Rotrou, Jean. "Le véritable Saint Genest." In his *Oeuvres*, vol. V. Paris: T. Desoer, 1820.

Salomon, Noël. *Recherches sur le thème "paysan" dans la "comedia" au temps de Lope de Vega*. Bordeaux: Institut d'Etudes Ibériques, 1965.

Sánchez de Lima, Miguel. *Arte poética en romance castellano*. Edited by R. de Balbín Lucas. Madrid: C.S.I.C., 1944.

Sannazaro, J. *Opere volgari*. Edited by A. Mauro. Bari: Laterza, 1961.

—— *Arcadia and Piscatorial Eclogues*. Translated with an Introduction by Ralph Nash. Detroit: Wayne State University Press, 1966.

Schack, A. F. von. *Geschichte der dramatischen Literatur und Kunst in Spanien*. 2 vols. Berlin, 1845. Translated by E. de Mier: *Historia de la literatura y del arte dramático en España*. 5 vols. Colección de escritores castellanos. Madrid: Tello, 1885 –1887.

Scudieri-Ruggieri, J. "Notas a la *Arcadia* de Lope de Vega," *Cuadernos hispanoamericanos*, nos. 161–162 (May–June 1963), 577–605.

Selig, Karl-Ludwig. Review of Edward Müller-Bochat, *Der allegorische Triumphzug: Ein Motiv Petrarcas bei Lope de Vega und Rubens* (Krefeld: Scherpe, 1957), *Bibliothèque d'Humanisme et Renaissance*, 20 (1958), 483–484.

Silva, Feliciano de. *Segunda comedia de Celestina*. Edited by J. A. de Palenchana. Madrid: Rivadeneyra, 1874.

Soto, Hernando de. *Emblemas moralizadas*. Madrid: Várez de Castro, 1599.

Southey, Robert. Review of H. R. Vassall Fox, Lord Holland, *Some Account of the Lives and Writings of Lope Felix de Vega Carpio and Guillen de Castro* (London, 1817), *Quarterly Review*, 18 (1817), 1–47.

Spitzer, Leo. *Classical and Christian Ideas of World Harmony*. Edited by A. G. Hatcher. Baltimore: Johns Hopkins Press, 1963.

––––– *Linguistics and Literary History*. Princeton: Princeton University Press, 1948.

––––– *Die Literarisierung des Lebens in Lope's "Dorotea."* Kölner Romanische Arbeiten. Bonn and Cologne: Rohrscheid, 1932.

––––– "A mis soledades voy . . .," *Revista de filología española*, 23 (1936), 397–400.

Stevens, Wallace. *Opus Posthumous*. Edited by S. F. Morse. New York: Alfred A. Knopf, 1957.

Suárez, Cipriano. *De arte rhetorica*. Paris: Officina Thomas Brumenni, 1573.

Suárez de Figueroa, C. *Plaça universal de todas artes, y ciencias*. Madrid, 1733.

Tasso, Torquato. *Poesie*. Edited by F. Flora. Milan and Naples: Riccardo Ricciardi, 1952.

Tayler, E. W. *Nature and Art in Renaissance Literature*. New York: Columbia University Press, 1964.

Téllez, Gabriel (Tirso de Molina). *Los Cigarrales de Toledo*. Edited by V. Said Armesto. Madrid: Renacimiento, 1913.

––––– *La mejor espigadera*. In his *Obras dramáticas completas*, edited by B. de los Ríos, vol. I. Madrid: Aguilar, 1946.

Templin, E. H. "The Exculpation of *yerros por amores* in the Spanish Comedia," *University of California at Los Angeles Publications in Language and Literature*, 1 (1933), 1–49.

Teresa, Saint. *Obras completas*. Edited by E. de la Madre de Dios and O. del Niño Jesús. 3 vols. Madrid: Biblioteca de Autores Cristianos, 1951–59.

Thomas, L. P. *Le Lyrisme et la préciosité cultistes en Espagne*. Halle: M. Niemeyer, 1909.

Ticknor, George. *History of Spanish Literature*. New York: Harper's, 1849.

Timoneda, Juan de. *Obras*. Edited by E. Juliá Martínez. Vol. II. Madrid: Sociedad de Bibliófilos Españoles, 1948.

Tomillo, A., and C. Pérez Pastor. *Proceso de Lope de Vega por libelos contra unos cómicos*. Madrid: Fortanet, 1901.

Torre, Alfonso de la. *Visión delectable de la filosofía y artes liberales, metafísica y filosofía moral.* In *Curiosidades bibliográficas,* edited by Adolfo de Castro, pp. 339–402. Biblioteca de Autores Españoles, XXXVI. Madrid: Hernando, 1926.

Torres Naharro, Bartolomé de. *Propalladia and Other Works of Bartolomé de Torres Naharro.* Edited by J. E. Gillet. 4 vols. Vol. II: Bryn Mawr, Pa., and Menasha, Wis.: George Banta Publishing Co., 1946.

Trueblood, Alan S. "The Case for an Early *Dorotea*: A Reexamination," *PMLA,* 71 (1956), 755–798.

—— "Lope's 'A mis soledades voy' Reconsidered." In *Homenaje a William L. Fichter: Estudios sobre el antiguo teatro hispánico,* edited by A. D. Kossoff and J. Amor y Vázquez, pp. 713–724. Madrid: Castalia, 1971.

—— "Masters and Servants: *La Dorotea* vis-à-vis the *Comedia,*" *Kentucky Romance Quarterly,* 16 (1969), 55–61.

—— "The *Officina* of Ravisius Textor in Lope de Vega's *Dorotea,*" *Hispanic Review,* 26 (1958), 135–141.

—— "Plato's *Symposium* and Ficino's Commentary in Lope de Vega's *Dorotea,*" *Modern Language Notes,* 73 (1958), 506–514.

—— "Role-Playing and the Sense of Illusion in Lope de Vega," *Hispanic Review,* 32 (1964), 305–318.

—— "'Al son de los arroyuelos': Texture and Context in a Lyric of *La Dorotea.*" In *Homenaje al Profesor Rodríguez-Moñino,* II, 277–287. Madrid: Castalia, 1966.

Valbuena Prat, Angel. *Literatura dramática española.* Barcelona: Labor, 1930.

Van Veen, O. *Amorum Emblemata.* Antwerp, 1608.

   Amorum Emblemata. Brussels: H. Swingen, 1667.

Vega Carpio, Lope Félix de. *El anzuelo de Fenisa.* In *Comedias escogidas,* vol. III.

—— *La Arcadia. OS,* vol. VI.

—— *La Arcadia (comedia). Obras escogidas,* vol. III.

—— *Belardo el furioso.* Ac., vol. V.

—— *Las bizarrías de Belisa.* Ac. N., vol. XI.

—— *Las burlas de amor.* Ac. N., vol. I.

—— *El caballero de Olmedo.* Edited by Francisco Rico. Salamanca: Anaya, 1967.

—— *El castigo sin venganza. OS,* vol. VIII.

—— *El castigo sin venganza.* Edited by F. A. Van Dam. Groningen: P. Noordhoff, 1928.

—— *Los celos de Rodamonte.* Ac., vol. XIII.

—— *La Circe. OS,* vol. III.

—— *La Circe, con otras Rimas y Prosas* [Madrid: Viuda de Alonso Martín, 1624]. Facs. ed. Madrid: Biblioteca Nueva, 1935.

—— *La Circe, poema.* Literary commentary, historical introduction, and annotated edition by C. V. Aubrun and M. Muñoz Cortés. Paris: Centre de Recherches de l'Institut d'Etudes Hispaniques, 1962.

—— *Colección de las obras sueltas, así en prosa como en verso, de don Frey Lope de Vega Carpio del hábito de San Juan.* 21 vols. Madrid: A. de Sancha, 1776–1779.

—— *Comedias escogidas de Frey* [also *Fray*] *Lope Félix de Vega Carpio.* Edited by J. E. Hartzenbusch. 4 vols. Biblioteca de Autores Españoles, XXIV, XXXIV, XLI, LII. Madrid: Hernando [for] Sucesores de Hernando, 1923–1925.

—— *La corona merecida.* Edited by J. F. Montesinos. Teatro Antiguo Español, V. Madrid: Centro de Estudios Históricos, 1923.

—— *La corona trágica. OS,* vol. XVI.

—— *El cuerdo loco.* Ac. N., vol. IV.

—— *La dama boba. Obras escogidas,* vol. I.

—— *El desdén vengado.* Ac., vol. XV.

—— *La Dorotea.* Edited by J. M. Blecua. Madrid: Ediciones de la Universidad de Puerto Rico—Revista de Occidente, 1955.

—— *La Dorotea.* Edited by E. Juliá Martínez. 2 vols. Madrid: Hernando, 1935.

—— *La Dorotea.* Edited by E. S. Morby. 2nd ed. rev. Published jointly by University of California Press, Berkeley, and Editorial Castalia, Madrid, 1968.

—— *La Dorotea: Acción en prosa* [Madrid, 1632]. Facs. ed. Madrid: Real Academia Española, 1951.

—— "Elogio en la muerte de Juan Blas de Castro." *OS,* vol. IX.

—— "Epístola a Don Fernando de Vega y Fonseca." Edited by J. de Entrambasaguas in his *Estudios sobre Lope de Vega,* III, 398–410.

—— "Epístola a Don Francisco López de Aguilar." *OS,* vol. I.

—— "Epístola a Don Matias de Porras." *OS,* vol. I.

—— "Epístola a Félix Quixada y Riquelme." *OS,* vol. I.

—— "Epístola a Fray Plácido de Tosantos." *OS,* vol. I.

—— "Epístola al Conde de Lemos." *OS,* vol. I.

—— "Epístola de Belardo a Amarilis." *OS,* vol. I.

—— *Epistolario de Lope de Vega Carpio.* Edited by Agustín G. de Amezúa under the sponsorship of the Real Academia Española. 4 vols. Madrid, 1935–1943. Individual volumes carry the following imprints: I: Tipografía de Archivos, 1935; II: Escelicer, 1940; III and IV: Artes Gráficas "Aldus," 1941 and 1943, respectively. The first two volumes are an introductory study; the last two, the letters proper.

—— *La escolástica celosa.* Ac. N., vol. V.

—— *Las ferias de Madrid.* Ac. N., vol. V.

—— *La Filomena. OS,* vol. II.

—— *Lo fingido verdadero o El mejor representante.* Ac., vol. IV.

—— *Flor nueva del Fénix.* Edited by J. de Entrambasaguas. Madrid: C.S.I.C., 1942.

—— *Fuente Ovejuna.* Ac., vol. X.

—— *El ganso de oro.* Ac. N., vol. I.

—— *La Gatomaquia.* Edited by F. Rodríguez Marín. Madrid: C. Bermejo, 1935.

—— *La hermosura de Angélica. OS,* vol. II.

—— *El Isidro* [Madrid, 1599]. Facs. ed. Madrid: Instituto de San Isidro, 1935.

—— *Jerusalén conquistada. OS,* vol. XV.

—— *El laberinto de Creta.* Ac., vol. VI.

—— *Laurel de Apolo*. *OS*, vol. I.

—— *Lope de Vega, poesías preliminares de libros*. Edited by F. Zamora Lucas. Madrid: C.S.I.C., 1961.

—— *El marido más firme*. Ac., vol. VI.

—— *El Marqués de las Navas*. Edited by J. F. Montesinos. Teatro Antiguo Español, VI. Madrid: Centro de Estudios Históricos, 1925.

—— *Los melindres de Belisa*. Ac. N., vol. XII.

—— *La moza de cántaro*. In *Comedias escogidas*, vol. I.

—— *El negro del mejor amo*. Ac. N., vol. XI.

—— *Obras de Lope de Vega*. Edited by Real Academia Española. 15 vols. Madrid: Sucesores de Rivadeneyra, 1890–1913.

—— *Obras de Lope de Vega*. Edited by Real Academia Española. New ed. 13 vols. Madrid: Tipografía de la Revista de Archivos, Bibliotecas y Museos, 1916–1930.

—— *Obras escogidas de Lope Félix de Vega Carpio*. Edited by F. C. Sainz de Robles. 2nd ed. 3 vols. Madrid: Aguilar, 1952–1962. (I: *Teatro*, I; II: *Poesías líricas, Poemas, Prosa, Novelas*; III: *Teatro*, II.)

—— *Obras poéticas de Lope de Vega*. Edited by J. M. Blecua. Barcelona: Planeta, 1969.

—— *Obras son amores*. Ac. N., vol. VIII.

—— *La oveja perdida*. Ac., vol. II.

—— *Los pastores de Belén*. *OS*, vol. XVI.

—— *El peregrino en su patria*. *OS*, vol. V.

—— *Peribáñez y el Comendador de Ocaña*. Edited by J. F. Montesinos and C. V. Aubrun. Paris: Hachette, 1943.

—— *Poesías líricas*. Edited by J. F. Montesinos. 2 vols. Madrid: Espasa-Calpe, 1941. (Originally published by La Lectura in 1925–26.)

—— *Porfiar hasta morir*. Ac., vol. X.

—— *El príncipe perfecto*, Second Part. Ac., vol. X.

—— "La prudente venganza." *OS*, vol. VIII.

—— *La prueba de los amigos*. Ac. N., vol. XI.

—— *Relación de las fiestas que la insigne Villa de Madrid hizo en la canonización de su Bienaventurado Hijo y Patrón San Isidro*. *OS*, vol. XII.

—— *Rimas* (1602). *OS*, vol. IV.

—— *Rimas humanas y divinas del licenciado Tomé de Burguillos* [Madrid: Imprenta del Reino, 1634]. Facs. ed. Madrid: Cámara Oficial del Libro, 1935.

—— *Rimas sacras*. *OS*, vol. XIII.

—— *El saber puede dañar*. In *Comedias escogidas*, vol. III.

—— *La selva sin Amor*. Ac., vol. V.

—— *El sembrar en buena tierra*. Edited by W. L. Fichter. New York: Modern Language Association of America, 1944.

—— *Servir a señor discreto*. Ac., vol. XV.

—— *Si no vieran las mujeres*. Ac., vol. XV.

—— *Soliloquios amorosos de un alma a Dios*. *OS*, vol. XVII.

—————— *El sol parado*. Ac., vol. IX.

—————— *Treinta canciones de Lope de Vega puestas en música*. Edited by J. Bal y Gay. Madrid: Residencia de Estudiantes, 1935.

—————— *Triunfo de la fe en los reinos del Japón por los años de 1614 y 1615* [Madrid: Viuda de Alonso Martín, 1618]. *OS*, vol. XVII.

—————— *Triunfos divinos*. *OS*, vol. XIII.

—————— *Ursón y Valentín*. Ac., vol. XIII.

—————— *La Vega del Parnaso*. 2 vols. *OS*, vols. IX–X.

—————— *El verdadero amante*. Ac., vol. V.

—————— *La viuda valenciana*. Ac., vol. XV.

Vélez de Guevara, Luis. *El diablo cojuelo*. Madrid: Sociedad de Bibliófilos Madrileños, 1910.

Vilanova, Antonio. *Las fuentes y los temas del Polifemo de Góngora*. 2 vols. Madrid: C.S.I.C., 1957.

Villegas, Alonso de. *Comedia Selvagia*. Libros españoles raros o curiosos, V. Madrid: Rivadeneyra, 1873.

Virgil. *Virgil*. With an English translation by H. R. Fairclough. Rev. ed. 2 vols. Cambridge, Mass.: Harvard University Press, 1954–56.

Vossler, Karl. *Algunos caracteres de la cultura española*. 2nd ed. Buenos Aires: Espasa-Calpe Argentina, 1943.

—————— *Escritores y poetas de España*. Buenos Aires: Espasa-Calpe Argentina, 1947.

—————— "*Euphrosina*," *Corona*, 8 (1938), 514–533.

—————— *Lope de Vega y su tiempo*. Translated by R. de la Serna. 2nd ed. Madrid: Revista de Occidente, 1940.

Wardropper, B. W. "La imaginación en el metateatro calderoniano." In *Actas del Tercer Congreso Internacional de Hispanistas*, edited by C. H. Magis, pp. 923–930. Mexico City: El Colegio de México, 1970.

Weisbach, Werner. *Trionfi*. Berlin: G. Grote, 1919.

Ximénez Patón, Bartolomé. *Mercurius Trimegistus, sive de triplici eloquentia sacra, Española, Romana* . . . Baeza: Pedro de la Cuesta, 1621.

Zamora Lucas, F. *Lope de Vega, censor de libros*. Larache: Artes gráficas Bosca, 1941.

I. Introduction

1. *La Dorotea*, 2nd ed. rev., ed. E. S. Morby (published jointly by University of California Press, Berkeley, and Editorial Castalia, Madrid, 1968), p. 49. Subsequent references are to this edition, by page number only, except in a few cases where I cite the facsimile edition, *La Dorotea: Acción en prosa* [Madrid, 1632] (Madrid: Real Academia Española, 1951), by folio number.

2. I have sometimes fallen back on the German term *Erlebnis* (Spanish *vivencia*) to suggest not simply experience but its living-through, its reshaping within the individual psyche. (There is no English equivalent.) It is obviously not events in themselves but events as seen, felt, and lived with by the creator that matter in *poiesis*.

3. *Epistolario*, III, 258. Lope here has in mind a Plutarchan *chria* (*Moralia* [London: Heinemann, 1931], III, 398), which he quotes in another private letter: "Quitaba un Lacón (en los Apophtegmas Griegos) las plumas a vn ruiseñor, y descubriendo tan débil carne, dixo: *Vox tu es, at nihil praeterea*" ("A Laconian [in the Greek Apophthegms] removed the feathers from a nightingale and finding such slight flesh, said: 'You're a voice and nothing more'") (*Epistolario*, IV, 88). Clearly the nightingale of the anecdote seemed an apt emblem of himself.

4. The studies of J. F. Montesinos cited in note 19 below are fundamental for the question of *Dichtung und Wahrheit* in Lope, as is Amado Alonso, "Vida y creación en la lírica de Lope," *Materia y forma en poesía* (Madrid: Gredos, 1955), pp. 133–164.

5. *Lope de Vega y su tiempo*, trans. R. de la Serna, 2nd ed. (Madrid: Revista de Occidente, 1940), p. 132.

6. *The Spirit of Romance*, rev. ed. (London: Peter Owen, 1952), p. 205.

7. *Epistolario*, IV, 189.

8. See the "Oraciones fúnebres pronunciadas en las exequias de Lope de Vega," *OS*, vol. XIX; the *Fama póstuma a la vida y muerte del doctor Frey Lope Félix de Vega*

Carpio y elogios panegíricos a la inmortalidad de su nombre escritos por los más esclarecidos ingenios, solicitados por el doctor Juan Pérez de Montalbán, OS, XX; and R. Menéndez Pidal, "Lope de Vega: El *Arte Nuevo* y la *Nueva Biografía*," *De Cervantes y Lope de Vega*, 2nd ed. (Buenos Aires: Espasa-Calpe Argentina, 1943).

9. The English poet Robert Southey in the *Quarterly Review*, 18 (1817), 43, was the first to speculate on the autobiographical character of *La Dorotea*. Two decades later Claude Fauriel, despite some insight into artistic structure, accepted the work's autobiographical value in toto and in detail, with no reservations (*Revue des deux mondes*, September 1, 1839, pp. 593–623; September 15, 1843, pp. 881–924). J. J. S. A. de Damas Hinard, dissenting, called the work pure fiction ("De quelques erreurs publiées touchant la vie et les ouvrages de Lope de Vega," introductory study to his *Chefs-d'oeuvre du théâtre espagnol: Lope de Vega* [Paris: C. Gosselin, 1842], pp. xlviii–xlix). A. F. von Schack, in 1845, more judicious than either of the Frenchmen, saw it as a compound of truth and poetry (*Geschichte der dramatischen Literatur und Kunst in Spanien*, 2 vols. [Berlin, 1845]; trans. E. de Mier: *Historia de la literatura y del arte dramático en España*, 5 vols. [Madrid: Tello, 1885–1887]; on *La Dorotea* see the Spanish edition, II, 304). George Ticknor, shortly afterward, rather noncommittally found in it "more or less of Lope's own youthful adventures and feelings" (*History of Spanish Literature* [New York: Harper's, 1849], II, 160).

10. The volume, *Nueva Biografía* [de Lope de Vega] (Ac., vol. I), because of the purportedly scandalous nature of some of Lope's private letters excerpted in it, was not published until 1890.

11. *Das Spanische Drama*, 5 vols. (Leipzig: T. O. Weidel, 1871–1876), II (1872), pp. 499–534.

12. "Lope de Vega," *Quarterly Review*, 79 (1894), 486–511.

13. *Historia de la literatura nacional española en la Edad de Oro*, trans. J. Rubio Balaguer (Barcelona: Sucesores de J. Gili, [1933]), pp. 499–507. German original: *Geschichte der spanischen Nationalliteratur in ihren Blütezeit* (Freiburg im Breisgau: Herder, 1929).

14. In his "Observaciones preliminares" to *Belardo el furioso*, Ac., V (1895), lxii–lxv.

15. A. Tomillo and C. Pérez Pastor, *Proceso de Lope de Vega por libelos contra unos cómicos* (Madrid: Fortanet, 1901). To be referred to subsequently as *Proceso*, or by page number only.

16. *The Life of Lope de Vega* (Glasgow: Gowans and Gray, 1904); *Vida de Lope de Vega (1562–1635)* (Madrid: Sucesores de Hernando, 1919); 2nd ed., with additions by Castro and F. Lázaro Carreter (Salamanca: Anaya, 1968). I cite the 2nd ed. as Rennert and Castro.

17. The *Spanischer Brief* (*Eranos* [Munich], February 1, 1924) appears in translation in Vossler's *Algunos caracteres de la cultura española*, 2nd ed. (Buenos Aires: Espasa-Calpe, 1943). My references are to this Spanish version as also to the Spanish version of *Lope de Vega und sein Zeitalter*: *Lope de Vega y su tiempo*.

18. *Lope de Vega y su tiempo*, p. 170.

19. First incorporated in Montesinos's introduction to Lope's *Poesías líricas*, 2 vols.

(Madrid: La Lectura, 1925–26), these insights are amplified in "Lope, figura del donaire," *Cruz y raya*, nos. 23–24 (February–March, 1935), 53–85. Both studies are reprinted in his *Estudios sobre Lope*.

20. Kölner Romanische Arbeiten (Bonn and Cologne: Rohrscheid, 1932).

21. *"La Dorotea" di Lope de Vega, studio critico seguito dalla traduzione delle parti principali dell'opera* (Bari: Laterza, 1940).

22. "Persistence and Change in the Formation of La Dorotea," *Hispanic Review*, 18 (1950), 108–125, 195–217. See also "A Pre-*Dorotea* in *El Isidro*," *Hispanic Review*, 21 (1953), 145–146; and "Reflections on *El verdadero amante*," *Hispanic Review*, 27 (1959), 317–323.

23. Published jointly by University of California Press, Berkeley, and Editorial Castalia, Madrid, 1968.

24. "The Case for an Early *Dorotea*," *PMLA*, 71 (1956), 755–798.

25. *La Dorotea* (Madrid: Ediciones de la Universidad de Puerto Rico—Revista de Occidente, 1955).

26. *"La Dorotea* de Lope de Vega," *Vox Romanica*, 16 (1957), 60–145.

27. *Opus Posthumous*, ed. S. F. Morse (New York: Alfred A. Knopf, 1957), p. 184.

28. See above, pp. 41, 93, 99.

29. *Philosophy in a New Key: A Study in the Symbolism of Reason, Rite and Art*, 3rd ed. (Cambridge, Mass.: Harvard University Press, 1957), chap. 4, "Discursive and Presentational Forms," especially pp. 86 ff.

30. Cf. Maurice Charney, *Shakespeare's Roman Plays: The Function of Imagery in the Drama* (Cambridge, Mass.: Harvard University Press, 1961), p. 8.

31. *Epistolario*, III, 293, and IV, 108. The first figure turns up, with a different application, in Lope's prologue to his account of the festivities for the canonization of San Isidro: "como algunas hierbas maltratadas dan más suave olor: assí la envidia a lo que piensa que destruye, añade fama" ("as some herbs when crushed give off a sweeter smell, so envy gives renown to what it thinks it is destroying") (*OS*, XII, 20).

32. Quoted in H. A. Rennert, "Sobre Lope de Vega," in *Homenaje a Menéndez Pidal*, 3 vols. (Madrid: Hernando, 1925), I, 466. E. Lafuente Ferrari writes: "There is no way of knowing what artist Lope is referring to; this Yaneti is unknown" (*Los retratos de Lope de Vega* [Madrid: Junta del Centenario, 1935], p. 15). I have not been any more successful in identifying this artist. The painting likewise is unknown.

33. In one of Lope's sonnets to Night (*Obras poéticas*, p. 105), he expresses resentment that "media vida es tuya" ("half a life is yours") and complains "Si velo, te lo pago con el día, / y si duermo, no siento lo que vivo" ("If I stay up, I pay you for it in daylight and if I sleep I am not aware of being alive"). Even burning the midnight oil will not give the day hours enough to satisfy his need to live life to the hilt.

34. Cf. p. 514 above.

35. *El peregrino en su patria* (*The Pilgrim of Castile*), *OS*, V, 116. The reference is to Isaiah 40:6.

36. See p. 387 above and note 15 to Chap. X.

37. *Obras poéticas*, p. 72.

38. "Lope de Vega: El *Arte Nuevo*." See p. 350 above.

39. On the subject of Lope's psychological make-up, on which valuable passing comments have been made by many critics (Castro, Montesinos, Amado Alonso, Lázaro Carreter, etc.), I have found no useful overall study except Amezúa's discussion in *Epistolario*, I and II, in connection with Lope's self-revelation in his private correspondence; and the first chapter of Agustín Albarracín Teulón, *La medicina en el teatro de Lope de Vega* (Madrid: C.S.I.C., 1954). Of little or no help are: H. R. Romero Flores, *Estudio psicológico sobre Lope de Vega* (Madrid: Sucesores de Rivadeneyra, 1936); and J. R. Beltrán, "El complejo psicológico de Lope de Vega," *Anales* (Instituto de Psicología, Facultad de Filosofía y Letras, Universidad de Buenos Aires), 3 (1941), 81–93.

40. *Lope de Vega y su tiempo*, p. 132.

41. "Silueta de Lope de Vega" in *Cuatro ingenios*, 2nd ed. (Buenos Aires: Espasa-Calpe Argentina, 1950), pp. 51–52.

42. Ac., XIII, 398a. Morley and Bruerton date this play before 1596. J. M. de Cossío, *Lope, personaje de sus comedias* (Madrid: Real Academia Española, 1948) cites this passage, p. 31.

43. Ac., XIII, 500a.

44. *Epistolario*, IV, 292.

45. He writes:

> Hauía juntado de mi pensión y estudios hasta mil ducados para pagar el dote de Marcela y alibiarme del censo de cinquenta ducados cada año, y cogióme la Premática, por ombre de bien, con ellos, pudiendo ocho días antes hauerlos dado a las Monjas. Hízeme un soneto a mí mismo, de que sólo enbío los tres últimos versos: "Que a mí, con ser de mis estudios partos, / Con mil ducados de bellón me coja, / Y a Carlos Trata con cinquenta quartos." (*Epistolario*, IV, 131)

From my pension and studies I had saved some thousand ducats to pay Marcela's dowry and avoid being levied fifty ducats a year, and the Decree caught me with them, as a man of means, when I could have given them to the Nuns a week before. I wrote a sonnet to myself, of which I will send only the last three lines: "That it should catch me with a thousand ducats in copper, and those the product of my mental labors, and Carlos Trata with fifty *quartos*."

46. *Epistolario*, IV, 88.

47. In "Los famosos 'libelos contra unos cómicos,' de Lope de Vega," *Boletín de la Academia de Bellas Artes de Valladolid*, 3 (1933), 460–491, J. de Entrambasaguas published five libelous compositions—four sonnets and a ballad—together with notes and commentary. The study is reproduced in vol. III of his *Estudios*, pp. 7–74. Two of the compositions had been published earlier by John M. Hill (see below, note 17 to Chap. II) without commentary, together with another libelous sonnet not among those published by Entrambasaguas. Though, as will be seen in the next chapter,

there was at least one other verse libel which has not turned up, the texts discovered by Entrambasaguas and Hill constitute an invaluable addition to our documentation.

48. The three letters, one of Lope to Liñán, the latter's reply, and Lope's reply to Liñán, are reproduced by Entrambasaguas as "Cartas poéticas de Lope de Vega y Liñán de Riaza," the first two from a *romancero* of 1605, the second from a contemporary *cancionero*, in *Fénix, revista del tricentenario de Lope de Vega*, 1 (1935), 225–261. Entrambasaguas reprints them in his *Flor nueva del "Fénix": Poesías desconocidas y no recopiladas de Lope de Vega* (Madrid: C.S.I.C., 1942), pp. 107–130; and in *Estudios*, III, 411–460.

II. Lope and Elena Osorio

1. *Proceso*, p. 46. Unless otherwise noted the *Proceso*, with accompanying data and documents, is the source of material used in this chapter.

2. See Father R. M. de Hornedo, "A propósito de una fecha: 1572. Lope en los Estudios de la Compañía de Jesús en Madrid," *Razón y fe*, no. 108 (1935), 52–78; and his "Lope y los jesuitas," *Razón y fe*, no. 166 (1962), 405–422.

3. At certain points in the exposition and for certain analyses of texts and poems in this chapter and the next, I have drawn on materials originally presented in my "Role-Playing and the Sense of Illusion in Lope de Vega," *Hispanic Review*, 32 (1964), 305–318.

4. On this motif, see E. S. Morby, "Persistence and Change in the Formation of *La Dorotea*," *Hispanic Review*, 18 (1950), 208–209; and "Two Notes on *La Arcadia*," *Hispanic Review*, 36 (1968), 112–113. Cf. note 42 to Chap. IV; p. 276 above; note 12 to Chap. VIII.

5. "Enamorada, siempre se toma en mala parte, como muger enamorada o amiga" ("'Enamorada' is always taken in a pejorative sense, as in an 'enamorada' woman, meaning a girl-friend"), states Covarrubias, s.v. *enamorado*.

6. Annotated text in Entrambasaguas, *Estudios*, III, 45–63.

7. An eighteenth-century adaptation of "Caballero de lejas tierras" ("Knight from distant lands") contains the lines: "No permita Dios del cielo / ni mi madre Santa Inés" ("May God in Heaven not allow, nor my mother St. Agnes"); they may also have figured in versions sung in Lope's day. The first published text, that of Juan de Ribera's broadsheet of 1605, does not contain these lines. Durán prints the two versions mentioned in *Romancero general* (Madrid: Atlas, 1945), I, 318. Cf. the remarks of R. Menéndez Pidal, *Romancero hispánico* (Madrid: Espasa-Calpe, 1953), II, 193–194.

8. The absence of further reference to these satires and sonnets may be due to the overriding concern of the plaintiffs with the compromising letter at this point.

9. W. Mayer-Gross, E. Slater, and M. Roth, *Clinical Psychiatry*, 2nd ed. (Baltimore: Williams and Wilkins, 1960), p. 135.

10. *Lope de Vega y su tiempo*, trans. R. de la Serna, 2nd ed. (Madrid: Revista de Occidente, 1940), p. 231.

11. "The Histrionic Sensibility: The Mimetic Perception of Action," in *The Idea of a Theater: The Art of Drama in Changing Perspective* (Garden City: Doubleday, 1953), pp. 250–255.

12. On this subject, see Américo Castro, "Algunas observaciones acerca del concepto del honor en los siglos XVI y XVII," *Revista de filología española*, 3 (1916), 1–50, 357–386 (reproduced in *Semblanzas y estudios espanoles*, ed. Juan Marichal [Princeton: Princeton University Press, 1956], pp. 319–382); W. L. Fichter, *Lope de Vega's "El castigo del discreto" together with a Study of Conjugal Honor in his Theater* (New York: Instituto de las Españas, 1925), pp. 43 and 236; and C. A. Jones, *"Honor in Spanish Golden Age Drama: Its Relation to Real Life and to Morals," Bulletin of Hispanic Studies*, 35 (1958), 199–210. An example of a public execution of adulterers by a vengeful husband is given by R. Schevill and A. Bonilla in a note to their edition of Cervantes, *Persiles y Sigismunda* (Madrid: Bernardo Rodríguez, 1914), II, 305.

13. One of the most damaging bits of evidence against Lope shows the conspirator in action. He steals into the patio of the house of a friend, Pedro de Moya, at nine one evening and slips a copy of the Latin satire through a cat-hole in his friend's door. Surprised by a servant as he is slipping out, Lope merely directs him to tell Moya he'll see him "en el juego de los trucos" ("at billiards") (p. 62). Moya tells (*Proceso*, p. 35) how Lope and Prado came to his house a few days later and how they stood about in the doorway a while talking until Moya brought up the question of Lope's possible authorship of the verse, only to meet with Lope's indignant denials.

14. Testimony of Francisco de Castro, gate-keeper of the royal prison. Substantially the same thing is said in the testimony of Francisco Gutiérrez, the keeper of the keys (*Proceso*, p. 73).

15. On this point consult R. Menéndez Pidal, "Lope de Vega: El *Arte Nuevo* y la *Nueva Biografía*," *De Cervantes y Lope de Vega*, 2nd ed. (Buenos Aires: Espasa-Calpe Argentina, 1943), pp. 77–78; and E. H. Templin, "The Exculpation of *yerros por amores* in the Spanish Comedia," *University of California at Los Angeles Publications in Language and Literature*, 1 (1933), 1–49.

16. Ac. N., I, 67a. Montesinos cites this passage in his edition of Lope's *Poesías líricas* (Madrid: Espasa-Calpe, 1941), I, 20n. Subsequent references to this work are all to the 1941 edition.

17. In the sonnet beginning "Angel almacigado que al Tudesco / rrindes tus entresacos y entresecos" ("You hothouse angel who give your seedlings and innards to the Teuton"), published by John M. Hill, Indiana University Studies, vol. X, no. 60 (December 1923), p. 81, from MS. 17556 of the Biblioteca Nacional. This supplement to the libels published by Entrambasaguas (two of which had already been printed from the same source by Hill, pp. 54 and 77) is considered by Montesinos "unquestionably by Lope" (*Estudios sobre Lope*, p. 248).

18. The young men's uncle, the Cardinal, had been viceroy of Naples for Philip II from 1571 to 1575 and had spent his last years, from 1579 to his death in 1586, in Madrid, as President of the Councils of Italy and of State. Their father Tomás, Count of Cantecroy, had been Philip II's Ambassador to Maximilian II of Austria from 1564 or 1565 to 1570. (See *Proceso*, pp. 130–131, and Rennert and Castro, pp. 52–56.) Pérez Pastor's identification rests on a note in an early seventeenth-century hand found in a *Romancero general* of 1604 opposite the Moorish ballad "De la armada de su rey"

("From his king's fleet"). As restored by Pérez Pastor (p. 127) after mutilation by a binder (the all-important first name is missing), the note identifies the protagonists of the ballad as follows: "Era don (Thomas) granue (la sob)rino del (card) Perrenoto (de Gr)anuela y esta felisalua es Elena Osorio la Philis de Lope, hija de Velezquez [*sic*] el representante" ("It was Don Thomas Granvela, a nephew of Cardinal Perrenot de Granvela and this Felisalva is Elena Osorio, the Filis of Lope, daughter of Velázquez the player").

19. The detail of the window recurs in one of the artistic ballads: "Pues mira, diosa cruel, / lo que me cuestas del alma / y cuantas noches dormí / debajo de tus ventanas" ("Just see, cruel goddess, what you are doing to my soul and all the nights I have slept beneath your windows"). From "Gallardo pasea Zaide" ("Boldly Zaide strides") in Montesinos, ed., *Poesías líricas*, I, 42.

20. See above, p. 301.

21. Entrambasaguas, *Estudios*, III, 70.

22. *Ibid.*, p. 71.

23. *Ibid.*, p. 435.

24. See note 17 above.

25. *Estudios*, III, 434. Nearly fifty years later we will find Lope writing, apropos of the rose, in his eclogue "Felicio" (1634):

y toda su lozanía
dura un día,
porque es, Lisis, la hermosura
una breve tiranía.

> (*Obras escogidas*, II, 266)

and all its fullness lasts one day because beauty, Lisis, is a short-lived tyranny.

26. *Vida de Lope de Vega* (Barcelona: Labor, 1936), p. 63.

27. Morby, for example, "Persistence and Change," p. 119, notes the references in *La hermosura de Angélica* (Angelica's Beauty) to "la inicua falsedad de los testigos" ("the iniquitous falsity of the witnesses") and to the Lope-figure's being "vendido de mis íntimos amigos" ("sold out by my intimate friends").

28. Cf. Lope's remarks in his second verse epistle to Liñán, quoted above, pp. 89–90. After stressing the clarity with which their "amorosas desventuras" ("misfortunes in love") can be read in the "glass" of their verse, Lope continues:

Y suelen, como tú, los más discretos
buscar un buen amigo que los canta
con el tono que alguno mis secretos.
Con esto el rudo vulgo se adelanta
y como el vidro tiene por antojos,
adonde dice *muero* dice *mata*.

> (*Estudios*, III, 453)

And like you, the cleverest ones usually seek out a good friend to sing them to the same tune to which a certain friend sings my secrets. Thereupon the coarse herd comes forward and since they think the glass eyeglasses, where it says "I die" they say "it kills."

Of interest is the evidence of close bonds between poets and musicians, and of the diffusion (and deformation) of the compositions by song. Montesinos has examined these questions in depth in "Algunos problemas del Romancero Nuevo," *Ensayos y estudios de literatura española*, ed. J. H. Silverman (Mexico City: De Andrea, 1959), pp. 75–98.

29. "Mirando estaba Lisardo" ("Lisardo was looking"). Cf. p. 82 above.

30. "Persistence and Change," p. 202.

31. For instance, Alda Croce, "*La Dorotea*" *di Lope de Vega, studio critico seguito dalla traduzione delle parti principali dell'opera* (Bari: Laterza, 1940), p. 127.

32. In his second epistle to Liñán we also find: "Filis ya está segura con su tío" ("Filis has settled down with her old boy") (*Estudios*, III, 459).

33. *Epistolario*, III, 120, and IV, 143. Cf. also the remarks in the epistle to the Count of Lemos (*OS*, I, 447–453), referred to above, pp. 514–515. In correspondence with Liñán, Lope is already exclaiming: "¿Siempre tengo de estar en una sala / más humilde que pollo presentado, / sufriendo más que si tuviera cala?" ("Must I always be hanging about an anteroom humbler than a chicken on a platter, suffering more than if I were wearing a suppository?") (*Estudios*, III, 457).

III. The Artistic Ballads: Moorish and Pastoral Masks

1. I shall occasionally glance also at a surviving composition in another lyric strophe, such as the *redondilla* or the *estancia*.

2. On the artistic balladry of this period and the complex questions of texts, attributions, style, chronology, etc., connected with it, see R. Menéndez Pidal, *Romancero hispánico* (Madrid: Espasa-Calpe, 1953), II, 117–168; J. F. Montesinos, "Algunos problemas del Romancero Nuevo," *Romance Philology*, 6 (1953), 231–247; and Montesinos's introductory study to his edition of *Primavera y flor de los mejores romances recogidos por el Licdo. Arias Pérez* [1621] (Valencia: Castalia, 1954). On Lope's artistic ballads in general and on similar questions concerning them, see: J. Millé y Giménez, "Apuntes para una bibliografía de las obras no dramáticas atribuidas a Lope de Vega," *Revue hispanique*, 74 (1928), 345–572; Montesinos, "Las poesías líricas de Lope de Vega" [1925–26], and "Para la bibliografía de las obras no dramáticas de Lope de Vega" [1932], in *Estudios sobre Lope*, pp. 129–213 and 279–291; María Goyri de Menéndez Pidal, *De Lope de Vega y del romancero* (Saragossa: Librería general, 1953); J. de Entrambasaguas, "Poesías nuevas de Lope de Vega, en parte, autobiográficas" and "Poesías de Lope de Vega en un romancero de 1605," in *Estudios*, III, 217–410. Studies referring to specific ballads are cited below. Regarding authorship, if no authority for attribution is cited, I am using Montesinos's inclusion of the poem in the selection of his *Poesías líricas*, 2 vols. (Madrid: Espasa-Calpe,

1941), as a criterion. For all poems included by him I give either in the text or in a note the page of the 1941 edition on which the poem is found.

3. *OS*, XII, 274.

4. Prologue to *Rimas* (1602), *OS*, IV, 176.

5. "Los hallo capaces, no sólo de exprimir y declarar qualquier concepto con fácil dulzura, pero de proseguir toda grave acción de numeroso Poema" ("I find them capable not only of expressing any thought, and bringing it out smoothly and sweetly, but of sustaining the weighty action of any long-metered poem") (*ibid.*).

6. Quoted from *Arte poética española* [1592] (Barcelona: Martí, 1759), p. 60.

7. *Cisne de Apolo*, ed. A. Porqueras Mayo (Madrid: C.S.I.C., 1958), I, 213.

8. *Ibid.*

9. My references to the *Flores* (Selections) will be to the facsimiles included in *Fuentes.*

10. On the connections between literary morophilia and the games of Christians and Moors, see María Soledad Carrasco, *El moro de Granada en la literatura* (Madrid: Revista de Occidente, 1956).

11. In countless *romances moriscos* one might match the descriptions of the quadrilles masquerading as Moors that participated in the *juegos de cañas* (reed-spear games) with which Burgos celebrated the arrival of Anne of Austria when she stopped there in 1570 on her way to marry Philip II: "Fue la primera [quadrilla] . . . la del corregidor, vestida de marlotas de terciopelo encarnado, con muchas lauores de franjas de plata, y unos penachuelos de argentería en los campos de ellas y con albornozes de damasco blanco, con la mesma lauor de franjas, y argentería, y rapacejos de plata" ("The first [quadrille] . . . the Corregidor's, was costumed in Moorish robes of deep red velvet, containing much silver-fringed embroidery and little tufts of silver-work in the open spaces; and in burnooses of white damask with the same fringed and tufted silver-work and silver edging"). Even more elaborate are the costumes of the quadrilles participating in the masquerade that greeted Margaret of Austria in Madrid nearly thirty years later.(J. Alenda y Mira, *Relaciones de solemnidades y fiestas públicas de España* [Madrid: Sucesores de Rivadeneyra, 1903], pp. 77b and 132.)

12. *Estudios sobre Lope*, p. 139.

13. *Ibid.*, p. 142.

14. Ed. Montesinos, I, 51. I follow *Fuentes*, II [1591], fol. 20v. This and the next ballad also occur, in less satisfactory texts, in *Fuentes*, I [1589].

15. Ed. Montesinos, I, 53. I follow *Fuentes*, II, fol. 22r.

16. See W. L. Fichter, "Color Symbolism in Lope de Vega," *Romanic Review*, 18 (1927), 223 and 230.

17. Lope's authorship is considered likely by Montesinos, *Estudios sobre Lope*, p. 282. Text in *Romancero general*, ed. A. Durán, 2 vols. (Madrid: Atlas, 1945), I, 25b; taken from G. Pérez de Hita, *Guerras civiles de Granada* (1595)—see the edition of P. Blanchard-Demouge (Madrid: Bailly-Baillière, 1913), I, 42. Not found in the *Flores* of the *Fuentes* or the *Romancero general* of 1600.

18. Ed. Montesinos, I, 6. I have numbered the quatrains. The ballad likewise appears in *Fuentes*, I and II. I follow Montesinos's text, from the *Romancero general* of 1600, including his modernization of spelling and punctuation, since neither of the texts of the *Flores* is satisfactory. In the discussion of this and several ballads to follow, I have made use of material first presented in my "Role-Playing and the Sense of Illusion in Lope de Vega," *Hispanic Review*, 33 (1964), 307–308, 310–315.

19. This was one of Lope's most famous ballads, remembered repeatedly by him and frequently imitated by others, as Montesinos remarks ("Notas a la primera parte de *Flor de romances*," *Bulletin hispanique*, 54 [1952], 404). The turtledoves became, in fact, one of Lope's trademarks, as a remark in the preface to the *Rimas* of 1602 shows: "Las tórtolas y Troya no es justo que las culpe nadie por repetidas" ("There is no reason for anyone to criticize the recurrence of the turtledoves and Troy") (*OS*, IV, 168). However, in the case of the turtledove motif, unlike that of Troy, reiteration does not occur in the sonnets of the *Rimas* but in ballads of the *Flores* and the *Romancero general*. There is a curious allusion by Lope, also, in his epistle from Valencia to the President of the Council of the Indies, Don Fernando de Vega y Fonseca (who held this post from 1584 to 1590), thanking him for trying—unsuccessfully—to obtain Elena's family's pardon and a lifting of the sentence of exile:

No es éste aquel amor tirano injusto
que un tiempo de las blancas tortolillas
me daba tantos celos y disgustos,
que ya juzgo a conciencia desasillas
del nudo regalado en que se besan,
antes procuro al mesmo reducillas.
Que limpio y conyugal amor profesan,
cual es el que me tiene con mil hierros,
que en cuello y manos, y en los pies me pesan.

This is not that unjustly tyrannical love that at one time made me so put out and jealous of the little white turtledoves. Now I would consider it wrong to untie the tender little knot of their kisses: on the contrary I try to keep them at it. For they profess a pure conjugal love, like that which has weighted me down, neck, hands, and feet, with a thousand iron shackles.

(From *Estudios*, III, 405; I have altered the punctuation of the seventh line.) There are similar references in the correspondence with Liñán, *Estudios*, III, 442 and 455. The subject is burlesqued in a ballad questionably attributed to Góngora, "Entre arenas de la gorda" ("Amidst coarse sands"), *Fuentes*, VI, 164.

20. The composition exemplifies both kinds of ballad mentioned in this description by Luis Carballo: "There are other ballads in the midst of which one finds sets of rhyming lines called *endechas*, which are complaints and laments, with the ballad resuming after them. Others have these rhyming lines at the very end of the ballad and then they are called *deshechas*" (*Cisne de Apolo*, I, 215).

21. The final line ("tronco, punto, vides, árbol") is not an instance of the enumerative line repeated at regular intervals which Menéndez Pidal finds in the artistry of balladry from 1589 on (see *Romancero hispánico*, II, 154) but a more subtle case of recapitulation comprising the two previous quatrains. Cf. D. Alonso, "Versos correlativos y retórica tradicional," *Revista de filología española*, 28 (1944), 139–153.

22. Cf., for example, the handling of the motif of the doves in Sannazaro's *Arcadia* (ed. A. Mauro [Bari: Laterza, 1961], pp. 50–51), which was soon to become a model for Lope's similarly named pastoral novel:

> Oh quante volte e' mi ricorda che vedendo per i soli boschi gli affetuosi colombi con suave mormorio basciarsi, e poi andare desiderosi cercando lo amato nido, quasi da invidia vinto ne piansi, cotali parole dicendo: "Oh felici voi, ai quali senza suspetto alcuno di gelosia è concesso dormire e vegliare con secura pace! Lungo sia il vostro diletto, lunghi siano i vostri amori; acciò che io solo di dolore spettaculo possa a' viventi rimanere!"

> Oh how often in solitary woods I can remember seeing amorous doves kiss one another with soft cooings and then, filled with desire, fly in search of their beloved nest, while I, weeping at the sight as if overcome with envy, spoke words like these: "Oh happy ones, to whom it is given to pass sleeping and waking hours in secure peace with no suspicion of jealousy. Long may your rapture last, long may your love endure so that I alone may stand as a spectacle of suffering to the living."

(See also Sannazaro's eighth eclogue, p. 64, ll. 55 ff.) The same pathos marks the response to the spectacle of vines embracing elms (p. 51), which in Lope, on the other hand, does not evoke any affective response at all. The motif of the doves runs through Lope's *Belardo el furioso*, as a poetic or rhetorical figure for a display of sensual love, usually in a context of jealousy (Ac., V, 669a, 683a, 686b, 690a). That the ballad treatment is not far from Lope's mind is plain from a reference at the end (p. 699a), after the lovers are reconciled:

> Que ya no es tiempo de andar
> del Tajo en las orillas
> espantando tortolillas
> y dando risa al lugar.

> The time for going around on the banks of the Tagus frightening turtledoves and making a laughing-stock of yourself is past.

Cf. p. 130 above and note 13 to Chap. V.

23. For the convention, see, for example, Sannazaro, *Arcadia*, ed. Mauro, pp. 61–62:

> Subitamente dal destro lato mi vidi duo bianchi colombi venire, e con lieto volo appoggiarsi alla fronzuta quercia che di sovra mi stava, porgendosi in

breve spazio con affettuosi mormorii mille basci dolcissimi. Dai quali io, sí come da prospero augurio, prendendo speranza di futuro bene, cominciai con più saldo consiglio a colpare me stesso del folle proponimento che seguire voluto avea.

Suddenly I saw two white doves approach on the right and fly happily till they alighted on the leafy oak that spread out above me, offering each other in a brief span a thousand very sweet kisses in the midst of amorous cooings.
Taking from them, as from a favorable omen, hope for future happiness, I began with sounder judgment to blame myself for the foolish intention I had attempted to execute.

24. We likewise find the familiar conviction "envidia me la quitó" ("envy deprived me of it") carrying a new corollary: "y envidia os quita la vida" ("and envy will deprive you of life").

25. See Montesinos, "Para la historia de un romance de Lope ('Una estatua de Cupido')," *Estudios sobre Lope*, pp. 251–266.

26. I follow the text of *Fuentes*, II (*Flor de varios romances nuevos . . . de Pedro de Moncayo* [1591]), fol. 8v. For Lope's authorship of this ballad, see Montesinos, *Estudios sobre Lope*, p. 284. See the description of the *Flor* of Villalta in *Romancero general* (*1600, 1604, 1605*), ed. A. González Palencia (Madrid: C.S.I.C., 1947), I, xv; and in *Romancero general*, ed. Durán, II, 683. María Goyri de Menéndez Pidal, in "Los romances de Gazul," *Nueva revista de filología hispánica*, 7 (1953), 414, dates the ballad around 1583 and links it with "Marfisa," not Elena Osorio. This she does on the basis of four lines written in at the end of the ballad "Mirando estaba Lisardo" ("Lisardo was looking") in a copy of the *Romancero general* of 1604, in which the connection of "Sale la estrella" with Elena is denied. In the version of "Mirando estaba Lisardo" found in *Ramillete de flores* (Lisbon, 1593), these lines, with slight variants, form part of the text; see *Fuentes*, V, fol. 42r. They are probably by Lope (see Montesinos, "Algunas notas sobre el romancero *Ramillete de flores*," *Nueva revista de filología hispánica*, 6 [1952], 364), but what do they prove? Simply that Lope is in a sour mood here, wilfully destroying the poetic worlds created in other ballads (cf. p. 82 above). He is no more to be taken at his word than when he tells Filis in another ballad of the *Ramillete*, "Mil años ha que no canto" ("I haven't sung for a thousand years"): "Ha tres años y más / que aun a solas no te nombro" ("For over three years I haven't spoken your name even to myself") (fol. 8r; for Lope's likely authorship, see Montesinos, "Algunas notas," p. 361). In support of the relevance to Elena of "Sale la estrella de Venus," one may point to the evidence of ballads like "Pues ya desprecias el Tajo" ("Since you now scorn the Tagus"), where Filis is assured "que ya no aurá razones / de tórtolas ni de estrellas" ("there will be no more talk of turtledoves or stars") (*Ramillete*, fol. 6v; see Montesinos, "Algunas notas," p. 361, for Lope's probable authorship). The ill-humored author of "Toquen a priessa a rebato" ("Sound the alarm-bell in a hurry"), whoever he was, certainly linked Filis-Elena with "Sale la estrella de Venus": "No me canse más Velardo / con

su Filis y su estrella" ("Let me not be pestered any longer by Belardo with his Filis and his star"), he writes (*Fuentes*, IX, fol. 108r). Since M. G. de Menéndez Pidal produces no evidence of versions of "Sale la estrella de Venus" antedating 1588, her assertions about the ballad strike me as unfounded.

27. Examples: "Sale de Sydonia ayrado" (l. 7); "Desesperado camina" (l. 13); "¿cómo permites, cruel?" (l. 29); "Dexas tu amado Gazul, / dexas tres años de amores" (ll. 37–38); "dexas vn pobre muy rico" (l. 41).

28. That Lope is building on a traditional formula is evident from the fact that this example is also invoked by Juan de Robles in speaking of periphrasis in *Primera parte del culto sevillano* [1631] (Seville: El Mercantil Sevillano, 1883), p. 130: "Hácense bien poniendo en lugar del nombre de la cosa que quieren decir . . . [sus] cualidades, como: *la enemiga del día*, por *la noche*" ("A good way to effect one is to replace the thing meant . . . by [its] qualities, as: *the enemy of day* for *the night*"). A ballad on the death of Alvaro de Luna (*Romancero general*, ed. Durán, II, 60) begins:

Tocaba las oraciones
la campana del silencio,
y tiende la noche oscura
al mundo su negro manto.

The bell of silence was ringing for vespers and the dark night spreads out its black mantle.

In *El Marqués de las Navas* (ed. J. F. Montesinos [Madrid: Centro de Estudios Históricos, 1925], p. 74) an apostrophe to Night includes the lines:

Noche de estrellas vestida,
cuyo manto escuro y negro
más hurtos que tienes luzes
ha concertado y cubierto.

Night dressed in stars, you whose black, dark mantle has brought off and concealed more thefts than you have lights.

The dark (or blue and star-studded) mantle of night is a common feature of iconographical tradition.

29. The rhetorical figures include correlative constructions and the hyperbolic comparisons (más . . . que) in ll. 25–26 and 27–28; the remonstrations, begun in the first two lines and completed in the last two of each subsequent quatrain; iteration— the strongly affirmative *dexas* of ll. 37, 38, 41, with emphatic dactylic stress, the last leading into a *commutatio*: "dexas vn pobre muy rico / y vn rico muy pobre escoges," the antitheses of which are spelled out in the contrasting terms of the following two lines. Then comes a series of imprecations, with Zaida involved as *enemiga* at the outset (hostility becoming more sharply focused), and a chain of contrasting or complementary clauses following. Verbs accumulate, nearly one to a line. The

situations invoked become more and more specific and finally are cut through by the alternative, all-inclusive imprecations: "y en batalla de Christianos / de velle muerto te asombres" (ll. 65–66) or "y si le has de aborrecer / que largos años la [su mano] gozes" (ll. 69–72), the latter the "greatest curse" conceivable.

30. "Aspectos folklóricos y literarios de la fiesta de moros y cristianos en España," *PMLA*, 78 (1963), 479.

31. In his earliest surviving play, *Los hechos de Garcilaso de la Vega, y el moro Tarfe* (The Deeds of Garcilaso de la Vega and the Moor Tarfe), dating probably from the early 1580's, an actual challenge is delivered onstage in the reenactment of a famous episode from the siege of Granada. Another play on the same subject, *El cerco de Santa Fe* (The Siege of Santa Fe), shows several soldiers affixing written challenges on the walls of Granada. As to why Lope selects a western Andalusian locale for the ballad rather than a Granadine one, and names his protagonist Gazul, Miss Carrasco kindly reminds me that the town of Alcalá de los Gazules, near Medina Sidonia, along with the whole Jerez region, was famous for its horses, considered to be the finest in Spain, and for its horsemen, whose prowess is extolled, for example, in a letter describing certain *juegos de cañas* and festivities of 1571 (cited by Alenda y Mira, *Relaciones de solemnidades*, p. 83). The festivities included quadrilles dressed in Moorish style and accompanying pageantry. The name Gazul, Miss Carrasco notes, was originally applied to the members of a cavalry troop made up of Africans serving the Christians on this frontier ("los moros fronterizos" of l. 77 of the ballad, perhaps). By Lope's day it was thought to be a family name.

32. That the kind of dramaticity found in this ballad was not necessarily transferable to Lope's stage is shown by his unsuccessful attempt some ten years later to string this ballad out in the subplot of *El sol parado* (The Sun Stopped Still) (1596–1603: Morley and Bruerton). Within the narrative framework of the ballad the "offstage" dramatic effects existed in a free state; they could arise from accumulated momentum followed by sudden compression. In the play (Ac., IX, espec. 59–61), Lope ran into problems of timing; the vertiginous pace of the ride, for example, could not be reproduced on the stage. By padding, the ballad meter is changed to *quintillas* and its pace slowed down to a walk; the interlarded glosses drain away all liveliness. It was probably the popularity of the ballad that led Lope to include it line by line instead of rethinking the total action in stage terms.

33. Emendation from ed. Montesinos, I, 46, for *Fuentes*, III, fol. 153r: "tercera."

34. *Fuentes*, III, fol. 146v: "fundas."

35. *Fuentes*, III, fol. 147v: "pusible."

36. *Ibid.:* "quiere."

37. Emendation from ed. Montesinos, I, 49, for *Fuentes*, III, fol. 147v: "hable."

38. *Fuentes*, III, fol. 148r: "del."

39. Ed. Montesinos, I, 44 and 47. I follow, with indicated emendations, the texts in Felipe Mey, *Flor de varios romances nuevos. Tercera parte* [Valencia, 1593]: *Fuentes*, III, fols. 152r and 146v, respectively.

40. The rhetorical character of the ballad is recognized by Lope's contemporaries.

Carballo (*Cisne de Apolo* II, 153) uses quotations from it to exemplify the figure *concessio*. Ximénez Patón, *Mercurius Trimegistus* . . . (Baeza: Pedro de la Cuesta, 1621), exemplifies this figure and *confessio* (fols. 119v and 129v) by quoting passages from an adaptation or imitation of the ballad.

41. Ed. Montesinos, I, 27. Like "Sale la estrella de Venus," this ballad appears in the *Flor* of Villalta (imprimatur, 1588); see *Romancero general*, ed. A. González Palencia, I, xvi. I follow Montesinos's modernized text, I, 47, taken from the *Romancero general* of 1600. The text found in *Fuentes*, II, is defective.

42. The mythic possibilities in the natural symbolism of the motif linked it in antiquity to the story of Cupid and Psyche. An inherent ambiguity helps explain its hold since Aeschylus on the imagination of artists and moralists: the flame that consumes the moth could represent either rational love or sensual passion; the moth's union with the flame could mean either the soul's regeneration or its submersion in carnality.

43. From a phenomenological point of view and in a broad context, the expressive power of the imagery is explored by Gaston Bachelard in *La Flamme d'une chandelle* (Paris: Presses Universitaires de France, 1961), especially in chap. 2, "La solitude du rêveur de chandelle."

44. The restlessness and the fixation which characterize the moth's flight and Filis's emotion are conveyed in lyrical trochaic octosyllables that gradually give way to other octosyllables of mixed rhythmic patterns. In the first quatrain three trochees are rounded out by one mixed line; in the second two trochees by two mixed lines; in the third, one trochee by a stray dactyl and two mixed lines, which are then followed by six more—the first six lines of Filis's address to the moth. The mixed rhythm with its balanced accents—on the second and seventh syllables—is the closest metrical equivalent to the circling flight, which it either specifically describes—"quemándose los extremos / y cerca de arderse toda" (ll. 7–8)—or suggests through alliterative devices—"la boca con que la besas / y el gusto con que la gozas" (ll. 15–16). As the speech builds toward its climactic end, the dactylic rhythm, more forceful, breaks in repeatedly (ll. 24, 25, 28, 29). In the rest of the ballad, when the thought of suicide arises, restlessness is heightened by the choppiness of a trochee such as "mucha falta y poca sobra" (l. 38), in effective contrast with the soothing repetition of *s*'s, *o*'s, and *e*'s in the more balanced mixed rhythms that follow: "y sólo el sosiego es bueno / adonde el alma reposa" (ll. 39–40). The growing irony of the sequel is pinpointed by sharp new alliterations: "corto cuchillo" (l. 50); "toda turbada" (l. 51); "Pero primero . . . / puesto . . . / probar . . ." (ll. 53–55); "quiso . . . / que" (ll. 55–56); "pide un paño . . ." (l. 61). The "picóse el dedo" of the needle prick (l. 58) fits naturally into these alliterative series.

45. Ed. Montesinos, I, 8. It is made clear that the tree beneath which Filis appears is the one in which Belardo destroyed the nest, although the species is now oak, not poplar. The poem is also found in *Fuentes*, VIII (*Sexta Parte de Flor de romances nuevos* [1594]), fol. 14r.

46. "Hice a los desdenes guerra, / guerra desdenes me hacen; / maté a Belardo con

celos, / celos es bien que me maten" (ll. 17–20); "Dejadme, pasiones locas, / locas pasiones, dejadme" (ll. 29–30).

47. The difficulty of the admission is underscored by the harsh alliterative *k*'s of ll. 27–28.

48. Attribution is particularly problematical with ballads of the different Moorish cycles. If "Azarque indignado y fiero" ("Azarque, indignant and fierce") is Lope's, as Millé ("Apuntes," p. 368) and González Palencia affirm, it may exemplify a stage in which the reversal of roles is still only a hoped-for eventuality: "Verás trocadas las suertes, / yo quexoso [at your importunity] y tú oluidada" ("You'll see our roles reversed, I objecting and you forgotten") (*Fuentes*, I, fol. 4r). Similarly, in "Las riberas del Genil" ("The banks of the Genil"), which Millé (p. 369) considers possibly Lope's, Muza warns of the day when "estando yo libre / aficionada te vea / donde me enfaden tus glorias, / y me burle de tus penas" ("being free of love myself, I'll see you in love and be irritated by your joys and mock your sufferings") (*Fuentes*, XI, fol. 98v).

49. *Epistolario*, III, 282.

50. Attribution to Lope by Montesinos in *Estudios sobre Lope*, p. 228; text in *Fuentes*, IX, fol. 37r ("A gustos de amor . . .").

51. *Estudios*, III, p. 405.

52. "Llenos de lágrimas tristes" ("Full of sad tears"), ed. Montesinos, I, 35.

53. *Fuentes*, V [1593], fol. 6v. Millé ("Apuntes," p. 460), González Palencia, and Montesinos ("Algunas notas," p. 361) believe the ballad Lope's.

54. Of a piece with the most abusive *romances de desamor* are the *redondillas* "Filis, las desdichas mías" ("Filis, my misfortunes") (*Poesías líricas*, ed. Montesinos, II, 4). The pastoral covering is laid aside as Lope heaps scorn and sarcasm on Filis for the meanness of her revenge: "Mucho de cuerpos entiendes / poco de las almas sabes" ("You understand a great deal about bodies, you know little about souls"). Embracing even here the fantasy of her suffering for his sake, he taunts her: "Dirás que contenta estás, / pues yo sé que, aunque lo doras, / algunas lágrimas lloras / y algunos suspiros das" ("You'll say you're satisfied; well, I know that, although you cover it up, you weep some tears and heave some sighs").

55. These are the lines referred to in note 26 above.

IV. Thematic Trends in Sonnet Cycles

1. Walter Mönch, *Das Sonnett: Gestalt und Geschichte* (Heidelberg: F. H. Kerle, 1955), p. 47.

2. *Ibid.*, p. 103. It was Montesinos who originally pointed out Lope's view of the sonnet as the form in which the conceit could best crystallize. See *Estudios sobre Lope*, p. 136.

3. *Obras de Garci Lasso de la Vega con anotaciones de Fernando de Herrera* (Seville: Alonso de la Barrera, 1580), p. 67.

4. "Yo quise hablar en el Rey de Francia; mas no de suerte alabarle, que hiciese las armas de España ynferiores a las suyas; y si los que contradizen esto consideraran

el artificio con que alabé al Rey, y de su misma alabanza saqué la nuestra, por ventura encarecieran este pensamiento, que fue el que yo tube para escriuirlo" ("I wished to speak of the King of France, yet not praise him in such a way as to render the arms of Spain inferior to his; and if those who dispute this would consider the artifice with which I praised the King and derived praise of ourselves from actual praise of him, they might perhaps extol this thought, which was the one I had for writing it") (*Epistolario*, III, 24). Of the sonnet Cascales observes: "[Tiene] por alma de su poesía un concepto como la lírica, y no [comprende] acción, como la heroica" ("[It has] as soul of its poetry a thought, like the lyric, and it does not [include] action, like the heroic"). From *Cartas filológicas* [1634], ed. J. García Soriano (Madrid: Espasa-Calpe, 1954), III, 240.

5. *Arte poética española* [1592] (Barcelona: Martí, 1759), p. 95.

6. *Tablas poéticas* [1616] (Madrid: Sancha, 1779), p. 222.

7. Viz., "Sirve para ... todo aquello, que sirven los Epigramas Latinos," Rengifo, *Arte poética*, p. 95; González de Sepúlveda, writing to Cascales, is more explicit: "El soneto siempre es epigrama" ("The sonnet is always an epigram"), he states, adding that its properties, like those of the epigram, are brevity, wit (*agudeza*), and smoothness. (From an epistle dated 1625 included in Cascales, *Tablas poéticas*, p. 218.) Herrera, more sweepingly, makes the sonnet equivalent in scope to the ode and elegy as well (*Obras de Garci Lasso*, p. 66). Mönch (*Das Sonnett*, p. 35) sees in the structure of the sonnet an affinity with the Pindaric order of strophe, antistrophe, and epistrophe.

8. *Arte poética en romance castellano*, ed. R. de Balbín Lucas (Madrid: C.S.I.C., 1944), p. 65.

9. *Cisne de Apolo*, ed. A. Porqueras Mayo (Madrid: C.S.I.C., 1958), I, 244.

10. *Obras de Garci Lasso*, p. 67.

11. Rengifo, *Arte poética*, p. 95.

12. "Haviendo este género de Poema de ser de conceptos, que son imágenes de las cosas, tanto mejores serán quanto ellas mejores fueren; y haviendo de ser las palabras imitaciones de los conceptos, como Aristóteles dice, tanto más sonoras serán, quanto ellos fueren más sublimes" ("Since this kind of poem should be made of concepts, which are images of things, the better the images, the better the concepts will be, and since words should be imitations of concepts, as Aristotle says, the more sublime the concepts are, the more sonorous the words will be") (*OS*, IV, 174).

13. A comment in *La Dorotea* on a recited sonnet states: "Tú le acabaste felizmente; no como algunos, que comiençan el soneto y van baxando en estilo y pensamiento, hasta que no dizen nada" ("You concluded it successfully, not like some who begin the sonnet and then fall off in style and thought till they say nothing") (p. 245). The demonstration is given in reverse in the sonnet of the *Rimas humanas y divinas del licenciado Tomé de Burguillos* (Human and Divine Verse of the Licentiate Tomé de Burguillos) entitled "Descriue vn Monte sin qué, ni para qué" ("He describes a mountain for no reason whatsoever"), which concludes: "Y en este Monte, y líquida laguna, / para dezir verdad como hombre honrado, / iamás me sucedió cosa

ninguna" ("And on this mountain and liquid lagoon, to tell the truth as a man of honor, nothing ever happened to me"). Quoted from a facsimile of the original ed. [1634] (San Sebastián: Manul, 1935), fol. 5v.

14. Ed. J. de Entrambasaguas in *Estudios*, III, 437; the succeeding quotation is from p. 453.

15. *Obras poéticas*, p. 23. Suggestive brief reflections on this sonnet within the context of Lope's creativity, broadly viewed, may be found in Amado Alonso, "Vida y creación en la lírica de Lope" in *Materia y forma en poesía* (Madrid: Gredos, 1955), p. 143. For an excellent detailed discussion of the poetics of this sonnet, see E. George Erdman, Jr., "Lope de Vega's 'De Absalón,' a *laberinto* of *conceptos esparcidos,*" *Studies in Philology*, 65 (1968), 753–756.

16. Texts of the two sonnets from *Rimas* in *Obras poéticas*, pp. 26–28, with earlier variant readings supplied; of the *Arcadia* sonnet in *OS*, VI, 221, with variant readings from a MS begun in 1593 in Entrambasaguas, *Estudios*, III, 339. In one of the sonnets from the *Rimas*, "De hoy más las crespas sienes de olorosa / verbena y mirto coronarte puedes" ("Henceforth you may crown your curly brows with fragrant vervain and myrtle") Filis becomes Lucinda (Micaela de Luján), Lope's mistress in 1602. The Manzanares, apostrophized in classical fashion as a river-god, is congratulated on the mistress's having dipped her foot into his waters, changing his sands to pearls. The other *Rimas* sonnet, "Estos los sauces son y ésta la fuente" ("These are the willows and this the fountain"), records the anniversary of the first meeting and deplores her mutability (*mudanza*) in conceits which vary the usual pledge couched in *impossibilia* to make these an accomplished fact: "Este llano, / entonces monte le dejé sin duda" ("Surely I left this plain a mountain then"). In this case there were two successive substitutions: in adapting the sonnet to his play *La pastoral de Jacinta* (Jacinta's Pastoral), Lope makes Filis Albania; in the *Rimas*, Albania becomes simply "mi sol" ("my sun") and by implication, Lucinda. In the case of the third sonnet, "Merezca yo de tus graciosos ojos" ("May I merit from your gracious eyes"), the Filis of the 1593 version becomes Alcida in *La Arcadia*. There is again a pledge with *impossibilia*, but a more cynical note is noticeable. Tirse's response, in the final tercet, to the lady's pledge is to write her words in water and call on the wind as his witness. While the occurrence of Tirse as Lope's pastoral name, instead of Belardo, is unusual and could raise doubts regarding the personal relevance of the sonnet, the cynical tone taken in regard to woman's constancy as well as the name Filis in the original version would seem to bring the sonnet into the emotional orbit of Elena.

17. Texts in *Estudios*, III, 240–242.

18. Mention may be made of two other sonnets of the *Rimas*, nos. 47 and 115— "Retrato mío, mientras vivo ausente" ("My portrait, while I am away") and "Maestro mío, ved si ha sido engaño" ("My master, see whether there was an error") (*Obras poéticas*, pp. 50 and 91)—presumably allusive to a critical stage in the development of the triangle Lope-Elena-Perrenot de Granvela. While not outstanding artistically, they appear to reflect beneath an anecdotal tone genuine uncertainty on Lope's part about how Elena will respond to the advances of his rival. This is particularly

the case with Sonnet 47, in which we read: "Mi bien es de las Indias combatido; / decid si el alma consintió en mi daño; / que el alma no la compra mortal precio" ("My love is besieged by the Indies; say whether her soul assented to my wronging; for no mortal price can purchase the soul"). (Cf. p. 250 above.)

19. On the ruins motif there are some perceptive remarks in Oreste Macrí, *Fernando de Herrera* (Madrid: Gredos, 1959), pp. 413–414, and A. Cioranescu, *El barroco o el descubrimiento del drama* (La Laguna: Universidad de La Laguna, 1957), pp. 81–83; and a more extensive treatment in E. Orozco Díaz, *Temas del barroco en poesía y pintura* (Granada: Universidad de Granada, 1947), 119–176.

20. See above, pp. 143–147, 151.

21. *OS*, VI, 441.

22. *Estudios sobre Lope*, 141.

23. Ed. Montesinos, I, 25.

24. Ed. Montesinos, I, 153, with modernized spelling and punctuation. Montesinos suggests that the sonnet may have been written in Valencia not long after 1588. It was not included in the *Rimas* of 1602, possibly because Lope was already reserving it for the appropriate geographical context in *El peregrino en su patria*, *OS*, V, 143.

25. *Das Sonnett*, p. 33. Cf. Carballo: "En los seys postreros versos conviene estar toda la sustancia del soneto, y tener en sí algún concepto delicado, y que los ocho de antes vayan previniendo y haziendo la cama, a lo que en estos seys postreros se dize" ("All the pith of the sonnet should be in the last six lines, which should contain some subtle thought; the eight preceding should lead up to and set the stage for what is said in these last six") (*Cisne de Apolo*, I, 245).

26. The most complete study of Sannazaro's sonnet, one which brings the earlier studies up to date, is J. Fucilla, "Notes sur le sonnet 'Superbi colli,'" *Boletín de la Biblioteca Menéndez y Pelayo*, 31 (1955), 51–93.

27. *Obras poéticas*, p. 80, gives the version from the *Rimas* of 1602 and the variant readings of an earlier version from a copybook begun in 1593 (published by Entrambasaguas, *Estudios*, III, 346). I reproduce Blecua's modernized text in *Obras poéticas* of the *Rimas* versions of this and subsequent sonnets, citing variants as required by the analysis.

28. *Epistolario*, III, 241. Amezúa calls these words "so little true that he would take it upon himself to prove them false shortly afterward" (*Epistolario*, II, 373).

29. "REVOLVER. Es ir con chismerías de una parte a otra y causar enemistades y quistiones" ("*Revolver* means to go around spreading stories and causing hostilities and quarrels") (Covarrubias). The connecting thread between the earlier and later versions of the two lines is perhaps the idea of liquidity in "sangriento lago" ("bloody lake") and "revolvía." The latter, in turn, is as applicable to ideas or memories as to liquids.

30. *Obras poéticas*, p. 96 (version of *Rimas* of 1602). Blecua also supplies the version of *Belardo el furioso* (c. 1588) from Ac., V, 698b.

31. The revisions of 1602 show the usual tendency to remove the more obvious

allusions to personal history in order to give the poem broader scope; ll. 3–4, for example, originally read:

> por quien fui Paris cuando fue mi diosa
> y agora el rey que despreció y destierra;
> for whose sake I was Paris when she was my divinity and now am the king ·
> whom she scorned and banished;

and ll. 7–8:

> de la troyana reina vitoriosa
> renace el fuego y la pasada guerra.

The fire and concluded war over the victorious Trojan queen are reborn.

32. The best reading of the ballad is a text printed in Valencia and reprinted by Raymond Foulché-Delbosc ("Les romancerillos de la Bibliothèque Ambrosienne," *Revue hispanique*, 45 [1919], 543); it is also found in the so-called *Romancero de Barcelona* (reprinted in *Revue hispanique*, 29 [1913], 124). Montesinos (*Estudios sobre Lope*, p. 227) considers it most likely Lope's.

33. See above, p. 552.

34. *Obras poéticas*, p. 43 (version of the *Rimas* of 1602), with variants supplied from the earlier version, copied by 1593, published by Entrambasaguas, *Estudios*, III, 339.

35. *Obras poéticas*, p. 53. The sonnet also appears in "El ganso de oro" ("The Golden Goose") (1588 1595), Ac. N., I, 169a, with only minor variants.

36. Lope's confidence in natural life processes is evident even when he is extolling those of art: "Y para esto no hay que aguardar las perezosas medicinas del tiempo, que aunque naturaleza por sí sola curaría qualquiera herida, aplicándole remedios el arte, se templa el dolor, y se cura más presto" ("And one should not await the slow-moving medicines of time for this, for although nature by herself would heal any wound, if art applies cures to it, the pain is alleviated and it heals more quickly") (*La Arcadia*, OS, VI, 225).

37. The unity of mood is sustained by sure stylistic control and technical mastery. Skillfully placed anaphoras hold the sonnet together, building tension without disturbing the measured tempo. Monotony is avoided by subtle yet balanced variations in the anaphorical terms and by decreasing the intervals between them: "Entre aquestas colunas" (l. 1), "entre éstas" (l. 5), "entre aquestas ruinas" (l. 7), "entre éstas" (l. 9). Contrasts between past and present are quietly brought out by other devices of poetic rhetoric: antithesis in l. 2: "frías cenizas de la ardiente llama" ("cold ashes of the burning flames"); adverbial correlation in ll. 5 and 6: "otro tiempo ... y ya" ("once and now"); and again, with order inverted, in ll. 9 and 10: "ya ... y ahora" ("once ... and now"); finally, by placing correlative initial verbs in the first two lines of the final tercet: "busco ... y hallo" ("I seek ... and find"). Contemplation crystallizes briefly in moral reflection at the conclusion of each of the sonnet's segments:

"ejemplo de soberbias acabadas" ("an example of extinguished pride") (l. 4); "la fama / por memoria dejó medio abrasadas" ("fame left half burned as a remembrance") (ll. 7–8); "despojos de la muerte rigurosa" ("the spoils of relentless death") (l. 11).

38. *Obras poéticas*, p. 125.

39. *Obras poéticas*, p. 40.

40. The source of this conceit is not Petrarch's Sonnet 19, from which the motif of "Contemplando estaba Filis" derives, but Sonnet 141, "Come talhora al caldo tempo sòle."

41. An *Auto de la oveja perdida* is among the schoolboy productions discussed by J. García Soriano in *El teatro universitario y humanístico en España* (Toledo: R. Gómez, 1945), p. 39.

42. In the first of his "Two Notes on La Arcadia," *Hispanic Review*, 36 (1968), 110–123, Morby points out (p. 113) that "an announcement of 'Querido manso mio'" and "the nucleus of 'Silvio a una blanca corderilla suya'" are found together in certain *quintillas* (presumably antedating both) spoken by Cristalina, the Marfisa-figure of *Belardo el furioso* (Ac., V, 675a). In them it is a *manso* (bellwether), not a *corderilla* (little she-lamb), as in the first of the sonnets under discussion, which has fled the master's anger when he throws his crook at the creature. Noting that the Lope-figure is the injured party and the violence is on the lady's side, Morby suggests that this was perhaps really the case, the roles being reversed in the literary elaborations. Yet the fact that elsewhere the Lope-figure is repeatedly the violent one, both in the allusions to a slap in *La Dorotea* (see p. 276 above and note 12 to Chap. VIII; also Morby's "Persistence and Change in the Formation of *La Dorotea*," *Hispanic Review*, 18 [1950], 208–209) and in motifs of other ballads ("Un tronco de ovas vestido," "Una estatua de Cupido") gives some grounds for presuming that the violence originated with Lope.

43. A different view of the chronology and interrelationship of these sonnets is most skillfully presented by Fernando Lázaro Carreter in "Lope, pastor robado: Vida y arte en los sonetos de los mansos," *Estilo barroco y personalidad creadora* (Salamanca: Anaya, 1966), pp. 184–194.

44. Ed. Montesinos, p. 116; from *La Arcadia*, OS, VI, 180. The sonnet is totally unconnected with its context in the pastoral novel. The name Silvio is not listed in S. G. Morley, "The Pseudonyms and Literary Disguises of Lope de Vega," *University of California Publications in Modern Philology*, 33 (1951), 421–484, nor in J. M. de Cossío's *Lope, personaje de sus comedias* (Madrid: Real Academia Española, 1948). However, in *La Arcadia*, the character of this name, although not the reciter of the sonnet, is the closest friend, confidant, and adviser of the protagonist, Amphryso-Alba. (Cf. p. 151 above.) Lope uses the pseudonym Silvio for himself in the "Egloga panegírica al epigrama del serenísimo infante Carlos," which appeared in *La Vega del Parnaso* (1637); OS, IX, 118). A Silvio is the subject of Sonnet 57 of the *Rimas* of 1602 (*Obras poéticas*, p. 57), and a sonnet which appeared in 1630 with the *Laurel de Apolo* (OS, I, 386) deals with a Silvio and a Filis.

45. In the dedicatory epistle of the *Ternario espiritual*, addressed to the Archbishop

of Valencia, Juan de Ribera, Timoneda likens himself to an "ovejuela que ha pascido algún tanto por los amenos y sonorosos bosques d'la sacra scriptura y ha gustado la sabrosa sal distribuyda d'tan facundíssima mano" ("little sheep that has grazed awhile in the pleasant and echoing woods of Holy Scripture and has tasted the delicious salt distributed by so abounding a hand") (*Obras de Juan de Timoneda*, ed. E. Juliá Martínez [Madrid: Sociedad de Bibliófilos Españoles, 1948], II, xvi). In the *auto* itself, Christ (the *mayoral* Christóbal Pascual) urging the sheep to return, tells it: "Vente, vente, y dart'he sal" ("Come, come and I will give you salt") (*ibid.*, p. 31). The sacrament of confession is also clearly alluded to by the forgiving shepherd of Lope's *La buena guarda* (*Obras escogidas*, II, 438b):

> Si ellas lloran y les pesa
> (que no hay cosa más suave
> para mí que ver llorar
> porque el corazón me parten)
> luego les doy sal . . .

If they weep and are sorry (there is nothing sweeter for me than to see them weep because they melt my heart), then I give them salt.

46. Fernando Lázaro, "Lope, pastor robado," p. 183, refers to Covarrubias, whose remarks, s.v. *manso*, are themselves suggestive of close physical contact: "De los animales, aquellos se llaman mansos que se dexan tratar y palpar con la mano, la qual amansa aún a la bestia cerril, trayéndole la mano por el rostro, cuello y lomo" ("Those animals are called bellwethers [lit., tame] which let themselves be touched and felt by the hand; even a recalcitrant animal can be tamed by running the hand over the face, neck, and back").

47. While the secular pastoral offers no precedent, so far as I am aware, for the characteristically violent act of this sonnet, it does perhaps provide a precedent for the anger. The emotion appears in the much more conventional form of a shepherdess's *furor* toward a shepherd who courts her. In Montemayor's *La Diana* (ed. F. López Estrada [Madrid: Espasa-Calpe, 1946], p. 54), a shepherd's song invokes the analogy of the fleeing sheep:

> Si la ovejuela simple va huyendo
> de su pastor, colérico y ayrado,
> y con temor, acá y allá corriendo,
> a su pesar, se alexa del ganado,
> mas ya que no la siguen, conociendo
> que es más peligro averse assí alexado,
> balando buelve al hato temerosa,
> ¿será no recibille justa cosa?

If the simple little sheep flees its aroused, angry shepherd and, running about in fear, unwittingly strays from the flock, but being no longer pursued and recognizing that there is greater danger in having thus strayed, comes bleating back timidly to the fold, would it be right not to receive it?

The unconventionality of the act of Lope's Silvio stands out by contrast with the norm seen in this analogue, in which it is the lady who is angry (though not violent) while the lover is wholly submissive.

48. *Obras poéticas*, p. 136 (version of the *Rimas* of 1602), with variants (unimportant) from the version of *Belardo el furioso* (Ac., V, 697b). In the play the sonnet is a lyric récitatif unconnected with its context, included perhaps because it was rooted in the same experience as the play's action and shared its pastoral convention.

49. In Lope's "La oveja perdida," Lucifer strikes the sleeping sheep in the inn of Deception (*Engaño*), but it cannot awaken until Memory reminds it to call on the Shepherd. When it does so and Lucifer flees, the sheep asks itself: "¿Qué encanto ha sido éste, que hechizada / mi razón ha tenido y mi albedrío?" ("What charm has this been, that has kept my reason and will under a spell?") (Ac., II, 620b).

50. "Selvatiquez," a reminiscence of Garcilaso's "salvatiquez" (Sonnet 28), is called a "voz toscana" ("Tuscan word") by Herrera (*Obras de Garci Lasso*, p. 198), who cites Boccaccio's "selvatichezza" (viz., *Ameto*, XXIX, 59). Cf. Tasso, *Aminta*, I, 80: "rozza salvatichezza." The abrupt initial cadence of "¿Qué furia os hizo condición tan loca?" the unexpected spondaic stress of which disrupts the rhythmically smooth texture, occurs likewise in the second sonnet of the *Rimas sacras* (*Obras poéticas*, p. 317), where Lope is apostrophizing the aberrant steps of his youth:

¡Oh pasos esparcidos vanamente!
¿qué furia os incitó, que habéis seguido
la senda vil de la ignorante gente?

Oh steps vainly squandered, what madness impelled you to take the base path of the ignorant?

51. "Dueño" in Lope's religious verse may of course connote love as well as reverence, as in "Pues te confieso por mi amor y dueño" ("Since I acknowledge you as my love and master"), a line of the sonnet "Pastor que con tus silbos amorosos" ("Shepherd, who with your loving whistling") (*Obras poéticas*, p. 322).

52. *Obras poéticas*, p. 135, with variants from the version copied by 1593, published by Entrambasaguas, *Estudios*, III, 340. Morby ("Two Notes," p. 114) plausibly sees, in addition to the theme of the Good Shepherd, a specific source for "Suelta mi manso" in Nathan's parable of the ewe lamb (II Samuel, 12:1–6).

53. "Lope, pastor robado," pp. 195–200.

54. See note 52 to Chap. VII.

55. See *OS*, VI, 31, 36, 96.

56. Not published by Lope. The sole text is that of the copybook begun in 1593, where Lope is given as author. Published by Entrambasaguas in *Estudios*, III, 242; discussion, pp. 293–299.

57. Belardo expresses himself in similar terms in *Belardo el furioso* (Ac., V, 670a):

No en balde, sino forzoso,
los pastores de este prado
me llaman pastor dichoso,
de todos siempre envidiado
y de ninguno envidioso.

Not hollowly but obligatorily the shepherds of this field call me a blissful shepherd, always envied by all, envious of none.

58. *Estudios*, III, 299.

V. *Belardo el Furioso*

1. The Marfisa-figure of the play, Cristalina, her relations with Belardo, and her encounter with Jacinta, are of interest mainly for the light they shed on analogues in *La Dorotea* and accordingly will be considered at appropriate junctures later rather than in the present chapter. For the same reason, I shall postpone discussion of the motif of Jacinta's attempted suicide.

2. *Ac.*, V, 670b. Subsequent references are by page to this edition.

3. In the first scene between Belardo and Jacinta (pp. 669–670), before any conflict has arisen, one already encounters this self-conscious staging of an act taken half-seriously, half in jest—again, a ludic manifestation. Jacinta feigns jealousy of Cristalina, Belardo reassures her, she relents—"¿Tú no ves que me he burlado?" ("Can't you see that it was only in fun?")—he pretends to be offended—"De burlas me has de matar" ("In fun you'll be the death of me")—and reconciliation follows. It leaves Belardo uneasy, however:

Jacinta: Pues, ¿qué temes?
Belardo: Tu desdén.
Jacinta: ¿Fingido?
Belardo: Aunque lo haya sido.
Jacinta: ¿Estás loco?

Jacinta: What are you afraid of, then?   *Belardo:* Your disdain.   *Jacinta:* Put on?
Belardo: Even so.   *Jacinta:* Are you out of your mind?

The coming action is foreshadowed by this make-believe; insecurity is hinted at in Belardo. The scene in which Jacinta self-consciously plays Eurydice to cure Belardo is also anticipated. Lope makes a collaborative sense of play a constant factor in their relationship.

4. See note 185 to Chap. X.

5. *Obras escogidas*, I, 1005a.

6. *Epistolario*, III, 29–30.

7. Despite the stress on Belardo's poverty, he had alluded in Act I (p. 674a) to a bit of inherited property:

Esa cuitada haciendilla
que mis padres en la villa
me dejaron, venderé
y el interés te daré.

That wretched bit of property that my parents left me in the village, I'll sell
and give you the proceeds.

The inconsistency is perhaps due to the intrusion of a real datum. Cf. in *La Dorotea*:
"Nací de padres nobles en este lugar, a quien dexaron los suyos poca renta" ("I was
born in this city of noble parents, who were left with little income by theirs");
and "Murieron mis padres y vn solicitador de su hazienda cobró la que pudo y
passóse a las Indias, dexándome pobre" ("My parents died and someone claiming
their inheritance collected what he could of it and went off to the Indies, leaving me
poor") (pp. 294–295).

8. José María de Cossío in *Lope, personaje de sus comedias* (Madrid: Real Academia
Española, 1948), p. 28, observes regarding *Belardo el furioso*: "Throughout the play
there is a veritable obsession with accusing Jacinta of self-interest. This may well not
have been the only grounds for Elena's breaking away, but it seems that Lope saw no
other reason for the break, and this will no doubt influence the judgments he passes on
women."

9. Noël Salomon, in *Recherches sur le thème "paysan" dans la "comedia" au temps
de Lope de Vega* (Bordeaux: Institut d'Etudes Ibériques, 1965), pp. 295–297, traces
back the descriptions of agrarian abundance (pp. 671a, 679b) to Virgil, Eclogue II;
and to the Polyphemus and Galatea story in Theocritus, Idyll XI, and in Ovid,
Metamorphoses, XIII, 789–869.

10. See p. 412 above.

11. I have changed the punctuation of the sixth line quoted, which begins a new
figure. Its source, as the phrasing suggests, is an emblem showing a torch turned
upside down, which originates, according to Mario Praz (*Studies in Seventeenth
Century Imagery*, 2nd ed. [Rome: Edizioni di Storia e Letteratura, 1964], p. 92) in a
device of the *Heroica Symbola* of C. Paradin and D. G. Simeoni (Antwerp: Plantin,
1562) bearing the motto: "Qui me alit, me exstinguit" ("What nourishes me,
extinguishes me"). The emblem reappears frequently in subsequent collections: viz.,
Daniel Heinsius, *Quaeris quid sit Amor, quid amare*, which shows a Cupid holding the
upside-down torch, with the motto "Qui me nourrist, m'estaind" ("What nourishes
me, extinguishes me"). Cf. *Emblemata: Handbuch zur Sinnbildkunst des XVI und
XVII Jahrhunderts*, ed. A. Henkel and A. Schöne (Stuttgart: J. B. Metzler, 1967),
col. 1365.

12. The *exempla* are condensations of the more detailed items found together under
the heading "Bruta, aliaque animalia honorata sepulchris aut statuis" ("Beasts and
other animals honored with tombs or statues") in the *Theatrum poeticum et historicum
sive Officina Johannis Ravisii Textoris* (Basel: Bryling, 1552), col. 195: "Ceruus
Syluiae qui . . . rosis & tumulo ornari meruit" ("The stag of Sylvia which . . . was

held worthy of being adorned with roses and a sepulchral monument"); "Alexander equum habuit Bucephalum nomine ... Rex defuncto duxit exequias" ("Alexander had a horse called Bucephalus ... When it died the King conducted the exequies"); "Romae fuit Coruus qui omnibus matutinis evolans in rostra Tyberium ... nominatim ... salutabat. Quem quum poster nescio quis ira percitus occidisset, a populo factum aegre ferente, saxis obrutus est" ("At Rome there was a crow that flew to Tiberius's tribunal every morning ... and greeted him ... by name. When subsequently in some fit of anger he impulsively killed it, the grieving people built it a mound of stones").

13. The most suggestive of the other allusions to the turtledove motif noted earlier (note 22 to Chap. III), is Belardo's (p. 683a):

¡Como paloma, tú con Nemoroso!
¡Tú ingrata, tú cruel, en nuevo nido!
¡Tu pico muerde tierno y amoroso,
un extraño pastor de ayer venido!

You, like a dove, with Nemoroso! You cruel, ungrateful one, in a new nest! A strange shepherd who arrived just yesterday is clipping your beak tenderly and affectionately!

14. Belardo goes on for another octave in lines (p. 683) markedly reminiscent of the *imprecatio* of the ballad:

¡Séase rico cuanto Craso [*sic*] o Midas,
y fáltete con él contento y gusto;
siempre tengáis a cenas y comidas,
por ser él importuno, algún disgusto;
jamás te dé las galas que le pidas,
respóndate colérico y robusto,
dete más celos que requiebros diga,
tráigate a casa hijuelos de su amiga!

May he be as rich as Croesus or Midas and may you lack pleasure and satisfaction with him; at suppers and meals may you always have some falling-out because of his importunities; may he never give you the finery you ask for, may he answer you angrily and sternly, may he give you more jealousy than fond words, and may he bring his mistress's children into your house!

15. In his commentary on the *Symposium*, Ficino actually makes the four types of madness of the *Phaedrus* (265b)—the prophetic, initiatory, poetic, and erotic— successive means for raising the soul to Unity. See *Commentary on Plato's "Symposium"*: *The Text and a Translation*, ed. S. R. Jayne, University of Missouri Studies, vol. XIX, no. 1 (1944), pp. 115–116. Cf. also *La Dorotea*, p. 327.

16. See O. H. Green, *Spain and the Western Tradition* (Madison: University of Wisconsin Press, 1963), I, 114 and 153–155.

17. Judging by the title of Lope's lost "Muza furioso," listed in *El peregrino en su patria* in 1604, Orlando may also have inspired a play with a Moorish setting; if the similarity in titles is any guide, perhaps with an autobiographical basis as well. In *La hermosura de Angélica*, which Lope states he began on the Armada expedition, Roland's going mad with jealousy and rage is imitated in the episode of Carpanto's raving insanity on discovering that Belcoraida has returned Lisardo's love (Canto XVII).

18. In comparison Belardo seemed still in possession of his senses when he told Jacinta angrily in Act I (p. 674a), after repeating sarcastically the *impossibilia* with which she had pledged fidelity:

Si a las palabras que dieses
el cielo obligar pudieses,
mudarían fundamentos
sol, noche, norte, elementos,
leones, hombres, y meses.

If you were able to make heaven hold to the words you pledge, sun, night, north, elements, lions, men, and months would shift their foundations.

19. The delirious Orlando forthwith decides that he is dead and wandering in hell. Belardo, however, continues with an intricate play of conceits in which his heart— unlike Orlando's, "ya consumido" ("already burned up")—becomes a silkworm suffocated within its cocoon that produces an "ave como fénix" ("phoenix-like bird") which he directs Siralbo to find.

20. Similar reproaches follow (p. 689b):

Fuiste Craso [*sic*] a quien el oro
abrasó las venas frías:
fuiste aquella vil mujer
del infelice Anfiarao,
fuiste en efeto tu mismo ser.

You were Croesus whose cold veins were burned up by gold; you were the vile wife of that unfortunate Amphiaraus, in a word you were simply yourself.

21. Salomon, *Recherches*, p. 295.

22. I discuss the point in "The Case for an Early *Dorotea*: A Reexamination," *PMLA*, 71 (1956), 792–793.

VI. The Years Between

1. See above, pp. 224–225.

2. See *Estudios sobre Lope*, pp. 202–203, and my "The Case for an Early *Dorotea*: A Reexamination," *PMLA*, 71 (1956), 759–798. I would today modify certain details and add others on the basis of Morby's documentation. I still find plausible the hypothesis of an early version dating from the 1590's, however, and have incor-

porated certain sections of my earlier treatment of the question into the present discussion.

3. Cf. Morby, p. 432, n. 122 and my "Case for an Early *Dorotea*," p. 764, n. 21.

4. *Estudios sobre Lope*, p. 221. The tendency of the two sources to fuse in the *romancero artístico* (artistic balladry) and the difficulty of determining out of which experience given ballads arose in the beginning is expertly treated by Montesinos in his study of the ballad "En el más soberbio monte," *Estudios sobre Lope*, pp. 267–277.

5. Montesinos, *Estudios sobre Lope*, p. 75.

6. *La Arcadia, OS*, VI, xxx. I cite henceforth from this edition, by page number.

7. Cf., for example, the much milder tone of a similar unfavorable view of a rival (Diana's husband) near the beginning of Montemayor's novel:

> Sylvano respondió: Dízenme algunos que le va mal y no me espanto, porque, como sabes, Delio, su esposo, aunque es rico de los bienes de fortuna, no lo es de los de la naturaleza, que en esto de la disposición, ya ves quán mal le va, pues de otras cosas de que los pastores nos preciamos, como son tañer, cantar, luchar, jugar al cayado, baylar con las moças el domingo, parece que Delio no a nacido para más que mirallo. (*La Diana*, ed. F. López Estrada [Madrid: Espasa-Calpe, 1946], p. 30)

> Sylvano answered: "Some people tell me that she is unhappy and I am not surprised, because Delio, her husband, as you know, although rich in the endowments of fortune, is not so in those of nature; in the matter of natural ability you are aware of how badly off he is, since in those things that we shepherds pride ourselves upon, such as strumming, singing, wrestling, games with the crook, dancing with the girls on Sunday, Delio seems to have been born to be a mere onlooker."

Not only is Sylvano's tone more restrained, more in keeping with the pastoral temper; the rivalry itself is measured in terms of conventional pastoral attainments.

8. The Neo-Platonic framework is visible in a passage like the following: "Es Belisarda tan celestial retrato de su hacedor, tan única perfección de la idea de su artífice, tan gran testigo de su poder, tan alta obra de naturaleza, tan rara suspensión de nuestros mortales ojos, y tan levantado éxtasis de nuestras almas, que en llegando a contemplar el divino todo de sus milagrosas partes, vano sería mi cuydado, si presumiesse resistirme" ("Belisarda is so celestial a likeness of her Maker, so unique a realization of the idea of her artificer, so great a testimony to his power, so lofty a work of nature, such a rare attraction to our mortal eyes, and so supreme an ecstasy of our souls, that when it comes to contemplating the divine whole of her miraculous parts, my efforts would be in vain if I tried to restrain myself") (p. 338; similar passages on pp. 14–15 and 81). Yet these views do not inform the outlook of those who express them, as do the discussions of Montemayor's characters on, for example, the two Venuses (vicious and virtuous love), derived from Ficino's commentary on the

Symposium (*La Diana*, ed. López Estrada, pp. 195–201). Lope's characters embroider on commonplaces while Montemayor's explore their implications.

9. Cf. also:

Si al amor llaman unión
de voluntades conformes,
donde hay zelos tan disformes,
temor, furia y confusión,
y donde en fin no hay razón
que gobierne la cabeza,
¿qué unión hará la belleza
con la envidia y el deseo?

(p. 334)

If love is called a union of conforming wills, where there is such deformed jealousy, fear, rage, perplexity and·where, in short, there is no reason ruling the head, what union can there be of beauty with envy and desire?

J. Scudieri-Ruggieri in "Notas a la *Arcadia* de Lope de Vega," *Cuadernos hispano-americanos*, nos. 161–162 (May–June 1963), 596–598, also finds the Neo-Platonic reminiscences of Castiglione, Ficino, and León Hebreo marginal and ornamental. Symptomatic, one may add, is Cardenio's inconsistent *a posteriori* attempt, once he has refuted many Platonic assumptions, to link his arguments to championship of the higher of the two Venuses of the *Symposium*. Cardenio refers to "el [amor] que Frondoso contaba el otro día en la contienda de las dos Venus" ("the [love] that Frondoso was telling about the other day in the struggle between the two Venuses") (p. 330), but this must be an afterthought, since Lope has not in fact included such a discussion in the novel.

10. P. 325. Amphryso does not stop here: "...desatinado ya de todo punto, con espantables ojos y cabello revuelto, comenzó a decir muchas cosas de las que entre los más entendidos del Arcadia se tenían por secretas" ("...completely out of his mind, with terrifying eyes and disheveled hair, he began to utter many of the things that the most knowledgeable persons in Arcadia considered secret") (p. 327). He is finally subdued by being manacled with a sling and thrown to the ground.

11. *La novela pastoril española* (Madrid: Revista de Occidente, 1959), p. 133.

12. Other instances on pp. 14 and 340.

13. When Lope adapted *La Arcadia* to the stage, he inserted complications from the outset and imposed as a happy ending the wedding of Amphryso and Belisarda.

14. *La Diana*, ed. López Estrada, p. 7.

15. *Orígenes de la novela* (Buenos Aires: Espasa-Calpe Argentina, 1946), II, 198.

16. Critics have even found it possible to hold that *La Arcadia* is conceived to a great extent like a *comedia de enredo* (play of intrigue): cf. Avalle-Arce, *La novela pastoril*, p. 138, and Scudieri-Ruggieri, "Notas a la *Arcadia*," p. 580. In an unpublished doctoral thesis, "*La Arcadia* de Lope de Vega: génesis, estructura y originalidad"

(Brown University, 1966), p. 297, Rafael Osuna has noted how closely the opening scene of Book II, laid in an *aldea* (village), is modeled on the typical night scene at a grilled window in a *comedia*.

17. *La Diana*, ed. López Estrada, p. 170.

18. The intimate relation between Amphryso and Silvio is best brought out in their long conversation, pp. 224–228, familiar in tone and unconventionally realistic, for the pastoral, in its amatory content. On Silvio, see note 44 to Chap. IV.

19. Quoted, respectively, from *OS*, II, 409, and *Obras escogidas*, II, 1381.

20. *Estudios sobre Lope*, p. 168.

21. Despite the critique of Huizinga's *Homo Ludens* in the work of subsequent students of the subject, such as Roger Caillois and Emile Benviste, and its theoretical invalidation by Jacques Ehrmann, I still find Huizinga's the most apposite approach to a consideration of the play-element in Lope's work and outlook. It is my point of reference in what follows. For the dissent to Huizinga see J. Ehrmann, "*Homo Ludens* Revisited," *Yale French Studies*, no. 41 (1968), 31–57. In succeeding pages I have drawn on material first presented in my "Role-Playing and the Sense of Illusion in Lope de Vega," *Hispanic Review*, 32 (1964), especially pp. 312–318.

22. On Lope's personas in his plays, see J. M. de Cossío, *Lope, personaje de sus comedias* (Madrid: Real Academia Española, 1948); and S. G. Morley, " The Pseudonyms and Literary Disguises of Lope de Vega," *University of California Publications in Modern Philology*, 33 (1951), 421–484.

23. *OS*, XII, xxii. I do not know the origin of the quotation.

24. *Literatura dramática española* (Barcelona: Labor, 1930), p. 134.

25. A case in point is the description of the exequies of Queen Marguerite in a letter of 1611 (*Epistolario*, III, 64–65). After declaring:

No sé cómo escriua a Vex.ª la muerte lastimosa de vn ángel, que me falta ánimo verdaderamente para referírsela . . . El es el fin de las cossas humanas, y la vltima raya a que puede llegar quien ha nacido, por altamente que sea . . .

I cannot find words to describe to Your Excellency the sorrowful death of an angel—I really lack the heart to relate it to you . . . This is the ending of all things human and the last limit to be reached by anyone born, no matter how highly . . .

Lope finds it perfectly easy to continue:

La segunda parte deste suceso es más templada, porque, realmente, si la lástima no fuera tan grande y el sentimiento tan justo, las figuras que andan por Madrid . . . con el luto sobre las cabezas, mouiera a rissa a todos, como passara en Yngalaterra. Vnos parezen alfaquíes; otros frayles benitos.

The second part of this tale is more restrained because, really, if the pity were not so great and the sorrow not so justified, the figures now going about Madrid . . .

with mourning over their heads, would make everyone laugh, if this were happening in England. Some look like fakirs, other like Benedictine friars.

26. One notes that the list of Lope's lost plays includes one by this title; cf. Rennert and Castro, p. 482.

27. For associations with *La Dorotea* and the ballad, see above, pp. 551 ff. The imagery occurs earlier in the play on pp. 498b and 503a.

28. Amphryso says (p. 523b): "De celos, Silvio, es el postrero efeto / volver a un hombre loco" ("The final effect of jealousy, Silvio, is to drive a man crazy").

29. Vossler find numerous such instances in Lope (*Lope de Vega y su tiempo*, trans. R. de la Serna, 2nd ed. [Madrid: Revista de Occidente, 1940], pp. 251–254). Montesinos had earlier touched on the same point in "Algunas observaciones sobre la figura del donaire en el teatro de Lope de Vega" (1925); reprinted in *Estudios sobre Lope*, see p. 62. See also C. Bravo-Villasante, "La realidad de la ficción negada por el gracioso," *Revista de filología española*, 28 (1944), 264–268.

30. See Ac., IV, xl.

31. "Other traits of Ginés's character make practically certain the assumption that Lope depicted himself to some extent in this character. In the instability of this actor there is something of the Fernando of *La Dorotea*. And does it not sound like a re-collection, a feeling of his own, and a joke, that Lope provides the mime and poet Ginés with a fickle mistress who two-times him with another actor, arousing wild bursts of jealousy in him, after which he gradually calms down, forgives and takes up all over again with the faithless woman." (*Lope de Vega y su tiempo*, p. 277).

32. Ac., IV, 1.

33. The suggested presence of the heavenly spectators at Genisus's martyrdom (Ac., IV, 78)—they are left out by Rotrou, as indeed is the martyrdom itself—exemplifies the strong medieval undertow in the Spanish theater. This example may be added to those E. R. Curtius has traced back to John of Salisbury (*European Literature and the Latin Middle Ages*, trans. W. R. Trask [New York: Pantheon, 1953], pp. 139–142).

34. See above, pp. 605, 622.

35. See Rennert and Castro, pp. 249–250. Texts in *OS*, IX.

36. *OS*, XII, 422–423.

37. On the dating, see Rennert and Castro, p. 312. My references are to the fac-simile of the original edition [1634]: Madrid: Cámara Oficial del Libro, 1935. The Advertimiento from which I quote is found in the unnumbered introductory folios.

38. The stoic view appears elsewhere also, as in the sonnet beginning "Don Juan, no se le dar a vn hombre nada" ("Don Juan, for a man to be indifferent") (fol. 77r). The *Rimas divinas*, far fewer in number, occupy a separate section at the end of the volume (fols. 142–160). They are written largely in Lope's popular vein and not interrelated with the *Rimas humanas* as the human and the divine are in *Lo fingido verdadero*. As might be expected, the comic possibilities of a naive religiosity are exploited, a tendency also prominent in Lope's earlier *Los pastores de Belén* (The

Shepherds of Bethlehem). This is especially the case with several shepherds' dialogues, miniature nativity plays like those of Juan del Encina and Lucas Fernández. Essentially, however, the difference between Lope and Burguillos in this section is one of degree only. Poems and glosses written in celebration of a certain image of Christ crucified carry echoes of Lope's *Rimas sacras* (cf. the sonnet beginning "Dulze Pastor que nuestro valle pisa" ["Sweet Shepherd that walks our valley"] [fol. 152r]). Their humor may be judged by the following sample (fol. 155r):

De vuestros pies gloria es
ser Burguillos Cordouán.
Pero no os salgan despúes
de las mançanas de Adán
sabañones en los pies . . .

It is Burguillos's glory to be the leather for your feet. But see you don't develop chilblains on your feet from Adam's apples as a result . . .

Lope also includes a ballad, "A San Ermenegildo en los Premios de la Iusta a la santa Madre Teresa de Iesús" ("To St. Hermengild on the Occasion of the Prizes in the Tournament for the Holy Mother Teresa of Jesus"), written for contests celebrating Teresa's beatification in 1614, in which Lope participated as a judge. One detects here (fol. 156r) the manner of Burguillos *avant la lettre*:

Pinten, Príncipe de España,
otros famosos Poetas
vuestra hermosura en la cárcel . . .
Yo poeta adozenado,
sólo tomaré licencia,
para pintar los Verdugos . . .

Prince of Spain, let others paint your beauty in prison . . . I, run-of-the-mill poet, will only permit myself to paint the executioners . . .

He proceeds to do so in a lavishly grotesque manner. Here, as in the subsequent contests, the fact that Lope was an official must have led him to assume another identity in order to participate. Although the poem is now included among those of Burguillos, it seems unlikely that Lope used this pseudonym on its original appearance.

39. Cf. these lines from fol. 33v:

Ver tanto gato, negro, blanco, y pardo
en concurso gallardo
de dos colores, y de mil remiendos,
dando juntos maúllos estupendos,
¿a quién no diera gusto
por triste que estuuiera . . .?

To see so many black, white, and brown cats in elegant array, two-colored and
with a thousand patches, uttering stupendous meows all at the same time:
Who would not be cheered up by it, no matter how sad he might be . . .?

40. See above, p. 7.

41. Nevertheless Rafael Osuna has found that *La Arcadia* "in contrast to standard
works of the kind reflects a heightened sense of temporality" ("*La Arcadia* de Lope de
Vega," p. 300). A close study of temporal references shows that the action takes somewhat over a year (the twenty-third in the life of the protagonist) as against the
conventional week or so current in most earlier pastorals. But as Osuna brings out,
"the mere establishing of dates does not necessarily indicate a sense of time" (p. 302).
There is little sense of time experienced as a dimension of living and Amphryso's
cure, in particular, is accomplished in a single day.

42. Osuna (*ibid.*, p. 220) notes the medievalism, the Plinian natural history connections, and the links with specific emblematic themes in this section of *La
Arcadia*.

43. *Obras completas*, ed. E. de la Madre de Dios and O. del Niño Jesús (Madrid:
Biblioteca de Autores Cristianos, 1951), I, 874.

44. *Vida del pícaro Guzmán de Alfarache*, ed. S. Gili Gaya (Madrid: La Lectura,
1926), I, 88.

45. *Sonetos completos*, ed. B. Ciplijauskaite (Madrid: Castalia, 1969), p. 239.

46. *Emblemas morales* (Saragossa: Alonso Rodríguez [for] Juan de Bonilla, 1603–
1604), II, fol 17v.

47. *Obras completas*, ed. J. M. Blecua (Barcelona: Planeta, 1963), I (*Poesía original*), 4.

48. Before his fiftieth year Lope is already referring to himself as having reached
old age: "Yo salí a reciuir a Doña Juana, de quien ya la vegez me ha hecho galán"
("I went to meet Doña Juana, of whom old age has now made me an admirer");
"a quien dé Dios más vida que a mí; que bien se puede creher este encarezimiento,
tiniendo yo tantos años" ("to whom may God grant more life than to me: and one
may well believe this hyperbole, considering how old I am") (*Epistolario*, III, 26
[1610?] and 39 [1611?]).

49. *Epistolario*, III, 58.

50. *Ibid.*, p. 95.

51. Barcelona: Sebastián de Cormellas, 1626. They are published under the
pseudonym of the R. P. Graviel Padecopeo, Lope appearing as their translator from
Latin into Spanish. My references are to page number in *OS*, XVII.

52. Lope was received into the third order of St. Francis on September 26 of that
year and there are references to the *Soliloquios* in two letters of October: *Epistolario*,
III, 68 and 71. The *Cuatro Soliloquios* were published in Valladolid by Francisco
Abarca de Angulo.

53. That Lope should have added three more, making a total of seven, is perhaps
explained by a passing remark in a letter of 1616: "De Barcelona tube el sábado un
pliego con siete cartas, escritas como soliloquios por los días de la semana" ("From

Barcelona I had an envelope on Saturday with seven letters, written like soliloquies, one for each day of the week") (*Epistolario*, III, 252).

54. I thus interpret what Lope writes in the Prologue about the alleged author, Padecopeo: "Grandes pruebas hizo de su constante ánimo este soldado de Christo antes de tomar el hábito, viviendo por aquellas soledades algunos días, en los quales escribió estos *Soliloquios* a Dios con la ternura y lágrimas, que ellos manifiestan" ("Before taking the habit, this soldier of Christ put his steadfast spirit to great tests, living in that wilderness a number of days, during which time he wrote these *Soliloquies* addressed to God with the tenderness and the tears which they reveal") (*OS,* XVII, xx).

55. I return on pp. 206 ff. to the transferral of this need to the esthetic sphere in *La Dorotea.*

56. Viz.: "¡Qué ira me da conmigo! agradézcame el cuerpo que hablo con vos" ("What rage I feel at myself! Let my body be thankful that I am talking with you") (p. 10).

57. Viz.: "Ni sé cómo puedo alzar los ojos de la tierra, acordándome, que a cuantas cosas hice contra vos estábades vos presente, porque de vos nadie puede huir" ("Nor do I know how I can lift up my eyes from the ground when I recall that you witnessed all the things I did against you, because no one can flee from you") (p. 27).

58. In his Prologue, he remarks of a certain sinner condemned to Hell: "¿Quién duda que sus pecados no eran de aquellos, que con facilidad los conoce el dueño, y como el autor deste libro, los siente y llora, sino de aquellos que disfrazados con el propio engaño, no ven la luz . . .?" ("Who can doubt that his were not the kind of sins that the sinner easily recognizes and that the author of this book laments and weeps over, but rather the kind that are disguised in self-deception and do not see the light of day . . .?" (p. xvii).

59. "El mayor Sabio" ("The wisest man") is presumably Solomon. In its general drift the passage is reminiscent of the Book of Wisdom; the initial sentiment could likewise derive from Proverbs, also ascribed to Solomon. I have found no specific reference in either case. For the image of the ship's plank, cf.: "Therefore do men entrust their lives to even the slenderest timber, and passing through the surge of a raft are come safely through" (Book of Wisdom 14:5, in the translation of Joseph Reider [New York: Harper, 1957], p. 169, where note is taken of a similar image in Diogenes Laertius [I, 8, 193]). The Book of Wisdom, in the Latin version (*Liber Sapientiae*), like that of Job, seems to have been one of the favorite readings of Lope's later years and to underlie certain of his formulations of sentiments of *desengaño.* For other presumed or evident references, see notes 62 and 72 to this chapter, and note 24 to Chap. XI.

60. The reference is to Psalms 25:7: "Remember not the sins of my youth, nor my trangressions."

61. Considerations of chronology rule out the possibility that this passage refers to the death of Marta de Nevares, as Helmut Hatzfeld suggests in his stylistic analysis

of the *Soliloquios amorosos*, chap. 8 of his *Estudios sobre el barroco* (Madrid: Gredos, 1964).

62. The second sentence quoted seems to carry echoes of the Book of Wisdom: "For it was he that gave me an unerring knowledge of things that be, to know the ordering of the world and the working of the elements, the beginning and end and middle of times, the turn of the solstices and changes of seasons, the cycles of years and the positions of stars" (7:17–19 in the Reider translation).

63. "It is hard to believe that the dominant note in his nature was sadness, yet his own testimony could not be more explicit and forthright" (*Epistolario*, II, 266). A. Albarracín Teulón, *La medicina en el teatro de Lope de Vega* (Madrid: C.S.I.C., 1954), p. 122, notes that melancholy is the most frequently and minutely described of any affliction in Lope's theater and sees in this fact a "faithful reflection of an inner life saturated with sadnesses and griefs."

64. *OS*, I, 418.

65. Amezúa, *Epistolario*, II, 269, cites these lines from *La Quinta de Florencia*, Ac., XV, 363; Albarracín Teulón gives this and other Lopean examples of the distinction, *La medicina*, pp. 126–129. Cf. also a remark to the Duke of Sessa: "Ya me pessa de hauer escrito a Vex.ª de esta materia [death]: pues me dize que está triste sin causa, y que le pareze que estarlo previene algún futuro sucesso" ("Now I am sorry to have written Your Excellency about this subject [death] since you tell me you're sad for no reason and that you think being so augurs some future occurrence") (*Epistolario*, IV, 47).

66. He writes, for example, to the Duke of Sessa, c. 1616: "Duque mi Señor, mucho me ha enternecido este papel de Vex.ª si bien me ha consolado el decirme que no sabe de qué causa prozeden estas tristezas, porque la diferenzia dellas a la melancolía es que las vnas nazen de los sucessos, y las otras de la falta de la salud y de la ynfluencia del cielo; y más vale que los humores corran desconpuestos que no los acaecimientos de las cosas" ("Duke, my Lord, I have been distressed by this letter of yours, although I have found some consolation in your saying that you don't know what is causing this sadness, since the difference between it and melancholy is that the one arises from things that happen and the other from lack of health and the influence of heaven, and it is better to have humors go out of joint than the course of events") (*Epistolario*, III, 224).

67. It is striking to see how Lope, writing about 1619 to the Duke, diagnoses in the tone of a letter the latter has received from Padre Juan de Mariana "melancolías de hombre sabio: tristezas que he leýdo en algunas Epístolas del Jovio, en sus vltimos días, donde dize que hasta los sueños le dauan yndicios de la partida" ("the melancholy of a wise man: sadness that I have read of in certain Epistles of Giovio in his final days in which he says that even dreams gave him indications of his departure") (*Epistolario*, IV, 47).

68. "Felicio," *Obras escogidas*, II, 266b.

69. In *Saturn and Melancholy: Studies in the History of Natural Philosophy, Religion and Art* (London: Nelson, 1964), the authors, Raymond Klitansky, Erwin Panofsky,

and Fritz Saxl, observe (p. 233) that it is in Elizabethan England and the Spain of Cervantes and Tirso (they might have added Lope) that we first encounter the view of "poetic melancholy" as "an ideal conception, inherently pleasurable, however painful—a condition which, by the continually renewed tension between depression and exaltation, unhappiness and 'apartness,' horror of death and increased awareness of life, could impart a new vitality to drama, poetry, and art." The development of the notion of melancholy as a condition of intellectual and creative achievement is subsequently traced by them from its Greek roots, through Italian humanism—Petrarch, Ficino—to Dürer's great etching.

70. *Si no vieran las mugeres* (If Only Women Didn't See), Ac., XV, 165a; cf. Cossío, *Lope, personaje de sus comedias*, p. 72. Blecua takes account of the relevance of this passage in the introduction to his edition of *La Dorotea* (Madrid: Ediciones de la Universidad de Puerto Rico—Revista de Occidente, 1955), p. 26.

71. *Obras escogidas*, II, 254. Playing on the concept of "loco de atar"—the madman fit to be tied—Lope tells Claudio that he speaks as a "loco que . . . intenta desatarse de sí mismo" ("a madman who . . . is attempting to untie himself from himself"). Inverting the usual sense of the expression—tying as restraining—Lope suggests that being bound to the self is the real madness. Yet just as he subsequently proceeds to smile rather than weep over the past, so the poem will reveal the hold of the self quite as much as his detachment from it. These shifting formulas of the opening point in fact to the balance Lope has achieved between engagement and disengagement vis-à-vis the world.

72. *Obras escogidas*, II, 255. Cf. p. 531 above. Once again there seem to be echoes of the Book of Wisdom in Lope's imagery. Cf. 5: 10–11: "As a ship that passes through billowy water, of whose passage there is no trace to be found, nor the track of her keel in the waves. Or as a bird that flies through the air, of whose passage no token is found; but the light wind being whipped by the stroke of her pinions, and divided by the force of her rushing, was traversed as her wings moved, and thereafter no sign was found of her passing through it" (Reider ed., p. 93). The figure of the stationary navigator on the moving sea appears, more perfunctorily, in Quevedo: "Como el que, divertido, el mar navega, / y sin moverse, vuela con el viento, / y antes que piense en acercarse, llega" ("Like one who, inattentive, sails the sea and, without moving, flies before the wind and before even thinking of approaching, arrives") (*Obras completas*, ed. Blecua, I, 11).

73. See Rennert and Castro, pp. 191, 251–252.

74. The phrase "póstuma de mis musas" for *La Dorotea* in the "Egloga a Claudio" is perhaps to be understood not as a metonymy but as the same metaphor as in the epistle to Lemos: the work is not a muse but the daughter of one.

75. The summer alluded to is probably that of 1627. The *aprobación* of *La corona trágica* is dated August 2 of that year and it appeared in print, say Rennert and Castro (p. 281), toward the end of September. The spring during which Lope is writing—cf. *OS*, I, 260—would be that of 1628.

76. *OS*, I, 466. S. G. Morley first drew attention to this passage in his "Pseudonyms

and Literary Disguises of Lope de Vega," pp. 427–428. Montesinos (*Estudios sobre Lope*, p. 197, n. 171) is certain the author is not Lope, and also believes with Ricardo Palma that the Peruvian poetess did not exist and that the epistle "smacks of literary mystification."

77. See Morby, "Persistence and Change in the Formation of *La Dorotea*," *Hispanic Review* 18 (1950), 201–202.

78. In *Los pastores de Belén*, for example:

Es amor un irracional excesso del deseo, y no como Platón lo define, un deseo de la inmortalidad, que quando tan puramente se ama, no da el espíritu parte de sus pensamientos al cuerpo; antes bien desasido desta corteza bárbara, vuela por superiores ayres a la región más alta. (*OS*, XVI, 59)

Love is an irrational excess of desire and not, as defined by Plato, a desire for immortality, since, when one loves so purely, the spirit does not inform the body of its thoughts; rather, freed from this coarse shell, it flies through the upper air to the highest region.

79. Quoted by Rennert and Castro, p. 227.

80. See *Epistolario*, II, 334.

81. *Epistolario*, II, p. 417. Lope, for his part, claims that he purposely sought to attach himself to Marta in order to free himself from Lucía de Salcedo (see pp. 322–323 above and *Epistolario*, III, 265). From Amezúa's masterly and exhaustive analysis in *Epistolario*, II, of the relationship of Lope and Marta I have largely drawn what follows.

82. On the basis of the eclogue "Amarilis," Amezúa (*Epistolario*, II, 424) conjectures Lope had first met Marta in 1608.

83. *Epistolario*, II, 426.

84. See *Epistolario*, II, 506.

85. *Poesía española: Ensayo de métodos y límites estilísticos* (Madrid: Gredos, 1950), p. 487.

86. "Epístola a Don Francisco López de Aguilar." The corresponding passage in the explanation of the sonnet in the play (*Obras escogidas*, I, 1106b) is much more general in its phrasing:

La intención o el argumento
es pintar a quien ya llega,
libre del amor que ciega,
con luz del entendimiento
a la alta contemplación
de aquel puro amor sin fin
donde es fuego el serafín.

The intention or argument is to paint one who, free of the love that blinds, through the light of his understanding attains the lofty contemplation of that pure endless love where the seraphim is fire.

87. *Poesía española*, p. 493n.

88. The quotation is from sec. 211E.

89. Lope de Vega, *La Circe, poema*, literary commentary, historical introduction, and annotated edition by C. V. Aubrun and M. Muñoz Cortés (Paris: Centre de Recherches de l'Institut d'Etudes Hispaniques, 1962), p. xviii.

90. The emphasis at the outset on the eyes as the channel of love is probably derived from Ficino's commentary on the *Symposium* and linked to his theory of spirits as carriers of love from the beloved's heart to the lover's (Oratio VII, cap. 4). As P. O. Kristeller points out (*The Philosophy of Marsilio Ficino*, trans. Virginia Conant [New York: Columbia University Press, 1943], p. 287), Ficino is the first to develop this "physiological" view of love's origin into a system. It is clear from *La Dorotea* that Lope knew this chapter of the *Symposium* well. Cf. p. 427 above and my "Plato's *Symposium* and Ficino's Commentary in Lope de Vega's *Dorotea*," *Modern Language Notes*, 73 (1958), 511–512.

91. In *La Dorotea*, apropos of the madrigal penned by Don Bela, we shall have occasion to return to the ladder of love in another of the sonnets published with *La Circe*.

VII. History and Poetry in *La Dorotea*

1. While literary characters conscious of being such are not unknown to Spanish literature of the Golden Age—see J. E. Gillet, "The Autonomous Character in Spanish and European Literature," *Hispanic Review*, 24 (1956), 179–181—for them to apply literary precepts as a standard of judgment to actions presented as real occurrences is unusual and highly sophisticated. The comments of Don Quixote and Sancho Panza, in contrast, are based on the written story of their exploits.

2. Cascales remarks in 1617: "If the actual events occurred the way they should have in order to be verisimilar . . . they constitute an action meriting the name of Poetry" (*Tablas poéticas* [Madrid: Sancha, 1779], p. 26).

3. *Cervantes's Theory of the Novel* (Oxford: Oxford University Press, 1962), p. 198.

4. Cf. Roy Pascal, *Design and Truth in Autobiography* (London: Routledge and Kegan Paul, 1960), p. 17. This suggestive study has helped me in the formulation of the remarks that follow.

5. This point of view is given a thorough airing in López Pinciano's *Philosophía antigua poética*, one of the speakers even going so far as to assert "that meter is not only not necessary for poetry but wholly opposed to it" (ed. A. Carballo Picazo, 3 vols. [Madrid: C.S.I.C., 1953], I, 206). This view (offered not without a trace of irony) does not go unchallenged but it is still agreed that what poetry gains in enjoyment ("deleyte") through its meter, it loses *qua imitación*.

6. *Epistolario*, IV, 81.

7. References to the practice of confession in the correspondence with the Duke of Sessa often reveal accompanying tensions: "Si Vex.ª le quiere [Cabrera de Córdoba's *De historia*], auise y enuiarémossele; que no es grande, aunque es pesado, y quédome aquí, porque hoy he confesado lo que del autor he sentido, y me dieron penitencia,

con ser verdades" ("If Your Excellency wishes it, just say so and we will send it to you; for it's not large, although it's burdensome, and I'll stop at that because today I confessed what I thought of the author and was given penance, even though what I think is the truth") (*Epistolario*, III, 79 [1611]). "¡Ay de quien tanto tiempo ha que hizo Carnestolendas, y que, aunque no quiera, se ha de confesar y arrepentirse! Mas Dios lo mereze todo; que quien no fuera El, no pudiera venzer tales inposibles" ("What a pity to have had one's Mardi Gras so long ago and, whether one likes it or not, to have to make confession and repent. But nothing is too good for God: no one else would be able to prevail against such tremendous odds") (*Epistolario*, IV, 31 [1619?]). ("Todos [los días] es fuerza confessarme" ("Every [day] I must make confession") (*Epistolario*, IV, 127 [1628]).

8. *Memorial de la vida cristiana* (Madrid: Hernando, 1925), p. 216a.

9. *The Spiritual Exercises of St. Ignatius Loyola*, ed. Joseph Rickaby, S.J. (London: Burnes and Oates, 1915), p. 33. The following quotation is from p. 52.

10. Introduction to the *comedia* version of *La Arcadia, Obras escogidas*, III, 493a.

11. For the distinction between recall and recollection, see M. L. Hunter, *Memory*, rev. ed. (London: Penguin Books, 1964), p. 27.

12. A contemporary of Lope, Garcilaso de la Vega el Inca, who had more reason than most to take note of this proclivity, observes: "La memoria guarda mejor lo que vio en su niñez que lo que passa en su edad mayor" ("Memory retains better what it saw in childhood than what happens in maturity"). (*Comentarios reales de los Incas* in *Obras completas*, III, ed. C. Sáenz de Santa María [Madrid: Atlas, 1960], 366.)

13. Hunter, *Memory*, p. 227.

14. For another example of this phenomenon, see note 83 below.

15. On this subject, see Hunter, *Memory*, p. 193.

16. See the examples above, pp. 240–243, 246.

17. One may recall Robortello's comment that the poet, as against the historian, "actionem mutat, auget, minuit, exornat, amplificat" ("modifies, augments, reduces, ornaments, enlarges upon the action"), *In Librum Aristotelis de Arte Poetica Explicationes* (Florence: In Officina Laurentii Torrentini, 1548), p. 90.

18. See my "The Case for an Early *Dorotea*: A Reexamination," *PMLA*, 71 (1956), 771.

19. The few references to the *comedia* amidst the lengthy discussion of the poetic *métier* in IV, 2—allusions to the inquiry (*escrutinio*) of 1599 (pp. 328–330)—and a handful of other references place on the characters' lips special concerns of the author's maturity; they have no bearing on the world in which the work is set.

20. On the derogatory meaning of "lindo" see Morby's n. 20, p. 70. Morby points out affinities with the colorful dress of soldiers, including Lope's own garb in 1588.

21. Cf. the detail of the "wretched bit of property" in *Belardo el furioso*, note 7 to Chap. V, above.

22. Nevertheless, there are three curious allusions (pp. 152, 302, 303) to pressures on Dorotea by "deudos" (relatives), quoted above, pp. 275, 277, 496. Possibly the

relatives had figured in the work at an earlier stage and Lope had neglected to eliminate these allusions, which point toward the butts of the satirical poems and the starving relatives of *Belardo el furioso*.

23. Fernando adds: "con más oro que el que te han traído" ("with more gold than was brought to you"). He may be thinking of the "señora deuda mía, rica y liberal, que tuuo gusto de favorecerme" ("lady, a relative of mine, rich and generous, who was kind enough to help me out"), of whose fifteen-year-old daughter and seventeen-year-old niece (Marfisa) he says: "Con qualquiera de las dos pudiera estar casado, pero guardáuame mi desdicha para diferente fortuna" ("I might have been married to either one, but my hard luck had a different fate in store for me") (p. 295).

24. Morby, p. 124, sums up evidence that the husbands of Micaela de Luján and Marta de Nevares, as well as of Elena Osorio, are alluded to.

25. Cf. the previously cited remark: "No es esta novela libro de pastores sino que han de comer y cenar todas las veces que se ofreciere ocasión" ("This story is not a shepherd-book; rather they are going to have dinner and supper whenever the occasion arises"), "La prudente venganza" (*OS*, VIII, 123). Morby cites this and similar statements from *comedias*, p. 186, n. 136.

26. Remarks like "Amarilis dize que con queso y rábanos y Duque de Sesa no a menester más para tener salud y vida, como sobre escrito de carta" ("Amarilis says that with cheese and radishes and the Duke of Sessa she needs nothing further in order to enjoy health and life, as they say in the address of letters") (*Epistolario*, IV, 139) connect the formal with the familiar, the elevated with the everyday, as does the dialogue of the *acción en prosa*. The effect is characteristic of the correspondence; one might cite many passages like the following: "Ya tengo la comedia del *Hermoso peligro*. Podrá Vex.ª venir a oyrla al anochezer, porque ya son las noches breues, y dice Antoñica que cenará Vex.ª con ellas guebos frescos de sus gallinas y vnos espárragos" ("I now have the play, *The Lovely Danger*, done. Your Excellency can come and listen to it this evening, because the nights are short now, and Antoñica says that these evenings Your Excellency will get fresh eggs from her hens and some asparagus for supper") (*Epistolario*, IV, 14). Of the *comedia*, on the other hand, Ricardo del Arco observes: "One was supposed to shy away from the daily routine," adding that the movement of the plot required the hero to be shown away from home and that even at home "he stands out amidst the small circle of flattering servants as he does amidst surrounding friends in the street, the gathering places, the theater and other places of amusement" (*La sociedad española en las obras dramáticas de Lope de Vega* [Madrid: Escelicer, 1941], p. 627). Montesinos had already pointed out: "In the Spanish theater, family life is scarcely suggested. The hero lives away from home and even when he is home, the pull of life outside is so strong that we almost never see him in an intimate circle" ("Algunas observaciones sobre la figura del donaire en el teatro de Lope," *Estudios sobre Lope*, p. 24).

27. Cf. Arco, *La sociedad española*, p. 636b, who cites *La Villana de Getafe* (The Village Girl of Getafe), Ac. N., X, 383b.

28. Dorotea's sentiments reflect Lope's: "De toda la crueldad del mal ninguna

hallo mayor que comer pollos" ("The meanest thing about this mean illness is having to eat chicken") (*Epistolario*, III, 58).

29. *Tragicomedia de Calixto y Melibea*, ed. M. Criado de Val and G. D. Trotter (Madrid: C.S.I.C., 1958), pp. 177 and 167.

30. In Lope's plays, we at most find the lady's maid doing needlework along with her mistress; cf. Arco, *La sociedad española*, p. 592.

31. Roldán is alluded to again, p. 429; Morby notes a reference of Lope to his own pet household dogs, Lobillo and Clavellina, *Epistolario*, IV, 141.

32. See Arco, *La sociedad española*, pp. 593–596 and 618–623.

33. As regards Bernarda and "la negra," Lope is uncharacteristically imprecise, for though he usually distinguishes between them—viz., "Le han visto Bernarda y la negra baxar reboçado por nuestra calle" ("Bernarda and the black girl have seen him come down our street muffled in his cloak") (p. 266)—once he seems to make them the same person: "Dame de comer, Bernarda . . . ¿Qué haze essa negra? ¿Por qué no sale de la cozina?" ("Give me something to eat, Bernarda . . . What is that black girl up to? Why doesn't she come out of the kitchen?") (p. 125).

34. Cf. "Y cuando las otras digan que hacen vainicas, si la preguntaren qué hace, diga que *comentarios, notas y escolios*, y sean a *Plinio*, si fuere posible" ("And when the other women say they are making open-work trimmings, if she is asked what she is making, she should say *commentaries, notes, and scholia*, and they should be on *Pliny* if at all possible"). Quevedo, "La culta latiniparla," *Obras completas*, ed. F. Buendía (Madrid: Aguilar, 1961), I, 374.

35. *Tragicomedia de Calixto y Melibea*, ed. Criado de Val and Trotter, p. 202.

36. The foreshadowing of Gerarda's death takes another form; cf. p. 563 above.

37. Even Fernando, after initiating his theatrical deception of Marfisa, gives thought to the practical arrangements for his flight to Seville (p. 117):

Fer.: ¿Quedaron las mulas a punto?
Iul.: Con sus maletas y cogines.
Fer.: ¿Qué pusiste en la mía?
Iul.: Vn vestido negro y alguna ropa blanca en vna manga verde que me prestó Ludouico.

Fer.: Have the mules been gotten ready? *Jul.:* The traveling-bags and cushions are already on them. *Fer.:* What did you put in my bag? *Jul.:* A black suit and some linen in a green portmanteau that Ludovico lent me.

Lope not only sees fit to mention this change of clothes and borrowed bag; for greater vividness he even notes their colors.

38. Marfisa and Clara, for example, resume their confidential exchange when they leave Dorotea and Celia in II, 3 (p. 151):

Cla.: ¡Qué bueno estaua Don Fernando!
Mar.: Tal es el pintor que le hizo. ¡Quién pudiera tomársele!
Cla.: Perdida queda. ¡Qué discreta has andado!

Mar.: Pocas vezes lo suelen ser los zelos.

Cla.: What a good picture that was of Don Fernando! *Mar.:* Just what you'd expect from such a painter. Oh, to have gotten it away from her! *Cla.:* She's completely done in. How cleverly you behaved! *Mar.:* Jealousy isn't usually very clever.

The only nonrealistic stage convention retained is the assumption that only the audience, and not the other characters, overhear them.

39. Cf. Julio's "Gente viene al Prado. Mejor es que nos vamos juntos, que en nuestra casa podéis hablar sin que os juzguen, y aueriguar estas quexas sin testigos" ("The Prado is beginning to fill up. We'd do better to go off together. At our house you can talk without being talked about and sort out your grievances without witnesses") (p. 316). Cf. also Julio's remark on arriving alone at the literary academy: "[Don Fernando] queda en casa en vna ocupación notable" ("[Don Fernando] stayed home on important business") (p. 337).

40. *Obras escogidas*, II, 888b. While Lope keeps the internal time of the work as close as possible to the reader's time-perception, these times are of course proportional rather than identical and we are aware of no inconsistency on learning that in the brief interval between Fernando's exit (end, I, 5, p. 113), and his re-entrance (p. 115), he and Julio have sought out Ludovico and begun preparations for the journey.

41. Mrs. Malkiel, discussing the treatment of time in *La Dorotea*, takes a different view: "As soon as one begins to examine the *acción en prosa* one is struck by the frequency of scenes unconnected in content and location which are conceived as simultaneous" (*La originalidad artística de "La Celestina"* [Buenos Aires: Eudeba, 1962], p. 195). She would appear, on this occasion, to have misread the evidence; by way of supplementing the presentation to follow, certain instances are here considered. Mrs. Malkiel does not sufficiently credit Lope's pains on the one hand to define realistically the spatial limits of each scene and on the other to account for his characters' movements from place to place when they are not before us. If Dorotea leaves her home at the end of I, 3, and reaches Fernando's at the beginning of I, 5, stumbling as she leaves and as she arrives, and later relates, "Toda fui lágrimas hasta tu casa, tan desatinada y ciega, que entre quantas cosas imaginé, ninguna fue tu ausencia ... Pensaua por el camino que hallaría consuelo en tu sentimiento" ("I went to your house all in tears, so dazed and blind that the last thing that crossed my mind was that you would desert me ... I thought as I walked along that I would find consolation in your distress") (p. 264), how can it be maintained that he thought of the intervening scene, between Fernando and Julio, at the end of which her steps are heard approaching, as simultaneous with those preceding her departure? In stating that scenes 1 and 3 of Act II are simultaneous, Mrs. Malkiel overlooks the fact that scene 2 (linked in unbroken sequence with scene 3) occurs in the afternoon and scene 1 in the morning. In Act III I fail to understand how she can call scene 5 (Don Bela and Laurencio before Dorotea's windows), scene 6 (Felipa and Dorotea inside), and scenes 7 and 8 (Fernando

and Julio before the windows) simultaneous. It is made clear that Don Bela has left (p. 263) when scene 6 begins, that Fernando has just arrived when scene 6 ends (p. 266). Why assume the conversation of scene 7 to be simultaneous with that of scene 6 when Lope so clearly wishes to suggest it is subsequent? The supposed simultaneity of scene 1 with scenes 2 and 3 of Act IV similarly does not stand up to analysis. Her statement that "the times at which César expounds the horoscope (V, 8), Dorotea arises in a good mood (V, 9), Gerarda performs her devotions (V, 10), and Don Bela goes down to the patio to be killed (V, 11) are all the same" confuses the time at which something occurred—Gerarda's devotions, Bela's death, both earlier that morning—with the time at which it is reported (scenes 10 and 11). It also makes scenes 8 and 9 simultaneous, although there is no compelling reason for so doing. Rather than a "marked impression of a flexible and multiple setting" (p. 161), *La Dorotea* suggests to me, as already noted, a limited number of fixed settings. Lope shifts from one to another as a director might today use lighting to focus successively on different areas of a single composite set representing, say, a whole city, yet leave the outlines of the remaining parts of the set barely perceptible through the darkness, so that we may feel them contained in the same temporal-spatial continuum.

42. See my "Case for an Early *Dorotea*," 779.

43. The timing is established by Fernando's placing the reconciliation on "vna mañana del abril passado" ("one morning last April") (p. 405) as well as by Julio's placing it pointedly "en el Prado y por abril" ("in April on the Prado") (p. 316). Julio mentions a few days after their arrival that they had left three months before (p. 236).

44. The lapse of time is suggested in the following remarks. Marfisa tells Fernando in Act IV: "Ocho días ha que estás en Madrid" ("You've been in Madrid a whole week") (p. 379). Ludovico says in III, 4: "Vltimamente, yo fui a visitarla ocho días antes que vos viniéssedes (que por estar en Illescas a vna nouena, hasta oy no os he visto)" ("Latterly I went to visit her a week before you arrived [I've not seen you till today because I've been at a novena in Illescas]") (p. 239). And Dorotea remarks to Marfisa in the Prado that Don Bela "está herido, aunque ya sin peligro" ("is wounded although no longer dangerously.") (p. 291).

45. *Lope, personaje de sus comedias* (Madrid: Real Academia Española, 1948), p. 31.

46. The opening of Dorotea's letter to him (p. 264) implies that he had been with her, and Clara tells Marfisa (p. 113) that she heard Fernando come in at four in the morning.

47. Gerarda tells Don Bela, as she is leaving, "A la tarde podrás ver a Dorotea, que ya está leuantada" ("This afternoon you'll be able to see Dorotea, who is now able to be up"), and Don Bela promises to be at her door at three (p. 137). In scene 2, Dorotea remarks of her mirror: "Ni esta mañana ni aora me ha engañado" ("Neither this morning nor now has it deceived me") (p. 139). Gerarda also makes it plain when she comes in (scene 4) that she has drunk wine copiously at lunch from the silver tankard given her by Don Bela the same morning (p. 158).

48. As the following exchange (p. 289) shows:

Mar.: ¡Qué solo está el Prado!
Cla.: ¿Cómo no quieres que lo esté si apenas lo acompaña el día?

Mar.: How alone the Prado is!   *Cla.:* What do you expect if it's hardly even accompanied by daylight?

49. On this subject, see Montesinos, *Estudios sobre Lope*, p. 77.

50. "Primavera, un género de velo o toca o tela de seda, a quien dieron este nombre por estar esparcido de flores" ("Springtime, a material for veils, headdresses, or silk cloth, which has been given this name because it is strewn with flowers"). Covarrubias, s.v. *primavera.*

51. Fernando himself observes: "Aunque me visto bien, no querría que fuesse con nota" ("Although I dress well, I would not wish to be thought ostentatious") (p. 413). His dress and appearance are described or suggested in general terms which make him typical of the "lindo" ("dandy") (p. 69) or the "pretendiente" ("suitor") (p. 299) or "galán tierno" ("soft-hearted lover") (p. 423). Lope does not particularize his appearance through distinctive features or bring him visually before the reader. The closest he comes is in a brief exchange over his portrait (p. 150):

Mar.: ¡Buena cara!
Dor.: No es lindo, pero todo junto es gentil hombre.

Mar.: A good-looking face!   *Dor.:* He's not handsome but all in all he's an attractive man.

52. Fernando Lázaro has adroitly noted the consistency of Dorotea's "escapulario azul sobre el hábito blanco" ("blue scapular on the white habit") with the "collarejo azul" ("blue collar") of the sonnet "Vireno, aquel mi manso regalado," seeing the latter as its bucolic equivalent ("Lope, pastor robado: Vida y arte en los sonetos de los mansos," *Estilo barroco y personalidad creadora* [Salamanca: Anaya, 1966], p. 180).

53. Morby (n. 191) notes Calepin's discussion of Virgil's (misquoted) "Dant sonitum rauci per saxa silentia cycni" ("Hoarse swans make sounds among the silent rocks"). (Cf. p. 511 above and note 165 to Chap. X.) Despite his capacity for drawing poetry out of familiar things, Lope could evidently see no poetic possibilities, save burlesque ones, in the sounds enumerated by César. His imagination was still bound by notions of propriety in the substance and diction of poetry. It would require the esthetic freedom assumed by the Romantics to discover the poetry of an ox-cart, as in Victor Hugo's famous line: "Les grands chars gémissants qui reviennent le soir" ("The great groaning carts that come back at evening"); or Juan Ramón Jiménez's "¡Cómo lloran las carretas / camino de Pueblo Nuevo!" ("How the carts are weeping on the way to Pueblo Nuevo!").

54. *"La Dorotea" di Lope de Vega, studio critico seguito dalla traduzione delle parti principali dell'opera* (Bari: Laterza, 1940), p. 37.

55. See the description of Marta quoted from the dedication to *La viuda valenciana* in Rennert and Castro, p. 227, and their remarks, p. 32, n. 3 (from which my citation

is taken), and p. 509. For Morby's reference to Propertius's Cynthia, see *La Dorotea*, p. 27. As I indicate in note 120 to Chap. X, the phrase in which Ludovico describes Dorotea's complexion—rose petals on *naterones cándidos* (milk-white curds) (p. 238)—originates in one of the Propertian passages (II, 3, 9–22) in which Cynthia's attractions are enumerated.

56. See Lope de Vega, *El sembrar en buena tierra*, ed. W. L. Fichter (New York: Modern Language Association, 1944), p. 21, n. 2.

57. Quoted from *OS*, V, 122, in Morby, "Persistence and Change in the Formation of *La Dorotea*," *Hispanic Review*, 18 (1950), 121.

58. *"La Dorotea" di Lope de Vega*, p. 40.

59. Ed. *La Dorotea* (Madrid: Ediciones de la Universidad de Puerto Rico—Revista de Occidente, 1955), p. 42.

60. Roy Pascal, *Design and Truth*, pp. 70 and 176.

61. See Maxime Chevalier, *L'Arioste en Espagne (1530–1650): Recherches sur l'influence du "Roland Furieux"* (Bordeaux: Institut d'Etudes Ibériques, 1966), p. 413. Carmen Bravo-Villasante, *La mujer vestida de hombre en el teatro español (Siglos XVI–XVII)* (Madrid: Revista de Occidente, 1955), p. 65, remarks: "No doubt Lope had no love for these pathological viragos whom Ariosto so admired, and preferred to reproduce a type of woman in love modeled on Bradamante or Herminia. Despite his preference, it was he who introduced this mannish type of woman into the Spanish theater." She discusses such characters on pp. 64–74, noting on p. 65 a reference to Ariosto's Marfisa in *Los palacios de Galiana* (Galiana's Palaces) (Ac., XIII, 200b), a play not later than 1602 (Morley and Bruerton). There is a similar reference in *El maestro de danzar* (The Dancing-Master) (1594): Ac. N., XII, 514. Ariosto's Marfisa is also alluded to in *Angélica en el Catay* (Angelica in Cathay) (Ac., XIII, 425b) dated 1599–1603 by Morley and Bruerton. The name, Marfisa, without the attributes, is used for feminine characters in two other plays of the period in question, a period in which I place the composition of the original *Dorotea*. Cf. S. G. Morley and R. Tyler, *Los nombres de los personajes en las comedias de Lope de Vega: Estudio de onomatología*, University of California Publications in Modern Philology, vol. LV, nos. 1–2 (1961), p. 244.

62. "Persistence and Change," pp. 202 and 124.

63. The Leonarda of *La prueba de los amigos* represents a somewhat later stage but the inevitable distance between her and Marfisa can be seen in their encounter with the respective Doroteas, a violent clash of virtue and vice in the play, a subtle confrontation of conflicting personalities in the *acción en prosa*.

64. "Muger fresca, la que tiene carne y es blanca y colorada y no de faciones delicadas ni adamada" ("Buxom [lit., fresh] woman: one on the heavy side, light-complexioned, ruddy, and not of delicate or refined features"). Covarrubias, s.v. *fresco*.

65. Cf. Ac., V, 700b, and Morby, "Persistence and Change," p. 210.

66. *América en el teatro de Lope de Vega* (Buenos Aires: Instituto de Filología, 1946), p. 149.

67. In the sonnet about Filis, "Retrato mío, mientras vivo ausente" ("My portrait,

while I am away"), *Obras poéticas*, p. 50. (See note 18 to Chap. IV.) In his play *El anzuelo de Fenisa* (Fenisa's Lures), the precious objects in a chest are called "Indias cifradas, / en escritorios de amor" ("Indies enclosed in love's writing-desks") (*Obras escogidas*, I, 896b). In a letter of 1617 Lope remarks to the Duke of Sessa: "Yo les doy a entender [he refers to Marta de Nevares and her family] quando no tengo qué dar, que de allí [Andalusia] espero las Yndias" ("I give them to understand, when I have nothing to give them, that I am expecting Indies from there [Andalusia]" (*Epistolario*, III, 287).

68. See Rennert and Castro, p. 251. With himself in mind Lope wrote his patron around 1617, for example, "que no tener que hacer, a quien oyr y con quien cunplir es la mayor bienauenturanza de todas" ("having nothing to be done, no one to listen to, no one to play up to is the greatest blessing of all") (*Epistolario*, III, 348).

69. "Persistence and Change," p. 202.

70. Hints of inferiority appear in Teodora's remark to Gerarda (p. 66), "Me truxistes de las andaderas en casa de mis padres" ("You took me about in the go-cart in my parents' house"); and in the fact that Felipa, Gerarda's daughter, serves Dorotea as maid.

71. In Teodora's account of her visit there may be an allusion to the birth of Antonia Clara to Lope and Marta de Nevares. Cf. Rennert and Castro, p. 57.

72. The irony behind the recalling of "Santa Inés," for example, is more mischievous than malevolent. One must recall that Agnes is the prototype of the virginal martyr, the betrothed of Christ, who spurns diamonds and riches, and is shielded by an angel when forced into prostitution.

73. *"La Célestine" selon Fernando de Rojas* (Paris: Didier, 1961), p. 240.

74. Bataillon, *"La Célestine,"* p. 239.

75. Besides Celestina's fate, her appearance—the prominent scar of a slash across the face—seems hinted at in the first proverb cited by Gerarda: "Galana es mi comadre si no tuuiera aquel Dios os salue" ("My crony would be fetching if she did not have that 'Here, take this' slash across her face") (p. 64). Morby (n. 3) recalls Lucrecia's remark about Celestina in Act IV: "Hermosa era con aquel Dios os salue que trauiessa la media cara" ("She was fetching with that 'Here, take this' slash covering half her face") (ed. Criado de Val and Trotter, p. 88). Since the trait is emphasized in *La Celestina* (both Lucrecia and Melibea also mention it in the same act), Lope perhaps expected his readers to be reminded of Celestina. Characteristically, in any case, the allusion hovers between Teodora, at whom it is aimed, and Gerarda, from whom it emanates; its import is of course purely associative and it is only a momentary hint, since the conversation quickly moves on.

76. Helmut Petriconi, "Trotaconventos, Celestina, Gerarda," *Die Neueren Sprachen*, 32 (1924), 232 ff.

77. The matters of Gerarda's covetousness and verbal opulence, as well as the significance of her self-awareness, will be treated more fully later, as will Lope's variations on certain specific Celestinesque motifs.

78. Vague imputations of sorcery are present in *Belardo el furioso* but are linked,

not with Pinardo, the uncle accused by Belardo of being Jacinta's procurer, but with Jacinta herself. Galterio, Belardo's father, even arranges (unsuccessfully) to have her jailed as a sorceress (Ac., V, 692–693). One wonders, with Alda Croce ("*La Dorotea*" *di Lope de Vega*, p. 129), whether Lope's experience of the magic arts practiced on him and others, by Jerónima de Burgos, the leading lady whom he nicknamed "La señora Gerarda," perhaps helps to account for Gerarda's name and this strain in her make-up. Amezúa, *Epistolario*, II, 33–34, discusses Lope's fascination with the world of magic and sorcery and his inability to disbelieve in it, notwithstanding many skeptical references in his works.

79. Cf. Fray Luis de Granada, *Memorial de la vida cristiana* (*Obras de Luis de Granada*, ed. J. J. de Mora [Madrid: Hernando, 1925], p. 230a), where the confessant is told: "Acúsese . . . si le da gracias a Dios por los beneficios que dél ha recebido. Y principalmente por le haber criado, redimido y hecho cristiano, no moro, ni hereje" ("Let him ask himself . . . whether he thanks God for benefits received from him. And principally for having created him, redeemed him, and made him a Christian, not a Moor or a heretic"). In *El Isidro*, facs. of the original ed. [1599] (Madrid: Instituto de San Isidro, 1935), Lope plays similarly on Moorish and Christian names: "Ramírez morís mejor, / que no viuiréis Zulemas" ("You'll do better to die as Ramirezes than live as Zulemas") (fol. 209r); "Que no deues de querer / trocar el Mendoza en Muza" ("You don't seem to want to exchange the Mendoza for a Muza") (fol. 209v).

80. Ed. Criado de Val and Trotter, p. 167.

81. "*La Dorotea*" *di Lope de Vega*, p. 55. The remarks on the servants in the following pages have appeared, in slightly distinct form, in my "Masters and Servants: *La Dorotea* vis-à-vis the *Comedia*," *Kentucky Romance Quarterly*, 16 (1969), 55–61.

82. There is a curious impersonality, for example, in the following exchange (p. 263):

> *Dor.:* Es discreción de los señores descuidarse algunos días de los criados que
> quieren bien, para que teman que pueden oluidarlos; que tratarlos siempre
> con igualdad no es seruirse dellos, sino seruillos.
> *Fel.:* Bien hazes en barajarnos como fueren las ocasiones de auernos menester;
> que salir siempre vno, es fullería de la condición y desprecio de la voluntad.

> *Dor.:* It's a smart move on the part of masters to neglect for a few days the
> servants they're fond of, so they'll fear they may forget them; always to treat
> them as equals is not to make use of them but to be used by them. *Fel.:* You
> are right to shuffle us according to the need that arises for us; for the same one
> always to turn up is cheating one's status and spurning one's will.

Elsewhere (p. 445) Dorotea reproves Celia: "Notables sois las que seruís. Todo lo aprouáis, que hechas tenéis las lisonjas para todo, aplicando el ánimo indiferente a lo bueno o a lo malo que se os propone" ("You servant-girls are extraordinary. You go along with everything and have your flattery ready for anything, disposing your spirits indifferently to the good or the bad that is proposed to you").

83. Claudio Conde nevertheless does not figure in the transcript of the hearings and only in 1595, in a statement of Porras (*Proceso*, p. 59), which Rennert and Castro (p. 65) consider false, is he mentioned as accompanying Lope. The actual occasion would have been Lope's return to Valencia after the Armada in 1589. Yet Lope himself later apparently confuses the two journeys, since he writes, c. 1619–20, in dedicating a *comedia* to Claudio Conde: "Esta comedia, intitulada *Querer la propia desdicha*, si no en la sustancia por lo menos en el título, conviene con aquellos sucesos notablemente, quando con tanto amor vuestra merced me acompañó en la cárcel, desde la cual partimos a Valencia" ("This play, entitled *To Seek One's Own Misfortune*, strikingly agrees, if not in content, at least in its title, with the events that happened at the time when you so devotedly kept me company in the prison from which we departed for Valencia") (quoted in Rennert and Castro, p. 49). This appears to be a case of retroactive interference in recall. Whether Claudio Conde did keep Lope company in jail is not important; that Lope remembered him as having done so is.

84. See *La Dorotea*, ed. Blecua, p. 62, and F. Monge, "*La Dorotea* de Lope de Vega," *Vox Romanica*, 16 (1957), 107. Cf. also this exchange (p. 236):

Fer.: ¡O, Ludouico, quán agradables son a mi deseo vuestros braços!
Lud.: Permitid que dellos me traslade a los de Iulio.

Fer.: Oh, Ludovico, how welcome your arms are to me! *Lud.:* Allow me to transfer from them to Julio's.

85. Another departure from decorum is acknowledged in a letter to Dorotea after a snowy vigil under her window: "Boluí a casa, donde me riñó Iulio, que estaua durmiendo al fuego, como si él truxera la nieue y yo fuera el dormido" ("I returned home, where I was scolded by Julio, who was dozing by the fire, as if he were the snowy one and I the one dozing") (p. 429).

86. For example, this passage from *En los indicios la culpa* (Everything Pointing to Guilt) (Ac. N., V, 259b):

Sólo vengo acompañado
de ti por ser mi criado,
pero no mi consultor.

I've brought you along to be my servant, not my adviser.

Or this excerpt from *El acero de Madrid* (The Mineral Waters of Madrid), in *Comedias escogidas*, III, 372a:

No es oficio de criado [to advise his master];
eso ha de hacer el amigo,
el superior y el que es viejo.

It's not a servant's place [to advise his master]; that the friend must do, the superior and the one who is old.

87. *Epistolario*, I, 398.

88. *Estudios sobre Lope*, p. 67n.

89. "Para con tu dotrina, Iulio, tengo por ignorante al Chirón de Aquiles" ("Compared to your learning, Julio, I consider Achilles' Chiron ignorant"), Fernando tells him (p. 294), and César comments to Ludovico on his "estremado ingenio" ("remarkable intellect") (p. 339). Indigent lower-class students served wealthy ones at the universities, as readers of Quevedo's *Vida del Buscón* will remember.

90. So Félix Monge does, "*La Dorotea* de Lope de Vega," p. 111.

91. An unflattering picture of Celia emerges when Laurencio scoffs at Gerarda's idea that he has designs on her: "¡Cierto que es Celia muy linda para dezirle amores! Buena era para alazán tostado . . . y llena de pecas" ("Celia is certainly a charming girl for paying court to! She'd do well as a brown sorrel . . . and all spotted, too!"). Gerarda answers, "Assí la quieren más de quatro; *que no ay olla tan fea que no tenga su cobertera*" ("Even so, she has her admirers: *there's no pot so ugly that it doesn't have a lid*"); and subsequently adds: "Pues ¿qué se puede presumir de Celia y de su recogimiento? *Desde la desgracia primera, ya soy donzella*" ("What can anyone insinuate against Celia and her being so retiring? *Since the first slip I've been a virgin*") (p. 235). One wonders if this humorous deformation in the picaresque manner does not, like the less caricaturesque word-pictures of Marfisa and Dorotea, conceal some specific recollection connected with Lope's quoted remark: "que la dicha Ana Velázquez es negra, y que por eso tiene mal término con las personas con quien trata" ("that the said Ana Velázquez is swarthy and that's why she has a hard time with the people she deals with") (*Proceso*, p. 57). Morby (n. 67) notes that *alazán tostado*—the reference is to the proverb "Alazán tostado, antes muerto que cansado" ("A brown sorrel will die before it gets tired")—is the darkest shade of sorrel and that another proverb cautions against marrying a *pecosa* (freckled) woman.

92. There is some suggestion in the last act that Celia is identified with Fernando's interests and Felipa with Don Bela's. Teodora blames Celia for covering up for her mistress (p. 371), while Julio and Fernando praise her for favoring his surreptitious relations with Dorotea despite his inability to reward her (pp. 408–409). They blame Felipa, whom they consider in league with her mother, for urging Dorotea to keep up the connection with Don Bela. In fact, however, Celia, for all her verbal opposition to her mistress, in the end always falls in with Dorotea's inclinations, following the convention of maid-servants in the theater. She had earlier accepted Don Bela when Dorotea did, something Dorotea manages to blame her for later, as Fernando remembers (p. 381). The partiality imputed to Felipa is at variance with her manifest favoring of Fernando in Acts III and IV and her defiance of her mother (IV, 6). It is perhaps to be understood as Fernando's slanted view, but it is more likely that Lope lost interest in Felipa once her part was played and forgot to be consistent.

Marfisa's servant, Clara, has too slight a role to stand out clearly. She is a foil for her mistress, a sharp interlocutor like Celia, whose inopportune remarks for or against Fernando invariably rub Marfisa the wrong way. She pointedly dissociates herself from her mistress's gullibility, telling Julio: "Pues, ¿qué pensauas? ¿Que era yo la mentecata de Marfisa, que paga los zelos de Dorotea con sus joyas?" ("Then what did you think? That I was that idiot of a Marfisa, who pays for his jealousy of Dorotea with her jewels?") (p. 119). (Celia never thus criticizes her mistress to others.) But she can also lend a sympathetic ear: "La traición es de suerte que no me permite consolarte. Antes bien quisiera añadir sentimientos a los que tienes" ("The betrayal is such that it doesn't permit me to console you. On the contrary, I should like to add further indignation to that which you already feel") (p. 375).

93. Cf. *Proceso*, pp. 269–279, and Rennert and Castro, p. 57. The name of César's lady, Felisarda (p. 417), suggests Lope's second given name, Félix.

94. See J. Millé y Giménez, "El horóscopo de Lope de Vega," *Humanidades* (La Plata), 16 (1927), 69–96. Its substance, given in Latin in the *Expostulatio Spongiae* (1618), is quoted by Pérez Pastor, *Proceso*, pp. 274–277. See also W. T. McCready, "Lope de Vega's Birth Date and Horoscope," *Hispanic Review*, 28 (1960), 313–318.

95. J. de Entrambasaguas ("Un amor de Lope de Vega desconocido: La 'Marfisa' de la 'Dorotea,'" *Fénix, revista del tricentenario de Lope de Vega*, 1 [1935], 457) links Ludovico with Luis de Vargas Manrique, apparently because of the resemblance in names and because Luis de Vargas was a ballad-writing intimate of Lope's. Still it should be recalled that, in contrast to the intensely loyal Ludovico, Luis de Vargas could have given one as susceptible as Lope grounds for thinking him disloyal by not categorically rejecting the possibility of Lope's authorship of the satirical ballads.

VIII. Action and Psychology

1. *Los melindres de Belisa* (Belisa's Squeamishness) (c. 1606–1608: Morley and Bruerton), Ac. N., XII, 654b.

2. *Obras escogidas*, II, 259.

3. For Amezúa's view, see *Epistolario*, II, 653–678.

4. *Epistolario*, II, 6. I am not convinced by the view of Alda Croce that Lope conceives love in *La Dorotea* in the same way as in his dramatic production generally ("*La Dorotea*" di Lope de Vega, studio critico seguito dalla traduzione delle parti principali dell'opera [Bari: Laterza, 1940], p. 57). This overlooks a tendency toward clear-cut formulations of sentiment and schematic delineation of character when Lope writes for *comedia* audiences. In the plays, as Félix Monge has observed, "sentiments are taken for granted" ("*La Dorotea* de Lope de Vega," *Vox Romanica*, 16 [1957], 77, n. 2). The characters' emotions are more or less predetermined by the plot and are not analyzed in such a way as to bring out aspects unfamiliar to the audience. "The important thing was to know what would, in given circumstances, be the attitude of a noble, plebeian, prince, peasant, saint, or hero," observe J. F. Montesinos and C. V. Aubrun (ed. *Peribáñez y el Comendador de Ocaña* [Paris: Hachette, 1943], p. ix). Though in fact there is not infrequently greater psychological subtlety and fuller characterization than such observations suggest, on the whole one may agree that on the stage Lope tends to deal in typed reactions. In *La Dorotea*, this is not the case and I would go further than Monge, who sees differences only in the extent of the psychological analysis, and find differences in its character and quality as well.

5. Cf. this passage from *El desdén vengado* (*Disdain Avenged*), Ac., XV, 404b:

Porque entiendan los que aman
que los amores descienden
de aquellas primeras causas
que, cuando nacemos, guían
la libertad de las almas.
No [digo] que el albedrío
fuerzan, pues ninguna basta,
sino que inclinan el gusto
y las voluntades llaman.

For those who love should understand that loves descend from those first causes which, at our birth, guide the freedom of souls. I do not [say] that they are binding on the will, since no bond could be, but that they affect one's tastes and attract desires.

6. The sonnet beginning "Angel almacigado" ends with the lines:

que vn poeta muy tuyo dice que heres
dura en el acto y blanda en el concierto.

a poet very much yours says that you are hard in the act and accommodating [lit., soft] in the approach.

The ballad is "Sentado en la seca yerba" ("Seated in the dry grass"), and the lines in question read:

Filis me ha muerto
que fue muy blanda en el primer concierto.

Filis has slain me, who was so accommodating when first approached.

See Morby, p. 449, n. 174, and Montesinos, *Estudios sobre Lope*, pp. 215–217, 247–248.

7. See Morby, "Persistence and Change in the Formation of *La Dorotea*," *Hispanic Review*, 18 (1950), 209.

8. The basis of the conceit is the Aristotelian and medieval commonplace which saw each of the four elements, impurely mixed with the others in the sublunary world, as tending toward its natural location, air and fire upward, earth and water downward. "All the elements have their spheres, and aspire to reach their proper spheres, where they find stability and rest; and when flame, for example, has soared to its own upper region it will be happy and contented, for here it can be still and can most endure" (Herbert Butterfield, *The Origins of Modern Science. 1300–1800*, rev. ed. [New York: The Free Press, 1965], p. 30). So Lope will write of nature: "En ella no sólo no produce flores el arte; pero estaría como el fuego sin combustible, ejercitando su actividad dentro de la misma esfera, de que sería necesario que hubiese

ingenios elementos [*sic*] próximos al cielo, donde por su raridad no fuesen vistos, ni tuviesen necesidad de nutrimento" ("in it not only does art not produce flowers; but it would be like fire without fuel, exercising its activity within the same sphere, whence it would be necessary for there to be mind-elements [*sic*] very close to heaven, where, because of their tenuousness, they wouldn't be seen or need nourishment") (dedication to *El marido más firme* [The Most Steadfast Husband], Ac., VI, 175). Juan de Horozco y Covarrubias, speaking in *Emblemas morales* (Saragossa: Alonso Rodríguez, [for] Juan de Bonilla, 1603–1604), III, fol. 120v, of the limited mind, says: "Es como el calor del fuego, que según la llama que concibe se estiende, y sino es que se añada materia y crezca el fuego, es impossible estenderse el calor a más de la esphera que dizen de su actiuidad" ("It is like the heat from a fire which extends outward in proportion to the flame produced, so that, unless material is added and the fire grows, it is impossible for the heat to extend beyond what they call the sphere of its activity").

9. "Me vi mil vezes con tal vergüenza y lástima, que no pudiendo cubrir aquellas hermosas manos con diamantes, las bañaua en lágrimas, que ella tenía por mejores piedras para sortijas que las que auía vendido y despreciado" ("Thousands of times I found myself so filled with shame and pity that, being unable to cover those beautiful hands with diamonds, I bathed them in tears, which she considered better stones for rings than those she had sold and scorned") (p. 303). Cf. p. 524 above.

10. Principally in the ballad "Por la calle de su dama," see above, pp. 55–56, 76. See also the intimations in *Belardo el furioso*, above, pp. 126–127.

11. Cf. Dorotea's later self-justification: "Es la condición de las mugeres tan temerosa, y imprímese en su cobardía tan fácilmente la más mínima amenaça, que ella tuuo la culpa de mi atreuimiento" ("Women's nature is so timorous and the slightest threat makes such an impression upon their cowardliness, that it was to blame for my audacity") (p. 264). Dorotea is voicing a conviction of Lope's: "La condición de la muger es naturalmente temerosa, y con poca falsedad la tendrá segura" ("Woman's nature is naturally timorous and with just a little falsity you can nail her down"), he remarks in a letter to his patron (*Epistolario*, III, 299).

12. This slap must once have resounded very loudly on Elena's cheek, judging from the many echoes in Lope's production. (See Morby, "Persistence and Change," p. 208, with the afterthoughts in "Two Notes on *La Arcadia*," *Hispanic Review*, 36 [1968], 110–115.) The Ovidian precedent (*Amores*, I, 7) noticed by Morby (ed. *La Dorotea*, p. 27) may from the start have mingled with the memory of an actual occurrence; and so also may the contrasting case of Heliodorus's characters pointed out by Dorotea.

13. "¡Iesús! Parece que tropecé en mi amor. ¡O amor, no te pongas delante! Déxame ir, pues me dexaste determinar" ("Heavens! I seem to have stumbled over my love. Oh love, don't block my way! Let me go since you let me make up my mind") (p. 81). "¿Qué traes, que tropieças?" ("What's the matter—you're stumbling?") (p. 93). The description of her progress which she later supplies (p. 264) creates a similar impression of groping and uncertainty.

14. *Die Literarisierung des Lebens in Lope's "Dorotea"* (Bonn and Cologne: Rohrscheid, 1932), p. 39.

15. Compare with these nuances the single passing remark of Jacinta in *Belardo el furioso* (p. 674a):

¿Esto había de durar
toda la vida, o cesar
como cesa cuanto vive?

Was this supposed to last a lifetime or to come to an end as everything living does?

Perhaps the presentation of Dorotea's attitude has been colored by sentiments of Marta de Nevares: "Dize Amarilis que los amores han de ... durar tres años ... pero que tratarse siempre, como es peligroso para el alma, es cansado para el gusto; que deue quedar vna honesta correspondencia, la qual se negocia con no haber echo agrauio durante el término" ("Amarilis says that love affairs should ... last three years ... but that to keep a relationship up forever is both dangerous for the soul and tiring for the taste; that an honest reciprocity should remain, which is managed by not having given cause for offense during the period"). *Epistolario*, IV, 125; letter of early July 1628, approximately.

16. Alfredo Hermenegildo, *Los trágicos españoles del siglo XVI* (Madrid: Fundación Universitaria Española, 1961), pp. 495–496, calls such dreams probably the most frequent device for arousing suspense, citing examples from Bermúdez's *Nise lastimosa* and the two tragedies of Pérez de Oliva. On the function of the dream in *El caballero de Olmedo*, see W. C. McCrary, *The Goldfinch and the Hawk* (Chapel Hill: University of North Carolina Press, 1966), pp. 113–124.

17. Cf. Dorotea's later denunciation:

¡O fementido, o falso, o cauallero indigno deste nombre! ¿A vna muger de mis prendas, ingrato, y que ha dexado por ti quanto puede atraer la hermosura, la gracia y el entendimiento en la Corte? ¿Esto merecía mi verdad? ¿Esto mis braços? ¿Esto lo que he padecido con mi madre y deudos, las necessidades que me han combatido, y que vencí con tan honrada resistencia? (p. 151)
Oh faithless one, oh deceiver, oh gentleman unworthy of this name! Is this a treatment for a woman of my attainments, ingrate, when she has given up for your sake all that beauty, charm and brains are capable of attracting in this Court city? Is this the reward for my faithfulness? For my caresses? For all I have suffered at the hands of my mother and my relatives, the financial pressures that have beset me and that I overcame with such honorable resistance?

18. Viz., "Sólo me dexa cuidadosa tu poca edad; no sea que el auerte enternecido naciesse de tus años, y no de tus sentimientos" ("Your youthfulness alone makes me uneasy, for fear your falling in love may be the result of your age and not of your feelings" (p. 106); and see p. 296 above.

19. Morby, "Persistence and Change," p. 210, gives another analogue from *La prueba de los amigos*.

20. Ac., V, 689b.

21. Morby, "Persistence and Change," pp. 207–208. The encounter likewise has an analogue in *La Arcadia, OS*, VI, 315–316.

22. Cf. Melchor Cano: "Los primeros movimientos son sin culpa, pues no es en nuestro libre poder el evitarlos" ("First movements carry no blame since it is not within our free power to avoid them") (*Tratado de la victoria de sí mismo* in *Obras escogidas de filósofos*, ed. Adolfo de Castro [Madrid: Sucesores de Hernando, 1922] p. 304b). Lope remarks in *El peregrino en su patria:* "Como no hay pared tan sólida, por donde el sol alguna vez no penetre, assí no hay voluntad tan firme por donde alguna vez el primer movimiento no entre" ("As there is no wall so solid that the sun does not at some time penetrate it, so there is no will so firm that a first movement does not enter into it at some time") (*OS*, V, 411). On the common recourse to the "primer movimiento" in the Golden Age, see the note of Rodríguez Marín in the *Quixote*, new critical ed. (Madrid: Atlas, 1947), II, 118. Further documentation in Morby, n. 49, p. 79.

23. *Belardo el furioso*, p. 698b.

24. As early as the quarrel Dorotea had begun to reject such considerations, for there she ascribes the argument based on *desengaño* to her mother (p. 99).

25. That this expression was itself current in Lope's day is evident from Juan de Robles's citing it in 1631 as an example of periphrasis: "No lo puede ver delante de sí, por aborrécelo" ("He cannot see him in his presence, for 'He hates him'"). *Primera parte del culto sevillano*, ed. J. M. Asensio (Seville: Sociedad de Bibliófilos Andaluces, 1883), p. 130.

26. This scene is discussed above, pp. 456–459.

27. As this exchange from the play (p. 678b) shows:

Bel.: Dame luego ese retrato.
Sir.: Rayalle quieres recelo.
Bel.: Tener pienso mejor trato;
     cava con la daga el suelo
     o el pecho a su dueño ingrato.

Bel.: Give me that portrait at once. *Sir.:* I'm afraid you'll deface it. *Bel.:* I have a better plan for it. Dig into the ground with your dagger or into the breast of its ungrateful subject.

28. See p. 371 above.

29. "Esse despertador [Don Bela] desvela más tu pensamiento que las gracias y hermosura de Dorotea" ("That alarm clock is keeping your thoughts awake more than the charms and beauty of Dorotea") (p. 224).

30. These images are developed in Act III, scene 4 (p. 241):

Lud.: Yo pienso que esta rabia de Fernando no es amor, ni este contemplar en
     Dorotea efeto suyo, sino que, como tocando la imán a la aguja de marear

siempre mira al Norte, assí la passada voluntad tocada en los zelos deste
indiano, le fuerça a que con viua imaginación la contemple siempre.
Iul.: Dessa manera le aurá sucedido lo que suele con los espejos cóncauos, que,
opuestos al sol, por reflexión arrojan fuego, que abrasa fácilmente la materia
dispuesta que se aplica, como cuentan del espejo de Arquímedes, con que
abrasó las naues enemigas; porque, reducidos los rayos solares a vn punto
solo, resulta dellos este ardiente efeto.
Lud.: De suerte, Iulio, que el sol es Dorotea, el espejo el indiano, y don Fernando
la materia opuesta.
Iul.: La hermosura de Dorotea passa por el cristal de los zelos al amor de don
Fernando; que no fuera tan ardiente si no passara por ellos.

Lud.: I think that this rage of Fernando is not love nor this fixation on Dorotea
an effect of it, but that, as the compass touched by a magnet always faces north,
so his former passion touched by jealousy of this *indiano* forces him always to
keep his mind on her with vivid imaginings. *Jul.:* According to that, the same
must have happened to him as happens to concave mirrors which, when set
facing the sun, by reflection give off fire which easily kindles suitable material
subjected to it, as is told of Archimedes' mirror with which he set the enemy
ships on fire; because when the sun's rays are focused on a single point, this
burning effect is the result. *Lud.:* So that the sun is Dorotea, Julio; the *indiano*,
the mirror; and Don Fernando the material set against it. *Jul.:* Dorotea's
beauty passes through the crystal of jealousy to Don Fernando's love, which
would not be so ardent if it did not pass through it.

31. See pp. 228 and 294 above.

32. His attitude prompts Dorotea to say, "Sin mirarnos passó de largo" ("Without
a glance at us, he walked on"), and makes Felipa exclaim, "¡Qué estraña melancolía!"
("What strange melancholy!") (p. 292).

33. See pp. 53 and 79 above.

34. "Auéis de entender, Ludovico, que es esto con tanta tristeza, que muchas
vezes se me queda casi muerto destos amorosos deliquios entre los braços" ("You
must understand, Ludovico, that so much sadness goes with this, that he frequently
falls into my arms practically dead from these amorous fainting spells") (p. 243).

35. See p. 192 and pp. 322–323 above.

36. See above, pp. 38, 207. The prototype of such repentance is the contrition of
St. Peter. A stanza of Tansillo's *Le Lacrime di San Pietro* quoted by Cervantes in
Spanish in "El curioso impertinente" (*Don Quixote*, I, 23) makes the same point that
Lope makes through Fernando:

Crece el dolor y crece la vergüenza
en Pedro, cuando el día se ha mostrado,
y aunque allí no ve a nadie, se avergüenza
de sí mesmo, por ver que había pecado:

que a un magnánimo pecho a haber vergüenza
no sólo ha de moverle el ser mirado;
que de sí se avergüenza, cuando yerra,
si bien otro no ve que cielo y tierra.

The grief increases and the shame increases in Peter when day appears and, though he sees no one there, he is ashamed of himself, seeing that he has sinned. For a noble spirit will not only be moved to shame by being observed; he is ashamed of himself when he errs, even if he sees nothing else but earth and sky.

37. Julio had hinted at this tactic immediately after the reconciliation, but Fernando had not listened: "Yo te daré la traça con que el amor de Marfisa te vaya quitando el de Dorotea" ("I'll give you a scheme whereby love of Marfisa will gradually free you of love of Dorotea") (p. 381).

38. Cf. above, note 18 to this chapter. Later Dorotea, from the same standpoint of greater maturity, will bitterly reproach herself: "¿Adónde estaua mi entendimiento quando me fié de diez y siete años? ¿Para qué criaba yo vn áspid en mi pecho?" ("Where were my wits when I put my trust in a seventeen-year-old? What was I nourishing a viper in my bosom for?"), etc. (p. 425).

39. Cf. in the monologue of I, 3: "Esse agrado tuyo, esse brío, esse galán despejo, essos regalos de tu boca, cuyo primero bozo nació en mi aliento, ¿qué Indias los podrán suplir, qué oro, qué diamantes?" ("That appeal of yours, that liveliness, that winning grace, those gifts of your mouth, whose first moustache was born of my breath—what Indies can ever replace them, what gold, what diamonds?") (p. 79).

40. The eight scenes in which Dorotea appears constitute only slightly more than two fifths of the length of the act. Even if the horoscope scene is reckoned in, the total length of the first three scenes of Act V still exceeds that of the remaining nine.

41. *Epistolario*, III, 197. Lope's relationship with Micaela de Luján exemplifies the confidence with which he could sometimes embrace the familiar.

42. Lope adds slyly: "si habemos de creher a Lope en su *Jerusalén*, que, a la cuenta, deuía de haber passado por lo que dize" ("if we can believe Lope in his *Jerusalem*—and he evidently would have experienced what he says") (*Epistolario*, III, 276).

43. *La moza de cántaro* (The Girl with the Water Jar), in *Comedias escogidas*, I, 552b. Lope's view is shared by Father Joseph de Aguilar: "Hermosura sin galas es descuido de los ojos; y gala sin hermosura es desprecio de la atención" ("Beauty without a fine wardrobe is neglect of the eyes; a fine wardrobe without beauty is lack of regard for the attention") (cited by M. Herrero García, "Ideas estéticas del teatro clásico español," *Revista de ideas estéticas*, 2 [1944], 89). But their taste is atypical since, as Herrero observes, the prevailing inclination was against the mixing of colors in dress.

44. *Epistolario*, III, 242. Covarrubias, p. 366b, calls "Consuetudo est altera natura" ("Habit is a second nature") a Latin axiom. Cf. also Morby, p. 433, n. 127.

45. *El peregrino en su patria*, OS, V, 84; cited by Morby, p. 433, n. 127, along with other similar passages.

46. *El Marqués de las Navas* (The Marquess of Las Navas), ed. J. F. Montesinos (Madrid: Centro de Estudios Históricos, 1925), pp. 50–51. Amezúa (*Epistolario*, II, 590) cites a similar passage from *El ingrato* (The Ingrate).

47. *Epistolario*, III, 241. Cf. p. 97 above.

48. *Epistolario*, IV, 123.

49. The topos of imprisonment, fundamentally Petrarchan, and a commonplace of fifteenth-century *cancionero* poetry, underlies Diego de San Pedro's *Cárcel de amor*. In Rodrigo Cota's "Diálogo entre Amor y un viejo," it appears in Love's threat: "Fenescerán tus viejos días / en ciega cautividad" ("Your old days will end up in blind captivity"). (I am indebted to Professor Robert H. Hathaway of Colgate University for these references.) The menacing tone here faintly anticipates Lope's attitude. On the stage Lope treated courtly "captivity" in a more restrained and traditional fashion, to good dramatic advantage, in his play on the troubador Macías, *Porfiar hasta morir* (Persist to the Death).

50. Behind Dorotea's figure there is surely a reminiscence of Garcilaso's Sonnet 27 ("Amor, amor, un hábito vestí") with its development of the Aristotelian commonplace on habit as second nature and its play on the double meaning of *hábito* (habit, garment). Herrera's annotation of Sonnet 7 ("No pierda más quien ha tanto perdido") explicates the same thought (*Obras de Garci Lasso de la Vega con anotaciones de Fernando de Herrera* [Seville: Alonso de la Barrera, 1580], fol. 100).

51. *El príncipe perfecto* (The Perfect Prince), Second Part, Ac., X, 513.

52. Marsilio Ficino, *Commentaire sur le Banquet de Platon*, ed. and trans. Raymond Marcel (Paris: Les Belles Lettres, 1956), p. 222.

53. *Epistolario*, III, p. 282. Cf. p. 79 above.

54. Cf., for example, the remark of Polinesta in *La Arcadia* quoted earlier (p. 144); the sonnet of *Rimas* (1602) beginning: "Si verse aborrecido, el que era amado / es de amor la postrera desventura" ("If for one who was loved to find himself hated is the ultimate mischance of love") (*Obras poéticas*, p. 123); and a passage in the *novela* "Guzmán el Bravo" (1624): "Pero es notable la condición de Amor, que al contrario de todas las cosas, que se corrompen para boluer a engendrarse, pocas veces dexa Amor de dar el vltimo passo, sin que el primero que le sigue no sea el del odio" ("But the nature of Love is remarkable. In contrast to everything else, which decays in order to be regenerated, it rarely fails that when Love takes its final step the next one following is the first step of hatred)." *La Circe, con otras Rimas y Prosas* [1624], facs. ed. (Madrid: Biblioteca Nueva, 1935), fol. 138r.

55. For Julio's rejection of the love-hate paradox, there was precedent in a theoretician of love frequented by Lope (see *Epistolario*, II, 573–574). Mario Equicola begins the section "Dell'amore et dell'odio" ("Of love and hate") of his *Libro de Natura de Amore* (p. 281 of the ed. revised by Thomas Porcacchi [Venice: Gabr. Giolito, 1562]) by insisting on the impossibility of their coexistence.

56. Franz Alexander, *Fundamentals of Psychoanalysis* (New York: W. W. Norton, 1948), p. 107.

57. In a letter he calls *agravio* "padre de la discordia y fuego de la pórbora de la

ira" ("father of discord and flame of the gunpowder of anger") (*Epistolario*, III, 285).

58. Entrambasaguas, *Estudios*, III, 436.

59. *Epistolario*, III, 206 (July 25–26, 1615), and III, 286 (spring of 1617?).

60. Ac. N., XI, 455b.

61. While Dorotea refers to her own sex, Lope elsewhere applies this commonplace to man (cf. Morby, n. 172). It is in fact rooted in the basic Thomistic division of the sensitive appetite into irascible and concupiscible powers (*Summa Theologica*, First Part, quest. 81, art. 2), each of which governs its own set of passions (Part I of Second Part, quest. 23, art. 1).

62. Quoted respectively from Part I of Second Part, quest. 35, art. 8; and Part II of Second Part, quest. 36, art. 1, in a translation derived from that of the Fathers of the English Dominican Province, 2 vols. (Chicago: Encyclopedia Britannica, 1952), I, 780, and II, 567. The second passage quoted continues, "Hence the Philosopher says that 'the old envy the young'" (the reference is to Aristotle's *Rhetoric*, sec. 1388a), an observation that perhaps explains the formulation of Dorotea's scornful jab at Teodora and Gerarda: "¡Qué propias virtudes de los años mayores, la malicia y la embidia!" ("What typical virtues of advanced years: malice and envy!") (p. 372).

63. *Epistolario*, III, 302 (the 1617 confession), and 141 (the self-analysis of 1614).

64. See Horst Baader, "Die Eifersucht in der spanischen Comedia des goldenen Zeitalters," *Romanische Forschungen*, 74 (1962), 322: "Lope de Vega [knew] that the advent of a rival automatically activates one's self-confidence and increases or awakens the feeling that one merits oneself the favor now being directed to another just as much or indeed much more: a jealous presumption that doubtless constitutes one of the most important psychological bases on which jealousy rests."

65. *OS*, II, 323.

66. *Epistolario*, III, 330.

67. While E. H. Templin notes the possibility of jealousy existing without love ("The Exculpation of *yerros por amores* in the Spanish Comedia," *University of California at Los Angeles Publications in Language and Literature*, 1 [1933], 29), as does Hyman Alpern ("Jealousy as a Dramatic Motif in the Spanish Comedia," *Romanic Review*, 14 [1923], 277–278), the reference is to *celos* understood as zeal for one's honor. Nor do Amezúa's masterly pages on the role of jealousy in Lope's life and art (*Epistolario*, II, 660–663) touch on its substitution for love. One must turn to Cervantes' "El celoso extremeño" for a similarly searching examination of the anatomy of jealousy.

68. *Summa Theologica*, Part I of Second Part, quest. 77, art. 4, p. 148.

69. Such honor is not a masculine prerogative. We have found Dorotea, for whom feminine honor in the usual conjugal sense is out of the question, laying claim to it in her letter to Fernando (III, 6): "Respondísteme con tanta seueridad y aspereza que le fue forçoso al alma esforçar mi natural flaqueza para no perder su honra" ("You answered me with such severity and asperity that my soul was forced to force my natural weakness into not losing my honor") (p. 264).

70. *Summa Theologica*, Part I of Second Part, quest. 77, art. 4, p. 148.

71. The contrast is striking with a figure like the Mengo of *Fuenteovejuna*. Although he originally takes the position that "nadie tiene amor / más que a su misma persona" ("No one feels any love except for his own person"), in practice, though only a peasant, he acts valiantly to defend Laurencia against the Comendador and holds out under torture to maintain his share in the honor of the community.

72. The narcissus is the first flower mentioned in the description of setting which opens Lope's *Arcadia*: "Allí estaba el blanco Narcisso listado de oro, oloroso testigo de la filautía y amor propio de aquel mancebo que engañó la fuente" ("The white narcissus streaked with gold was there, bearing fragrant witness to the philautia and self-love of that youth whom the fountain misled") (*OS*, VI, 2).

73. *Rimas . . . de Burguillos* [1634], facs. ed. (Madrid: Cámara Oficial del Libro, 1935), fol. 34v.

74. *Ibid.*, fol. 68r.

75. *El negro del mejor amo* (The Negro Slave of the Best Master), Ac. N., XI, 91a. Morley and Bruerton date it 1599–1603. Covarrubias, s.v. "Narciso," writes:

> Su olor es tan grave, que causa pasmo y estupor, y assí se dixo de νάρκη, *latine stupor*, según Plinio, lib. 21, c. 19 [i.e., c. 75]. Temo que oy día ay muchos destos Narcisos, que en la fuente de sus espejos se enamoran de sí mismos y con justa razón se les puede dar el nombre de estúpidos.

> Its fragrance is so heavy that it overwhelms one and throws one into a stupor and thus the name comes from νάρκη, the word that in Latin is *stupor*, according to Pliny, Book 21, Chapter 19. I fear there are many of these Narcissuses about today who in the fountain of their mirrors fall in love with themselves and who may quite rightly be called stupid.

In Lope's *Jerusalén conquistada*, we find "narciso loco en flor" ("narcissus madly in flower") (*Obras escogidas*, II, 830b). Lope begins the tenth *silva* of his *Laurel de Apolo* (1630) with a leisurely excursus relating the story of Echo and Narcissus and again condemning *philautia* as an aberration (*OS*, I, 203):

> pues a tanto llegó su philautía,
> que fuera de sí mismo y en sí mismo
> buscaba la hermosura que tenía.
> ¡O ciego barbarismo! . . .

> for his philautia reached the point where outside himself and inside himself
> he sought the beauty he possessed. Oh blind barbarity!

He goes on to extend *philautia* to conceited poets and, elsewhere, applies the term to other forms of conceit; cf. *OS*, I, 442, and *OS*, XII, 411.

76. *Epistolario*, II, 647 ff.

77. *Epistolario*, III, 339.

78. *Epistolario*, III, 277.

79. *Ibid.*

80. *Epistolario*, IV, 117.

81. Other instances of reassurance extinguishing love are noted by D. K. Petrov in "El amor, sus principios y dialéctica en el teatro de Lope de Vega," *Escorial*, 16 (1944), 14–15.

82. *Epistolario*, III, 265: October–November (?) 1616.

83. *Epistolario*, III, 267: November (?) 1616.

84. *Remedia amoris*, ll. 401–404.

85. *Epistolario*, III, 266: autumn (?) 1616.

86. *Epistolario*, II, 386.

IX. Dramatic and Lyric Aspects of Form

1. Lope has in mind the *letrados* (lettered) and *científicos* (learned), "this new class of scholars, licentiates, and degree-holders in all the faculties, which in a certain sense constituted the intellectual aristocracy." (Ricardo del Arco y Garay, *La sociedad española en las obras dramáticas de Lope de Vega* [Madrid: Real Academia Española, 1942], p. 661.) In the dialogued Prologue to Part XVI of his *Comedias* (1621) (*Comedias escogidas*, IV, xxx–b), he makes clear that he would like to cater to their tastes in his plays but cannot:

> *Teatro:* ... Pues nadie se podrá persuadir con mediano entendimiento, que la mayor parte de las mujeres que aquel jaulón encierra, y de los ignorantes que asisten a los bancos, entienden los versos, las figuras retóricas, los conceptos y sentencias, las imitaciones y el grave o común estilo.
> *Forastero:* Algunos doctos y cortesanos habrá también que agradezcan a los poetas sus estudios, con diferencia de los buenos a los no tales, de los legos a los científicos ...
> *Teatro:* ¿Qué importa, si no puede vivir el autor del parecer y singular voto de los que saben?

> *Theater:* No one who is halfway intelligent can possibly believe that the majority of the women whom that big cage contains and of the ignoramuses who sit on the benches, understand the lines, the rhetorical figures, the conceits and dictums, the imitations and the lofty or ordinary style. *Foreigner:* There must also be some men of learning and breeding who will appreciate the poets' cultivation and differentiate between the good ones and those who aren't so, between the lay and the scholarly ... *Theater:* What difference does that make if the author cannot make a living out of the opinions and the single votes of those who are knowledgeable?

2. J. García Soriano notes in *El teatro universitario y humanístico en España* (Toledo: R. Gómez, 1945) that one often finds, in the same work, erudite and popular elements, borrowings from the Latin humanistic drama, imitations of Seneca and Plautus, elements taken from medieval allegorical and religious drama and from the interludes and eclogues of the popular stage (p. 34). Though they all have Latin titles, the plays are generally written in both Spanish and Latin; by the seventeenth century usually in

Spanish alone (p. 32). They combine verse and prose and are commonly in five acts, often subdivided into scenes, and often with moralizing choruses (p. 41). While the moral and didactic emphasis is strong, the plays are not sanctimonious (p. 81). They reflect everyday life, often in vivid colloquial dialogue; feminine characters, including prostitutes (though excluded by the *ratio studiorum*) are present. On the other hand, allegorical figures (*moralidades*) are also common: Desire, Zeal, Love of Learning, Honor, Sensual Love, Mercenary Love, for example, in a play on Hercules as conqueror of ignorance, performed in 1580; Time, Experience, Illusion, Disillusionment, Truth are other typical figures (p. 28). It is not impossible that, besides the designation *acción en prosa*, formal aspects, atmosphere, perhaps even themes of *La Dorotea*, may reflect Lope's experience of school drama. García Soriano (p. 43), recalling that Lope attended the Jesuit school in Madrid, suggests that this drama (written by both students and teachers) must have influenced his own and that his first plays may have been of this type. See below, note 54 to Chap. X.

3. Addressing Marta de Nevares in his *novela* "La prudente venganza" on the subject of writing short stories, Lope remarks: "No sirvo sin gusto a V.m. en esto, sino que es diferente estudio de mi natural inclinación, y más en esta Nouela, que tengo de ser por fuerça Trágico, cosa más aduersa, a quien tiene como yo, tan cerca a Iupiter" ("I am not unhappy to do as you ask in this, only it is a pursuit different from my natural bent, and particularly in this tale in which I am obliged to be a tragedian, something that goes very much against the grain when one has Jove so near one"). From *La Circe, con otras Rimas y Prosas* [1624], facs. ed. (Madrid: Biblioteca Nueva, 1935), fol. 122v.

4. The phrase, which Lope used apropos of the adventures of *El peregrino en su patria* (*OS*, V, 26), is equally applicable to his dramatic production.

5. The *Novelas a la señora Marcia Leonarda* (Marta de Nevares) are full of reservations on the order of that quoted in note 3 above. The opening of "La prudente venganza" is explicit:

> Prometo a V.m. que me obliga a escriuir en materia, que no sé cómo pueda acertar a seruirla, que como cada escritor tiene su Genio particular a que se aplica, el mío no deue de ser éste . . . Es Genio . . . aquella inclinación que nos guía más a vnas cosas que a otras: y assí defraudar el Genio, es negar a la naturaleza lo que apetece. (*La Circe*, facs. ed., fol. 122v)

> I assure you that you are making me do a kind of writing in which I don't know how I can manage to satisfy you, for as every writer has his own particular genius which he cultivates, this can't be mine . . . Genius is . . . that inclination which leads us more toward some things than toward others: and so, to cheat genius is to deny nature what it craves.

6. On these distinctions, which pertain to different interpretations of the Aristotelian "mode of imitation," and on the divergent views which Lope's contemporary, Francisco Cascales, and the latter's correspondent, González de Sepúlveda, took of

them, see Claudio Guillén, *Literature as System: Essays toward the Theory of Literary History* (Princeton: Princeton University Press, 1971), pp. 390–394.

7. "Su voluntad de que las apariciones de Belardo deban tomarse por reales apariciones suyas tampoco es dudosa" ("His desire to have Belardo's appearances taken as actual appearances of his own is also beyond question"). *Lope, personaje de sus comedias* (Madrid: Real Academia Española, 1948), p. 74.

8. I am adapting concepts borrowed from the fourth essay, "Rhetorical Criticism: Theory of Genres," in Northrop Frye's *Anatomy of Criticism* (Princeton: Princeton University Press, 1957).

9. About 1630 Lope writes to his patron:

> Nueuo le parezerá a Vex.ª este pensamiento, aunque en la verdad no lo es, ni tiene de serlo más que la calidad que le faltaua. Días ha que he desseado dexar de escriuir para el teatro, así por la edad, que pide cosas más seueras, como por el cansancio y aflicción de espíritu en que me ponen ... Aora, señor exm.º, que con desagradar al pueblo dos historias que le di bien escritas y mal escuchadas e conocido, o que quieren verdes años, o que no quiere el cielo que halle la muerte a vn sacerdote escriuiendo lacayos de comedias, e propuesto dexarlas de todo punto. (*Epistolario*, IV, 143)

> This idea will appear strange to Your Excellency, although it actually isn't, and the only thing strange about it is its present force. For some time I've wanted to give up writing for the stage, both because of my age, which demands graver things, and because of the fatigue and spiritual affliction that [plays] cause me ... Now, Excellency, when two stories I gave the people well written and not well received have turned out not to be to their liking, I've recognized that either plays require one to be in his prime or heaven does not want death to overtake a priest creating comedy valets, so I've decided to give them up completely.

In the already cited dialogued Prologue to Part XVI (1621), Lope complains of the hazards to which a play is subject in performance,

> accidentes como mandar algún poderoso inquietarla [la comedia], herir un representante, parir una mujer, caerse una apariencia, errarse el que no estudia o el desairado ser odioso al pueblo, cosas que no están en las márgenes [*sic*] del poeta, sin esto, muchos van a la comedia más como figuras que como oyentes; y se hacen allí mayores papeles que los representantes.
>
> (*Comedias escogidas*, IV, xxv–b)

> accidents like some powerful individual ordering a disturbance, an actor wounding someone, a woman giving birth, a set falling over, someone tripping up who hasn't learned his lines or a booed actor turning on the audience, things not in the poet's script; besides which, many go to the theater more to be seen than to listen and put on a bigger act there than the actors.

10. The example of *La Euphrosina* (see above, p. 331), unlike *La Celestina* divided into five acts and subdivided into scenes, may also have influenced Lope, although the act division of that work, as Eugenio Asensio notes, is completely capricious.

11. The acts of Seneca's plays were simply the five divisions created by the four appearances of the chorus, whose interventions brought all acts but the last to a close. In Spain, only Carvajal, Bermúdez, and Virués in *Elisa Dido* retained this five-part division and only the last used Lope's term "acto." (See Alfredo Hermenegildo, *Los trágicos españoles del siglo XVI* [Madrid: Fundación Universitaria Española, 1961], p. 445.) Probably the models Lope has most immediately in mind are Bermúdez's *Primeras tragedias españolas* published in 1577 and not written for public performance. *Nise lastimosa*, a close imitation of Antonio Ferreira's "A Castro," based on Greek, not Senecan models, is more restrained in tone than Bermúdez's markedly Senecan sequel, *Nise laureada*. However, the chorus appears only at the act endings of *Nise lastimosa*, as in *La Dorotea*, while in *Nise laureada* it also engages in dialogue during the acts. Several terms used to designate the classical type of meter of both plays are echoed by Lope as descriptions of the meters of his own choruses. That Lope also has Seneca directly in mind is seen in the specific allusion to the latter's *Hippolytus* when Laurencio appears as a "trágico y desdichado nuncio" ("tragic and hapless messenger") at the end of the *acción en prosa* (p. 455).

12. The phrases are from Lope's Prologue to *El castigo sin venganza, OS*, VIII, 384.

13. Cf. Hermenegildo, *Los trágicos españoles*, p. 445. There are none in Virués's five-act *Elisa Dido*, for example, and only two or three to an act in Bermúdez's tragedies, which are far shorter than *La Dorotea*.

14. Another instance of segmentation with continuity is the division between scenes 7 and 8 of Act IV, pp. 378–379. See above, p. 222.

15. Elsewhere Lope paraphrases himself: "Calla, Iulio; que algún ingenio sagrado dixo que la lengua del amor es bárbara para quien no le tiene" ("Hush, Julio, for some sacred writer said that the tongue of love is barbaric to anyone not in love") (p. 257). The "calla" (hush) reinforces the finality of the line. One finds variations on this sort of ending in scenes 2, 8, and 9 of Act V.

16. Dorotea's "Déxame, Celia, vete a tu labor; que más me quiero estar sola, que con quien me pone en las heridas cáusticos para matarme" ("Leave me, Celia, go and do your sewing. I'd rather be alone than with someone who puts caustic on my wounds to kill me") (p. 147); Gerarda's cynical "Piensa en lo que has de tomar, que esto ya lo tienes" ("Think of what you're going to take in; this you already have") (p. 188). When an actual exit is involved, it is sometimes even briefly indicated, as in Gerarda's "Esso me deues, que te he enseñado a hablar. Adiós, don Bela" ("You have me to thank for that, I taught you how to speak. Goodbye, Don Bela") (p. 236). Cf. also pp. 279 and 125.

17. In V, 7, Laurencio merely adds a little to our knowledge of Don Bela's troubles over the horse, Pie de Hierro (Iron Foot), when he comes to deliver a note of which we hear nothing more.

18. Instances of such scenes between Fernando and Julio are: I, 4; III, 1 and 7; between Dorotea and Celia: II, 2, and V, 9; between Don Bela and Laurencio: III, 2 and 5; and V, 1.

19. See K. Vossler, "*Euphrosina*," *Corona*, 8 (1938), 517. "Konversationsstuck" unaccountably appears as "drama convencional" in the Spanish version of the essay included in Vossler's *Escritores y poetas de España* (Buenos Aires: Espasa-Calpe Argentina, 1947), p. 135.

20. Vossler, *Escritores y poetas*, p. 133. Vossler (p. 134) sees Seneca's closet drama and his dictum "Satis enim magnum alter alteri theatrum sumus" ("Each of us is a big enough theater for the other") behind the idea of this kind of nonstageable play. *La Dorotea* goes further, of course, since, unlike *La Celestina*, and also unlike *La Euphrosina*, whose Prologue clearly suggests declamation in public (see introduction to E. Asensio's edition [Madrid: C.S.I.C., 1951], I, lxvii ff.), it is not intended for any kind of declamation.

21. See, for example, M. R. Lida de Malkiel, *La originalidad artística de "La Celestina"* (Buenos Aires: Eudeba, 1962), pp. 19ff.

22. *Escritores y poetas*, p. 137.

23. "*La Célestine" selon Fernando de Rojas* (Paris: Didier, 1961), p. 80.

24. Affinities with the *comedia* as regards situations and motifs are pointed out by Alda Croce, *La "Dorotea" di Lope de Vega, studio critico seguito dalla traduzione delle parti principali dell'opera* (Bari: Laterza, 1940), pp. 132–141; and in matters of style and expression by F. Monge, "*La Dorotea* de Lope de Vega," *Vox Romanica*, 16 (1957), 116–117.

25. It is this attitude which best defines the spirit of a passage like the following (p. 101) in which Julio apes his master:

Iul.: ¡A Celia, Celia!
Cel.: ¿Qué quieres, Iulio?
Iul.: Háblame tú a mí, y no me niegues el postrero abraço, si no es que te ha
     venido alguna carta de las Indias con los criados del indiano.
Cel.: Déxame baxar, que se va mi señora sola.

Jul.: Oh, Celia, Celia! *Cel.:* What is it, Julio? *Jul.:* At least you speak to me and don't deny me a final embrace, unless some letter has come for you from the Indies with the *indiano*'s servants. *Cel.:* Let me go down, my mistress is going off alone.

26. Lida de Malkied, *La originalidad artística de "La Celestina,"* chap. 2, "La acotación."

27. Quoted from the sonnet entitled "A la muerte de vna dama, representanta vnica" ("On the death of a lady, unique as an actress"), where Lope also refers to: "la graue del coturno compostura, / que ya de zelos, ya de Amor suspira" ("the grave bearing of tragedy, sighing now for jealousy, now for love") (*Rimas . . . de Burguillos* [1634], facs. ed. [Madrid: Cámara Oficial del Libro, 1935], fol. 23r).

28. Dedication to *El sol parado* (The Sun Stopped Still), published in Part XVII (1621); Ac., IX, 41.

29. *La originalidad artística de "La Celestina,"* p. 104.

30. Comparison with a somewhat similar sequence in *¡Si no vieran las mujeres!* (If Only Women Couldn't See) (Ac., XV, 177b) will bring out for the reader the difference in technique mentioned.

31. Felipa's words indicate similarly impulsive behavior in Dorotea when she hears Fernando is outside: "*¿De qué te alteras? ¿Adónde vas? Detente, que anda don Bela por la calle*" ("What is agitating you? Where are you going? Restrain yourself, Don Bela is in the street") (p. 266). Or when Fernando faints and she threatens to go mad: "*Quedo, que ya lo estás, Dorotea. Dexa el cabello, dexa las manos*" ("Quiet, you already are, Dorotea. Let your hair alone, let your hands be") (p. 312).

32. While the motto is Virgilian (Eclogue X, 69), the context suggests an immediate pictorial source. The same motto adorns a somewhat similar emblem in an early seventeenth-century collection which shows, in Mario Praz's words, "a Cupid in the act of bridling a lion." (*Studies in Seventeenth Century Imagery*, 2nd ed. [Rome: Edizioni di Storia e Letteratura, 1964], p. 29.)

33. Another meaningful prop is the hair torn from Dorotea's head by her mother (see above, p. 454). Even when properties have less significance, the attention paid to them bespeaks the dramatic craftsman. Lope thinks ahead, for example (p. 257) to the guitar Fernando will be playing in the last scenes of Act III:

Iul.: ¿Llevaré el instrumento?

Fer.: Lléuale; que si se ofreciere sacar la espada, poco importará perderle.

Jul.: Shall I take along the instrument?   *Fer.:* Take it; if there is occasion for swordplay, it won't matter much if it's lost.

Julio eventually hands it to him: "*Toma el instrumento y canta*" ("Take the instrument and sing") (p. 272). And later, when swordplay threatens, Fernando hands it back with the order: "*Arrima esta guitarra a essa reja*" ("Put this guitar over by that grillwork") (p. 285). Lope plans the disposition of the article as carefully as if he had performance in mind.

34. On the role of the chorus in these dramatists, see Hermenegildo, *Los trágicos españoles*, pp. 178–179, 276–278, and 446–448.

35. The presence of a chorus at the end of the last act is not Senecan but we find parallels to Lope's moralizing Coro del Exemplo in Virués's *Elisa Dido* ("Ay, humana esperança . . .," *Poetas dramáticos valencianos*, ed. E. Juliá Martínez [Madrid: Revista de Archivos, 1929], I, 177) and also at the end of Bermúdez's *Nise laureada*, where the subject is fortune's mutability and the misery of the human condition. Lope's thematic and not merely moralistic use of his choruses reminds us that in earlier works like *El peregrino en su patria* and *La Arcadia* he occasionally placed at the end of one of the books a lyric that stands outside the story, coming from the author rather than from a character and relevant to the sense or subject of the book as a whole. A sonnet on love, for example, ends Book I of *El peregrino* (OS, V, 87). Its relevance to the pilgrim's

case is made plain in the author's remarks introducing it. It describes love's universality, deceits, and destructiveness in a manner not unlike the Coro de Amor at the end of Act I of *La Dorotea*. At the end of *La Arcadia* the *canción* "La verde primavera" ("The green springtime") (*OS*, VI, 451), ostensibly given to Amphryso, is in fact the author's lyric epilogue set apart from the preceding narrative. As Montesinos notes (*Estudios sobre Lope*, pp. 170–171), it had originally been written about Lope and Elena Osorio, but Lope now makes it refer to the total experience of Amphryso related in the previous five books and, beyond this, to the whole period of his own youth. More personal and expressive, less sententious and admonitory in tone, it nevertheless, like the Coro de Exemplo, subsumes in one appended poetic statement the sense of the whole work.

36. *OS*, XVII, 102.

37. Juan de Jáuregui speaks of "la mansedumbre y lisura que piden algunos a los versos, deseándolos tan senzillos i fáciles como la prosa. Mucho deven diferenciarse" ("the tameness and evenness which some demand of verse, wishing it to be as simple and easy as prose. The two must differ greatly"). (*Discurso poético* [1624], ed. A. Pérez Gómez [Valencia: Tipografía Moderna, 1957], p. 59.) Lope's attitude is patent in this passage from the introduction to the *Rimas* (1602): "Los que no han estudiado ... quisieran que todo estuviera lleno de cuentos y novelas, cosa indigna de hombres de letras; pues no es justo que sus libros anden entre mecánicos e ignorantes." ("Untutored people ... would like to have everything full of stories and tales, something unworthy of men of letters, since it is not right that their books should circulate among workmen and ignoramuses") (*OS*, IV, 167).

38. The lyrics of *La Dorotea* are the "culmination of a development," as Montesinos notes in his remarks on them (*Estudios sobre Lope*, p. 203). The possible exception is the sonnet on the marriage of Vittoria Colonna (*La Dorotea*, p. 420), which took place on December 31, 1587: it may be an occasional piece preserved from the early period.

39. Besides the wedding sonnet, there are two burlesque poems: the mock-*culterano* sonnet commented on in IV, 2 and 3, and the ode of Tomé de Burguillos to a flea (IV, 3).

40. The only full lyrics in *La Celestina* are the brief verses in the style of Galician *canciones de amigo* (songs for the lover) sung by Lucrecia and Melibea in the second garden scene (Act XIX). *La Euphrosina* contains only two lyrics and in other *Celestinas* they are similarly rare. Of course the inclusion of lyrics in narrative prose is not limited to the pastoral, although for various reasons, not the least his own experience with the mode in his *Arcadia*, I judge that Lope had the pastoral particularly in mind. One finds verse insertions in antiquity—viz., Petronius's *Satyricon*—and in Hispano-Mauresque literature—see A. Castro, *La realidad histórica de España* (Mexico: Porrúa, 1954), pp. 416–417; and *Hacia Cervantes*, 2nd ed. (Madrid: Taurus, 1960), pp. 350–351. An early Spanish example is *Cuestión de amor* (c. 1513), which contains a generous sprinkling of lyrics, not only *letras* and *villancicos* but extensive *coplas* and an eclogue.

41. Montemayor relates in a verse flashback an earlier episode of the action of

La Diana, the leave-taking of Sireno and Diana, in the "Canto de la Nimpha" (ed. F. López Estrada [Madrid: Espasa-Calpe, 1946], pp. 73–87). The verse narrative of the nymph Dorida forms an account into which are inserted the farewell songs of the shepherd and the shepherdess. In Lope's *La Arcadia* the life and love story of a shepherd, Celio, are told in a long narrative poem in Book I (*OS,* VI, 63–73). Moreover, Lope turns to verse to relate the final leave-taking of Belisarda and Amphryso after their tardy reconciliation. "Fue tanto su sentimiento, que no es posible, pastores del Tajo, poder ahora escribírsle . . . Lo que ahora puedo decir es, que Belisarda se despidió de Amphryso, diciendo assí" ("Their sorrow was so great, shepherds of the Tagus, that there is no possibility of describing it to you . . . What I can say is that Belisarda took leave of Amphryso with these words"). To her poem of farewell he replies with his own. (*OS,* VI, 360–374).

42. When a song produces a similar effect in a play, the lyric mood is inevitably more evanescent:

> *Conde:* Cantad algo, que estoy muerto.
> (*Siéntese en una silla, y canten los Músicos*)
> *Mús.:* Antes que amanezca,
> sale Belisa;
> cuando llegue al soto,
> será de día.
> *Conde:* Cuando ese estribo escribí
> ¡qué bizarra la miré!
> Cantad la copla y haré
> una endecha para mí.
>
> (*Las bizarrías de Belisa,* Ac. N., XI, 454b)

Count: Sing something, for I am slain. (*Sits in a chair and musicians sing*) *Mus.:* Before it dawns, Belisa comes forth; when she reaches the grove, it will be day.   *Count:* When I wrote that refrain, how fetching she was in my eyes! Sing the verses and I'll make up a mournful ditty for myself.

With the singing of the *copla* ("Mañanicas de mayo . . ."—"May mornings . . ."), the brief sequence ends.

43. The more important characters—Sireno, Sylvano, Selvagia, Belisa in *La Diana,* for example; Celso and Olympia in *La Arcadia*—sing more often but hardly more perfectly than the others.

44. Appreciation of the kind one sometimes finds in Sannazaro's *Arcadia* is rarely to be observed in Spanish pastoral novels:

> Piacque maravigliosamente a ciascuno il cantare di Galicio, ma per diverse maniere. Alcuni lodarono la giovenil voce piena di armonia inestimabile; altri il modo suavissimo e dolce, apto ad irretire qualunque animo, stato fusse più ad amore ribello; molti comendarono le rime leggiadre et tra rustici pastori

non usitate; e di quelli ancora vi furono, che con più ammirazione estolsero la acutissima sagacità del suo avvedimento . . .

(ed. A. Mauro [Bari: Laterza, 1961], p. 25)

Galicio's singing was marvelously pleasing to everyone, but to each in his own way. Some praised the youthful voice rich in priceless harmony; others the manner so soft and sweet, calculated to ensnare any heart, no matter how refractory to love; many commended the graceful verses, not usual among rustic shepherds; and there were still others who with greater admiration extolled the keen and clever way he managed . . .

(On this subject see E. C. Riley, *Cervantes's Theory of the Novel* [Oxford: Oxford University Press, 1962], pp. 33–34.) On the other hand, despite the paucity of interpolated lyrics in *La Euphrosina*, there is refinement in the attitude toward music and poetic composition:

Euphrosina: E elle se estará em casa?
Siluia: Dizme minha tia que todo o dia está recolhido na sua posada. E o seu passatempo he tomar uma viola, que elle tange e canta marauilhosamente quanto quer, e troua muyto bem, e nisto se ocupa o mais do tempo.
Euphrosina: Noutro dia diz que cantauão umas moças uma cantiga com sua irmã. E elle fezlhe uns pes que me ella mandou e que lhos tornasse logo, mas eu não lhos torney mais, e aquí cuydo que as trago.

(ed. Asensio, I, 256)

Euphrosina: And he simply stays home? *Silvia:* My aunt tells me that he shuts himself up in his room the whole day long. And his pastime is to take a viol and play it and he sings marvelously well whatever he wishes and composes very good verse, and this is how he spends most of his time. *Euphrosina:* The other day she says some girls were singing a melody with his sister. And he made up some refrains for it which she sent me. I was to return them to her directly but I never did and I think I have them here with me.

45. The burlesqued *culto* sonnet and the sonnet on the marriage of Vittoria Colonna are both presented by César, the latter as his own composition, while the burlesque ode of IV, 3, is recited by Julio.

46. With the exception of "Corría vn manso arroyuelo" ("A gentle little stream was flowing") (II, 5), the lyrics of unspecified authorship are the least distinctive and least significant.

47. Morby, who points to the passage in the *Phaedo*, also refers to Aristotle, *De Anima*, sec. 407b–408a, and gives other references (p. 403, n. 54). One may add that in *Politics*, sec. 1340, Aristotle writes: "Music has a natural sweetness. There seems to be in us a sort of affinity to harmonies and rhythms, which makes some philosophers say that the soul is a harmony, others, that she possesses harmony" (trans. B. Jowett [Oxford: Clarendon Press, 1920]).

48. Marsilio Ficino, *Commentaire sur le Banquet de Platon*, ed. and trans. Raymond Marcel (Paris: Les Belles Lettres, 1956), p. 163.

49. *Divini Platonis Opera Omnia quae Exstant*, trans. Marsilio Ficino (Frankfurt: C. Marnium et haeredes J. Aubrii, 1602), p. 1181D (sec. 187). I quote this version (in an edition which Lope could have seen) because of the closeness of Ficino's Latin version to Lope's Spanish.

50. See Leo Spitzer, *Classical and Christian Ideas of World Harmony*, ed. A. G. Hatcher, Baltimore: Johns Hopkins, 1963. I have treated Lope, Ficino and Plato in "Plato's *Symposium* and Ficino's Commentary in Lope de Vega's *Dorotea*," *Modern Language Notes*, 73 (1958), 506–514.

51. The two passages are in *OS*, XVI, respectively on pp. 396–397 and 80.

52. *OS*, V, 207. The reference should be to the eighth, not the seventh, book of the *Politics*, loc. cit.

53. See *La Diana*, ed. López Estrada, p. 229. There is a brief discussion in Agustín Albarracín Teulón, *La medicina en el teatro de Lope de Vega* (Madrid: C.S.I.C., 1954), pp. 142–144, in which the diverse effects of music—intensification or relief—are noted. Lope's contemporary, Tirso de Molina, once at least coincides with Montemayor: "Cantad: mas nunca el canto el mal resiste, / que al alegre da gusto, y pena al triste" ("Sing: but singing never is proof against trouble, for it gives pleasure to the joyous and pain to the sad"). (*La mejor espigadera* in *Obras dramáticas completas*, ed. Blanca de los Ríos [Madrid: Aguilar, 1946], I, 989b.) On the other hand, in Gil Vicente, of all Lope's precursors probably the most sensitive to musical values and their relation to poetry and drama, the same duality appears as in Lope. See A. E. Beau, "A música na obra de Gil Vicente," in his *Estudos*, I (Coimbra: Universidade de Coimbra, 1959), 219–249. (I am indebted to Professor Alice R. Clemente of Smith College for bringing this study to my attention.)

54. As the following passage from *El peregrino en su patria* (*OS*, V, 309) demonstrates:

> ¿En qué se divide la música? En Theórica y práctica, dixo el loco, según Boecio; o sea en natural y artificial, en celestial y humana. La natural celestial es la que se considera de la harmonía de todas las partes del mundo: la humana es la que trata de las proporciones del cuerpo y del alma y de sus partes . . . se sigue la artificial dividida en instrumentos y órganos musicales.

> How is music divided? Into theory and practice, according to Boethius, said the fool; that is, into natural and artificial, celestial and human. Natural celestial music is that which is derived from the harmony of all parts of the world; the human is that which treats of the proportions of the body and the soul and of their parts . . . then comes the artificial, divided into musical instruments and organs.

55. Rafael Mitjana, "Comentarios y apostillas al 'Cancionero poético y musical del siglo XVII,' recojido por Claudio de la Sablonara y publicado por D. Jesús Aroca," *Revista de filología española*, 6 (1919), 20 and 26. Mitjana cites (p. 29) Cristóbal Mosquera de Figueroa's remarks about Francisco Guerrero in his preface to the latter's

Canciones y villanescas espirituales (1589): "Fue de los primeros que en nuestra nación dieron en concordar con la música el ritmo y espíritu de la poesía, con ligereza, tardanza, rigor, blandura, estruendo, silencio, dulzura, aspereza, alteración, sosiego; aplicando al vivo, con las figuras del canto, la misma significación de la letra" ("He was one of the first in our nation to think of bringing the rhythm and spirit of poetry into accord with the music, bringing in quickness, slowness, severity, mildness, noise, silence, sweetness, harshness, agitation, tranquillity; bringing out, to the life, through the figures of the melody, the meaning of the words").

56. *Obras poéticas*, p. 325.

57. In *Treinta canciones de Lope de Vega puestas en música* (Madrid: Residencia de Estudiantes, 1935), p. 98, Bal comments: "What constitutes the genius of our music? One has to answer with an English word: 'directness.' This is the word that sums up the best qualities of the most authentic Spanish music, the one which says most succintly what we know familiarly as 'coming to the point,' 'not beating around the bush.'"

58. See, respectively, the dedication to Marta of *La viuda valenciana* (Part XIV, 1620), cited by Rennert and Castro, p. 227, and a sonnet beginning "Cuando con puntas de marfil labrado" ("When with carved ivory tips") published with *La Circe* (1624), *Obras poéticas*, p. 1288. I follow Amezúa (*Epistolario*, II, 434) in interpreting "lira" as lute.

59. Fernando remarks (p. 206) that he has "puesto en famosos tonos" ("set to memorable melodies") the two elegiac ballads he later sings (III, 7 and 8). The wording is ambiguous, "famoso" meaning both famous and deserving of fame. Fernando asks Julio for a copy of the other two ballads, "que si fueran breues, las estudiara para cantarlas" ("if they were short, I would study them in order to sing them") (p. 223). Again he could have in mind original composition or use of existing settings. His remark, in any case, shows that musical attainment is a product of effort, not an automatic possession.

60. "El que dixo que fuera comodidad hallar a comprar cartas y barbas hechas, ¿por qué no dixo instrumentos templados?" ("Why didn't the person that said it would be a convenience to find ready-made letters and beards on sale, add tuned instruments?") (p. 86).

61. This obvious response to tuning is the one most natural to the *comedia* stage:

Que a un ynquieto corazón
oír templar vn instrumento
es darle mayor tormento
y doblarle la pasión.

For it is adding further torture to a restless heart and doubling its suffering to hear an instrument being tuned.

(From *La corona merecida* [The Crown Deserved], ed. J. F. Montesinos [Madrid: Centro de Estudios Históricos, 1923], p. 62.) Tuning the viol aroused the real ire of Juan de Robles: "Ni hay enfado como estar oyendo en una vihuela *tan, tin, ton, tin,*

tin dos horas, y viendo bajar y subir cuerdas, y comenzando a tañer y volver a refinarlas" ("There is nothing so annoying as to have to listen to a viol going *tan, tin, ton, tin, tin* for two hours and seeing strings slackened and tightened, and someone starting to play, and going back to tuning"). (*Primera parte del culto sevillano,* ed. J. M. Asensio [Seville: Sociedad de Bibliófilos Andaluces, 1883], p. 250.)

62. For a fuller treatment than is here possible of this and other aspects of the song, see my "'Al son de los arroyuelos': Texture and Context in a Lyric of *La Dorotea,"* *Homenaje al Profesor Rodríguez-Moñino* (Madrid: Castalia, 1966), II, 277–287. It is noted there that the instrument designated *clavicordio* in Spanish is equivalent to the English spinet, while the English term "clavichord" corresponds to the Spanish *manicordio* or *monicordio.* I have drawn on this study for many of the remarks that follow.

63. This lyric and its context are treated above, pp. 556–557.

64. See the examples cited by Morby, p. 306n., and by C. F. A. Van Dam, ed., *El castigo sin venganza* (Groningen: P. Noordhoff, 1928), p. 215.

65. The swain exonerates himself in these lines (p. 108):

Por hablar con las serranas
acaso y sin detenerme,
¡ay Dios, qué duras venganzas
de culpas que no te ofenden!

For talking with the mountain girls casually and just in passing, heavens, what a harsh revenge for faults that don't offend you!

66. *Die Literarisierung des Lebens in Lope's "Dorotea"* (Bonn and Cologne: Rohrscheid, 1932), p. 32, n. 28.

67. See Morby's nn. 39 and 40, p. 224, with reference to Horace, *Odes,* I, 26, 1–3, and to Theocritus, Idyll XI, which begins proclaiming that there is no balm for love except the muses, but ends with Polyphemus's reminding himself that there are maids ashore to replace the inflexible Galatea and with the poet stating in his own voice: "Thus did Polyphemus tend his love-sickness with music, and got more comfort thereout than he could have had for any gold" (trans. J. M. Edmonds, *The Greek Bucolic Poets* [Cambridge, Mass.: Harvard University Press, 1950], p. 147).

68. Lope adopts in it the poetic name of Fabio, one sometimes coupled with Amarilis, as in the piscatory elegies. Its setting, a cliff above a rocky coast, links it with Fernando's similar situation, though the latter may have been contrived to accommodate the poem.

69. He has approached the re-reading of Dorotea's letters in Act I with the same solemnity: "Hagamos con toda solenidad las honras a esta ausencia" ("With all due solemnity, let's do the honors to this separation") (p. 109). The mention of Dorotea's name in a rhyming position and the perfect aptness of the sonnet to its context suggest that in this case Lope may exceptionally have composed the poem along with the surrounding dialogue, elaborating magniloquently upon the scheme of the corresponding sequence in *Belardo el furioso.*

70. Cf. Amphryso's "Haviendo tomado el tósigo de amor, cruelíssimo veneno, el de los zelos, ahora le han resistido, y procurando consumirle a él, me tienen vivo a mí" ("The toxin of love, a most cruel poison, having taken that of jealousy, the latter has now resisted it and in trying to consume it, keeps me alive") (*La Arcadia*, *OS*, VI, 326). Morby (n. 254) notes the Plinian roots of this motif and other metaphorical applications in Lope.

71. Fernando surely coincides with his creator subsequently when he makes the observation already noted: "Aduierte cómo parece que se hizieron los versos para descansar los que aman ... y deue de ser porque [las musas] aliuian sus tristezas [del amor] quexándose, que no porque le curen; y son exemplo los versos referidos" ("Observe how verse seems to have been invented to afford some respite to those in love ... and it must be because [the muses] alleviate [love's] sufferings by lamenting them, not because they cure it. And the verse you recited is a case in point") (p. 224). Yet a moment later Fernando returns to his private *leitmotiv*: "Pero ni el escriuirlos ni el cantarlos sossegará las tempestades del mar de mis pensamientos" ("But neither writing them nor singing them will still the storms on the sea of my thoughts") (p. 224).

X. Style and Literary Stylization

1. See the introduction to his edition (Madrid: C.S.I.C., 1951), pp. lii ff. Asensio thus describes the styles: the sublime for heroic monologues and scenes of love and despair, characterized by symmetrical periods, musical intonation, repetitions, copiousness, exclamations; a medium style, corresponding to the conversations of cultivated speakers, with *sententiae*, displays of wit, proverbs, little recourse to mythology; the lowly for the conversation of popular types. Stephen Gilman discusses stylistic level in *La Celestina* in *The Art of "La Celestina"* (Madison: University of Wisconsin Press, 1956), pp. 43–55.

2. *Cisne de Apolo*, ed. A. Porqueras Mayo (Madrid: C.S.I.C., 1958), II, 120.

3. Juan de Jáuregui in his *Discurso poético* [1624] brands *desigualdad* "feíssima" ("extremely unpleasant") (ed. A. Pérez Gómez [Valencia: Tipografía Moderna, 1957], p. 61).

4. In this case Juan de Robles provides a helpful distinction between varieties of the low style:

Lo que no he visto advertido por otro ninguno ... es que al primer estilo se le dan diversos nombres de humilde, bajo, ínfimo, delgado y otros, los cuales no son sinónimos, sino significadores de diversas especies dél; porque ínfimo o bajo significará el grosero y rústico, el que tratare cosas humildes y con simplicidad; delgado el usual que (según Quintiliano [XII, 10, 58–59]) es para enseñar: y así servirá todo género de doctrinas convenientes a la república, y para historias, relaciones y novelas, y para cartas familiares de personas bien entendidas, y para ello ha de ir compuesto con pureza, en que admite hermosura y sonoridad, y sentencias breves, y otras cosas así. (*Primera parte del culto sevillano,* ed. J. M. Asensio [Seville: Sociedad de Bibliófilos Andaluces, 1883], p. 226)

What I haven't seen pointed out by anyone else . . . is that the first style is given different names—lowly, base, bottom-most, plain, and others—which are not synonymous but indicative of different varieties of it: because bottom-most or base will mean the coarse and rustic, a style treating humble things in a simple way; plain, the ordinary one which (according to Quintilian [XII, 10, 58–59]) is for instructing: hence it will serve for every kind of doctrine beneficial to the state, and for histories, accounts, and tales, and for familiar letters between cultivated people, and for these purposes it should be written purely, be open to beauty and sonority and brief dictums and other things of this kind.

5. The term "conversación" carried meanings ranging from social to carnal intercourse. Nebrija confines it to its Latin sense of "living in the company of." But Melibea protests the "cruel conuersación" of Calixto at the outset of the first garden scene in *La Celestina* and a century later we hear in *Rinconete y Cortadillo* of a proscription against "conversación con mujer que tenga nombre de María en días de viernes" ("any intercourse with women named Mary on Fridays"). In a letter Lope speaks of the "conuersación de la Corte" (*Epistolario*, III, 70); the sense is clearly equivalent to "trato," social intercourse.

6. *La originalidad artística de "La Celestina"* (Buenos Aires: Eudeba, 1962), p. 133.

7. "El lenguaje de Lope de Vega" in *El padre Las Casas y Vitoria* (Madrid: Espasa-Calpe, 1950), p. 103.

8. Dialogued Prologue to Part XVI (Madrid, 1621), quoted in *Comedias escogidas*, IV, xiv–b.

9. There are complaints along these lines by Lope in the dialogued Prologue to Part XVI just quoted. Vélez de Guevara, for his part, in the "Prólogo a los Mosqueteros de la Comedia de Madrid" of his prose narrative, *El diablo cojuelo* (Madrid: Sociedad de Bibliófilos Madrileños, 1910), p. 5, rejoices in the fact that the work "comes into the world conceived without original Theater" (the conceit alludes to original sin), out of their reach, for they are too illiterate to read it, and even in the theater wait, "gaping, for the idea to hit them via the ears or through a slap of the actor's hand, and not through their heads."

10. The Lisbon edition is described by Margherita Morreale in her edition of the *Galateo español* (Madrid: C.S.I.C., 1968), pp. 72–73. Lope's sonnets are reproduced on p. 102 and may also be read in *Lope de Vega, poesías preliminares de libros*, ed. F. Zamora Lucas (Madrid: C.S.I.C., 1961), pp. 5–6. The earliest surviving edition of the *Galateo español* is 1593, although it probably had appeared before 1586; cf. ed. Morreale, p. 5. My quotations are from this edition, as reproduced by Miss Morreale.

11. Pinheiro relates, for example, an encounter on St. Peter's night, June 27, 1605, in Valladolid, with a veiled lady, who turns out to be Ana de la Mata, a noblewoman with a lurid past. She sets up a game in which Pinheiro and his two companions (one

of whom was sitting on a clog) are to vie in giving her nicknames, the winner to get a favor:

> a medida de su boca (contando que no pase della), y el que peor diere, envíe por colación. Dije yo: "Parécesme bruja en encrucijada." Dijo Diego Sodré: "Parécesme reunión de San Francisco, con dos cruces y una delante, porque no se meen en él." Dijo Constantino de Menelao: "No, sino Santa Elena haciendo elección de las cruces." Y ella: "No parezco sino Magdalena la buena entre ladrones." Repuso Diego Sodré: "Condenada, porque me deja sin figura." Respondí: "No, tú eres Longinos, que está delante caballero en un chapín." A esto dijo ella: "Desa suerte, yo daré la lanzada." Proseguí yo: "Y yo, como Tomás, meteré la mano." Y Menelao: "Y yo, como Menelao, gozaré la Elena." La bellaca, sin pensar, dijo muy a prisa: "Condenado en la colación, porque ha salido del brevario y dejó los Evangelistas por los poetas." (Thomé Pinheiro da Veiga, *Fastiginia o fastos geniales*, trans. N. Alonso Cortés [Valladolid: Colegio de Santiago, 1916], pp. 117–118)

> whatever his mouth desires (provided it doesn't get beyond the mouth), and the one giving the poorest [nickname] will send for supper. I said: "To me you look like a witch at a crossroads." Diego Sodré said: "To me you look like a group with a St. Francis, with two crosses and one in front so they won't make water on him." Constantine de Menelao said: "No, not that but St. Helen choosing the crosses." And she: "I simply look like the good Magdalene between the thieves." Diego Sodré replied: "You lose, because that leaves me out." I answered: "No, you are Longinus, who is up in front mounted on a clog." To this she said: "At that rate, I will deliver the stab with the lance." I continued: "And I, like Thomas, will put my hand in." And Menelao: "And I, as Menelaus, will have my way with Helen." The crafty thing, without stopping to think, said very quickly: "You will have to pay for supper, because you went beyond the breviary and gave up the evangelists for the poets."

12. I am referring to works written entirely in dialogue, not to the dialogues one finds in narrative prose, though the remark applies there also. Cervantes is, of course, the great exception. See Luis G. Murillo, "Diálogo y dialéctica en el siglo XVI español," *Revista de la Universidad de Buenos Aires*, 5th ser., 4 (1959), 56–66; and "Cervantes' *Coloquio de los Perros*, a Novel-Dialogue," *Modern Philology*, 58 (1961), 174–185.

13. In the *Diálogos de apacible entretenimiento* some attempt is made to suggest a domestic atmosphere, there are occasional bits of repartee, yet no real conversational movement becomes established and the mechanics of the conversation are painfully obvious: "Señores, vamos a conversación entretanto que nos avisan de nuestros convidados" ("Ladies and gentlemen, let's have a conversation until the guests are announced") (ed. A. de Castro in *Curiosidades bibliográficas* [Madrid: Hernando,

1926], p. 293a); "Señores, vamos a la sala y pongan sillas a la lumbre, y a quien no acudiere con algo de gusto, quitarémosle la silla y pondrémosle una albarda" ("Ladies and gentlemen, let's go to the living room and have chairs drawn up by the fire and anyone not contributing something amusing will have his chair taken away and a packsaddle put on him") (p. 281a).

14. *La originalidad artística de "La Celestina,"* pp. 114–116.

15. "Como a mí no me toca el disculparla sino la prosecución de la narración propuesta, para volverme a ella, sólo digo . . ." ("As my job isn't to find excuses for her but to go ahead with the narrative in progress, in order to get back to it, I merely say . . .") (*El peregrino en su patria, OS,* V, 390). Or "Respondida pues esta objeción, nuestra historia, cuyo fin es mover con los trabajos de este hombre, prosigue assí . . ." ("With this objection taken care of, then, our story, whose goal is to arouse sympathy through the trials of this man, continues thus . . ." (*ibid.,* p. 300).

16. For instance, in "La desdicha por la honra," in *La Circe, con otras Rimas y Prosas* [1624], facs. ed. (Madrid: Biblioteca Nueva, 1935), fol. 109v:

En este género de escritura ha de auer vna oficina de quanto se viniere a la pluma sin disgusto de los oydos, aunque lo sea de los preceptos, porque ya de cosas altas, ya de humildes, ya de Episodios y Paréntesis, ya de Historias, ya de Fábulas, ya de reprehensiones y exemplos, ya de versos y lugares de Autores, pienso valerme.

In this type of writing there should be a miscellany of whatever comes to the pen without displeasing the ears, even though it may [displease] the rules, because I intend to make use now of lofty things, now of lowly ones, now of episodes and digressions, now of historical anecdotes, now of myths, now of reprimands and *exempla,* now of verse and citations of authors.

17. *OS,* VI, 227. I cite another passage of this kind from the same work (pp. 110–111) in "The Case for an Early *Dorotea*: A Reexamination," *PMLA,* 71 (1956), 770; other examples: *OS,* VI, 14–15 and 315, and, in *El peregrino en su patria, OS,* V, 199.

18. *Epistolario,* III, 79, 325, 197, 257.

19. *Epistolario,* IV, 55, 127, 131.

20. *Epistolario,* III, 264.

21. Examples: Lope as narrator: "Cortándolo [el hilo] a esta digressión, que siendo larga, es contra las leyes de la buena Rhetórica, pues en la Poética misma divierten los episodios, digo, que Pánfilo en Zaragoza entró . . ." ("Cutting [the thread] of this digression which, being long, is contrary to the rules of good rhetoric, for even in poetry episodes are distracting, I say that Pánfilo entered Saragossa . . .") (*El peregrino en su patria, OS,* V, 411). A character speaking: "De estas [enigmas] os diré algunas a su tiempo, dixo Aminadab, mas volviendo a atar el hilo de nuestra narración, sabed . . ." ("I'll give you a few such [enigmas] at the proper time, said Aminadab, but, to tie the thread of our narrative together again, be informed . . .")

(*Los pastores de Belén, OS*, XVI, 159). The reference in the first passage to "the rules of good rhetoric" salutes a norm often honored by Lope in the breach though repeatedly affirmed. Whatever his practice, Lope wishes it understood that he has the precepts in mind. The allusion to a basic distinction between poetry and rhetoric in respect to digressions is characteristically hasty and vague. Even in poetry, Lope says, episodes are distracting. But episodes are not, properly speaking, digressions; Aristotle insists on the need to knit them organically to the plot. Moreover, Quintilian allows long rhetorical excursuses in certain cases (IV, 3, 12–13 and 17), though these are epideictic in nature, to be sure, and thus of a type germane to poetry. In both passages cited and in similar ones of *La Dorotea*, Lope makes use of established formulas for a clear-cut *reditus ad rem*, as prescribed by Quintilian—IX, 1, 28; IX, 3, 87.

22. Except parataxis, more easily demonstrated in particular contexts; cf. pp. 421–422 above. Nor do I consider proverbs here. For the most part they are a stylized mode of expression peculiar to Gerarda or provoked by her in her interlocutors. Instances of genuine colloquial proverbs may more easily be noted separately.

23. *Obras completas*, ed. Felicidad Buendía (Madrid: Aguilar, 1961), I, 367.

24. Gerarda uses the phrase two other times: "Aora bien, voy a darle este búcaro" ("Very well then, I am going to give her this *búcaro*") (p. 133); and "Aora bien, yo quiero contentarte" ("Now then, I want to make you happy") (p. 396). Fernando once: "Aora bien, tomaremos, por lo que sucediere, dos broqueles . . ." ("Now then, just to be prepared, we'll take two bucklers . . .") (p. 256). Julio once: "Aora bien, éstos son males que sólo el tiempo tienen por Auicena" ("Well now, these are troubles that have only time as their Avicenna") (p. 269). And Don Bela once: "Aora bien, ¿a qué vienes, Gerarda?" ("Now tell me, why have you come, Gerarda?") (p. 234).

25. "'Tanto monta,' dijo la mozuela. Y replicó la pupilera: 'No, sino el alba'" ("'It's all the same,' the young girl said. And the boarding-house woman replied: 'Oh yes, no doubt'") (Quevedo, *Obras completas*, ed. Buendía, I, 369). "No, sino el alba" is short for "No es sino el alba que anda entre los coles," a phrase which Covarrubias (s.v. *alva*) explains by noting that the ancients held the dawn to be a beautiful nymph-like goddess. A peasant woman, having retained her lover overly long, was asked by her husband, as the lover was slipping out at dawn through the vegetable garden: "Is that someone there making that noise?" To which she replied: "No, it's just the dawn going about among the cabbages."

26. The phrase comes in a defiant aside of Hernando del Pulgar to the Granadine Moors (*Romancero general*, ed. A. Durán [Madrid: Atlas, 1945], II, 124b):

Rióse d'eso Pulgar,
Y dice: — ¡Perra canalla,
No os veréis en ese gozo,
Si Dios me guarda mañana!

Pulgar laughed at that and says: "Slimy curs, you'll never know such delight, if God spares me tomorrow."

27. Not surprisingly one finds repetitions of the type noted in Lope's familiar letters (*Epistolario*, III), viz.:

que a ffe, a ffe que si vna vez fuessen verdaderas [resoluciones], que saliesse . . . esse desatinado amor   (p. 264)

y, al fin, al fin, se ha de llegar al [puerto] que promete vna onrrada resistencia en vn amor mal empleado   (p. 302)

Apurando un día a cierta vellaca . . . sobre los regalos de vna merienda, me dixo sonrriéndose: "—Lope, Lope, no lo han de saber todo los hombres."

(p. 325)

believe me, believe me, if those were ever real [resolves], that misguided love . . . would depart

and, when all is said and done, you'll end up just where you'd expect when there is honorable resistance to a misplaced love

Pressing a certain rascally woman one day . . . about the tasty things at a snack, she said to me, smiling: "Lope, Lope, there are some things men shouldn't know."

Such repetitions are of course also found in the *comedias*, viz.: "¡Ah, Patricio, Patricio! Que con ella / hiciste aqueste indigno casamiento" ("Oh, Patricio, Patricio! That you should have made that unworthy match with her"). (*Las ferias de Madrid* [*The Fairs of Madrid*], Ac. N., V, 621a)

28. Cf. "¿Qué dirás a esto, Pármeno? ¡Nesçuelo, loquito, angelico, perlica, simplezico! ¿Lobitos en tal gesto? Llégate acá, putico . . ." (*Tragicomedia de Calixto y Melibea*, ed. M. Criado de Val and G. D. Trotter [Madrid: C.S.I.C., 1958], p. 49). "¡Bendígaos Dios, cómo lo reys y holgáys, putillos, loquillos, trauiessos! ¿En esto auía de parar el nublado de las questioncillas que auéys tenido?" (*ibid.*, p. 173). (The effect of these accumulated diminutives cannot be reproduced in English.)

29. "Noción, emoción, acción y fantasía en los diminutivos," *Estudios lingüísticos: Temas españoles* (Madrid: Gredos, 1954), pp. 195–229. My designations of different categories of diminutives follow those of Amado Alonso.

30. Thinking aloud—but directing her thoughts to Clara. Though Lope lets Marfisa go on at length while Clara merely listens, the speech is not a soliloquy but an appeal to the latter as witness. The second person is established in the vocative of the opening exclamation: "¡Don Fernando en Madrid, Clara, y tantos días sin verme!" ("Don Fernando in Madrid, Clara, all these days without coming to see me!"), a close analogue in spontaneity to Dorotea's "Dama Fernando . . ." ("A lady, Fernando . . .").

31. In speaking of life styles, I am supplying a modern equivalent for one of the meanings already assumed by *estilo* in the Golden Age. Fray Luis de León, speaking of the Scriptures, observes: "Algunas veces *camino* en ellas significa la condición y el ingenio de cada uno, y su inclinación y manera de proceder, y lo que suelen llamar *estilo* en romance o lo que llaman *humor* agora" ("In them *camino* [way] sometimes

means the nature and make-up of a person, and his tendencies and way of behaving and what is usually called *estilo* in the vernacular or what is now called *humor*"). (*De los nombres de Cristo*, ed. F. de Onís [Madrid: La Lectura, 1914], I, 108.) I am indebted to José Manuel Blecua for this reference. Cf. "Una mediana vida yo posea, / Un estilo común y moderado" ("Let mine be a medium way of life, an ordinary, moderate style") (*Epístola moral a Fabio*). It is in this sense, in reference to both literary conventions and reality, that the Prologue to the *acción en prosa* commends "el estilo de los criados" ("the servants' style").

32. Of course in an absolute sense, as a work of "poesía, aunque escrita en prosa" ("poetry, although written in prose"), *La Dorotea* is of necessity conceived by Lope in the literary medium proper in his eyes to all such works, an artistic language of which rhetorical and poetic diction and even conventionalized techniques of repartee and argumentation are inseparable constituents. To this extent conventional stylization necessarily imposes itself upon naturalism in the formal treatment of the material; one cannot press the concept of stylistic realism to extremes. But in Lope's own terms the issue of art versus nature is clearly a central one to *La Dorotea*.

33. "Si alguno pensasse que consistía en los números y consonancias, negaría que fuesse ciencia la poesía" ("If anyone were to think that it consisted simply of meter and rhyme, he would deny that poetry was a matter of learning") (p. 51). Menéndez Pidal sees El Pinciano as reviving this view, prevalent in the fifteenth century, and passing it on to Cervantes (*Don Quixote*, II, 18) and to Lope (*La Arcadia, Laurel de Apolo*, etc.). See "El lenguaje de Lope de Vega," pp. 105–106.

34. *Las fuentes y los temas del Polifemo de Góngora* (Madrid: C.S.I.C., 1957), I, Introduction.

35. Dedication to *El cuerdo loco* (The Sane Man Mad), Ac. N., IV, 374.

36. In Lope's plays, on the other hand, as R. D. F. Pring-Mill brings out, one not infrequently finds "aphoristic commonplaces" consistently linking "abstract universal principles and the particular situations facing the characters in the play." ("Sententiousness in *Fuente Ovejuna*," *Tulane Drama Review*, 7 [1962], 6.)

37. Of course, as readers, we are free to extract the "tantas partes de filosofía natural y moral" ("so many aspects of natural and moral philosophy") of which the prologuist speaks, irrespective of the contexts in which they are embedded. We will then come up with nuggets of "natural philosophy" like those relating to dream-lore in I, 4, or to gold, mercury, and alchemy in III, 4; with kernels of "moral philosophy" in the sanctimonious strictures on drunkenness suddenly injected into the supper scene (II, 6, p. 193) by Teodora and Dorotea, the condemnations of make-up in V, 2, and of sorcery in V, 6. When the prologuist speaks of "la erudición tan ajustada a su lugar" ("the erudition so well suited to its context"), he perhaps has in mind sequences like the supper scene in which "natural" wine-lore is spouted by Gerarda and moral evaluation offered by Dorotea and Teodora in the midst of the conviviality and talk of the meal. This is clearly not done without considerable strain, however; the miscellaneous tags of learning scattered throughout the *acción en prosa* in the end provide only a smattering of culture and knowledge.

38. C. Suárez de Figueroa, *Plaça universal de todas artes, y ciencias* (Madrid, 1733), fols. 319v and 321r. Subsequent references will be given in the text by fol. no.

39. Juan de Jáuregui is even more emphatic in his disapproval than Suárez de Figueroa:

> Reparemos en la voz *curiosus*, que en el más notorio sentido de los latinos, significa el demasiado diligente en inquirir novedades; es vicio la curiosidad, vicio que excede todo límite en la diligencia, i se distingue della tanto, como la superstición de la religión: "ut a diligenti curiosus, a religione superstitio distat." (*Discurso poético*, p. 48)

> Let us note the word *curiosus*, which in the best-known Latin sense means one too industrious in seeking out new things; curiosity is a vice, a vice which exceeds all the bounds of industry and is as distinct from it as supersition is from religion; "curiosity is as far from industry as superstition is from religion."

Both writers, in their eagerness to condemn freedom of inquiry, insist on ignoring the fact that *curioso* still could carry the simple neutral meaning "careful," "painstaking."

40. The epitome of inappropriate curiosity for Lope is that of the *culteranos*. The indiscriminate pursuit of words, learned or humble, which he imputes to them, he characterizes as "curiosa temeridad" ("fastidious temerity"), with acerbity invoking Titelmans on the subject of *detestanda curiositas*, in *Epistolario*, IV, 89. It is significantly a literary polemic that rouses him in this fashion; otherwise his attitude toward *curiosidad* is more equable.

41. See the edition included in his *Mercurius Trimegistus, sive de triplici eloquentia sacra, Española, Romana* (Baeza: Pedro de la Cuesta, 1621), fol. 56r.

42. *Obras poéticas*, p. 1294, sonnet published with *La Circe*, 1624. The preceding reference is from the earlier cited preface written for the *comedia* version of *La Arcadia* included in Part XIII (1620), as quoted in *Obras escogidas*, III, 493a. Lope's reservations coincide with those of his contemporary, Huarte de San Juan, who remarks, surely from experience, on those who "grasp what is taught and retain it firmly in their memory . . . and when asked the reason for what they know and understand, clearly reveal that their learning is merely a matter of taking in the words and statements contained in what was taught with no understanding or knowledge of why and how it is so" (*Examen de ingenios*, in *Obras escogidas de filósofos*, ed. Adolfo de Castro [Madrid: Sucesores de Hernando, 1922], p. 414a).

43. There appeared on the market some years ago a copy of the first edition of Levinus Lemnius, *Occulta naturae miracula* (Antwerp: G. Simonem, 1559), once owned by Lope, with numerous marginal notes in his hand—"q.bien," "Nota" ("How good," "N.B.") etc.—and underlinings of certain passages, for instance, a sentence (fol. 17v): "Mulier in congressu . . . viro plus voluptatis concipiat" ("The woman in intercourse . . . conceives more pleasure than the man"). I am indebted to my colleague, W. L. Fichter, for this information.

44. Quoted by Vilanova, *Las fuentes y los temas*, p. 33.

45. See Amezúa, *Epistolario*, II, 594–600.

46. *OS*, IX, 388.

47. *OS*, IV, 470–471. Ximénez Patón identifies rhetoric with the style of public speaking on the one hand ("lo mismo es Eloqüencia que Rhetórica") and on the other observes that the poet "sino es en la acción corporal en todo corre parejas con el Orador" ("in everything except movements of the body is equivalent to the speaker") (*Mercurius Trimegistus*, fols. 53v and 56r). Significantly he observes that "los poetas que escriben para ellos solos, y no para todos, a nadie dan gusto, y assí quedan burlados del fin para que escriben" ("poets who write for themselves alone and not for everyone, please no one and thus are cheated of the purpose for which they write") (fol. 58v). On the fusing of epideictic rhetoric and poetry, see Heinrich Lausberg, *Handbuch der literarischen Rhetorik* (Munich: Max Hueber, 1960), I, 555; and O. P. Hardison, Jr., *The Enduring Monument* (Chapel Hill: University of North Carolina Press, 1962).

48. In *El culto sevillano* (p. 67) Juan de Robles takes exception to the view that the forensic rhetoric of the ancients is now out of date "because the system of trials has changed and that sort of speech is no longer in use." He still considers it the most necessary of the three because "it is common to all human affairs, in which one is always trying to find out whether something is this way or that way, whether it was rightly or wrongly done . . . for the determination of which one should adopt the method and manner of what is said in this branch; a great deal of this one inevitably enters also into the other two."

49. *Institutio Oratoria*, IV, I, 51; Cipriano Suárez, in whose manual *De arte rhetorica* (Paris: Officina Thomae Brumennu, 1573) Lope as a schoolboy probably received his introduction to the subject, echoes this phrase of Quintilian: "Exordium est oratio, animum auditoris idonee comparans ad reliquam dictionem. Id fieri tribus maxime rebus inter auctores plurimos constat, si beneuolem, attentum, docilem auditorem fecerimus" ("The exordium is a speech that puts the auditor in a state of mind favorable to what is to follow. Most authors agree that this is accomplished in three main ways: by making the auditor well-disposed, attentive and receptive") (fol. 20r).

50. Among figures for proposing, continuing and concluding, his second type of *figuras de sentencias*, Juan de Robles includes "metastasi o transición, cuando se resume lo dicho y se previene lo por decir; como: 'Pero porque hasta aquí se ha dicho del género de la guerra, ahora me parece que conviene tratar de su grandeza'") ("metastasis or transition, when one sums up what has been said and anticipates what remains to be said, as: 'But since up to now we have spoken of the kinds of warfare, it now seems appropriate to me to treat its greatness'") (*El culto sevillano*, p. 208).

51. Cf. Quintilian, IX, 3, 34; Lausberg, *Handbuch*, I, sec. 625. In her next speech (p. 64), Teodora makes the proper contraposition of *naturaleza* and *crianza*. The justificatory *exemplum* that she cites for the fact that "aquel señor extrangero regaló a mi hija . . . con mucha honra" ("that foreign gentleman was kind to my daughter . . . much to her honor") (p. 67), namely that "el rey don Rodrigo forçó a la Caua"

("King Roderick violated La Cava") is, as earlier noted, ludicrously inept both on the usual ground of decorum and because it fails to support her argument.

52. *Mercurius Trimegistus*, fol. 58r (erratum for 54r).

53. *Emblemas morales* (Saragossa: Alonso Rodríguez, 1604 [for] Juan de Bonilla, 1603–1604), III, fols. 162r and 127r.

54. Lope most probably entered the Jesuit school in Madrid in 1573, the year after its opening, according to R. M. Hornedo ("Lope y los jesuitas," *Razón y fe*, no. 166 [1963], 409), having been enrolled there either on the initiative of D. Jerónimo Manrique, in whose household he would have been a page at this time, or on that of his uncle, Don Miguel del Carpio. Noting Pérez de Montalbán's statement that at this school Lope mastered grammar and rhetoric in two years, Hornedo considers "the humanistic cast of his 'culture'" the most lasting trace on Lope of his years there. He notes two references in the *Epistolario* (IV, 62 and 83) which indicate Lope's familiarity with the text used by the Jesuits in their rhetoric classes, the already noted *De arte rhetorica, Libri III*, of Cipriano Suárez, mentioned also by César in *La Dorotea* (p. 357), although, as pointed out by Hornedo in an earlier article ("Lope en los estudios de la Cía. de Jesús," *Razón y fe*, no. 108 [1935], 52–78), there was probably no course in rhetoric as yet during Lope's two-year stay. Fernando's assertion "no ygnoraua la retórica" ("I was not unfamiliar with rhetoric") (p. 294) is to be understood on the basis of the "metrics and perfecting of Latin style," which probably included some study of poetic genres (Hornedo, "Lope en los estudios," p. 68) as part of a course in *humanidades* that followed the three in grammar.

55. Among the many debating propositions we find mentioned in the accounts of the debates, one in particular, "cuál era la cosa más fuerte" ("which was the strongest thing")—wine, king, woman, the truth, etc.—offers a clue to the habit of mind visible in Fernando's query, "¿Cómo la primera palabra ha sido las dos cosas más poderosas, Dios y la muerte?" ("How is it that your first words have been the two most powerful things: God and Death?") (p. 95; cf. p. 452 above); or to the way of thinking behind his similar observation that "la cosa más fuerte siempre fue la honra—perdone aquel antiguo problema del vino, la verdad y la muger" ("the strongest thing always was honor—despite that old problem of wine, truth, and woman") (p. 304). On such school debates see J. García Soriano, *El teatro universitario y humanístico en España* (Toledo: R. Gómez, 1945), p. 19.

56. In his already quoted strictures on "bachilleres," Horozco y Covarrubias writes (*Emblemas morales*, III, fol. 127r): "They're forever wearing themselves out and pestering those in whose company they are until they tell them they are right. And if this is done out of politeness, they are offended; and other times they won't be satisfied with having what they wish conceded to them; and, letting it be understood, as it were, that the other was merely a form of disputation, they want to go back and maintain the opposite . . . and all they ever do is contradict, so as to make everything incomprehensible."

57. Quintilian, IV, 1, 49; cf. Lausberg, *Handbuch*, I, sec. 855.

58. The quasi-technical performance of Julio in prying Fernando's secret out of

him contrasts notably with Sempronio's in an analogous situation (*Tragicomedia de Calixto y Melibea*, ed. Criado de Val and Trotter, pp. 25–28). When Sempronio asks, "¿Qué cosa es?" ("What's the trouble?"), and Calixto orders him to leave, threatening him, Sempronio, though perplexed and in conflict, goes off and leaves his master alone. When Calixto recalls him, he simply bides his time till the secret comes out by itself. His tactics are psychological, not verbal.

59. Lausberg, *Handbuch*, I, sec. 663.

60. The exchange continues:

> *Fer.:* ¿Pero cómo saldrás a oírme, aunque tengas allá mi alma que te lo aduierta, si tienes también la de don Bela, que no te dexe?
> *Iul.:* Impossible es que vn sujeto tenga más de vna forma. Si el amor de Dorotea ocupa el alma de don Bela, ¿dónde ha de estar la tuya?
> *Fer.:* Allí junto a Dorotea.
> *Iul.:* También es impossible estar la forma sin la materia.
> *Fer.:* ¿Quién te lo dixo?
> *Iul.:* Aberrois quando menos.
> *Fer.:* Pues tú y Aberrois os id noramala, que me tenéis quebrada la cabeça.

> *Fer.:* But how will you come out and listen to me, even though you have my soul there telling you to, if you also have Don Bela's not allowing you to? *Jul.:* Impossible for one subject to have more than one form. If the soul of Don Bela occupies Dorotea's love, where is there room for yours? *Fer.:* Right there beside Dorotea. *Jul.:* It's also impossible for the form to exist without the matter. *Fer.:* Who told you so? *Jul.:* Averroes at least. *Fer.:* Well, you and Averroes can go hang, you've pummeled my brains so.

Absorbed in his appeal to Dorotea, Fernando first takes no notice of Julio's carping, then lets himself be sidetracked and exasperated.

61. The scene continues (p. 230):

> *Lau.:* Pero mira, assí Dios te guarde, de qué manera declaró Marsilio Ficino el pintar los antiguos al dios Pan medio hombre y media bestia.
> *Bel.:* ¿Quál fue la causa?
> *Lau.:* Como era hijo de Mercurio, significaron las dos maneras de hablar en sus dos formas: quando verdadera, hombre; y quando falsa, bestia.
> *Bel.:* Por buen camino me lo llamas.
> *Lau.:* No digo tal, sino que te aprouechas mal de la parte superior en tus argumentos.

> *Lau.:* But, God preserve you, listen to how Marsilio Ficino explained the ancients' depicting the God Pan as half-man, half-beast. *Bel.:* What was the reason? *Lau.:* As he was Mercury's son, they indicated the two ways of speaking in his two forms: if truly, a man; if falsely, a beast. *Bel.:* You've found a fine way to call me one. *Lau.:* I don't mean that, only that you make little use of your superior side in your arguments.

The reference is to the commentary on the *Cratylus*; cf. Morby, n. 49. While the erudition is more recondite, the roundabout procedure is similar to that of the *motes* (cracks) we find anecdotally exemplified in the *Diálogos de apacible entretenimiento* of Bartolomé Lucas Hidalgo. Much closer to the popular level of the *Diálogos* is another case in which Julio obliquely calls Fernando a "rozín" ("nag") (p. 227).

62. On *fábulas* as *moralidades*, see also Gracián Dantisco, *Galateo español*, ed. Morreale, p. 155, and the examples adduced to this text by Miss Morreale, note to fol. 70r, pp. 198–199.

63. *Mercurius Trimegistus*, fol. 125v. Ximénez Patón may be recalling Socrates in the *Phaedrus* (sec. 267): "But shall I to dumb forgetfulness consign Tisias and Gorgias, who are not ignorant that probability is superior to truth, and who by force of argument make the little appear great and the great little, disguise the new in old fashions and the old in new fashions . . .?" If so, he has passed over Socrates' irony in evaluating favorably as *gracia* what Socrates ridicules as sophistry.

64. *Galateo español*, ed. Morreale, p. 152. See also a passage from Lope's *La mayor virtud de un rey* (The Greatest Virtue of a King), *Comedias escogidas*, III, 77a, quoted by Morby, pp. 226–227, n. 43.

65. Cf. "Y aunque es semejanza nueva, / es linterna su costumbre / que vemos mover la lumbre / y no vemos quien la lleva" ("And, although this is a new comparison, her habits are a lantern, where we see the moving light well but we don't see who is carrying it") (*La escolástica celosa* [The Jealous Scholastic Girl], Ac. N., V, 446b). Cf. also this gloss on jealousy: "Tiene a la linterna igual, / su incertidumbre también, / que se ve la lumbre bien, / pero quien la lleva mal" ("It has also in common with the lantern its uncertainty: you see the light well but the one carrying it poorly") (*La Arcadia, OS*, VI, 113).

66. "*La Dorotea* de Lope de Vega," *Vox Romanica*, 15 (1957), 118.

67. As this passage shows, Fernando's ingenuity also expends itself upon puns, a tendency which he shares with Gerarda and the servants. Commonplace plays— *locura-cuerdas, hierro-yerro*—are tossed off effortlessly enough by all of them, but Fernando goes considerably further in his juggling with the language: "La auía caído en gracia o mi persona o mi donaire, o todo junto. Y fue gracia con que he caído en tantas desgracias" ("My person or my appeal or both together had fallen into her good graces. So it was with good grace that I fell into so many ill graces" ["desgracias," lit., misfortunes]) (p. 298).

68. Laurencio's comment on Felipa's statement that Dorotea is composing a ballad to send to Don Bela—"How much do you want to bet that the ballad is to the tradesman and the refrain to your money?" (p. 259)—is interpreted by Felipa to mean "que sería alguna prosa dedicada a tus galas" ("that it was probably some piece of prose dedicated to your wardrobe") (p. 263). The term "prosa" here clearly suggests the stale terminology of the commercial transaction.

69. Morby, p. 85, n. 66, traces this particular *chria* to Polydorus Vergilius and Diogenes Laertius and locates it in Pedro Mexía, *Silva de varia lección*. In the *Polyanthea* of Nanni Mirabelli (ed. Savona: F. de Silva, 1503), one also reads, s.v. *aurum* (col.

315): "Physicus quiddam interrogauit Diogenem, cur aurum palleret? Quoniam, inquit, plurimos habet sibi insidiantes. Pallent autem qui metuunt" ("Some natural philosopher asked Diogenes why gold was yellow. Because, he said, it has so many people after it. Those who are afraid turn yellow").

70. Terence's "Amantium irae amoris integratio" ("Lovers' spats are a reaffirming of love") clearly struck a responsive chord in Lope: it summed up in a succinct formula a conviction based on long experience and, as Morby's n. 89, p. 417, makes clear, one that is expressed repeatedly throughout his work. The tag was already common a century earlier, viz., in Feliciano de Silva, *Segunda comedia de Celestina* [1534], ed. J. A. de Palenchana (Madrid: Rivadeneyra, 1874), p. 132. It also is the subject of at least one emblem—the fifty-ninth in Jacob Cats, *Emblemata moralia et aeconomica* (Rotterdam: P. van Waesberge, 1627). One notes that Fernando's version of the saying is an exact translation of the caption of this emblem—"Irae amantium redintegratio amoris" (down to the form "redintegratio" instead of "integratio") —rather than of the original Terentian version. This could mean that Lope knew, in this or an earlier collection, this pictorial form of the commonplace, which shows Cupid putting away his arrows against the backdrop of a clearing sky.

71. *OS*, IV, 167.

72. *Obras completas (Prosa)*, ed. L. Astrana Marín (Madrid: Aguilar, 1932), p. 150. A character in Lope's *Los melindres de Belisa* makes a similar remark (Ac. N., XII, 658a).

73. Venus, Apollo, and Juno, for example, when Isabel of Valois entered Toledo in 1560; coachmen dressed as Midas and the satyr Marsyas at games in Valladolid in 1590, with Bacchus and Silenus following them. Neptune and the Muses and the Seven Liberal Arts took part in the observance of the queen's entry into Madrid in 1599; mythological scenes and the taking of Troy in pyrotechnics, the nine peers of Fame, Neptune riding Pegasus at the head of a troop of sea-gods, Diana as huntress, and countless others figured on later occasions. Descriptions of such festivities are reproduced in the chronologically arranged *Relaciones de solemnidades y fiestas públicas de España* of J. Alenda y Mira (Madrid: Sucesores de Rivadeneyra, 1903), pp. 101a, 130b, etc.

74. One may perhaps see in such invoking of anonymous books an effect of the popularity in the Spanish Golden Age of the symbolic imagery of the book; cf. E. R. Curtius, *European Literature and the Latin Middle Ages*, trans. W. R. Trask (New York: Pantheon, 1953), pp. 340–346.

75. In a letter of 1611, Lope writes to the Duke of Sessa: "La carta de don Lorenzo tengo sola de Vex.ª, y assí, va inserta en estos renglones; en oyendo dezir *indecoro* vi que era suya, porque es el más afficionado a vocablos nuebos de cuantos archidiscretos tiene la Corte" ("Don Lorenzo's letter is the only one I have of Your Excellency's, and so I am including it with these lines; as soon as I heard *indecoro* [indecorous] I realized it was his because he is the most given to new words of any of the supersophisticates of this Court city") (*Epistolario*, III, 40). On the vogue of new words of every kind, see Lucien-Paul Thomas, *Le Lyrisme et la préciosité cultistes en Espagne* (Halle: M.

Niemeyer, 1909), pp. 139–140; and M. Romera-Navarro, *La preceptiva dramática de Lope de Vega* (Madrid: Ediciones Yunque, 1935), p. 271.

76. "Epístola a Angulo," *OS*, I, 425.

77. Horozco y Covarrubias, *Emblemas morales*, II, fol. 70v.

78. Lope's fancy was clearly struck by the term "bagatelas." In *La Gatomaquia*, Silva VI, he refers to "niñerías que en Italia se llaman *bagatelas*" ("inconsequentialities [lit., childish things] that in Italy are called bagatelles") (ed. F. Rodríguez Marín [Madrid: C. Bermejo, 1935], p. 67). In *El anzuelo de Fenisa* (Fenisa's Snare) (*Comedias escogidas*, III, 369b), in a scene set in a Palermo home, an *escritorio* (writing-box) is brought out and it is explained that its contents "bagatelas son, que allá soléis llamar niñerías" ("are bagatelles, which over there you customarily call inconsequentialities"). There may be a connection between this scene and that of *La Dorotea* (II, 3). The play is dated by Morley and Bruerton 1602–1608 (probably 1604–1606), and the sequence could conceivably have been expanded upon by Lope when revising *La Dorotea*, although in view of the uncertain chronology of the *acción en prosa*, the order of priority could also be the reverse.

79. Lope may never have seen a banana or alligator pear since, as Morby points out (p. 133, n. 11), they had not yet been widely introduced in Europe. He must have seen reproductions in illustrated histories or chronicles. The fascination with the sound and exotic associations, the sheer verbal substance of the names of New World flora, is plain in the *Laurel de Apolo* (*OS*, I, 34):

> . . . algunos Indianos viendo el leño
> de mil árboles Indios enramado,
> bexucos de guaquimos,
> camayronas de arroba los razimos,
> aguacates, mageyes [*sic*], achiotes,
> quithayas, guamas, tunas y zapotes,
> preguntaban, de dónde havía trahido
> árboles, que en la India havían nacido,
> tan frescos a Sevilla. . . .

Some *indianos* seeing branches of a thousand trees of the Indies festooning the masts, filaments of *guajimos*, *camaironas* with twenty-five-pound fruit clusters, alligator pears, magueys, heart-leaved *bixas*, *quithayas*, *guamo* fruit, prickly pears, and *zapote* fruit, asked how it [the ship] had brought trees that had grown in the Indies to Seville in such fresh condition.

80. Cf. L. Spitzer, *Die Literarisierung des Lebens in Lope's "Dorotea"* (Bonn and Cologne: Rohrscheid, 1932), p. 28. In "mager" (maguer) Gerarda has picked up an archaism that had been partially restored to use by the *romances en fabla* (ballads in antiquated language). (See R. Menéndez Pidal, *Romancero hispánico* [Madrid, Espasa-Calpe, 1953], II, 157.) In his *Mercurius Trimegistus*, Ximénez Patón, after including the word among "the very ancient ones," observes that on occasion such a word may

be "more expressive . . . more efficacious and weighty [than modern ones]." He notes that *comedias* "such as those about the Cid Ruy Díaz" as well as *romances* were bringing about the reintroduction of old words (fol. 60v). Carballo in his *Cisne de Apolo* (II, 134) includes *maguer* among words used by Juan de Mena which are now archaic and to be avoided, except when used "on purpose." "Primorosa" Lope apparently considered a contemporaneous *cultismo*.

81. The fun here is at the *culteranos'* expense. Lope connected *morigerado* and presumably *educación* (like *primoroso*) with the *culterano* lexicon. The first word appears in a list of *culterano* words in the "Epístola a Angulo," *OS*, I, 425. (This, however, did not prevent his employing it in *El Caballero de Olmedo*.) The comparison of language, in its catchiness, to a rash, is a dig at the *culteranos*: "y aun un médico decía / que era esta negra poesía / especie de enfermedad. / Sarna, dijo, a lo divino" ("and a doctor also said that this black poetry was a kind of illness. The itch gone godly, he said"). (*Servir a señor discreto* [Serving a Clever Master], Ac., XV, 576b)

82. The term *simpatía* was in style. Cf. this passage from Juan de Robles:

> Lo mismo le sucedió a un criado del Cardenal de Castro, mi señor, que, oyendo una comedia en Valencia, dixo un galán que ningún amor tenía simpatía con el de su dama. Salimos del corral y encontramos un hombre vendiendo peines de Tortosa, que son muy buenos; y queriendo comprarlos, dijo aquel criado: "¿Para qué queremos ir cargados destos? Hay peines en el mundo que tengan simpatías con los de Sevilla?" (*El culto sevillano*, p. 239)

> The same thing happened to a servant of my lord, Cardinal Castro, when he was at a play in Valencia. One of the players said that no love was in sympathy with that of his lady. We left the theater-yard and met a man selling Tortosa combs, which are very good ones, and when [my lord] wished to buy some that servant said: "Why should we load ourselves down with these? Are there any combs in the world in sympathy with those of Seville?"

The anecdote shows the part the stage could play as a medium of stylistic leveling. Don Bela (p. 233) and Julio (p. 92) also use the word *simpatía*.

83. Maurice Charney notes (*Shakespeare's Roman Plays: The Function of Imagery in the Drama* [Cambridge, Mass.: Harvard University Press, 1961], p. 222) apropos of Cleopatra's speech to the asp (*Antony and Cleopatra*, V, ii, 306–309: "Come thou mortal wretch / with thy sharp teeth this not intrinsicate / of life at once untie"): "'Intrinsicate' was considered a pedantic 'inkhorn' term in its time, a fit object for satire in Marston's *The Scourge of Villanie* (1599). 'When his poem shall come into the late perfumed fist of judiciall Torquatus . . . he will vouchsafe it some of his new-minted Epithets (as Reall, Intrinsicate, Delphicke . . .).'" In Spain the word is known from the mid-fifteenth century; we find it on Celestina's lips (*Tragicomedia de Calixto y Melibea*, ed. Criado de Val and Trotter, p. 48), and Lope himself uses it in *La Arcadia* (*OS*, VI, 409). It nonetheless clearly retains a learned ring and it is unfamiliarity as well as wine that trips Gerarda up. The contrast between the ease with which

Celestina utters it and Gerarda's difficulty with it is an indication of the increased stylistic realism of the *acción en prosa*.

84. See Morby, p. 367, n. 235, and my "The *Officina* of Ravisius Textor in Lope de Vega's *Dorotea*," *Hispanic Review*, 26 (1958), 127.

85. Although it is hardly necessary to cite precedents for greeting a victory in love with exaggerated expressions of jubilation, Lope may have recalled those which Ferreira de Vasconcelos gives his protagonist, Zelotypo, when he finally wins Euphrosina toward the end of the work of the same name (*Comedia Euphrosina*, ed. E. Asensio [Madrid: C.S.I.C., 1951], I, 302):

> Se he verdade que morrem as pessoas antes de prazer que de pesar,
> verdadeiramente eu não sey como sou viuo, nem hey minha vida por segura . . .
> Porque o meu contentamento assí como nunca ouue outro tal, assí deue fazer
> diferentes mostras e efeytos dos que se ja viram, nem creyo que quando
> Hércules alcançou a sua amada Jole, Demofom a Hisiphile, Paris a Helena,
> Horestes a Hermione, e Martes aa fermosa Venus algum deles teue a terça parte
> da gloria que eu tiue.

> If it is true that people die more easily from pleasure than from grief, I really
> don't know how I am alive nor do I consider my life safe . . . Because just as
> there never was any happiness like mine, so it must have different manifestations
> and effects from those hitherto known, nor do I believe that when Hercules
> won his lady Iole, Demophon Hypsipyle, Paris Helen, Orestes Hermione, and
> Mars the beautiful Venus, any of them knew one third the bliss that I knew.

A comparison of this soliloquy (to which the unseen Cariophilo supplies sarcastic asides *sotto voce*) with the collaborative performance of Fernando and his peers serves to highlight the contrast between the highly ornate rhetorical and theatrical character of the latter and the simpler decorative effect of the *exempla* cited in the mid-sixteenth-century work.

86. See Werner Weisbach, *Trionfi* (Berlin: G. Grote, 1919), *passim*.

87. Of the Carriage of Virginity Lope writes, for example: "Aquí varias *historias engastadas* [emphasis mine] / formaban tantos arcos y molduras / en oro, plata y piedras relevadas / Que solas las divinas hermosuras, / de quien eran assiento, no pudieran / dejar de ser entre su luz oscuras" ("Here several enchased stories formed so many arches and moldings, embossed in gold, silver, and precious stones, that only the divine beauties for whom they served as a support could have failed to appear dark amidst their light") (*OS*, XIII, 51). Not only the triumphal carriages file by; there are also processions of saints and other holy figures both in and out of them. Among the "spoils of war" secured to the carriage representing the Triumph of the Victorious Angels (p. 12) is Lucifer; Erasmus "atado, maltratado y roto, / dio fin a los despojos" ("bound, battered, and tattered, was the last of the booty") tied to the carriage of the Triumph of Religion (p. 50); while behind the Carriage of Virginity is found "incontinence bound by the neck with an iron" (p. 56). This allegorical depiction of a moral quality in the form of a captive figure is similar to the case of

"the pretended disdain of Dorotea." According to Edward Müller-Bochat, the publication of Lope's *Triunfos divinos* in 1625 gave the Infanta Clara Eugenia the idea of commissioning Rubens to execute the tapestries on the same subject which now adorn the Convent of the Royal Discalced Nuns in Madrid; Rubens's cartoons are in the Prado. See *Der allegorische Triumphzug: Ein Motiv Petrarcas bei Lope de Vega und Rubens* (Krefeld: Scherpe, 1957). Karl-Ludwig Selig, reviewing Müller-Bochat's monograph in *Bibliothèque d'Humanisme et Renaissance*, 20 (1958), 483–484, considers the relationship with Rubens still to be demonstrated. In any case, the pictorial and plastic cast of Lope's imagination is clearly seen in the *Triunfos divinos*. In *La Dorotea*, he has in mind, rather than the Christian allegorical triumph, the original Roman form of the motif, with the return of the victorious consul or general, also a favorite pictorical and decorative subject. This he also alludes to at the end of the Coro de Interés (p. 202).

88. *Tragicomedia de Calixto y Melibea*, ed. Criado de Val and Trotter, p. 24.

89. At this stage Belardo had dismissed the portrait with scorn, "que aun no quiero ver pequeño / dueño de tan bajo trato" ("I don't even want to see in miniature a mistress who acts so basely") (p. 677b).

90. The marriage of histrionism and rhetoric is of long standing and the extremes to which Fernando goes need no other measuring stick than the sober warning of Quintilian: "The comic actor will also claim a certain amount of our attention, but only insofar as our future orator must be a master of the art of delivery . . . Nor yet again must we adopt all the gestures and movements of the actor. Within certain limits the orator must be a master of both, but he must rigorously avoid staginess ["aberit a scenico"] and all extravagance of facial expression, gesture, and gait. For if an orator does command a certain art in such matters, its highest expression will be in the concealment of its existence." *Institutio Oratoria*, I, 11, 1–3, trans. H. E. Butler (Cambridge, Mass.: Harvard University Press, 1959), pp. 183, 185.

91. See above, note 55 to this chapter.

92. *Die Literarisierung*, p. 33n.

93. I follow the punctuation of the facs. ed., fol. 21r.

94. See above, pp. 470–471, 478.

95. There seems to be some inconsistency between Marfisa's telling Dorotea when they meet in the Prado (IV, 1) that Fernando "auráos engañado; que sabe fingir vna muerte con gran donaire" ("must have deceived you because he knows how to feign a murder in a most accomplished way") (p. 291) and the implication six scenes later (p. 376), as she waits at his door to denounce him, that she has only then learned of his duplicity, an implication consistent with her remark to Dorotea on the earlier occasion that Fernando is still in Seville. But perhaps Marfisa is merely alluding to what she believes to be Fernando's restaging of an actual occurrence, extolling, that is, his histrionic powers. Or are we to see, on the contrary, in the remark, a first tentative acknowledgment of disbelief originally suppressed under the spell of Fernando's theatrics? Neither explanation seems wholly satisfactory and one cannot discount the possibility of a plain oversight on Lope's part.

96. Lope frequently uses this formula—for example, in "Felicio," the elegiac piscatory eclogue on the death of his son Lope Félix written in 1634 or 1635, to describe the reaction of Eliso (his persona in the poem) to the news: "Cayó no de otra suerte desmayado, / que suele a la segur robusta encina" ("He fell down in a faint, not otherwise than a robust oak is wont to fall under the ax") (*OS*, X, 378). He uses it burlesquely in *La Gatomaquia* to introduce comically prolonged similes for cats in flight: "No de otra suerte, que en sereno día / balas de nieve escupe" ("Not otherwise than on a clear day [a storm] spits pellets of snow"); "No de otra suerte el jugador ligero / le vuelve la pelota" ("Not otherwise does the nimble player return the ball") (ed. Rodríguez Marín, pp. 8 and 19). Besides underscoring the impropriety of Fernando's simile, Marfisa's comment ridicules the irrationality, which Lope found irresistibly comical, of expecting an angry bull to stop for questions. Cf. this passage from *La Gatomaquia* (p. 36):

Aquí Marramaquiz, desatinado
cual suele arremeter el jarameño
toro feroz, de media luna armado,
al caballero, con airado ceño
(andaluz o extremeño:
que la patria jamás pregunta el toro) . . .

At this point Marramaquiz, beside himself, just as a fierce bull of the Jarama armed with his half-moon, will lunge with an angry scowl at the horseman (Andalusian or Extremaduran: the bull never asks where he comes from) . . .

97. Cf. the following passage from Lope's "La rosa blanca" ("The White Rose") [1624], *Obras poéticas*, p. 1064:

No de otra suerte dos valientes toros
celosos riñen por la vaca amada,
y por el monte van bramando a coros,
a la dura palestra y estacada
donde vertiendo los abiertos poros
sangre, y furor, en tanto, conquistada
del más cobarde y flaco, está rendida,
él puesto en posesión y ellos sin vida.

Not otherwise two brave bulls from jealousy fight over the beloved cow and go bellowing back and forth over the mountain to the hard wrestling-floor and stockade where, as blood and fury gush from their open pores, the cow meanwhile, a conquest of the weakest and most cowardly bull, has given in to him—he in possession and they lifeless.

At the basis of this and similar figures involving a bull losing the cow to a rival is probably Ovid's description of Polyphemus: "ut taurus vacca furibundus adempta / stare nequit silvaque et notis saltibus errat" ("as a bull, raging when the cow has been taken away from him, cannot stand still but wanders through the woods and familiar pastures") (*Metamorphoses*, XIII, 871–872). (One notes how characteristically Lope builds a dramatic and novel situation out of the motif in "La rosa blanca.") The germaneness of such figures to lofty poetic style may be gauged by an example in the *Fábula de Atis y Galatea* of Carrillo y Sotomayor [1611] (ed. P. Henríquez-Ureña and E. Moreno [La Plata: Cuadernos de *Don Segundo Sombra*, 1929], p. 22):

> Cual el valiente toro, que ha perdido
> de la vacada el reino, que enojado
> espanta el bosque con feroz bramido,
> desafía al contrario . . .

> As the brave bull which has lost sway over the herd of cows, and angrily terrifies the woods with his fierce bellowing, challenges his adversary . . .

Fernando's "comparación" is a sign of the practice not only of verse, as Marfisa says, but of the poetic prose of the pastoral, where the leisurely cadence and bucolic content of his comparison, notwithstanding the incongruous venatory note which he injects into it, are clearly at home. Amphryso indeed applies such imagery to himself in *La Arcadia*: "Si un toro como tú sabes, vencido de su competidor, huye la vista de la amada vaca, y si segunda y tercera vez es vencido, metiéndose entre asperíssimos bosques, miserablemente perece, ¿cómo podré yo, triste, vencido de mi competidor, vivir entre hombres?" ("If a bull, as you know, when vanquished by his competitor, flees the sight of the beloved cow, and if he is vanquished a second and third time, penetrating the thickest woods, dies wretchedly, how shall I, miserable one that I am, vanquished by my competitor, live among men?") (*OS*, VI, 318).

98. See p. 452 above and the analysis on pp. 477–478 above.

99. *Die Literarisierung*, p. 30.

100. When those around Fernando adopt his language, they invariably come up with imagery of this kind, Teodora in sarcasm, Dorotea imploringly (see above, p. 454), Ludovico as a poetic confrère and fellow spirit (see above, p. 475), Julio voicing Lope's own irony:

Teodora (to Dorotea, after pulling her hair): "Dile a don Fernando que haga versos a este sujeto, y que me llame Nerona, sacrílega, atreuida a la cabeça del sol" ("Tell Don Fernando to write a poem about this and call me a female Nero, a sacrilegious woman making bold with the head of the sun" (p. 77).

Julio (reacting to Fernando's description of Dorotea's swoon): "Celia, encender quiero vn acha" ("Celia, I'd like to light a flare") (p. 94).

101. "Musa" here is not a personification but a personalizing of poetic inspiration, as often for Lope: "mi mejor musa, Amarilis" ("my best muse, Amarilis"), "póstuma de mis musas, Dorotea" ("the posthumous one of my muses, Dorotea"), etc.

102. The already noted formality with which Fernando introduces his account of the cooling of his love suggests the reading of a poem not only entertaining but edifying: "Os suplico que no os tengáis por deseruido de estarme atento; por ventura daréis por bien empleado el silencio" ("I beg you not to consider it a disservice if I

ask you to heed what I say; you will perhaps consider the silence well employed")
(p. 404).

103. "Illa quoque vocatur *aversio*, quae a proposita questione abducit audientem" ("That is also called *aversio* which takes the hearer away from the subject at hand"). Quintilian, IX, 2, 39.

104. "Levinus Lemnius and Leo Suabius in *La Dorotea*," *Hispanic Review*, 20 (1952), 108–122.

105. On this subject, I have found helpful H. H. Hudson, "Rhetoric and Poetry," in *Historical Studies of Rhetoric and Rhetoricians*, ed. R. F. Howes (Ithaca: Cornell University Press, 1961), pp. 369–379.

106. The differences affecting imagery will be treated in the context of the individual passages.

107. "Mejor me parece se aplican a su dulzura [*scil.*, of music] los versos líricos, que los heroicos" ("Lyric verse seems to me to suit its [music's] sweetness better than the heroic") (*Los pastores de Belén*, OS, XVI, 363). "Canto a Dios sus inefables glorias, / a quien los corazones encendidos / de mi dulzura erigen sus memorias" ("I sing His ineffable glories unto God, to whom hearts inflamed by my sweetness raise their paeans"); "Música," *La Arcadia*, OS, VI, 417 (Music speaking). "Canta Amarylis, y su voz levanta / mi alma desde el orbe de la luna / a las inteligencias, que ninguna / la suya imita con dulzura tanta" ("Amarilis sings and her voice lifts my soul from the orb of the moon to the intelligences, none of which can imitate the sweetness of her voice") (*OS*, I, 378).

108. *Epistolario*, III, 310.

109. *Obras de Garci Lasso de la Vega* (Seville: Alonso de la Barrera, 1580), p. 293.

110. *El culto sevillano*, p. 237.

111. *El peregrino en su patria*, OS, V, 132.

112. *Obras de Garci Lasso*, p. 131.

113. *El culto sevillano*, p. 125. The reference to Aristotle should be to *Rhetoric*, sec. 1406a: "That is why the epithets of Alcidamas leave us so cold; he does not use them as sauce for the meat, but as the meat itself."

114. *Obras de Garci Lasso*, p. 85.

115. *Cisne de Apolo*, II, 56.

116. *De arte rhetorica*, fol. 34v. The proscription against far-fetched metaphors goes back to Aristotle, *Rhetoric*, sec. 1405a; Suárez refers it marginally to Quintilian, VIII, 6, 17 and Cicero, *De Oratore*. His first sentence is in fact simply quoted from Cicero, *De Oratore*, III, 41, 163.

117. Cf. Morby's n. 183, p. 349, and also Quintilian, IX, 4, 72.

118. *De arte rhetorica*, fol. 31r, with marginal reference to Quintilian, I, 6, 32.

119. The image appears to derive from a description of Olimpia in the *Orlando furioso* (XI, 65):

Era il bel viso suo, quale esser suole
da primavera alcuna volta il cielo,

quando la pioggia cade, e a un tempo il sole
si sgombra intorno il nubiloso velo.

Her beautiful face was as the sky is wont to be sometimes in spring when rain
falls and the sun at the same time clears away the cloudy veil surrounding it.

120. Antonio Vilanova sees a possible reminiscence of this strain of imagery in
Góngora's lines: "Purpúreas rosas sobre Galatea / la Alba entre lilios cándidos deshoja"
("Dawn sheds petals of purple roses and white lilies upon Galatea") (*Polifemo*, XIV,
1–2). He traces it back to Propertius—"Utque rosae puro lacte natant folia" ("And
as rose petals float on pure white milk") (II, 12)—and suggests that Góngora's
"deshoja" ("sheds petals of") shows conflation with the passage I have quoted from
Lope's *Arcadia* as well, "where the expression 'deshojar' appears for the first time."
In Góngora's lines, however, other strains—Ovidian and Virgilian—in which milk
or curds do not appear, are much more prominent. (*Las fuentes y los temas*, I, 625–626
and 629). In any case, behind Propertius we find Anacreon (XXVII, 21–22):

γράφε ῥῖνα καὶ παρειάς,
ῥοδὰ τῷ γάλακτι μίξῃς

Paint the skin and the cheeks, mingling roses with milk.

Theocritus's treatment of Polyphemus and Galatea, in which the motif of milk
(curd)-like whiteness appears, may also be recalled. (The sea-nymph's name may
itself be linked to γάλα—"milk"—perhaps alluding to the whiteness of sea-foam.)
Theocritus's Polyphemus calls Galatea: 'Ω λευκὰ Γαλάτεια . . . / λευκότερα πακτᾶς
ποτιδεῖν ("Oh fair Galatea . . . fairer to look upon than creamy curds") (XI, 19–20).
In the second eclogue of Sannazaro's *Arcadia*, the motif recurs rather routinely:
"Tyrona mia, il cui color aguaglia / le matutine rose e 'l puro lacte" ("Tyrona of
mine, whose complexion is like early morning roses and pure white milk") (ll. 109–
110). Lope must have Anacreon or Propertius as well as, possibly, Sannazaro in mind
in *La Arcadia* and *La Dorotea* and also in *El peregrino en su patria*: "Las colores que a
Nise le salieron, amigo Peregrino, quando oyó las palabras de Pánfilo, bien se pueden
comparar a las rosas deshojadas acaso sobre la leche cándida, aunque esto sea término
poético" ("The color that came to Nise's cheeks, friend Pilgrim, when she heard
Pánfilo's words, may well be compared to rose-petals dropped perchance on pure
white milk, even if the expression is poetic") (*OS*, V, 212). Because *El peregrino en
su patria* is presented as a *historia*, Lope feels obliged here also to remark on the poetic
character of the image. In Pérez de Montalbán's *Orfeo en lengua castellana* (1624),
sometimes attributed to Lope, a description of Eurydice contains the lines: "Eran
las dos mexillas amorosas / en pura leche deshojadas rosas" ("The two loving cheeks
were rose petals dropped on pure white milk") (Juan Pérez de Montalbán, *Orfeo en
lengua castellana*, ed. P. Cabañas [Madrid: C.S.I.C., 1948], p. 32).

The detail of the "texidas encellas" ("wattle baskets") reappears frequently in
Lope, evidence of his sensitivity to the subtlest combinations of plastic, tactile, and

visual impressions. In *La Arcadia* we find, albeit with characteristic epithets, a direct perception: "en texidas encellas de torcidos mimbres, los naterones cándidos" ("in wattle baskets of twisted osiers, pure white curds") (*OS*, VI, 120). In *Jerusalén conquistada* (1609) the detail is even more naturalistically presented and, again, is not the vehicle of a metaphor: "La cena se apercibe en pobre mesa, / con negro pan y cándida cuajada, / tan fresca que por ella se ve impresa / mimbrosa encella, en torno dibujada" ("Supper is prepared on a poor table, with black bread and pure white curds, so fresh that one can see imprinted on them an osier basket, impressed all about") (*OS*, XV, 166). In *La Circe* Lope noticeably embroiders on Theocritus (and, in his own way, on Góngora): "O más hermosa y dulce Galatea, / que entre las mimbres de la encella elada / cándida leche pura de Amalthea" ("Oh Galatea, more beautiful and sweet than pure white milk of Amalthea among the osiers of the ice-cold wattle basket") (*OS*, III, 44). Lope would also surely have been struck, in Tasso's *Aminta*, by the description of the naked Silvia tied to a tree: "quelle membra belle, / che, come suole tremolare il latte / ne' giunchi, sì parean morbide e bianche" ("those beautiful limbs which appeared as soft and white as milk trembling in rushes") (III, 1, 74–76). One may judge from these various instances how vividly Lope reinvigorated inherited imagery through direct observation.

121. *La Diana*, ed. F. López Estrada (Madrid: Espasa-Calpe, 1946), p. 246.

122. P. 242. Morby, n. 86, sees a possible reference to the sonnet "Datemi pace, o duri miei pensieri" ("Give me peace, oh harsh thoughts of mine").

123. My analysis disregards the introductory words "A recibir ..." since the four syntactically similar members of the succeeding appositive series are clearly felt as a rhetorical and poetic unit.

124. *Mercurius Trimegistus*, fol. 108v.

125. *Obras completas*, ed. Buendía, I, 363. There is, of course, similar mockery by Cervantes in the *Adjunta al Parnaso*.

126. *Rimas de Bartolomé y Lupercio L. de Argensola*, ed. J. M. Blecua (Saragossa: C.S.I.C., 1951), II, 373, and II, 375.

127. Preface to *Rimas* of 1602, *OS*, IV, 171.

128. *OS*, IV, 508.

129. Cf. Julio's "recipe" for the lovers' reconciliation, "Recipe la yerua Dorotea" ("Take the herb Dorotea"), and Morby's note, p. 313.

130. *OS*, VI, 364.

131. The paradoxical confounding of the senses of sight and taste is not of course original with Lope. Earlier, in Torres Naharro, for example, we find: "Es mi mal / ... / vna ponçoña real / que por los ojos beuí" ("This affliction of mine ... is a royal poison that I drank in through the eyes") (*Propalladia and Other Works of Bartolomé de Torres Naharro*, ed. J. E. Gillet [Bryn Mawr, Pa., and Menasha, Wis.: George Banta Publishing Co., 1946], II, 518). Compared to this simple conceptual kernel, the passage of *La Arcadia* seems as highly elaborated as it seems straightforward by comparison with that of *La Dorotea*. In truth, there is a progressive unraveling of conceptual possibilities: drinking remedies or poisons, through eyes or ears, etc.

132. *OS*, I, 259. In a sonnet to Van der Hamen (*OS*, I, 399) Nature complains to Jupiter:

Dixo, que vuestro ingenio peregrino
le hurtó para hacer frutas sus pinceles;
que no pintáis, sino criáis claveles,
como ella en tierra, vos en blanco lino.

She said that your remarkable talent stole her brushes from her in order to paint fruit; that you don't paint but grow carnations—as she does in the earth, so you do on white canvas.

133. Madrid: Francisco Martínez, 1633, fol. 82v.

134. The fact that painting was not one of the liberal arts did not preclude ascribing a divine character to it, especially in the art theory of Spain. Lope is in fact alluding to one of the key tenets of Carducho's work. The subject is discussed by Curtius, *European Literature and the Latin Middle Ages*, excursus 23, espec. p. 561.

135. Morby notes that "escultura de Michael Angel" is not appositive with "mármol de Lucrecia," there being no such statue by the Italian artist. Perhaps the phrase should be associated with the "aurora de jazmines," as an allusion to the famous Dawn of the Medici tombs.

136. Samples of such verse are, as we know, included in *La Dorotea*, viz., the "versos que le hize al brío y gracia con que anduuo aquel día" ("lines I wrote for her about the verve and elegance she displayed that day") (p. 109); and more is alluded to: "dézimas concetiles, soneto releuante, o romance brillador con su villancico a la postre, o lamentable estriuo como aquello de 'Filis me ha muerto'" ("conceit-packed *décimas*, a showy sonnet or a flashy ballad with its popular air at the end or its mournful refrain like the one that goes 'Filis killed me'") (p. 449), as Gerarda disparagingly calls them. She also describes Dorotea as "muy desvanecida de que se canten por el lugar a bueltas de sus gracias, sus flaquezas" ("all stuck up at their singing about town her foibles along with her charms") (p. 70).

137. Ficino (Fifth Speech, chap. 2) sets the higher "spiritual" senses, oriented toward the soul (seeing, the highest, then hearing), apart from the lower, which pertain to the body: in descending order, smell, taste, touch. In modern terms he sets apart the "distance receptors" from the "contact" senses, making the former characteristic of the noble, the latter of the plebeian nature. The keen responsiveness of Lope to percepts of the contact as well as the distance senses, a characteristic trait of his own nature, is quite capable of superseding the traditional distinction in as personal a work as *La Dorotea*, where it is manifest also in Fernando's already discussed elaboration of the "vista-bebida" ("sight-drink") conceptual paradox. One notes that in *Lo fingido verdadero* a verse-writing recipe includes the provision: "Revuelva las olores, las especias / de las dos Indias" ("Let him run through the fragrances, the spices of the two Indies") (Ac., IV, 58a). A passage in *Las ferias de Madrid*, while pointedly associating the sense of smell with the lackey, in the master's response suggests the kind of olfactory distinction elaborated upon in *La Dorotea*:

Lucrecio: ¡A mí me cabe el oler
            por Dios, bellaco sentido!
            si por la noche, a las diez,
            va a la calle de Santiago.
Claudio: Hame llovido su estrago,
            Lucrecio, más de una vez.
            De trabajos semejantes
            es de noche peligrosa;
            pero de día olorosa
            porque allí se adoban guantes.

(Ac. N., V, 609a)

Lucrecio: Smelling is my lot, a ruffianly sense by God, if at ten o'clock in the evening you go to Santiago Street. *Claudio:* More than once its damage has rained down on me, Lucrecio. There's always the danger of having to put up with such things there at night but by day it's fragrant because gloves are treated with scent there.

138. The scatological implication of Góngora's lines is not evident in Julio's reference to them.

139. See Morby's n. 150, p. 267.

140. The gaucheness and plainness of Don Bela's style become evident when contrasted with a conceptual elaboration of these same materials in verse in *El saber puede dañar* (Ignorance Is Bliss):

Camilo: Son las joyas que le das
          conformes a tu valor.
Principe: Si se las diera mi amor,
          Camilo, valieran más,
          porque es menester que críes,
          Naturaleza, diamantes,
          en la China más brillantes
          y en Ceilán nuevos rubíes;
          y aún con cambios diferentes,
          en que ella recibe agravios,
          con las rosas de sus labios
          y las perlas de sus dientes.
Camilo: ¡Bravo pintor es amor!

(*Comedias escogidas*, III, 123)

Camilo: The jewels you are giving her are in keeping with your worth.
Prince: If my love could give them to her, Camilo, they would be worth more because, Nature, in China you will have to produce diamonds more sparkling,

and in Ceylon new rubies, different scintillations also, to put the roses of her lips and the pearls of her teeth to shame.   *Camilo:* What a superb painter love is!

141. As Morby notes (p. 133, n. 10), in the term *energía,* a rhetorical quality (*energeia*) and a rhetorical device (*enargeia*) had become confused, the first referring to vigor in the manner of putting across one's thought (related to *subiectio*; see Lausberg, *Handbuch,* I, sec. 772), the second to visual vividness in description (*perspicuitas, evidentia*). Morby extensively documents the confusion and notes the difficulty of ascertaining which sense Lope had in mind. Don Bela would scarcely be thinking of both, in any case; it is the first which better suits his whole manner and practice. In the two instances of Lope's own use of the term in the *Epistolario,* one is similarly in doubt, as Morby notes, though I incline to believe that one (III, 24) exemplifies *energeia* and the other (III, 336) *enargeia*. In any case, contrary to the view of J. de Entrambasaguas ("Las 'hipérboles' y 'energías' de *La Dorotea* de Lope de Vega," *Romanica et occidentalia: Etudes dédiées à la mémoire de Hiram Peri [Pflaum],* ed. Moshe Lazar [Jerusalem: Magnes Press, Université hébraïque, 1963], p. 148), in my opinion something more than a comical effect is involved.

142. Compare Dorotea's "Supo [mi madre] que auía vendido los passamanos del manteo de tela el mes passado, y antiyer el de primauera de flores" ("[My mother] found out that I had sold the gilt lace edgings of the fabric cloak last month and the flowering spring one the day before yesterday") (p. 99) with Gerarda's words to Teodora: "Ayer vendió [Dorotea] vn manteo a vna amiga suya, y dize que por deuoción y promessa trae vn ábito de picote la que solía arrastrar Milanes y Nápoles en passamanos y telas" ("Yesterday [Dorotea] sold a cloak to a friend of hers and she says that out of piety and to keep a vow she is wearing a goathair habit, she who used to trail Milans and Naples after her in gilt lace trimmings and in fabrics") (p. 69).

143. The underlying concept belongs to the Platonic framework of the pastoral. Cf. Filemón in Montemayor's *La Diana* (ed. López Estrada, p. 261): "Quando yo nací y aún ante mucho que naciesse, los hados me destinaron para que amasse a esta hermosa pastora" ("When I was born and indeed much before I was born, the fates destined me to love this beautiful shepherdess").

144. *Die Literarisierung,* p. 25.

145. The Spanish greeting is both Celestinesque and traditional—cf. *Tragicomedia de Calixto y Melibea,* ed. Criado de Val and Trotter, p. 82—but the addendum is her own. The garbling of Latin by ignorant old women, of which Lope made such effective comic use also in the Fabia of *El caballero de Olmedo,* was a commonplace form of sanctimoniousness. Cf., for example:

Fabricio: Siempre tuvieron pasión las viejas de meterse latinas y aun pienso que se debe de fundar en algo desto lo que suelen decir a las tales: "Puta vieja, ¿latín sabéis?"

Castañeda: De veras lo diríades si hubiérades oído, como yo, algunas destas

viejas rezadoras, que en las iglesias levantan la voz sobre todos los
circunstantes, interpretando las palabras del oficio divino a su modo.

(Hidalgo, *Diálogos*, p. 299a)

Fabricio: Old women have always had a passion for spouting Latin: in fact
I think something of this kind must be at the bottom of what people commonly
say to them: "You old whore, so you know Latin?" *Castañeda:* You'd really
say it, too, if you had heard some of these old women at their prayers, as I
have, raising their voices in church above all those around them and
interpreting the words of the divine services in their own way.

146. *Tragicomedia de Calixto y Melibea*, ed. Criado de Val and Trotter, p. 47.

147. On Gerarda's "trivializing," cf. Spitzer, *Die Literarisierung*, p. 30.

148. Juan de Robles, *El culto sevillano*, p. 241, provides perspective on the specific
impropriety. When one is addressing "los señores, a quien ha puesto Dios en la
tierra en su lugar" ("masters, whom God has placed on earth in their appointed
station"), he proscribes the use of "comparaciones de cosas bajas, como el que dijo a
un príncipe que sus favores eran chapines que levantaban . . ." ("comparisons with
base things, like the person who told a prince that his favors were clogs that
elevated . . .").

149. As Morby notes (n. 163), " ¡Gragea a Guinea!" is incorrectly underlined in the
original edition, since it is not a proverb but a coining of Gerarda, prompted by an
association of black with black as well as by the play of sound. In the amplifying
sequence, "Vn testimonio, zelos de casadas, embidia de donzellas, malas lenguas
de mugeres libres" ("A piece of slander, pure jealousy on the part of married women,
envy on that of single, loose tongues of loose tarts") (p. 137), one notes the echo effect
of the repeated *m* and *l* in the final phrase.

150. "Proverbs in *La Dorotea*," *Romance Philology*, 8 (1955), 246, 249.

151. Gerarda's Latin benedictions before and after supper (pp. 190, 198) also gain
comicity from the play of rhyme and assonance.

152. "*La Célestine*" *selon Fernando de Rojas* (Paris: Didier, 1961), pp. 97ff.

153. *Die Literarisierung*, p. 25.

154. The usual ornamentality of the proverbs of *La Dorotea* does not preclude on
occasion a noticeably natural ring and a simple aptness: Teodora's already noted
remonstration to Gerarda, "Vieja que baila mucho poluo levanta" ("An old woman
dancing raises a lot of dust") (p. 121); Gerarda's "La coz de la yegua no haze mal al
potro" ("The mare's kick doesn't hurt the colt") (p. 372) in justification of scolding
her daughter; the "Adonde ay voluntad, mejor es entrarse que llamar" ("Where
there is good will, better enter than knock") (p. 231) with which she enters Don
Bela's quarters; Julio's rejoinder to Fernando's perfumed idealization of Dorotea's
street, "El poluo de la oueja alcohol es para el lobo" ("The dust of the sheep is
alcohol to the wolf") (p. 267). In at least two cases—"Contigo me entierren, que sabes

de cuentas" ("They can bury me with you—you're good at accounts") (p. 158) and "Aunque dizen que *el moço puede morir y el viejo no puede viuir*, lo cierto es ir con las leyes de la naturaleza" ("Though they say that *the young man may die and the old man cannot live*, the truth is that things go according to the laws of nature") (p. 160)—successive proverbs quoted more glibly than feelingly by Gerarda, there is marked verbal irony (see above, pp. 569, 573–574).

155. *"La Dorotea* de Lope de Vega," p. 139.

156. Dorotea's assessment of Gerarda's performance in I, 1—"Y ¡qué bien supo apocar y disminuir las partes de Don Fernando!" ("And how well she managed to minimize and diminish Don Fernando's assets!") (p. 77)—has the same professional ring.

157. I cite this study from the volume *De Cervantes y Lope de Vega*, 2nd ed. (Buenos Aires: Espasa-Calpe Argentina, 1943). For the broader background I have also drawn upon E. W. Tayler, *Nature and Art in Renaissance Literature* (New York: Columbia University Press, 1964).

158. Menéndez Pidal, *De Cervantes y Lope*, pp. 72–73, 99.

159. "Egloga a Claudio," *Obras escogidas*, II, 258.

160. "Silva a la ciudad de Logroño" ("Silva to the City of Logroño"), cited by Menéndez Pidal, *De Cervantes y Lope*, p. 31.

161. *OS*, V, xvii; cf. Menéndez Pidal, *De Cervantes y Lope*, pp. 73 and 130, n. 8.

162. The single form "perfecta" ("executed," "carried out") used by Cicero in "Meliora sunt ea, quae natura, quam illa quae arte perfecta sunt" ("Those things carried out by nature are better than those carried out by art") (*Natura Deorum*, II, 87) is given noticeably different renderings by Lope in referring to nature and to art: "hacía" ("made") and "perficiona" ("perfects"), respectively. Cervantes' "El arte no se aventaja a la naturaleza, sino perficiónala" ("Art does not surpass nature, it improves upon it") (*Don Quixote*, II, 16) places the emphasis on improving, refining.

163. Andrée Collard has recently emphasized this distinction in her *Nueva poesía: Conceptismo, culteranismo en la crítica española* (Madrid: Castalia, 1967), pp. 2–10.

164. Robles, *El culto sevillano*, p. 34; cf. the discussion in Thomas, *Le Lyrisme et la préciosité*, pp. 147–163, 167–168.

165. The Virgilian reference is to *Aeneid*, XI, 458: "Dant sonitum rauci per stagna loquacia cycni" ("Hoarse swans make sounds among the lapping pools"). It is misquoted "per saxa silentia" ("among the silent rocks") by Calepin, s.v. *raucus*, *Dictonarium septem linguarum* (Lyons, 1581).

166. Morby's n. 217, p. 361, and Dámaso Alonso's discussion in *La lengua poética de Góngora (Parte primera)* (Madrid: S. Aguirre, 1935), pp. 165–166, substantiate Góngora's special fondness for the Greek accusative construction with the verbs *calzar* (to put on the feet) or *vestir* (to dress).

167. *OS*, IV, 459 ff.

168. *OS*, VI, 411. The description of Rhetoric's room in the Temple of Learning is without originality, the source being the medieval *Visión delectable* of Alfonso de la

Torre: in *Curiosidades bibliográficas*, ed. Adolfo de Castro (Madrid: Hernando, 1926), pp. 346–347; the verse, however, has no exact equivalent in the *Visión*.

169. *OS*, V, 130–131. The reference is probably to *Institutio Oratoria*, III, 2, 2. Lope may also have been aware of Aristotle's observation on "the necessity of disguising the means we employ, so that we may seem to be speaking not with artifice, but naturally. Naturalness is persuasive, artifice is just the reverse . . . In style, the illusion is successful if we take our individual words from the current stock, and put them together [with skill]." (*Rhetoric*, III, 2, 1404b; from *The Rhetoric of Aristotle*, an expanded translation by Lane Cooper [New York: D. Appleton, 1932], p. 186.)

170. In the Prologue to Part XV (Madrid, 1621) as quoted by Romera-Navarro, *La preceptiva dramática de Lope de Vega*, p. 106. The context is anti-*culterano*.

171. *Mimesis: The Representation of Reality in Western Literature*, trans. W. R. Trask (Princeton: Princeton University Press, 1953), p. 71. In Lope's own day, Huarte de San Juan makes comments in a noticeably similar vein: "Saint Paul's talent was appropriate to this ministry because he had great ability at upholding and proving in the synagogues and among the Gentiles that Jesus Christ was the Messiah promised by the Law and that no other should be expected, this despite a poor memory, which made him unable to learn how to speak in an elaborate way with soft, sweet words, and this is just what the divulgation of the Gospel needed." The last phrase refers to the preceding remark that the mission of St. Paul was to "preach but not in an oratorical manner, so that the audience would not think that Christ's cross was some empty thing of the type that orators are always urging on us." (*Examen de Ingenios*, p. 452a.)

172. *OS*, XVII, 85. The extreme simplicity of Lope's position stands out by contrast with the reservations of Juan de Robles, who cautions on the need to "be careful about divine matters and the way the human are connected with them," citing and censuring expressions like "tiene golosina de hablar de Dios" ("he has a sweet tooth where talking of God is concerned") or references to God's "*caricias y halagos* a los hombres" ("caresses and fondling of men") ". . . because even if his Divine Majesty employs unusual similes and words in the Scripture, similar to these, it is not proper for us to use them; rather, when they are repeated, we must build them up and set them off with others of greater magnitude") (*El culto sevillano*, p. 240).

173. *OS*, XIII, 78. A corresponding devaluation of elaborate religious oratory appears very early. In the same excursus of *El peregrino* the story is told of a worldly youth converted by a sermon—"not one of those that with oratory and rhetoric appeal to the mind but one of those that with keen words come knocking at the heart . . . He embraced a cross and with some tears spoke four or five disorderly words (I mean not arranged so as to fit smoothly together; in everything else they were most chaste) which, interrupted by his moans and sighs, seemed like a child's when he is feeling sorry for himself after being punished" (p. 134). God leads him to salvation in a monastery "of the silent St. Bruno." Carthusian silence is the ultimate version of genuine inarticulateness.

174. Cf. Lausberg, *Handbuch*, I, sec. 916.

175. *Epistolario*, III, 65, Cf. also the following passage, which Lope wrote on one occasion when he had fallen out of favor: "Con temor y respeto escriuí aquel papel, que no con sequedad; porque, aunque Vex.ª me tratara como a vn perro, no la tuuiera yo, ni me dexaran tanto de su mano mi amor y obligaciones" ("I wrote that note with fear and respect, not with sarcasm, because, even though Your Excellency were to treat me like a dog, I wouldn't show any, nor would my love and indebtedness allow me to go so far astray") (*Epistolario*, IV, 81).

176. *Epistolario*, III, 19. Cf. "Mas porque Vex.ª se rinde [a] tan grosera comparación, si bien todas las permite la familiar correspondenzia, sepa Vex.ª que yo imaginé siempre a los hombres altos y bajos, grandes y chicos, como están los pasteles de diuersos precios en los mostradores de las tiendas" ("But because Your Excellency has a fondness for such crude comparisons, although it's true that informal correspondence allows them all, please understand that I have always imagined tall men and short, large and small, like meat-pies of different prices displayed in shop windows") (*Epistolario*, III, 194).

177. *Epistolario*, III, 286.

178. *Epistolario*, III, 323–324.

179. *Ibid.*

180. *Epistolario*, III, 113.

181. *Epistolario*, III, 278. A similar explanation is in *Epistolario*, IV, 140.

182. *Epistolario*, III, 284.

183. In another instance, the combination of hyperbole and apparent directness surely also betrays ambivalence: "Tenía tanto que decir en materia de las merzedes reciuidas aquel gran día, que ni prossas ni versos fueran suficientes, ellas con sus retóricas y ellos con sus energías" ("There would be so much for me to say on the subject of favors received that great day that neither prose nor verse would be adequate, the former with its rhetoric and the latter with its *energeias*" (*Epistolario*, III, 336).

184. As Morby shows, n. 141, Ludovico's example is based on a Latin distych given by the rhetorician Antonio Spelta to exemplify the figure *brevitas* or *brachylogia*.

185. W. C. Atkinson calls *La Dorotea* "the protest of genius against a mercenary world" ("*La Dorotea*, acción en prosa," *Bulletin of Spanish Studies*, 12 [1935], 212). Lope's is of course not the only protest. The traditional strictures of moralists are much insisted on in his day in sermon, emblem, disquisition, prose, and verse; examples are endless. No doubt such insistence corresponds to the situation of a society in which the corrosive effect of New World gold and silver is noticeable on every side. In the mid-sixteenth century Melchor Cano is already observing: "The insatiable greed for money ... today dominates most men and they are as set on this today as if no other happiness existed. Parents indoctrinate children with this and from early infancy make them worshippers of gold" (*Tratado de la victoria de sí mismo* [1550], *Obras escogidas de filósofos*, ed. Adolfo de Castro [Madrid: Sucesores de Hernando, 1922], 314a). In the *Emblemas moralizadas* of Hernando de Soto (Madrid:

Várez de Castro, 1599), fol. 108v, an emblem of Mercury and Argos (the latter not asleep but open-eyed) is glossed as follows:

Argos bien puede velar
con los cien ojos que suele,
que por más que se desuele
Mercurio le ha de engañar.
Porque ha hecho el inuentor
de aquel metal poderoso
un instrumento amoroso
que aduerme con gran sabor.

Let Argos keep awake as is his wont, with all his hundred eyes; for all his exertions, Mercury will dupe him. Because the inventor of that powerful metal created an instrument for love that shuts one's eyes most agreeably.

Another emblem of Soto (fol. 13) illustrates through the example of Venus and an ugly satyr the truth that "money makes the ugly beautiful." The satiric muse of Quevedo notes that "Mr. Money is a powerful gentleman" and that of Góngora (*Obras completas*, ed. J. and I. Millé y Giménez, 5th ed. [Madrid: Aguilar, 1961], p. 113) exclaims:

¡Oh interés, y cómo eres,
o por fuerza o por ardid,
para los diamantes, sangre;
para los bronces, buril!

Oh covetousness, how you are, by force or by guile, blood for diamonds, burin for bronze!

Tirso laments: "Wretched avaricious century of ours that doesn't value the quality of nobility without the quantity of gold, equating the soul's merits with greed for a metal which, as unworthy of seeing the light of day, Nature kept buried in the barbaric bowels of the rough mountains of the Indies!" (*Los Cigarrales de Toledo*, ed. V. Said Armesto [Madrid: Renacimiento, 1913], p. 225). The Spanish gloss on O. van Veen's emblem of Ovid's "Auro conciliatur amor" ("Love is procured by gold") declares that Love:

por nueuo norte en nuestra edad se guía
que no lleva otro fin sino su prouecho.
Sólo tiene interés la monarchía
de Amor puesta en costumbre y no en derecho.

is guided in our age by a new rule which has no other aim than profit. Self-interest alone holds sway over love as a matter of habit, not of right.

(I quote from *Amorum Emblemata* [Brussels: H. Swingen, 1667], p. 128; the original polyglot edition [Antwerp, 1608] includes glosses in Latin, French, and Italian only.) The appeal of the subject to writers of emblem books is inexhaustible.

The effectiveness of gold as an amatory weapon in consequence of its particular appeal to women (Lope knew well, of course, Ariosto's eloquent formulation of this aspect of *interés* in the exordium to Canto XLIII of the *Orlando furioso*) is echoed at all levels by Lope's contemporaries, often through a debunking of classical exempla: "All [women's] feats come down simply to pointing out that they are not being spoken to with money in hand; upon my faith as an honorable man, as a poet says, 'if Lucrecia were given a thousand *reales*, she would be more receptive and less silly'") (Hidalgo, *Diálogos*, p. 304a); "Ya no son las damas Eros / ni los galanes Leandros / si no dan como Alejandros" ("Ladies are no longer Heros nor gentlemen Leanders, unless money is given the way it was by Alexander") (*ibid*.)—quoted from a masquerade motto. Lope spins endlessly his own variations on this theme: "Son mujeres / gente que sólo en interés repara" ("Women are creatures who are interested only in making a profit") (*El marido más firme*, Ac., VI, 200); "Mi Jesús, el amor humano es un engaño de dos fundado en interés" ("My Jesus, human love is a mutual deception based on self-interest") (*Cien jaculatorias a Christo nuestro señor, OS*, XVII, 80); "Como Venus sin Baco y Ceres se resfría, assí el amor de las cosas de la tierra sin plata, quiero decir, sin interés, se hiela" ("As Venus cools off without Ceres and Bacchus, so love of earthly things without silver, I mean without self-interest, freezes up") (*Los pastores de Belén, OS*, XVI, 319)—Lope is paraphrasing Terence, *Eunuch*, 732, "Sine Cerere et Libero friget Venus" ("Without Ceres and Bacchus, Venus flags"), a line that had become proverbial; "Sin algun interés no se obligará esta persona, según la Astrología del Doctor Dando" ("Without some offer of money that person will not come round, according to the astrology of Dr. Giving") (*Epistolario*, IV, 95). Cf. the already noted condemnation in "A mis soledades voy" of the corrupting effect of wealth on the age.

186. The Academia dictionary does not list this meaning but the Diccionario de Autoridades does, s.v. *nácar*, with the Latin equivalent "roseus color" ("rosy color"), citing this passage of *La Dorotea* and one of Quevedo's: "infinito nácar para las mejillas" ("infinite nacre for cheeks"). An outright red is clearly meant in Góngora's description of the turkey's wattles: "penda el rugoso nácar de tu frente / sobre el crespo zafiro de tu cuello" ("suspend the wrinkled nacre of your brow over the curly sapphire of your neck") (*Soledad primera*, ll. 312–313).

187. We subsequently discover (p. 265) that the ring had been given to Dorotea by Fernando, a detail which adds to the pathos of her situation but is curiously at odds with his poverty and her sacrifices to it.

188. Even in the detail of Dorotea's description of the writing-box containing Fernando's letters—"el escritorillo de los embustes . . . que le llamo assí por las bagatelas que tiene, vocablo de vn señor italiano, que me le ferió a vn instrumento que yo tenía" ("the little writing-desk with the fibs . . . a name I give it on account of the bagatelles it contains, a word of an Italian gentleman who gave it to me in

exchange for an instrument I had") (p. 52)—there is a passing ambiguity—that of the final pronominal complement, "le," which couples object and word as equivalent gifts.

189. *Obras escogidas*, II, 194b.

190. *Obras escogidas*, II, 981b. The reference is to the final line of an epigram to Cirinius (VIII, 18): "Gold, wealth and estates, many friends will yield; anyone willing to yield in talent will be most unusual." Lope's contemporaries remark on the same trait in human nature, also with classical substantiation. Huarte de San Juan, *Examen de ingenios*, p. 412b, falls back on Aristotle and Cicero:

> Una de las mayores injurias que al hombre le pueden hacer de palabra estando ya en edad de discreción, dice Aristóteles, es llamarle falto de ingenio: porque toda su honra y nobleza, dice Cicerón, es tener ingenio y ser bien hablado: *Ut hominis decus est ingenium, sic ingenii lumen est eloquentia* . . . Por lo contrario, el que nació sin ingenio . . . forzosamente se ha de contar en el número de los brutos animales y estimarle por tal; puesto caso que en los demás bienes, así naturales como de fortuna, sea hermoso, gentil hombre, rico, bien nacido y en dignidad, rey o emperador.

> One of the most insulting things you can say to a person when he has already reached the age of reason, says Aristotle, is that he is lacking in intelligence; because all his honor and nobility, says Cicero, consists of having brains and being well spoken: "As the pride of man is his mind, so the light of the mind is oratory" . . . On the contrary, one born without intelligence . . . must of necessity be ranked among the brute beasts and be considered one himself, even though, in respect to other endowments, those both of nature and of fortune, he may be handsome, gentlemanly, rich, well born and in status, a king or emperor.

Huarte goes on to cite scriptural statements of the same idea. Horozco y Covarrubias, for his part, observes: "De la riqueza y la salud de la honra [*sic*] fácilmente juzgarán todos . . . mas en lo que es saber y entendimiento, ninguno piensa que otro le excede" ("Anyone may pass judgment on wealth and the state of someone's honor . . . but where knowledge and intellect are concerned, no one thinks anyone else surpasses him") (*Emblemas morales*, III, fol. 120v).

XI. *Desengaño*

1. Part XVI, 1621; Morley and Bruerton: 1610–1615 (probably 1612–1615). The concept of the labyrinth is touched on with reference to the sonnet of the *Rimas* (1602) in E. G. Erdman, Jr., "Lope de Vega's' De Absalón,' a *laberinto de concetos esparcidos*," *Studies in Philology*, 65 (1968), 73–74; with reference to the sonnet of the *Rimas sacras* in E. Glaser, *Estudios hispano-portugueses* (Valencia: Castalia, 1957), pp. 83–85. It naturally figures more or less incidentally elsewhere in Lope, viz., in this passage of *El peregrino en su patria* (1604) (*OS*, V, 127): "El Alva traxo la luz, la luz el día, el día al sol, y ninguno de todos estos me desengañó: que mal se desengaña

quien ama, ni en tanta escuridad de laberintos y vueltas de fingimientos halla principio la razón, en que poner el hilo de Theseo" ("Dawn brought light, light day, day the sun, and none of these disabused me: for one who loves is not easily disabused nor in such darkness of labyrinths and twists of deceptions does reason find a starting point on which to affix the thread of Theseus").

2. Madrid: Francisco López, 1585; subsequent editions 1599, 1611, etc. The quotation to follow is from the edition by E. Gómez de Baquero (Madrid: C.I.A.P., 1928), II, 148.

3. There is no suggestion of moral allegory, much less a personal overtone, despite rhetorical flourishes by the *gracioso* in which the minotaur is found no worse than many offspring of women—anger, flattery, lies, double-dealing—and definitely less bad than monsters like jealousy and ingratitude; in which also the gold thread, with the stress on gold, is the key not only to "monstruo de mujer" but to all human affairs (Ac. VI, 126a–b).

4. *Epistolario*, III, 306.

5. Read in this light, with only a shift in emphasis, Don Bela's declaration in II, 5, seems less frivolous: "que si la hermosura del cuerpo es lo visible por quien lo inuisible se conoce, cada vno destos dos indiuiduos se ha de gozar amando, el vno por los braços y el otro por los oídos" ("for if the beauty of the body is the visible through which the invisible is known, each one of these two individuals is to be enjoyed in love, the one with embraces and the other through the ears") (p. 174).

6. Quotations respectively from *Epistolario*, III, 339 and 277, and *El peregrino en su patria*, OS, V, 411.

7. *Poesías líricas*, ed. J. F. Montesinos (Madrid: Espasa-Calpe, 1941), I, 153; subsequent quotation, *ibid.*, I, 27.

8. OS, IV, 168.

9. Regarding the conflation of images in the metaphor, see above, p. 12.

10. At most we might see an analogy to the actions of a person casting about in a *maze* in Fernando's account of the vicissitudes of his relations with Dorotea in the interval between reconciliation and rupture: disorientation, deviousness, restiveness under an old yoke, an ultimate chance delivery.

11. "Después que acabó Belardo" ("After Belardo finished"), *Poesías líricas*, ed. Montesinos, I, 17. The turn from one form of destruction to another—from tearing up to burning—should perhaps even be linked with the impression left on Lope by the backfiring of the stratagem of the forged letter (signed Elena), which is recorded for us in Juana de Ribera's testimony: "Señor, dejalde que hecho está pedazos, y él [Lope] le decía que le quemase en su presencia, y como esta testigo le metió en los pechos y le guardaba, el dicho Lope de Vega arremetió a esta testigo y por fuerza se le quitó y le tomó, diciendo que le quería rasgar y hacer pedazos" ("Sir, forget about it, it's torn to shreds; and he [Lope] kept telling her to burn it in his presence, and when this witness put it in her bosom to save it, the said Lope de Vega grabbed this witness and forcibly took it away from her, saying that he wanted to tear it up and reduce it to shreds") (*Proceso*, p. 76).

12. Taking a cue from Spitzer's impression (*Classical and Christian Ideas of World Harmony*, ed. A. G. Hatcher [Baltimore: Johns Hopkins Press, 1963], p. 98) that "*Hamlet* and some of the Shakespeare sonnets read like a Spanish *comedia* or the poetry of Lope," one may note the similarities in theme and dramatic technique between this Lopean sequence and Richard II's words (V, v), which Spitzer goes on to quote:

> Music do I hear?
> Ha, ha! keep time! How sour sweet music is,
> When time is broke and no proportion kept!
> So is it in the music of men's lives.
> And here have I the daintiness of ear
> To check time broke in a disorder'd string;
> But for the concord of my state and time
> Had not an ear to hear my true time broke.
>
> (V, v, 41–48)

In the *acción en prosa*, of course, there is no political sphere bound up with the personal as in the words of the imprisoned king: the epic dimension is missing as it was in Dorotea's reworking of the Ovidian Dido's epistle. But Shakespeare, like Lope, knows the presentational effectiveness of music as an index of character and mood. Toward the end of the monologue, the king reverts to the music:

> This music mads me; let it sound no more;
> For though it have holp madmen to their wits,
> In me it seems it will make wise men mad.

The music has clearly gone on working its jarring effect while the king spoke of other things but he himself recognizes that this effect depends as much on subject as object. Again parallels with Lope are evident.

One may add that the author of Act I of *La Celestina* (*Tragicomedia de Calixto y Melibea*, ed. M. Criado de Val and G. D. Trotter [Madrid: C.S.I.C., 1958], p. 26) was no stranger to these possibilities:

> *Cal.:* Dame acá el laúd.
> *Sem.:* Señor, veslo aquí.
> *Cal.:*   ¿Quál dolor puede ser tal
>   que se yguale con mi mal?
> *Sem.:* Destemplado está esse laúd.
> *Cal.:* ¿Cómo templará el destemplado? ¿Cómo sentirá el harmonía aquel que
>   consigo está tan descorde . . .? Pero tañe, y canta la más triste canción que
>   sepas.

> *Cal.:* Give me the lute. *Sem.:* Here it is, sir. *Cal.:* "What pain can be so
> great as to equal my suffering?" *Sem.:* That lute is out of tune. *Cal.:* How
> shall one unattuned tune? How shall one in such discord with himself know
> harmony . . .? But play and sing the saddest song you know.

13. As this exchange (p. 448) indicates:

Cel.: Nunca te he oído estos versos ni este tono. ¿Quién los hizo?
Dor.: Los versos, Celia, yo: y el tono, aquel excelente músico, Iuan de
   Palomares . . .

Cel.: I've never heard this verse nor this music from you. Who wrote them?
Dor.: The verse, Celia, myself; the music, that excellent musician Juan de
   Palomares . . .

Dorotea goes on to note that the lines of the poem "hablan en nombre de mujer"
("are spoken by a woman"). The reference is to lines "Que fuera a mi pena ingrata /
si menos gloria me fucra" ("I would be unworthy of my pain if it were any less of a
glory to me").

14. *Guzmán de Alfarache*, ed. S. Gili Gaya (Madrid: La Lectura, 1926), I, 108.
15. *Epistolario*, III, 199.
16. *Epistolario*, III, 257.
17. Cf. this passage from *Los pastores de Belén* (*OS*, XVI, 431):

Estos [versos] son, dixo Dositea, de Damón el viejo. Conformes son, replicó
Aminadab, a sus años y desengaños, que cierto se pudieran llamar desengaños
los años, sino se llamaran años hasta que fueran desengaños.

"This [verse]," said Dositea, "is by old Damon." "It is appropriate,"
Aminadab replied, "to his burden of years and unburdening of illusions [lit.,
his years and disillusions], for years could certainly be called disillusions if
they weren't called years until they turned into disillusions."

18. *Die Literarisierung des Lebens in Lope's "Dorotea"* (Bonn and Cologne:
Rohrscheid, 1932), p. 22.
19. The parallel with a dialogue between two old crones, Valera and Dolosina, in
another work influenced by *La Celestina*, the *Comedia Selvagia* of Alonso de Villegas
[1554] (Madrid: Rivadeneyra, 1873), may be purely coincidental. On the other hand,
Lope could have found in it suggestions to be unraveled: the casual manner of
introducing the reference to the crony's young days, the color of the cheeks, the
baptismal record, the exchange of digs:

Val.: Y aún con eso tienes en el rostro tales colores, que por mi salud en tu
   mocedad no las podías tener tales.
Dol.: Malo va esto, vieja me ha llamado; mas no se me irá con ella.
Val.: ¿Qué dices, comadre?
Dol.: Digo que como ya tú, de vieja, estás en los huesos, que no has podido
   tomar color como yo . . .
Dol.: . . . Verás que mis colores son de mío, y no causados por la bebida; que
   sabe, si no lo sabes, comadre, que toda mi vida he sido fermosa y fresca

mujer, y como agora en lo mejor della esté, mira qué maravilla si tengo colores.

Val.: ¿Qué años habrás, comadre?

Dol.: Este otro día hice esa cuenta, y hallé en el libro de la perrochia que tengo hasta cuarenta años.

Val.: De la mitad arriba, y aun Dios y ayuda.

(pp. 240ff.)

Val.: And despite this you have such color in your cheeks that, so may I be saved, you couldn't have had anything like it in your youth.   *Dol.:* This is not so good, she's calling me an old woman, but she won't get away with that.

Val.: What are you saying, gossip?   *Dol.:* I say that because you, from sheer age, are skin and bone, you haven't been able to acquire color like me . . .

Dol.: . . . You'll see that my color is my own and not the result of drink; understand, gossip, in case you don't, that I've been a handsome ruddy woman all my life, and since now I'm in the prime of it, what's so surprising about my having color?   *Val.:* What would your age be, gossip?   *Dol.:* The other day I figured it out and I found in the parish-book that I'm something like forty.

Val.: Halfway there and then some.

20. With less trust than Gerarda in "the laws of nature," Celestina, in conversation with Melibea, embraces without reservations the proverbial thought rejected by Gerarda (*Tragicomedia de Calixto y Melibea*, ed. Criado de Val and Trotter, p. 88):

Mel.: Siquiera por biuir más, es bueno dessear lo que digo [la mocedad].

Cel.: Tan presto, señora, se va el cordero como el carnero. Ninguno es tan viejo que no pueda biuir vn año, ni tan moço que oy no pudiesse morir. Assí que en esto poca ventaja nos lleuáys.

Mel.: If only in order to live longer, it's good to want what I say [youth].

Cel.: The lamb goes as quickly as the ram, madam. No one is so old that he can't live a year, nor so young that he couldn't die today. So you're not much better off in this than we.

21. Occasionally even a youthful character unexpectedly betrays Lope's preoccupation with old age; cf. Dorotea's "Los encarecimientos mentirosos más son consuelo de las partes defetuosas que alabanças; como quando a vna persona de mayor edad le dizen que no passa día por él" ("An untruthful build-up is more a consolation for shortcomings than praise—as when they tell an elderly person that he doesn't look a day older") (p. 139).

22. This attitude persists until very shortly before her death. There is real complacency, for example, behind the jocularity of her already quoted words to Dorotea in V, 10: "I, my darling child, got up feeling well. I gave God thanks for my good health and for having been born in Christendom. Now just think if I were Jarifa

Rodríguez or Daraja González ... what would become of me? Why it's beyond any doubt that this misfortune would take me straight to hell, wrapped up in one of those Moorish robes" (p. 449).

23. *OS*, XVII, 73.

24. The traditional idea of the world as a hostelry, for example, is linked by Lope himself in 1631 to the Book of Wisdom [5:14]: "El nombre de *Mesón* para descrivir el viaje de la vida es muy conforme a las palabras de la Sabiduría *Tanquam memoria hospitis unius diei praetereuntis*" ("The name of *Hostelry* to describe the journey of life is very much in keeping with the words of Wisdom: *Like the memory of a guest staying a single day and moving on*"). (From the approbation by Lope, as censor, of the work by Rodrigo Fernández, *Mesón del mundo* [Madrid, 1631], reproduced in F. Zamora Lucas, *Lope de Vega, censor de libros* [Larache: Artes gráficas Bosca, 1941], p. 59.) (There is a verse on the same subject in *OS*, XVII, 274.) Tirso writes: "Todos cuantos viven / son de la vida correos, / la posada donde asisten / con más agasajo es patria / más digna de que se avise" ("All who live are couriers of life; the hostelry [i.e., country] where they are best received should be considered their true fatherland") (*Obras dramáticas completas*, ed. B. de los Ríos [Madrid: Aguilar, 1946], I, 1007a). This and similar commonplaces of ascetic literature can be found exemplified in a sample from the *Discurso de la paciencia* of Fray Hernández de Zárate quoted by Stephen Gilman, *Cervantes y Avellaneda* (Mexico: El Colegio de México, 1951), pp. 20–21, while typical perfunctory variations on the *memento mori* theme, presumably from Lope's own pen but without the personal force of *La Dorotea*, are the *décimas* "Diferencia entre lo temporal y lo eterno" ("Difference between the Temporal and the Eternal" (*OS*, XVII, 217–222).

25. *OS*, XVII, 63. The clipped asyndeton and the rapidity of tempo it produces can sometimes be found in the correspondence, viz.: "Pasa el tiempo, múdase la voluntad; estrágase el gusto, diuiértese la memoria; conózense los defectos y aborrézense las desigualdades" ("Time passes, the will changes; pleasure is spoiled, memory strays; flaws are discovered and inequalities are detested") (*Epistolario*, IV, 37). Lope is reproaching his patron for what he considers unjust neglect.

26. In a letter of 1621, Lope writes: "Señor Don Diego, yo estoy desengañado, viejo, aunque brioso, que es lo que todos los que lo son dizen" ("Don Diego, I am disillusioned, old, but lively, which is what all those who are so say") (*Epistolario*, IV, 67).

27. Cf. Montesinos, *Estudios sobre Lope*, p. 258.

28. In one of Lope's early plays, *El verdadero amante* (The True Lover), dated by Morley and Bruerton before 1596 (probably 1588–1595), we find the following lines (Ac., V, 605a):

Siempre se debe a la muerte
el llanto de cualquier suerte,
aunque muera un enemigo;
porque allí nos acordamos

que nos falta aquella pena,
y llorando por la ajena,
por nuestra muerte lloramos.

Weeping in any case is always owed to death, even if an enemy dies, because we then remember that that penalty is still to come for us and in weeping for another's death, we weep for our own.

29. I am unable to see in the *soledades* of the ballad, as Leo Spitzer did (*Die Literarisierung*, p. 16), a radical loneliness of Fernando which the word play of the previous scene had covered over. Nor am I convinced by Spitzer's equation of the poem's purported dialectical structure with that of the preceding discussion of Fernando's dream.

30. In the remarks to follow I have drawn, especially for the poem of Act I, on the fuller material included in my study "Lope's 'A mis soledades voy' Reconsidered," *Homenaje a William L. Fichter: Estudios sobre el antiguo teatro hispánico* (Madrid: Castalia, 1971), pp. 713–724.

31. *Epistolario*, IV, 67.

32. *Epistolario*, III, 193.

33. *Epistolario*, IV, 107.

34. *Algunos caracteres de la cultura española*, 2nd ed. (Buenos Aires: Espasa-Calpe, 1943), p. 44.

35. I do not subscribe to Spitzer's view of the poem as didactic in a lyric frame, nor would I distinguish, as do W. L. Fichter and F. Sánchez y Escribano, between "two main themes—longing for solitude and criticism of worldly cares, hopes and ambitions . . . sharply separated, that of solitude appearing only in the opening and closing quatrains" ("The Origin and Character of Lope de Vega's 'A mis soledades voy,'" *Hispanic Review*, 11 [1948], 304–313). While there is no reason to believe that Lope composed "A mis soledades voy" for the context in which it has come down to us, the critical consensus—cf. Fichter and Sánchez y Escribano, p. 307—which places its composition toward the end of his life, is surely well grounded. If ll. 53–56—"En dos edades viuimos / los propios y los agenos: / la de plata los estraños, / y la de cobre los nuestros" ("Our people and other people live in two different ages: foreigners in that of silver, ourselves in that of copper")—refer to the Pragmática of August 1, 1628, which halved the value of the copper coinage, that date would provide a *terminus a quo*. This devaluation was a matter that greatly preoccupied Lope, as his correspondence shows, e.g., *Epistolario*, IV, 119, 128, 129.

36. Ditty quoted by Fichter and Sánchez y Escribano, "The Origin and Character," p. 305. It forms the coda of an anonymous hexasyllabic ballad beginning "Una zagaleja" ("A little shepherd-girl") included in *Romancero general*, ed. A. Durán (Madrid: Atlas, 1945), II, 620e.

37. Examples: "Entiendo . . . y no entiendo," ll. 13–14; "me defiendo; pero no puedo guardarme," ll. 18–19; "Adonde lo más es menos," l. 36; "Vnos por carta de más / otros por carta de menos," ll. 47–48; "Señales son del juizio / ver que todos

le perdemos," ll. 45–46; "lugar de tantas cruzes," l. 83 ("I understand . . . and I don't understand"; "I defend myself, but I can't protect myself"; "Where what is most is least"; "some for one card too many, others for one card too few"; "It's a sign of the Judgment that we are all losing ours"; "a place with so many crosses").

38. The image is so striking that it tends to "seed" the reader's mind and reecho for him in more limited contexts, i.e., a response of Dorotea to Gerarda when the latter urges Don Bela's suit: "¿Este hombre me alabas, tía? Lo que auía menester vn vidriero era vn gato que le anduuiesse retozando con los vidros" ("Is this the man you are holding up to me, mistress? All a glazier would need is a cat to play around with his glassware") (p. 162).

39. *Epistolario*, IV, 326 (August [?] 1621).

40. "A mis soledades voy . . .," *Revista de filología española*, 23 (1936), 400.

41. Well exemplified for example, in Alciatus's emblem of Invidia.

42. E. Juliá Martínez recalls (ed. *La Dorotea* [Madrid: Hernando, 1935], I, 36n), in connection with the first two lines of the last quatrain, the two types of envy (invidiousness and emulation) alluded to by Cervantes in the Prologue to *Don Quixote*, Part II. But Lope clearly does not have this distinction (which stems from Aristotle and St. Thomas) in mind. He says "lo que passo" ("what I suffer"), not "la que passo" ("the one I suffer"), and in the preceding quatrain the "ugly" envy which he acknowledges feeling contains elements of both animosity and admiration.

43. The image had long since entered Lope's ordinary expressive idiom. Cf. a letter of 1616 (*Epistolario*, III, 261): "No es mucho, que si en el mar de la murmuración se pierden baxeles de alto borde, se anegue mi barquilla, tan miserable, que apenas se ve en las aguas, y que por cosa ynútil, la pudieran perdonar las olas de la ociosidad y los vientos de la enbidia" ("It's not surprising that if high-riding vessels are lost in the sea of slander, my little boat should go down, being so wretched that it can hardly be seen in the waters and something so useless that it could well be spared by the waves of idle speculation and the winds of envy"). In "A Footnote on Lope de Vega's *Barquillas*" (*Romance Philology*, 6 [1953], 289–293), Morby has surveyed the classical sources and subsequent cultivation of the metaphor of the ship, concurring in Menéndez y Pelayo's judgment that Lope derived it from Horace himself and noting also the links of the *barquillas* with Virgil and Sannazaro.

44. Fernando confirms the influence when he notes that "Sanazaro escriuió en latín poema y églogas" ("Sannazaro wrote a long poem and eclogues in Latin") (p. 244). A listing of writers of eclogues included in a prose epistle of 1621 concludes with the name of Sannazaro (*OS*, IV, 481). Lope speaks in the same context of the "mixed" style of the eclogue and calls this type of poem, "por esta varia elocución, gracioso y agradable a todos" ("because of all this variation in style, charming and pleasing to all"). He must have found the eclogue, like the ballad, to which he here assimilates it metrically, particularly congenial in its flexibility, its capacity to absorb free-ranging movements of sensibility and imagination.

45. When Fernando in a passage quoted earlier tells Julio that he would learn to sing the first two ballads "if they were short," Julio answers: "Las otras dos que tienes

son más a propósito" ("The other two which you have are more suitable") (p. 223).

46. See Morby, "A Footnote," p. 292, n. 16. Horace himself makes the ship a metaphor of the self at the beginning of "Rectius vives" (II, 10), an ode which has also left certain traces in the *barquillas*.

47. Cf. "En tanto que las olas / por estas rocas trepan; / pues viuen retiradas / las barcas y las pescas . . ." ("While the waves scale these rocks, since fishing boats and fishing are holding off . . .") (ll. 75–78) with the opening of Sannazaro's third eclogue: "Dic mihi (nam Baulis, verum si rettulit Aegon / bis senos vos, Mopse, dies tenuere procellae) . . ."—"Tell me (for storms detained you twice six days at Bauli, Mopsus, if Aegon is correct) . . ."

48. An emendation by later editors—"si puede ser que sea" ("if such is possible") for "que muero de tristeza" ("for I am dying of sadness") (p. 211, l. 10)—to avoid the consonantal rhyme *gentileza-tristeza*, makes l. 12 mean "I do not wish to lose Amarilis," instead of "I do not wish to lose my sadness." Unlike Morby, I find the line decidedly more coherent and expressive as originally written. It is shadows, likenesses, memories of Amarilis that Fabio clings to, along with the sadness that keeps them intact. Amarilis herself he knows to be irrevocably lost.

49. The last time this becomes:

Mas tanto pueden desdichas
que obligan si porfían
a no estimar la muerte ni la vida.

But misfortunes are so powerful that, if they persist, they force one not to value death or life.

The removal of the nonassonating word and the reduction to three lines suggest a musical resolution indicative of the close. Perhaps Fernando's statement "I've set them to memorable melodies" means that Lope had indeed had the last two eclogues set to music. A text accompanying the polyphonic version found in the mid-seventeenth-century MS *Tonos humanos* uses the three-line refrain throughout. (See J. Bal y Gay, ed., *Treinta canciones de Lope de Vega puestas en música* [Madrid: Residencia de Estudiantes, 1935], pp. 11–14 and 103.) As Morby notes (p. 282, n. 187), there may be a reminiscence of Dante's well-known lines on Paolo and Francesca (*Inferno*, V, 121–123) in the four-line refrain.

50. In "Pobre barquilla mía" Lope will merely suggest unconcern: "Mas ¡ay que no me escuchas!" ("But alas, you are not listening to me!") (p. 277). A precedent for the sharpened contrast of the ending of "Gigante cristalino" is the "Canción a a la muerte de Carlos Félix" ("Song on the Death of Carlos Félix"): "Y si mi llanto vuestra luz divisa, / los dos claveles bañaréis en risa" ("And if your light catches a glimpse of my weeping, you will bathe your two carnations in laughter") (*Obras poéticas*, p. 490). Cf. Petrarch, "E se cosa di qua nel ciel si cura" ("And if there is any care in heaven for anything here below") (Canzone IV, *in morte*); Sannazaro, "Lieta ivi schernendo y pensier nostri / quasi un bel sol ti mostri" ("Joyfully mocking our

thoughts there, you appear as a beautiful sun") (*Arcadia*, Eclogue V). The reversal of mood caused by thoughts of the beloved's bliss is derived from the shift to rejoicing found at the end of the classical pastoral elegy, and more remotely from the underlying vegetation myth in which the god—Daphnis, Linus, etc.—whose death symbolizes the dying out of greenery at the onset of the hot summer is to be reborn with the new season, turning grief to joy. A *locus classicus* is Virgil's fifth eclogue, ll. 56–59:

Candidus insuetum miratur limen Olympi
sub pedibusque videt nubes et sidera Daphnis
ergo alacris silvas et cetera rura voluptas
Panaque pastoresque tenet Dryadasque puellas.

Daphnis, in radiant beauty, marvels at Heaven's unfamiliar threshold, and beneath his feet beholds the clouds and stars. Therefore frolic glee seizes the woods and all the countryside, and Pan, and the shepherds, and the Dryad maids.

(I quote from the translation by H. R. Fairclough, *Virgil: Eclogues, Georgics, Aeneid 1–6*, rev. ed. [Cambridge, Mass.: Harvard University Press, 1956].)

51. This echoes Horace in Odes, II, 10:

Rectius vives, Licini, neque altum
semper urgendo neque, dum procellas
cautus horrescis, nimium premendo
litus iniquum.

You will live better, Licinius, if you neither press constantly out to sea, nor, cautiously fearing storms, hew too close to the treacherous shore.

52. Lope remembers here not only Virgil's "sub pedibusque videt nubes et sidera Daphnis" but Garcilaso's "Egloga Primera" (ll. 394ff.):

Divina Elissa, pues agora el cielo
con inmortales pies pisas y mides
y su mudança ves, estando queda,
¿por qué de mí te olvidas y no pides
que se apresure el tiempo en que este velo
rompa del cuerpo, y verme libre pueda ...?

Divine Elissa, since you now tread heaven's floor and pace it with immortal feet and, yourself unmoving, behold its movement, why do you forget me and not ask that the time be hastened when I shall break out of this bodily coil and become free ...?

53. Francesco Petrarca, *Prose*, ed. G. Martellotti et al. (Milan and Naples: Ricciardi, 1955), p. 296.

54. Morby, p. 386, n. 2.

XII. The Meaning of *La Dorotea*

1. See "Pour une phénoménologie du baroque littéraire: Essai sur la tragédie européenne au XVIIe siècle," *Publications de l'Université de l'Etat à Elisabethville*, 5 (1963), 25–65.

2. *Los Cigarrales de Toledo*, ed. V. Said Armesto (Madrid: Renacimiento, 1913), p. 92.

3. See "The Making of *The Magic Mountain*," *The Atlantic*, January 1953, pp. 41–45.

4. Amezúa (*Epistolario*, II, 644–650) provides background for a perspective on the presentation of the final stages of love—*desamor*, revenge, forgetting—in *La Dorotea*, permitting us to see the distinctiveness and subtlety of Lope's treatment. He notes, as I earlier observed, the relative infrequency of these stages in the plays, notes also the Ovidian cast of the philographic framework: contributing causes are seen as absence, the passage of time, and especially, as I earlier noted, aggrievement. Lope also characteristically brings in publicity.

One may add that, as against the simple, yet unique, postulation in *La Dorotea* of indifference, forgetting, as the real sign of love's demise, Lope returns again and again throughout his career, with personal insistence, to hatred and vituperation. Cf. the strikingly personal remark of Polinesta in *La Arcadia* quoted above (p. 144) and the sonnet of the *Rimas humanas* beginning: "Si verse aborrecido el que era amado, / es de amor la postrera desventura" ("If for one who has been loved to find himself hated is the ultimate mischance of love") (*Obras poéticas*, p. 123). In *Obras son amores* (Handsome Is As Handsome Does), dated 1613–1618 by Morley and Bruerton, we read:

Que no hay amor que no vuelva
todo su vino vinagre;
porque en efeto comienza
en anillos, como dizen,
flores, cintas, cartas, letras,
y acaba en dagas, deshonras,
celos, sátiras y quejas.

(Ac. N., VIII, 174a)

There is no love that doesn't turn all its wine into vinegar, because a love
begins, in fact, as they say, with rings, flowers, ribbons, letters, songs, and ends
in daggers, dishonoring, jealousy, satires, and complaints.

The mention of *sátiras* is surely significant. As narrator we have seen Lope remark in the *novela* "Guzmán el Bravo" (1624): "it rarely fails that when Love takes its final step, the next one following is that of hatred" (*La Circe, con otras Rimas y Prosas* [1624], facs. ed. [Madrid: Biblioteca Nueva, 1935], fol. 138r). By the time we come to the *Rimas de Burguillos*, hatred and vituperation have been softened to a simple recantation. The *licenciado* chooses a laundress as his lady, says the foreword, because 'siendo tan cierto en el fin de todo Amor el arrepentimiento, menos tendrá que sentir el que perdió menos" ("since repentance is so sure to come at the end of every love, one who has lost less will have less to regret") (facs. ed. [Madrid: Cámara Oficial del Libro, 1935], unnumbered preliminary pp.). More subtle than any of these statements is Dorotea's well-reasoned but unrealistic formulation of the premise on which she acts at the outset:

> No quiero aguardar al fin que tienen todos los amores; pues es cierto que paran en mayor enemistad quanto fueron más grandes. Si auemos de ser enemigos después, más vale que aora nos concertemos con amistad; que quando el trato cessa sin agrauio, bien se puede conseruar en llaneza sin reprehensión, y en voluntad sin miedo.   (p. 80)

> I don't want to wait for the end in store for all love, since it's certain that the greater it has been, the greater enmity it turns into. If we must be enemies later, it is better for us to come to an agreement now in friendship; for when a connection ends without offense, it is quite possible to preserve it in a straightforward way with no reproaches and in good will with no fears.

On *desamor* and the dissolution of love, see also R. del Arco y Garay, *La sociedad española en las obras dramáticas de Lope de Vega* (Madrid: Escelicer, 1941), pp. 368–370.

5. "¡Quán sabios que son en ellos [los ojos de Dios] los que al mundo le parecen ignorantes! el que os alaba, el que os imita, el que os sigue, el que vive por vuestros preceptos, *el humilde a los agravios*" ("How wise in [God's eyes] are those who appear ignorant to the world! one who praises you, one who imitates you, one who follows you, one who lives by your precepts, *one who is humble in the face of offenses*" (*OS*, XVII, 53). (I have supplied the italics and changed the question marks, plainly erroneous, to exclamation points.) We see here how Lope, in imitation of Christ, seeks to make a virtue of the inborn streak of humbleness in his nature.

6. Ed. C. V. Aubrun and M. Muñoz Cortés (Paris: Institut d'Etudes Hispaniques, 1962), p. 20.

7. *Epistolario*, IV, 145.

8. Cf. this passage from "La desdicha por la honra" ("Misfortune Caused by Honor"), in *La Circe*, facs. ed., fol. 113r:

> ¡Qué cierto será que estés aora contando a otra más dichosa que yo, pero tan cerca de ser tan desdichada, las locuras que me has visto hazer y las penas que me has hecho sufrir: pues no se burle aora de mí la que te cree y te escucha, que presto me ayudará a quexarme de ti, y sabiendo quién eres, me disculpará porque te quise, y me tendrá lástima porque te quiero!

> How certain it is that you must now be telling another woman luckier than I but so close to being as unlucky, about the crazy things you have seen me do and the pains you have caused me to suffer! Well, let the woman who now believes you and listens to you not make fun of me now, for she will soon be helping me to complain about you and, knowing what you are like, will excuse me because I loved you and will pity me because I love you!

9. This does not prevent Lope, nevertheless, from also allowing César (p. 406) to interlard Fernando's account with data on cures for love lifted from Ficino's commentary on the *Symposium*, data which, especially out of context, are more "curious" and suggestive than edifying. (See Morby's documentation and my "Plato's *Symposium* and Ficino's Commentary in Lope de Vega's *Dorotea*," *Modern Language Notes*, 73 [1958], 509–511.) Moreover, when César subsequently relays Fernando's horoscope to him (V, 8), he even drops the viewpoint of Lope's maturity and adopts that of Fernando-Lope to tell Fernando "your honor" and "your revenge" will prevent Dorotea's winning him as husband (p. 440). Such shifts, effects of Lope's domination and appropriation of the characters, also reflect his shaping of the dialogue to suit the freely associative character of his mind.

10. By the end of *La Dorotea* the contrast between Fernando and Don Bela is, *grosso modo*, a contrast between different avatars of the self. Its roots lie, as we know, in Lope's *Erlebnis*. If any specific precedent suggested the polarizing of the contrast in a pair of characters, it could have been the *Comedia Euphrosina*, where its derivation, as with Lope, is ultimately from the Platonic two Venuses. It would have been only a suggestion, since in Ferreira de Vasconcelos's work the contrasting attitudes are more verbalized than dramatized. Cf. Zelotypo's words to Cariophilo:

> Essa ley tendes os autivos d'amor, que não temos os contemprativos,
> verdadeiros mártires de Cupido, os quais pretendemos antes o proueito de
> quem amamos que nosso interesse . . . E assí deuemos antes amar a fermosura
> do ánimo que a do corpo, porque mais durável gosto he contemprar os bens
> racionais sem o defeito que a idade causa no rosto: os que amam o corpo mais
> sam cobiçosos médicos que verdadeiros amadores. (ed. E. Asensio [Madrid:
> C.S.I.C., 1951], I, 158)

> That is a law that you active lovers follow, which we contemplative ones, true
> martyrs to Cupid, don't. We seek rather the good of the one we love than our
> own advantage . . . and thus we must love the beauty of the soul rather than
> that of the body, because it is a more enduring pleasure to contemplate a
> rational good without the flaw that age causes in the countenance. Those who
> love the body are grasping doctors rather than true lovers.

11. The ludic turn of phrase in these instances shows increased equanimity of outlook vis-à-vis the earlier noted passage of *El peregrino en su patria* on the brevity of life (above, pp. 168–169). One finds the same turn of phrase in the *Epistolario:* "Los enamorados . . . para desapassionarse buscan otras mugeres, y en acabándose el juego, quedan más tristes" ("Lovers . . . seek other women in order to cool their passion and when the game is up end up sadder") (III, 113 [1628]).

12. To observe the play-spirit in all its gratuitous spontaneity, we need only look again at the supper scene (II, 6). Flushed with success now that Dorotea has yielded, Gerarda gives her native ebullience free rein. When the food is brought on, she strikes a chaplain's pose—"De capellana os tengo de servir" ("I must be your she-chaplain"). The humor of her macaronic Latin grace derives from the not

wholly ingenuous deformation of a serious sentiment under uncertain linguistic control. This is even more the case with the blessing at the end, in which the addition of rhymes makes the wobbling language a reflection of Gerarda's by now hopeless unsteadiness on her feet. Dorotea, though she has earlier decried the vice of drunkenness, cannot restrain a smile: "No se le puede negar que tiene gracia" ("It can't be denied that she is amusing") (p. 198).

Gerarda is her own most appreciative spectator as she makes this exhibition of herself. Teodora and Dorotea attempt to maintain a certain composure but the maids are unable to suppress their merriment at the increasingly urgent play of gesticulation directed at Celia and the wine jug. She becomes as intoxicated with her own comical loquacity as with the wine: "Madre Gerarda, come más y bebe menos; que con la sal de tus gracias te brindas a ti misma" ("Mother Gerarda, eat more and drink less; you're toasting yourself with the saltiness of your witticisms"), Teodora remarks (p. 194). The panegyric of Nuflo Rodríguez is succeeded by the panegyric of wine, which, as has already been noted, weaves the gayest of festoons around Celestina's *laus vini.*

13. La Barrera, *Nueva biografía,* Ac., I, 669b.

14. The sonnet is the *soi-disant* profession of faith of one of these presented in the first person, and the commentary upon it is a parody of Pellicer's *Lecciones solemnes.* See Morby, p. 320, n. 73.

15. "Porque no digáis que os quiero cansar con el tal Columela" ("So that you won't say I'm seeking to bore you with that Columela"), César maliciously cites parallels: "*çabullome de pato, anda de reboço, viue de milagro, viste de verde, habla de enfermo, sale de juizio*" ("I plunge like a duck, he goes about in a cape, she lives by miracles, she dresses in green, he speaks like a sick man, he goes out of his mind"). Referred back to the phrase being commented on—"pululando de culto"—these speak for themselves. (Cf. Morby, p. 336, nn. 135, 136.)

16. The total effect, one of shifting irony, is already present in César's words early in scene 2: "Sin passión digo que muchos dellos [los que comentan] no son dignos de alabança, aunque yo lo quiero ser deste soneto" ("With no hard feelings, I say that many [commentators] are not worthy of praise, although I want to be so of this sonnet") (p. 320). To do justice to a ridiculous sonnet means to make the commentary upon it equally ridiculous, although at first glance César's words seem to be saying the opposite.

17. The personal acquaintance of the speakers with Burguillos and the retention of the name of Claudio [Conde], Lope's lifelong friend and the original addressee of the sonnet (cf. *Epistolario,* IV, 147) are indications of Lope's solidarity with the literary credo of Fernando's friends, as also with the ludic spirit of their commentary.

18. *Lope de Vega y su tiempo,* trans. R. de la Serna, 2nd ed. (Madrid: Revista de Occidente, 1940), p. 206.

19. Because of the ultimate improvisatory and even amateurish character of the role-playing in *La Dorotea,* its intermittencies and changes of direction, I do not find particularly relevant to the work the concept of metatheater developed by Lionel

Abel in his book of the same title (New York: Hill and Wang, 1963). This concept rests on a view of dramatic characters not merely as self-conscious actors but as dramatists, agents of dramas of their own, by which they take into their hands the action of the plays in which they appear, generating new actions out of the conflict with wills and ordinances more powerful than their own that inevitably ensues.

20. "La imaginación en el metateatro calderoniano," *Actas del Tercer Congreso Internacional de Hispanistas*, ed. C. H. Magis (Mexico City: El Colegio de México, 1970), pp. 923–930. Wardropper notes Lope's use of the term "imaginaciones" to designate his *comedias*.

21. Cited by Wardropper, *ibid.*, p. 924, from *Examen de ingenios*, in *Obras escogidas de filósofos*, ed. Adolfo de Castro (Madrid: Sucesores de Hernando, 1922), p. 447a.

22. Fernando's assertion is made purely at the worldly level. In the *Soliloquios amorosos de un alma a Dios*, however, to recall phrases cited earlier, disillusionment with the imagination became a more far-reaching *desengaño*:

> ¡Qué engañosos deleites! ¡qué grandes en la imaginación! ¡qué pequeños en el efecto! Gigantes parecen a la idea del miserable entendimiento que los fabrica, pero llegados a tocar con las manos, son vanas sombras, sueños phantásticos, oro de alchimia, cometas breves. (*OS*, XVII, 62)

> What deceitful delights! How great in imagination! How small in fact! They seem gigantic in the eyes of the miserable mind that invents them, but when they come within hand's reach, they are empty shadows, fantastic dreams, alchemist's gold, short-lived comets.

23. I prefer to place a more restricted and literal construction on this problematical term than Manuel Durán does, following Walter Friedlaender, Wylie Sypher, Gustav R. Hocke, and others, in his study "Lope de Vega y el problema del manierismo" (*Anuario de letras*, 2 [1962], 76–98). While Durán considers that "the essential, permanent stance of Lope in artistic matters is not manneristic" (p. 95n), he finds *La Dorotea* (like the *Soliloquios*) an exception that reflects this epochal style: "The contrast between the lyric and the prosaic lends the characters a dimensional *chiaroscuro* and helps to present them in their intimacy, an offhand intimacy in which they are concerned not with the impression they may be creating but with the free expression of their subjectivity." He sees as manneristic features the "instability" of their world, its subjection to temporal and material forces, the interaction between poetry and truth, and finds the work reminiscent in its general tone and effect of "the luminous intimacy of Vermeer," or "the restless and somber 'realism' of Caravaggio" (p. 97). While I do not follow him in these artistic parallels, nor would I agree that the characters are unconcerned with the impression they are making, there is of course no doubt about the significance of the elements which Durán singles out for notice. It is a matter of definition whether one considers them manneristic or not. In any case, I would confine the manneristic attitude to the characters and see the author and consequently the spirit of the work as transcending it. The "instability" of the characters' world does not define Lope's outlook. Their vacilla-

tions and dilemmas, the imbalance between their reality and their aspirations, from his vantage point become a range of possibilities, all attractive, none to be necessarily foregone until all must be foregone together. Or else the dilemmas are deflated and resolved by the antidote of humor: the comic outlook seems incompatible with the mannerism Durán postulates. Lope's secure overlordship, his firm hold on this life and the next seem to me much more in the spirit of the baroque, if they are to be fitted into an epochal category, than of mannerism. *La Dorotea* is an act of acquiescence in life, a celebration of the world, not an uneasy interrogation of them. Its spirit is not problematical despite its suggestions of the elusive and indeterminate areas of experience.

To turn to matters of detail: if one thinks of the characters' mannerism in terms of noncanonical effects, attitudes expressive of emotional and spiritual distress or willful self-delusion, one may cite, in Dorotea, for example, the pallor which gives her an unwonted charm in convalescence (p. 138); the peculiar appeal of her glance: "Miras por lo condolido con tan garabatosa suauidad que prouocas a amor y lástima, dos efetos que atraen la voluntad entre la piedad y el gusto" ("your air of injury makes you look about with such provocative gentleness that you arouse love and pity, two effects that appeal to the will half pityingly and half pleasurably") (p. 139); the play of perspectives, actual and reflected, created when she consults the mirror, "espejo de las facciones del alma" ("mirror of the features of the soul"), which reveals to her not the "blended harmoniousness" her maid had claimed to see in her face, but "accidentes del espíritu" ("disturbances of the spirit") (p. 139). There is also the studied casualness of her appearance as noted by Ludovico: "low headdress, a wimple that encircled the whole face the first days and after that, the hair showing a bit as if unintentionally" (p. 238). Cf. the presentation of Circe as she tries in vain to seduce Ulysses: "y como hazía / efetos de muger desesperada / la nieue de los brazos descubría, / artificiosamente descuydada" ("and as she was behaving like a desperate woman, she uncovered the snow of her arms, artfully casual") (*La Circe, poema*, literary commentary, historical introduction, and annotated edition by C. V. Aubrun and M. Muñoz Cortés [Paris: Centre de Recherches de l'Institut d'Etudes Hispaniques, 1962], p. 78). This contrived negligence contrasts with the spontaneous and nonmanneristic negligence which Lope also found attractive. Cf. the sonnet "A una dama que salió rebuelta vna mañana" ("To a lady who came out disheveled one morning") (*Rimas de . . . Burguillos*, facs. ed., fol. 21r), in which the lady's disheveled state is considered as natural as that of a "turbada Aurora" ("ruffled dawn"). A naive touch of *aspereza* is being appreciated here.

In the instances cited from *La Dorotea* (one could add others) the touches I would call manneristic involve accidental or studied deviation from a norm. The abandonment of the norm, on the other hand—viz., Marfisa "para dama con demasiada frescura" ("too buxom for a lady") (p. 154)—seems simply naturalistic.

24. *OS*, I, 456. The epistle was published with *La Filomena* in 1621.

25. See *Linguistics and Literary History* (Princeton: Princeton University Press, 1948), pp. 68–73.

Index